Applied Phonetics

Applied Phonetics

by

CLAUDE MERTON WISE

Chairman, Department of Speech
Louisiana State University

Illustrated by

H. S. Wise, M.D.

U. S. Public Health Service
Seattle, Washington

Englewood Cliffs, N. J.
PRENTICE-HALL, INC.

PE 1135
W57

Third printing......March, 1965

PRINTED IN THE UNITED STATES OF AMERICA

04154–C

Preface

The title *Applied Phonetics* has been given to this book to suggest its main intent: to apply phonetic symbols and nomenclature to the description of the principal varieties of the English language in America and the British Isles. Actually, the name is not entirely accurate in respect to the first part of the book, where phonetic modes of thought and phonetic symbols are given preliminary presentation without specific application. However, the presentation is reasonably selective, so that although the material is of the nature of general, rather than applied, phonetics, it is less extended than in most general discussions. The remainder of the book can without qualification be called *applied* phonetics.

An applied phonetics book is by definition a practical book. It is also a highly eclectic book. Its eclecticism lies in part in its plan of selection from the informational and theoretic material available. As of this date, such selection is a matter for much thought. In the days of Franklin, Ellis, and Bell, and of Sweet, Passy, and Viëtor, the known items of phonetic information seemed very final and were certainly very sparse; nowadays little information can be trusted to be final and the items are certainly not sparse. Instead, there is a welter of many kinds of information: the theories of de Saussure, Trubetzkoy, and Bloomfield have burst upon us; and the X-ray, slow-motion photography, and the spectrograph have heaped their findings before us. With this great wealth of material at hand, writing on any phase of phonetics has become a difficult undertaking, and, critical opinion being what it is, a dangerous one.

Of the phases of study suggested above, this book contains selected material somewhat as indicated in the following list:

1. *Anatomy.* Confined to the gross features that can be comprehended from pictures, charts, models, and discussions.
2. *Physics.* Confined to information that is demonstrable by illustrations, drawings, and simple apparatus.
3. *History of the English language.* Very little.
4. *The phoneme.* The phonemic concept is used many times, as required. Any impulse to use extensive phonemic transcription, however, is herein firmly resisted; the purposes of this book are better served by phonetic transcription.
5. *Close transcription.* This book avoids the overweening specificity of too great a clutter of diacritics and special phonetic symbols. The transcription

undertakes to strike a usable mean between the extremes of generalization and particularization.

6. *Instruments*. The new instrumentation is referred to, but sparingly, since the emphasis of this book is on practical phonetics.

7. *Isolation of sounds vs. sounds in context*. The differences between sounds in isolation and sounds in context are recognized, but for the most part it is necessary herein to discuss sounds in their isolated forms.

8. *Standards of correctness*. All educated people recognize standards of correctness in personal practice—even those who affect to scorn them in principle. Such contradicting attitudes must surely arise from confusion between the functions of phonetics *per se*—that is, general phonetics, which has no opinions on correctness—and the functions of applied phonetics, which is regularly used as an instrument for inculcating standards of speech. This book describes both standard and substandard speech. Despite all attempts to find out what is believed to be acceptable generally, there will be some statements reflecting the writer's own practice or predilection. These are certain to differ with the practices, predilections, or perhaps the more accurate knowledge of some other people. We shall doubtless hear from these people, often with profit. Any statement concerning standard or substandard speech runs the risk of being called *prescriptive*—a term of negative, even scornful, connotation. But those who insist that what is called substandard is actually as "standard" as what is called standard are being prescriptive too. Perhaps the two prescriptions will balance each other.

Baton Rouge, La., 1957

C. M. WISE

Acknowledgments

Through the years of the development of *Applied Phonetics*, so many people have lent assistance that proper acknowledgment to all of them is impossible. But to every one of them, my grateful thanks. Certain people read the book in manuscript and rendered such other equal services that I shall attempt a partial list here, with an indication of the portion of the book on which they were consulted.

Dr. Gordon E. Peterson, Bell Telephone Laboratories and University of Michigan. Chapter 3, Production and Classification of Speech Sounds.

Dr. A. A. Hill, formerly of the University of Virginia and the Georgetown Institute of Languages and Linguistics, now of the University of Texas. Chapter 5, Sound Change.

Dr. Raven I. McDavid, Linguistic Atlas of the United States and Canada, and University of Michigan. Chapter 6, Speech Regions of America.

Dr. Malcolm S. Coxe, Brooklyn College. Chapter 14, Speech of New York City.

Brother Nicholas Grahmann, De La Salle Juniorate; Dr. Elliott D. Healy, Louisiana State University; and Dr. John J. Guilbeau, Louisiana State University. Chapter 17, French.

Dr. Martin Joos, Linguistic Atlas of the United States and Canada, and University of Wisconsin; and Dr. Herbert Penzl, Linguistic Atlas of the United States and Canada, and University of Illinois. Chapter 18, German.

Dr. J. William Frey, Lancaster College. Chapter 19, Pennsylvania German.

Dr. Einar Haugen, University of Wisconsin. Chapter 21, Norwegian.

Dr. Robert A. Hall, Jr., Cornell University. Chapter 22, Italian.

Dr. Floyd G. Lounsbury, Yale University. Chapter 25, Portuguese.

Dr. A. A. Hill, complete manuscript.

The advice of these scholars was usually heeded, but it would be unfair to hold them responsible for my interpretation of the material or for omission of this or that specific item; the responsibility, of course, is mine.

ACKNOWLEDGMENTS

Credit is also due the faithful people who have for years sustained the arduous task of typing and retyping so long and detailed a work. Particular credit must go to Roberta Fluitt White, Ernestine Heard Jensen, Edith Holloway Stevens, Dr. Lynn Earl Orr, Leborah Alfonso Carnovale, Patsy Heidt Grubbs, Dr. Albert Donald George, Dr. Clinton William Bradford, and Dorothy Holbrook.

Special gratitude is expressed to Dr. Cj Stevens, research assistant and amanuensis; to my colleague, Dr. C. L. Shaver, and to Minoru Tomura, of the Japanese Ministry of Education, Tokyo, who proofread the entire book; and to my wife, Shirley Gorrell Wise, who comments that now, for the first time in twenty years, there will be no manuscript to carry along on vacations.

Contents

PART ONE

1. The Purpose of This Book   3

2. Sounds and Symbols: A Preliminary View of the Sounds of English
and the Phonetic Symbols Representing Them   5

   Observations on "silent letters" in English, 6
   Stressing and unstressing, 13
   Summary of the sounds of English: Key words, 24

3. Production and Classification of Speech Sounds   33

   The need for a special nomenclature, 49
   Consonant, vowel, and phoneme defined, 65

4. Detailed View of the Sounds of English Speech   81

   Résumé, 81
   English vowels, 90
   English diphthongs, 95
   Unstressing in sentences, 110
   Some stressed and unstressed pairs of vowels, 115
   Duration of stressed vowels in English, 117
   English consonants, 120
   Observations on distinguishing between voiced and voiceless plosives, 123
   An observation on the vocal component of voiced consonants, 123
   The glottal stop and its functions, 127
   Nasals, 128

5. Sound Change   146

   Physiological causes of sound change, 151
   Psychological causes of sound change, 152
   Sociological causes of sound change, 152
   Specific sound changes, 152
   Special cases of assimilation, 155

PART TWO

6. Speech Regions of America 171

7. General American English: Standard and Substandard 182

   Standard General American English, 183
   Deviations from standard General American speech, 189
   Southern-General American Border substandard pronunciation, 192
   Urban substandard speech, 193
   Deviations from standard General American, Southern, and Eastern
   speech, 193

8. Southern American English: Standard and Substandard 205

   Standard Southern speech, 205
   Deviations from standard Southern American speech, 212
   Miscellaneous substandard pronunciations, 220

9. Eastern American English: Standard and Substandard 221

   Standard Eastern speech, 222
   Deviations from standard Eastern speech, 233
   Urban substandardisms, 235

10. Standard Southern British: "Stage Speech" 239

    Plays requiring or permitting stage speech for the grammatically accurate
    portions, 239
    Sound system of Southern British (stage) speech, 240

PART THREE

11. Cockney 247

    Some important pronunciation features of Cockney vowels, 251
    Some important pronunciation features of Cockney consonants, 252
    Characteristics of standard Southern British speech peculiarly necessary
    to the pronunciation of Cockney, 254

12. Scottish 256

    Some characteristics of standard Scottish pronunciation, 258
    Deviations from standard Scottish, 262
    Some dialectal features evident in spelling, 262

13. Irish 273

14. Speech of New York City: Standard and Substandard 280

Deviations from standard New York speech, 281

15. Substandard Southern Negro Speech 293

Features of substandard Negro speech held in common with substandard
American speech in general, 297
Features of substandard Negro speech held in common with substandard
Southern white speech, 298
Specific features of substandard Southern Negro speech, 299

16. Mountain Speech 303

Features of Mountain speech held in common with substandard General
American, Southern, and Eastern speech, 305
Features of Mountain speech held in common with substandard Southern
speech, 309
Pronunciation features regarded as peculiar to Mountain speech, 310
Pronunciation features classified according to certain linguistic formulae,
314
Stressing and unstressing, 315

PART FOUR

17. French: Including Louisiana French and French-Canadian 325

Notes on pronouncing French sounds, 326
Silent letters in French, 331
"Open" and "close" vowels; "open" and "closed" syllables, 334
The sounds of French, 335
Sounds of French not in English, 349
English sounds not in French, 349
French-English dialects, 350
French-Canadian, 352
Louisiana French-English, 354

18. German 364

Non-English sounds in German, 366
The spelling of German sounds, 367
Comparison of German and English sounds, 393
German substitutions in English, 394

18. German: (continued)

Some of the problems of foreign dialect in English, 397
Exercises in German dialect, 398

19. Pennsylvania German ("Pennsylvania Dutch")   403

20. Yiddish   411

Models for Yiddish speech, 412
Yiddish as it is written, 413

21. Norwegian   419

Intonation, 420
Sounds of Norwegian, 421
Sounds of English not found in Norwegian, with probable Norwegian substitutions, 427

22. Italian   431

Some important pronunciation features of the Italian language, 432
The sounds of Italian, 435
Some characteristics of Italian contexts and their effects on English pronunciation, 447

23. Spanish: Including Mexican   455

Sounds of Spanish, 456
Reduction, 466
Spanish dialect, 467

24. Russian   475

The English and Russian sound systems, 477
Pronouncing Russian vowels, 478
Pronouncing Russian consonants, 481
Russian pronunciation of English vowels, 504
Russian pronunciation of English consonants, 507

25. Brazilian Portuguese Dialect: The Sounds of Brazilian Portuguese; the Brazilian Dialect of English   512

Detailed account of Brazilian Portuguese sounds, 514
Brazilian Portuguese sounds not in English, 530
English sounds not in Brazilian Portuguese, 530

Index   533

PART ONE

CHAPTER 1

The Purpose of This Book

Stated in the broadest possible terms, the purpose of this book is expressed in the following outline:

To introduce the student rapidly to the use of the International Phonetic Alphabet (IPA) as a tool applied to

English.
Certain foreign languages.

To explain the more important characteristics of

General American speech.[1]
Standard.
Substandard.
Southern American speech.
Standard.
Substandard.
Eastern American speech.
Standard.
Substandard.
Standard Southern British speech.

---

[1] The designations General American, Southern, and Eastern for the great English speech regions of North America are those common to the phonetic literature of the past half-century. The term General American does not mean general for the whole area, but belongs rather to that area not designated Southern or Eastern. (See full discussion, Chapter 6.) All three terms refer to pronunciation rather than to word selection or syntax. Hans Kurath, in *Word Geography of the Eastern States* (Ann Arbor: The University of Michigan Press, 1949), a book on word selection, not pronunciation, uses the terms Northern, Midland, and Southern. (See discussion, Preface, q. v., and Chapter II, pp. 11 ff.) Kurath's excellent maps trace word boundaries from the coast inland approximately to the western edge of the Appalachians. The boundary between Northern and Midland has since 1949 been continued, though with less definiteness, across northern Pennsylvania, central Ohio and Indiana, and a part of south-central Illinois. Until such boundaries have been projected as far west as possible, and attested throughout in terms of pronunciation as well as lexicon, it seems necessary to continue using the already established names for the speech areas of the country as a whole. The older boundaries can, of course, be corrected as newer information is available. (See Chapter 6.)

3

To explain the more important characteristics of

British regional dialects, including Scots, Irish, and Cockney.

American provincial dialects, including Mountain, Negro, and New York.

To explain the more important characteristics of dialects of English spoken by foreigners or related to foreign languages. These dialects include German, Pennsylvania German, Norwegian, French (including Louisiana French and French-Canadian), Spanish (including Mexican), Italian, Brazilian Portuguese, and Russian.

Persons for whom this book is intended. The information imparted in the pursuit of these purposes is intended primarily to be useful to any speaker of a standard American or British dialect; and to teachers, speech correctionists, actors, play directors, interpretative readers, radio and television speakers, and all others to whom information on dialects would be valuable. Secondarily, it is intended that the material of the book be of service to students of some foreign languages, to foreign students of English, and to students of the phonetic aspect of contemporary languages in general.

Limitation of scope of this book. As stated in the preface, this work does not permit itself extensive excursions into linguistic history, phonemics, or even theoretic or pure phonetics. Such references as are made to these and related fields of thought are intended only to support the aim epitomized in the title *Applied Phonetics*.

Intentional delay in presenting most phonetic theory, technical nomenclature, and definitions. It is important to note that most of the theoretic material and technical nomenclature included herein, as well as many of the definitions, are delayed until enough of the phonetic alphabet has been presented to constitute a vocabulary for discussion and illustration. This is not the usual arrangement; but it has been found rewarding, in that each item of information is seen to be serviceable when it finally appears.

Students are particularly gratified when they are not asked to use, or even to read, phonetic symbols to which they have not been formally introduced. The progressive introduction of an exclusive few symbols at a time greatly facilitates the orderly learning of the phonetic alphabet, which, though it need not be a serious task, sometimes becomes one when approached in some other fashion.

CHAPTER 2

Sounds and Symbols

A Preliminary View of the Sounds of English and the Phonetic Symbols Representing Them

The need for a phonetic alphabet. It has become traditional to explain the need for a phonetic alphabet by calling attention to the inconsistent spelling of most languages. These inconsistencies are indeed bewildering. They take two opposing forms: (1) the representation of the same sound by a variety of spellings, and (2) the use of the same spelling for a variety of sounds. For illustration of (1), observe the following list, where each line shows the same sound spelled in a different way. (Beginners may disregard the phonetic symbols until after finishing the chapter.)

English [eɪ]: n*a*me, n*ay*, br*ea*k, br*ai*d, *eigh*t, th*ey*.
German [i]: *I*gel, *ih*n, v*ie*l.
Norwegian [ɔ]: kl*o*kke, *Aa*se, *å*tte.
French [ɛ]: ch*ai*se, r*ei*ne, c*e*tte.
Spanish [b]: *v*oz, *b*oca.
Italian [k]: *ch*e, *c*asa.
Portuguese [ʒ]: *g*erais, *j*ota.
Russian [ʃ]: *ш*аг, му*ж*.

For illustration of (2), observe in the following that each line shows the same letter representing a different sound:

English: c*o*ld [oʊ], c*o*t [ɑ, ɒ], c*o*rn [ɔ], pr*o*ve [u], l*o*ve [ʌ], w*o*man [ʊ], w*o*men [ɪ].
German: i*ch* [ç], a*ch* [x], wa*ch*sen [k], s*ch*ön (*sch* = [ʃ]).
Norwegian: *g*ud [g], *g*ifte [j].
French: donn*er* [e], f*e*mme [a], l*e* [ə], cli*en*t (*en* = [ɑ̃]).
Spanish: *c*errar [s, θ], *c*ada [k], *ch*ico (*ch* = [ʧ]).
Italian: *s*pecie [s], *s*gelare [z].
Portuguese: *c*ama [k], *c*inco [s], *ch*apeu (*ch* = [ʃ]).
Russian: *х*орощо [ə-a-ɔ].

5

Conditions such as these examples show establish the need for an alphabet constructed on the plan of one sound per symbol and one symbol per sound.[1] Such an alphabet is the IPA, or International Phonetic Alphabet, to be taken up a few paragraphs farther on.

The need for a consideration of speech sounds as such. Even greater than the need for a simple, consistent alphabet is the need to consider speech sounds as such, apart from symbols. A speech sound[2] is an entity in itself, entirely separate from any letter or letters representing it. It comes first both phylogenetically, i.e., in the development of the race; and ontogenetically, i.e., in the development of the individual. The symbol is an afterthought, growing out of the need (before telegraph, telephone, or radio) to communicate at a distance, either in time or space.

But in our modern educational experience, we often confuse sound and symbol, and we fail to separate sound combinations or complexes into their individual parts. A written or printed word becomes a unit configuration recognized as a whole, and we take no thought of its components, either functional or non-functional. For silent reading this is as it should be, but not for accurate or perfected speech. It may not usually be realized, for example, that of the six letters in *knight*, only three are pronounced, viz., *n*, *i*, and *t*, and that, paradoxically, two of the four sounds in the word as pronounced are represented in the spelling by only one letter, the letter *i*. But this is true, and from the viewpoint of developing good audible speech it must be realized.

Observations on "Silent" Letters in English

English orthography (spelling) is characterized by the presence of numerous unused letters, many of which were formerly pronounced and, as in the case of the *t* in *listen* [ˈlɪsn̩], have been carried along in the spelling after their day of usefulness was past. Others have been added by analogy, as when Middle English (ME) *delit* was respelled *delight* by analogy with *light*. Still other words had extra letters added as a kind of learned gesture; for instance, the Old French (OF) loan word *dette* was respelled *debt*, as if it had been borrowed directly from the Latin *debitus* instead of from the OF.

In the case of loan words, some of the currently silent letters have never been pronounced in English; for example, *p* in *pneumonia*.

---

[1] Later to be explained as either one *phone* (sound) per symbol or one *phoneme* (to be discussed) per symbol, according to the requirements of a given time. As is the usual custom, phonetic symbols in this book will be enclosed in square brackets, [ ], and phonemic symbols in diagonals or virgules, / /.

[2] The distinction between a speech sound from the point of view of physics and from the point of view of psychology will be made later.

Exercise

Show that the word *reading* has two more letters than sounds.
Show that the word *cure* has one unpronounced letter, yet allocates two sounds to one of the letters.
Show that the words *mints* and *mince* may be pronounced exactly alike.
Show that the word *through* contains only three sounds.

If any statement in the exercise above does not seem reasonable or self-evident, it is of no great matter at the moment. It merely demonstrates that sound and spelling many times disagree, and that the beginner often finds it difficult to isolate the sounds in a word. Once the concept of each sound as a separate entity is established, it will soon become clear that every statement in the exercise is quite accurate. The development of sensitivity to sound, so that the speaker can be conscious of what he utters, can compare the sounds he uses with those of other people, and can contrast the sounds of his language with those of other languages, is a paramount need in the life of every educated person.

Definition of phonetics. The developmental process envisioned above involves an activity which could very well be called the study of phonetics. Since phonetics ordinarily disregards non-significant sounds, and since this developmental process is essentially a process of abstracting from the continuum of what we call "speech sounds" the individual fractions of sound which have significance, we may say that *applied phonetics is the study of significant speech sounds.* Such a study recognizes, but does not deal at length with, the following in sequence: (1) stimuli to the nervous system; (2) neural response; followed by (3) muscular action of frequently very generalized nature, but typically centered in what are called the organs of speech; (4) resultant sound waves, (a) in the air, (b) in the tympanum of the listener's ear, (c) in the ossicular chain of the middle ear, (d) in the endolymph of the cochlea; (5) nerve current to the brain, interpreted there as acoustic phenomena (speech as heard). Phonetics may be redefined as a study of (3) above, the action of the vocal organs in speech, and of (5) above, speech sounds as heard. (Chapter 3 gives minimal details relating to this definition.)

The International Phonetic Alphabet. The IPA is one of many alphabets which have been devised to fill the needs we have indicated. One such alphabet was invented (*circa* 1867) by Alexander Melville Bell (1819–1905), of Edinburgh, Scotland (later of Washington, D.C.), father of the inventor of the telephone, Alexander Graham Bell (1847–1922). Alexander Melville Bell called his alphabet *Visible Speech.*[3] *Visible Speech* had the remarkable quality of showing by the

---

[3] Cf. Henry Sweet, *Primer of Phonetics*, Second Edition (Oxford: The Clarendon Press, 1902), pp. 1–88. The symbols used on page 8 are those of the Organic (revised *Visible Speech*) notation. Cf. also *Handbook of Phonetics* (Oxford: The Clarendon Press, 1877).

structure of its symbols the most important facts concerning how the sounds are produced. The words *Visible Speech* in Bell's alphabet follow.[4]

⟩ʃʃᵣɵꞷ ꜱɒʃꞔꝺꞙ

This alphabet is still used in some schools for teaching the deaf.

The forbidding, unfamiliar appearance of *Visible Speech* induced Henry Sweet (1845–1912), a British phonetician and a pupil of Bell, to devise an alphabet on the basis of the more familiar Latin or Roman alphabet. Sweet called his alphabet *Romic*, which he used in two forms, *Broad Romic* and *Narrow Romic*.[5] Here are the words *Broad Romic* in Sweet's alphabet: [brɔd ˈroumik]. In 1886, when the International Phonetic Association was founded, it based its alphabet on *Broad Romic*. The IPA, with remarkably few modifications, is still in use, and is employed by more people than is any comparable alphabet. It may be found in many books and in many scholarly periodicals, among which is the official organ of the International Phonetic Association, *Le Maître Phonétique*.[6]

The identity of many IPA symbols with orthographic symbols. Many of the IPA symbols are identical with the orthographic symbols used as the letters of ordinary spelling. This fortunate situation greatly facilitates rapid learning of the alphabet. Some sixteen of the letters of the English orthographic alphabet, taken in their most common interpretation, are identical with an equal

[4] Other alphabets of early date (Cf. Alexander J. Ellis, *Early English Pronunciation*, E.E.T.S. Extra Series, Parts I and II, pp. 31–48): (a) Those attempted by Orm (circa 1200); Sir Thomas Smith, John Hart, William Bullokar (16th Century); Alexander Gill, Charles Butler, John Wilkins (17th Century). (b) That of James Buchanan (1776); also of Benjamin Franklin (1706–1790), who in 1768 devised a reformed spelling alphabet that was essentially phonetic. (He would have transcribed his own name as [bendʄʌamin fraŋklin].) Cf. Jared Sparks, *The Works of Franklin*, Vol. VI, pp. 295–303; also C. M. Wise, "Benjamin Franklin, Phonetician," *Speech Monographs*, 1948. (c) That of S. S. Haldeman (1860); also of Alexander J. Ellis, called Paleotype. (Ellis would have transcribed the word *Paleotype* thus: [peeliotəip]. Cf. Ellis, *op. cit*, pp. 3–12, 1869.) Ellis made another alphabet called Glossotype, which he used for compiling glossaries of dialectal speech. Cf. Ellis, *op. cit*, pp. 13, 607 ff. (d) A. J. Ellis and Isaac Pitman (1845) combined forces to make an alphabet which developed into several forms. Ellis, *op. cit*, pp. 24, 607. (e) The alphabets of continental scholars, such as Lepsius (1863), Max Müller, Rapp, Brücke, Merkel, *et al.*

[5] Sweet, *Primer of Phonetics*, pp. 76–88.

[6] As of this date, published at University College, London, W. C. 1, A. C. Gimson, Editor. First published, 1886.

number of the symbols of the phonetic alphabet. These letters are *p, b, t, d, k, g, l, m, n, r, f, v, s, z, h, w.* By placing these in square brackets, we have the corresponding phonetic symbols, thus: [p, b, t, d, k, g, l, m, n, r, f, v, s, z, h, w]. Here we have sixteen of the twenty-three commonly designated consonant symbols of English phonetics,[7] already learned, as it were. The remaining seven will be taken up at suitable points later.

How to transcribe. If to these already known consonant symbols, certain of the seventeen commonly designated vowel symbols of English phonetics are added, we can transcribe English words in phonetics, i. e., write them in phonetic symbols rather than in ordinary orthographics, and thus make a beginning in developing the necessary sensitivity to isolated speech sounds as such. Transcription will be found to be essentially a process of setting down one symbol for each sound.[8]

[i] *and* [ɪ]

It is simplest to begin with the two vowel symbols [i] and [ɪ].[9] The symbol [i] is used to represent the vowel sound in the second syllable of each of the following three words: *police, machine, cerise.* It likewise represents the vowel sound in each of the four words: *meet, beat, seem, brief.* We can now transcribe these four words respectively as [mit, bit, sim, brif].

> *Transcribe:* bead, beads, beast, beasts, beet, beets, bee, bees, bean, beans, ceil, ceils, deed, deeds, deal, deals, eat, eats, eel, eels, ease, feat, feats, feet, feel, feels, feed, feeds, geese, heed, heeds, heel, heels, he's, keel, keels, keen, key, keys, keyed, lea, leas, Lee, Lee's, leek, leeks, leaks, lean, leans, leaned, leal.

The symbol [ɪ] is used to represent the vowel sound in *it, bit, sill.* These may be transcribed respectively as [ɪt, bɪt, sɪl].

> *Transcribe:* bin, bins, bill, bills, billed, bid, bids, bits, Billy, Billy's, did, din, dizzy, Dick, Dick's, dim, dims, fin, fizz, gill (of a fish), gig, gigs, gigged, him, his, hid, hill, hills, hilly, kid, kids, kid's, kiss, kissed, kill, kills, killed, lit, lid, lids, list, lily, lilies.

Suggestions on problems encountered in the foregoing. It may be surmised that certain problems have arisen in the preceding work with [i] and [ɪ]. The following are suggested solutions to some of these, and answers to some related questions:

---

[7] The definition, description, and classification of consonants is being delayed (in accordance with the plan indicated on page 4) until a minimum familiarity with a number of the symbols is established.

[8] But see footnote 1, page 6.

[9] As in the case of the consonants, definition and classification of vowels will be delayed until a minimum familiarity with a limited number of symbols is established.

1. What names shall be used in speaking of phonetic symbols? The accepted practice is an arbitrary one; some symbols are referred to by their common letter names and some by their actual sounds. The sixteen consonants already given are simply called by their letter names, largely because the actual sounds of some of them, especially [p, b, t, d, k, g], are difficult to pronounce in isolation loudly enough to be easily heard in conversation. The symbols [i] and [ɪ], on the other hand, are referred to by their actual sounds, never by their letter names. As new symbols are introduced, the customary names used in speaking of them will be given. *Note the next paragraph closely.*

2. But whether a symbol is spoken of by its letter name or by its sound, in transcription *it must be thought of by its sound only.* Thus we must think of the sounds in *bid* so as to transcribe them [bɪd]; it would be ridiculous if we thought of them as *bee-eye-dee* and tried to transcribe them thus.

3. In *beads* it becomes evident for the first time that *s* is often pronounced [z]. The change from [s] in *beats* [bits] to [z] in *beads* [bidz] is a quite orderly one, which will be discussed in due course. Meanwhile, listen for the sound when each word is pronounced. If the sound is [s], set it down; if [z], set down [z].

4. *Ceil* [sil] presents the problem of [s] spelled with *c*. This is a frequent occurrence, as in *cease* [sis], *cystic* [ˈsɪstɪk], *cede* [sid].

5. The transcription [ˈsɪstɪk] introduces the matter of accent, usually called "stress" in this book. In IPA, primary stress is marked by a vertical stroke above and to the left of the stressed syllable, as in the preceding example. The mark for secondary stress is a vertical stroke below and at the left of the syllable, while weak stress has no mark at all.[10]

6. It is continually evident that it is impossible to represent each letter of the spelling with a phonetic symbol. Do not try to do so. Disregard the spelling entirely and listen for the sounds as you pronounce the words. Write a symbol for each sound you can distinguish, no matter whether in the end you have more phonetic symbols than letters in the original word, or the same number, or fewer. In *it* [ɪt], the number of phonetic symbols and the number of letters are the same; in *geese* [gis], there are five letters but only three symbols. The word *keyed* illustrates unusually well the necessity to transcribe only enough phonetic symbols to represent the sounds present; despite the five letters, there are again only three phonetic symbols, [kid], and the visual appearance of two syllables is contradicted by the sound of the word as pronounced, which shows that there is only one syllable.

7. The word *Billy* may present a particular problem. Some may hear the *y* as

---

[10] It is important to note here that in modern descriptive linguistics four stress phonemes are recognized, *viz.*, primary, secondary, tertiary, and weak, marked thus: [ˊˆˋ˘]. The following words illustrate the four: *lóng-bòw*, *a lông bów* (i.e, not a long arrow), *lóngĭsh*. Phonemic secondary stress is included under IPA primary, and phonemic tertiary stress is identical with IPA secondary.

[ɪ] and some as [i]. As a matter of fact, good argument can be adduced for either sound. For the present, it is recommended to use [ɪ]. Explanations will be given in due course. The word will, accordingly, be transcribed [ˈbɪlɪ]. The same suggestion will apply to *Billy's, dizzy, hilly, lily, lilies.*

8. Do not use capital letters at any time in phonetic symbolization in English; some capital letters are symbols for sounds in other languages.

Most people print all the phonetic symbols given so far, except [g], which is rather difficult to print, and which is therefore done in script. However, [p, b, t, d, k, h] are very acceptable in script. [z] has to be printed, since [ʒ] is a separate symbol, as will be seen later.

9. Punctuate as usual, but do not use the apostrophe in contractions like *he's* [hiz] nor in possessives like *Lee's* [liz].

With the foregoing nine explanations and directions in mind, we may turn to a word list wherein [i] and [ɪ] are both used.

Transcribe: mean, means, Minnie, Minnie's, meed, mid, meal, mill, miss, meek, Mickey, Mickey's, neat, nick, knee, knees, knit, knits, pit, Pete, pits, Pete's, peel, pill, peal, peels, peals, pills, peeled, pealed, peek, pick, peeks, peak, picks, peaks, peeked, picked, pin, pins, pinned, rid, reed, read, rick, reek, reel, rill, rims, ream, rib, silly, seal, seed, Sidney, seedy, sieve, easy, see, sea, tea, teak, tick, teal, till, Tim, 'tis, tinny, physics, vim, veal, wit, weal, zeal.

[ε] *and* [æ]

The phonetic symbol [ε] is used to represent the vowel sound in such words as *set* [sεt], *met* [mεt], *guest* [gεst], *wed* [wεd]. Its own sound is used as a name in speaking of [ε]. Some speakers unconsciously change [ε] to [ɪ] when it occurs before *m, n,* or *ng.* Thus, instead of *went* [wεnt], *fence*[fεnts],*friend* [frεnd] they may fall into the habit of saying [wɪnt],[fɪnts],[frɪnd]. Some may take the opposite direction, pronouncing *since* [sɪnts] as if it were *sense.* In the paragraph of transcription immediately following, there is no word containing [ɪ].

Transcribe: bet, bed, Ben, best, bend, bent, bread, breast, beg, Bess, bell, beck, best, cell, cent, dead, desk, dell, den, dens, dents, dense, ell, end, fen, fend, fenced, guessed, get, head, Hess, help, kelp, kept, let, lend, led, lest, lead (a metal), tempt, tempts.

Suggestions. 1. Remembering that there is no vowel except [ε] in the foregoing, be sure to pronounce that vowel and no other in each word. Let the first two words, *bet* [bεt], *bed* [bεd], set the vowel pattern, and hold to that vowel throughout the list.

2. The two words *dents* and *dense* raise a particular problem. Pronounce them in succession. It will be observed that, in the pronunciation of nearly every speaker, they sound exactly alike. Any feeling that they are different is usually due to the spelling, and is therefore the report of the eye, not the ear. Since *dents* obviously contains [t], and since *dense* is usually pronounced identically,

it likewise usually contains [t]; both words are then pronounced [dɛnts]. There are arguments both for and against transcribing words like *dense* and *fence* with [t]. These will be taken up later. In the meantime, the student is advised to insert the [t].

The phonetic symbol [æ] is used to represent the vowel sound in words such as *bat* [bæt], *sat* [sæt], *fat* [fæt]. Exactly the same vowel is used in all the words in the next list. The name used in speaking of [æ] is the actual sound represented.

Transcribe: add, adze, adds, axe, bad, cad, cab, cat, cam, can, catch, dab, fad, gas, have, has, had, ham, hand, hands, lamb, lad, lack, lass.

Transcribe with [i, ɪ, ɛ, æ]: Bessie, east, paddy, empty, met, mats, fits, reedy, risk, man, man's, men, men's, rick, ready, net, knack, neck, nick, peeve, peg, pad, pewee, wrist, rest, wreck, wrack, quick, wrecked, racks, friendly, sweep, swept, quiz, west, quest, weed, win, swim, swam, sweet, sweat, zest.

[ɑ] *and* [ɔ]

The symbol [ɑ] is used to represent the vowel sound in words like *calm* [kɑm]. The symbol [ɔ] is used to represent the vowel sound in words like *wall* [wɔl]. The names for these symbols are the actual sounds represented.

Transcribe: psalm, call, hawk, alms, caught, cause, awe, awl, fawn, ball, balk, gall, gauze, haul, gauzy, halls, spawn, tall, raw, vault, saw, qualm, Paul, palm, malt, haw, fraud, bald, aught, augment, ought, bought.

[ʊ] *and* [u]

The phonetic symbol [ʊ] is used to represent the vowel sound in words like *full* [fʊl], *good* [gʊd]. The phonetic symbol [u] is used to represent the vowel sound in words like *boom* [bum], *rude* [rud], *food* [fud]. The names for these symbols are the actual sounds represented.

Transcribe: boost, rule, put, cool, stood, could, tool, would, ooze, foot, book, boon, ream, rib, scrap, look, soon, brim, loose, hood, sprawl, blue, crude, school, rune, rook, cook, cookie, wooed, wood, rue, roost, took, brisk.

[ʌ] *and* [ə]

The phonetic symbol [ʌ] is used to represent the vowel sound in words like *up* [ʌp], *cut* [kʌt], *ton* [tʌn]. The phonetic symbol [ə] is used to represent the vowel sound in the unstressed syllable of words like *above* [əˈbʌv], *commit* [kəˈmɪt], *command* [kəˈmænd, kəˈmɑnd]. The name of the symbol [ʌ] is its actual sound, but the actual sound of [ə] is so brief and insubstantial that it does not serve well for use as a name. Accordingly, the word *schwa*, a German modification of the Hebrew word *sheva*, is customarily used.

Transcribe, using [ə] *in all the unstressed syllables and marking all stressed syllables:* love, lug, bun, bust, cub, attack, attend, assist, run, son, sun, dove, commend, complete, applaud, appall, cull, cusp, stomach, approve, abut, stubbed, condemn, collect, consist.

Suggestion: Note that although the consonants are often doubled in the spelling of the words above, they are not doubled in the pronunciation. In fact, the doubling of a consonant in the spelling is a positive indication of a single consonant in the pronunciation. For example, to say [kəm-ˈmɪt], or [ət-ˈtɛnd], is at once seen to be wrong.

Stressing and Unstressing

The use of [ə] in unstressed syllables in words like *upon* [əˈpɔn] and the use of [ɪ] in words like *seedy* [ˈsidɪ] in various transcription lists preceding make it necessary to interrupt here the process of introducing the phonetic alphabet to explain a very old and very characteristic peculiarity of the English language called *"unstressing."* The word *"unstressing"* is, of course, a derivative of the word *"stress."*[11]

Stress defined. *Stress* is a word designating the relative loudness (force, intensity) with which a syllable is uttered.[12] The effect of this factor of loudness is to give to a syllable a relative prominence which distinguishes it from other syllables. And although stress affects the whole syllable, for the purposes of this discussion we may say that stress is the loudness (force, intensity) with which the *vowel* (or diphthong) of a syllable is uttered.

Degrees of stress. As will be developed at the proper point, there are several degrees of vowel force in English, ranging from primary, or strong, stress (for example, the vowel of the first syllable of *button* [ˈbʌtn̩]) to weak stress (as in the second syllable). Note: When a syllable does not contain one of the usually recognized vowels, as in the case of the second syllable of [ˈbʌtn̩], a stroke is placed under the appropriate consonant symbol to indicate that it is a vowelized consonant, and hence functionally a vowel, though often called a syllabic consonant. (See discussion, page 73.)

---

[11] Unstressing, as a natural corollary to stressing, was a feature of Indo-European, the ancient parent language of most European tongues. From Indo-European it descended via Primitive Germanic to West Germanic to Old English to Middle English to Modern English. By an analogous path it descended through West Germanic to Old High German to Middle High German to Modern High German. From Indo-European, through Italic and Latin it descended to French, and through Old Slavic to Russian. In English and Russian it affects every vowel sound, in German and French usually only the sound of the vowel *e*.

[12] In modern phonemics, as noted in footnote 10, p. 10; the four stress phonemes, /ˊˆˋˇ/, designated primary, secondary, tertiary, and weak, respectively, are regarded as being distinguished from each other by loudness, which may be roughly correlated with force or intensity.

Cf. H. A. Gleason, *Introduction to Descriptive Linguistics*, Chapter IV; Bernard Bloch and George L. Trager, "Outline of Linguistic Analysis," *Special Publications of the Linguistic Society of America*, 1942, sec. 37–(2), pp. 27–8; and George L. Trager and Bernard Bloch, "The Syllabic Phonemes of English," *Language*, July–Sept., 1941, p. 231. Trager and Bloch equate primary with *loud*, secondary with *reduced loud*, tertiary with *medial*, and weak with *weak*.

Our concern at this point is with the degree of stress in the lightly stressed vowel of the first syllable of *approve* [ə'pruv].[13] A vowel with this degree of stress is rather inconsistently called *unstressed*, which must not be understood to mean *without* stress, but rather with the *lightest* stress found in language, short of zero. In other words, what is more properly called in historical linguistics a vowel of *reduced grade*, is in phonetics customarily called an *unstressed* vowel.

Pronunciation of unstressed vowels. Some unstressed vowels in English take the form of [ɪ], as in the second syllable of *pity* ['pɪtɪ]; some of [ɪ] or [ə], according to dialect or community custom or individual habit, as in *reflect* [rɪ'flɛkt, rə'flɛkt]; some of [ə] only, as in *approve* [ə'pruv]. In far the larger number of instances an unstressed vowel is pronounced [ə].

There is, unfortunately, no letter in the ordinary alphabet to represent the sound of [ə]. Accordingly, it is represented, at one time or another, by every one of the vowel letters *a, e, i, o, u, y.*

The unstressed sound [ɪ] is basically represented by *i* or *y*, but nevertheless, if we draw upon the various dialects of English, we may find it used to pronounce every unstressed vowel letter except *o.*[14]

Vowel letter		Pronounced [ə]	Pronounced [ɪ]
a	pal*a*ce	['pæləs]	['pælɪs]
e	r*e*spect	[rə'spɛkt]	[rɪ'spɛkt]
i	Al*i*ce	['æləs]	['ælɪs]
o	*o*ppress	[ə'prɛs]	
u	lett*u*ce	['lɛtəs]	['lɛtɪs]
y	anal*y*sis	[ə'næləsəs]	[ə'nælɪsɪs]

The "correctness" of unstressed vowels. Let it be understood that there is nothing reprehensible in the use of [ə] and [ɪ] in unstressed syllables. On the contrary, it is incorrect not to use these unstressed forms in their proper places. The stage director who forces the actor to say [æ'pɔld] for *appalled* [ə'pɔld], and the teacher who requires her pupils to say [ɛk'spɛkt] for *expect* [ɪk'spɛkt] or [ɛk'sɪst] for *exist* [ɪg'zɪst] are violating one of the most important historical principles of the English language, and exemplifying a common form of pedantry and affectation.

---

[13] Corresponding to the various degrees of stress are modifications of pronunciation, which, taken together with the shifts of stress themselves (and particularly of duration factors), correspond in a general way to what in Indo-European linguistics is called *grade.* Indo-European had lengthened (prolonged) grade, or *Dehnstufe*; normal (full) grade, or *Vollstufe*; reduced grade, or *Schwundstufe*; and zero grade, or *Nullstufe*. Two of these degrees are exemplified above, viz., normal grade (first vowel of *button* ['bʌtn̩]), and reduced grade (first vowel of *approve* [ə'pruv]).

[14] Even *o* is pronounced [ɪ] in the substandard pronunciation of *alcohol* ['ælkə,hɔl] as ['ælkɪ,hɔl]. (See explanation of secondary stress mark [,] on p. 18.)

The need for foreign students to learn the English unstressing system.
It should be added for foreign students that the mastery of the English system
of unstressing is one of the most important ways of acquiring what is known
as a good English accent. Such students must bear in mind that only in stressed
syllables are vowels pronounced with what may be called normal value. In
unstressed syllables, vowels are reduced to [ə] or [ɪ]; as an inevitable concomitant, they are also reduced in intensity, i. e., loudness. Such pronunciation
will sound careless to the foreign student; but, paradoxically, in English the
speaker must be exceedingly *careful* to observe this apparent *carelessness* in
unstressed syllables.

**The need for English-speaking students to learn foreign stressing
systems.** Conversely, the English-speaking student must not let his habit of
using [ə] and [ɪ] in unstressed syllables carry over into other languages' except
in strict accord with the nature of the languages themselves. In Spanish and
Italian, this fashion of pronouncing unstressed syllables does not apply at all,
though there is an approach to it in the pronunciation of, e.g., lightly stressed
final *a* in Spanish *casa* [ˈkasa], and Italian [ˈkaza, ˈkasa]; in French and German,
it applies with the rarest exceptions only to the pronouncing of unstressed *e* as
[ə]; in Russian, it applies to the use of both [ə] and [ɪ] for a variety of vowel
letters, but in a complicated way only roughly comparable to the plan in English.

> *Transcribe and pronounce:* (Use [ə] or [ɪ] in the unstressed syllables according
> to your personal practice. Be sure to use [ə] only in unstressed syllables, and
> [ʌ] only in stressed syllables. Put in all appropriate stress marks.) atone,
> applaud, added, Adam, axle, affect, antic, attic, atlas, adzes, awful, boosted,
> Blundon, comma, corrected, ceaseless, candy, convicted, company, custom,
> comical, committed, devil, defend, digress, dismiss, exhibit, effected, extend,
> evince, evil, expand, faddist, facile, facade, gallant, gallop, haddock, headed,
> happily, Hazlitt, harass, husky, hovel, hoodlum, impact, impacted, levels,
> London, listed, limited, lucky, remove, ribald, refund, redeemed, rebuffed,
> reckless, repeal, risky, rusted, rabbit, suspend, submit, saloon, timid, timorous,
> Tilly, tooted, Upton, ugly, villain, vista, valley, vaulted, wonted, Walton,
> wistful.

The *diphthongs* [eɪ] *and* [oʊ]

We may temporarily define a diphthong as a complex of vowel sounds beginning with one easily identifiable sound and ending with another. A diphthong
functions as does a single vowel. At this point in our discussion it is pertinent
to consider only two diphthongs, [eɪ] and [oʊ]. When referred to in speaking,
these sounds are designated by their actual sounds, with sometimes the adjective
diphthongal prefixed.

The diphthong [eɪ] occurs in English in monosyllables and stressed syllables
like *weigh* [weɪ] and *today* [təˈdeɪ]. The diphthong [oʊ] occurs in such words as
dough [doʊ] and *below* [bɪˈloʊ, bəˈloʊ]. It may come as a surprise to beginners

that [eɪ] and [ou] are regarded as diphthongs, and are so pronounced by nearly every speaker. The impression that they are monophthongs (single, pure sounds) arises from the fact that they are sometimes spelled with the single letters *a* and *o*, as in *able* [ˈeɪbəl] and *so* [sou]. Actually, such spellings are not typical; on the contrary, they are the exception rather than the rule. Some spellings have a letter for [o] and a letter for [u], as in *poultry* [ˈpoultrɪ], or a letter for [e] and a letter for [ɪ], as in *eight* [eɪt], *braid* [breɪd]; or, failing in indicating the diphthong so completely by the spelling as do the foregoing, many words give notice of its presence by some other orthographic element, such as the *a* in *boat* [bout], the *a* in *break* [breɪk], or the final *e* in *trade* [treɪd] and *alone* [əˈloun]. The most frequent pronunciations of single orthographic *a* and *o* are entirely different sounds, as in *hat, hard, wall, hot, love, moss.*

In this use of the diphthongal [eɪ] and [ou] in monosyllables and stressed syllables, the English language differs sharply from most of the other languages of the world, where the pure vowels [e] and [o], as in French *été* [eˈte] and Spanish *como* [ˈkomo], are used instead. These sounds are referred to as *pure* [e] and *pure* [o].

It is partly this contrast of diphthongs with pure vowels in English and foreign languages that makes it necessary to show the difference in transcription. Foreigners are misled by English transcriptions using [e] and [o] for [eɪ] and [ou], and are thus confirmed in continuing to use their pure vowels in English, thereby pronouncing the English words with a conspicuous foreign accent.[15] Conversely, speakers of English who are not strongly sensitized to the presence of [eɪ] and [ou] in English will carry them over into foreign languages, and so make themselves correspondingly conspicuous for their heavy English accent. Compare the following:

English	*day*	[deɪ]	French	*des*	[de]
English	*lay*	[leɪ]	French	*les*	[le]
English	*say*	[seɪ]	Spanish	*se*	[se]
English	*bait*	[beɪt]	German	*Beet*	[be:t][16]
English	*low*	[lou]	Spanish	*lo*	[lo]
English	*know*	[nou]	Italian	*no*	[no]
English	*zone*	[zoun]	German	*Sohn*	[zo:n]

[eɪ] and [ou] in stressed syllables in English. Pursuant to the foregoing discussions, numerous examples of [eɪ] and [ou] in stressed syllables are to be

---

[15] In this connection it must be admitted that a single symbol does not always completely solve the foreigner's problem; Spanish pure [i] is an inaccurate substitute for the frequently diphthongal English allophones. Moreover, Spanish [i], being seldom as close (high) as English [i], and often nearly as open (low) as English [ɪ], is poorly adapted for distinguishing between English [i] and [ɪ], as in *seat* [sit] and *sit* [sɪt].

[16] The symbol [:] is a mark of extra length or duration.

found in the next paragraph. Students should take care to transcribe them as diphthongs, i.e., using two symbols for each.

Transcribe: ate, abate, await, abode, aweigh, approve, avail, bacon, bolted, baste, bone, bales, bane, boast, coast, cake, acclaim, code, coal, comb, deceive, distant, condole, dale, deign, desperate, debt, debit, deface, depose, fail, feign, faddist, gazes, gall, haul, hostess, hold, hailed, hale, hut, honey, hyssop, home, hook, lake, look, loom, lame, lucky, lovely, loosely, lazily, lonely, moan, mode, mould.

[e] and [o] in unstressed syllables in English. We may now return to the matter of unstressing. If a diphthong of English is unstressed, the usual result is the loss of the final element. In the case of [eɪ] and [oʊ], the loss of the final element reduces the diphthong to the pure vowels [e] and [o]. In addition, then, to the incessant use of [ə] and [ɪ] in unstressed syllables, there is an occasional use of [e] and [o] in such syllables in words such as *fatality* [feˈtælətɪ], *obey* [oˈbeɪ]. The use of [e] and [o] occurs only in syllables of very light stress, i.e., stress closely approaching that in unstressed syllables where [ə] and [ɪ] are appropriate, as in *sofa* [ˈsoʊfə], *intend* [ɪnˈtɛnd]. Words containing [e] are infrequent; those containing [o] are plentiful, but the [o] is often further reduced to [ə] in casual conversation. Cf. *window* [ˈwɪndo, ˈwɪndə].[17]

Transcribe: pillow, follow, potato, proceed, orate, rotate, bellow, mellow, hollow, opacity, opaque.

Level stress; secondary stress. The stress habits of the English language present two other patterns in addition to the simple contrast of stressed and unstressed syllables. These are called *level stress* and *secondary stress. Level stress* may be defined as a close succession of (usually two) primary or strong stresses. It occurs most typically in certain pairs of words where the force accorded the elements of the compound remains approximately balanced, i.e., approximately equally distributed. Thus, whereas in *postman* [ˈpoʊstmən] the first element appears to have absorbed attention at the expense of the second element so that the compound has come to be regarded as a single word with one stressed and one unstressed syllable, in the case of *handmade* [ˈhændˈmeɪd], each element is regarded as of equal importance, with level stress on each one.[18] Since the English language has, as yet, no invariable rule for hyphenation, sometimes words of level stress are written as one word, like *handmade*, sometimes with

---

[17] Note that [ɪ] can be used in stressed syllables as well as unstressed ones, as in [ˈwɪndo] above. (*Kitty* [ˈkɪtɪ] illustrates both uses.) An intermediate stage between [ˈwɪndo] and [ˈwɪndə] may be transcribed [ˈwɪndʊ].

[18] As indicated in footnote 10, p. 10, the stress on the first syllable of *handmade* is in phonemics called secondary stress, and the word is marked thus: *hândmáde.* But in phonetics it is convenient to consider *hand* as carrying a variant of primary stress, especially as the standard dictionaries so mark it.

a hyphen, like *twenty-twenty* [ˈtwɛntɪ-ˈtwɛntɪ], and sometimes with the elements entirely separate, like *baked beans* [ˈbeɪkt ˈbinz]. In combinations like *baked beans*, the use of level stress within words begins to overlap the stress patterns of sentences, which will be discussed later. In terms of exact mathematical measurements, such as might be made in a physics laboratory, level stress is not "level": i.e., the factor of loudness (intensity or force) is not precisely equal in the two words, e.g., in the combination *tin pan* [ˈtɪn ˈpæn]. But under the conditions of casual conversation, where close, overt differentiation of the degrees of stress are wanting, the two stress effects on *tin* and *pan* seem about equal acoustically, and that is all that is necessary in applied phonetics to justify the term, *level stress.*

Secondary stress is a degree of stress lying between primary stressing and unstressing. It shows most typically in words of three or more syllables, as in the last syllable of *aggravate* [ˈægrəˌveɪt], where the convenient contrast with primary stressing in the first syllable, [æg], and unstressing in the second syllable, [rə], makes its intermediate value clear. Secondary stress occurs also in a considerable number of words of two syllables, such as *canteen* [ˌkænˈtin]. It also occurs in many compounds, such as *railroad* [ˈreɪlˌroʊd], *roadway* [ˈroʊdˌweɪ], where the lesser element appears to have kept its identity better than in *postman*, but not so well as in *handmade*.

Since these matters of stress have been introduced at this point for their bearing on transcription, it is now pertinent to re-emphasize the fact that as to the diphthongs [eɪ] and [oʊ] and their opposite pure forms, [e] and [o], the pure forms occur in the generality of English speech only in unstressed syllables; conversely, [eɪ] and [oʊ] are used in syllables of both primary stress and secondary stress, as in *Ada* [ˈeɪdə] and *irritate* [ˈɪrəˌteɪt, ˈɪrɪˌteɪt], and in *Ora* [ˈoʊrə] and *semitone* [ˈsɛməˌtoʊn, ˈsɛmɪˌtoʊn]. In words of level stress, [eɪ] and [oʊ] will likewise be used, since the strong stresses are merely successive primary stresses, as may be seen in *day's pay* [ˈdeɪz ˈpeɪ] and *old rose* [ˈoʊld ˈroʊz].

Marking the three stresses. It has been noted in the examples preceding that secondary stress has been marked with a vertical stroke to the left and below the syllable in question. This distinguishes syllables of secondary stress visually from those of primary stress, which, as already explained, are marked with a vertical stroke to the left and above the syllable, and from unstressed (i.e., weakly stressed) syllables, which are unmarked. In the exercise which follows, it is necessary to distinguish primarily stressed syllables (including those of level stress), secondarily stressed syllables, and unstressed syllables, and to mark them accordingly.

NOTE: Dictionaries often omit marking certain secondary stresses, as in *im′itate* and *ex′tract* (noun), or are apparently inconsistent, as in *cat′mint′* and *cat′nip*. This book employs the narrower practice of marking all secondary stresses. Thus, [ˈɪməˌteɪt, ˈɪmɪˌteɪt], [ˈɛkˌstrækt], [ˈkætˌnɪp].

Transcribe, using [i, ɪ, eɪ, ɛ, æ, ɑ, ɔ, ou, ʊ, u, ʌ] *in syllables of primary and secondary stress, and* [ə, ɪ, e, o] *in unstressed syllables:* gold coast, sulphate, aggravated, easily, episode, prorate, propend, abbreviate, almsman, oatmeal, oatcake, oboe, lemon, sixteen, bedpost, fall rains, hatrack, back step, two-step, seventeen, cold roast, aerate, handball, handbook, handcuff, pitiful, bystreet, byway, bylaw, eightfold, eminent, two-faced, two-fisted, twopence, twosome, Negro, aorta.

[o] *or* [ə] *in polysyllables*

Choices between pure vowels and [ə] are not fixed, but vary according to rate of speaking. In the case of a number of words, such as *advocate*, a slow rate will permit the pronunciation of [o], while a rapid rate will reduce the vowel to [ə]. Thus we have two acceptable pronunciations of the same word, viz., [ˈædvoˌkeɪt, ˈædvəˌkeɪt].

Transcribe with both [o] *and* [ə], *and pronounce the words both ways:* accolade, abrogate, hemostat, neoplastic, electro-plate, phonograph, undemocratic, reprobate.

The sound [ŋ]

The phonetic consonant symbol [ŋ] represents the sound *ng* in *sing* [sɪŋ] or the sound of *n* in *ink* [ɪŋk] or *single* [ˈsɪŋgəl]. This sound is referred to in speaking by its actual sound, or by the name *eng*.

Transcribe and pronounce: (In pronouncing, be sure to use [ŋ] wherever it occurs, being careful never to substitute [n], nor to add a superfluous [g] or [k]. In some of the words, the *g* of the spelling is, of course, to be pronounced, as in *tingle* [ˈtɪŋgəl].) singing, swing, sang, sung, sink, sunk, mingle, Mengel, Kris Kringle, spangles, calibrating, photographing, safe playing, brink, Bronx, monkey, donkey, ankle, springing, hung, hungry, uncle.

[θ] *and* [ð]

The phonetic consonant symbol [θ] represents the sound of *th* in *thing* [θɪŋ]; the consonant symbol [ð] represents the sound of *th* in *this* [ðɪs]. The reasons for pairing the two together will be taken up on page 63 along with analogous pairs. It is sufficient to state at this point that the descriptive words *voiceless* and *voiced* apply to [θ] and [ð] respectively, [θ] consisting only of a whisper-like rush of air, and [ð] of a similar rush of air plus voice or tone. Pronouncing *thing* and *this* in succession will illustrate the contrast of the voiceless [θ] and the voiced [ð]. These sounds are referred to in speaking as *theta* [ˈθeɪtə] and *crossed d* respectively.

Transcribe: thin, thronged, they, them, thole-pin, that, those, thalamus, theory, theoretical, Methuselah, with, thwack, pithy, throes, throwing, threw, rhythmic, seethe, soothing, homeopath, athletic, broth, truths, booths, through road, lathe, bathe.

[ʃ] and [ʒ]

These phonetic consonant symbols are a voiceless-voiced pair like [θ] and [ð]. The symbol [ʃ] represents the sound of *sh* in *she* [ʃi], the *ssi* in *mission* [ˈmɪʃən], the *ti* of *action* [ˈækʃən], the *s* of *sure* and *sugar*, and the like; [ʒ] represents the *si* of *aphasia* [əˈfeɪʒə], the *z* of *seizure*, and the like. The sound [ʃ] is referred to in speaking by the name *esh;* [ʒ] by its actual sound.

> *Transcribe:* shame, sash, fishing smack, shackle, garage, prestige, casual,[19] profession, fission, adhesion, caution, visual, passion, menage, rouge, phonetician.

[tʃ] and [dʒ]

By combining [t] and [ʃ] to make the phonetic symbol [tʃ], and [d] and [ʒ] to make [dʒ],[20] we have another pair of voiceless-voiced consonant sounds. The symbol [tʃ] represents the sound of *ch* in *chalk* [tʃɔk], and [dʒ] represents the sound of *j* in *joke* [dʒoʊk], of *g* in *gem* [dʒɛm], and of *dg* in *ledge* [lɛdʒ]. These symbols are referred to in speaking by their actual sounds.

> *Transcribe:* chance, change, chisel, James, Jack, jewel, gentle, just, chuckle, chicken, judge, choke, catch, fetch, edge, fidget, gadget, chicory, chimney, digit, midget, itch, latch, ridge, hatchet, coach, cello, champion, chewing.

The sound [ʍ]

The phonetic consonant symbol [ʍ] represents a sound which is an approximate[21] voiceless counterpart to the voiced sound [w]. The sound represented by [ʍ] is that of *wh* in *which* [ʍɪtʃ]. Sometimes [hw] is used for [ʍ]. Though inaccurate, [hw] has some value to the beginner in helping to distinguish [ʍ] and [w]. In southern England and in parts of the eastern United States and Canada [ʍ] is not used. In these areas *which* and *witch* are homonyms, both being pronounced [wɪtʃ]. In other areas, the words are respectively [ʍɪtʃ] and [wɪtʃ]. Almost all words spelled with *wh* except *who* and *whole* and their derivatives may be pronounced with [ʍ]. This sound is referred to in speaking as voiceless [w].

> *Transcribe, using both* [ʍ] *and* [w]: (If your dialect does not use [ʍ], transcribe the words in *wh* a second time according to your own pronunciation.) whey, way; whale, wail; wheel, weal; Whig, wig; whinny, Winnie; whet, wet; wheat, whistle, whittle, wheeze, whimsy.

---

[19] The question of the reduction of [u] to [ʊ] or [ə] will recur on page 110.

[20] In English phonemics, [tʃ] and [dʒ], though phonetically separable, are shown structurally to be the single phonemes /tʃ/ and /dʒ/ (see discussion, page 138). The phonemic indivisibility of these sounds is expressed in this book by writing the symbols with a ligature joining them, thus [tʃ], [dʒ].

NOTE: Remember that phonemic symbols are enclosed in virgules, / /.

[21] See explanation, page 145.

The sound [ɾ]

The phonetic consonant symbol [ɾ] is used to represent the sound of *r* or *rr* between vowels as it is pronounced in parts of eastern United States and Canada and in southern England. In this use it is called the *linking r;* it is also called the *one-tap trill*, since it is made with a single flap of the tip of the tongue. It is used either within a word, as in *very* [ˈvɛɾɪ], or at the end of a word followed by another word beginning with a vowel, as in *hear it* [hɪɾ ɪt]. In the greater part of the United States and Canada, the ordinary [r], similar to the initial [r] in *row* [roʊ], is used instead of [ɾ].

NOTE: Many words spelled with *air, are, arr,* and *ear* are correctly pronounced with either [æ] or [ɛ] according to regional, community, or individual custom. Such words as occur in the exercise below, or later, may be transcribed either way, according to individual preference.

Transcribe both with [ɾ] *and* [r] *and pronounce both transcriptions:* carry, merry, cheery, cherry, fairy, ferry, hairy, Harry, hoary, fearing, bearing, marrying, endearing, searing, touring, tourist, luring, their uncle, their own, they are all gone, whereas, where is it, there it is, for England, for Africa, clear every stone, caring, story for adults, sure of himself, pour it, hear it, the care of it.

[ɜ], [ɝ], *and their alternation*

The phonetic symbol [ɜ] is used to represent the vowel sound in the Eastern and Southern American, and the British pronunciation of *bird* [bɜd]. There is no *r*-quality in [ɜ]; [ɝ], on the contrary, possesses *r*-quality, as is indicated by the portion of the *r* attached to the upper right of the symbol. Until proper explanations can be given regarding the pronunciation of [ɜ] and [ɝ], it is suggested that those to whom either sound is unfamiliar may defer trying to pronounce it.

The spellings for the two sounds are identical, and very diverse, including every vowel letter (plus *r*) in the conventional alphabet, except *a*, viz., *er, ir, or, ur, yr*, as well as the combinations *ear* and *our* and the isolated peculiarity *olo*. The sounds [ɜ] and [ɝ] are always stressed.

herd	[hɜd, hɝd]	*myrrh*	[mɜ, mɝ]
whirl	[ʍɜl, wɜl, ʍɝl]	*heard*	[hɜd, hɝd]
word	[wɜd, wɝd]	*journey*	[ˈdʒɜnɪ, ˈdʒɝnɪ]
turn	[tɜn, tɝn]	*colonel*	[ˈkɜnl̩, ˈkɝnl̩]

The sounds [ɜ] and [ɝ] are referred to in speaking either by their actual sounds or by the rather awkward designations *reversed epsilon* and *hooked reversed epsilon*.

Transcribe with [ɜ] *and* [ɝ] *according to your dialect:* pearl, journal, squirm, worm, twirl, curse, myrtle, worst, fern, colonelcy, journeyman, hurtful, worse, aspersion, disburse, reverse, cut-purse, curbstone, earnestly, burst, immerse, firstly, workable, burnished, furnace, attorney, occurrence.

[ɚ] *and its alternation with* [ə]

The phonetic vowel symbol [ɚ] is used to represent the sound of *er* in *sister* [ˈsɪstɚ] in the general American pronunciation. The sound [ɚ] has *r*-quality, as indicated by the hook at the upper right, from which arises its name, *hooked schwa*. Until such time as proper explanations can be made concerning the pronunciation of [ɚ], it is suggested that those to whom it is unfamiliar may defer trying to pronounce it.

The sound [ɚ] corresponds to [ə] as in *sister* [ˈsɪstə] in Eastern, Southern, and British speech. The spelling for the two sounds is identical, and largely duplicates the spellings for [ɜ] and [ɝ], consisting as it does of every vowel letter in the Latin alphabet plus *r*, viz., *ar, er, ir, or, ur, yr*, with some instances of the combination *our*, and with the alternate spelling *re* for *er* in some words derived from or through the French. The sound [ɚ], like [ə], occurs only in unstressed syllables.

attar	[ˈætɚ, ˈætə]	*lemur*	[ˈlimɚ, ˈlimə]
paper	[ˈpeɪpɚ, ˈpeɪpə]	*satyr*	[ˈseɪtɚ, ˈseɪtə]
tapir	[ˈteɪpɚ, ˈteɪpə]	*flavour* (Br., Can.)	[ˈfleɪvɚ, ˈfleɪvə]
actor	[ˈæktɚ, ˈæktə]	*center, centre*	[ˈsɛntɚ, ˈsɛntə]

Transcribe in your own dialect, taking care to use [ɜ, ɝ] *only in stressed syllables, and* [ɚ, ə] *only in unstressed syllables:* mercer, shirker, merger, further, murmur, murder, curler, worker, hurler, Turner, burner, learner, twirler, server, firmament, merganser, churn, Germany, urgency, fancier, squirrel, perfectly, imperfection, emerge, erosion, reactor, resurgence, pursue, ferment, factor, favor, odor, color, savor, odour, colour, mortar, martyr, favour, fakir, vector, sector, bachelor, theater, theatre, tartar, alternator, acceptor, juror, astylar, axilar, calendar, zephyr, Ophir.

The alternation of [ɒ] *and* [ɑ]

The phonetic vowel symbol [ɒ] is used to represent certain Eastern and British pronunciations. The sound [ɒ] suggests the sound [ɔ] in *vault* [vɔlt], but is noticeably briefer. Other differences can be noted, which will be taken up in due course. Until proper explanations are given, it is suggested that those to whom [ɒ] is unfamiliar defer trying to pronounce it. The sound in General American and Southern speech corresponding to [ɒ] is [ɑ] as in *balm* [bɑm]. The spellings for [ɒ] and [ɑ] are identical, consisting principally of instances of what is sometimes loosely called "short *o*," as in *got* [gɒt, gɑt], and sometimes of *a* after [w] or [ʍ], as in *what* [ʍɑt, wɒt], *waddle* [ˈwɑdḷ, ˈwɒdḷ], *watch* [wɑtʃ, wɒtʃ], *squab* [skwɑb, skwɒb].

Transcribe according to your own dialect: lot, folly, watch, wander, hotter, toddle, cotter, knotty, Polly, modesty, cobweb, oddity, wasn't, wad, wasp, possibility, abominate, comparable, qualify, totter, sod, besotted, wattle, watt, wallaby, wallow, wallop, whatnot.

The alternation of [a] and [ɑ]

The phonetic vowel symbol [a] is used in New England to represent, typically, the pronunciation of *ar* as in *hard* [had]. However, many New Englanders, and all other speakers, use [ɑ] in words like *hard*. For present purposes it may be said that [a] is intermediate between [ɑ] and [æ]. Full explanation will be given in due course. Until such explanation is given, it is suggested that those to whom [a] is unfamiliar defer trying to pronounce it. However, the instructions given under [aɪ] below may help most students to a correct pronunciation of [a].

Transcribe according to your own dialect: far, farther, ardent, army, article, parchment, parcel, tarpaulin, carpet, watchman, cartilage, charming, startled, harmony, archangel, partake, Arctic, fardels, parliament.

The sound [j]

The phonetic consonant symbol [j] is used to represent the sound of *y* in *yes* [jɛs]. The sound [j] functions in the combination [ju], which is the pronunciation of the spellings *u*, *eu*, *ew* (with variants), after [f, h, k, m, p, v] or initially, as in *feud* [fjud], *hew* [hju], *cute* [kjut], *mule* [mjul], *pew* [pju], *view* [vju], *use* [jus] (noun), [juz] (verb).

Transcribe: yellow, yesterday, yew, you, ewe, yule, mute, beauty, feudal, fume, useful, exude, cube, cue, culinary, queue, accuse, cupola, Cupid, accumulate, cumulative, accusation, yell, yawl, yacht, yaws, humor, humorous, hue, Hugh, huge, humanity, mew, muse, musical, fuse, abuse, abuses.

[aɪ], [aʊ], and [ɔɪ]

We may now close our preliminary survey of the sounds of English speech with the remaining diphthongs, [aɪ], [aʊ], and [ɔɪ].

NOTE: All of these diphthongs, as well as the diphthongs [eɪ] and [oʊ] already introduced, may be represented by several different combinations of symbols. The symbols used here are very commonly employed, and will serve until the progress of discussion brings up the need for others.

The symbols [aɪ] constitute the phonetic representation of the pronunciation of *ei* in *height* [haɪt], the *i* in *pride* [praɪd], the *y* in *fly* [flaɪ], and the like. Beginners can discover its diphthongal character by sustaining the pronunciation of the pronoun *I* over several seconds, whereupon the sound of the closing vowel, [ɪ], will be clearly heard; thus, [a::::::ɪ]. (The colon [:], as indicated on page 25, is used as a sign of lengthening or duration in phonetics. Its repetition here represents exaggerated lengthening.) The sound of the opening vowel, [a], can be isolated by pronouncing the same sustained tone but cutting it off suddenly and sharply without using the closing sound, [ɪ]; thus, [a::::::]. The sound [a] is also the first element of the diphthong [aʊ].

The symbols [aʊ] represent the diphthongal sound of *au* in *Faust* [faʊst], *ou* in *loud* [laʊd], *ow* in *crowd* [kraʊd], and the like.

The symbols [ɔɪ] represent the diphthongal sound of *oi* in *oil* [ɔɪl], *oy* in *boy* [bɔɪ], and the like.

> *Transcribe:* ride, round, roily, rail, roll, find, found, foil, frail, roach, ice, idle, idol, ivory, owl, ouster, oyster, oval, ace, age, chain, Jane, jounce, jolt, chowder, rice, broil, jowl, loin, scout, skate, foist, foul, roustabout, pounce, mountain, mighty, sleight, slate, heighten, frighten.

Summary of the Sounds of English: Key Words

A summary of the sounds of English as treated in this chapter follows, with key words in English and in various foreign languages. It must be understood that key words are at best a makeshift, helpful only to the degree in which the maker of the key word list and the reader pronounce alike. This is especially true of key words in languages other than the one being discussed. While it has seemed necessary to include non-English key words here for the benefit of non-English-speaking students, such students must be warned against assuming that the English sounds and the corresponding or analogous sounds are exactly alike; they are almost never exactly alike. Differences will be indicated in footnotes by numerals referring to later pages where detailed discussions will clarify matters. English-speaking students may for the time being disregard the foreign key words entirely.

In Chapter 3, more universal ways of explaining sounds than by key words will be suggested. Following the key word list is a chart of the IPA, including symbols for the sounds of a great many languages. This chart will be of frequent use throughout this book.

KEY WORD LIST FOR THE PRINCIPAL SOUNDS OF ENGLISH

With Certain Corresponding and Approximate Sounds
in German, Norwegian, French, Spanish, Italian, Russian, and Brazilian Portuguese

Notes

1. The numerals accompanying the symbols refer to later pages where the sounds are discussed in detail.

2. The asterisks refer to footnotes where gross differences between English and foreign sounds are mentioned, pending detailed discussions later. Foreign students should give close attention to these footnotes, to avoid establishing wrong habits of pronouncing the English sounds involved.

3. The only diacritic occurring in the following list is the symbol [:], placed after certain vowel and consonant symbols. This symbol indicates that the sound to which it applies is of longer duration than other corresponding sounds. Thus [ɑ:] is of longer duration than [ɑ], [i:] than [ɪ], [ɪ:] than [ɪ], etc. (see page 23). In the transcription of English in this book, [:] is used with vowels only in the rare instances when it is significant (i.e., used to distinguish between words of different meaning), but in the transcription of French, German, and Norwegian, phoneticians use it regardless of whether it is significant.

Sounds of English		Corresponding Sounds and Approximate Sounds in Other Languages						
IPA Symbols	English	German	Norwegian	French	Spanish	Italian	Russian	Brazilian Portuguese
[a][224]	E. *large* [lɑdʒ] First sound of [aɪ] in *fly* [flaɪ] and of [aʊ] in *how* [haʊ]	First sound in [aɪ] (variant of [ɑɪ])[392] in *Zeit* [tsaɪt, tsɑɪt]		*glace* [glas][337]	*pan* [pan][459]	*mano* ['mano][439]	да [da][480]	*pá* [pa][517]
[aɪ][103]	*lie* [laɪ]	Variant of [ɑɪ] in *Zeit* [tsaɪt, tsɑɪt]			Analog, [ɑɪ][461] in *hay* [ɑɪ]	Analog, [aɪ] in *mai* [maɪ][441]	Analog, [aɪ] in трамвай [tramˈvai][480]	Analog, [aɪ] in *pai* [pai][520]

Sounds of English

Corresponding Sounds and Approximate Sounds in Other Languages

IPA Symbols	English	German	Norwegian	French	Spanish	Italian	Russian	Brazilian Portuguese
[aʊ][104]	loud [laʊd]	Variant of [aʊ][392] in Haus [haʊs], haʊs	Analog, [æʉ][424] in sau [sæʉ]		Analog, [au][461] in causa ['kausa]	Analog, [au][441] in causa ['kausa]		Analog, [au][520] in auto ['autu]
[ɑ][104]	palm [pɑm]	Paar [pɑːr][390]	goddag [go'dɑːg][423]	âme [ɑːm][338]	mal [mɑl][460]		палка ['pɑlka][488]	mal [mɑl][517]
[ɒ][104]	E., Br. hot [hɒt]							
[æ][101]	mat [mæt]		være ['væːrə][423]				пять [pæt][488]	
[b][122]	be [bi]	Bett [bɛt][371]	blind [blinː][425]	bête [bɛːt][341]	boca ['boka][462]	barca ['barka][442]	борщ [bɔrʃtʃ][493]	baile ['baili][523]
[d][124]*	do [du]	du [duː][373]	·derfor ['dærfɔr][425]	des [de][341]	de [de][462]	dente ['dɛnte][442]	дом [dɔm][488]	dedo ['dedu][524]
[dʒ][138]	Jew [dʒu]				[dʒo][466] dialectal variant of yo [jo]	gente ['dʒente][447]		bonde ['bõndʒi][529]
[e][98]	vacation [ve'keɪʃən]	Deponent [depo'nɛnt][387]	sted [steː][423]	chez [ʃe][335]	se [se][458]	che [ke][437]	день [den][487]	beco ['beku][516]

* English [d] is alveolar, i.e., made with the tongue against the alveolar ridge somewhat back of the upper front teeth. (See page 48.) In the other languages, especially the Romance and Slavic languages, [d] is dental, i.e., made with the tongue against the upper front teeth. (See page 48.)

Sounds of English | Corresponding Sounds and Approximate Sounds in Other Languages

IPA Symbols	English	German	Norwegian	French	Spanish	Italian	Russian	Brazilian Portuguese
[eɪ][98]†	date [deɪt]		Analog, [ei][424] in grei [grei]		Analog, [ɛi][461] in ley [lɛi]	Analog, [ɛi][441] in pei [pei], Lei [lɛi]	Analog, [ei] in мужей [muˈʒei][491]	Analog, [ei] in lei [lei][520]
[ə][115]	soda [ˈsoʊdə]	knabe [ˈknɑːbə][392]	gjerne [ˈjæɜnə][424]	le [lə][339]			это [ˈɛtə][487]	
[ɛ][100]	met [mɛt]	des [dɛs][388]		tête [tɛːt][336]	el [ɛl][459]	bello [ˈbɛlːo][437]	этот [ˈɛtat][487]	fé [fɛ][516]
[ɜ][118]	E., S., Br. fur [fɜ]							
[ɝ][119]	G. A. fur [fɝ]							
[ɚ][119]	G. A. sister [ˈsɪstɚ]	Analog, [ɐr] in Vater [ˈfɑːtɐr]	Analog, [ər] in eller [ˈɛlar]					
[f][133]	face [feɪs]	fahren [ˈfɑːrən]	for [fɔr][426]	femme [fam][345]	fue [fwe][164]	facile [ˈfatʃile][144]	фуга [ˈfuga]	fim [fĩ][527]
[g][126]	get [gɛt]	Gabel [ˈgɑːbəl][374]	glad [glɑː][425]	guide [gid][342]	gota [ˈgota][462]	golfo [ˈgolfo][143]	бумага [buˈmaga][496]	gas [gaɾ][524]
[h][139]	heel [hil]	hat [hɑt][382]	heller [ˈhelar][127]					
[i][90]	seed [sid]	viel [fiːl][384]	fri [fri][422]	fils [fis][335]	sí [si][457]	sì [si][436]	один [aˈdʲin][486]	frito [ˈfɾitu][514]

† In all syllables of primary or secondary stress, English uses the diphthongal [eɪ] instead of [e]. (See pages 17, 18.) The monophthongal [e], such as the other languages use, is found regularly in English only in unstressed syllables. (See [e] immediately above; also pages 17, 18.)

Sounds of English		Corresponding Sounds and Approximate Sounds in Other Languages						
IPA Symbols	English	German	Norwegian	French	Spanish	Italian	Russian	Brazilian Portuguese
[ɪ][92]	bit [bɪt]	bis [bɪs][385]					улица ['uɪɪtsə][487]	
[j][139]	yet [jet]	ja [jɑː][382]	jord [joːr][427]	ciel [sjɛl][348]	ya [ja][465]	ieri ['jɛri][441]	Ялта ['jɑltə]	freio ['frei(j)u][528]
[k][125]‡	king [kɪŋ]	König ['køːnɪç][373]	kort [kɔrt][425]	que [kə][343]	que [ke][462]	che [ke][442]	кто [kto][495]	crime ['krimi][524]
[l][131]§	lie [laɪ]	legen ['leːgən][376]	lov [lɔːv][426]	les [le][344]	la [la][463], mal [mal]	la [la][444]	лоша ['lɔʃə][497]	lei [lei][525], cal [kaɫ][525]
[m][129]	meet [mit]	Mann [man][376]	merke ['mærkə][425]	ma [ma][344]	mi [mi][463]	membro ['mɛmbro][443]	май [mai][496]	ma [ma][524]
[n][130]§	nest [nɛst]	nein [nɑin][376]	ned [neː][425]	nez [ne][344]	no [no][463]	no [no][443]	нош [nɔʃ][497]	po [pɔ][524]
[ŋ][131]	sing [sɪŋ]	ring [rɪŋ][376]	langsom ['laŋsɔm][426]		banco ['baŋko][463]	banco ['baŋko][443]		banco ['beŋku][525]
[o][107]	notation [noˈteɪʃən]	so [zoː][390]	nord [noːr][424]	côte [koːt][338]	como ['komo][460]	otto ['otːo][439]		gôlfo ['golfu][518]

‡ English [p] and [k] are more aspirated (i.e., more plosive, especially in initial positions) than in the other languages.
§ English [l] and [n] are alveolar (except [l] in E., S., and Br. before front vowels), while in the other languages, especially the Romance and Slavic languages, they are dental, except final in a syllable in Portuguese.

Corresponding Sounds and Approximate Sounds in Other Languages

IPA Symbols	English	German	Norwegian	French	Spanish	Italian	Russian	Brazilian Portuguese
[ou][107] //	toe [tou]							
[ɔ][106]	law [lɔ]	Morgen ['mɔrgen][391]	norsk [nɔrsk][424]	coq [kɔk][338]	dos [dɔs][460]	motto ['mɔt:o][439]	Бог [bɔk][489]	golpe ['gɔłpi][517]
[ɔɪ][107]	toy [tɔɪ]	Analog, [ɔɪ] in Feuer ['fɔɪər][392]			Analog, [ɔɪ] in soy [sɔɪ][461]	Analog, [ɔɪ] in poi pɔi][441]	Analog, [ɔɪ] in тройца ['trɔɪtsə][492]	Analog, [ɔɪ] in sói [sɔɪ][520]
[p][120]	peel [pil]	pressen ['presen][369]	par [par][424]	pas [pɑ][341]	por [por][461]	pei [pei][442]	пол [pol]	padre ['padɾi][523]
[r][132] #	reel [ril]	reiten ['rɑitn][377]	rent [re:nt][426]	respect [rɛs'pɛ][345]	rey [rei][464]	ricco ['rik:o][444]	рас [ras][498]	
[ɾ][132]	E., Br. cherry ['ʧɛɾɪ]							caro ['kaɾu][526]
[s][135]	see [si]	das [das][380]	selv [sel:][426]	ses [se][346]	se [se][465]	si [si][444]	стол [stɔl][500]	sim [si][527]
[ʃ][136]	she [ʃi]	Spass [ʃpas][381]	ski [ʃi:][426]	crèche [krɛ:ʃ][348]	2nd element of [ʧ] cheque ['ʧɛke]	fascisti [fa'ʃisti][445]	Analog, retracted [ʃ] in что [ʧto, ʃtə]	chave ['ʃavi][528]
[t][124] **	tea [ti]	Tal [tɑ:l][371]	takk [tɑk:][425]	ta [ta][342]	tu [tu][462]	tempo ['tempo][442]	толк [tɔlk][494]	telha ['teʎa][524]

// In all syllables of primary and secondary stress English uses [ou] instead of the [o] which is used in other languages. Pure [o] is found regularly in English only in unstressed syllables. (See [o] above; also pages 17, 18.)

English [r] is retroflex (i. e., made typically—see page 132—with the tip of the tongue turned back) and is not trilled, while in Spanish, Italian, Norwegian, and Russian it is trilled with the point of the tongue, and in French and German, with either the point of the tongue or the uvula, symbols [r] and [R] respectively. Brazilian Portuguese has trilled [r] in some contexts. (See page 526.)

** English [t] is alveolar, while in the other languages, especially the Romance languages, it is dental. It is also more aspirate in English than in other languages, especially in initial positions.

Sounds of English   Corresponding Sounds and Approximate Sounds in Other Languages

IPA Symbols	English	German	Norwegian	French	Spanish	Italian	Russian	Brazilian Portuguese
[tʃ][138]	chew [tʃu]	Klatch [klatʃ][383]			chico ['tʃiko][465]	cera ['tʃera][447]	Чехов ['tʃexəf][447]	Analog, [tʃ'] in sete ['setʃ'i][529]
[θ][134]	thing [θiŋ]				Castilian cinco ['θiŋko][464]			
[ð][134]	this [ðɪs]		Not in Nor., but cf. Dan. hentet ['hɛntəð]		Colonial nada ['naða][465]			
[u][109]	tool [tul]	tun [tuːn][390]	uten [ɯːtn̩][424]	fou [fu][399]	cura ['kura][460]	cura ['kura][440]	рука [ru'ka][489]	soluço [so'lusu][518]
[ʊ][109]	took [tʊk]	Mund [mʊnt][390]			culpa ['kʊlpa][460]			
[ʌ][115]	up [ʌp]							
[v][133]	vain [vein]	was [vas][380]	ved [veː][426]	vous [vu][345]		verso ['vɛrso][440]	Ваш [vaʃ][493]	vaso ['vasu][527]
[w][144]	woe [wou]			oui [wi][348]	fuego ['fweɣo][466]	uomo ['wɔmo][441]		agua ['agwa][528]
[ʍ][145]	when [ʍɛn]							
[z][136]	zest [zɛst]	Seele ['zeːlə][381]		zèle [zeːl][346]		casa ['kaza][445]	зафтра ['zaftrə][500]	zona ['zõna][527]
[ʒ][137]	casual ['kæʒʊəl]	Fr. loanword charge ['ʃarʒə]		jamais [ʒa'mɛ][348]	Dialectal ['kaʒe] for colonial calle ['kaje]	2nd element of [dʒ] in giorno ['dʒorno][446] also dialectally in Tuscan regina [re'ʒina]	жив [ʒif][501]	geral [ʒe'raɫ][528] as lagos [aʒ 'laguʃ']

THE INTERNATIONAL PHONETIC ALPHABET

(Symbols ɜ and ɔ included)

CONSONANTS

	Bi-labial	Labio-dental	Dental and Alveolar	Retroflex	Palato-alveolar	Alveolo-palatal	Palatal	Velar	Uvular	Pharyngal	Glottal
Plosive	p b		t d	ʈ ɖ			c ɟ	k g	q ɢ		ʔ
Nasal	m	ɱ	n	ɳ			ɲ	ŋ	ɴ		
Lateral Fricative			ɬ ɮ								
Lateral Non-fricative			l	ɭ			ʎ				
Rolled			r						ʀ		
Flapped			ɾ	ɽ					ʀ		
Fricative	ɸ β	f v	θ ð s z	ʂ ʐ	ʃ ʒ	ɕ ʑ	ç j	x ɣ	χ ʁ	ħ ʕ	h ɦ
Frictionless Continuants and Semi-vowels	w ɥ	ʋ	ɹ				j (ɥ)	(w)	ʁ		

VOWELS

	Front	Central	Back
Close	(y ʉ u) (ʏ ʊ) (ø o)	i y ɪ ʏ	ɯ u ʊ
Half-close	(ø o)	e ø	ɵ o
Half-open	(œ)	ε œ	ʌ ɔ
Open	(ɒ)	æ œ	ɑ ɒ
		a ɐ	

(Secondary articulations are shown by symbols in brackets.)

OTHER SOUNDS.—Palatalized consonants: ƫ, ᶁ, etc. Velarized or pharyngalized consonants: ɫ, d̶, ẕ, etc. Ejective consonants (plosives with simultaneous glottal stop): p', t', etc. Implosive voiced consonants: ɓ, ɗ, etc. ř fricative trill. ơ, ǫ (labialized θ, ð, or s, z). ʓ, ʒ (labialized ʃ, ʒ). ʇ, ʖ, ʗ (clicks, Zulu c, q, x). ɫ (a sound between r and l). ʍ (voiceless w). ɪ, ʏ, ʊ (lowered varieties of i, y, u). ɜ (a variety of ə). ə (a vowel between ø and o).

Affricates are normally represented by groups of two consonants (ts, tʃ, dʒ, etc.), but, when necessary, ligatures are used (ʦ, ʧ, ʤ, etc.), or the marks ⁀ or ‿ (ʦ or ʧ, etc.). c, ɟ may occasionally be used in place of tʃ, dʒ. Aspirated plosives: pʰ, tʰ, etc.

LENGTH, STRESS, PITCH.—ː (full length). ˑ (half length). ˈ (stress, placed at beginning of the stressed syllable). ˌ (secondary stress). ˉ (high level pitch); ˍ (low level); ´ (high rising); ˏ (low rising); ` (high falling); ˎ (low falling); ˆ (rise-fall); ˇ (fall-rise). See Écriture phonétique internationale, p. 9.

MODIFIERS.—˜ nasality. ˳ breath (l̥ = breathed l). ˬ voice (ş = z). ˈ slight aspiration following p, t, etc. ˳ specially close vowel (ẹ = a very close e). ˓ specially open vowel (ẹ = a rather open e). ˷ labialization (n̫ = labialized n). ̪ dental articulation (t̪ = dental t). ˒ palatalization (ż = z). ˔ tongue slightly raised. ˕ tongue slightly lowered. ˒ lips more rounded. ˓ lips more spread. Central vowels ï (= ɨ), ü (= ʉ), ë (= ə⏑), ë (= ɵ), ö (= o̶). ˌ (e.g. ṇ) syllabic consonant. ˘ consonantal vowel. ʃ variety of ʃ resembling s, etc.

It will be remembered that this chapter set out to introduce the phonetic alphabet in the simplest possible terms. That has now been accomplished. The student should now be able to read material in phonetic transcription without much difficulty. He has, then, a body of necessary elementary knowledge at hand which will make the approaching more complete discussions intelligible, interesting, and useful.

CHAPTER 3

Production and Classification
of Speech Sounds

The preceding chapter has undertaken to present the sounds of English in the simplest possible fashion, for the principal purpose of establishing a working vocabulary of the sounds themselves, with the corresponding symbols and the names of the symbols. The function of this vocabulary is to facilitate further discussion, more analytic and definitive, ranging over the same sounds. The presentation has been deliberately limited thus far, thereby drawing upon little more than the student's conscious or subconscious recognition of the sounds of spoken English. It has, it is hoped, somewhat sharpened his sensitivity to sounds as such, whether in isolation or in the context of fluently uttered speech. We may now proceed to the more detailed consideration.

Speech as an overlaid function. It is a startling fact that, considering the paramount importance of speech, there are no organs of speech. That is, there are no organs whose primary function is speech. On the contrary, speech is an overlaid function,[1] achieved by means of organs whose primary functions are the vital ones of eating, drinking, and breathing.

The organs of eating, drinking, and breathing include the mouth, nose, pharynx, larynx, and lungs, with all the related parts of the nervous, glandular, circulatory, muscular, and skeletal systems, comprising actually a considerable part of the body. If passive parts of the body are included, such as the abdominal viscera, which, when compressed by the abdominal muscles, push upward on the diaphragm to force the air from the lungs in expiration, a very large part of the body indeed is involved in speech. If we include such special cases as those of people who have had the larynx removed, and who have learned to swallow air and expel it through the esophagus in such a way as to provide

---

[1] V. E. Negus, *The Mechanism of the Larynx* (London: Heineman, 1929), p. 7. T. P. A. Stuart, "On the Mechanism of the Closure of the Larynx," *Proceedings of the Royal Society*, V. 50, 1892, p. 323. H. S. Wise, "Speech—'The Overlaid Function?'" *Quarterly Journal of Speech*, February, 1938, p. 11.

some of the necessary speech sounds in what we loosely term *esophageal speech*,[2] we may even include the esophagus and the stomach as organs actively used in speaking.

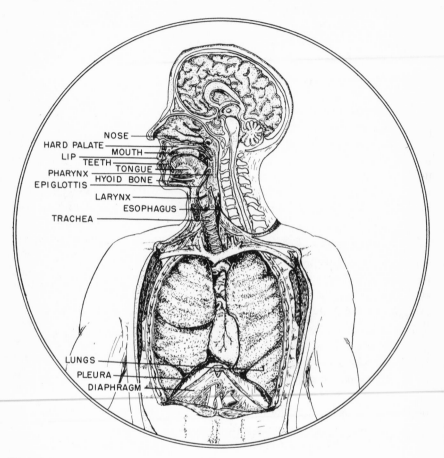

Figure 1. Location of the organs of eating, drinking, and breathing, which are used in speech.

Man not the sole possessor of the organs used in speech. Man is not alone in the possession of the organs used in speech. Other mammals possess them in all sorts of variations. Some mammals, e.g., cats,[3] have them in forms well adapted to speech, but lack the intelligence to make use of them in any but the most primitive and generalized fashion. It is possible, of course, to debate whether the communicative voice-sounds of animals constitute what may

---

[2] In esophageal speech some sounds have to be produced by means of air within the mouth and pharynx. Hence, the term esophageal speech, though convenient, is a loose one, just as pulmonic or lung speech is a loose term for ordinary speech.

[3] V. E. Negus, *The Mechanism of the Larynx* (London: Heineman, 1929), p. 284.

be called speech, just as it is possible to debate the related question of whether animals think. Such questions are beside the point here, since it is evident that no animal uses his voice in anything approaching human speech with its striking intellectual attributes. It may be added that birds, vultures excepted,[4] do possess an organ of voice, the syrinx, a membranous instrument located at the fork of the trachea.

Hearing as the complement to speaking. As a corollary to these comparative facts concerning birds, the lower mammals, and human beings, it may be speculated that the function complementary to producing vocal sounds, that of hearing, was first developed in all living beings to report to consciousness the sounds of nature, such as those of wind, water, and moving objects and creatures, rather than the sounds of each other's voices. Exception may be made for the hearing of what can be termed involuntary vocalization, such as accompanies the acts of eating, drinking, and breathing; indeed, since these involuntary vocalizations no doubt imperceptibly merged into voluntary ones, they probably constituted a bridge toward those intentional and meaningful vocalizations which have become the most important sounds ever to be heard. With birds, the development of hearing to report to consciousness the sound of other birds' voices, together with all other sounds, probably came about as a single process. In any case, it is evident that, as mammalian intelligence increased, the voluntary use of the borrowed organs for vocal signaling developed and increased also. It finally climaxed with the human achievement of making audible signals into a code capable not only of sustaining communication on the primitive level, concerning such elemental things as food, danger, and sex, but also on levels reaching progressively higher, up to that of philosophical abstraction.

The varieties of speech sounds and non-speech sounds. The range of sounds that can be made by the organs of eating, drinking, and breathing is a surprisingly wide one, reaching far beyond the single act about which the average layman has heard, viz., the vibration of what are inexactly called vocal cords (hereinafter called vocal bands). The largest number of these sounds are made with the outgoing breath, but a great many can be made with the intake of breath. A limited number (certain clicks) can be made with air found normally in the mouth but not necessarily a part of the breath. A few, such as the clashing of the teeth, can even be made without developing air pressures at all. The outgoing breath, or expiration, helps, typically, to produce all of what in the preceding chapter were tentatively and loosely called the vowels and consonants of English. The outgoing breath can, and for other languages does, help to produce many other comparable sounds. The intake of breath, or inspiration, whether the air reaches the lungs or only the mouth, helps to produce some English-language interjections, like the one spelled *tut-tut* or *st-st-st*, along with

---

[4] Negus, p. 351.

the Japanese hiss of polite appreciation, and in the African languages, a considerable number of so-called clicks. The sounds made otherwise than by the vocal bands are produced in groups wherever the inspired or expired breath stream can be constricted, either completely, by blocking, or partially, by narrowing.

By no means do all these sounds occur as speech sounds in English, or in any other single language, but nearly every one of them occurs in some of the many languages in the world. A glance at the IPA chart, page 31, will reveal symbols for a large number of the possible sounds. To cover the ground completely, numerous other symbols would have to be invented.

Modes of utterance. Any system of sounds taken from the whole gamut of sounds and constituting a given language can be spoken in a number of different ways. First, a speaker can utter the sounds at what he regards as his normal pitch, or at several other higher or lower pitches, still within his normal range.[5] Second, he can speak in falsetto, an abnormally high pitch to which reference will be made later. Third, he can speak in a whisper, a phenomenon which will presently demand explanation. Whispering, it must be added, can scarcely be classified as abnormal, since it is incessantly used in all sorts of situations and is regarded as perfectly natural by all concerned, both users and observers.[6]

The sound-making and sound-modifying mechanisms. It is now in order to direct attention to the mechanisms borrowed from the vital functions of eating, drinking, and breathing, and used (1) for the making of sound, and (2) for the modification of sound for communicative purposes. Since sound results from vibration in the air (ordinarily), and since the air vibrations which form the basis of speech sounds originate in the larynx, pharynx, and mouth, our interest will for the time being focus at these points.

The motive power for vibration. No vibration can take place without a motive power to actuate it. The vibrations in the instance of a violin are actuated by the bow, of a piano by the hammers, of a clarinet or French horn or flute by the lungs of the player, and of a pipe organ by its lung-like bellows.

The vibrator. For each of these instruments there is some kind of vibrator which serves as an intermediary to transform the power of the motor into air vibration. For the violin and piano it is (initially) the strings; for the drum,

---

[5] In descriptive English linguistics these pitches are gathered into four groups, *viz.*, 1, low pitch; 2, average pitch, 3, high pitch; 4, very high pitch. These are significant in the differentiation of meanings, and constitute the pitch phonemes of English. They are written /1/, /2/, /3/, /4/, and are read "pitch phoneme one," "pitch phoneme 2," and so on.

[6] Kenneth Pike, *Phonetics* (Ann Arbor: University of Michigan Press, 1943), pp. 96, 126–128. Pike writes of several other types of voice, the glottal trill, falsetto glottal trill, and so on, all of which are appropriate for the consideration of the research worker.

the drumhead; for the clarinet, the reed; for the French horn, the vibrating edges of the player's lips; for the flute and pipe organ, the moving airstream itself, agitated at the lip of the sound aperture of the instrument.

The motors for vocal vibration. For most of the sounds originating in the larynx, pharynx, and mouth, the lungs (Figure 2) constitute the motor,

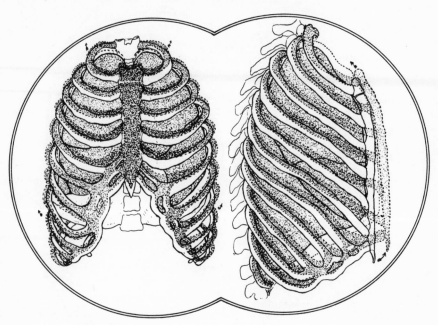

Figure 2. The lungs. (Dotted lines show expansion after inspiration.)

furnishing opportunity for a limited number of sounds on inspiration of breath and a great many on expiration of breath. In the case of sounds made by the teeth, the lower jaw is the motor. In the case of many clicks and some hisses, the tongue (or the tongue and lower jaw) constitutes the motor, which, by enlarging the mouth cavity to create a partial vacuum, promotes an inrush of air which can produce a hiss, or a labial, lingual, or velar click, occurring as the air finally is admitted through the front of the mouth or, by way of the nose, through the rear. Conversely, the tongue as a motor can be made to lessen the size of the mouth cavity and thus compress a quantity of air which, when released at lips, tongue-tip, or velum, will produce a bilabial or lingual trill, or a variety of ejective clicks.

The vocal vibrators. As in the case of the musical instruments, there is for every vocal sound a vibrator, which acts as intermediary to transmit or control power from the appropriate motor in such a way as to set the atmospheric molecules into vibration. For the sounds which we call *voiced*, i.e., vowels and voiced consonants, this intermediary is the vocal bands of the larynx (Figures 3–11).

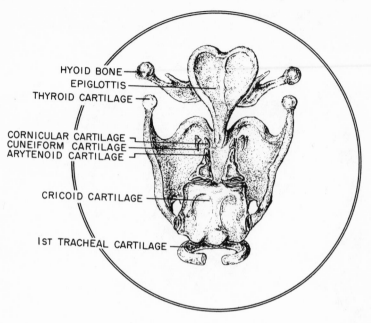

Figure 3. Cartilages (assembled) that form the skeleton of the larynx (rear view).

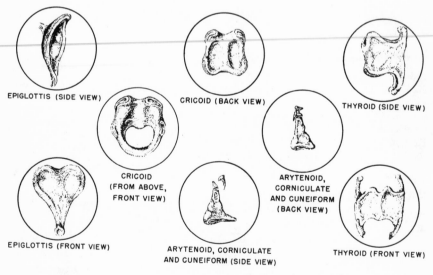

Figure 4. Cartilages (separated) that form the skeleton of the larynx.

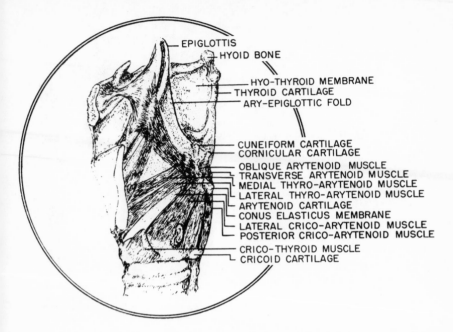

Figure 5 a. The larynx with its muscles (side view left).

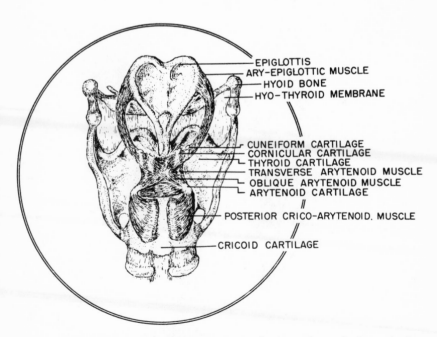

Figure 5 b. The larynx with its cartilages, membranes, and muscles (rear view).

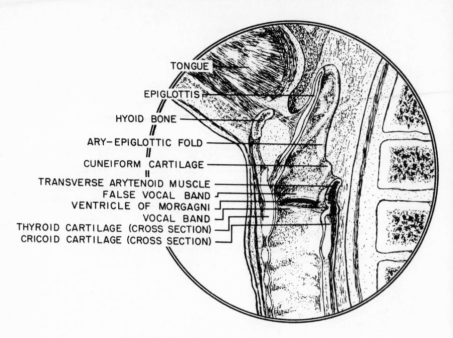

TONGUE
EPIGLOTTIS
HYOID BONE
ARY-EPIGLOTTIC FOLD
CUNEIFORM CARTILAGE
TRANSVERSE ARYTENOID MUSCLE
FALSE VOCAL BAND
VENTRICLE OF MORGAGNI
VOCAL BAND
THYROID CARTILAGE (CROSS SECTION)
CRICOID CARTILAGE (CROSS SECTION)

Figure 6. Sagittal section of larynx (right).

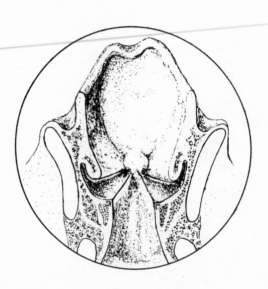

Figure 7. Schema of larynx showing front half.

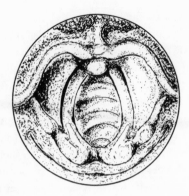 

Figure 8. Top view of larynx open for breathing.

Figure 9. Top view of larynx almost closed, as at one phase of phonation.

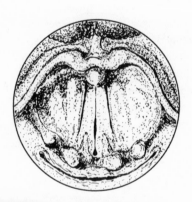

Figure 10. Schema of larynx with vocal bands adjusted for falsetto.

Briefly, tone is produced in the larynx in the following-described manner. As the vocal bands are closed or partially closed, air pressure is created in the trachea immediately beneath. This pressure forces the bands apart and allows air to flow rapidly between them. The direction of the force of the vocal bands themselves in this open position is nearly perpendicular to the direction of flow of the air stream through the glottis. It is known, from the principles controlling fluid motion in physics, that the greater the velocity of the air, the less will be its resisting pressure in this perpendicular direction. Thus the vocal bands are permitted to be drawn together by their own elasticity, and the entire process is again repeated. These regular interruptions in the breath stream produce the larynx tone.[7]

Such voiced sounds may be produced in a limited way by the inspired breath, but are usually produced by the expired breath. All vowels, such as [i], [ɑ], can be produced in both these ways, and all the voiced consonants as well, such as [v], [d]. Voiced sounds are customarily defined, accordingly, as sounds produced with accompanying vibration of the vocal bands; conversely, voiceless sounds, such as [f], [t], lack the vibration of the vocal bands.

The vibratory intermediary for whispered sounds. The vibratory intermediary for whispered vowels, whispered sonorant consonants, such as [m, n, ŋ, l, r, w, j], and perhaps to a slight extent for what in whispering corresponds to the voiced components of such voiced plosives as [b, d, g] and of such voiced fricatives as [v, ð, z, ʒ], is the breath stream itself, which is constricted at the glottis by a partial closure of the vocal bands. Under such stricture, vibrations are set up in the air which serve the whispered speech in the same way that the vibrations set up by the vocal bands serve vocalized speech.

Interestingly enough, whispered speech, contrary to vocalized speech, can be carried on practically as well with the inspired breath as with the expired breath. Whispered speech lacks, however, the pitch range of vocalized speech. Whispering will not serve for making the simplest tune recognizable. A tone language is at great disadvantage when whispered. The tones cannot be satisfactorily distinguished, and the hearer has to rely principally on context to reveal the meanings of what tend to become, by the lack of pitch variation, homonyms. When context fails, the hearer has to rely on differences of force and duration, which, with differences of onset and vowel completion, give him clues to the missing pitch characteristics. There is, too, a much smaller quality range in whispering than in vocalized speech. This can be better understood after the discussion of resonance.

---

[7] In many instances the vibrator does not transmit the major portion of the energy to the air, but simply serves as a rapidly opening and closing valve to control the energy. It is now rather clear that tones in the vocal cavities which result from vocal band vibration are created by the recurrent puffs of air: this is true whether the bands achieve partial or complete closure during the vibration. The bands are maintained in vibration in accordance with certain principles of fluid dynamics. When the air has a high velocity through the glottis, pressure against the bands is reduced and they tend to fall together, approximately perpendicular to the direction of air flow. The sound is not created by the lips or bands pushing on the air, but by the puffs of air striking into the cavities beyond. This appears to raise the old controversy about puff versus harmonic theory of voice production. Actually there is no reason for controversy, and both theories are in essence correct. While the muscle does not push on the air in such a way as to produce appreciable sound, the cavity vibrations are periodic, or nearly so. Since Fourier showed that any single-valued wave form, no matter how irregular, if regularly repeated can be analyzed into a series of simple harmonic motions—the puff theory and the harmonic theory are at once correct. This view is that held, apparently unanimously, by the present-day experts on acoustics who have studied the nature of vocal band movements.—Excerpt from letter from Gordon E. Peterson of Bell Laboratories and the University of Michigan.

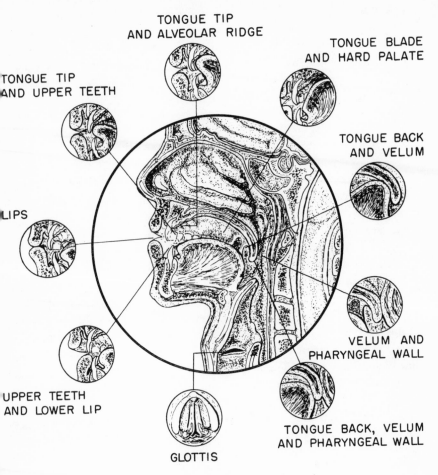

TONGUE TIP
AND ALVEOLAR RIDGE

TONGUE BLADE
AND HARD PALATE

TONGUE TIP
AND UPPER TEETH

TONGUE BACK
AND VELUM

LIPS

VELUM AND
PHARYNGEAL WALL

UPPER TEETH
AND LOWER LIP

TONGUE BACK, VELUM
AND PHARYNGEAL WALL

GLOTTIS

Figure 12. The valves capable of producing stricture.

The vibrator for the voiceless sounds. (Figure 12.) The vibrator for the remaining sounds, i.e., the voiceless sounds of the order of [p, t, k, f, θ, s, ʃ], is either the breath stream or the analogous stream of mouth air. Either stream may be inspired or expired, expiration being typical. Either stream sets up molecular vibrations in the atmosphere at some point where it is constricted (Figure 12). The stricture, as indicated earlier, may be a complete block or simply a narrowing. The locations of the strictures may be very numerous, considering the great mobility of the tongue. The commoner ones are at the lips, the lower lip and the tips of the upper front teeth, the tongue tip and the backs of the upper front teeth, the tongue tip and the alveolar ridge, the tongue blade and the hard palate, the back of the tongue and the velum, the back of the tongue and the back wall of the pharynx, and the glottis.

The chart on pages 46 and 47 names the valves which can produce strictures by blocking or narrowing, and shows what sounds can be produced at each point of stricture. The chart shows both primary and secondary articulation. The latter is made by a valve forming a stricture that supports the active mechanism by (1) narrowing an aperture (e.g., the lip-rounding for [w, o, ʊ, ɔ]), or (2) blocking an aperture (e.g., the velar closure for [k, g, ɪ]).

Explanation of Terms in First Column of Chart

Valves. A valve is a movable organ capable of narrowing or blocking the breath stream. The valves used for English are the lips, tongue, velum, and glottis (see Figure 12, page 43), with the variations indicated across the top of the chart. The valves of speech are fleshy and flexible.

To effect a closure which will block the breath stream, a valve must have—to borrow a word from mechanics—a "seat" against which to fit itself; to narrow the breath stream, it must approach such a seat. In a case where the valve consists of two fleshy members, these approach, or seat against, each other; e.g., the lips, the vocal bands, and the back of the tongue and the velum. In a case where the valve consists of only one fleshy member, it must seat itself against something solid; e.g., the lower lip against the upper teeth, the tongue tip and tongue blade against the hard palate, and the back of the tongue against the pharyngeal wall.

Strictures. A stricture is any degree of narrowing in the passage through which the air stream passes. A completely open passage has no stricture. A partially closed passage or a completely closed passage has been subjected to stricture.

Plosives. The term *plosive* is a short name for such consonants as [p-b, t-d, k-g, ʔ], which might more completely be called *stop-compression-plosives*. From the first word of the compound above, these sounds are also very often called *stops*.

The production of a plosive consists of three events in rapid sequence, viz., implosion, compression, and explosion. Implosion here means the taking of position by the articulators. With the first six consonants on the chart, this involves the closure of the nasal passages at the rear with the velum, and closure of the mouth by the lips, by the tongue tip and alveolar ridge, or by the tongue-back and velum (see Figure 12, page 43). Compression involves action of the abdominal and thoracic muscles of exhalation to force air at more than atmospheric pressure into the pharynx or pharynx and mouth. Plosion means the explosion of the compressed air through the mouth (ordinarily). With the glottal stop [ʔ], the necessary and characteristic closure is at the glottis; the velum may or may not be closed. In the case of [b, d, g], the vocal bands are vibrating during the compression period.

Nasals. A nasal consonant is one characterized by the escape of the air stream through the nasal passages, the mouth passage being entirely blocked, either by the lips, by the tongue tip and alveolar ridge, or by the tongue back and velum (see Figure 12, page 43). The English nasals are [m, n, ŋ]. Nasal vowels, found typically in French and Portuguese, are made with simultaneous exit of air from mouth and nose.

Laterals. A lateral consonant is a consonant made by permitting the exit of the breath on one or both sides of the tongue, the tongue tip or blade being against the upper teeth or the roof of the mouth. The basic lateral in English is [l], made with the tip of the tongue against the alveolar ridge or the back surfaces of the upper front teeth.

One-tap trill. The one-tap trill [ɾ] is a member of the r-family, made with a single vibration of the tongue tip against the alveolar ridge, or with a gesture of the tongue tip in that direction.

Retroflex sounds. A retroflex sound is made with the tip of the tongue pointing upward or upward and backward. It is possible to pronounce many sounds with retroflexion, but the only standard retroflex sounds in English are [r] (with variant [ɹ]), [ɜ˞], and [ɚ].

Fricatives. A fricative is a sound consisting basically of a speech noise (see page 61) originating in the friction of the breath stream against the walls of the aperture through which the breath exits or, in the case of inspired fricatives, through which it enters. A voiced fricative consists of the same noise, accompanied by vocal band vibration. The voiced fricatives of English are [v, ð, z, ɹ, ʒ]; the voiceless ones are [ʍ, f, θ, s, ʃ, h]. The strictures for these will be taken up in connection with the respective sounds.

Glides. A glide is a sound which has a constant point of beginning, but which is for the remainder of its duration a changing series of sounds, modulating or gliding toward whatever vowel follows. There are three such glides which are phonemes in English, [j], [ʍ], and [w].[8] The sounds [ʍ] and [w] start from the position of [u] (often [ʊ]) and glide toward whatever vowel follows; the sound [j] starts with [i] (often [ɪ]) and glides similarly.

The shifting or modulating portion of a so-called glide appears to be of little consequence in distinguishing the sound; it appears to be a phenomenon of close juncture, a smear[8] of too great brevity and indeterminacy for the ear to

---

[8] The definition given here is intentionally limited to the consonant phonemes [ʍ, w, j], which are of the nature of off-glides in that they "take off" from [ʊ] and [ɪ]. This definition does not include the weak second element of any diphthong, nor any sort of on-glide. For discussion of smear, or perception indeterminacy, see Martin Joos, "Acoustic Phonetics," *Language Monograph* No. 23, Vol. 24, No. 2, Supplement to *Language*, April–June, 1948, Chap. III.

Valves forming strictures / Classes of sounds formed	Upper and lower lips (Bilabial)		Upper teeth and lower lip (Labiodental)		Upper teeth and tongue (Dental)		Alveol... and tongu... (Alve...)
	Glottis vibrating (Voiced)	Glottis not vibrating (Voiceless)	Glottis vibrating (Voiced)	Glottis not vibrating (Voiceless)	Glottis vibrating (Voiced)	Glottis not vibrating (Voiceless)	Glottis vibrating (Voiced)
CONSONANTS							
Plosives	b	p					d
Nasals	m						n
Laterals........					ḷ		l
One-tap trill ...							ɾ
Retroflex.......							
Fricatives		ʍ	v	f	ð	θ	z
Glides	(w)						
VOWELS							
HIGH.........	(u)						
Low-high	(ʊ)						
High-mid	(o)						
MID..........	ɱ						ŋ ļ
Low-mid.......	(ɔ)						
High-low	(ɒ)						
LOW..........							
DIPHTHONGS							
HIGH.........							
Low-high	(ʊ)						
High-mid	(o)						
MID							
Low-mid.......							
High-low	(ɔ)						
LOW..........							

Palato-alveolar boundary and tongue blade		Hard palate and tongue blade	Velum and back of tongue		Velum and pharyngeal wall			Glottis
Glottis vibrating	Glottis not vibrating	Glottis vibrating	Glottis vibrating	Glottis not vibrating	Velum open Gl. vib.	Velum closed Gl. vib.	Gl. not vib.	Glottis not vibrating
ato-alveolar		Palatal	Velar					Glottal
Voiced	Voiceless	Voiced	Voiced	Voiceless	Voiced	Voiced	Voice-less	Voice-less
			g	k		(b,d,g)	(p,t, k,ʔ)	ʔ
			ŋ		(m,n,ŋ)			
						(l̩,l)		
						(ɾ)		
						(r)		
ʒ	ʃ			(ʍ)		(v,ð,z, ɹ,ʒ)	(ʍ,f,θ s,ʃ,h)	h
		j		(w)		(w,j)		
		i						
		ɪ						
		e		u		(i,u)		
				ʊ		(ɪ,ʊ)		
				o		(e,o)		
		(ɝ,ɚ) ɜə		ɒ	(m̩ŋ̩)	(l̩,ɝ,ɚ, ɜ,ə)		
		ɛ	Λ			(ɛ,Λ,ɔ)		
		æ		ɔ		(æ,ɒ)		
		a		ɒ		(a,ɑ)		
				ɑ				
		ɪ						
		e				(ɪ,ʊ)		
			●	ʊ				
				oᵒ		(e,o)		
				ɔ		(ɔ)		
		a		ɔ		(a)		

analyze effectively, and hence of no more significance than the modification of any other sound approaching a second sound. It is the beginning portion of the glide, along with the characteristic extreme rapidity of its utterance, that is important.

Terms Used Across the Top of the Chart

Bilabials. In English, a bilabial sound is made by closing the lips at some point in the production of the sound. The typical English bilabials are [p, b], for which the lips are closed during compression, and [m], for which the lips are closed throughout. In the sense that the lips are rounded, the consonants [ʍ] and [w] are also bilabials, as are the rounded vowels [u, ʊ, o, ɔ].

Labiodentals. Labiodentals are sounds made with the upper teeth resting lightly on the lower lip. The English labiodentals are [v, f]. Spanish has a labiodental nasal, [ɱ]. German has [ʋ] and [F], which may be called labiodental in view of the fact that the lower lip makes a lax gesture toward the upper teeth, though it may seldom touch the teeth.

Dentals. Dentals are sounds made with the tip of the tongue against the posterior surfaces of the upper teeth. In English only [θ, ð] are regularly dental, though [t, d, n, l] can be on occasion, as will be shown later. (It is possible for [θ, ð] to be interdental, that is, made with the tongue between the teeth, but they are seldom made in this fashion.)

Alveolars. Alveolars are sounds made with the highest part of the tongue (tip or blade) touching or approaching the alveolar ridge, which is the rough ridge on the hard palate, just behind the upper teeth. The tongue (tip or blade) touches the alveolar ridge for [d, t, n, l, ɾ], and approaches it for [z, s].

Palato-alveolars. Palato-alveolar sounds are made with the tongue tip or blade approaching the boundary between the alveolar ridge and the hard palate proper. The English palato-alveolars are [r, ɹ], made typically with the tongue tip, but, with some individuals, with the blade; and [ʃ, ʒ], made with the tongue blade only.

Palatals. Palatals are sounds made with the tongue tip or blade approaching the hard palate. In English the front palatals are [j, i, ɪ, e, ɛ, æ, a], made with the tongue blade. The central palatals, made with the tongue blade, are [ɨ, ɪ, ʉ, ʊ, ɝ, ɚ, ɜ, ə]. The front palatal vowels are usually called simply front vowels, and the central palatals, central vowels.

Velars. Velars are, in English, sounds made with the back of the tongue against or approaching the soft palate or velum. The English velars are, with the tongue touching, [g, k, ŋ]; with the tongue approaching, [u, ʊ, o, ɔ, ɒ, ɑ]. These vowels are usually called merely back vowels, not velars.

Glottals. Glottals are made with the glottis (the chink between the vocal bands) closed or almost closed. The English glottals are, with the glottis closed,

[?], and with the glottis nearly closed, [h]. Whispered vowels, as distinguished from regularly voiceless consonants except [h], have a glottal component.

The Need for a Special Nomenclature

Up to this point discussions have been carried on by relying upon the student's general knowledge, on the theory that few definitions could be made until the student had gained a certain facility in dealing with elementary phonetic concepts. Even so basic a thing as speech sound, and so basic a classification as the separation of speech sounds into vowels and consonants, has remained without complete definition, as if they could be taken for granted. Fortunately, the notion which one may almost subconsciously possess concerning these matters is not far removed from that resulting from careful thinking, and so it has been possible to proceed thus far without great difficulty. But the more detailed discussions which are to follow demand a more technical vocabulary. The pages following will therefore be devoted to the definition and explanation of a considerable number of terms, beginning with certain ones dealing with sound itself.

What sound is. It has been stated earlier that sound is produced when some vibrator, actuated by a motor, sets the molecules of (ordinarily) the air in motion. The preoccupation of the physicist is with this vibration. Sound as perceived, however, may be thought of as the interpretation in consciousness of these vibrations after the disturbed molecules of air have set into vibration the tympanic membrane (eardrum), which sets into vibration the ossicular chain (hammer, anvil, and stirrup)[9] of the middle ear, which acts upon the lymph in the cochlea (inner ear), and through it upon the organ of Corti, setting up stimuli at the terminals of the auditory nerve (N. VIII), which carries nerve impulses to the brain for such interpretation (Figure 13). The preoccupation of the psychologist is with the interpretation of the neural impulses. At this juncture, we shall briefly consider sound from the physicist's viewpoint.

Sound waves. From any point where vibrations are set up, a disturbance in the molecules of the surrounding air is propagated outward in all directions. This disturbance consists of vibrations of the molecules themselves, the rate of vibration being identical in frequency with that of the vibrator. Vibrating molecules set adjacent molecules into vibration, producing a configuration of vibratory motion, moving outward from the source. This pattern, called a sound wave, travels through the air at a speed of approximately 1100 feet per second. (Sound waves travel through denser media, such as wood or metal, at much greater speed. The electric impulses into which sound waves in the air may be

---

[9] Also called malleus, incus, and stapes.

converted for transmission by wire or wireless travel very much faster, viz., with the speed of light, about 186,000 miles per second.)

Fundamental and overtones. It is characteristic of many vibrators, such as strings, to be able to carry on several modes of vibration simultaneously: a string may vibrate as a whole, producing a basic sound called the *fundamental;* and it may vibrate in segments, such as halves, thirds, and fifths, producing

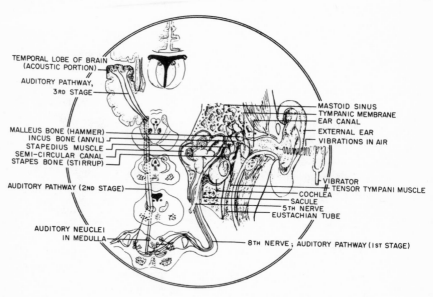

Figure 13. Schema showing progress of sound from vibrator through ear to brain.

accompanying sounds called *overtones*.[10] The halves vibrate at double the frequency of the whole vibrator, and produce a tone an octave higher than the fundamental, while the fourths produce a tone two octaves higher, and the thirds, fifths, sevenths, and the like, produce tones distributed mathematically through the whole tone complex. This tone complex (if we turn momentarily to the psychologist's point of view on sound) is regarded by the ear as a single sound.

Graphing a complex sound. Any pure tone, such as the fundamental of a tone complex, can be graphed as a simple sine curve (Figure 14). Likewise each overtone can be so graphed. One sine curve can represent the pattern of simple harmonic motion[11] described by the whole vibrator; another can repre-

---

[10] The term *partial* is likewise often used in this connection. Partial and overtone are not equivalent terms, in that the fundamental itself is the first partial, the first overtone the second partial, and so forth.

[11] *Simple harmonic motion* may be defined as the projection upon a plane surface of the motion of a point on the circumference of a circle revolving at constant speed in a second plane at right angles to the first.

sent one of its segments considered as vibrating independently. For that matter, a sine curve can represent equally well the vibration of the tympanic membrane (eardrum), the ossicular chain, or any of the responsive membranes or liquids of the inner ear. It can also represent a pattern of fluctuating pressure in the atmosphere, as exercised against the eardrum by each segmental vibration.

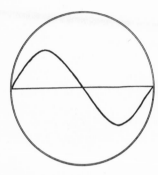

Figure 14. Sine curves for the
fundamental.

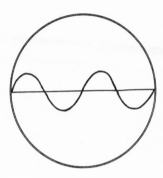

Figure 15. Sine curves for the
first overtone.

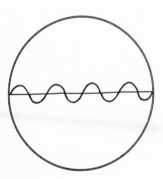

Figure 16. Sine curves for the
third overtone.

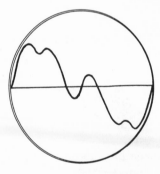

Figure 17. Composite of the three
curves in figures 14, 15, and 16.

A combination of the individual curves for the fundamental and for the various overtones produces a complex curve which represents certain components of the actual motion of the vibrator involved. This curve represents also the composite pressure patterns of fundamental and overtones as present in the atmosphere and impinging on the eardrum. Figures 14–17 illustrate the foregoing.

Significance of the presence of overtones. Two factors govern the quality or timbre of a tone: (a) the nature of the tone complex delivered by the vibrator, and (b) effects in the transmission of the sound. These two factors together will usually result in the dominance of certain overtones and the subordination of others; that is, the concentration of energy in some overtones at the expense of others. These give the characteristic quality to the tone of a given musical instrument, or to the voice of a given person. Differences in the overtone structure make the tones of different instruments and the voices of different people distinguishable from each other. From the point of view of phonetics, this is a very important matter, for it accounts for the different vowels. Were it not possible to shift the factors of dominance and subordination among the overtones in the human voice, it would not be possible, indeed, to make different vowels.

Resonance. The mechanism by which a given combination of the fundamental and overtones is selected for emphasis and subordination to produce a given tone quality or vowel quality is the resonator. Its action in emphasizing some tones and subordinating others in the fundamental-overtone complex is a resonating process. Resonance is a process of transmission by which those frequencies to which the resonator is "in tune" are freely passed, while those to which the resonator is not "in tune" are not. It is by this selective transmission that the resonator contributes to the timbre or quality of the tone as a whole.

Resonators. Common acoustical resonators are of two types, cavities and sounding boards. Major attention herein is given to cavity resonators. When cavities and sounding boards are acted upon by sound waves from a vibrator they will respond well to certain frequencies within the sound complex, but not to others. Such resonators usually make possible a more effective transfer of energy from the vibrator producing the sound to the surrounding air, so that the frequencies resonated may appear in the air with much greater strength than when the resonator is not present. The selectivity of a sounding board is fixed, according to its size, mass, and texture; that of a cavity may likewise be fixed, or it may be variable, if its dimensions, openings, and texture are variable.

Resonating cavities and pitch. The effects of the factors of variability in cavity resonators can best be seen by considering them first in their application to laboratory types of resonators, and then to cavities of the head, neck, and chest. It is well known that ordinary spherical Helmholtz resonators are selective according to the following principles:

The larger the cavity of the resonator, the dimensions of aperture and neck remaining constant, the lower the pitch to which it is best adapted (Figure 18 a).

The larger the aperture of the cavity, the size of cavity and length of neck remaining constant, the higher the pitch to which it is best adapted (Figure 18 b).

The longer the neck of the aperture, the dimensions of aperture and cavity remaining constant, the lower the pitch to which it is best adapted (Figure 18 c).

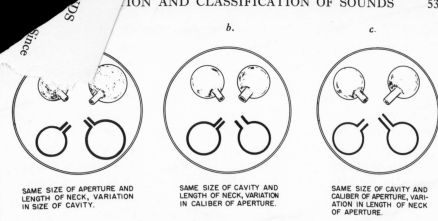

b.   c.

SAME SIZE OF APERTURE AND
LENGTH OF NECK, VARIATION
IN SIZE OF CAVITY.

SAME SIZE OF CAVITY AND
LENGTH OF NECK, VARIATION
IN CALIBER OF APERTURE.

SAME SIZE OF CAVITY AND
CALIBER OF APERTURE, VARI-
ATION IN LENGTH OF NECK
OF APERTURE.

Figure 18. Hemholtz resonators.

In addition, the softer the texture of the cavity walls, the more the cavity emphasizes low overtones.

The identifying pitch characteristics of vowels. It is likewise well known that for every vowel there are characteristic concentrations of energy, evidencing themselves in pitch patterns which identify the vowel. These patterns are found in limited regions of frequency, within which they must remain. This is another way of saying that the identifying pitch characteristics of a vowel are relatively constant. It is possible, to be sure, to speak or sing a given vowel at several different pitches without distorting it beyond recognition. But if the pitch is changed so much as to go above the regions wherein are found the pitches of the components which identify the vowel, the resultant sound will actually be some other vowel. Note the concentrations of energy in the following vowel spectra (Figure 19). These are the identifying characteristics of the vowels.

[ɪ]   [æ]   [ʊ]

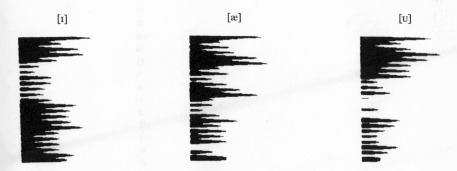

Figure 19. Vowel spectra as shown by the Spectrograph: [ɪ, æ, ʊ].

Cavity resonance in the human body. The applicability to the human structure of the principles governing cavity resonance is fairly obvious. The cavities available for resonation are the mouth, nose, pharynx, and laryngo-trachea. little information is as yet available on infra-glottal resonance, major attention here will be given to resonance above the glottis, viz., resonance in the mouth, nose, and pharynx. The walls of the mouth and pharynx can be changed in texture by changing the tension of the musculature of the lips, tongue, and pharyngeal walls. As a result, the reflection of selected overtones is modified, so that the timbre of the vowel tone being uttered is itself modified, or even shifted in the direction of a different vowel. The difference between [i] and [ɪ], for example, and between [u] and [ʊ] are apparently achieved partly by a change of muscular tension in the tongue, though typically there is also change in the size of the mouth cavity. This change of lingual tension can easily be detected by placing the thumb and forefinger under the lower jaw and pressing firmly against the tissue below the tongue while pronouncing [i-ɪ] and [u-ʊ]. It may be concluded that when the inner surface of the mouth cavity, especially the floor, is firm, the cavity selects from the tone complex the proper combination of fundamental and overtones to produce [i], while when the musculature is soft, the cavity selects the combination appropriate for [ɪ]. In similar fashion, firm cavity surface helps to produce [u], soft surface to produce [ʊ]. Accordingly, [i], [u], and the like are called tense vowels, and [ɪ], [ʊ], and the like, lax vowels.

The cavities concerned in speech vary considerably in adaptability to change of size, change of size of aperture, and change of length of neck of aperture—the changes common with Helmholtz resonators. The nose is the least amenable to change. A slight narrowing of the nostrils is possible, but it is doubtful whether this affects resonance greatly. No general change of size is possible at all.

The mouth is the most amenable to change. The size of the mouth cavity can be varied greatly by the widening and narrowing of the angle of the jaw and by the elevation and depression of the tongue. With the lips closed and the velum drop-

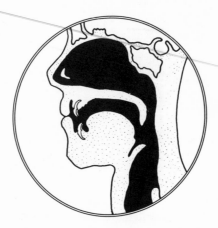

Figure 20. Pharynx and mouth as resonators, with nose as aperture.

ped, the nose serves as the aperture of a resonating cavity consisting of the mouth and pharynx combined, with a divided neck of considerable length (Figure 20). The size of the mouth-pharynx cavity can then be progressively decreased by

Figure 21. Pharynx and mouth, from the lips back, as resonators, with nose as aperture.

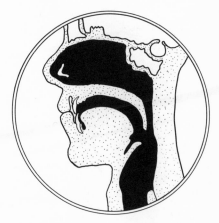

Figure 22. Pharynx and mouth, from the teeth back, as resonators, with nose as aperture.

Figure 23. Pharynx and mouth, from alveolar ridge back, as resonators, with nose as aperture.

Figure 24. Pharynx and mouth, from the alveolo-palatal border back, as resonators, with nose as aperture.

closing the lips (Figure 21), by touching the tip of the tongue at the teeth (Figure 22), at the alveolar ridge (Figure 23), at the alveolo-palatal border (Figure 24), or at the hard palate (Figure 25), etc. The lips may serve as the aperture, which can be adjusted to several different sizes. By pursing the lips, the neck of the aperture can be made longer.

The pharynx and nose function as a resonator when the tongue is raised at the rear, as for [ŋ] (Figure 26). In this case the nose again serves as the aperture, with

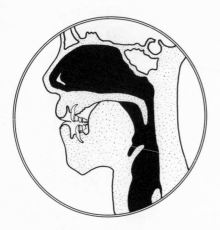

Figure 25. Pharynx and mouth, from the hard palate back, as resonators, with nose as aperture.

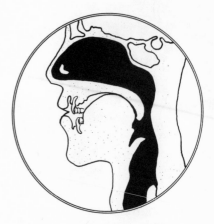

Figure 26. Pharynx as resonator, with nose as aperture.

a long, divided neck. When the velum is closed, the pharynx can serve as a resonator with a very long-necked aperture, consisting of the mouth and lips, the mouth being modified into a tube by the elevation of the tongue.

Open-tube and closed-tube resonators. The foregoing discussion has disregarded the fact that in some of the instances considered, the cavities are open at one end, and at other times at both ends. When speech is produced, any cavity which serves an important part in the production of tone clearly must be partially or completely open at the end toward the lungs. Thus, when employed in speech, the nose is always open at both ends. During the production of sound, the pharynx is likewise always open at both ends, except that during phonation the glottis reduces the lower opening to a very small one. The mouth is usually open at both ends, but may be closed at one end by the lips. The laryngo-trachea is in a rather ambiguous situation at the lower end, with its multiple divisions and subdivisions into the bronchi, bronchial tubes, bronchioles, and alveoles of the lungs; it is therefore difficult to know whether it behaves as a closed tube or an open tube. Pending convincing experimentation, it is usually thought of as open. If it proves to have no more effect on resonance than is now known, the matter is of little importance.

The significance of all this becomes evident when we consider that the pitches to which a resonating tube is adapted vary, not merely according to the length of the tube, but also according to whether it is an open tube or a closed tube. It is a fact of physics that an open tube is best adapted to resonate a sound whose wave length is twice the length of the tube (Figure 27a), whereas a closed tube is best

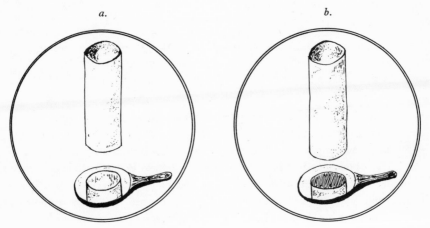

Figure 27. Open and closed resonating tubes.

adapted to resonate a wave length four times the length of the tube (Figure 27b).

When it is recalled that the wave length for C^1 is about four feet, it will be seen that it would take an open tube two feet long or a closed tube one foot long to act as resonator for it. If the mouth plus the pharynx may be considered as a single open tube, the total length would amount to no more than one-half foot, and the fundamental of middle C could not be resonated. But the upper partials of middle C could be resonated, if not the fundamental. The second overtone, C^2, could use a tube one-half foot long, and all the higher overtones still shorter tubes in rapidly decreasing proportion.

However, since the mouth and pharynx are often adjusted to be more like Helmholz resonators than like tubes, i. e., more bottle-shaped than strictly cylindrical, the longer wave lengths can be accommodated. The tubes and other cavities of the mouth, nose, and throat can resonate tones of a great many wave lengths, longer as well as shorter, especially from the middle tones to the high ones. A number of the foregoing facts are summarized and certain conclusions drawn in the following quotation:

> It will readily be seen that the mouth can operate as either a closed tube
> or an open tube by reason of the adjustability of the lips, and that the pharynx
> can have two outlets or only one because of the adjustability of the soft palate,
> which adds or cuts off at will the nasopharynx and the nose as extensions of

the pharyngeal tube. When with these adjustments are compounded the many adjustments of length of tube, diameter of tube, diameter of aperture and length of aperture, it will be seen that by sheer application of ... mathematical principles ... the number of different pitches ... to which the pharynx is adapted for resonation is very large.

It becomes evident, then, that when the tone-complex consisting of fundamental and numerous overtones—sometimes as many as fifty or more, each overtone necessarily of higher pitch than its predecessor—emanates from the glottis, the possibilities for the selection of overtones for emphasis and the possibilities for change in the selection are almost innumerable. Hence arise the many shadings of each vowel sound, and the myriad nuances that make voices different from each other, and individual voices expressive of such a myriad of meanings.[12]

Sounding boards and "registers." Much speculation and some experimentation have been applied to the question of whether the human body possesses effectual sounding boards. The possible sounding boards are the hard palate, teeth, facial bones, cranial bones, and thoracic bones. Related to the concept of sounding boards is that of the so-called "registers," of the peculiar term "placement," and of the terms "head tone" and "chest tone." It has been popularly believed that the bones of the head, particularly of the face, are best suited to the resonation of the higher tones ("head tones"), and that the bones of the chest are best suited to the resonation of the lower tones ("chest tones"). Some understanding of the degree to which sounding board effects may be expected can be obtained from the fact that to be effective the dimensions of a sounding board must, as a minimum, be great enough to accommodate the wave lengths of the frequencies radiated.

It has been demonstrated by experiments that glottal vibration readily communicates itself through both the hard and soft tissues of the body so as to be readily detectable, e. g., on the sternum, by touch, by the stethoscope, and by the microphone.[13] These experiments appear to show that solid fastenings by means of dense material connecting the vocal bands with the so-called sounding boards are not necessary, though such connections between, e. g., piano string and piano sounding board, violin string and violin body, are customary. It has also been demonstrated by experiment that there is no appreciable emanation of sound through the chest wall into the external air.[14]

It apparently remains to be investigated whether (1) the impression of a speaker or singer that there are effectual sounding board vibrations from his chest is

---

[12] Giles W. Gray and Claude M. Wise, *The Bases of Speech* (New York: Harper, 1946, p. 191).

[13] C. M. Wise, "Chest Resonance," *Quarterly Journal of Speech*, June, 1932, pp. 446–452.

[14] Charles Mudd, *The Effect of Chest Resonance Upon the Quality of the Voice* (Unpublished M. A. thesis, Louisiana State University, 1948).

merely subjective, or (2) whether some reciprocal effect of resonation by the chest bones is communicated to the hearer through the air of the breath stream. Corresponding investigations relative to the vibration of the bones of the skull likewise remain to be made.

Resonance in whispering. Now that resonance has been introduced, it may be applied to the problem of distinguishing vowels in whispering, mentioned earlier. It has already been stated that, so far as whispered vowels are concerned, the essential vibrations are set up at the glottis, where the partially closed vocal bands, while not themselves vibrating, present a sufficient stricture to the outgoing breath stream to produce light air vibrations. These vibrations are very similar to, if not identical with, the vibrations for [h]. Indeed, it is possible to say that whispered vowels are based on the sound [h].[15] Whereas the mouth (lips, tongue, mandible) is in a neutral position for isolated [h], it is in the characteristic position for resonating an ordinary voiced vowel when producing a corresponding voiceless or whispered vowel. If [h] itself were regarded as a whispered vowel,[16] it would be whispered neutral vowel [ə]. If this [h] is given, e. g., the characteristic tongue position of [u], the neutral [ə] quality will at once be changed to [u] quality. The important point here is that the vibrations in the breath stream, set up as the result of glottal stricture, though voiceless and aperiodic, are as readily seized upon by the supraglottal resonance cavities and treated selectively as if they were voiced and periodic. These cavities pass selected frequencies and fail to pass others, so that the vowel, though constructed from noise components, is perfectly intelligible as a vowel. Whispered vowels may be classified as resonant whispers. (See Figure 28. Whispered vowels and consonants compared with voiced vowels and consonants.)

It seems probable that there is little vibration set up at the glottis for the whispered [b, d, g]; these appear to be distinguished from [p, t, k] mainly by lighter puffing of the released air stream; but the whispered [m, n, ŋ, r, l, j, w] seem to draw upon the same sort of basic [h]-formation as do the whispered vowels. Accordingly, they are characterized by resonance effects more like those of vowels than are the remaining consonants, whose identifying features have to be derived mainly from the fricative or plosive sounds made at their respective points of stricture. Whispered [v, ð, z, ʒ], with probably little glottal vibration, appear to distinguish themselves from [f, θ, s, ʃ] mainly by contextual clues, such as the

---

[15] Pike, pp. 71–72. A difference, interesting even if lacking in significance, is that whereas [h] begins without initial closure of the glottis, a whispered vowel, if initial and stressed, practically always begins with a glottal stop. However, so does an initial voiced vowel, though usually the stop is not symbolized, since it is non-significant.

[16] It can be so regarded, especially if sustained. See discussion of the distinction between vowels and consonants, pp. 65 ff. Pike (p. 72) has contrived an interesting statement of the relationship, not merely of the familiar voiceless [h], but also of the voiced [ɦ], to whispered and voiced vowels. He uses the mathematical statement of proportion, [h]: whispered vowel :[ɦ]: voiced vowel.

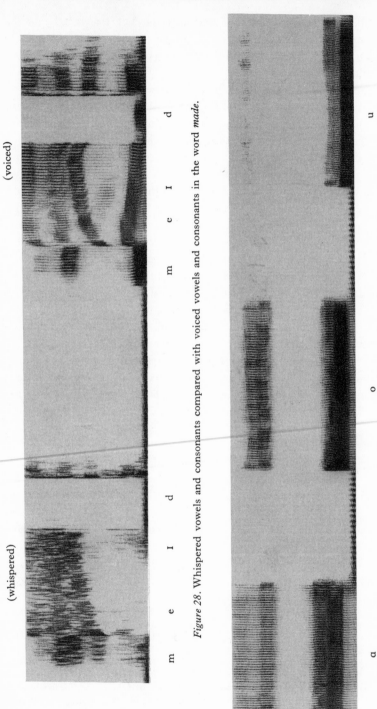

Figure 28. Whispered vowels and consonants compared with voiced vowels and consonants in the word *made*.

Figure 29. Bar one (lowest resonance band) is succesively lowered as sonority decreases through [ɑ], [o], [u].

greater length of preceding vowels before [v, ð, z, ʒ], or by less audible friction at the point of oral stricture; whispered [w], with some glottal vibration, distinguishes itself additionally from [ʍ] by its lack of labial and oral fricative features as compared with [ʍ].

Tone and noise. Speech sounds consist of tone, or of noise, or of a combination of the two. Tone is defined as sound resulting from periodic or regular vibrations, noise as sound resulting from aperiodic or irregular vibrations.

Considered broadly, all vowels consist of tone, as do the so-called liquid consonants [m, n, ŋ, l, r] and the glides [w] and [j].[17] The voiced plosive consonants [b, d, g] and the voiced fricative consonants [v, ð, z, ʒ] consist of a mixture of tone (the glottal component) and noise (the fricative component). The voiceless consonants consist only of noise. Considered more narrowly, very close (that is, high) vowels, such as [i] and [u], are made with a certain amount of friction, which produces noise.

Sonority. Sonority may possibly be defined as the degree of resonant tonality possessed by a sound. Low vowels, mid vowels, high vowels, the glides [w] and [j], "liquids" (nasals, laterals, and retroflexes) and voiced plosives and fricatives may be said to possess sonority in a decreasing series, while voiceless consonants possess none at all. Whispered vowels and whispered [m, n, ŋ, l, r, j, w] perhaps possess some feature which corresponds to sonority. Spectrograms appear tentatively to indicate that sonority decreases as bar one, representing the first resonance, is lowered (see Figure 29).

Tense and lax vowels. It has been mentioned (page 53) that a major difference between certain vowels is that resulting from the difference of cavity texture produced by tension of the muscles of the mouth and throat. This difference sharply distinguishes high and mid vowels, but dwindles to negligibility with low vowels. It follows that tense-lax pairs may be listed as follows:

Front		Back	
Tense	*Lax*	*Tense*	*Lax*
i	– ɪ	u	– ʊ
e	– ɛ	o	– ɔ

A modification of the conventional vowel diagram (see page 86) can be drawn to show the same facts (Figure 30).

As indicated, the distinction between tense and lax vowels seems to diminish toward insignificance for low vowels. Hence in the diagram above no attempt is made to distinguish between tense and lax vowels below [ɛ] and [ɔ]. The sounds [æ, a, ɒ, ɑ] are arbitrarily, but probably justifiably, considered lax. (In substandard speech there is actually a tense [æ] also, made with the tongue in contact with the

---

[17] The reference here is to the frictionless [j] of English, not the fricative final [j] of French.

inner surfaces of the upper molars. This [æ] contrasts sharply with the standard lax [æ], which is made with the tongue much lower, out of contact with the upper teeth. Tense [æ] is not socially approved of, and so is felt to be harsh, flat, and unmusical, and subject to objectionable nasalization.)

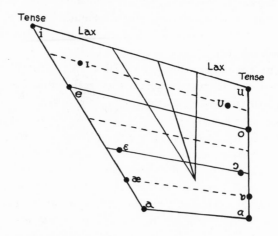

Figure 30. Tense and lax vowels.

Voiced and voiceless sounds. It may be said that some consonants are always whispered. These are the ones which, even in ordinary non-whispered speech, are unaccompanied by vibrations of the vocal bands. In English, every such sound except [h] and [ʍ] has a closely analogous voiced counterpart, which is made with essentially the same positions of the organs except that the vocal bands vibrate. Even [ʍ] has an analog, [w], which, besides being voiced, lacks the mildly fricative feature of [ʍ]; and [h] has a voiced analog [ɦ] (a standard sound in the South African form of Dutch called Afrikaans), which bears a peculiar relation to all vowels,[18] as may be seen in footnote 16, page 59.

Affricates. The symbols [tʃ, dʒ] represent two members of a class of consonants called affricates. An affricate is a consonant sound made by beginning with the vocal organs in the position of a plosive, and with the air-compression for that plosive, but exploding the compressed air through the aperture of a fricative continuant, instead of through the aperture normal for the plosive. Thus [tʃ] begins with the position and compression appropriate for [t], but the compressed air explodes through the aperture appropriate for [ʃ]. So with [dʒ], which begins like [d] but ends like [ʒ]. Thus an affricate, although it may be shown by structural analysis to be a phoneme, and hence functionally indivisible, may be seen to consist of phonetically separable parts. What may pass in auditory aspects

---

[18] Pike, pp. 140, 142.

as affricates can be artificially constructed in large numbers by combining the initial position of any plosive with the position of any fricative continuant that can conveniently be uttered in connection with it. These combinations of plosive plus fricative, such as the [ts] of *cats*, are not in English regularly called affricates nor written and considered single sounds with inseparable parts. For in the phonemic structure of English, the [t] and [s] of *cat* and *cats* belong to two different phonemes and are quite separable, whereas /ʧ/, as distributed in *chin* [ʧɪn], *kitchen* ['kɪʧən] and *catch* [kæʧ], is a single phoneme, incapable of separation. In German *Zeit* [t͜sait] and Russian отец (otets) [a'͜tɛt͜s], /t͜s/ is indeed a single phoneme, quite inseparable, even represented by the single letters *z* and *ц*. In these languages, /t͜s/ is regularly called an affricate, and should be represented by a single symbol. Throughout this book only affricates which are phonemes will be referred to as affricates. In English only /ʧ/ and /ʤ/ are so classified. Merely auditory affricates will be referred to by the names of their components. In other languages, the affricates peculiar to each language will be so designated.

Diphthongs. A diphthong has already been defined (page 15) as a gliding complex of sounds beginning with a recognizable vowel and ending with another. The "two sounds" implied by the word diphthong are these same initial and final sounds. The intervening glides are too brief to attract auditory attention. Like the affricates, the diphthongs are single units phonemically, but each is separable phonetically into two units. This book usually recognizes only "rising" diphthongs in English, i. e., only those diphthongs beginning at some point below the "high" area of the vowel diagram (page 86) and rising typically to [ɪ] or [ʊ]. These diphthongs are all stressed on the initial element. They are, specifically, [eɪ, aɪ, ɔɪ, aʊ, oʊ].

Pairs of voiceless-voiced consonants. The conventional pairings of voiceless-voiced consonants, including glides and affricates, are as follows:

	PLOSIVES		CONTINUANTS	
Voiceless	*Voiced*	*Voiceless*	*Voiced*
p	b	f	v
t	d	θ	ð
k	g	s	z
		ʃ	ʒ
	Glides		*Affricates*	
ʍ	w	ʧ	ʤ

Of the English consonants not appearing above, only one, [h], is voiceless; all the others, viz., [m,n,ŋ,l,r,ɾ,j], are voiced.

Tests for voicelessness and voicing. Some persons appear to have difficulty in distinguishing between voiceless and voiced consonants. Here are a number of tests to aid in developing the concept of voicelessness and voicing.

Close the ears with the fingers and pronounce the pairs [f-v], [s-z], [ʃ-ʒ]. Note the ringing in the ears for the voiced sounds. Similar tests can be made with the remaining pairs, but with less satisfaction, since each sound in these pairs, when spoken in isolation, is so brief that it is difficult to get a good impression of it. Moreover, it is difficult for the beginner to inhibit the appearance of an extraneous vowel, such as [ʌ], which may cause an intended [b] to appear as [bʌ], [p] as [pʌ], and so on, in such a way as to becloud the auditory impression and confuse the experimenter.

Place the hand against the throat with the crotch of the thumb and forefinger astride the larynx and pronounce [f-v, s-z, ʃ-ʒ]. Note the sensation of vibration with the voiced sounds.

Pronounce, noting the contrasts:

[p-b] in [pɛt, bɛt; rɪp, rɪb]
[t-d] in [tɛn, dɛn; sɛt, sɛd]
[k-g] in [kɪl, gɪl; hæk, hæg]
[f-v] in [fɔlt, vɔlt; rif, riv]
[θ-ð] in [ˈθɪsəl, ðɪs; wɪθ, wɪð]
[ʃ-ʒ] in [rʌʃ, ruʒ]
[tʃ-dʒ] in [tʃouk, dʒouk; kætʃ, kædʒ]
[ʍ-w] in [ʍɪtʃ, wɪtʃ]

Most, if not all, hisses and clicks are voiceless, whether on inspired or expired breath.

Continuants. The term continuant is arbitrarily narrowed in phonetics to apply only to consonants of more than momentary duration. Vowels, which, so far as duration is concerned, would qualify as continuants, are arbitrarily excluded from classification as such, so that the word continuant can be reserved to apply to consonants. The following consonants are continuants: [m, n, ŋ, l, r, f, v, θ, ð, ʃ, ʒ, s, z, h]. The glides [j], [w], and [ʍ], and the trill [ɾ] are by definition (pages 139, 144, 132) so rapidly uttered that the word continuant does not well apply.

Aspirates, spirants, aspiration. In the most general terms, any breathy sound is an aspirate (Lat. *spirare*, to breathe) or a spirant (Lat. *spirans*, breathing). More narrowly, an aspirate is, in English, a voiceless plosive, characterized by a strong puff of air at the moment of plosion. In this narrower sense, the aspirates in English are [p, t, k]; the corresponding voiced sounds [b, d, g], having very light aspirate puffs, are arbitrarily regarded as unaspirate. Spirant, more narrowly defined, is a breathy continuant. The voiced spirants in English are [v, ð, z, ʒ]; the voiceless spirants are [f, θ, s, ʃ, h].

Aspiration, then, as used here, refers to the degree of plosion accompanying a plosive consonant. The voiceless plosives [p, t, k] have strong aspiration in English; the voiced plosives [b, d, g], weak aspiration. Considered loosely, [p, t, k] are said to be aspirated, [b, d, g] unaspirated—but this classification is not invariable. (See further consideration under *fortis* and *lenis*, following.)

Fortis and lenis. *Fortis* means strong; *lenis* means weak. The reference is to muscle tension in the pronunciation of consonants. In general, the English voiceless plosives [p, t, k] are fortis, the voiced plosives [b, d, g] lenis. However, fortis and lenis conditions are not always accompanied by aspiration-voicelessness and unaspiration-voice respectively, as seems natural, though the simultaneous appearance of fortis-aspirated-voiceless consonants and lenis-unaspirated-voiced consonants is the usual thing. Note the following:

> Any number of variations are possible. For example, [p] in *pat* is fortis, aspirated, and voiceless; in *flapper*, [p] is still fortis, but comparatively unaspirated; in *spatter*, [p] is lenis and unaspirated; in *bat* [b] is lenis and unaspirated, voiced.

Falsetto. Etymologically, falsetto is an Italian diminutive, which may be translated as "little false voice." *Little* must be taken here to mean high-pitched, and to suggest, without more than fanciful justification, the voice of a little child. Falsetto is uttered with the glottis completely closed at the front. Most men can produce the falsetto; few women can. A falsetto whisper is possible with the glottis adjusted as for falsetto voice. The falsetto whisper, though seemingly higher-pitched than the normal whisper, is like it in being capable of no change of pitch.

Other Terms Sometimes Used

Sibilants. A sibilant is any *s*-like sound. The sounds usually spoken of as sibilants are [s, z] and sometimes [ʃ, ʒ].

Liquids. Sometimes, especially in older books, [m, n, ŋ, l, r] are figuratively called liquids. The French use *mouillé* (moist, wet—hence, liquid) in the same sense.

Gutturals. The term guttural is sometimes applied to back consonants. In English, these are [k, g, ŋ].

Consonant, Vowel, and Phoneme Defined

Consonant, vowel, and phoneme. Consonant, vowel, and phoneme can be defined for only one language at a time. Formal definitions of these for English have been deferred to this point in order to give the student a frame of reference into which to fit them. For consonant and vowel, at least, the student has had serviceable, if unformulated, definitions already in mind from ordinary school experience, which have been sufficient for the time. Actually, the formulation of exact definitions, even of consonant and vowel, is a difficult matter, and a very controversial one. The student must understand that the definitions in this book will not necessarily be approved by critics and other writers of phonetic texts. On that account, a certain amount of historical matter will be included in the ensuing discussion.

Distinguishing between consonant and vowel. *Definitions:* all of us use the terms consonant and vowel as opposites, the implication being that we can divide our forty-odd English speech sounds into two groups, with every sound fitting into the one group or the other. Yet when we come to the problem of fixing upon that indispensable factor in making any exact division, viz., the *basis* of the division, we find ourselves in a quandary. Since we shall have to name such a basis within a few paragraphs, it will be well to examine a few of the bases that have at one time or another been tried.

Pronounceability in isolation as a basis for separating vowels and consonants. First we may note the implications of the word, consonant, which is derived from Lat. *con* (with) + *sonare* (to sound). Evidently the early coiners of the word meant to say that a consonant is a sound used with another sound, i. e., with a vowel. The reverse meaning appears to have been understood to obtain, viz., that a consonant cannot be pronounced in isolation. Early writers boldly said as much, and defined a consonant as a sound which had to be used with another sound, whereas a vowel was a sound which could be pronounced alone.[19] Obviously, these definitions cannot hold, for any sound whatever can be pronounced alone.

Exercise

Pronounce aloud:

Front – [i, ɪ, e, ɛ, æ, a]

Back – [ɑ, ɒ, ɔ, o, ʊ, u]   ([ɒ] is brief, lax and halfway between [ɔ] and [ɑ])

Central – [ə, ɜ, ɚ, ɝ, ʌ]

Plosive – [p, b, t, d, k, g, ʧ, ʤ]   (Do not say [pʌ, bʌ], and the like. Do not pronounce any vowel after the consonant)

Nasal – [m, n, ŋ]

Lateral – [l]

Retroflex – [r]

Trilled – [ɾ]

Fricative – [ʍ, f, v, s, z, θ, ð, ʃ, ʒ, h]

Glide – [w, j]   (Try pronouncing *we* [wi] and *you* [ju]. Then leave off the vowels [i] and [u])

---

[19] An example of such a statement applying to one group of consonants is to be found in the introduction to Joseph Emerson Worcester's *Dictionary of the English Language* (Boston: Hickling, Swan and Brewer, 1860), p. XVII, as follows: "The consonants are divided into *mutes and semivowels.* The mutes cannot be sounded at all without the aid of a vowel. They are *b, d, k, p, t* and *c* and *g* hard."

Transcribe each of the following words forward and backward and pronounce aloud; example, *king* [kɪŋ – ŋɪk]: cats, kits, coats, last, chin, niche, valley, ding-dong, fling, oats, Alps, flood, mid, middy, Malone, mists, mosques.

Sonority as a basis for separating vowels and consonants. Attempts have also been made to divide speech sounds into vowels and consonants on the basis of sonority, or tonal effect, the technical opposite of which is noise. But tone and noise overlap each other in such a way as to handicap any effort to make the division. Note the following:

Sounds of complete sonority* (produced by periodic or regular vibration)	Sounds of mixed sonority and noise	Sounds of complete noise (produced by aperiodic or irregular vibration)

	Sonority		
i, ɪ, e, ɛ, æ, a		Noise	
ɑ, ɒ, ɔ, o, ʊ, u			
ə, ɜ, ɚ, ɝ, ʌ		b, d, g	p, t, k
m, n, ŋ		v, z, ð, ʒ	f, s, θ, ʃ
l		ʤ	tʃ
r, ɾ			ʍ
w, j			

* This classification disregards the fact that some friction may be present in close vowels such as [i] and [u]. It also disregards cavity friction, except in whispering. (Cavity friction is defined by Pike in *Phonetics*, p. 138, as "voiceless resonance of a chamber as a whole.")

It is evident above that some of the sounds traditionally called consonants are scattered throughout the chart. Some of the sounds contain both tone and noise, and the purely tonal sounds vary greatly in degree of sonority. It follows, therefore, that sonority cannot be used for dividing English speech sounds into two classes, whether along traditional lines or any other.

Exercises

Pronounce all the sounds symbolized in the chart above, noting: (1) that in the first section there is only tone, (2) in the second section a mixture of tone and noise (plosion and/or friction), and (3) in the third section only noise (plosion and/or friction).

Transcribe: seal, beast, fretting, faster, shrine, crowd, almshouse, tot, hood, cruise, abutted, firmer, churner, multiply, nobody, bringing, liver, raucous, story, wall, young, bamboo, daughter, goiter, bridegroom, visible, whether, prestige, journey, patch, tandem, cauliflower, fistula, soon, thatch, shoal, gelatin, whale.

Context as a basis for separating vowels and consonants. Still other attempts have been made to effect division by using context as a basis. As will be seen, this proves, for the English language, to be the most satisfactory of the bases mentioned thus far. The contexts which can be used as tests in English are strictly limited. They consist in taking a word beginning with the sound to be tested, and placing before it successively *a* [ə], *an* [ən]; *the* [ðə], [ðɪ]; and *to* [tə], [tʊ]. If the first of each pair, i.e., [ə, ðə, tə], accommodates itself to the succeeding sound in such a way as to satisfy the sense of fitness of an English-trained hearer, then the sound being tested is a consonant; if [ən, ðɪ, tʊ] seem better, the sound is a vowel. That is, if [ə ˈjild, ðə ˈjild, tə ˈjild] sound better than [ən ˈjild, ðɪ ˈjild, tʊ ˈjild], [j] is a consonant; if [ən ˈɔl, ðɪ ˈɔl, tʊ ˈɔl] sound better than [ə ˈɔl, ðə ˈɔl, tə ˈɔl], [ɔ] is a vowel. In addition, if there is a tendency for the glottal stop [ʔ] to develop when [ə, ðə, tə] are arbitrarily used, as in [əʔˈɔl, ðəʔˈɔl, təʔˈɔl],[20] we may be further confirmed in calling [ɔ] a vowel.

Perhaps it might as well be confessed at this point that the average phonetician, however objective he may ordinarily wish to be, in the matter of dividing vowels from consonants is anxious to find a basis of separation which will not disturb too much the division already well established and continually used. Context appears to constitute such a basis.

The tests of context are in most cases easy to apply, but they prove difficult to apply to a sound which ordinarily is found only in final position, such as the [ɚ] of *sister* [ˈsɪstɚ]. There is also the problem of some sounds that exist in closely related pairs, one member of each pair being syllabic and the other non-syllabic, or, as we shall presently consider it justifiable to say, one seeming to be a consonant and the other a vowel; e.g., [n, n̩] in *ton* [tʌn] and *button* [ˈbʌtn̩], [m, m̩] in *rip them* [ˈrɪp ðɛm] and *rip 'em* [ˈrɪpm̩], [l, l̩] in *sell* [sɛl] and *battle* [ˈbætl̩], [ŋ, ŋ̍] in *ing* [ɪŋ] and *I can go* [ˈaɪ kŋ̍ gou], [r, ɚ] in *for* [fɔr] and *debtor* [ˈdɛtɚ] (see Figures 31, 32, and 33). These matters will come up for consideration in the approaching discussions of the sounds respectively involved.

It is somewhat ironic that in seeking for a basis of division which will confirm a division already made, we do not find a true basis in context, but only a condition detectable by the ear, or by the muscular "feel" or kinesthesia, of the skilled speaker of English. This condition is, of course, the mutually exclusive appropriateness of [ə, ðə, tə] to precede consonants, and of [ən, ðɪ, tʊ] to precede vowels. The *basis* of this appropriateness lies still farther back and is the true basis. Just what it is, is probably debatable. It may actually be several things, one operative at one time, another at another, and sometimes more than one operating at the same time. Bloomfield, e.g., says, "Vowels are modifications of the voice-sound that involve no closure, friction or contact of the tongue

---

[20] A better transcription would be [əʔːˈɔl], since the glottal stop appears to be lengthened by a period of time between the implosion and the explosion.

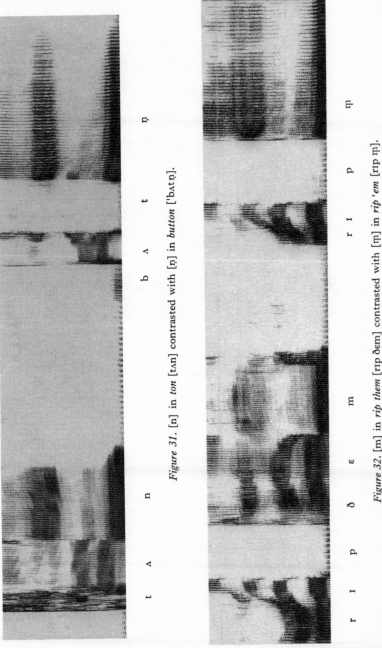

Figure 31. [n] in *ton* [tʌn] contrasted with [n̩] in *button* ['bʌtn̩].

Figure 32. [m] in *rip them* [rɪp ðɛm] contrasted with [m̩] in *rip 'em* [rɪp m̩].

or lips."[21] In a footnote[22] he goes on to say, "In contrast with vowels, stops, trills, spirants (fricatives), nasals, laterals are sometimes [!] called *consonants*." Here closure with lips or tongue, as with [p, g, n], friction, as with [v], and

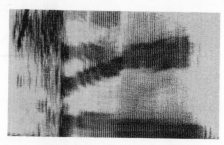

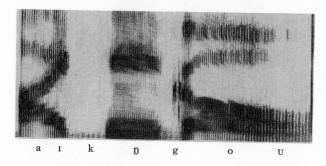

a   ɪ   k   ŋ   g   o   u

Figure 33. [ŋ] in *sing* contrasted with [ŋ] in [aɪ kŋ goʊ].

contact of lips or tongue, as with [m, l], are taken as bases for separating consonants from vowels.[23] Jones[24] and Kenyon[25] mention relative rapidity of utterance as identifying characteristics of [w] and [j].

---

[21] Leonard Bloomfield, *Language* (New York: Henry Holt and Co., Inc., 1933), p. 102.

[22] *Ibid.*, p. 102n.

[23] That Bloomfield had trouble with his bases is evident when, on the same page, he is obliged to call [r] as in *red* a vowel, since it presents neither closure, friction, nor contact.

[24] Daniel Jones, *An Outline of English Phonetics* (Leipzig and Berlin: B. G. Teubner, 1922), pp. 102, 800.

[25] J. S. Kenyon, *American Pronunciation* (Ann Arbor: G. Wahr, 1924), p. 155.

Grouping English consonants according to acoustic features mentioned by Bloomfield, Jones, and Kenyon:
Closure (by means of lips or tongue): [p, b; t, d; k, g].
Friction: [f, v; s, z; θ, ð; ʃ, ʒ; h*; ʍ].
Relative rapidity of utterance (plus closure or contact): [w, j,* m, n, ŋ, l, r] (as contrasted with [u, i, m̩, n̩, ŋ̍, l̩, ɚ, ɝ]).

* N.B. The letter *h* as in *a hand, a historical novel, a Hawaiian flower*, is the consonant [h]. The letter *u*, when pronounced [ju], as in *a useful book, a union*, has the consonant [j] as its initial sound. (See page 112 for the mistaken use of *an* before initial *h* and initial *u*.)

Pending some possibly more definitive final pronouncement not yet available,[26] we had as well be content, then, with the apparent truth that the quasi-instinctive use of [ə, ðə, tə] preceding certain sounds identify them as consonants and separate them from vowels. Following are Chart A illustrating the separation of consonants and vowels on the basis of context, and Chart B illustrating the separation of consonants and vowels in the traditional fashion.[27]

TWO CHARTS ON DISTINGUISHING CONSONANTS AND VOWELS

A. Separated by test of context [ə-ən, ðə-ðɪ, tə-tʊ] (only [ə-ən] employed below).

I. [ə ˈpæt, ə ˈbæt; ə ˈtæb, ə ˈdæb; ə ˈkoʊst, ə ˈgoʊst; ə ˈjoʊk, ə ˈʍɪp; ə ˈwɔl; ə ˈmæn, ə ˈneɪl, ə ˈŋɑlɑn (Tagalog), ə ˈloʊd, ə ˈroʊd; ə ˈfæn, ə ˈvæn, ə ˈsid, ə ˈzibrə, ə ˈθɪŋ, ə ˌdʌs tə bi ʌnˌnoʊn, ə ˈʃu, ə ˌʒɑːnˈdark, ə ˈhaʊs.]

II. [ən ˈil, ən ˈɪmp, ən ˈeɪs, ən ˈɛdʒ, ən ˈæks, ən ˈant (N.E.), ən ˈuz, ən ˈʊmlaʊt, ən ˈoʊk, ən ˈɔl, ən ˈɒpərə (Br.), ən ˈɑsp (Br.), ən m̩ˈbɑsi (nonsense word, constructed to place [m̩] initially; see also [n̩, ŋ̩, l̩] following), ən n̩ˈdɑsi, ən ŋ̩ˈgɑsi, ən l̩ˈfɑsi, ən ɚˈgɑstərɔl, ən ˈɝdʒ (G.A.), ən əˈplaɪənts, ən ˈɜdʒ (Br.), ən ˈʌŋkəl.

CONSONANTS   VOWELS

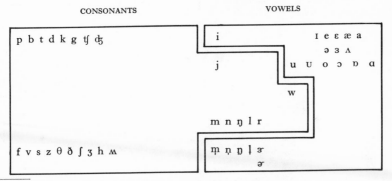

[26] It has become customary to look to instruments for information not readily discernible through the senses. There are truly instances where instruments aid, especially in the interpretation of transient phenomena. This book uses the findings of such instruments as the Spectrograph. But it is dubious whether instruments could help in this instance. The information needed here must be within the range of sensory perception, and no record or demonstration of extrasensory evidence will be of value in speech between person and person. For speech *is* between person and person, not between instrument and instrument.

[27] The "context test," which is to follow, for distinguishing between vowel and consonant is essentially structural. It proves that English divides its phonemes into two groups which receive different treatment in syntax. The correspondence of these classes with physical facts can be established, as will be seen, only at the expense of a number of awkward arrangements. This test does not undertake to distinguish vowels from consonants in any language other than English. Any attempt to make the distinction for all languages at once in terms of physical characteristics is certain to fail.

OBSERVATIONS

1. Note that [j] is placed below [i] to call attention to the fact that [j] is derived from [i].

2. Likewise [w] is placed below [u] to call attention to the fact that [w] is derived from [u].

3. Note that [m̥, n̥, ŋ̥, l̥, ɚ, ɝ] are placed below [m, n, ŋ, l, r] to call attention to the fact that [m̥, n̥, ŋ̥, l̥, ɚ-ɝ] are derived from [m, n, ŋ, l, r] by lengthening, thus making them technically classifiable as vowels. (Bear in mind that only nasal, lateral, and retroflex consonants can be given vowel characteristics by lengthening them. Other consonants remain consonants when lengthened.)

4. Note that using syllabicity as a basis of division would result in precisely the same division as above, for every sound designated as a vowel can be used either as a syllable or as the nucleus of a syllable.

5. It will be remembered from page 13 that [m̥, n̥, ŋ̥, l̥] are needed for such transcriptions as ['kipm̥, 'bɪtn̥, 'θɪŋkn̥, 'fɪdl̥].

B. Separated by test of traditional usage, using as bases of division plosion, friction, nasality, laterality, retroflexion, rapidity of motion, etc., none of which applies to all cases.

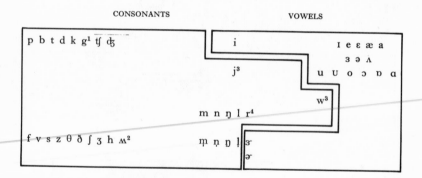

CONSONANTS   VOWELS

Explanation of numbers on chart:
[1] [p, b, t, d, k, g] are traditionally called consonants by reason of plosion.
[2] [f, v, s, z, θ, ð, ʃ, ʒ, h, ʍ] are so called by reason of friction.
[3] [j, w] by reason of rapidity of motion.
[4] [m, n, ŋ] by reason of nasality; [l] by reason of laterality; [r] by reason of retroflexion.

1. Note that, contrary to Chart A, there is no single basis of division. It would not help to group plosion, friction, and rapidity of motion together under some such name as non-vowel characteristics, since none of them applies to all the consonant sounds of English.

2. Chart B differs from Chart A only in the fact that [m̥, n̥, ŋ̥, l̥] are included with the consonants. This is by reason of their relation to [m, n, ŋ, l] and additionally because normally they are never used initially. To avoid

referring to them as vowels (according to Chart A they would be called vowel [m̩], vowel [n̩], vowel [ŋ̩], and vowel [l̩]), they are referred to in Chart B as syllabic consonants, viz., syllabic [m̩], syllabic [n̩], syllabic [ŋ̩], syllabic [l̩].

3. To be consistent, this chart should include [ɝ] and [ɚ] with the consonants, since, like [m̩, n̩, ŋ̩, l̩], they are derived from a consonant, viz., [r], mainly by lengthening, [ɝ] being equal to [r:], and [ɚ] to half-long [r·]. But the habit of calling them "vowel [r]" and "hooked schwa" (schwa being a vowel), largely because of their syllabicity, no doubt, has made it traditional to group them with the vowels. Besides, the fact that an [ən] is used preceding [ɝ] constantly and preceding [ɚ] in the rare instances when it is initial (something that, as noted above, never happens in English to [m̩, n̩, ŋ̩, l̩]) is an added strong traditional urge to call them vowels.

4. Chart B lacks technical consistency, but, since its inconsistency never shows up ([m̩, n̩, ŋ̩, l̩] never being used initially), Chart B can be used in a practical way without serious difficulty.

Now that we have examined the situation more closely than is usually done, it will be possible when necessary to use the traditional classification understandingly, and so interpret other phonetic literature readily. Within this book, however, Chart A will be followed.

Many phoneticians have traditionally called [w] and [j] semivowels, in view of the fact that they are related to the vowels [u] and [i]. The term semivowel is, however, confusing, since [w] and [j] behave, not as vowels, but as consonants, thus: a wish, the wish, to wish [ə wɪʃ, ðə wɪʃ, tə wɪʃ], a yield, the yield, to yield [ə jild, ðə jild, tə jild]. In terms of the thinking in this book, it would be equally appropriate to call [m̩, n̩, ŋ̩, l̩, ɝ-ɚ] semivowels because of their relation to [m, n, ŋ, l, r], and equally confusing, because [m, n, ŋ, l, r] behave like consonants. In any case, the term semivowel appears to be unnecessary, and will not be used further in this book. It is clear, however, that [m̩, n̩, ŋ̩, l̩] could be called "vowel [m̩]," "vowel [n̩]," "vowel [ŋ̩]," "vowel [l̩]," equally as well as "syllabic [m̩]," "syllabic [n̩]," "syllabic [ŋ̩]," "syllabic [l̩]." Stetson appears to confirm the validity of using such terms as "vowel [m̩]" when he says, "the chest pulse constitutes the essential syllable; the consonants have no independent existence, they function only in the syllable."[28] A syllabic, in this way of thinking, can be only a vowel, which may or may not be accompanied by one or more consonants. Vowel [m̩] is unaccompanied.

Definitions. In view of the evidence of Chart A, ante, and the accompanying discussion, we may now define vowel and consonant in English as follows:[29]

A vowel is a speech sound which may constitute a syllable or the nucleus of a syllable. Alternately, a vowel is a speech sound which may be preceded in context by an [ən], the when pronounced [ðɪ], and to when pronounced [tʊ].

---

[28] R. H. Stetson, *Bases of Phonology* (Oberlin, Ohio: Oberlin College, 1945), p. 6.

[29] Pike's definition may be examined for comparison. "Vowels and consonants are then categories of sounds, not as determined by their own phonetic nature, but according to their grouping in specific syllable functions." *Phonetics*, p. 76.

A consonant is a speech sound which is used marginally with a vowel or diphthong to constitute a syllable. (But see page 82 for such sounds as *pst*.) Alternately, a consonant is a speech sound which may be preceded in context by *a* [ə], [ðə] (a pronunciation of *the*), and [tə] (a pronunciation of *to*).

The phoneme.[30] The concept of the phoneme is an indispensable one, in phonetics no less than in its related discipline, phonemics. Yet the phoneme has never been finally and consistently defined. Probably some of the attempted definitions are even more likely to lead their users into difficulties—including occasional absurdities—than some of the definitions of vowel and consonant. The specific phonemes of the English language have never been completely agreed upon; on the contrary, those who have thought most deeply and effectively on designating them still change their minds occasionally as to what the phonemes are and what they include.[31] Yet the concept remains indispensable despite all this.

For a book on applied phonetics (which is practical, as distinguished from exhaustively theoretical phonetics), an error-proof definition is fortunately not necessary. Just as we have for centuries profited from a concept of vowel and consonant without being able to formulate a statement of precisely what they were, so we have unconsciously used some aspects of the phonemic concept even before we had the word phoneme, not to mention its definition. But a conscious application of the phonemic principle is more useful than an unconscious one, and so a definition of sorts is valuable.

In 1935 Twaddell[32] summarized the extant opinions and knowledge on the phoneme, adding a definition of his own.[33] Of all the definitions up to 1935, two have proved more useful in applied phonetics than any others; viz., Jones'

---

[30] R-M. S. Heffner, "The Program of the Prague Phonologists," *American Speech*, April 1936, p. 108. "It seems that the term 'phoneme' was introduced into linguistic science by Ferdinand de Saussure, who defined it as 'the sum of the acoustic impressions and the articulatory movements, of the unity heard and the unity spoken, the one conditioning the other.' Although first published in 1916 (in *Cours de linguistique genérale*), his definition is older than that of Baudoin de Courtenay, published in 1894."

[31] Cf. George L. Trager and Bernard Bloch, "The Syllabic Phonemes of English," *Language*, Vol. 17, No. 3 (July-September, 1941), pp. 223–246, and George L. Trager and Henry Lee Smith, *An Outline of English Structure* (Norman, Okla.: Battenburg Press, 1951).

[32] W. Freeman Twaddell, "On Defining the Phoneme," *Language Monographs*, No. XVI, March, 1935. Anyone wishing to investigate the thinking on the phoneme should begin with this monograph, and should supplement it from the writings Twaddell cites, particularly Bloomfield's *Language*, Chapters. V and VI; thence the student can proceed to such later writings as are available. Actually, the crest of scholarly excitement over the phoneme was in August, 1935, five months after the publication of Twaddell's monograph. The occasion was the Second International Congress on Phonetic Sciences, held in London. Here the phoneme was discussed by so many of the speakers that it finally became a matter of amusement when yet another paper on the subject was announced. The later years have, of course, produced other views on the phoneme, some of which will be cited.

[33] *Ibid.*, "...an Abstractional Fictitious Unit," p. 37.

statement that a phoneme is a family of sounds,[34] and Bloomfield's that a phoneme is "a minimum unit of distinctive sound feature."[35] We may illustrate Jones' definition thus:

Consider [t] in each of the following words, noting that each phonetic [t] or [t]-phone is different from the others, yet each conforms to the general concept and function of the phoneme /t/ which we have in our minds as a result of our experience with the English language.[36]

WORD	PRONUN-CIATION	KIND OF /t/ —OR SUBSTITUTION FOR CONVENTIONAL /t/.
tea	[ti]	Aspirated alveolar [t], tongue touching alveolar ridge some distance back of upper front teeth; strong explosion is sometimes indicated by raised [h], or by [ʻ].
stay	[steɪ]	Unaspirated alveolar [t]; weak explosion; un-aspiration sometimes indicated by ['].
pit	[pɪt]	Unreleased alveolar [t]; no explosion.
mutton	['mʌtn̩]	Alveolar nasal [t̃], exploded through nose in-stead of through mouth; the symbol [˜] in-dicates nasality.
battle	['bætl̩]	Alveolar lateral [t]; exploded at sides of tongue instead of over top of tongue.
that time	[ˌðæt 'taɪm]	Aspirated long alveolar [t]; explosion delayed, as indicated by symbol [:] or by doubling.
eighth	[eɪt̪θ]	Unaspirated dental [t̪]; tongue touching backs of upper front teeth. Symbol of dentality [ˌ].
sentence	['sɛnʔn̩s]	Glottal stop substituted for [t] between [n]'s, used and heard by speakers of standard

<hr>

[34] Daniel Jones, in *Proceedings of the International Congress of Phonetic Sciences*, Amsterdam, 1932. "Definition of a phoneme: A family of sounds in a given language, which are related in character, and are such that no one of them ever occurs in the same sur-roundings as any other in words."

———— "On Phonemes," in *Travaux du Cercle Linguistique de Prague*, p. 74. "A phoneme may be defined as a family of sounds in a given language, consisting of an important sound of the language together with other related sounds, which take its place in particular sound-sequences." (This is not to be confused with the definition of *le Cercle* itself, which describes a phoneme as a phonological unit [a differentiator of meaning] not divisible into smaller units. Cf. *Journal de Psychologie Normale et Pathologique*, XXX, 1933, p. 229.)

V. Trofimov and Daniel Jones, *The Pronunciation of Russian* (Cambridge: The University Press, 1923), pp. 49ff. "A phoneme is a group of sounds consisting of an important sound of the language (i.e., the most frequently used member of that group) together with others which take its place in particular sound-groups."

[35] Bloomfield, p. 79.

[36] George Trager in "The Phoneme 'T': A Study in Theory and Method," *American Speech*, Vol. XVII, October, 1942, cites certain other varieties of /t/, found in the speech of Northern New Jersey, which are not included here.

WORD	PRONUN- CIATION	KIND OF /t/ —OR SUBSTITUTION FOR CONVENTIONAL /t/.
		American English without consciousness of substitution.
little	['lɪʔļ]	Glottal stop substituted for [t]; substandard.
patty	['pærɪ]	One-tap trill substituted for [t], but used and heard by speakers of standard American English without consciousness of substitution.

Since all of these kinds of [t]'s (and substitutions) serve the single purpose of /t/ in the communication process, and since the non-phonetically-trained speaker of English would be surprised indeed to learn that there are any differences among those which he as an individual uses, it can be readily seen why Jones refers to the group as a family of [t]-sounds constituting (with the addition of any others common to the English language as a whole) the English /t/ phoneme. The various constituent [t]'s are called allophones of the /t/ phoneme.

Bloomfield's definition of the phoneme as "a minimum unit of distinctive sound-feature" must be approached in a different way. For the student of applied (practical) phonetics, the most important word in the definition is *distinctive*. Bloomfield is saying that a phoneme is a sound-feature which makes a distinction, or distinguishes, between words regarding their meanings. Note that in the following list each word is distinguished from the others by a single initial sound-feature (really a collection or complex of the sound-features which make up [t], [d], [f], and so on), thus:

till	[tɪl]	mill	[mɪl]	gill	[dʒɪl]
dill	[dɪl]	nil	[nɪl]	hill	[hɪl]
fill	[fɪl]	kill	[kɪl]	sill	[sɪl]
pill	[pɪl]	gill	[gɪl]	rill	[rɪl]
bill	[bɪl]	chill	[tʃɪl]		

We must understand, when reading this list, that for any initial sound, say the [t] of *till*, any other [t] may be *substituted* if it can be used initially. For example, the dental [t], i.e., [t̪], may be substituted without changing the meaning. But as soon as something is used, e.g., [d], which changes the meaning, in this case from *till* to *dill*, we know that we have crossed the boundary of the /t/-territory, and that we are in /d/-territory, for there has been introduced another distinctive unit of sound-feature. By it, *till* is distinguished from *dill*. We can see, then, that any initial sound which may be used without changing the meaning of the word *till* is a member of the /t/-phoneme, but that any sound which changes *till* to some other word, or even to a nonsense-syllable, such as *vill* or *zill*, is a member of some other phoneme.

It must be evident that we can follow the same process of thinking in respect to the middle sound of [tɪl], [ɪ], by considering it in the series *till, tell, toll, tall, tool, teal, tile, toil,* and of the final sound, [l], by considering it in the series *till, tib, tiff, tick, Tim, tin, tip, tit.* The total effect of these considerations is to demonstrate that *till* is made up of three phonemes, /t/, /ɪ/, and /l/, each of which may exist in a number of constituent allophones.

Since 1934, when Bloomfield's *Language* appeared, there have been many formulations of the phonemic concept. In that same year, Swadesh[37] called attention to *complementary distribution* and *pattern congruity* as necessary criteria for designating a phoneme. Trager and Bloch[38] in 1941 used these terms and added that a phoneme "class thus composed must be in contrast and mutually exclusive with every other such class in the language." In 1942, Trager composed a formal definition thus:

A phoneme is a selectional class of complementarily distributed, phonetically similar, and congruently patterned sound-types; it contrasts and is mutually exclusive with every similar class in the language, with some or all of which it enters into juxtapositional classes. [See definitions in footnote below.][39]

The principal features of this definition are explicit or implicit in other writings of these authors and their associates down to the present date.[40]

It remains to add that once having grasped the phonemic concept, it is possible, in phonetics, to view with complacency the fact that no sound is ever pronounced in exactly the same way twice, either by an individual or by dif-

---

[37] Morris Swadesh, "The Phonemic Principle," *Language*, June 1934, pp. 117–118.

[38] George L. Trager and Bernard Bloch, "The Syllabic Phonemes of English," *Language*, July-September 1941, p. 223.

[39] G. L. Trager, "The Phoneme 'T': A Study in Theory and Method," *American Speech*, October 1942, p. 145. Trager continues with definitions of terms (by [B] and [G] he means lenis [p] and [k] respectively):

In this definition, *selectional* refers to the process of selection discussed above. *Complementarily distributed* means that the sound-types never occur in contrast in the same situation; thus in English [pʻ] occurs initially and in certain other cases, while non-aspirated [p] occurs after stressed vowels internally, and lenis [B] is found only after [s]. *Phonetically similar* means involving at least one sound-feature in common: the sounds just mentioned are all voiceless labial stops (three sound-features in common). *Congruently patterned* refers to arrangement in the juxtapositional classes mentioned at the end of the definition: thus the three kinds of labial stops mentioned occur in similar sequences and combinations to three kinds of velar stops ([kʻ, k, G]). *Contrasts with* means that meanings may be distinguished; for example, in English [pʻ] and [b] contrast (*pit, bit*), while [pʻ] and [p] do not; in Chinese [pʻ] and [p] contrast, but [b] is just a nondistinctive variety of [p]. *Mutually exclusive* refers to the fact that no one sound-type occurring in any given situation may belong to more than one phoneme; cf. B. Bloch, "Phonemic Overlapping," *American Speech*, 16: 278–284 (1941). The order of the statements in the definition is also the order of procedure and importance: if complementary distribution does not completely determine the phonemic appurtenance of a sound-type, we next try phonetic similarity, and then congruent patterning.

[40] E. g., Bernard Bloch, "A Set of Postulates for Phonemic Analysis," *Language*, January-March 1948, pp. 3–46; G. L. Trager and Henry Lee Smith, Jr., *An Outline of English Structure.*

ferent individuals. Considering mechanical maladjustment and wear and tear, no sound is ever produced in the same way twice, even by a machine. But so long as a given utterance does not at any point take on the distinctive sound-features of a different phoneme, it will be understood as belonging to its own phoneme.

Strictly speaking, a phoneme can best be defined for a single individual or for a relatively homogeneous group. But with proper warning, it can be defined for a whole language. In the foregoing, it has been so defined.

A sound belonging to a given phoneme in one language does not necessarily belong to the same phoneme in another language; /l/, which is a separate phoneme in English, belongs to the /r/ phoneme of Japanese; and /t/, which is a separate phoneme in English, belonged, incredible as it may seem, to the /k/-phoneme of Hawaiian as that language was spoken when the Hawaiian Islands were discovered, and for more than half a century thereafter.[41] These matters and many related ones will come into subsequent discussions at the proper places, as the phonemic principle is applied to the phonetic material to follow.

Transcription in this book. It is often said, and well said, that we cannot set down every phone, or recognizable sound, of a language, (a) without including non-distinctive or non-significant features, and (b) without burdening the phonetic alphabet used with an unwieldy number of symbols. In contrast, it can be said that a purely phonemic transcription omits many features which are necessary to record in a book on applied phonetics. A purely phonemic transcription is serving one of its most practical purposes when it is used in developing an alphabet for a language which has none, or for reforming an alphabet already existing. Pike expresses this well when he says, "The purpose of practical phonemics...is to reduce a language to writing."[42] The transcriptions in this book will not be cumbersomely phonetic or starkly phonemic. This being a phonetics text, the transcriptions will be basically phonetic; but they will draw upon the phonemic principle wherever the results promise to be illuminating.

Phonetics is like arithmetic, which draws on algebra, geometry, and related

---

[41] But it must be admitted that [tl] may be found as a substitute for [kl] in English when some speakers pronounce *class* [klæs] as [tlæs]. Congruently, [dl] may be found a substitute for [gl], as when *glass* [glæs] is pronounced [dlæs]. These substitutions are conditioned by the lack of opposition between the clusters [tl] and [dl] and between [kl] and [gl].

[42] Kenneth L. Pike, *Phonemics* (University of Michigan Press, 1947), p. 57. The complete statement is as follows:

Phonetics gathers the raw material. Phonemics cooks it. Practical phonetics provides a technique for describing sounds in terms of movements of the vocal apparatus, and for writing them in terms of articulatory formulas, i.e., as letters of a phonetic alphabet. Practical phonemics provides a technique for processing the rough phonetic data in order to discover the pertinent units and to symbolize them in an alphabet easy for the native to read. The purpose of practical phonemics, therefore, is to reduce a language to writing.

fields, but does not use their nomenclature or processes. Phonetics is to phonemics as arithmetic is to higher mathematics.

In phonetics for speech, transcription can usually be in simple, unmodified symbols, without frequent diacritics or other modifications. Such transcription is, in a sense, essentially phonemic. But when a modification is necessary—a dental sign, a raising, lowering, fronting, or backing sign, a nasal sign, or an aspiration sign—it can be used for the purpose of the moment. Extreme use of phonemics will not serve in practical phonetics. Extreme over-burdening of a phonetic transcription with diacritics likewise will not serve.

The user of this book may well now recall that he knows all the basic symbols of the phonetic alphabet as applied to English, and that he knows how the sounds of English are produced and classified. He may now proceed to a more detailed view of the English sound system.

Bibliography

Phonetics–Phonemics

Books

Armstrong, L. E. and I. C. Ward, *Handbook of English Intonation* (2nd Ed.) (London: W. Heffer and Sons, Ltd., 1931).

Bloomfield, Leonard, *Language* (New York: Henry Holt and Co., Inc., 1933).

Gleason, H. A., *An Introduction to Descriptive Linguistics* (New York: Henry Holt and Co., 1955).

Gray, Giles Wilkeson and Claude Merton Wise, *The Bases of Speech* (Revised Ed.) (New York: Harper & Brothers, 1946).

Harris, Zellig S., *Methods in Structural Linguistics* (Chicago: University of Chicago Press, 1951).

Heffner, R-M. S., *General Phonetics* (Madison: The University of Wisconsin Press, 1949).

Jespersen, Otto, *Lehrbuch der Phonetik* (Leipzig and Berlin: B. G. Teubner, 1926).

Jones, Daniel, *The Pronunciation of English* (London: Cambridge University Press, 1950).

Kantner, Claude E. and Robert West, *Phonetics* (New York: Harper & Brothers, 1941).

Kenyon, J. S., *American Pronunciation* (8th Ed.) (Ann Arbor: George Wahr, 1940).

Negus, V. E., *The Mechanism of the Larynx* (London: Heineman, 1928).

Noël-Armfield, G., *General Phonetics* (Cambridge: W. Heffer and Sons, Ltd., 1931).

Paget, Sir Richard, *The Principles of the International Phonetic Association* (London: International Phonetic Association, 1949).

————, *Vowel Resonances* (London: International Phonetic Association, 1922).

Palmer, H. E., *English Intonation with Systematic Exercises* (New York: Appleton, 1922).

Pike, Kenneth, *Phonemics* (Ann Arbor: University of Michigan Press, 1947).

————, *Phonetics* (Ann Arbor: University of Michigan Press, 1943).

————, *The Intonation of American English* (Ann Arbor: University of Michigan Press, 1945).

Potter, Ralph K., George A. Kopp, and Harriet C. Green, *Visible Speech* (New York: D. Van Nostrand Co., Inc., 1947).

Russell, G. O., *Speech and Voice* (New York: The Macmillan Co., 1931).

————, *The Vowel* (Columbus: The University of Ohio Press, 1928).

Stetson, R. H., *Bases of Phonology* (Oberlin, Ohio: Oberlin College Press, 1945).

————, *Motor Phonetics* (Oberlin, Ohio: Oberlin College Press, 1945).

Stuart, T. P. A., "On the Mechanism of the Closure of the Larynx" in *Proceedings of the Royal Society*, V. 50, 1892.

Sweet, Henry, *Handbook of Phonetics* (Oxford: Clarendon Press, 1877).

————, *A Primer of Phonetics* (2nd Ed.) (Oxford: Clarendon Press, 1902).

————, *The Sounds of English* (Oxford: Clarendon Press, 1908).

Thomas, C. K., *An Introduction to the Phonetics of American English* (New York: The Ronald Press Co., 1947).

Trager, G. L. and Henry Lee Smith, Jr., *An Outline of English Structure* (Norman, Okla.: Battenburg Press, 1951).

Viëtor, Wilhelm, *Deutsches Aussprache-Wörterbuch* (Leipzig: O. R. Reisland, 1915).

Periodicals

Andrade, Manuel J., "Some Questions of Fact and Policy Concerning Phonemes," *Language*, January-March, 1936.

Bloch, Bernard, "A Set of Postulates for Phonemic Analysis," *Language*, January-March, 1948.

————, "Phonemic Overlapping," *American Speech*, December, 1941.

Caffee, Nathaniel M., "The Phonemic Structure of Unstressed Vowels in English," *American Speech*, May, 1951.

Fries, Charles C., and Kenneth L. Pike, "Coexistent Phonemic Systems," *Language*, January-March, 1949.

Graff, W. L., "Remarks on the Phoneme," *American Speech*, April, 1935.

Hall, Robert A., Jr., "French," Language Monograph No. 24, Structural Sketches 1, *Supplement to Language*, July-September, 1948.

Hayden, Rebecca E., "The Relative Frequency of Phonemes in General-American English," *Word*, V. 6, No. 3, December, 1950.

Heffner, R-M. S., "Program of the Prague Phonologists," *American Speech*, April, 1936.

Hill, A. A., "Phonetic and Phonemic Change," *Language*, January-March, 1936.

Hubbell, Allan F., "The Phonemic Analysis of Unstressed Vowels," *American Speech*, May, 1950.

Joos, Martin, "Acoustic Phonetics," Language Monograph No. 23, *Supplement to Language*, April-June, 1948.

Locke, W. N., and R-M. S. Heffner, "Notes on the Length of Vowels (II)," *American Speech*, February, 1940.

Malone, Benjamin, "The Phonemic Structure of English Monosyllables," *American Speech*, October, 1936.

Peterson, Gordon E., "The Phonetic Value of Vowels," *Language*, October-December, 1951.

Pike, Kenneth L., "Grammatical Prerequisites to Phonemic Analysis," *Word*, December, 1947.

————, "On the Phonemic Status of English Diphthongs," *Language*, April-June, 1947.

Trager, George L., "The Phoneme 'T'," *American Speech*, October, 1942.

————, "What Conditions Limit Variance of a Phoneme," *American Speech*, September, 1934.

————, "The Pronunciation of 'Short-a' in American Standard English," *American Speech*, June, 1930.

Trager, George L. and Bernard Bloch, "The Syllabic Phonemes of English," *Language*, Vol. 17, No. 3, 1941.

Twaddell, W. Freeman, "On Defining the Phoneme," *Language Monographs*, No. XVI.

Vachek, J., "Some Remarks on Writing and Phonetic Transcription," *Acta Linguistica*, Vol. V, No. 2, 1941.

Wells, Rulon S., "The Pitch Phonemes of English," *Language*, January-March, 1945.

CHAPTER 4

Detailed View of the Sounds of English Speech

Résumé

We have seen that the sounds of speech are produced in four ways:

1. A motor (the lungs) puts into motion a pair of vibrators (the vocal bands) setting up periodic (regular) vibrations in the air at the level of the glottis. These vibrations are modified selectively by the resonating surfaces and cavities of the throat, mouth, and nose. Here some are freely transmitted and the others are not, producing complex periodic (regular frequency) wave motions in the air. These are received by the ear and interpreted by the brain as speech tones of given quality (timbre). The sounds thus produced are for English the sonorous sounds [i, ɪ, e, ɛ, æ, a; ɑ, ɒ, ɔ, o, ʊ, u; ə, ɚ, ɜ, ɝ, ʌ; m, ɱ, n, ṇ, ŋ, ɲ; l, ḷ; r, ɾ; w, j].

2. A motor (the lungs) forces the breath stream through strictures (closed or narrowed valves, viz., glottis, back of tongue and soft palate, blade of tongue and hard palate, tip of tongue and alveolar ridge, upper lip and lower teeth, both lips) to produce aperiodic (irregular frequency) vibrations in the air. The resultant complex wave motions are received by the ear and interpreted by the brain as speech noise. These sounds are for English the voiceless plosives [p, t, k, ʔ] and the voiceless fricatives [f, s, θ, ʃ, h, ʍ].

NOTE: If a voiceless plosive is exploded through the aperture characteristic of a voiceless fricative, a voiceless affricate results. In English, the only commonly recognized voiceless affricate is [tʃ].

3. By a combination of No. 1 and No. 2, there are produced for English certain sounds characterized by both tone and noise, viz., the voiced plosives [b, d, g] and the voiced fricatives [v, z, ð, ʒ].

NOTE: If a voiced plosive is exploded through the aperture characteristic of a voiced fricative, a voiced affricate results. In English, the only commonly recognized voiced affricate is [dʒ].

4. By a particular form of No. 2, with, typically, only the posterior or cartilage glottis being open enough to constitute a functional stricture,[1] there are produced for English the whispered sounds corresponding to all sonorous sounds and to voiced plosives and fricatives.

We have found further that the English sounds are divisible on the basis of syllabicity (or of context, which leads to the same result) into two categories, traditionally called vowels (syllabics) and consonants (non-syllabics), thus:

1. Vowels: [i, ɪ, e, ɛ, æ, a; ɑ, ɒ, ɔ, o, ʊ, u; ə, ɚ, ɜ, ɝ, ʌ; m̩, n̩, ŋ̍, l̩]²
2. Consonants: [p, b, t, d, k, g; m, n, ŋ; l, r, ɾ, f, v, s, z, θ, ð, ʃ, ʒ, h, ʍ, w, j, ʧ, ʤ]

As indicated above, every sound classified here as a vowel is also a syllabic; that is, it is capable of supplying the peak or crest of sonority necessary to make it the nucleus of a syllable. We have already had discussion (pages 65–74) as to whether the ability to serve as a syllabic constitutes a test for a vowel. Evidently it does, if we disregard such quasi-syllables as the interjections *s-s-s* [s:], *sst* [st], *pst* [pst].

We are now ready to make a more detailed study of speech sounds in the light of all the discussion and practice which has preceded this point. New principles, nomenclatures, and suggestions will be considered as occasion demands. Note references to matters already discussed in Chapter 2.

The vowel diagram. It has long been the custom to explain the relationship of vowels to each other by means of a diagram, such as the one below. This diagram originated as a vowel triangle and gradually evolved in various publications on phonetics as a four-sided figure, geometrically described as a trapezium. Its approximate present form has been widely popularized by Daniel Jones of University College, London, and by his pupils, colleagues, and critics, in the form known as the cardinal vowel diagram.[3] The method of developing the diagram was as follows:

1. A series of eight X-ray photographs was made to show the position of the tongue for each of the vowels [i, e, ɛ, a, ɑ, ɔ, o, u], the arch of the tongue being outlined by a very small chain draped from front to back along its center line. These eight photographs, superimposed upon each other, gave a composite effect, thus (Figure 34):

---

[1] Pike, *Phonetics*, p. 136, "with whisper the anterior part of the glottis may be closed." See also Heffner, pp. 20, 22 (diagram), 85, 86.

[2] It is not traditional, of course, to regard [m̩, n̩, ŋ̍, l̩] as vowels; but it seems as reasonable as the well-established practice of regarding [ɝ] and [ɚ] as vowels. All of them will stand the test of context with a preceding [ən], [ðɪ], or [tʊ], as has been seen (pages 71–73), as well as the test of syllabicity (pages 65–74).

[3] See Daniel Jones, *Pronunciation of English* (London: Cambridge University Press, 1950), pp. 21–23, and *An English Pronouncing Dictionary* (New York: E. P. Dutton, 1937), Frontispiece. Also Ida C. Ward, *The Phonetics of English* (Cambridge, Heffer, 1929), pp. 55 ff., and R-M. S. Heffner, *General Phonetics* (University of Wisconsin Press, 1950), p. 84.

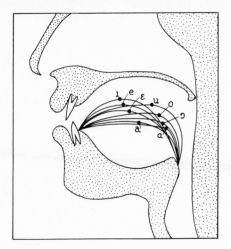

Figure 34. Composite diagram showing height of the tongue for each of eight vowels.

The small phonetic symbols in the picture represent the highest point of each arch respectively.

Lifting the pattern of symbols from the pictures and enlarging it, we have a roughly oval figure, thus:

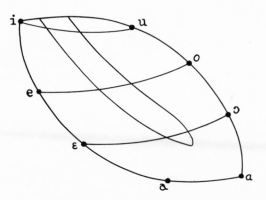

Figure 35. Enlargement of pattern of vowel distribution in Figure 34.

Since this figure is of awkward shape and difficult to reproduce, it is conventional to straighten its boundaries into the form of trapezium:

Years after this establishment of the vowel diagram on the basis of X-ray evidence, a remarkably similar diagram evolved from the patterns produced by the spectrograph or visible speech machine. By plotting formant No. 1 against formant No. 2 in pictures of vowels such as the one below (Figure 37), a diagram

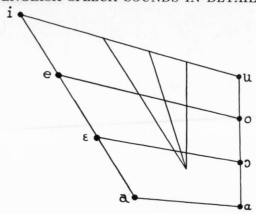

Figure 36. Preceding diagram conventionalized to form the cardinal vowel diagram.

like the following results (Figure 38). The resemblance to the Jones diagram is striking.[4]

Cardinal vowels.[5] The word *cardinal* as used here is taken from the nomenclature of the mariner's compass, on which the principal directions are called the cardinal points of the compass. These are points of reference to which all other

---

[4] Gordon Peterson, "Vocal Gestures," *Bell Laboratories Record*, November, 1951, p. 501. See also Martin Joos, "Acoustic Phonetics," *Language Monograph* No. 23, April-June, 1948, p. 52.

[5] Throughout this discussion of the cardinal vowel concept it must be borne in mind that the cardinal vowel diagram is, as indicated in the title of Figure 36, a conventionalization, and that the cardinal vowels are, as stated above, theoretic vowels. Both the concept and the diagram have long proved valuable as a teaching device. The fact that the diagram and the descriptions of vowel positions derived from it are normalized does not lessen their value, since any visual image of tongue position has to be corrected in practice by the ear.

Perhaps it should be said once for all that the possibilities of cavity adjustment within the mouth are very great, so that satisfactory vowels can be made despite astonishing handicaps: e.g., [i] can be made with the jaws widely opened, [ɑ] with teeth clenched; all the English vowels except [ɝ, ɚ] can be made with the tongue protruded and held tightly between the teeth; Demosthenes appears to have done very well with his mouth full of pebbles.

G. Oscar Russell in *Speech and Voice* (New York: Macmillan, 1931) concluded long ago from his X-ray studies that the vowels could be made with the tongue in various unexpected positions. Even after his methodology had been improved by C. E. Parmenter and S. N. Treviño ("Vowel Positions As Shown by X-Ray," *Quarterly Journal of Speech*, 18–351, 1932), the fact still remained that the mouth can make compensations for abnormal highness or lowness of tongue position and produce vowels approved by the ear notwithstanding. H. K. Dunn ("The Calculation of Vowel Resonances, and an Electrical Vowel Tract," *Journal of the Acoustical Society of America*, 22, 740–753, 1950) demonstrated that in his artificial vocal tract there was, for back vowels, evidence of "the extension of the tongue downward toward the larynx." But since only gross movements of the tongue are under easy control of the will, teaching processes are promoted by considering that vowel positions are typical or normal positions, remembering that the cardinal references are for positions of the tongue within its normal constraints inside the mouth.

directions are related. In the same way, the cardinal vowels are points of reference, as will be developed below. They are not necessarily, it must be added, the standard sounds of any language or dialect. They are made arbitrarily, as has been seen.

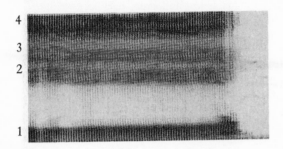

Figure 37. Spectrogram of [ɪ], showing formants corresponding to the first four resonances.

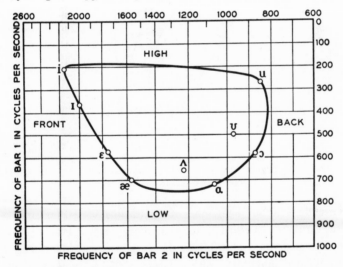

Figure 38. Diagram resembling cardinal vowel diagram, derived by plotting formant No. 1 against formant No. 2 of the Spectrograms of [ɪ], [ɛ], [æ], etc.

The cardinal vowel concept is a valuable one, as is the definition of a cardinal vowel. A cardinal vowel may be defined as a theoretic vowel made with a tongue-position that is invariable, easily described in writing or printing so as to be communicable at a distance. By referring to this tongue-position of the theoretic vowel as a point of reference, other vowels can be described as higher, lower, farther front, or farther back.

Actually, only the vowels at the corners of the diagram, viz., [i, a, ɑ, u] can properly be called cardinal vowels, for they and they alone can be reproduced invariably with the same tongue positions. That is:

[i] is made with the tongue as high and as far front as possible.

[a] with the tongue as low and as far front as possible.

[ɑ] with the tongue as low and as far back as possible.

[u] with the tongue as high and as far back as possible.

When [e] is placed one-third of the vertical distance downward from [i] toward [a], [o] one-third of the distance downward from [u] toward [ɑ], and when [æ] and [ɔ] have been placed respectively two-thirds of the same distances downward, the number of vowels has been doubled to make up the form of the

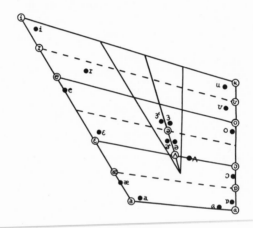

Figure 39. Diagram showing cardinal vowels (at intersections of lines) and positions of author's vowels (in heavy dots).

diagram usually seen; but the number of true cardinal vowels remains the same—four. However there is a visual, if not an auditory, value in placing the extra four vowels on the diagram. And it follows that if the space on the trapezium can be arbitrarily divided into thirds with resulting visual advantage, it can just as well be divided into sixths to equally great advantage, permitting the placing on it of the complete list of English vowels. The diagram above is so divided, and all the English vowels are placed upon it. The four at the corners may truthfully be called cardinal vowels, and the remainder may be called theoretic vowels, or, continuing in the terminology of the compass,[6] collateral vowels. Reproducing

---

[6] Names of directions on the compass: Corresponding vowel names:

Cardinal points—N, S, E, W.   Cardinal vowels—i, a, ɑ, u.

Collateral points—NW, NE, SW, SE.   Collateral vowels—ɪ, e, ɛ, æ, ɒ, ɔ, o, ʊ.

them requires accuracy in lowering or raising the tongue by thirds and sixths of the normal opening of the jaws—a feat which is impossible of precise achievement, but which can be improved with practice. Actually, the ear is probably the principal guide in locating all but the four cardinals, the kinethesia of tongue position being probably of secondary value. In the diagram the cardinal and theoretic vowels are shown in small circles, and vowels of daily use, as the author of the book believes he pronounces them, are shown by heavy black dots (Figure 39). The total diagram may be taken as a conventionalized representation of the human mouth, with the lips to the left and the pharynx to the right, with the height of the tongue represented in six degrees, and with the symbols for the English vowels written at the highest point of the tongue-arch for each.

Front, back, and central vowels, at high, low, and mid elevations. It has already been made clear that a front vowel is one made with the highest part of the tongue-arch in front. Conversely, a back vowel is made with the highest part of the tongue-arch at the back. One may get a kinesthetic impression of front and back positions by pronouncing a sustained [i:::] with the tip of the forefinger touching the tip of the tongue, and immediately thereafter pronouncing [u:::]. The sensation of the tongue jerking from the front to the back position is a startling demonstration of the back position of [u] as compared with the front position of [i]. The same experiment may be performed with [ɪ-ʊ], [e-o], [ɛ-ɔ], [æ-ɒ], and [a-ɑ]. It will be noticed that as the pairs of vowels are lower, the backward excursion of the tongue becomes shorter. This reduced distance is reflected in the shortness of the lower line of the vowel diagram, as compared with the upper.

If, now, the finger be placed on the top of the tongue-tip while [i] is being pronounced, and if the tongue be followed backward by the finger as the shift is made to [u], the contours and position of the tongue-arch can be further discovered and understood. This experiment, too, can be repeated for [ɪ-ʊ], [e-o], [ɛ-ɔ], [æ-ɒ], and [a-ɑ].

The term *central* indicates that the tongue-arch is in the center of the mouth, i.e., midway between front and back. Exploring with the finger while pronouncing [ə] or [ɜ] will demonstrate this.

High, low, and *mid* refer to degrees of tongue elevation. *High* applies to the space at the top of the diagram bounded by the small symbols [i, e, o, u]. *Low* applies to the space bounded by [ɛ, a, ɑ, ɔ], and *mid* to the space bounded by [e, ɛ, ɔ, o]. If the finger is held horizontally under the lower jaw while the vowels [i, ɪ, e, ɛ, æ, a] are successively pronounced, the dropping of the jaw, registering a similar dropping of the tongue from high to low, will readily be felt. The same effect, but in reverse, can be noted by pronouncing [ɑ, ɒ, ɔ, o, ʊ, u] with the finger under the jaw.

All of these terms prove useful in describing vowels, as will presently be seen. The combinations sometimes used are somewhat paradoxical, such as low-high and high-low. But they are easily understood in context.

Nasality. For all English vowels, the velum is theoretically closed, preventing all exit of air through the nose. Slight opening of the velum is to be disregarded, unless the resultant effect of nasality is great enough to attract unfavorable attention. It should be added that no one listening to his own voice is a reliable judge as to whether he speaks with a degree of nasality which might be classed as offensive. A much more reliable judgment may be had from a phonetically-trained colleague or teacher. This judgment may well be supplemented by listening to a record of the speaker's own voice. Such a record often reveals startlingly an unsuspected nasality too conspicuous for agreeable effect.

Conspicuous nasality in cases where it does not pervade the whole speech pattern of an individual usually shows up on stressed vowels preceeding the nasals [m], [n], [ŋ]. It is particularly likely to affect [æm], [æn], [æŋ] as in *Sam* [sæm], *man* [mæn], *clang* [klæŋ]. (See page 62.)

Some languages, such as French and Portuguese, have extensive systems of nasal vowels. Such vowels are in perfectly good standing. But in English, nasal vowels are theoretically not in good standing. However, it has been demonstrated by X-rays,[7] and by tests to determine whether any part of the breath stream passes out through the nose during the utterance of vowels, that there is very often a partial opening of the velum during such utterance. This does not necessarily prove that the person being X-rayed or being tested for escape of air through the nose is producing an unacceptable vowel. It may only prove that he was producing a vowel with some degree of nasal resonance. For it is a matter of common observation that some speakers, pronouncing with a degree of nasality, still produce quite acceptable vowels. It is further well known that teachers of singing often advise their pupils to introduce a controlled degree of nasality into the tone for the purpose of improving it. It is probably tolerant and reasonable to say that if the velum drops slightly, without resultant offensiveness in the vowel tone, no harm has been done. On the other hand, probably no harm is ever done in speaking by keeping the velum completely closed during the phonation, that is, the vocal utterance, of vowels.

Exercise

Memorize the vowels on the diagram, reciting them in order down the front from [i] to [a] and up the back from [ɑ] to [u]. Include the central vowels as a final group. Draw the vowel diagram freehand and write the English vowels upon it.

---

[7] Russell, *Speech and Voice*, pp. 121–176.

Use of the dictionary in transcription work. The student is encouraged to use the dictionary on unfamiliar words. Several such words are deliberately included in the transcription lists. Excellent standard dictionaries for student use are *The American College Dictionary*,[8] *Webster's New Collegiate Dictionary*,[9] and *The Thorndike-Barnhart Dictionaries*.[10] *The American College Dictionary* and *The Thorndike-Barnhart Dictionaries* have the great advantage of using [ə] where it is needed, whereas *Webster's New Collegiate Dictionary* uses, apparently, seven different symbols with the value of [ə]. All these dictionaries use *r* in the post-vocalic position in the quasi-phonetic respellings of words for pronunciation, leaving it to the user to pronounce the *r* or omit it, according to his dialect. For example, *ACD* and *Thorndike-Barnhart* (sist'ər) and *Webster* (sĭs'tẽr) are both intended to be pronounced either ['sɪstɚ] or ['sɪstə]. Standard dictionaries are valuable to students of phonetics mainly for stress markings and for broad distinctions in pronunciation. They are often confusing in respect to details by reason of the use of ambiguous symbols, meant to cover the pronunciations in more than one dialect. For example, the middle vowel of the *Webster* (ĭm'ĭtāt) is intentionally ambiguous, indicating that the word may be pronounced ['ɪmɪ‚teɪt] or ['ɪmə‚teɪt].

Phonetic dictionaries. There are two valuable pronouncing dictionaries available, as of this date, which use phonetic symbols based on IPA. These are the Kenyon and Knott *Pronouncing Dictionary of American English*[11] and the Jones *English Pronouncing Dictionary*.[12] The first gives American pronunciations, including many regional pronunciations, while the second gives only standard southern British pronunciations.

The user of any phonetics book is obliged to become accustomed to the personal biases of the author, and to change the transcriptions affected by these biases to the form which he, by reason of his own biases (or those of his teacher), wishes to use. For example, from the standpoint of this book, the use in Kenyon and Knott of [e] = [eɪ] and [o] = [oʊ], as in *day* [deɪ] and *dough* [doʊ] is unfortunate, notwithstanding the explanation[13] that [e] and [o] are intended to include [eɪ] and [oʊ]. Foreigners, especially, are misled. And in Jones, an individualized form of IPA, called "broad transcription," is used, which, among

---

[8] *The American College Dictionary* (Edited by Clarence L. Barnhart) (New York: Random House, Inc., 1953).

[9] *Webster's New Collegiate Dictionary* (Springfield, Mass.: G. and C. Merriam Company, 1953).

[10] *The Thorndike-Barnhart Dictionaries* (Edited by Clarence Barnhart) (Garden City: Doubleday and Co., Inc., 1951–1954).

[11] J. S. Kenyon and Thos. A. Knott, *A Pronouncing Dictionary of American English* (Springfield, Mass.: G. and C. Merriam Company, 1944).

[12] Daniel Jones, *An English Pronouncing Dictionary*, Rev. Ed. (New York: E. P. Dutton, 1937).

[13] Kenyon and Knott, pp. viii-xix.

other things, employs the sign [:] as a means of distinguishing otherwise identical symbols, rather than for its proper purpose of indicating length. To use Jones understandingly, it will be necessary for the student to learn the following table of equivalences:

Jones — IPA	Jones — IPA
i: = i	ɔ = ɒ
i = ɪ	u: = u
e = ɛ	u = ʊ
ɔ: = ɔ	ə: = ɜ

English Vowels

[i]

The vowel [i] is a high-front, tense, unround vowel. The terms *high* and *front* have been sufficiently explained in the paragraphs just preceding. The term *unround* refers to the neutral spreading position of the lips during the utterance of [i]. Since the tongue is high in the mouth, the air passage over the top, between tongue and palate, is vertically narrow, but horizontally wide. The tongue is in contact laterally with the upper teeth almost to the front of the mouth. The term *tense*, referring to the strong contraction and hard tensity of the muscles of (principally) the tongue, was explained briefly on page 61. This tensity can easily be detected by holding the thumb and forefinger beneath the lower jaw in such a way as to touch only the fleshy underside of the tongue while pronouncing a sustained [i:::]. The effect is heightened if [i] and [ɪ] are pronounced alternately, thus, [i::——ɪ], [i::–ɪ], so that the contrast between the tense [i] and the lax [ɪ] is strongly palpable. The velum is closed.

The sound [i] has many spellings in English. Certain French loan-words use the orthographic symbol *i*, which is identical with the phonetic symbol; cf. *prestige, clique, marine*. Other spellings of [i] are *ae* as *Caesar, ay* as in *quay, ea* as in *league, e* as in *concede, ee* as in *proceed, ei* as in *receipt, eo* as in *people, ey* as in *key, ie* as in *relieve, oe* as in *phoenix*.

It is often of value to consider the positions in which a sound can be used in a given language. May the sound be used initially, medially, and finally in a word? And in what contexts with other sounds? If it cannot be used in a certain position, such position is called for that language a "forbidden" position.

The sound [i] may be used initially as in *eat* [it], medially as in *redeemer* [rɪˈdiməˌ, rɪˈdimə], or finally as in *tree* [tri]. It is not normally used before *r* in the same syllable; historical [i] in this position has become [ɪ].

Transcribe, marking primary stress with [ˈ] before the syllable, and secondary stress with [ˌ] before the syllable, as in *hemiplegia* [ˌhɛməˈplidʒɪə, ˌhɛmɪˈplidʒɪə]: reprieve, esteem, chic, meaty, paraplegia, chiefly, precede, displeasing, freedom, creation, Phoebus, quay, relay (n), beleaguer, breezy, unfeeling, keyed, peopled, Caesar, perceive, feet, Aeolian, daemonic, Aegean, abbreviate, creamery, daedal, defeat, marine, idea, prestige, Phoebe, evade, leisure, Egypt, Piraeus, cerise, grease, greasy, Queen Mab, subpoena, priesthood, pristine, primeval, Phaedrus, Tahiti, pleaded, replete, cliché, frieze, achievement, Aeneas, coenobite, teapot, leisurely, Wheeling, geyser (Br., hot water heater), suite, been (Br.).

Transcribe:
1. There is no more real difference between the two than between Tweedle-dum and Tweedle-dee.
2. At the very least he could appeal to the Supreme Court.
3. He committed a really egregious error.

Suggestions. The following are some suggestions designed to help in solving particular problems arising in the transcription of the foregoing:

1. *Final unstressed y.* Words like *meaty, chiefly,* and *breezy* bring back the question whether to use [i] or [ɪ] in the unstressed final syllables. When we compare the two syllables of *meaty,* the vowels sound much alike, yet not exactly so. We might say the same of the two vowels of *misty.* Aside from the question of what phoneme the final vowels belong to, there is the question, in applied phonetics, of whether [i] or [ɪ] is the more practical to use. Usually there is little choice. In a few cases, words can be partially distinguished by using [ɪ], as in *guaranty-guarantee* ['gærəntɪ-ˌgærən'ti], *warranty-warrantee* ['wɔrəntɪ-ˌwɔrən'ti]. In view of instances like these, and in view of the practice of many publications, it seems best to use [ɪ],[14] e. g., ['mitɪ], ['mɪstɪ], ['tʃiflɪ]. Variations of this problem of choice occur also in *reprieve* and *abbreviate,* where [ɪ] is probably the most practical symbol to use in the unstressed syllables spelled with *e* and *i;* thus [rɪ'priv], [ə'brivɪeɪt]. In *reprieve* [ə] can also be used in the first syllable, thus [rə'priv]; in *abbreviate,* [ə] cannot be used in the third syllable, by reason of the vowel immediately following.

2. *The vowel [l̩] (also called syllabic [l̩]).* The nonsense words *Tweedle-dum* and *Tweedle-dee* present a problem of transcription commonly solved by use of [l̩], called vowel [l̩] or syllabic [l̩], thus: [ˌtwidl̩'dʌm, ˌtwidl̩'di]. To understand the typical occurrences of syllabics like this, it is necessary to understand the term *homorganic sounds.* Accordingly, a discussion of these sounds is interpolated at this point.

Homorganic sounds: the vowels (syllabics) [l̩, m̩, n̩, ŋ̩]. Homorganic sounds are two or more sounds made with at least a part of the speaking mechanism in the same position. The sounds [p, b, m] have the closed position of the lips

---

[14] All of the dictionaries named earlier use symbols meaning [ɪ]; viz., [ɪ] (Kenyon and Knott), [i] (Jones), [i] (*ACD*), [i] (Thorndike-Barnhart) and [i] (*Webster*). For opinions concerning [i] in the context of No. 3 above, see C. K. Thomas, *An Introduction to the Phonetics of American English* (The Ronald Press, 1947), p. 48; Allan F. Hubbell, *The Pronunciation of English in New York City* (Columbia University Press, 1950), p. 87.

in common and are therefore called homorganic. The sounds [t, d, n] have the alveolar and bilateral dental contact of the tongue in common, and the sounds [k, g, ŋ] have the velar contact of the tongue in common. All three groups are thus homorganic among themselves. It therefore follows that from [t] or [d] it is possible to proceed to the pronunciation of [n] without any intervening vowel, so that [n] becomes a syllabic (i. e., vowel) itself, as in *kitten* ['kɪtn̩], *hidden* ['hɪdn̩]. Likewise from [p] or [b] we can proceed without an intervening vowel to syllabic [m̩], as in *grip 'em* ['grɪp m̩]; and from [k] and [g] we can proceed without an intervening vowel to syllabic [ŋ], as in *kicking high* [ˌkɪkŋ̩ 'haɪ] and *digging sand* [ˌdɪgŋ̩ 'sænd]. In every case, the consonant preceding the syllabic does not have its usual forward explosion, or, indeed, any proper explosion at all. Instead, the air which might have exploded forward is conserved and passed out through the nose as a part of the out-going breath for the production of the syllabic. Observe this effect in pronouncing ['kɪtn̩].

Now the case of syllabic [l̩] is slightly different. The sound [l] is homorganic with [t] and [d], but in a somewhat different way. In [twidl̩], the air for [d] does not explode through the nose, as in *hidden* ['hɪdn̩], and of course it does not explode over the tip of the tongue in typical fashion; instead it escapes bilaterally when the sides of the tongue drop for [l̩]. As before, there is no intervening vowel between [d] and [l̩].

Occasionally we shall find other combinations of sounds with [m, n, ŋ, l], each of which permits the pronunciation of one or another of these sounds with no vowel intervening between it and the preceding consonant. Such instances may allow us to designate [m, n, ŋ] or [l] as syllabic. But it is wise to be cautious with any other sequences than [pm]; [bm]; [tn], [dn]; [tl], [dl]; [kŋ], [gŋ].

Transcribe: mitten, Eden; fiddle, kettle; ribbon (i. e., colloq. rib'm).

[ɪ]

The sound [ɪ] is low-high-front, lax, unround. All these terms have been explained (pages 87–88) except the apparently contradictory term "low-high." By reference to the vowel diagram (page 86), it will be seen that "low-high" refers to the lower portion of the space bounded by [i] [e] [o] [u]. *Low-high-front*, then, means the tongue is in a position just below the position of [i], which has been designated as high. As the diagram further indicates, the highest part of the tongue-arch is slightly farther back than for [i]. Obviously the air passage over the tongue, while only a little wider than for [i], is considerably greater in a vertical direction. The lateral contact of the tongue with the upper teeth is essentially the same as for [i]. The velum is closed.

Like [i], the sound [ɪ] has many spellings in English. The basic spelling is with *i* as in *bit*. Other spellings in stressed syllables are *e* as *pretty*, *here*, and *England;* *ea* as in *hear;* *ee* as in *been* (Am.) and *queer;* *ei* as in *weird;* *ie* as in *sieve;*

o as in *women; u* as in *business; ui* as in *built;* and *y* as in *gypsum*. In unstressed syllables, if we draw upon several dialects, we can find [ɪ] spelled with all the vowel letters of the alphabet, except *o*, and with several combinations of these letters. Compare the following:

> *a—character* ['kærɪktɚ],[15] *courage* ['kɜɪʤ], *palace* ['pælɪs] (Eastern, Southern, British), *salad* ['sælɪd] (E., S., Br.), *Dallas* ['dælɪs] (E., S., Br.), *palate* ['pælɪt] (E., S., Br.).
> *ay—Thursday* ['θɜzdɪ].
> *e—example* [ɪg'zæmpl], *devote* [dɪ'vout], *pushes* ['puʃɪz] (E., S., Br.), *counted* ['kauntɪd] (E., S., Br.), *kitchen* ['kɪtʃɪn] (E., S., Br.), *hostess* ['houstɪs] (E., S., Br.), *cricket* ['krɪkɪt] (E., S., Br.).
> *ei—forfeit* ['fɔfɪt] (E., S., Br.).
> *i—malice* ['mælɪs] (E., S., Br.), *pallid* ['pælɪd] (E., S., Br.), *Baffin* ['bæfɪn] (E., S., Br.), *Phillip* ['fɪlɪp] (E., S., Br.), *deposit* [dɪ'pɒzɪt] (E., Br.), *imitate* ['ɪmɪˌteɪt] (Br.).
> *u—lettuce* ['lɛtɪs] (E., S., Br.), *minute* ['mɪnɪt] (E., S., Br.).
> *ui—biscuit* ['bɪskɪt] (E., S., Br.).
> *y—truly* ['trulɪ].

Most foreign languages do not contain [ɪ] as a separate phoneme. Of the Western European languages, only Germanic languages do so, viz., English, German, etc. It follows that speakers of French, Spanish, Italian, Portuguese, Russian, and numerous other languages substitute in stressed English syllables their nearest sound, which is [i]. If such speakers are taught that [i] is pronounced with tense glossal muscles and [ɪ] with lax glossal muscles, they usually have little further trouble. As explained on page 90, the contrast between the tenseness of [i] and the laxness of [ɪ] can be detected by placing the thumb and finger against the fleshy central portion of the underside of the lower jaw and phonating [i-ɪ] successively.

In some languages, such as Spanish, the foreign [i] is lower and more lax than the English [i], but higher and more tense than English [ɪ]. When the lowered [i] is used indiscriminately for English [i] and [ɪ], English-speaking listeners often get the effect of exact reversal, that is, of [i] used for [ɪ] and [ɪ] used for [i]. A good drill for all speakers who have trouble with English [ɪ] is to pronounce pairs of words such as *fill-feel, sin-seen, it-eat*.

The [ɪ] phoneme contains many slight variants or allophones. We have noted (page 91) the difference between the two vowels of *pity* and have recommended that, despite this difference, the second vowel, as well as the first, be transcribed [ɪ]. Observe also the differences in the varieties of [ɪ] in *carrying* ['kærɪɪŋ], *sleepiest* ['slipɪɪst] (E., S., Br.), *fiftieth* ['fɪftɪɪθ] (Br.), *finality* [ˌfaɪ'nælɪtɪ] (Br.), *excoriate* [ɪks'kourɪˌeɪt], *Wednesday* ['wɛnzdɪ].

---

[15] Transcriptions in these illustrations, unless otherwise indicated, are in the General American dialect.

Transcribe: (Note that some of the following words do not contain [ɪ] in all dialects.) pitiful, mystery, business, busyness, springing, pretty, fearsome, sieve, womenkind, hereafter, pigeon, pier, prettiest, been (Am.), exult, sinfully, sheer, pierce, shear, building, cryptic, guiltiest,[16] seer, mere, crystalline, expand, built, quilter, tier, discipline, extend, sixtieth, actuality, terrier, tierce, tarrying, noisiest, existence, busiest, dizzily, bier, deer, dear, abysmal, rhythmic, interest, interpret, frigidly, exhilarate, biscuit, Baffin, chalice, leer, stolid, chicken, closes, exact, prelate, cheer, Pallas, direct, fitted, executrix, counterfeit, rocket, actress, abdicate, possible, exhibit, sit-seat, pit-Pete, bin-bean, mill-meal, pill-peal, sill-seal, kill-keel, bit-beet.

Commentary

1. Words such as *fear*(some), *here*(after), *sheer,* and *shear,* where the vowel is followed by *r,* were at one time marked in most dictionaries as if pronounced with [i]. As indicated (page 211), it is now recognized that the historical [i] in these words has been lowered to [ɪ] by the *r.* This lowering is a type of assimilation (see pages 152ff.), whereby the vowel has accommodated itself to the following consonant. With the subsequent loss of the post-vocalic *r* in the southern British dialect, the previously completed lowering effect remained.

2. Several of the words above, such as *chalice, stolid, prelate, palace, actress,* in the speech of many people, especially in the General American area, do not contain [ɪ] (see page 187). The standard General American pronunciation of the vowel in the final syllable of each of these words is [ə].

3. In all dialects, the vowel of the initial syllable of a word such as *direct* is [ə] or [ɪ] interchangeably.

4. In most American dialects, the medial vowel of such words as *imitate* and *beautified* is predominantly pronounced [ə], but occasionally [ɪ].

5. See pages 193, 217 for the substandard substitution of [ɛ] for [ɪ] in such words as *since, rinse, lynch.*

6. See pages 193, 217 for the substandard use of [ɪ] for [ɛ] before nasals, as in *when.*

7. See page 198 for the substandard substitution of [i] for [ɪ] in stressed medial syllables, as in *addition.*

8. See pages 198, 204 for substandard use of [ɛ] before [r] in *miracle, spirit.*

9. Under the assimilative influence of the retroflexion of a following *r,* [ɪ] may in dialectal speech be shifted to [ɝ], as in *spirit* [ˈspɝət]. Under the influence of an adjacent "dark" [ɫ], [ɪ] may be centralized, as in *bill* [bɨɫ], *little* [ˈlɨtɫ].

10. The word *exact* in the transcription list above raises the problem of the pronunciation of the initial vowel. Such words as *expect, example, exist,* present the same problem. It is safe to say that most speakers of most American dialects

---

[16] Here the *u* has the effect of a diacritical marking used to "harden" the *g,* and so is not strictly a part of the spelling of [ɪ].

use [ɪ] in the initial syllable of these words. In very slow utterance, or in speaking the words in isolation, the vowel [ɛ] may appear as a spelling pronunciation. (Note that in words beginning with *ex-* followed by a stressed orthographic vowel, the expected [ks] as a pronunciation of *x* does not appear; instead, the consonants are voiced to [gz]. Thus, *exist* [ɪgˈzɪst].) (Cf. Verner's Law, page 147.)

English Diphthongs

In the sequence which we are following (that is, in the order of the arrangement of the vowels on the front of the vowel diagram), the next sound to be taken up is the pure vowel [e]; but since a discussion of [e] involves a discussion also of the diphthong [eɪ], it is necessary to interrupt our sequence for some observations on diphthongs in general.

An English diphthong has been defined (page 15) as two vowels pronounced in quick, unbroken succession within a syllable, and connected by a gliding series of related sounds. As noted earlier, it is easy for us to regard the sounds intervening between the beginning and the end of the diphthong with an emphasis disproportional to their importance. For they are rapid and indistinguishable, subordinated in the listening process to the vowels on either side. They are phenomena of close juncture,[17] and do not contrast meaningfully (significantly) with other such phenomena or with the absence of any sound at all, and so do not attract primary attention. The fact that the word diphthong itself comes from Greek *di* (two) + *phthongos* (sound) indicates that the coiners of the name were hearing the two vowels, that is, the initial and final vowels, which are the important parts of the sound complex.

One reason for the subordination of the glides in English diphthongs is their extreme brevity. When the diphthongs of English are compared with those of certain other languages, this brevity is quite noticeable: [ɑi] of Spanish *baile* [ˈbɑile], contrasted with the [aɪ] of English *bile* [baɪl], reveals a spacing thus,

---

[17] G. L. Trager and Bernard Bloch, "The Syllabic Phonemes of English," *Language*, Vol. 17, No. 3, July-September 1941, p. 244:
"*Juncture:* These (phonemes) that relate to the way in which utterances begin and end (or secondarily to the way in which elements of utterance are joined together) we call juncture phonemes... (They) are usually recognizable only as modifications of other sound types; they are suprasegmental. Segmental phonemes, following one another in sequence, are typically the vowels and consonants. In the structure of the syllable, vowels are nuclear, consonants marginal."
Ibid., p. 225. *Open juncture.* "The transition from the pause preceding an isolated utterance to the first segmental phoneme, and from the last segmental phoneme to the following pause, we call open juncture."
Loc. cit. Close juncture. "By contrast (with open juncture) the transition from one segmental phoneme to the next within the utterance we call close juncture."
Robert A. Hall, Jr., *Descriptive Italian Grammar* (Ithaca, N.Y.: Cornell University Press, 1948), p. 12. "Close juncture is the absence of any interruption between linear symbols."

[ɑ-i], while the English diphthong is contracted thus, [aɪ]; so with the [ɑ-o] of Hawaiian *hao* (iron), as contrasted with [aʊ] of English *how*.

The typical English diphthongs, the ones most spoken in America, are [aɪ, aʊ, eɪ, oʊ, ɔɪ]. They are all rising diphthongs; i. e., the tongue rises from a lower to a higher position in making each, as may be seen from the following diagram.

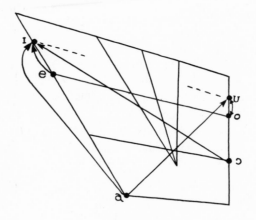

Figure 40. Rising diphthongs.

In such diphthongs, the greater stress is on the beginning vowel in each instance. This stress consists not merely of greater loudness, but also of longer duration. Thus in [eɪ], [aɪ], [aʊ], [ɔɪ], [oʊ], [e] has greater loudness and duration than [ɪ], [a] than [ɪ], [a] than [ʊ], [ɔ] than [ɪ], and [o] than [ʊ].

Sometimes the sequence [ju], stressed on the second element, as in *cube* [kjub], or as one of the alternatives or non-significant optional variants [u-ju] in [tun-tjun], is called a diphthong. However, there seems little more reason for calling [ju] a diphthong in *cube* than [ju] in *you* [ju], [jɛ] in *yes* [jɛs], or [ji] in *yield* [jild], where each pair of sounds consists, according to the viewpoint of this book, of a consonant plus a vowel. Similarly, [oə] in S. *four* [foə] (note the common use of [oə] instead of [oʊə]), [ɪə] in *fear* [fɪə], are sometimes referred to as diphthongs. But since *boa* [ˈboə] is regularly regarded as a word of two syllables and therefore containing no diphthongs, there seems no sufficient reason why *boar* [ˈboə], pronounced in exactly the same way in Southern speech, should not be so regarded also. In any case, in applied English phonetics, it is a matter of worth-while convenience to limit the basic list of diphthongs to [eɪ, aɪ, aʊ, ɔɪ, oʊ]. This is especially true in view of the fact that we have committed ourselves in this book to classify [j] as a consonant, by reason of its non-syllabicity, and in view of the fact that by our definition, a diphthong is made up of vowels only.

There is a question as to whether the vowels of *raid* and *road* ought not to be regarded as the pure vowels [e] and [o]. It is undeniable that there is no phonemic difference between [o] and [oʊ], since [rod] and [roʊd] signify the same thing, as do [de] and [deɪ]. But stylistically the differences are very great, for [rod] and [de] at once suggest the dialect of a foreigner, or of a native of a sharply marked dialectal area, such as the Bayou Têche section of Louisiana, or the city of Charleston, South Carolina. Whatever the basic phonemes may be thought to be—and most linguists regard them as diphthongs, not pure vowels[18]—the general practice throughout America is to use diphthongal [eɪ] and [oʊ] in all positions of primary and secondary stress, reserving [e] and [o] for lightly stressed syllables, such as the first syllables of *obey* [oˡbeɪ] and *nativity* [neˡtɪvətɪ].

There are numerous variations in the pronunciation of all the diphthongal phonemes, and these reflect themselves in many variant transcriptions. Some of these will be given with the discussions in connection with the diphthongs themselves. Most students, even if not far advanced in reading phonetic literature, will be able to understand them. But there is one method of transcribing diphthongs which beginners will have trouble in making out, viz., [aɪ] as [aj], [aʊ] as [aw], [eɪ] as [ej], [ɔɪ] as [ɔj], [oʊ] as [ow]. The uninitiated, trying to pronounce these transcriptions according to their previous experience with [j] and [w], are likely to pronounce [aj] as [ˡa-jə], [ow] as [ˡo-wə]. Those interested in weighing the validity of these transcriptions may consider at this point the footnote below.[19]

---

[18] Bloomfield, p. 51, records the two under consideration /ej/ and /ow/ and designates them as compound primary phonemes. According to his system, the pronunciation he intends is [eɪ] and [ʌʊ]. Bloch and Trager, on the contrary, p. 245, designate them as /ej/ and /əw/, to be pronounced [eɪ] and [ɜʊ]. Kenyon and Knott (pp. VII ff.) designate them as /e/ and /o/, to be pronounced indifferently as [e, o] or as [eɪ, oʊ].

[19] Phonemicists, thinking through the problem of transcribing diphthongs phonemically, may decide that [j] and [w] are the proper and inevitable final symbols for use in the five common diphthongs. They would be the last, however, to insist that phoneticists should feel obliged to use them in practical transcriptions.

Nevertheless, some phonetic literature, even when the transcriptions are intended to be more nearly impressionistic than phonemic, uses [ej, aj, ɔj, aw, ow]. An explanation is frequently asked for.

On the side of using [j] and [w] is an interesting item of fact: when a recording is made of *woe* [woʊ] and *yea* [jeɪ] and played backward, the acoustic result is the same thing— [woʊ], [jeɪ] (see Figure 41). This evidence would seem to demonstrate that the beginning and end of each word are identical, and that they should be transcribed [wow], [jej]. But spectrograms of the words show that the two words as pronounced are not symmetrical, i. e., not identical at the two ends respectively; therefore, the first and last sounds of each are not mathematically the same (see Figure 41). More to the point, it can be shown that a glide sound, not being of steady state, is not the same acoustical entity when played backward.

Consider the syllable [jɑi]. When recorded and played forward or backward, it is acoustically the same thing—[jɑi] (see Figure 42). But [ɑi], consisting of two vowels with a rising glide between them is not the same thing when played in reverse, but only the mirrored image of itself (see Figure 43). The pressure patterns in the air for [ɑi] impinge on the ear in reverse order to those of [jɑ]. Though [ɑi] sounds like [jɑ] when turned about, and may be said to become [jɑ], and though [jɑ] turned about becomes [ɑi], they are not on that account identical; they become identical only when one of them is reversed. Thus [ɑi] and [jɑ] resemble each other only as the right and left hands resemble each other, and are plainly not of identical pattern. We are, then, not justified in using [j] as the phonetic transcription of the diphthong represented in some cases as [ɑi] and in this book as [aɪ]. Similarly, [wow] and [jej] are unsatisfactory for [woʊ] and [jeɪ].

French has a [j] which is used finally, as in *fille* [fij], but this is the fricative [j], not present in English as a standard sound. Initially in a syllable, French uses the non-fricative [j] just as in English; cf. *nation* [nasˈjɔ̃].

[e] *and* [eɪ]

The sound [e] is high-mid-front, tense, and unrounded. Reference to the vowel diagram will serve to remind us that the mid-space is bounded by [e], [ɛ], [ɔ], [o]. Since [e] is high-mid-front, it is therefore to be found in the upper-left portion of this space. This position on the diagram indicates, of course, a high-

[19] (Continued)

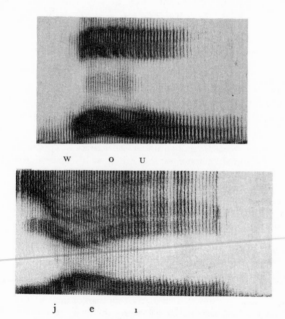

Figure 41. Spectrograms of [woʊ] and [j e i].

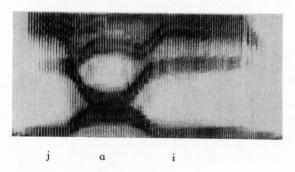

Figure 42. Spectrogram of [j ɑ i].

mid-front position of the tongue-arch in the mouth. Although the tongue is lower than for [ɪ] and drawn slightly farther back, bilateral contact of the tongue with the upper teeth is maintained. The tensity of the glossal muscles is noticeable, but less so than for [i]. The lips remain neutral and the velum is closed.

As noted in the description on page 15, [eɪ] is a complex of sounds beginning with [e], ending with [ɪ], and used in syllables of primary and secondary stress by a large majority of the speakers of American and southern British English.

The pure [e], being excluded from syllables of primary and secondary stress, is found only in syllables of light stress (usually called unstressed), apparently lying somewhere between syllables of secondary stress and syllables containing [ə]. That is to say, the first syllable of *chaotic* [keˈɑtɪk] has less stress than the last syllable of *initiate* [ɪˈnɪʃɪˌeɪt] and greater stress than the first syllable of *above* [əˈbʌv]. Its stress is comparable to that of the first syllable of *react* [rɪˈækt]. The sound [e] is spelled in English with the letter *a* only, as in *nativity* [neˈtɪvətɪ].

The sound [eɪ] is spelled with *a* as in *fate*, *ae* as in *brae* (Sc.), *ai* as in *rain*, *ao* as in *gaol* (Br.), *au* as in *gauge*, *ay* as in *pray*, *e* as in *sachet*, *ea* as in *steak*, *ei* as in *veil*, *eigh* as in *eight*, *ey* as in *prey*. NOTE: Throughout this book, the spellings of words are indicated impressionistically, as probably seen by a linguistically naive person, rather than otherwise. Obviously the *gh* of *eight* can be regarded as silent; so can the *o* of *gaol*, the *u* of *gauge*, and the *a* (or is it the *e*?) of *steak*. It appears to be a more useful practice here not to try too precisely to name the silent letters in such an illogically spelled language as English.

It may be noted in passing that, aside from proper names, there are only four common words in which the sound [eɪ] is spelled with *ea*. These are *break*, *steak*, *great*, *yea*. Large numbers of other words formerly pronounced with [eɪ], such as *tea* and *sea*, have been pronounced with [i] since about the eighteenth century.

---

[19] (Continued)

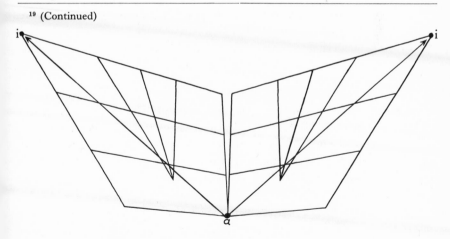

Figure 43. Mirrored diagrams of the diphthong [ɑi].

In reading phonetic literature, we come upon many variant transcriptions for the dipthong [eɪ]. Some of these are [ei], [ɛi], [ɛɪ], [ɛj], and [ej]. Sometimes these represent the sounds of a foreign language, sometimes the sounds of a dialect of English, and sometimes the central tendency or average pronunciation of the diphthong according to the opinion of a given writer. Students of phonetics have to learn to adapt themselves to whatever symbols are used in a given book or article and to try to understand them according to the intention of the individual writer. Some assistance in interpreting diphthongs ending in [j] is found *ante*, pages 97–99.

For the practical purposes of this book, [eɪ] is used as a generalization on the pronunciation of this diphthong, and variations from it will, in the later parts of the book, be used as needed. This generalization will agree with the symbolization in more phonetic literature than any other and will thus facilitate reading of references with a minimum of reorientation.

> *Transcribe:* alteration, appliqué, palpitate, fatality, brae (Sc.) brainy, gaol (Br.), jail, gauged, today, fiancée, holiday, steak, greatest, weight, whey, sachet, they, eighty-eight, breakers, prey, saying, drained, gayety, braille, Gaelic, co-operation, incorporate, neighborhood, sane, seine, faint, Australia, feint, persuade, foray, locate, veiling, maelstrom.
>
> "I hurry amain to reach the plain."
>
> "In there stepped a stately raven of the saintly days of yore. Not the least obeisance made he; not a minute stopped or stayed he; but, with mien of lord or lady, perched above my chamber door."
>
> "Much I marveled this ungainly fowl to hear discourse so plainly."

Suggestions. 1. Note that the syllable *tate* of *palpitate*, *rate* of *incorporate* (v.) and the *cate* of *locate* have secondary stress and by most speakers of English will be pronounced with the diphthong [eɪ] equally with syllables of primary stress.

2. Note that the vowel on the first syllable of *fatality* has weak stress, weaker at least than secondary stress, and will, therefore, be pronounced with the pure vowel [e]. (Some will even use [ə].)

3. In the pronunciation of some speakers, the last syllable of *holiday* may be unstressed to [ɪ].

[ɛ]

The sound [ɛ] is low-mid-front, lax, and unround. The tongue is lower but nearly as far front as for [e]. The sides of the tongue maintain contact with the inner surfaces of the upper molars. The air passage over the tongue is larger in both vertical and horizontal dimensions than for [e]. The velum is closed. The symbol [ɛ] is sometimes referred to as epsilon, since it is shaped like the Greek letter of that name.

The sound [ɛ] is spelled basically with the letter *e* before a final consonant or a consonant cluster as in *bed*, *swept*, and before doubled orthographic consonants as in *merry*. Other spellings are *a* as in *any* and *secondary*, *ai* as in *said*, *ae* as in

aesthete, ay as in *says, ea* as in *bread, ei* as in *heifer, eo* as in *leopard, ie* as in *friend,*
u as in *burial.*

Along with [æ], [ɛ] is standard in a number of words in which the vowel is
followed by *r* in a syllable of primary and secondary stress. The customary spellings are *-are, -air, -ear,* and *-eir,* as in *rare, fair, pear, heir.*

For the substandard substitution of [ɛ] for [eɪ] before voiceless plosives, as
in [mɛk] for [meɪk], see page 215.

See pages 211 and 243 for the alternate pronunciation of *again* as [əˈgɛn,
əˈgeɪn] in Southern speech and in British speech.

For the substandard substitution of [ɪ] for [ɛ] before nasals, as in [ʌɪn] for
when, see page 217.

For the substandard substitution of [eɪ] for [ɛ] before voiced sounds, as in
[eɪg] for *egg,* and [ˈpleɪʒɚ] for *pleasure,* see page 203.

> *Transcribe in your own dialect:* many, again, binary, aesthete (also esthete),
> credit, expect, raspberry, says, entering, interval, breathless, breather, heifer,
> leopard, friendless, bury, pare, pair, parry, pear, get, guitar, bedspread, cleft,
> berry, any, said, cleanly (adj.), cleanly (adv.), genuine, inevitable, benefit, ferry,
> fairy, questionable, Thames, headship, eggplant, missionary, spreading, peni-
> tentiary, plenipotentiary, feather, aesthetic (esthetic), expectorate, exemption,
> breakfast, Leicester, Frenchmen, Glastonbury, where, bear, bare, more, mayor,
> liar, layer.
> The guest had the best of everything.
> The empire of Frederick the Great.
> There is an element of chance in it.
> It is expected that *Great Expectations* will make a good film.
> Benjamin Franklin has been said to have had the most inquiring mind of
> his generation.

Suggestions. 1. Remember the caution (page 11) not to transcribe [ɪ] for
standard [ɛ] in words such as *many, friendless, genuine, benefit,* where [ɛ] precedes
a nasal, except in certain dialects, such as Irish and substandard Southern speech.

2. Note that the *h* of *his, has,* and similar pronouns and auxiliary verbs in
sentence contexts drops out when the words are unstressed (see full discussion
later, page 114).

3. Note that the *a* in syllables of secondary stress spelled *ary,* as in *apothecary*
[əˈpɑθəˌkɛrɪ], is pronounced with [ɛ] only, never [æ].

[æ]

The sound [æ] is high-low-front, lax, and unround. The velum is closed.
Aside from the fact that it differs from [ɛ] in a general lowering of the tongue,
[æ] differs from all the sounds above it in the important feature that the lateral
contact of the tongue with the upper teeth is definitely broken. It is the attempt to maintain this contact that produces the [æ] raised in the direction of [ɛ].
This raising characterizes the speech of some individuals and communities.

The raised [æ], pronounced with the tongue higher than it should be and with consequent inadequate air passage above the tongue, seems in the speech of many individuals to invite the dropping of the velum, with resultant nasalization of [æ]. (See page 101, *ante*, for discussion of the alternate use of [æ-ɛ] in words spelled with *air, are, ear, eir,* such as *chair, fare, bear, heir.*)

The basic spelling of [æ] is *a* followed by a single consonant in a monosyllable, or by a doubled orthographic consonant or a consonant cluster in any word, as in *sat*,[20] *gaff, battle,* and *catch.* Other spellings are *a* before *r(e)*, as in *fare; a* before *rr* plus unstressed vowel, as in *narrow; ai* before *r*, as in *hair,* *ea* before *r,* as in *bear; ei* before *r,* as in *heir; ai* as in *plaid, i* as in *meringue, au* as in *laugh* (Am.).

> *Transcribe in your own dialect:* catching, thatching, characterize, gladden, blacken, airplane, bearings, heiress, gnat, meringue, wrap, airship, heirship, farewell, guaranty, guarantee, chairmanship, atom, Adam, heirloom, fraternization, absolute, platitude, congratulations, average, candidate, indefatigable, plastic, neoplasm, bear, algebraical, catastrophe, fair, Caribbean, Capulet, caramel, Capricorn, blanket, lair, blackboard, battery, baritone, barrel, pusillanimous, Pandora, napkin, narrow-gauge.

[a]

The sound [a] is low-front, lax, and unround. The velum is closed. A commonly used name for [a] is "French *a*." Like pure [e] and pure [o], [a] in English is used in isolation relatively infrequently. Many people find it difficult to isolate it. Easterners may locate it as an allophone of [ɑ] in "broad *a*" words (see page 222), such as *path* [paθ], and in the pronunciation [a] for *are*, or [ban] for *barn*, as used by many Eastern speakers. Southerners may be able to isolate it by noting the substandard pronunciation of the pronoun *I*, viz., [a], or by abstracting it from the Southern substandard pronunciation of *fine* as [fan]. Many people can isolate the sound [a] by drawling the standard pronunciation of the pronoun *I*, hence delaying the second element [ɪ] until the very last, thus [a:::ɪ]. By dropping off the [ɪ], the remaining portion will be an isolated [a], thus [a:::]. The sound [a] is widely used in the standard diphthongs [aɪ] and [aʊ], discussion of which follows presently.

Commentary

The now almost abandoned attempt by some textbook writers, dictionaries, and teachers to inculcate the sound [a] as a "compromise" between [ɑ] and [æ]

---

[20] Exception must be made for a number of so-called "broad *a*" words, such as *pass* and *ask*, which in British and to a limited extent in Eastern speech are pronounced with [ɑ] instead of [æ], thus: [pɑs], [ɑsk]. See page 240. Such words are in New England also pronounced with [a]. See page 222.

in "broad *a*" words such as *ask*, and even as a substitute for [æ] in words such as *man* and *cat*, had for its foundation mainly an arbitrarily held subjective impression that there was something vulgar or otherwise unacceptable about the sound [æ]. It may be supposed that proponents of [a] in these words had in mind to substitute it for the raised [æ] (see pages 101–102), made with the tongue in lateral contact with the upper molars. The sound made in this position is not generally accepted as standard, being described as "flat" and often as nasal. But the sound [æ] produced with the tongue lower in the mouth, and without lingual contact laterally with the upper teeth, is almost sure to be free from these objections, rendering recourse to [a] unnecessary.

[aɪ]

The diphthong [aɪ] begins with the vowel [a] and ends with the vowel [ɪ]. There is a brief complex of gliding intermediate sounds, apparently negligible in the hearing process. The velum is closed.

Beginning students are often surprised to find that [aɪ] is a diphthong, having been deceived by the fact that it is so often spelled with the single letter *i*, as in *ride*, or by the single letter *y*, as in *nylon*. Actually, it is sometimes spelled with two letters, suggesting its diphthongal character, as in *aisle*. Besides the spelling *i*, *y*, and *ai*, as just indicated, [aɪ] is also spelled with *ay(e)* as in *ay* or *aye* (yes), *ey* as in *eye*, *ye* as in *dye*, *ie* as in *die*, *uy* as in *buy*, *ei* as in *height*. We might add *ui* as in *guile* were it not that the *u* is used merely diacritically, to indicate that the *g* is pronounced "hard." Similarly *oi* as in *choir* might be considered a spelling of [aɪ] were it not that the *o* probably represents *w* in the pronunciation. Certain foreign spellings of [aɪ] are common in America, such as the German *ey* and *ay* as in *Meyer* and *Mayer*.

For the reduction of [aɪ] to [a] in Southern speech, see page 215. For the rustic substitution of [aɪ] for [ɔɪ] as in [paɪnt] for *point* [pɔɪnt], see pages 194 and 307. For the rustic New England substitution of [ɜɪ], see page 234. For the substitution of [ɔɪ] for [aɪ], see page 275. For [ɑɪ] in cockney and [ʌɪ] in Irish, see pages 251 and 275 respectively.

Various transcriptions are used in phonetic literature to express the diphthong [aɪ], such as [ɑi], [ɑɪ], [ɑe], [æɪ], [ææ], [æj], [ai], [ay], [ɑj], [aj], [əj], [ʌi], [ʌe], [əe], and [ɜe]. They are used to represent what corresponds to [aɪ] in various languages and various dialects of English, or to express the opinion or bias of a given writer. The transcription [aɪ] is used more than any other single transcription in practical phonetics as applied to English, and will be used in this book except when some deviation from central tendencies of the pronunciation of [aɪ] is under discussion.

Transcribe: applied, applying, lie, lying, beguile, guide, aisle, height, playwright, daylight, ice cream, flight, despite, awry, rye, buy, sleight, slight, idea, splicing, silo, nigh, Nye, why, diamond, psychology, diameter, dianoetic, capsize, bison, spice, highway, pride, deride, slimy, pliable, bride, dialect, Christ-like, misfire, pry, prize, my, mine, lyceum, lichen, liable, license, life-boat, choir, Ainu, ay, aye, aye-aye (an animal), Myers, Meyer's, Mayer's, mires, nightingale, lifeline, mankind, stylistically, birdlime, wire, bright, bite, Crimea, splice, decry, bile, giant, Skye, quiet, Schuyler, island, rhyme, rime, percentile, skylight, firefly, quire, squire, esquire, biography.

In applied phonetics, we strive to find methods of using sound symboliza-tion as an instrument of the highest usefulness.

[aʊ]

The diphthong [aʊ] consists of the vowel [a] (variant [ɑ]) and the vowel [ʊ] spoken in quick succession with an intervening complex of glide sounds which appears to be relatively negligible in the hearing process. As with other English diphthongs, the diphthongal character of the sound appears to lie in the rapidity with which the two elements are spoken together, and in the totality of their effect as a singly heard sound. Like all major English diphthongs, [aʊ] is stressed on the first element, in this case [a]. Other symbolizations which the student is likely to encounter in phonetic literature are [ɑu], [æʊ], [ɑw]. (For discussion of the inappropriateness of *w* in this diphthong, see page 97. For discussion of substandard [æʊ], see page 216. For the Virginia [ɜʊ] before voiceless conso-nants, and [æʊ] before voiced consonants and finally, see page 207. For the cockney [ɑ:] for [aʊ], see page 252.) For substandard [æʊ], [æ̃ʊ], [jæ̃ʊ], see page 200.

The basic spellings of [aʊ] in English are two in number: *ou* as in *out, ow* as in *cow*. Other spellings are *au* from the German, as in *Faust; eo,* as in the Scottish *Macleod;* and *ough,* as in *bough.*

Transcribe: cowl, Faust, Macleod, county seat, bounce, bounty, rebound, downward, howler, oust, ouch, Hauptmann, grouse, carouse, frown, Browning, prowler, proud, trowel, scout, bough, bow, rowdy, crowd, crowned, shroud, around, sounding, flounder, chowder, gouge, gown, douse, sprout, couch, sauer-kraut, loudly, mountainous, wound (v.), sow (animal), towel, trout, stout, frowzy, ounce, ourselves, outboard, hour, outcast, outburst, out-frown, plough, plow, drought, drouth, bow-wow, southeast, sourdough, roustabout, doubtful, merry-go-round, cauliflower, abounding, allowable, now, housekeeper, downspout, devout, flour, tousled, trauma, shout, pout, gout, expound, resound, redound, drown, drowned, counterfeit, counterbalance, mouth (n.), mouth (v.), mouse.

[ɑ] *and* [ɒ]

The sound [ɑ] is low-back, lax, unround; i.e., [ɑ] is made with the tongue low in the mouth, with the tip behind the lower teeth, and the highest part arched at the back of the mouth. The glossal muscles are lax and the lips are unround; the velum is closed.

It is difficult to find a key word for the sound [ɑ] which will be pronounced the same in the several regional dialects of America. Probably the most commonly used key word is *father*, but it is likely that few words are pronounced in more different ways than *father*. *Calm* is a fairly useful key word, since it is pronounced with [ɑ], i.e., [kɑm], by General American, Southern, and British speakers, and by some Eastern speakers. But other Eastern speakers pronounce it [kam], not to mention some in all sections who use the archaic or rustic [kæm]. Those who know the Latin hymn *Ave Maria* will recognize the sound [ɑ] at every point where the letter *a* occurs, thus [ˈɑwe mɑˈriɑ]. For a great many people, the use of *h* after *a* connotes [ɑ], so that the word *ah* [ɑ] becomes a useful key word. Those who pronounce the formerly much-used word *Nazi* as [ˈnɑtsi] rather than the Churchillian [ˈnæzi] may use that word as a key word.

The sound [ɒ] is high-low-back, lax, and round. It is sometimes called the British "short *o*," since it is used in southern British speech to correspond to the American "short *o*" in words like *hot* and *not*. It is also used by considerable numbers of people in New England in essentially the same words in which it is found in southern British. It is typically spelled with *o* followed by a single consonant in a monosyllable, as in *got;* or by two or more consonants, as in *rotten, blocks;* but it is also spelled with *a* preceded by [w], as in some words like *was, quality, squabble*.

The tabulation below presents the several spellings of [ɑ] in the standard American English and in the southern British, with alternate pronunciations of these spellings in these same dialects.

Spellings	Standard Pronunciation in G. A., S.	Standard Eastern	Standard Southern British
a as in *calm*	ɑ	a, ɑ	ɑ
a as in *barn*	ɑ	a, ɑ	ɑ
aa as in *bazaar*	ɑ	a, ɑ	ɑ
a (al, au) as in the "broad *a*" *calf, calves, bath, aunt, class, can't*	æ	æ, a, ɑ	ɑ
e as in *sergeant*	ɑ	a, ɑ	ɑ
ea as in *hearth*	ɑ	a, ɑ	ɑ
a as in *was, watch*	ɑ	ɒ, ɑ	ɒ
o as in *hot*	ɑ (shorter than above)	ɒ, ɑ	ɒ
ow as in *knowledge*	ɑ (shorter than in *was*)	ɒ, ɑ	ɒ
a, o as in *wash, horrid, fog*	ɔ, ɑ	ɑ, ɔ, ɒ	ɒ

Transcribe each of the following with [ɑ], for practice, regardless of whether this transcription agrees with your own pronunciation. This transcription will indicate the pronunciation of the majority of people in the United States and Canada. If you pronounce any of the words with a different vowel, transcribe such words a second time using [a], as seen by the preceding chart. This will represent one of the standard New England pronunciations.

palm, part, argument, calm, bazaar, sergeant, barn, car, farm, hearth, Palmer, Parmelee, arbitrary, army, heart, pharmacy, cart, Arlington, yard, card, hard, psalm, article, balm, farther, martial, alms, qualms, quandary, particle, quadratic, partial, chard, guard, lard, guardian.

Transcribe the following with [æ] for practice. If in your pronunciation you use a different vowel, transcribe again with [a] or [ɑ], according to your choice. The sound [a] represents one of the standard New England pronunciations, and [ɑ] another standard New England pronunciation as well as the standard southern British pronunciation. (The words in this group belong to the so-called "broad *a*" class. See page 240 for discussion and definition of broad *a*.)

calf, calves, laugh, staff, shaft, waft, crafty, rafter, bath, baths, rather, grass, pass, blaspheme, mask, task, casket, rascal, hasp, rasp, raspberry, repast, pasture, plaster, example, sample, remand, reprimand, prance, trance, answer, lance, can't, shan't, slant, advantage, branch, Frances.

Transcribe the following with [ɑ] for practice. This will represent the pronunciation of the majority in the United States and Canada. If your pronunciation disagrees on any word, transcribe it a second time using [ɒ]. This will represent one of the standard New England and Canadian pronunciations as well as the standard southern British pronunciation.

hot, not, dot, lot, plot, prompt, impossible, orthography, geography, was, watch, wallop, Wallace, Scott, doll, apologize, Polly, follow, abolish, college, colloquy, mollify, common, rotten, spot, God, rod, sorrow, prominent, expostulate, frolic, comical, comparable, abominate, predominant.

Commentary

See pages 216, 282 for the substandard use in New York City and the South of [ɔ] for [ɑ] in stressed syllables spelled with *ar* not preceded by [w], as in *charm*.

[ɔ]

The sound [ɔ] is low-mid-back, lax, and round. The velum is closed. This sound is typically longer in duration than [ɒ], to which it is closely related. Its most recognizable spellings are probably *au* as in *taut*, and *aw* as in *yawn*. Other spellings are *o* as in *cloth* and *cord; ough* as in *brought; a* before *l* as in *all* and *talk; a* preceded by [w] as in *warm, wash*, and *quarter; eo* as in *George;* and *oa* as in *abroad*. The spellings *or, oar, our*, as in *port, coarse*, and *course*, vary in pronunciation between [oʊ] and [ɔ], according to individual or community choice, or according to dialect. (See pages 185, 207, 226.) Some of the words following are transcribed with [ɑ] as well as with [ɔ]. Usually, these pronunciations are regarded as standard also. Transcribe all the words with [ɔ] for practice. If your pronunciation differs from this, transcribe the affected words a second time, this time using [ɑ].

The pronunciation of many of these words, including most words in -og, with [ɑ] is a strong characteristic of much Rocky Mountain speech, especially in the area centering on Utah and Idaho, while the use of [ɑ] in words of the type of *forest* and *orange* characterizes considerable Southern speech as well as that of certain sections (see page 225) in New England and in the Eastern parts of the General American area. For the substandard excrescent [r] after [ɔ], see page 192.

Transcribe: awe, ought, audible, auction, war, salt, fog, squaw, haul, hall, Paul, pall, fought, caught, cloth, talk, cord, George, taut, yawn, warm, quarter, abroad, brought, log, all, awl, sprawl, vault, gall, drawing, hospitable, audiometer, coffee, foreign, cough, Boston, torrid, laurel, cost, dog, loft, origin, wrong, gone, strong, lost, soft, off, often, small, offer, orange, office, stalk, mortal, important, hog, quarrel, quarantine, haunt, warrior, gauntlet, corpse, catalog, laundry, jaunt, sawmill, warrant, swath, cork, corn, vaunt, fortune, horse, forward.

[ɔɪ]

The diphthong [ɔɪ] begins with [ɔ] and ends with [ɪ]. Between the two is a complex of gliding sounds, negligible in the hearing process. The velum is closed. The sound [ɔɪ] is spelled with *oi* as in *oil*, *oy* as in *oyster*, *uoy* as in one pronunciation of *buoy*.

For the substitution of [ɝ] for [ɔɪ], see page 237; of [ɝɪ] for [ɔɪ], see page 237; of [ɔ] for [ɔɪ], see page 216; of [ɑɪ] for [ɔɪ], see page 194.

Transcribe: boycott, coyly, oiler, Detroit, voiceless, soiled, sirloin, moisten, poignant, hoist, foil, Roycroft, thyroid, toiler, mastoid, purloined, record (v.), cloy, oyster, buoy, boisterous, toy, ointment, anoint, doily, Doyle, Hoyle, hoity-toity, appointment, goiter, hyoid, rhomboid, royal, roil, royally, roily.

[o] *and* [oʊ]

The sound [o] is high-mid-back, tense, and round. The highest part of the tongue-arch is at the back, at an elevation approximately one-third of the distance down from the highest possible point to the lowest possible point. The velum is closed.

As noted in the description on page 15, the diphthong [oʊ] is a complex of sounds, beginning with [o] and ending with [ʊ]. In addition to the common transcription [oʊ], the student will find in phonetic literature [ou] and [ow]. (For discussion of [ow], see page 97.) The diphthong [oʊ] is used in syllables of primary and secondary stress by a large majority of speakers of American English and of southern British English.[21] It is more prominently diphthongal

---

[21] Eilert Ekwall, *Historische neuenglische Laut- und Formenlehre* (Berlin: de Gruyter, 1922), notes the diphthongal character of both [eɪ] and [oʊ]:
p. 40. "In vier Wörtern — *break, great, steak, yea* — sich me. e zu heutigen [ei] entwickelt."
p. 52. "Spätme. o hat ausser vor *r* in der Regel [ou] ergeben. Beispiele: *boat* [bout], *coach* [koutʃ]."

in an open syllable, as in *ago*, or in a syllable closed with a voiced consonant, as in *abode*, than in a syllable closed with a voiceless consonant, as in *goat*. Pure [o], being excluded from syllables of primary and secondary stress, is found only in syllables of light stress, apparently lying somewhere between syllables of secondary stress and syllables containing [ə]. These syllables are possibly analogous, in degree of stress, to another group of lightly stressed syllables, those containing [ɪ]; that is to say, the first syllable of *obey* [oˈbeɪ] has less stress than the first syllable of *Roman* [ˈroʊmən], but greater stress than the first syllable of *about* [əˈbaʊt]. Its stress is comparable to that of the first syllable of *react* [rɪˈækt]. It is, however, along with [ə], pure [e], and the [ɪ], called unstressed.

Pure [o] is spelled in English with *o* and *ow*, as in *opinion* [oˈpɪnjən] and *window* [ˈwɪndo]. Words ending with lightly stressed [o] are sometimes pronounced with the still more lightly stressed [ʊ], as well as with the relatively unstressed [ə]. All of these pronunciations are usually regarded as standard, the first, [ˈwɪndo], being regarded as the more suitable for careful speech and formal occasions, and the other two, [ˈwɪndʊ] and [ˈwɪndə], being allocated to casual and colloquial speech.

The sound [oʊ] is spelled basically with *o*, as in *cold*, *port* (see alternative [ɔ] below). Other spellings are *eau* as in *beau*, *oe* as in *hoe*, *oo* as in *brooch*, *ou* as in *mould*, *ow* as in *throw*, *ough* as in *though*, *ew* as in *sew*, *oa* as in *boat*, *eo* as in *yeoman*.

Commentary

Several of the spellings of [oʊ], particularly *ou* and *ow*, indicate very well the diphthongal character of the sound. In *sew*, the spelling, selected from one ME dialect and pronounced in another, chances to agree roughly with the pronunciation of the current southern British diphthong [ɜʊ], thus [sɜʊ]. In the King James Bible, there are other similar spellings, such as *shew* for *show*.

In the case of certain words where various spellings of [oʊ] occur before *r*, some individuals, communities, and sections use [ɔ]. Some examples spelled with *o* and pronounced both [oʊ] and [ɔ] are *ford*, *horde*, *sword*, *port*, *sport*, *forth*, *core*, *score*, *tore;* some spelled with *oa* are *coarse*, *hoarse*, *board*, *soar*, *roar;* some with *ou* are *court*, *four*, *mourn*,[22] *source*. Some with *oo* are *door*, *floor*. In the list below, transcribe such words according to your own pronunciation. For the standard British use of [ɜʊ] for [oʊ], see page 241. For the Cockney substitution of [aʊ] for [oʊ], see page 252.

Transcribe: Beaumont, yeoman, sew, boast, stone, toes, soul, crow-bar, gold, groan, mistletoe, moulting, owner, follow, whole, program, roast, shoulder, sophomore, sword, fourteen, coarse, course, porch, gory, story, more, poor,

---

[22] See Kuṛath, "Mourning and Morning," in *Studies for William A. Read*, ed. by N. M. Caffee and T. A. Kirby (Baton Rouge: Louisiana State University Press, 1940).

pore, only, snore, home, report, both, Roosevelt, rose, coat, omission, alto, polo, holy, potato, alone, wallow, tomato, chromatic, obese, chromosome, fellow, quotation.

> The chestnut, the oak, the walnut, the pine
> Over-leaning with flickering meaning and sign,
> Said "Pass not so cold
>   These manifold
> Deep shades of the hills of Habersham,
> These glades of the valleys of Hall."

[ʊ] *and* [u]

The sound [ʊ] is low-high-back, lax, and round. The velum is closed. The tongue-arch is highest at the back of the mouth, being approximately one-sixth of the distance down from [u] toward [ɑ]. The muscles of the tongue, as compared with their condition for [u], are quite lax.

As in the case of [ɪ], page 93, foreign students will find it helpful to place the thumb and finger under the jaw in such a way as to press against the musculature of the tongue while pronouncing [u] and [ʊ] alternately; thus, [u-ʊ, u-ʊ, u-ʊ]. The purpose of this exercise is to demonstrate the difference between the tenseness of the muscles for [u] and their laxness for [ʊ]. The student should try to memorize the kinesthesia or "feel" of the muscles, so as to be able to distinguish [ʊ] from [u] by muscular sensation. Since many foreign languages do not contain [ʊ], a good exercise for foreign students is to pronounce words with [u] and [ʊ] in pairs, in order to fix in mind the distinctions between them. Suitable pairs are *pool-pull, fool-full, root-rook, shoot-shook, tool-took, boot-book, Luke-look.* The sound [ʊ] is spelled with *o* as in *bosom, oo* as in *book, ou* as in *would*, and *u* as in *full.*

The sound [u] is high-back, tense, and round; i.e., the highest part of the tongue-arch is in the back of the mouth at a point usually somewhat below the extreme possible height. The musculature of the tongue is tense, the lips are round, and the velum is closed.

The [u] is spelled with *au* as in *Sault (Ste. Marie), eau* [(j)u] as in *beauty, ew* as in *crew, eu* as in *rheumatism, o* as in *do, oe* as in *shoe, oo* as in *cool, ou* as in *croup, iou* as in *Sioux, u* as in *rude, ue* as in *true*, and *ui* as in *fruit.*

Since both [ʊ] and [u] are spelled with *oo*, it often becomes a problem as to which sound to use.[23] Some words are practically invariably pronounced with [u], as in *boom* and *moon;* others with [ʊ], as in *foot* and *book* (and nearly all words in *ook*). A number of words, however, lie in a middle ground and are often pronounced indifferently with both [u] and [ʊ]. Some of the commonest of these are *broom, coop, food, hoof, roof, room, root.*

---

[23] C. H. Grandgent, "English in America," *Die Neueren Sprachen.* Stechert, 1895, Vol. 2, p. 457.

The spellings *ue, u, eu,* and *ew* in non-foreign words present a special problem in that they are pronounced either with [u] or [ju],[24] sometimes according to phonetic context, sometimes according to individuals, communities, or speech regions. These spellings are invariably (where the choice is between [u] and [ju]) pronounced [ju] after *b, c, f, h, m, p, qu,* as in *abuse, Beulah cue,* (exceptions *pharmaceutical* and similar words), *few, fuse, feud, hew, hue, music, mew, pew pupil, queue.*

After [t, d, n], [θ, ʃ, ʒ], and [l] there is a great variation between [u] and [ju] according to individuals, communities, and regions (see pages 186, 208, 226, and 243), as suggested above; thus, *tune* [tun—tjun], *duly* [ˈdulɪ—ˈdjulɪ], *due* [du—dju], *dew* [du—dju], *deuce* [dus—djus], *nude* [nud—njud], *neutral* [ˈnutrəl —ˈnjutrəl], *new* [nu—nju], *nuisance* [ˈnusənts—ˈnjusənts], *suit* [sut—sjut], *resume* [rɪˈzum—rɪˈzjum], *lute* [lut—ljut], *enthusiastic* [ɪnˌθuzɪˈæstɪk—ɪnˌθjuzɪˈæstɪk].

In the transcriptions below, transcribe any words in the classes discussed in the paragraph above according to your own pronunciation. With words spelled with *oo*, where there is doubt whether to use [u] or [ʊ], it is usually safest to use [u]. In unstressed syllables where *u* follows *c* or *g*, as in *accurate, regulate,* use [ju, jʊ, jə].

> *Transcribe:* book, cook, boost, roost, do, food, good, Sioux, moor, pull—pool, hood, groom, broom, full—fool, accumulate, bruise, room, nook, roof, look, recruit, brook, wooed—would, cooed—could, coop, lieu, regulate, root, crude, hoof, shooed—should, view, troop, sue, shoe, rheumatic, drew, you, bosom, Sault Ste. Marie, bruit, to, accurate, fruit, Tuesday, mule, musical, tulip, dubious, beautiful, fusible, cute, duke, Beulah, huge, newspaper, neutral, ewe, February, feud, purify, curable, queue, hew, enthusiasm, suitable, presume, constitution, union, adduce, enumerate, gratitude, durable, remunerative, innumerable, nuisance, sewage, European, knew, United States, thews.
> What would you say is a good definition of "goods"?
> The boom has caused the price of crude oil to move upward.
> "School days, school days, dear old golden rule days."

NOTE: Under conditions of progressive unstressing, [u] may shift successively to [ʊ] and [ə]. Cf. *educate* [ˈɛdʒuˌkeɪt, ˈɛdʒʊˌkeɪt, ˈɛdʒəˌkeɪt].

Unstressing in Sentences

Before proceeding with the discussion of vowels, it is necessary to take up the special problem of unstressing in sentences. In Chapter 2, pages 13 ff., it has been explained that we ordinarily recognize three degrees of stress within

---

[24] According to the discussion of vowels and consonants in this book, especially p. 96, [j] is considered a consonant, and [ju], therefore, is not a diphthong (see definition p. 15) but a combination of consonant plus vowel. A variant of [u] is [ɪu], which is a manifestation of a drawl (e.g., [tɪu] for *too* in New England and the South, and [nɪu] for *new* in the Western Reserve area). It is effected by lengthening the [ɪ] upon which [j] is based until its character as a vowel is restored.

isolated words, viz., primary stress, secondary stress, and light stress. It was further stated: (1) that a vowel of light stress, i.e., carrying any degree of stress weaker than secondary, is arbitrarily referred to as an unstressed vowel; and (2) that whereas under conditions of primary or secondary stress a vowel or diphthong retains its full or typical quality, under conditions of unstressing, the diphthongs [eɪ] and [oʊ] are reduced to pure vowels, and single vowels are reduced to shortened forms of themselves, or, in the greatest number of cases, to [ə] or [ɪ]. The following lists constitute a résumé of the foregoing. Note that primary stress is, as specified earlier, marked with [ˈ], secondary stress with [ˌ], and unstressing without any qualifying mark. NOTE: Dictionaries ordinarily do not indicate secondary stress in a noncompound word unless it contains four or more syllables, and even then only if the secondary stress is quite strong. Thus [ˈsɛkrəˌtɛrɪ] for *secretary*, but [sɛkˈtɛrɪənɪzm̩] for *sectarianism*.

Words containing primary and secondary stress only: *abstract* (n.) [ˈæbˌstrækt], *conduct* (n.) [ˈkanˌdʌkt], *bookshelf* [ˈbʊkˌʃɛlf], *abstract* (v.) [ˌæbˈstrækt], *upheave* [ˌʌpˈhiv].

Words containing unstressed syllables and syllables of primary stress only: *repeat* [rɪˈpit, rəˈpit], *abode* [əˈboʊd], *detract* [dɪˈtrækt, dəˈtrækt], *tapping* [ˈtæpɪŋ], *vantage* [ˈvæntɪʤ], *ribbon* [ˈrɪbən].

Words containing all three types of stressing: *ratify* [ˈrætəˌfaɪ, ˈrætɪˌfaɪ], *dictionary* [ˈdɪkʃənˌɛrɪ], *amputate* [ˈæmpjuˌteɪt]. NOTE: In *amputate*, we have the syllable *pu*, which illustrates both the shortening of a vowel, and its progressive reduction to [ə], as when we transcribe the word successively [ˈæmpjuˌteɪt, ˈæmpjʊˌteɪt, ˈæmpjəˌteɪt].

Diphthongs stressed and unstressed: *open* [ˈoʊpən], *willow* [ˈwɪlo]; *ailing* [ˈeɪlɪŋ], *chaotic* [keˈatɪk]; *mileage* [ˈmaɪlɪʤ], *give me my hat* [ˌgɪv mɪ mə ˈhæt]. Note that the diphthongs [aʊ] and [ɔɪ] do not occur in unstressed positions, though they may be found in positions of secondary stress, as in *outplay* [ˌaʊtˈpleɪ], *bell-buoy* [ˈbɛlˌbɔɪ].

Unstressing in word groups. From the standpoint of phonetics as considered apart from meaning, there are no necessary or obligatory pauses within certain word groups, i.e., sense-groups and breath-groups, any more than between the syllables of a word. It follows, then, that such word groups are, speaking again of sounds only and not of meanings, simply long "phonetic words." This is particularly true of languages of the types called incorporative and agglutinative, where "word" and "phrase" or "sentence" may become essentially identical; but it is scarcely less true in English. Accordingly, it follows still further that in such a word group in English certain monosyllables found among its components are subject to stressing and unstressing within the "phonetic word," exactly as syllables are subject to stressing and unstressing within an ordinary word. Thus the word group "up to the top of it" and the word "multicylindrical" actually have identical stress patterns, thus: [ˌʌptəðə ˈtapəvət], [ˌmʌltəsəˈlɪndrɪkəl].

As stated above, the important fact here is that certain of the monosyllable of the word groups appear in unstressed forms. That they do so is an importan characteristic of the English language. Foreigners whose languages lack wholly or in part an unstressing system comparable to that of English will find that their careful utterance of each word as if each were in isolation, [ʌp tu ði tɑp ɑv ɪt], will give the effect of foreign accent, even though each individual word is ever so accurately pronounced with true English sounds.

What monosyllables are subject to unstressing in word groups? The monosyllables most consistently subject to unstressing in word groups are the definite and indefinite articles, prepositions, conjunctions, personal and relative pronouns, copulative and auxiliary verbs, some adverbs, and some occasional words not easily classifiable.[25]

The following lists are classified according to the parts of speech concerned.

Word	Stressed Pronunciation	Unstressed Pronunciation	Illustration
ARTICLES:			
a (used only before a consonant sound)*	[eɪ]	[ə]	[ə 'bʊk, ə hɪs'toʊrɪkəl ˌbʊk, ə 'junjən]†
an (before a vowel sound)	[æn]	[ən], [n̩] (after [t, d])	[ən 'aɪlənd, ən 'ɑnərəbəl‡ mæn, ˌæd n̩ 'ɪntʃ, baɪt n̩ 'ɔrɪndʒ]

---

[25] Lee S. Hultzén, "The Pronunciation of Monosyllabic Form-Words in American English," in *Studies in Speech and Drama in Honor of Alexander M. Drummond* (Ithaca: Cornell University Press, 1944), pp. 255–284. See also J. S. Kenyon, *American Pronunciation*, Fourth Ed. (Ann Arbor: George Wahr, 1930), pp. 150–159.

* In earlier times in England, when "h-dropping" was commoner than now, a rule became established requiring the use of *an* before *h* as well as before vowels. The rule still applies if the *h* is silent, as in *an honor*, and it would apply if *historical novel* were still pronounced *'istorical novel*. Since, however, the *h* is now regularly pronounced, the word begins with a consonant and so requires *a* instead of *an*. Interestingly enough, the erroneous use of *an* attached itself to very few other words aside from *historical*. No one, for example, appears ever to have said "*an hand*."

† Following the customary rule for using *an* before vowels, many unphonetically trained writers have written *an union* under the misapprehension that the word *union* begins with a vowel. Obviously the rule should read "before vowel sounds," not "before (merely orthographic) vowels." Since *union* actually begins with the consonant [j], it is obvious that it should be preceded by *a*. Paralleling the almost isolated instance of *an historical*, *an union* is the most frequently occurring instance of mistakenly using *an* before a word beginning with [j].

‡ It is worthy of passing note that the word *honor* (Br.- Can. *honour*) and its derivatives encompass almost all the instances of silent initial *h* in modern English. The word *humble* vacillates between silent *h* and pronounced *h*, with apparent leanings toward the latter; *humor* vacillates similarly.

Word	Stressed Pronunciation	Unstressed Pronunciation	Illustration
the	[ði]	[ðə] (before consonant sounds)	[ðə 'deɪ]
		[ðɪ] (before vowel sounds)	[ðɪ 'oʊʃən]

CONJUNCTIONS:

Word	Stressed Pronunciation	Unstressed Pronunciation	Illustration
and	[ænd]	[n̩, ən, n̩d, ənd]	[ˌeɪməs n̩ 'ændɪ, ˌkæʃ ən 'kærɪ, ˌgʊd n̩d 'ivəl, ˌtu ənd 'eɪt]
		[m̩] (after labials)	[gɛt ˌʌp m̩ 'wɔk]
		[ŋ̩] (after velars)	[ˌbæg ŋ̩ 'bægɪʤ]
that	[ðæt]	[ðət]	[ˌsi ðət ɪ 'goʊz]
but	[bʌt]	[bət]	[bət iz 'gɔn]
or	G. A. [ɔr]	[ɚ]	[ˌθri ɚ 'foʊr]
	E., S., Br. [ɔ, ɔə] before consonant sounds and finally	[ə] before consonant sounds	[ˌwʌn ə 'tu]
	E., S. [ɔr, ɔər] before vowel sounds	[ər] before vowel sounds	[ˌsɛvən ər 'eɪt]
	Br., alternate E. [ɔɾ] before vowel sounds	[əɾ] before vowel sounds	[ˌsɛvən əɾ 'eɪt]
for	See *for* under *prepositions* below. Cf. also *or* above.		

PREPOSITIONS:

Word	Stressed Pronunciation	Unstressed Pronunciation	Illustration
to	[tu]	[tə] before consonant sounds	[tə 'kʌm, tə 'wɔk, tə ju'naɪt, tə 'taʊn]
		[tʊ] before vowel sounds	[tʊ 'ʌs, tʊ 'it, tʊ 'oʊpən]
for	G. A. [fɔr]	[fɚ]	[fɚ 'ðɪs, fɚ 'ɔl, fɚ 'mi]
	E., S., Br. [fɔ, fɔə] before consonant sounds and finally	[fə] before consonant sounds	[fə 'ðɪs, fə 'hɪm, fə 'mi]
	E., S. [fɔr, fɔər] before vowel sounds	[fər] before vowel sounds	[fər 'ɔl]
	Br., alternate E. [fɔɾ] before vowel sounds	[fəɾ] before vowel sounds	[fəɾ 'eɪʤɪz, fəɾ 'ɛvəɾɪˌbɒdɪ]
from	[fram], Br. [frɒm]	[frəm]	[frəm ˌdeɪ tə 'deɪ]
by	[baɪ]	[bə]	[ˌtu bə 'sɪks]
of	[ɑv], Br [ɒv]	[əv, ə] before vowel and consonant sounds respectively	['ɔl əv əs, ə ˌpær ə 'sɪksəz]
at	[æt]	[ət]	[ət 'wʌnts]
but	[bʌt]	[bət]	[ˌɔl bət 'wʌn]

Word	Stressed Pronunciation	Unstressed Pronunciation	Illustration
PRONOUNS:			
I	[aɪ]	[a, ə]	[a ˈθɪŋk ˌsoʊ, ə ˈθɪŋk ˌsoʊ]
me	[mi]	[mɪ]	[ˌdɪd ɪ ˈsi mɪ?]
my	[maɪ]	[mə]	[ˌgɛt mə ˈbuts]
you	[ju]	[jʊ] before vowel sounds	[du ju ˌɔfən ˈgoʊ?]
		[jə] before consonant sounds	[ˌdɪd jə ˈgoʊ?]
he	[hi]	[i, ɪ]	[ˌkæn i ˈgoʊ? ˌkæn ɪ ˈgoʊ?]
his	[hɪz]	[ɪz]	[ˌbrɪŋ ɪz ˈbʊks]
him	[hɪm]	[ɪm]	[ˌkɔl ɪm ˈɪn]
her	G.A. [hɝ]	[ɚ]	[ɪn,vaɪt ɚ ˈɪn]
	E., S., Br. [hɜ] before consonants and finally	[ə] before consonant sounds	[ˌgɪv ə ˈtaɪm]
	E., S. [hɜr] before vowel sounds	[ər] before vowel sounds	[ˌlid ər ˈaʊt]
	Br., alternate E. [hɜɾ] before vowel sounds	[əɾ] before vowel sounds	[ˌlid əɾ ˈaʊt]
their	G.A. [ðɛr]	[ðɚ]	[ˌhoʊld ðɚ ˈbʊks]
	E., S., Br. [ðɛə] before consonant sounds and finally	[ðə]	[ˌhoʊld ðə ˈbʊks]
	E., S. [ðɛr] before vowel sounds	[ðər]	[ðeɪ ˌlʊk ðər ˈeɪʤ]
	Br., alternate E. [ðɛɾ]	[ðəɾ]	[ðeɪ ˌlʊk ðəɾ ˈeɪʤ]
them	[ðɛm]	[ðəm] [əm] colloquial	[ˌteɪk ðəm ˈhoʊm]
VERBS:			
shall	[ʃæl]	[ʃəl]	[ʃəl aɪ ˈwɔk?]
should	[ʃʊd]	[ʃəd]	[ʃəd aɪ ˈwɔk?]
would	[wʊd]	[wəd], [d]	[aɪ ˌθɪŋk i wəd ˈgoʊ]
are	G.A. [ɑr]	[ɚ]	[ɚ ˈju ˌgoʊɪŋ?]
	E., S., Br. [ɑ] before consonant sounds and finally	[ə] before consonant sounds	[ə ˈju ˌgoʊɪŋ?]
	E., S. [ɑr] before vowel sounds	[ər] before vowel sounds	[ˌhuz ər ˌænɪ ˌgʊd?]
	Br., alternate E. [ɑɾ] before vowel sounds	[əɾ] before vowel sounds	[ˌhu əɾ ɪn ˈtaʊn?]
was	[wɑz], Br. [wɒz]	[wəz]	[ˌʃi wəz ət ˈhoʊm]

Word	Stressed Pronunciation	Unstressed Pronunciation	Illustration
were	G.A. [wɜ˞]	[wə˞]	[ˌmaɪ wə˞ ðeɪ ə'weɪ?]
	E., S., Br. [wɜ] be-fore consonant sounds and finally	[wə] before conso-nant sounds	[ˌwi wə 'gɔn]
	E., S. [wɜr] before vowel sounds	[wər]	[ˌwi wər 'aʊt]
	Br., alternate E. [wɔɾ] before vowel sounds	[wəɾ]	[ˌwi wəɾ 'aʊt]
can	[kæn]	[kən]	[ˌhi kən 'sɪŋ]
could	[kʊd]	[kəd]	[ˌhi kəd 'sɪŋ]
ADVERBS:			
so	[soʊ]	[sə]	[ˌdoʊnt bi sə 'rud]
as	[æz]	[əz]	[əz ˌgʊd əz 'goʊld]

Some Stressed and Unstressed Pairs of Vowels

We have found that certain diphthongs, viz., [eɪ] and [oʊ], maintain their identity as diphthongs under conditions of either primary or secondary stress, but are reduced to [e] and [o] when unstressed. It is possible, therefore, to make the following pairs according to stress:

Stressed	Unstressed
[eɪ]	[e]
[oʊ]	[o]

We are approaching the discussion of three pairs of sounds which bear a relation to each other in point of stress analogous to that in the pairs above:

Stressed	Unstressed
[ʌ]	[ə]
[ɜ]	[ə]
[ɝ]	[ɚ]

The student is urged to refer to this tabulation again and again, until he has well fixed in his mind the fact that the vowels in the first column are always used in stressed syllables, while those in the second column are always used in unstressed syllables. These three pairs will now be taken up in order.

[ʌ] *and* [ə]

The sound [ʌ] is low-mid, back-central, lax, and unround. The velum is closed. In American speech, [ʌ] is much higher than in British speech. In the latter, it is so low as to be heard as almost [ɑ] by Americans and very often as [ɑ] by non-English speakers, as is evidenced in their dictionaries and other writings. Since the sound [ʌ] occurs in very few foreign languages, foreign students will be obliged to learn it more or less mechanically in some such way as by pronouncing it as an unround [ɔ] or as an [ɑ] raised and fronted Knowledge of the position of the tongue for [ʌ] should be supplemented whereve possible by hearing the sound spoken by English-speaking people and imitatin, it. Since foreigners incline to substitute either [ɑ], [ɔ], or [u] for [ʌ], it is wel for them to practice the pronunciation of pairs of words in which [ʌ] is con- trasted with these other sounds; such pairs are *cup—cop* [kʌp—kɑp], *cuff—cough* [kʌf—kɔf], *cull—cool* [kʌl—kul].

The sound [ə] is mid-central lax. The lips are neutral, or often, as when the sound is sustained, very slightly round. The velum is closed. The sound [ə] is produced with the tongue lying almost inert in the floor of the mouth, but with a slight arch in the center. It differs from [ʌ] in several characteristics: the lips may on occasion be slightly round instead of unround as for [ʌ]; though both sounds are lax, [ə] is probably the more so; the tongue-arch is central instead of back of central; [ə] is always unstressed, whereas [ʌ] is always stressed; and, as a result of this unstressing, [ə] is typically brief in the extreme, whereas [ʌ] has a duration comparable to that of any other vowel in a given stressed context. Nevertheless, beginning students confuse [ə] and [ʌ] very often because of the acoustic similarity of the two sounds when length and stress are disregarded. It is helpful for beginners to observe these sounds in contrast in words such as *above* [əˈbʌv], *abut* [əˈbʌt], *butter* [ˈbʌtə] (E., S., Br.).

The basic spelling for [ʌ] is *u* followed by a single orthographic consonant in a monosyllable, or by a doubled orthographic consonant or a consonant cluster in either a monosyllable or a stressed syllable in a polysyllable, as in *cut, muff, buck, abut, butter, buckle.* Other spellings are *o* as in *dove*, *oe* as in *does*, *oo* as in *blood*, *ou* as in *rough*.

The sound [ə] is spelled by every one of the orthographic vowels of English, as well as by many combinations of these orthographic symbols. It has been stated earlier (page 17) that except for numerous instances of the occurrences of [ɪ] as an unstressed form, and a relatively small number of instances of the occurrence of [e] and [o] from [eɪ] and [oʊ], nearly every vowel in an unstressed syllable in English is pronounced [ə].

Note the following list (the abbreviations for Southern, Eastern, General American, and British indicate the dialects in which the pronunciations listed are to be found):

1. *a* as in *await* (S., E., G.A., Br.)
2. *aa* as in *Canaan* (S., E., G.A., Br.)
3. *ae* as in *Michael* (S., E., G.A., Br.)
4. *ai* as in *mountain* (S., E., G.A., Br., when [n̩] is not used)
5. *au* as in *authority* (S., E., G.A., Br.)
6. *e* as in *tangent* (S., E., G.A., Br.)
7. *ea* as in *sergeant** (S., E., G.A., Br.)
8. *eo* as in *pigeon** (G.A.,—[ɪ] in S., E., Br.)

9. *eou* as in courag*eou*s* (S., E., G.A., Br.)
10. *i* as in im*i*tate (S., G.A.—[ɪ] in E., Br.)
11. *ie* as in consc*ie*nce (S., E., G.A., Br.)
12. *io* as in relig*io*n* (S., E., G.A., Br.)
13. *iou* as in relig*iou*s* (S., E., G.A., Br.)
14. *o* as in bloss*o*m (S., E., G.A., Br.)
15. *ou* as in vigor*ou*s (S., E., G.A., Br.)
16. *u* as in radi*u*m (S., E., G.A., Br.)
17. *y* as in paral*y*sis (S., G.A.,—[ɪ] in E., Br.)
18. *'* as in Jones's (S., E., G.A., Br.)

Note that, as stated on page 14, there is frequently a choice between [ɪ] and [ə] in unstressed syllables, according to the regional dialect spoken. Such syllables include medial *e*, *i*, and *y*, as in *telephone, possible*, and *analysis*, as well as many suffixes, such as *ace, ad, as, ase, ate, ed, en, eon, es, ess, et, eit, ice, id, in, ip, is, it, ite, uce, ute*. Words containing these syllables, when encountered in the transcription list to follow, are to be transcribed according to the pronunciation of the individual.

> *Transcribe the following in your own dialect:* above, does, flood, couple, touch, blood, stuff, tough, abate, Canaan, dove, pavement, telegraph, amount, breakfast, woman, women, gentleman, gentlemen, hiccough, money, sunshine, son-in-law, honey, coming, somewhere, frontiersman, Christmas, possession, difficulty, principality, qualitative, disability, enough, clump, clucking, tufted, rutted, lucky, solace, myriad, ballast, purchase, delicate, sprinted, written, foxes, countess, locket, forfeiture, chalice, frigid, pippin, fillip, crisis, tourist, tourists, visit, opposite, encompassing, doublet, shovel, coverlet, won, one, specimen, complete, ration, suspect, Christendom, purposeful, unwelcome, ruddy, sup—sop, muss—moose, mull—maul, confession, purpose, tongue, ton, added, fundamental, righteous†, callous, abacus.

Duration of Stressed Vowels in English

Duration is not significant in English except in very rare instances, such as may be seen in *cot—cart* [kɑt—kɑːt] in Southern American English. In nearly all instances a change in duration will only change the style of the moment's utterance, or will result automatically from certain phonetic contexts; for example, a voiced consonant following a vowel will lengthen it so that it will contrast with the same vowel followed by a voiceless consonant. (Cf. pot – pod, hop – hob, tack –

---

* It may be questioned whether the *e* in the unstressed syllable of *sergeant*, the *e* of *pigeon*, the *e* of *courageous*, and the *i* of *religion* and *religious* should be considered a part of the spelling of [ə], since in each case the *e* or *i* serves to "soften" the preceding *g*, causing it to be pronounced [dʒ] instead of [g]. It may be said that *e* and *i* here are more nearly diacritics, indicating the pronunciations of *g*, than symbols to be themselves pronounced. However, as seen impressionistically by the naive reader, these letters seem to be a part of the vowel spellings.

† The letter *e* may here be thought of as a diacritic indicating that [t] has been palatalized to [tʃ]. Cf. footnote above.

tag, date – dame, bate – bale, boat – bone.) Since changes of length, such as the foregoing illustrate, take place in the utterance of English-speaking people automatically and without significance, it is of little value to the laymen even to know of the changes; but to the foreigner in whose language such changes do not always parallel those of English, knowledge of these differences of length is very valuable in gaining a spoken style more nearly like that of the English speaker.

[ɜ] *and* [ə]

The sounds [ɜ] and [ə] exist in a stressed-unstressed relationship to each other analogous to that in the case of [ʌ] and [ə], as will be seen in the following discussion.

The sound [ɜ] is mid-central, tense, and unround—or slightly round. The velum is closed. The sound [ɜ] differs from [ə] in that the arch of the tongue is higher, in being tense rather than lax, and in being of longer duration. These characteristics go hand in hand with the use of [ɜ] in stressed syllables, and of [ə] in unstressed syllables, as indicated above and on page 115. Like most vowels, [ɜ] is referred to by its sound. Sometimes speakers who are not sure of pronouncing [ɜ] accurately in isolation refer to it as "reversed epsilon."

Speakers of General American English, who pronounce the word *err* with the tip of the tongue retroflexed, can learn [ɜ] by pronouncing *err* with the tip of tongue lying behind the lower teeth and the body of the tongue only slightly arched.

The sound [ɜ] is used by Eastern, Southern, and British speakers in such typical words as *bird* and *turn*. The various spellings follow: *er* as in *herd* [hɜd], *ear* as in *search* [sɜtʃ], *eur* in one of the pronunciations of *amateur* [ˈæməˌtɜ], *ir* as *firm* [fɜm], *or* as in *word* [wɜd], *our* as *journey* [ˈdʒɜnɪ], *ur* as in *curd* [kɜd], *yr* as in *myrtle* [mɜtl̩]. Besides these there is the irrational spelling *olo* as in *colonel* [ˈkɜnl̩]. Variants of the spellings listed above are *ere* as in *were* [wɜ], *err* as in *err* [ɜ], and *urr* as in *purr* [pɜ].

Before intervocalic *r* or *rr*, Southern, British, and some Eastern speakers use [ʌ] instead of [ɜ]. This use is explained by the fact that these speakers use the *r* as the first sound of the succeeding syllable, thus removing the *r* coloration from the preceding vowel. (Cf. *courage* [ˈkʌ-rɪdʒ, ˈkʌ-rɪdʒ], *hurry* [ˈhʌ-rɪ, ˈhʌ-rɪ].) As will be seen on page 119, General American speakers include the *r* value in the stressed syllable, as may be noted in [ˈhɝ-ɪ].

Almost exactly paralleling the spellings recorded above for the stressed [ɜ] are the following unstressed spellings, which in Southern, Eastern, and British are pronounced [ə]:

1. *ar* as in mort*ar* [ˈmɔtə].
2. *er* as in bett*er* [ˈbɛtə].
3. *ir* as in tap*ir* [ˈteɪpə].

4. *or* as in lab*or* ['leɪbə] (S., E.).
5. *oar* as in cupb*oard* ['kʌbəd].
6. *our* as in lab*our* ['leɪbə] (Br., Can.).
7. *re* as in thea*tre* ['θɪətə].
8. *ur* as in murm*ur* ['mɜmə].
9. *ure* as in past*ure* ['pæstʃə].
10. *yr* as in mart*yr* ['mɑtə].

Additionally there is the illogical spelling *ron*, as in *iron* ['aɪən], resulting from a metathesis (see definition, page 165) of *iron* to *iorn*.
For the substandard substitution of [ɜɪ] for [ɜ], see page 214.

> *Transcribe* the following in Southern, Eastern, or British, using [ɜ] in monosyllables, [ɜ] or [ʌ] as required in the stressed syllables of polysyllables, and [ə] in unstressed syllables: sirloin, earnest, hurler, were, worry, worker, cur, courage, Turner, urn, fur, furry, earlier, insert, curve, wordy, her, hurry, curvature, absurd, earl, rehearse, bursting, impersonate, hurtful, sunburn, impertinent, heard, Bertram, pearly, fern, blackbird, bur, burry, worldly, wormwood, curly, cutpurse, purr, worst, server, colour (Br., Can.), irksome, termite, journey, journal, colonel, kernel, furrow, first, thoroughfare, mirthful, thirdly, burner, tartar, faker, neighbor, honour (Br., Can.), center, centre, sulphur, satyr, attar, Kaffir, burglar, vector, muster, Castor, zephyr, saber, sabre.

[ɝ] *and* [ɚ]

The paired sounds [ɝ] and [ɚ] are exactly analogous in General American to the paired sounds [ɜ] and [ə] in Southern, Eastern, and British. The spellings for each are, respectively, nearly the same; that is, [ɝ] is spelled by stressed *er, ear, eur, ir, or, our, ur, yr*, and [ɚ] by *ar, er, ir, or, oar, our, re, ur, yr*.
Note the following:

Spellings	[ɝ] (always stressed)	[ɚ] (always unstressed)
ar		mortar ['mɔrtɚ]
er	herd [hɝd]	better ['bɛtɚ]
re		theatre ['θiətɚ]
ear	search [sɝtʃ]	
eur	amateur ['æmə,tɝ]	
ir	firm [fɝm]	tapir ['teɪpɚ]
or	word [wɝd]	labor ['leɪbɚ]
oar		cupboard ['kʌbɚd]
our	journey ['dʒɝnɪ]	favour ['feɪvɚ] (Can.)
ur	curd [kɝd]	murmur ['mɝmɚ]
ure		pasture ['pæstʃɚ]
yr	myrtle ['mɝtl̩]	martyr ['mɑrtɚ]

The sound [ɝ] is mid-central, tense, and unround. The velum is closed. In addition to the generalized arching of the tongue in the center of the mouth for [ɝ], there is an elevation and retroflexion of the tip of the tongue toward the center of the hard palate. Alternatively, instead of the elevation of the tip, there may be an elevation of the blade of the tongue without retroflexion. The acoustic effects of these two ways of making [ɝ] are identical.

The sound [ɚ] is mid-central, lax, and unround. The velum is closed. As with [ɝ], [ɚ] may be made either with elevation and retroflexion of the tip of the tongue or elevation of the blade of the tongue. The acoustic effect in either case is the same. Transcription: Turn to page 119 and transcribe the list there in General American.

Suggestions. 1. The sound [ɚ] is not a consonant but a vowel. (See discussion under [r], page 72.) Accordingly, do not use [ɚ] instead of a final consonant in a stressed syllable, as in [fɔr], *fortify* [ˈfɔrtəˌfaɪ], *form* [fɔrm]. (In *form* the [r] is not itself final, but is a part of the final consonant cluster [rm].)

2. Remember that [ɚ] is used only in unstressed syllables spelled as indicated earlier. Such syllables are not necessarily final. (Cf. *sisterly* [ˈsɪstəlɪ], *fluttering* [ˈflʌtərɪŋ], *ersatz* [ɚˈzɑts].) Students are often confused with words like *fluttering*, not being sure whether to use [ɚ] or [r]. The proper use can be quickly determined in this instance by remembering that the root word is *flutter* [ˈflʌtɚ]. In any case where the spelling is vowel plus *r*, unstressed and constituting the nucleus of a complete syllable, the transcription will be [ɚ]. If the orthographic *r* is the first sound of a syllable, as in *very* [ˈvɛrɪ], it is a consonant and should be transcribed as [r] (see pages 72–73).

> *Transcribe* in General American: scatter, scattering, scatterer, mirror, mirrored, mirroring, story, storied, carrier, murder, murdering, murderer, order.

3. The use of [ɝ] when followed by a vowel perhaps needs illustration. Note the following: *stir* [stɝ], *stirring* [ˈstɝɪŋ], *stirrer* [ˈstɝɚ], *hurry* [ˈhɝɪ].

> *Transcribe* in General American: furry, purring, deferring, demurrer, erring, recurring, her, burr, occurrence, scurrilous, scurry, churlish.

English Consonants

[p]

The sound [p] is voiceless, bilabial, aspirate, and plosive. It is made typically by three successive acts: (1) by closing the lips and blocking the nasal passage with the soft palate; (2) by forcing unvocalized air upward from the lungs to build up considerable air pressure in the mouth; and (3) by opening the lips to explode the air over the top of the tongue.

It is possible to omit the explosion by remaining silent with lips closed after pronouncing a word ending in [p]. (The velum, naturally, will drop after a moment for the resumption of breathing.) Such a [p] is called an unreleased [p]. The change from [p] with plosion to [p] without plosion is not significant in English, though it is in certain other languages, e.g., the language of the Marshall Islands.

In the case of a compound word, or of any two adjacent words where the final sound of the first member of the pair is [p] and the first sound of the second member is also [p], we have the phenomenon of a long [p]. The extra length is achieved by delaying the explosion, as in *stop pushing* [ˌstɑpˈpuʃɪŋ]. Note that although there are two *p*'s in the spelling of the words, there is only one in the normal pronunciation, viz., the long sound [p:] or [pp]. Students must be warned that long [p] does not occur within an uncompounded word, even if there are two *p*'s in the spelling; thus, *happy* [ˈhæpɪ] is pronounced with a short [p]. Only adjacent words or compounds, as described above, produce long [p].

Orthographically doubled consonants, as in *happy*, or orthographically repeated consonants as in *stop pushing*, are to be distinguished from phonetically repeated sounds, as in *such children* [ˌsʌtʃ ˈtʃɪldrən]. Here the similar spellings are spoken as individual and complete sounds, whereas in the case of *happy* and *stop pushing*, the orthographically identical symbols are together pronounced as a single sound.

In many foreign languages, particularly the Romance languages and some dialects of German, [p] lacks the strong aspiration characteristic of the typical [p] in English. Such an unaspirated [p], though voiceless, sounds to English ears like [b]. Foreign students of English should learn to aspirate [p] as explained below.

English voiceless plosives are aspirated most strongly when initial, as in *pad* [pæd]; less strongly when final and released, as in *nap* [næp]; weakest intervocalically, as in *ripping* [ˈrɪpɪŋ], where the aspiration is comparable to the weak aspiration of a voiced plosive; and with no aspiration at all when unreleased. In a general discussion of an English voiceless plosive, the initial, strongly aspirated variety is thought of as typical.

The sound [p] is spelled with *p* as in *pet*, and *pp* as in *ripple*, *gh* in the single irrational *hiccough*. The sound [p] appears as a homorganic glide between [m] and other consonants, as follows:[26]

1. between *m* and *f*, as in *comfort* [ˈkʌmpfɚt, ˈkʌmpfət].
2. between *m* and *ph*, as *lymph* [lɪmpf].
3. between *m* and *t*, as in *dreamt* [drɛmpt].
4. between *m* and *th*, as *warmth* [wɔrmpθ, wɔmpθ].
5. between *m* and *s*, as in *Samson* [ˈsæmpsən].
6. between *m* and *k*, as in *Tomkins* [ˈtɑmpkənz].

Dictionaries usually do not recognize the glide [p] in words such as those above; many people, some of whom are doubtless influenced by the visual aspects of the words, do not believe they pronounce the glide. However, the presence of the glide [p] has been prominent enough to cause it to appear orthographically

---

[26] R-M. S. Heffner, *General Phonetics* (Madison: University of Wisconsin, 1949), pp. 185–186.

in numerous words where it formerly was not present. Examples are *empty* from ME *emti, glimpse* (v.) from ME *glymsen, Sampson* from Biblical *Samson, Thompson* from *Thomson, bumpkin* from *bumkin.*

> *Transcribe:* palate, planet, applicator, troop-passage, stopper, top part, topple, purser, pitter-patter, implement, planetary, display, stop playing, planograph, ripple, flapper, upper, upon, amplify, Pleiades, occupy, palmistry, hiccough, pioneer, pleasurable, clap-trap, polyp, camp, capitol, pillory, skip playfully, depression, depreciate, replevin, grapple, hippopotamus, epic, epoch.

[b]

The consonant [b] is a voiced bilabial unaspirate plosive. The production of [b] is identical with that of [p] with two exceptions: (1) the vocal bands are in vibration during the compression period to produce a voiced consonant; (2) because it is unaspirated, the sound glides into the following sound with a much weaker puff of air than that which characterizes [p]. In the pronunciation of adjacent words where the first word ends and the second begins with [b], the explosion is delayed to produce a long [b:] or [bb]; thus, *scrub brush* [ˈskrʌbˌbrʌʃ]. Long [b] is produced only under these conditions. If [b] ıs orthographically doubled within a word, it is pronounced short, as in *rabble* [ˈræbḷ].

The sound [b] is spelled with *b* as in *bat, bb* as in *pebble, pb* as in *cupboard* [ˈkʌbɚd, ˈkʌbəd].

> *Transcribe:* absent, barbarous, carbonate, dabble, feeble, grab Ned, habitable, jumble, cobblestones, lobe, mandible, nibble, parboil, squabble, tambourine, Wilberforce, zombie, edible, barley, horseback, rebuff, raspberry, bobbin, cub bear, rubble, ribbon.

Note the following observations on the juncture of plosives with succeeding consonants: In a combination like *grab Ned*, the [b] is not exploded over the tip of the tongue in typical fashion, but is momentarily unreleased, after which the impounded air is released through the nose at the beginning of the utterance of the [n] of *Ned*. Analogously, the [b] of *rub clothes* is momentarily unreleased, then exploded as a part of the following [k], so that for the two orthographic plosives there is only one actual plosion. A similar single plosion takes place whenever two plosives are pronounced in close succession, as in *Bob Thomas, black gold, bad boys*. Any plosive followed by any continuant presents a similar situation, as in *that fan, good men, pig Latin, drag me, back through, top man, cabman.*

> *Transcribe* all the examples in the paragraph above plus the following, which are illustrations of the juncture phenomena just described and at the same time illustrations of vowel [ḷ] and vowel [n̩], often called syllabic consonants: brittle, Britain, bridle, widen, quibble, couple.

Observations on Distinguishing Between
Voiced and Voiceless Plosives

It may be observed that whereas we divide the six English plosives into the voiceless-voiced pairs [p-b], [t-d], [k-g], it is likely that in many instances native speakers of English distinguish them more by differences of aspiration than by differences of voicing. Two instances show evidence of the probable truth of this statement: (1) when foreigners, e.g., speakers of Romance languages, pronounce initial [p], [t], [k] with the weakened aspiration characteristic of these consonants in Romance languages, speakers of English are likely to hear the sounds as [b], [d], [g]; (2) in medial positions, where the English regularly has unaspirated [p], [t], [k], speakers of English will use and hear others use [b], [d], [g] without being conscious of the discrepancy. Thus, [ˈnoʊdəs, ˈnoʊdɪs] is accepted for *notice* [ˈnoʊtəs, ˈnoʊtɪs],[ˈprɑdəstənt] for *Protestant*, and [ˈbæbtəst, ˈbæbtɪst] for *Baptist* [ˈbæptəst, ˈbæptɪst] without question.

An Observation on the Vocal Component
of Voiced Consonants

It may be observed that the vocal component of nearly any voiced consonant, such as [b], consists of a sound which suggests some sort of indefinite vowel. The actual sound of [b], aside from the explosion, is difficult to isolate. However, if one will close the lips and velum and make a vocal component of [b] without confusing it with the explosion or with preceding or following sounds, one can so isolate it. If the sound is repeated at greater length so that the cheeks are puffed outward with the accumulation of air, the vocalic effect can be heard and studied more effectively; but care must be taken not to open either the lips or velum lest the vocal sound be obscured by the explosion. Voiced continuant consonants can be studied more easily, since they can be sustained for a greater length of time and can be compared with their voiceless counterparts. To illustrate, sustain [s] for a considerable length of time, thus [s:::], then sustain [z] for an equal length of time, thus [z:::]. Again the vocal component of [z], if the fricative component be disregarded, will seem to suggest the same vowel as does [b]. This observation will hold good also for the vocal components of [d], [ð], [ʒ], [l], [m], [n], and indeed most voiced consonants, with the notable exceptions of [j] and [w], whose vocal components are related to [ɪ] or [i] and [ʊ] or [u] respectively.

It should almost go without saying that the sounds [bʌ], [dʌ], etc., which are often used to represent [b], [d], etc., are by no means true representatives of the sounds, since each includes the vowel [ʌ]. When [tʌ] is used for [t], the discrepancy is even greater, since a vowel is thus added to what is actually a voiceless sound.

[t]

The sound [t] is a voiceless, alveolar, aspirated plosive. It is produced by (1) closing the velum and placing the tip of the tongue against the alveolar ridge a short distance back of the upper teeth, (2) filling the mouth with compressed air from the lungs, and—typically—(3) allowing that air to escape suddenly and violently over the tip of the tongue. The strong explosion of [t] constitutes its aspiration. This aspiration is strongest in initial positions, next strongest in final positions (except when unreleased), and weakest in medial positions where [d] or the one-tap trill, viz., [ɾ] (page 76), is often substituted. (See page 123 for examples of [d] substituted for medial [t].) Foreigners, especially speakers of Romance languages, will need to aspirate [t] in initial and final positions more strongly than in their native languages, and to place the tongue in the alveolar position, not the dental position. The /t/ phoneme contains many allophones, especially in American English (see page 76, under the discussion of the phoneme, for a list). Note long [t] in *that time* [ðætˈtaɪm].

The sound [t] is spelled with *t* as in *too* [tu], *pt* as in *ptarmigan*, *th* as in *Thompson*, *bt* as in *doubt*, *tt* as in *written* [ˈrɪtn̩], *d* as in *walked* [wɔkt]. As often noted, the suffix *ed* as an ending for the past tense and past participle of verbs is pronounced [d], [t], [əd, ɪd], according to the following conditions: (1) If the stem of the verb ends in [t] or [d], the suffix will be pronounced [əd-ɪd], as in *waited* [ˈweɪtəd-ɪd], *ceded* [ˈsidəd-ɪd]; (2) if the stem ends in a vowel or a voiced consonant other than [d], the suffix will be pronounced [d], as in *wooed* [wud], *robed* [roʊbd]; (3) if the stem ends in a voiceless consonant other than [t], the suffix will be pronounced [t], as in *capped* [kæpt]. Foreign students of English should master the foregoing.

Transcribe: Tamerlane, temperament, attain, bettering, calculate, debtor, batted, fetters, ghostly, Hottentot, intimation, pleaded, jetty, Cotswold, lantern, mitten, kicked, waded, natty, otter, pottage, tattered, stemmed, quantity, right time, rotation, horn-rimmed, what taste, tension, notice, little, rock-ribbed, Protestant, catty, stumped, stabbed, clipped, haunted, crowed, brewed, stayed.

[d]

The sound [d] is produced in a manner paralleling that of [t], with two exceptions: (1) the vocal bands are in vibration, (2) there is no strong aspiration. The /d/ phoneme in English contains several allophones and one substitute:

1. Dental [d], that is, [d̪] as in *width* [wɪd̪θ]. (Since *d* is never pronounced with the tongue in the dental position except before *th*, foreigners, especially speakers of Romance languages, must in all other cases take care to place the tongue against the alveolar ridge for [d].)

2. Unreleased [d], as when *mad* [mæd] is spoken without immediately moving the tongue from contact with the alveolar ridge.

3. Alveolar [d], which is regarded as the normal English pattern. It is made with the tongue in contact with the alveolar ridge.

4. [d] with bilateral plosion, when followed by syllabic [l̩], as in *riddle* ['rɪdl̩].

5. [d] with nasal plosion when followed by syllabic [n̩], as in *ridden* ['rɪdn̩].

6. Medial [d] between pronounced vowels is often heard in standard American English as [ɾ], as in *ladder* ['læɾɚ, 'læɾə].

Long [d], that is, [d:] or [dd], occurs as a juncture phenomenon when a word ending in orthographic *d* is followed immediately by another word beginning with orthographic *d*, as in *sad day* [ˌsæd'deɪ]. On the other hand, *dd* medially in a word is always pronounced short [d], as in *padded* ['pædəd, 'pædɪd].

The sound [d] is spelled with *d* as in *day*, *dd* as in *odd* [ɑd, ɒd], *ed* as in *opened*.

> *Transcribe:* dandelion, madder, conditioned, mad day, and then, debatable, receded, relayed, Daphne, dangerously, mid-day, dived, derivative, abdicated, resounding, middle, Broadway, tread, trod, additive, doleful, dolls, herded, bleed, mandate, mandatory, found, behind, braised, send, cleansed.

[k]

The sound [k] is a voiceless, aspirated, velar plosive. It is produced by (1) closing the nasal passage with the velum and blocking the oral passage with the back of the tongue placed against the velum, (2) building up air pressure in the pharynx, (3) exploding the air through the mouth sharply. The plosion, or aspiration, of [k] is strongest initially, next strongest finally (except when un-released), and weakest medially. English [k], especially initially and finally, is much more aspirate than the [k] of many foreign languages, such as the Romance languages. Speakers of those languages should aspirate [k] much more strongly than they are accustomed to do.

The /k/ phoneme has relatively few allophones:

1. The velar [k] exploded over the tongue as described above, as in *can* [kæn].

2. A nasally exploded [k], as in *I can go* when pronounced [aɪ kŋ goʊ].

3. The bilaterally exploded [k] before [l] as in *class* [klæs].

4. Unreleased [k], as when *lack* is pronounced without immediately removing the tongue from the velum.

5. A front [k] as in *keen* [kin]. The close transcription symbol is [c]; *keen* with this symbol is transcribed [cin].

6. A back [k] as in *cool* [kul]. The difference between front [k] and back [k] is non-significant, since the change from one to the other happens automatically, according to whether a front or back vowel follows; but the distinction between the two constitutes valuable information, since in some dialects (Virginia tide-water, Irish), the attempt to use a front [k] with a back vowel results in the insertion of an excrescent [j] as [kjɑ(r)] for [kɑ(r)].

For substitution of the glottal stop, [ʔ], for [k] in Cockney and New York speech, see pages 127 and 128. For the substitution of [t] for [k] before [l], as in [tlæs] for *class* [klæs], see page 78, footnote 41. Note intrusive [k] in *length* [lɛŋkθ].

Long [k], i.e., [k:] or [kk], occurs as a juncture phenomenon when one of the spellings of [k] at the end of a word is followed by any spelling of [k] at the beginning of the next word, as in *black cats* [ˌblækˈkæts]. When any two spellings of [k] are found in the middle of a word, the pronunciation is invariably that of a short [k], as in *cackle* [ˈkækl̩], *Rebecca* [rɪˈbɛkə]. (The apparent exception in *coccidiosis* [ˌkɑksɪdɪˈousɪs], where the second *c* of the medial pair is pronounced as [s], is not really an exception, since *c* before *i* (or *e*) is normally pronounced [s].

The sound [k] is spelled with *k* as in *Kate; kh* as in *Khan; c* as in *call, cool, cull, clean, Atlantic; cc* as in *staccato; ch* as in *character; ck* as in *click; q* as in *squall, qu* as in *quay, que* as in *saque;* and as the first sound of orthographic *x* (when equal to [ks]) as in *lax*.

NOTE: As may be observed above, *c* before *a, o,* or *u* in native English words, as in Romance words, is pronounced [k] with great regularity. The French loan word *façade* [fəˈsɑd] is an exception, but is marked with the cedilla.

> *Transcribe:* kittenish, Khan, cold, cut, liquor, pique, thickness, sackcloth, fix, queue, cue, bookkeeper, fickle, scales, escape, creek, Basque, crackle, squash, ask, asked.

[g]

The sound [g] is a voiced, unaspirated, velar plosive. The manner of producing it parallels that of [k], with two exceptions: (1) the breath stream is vocalized; and (2) the sound is relatively unaspirated. The /g/ phoneme contains several allophones:

1. The velar [g], as described above. When this [g] is exploded over the tongue, the pronunciation is considered typical.

2. A front [g], as in *geese* [gis]. The close transcription symbol is [ɟ]; transcribed with this symbol, *geese* would appear as [ɟis].

3. A back [g], as in *gold* [goʊld]. The difference between front [g] and back [g] is non-significant, in that the change from one to the other occurs automatically, according to whether a front or back vowel follows; but the distinction between the two constitutes valuable information, since in some dialects (Virginia tidewater, Irish), the attempt to use a front [g] with a back vowel results in the insertion of an excrescent [j], as in [ˈgjɑ(r)dn̩] for [ˈgɑ(r)dn̩].

4. [g] nasally exploded, as when the sequence *pig and goat* is pronounced [pɪg ŋ goʊt].

5. [g] with a bilateral explosion, as in *glass* [glæs].

6. [g] without plosion, i.e., unreleased, as in *dig* [dɪg] pronounced without immediately removing the tongue from contact with the velum.

Long [g], i. e., [g:] or [gg], occurs when a word ending in [g] is followed immediately by another word beginning with [g], as in *big game* [ˌbɪgˈgeɪm]. When [g]
is orthographically doubled within a word, the sound is invariably short, as in
wriggle [ˈrɪgl].

The sound [g] is spelled with *g* as in *go, gay, gull, glow, gear, gill* (of a fish),
gu as in *guess*, *gg* as in *egg*, *gh* as in *ghost*, *gue* as in *vogue*, and as the first
element of *x* (when equal to [gz]) as in *exist* [ɪgˈzɪst].

NOTE: As may be observed above, *g* before *a, o,* or *u* in native words, as in
Romance words, is pronounced [g] with great regularity. British *gaol* [ʤeɪl] is a
rare exception.

> *Transcribe:* gain, finger, rigged, rugged, struggle, ungainly, bigoted, doggone,
> brogue, guilty, guest, mingle, aggregation, suggest, granulated, regulate, grime,
> integration, exhibit, existence, regain, aground, catalog, gadget, example,
> tangles, wrangle.

The Glottal Stop [ʔ] and Its Functions
Alternatives for [ʔ]

The glottal stop [ʔ], made by closing the glottis, compressing the air below,
and then opening the glottis to release the air, is not significant in English.
That is to say, using it or omitting it does not change the meaning of any
word. Instead, it is stylistic, giving to a word an effect which is emotionally
different because of its use. Thus *oh* pronounced [ʔou] differs from [ou]. The
glottal stop sometimes serves a useful purpose in English by way of distinguishing between what would otherwise be ambigous expressions. It is possible,
for instance, to distinguish between *some mice* [səmˈmaɪs] and *some ice* [səm ˈʔaɪs]
by using the lengthening sign and the glottal stop in contrast.

A very convenient use of the glottal stop is to separate successive vowels
between which no natural glide develops to bridge the hiatus, as in *Anna asks*
[ˈænə ˈʔæsks]. This appearance of [ʔ] to separate vowels is quite orderly and is
severely limited. The glottal stop is not needed when a word ending in one of
the front vowels [i], or [ɪ] (including the diphthongs [eɪ], [aɪ], and [ɔɪ]) precedes
a word beginning with a vowel. With such words, the consonant [j] develops as
an off-glide of the final vowel and bridges the hiatus between the vowel and the
succeeding vowel. This [j] may be so slight as to be exceedingly inconspicuous;
some speakers may doubt that they use it; certainly it is non-significant; but it
is sufficient to render a glottal stop unnecessary. Examples: *see it* [ˈsijɪt], *the
ultimate* [ðɪˈjʌltəmət], *stay out* [ˌsteɪˈjaʊt], *die out* [ˌdaɪˈjaʊt], *toy auto* [ˌtɔɪˈjɔto].

Since, in standard English, words do not end in [ɛ], [æ], or [a] (except for the
[a] in New England speech), the problem of hiatus does not present itself in
connection with those vowels. Similarly, the glottal stop is not needed when a
word ends in one of the back vowels [u], [ʊ], [ɔ] (including the diphthongs [ou]

and [aʊ]). The non-significant off-glide from these vowels, [w], however slight, is sufficient to render [ʔ] unnecessary to bridge the hiatus between the vowel and a succeeding vowel. Examples: *too easy* [tuˡwizɪ], *to eat* [tuˡwit], *raw apples* [ˌrɔˡwæpəlz], *go on* [ˌgoʊˡwɔn], *bow out* [ˌbaʊˡwaʊt]. Since, in standard English, words do not ordinarily end in [ʌ], or [ɒ], the problem does not arise in connection with these sounds.

In dialects where the linking *r*, [ɾ, r], is prevalent, the problem of bridging hiatus does not arise in words ending in *r*, since the *r* serves as a bridge; naturally, in dialects where [ɝ, ɚ] are used, there is likewise no problem. It follows, then, that the necessity for bridging hiatus with [ʔ] occurs only between [ə] and a succeeding vowel, as in *Ada Adams* [ˌeɪdəˡʔædəmz]. In such instances, there is no natural glide in the form of either [j] or [w].

In British, Eastern, and, occasionally, Southern speech, the hiatus after [ə] is often bridged with an excrescent and hence unjustified linking *r*, as in *Ada Adams* [ˌeɪdər ˡædəmz, ˌeɪdəɾ ˡædəmz]. In the South, where the linking *r* is not universally established, [ʔ] may be substituted, as in *better apples* [ˌbɛtə ˡʔæpəlz].

The glottal stop is dialectally used (see Cockney, page 253, and New York speech, page 286) as a substitute for [t] and [k] as in *little* [ˡlɪʔl̩] and *bacon* [ˡbeɪʔn̩]. The substitution for [t] is much the more frequent.

In standard conversational American English, the glottal stop is regularly used instead of [t] between [n] and [n̩] in words like *Benton* [ˡbɛnʔn̩]. This contrasts with the British pronunciation [ˡbɛntən].

In German the stylistic use of the glottal stop is much more definite than in English. In poetry and oratory particularly, the glottal stop is used to introduce any stressed syllable beginning with a vowel. Thus *die einzige* [di ˡʔaɪntsɪgə], *verehrt* [fɛrˡʔeːrt].

In the Hawaiian language the glottal stop is significant and ranks as a regular consonant phoneme. It constitutes the difference between *pau* [pau] (finished) and *pa'u* [ˡpaʔu] (soot). In this branch of Polynesian, the glottal stop is apparently a vestigial [k], since in Tahitian, for example, the word cognate with *ali'i* appears as *aliki*.

> *Transcribe each of the following twice*, once as in conversational American English with the glottal stop where *t* appears in the spelling, and again as in formal American English or British English: sentence, Denton, Winton, Canton, Brenton.

Nasals

We have said that the consonants [m, n, ŋ] (with which we must include, of course, their derivatives, the vowels [m̩, n̩, ŋ̩]) are the only standard nasals in the English language (see page 45). They are also the only nasals made with the mouth passage completely blocked so that the air can escape solely through the nose. In French and Portuguese, where there is a set of standard nasal vowels, the air escapes simultaneously through the mouth and nose.

It has been proved by the experiment of plugging the nasal passages both front and rear that the characteristic quality which we call nasal is mainly from nasopharyngal resonance rather than nasal resonance proper.[27] In other words, the nasal passages appear to have in reality little to do with producing nasal resonance. Instead, the nasopharynx is the more important resonating cavity.

When combined with a vowel to form a syllable, as in *me* [mi], *on* [ɔn], or *ing* [ɪŋ], [m, n, ŋ] are indubitably consonants. When themselves syllabic, as in [ˈrɪbm̩] for *ribbon, button* [ˈbʌtn̩], and [ˈθɪŋkŋ̩ ˌɑv ɪm] for *thinking of him*, [m̩, n̩, ŋ̩] are regarded in this book as vowels, since they fulfill every requirement of being vowels except that as syllabics they never occur initially in English so as to permit the test of being preceded by *an* [ən], *the* [ðɪ], and *to* [tu] (see page 71). Some find it convenient to refer to these syllabics as syllabic consonants (see page 73). As consonants, [m] and [n] can be used initially or finally in a syllable; [ŋ] can be used only finally—the initial position is what is called a forbidden position for [ŋ] in English, although in such languages as Tagalog and Visayan it appears initially regularly.

[m]

The consonant [m] is a bilabial, non-fricative, nasal continuant. It is made by closing the lips, the velum being open, and sending the vocalized breath stream into the mouth and pharynx, from which it finally makes exit through the nose. As indicated above, the principal resonance for [m] appears to take place in the nasopharynx. The mouth itself, however, must function also as a cavity resonator, and because it is used as a whole for [m], only in part for [n], and not at all for [ŋ], the mouth must furnish the acoustic characteristics which enable us to distinguish [m] from [n] or [ŋ]. (See Figs. 21–26, pages 55–56.)

The only variant of [m] in English is an occasional labiodental [m] made by resting the upper teeth on the lower lip rather than by closing the two lips. The symbol for this [m] is [ɱ]. It is an allophone of /m/ and has no separate significance. People with protruding upper teeth sometimes use it regularly and others will use it if speaking when smiling. It occurs regularly in Spanish when *n* is followed by *f* (see page 463). [m] may be long, as in *Sam* Miles [ˌsæmˈmaɪlz].

The sound [m] is spelled with *m* or *mm* as in *made* and *hammer*, *chm* as in *drachm*, *mb* as in *comb*, *gm* as in *phlegm*, *mn* as in *hymn*. By assimilation, [n] after [p] or [b] may change to [ɱ], as in the phrase *up and over* pronounced [ˌʌp ɱ ˈoʊvɚ, ˈoʊvə], or to [ŋ], as in *fog and rain* [ˌfɔg ŋ ˈreɪn].

Transcribe: medial, membraneous, mobility, ambidextrous, criminal, Rembrandt, ruminant, illuminate, buckram, doldrums, syndrome, some, cam, lamb,

---

[27] C. M. Wise, "Is Nasal Resonance Really Naso-Pharyngal Resonance?" *Le Maître Phonétique*, Janvier-Juin, 1948.

ambulatory, dumb, drum, comb, climb, clime, crumb, crumble, clamber, numeration, number, column, volume, similar, simulate, Cambrian, malocclusion. Up 'n at 'em, keep 'em busy, rhythm, bottom, some men, immobilize, big and bigger.

[n]

The consonant [n] is a lingua-alveolar, non-fricative, nasal continuant. It is made by closing the mouth cavity in front with the tongue on the alveolar ridge, and on the sides with the tongue in contact with the inner surfaces of the upper teeth. The vocalized breath stream rises through pharynx and oral cavity, and thence passes out through the nasal passages. The acoustic differences between [n] and [m] are the result of the shortening of the oral cavity by the distance from the lips to the alveolar ridge. It is likely that the cavity is also made smaller by the rising of the tongue to touch the alveolar ridge. (See Figs. 21–26, pages 55–56.) Even with these changes in the resonance cavity, the difference between [m] and [n] is probably more visual than auditory. This can be demonstrated by making [n] with the tongue in the usual position but with the lips closed. Listeners who observe the closed lips are very likely to mistake the [n] for [m]. Note that long [n] occurs in contexts like *ten nights* [ˌtɛnˈnaɪts].

In most foreign languages [n] is dental rather than alveolar. Foreign students of English will, therefore, need to abandon their dental [n]'s and use the alveolar [n] of English. To effect this change they must not let the tip of the tongue touch the backs of the upper teeth, but must instead touch the tongue to the alveolar ridge, approximately one-fourth inch back of the front teeth. In Spanish, *n* before *v* is pronounced [m], as in *invitar* [imbiˈtar]. Spanish-speaking students will need to take care to pronounce English words like *invite* and *environment* with *nv* as spelled, rather than [mb] as practiced in Spanish.

The sound [n] is spelled with *n* or *nn* as in *no* and *cunning*. It is often preceded by an initial silent *k*, *g*, or *p*, as in *knee, gnome, pneumonia*. The sound [n] has a very powerful assimilative influence on the vowel [ɛ]. The tongue, anticipating the alveolar position of [n], tends to rise while the vowel is being pronounced, thus changing the [ɛ] to [ɪ]. In the Irish dialect and in substandard Southern American English, *ten* becomes [tɪn], *when* becomes [ʌɪn], *any* becomes [ˈɪnɪ]. To avoid this shift the speaker should hold the tongue in the position for [ɛ] until the vowel is finished, and then let it rise to the position for [n].

The nasal factor of [n] also exerts a strong assimilative influence on preceding vowels, tending to make nasal vowels of them. As noted (page 217), this is particularly noticeable with the vowel [æ] and the diphthong [aʊ]. Under this influence, *man*, e.g., may be heard as [mæ̃n] and *down* as [dæ̃ũn]. In *down*, the [n] has performed both the assimilative functions referred to, having both raised and nasalized the [a] of the diphthong.

Transcribe: knitting, neighborly, Nash, gnash, Ann, kitten, gnarled, bitten, knapsack, knighthood, cotton, inn, spinning, kneaded, pine knots, spanned, funny, explain, penknife, batten, candidate, anaconda, green, bantam, mandate, commander, annotate, fanciful, landlady, antedate, rancid, kneel, knell, knoll, pneumatic.

[ŋ]

The consonant [ŋ] is a lingua-vela r, non-fricative, nasal continuant. It is made by raising the back of the tongue into contact with the open velum, and sending the vocalized breath stream through the pharynx and out through the nasal passages. The acoustic quality of [ŋ] differs considerably from that of [m] and [n] because of the fact that the mouth cavity is completely eliminated as a resonator. The sound [ŋ] is phonemic in English, but in Spanish and Italian it occurs only as an allophone of /n/ before [g] and [k], as in Spanish *mango* [ˈmaŋ-go] and Italian *cinque* [ˈtʃiŋkwe]. The sound does not occur in French or Russian and must simply be learned by speakers of these languages from the description of the way it is made, or by imitation.

In nearly all the substandard dialects of English, [ŋ] in the final *ing* of participles, and in a few other words like *something* and *nothing*, is exchanged for [n], as in *comin* [ˈkʌmɪn] for *coming* [ˈkʌmɪŋ]. This process is popularly known as "*g* dropping," but the term can be applied only to the spelling, since there is no such sound as *g* in the pronunciation. Actually what happens is that [n] is substituted for [ŋ], as stated above.

The sound [ŋ] is spelled (1) with *n* before a pronounced [k] in the same syllable, and before [g] initial in the succeeding syllable, as in *link* and *angry*, and (2) with *ng* as in *bring*. To avoid confusion, it must be noted that *ng* often contains both [ŋ] and[g], as in *mingle* [ˈmɪŋgl]. It may be further noted that *n* before [k] in a succeeding syllable may become [ŋ] by assimilation, as in *include* [ɪnˈklud, ɪŋˈklud].

Transcribe: ink, single, singing, bang, bangle, hang, mangle, thing, jingle, tangle, bank, thank, thinking, stringing, singer, finger, linger, bringer, wringer, wrangle, Thanksgiving, long, longer, length, strong, stronger, strength, Concord, income tax.

[l]

The consonant [l] is a voiced, bilateral, dental, or alveolar continuant. It is made by establishing contact of the tip of the tongue against the teeth or the alveolar ridge and passing the vocalized breath stream out over both sides of the tongue. (This sound may be made unilaterally as well as bilaterally.) The velum is closed.

When [l] is made with the tongue against the teeth, it is referred to as dental [l], or, more often, as clear [l]. When it is made alveolarly, it is called "dark [l]." In Southern, British, and Eastern English, [l] before a front vowel, particularly a high front vowel, is clear. In General American all [l]'s are dark. In this book when it is necessary to distinguish between clear [l] and dark [l], the symbol [ļ] will be used for clear [l] and the symbol [ł] for dark [l]. Otherwise the unmodified symbol [l] will be used for both.

Foreign students of English should be on guard to use [l] in the various dialects of English as indicated above. Since many foreign languages do not contain dark [l], such students will have to be particularly on the alert to use dark [l] in all positions in General American, and in all positions except before front vowels in the other major dialects of English.

The sound [l] is spelled with *l* as in *leave*, *ln* as in *kiln*, and *ll* as in *fall*. It occurs regularly either at the beginning or end of a syllable.

When [l] occurs in an unstressed syllable following a sound with which it is essentially homorganic, particularly [t, d, n], it becomes a syllabic [ḷ], as in *bottle* ['baṭḷ]. In this book, [ḷ] is regarded as a vowel, called vowel [ḷ].

> *Transcribe:* welt, whelp, pulpit, wealthy, dissolution, disillusionment, indissoluble, twelve, help, myself, themselves, million, billion, college, salvage, alignment, revolving, solving, shelf, livable, valuable, befall, recall, milk, sulky, battle, little, middle, funnel, fault, brittle, riddle, kennel, calculation, elm tree, all laws, call Laura.

[r]

The consonant [r] is a voiced, retroflex, alveolar continuant. It is made by pointing the tongue-tip toward the roof of the mouth at about the point where the palatal arch joins the gum ridge, and passing the vocalized breath through the aperture between the tongue and the hard palate. The velum is closed. Alternately the blade of the tongue can be arched toward the hard palate with the tip pointing downward; the space over the tongue is about the same as with the tongue-tip position just described and the acoustic effect is identical. Many students of this book will have probably been unconscious of which way they place the tongue for [r] until the present moment. While the tongue-tip [r] is regarded as typical, there is no reason for changing if a given individual makes the [r] in the alternate position.

As indicated in the discussion on page 72, the characteristic of the consonant [r] which distinguishes it from the two vowel *r*'s, viz., [ɜ], and [ɚ], appears to be rapidity of motion; or, approaching the matter from another point of view, it is the inability of the consonant *r* to be syllabic. Conversely, the greater duration of [ɜ] and [ɚ], coupled with their syllabicity, constitutes the vowel characteristic of these two sounds. The sound /r/ has three allophones in English, none of them being significant. These three sounds are [ɹ], [ř], and [ɾ]. The first one, [ɹ], has been described above. It is called the fricative *r* and tends to occur automatically after [t] or [d], as in *try* [tɹaɪ] and *dry* [dɹaɪ]. The sound [ř] is the trilled *r*, characteristic of various dialects and likely to occur automatically in standard English after [θ], as in *three* [θři]. The sound [ɾ] is the one-tap trill, which is regularly used intervocalically in British English, either within a word, as in *very*

[ˈvɛɾɪ], or at the end of a word followed by another word in the same breath group beginning with a vowel, as in *far away* [ˌfɑɾəˈweɪ]. (For the varieties of *r* found in foreign languages, see pages 329, 377.)

The sound [r] is spelled with *r* as in *ring*, and *rr* as in *ferry*, *rh* as in *rhythmic*. A single *r* can be used either at the beginning or end of a syllable; *rr* occurs only medially and finally.

After a voiceless consonant, [r] tends to be voiceless—at least near the point of juncture. Pronounce *treat* and note when the [r] begins to be voiced. This unvoicing is, of course, non-significant.

> *Transcribe in your dialect,* using [ɾ] intervocalically if you customarily pronounce intervocalic *r*'s in that manner; otherwise use [r]: reasonable, trilling, bringing, friendly, crier, brawn, brilliant, trial, fairly, freely, forested, horribly, corrupted, carrier, verily, priestly, braise, for, more, abhor, confer, deter, detour, referable, mysteriously, curious, furious, chores, more reasons, her rights.

[f]

The consonant [f] is a voiceless, fricative, labiodental continuant. It is made by bringing the upper front teeth and the lower lip into light contact and passing the unvocalized breath stream through the constricted spaces between the teeth and the lip. The velum is closed. (For other types of [f] in foreign languages, see pages 378, 379.)

In English, [f] is spelled with *f* as in *fun*, *ff* as in *cuff*, *ph* as in *philosophy*, and *gh* as in *enough*.

The sound [f] occurs initially, medially, and finally, as in *foe*, *effect*, and *if*. The orthographic *f* is as nearly a true phonetic symbol as occurs in the English language, since it is never silent and never pronounced anything but [f], with the single exception of the *f* in the word *of* [ɑv]. A similiar voicing occurs for the spelling *ph* in *Stephen* [ˈstivən] and the British [ˈnɛvju] (from ME *nevew*, OF *neveu*) for *nephew* [ˈnɛfju]. There is sometimes found a dialectal pronunciation of *trough* [trɔf] as [trɔθ].

> *Transcribe:* failure, phraseology, defect, affect, reef, reefs, effect, rift, traffic, tariff, laughter, quaff, thief, thieves, physiognomy, trough, rough, tough, cough, half fare, half, halves, framework, flail, cliffs, roofs, safe philosophy, wife, wives, enough facts, diphthong, diphtheria, staff, waif, leaf, leaves, grief, sift, myself, muffed, fricative, self, selves, drafty, fife, fifes.

In many inflected forms in English [f] becomes [v] through the assimilative influence of adjacent vowels or voiced consonants on either side, as in *life – lives*, [laɪf—laɪvz], *elf – elves* [ɛlf—ɛlvz]. This change does not, however, take place invariably; cf. *grief – griefs*.

[v]

The consonant [v] is a voiced, fricative, labiodental continuant. It is made by resting the upper teeth lightly on the lower lip, closing the velum, and passing the vocalized breath stream through the constricted spaces between lip and teeth. Like orthographic *f*, the orthographic *v* of English is truly phonetic. It is never silent, and never pronounced anything other than [v]. For other varieties of [v] found in foreign languages, see page 380.

Spanish-speaking students of English, as indicated on page 469, are likely to have trouble with English words containing *nv*. Since in Spanish this orthographic combination is pronounced [mb], the Spanish-speaking student will have a tendency to use [mb] in English, so that *invitation*, e.g., would be pronounced *imbitation*, and *environment* would be *embironment*. It will be necessary for such students to take care to pronounce orthographic *nv* as [nv].

The sound *v* is spelled with *v* as in *view*, *vv* in *savvy*, *f* as in *of*, *ph* as in *Stephen*.

Transcribe: brevity, bravery, vanguard, fever, fervor, loaf, loaves, knife, knives, voluble, salve, bereave, visual, volition, heavy, Livy, vicious, universal, sheaf, sheaves, salvation, forgive, grove, prove, shove, enclave, derive, vivisection, envisage, reveal, revelation, elevation.

[θ]

The consonant [θ] is a voiceless, dental, fricative continuant. It is made by placing the tip of the tongue in light contact with the back surfaces of the upper teeth and passing a stream of unvocalized air through the constricted spaces between the teeth and tongue. The velum is closed and the sides of the tongue are in contact with the upper molars. Among the prominent western European languages, only English and Spanish contain [θ]. It is found also in Celtic tongues, as in Welsh. Most foreign students of English, lacking [θ] in their native speech, find it difficult. Such students will need to follow the foregoing directions carefully, to avoid substituting [t] or [s] for [θ]. They will need also to avoid forming a habit of protruding the tongue in an interdental position.

The sound [θ] is spelled regularly only with *th*, as in *breath*, though there is a rare pronunciation of *ght* as [tθ] in [haɪtθ] for *height* [haɪt].

Nearly all initial *th*'s are pronounced [θ]; some exceptions are found in *the*, *this*, *that*, *these*, *those*, and similar words. There is no invariable rule for determining when medial *th* is pronounced [θ] except as indicated in the discussion of [ð]. In final clusters, however, [θ] almost regularly changes to [ð] in plurals, as in *path—paths*. Final *th* is usually [θ]; some exceptions are *smooth*, *soothe*, *breathe*, *seethe*.

Transcribe: wreath, wraith, wrath, thesis, thing, third, pathway, both, cloth, birth, thoughtful, thirsty, methodical, truth, mouth, theme, thrilled, thin, booth, earthy, ethereal, lath, thigh, withy, something, anything, beneath, faith, ethics, Catholic, three, both things, fifth, sixth.

[ð]

The consonant [ð] is a voiced, dental, fricative continuant. It is made by placing the tip of the tongue in light contact with the back surfaces of the front

teeth and passing a stream of vocalized air through the constricted spaces between the tongue and teeth. The velum is closed and the sides of the tongue are
in contact with the upper molars.

The sound [ð] is invariably spelled with *th*. However, it occurs initially, as
indicated earlier, in only a limited number of words, particularly *the*, *this*, *that*,
these, *those*, *they*, *them*, *their*, *there*, *then*, *than*, *thus*, and *though*. *Th* in the intervocalic position when followed by *er* is pronounced [ð], as in *rather*, *lather*,
father, *other*, (exceptions are *zither*, *ether*).

Final *th* followed by *e* is generally [ð] as in *bathe*. Plurals of most words (but
not all) ending in *th* are pronounced with [ð], as in *bath*, *baths*.

Since [ð] occurs in the western European languages only in English, Spanish,
Danish, and the Celtic languages, foreign students of English will need to take
particular care to pronounce [ð] as described above. Particularly they will need
to avoid substituting [d] or [z] for it. They should also avoid protruding the
tongue in an exaggerated interdental position.

> *Transcribe:* the, this, these, that, those, they, there, them, than, thigh, thine,
> thus, though, then, smooth, sooth, writhe, seethe, heath, heathen, cloth, clothes,
> path, paths, bath, baths, lath, laths, oath, oaths, worthy, clothe, breathe, scathe,
> hither, weather, whether, father, other, brother, rather, lather, feather, either,
> southern, with them, smooth these.

[s]

The consonant [s] is a voiceless, alveolar, fricative continuant. It is made by
simultaneously closing the nasal passages with the velum and placing the sides
of the tongue in close contact with the inner surfaces of the upper molars, leaving
open a narrow groove over the top of the tongue in front, typically in the region
of the alveolar ridge. The unvocalized breath stream is passed at relatively high
pressure through the narrow space between the tongue and alveolar ridge, whence
it is deflected downward and cut into two eddies by the lower teeth, one inside
the teeth and one outside. Alternately, instead of the tip of the tongue approaching
the alveolar ridge, the blade of the tongue may approach it, the tip being down
behind the lower teeth. The acoustic effect in both cases is the same and there
is no reason why an individual who has learned to make [s] in either fashion
should change his habit. However, the tongue-tip [s] is usually regarded as
typical.

The sound [s] is of very high frequency (6000–7800 double vibrations per
second).[28] Any shift of tongue position which has the effect of enlarging the
aperture through which the breath stream exits will lower the air pressure,
reduce the frequency necessary to give [s] its identifying characteristics, and
produce some type of lisp such as [θ, ʃ].

---

[28] Heffner, p. 157.

The sound [s] is spelled by *s* as in *so*, *ss* as in *miss*, *c* as in *cent* (and before *e*, *i*, and *y* generally), *sc* as in *scent*, *z* as in *waltz*, *sch* as in *schism*, *ps* as in *psychology*, and in *x* pronounced [ks], as in *six* [sɪks]. The orthographic *s* is pronounced in many ways, as will be developed especially under [z], [ʒ], and [ʃ]. The most frequent shift of pronunciation occurs when *s* in an inflectional ending follows a voiced, non-sibilant consonant. In such cases it is pronounced [z] as in *beads* [bidz], *clothes* [klouðz]. After the sibilants [s], [z], [ʃ], and [ʒ], *es* is pronounced [ɪz] or [əz] regardless of whether the preceding consonant is voiced. Thus, *Mrs.* [ˈmɪsəz, ˈmɪsɪz], *buzzes* [ˈbʌzəz, ˈbʌzɪz], *bushes* [ˈbuʃəz, ˈbuʃɪz], *garages* [gəˈrɑʒəz, gəˈrɑʒɪz].

> *Transcribe:* secession, submarine, surplus, this soap, pass, force, fence, since, confess, abyss, coastline, cerebral, symbolism, Chase, place, peace, misty, aspiration, inspiration, expiation, resist, unless, compass, mercy, close, mass, increase, race, post, pencil, ceiling, encyst.

[z]

The consonant [z] is a voiced, alveolar, fricative continuant. It is made by simultaneously blocking the nasal passages with the velum and placing the tongue into occlusion with the inner surfaces of the upper teeth, except for a narrow passage over the tip of the tongue in front. The vocalized breath stream is passed through this constricted passage, whence it is deflected downward and cut into two eddies by the lower teeth. Alternately, the blade of the tongue is elevated and the tip turned downward behind the lower teeth. The acoustic effects of the two methods of production are identical, and there is no need for an individual who has learned to produce [z] by one of these methods to change to the other. However, the tongue position with the tip elevated is regarded as typical.

The sound [z] is spelled with *z* as in *glaze*, *zz* as in *blizzard*, *s* as in *rose*, *ss* as in *scissors*, *sc* as in *discern*, *x* as in *Xanadu*. (See discussion in section on [s], page 135, for explanation of [s] pronounced [z] in inflectional endings after voiced consonants, as in *ebbs* [ɛbz].) The sound [z] also appears in *x* pronounced *gz*, as in *examine* [ɪgˈzæmən].

> *Transcribe:* is, was, his, hers, theirs, roses, closes, abysmal, chasm, cosmos, crazed, frieze, breeze, Xerxes, xylophone, zebra, zipper, zoological, Zulu, puzzle, muzzle, nozzle, dazzle, drizzle, bruise, amuse, roads, bridges, ribs, rags, rushes, rouges, masses, fizzes, exert, existence, exaggerate.

[ʃ]

The consonant [ʃ] is a voiceless, palato-alveolar, fricative continuant. It is made by simultaneously blocking the nasal passages with the velum and raising the tongue against the lateral inner surfaces of the upper teeth with the tongue directed toward a point just back of the alveolar ridge. The unvocalized breath stream is forced through the close stricture between the blade of the tongue and the roof of the mouth. The opening is wider horizontally than for *s*.

The Russian [ʃ] and one kind of Brazilian [ʃ] are farther back than the English [ʃ], and, relative to the English sound, may be written [ʃ˖]. German and French [ʃ] are made with the front, rather than the tip, of the tongue approaching the palate. The German [ʃ] is accompanied by marked rounding and protrusion of the lips; the French [ʃ] by more protrusion than the English, but less than the German.

The sound [ʃ] is spelled by *sh* as in *shame, s* as in *sure, ti* as in *action, ce* as in *ocean, ch* as in *Chicago, ci* as in *specious, ssi* as in *passion, ss* as in *tissue, sch* as in *Schick, chsi* as in *fuchsia, sc* as in *Fascist* (one pronunciation), *se* as in *nauseous*.

Transcribe: oceanic, machinery, spacious, facetious, sugar, sumac, surety, insurance, sugary, assurance, shovel, shoulder, sheath, sheathe, sharpen, shibboleth, shepherd, imagination, fashion, faction, reactionary, fissure, fraction, expectation, confection, relation, sebaceous, nauseous, fractious, congressional, specious, specie, crochet, ferocious, fuchsia, schist, schwa, pshaw, schnapps, issue, session, mission, fascism.

[ʒ]

The consonant [ʒ] is a voiced, palato-alveolar, fricative continuant. It is made by simultaneously blocking the nasal passages with the velum, raising the tongue against the lateral inner surfaces of the upper molars with the tip directed toward a point just back of the alveolar ridge, and passing the vocalized breath stream through the close stricture between the blade of the tongue and the palate. The passage is wider horizontally than for [z].

The sound [ʒ] is found in recent French loan-words in English, in a number of words of Greek derivation where palatalization has taken place in the endings, and in many words of Latin origin in which spellings such as *-sion* and *-sian* in the endings have developed palatalization. The sound [ʒ] is the least frequently used of all the sounds of English.[29] Actually it is not originally an English sound, having come into English partly by adoption from Norman French and partly by assimilation within the older cluster [zj].

The sound [ʒ] is spelled with *g* before *e* in French loan-words like *rouge; j* as in *bijou;* and *s* as in *pleasure; z* as in *azure; si* as in *aphasia;* and *zi* as in *brazier*. It appears in [dʒ], as in *jury, gist,* and *procedure*.

Transcribe: garage, anesthesia, prestige, camouflage, beige, Asiatic, ambrosia, measure, leisure, osier, visual, derision, occlusion, jabot, jalousie, casual, menagerie, menage, seizure, enclosure, conclusion, precision, delusion, illusion, occasion, inclusion, diffusion, persuasion, collision, collusion, verdure, grandeur, jerk, geminate.

---

[29] Jeannette Laguaite, *Rules for the Pronunciation of English Orthographic Symbols.* Unpublished doctoral dissertation, Louisiana State University, 1952.

[tʃ]

The sound [tʃ] is a voiceless affricate (see page 62 for definition of affricate). Although [tʃ] can be dissected into the plosive [t] and the fricative [ʃ], it is phonemically regarded as a single sound.[30] It is made by placing the tongue in the position for [t] as described on page 124, that is, with the sides in contact with the upper molars, the tip in contact with the alveolar ridge, and the velum closed. The voiceless breath stream is now forced upward as for [t]; but instead of free plosion over the tip of the tongue, there follows constricted plosion with the tongue in the position for [ʃ], that is, with the blade elevated nearly to the hard palate. It is, accordingly, possible to think of [tʃ] as resembling [t] but having an impeded plosion. Thinking of it in this way, it is possible to regard it as a single sound rather than a succession of the two sounds, [t] and [ʃ].

The sound [tʃ] is spelled basically with *ch* as in *church*. It appears also as *c* in the Italian loan-word *cello*, *tch* as in *catch*, *te* as in *righteous*, *ti* as in *question*, *t* as in *adventure*, and *si* as in *mansion* (also ['mænʃən]).

> *Transcribe:* children, chalice, chocolate, watch, scratch, wretch, bastion, pension, mention, tension, catcher, virtue, ritual, fracture, factual, obituary, mortuary, cherry, chicken, chisel, choke, charcoal, charter, chariot, checkers, cherub, bachelor, Atchison, fatuous, nature, natural, cellist.

[dʒ]

The sound [dʒ] is a voiced affricate (see page 62 for definition of affricate). The sound [dʒ] can be dissected into the plosive [d] and the fricative [ʒ], but it is phonemically regarded as a single sound.[31] The tongue is placed in the position for [d], that is, with the sides in contact with the upper molars, the tip in contact with the alveolar ridge, and the velum closed. The voiced breath stream is forced upward as for [d], but instead of free plosion over the tip of the tongue, there follows constricted plosion with the tongue in the position for [ʒ]; that is, with the blade elevated nearly to the hard palate. Thus [dʒ] resembles [d] with an impeded plosion.

The sound [dʒ] is spelled with *j* as in *judge*, *dj* as in *adjacent*, *d* as in *gradual*, *dg* as in *ridge*, *di* as in *cordial*, *g* as in *cogitate*, *ge* as in *George*, *gg* as in *exaggerate*.

> *Transcribe:* tragical, jurisprudence, gyrate, gem, generalization, July, grudge, longevity, average, gill (1/4 pint), suggest, exaggeration, magic, agenda, giraffe, gelatin, religious, sacrilegious, jewels, adjure, justice, perjury, jail, jealous, jelly, jerk, agitate, midget, badger, geopolitics, Virginia, incorrigible, juice.

---

[30] A possible argument against regarding [tʃ] as a single phoneme is the fact that, unlike other plosives, it cannot be lengthened; it must be repeated; thus, *such children* [ˌsʌtʃ 'tʃɪldrən].

[31] A possible argument against regarding [dʒ] as a single phoneme is the fact that, unlike other plosives, it cannot be lengthened; it must be repeated; thus, *Madge Jones* [ˌmædʒ 'dʒoʊnz].

[h]

The consonant [h] is a voiceless, fricative, glottal continuant. It is made by forcing the unvocalized breath stream between the almost closed vocal bands. The velum is closed.

The sound [h] is spelled in English solely by initial *h* as in *how* [haʊ], and *h* initially with silent *w*, as in *whole* [hoʊl]. All other *h*'s are either silent or pronounced in some other way; e.g., *h* in *oh* [oʊ] is silent, while in such words as *child* [tʃaɪld], *thing* [θɪŋ], *this* [ðɪs], *dough* [doʊ], *enough* [ɪˈnʌf], it is used in orthographic clusters to express a variety of sounds.

Occasionally [h] is voiced (symbol [ɦ]), as in *oho* [oˈɦoʊ], but the voicing is non-significant. (Voiced [h] occurs regularly in Arabic, Dutch and Afrikaans.)

Sometimes the voiceless [ʍ] is symbolized by [hw] or [ʜ]. This is misleading, since there is no sound of [h] in [ʍ]. The friction of [ʍ] is in the mouth (see page 145) and not in the glottis.[32]

The former practice of allowing *h* to be silent in *humor* and *humble* is waning, and the spelling pronunciations [ˈhjumɚ, ˈhjumə] and [ˈhʌmbəl] are growing in frequency. But *honor* [ˈɑnɚ, ˈɑnə] and its derivatives continue to be pronounced without [h].

The [h] of combination [hj], as in *hue* [hju], can be and often is absorbed to the [j] by progressive assimilation (see page 153), producing [ju]. When the [h] is retained, the [j] is largely unvoiced by the progressive assimilation exercised by the [h]. The reciprocal action of the two sounds upon each other often produces a third sound, [ç], which is the *Ichlaut* of German; thus, *hue* [çu]. The change from [hj] to [ç] is non-significant; it takes place automatically whenever [hj] is spoken tensely or breathily. (This [ç] can readily be transferred to German, as in *dich* [dɪç], by English-speaking students of that language. The presence of a preceding back vowel in German automatically produces the corresponding *Achlaut* [x], as in *Bach* [bɑx].)

Transcribe: hound, haven, hah, ahead, hatchet, bath, Houghton, rough, although, howdah, through, cough, Callaghan, bough, trough, chowder, chic.

[j]

The consonant [j] is a frictionless, voiced palatal. It is often called also a continuant, but its duration is so brief as to preclude adequate justification of the term. As used in this book it occurs always initially in a syllable and always immediately before a vowel. It is made by starting from a high-front position,

---

[32] For [h] regarded as a variety of vowel onset, see Heffner, pp. 150–152. See also George Trager and Henry Lee Smith, Jr., *An Outline of English Structure* (Norman, Okla.: Battenburg Press, 1951, pp. 21–22.)

For [h] as the basic material of vowels, see Pike, pp. 71–72, 76. "Voiceless vowel: whispered vowel:: voiced vowel: voiced [h]."

probably typically as high as that of cardinal [i], but somewhat farther back. Possibly the start can be from any high-front point provided it is higher than that of the vowel to follow, or otherwise distant from it, as when [j] precedes a back vowel. Apparently the indispensable positional feature in English is a location sufficiently "close" to constitute a rather narrow stricture, but not close enough to produce a fricative sound.

The identifying acoustic feature of [j] appears to be the quick shift of sound attendant on a very rapid departure of the tongue from the starting point; the direction the tongue travels (except as limited above), which varies according to whatever vowel follows, is evidently non-significant, since [j] before any vowel registers with the ear as the same sound. See spectrograms of [ji, jɪ, jeɪ, jɔ, joʊ, jʊ] below (Figure 44). It seems that the first or highest part of the glide carries the essential identification of [j] acoustically. Or if the whole glide does so, then it is the *fact* of the glide that counts, and not the vowel complex which composes it, for, as implied above, the ear does not attend to the vowel sounds after the starting point, since these sounds veer off accordingly in other directions as we say [ji], [jɪ], [je], [jɛ], [jæ], [jɑ], [jɔ], [jo], [jʊ], or [ju]. Note the starting points and the glides of the spectrograms in Figure 44.

The name semi-vowel has traditionally been given to [j], presumably because the sound is based on a vowel, typically [i]. Actually, [j] fails the first test of being a vowel, viz., syllabicity—in other words, it cannot be used as the essential nucleus of any syllable. Calling it a semi-vowel here would therefore indicate lack of consistent basis for dividing vowels from consonants. This book maintains that syllabicity is such a basis, using as additional supporting evidence the fact that all syllabics (vowels) can be preceded by the vowel-sign article *an*, as in *an eel* [ən il], while non-syllabics (consonants) can be preceded only by the consonant-sign article *a*, as in *a yield* [ə jild]. When [j] precedes [i], there is simply a variation in the muscular tension of the tongue, marking the boundary between [j] and [i].[33]

The frictionless [j] of English must be distinguished from the fricative final [j] of French, as in *fille* [fij]. It is this [j], not the frictionless [j], which is the voiced counterpart of [ç].

The name customarily used in speaking of [j] is *yot* [jɔt]. The sound [j] is spelled with initial *y* as in *you* [ju], prevocal *i* as in *pinion* [ˈpɪnjən], and *j* in *hallelujah* [ˌhælɪˈlujɑ]. It appears also as the first element in the *u* of *use* [jus] and in the *ew* and *eu* of *few* [fju] and *feud* [fjud].

When another palatal precedes [u], [j] is not used in transcription, even though the listener hears an acoustic approximation of it; cf. *shoe* [ʃu], *chew* [tʃu], *July* [ˌʤuˈlaɪ].

> *Transcribe:* usual, humanity, huge, ewe, European, capitulate, few, jewel,
> surely, peculiar, onion, canyon, queue, yielding, Yiddish, yam, yellowish, June,

---

[33] Cf. N. S. Trubetzskoy's *Grenzsignal,* or boundary sign.

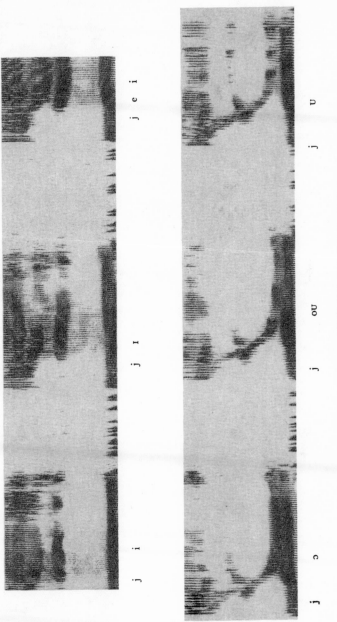

Figure 44. Spectrograms of [ji], [jɪ], [jei], [jɔ], [jou], [jʊ].

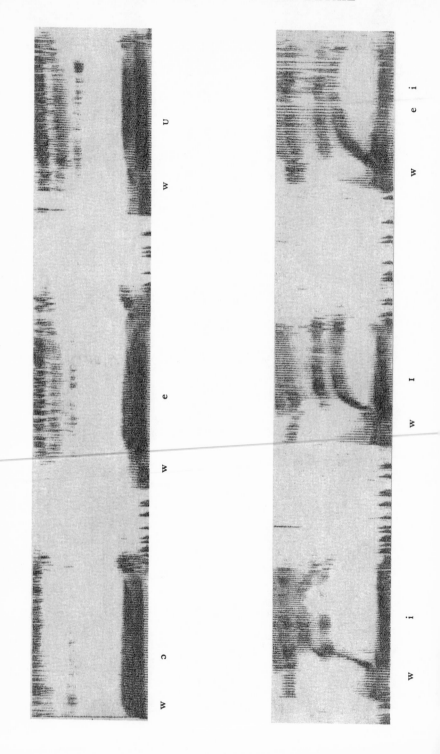

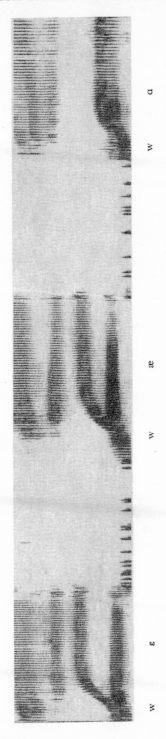

Figure 45. Spectrograms of [wɔ], [we], [wʊ], [wɪ], [weɪ], [we], [wæ], [wɑ].

Williamson, millionth, calculation, youthful, yodel, New York, yardarm, yak, yearn, juice.

[w]

The consonant [w] is a voiced labial and velar non-fricative. It is also often called a continuant, but its duration is so brief that it hardly justifies the term. A true continuant can be held as long as the breath lasts. As used in this book, [w] is always initial in a syllable, alone or in a cluster, and always precedes a vowel. It is made: (1) by placing the lips, tongue, and velum in the position of a back rounded vowel, typically probably [u]; (2) beginning the utterance of [u] and quickly shifting from the [u] position to that of the succeeding vowel. As in the case of [j], the quick shift of sound attendant on the rapid departure from the starting point appears to be the feature which identifies [w]. The vowel complex composing the glide is a negligible factor, comparable to non-significant juncture phenomena between many sounds which are adjacent to each other. Apparently the ear does not attend to the vowels nor to the direction (except that it cannot be upward) of the glide, for the glide is different for every succeeding vowel (cf. [wi, wæ, wɑ, wɜ], etc.). When [w] is before [u], there is simply a variation of muscular tension in the lips, marking the boundary between [w] and [u]. See spectrograms for [wɔ], [wo], [wʊ], [wi], [wɪ], [wei], [wɛ], [wæ] and [wɑ] (Figure 45).

As with [j], the designation semi-vowel has long been applied to [w], probably because the sound is based on [u]. But [w] does not conform to the first requirement of being a vowel, i.e., syllabicity, or the ability to serve as the essential nucleus of a syllable. Designating it as a semi-vowel here would therefore indicate lack of a consistent basis for dividing vowels from consonants. This book adheres to syllabicity as such a basis, using as additional supporting evidence the fact that all syllabics (vowels) can be preceded by the vowel-sign article an, as in an oozing wound [ən ˌuzɪŋ ˈwund], while non-syllabics (consonants) can be preceded by the consonant-sign article a, as in a weeping woman [ə ˌwipɪŋ ˈwumən].

Since the sound of [w] is difficult to make or hear in isolation, it is spoken of as double-u [ˈdʌbəlju, ˈdʌbəljə].

The sound [w] is spelled with initial prevocal w as in wish [wɪʃ], u in queen [kwin], o as in choir [kwaɪr, ˈkwaɪə], and as the first element of the pronunciation of o in one [wʌn].

Preconsonantal w is silent, as in who [hu], whole [hoʊl], wreck [rɛk], wring [rɪŋ], write [raɪt], and in sw in an occasional word like sword [soʊrd, ˈsoəd, sɔd]. In many other orthographic combinations, it is thought of as helping to express a variety of vowel sounds; cf. crew [kru], crow [kroʊ], cow [kaʊ].

As shown in queen above, the letter u before another vowel letter in the same syllable, unless combined orthographically with that letter as the spelling of some vowel sound, is pronounced [w], as in quick [kwɪk], quaint [kweɪnt], guava [ˈgwɑvə], assuage [əˈsweɪdʒ], pueblo [ˈpwɛblo].

Transcribe: walnut, wastage, weasel, quicken, quill, quail, memoirs, persuasion, languish, Guelph, Gwendolyn, guano, Dwight, swell, answerable, sword-play, toward, Greenwich, exquisite, quench, quizzical, won, once, wizard, quaint, swallow, swelling, wrought, bewray, waken, underwriter, wrinkle.

[ʍ]

The consonant [ʍ] is a voiceless labial and velar fricative. It is sometimes also called a continuant, but it is so brief that it hardly justifies the term. It is regarded as roughly the voiceless counterpart of [w], but it does not parallel [w] completely, especially in that [w] is frictionless, while [ʍ] is fricative.

The sound [ʍ] is made by placing tongue and velum in the position for [u], but with tenser lips and narrower stricture between the back of the tongue and the velum than for [w]. The unvocalized breath stream is then forced vigorously through the passage over the tongue and between the lips, its friction in the mouth and at the lips producing a fricative noise which is characteristic of [ʍ]. Immediately after the onset of this sound, the whole mechanism glides toward the position of whatever vowel succeeds, the fricative sound continuing through the glide.

In the normal production of [ʍ], the glottis is open and produces no [h] sound. Accordingly, the symbols [hw] and [h̯] for [ʍ] are inaccurate, especially as the symbol [w] connotes voicing. However, students learning [ʍ] for the first time sometimes make a beginning more easily by thinking of the sound as [hw].

The sound [ʍ] is spelled solely by initial *wh*, as in *which* [ʍɪtʃ]. Conversely, all words spelled with *wh* may be pronounced with [ʍ], with the exception of a very few, of which *who* [hu] and *whole* [hoʊl] and their derivatives are the principal ones. Some dialects, most notably the southern British dialect, do not contain [ʍ]. In such dialects, [w] is used for the *wh*-spellings. (See pages 230–243.)

Transcribe: which—witch, why—Wye, whether—weather, whither—wither, when—wen, whine—wine, wheel—weal, whack—Wac, while—wile, what—Watt, whist—wist, where, wheel, wheat, whistle, whimsy, whinny, whelk, whelp, whippersnapper, whirligig, whey—way, whale—wail, white—wight, whoa, whoever, whom, wholewheat.

CHAPTER 5

Sound Change

It is a matter of common observation that the sounds of a language change with the passage of time. Through such changes, the pronunciation of a word, or of a class of words, shifts to something recognizably different.

A basic distinction applying to types of sound change is that between non-systemic and systemic change. A non-systemic change is a distribution, among the vocables of a language, of familiar sounds in a new way. The layman notes this when he hears an aged or unlettered person in a rural community say [paɪnt] for *point* or [spaɪl] for *spoil*. Here is an instance where an old pronunciation persists alongside a new one.

These non-systemically evolved, contrasting pronunciations are the types of which the layman is most conscious, for such contrasts present to him the problem of which one to choose for his own use. Since it is the function of this book to deal often with such choices, it follows that many of the sound changes discussed in this chapter are of the non-systemic order. As an example of the appearance of a non-systemic change, and of an unusually arbitrary choice between pronunciations, we may note the instance of the *gladiolus,* once called [gləˈdaɪoləs] by learned folk, and still so-called when botanists speak of the genus name of the flower. But folk in general balked at the unusually placed stress and substituted the pronunciations [ˌglædɪˈoʊləs] and [ˌglædɪˈoʊlə]. The former has come to be recognized by dictionaries, but the latter is proving to be the people's final choice, and as a result will probably also appear in dictionaries in time. It is said that a certain florists' organization legislated specifically to the effect that its members should use *gladiola.* Thus within a few years a Latin masculine noun, *gladiólus* (little sword, from the shape of the leaf), plural *gladióli,* was changed to the form of a Latin feminine noun, *gladióla,* with an anglicized plural, *gladiólas.* Here we have an example of consciously directed change by deliberately exercised choice.

Systemic change, on the other hand, is a change in any one of the systems of contrasting sounds by which meanings are distinguished. This change may entail loss of contrast, or the setting up of new contrasts, or the preservation of the same number of contrasts made in a new way. The great sound shifts of the

146

past, such as the English vowel shift culminating in the fifteenth century, or the slow and profound Germanic shifts observed and formulated by Jacob Grimm in the series of statements designated by the term Grimm's law—these are systemic shifts.

Speakers have little opportunity to exercise choice between the sounds used before and after these shifts, for the changes take place so gradually that no one is likely to be conscious that they are in process. It is only in the fullness of time, when the end results of two long-continuing drifts are suddenly brought face to face, that the contrasts finally established attract attention. Thus when we place tenth century Old English hāl [hɑːl] beside Modern English whole [houl], and Old English ham [hɑːm] beside Modern English home [houm], we become conscious of the great English vowel shift, and can make up those formulae describing its sound changes which linguists have often called "laws."[1] Likewise, when we place side by side the Modern English and new High German words bite [baɪt]—beissen ['baisən], book [bʊk]—Buch [buːx],[2] ten [tɛn]—zehn [tseːn], dale [deɪl]—Tal [tɑːl], thick [θɪk]—dick [dɪk], we observe contrasts respectively between [t-s], [k-x], [t-ts], [d-t], [θ-d], which are features of Grimm's law.[3] For since English, originating in a cluster of Low German dialects, is known to have shared with them the first, or common, Germanic shift observed by Grimm (whereas High German moved on into a second shifting), English and German show contrasts comparable to those in the earlier Germanic of any two chronologically adjacent stages of development. So gradual were all these changes and so ancient were their beginnings, that Verner's formula[4] to explain why certain changes expected under Grimm's law did not take place is considered to apply to a time as far back as the beginning of the Christian era.

Systemic sound changes like the foregoing are of far greater interest to the linguist than to the layman, but there are, nonetheless, systemic changes nearer our own times which arrest the layman's attention sharply. Among these are the New Orleans and New York [pɜɪnt, pɜnt] for point [pɔɪnt] and [spɜɪl, spɜl] for spoil [spɔɪl]; the Virginia and rural southern New England [wɜɪf] for wife [waɪf]; the Southern [oun] for on [ɔn] and [fan] for fine [faɪn]; the Rocky Mountain [mad] for Maude [mɔd]; and many other pronunciations which will come in for discussion later in this chapter or in later chapters. As the foregoing illustrates,

---

[1] Ger., Lautgesetze (sound laws), as in the famous challenge of the nineteenth century group called Junggrammatiker, "Giebt es Lautgesetze?" (Are there sound laws?)

[2] The sound [x] is the German Achlaut, a voiceless, velar spirant, made by closing the velum and raising the back of the tongue almost into contact with it, so that there is friction when the breath stream passes through the constricted opening between the tongue and the velum.

[3] See E. Prokosch, A Comparative Germanic Grammar (Philadelphia: University of Pennsylvania, Special Publications of the Linguistic Society of America, 1939), p. 46.

[4] For Verner's law, see E. Prokosch, An Outline of German Historical Grammar (New York: Oxford University Press, 1933), p. 36 ff.

the usually accepted pronunciation may be either older or younger than its opposite number; our point here is that contrasting pronunciations belonging to the systemic category do come face to face. As before, if the contrasting sounds are of recent development, speakers often have to choose between them, much as in the case of non-systemic contrasting sounds.

The beginning student of languages sees a similar evidence of systemic change when he encounters the obviously related English *boor* [bʊr, ˈbʊə] (an unmannerly person), the Dutch *boer* [buř] (farmer), and the German *Bauer* [ˈbauəř, ˈbɑuəR, ˈbɑuə] (farmer); or the French *bouche* [buʃ], the Spanish *boca* [ˈboka] and the Italian *bocca* [ˈbokːa], all meaning *mouth.* These parallelisms and the changes that have produced these differences never cease to challenge and intrigue. Scholars use them in tracing languages of observable kinship backward into time, even beyond the earliest records, and reconstruct theoretic vocabularies belonging to ages past, before the changes now evident had taken place. Thus most of the Western European languages and certain of the Asiatic languages (the Indo-European family) can be shown to fall into relation with each other according to the following condensed outline:[5]

Indo-European
  I. Germanic
    1. West Germanic
      a. German
      b. Dutch
      c. English
    2. North Germanic
      a. Dano-Norwegian
      b. Swedish
      c. Icelandic
    3. East Germanic
      a. Gothic (extinct)

  II. Italic
    1. French
    2. Spanish
    3. Italian
    4. Portuguese
    5. Roumanian

  III. Celtic
    1. Irish
    2. Scotch Gaelic

    3. Welsh
    4. Breton

  IV. Baltic
    1. Lithuanian
    2. Lettish

  V. Slavic
    1. East Slavic
      a. Russian
      b. White Russian
      c. Ukrainian
    2. West Slavic
      a. Polish
      b. Czech
    3. South Slavic
      a. Bulgarian
      b. Serbo-Croatian
      c. Slovene

  VI. Albanian

  VII. Greek

[5] For an expanded and more nearly complete outline, Leonard Bloomfield, *Language* (New York: Holt, 1933), Chap. IV; also C. M. Wise and G. W. Gray, *The Bases of Speech* (New York: Harper, 1946), pp. 459 ff.

VIII. Armenian

IX. Indo-Iranian
  1. Indic
    a. Early forms—Prakrit (Middle Indic),
      Pali, Sanskrit (Old Indic)
    b. Modern forms—Hindi, Panjabi,
      Bengali, Romani (Gipsy)

2. Iranian
  a. Persian
  b. Afghan
  c. Kurdish
  d. Pamir
  e. Baluchi
  f. Avestan (extinct).

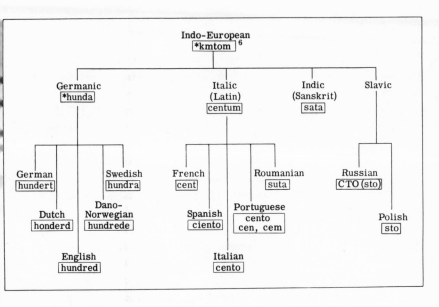

Figure 46. The evolution of the Indo-European word for *one hundred*.

Such a statement of the relationships of the Indo-European group of languages could never have been made without first observing the relationships among individual words, such as are shown in the fragmentary outline of variants above, which sketches briefly the results of extremely slow and profound systemic changes. These are much more regular and much more complex than most of the relatively rapid and often conscious and irregular changes which make up the body of this chapter.

Once these evidences of sound change have been observed, it is natural (a) to seek the cause of change and (b) to try to discover whether there is any regularity or system observable. Since the human life-span is so short relative to

---

[6] Reconstructed forms, i.e., theoretic forms not attested by being found in any manuscript or inscription, are customarily marked by asterisks.

the time it takes for general sound changes to take effect, our observations are more often after the change rather than during its onset and progress. In fact, we should often never know of the changes were it not that, as noted earlier, old and new forms do for a time exist side by side, or that someone records the pronunciation of his time in some such positive and unmistakable ways (spelling, unfortunately, not being by any means uniformly reliable) that comparisons can ultimately be made. A few such fortunate observations have been made during the recorded history of the English language. An early example is that of Orm, who, about 1200, developed a system of spelling using single consonants after long vowels and double consonants after short vowels,[7] thus preserving a record of which vowels were long and short in his time. In the 16th century William Salesbury (1547), Sir Thomas Smith (1568), John Hart (1569), William Bullokar (1580), and numerous others wrote dictionaries, orthographies, and treatises which preserved many features of pronunciation. In the 17th century, comparable works were written by Ben Jonson (1640), John Wallis (1653), John Wilkins (1668), and others; and in the 18th century by Thomas Dyche (1710), James Buchanan (1766), Benjamin Franklin (1768), and Thomas Sheridan (1780). Sheridan's *General Dictionary of the English Language*, "One main Object of which, is, to establish a plain and permanent Standard of Pronunciation," was the first example of a type thereafter universal: the pronouncing (as well as the defining) dictionary.[8]

By the middle of the 18th century, phonetic alphabets began to assume dominance as a means of preserving pronunciation and thus making sound change traceable. Franklin[9] invented an excellent phonetic alphabet as a reformed spelling device in 1768. This was followed by the visible speech alphabet of Alexander Melville Bell,[10] the paleotype of A. J. Ellis,[11] the broad Romic of Henry Sweet,[12] and the International Phonetic Alphabet. None of these, since they all depend on print, could by any means preserve human speech as accurately as do present-day phonographic recordings of the human voice. Now that we have such recordings already more than half a century old, we shall in time know much more about the processes, and hence the causes, of sound change.

---

[7] Orm (or Orme or Ormmin), *The Ormulum*, a paraphrase of gospel lessons. See Wm. J. Long, *English Literature* (New York: Ginn & Co., 1909), p. 60.

[8] All the foregoing, as well as numerous others of similar date and import, are admirably discussed in A. J. Ellis, *Early English Pronunciation*, Part II (London: Trübner, 1869), Ch. II.

[9] Jared Sparks, ed., *The Works of Benjamin Franklin*, 10 vols. (Boston: Tappan and Whittemore, 1836), VI, pp. 295–303. See also C. M. Wise, "Benjamin Franklin as a Phonetician," *Speech Monographs*, 1949, pp. 99–120.

[10] Henry Sweet, *A Primer of Phonetics* (Oxford: Oxford University Press, 1902), pp. 24–25, 41.

[11] Ellis, *Early English Pronunciation*, Part II, pp. 3–13.

[12] Henry Sweet, *The Sounds of English* (Oxford: Oxford University Press, 1908), pp. 22–48.

But up until the beginning of the present century, our knowledge of what has happened has been inaccurate, and our knowledge of the causes at least partly speculative.

Nevertheless, we can set down some of the causes which we can reasonably believe to have been operating.

Physiological Causes of Sound Change

Physiological (somatic) causes of sound change are those which bring about changes through the limitations or characteristics of those parts of the human body having to do with speech. These are, particularly, those concerned with the act of utterance and the act of hearing. Among them we may enumerate the following:

1. The lack of a uniform capacity among individuals in auditory perception, preventing people from hearing sounds alike, from distinguishing between them precisely,[13] and from repeating them accurately.

2. The fading of the neurograms or neuromuscular patterns which constitute the memory of speech sounds, so that repetitions of the sounds deviate more and more from the originally learned sound.

3. The natural tendency toward economy of effort,[14] resulting in the simplification of sound combinations which, in a given language, are difficult for the speakers of that language.

NOTE: It must be emphasized here that difficulty and ease in utterance are relative matters, depending largely upon a speaker's familiarity from childhood with the sound combinations of his mother tongue. Thus Russians appear to be at home with such extended consonant sequences as [rʃtʃ] in борщ [bɔrʃtʃ], while the Spanish find initial [st] so difficult as to demand a preceding *e* to break it up (cf. *estado*—state—from Latin *status*); and the Hawaiians, in whose language no two consonants are ever adjacent, have had to adjust the borrowed English word *plow* to *palau* [paˈlau] in order to render easy the (to them) exceedingly difficult combination [pl]. For a case similar to the Hawaiian, see the Portuguese colloquial pronunciation [abisoˈlutu] for *absoluto*—absolute. Speakers of every one of these languages find English [ʌ] in *but* extremely difficult, however easy it may seem to the speaker of English. Nevertheless, it must be conceded that even within a single language there are degrees of difficulty of utterance. Speakers of English find [sts], [sks], and [skt] difficult despite being used to them from childhood, and often omit one consonant each in *consists, asks, asked* as a measure of ease and convenience.

---

[13] Louis H. Gray, *Foundations of Language* (New York: The Macmillan Co., 1939), p. 85.
[14] Gray, p. 84; Leonard Bloomfield, *Language* (New York: Henry Holt and Co., 1933), p. 320; Hermann Paul, *Principles of Language* (tr. by H. A. Strong) (New York: Longmans, Green and Company, 1891), p. 46.

Psychological Causes of Sound Change

The difficulty of coordinating the rapidly flowing nerve current with the more slowly moving muscular system constitutes a handicap in the development of most skills; for instance, musical, terpsichorean—and articulatory. Just as the fingers may err in running a rapid scale, so the articulators may err in producing a rapid series of sounds, and, by repetition, habituate themselves in some sort of change. Some such changes are as follows:

1. The exchange of the positions of two sounds (see page 165, metathesis).
2. The modification of a sound through the influence of an approaching sound or of a sound just uttered (see below under assimilation).
3. The falling together of similar-sounding words, and the drawing together by analogy of differing inflectional forms.
4. The rejection of one of two duplicative or nearly duplicative sounds or syllables (see pages 157, 165, dissimilation, haplology).

Sociological Causes of Sound Change

1. Failure within a group to gain uniformity of speech and hearing experience because of geographical separation, class stratification, non-uniform educational experience, and political, economic, and religious influences.[15]
2. Language blends and substrata.
3. Popularity or unpopularity of a prominent individual or group, whose speech might become a model for imitation, or an example of what not to imitate.
4. Popularity or unpopularity of a dialect.
5. Drift or chance.

Obviously the foregoing varieties of influence can not be kept in complete separation. They not merely overlap, but they augment or neutralize each other according to, e.g., the prevalence of a tendency toward change in popular or unpopular circumstances.[16]

Specific Sound Changes

Assimilation. Assimilation is the most frequently occurring of all phonetic changes. In addition to its appearance in forms specifically designated by the word assimilation itself, it is the basis of various changes designated by other names. It is well, then, to begin the enumeration of sound changes with a definition and discussion of assimilation.

---

[15] Gray, pp. 86–87.

[16] Illustration: In the Midwest, the pronunciation [strɛnθ] for *strength* [strɛŋkθ], which is limited to rustic illiteracy, is unpopular among even moderately educated people; in the South and East, the prevalence of [strɛnθ] among people of considerable schooling and often high position makes the pronunciation quasi-popular.

Assimilation is a change in a given sound made under the influence of other sounds near by. The position assumed by an organ or organs, or the action taken by an organ or organs in making a sound, is modified toward agreement with the position or action of the organs in making a neighboring sound.[17] Assimilation is a simplification of the motions of the organs, a change in the direction of least resistance, greater simplicity, and greater ease within a given language in terms of the neuro-muscular habits of a speaker of that language. (See note under No. 3, page 151.) Assimilation is usually considered in three different manifestations, according to the direction in which the assimilative influence travels: viz., progressive assimilation, regressive assimilation, and progressive-regressive, or reciprocal, assimilation.[18]

Progressive assimilation. Progressive assimilation is assimilation characterized by the movement forward of the assimilative influence from the sound which generates it to a sound occurring later in the series of sounds being uttered. "Forward" or "progressive," as used here, means, then, toward a point later in time; in written English, it means farther to the right on the page.

When the phrase *Up and at them* is reduced by speed and unstressing to what would be printed *Up 'n' at 'em*, it is pronounced [ˌʌp m̩ ˈæt m̩]. Here we have an example of progressive assimilation. The influence of the bilabial characteristic of [p] in [ʌp] progresses forward and bilabializes the [n] of *and*, changing it to [m̩]. When the colloquially spoken *Gwan ina house* [ˌgwɑn ɪnə ˈhaʊs] is used for *Go on into the house*, the characteristics of voicing and nasality inherent in the [n] of *in* proceed forward to change the [ð] of *the* by completely absorbing it into itself. At a slower rate of utterance, the absorbed [ð] may show up as a time value in the [n], so that the pronunciation will take the form [ˌgwɑn ɪn:ə ˈhaʊs]. Conversely, with accelerated utterance, the [n] of *gwan* may by progressive assimilation absorb the vowel in *in*, whereupon the two [n]'s coalesce into a long [n], i.e., [n:], and absorb the [ð] as before, so that the pronunciation [gwɑn:ə haʊs] results.

In one pronunciation of *absorption* and *absurdity*, the factor of voice in the [b] of the first syllable of each word proceeds forward to effect the voicing of the succeeding [s] in each, so that the words come to be pronounced [ˌæbˈzɔrpʃən, ˌæbˈzɔpʃən] and [ˌæbˈzɝdətɪ, ˌæbˈzɜdɪtɪ]. Instances of progressive assimilation are relatively rare.

Regressive assimilation. Regressive assimilation is assimilation characterized by the anticipation of an approaching sound in such a way that the sound being uttered is modified by the approaching sound. In other words, the organs

---

[17] Bloomfield, p. 372; Albert H. Marckwardt, *Introduction to the English Language* (New York: Oxford University Press, 1942), pp. 39–40.

[18] T. L. Papillon, *A Manual of Comparative Philology* (London: 1877), pp. 73–74; J. Vendryes, *Language: A Linguistic Introduction to History* (New York: Knopf, 1931), pp. 61–62.

concerned with the utterance of a given sound anticipate the position or action required for a later sound and partially or completely assume that position or perform that action prematurely, thus modifying the sound being uttered. It can be seen, then, that the word "regressive" may reasonably be used here, since the assimilative influence of a later sound travels backward, or regressively, to modify an earlier sound.

When a combination such as *this shield* is spoken rapidly, the tongue, about to make the approach to the alveolar ridge for the production of the [s] of *this*, anticipates the approach to the palate for the production of the [ʃ] of *shield*, and approaches too soon, with the result that the [s] also becomes [ʃ], whereupon the two [ʃ]'s fall together as a single long [ʃ], thus, [ˌðɪʃˈʃild]. We may say, then, that the palatal characteristic of the [ʃ] of *shield* has reached backward, or regressively, to palatalize the [s] of *this*. In the same way, *his shield* may be pronounced [hɪʒ ʃild], the [ʃ] having functioned to palatalize the [z] of *his*. Many English words of Latin derivation show evidences of regressive assimilation which took place long before the words were borrowed into English; e.g., Latin *ad* plus *sumere* gives us *assume* [əˈsum], the [d] of *ad* having been absorbed by regressive assimilation into [s] of *sumere*.[19] Those who say *dleam* for *gleam*, *dlide* for *glide*, *dlory* for *glory*, etc., have allowed the position of the [l] to front the [g] to the extent that it is actually [d]. In the (usually) jocular pronunciation of *sandwich* as *samwich*, the bilabial characteristic of the [w] has acted regressively to labialize the [n] ([d] having dropped out earlier) to [m]. Here we have the peculiar fact that the mere lip rounding of the [w] has generated sufficient influence to effect a complete lip closure for the [m].[20]

Progressive-regressive, or reciprocal, assimilation. Progressive-regressive assimilation is typically characterized by the mutual modification of each other by two adjacent sounds, with the result that both sounds disappear as such and a third sound emerges in their place. Thus, in ME *pacience* [ˈpasiˌɛns], the [i] first became the consonant [j] by the increasing of the rapidity of utterance, producing [ˈpasjənts]. The sounds [s] and [j] then affected each other mutually so that a third sound emerged with something of the palatalization of the [j] and something of the sibilance of the [s]. This sound approximated the already known [ʃ] and fell in with it, with the result that the word (including the 15th

---

[19] Consider also *assent* from *ad* plus *sentire*, *assimilate* from *ad* plus *similare* (or *simulare*).

[20] If this book were written in phonemic terms rather than in phonetic terms, the situation might be analyzed with somewhat different nomenclature, thus: Vowel plus nasality plus consonant may be interpreted as vowel plus whatever nasal consonant is homorganic with the succeeding consonant. Phonetic [kræk] can then be interpreted as phonemic /kræŋk/ and phonetic [sæd] as phonemic /sænd/. It would follow, then, that upon the loss of [d] of *sandwich*, the [n] would be reinterpreted as [m], a bilabial nasal homorganic with the bilabial [w]. Hence [ˈsændwɪtʃ] minus [d] is [ˈsæmwɪtʃ]. This explanation assumes another regressive assimilation, the nasalizing of the [æ], which, though likely to happen, conceivably might not do so.

century shift of [a] to [e] and later to [eɪ]) appeared as ['peɪʃənts]. There are many similar words from ME which now appear in MnE with evidences of progressive-regressive assimilation; e.g., *discrecion* > *discretion*, *nacion* > *nation*, *sauvacion* > *salvation*. The rapidly spoken [ˌðɪʃːʌŋ 'mæn] for *this young man* shows a similar assimilation; so does *nature* ['neɪtʃɚ, 'neɪtʃə]. In some words the assimilation can be observed in action, since the unassimilated and assimilated forms exist side by side; e.g., ['vɝˌdjʊr, 'vɝˌdjʊə] alongside ['vɝdʒɚ, 'vɝdʒə] for *verdure*. Sometimes three stages can be found simultaneously, as with British [ɪ'midɪətlɪ, ɪ'midjɪtlɪ, ɪ'midʒɪtlɪ] (the last being substandard).

Special Cases of Assimilation

Distant assimilation (also called incontiguous or dilated assimilation). The examples of distant assimilation following are all instances of umlaut or mutation, a form of regressive assimilation indigenous in Germanic languages. They do not appertain to MnE except as they explain certain plurals, comparatives, and derivatives which have different vowels in their related forms. Umlaut is, typically, a change in the stem vowel of a word under the influence of the vowel of the ending. So-called i-umlaut is seen in **fōtiz* > OE *fēt* > MnE *feet*. There is no comparable change in the singular **fōt* > *foot*, there being no vowel ending to cause change in the stem vowel. Modern English contains evidence of a number of such mutations; e.g., *louse–lice, mouse–mice, gold–gild, goose–geese, old–elder, long–length, strong–strength, foul–filth, full–fill, hot–heat.*

Partial assimilation (accommodation) and complete assimilation (equalization). When *rub and scour* becomes [rʌb m̩ skaʊr], we have partial assimilation, since the [n] of *and* has accommodated itself to the [b] of *rub* by becoming bilabial. Again there is partial assimilation when the final [b] of *absorb* becomes voiceless to accommodate itself to the voicelessness of [ʃ] in the suffix *tion* [ʃən] in *absorption* [æb'sɔrpʃən]. In *man-killer* ['mæŋˌkɪlɚ, 'mæŋˌkɪlə] there is partial assimilation of [n] to [k]; in *raspberry* ['ræzˌberɪ], of [s] to [b]. In the French immigrant's [ðiz dɔg] for *this dog* there is partial assimilation of [s] to [d].

On the other hand, when the Latin *con* plus *mittere* gave us *commit*, there was complete assimilation of [n] of *con* to the [m] following. There is complete assimilation of [s] to [ʃ] in *this shawl* [ˌðɪʃ'ʃɔl]; and of [p] to [b] in *cupboard* ['kʌbɚd, 'kʌbəd]. The present-day pronunciation of *autumn, column, damn, hymn, kiln* illustrates complete assimilation of the final [n] of each word to the preceding consonant. But even though there is no [n] in the pronunciation of these forms, the sound can still be said to belong in some sense to the morphemes in question,

---

* Asterisks indicate reconstructed forms.

since it reappears in *autumnal, columnar, damnation, hymnal*.[21] In the spelling of many English words there are *l*'s, *k*'s, and *w*'s which often appear where no analogous sounds occur in the modern pronunciation. Such letters are usually relics from the time when the words in which they appear did indeed contain the sounds for which the spellings still persist. These sounds have long since been obliterated by complete assimilation; cf. *calf, calm, half, palm, psalm, balk, calk, folk, should, talk, walk, would, yolk, knave, kneel, knead, knight, knit, knock, know, wrath, wrist, wretch, wrench, wring, write, wrong.*

Voicing. Voicing has already been used to illustrate a form of assimilation. It appears in the progressive form in the change of [s] to [z] in [æbˈzɝd, æbˈzəd] for *absurd*, and in the change from [ʃ] to [ʤ] in *cartridge* (via *cartrage*) from F. *cartouche*. It appears in the regressive form in *gosling* [ˈgɔzlɪŋ] from *goose* and in *husband* [ˈhʌzbənd] from *house*. It appears intervocally where the second syllable is unstressed, as in [ˈnoʊdəs, ˈnoʊdɪs] for *notice*, in [ˈkɪdɪ] for *Kitty*, in [ˈpædɪ] for *Patty*, in [ˈsædəsˌfaɪ, ˈsædɪsˌfaɪ] for *satisfy*, [ˈprɑdəstənt] for *Protestant*, and in *Louisiana* [ˌluɪziˈænə, ˌluəziˈænə] from *Louis*. The appearance of [d] as in the foregoing is relatively rare. Intervocalic voicing may be called a kind of progressive-regressive assimilation, since the vowels on either side of the consonant undoubtedly cause the voicing.

Intervocalic voicing of [t] does not always produce [d] as in *Kitty* above; it is much more likely to produce the one-tap trill [ɾ], as in [ˈkɪɾɪ], *betting* [ˈbɛɾɪŋ], *water* (G.A.) [ˈwɑɾɚ]. This exchange of [t] for the one-tap [ɾ] inadvertently produces certain homonyms between American and British English, as in Am. *petty* [ˈpɛɾɪ], Br. *Perry* [ˈpɛɾɪ]; Am. *Betty* [ˈbɛɾɪ], Br. *berry* [ˈbɛɾɪ].

Voicing is in certain cases employed as a device to distinguish parts of speech, such as *close* (adj.) [kloʊs], *close* (v.) [kloʊz]; *use* (n.) [jus], *use* (v.) [juz]; *cloth* (n.) [klɔθ], *clothe* (v.) [kloʊð]. It also illustrates Verner's addendum to Grimm's law, in words where the stress does not fall on the syllable preceding the consonant or consonants being considered, as may be seen in English by comparing *exist*, [ɪgˈzɪst], *exhibit* [ɪgˈzɪbɪt, ɪgˈzɪbət], *example* [ɪgˈzæmpəl] with *exercise* [ˈɛksɚˌsaɪz, ˈɛksəˌsaɪz], *exit* [ˈɛksət, ˈɛksɪt].

Voicing and unvoicing alternate according to assimilative influences in the inflectional endings *s* and *ed*. The *s* of nouns in the plural and verbs in the present tense is pronounced [s] after voiceless consonants as in *bets* [bɛts], but [z] after voiced consonants or vowels as in *beds* [bɛdz], *sees* [siz]. After voiceless consonants, *ed* is pronounced [t] as in *walked* [wɔkt], but [d] after voiced consonants or vowels, as in *rubbed* [rʌbd], *cooed* [kud]. Note: Both *es* and *ed* are pronounced as separate syllables under certain conditions: viz., *es* after [s], [z], [ʃ],

---

[21] This situation involves the concept of morphophonemics. See Zellig S. Harris, *Methods in Structural Linguistics* (Chicago: University of Chicago Press, 1951), Chapter XIV.

[ʒ], [tʃ], [ʤ], as in *passes* [ˈpæsəz, ˈpæzɪz], *fizzes* [ˈfɪzəz, ˈfɪzɪz], *sashes* [ˈsæʃəz, ˈsæʃɪz], *rouges* [ˈruʒəz, ˈruʒɪz], *witches* [ˈwɪtʃəz, ˈwɪtʃɪz], *ridges* [ˈrɪʤəz, ˈrɪʤɪz]; *ed* after [t], [d], as in *wanted* [ˈwɒntəd, ˈwɒntɪd], *banded* [ˈbændəd, ˈbændɪd]. All these pronunciations are normal, of long standing, and as seen above, of quite orderly arrangement.

Unvoicing. Unvoicing of [d] in *ed* by assimilation has already been illustrated in the paragraph above. We have also seen the assimilative unvoicing of [b] in *absorb* > *absorption*. In addition we often hear [ˈhæf tu] for *have to*, [ˈjust:u] for *used to*.

The theory is sometimes advanced that the unvoicing of originally voiced final plosives and fricatives in Russian and German is caused by the assimilative influence of the silence which follows the word.[22] Compare Russian муж (*muzh*, husband), pronounced [muʃ], and German *Tod* (death), pronounced [tot].

Dissimilation. When the same sound or similar sounds appear repeatedly in an utterance, there is set up a difficulty in pronouncing all the instances of it. This is the difficulty we recognize under the name "tongue-twister," as in the familiar "six thick thistle sticks." Even within a single word the difficulty arises, and there is a tendency to drop one instance of the sound, or to change it so as to break up the similarity—the sounds are "dissimilated." Dissimilation is, then, (1) the dropping or (2) the changing of one of two non-adjacent duplicative or similar sounds within a word. Dissimilation does not necessarily work alone; other influences often operate, making the reasons for change quite complex; e.g., as noted later (page 166), the pronunciation [ˈfɛbjuˌɛrɪ] is influenced by the analogy of January as well as by dissimilation.

Examples of (1) above: substandard [ˈartɪk, ˈatɪk] for *arctic* [ˈarktɪk, ˈaktɪk]. [ˈfɛbjuˌɛrɪ] for preferred *February* [ˈfɛbruˌɛrɪ], substandard [ˈgʌvɚmənt, ˈgʌvə-mənt] for *government* [ˈgʌvɚnmənt, ˈgʌvənmənt], substandard G.A. [pəˈtɪkjələ-] for *particular* [pɚˈtɪkjələ-], substandard Southern [ˈrɛkəˌnaɪz] for *recognize* [ˈrɛkəgˌnaɪz], substandard G.A. [səˈpraɪz] for *surprise* [sɚˈpraɪz] and [θəˈmɑmətɚ] for *thermometer* [θɚˈmɑmətɚ].

A most striking example of (2) is the tendency which is general in Latin, whereby the two series [. . . r . . . r . . .] and [. . . l . . . l . . .] are dissimilated so as to give [. . . r . . . l . . .] or [. . . l . . . r . . .]. This tendency is found in Classic Latin (note the ending -*aris* in *militaris*, which contains an [-l-] in the stem, beside -*alis* in *Quirinalis*, which contains an [-r-]), but is carried even farther in English forms which are derived from later forms of Latin (note *purple* from Classic Latin *purpur* and *turtle* from *turtur*). Within the English language we find *Annabel* and *Arabella* from *Amabel*, the bilabials [m] and [b] having opposed each other; and *irreploachable* for *irreproachable*.

Fronting and Backing. Fronting is a vowel change produced by arching the tongue at the front of the mouth instead of at the back or center, as with

[22] Margaret Schlauch, *The Gift of Tongues* (New York: Modern Age Books, 1942), p. 176.

drap for *drop*; [ær] for *are*; substandard *bresh, jist* or *jest, resh, shet, sech* or *sich, tech* for *brush, just, rush, shut, such, touch.*

Backing is a change produced by arching the tongue at the back of the mouth instead of at the front or center, as with substandard [ˈtɔsl̩] for *tassel,* [rɑp] for *wrap,* [ˈtʃuldrən] for *children.*

Raising. Raising is a vowel change caused by elevation of the tongue. It is often a form of assimilation, the rise of the tongue being in anticipation of a succeeding sound. When *ten* [tɛn] is dialectally pronounced [tɪn], the anticipation of the [n] has caused the tongue to rise too soon and has thus placed the vowel at the higher [ɪ]-position instead of at the standard [ɛ]-position. Examples: substandard Southern [jɔd] for *yard* [jɑd], substandard Eastern *hev, hed, thet* for *have, had, that,* colloquial *git, ketch* for *get, catch,* [eɪg], [leɪg] for *egg* [ɛg], *leg* [lɛg].

Lowering. Lowering is a vowel change caused by depressing the tongue. Examples: colloquial *kag* for *keg* and [rʊt] for *root* [rut], Rocky Mountain [lɑg] and [ˈɑdətɚ] for *log* [lɔg] and *auditor* [ˈɔdətɚ]; substandard Southern [ˈsɛmpəl] and [ˈɛntərəst] for *simple* [ˈsɪmpəl] and *interest* [ˈɪntərəst]; colloquial *pore* and *shore* for *poor* and *sure*; substandard Eastern [sʊn] and [spʊn] for *soon* [sun] and *spoon* [spun].

Centralization. Centralization is a sound change resulting from arching the tongue in the center of the mouth instead of the front or back, as with colloquial *tuck* for *took, shuck* for *shook*; New York and New Orleans substandard [tʃɝs] for *choice*, substandard G.A. [ˈvɝɪ] for *very*, [əˈmɝəkən] for *American, purty* for *pretty*;[23] Southern [ˈprʌzədənt] for *president*, [ˈsʌnətə] for *senator*; universal substandard *bust, nuss, cuss* for *burst, nurse, curse*. The reduction of all sorts of vowels to [ə] and [ɚ] in unstressing may be regarded as a form of centralization, as with *about* [əˈbaut], *upon* [əˈpɔn], *alcohol* [ˈælkəˌhɔl], *paralysis* [pəˈræləsəs], *sulphur* [ˈsʌlfɚ], *odor* [ˈoʊdɚ], *sleeper* [ˈslipɚ].

Unrounding. Unrounding is a sound change whereby rounded vowels are modified by unrounding the lips. Some individuals and some groups, speaking in what, superficially at least, seems to be a languid manner, habitually unround certain vowels, usually high back vowels, as in the classic example of substandard General American *a good book*, pronounced [ə gɤd bɤk].[24]

Vowelization (Vocalization). Vowelization is a name given to the change of a consonant into a vowel. The syllabics [l̩, m̩, n̩, ɚ] may be thought of as having been vowelized from [l, m, n, r] when they appear in [ˈbætl̩], *stop'em* [ˈstɑp m̩], [ˈmʌtn̩], [ˈbɪtɚ]. [ɪ, o, u,] appear for Cockney and Southern [l] in *silk* [sɪək, sɪuk, sɪok], *milk, will, bill, fill, fail, sill, sale*, etc. Eastern, Southern, and

---

[23] Metathesis operates here as well as centralizing.

[24] The symbol [ɤ] represents unrounded [u], i.e., [u] made with the tongue in the usual position, but the lips unrounded.

British unstressed postvocalic *r* is represented in pronunciation by [ə], which may be thought of as a vowelized residuum of the consonant. Examples: *here* [ˈhɪə], *where* [ˈʍɛə, ˈwɛə], *fire* [ˈfaɪə], *tour* [ˈtʊə], *four* [ˈfoə], *hour* [ˈaʊə].

Diphthongization. Diphthongization is the expansion of a single or pure vowel into the gliding complex of sounds which, from the two vowels at the beginning and end, we call a diphthong. Historically, there has been much diphthonging in English, as when ME *a* [ɑ] in *make* [ˈmɑkə] changed to MnE [e] and acquired the off-glide [ɪ] to produce the diphthong [eɪ] as in [meɪk]. Similarly ME [ɔ] in *holy* [ˈhɔlɪ] changed to [o] and took on the off-glide [ʊ] to produce the diphthong [oʊ] in [ˈhoʊlɪ]; and [i] as in ME *pride* [ˈpridə] took the on-glide [a] and produced the diphthong [aɪ] in [praɪd].

Quite often the two elements of the diphthongs are represented in the spelling, as in *say, eight, blow, though, aisle, sleight*, but not in *rate, note, ride*.

Diphthonging is a continuing phenomenon in English. In New York City and in the South [ɜ > ɜɪ] as in *heard* [hɜɪd], with occasionally even [ɜ > ɔɪ] in New York City and New Orleans. In the South [ɔ > ɔo] in some words (see page 214), as in *walk* [wɔk > wɔok]; and in a few words [ɔ > ɔo > oʊ], as in *on* [ɔn > ɔon > oʊn]. Also we have in the South [ɔ > aʊ], as in *long* [lɔŋ > laʊŋ]; [æ > æɪ] before [s] and [n], as in *class* [klæs > klæɪs], *chance* [tʃænts > tʃæɪnts]; [æ > eɪ], as in *can't* [kænt > keɪnt]. In General American speech [ʊ] and [ɔ] before [ʃ] take the off-glide [ɪ] to produce [bʊɪʃ] for *bush* and [wɔɪʃ] for *wash*. In New York City, stressed final [i] may take on [ɛ] to produce [ɛi] in *degree* [dɪˈgri > dɪˈgrɛi].

As indicated in the discussion on page 213, in the South any vowel may break into three or four sounds, the front vowels developing [j] within the group, and the back vowels [w]. Thus *that* may be heard as [ˈðæjət] or [ˈðæɪjət], and *fall* as [ˈfɔwəl] or [ˈfɔowəl]. The more recent such a change, the more resistance it meets from educational forces. Some diphthongizations are completely accepted, while others, such as [ɜɪ], [ɛi], [ɔo], [æɪ], and [ʊɪ] are opposed.

Monophthongization. It has often been observed that any given tendency toward sound change in a language is, under certain conditions, balanced by an opposite tendency. Thus we have monophthongization, the reducing of a diphthong to a pure vowel, opposed to diphthongization. We have seen (page 159) [ɔ] expand to [ɔɪ] in General American *wash* [wɔʃ > wɔɪʃ]; conversely, in Southern *oil* [ɔɪl > ɔl], we have [ɔɪ] contracting to [ɔ]. Likewise Southern [æ] expands to [æɪ] in *dance* [dænts > dæɪnts], while [aɪ] contracts to [a] in *fried* [fraɪd > frad]; and in Cockney, the [i] of *me* [mi] becomes [ɜɪ] in [mɜɪ], while the [aʊ] of *about* becomes [a] or [ɑ] in [əˈbat, əˈbɑt].

Palatalization. Palatalization is effected by bringing the broad upper surface of the tongue into loose contact with the middle of the hard palate. If the non-distinctive front [k] and [g] (viz., [c] and [ɟ], which ordinarily appear automatically by regressive assimilation before front vowels, as in *keen* [cin] and *geese* [ɟis]) should be introduced before back vowels, the palatal [j] at once appears, as in Virginia *card* [cjɑd] and *garden* [ˈɟjɑdn̩], more simply transcribed as [kjɑd], [ˈgjɑdn̩].

Many MnE words represent palatalizations of OE, as in *drench* from *drencan* (prehistoric OE *drankjan*). Through the French, many others have come into English from the Latin, as with *chapter*, *chief*, and *chef* from *caput* (head); and *gender* from *genus*. Often derivatives of the same Latin words, coming directly from the older language without the intervention of the French, avoid the palatalization, as when *caput* yields *capital* and *captain*.

Front vowels tend by nature to generate palatalizations, as when *Indian* [ˈɪndɪən] comes to be pronounced first [ˈɪndjən] and then [ˈɪnd͡ʒən], or when we have the sequence [ɪnˈdus > ɪnˈdjus > ɪnˈd͡ʒus]—the last not usually approved. Some palatalizations have won approval, but slowly; whereas *nature* [ˈneɪtʃə, ˈneɪtʃɚ] has long been established, and [næt͡ʃərəl] almost as long, *don't you* [ˈdoʊntʃə] is still sometimes displaced for the pedantic [ˈdoʊnt ˌju].

Unstressing. Unstressing, especially in a language such as English, where only stressed vowels consistently have their normal values, causes many sound changes. These have been summarized in Chapter 2, pages 13–17, as the reduction of the diphthongs [eɪ, oʊ, aɪ] to [e, o, a], and of all other vowels to [ə] or [ɪ], according to context within words or phrases, or according to regional or community habit. For details turn to the pages just indicated.

Restressing. Restressing is a name given to the effect produced on a sound when, having once been unstressed, it again receives the stress. Normally, the original sound is merely restored. But since the unstressed sound, no matter what its origin, is oftener than not [ə], the restressing frequently does not restore the original sound, but instead the sound most closely related to [ə], viz., [ʌ]. Thus the preposition *of* [ɑv], having first been unstressed to [əv], reappears, when restressed, as [ʌv]. Instead of *He said* OF *the people, not* FOR *them* [hi sɛd ˈɑv ðə pipəl, nɑt fɔr ðəm], we often hear [hi sɛd ˈʌv ðə pipəl, nɑt fɔr ðəm]. Similarly we find [fə, fɚ], the Eastern-Southern and General American unstressings respectively of *for*, reappearing restressed as [fɜ, fɝ]. A tabulation of some of the most frequently encountered restressings follows:

Word	Original Pronunciation	Unstressed Pronunciation	Restressed Pronunciation
from	frɑm	frəm	frʌm
of	ɑv, ɒv	əv, ə	ʌv
what	ʍɑt, wɒt	ʍət, wət	ʍʌt, wʌt
was	wɑz, wɒz	wəz	wʌz
for	fɔr, fɔə, fɔ	fɚ, fə	fɝ, fɜ, fʌ

All of these restressed pronunciations, with the possible exception of [frʌm], are regarded as substandard.

In the South the peculiar tendency to relocate on the initial syllable the stress of a dissyllable normally stressed on the final syllable produces some unique unstressings analogous to those above:

Word	Original Pronunciation	Pronunciation After Relocation of Stress
Monroe	mən'roʊ	'mʌn,ro
pecan	pə'kɑn	'pʌk,ɑn, 'pʌk,ɔn
pecan	pɪ'kɑn	'pi,kɑn
police	pə'lis	'poʊ,lis

The treatment of *pecan* in the second instance above illustrates the pattern followed by the restressing of certain other words throughout the United States and Canada:

Word	Original Pronunciation	Pronunciation After Relocation of Stress
research	'ri,sɝtʃ, 'ri,sɜtʃ	rɪ'sɝtʃ, rɪ'sɜtʃ
recess	rɪ'sɛs	'ri,sɛs
Detroit	dɪ'trɔɪt	'di,trɔɪt

This type of restressing does not call for so drastic a vowel shift as in [wəz > wʌz], and so is more easily accepted. Dictionaries have begun to recognize the restressed pronunciations immediately above, along with analogous stress shifts in such words as *adult* [ə'dʌlt > 'æd,ʌlt], *address* [ə'drɛs > 'æd,rɛs], *allies* [ə'laɪz > 'æl,aɪz].

The rhythms of song often disturb the normal stresses of words. When the musical stress falls on an ordinarily unstressed syllable, the basic rule (subject to notable modifications) is to return to the original vowel in its stressed form. Thus in the spoken *Saint Joseph and Mary to Bethlehem did go* [seɪnt 'dʒoʊzəf-] is normally sung [seɪnt dʒoʊ-zɛf—]; but it may be heard [seɪnt dʒoʊ-zʌf]. Similarly we may hear *Where seldom is heard a* [dɪskɝ-rʌd-dʒɪŋ] *word*, instead of the normal [dɪskɝ-ɪdʒ-ɪŋ].

Compensatory lengthening. In Southern and Eastern American and in British speech the dropping of the postvocalic *r* has the effect of lengthening the preceding vowel. Since this lengthening is ordinarily non-significant, it is seldom necessary to indicate it in transcription. But in Southern speech it is sometimes significant; i.e., it identifies words, and should be marked as a means of distinguishing otherwise ambiguous homonyms. Compare the following:

hod [hɑd]	hard [hɑ:d]
shod [ʃɑd]	shard [ʃɑ:d]
lock [lɑk]	lark [lɑ:k]
pot [pɑt]	part [pɑ:t]

In Eastern and British the indication of contrasting length is unnecessary, since such length is non-significant. The actual distinction between the members of the pairs above is a vowel distinction, as in *hod* [hɒd], *hard* [hɑd].[25]

Compensatory lengthening may be found in various languages. The loss of a Latin nasal consonant had the effect of lengthening as well as nasalizing the preceding vowel, as in Latin *cantare* > Fr. *chanter* [ʃɑ̃ˈte]. The dropping of [ç] from OE *niht* [nɪçt] had the effect of lengthening the [ɪ] and changing its quality to [i], the length of which shows in the total length of [aɪ] in MnE *night* [naɪt].

Anaptyxis. Anaptyxis is the insertion of a vowel, most frequently [ə], between two consonants,[26] one of which is either derived from a vowel (e. g., [w < u]), or can be made into a vowel (e.g., [l > ḷ, r > ɚ, m > m̩]. This insertion is promoted by slow utterance. Compare [kəˈræʃ] from *crash*, [skəˈwil] from *squeal*, [ˈæləkəˌlaɪn] from *alkaline*, [bəˈreɪv] from *brave*, [ˈæθəˌlit] from *athlete*, [ˈfɪləm] from *film*, [ˈɛləm] from *elm*, [ˈðɪsəˌweɪ] from *this way*.

Simplification of consonant clusters. Complex consonant clusters, initial, medial, and final, are likely to be simplified, especially if they are foreign to the language patterns in which they are being used, as with the Greek derivative *psychology* [saɪˈkɑlədʒɪ], [saɪˈkɒlədʒɪ], the Greek derivative *pneumonia* [njuˈmoʊnjə], [nuˈmoʊnjə], *knight* [naɪt] from O.E. *cniht* [knɪçt], substandard [ˈpɪkʃɚ, ˈpɪkʃə] from *picture* [ˈpɪktʃɚ, ˈpɪktʃə], substandard [kənˈsɪs:] from *consists*, *dip'thong* and *dip'theria* for *diphthong* and *diphtheria*.[27]

Prothesis. Prothesis is a method of breaking up unfamiliar sound clusters by prefixing a vowel. Spanish furnishes many examples of the breaking up of [s] plus a plosive, as when the (to the natives of the Iberian Peninsula) unfamiliar Lat. *stylus, stilus* > Sp. *estilo*; Lat. *statua* > Sp. *estatua*; Lat. *scala* > Sp. *escala*; Lat. *scribere* > Sp. *escribir*; Lat. *stare* > Sp. *estar*. French furnishes examples of first breaking up the cluster [s] plus plosive, and then dropping the [s], as in *sponsare* > *espouser* > *épouser*. English sometimes acquired doublets, one member being derived from OF and the other directly from Latin, as with *estate–state, established–stable, espouse* (v.)–*spouse* (n.). (Complex final clusters are often broken up if they lend themselves to the insertion of a vowel, as with substandard *nestes* from *nests*, and substandard *ghostes* from *ghosts*.)

Aphesis. Aphesis may be defined as the dropping of an unstressed initial

[25] To avoid complicating English phonemics by the introduction of vowel length as a significant feature or phoneme, we may explain the situation here as follows:

If it may be conceded that loss of postvocalic /r/ always produces schwa (which is already set up as a phone) after /a/, as it obviously does after /ɪ, ɛ, ʊ/, usually after /ɔ/ and occasionally after /a/ itself, this schwa can be described as having an allophone consisting of length alone. Thus in those dialects in which the only audible distinction between *hod* and *hard* is one of time, the phonemic transcriptions would be /had/ and /haəd/, though of course a phonetic transcription could be separately given as [hɑd] and [hɑ:d].

[26] Bloomfield, p. 384.

[27] Note the probability of dissimilation: – – fricative + fricative – –> – – plosive + fricative; i.e., [– – f + θ – –> – – p + θ – –].

vowel or syllable, as in *assize* > *size, escheat* > *cheat, espice* > *spice, esquire* > *squire, escallop* > *scallop, estop* > *stop, estrange* > *strange, estray* > *stray, ensample* > *sample, opossum* > *possum.* Aphesis is obviously a process of opposite nature to that seen in prothesis, and may on occasion result in the undoing of what prothesis has accomplished. In Lat. *sponsare* > OF *espouser* > E. *espouse* (v.) > E. *spouse* (n.) we have such a completed cycle.

Excrescent sounds. Excrescent sounds appear in English under a variety of conditions, some of which may be explained as follows:

1. There is a habit of English articulation whereby the normal explosion of a plosive consonant is suppressed if another plosive or a fricative or a nasal follows in close juncture. For instance, the [k] in *doctor* is reduced to closure only, whereupon, by diadochokinetic movement, the tongue exchanges velar contact for alveolar contact, thereby preparing the way for the plosion of the air originally accumulated for the [k] through the stricture for [t]. Again, the [t] of *plants* is reduced to mere closure, and the air accumulated for it is expelled through the stricture appropriate for the [s]. Repetition of events like these has the tendency to minimize the contrast between plosive consonants and zero in certain homorganic sequences. Thus *tents* may conceivably be pronounced indifferently with [t] as [tɛnts] and with zero as [tɛns]. By extension of this pattern of loss and gain, *tense* may also be pronounced [tɛns, tɛnts]. The excrescent [t] thus developed does indeed very often appear, as in many people's pronunciation of *fence* [fɛnts], *once* [wʌnts]. Frequently it accounts for homonyms, as in *prince* [prɪnts]–*prints, chance* [tʃænts]–*chants, quince* [kwɪnts]–*quints, mince* [mɪnts]–*mints, dense* [dɛnts]–*dents.*

2. The same reduction of plosives to closure only, which is seen above within such a word as *doctor,* occurs also where the juxtaposition of two words places a final plosive of the first in close juncture with an initial plosive of the second. Compare *black top, rag doll.* In *round top,* the [d] of *round* is reduced to closure (which attaches itself as a length augmentative to the homorganic [t] following), plus a modicum of voicing (which often is not perceived at all), whereupon the [d] seems to disappear entirely. Since it does not so disappear in *round orange,* the word *round* seems to have two morphonemically alternate forms, *roun'* and *round.* By a similar process of reasoning, *first day,* contrasted with *first act,* appears to have the morphophonemic alternates *firs'* and *first.*[28] By extension of the pattern of loss and gain, *gown* may be thought

---

[28] Obviously, the concepts discussed in this paragraph are all laymen's concepts, and the conclusions (that these words have two forms each) are laymen's conclusions. For none of the consonants really disappear; each remains as a combination of length and voicing, or as length alone. C. K. Thomas cleverly diagrams the situation, using wavy lines for voicing and straight lines for voicelessness:

For voiced con. + same voiced con., as in *sad day* [sæd:eɪ]

For voiceless con. + same voiceless con., as in *that time* [ðæt:aɪm]

For voiceless con. + homorganic voiced con., as in *that day* [ðætdeɪ]

For voiced con. + homorganic voiceless con., as in *sad time* [sædtaɪm]

by the layman to have two forms, *gown* and *gownd*, and *across* the two forms *across* and *acrost*. Compare also standard *against* from earlier *agains*, *betwixt* from earlier *betwix*, *whilst* from *while(s)*, *amongst* from *among(s)*, and the standard-substandard pairs *close–clost*, *once*–[wʌnst], *twice*–[twaɪst], *drown*–[draʊnd], *orphan–orphant*.

3. When excrescent plosives develop in close juncture after nasals, they do so according to a rule of English morpheme construction by which such plosives should be homorganic with the nasals, so that [m] calls for a succeeding [b, p], [n] for [d, t], [ŋ] for [g, k]. Thus a certain professor who was much given to filling moments of hestitation in his lectures with *uh*, invariably developed [b] before *uh* after *from*, and [d] after *in*, viz., *from-buh*, *in-duh*. Such excrescent plosives may develop before vowels, but are even more likely to develop as glides to smooth the pathway between the nasal and any non-homorganic consonant already succeeding. Compare [p] in *empty* from ME *emti*, [b] in *nimble* from ME *nimel*, [b] in *ember* from ME *emer*, [b] in *number* from Lat. *numero*; [p] in [ˈsʌmpθɪŋ] from *something*, [k] in [lɛŋkθ] from *length*, [k] in [strɛŋkθ] from *strength*, [b] in *fambly* from *family* (the *i* having first dropped out). In some measure, words of the order of *tense* (when pronounced [tɛnts]) belong also in this category, since [n] and [s] in [tɛns], while almost homorganic, are not completely so; hence the [n] often calls for [t] to make the sequence entirely homorganic. Furthermore, considering the situation of [nts] purely as a sequence of events, it can readily be seen that when the tongue is in the [n]-position, it completely closes the month as an exit of air. If, thereupon, the velum closes in anticipation of the [s] even a small fraction of a second before the tip of the tongue can break contact with the alveolar ridge, enough air pressure will build up to produce the plosion of a [t] when the tongue does break contact.

4. The reverse of the situation described at the beginning of No. 3 above can and often does prevail, as when the [k] of *ink* demands that the nasal preceding be the homorganic [ŋ], so that we have [ɪŋk]. Compare also [ŋ] in *sank* [sæŋk], *trunk* [trʌŋk], etc.; and [m] in Sp. *un peso* [um ˈpeso], [ŋ] in *un coco* [uŋ ˈkoko], [n] in *un tono* [un ˈtono]. In the case of *length* and *strength*, if the excrescent [k] fails to develop to form the homorganic sequence [ŋk] of [lɛŋkθ, strɛŋkθ], then the [θ] will usually demand that [ŋ] change to the more nearly homorganic [n], so as to produce [lɛnθ, strɛnθ], and later, [lɛntθ, strɛntθ].

Throughout the foregoing discussion of excrescent sounds there can be seen evidences of the principle of assimilation, sometimes clearly shown, as in No. 4 above, and sometimes less typically shown, as in No. 3.

Syncope.[29] Syncope is the elimination of medial vowels, usually syllabics—hence the related term syllabic syncope.[30] Examples: ME *legges* > *legs*; modern

---

[29] Hans Oertel, *Lectures on the Study of Languages* (New York: Scribner's, 1901), p. 207.
[30] Bloomfield, *Language*, p. 382.

bstandard *med'eval, hick'ry, Dan'l, comp'ny, fam'ly, reg'lar, acc'rate,* and of
e *vet'ran, batt'ry;* Southern substandard *var'able, assoc'ation, exper'ence,*
'ously; standard British *secret'ry, cemet'ry, confection'ry.* Expanding the term
include consonants,[31] we can apply it to the loss of [t] in *hasten, glisten, thistle,*
istle, listen, christen, fasten, often.

Word shrinkage. Word shrinkage is a term applied to many kinds of irregu-
· shortenings of words. Proper names and other frequently used words, if at
long, are always liable to shrinkage, as with [ˌmeɪˈræn] from *Mary Ann,*
nɛlənɚ, ˈmɛlənə] from *Mary Eleanor,* [ˈtʃʌmlɪ] from *Cholmondeley, bedlam* from
thlehem, sexton from *sacristan,* [ˈboʊsən] from *boatswain, weskit* from *waistcoat,*
nɔdlən] from *Magdalen.*

Metathesis. Metathesis is the reversal of the position of sounds. Examples:
ɔdren for *modern, persume* for *presume, hunderd* for *hundred, prespiration* for
rspiration, westren for *western, pattren* for *pattern, aporn* for *apron, ax* for *ask,*
rty for *pretty, asterix* for *asterisk, larnyx* for *larynx.* When the exchange of
unds takes place at some distance, it is called a "spoonerism." Examples: *no*
ut a doubt it for *no doubt about it, sues and shocks* for *shoes and socks, dit of*
fference for *bit of difference.* No doubt analogy often plays a part in metathesis;
g., *modren, pattren,* perhaps from *brethren.*

Apocope. Apocope can be defined as the loss of final sounds or syllables.
he strong stresses characteristic of English have promoted the loss of many
ⅼE final *e*'s, as may be seen by comparing MnE *complaint, sun, yellowness, had,*
ver, peer with the corresponding words from Chaucer's *Compleinte to His*
mpty Purs.

> Or see your colour lyk the sonne bright
> That of yelownesse hadde nevere pere.

The dropping of final *t*'s and *d*'s, as with *firs'* for *first, nex'* for *next, lan'* for
nd, illustrate the concept of apocope as applied to consonants. If the concept
expanded to admit the loss of considerable portions of words, what are some-
mes called clipped words may be included, provided only that the loss is at
ⅼe latter part of the word. Examples: *pro* for *professional, mon'* for *money, monk*
r *monkey, Mississip'* for *Mississippi, Alabam'* for *Alabama, Fred* for *Frederick,*
iss for *mistress, mob* for *mobile vulgus, auto* for *automobile, gas* for *gasoline,*
ıb for *cabriolet, zoo* for *zoological garden, medico* for *medical physician, vet* for
) *veteran* and (b) *veterinary surgeon, Cap* for *Captain, Doc* for *Doctor, gym* for
ymnasium, polecon for *political economy, co-ed* for *co-educational* (also a girl
tudent in a school for both sexes).

Haplology. Haplology is syncope of one of two duplicative or nearly dupli-

[31] Albert H. Marckwardt, *Introduction to the English Language* (New York: Oxford University Press, 1942), pp. 29–30.

cative elements. It could also be described as syllabic dissimilation. Examples: *Mis'sippi* for *Mississippi*, *cal'late* for *calculate*, *prob'ly* for *probably*, [ˈkoukˈkoulə] for *Coca-Cola*, *miz* for *mistress* [ˈmɪsɪz, ˈmɪsɪs], *Posties* for *Post-Toasties*,[32] interpretive for *interpretative*.

Analogy. Analogy as used here is a sound change resulting from comparison with some superficially similar utterance. Examples: *seed* (past tense of *see*) by analogy with *freed, these cheese–these peas, lawr and order–war and peace, heared–feared, Feb'uary–January* (also by dissimilation), *some license–some hyphens, knowed–flowed, cherubims–rims, seraphims–limbs.* (*Cherubim* and *seraphim* are already plural.)

Folk etymology (popular etymology). Folk etymology is an analogical substitution of a similarly sounding familiar word or syllable for a new or complex word or syllable. Examples: *penniwinkle* for *periwinkle, wrench* for *rinse, Westminister* for *Westminster, telefoam* for *telephone, Bushway* for *Bourgeois, sparrow grass* for *asparagus, cold slaw* for *coleslaw* (from Ger. *Kohl–cabbage*), *lie bill* for *libel, mad axe* for *mattock, broom sage* for *broom sedge, flatform* for *platform, frog lights* for *fog lights, cow buckle* for *carbuncle,* Fr. *pomme d'amour* (whence E. *love apple*) from Ital. *pomo dei Moro* (Moor's apple), *primrose* from OF *primerole* (first little flower), *cockroach* from Sp. *cucaracha.*

Hyperurbanism (over-correction). A sound change resulting from a misguided attempt to speak correctly. Examples: *mounting* for *mountain,* kitching for *kitchen,* [ˈlɪnɪŋ] for *linen, Cincinnata* for *Cincinnati, Missoura* for *Missouri, Miama for Miami.*

Spelling pronunciation. Spelling pronunciation is the tendency to remake pronunciation in accord with spelling. It may often restore an older form which the spelling happens to preserve, but may also, if the spelling is unetymological, or is misunderstood, give forms quite without historical justification. Examples: [ˈgrɪnwɪtʃ] for *Greenwich* [ˈgrɪnɪtʃ, ˈgrɪnɪdʒ], [ˈhɑɪwɪtʃ] for *Harwich* [ˈhærɪdʒ], [ˈɔftən] for *often* [ˈɔfən], [ˈfoUrˌhɛd] for *forehead* [ˈfɔrəd, ˈfɔrɪd], [ˈɑrtʃˌeɪndʒəl, ˈɑːtʃ ˌeɪndʒəl] for *archangel.*

Portmanteau words (blend-words, contamination). A portmanteau word is a word made up of parts of two words having some real or fancied relation in meaning. Examples: *Reno-vate* [ˈrinoˌveɪt] from *Reno,* Nev., and *renovate, cinemactress* from *cinema* and *actress, dictaphone* from *dictate* and *graphophone, novocaine* from Lat. *novus* and *cocaine, globaloney* from *global* and *baloney, bellocution* from *bellow* and *elocution, brunch* from *breakfast* and *lunch, Amerindian* from *American* and *Indian.*

Invention. The invention of words is so infrequent that one wonders how languages acquire so many words. Every new word seems to have to have a

---

[32] E. H. Sturtevant, *Linguistic Change* (Chicago: University of Chicago Press, 1947), p. 55.

beginning, and the beginnings themselves have to have beginnings, so that we ultimately trace each word back to some event of human experience. The origin of language[33] and the origin of words within a language illustrate as well as anything could the necessity of stimulus before there can be response. Invention of words, then, can only be the response to some stimulus which creates a desire for a new vocable.

Sometimes the stimulus is a sound which can be named imitatively. The *pow*, *zowie*, *sock*, *blam* of the comic strip and the *boom*, *gurgle*, and *crash* of natural objects in motion account for a large group of onomatopoeic words. The current times have brought on a spate of words made up from initials—*Nato* (North Atlantic Treaty Organization), *Unesco* (United Nations Educational, Scientific, and Cultural Organization), *Wac* (Women's Army Corps), *Anta* (American National Theater and Academy), *Waves* (Women's Auxiliary Volunteer Emergency Service). Much like these are the acrostics—*Benelux* (Belgium, Netherlands, Luxembourg), *Spar* (*semper paratus*, always ready), *Nabisco* (National Biscuit Company). *Kodak* is said to have been suggested by the click of the camera shutter; Lewis Carroll's *chortle* may be based on *snort* and *chuckle* and his *gallumphing* may be a blend of *gallop*, *jump*, and *puff*; Gelett Burgess' *blurb* must have had some onomatopoeic origin; Helmont's *gas* undoubtedly did; *gimmick*, *gismo*, and *gremlin* still await adequate explanation of what suggested them. Latin and Greek, particularly Greek, continually contribute to the language of science, as in *psychotherapy*, *thermodynamics*; both languages contribute to *pericardium* and *altimeter*.

Language substrata.[34] When foreigners learning English live together in large groups, they become bilingual, and the phonetic patterns of the foreign language often assert themselves so as to effect changes in the English itself. (Of course there is a reciprocal effect on the foreign language as well.) Descendants of such groups often sound as if they could speak the foreign tongue, even though in time many of them know no other tongue than English. Thus in the United States there are dialects such as the Pidgin of Hawaii, the English of the Pennsylvania Germans and the Milwaukee Germans, the English of the north-middle-states Scandinavians, the Louisiana French-English, and the Yiddish of New York. The foreign-language substratum evidences itself in such features as pure vowels instead of English diphthongs, trilled *r*'s, unvoicings, characteristic assimilative patterns, and the substitution of foreign sounds for unfamiliar English sounds, together with foreign rhythms and intonations. When any of these features are used in any large area for a long time, they cease to be thought of

---

[33] See Gray and Wise, *The Bases of Speech* (New York: Harpers, 1946), Chap. VII, "The Genetic Basis of Speech."

[34] See Einar Haugen, *The Norwegian Language in America* (Philadelphia: University of Pennsylvania Press, 2 vols., 1953), Vol. I, pp. 10–12. Haugen uses the terms "substrata" and "substratum theory," following Bloomfield (p. 286), *et al*, but appears to prefer the more nearly self-defining terms "confusion of patterns" and "confounding of patterns."

as foreign, and are accepted as features of the English of that region. Thus the characteristic speech of Scotland and Ireland is not often thought of as being influenced by the other language in these areas, viz., Gaelic. Yet when one studies Gaelic, one can thereafter trace certain of its features in the current English—even when, as indicated above, a given speaker has no knowledge of Gaelic whatever.

There are various other formulae for describing sound change which have not been taken up here, e.g., Grimm's law,[35] with its corollary Verner's law, which, applying originally to Primitive Germanic and subsequent German dialects, has only marginal application to Modern English. Besides, there are language changes which are not phonetic (some of the foregoing are only distantly so), and hence are not included in this work. Prominent among these are semantic changes,[36] some of which are designated as connotation, pleonasm (redundancy), metaphor, synecdoche, metonymy, widening (generalization), narrowing (specialization), litotes, elevation (amelioration), degeneration (pejoration), and hyperbole.

---

[35] See E. Prokosch, *An Outline of German Historical Grammar* (New York: Oxford University Press, 1933), pp. 13–45.

[36] See Bloomfield, Chapter 24, and Gray and Wise, pp. 499–504.

PART TWO

CHAPTER 6

Speech Regions of America

The larger regions—their names and extent. Ever since the American colonies acquired a considerable population, there has been a continuing search for names for the speech regions, large and small, into which the United States and Canada are divided. With the ultimate expansion of the United States to the central areas and to the Pacific coast, it seemed to travelers and other observers that the great inclusive speech regions must be three in number, including, roughly, (1) New England, (2) the South, and (3) the remainder of the country. For New England, the term *Eastern speech* seemed obvious and satisfactory, and for the South, *Southern speech.* Eastern and Southern *dialect* were alternative terms, dialect being used not in the sense of foreign or substandard, but only as a division under the general head, American English.

But for the speech of the remainder of the country, no obvious name appeared. The South was inclined to call it *Northern speech,* an obvious misnomer, since New England also lies far north, and since that part of the "northern" area itself from Texas to California lies far south. *Western speech* was also used, but the term applied poorly, even from an eastern point of view, to New Jersey, New York State, and Pennsylvania. *Midwestern speech* had even wider currency, but was no better, in that the term could hardly apply either to New Jersey, New York State, and the Alleghenies, or to the Rocky Mountains, the Pacific Coast, and the Southwest.[1] A quarter of a century ago, North-and-West was suggested,[2] but though it had the merit of being nearly consistent with the other geographical designations, East and South, it did not catch on. Unfortu-

---

[1] See parallel discussion by Albert C. Baugh, *History of the English Language* (New York: Appleton-Century, 1935), Footnote 2, p. 446. Baugh uses the term general American here and on his map of the speech areas of the United States, p. 447.

[2] Hans Kurath, "Dialectal Differences in Spoken English," *Modern Philology,* Vol. 26, May, 1928, p. 387. "To my mind, most of the dialectal differences existing at present between New England, the South, and the North-and-West did not develop out of a uniform Southern English standard, but have their bases partly in the regional varieties of the standard and partly in the strongly dialectal speech which the early settlers of these regions brought with them from England and Scotland. This conclusion seems to me unavoidable to one tracing the treatment of the *r* and the vowels preceding an original *r* in the three sections mentioned."

171

nately, no geographical term existed which was convenient to apply. Accordingly, General American speech, notwithstanding its false suggestion of applying to the whole North American Continent,[3] and notwithstanding its illogical lack of a geographical basis such as that of Eastern and Southern, became a common designation.

In spite of the inherent challenge to invent a better name than General American, no one did so. At least, no better term came into general use. The three great speech regions of America have long been called, then, in order of size and population, General American, Southern, and Eastern. These terms are still subject to revision. Some indications of change are discussed later in these pages.

Boundaries and extent of the speech regions. It is far easier to name speech regions than to define the boundaries that separate them. Until the advent of the surveys of the Linguistic Atlas of the United States and Canada,[4] the boundaries could not be determined with any accuracy at all, although

---

[3] Hans Kurath, *A Word Geography of the Eastern United States* (Ann Arbor: U. of Mich. Press, 1949), p. VI. "The widely accepted assumption that there is a 'General American' type of English proves to be ... unfounded in fact; no Southerner or New Englander would ever have made such a generalization." Here Kurath appears to be using "General American" to refer to the whole country. Singularly enough, it was a New Englander, Windsor P. Daggett, of Maine, whom this writer first heard use the term *General American* in a public manner. Addressing the National Association of Teachers of Speech in New York in the early 1920's, he exhibited charts dividing the country into three mutually exclusive areas, Eastern, Southern and General American. George Philip Krapp used "western or general type of American speech" continuously in his *The English Language in America* (New York: Century, 1925), referring to the area outside the East and South. J. S. Kenyon uses the term in the many editions of his *American Pronunciation* (Ann Arbor, Michigan: George Wahr, 1925, *et seq.*); see preface to fourth edition, p. v.

[4] Some of the principal events in the history of the *Atlas* to date are as follows:
1928 (December). First proposed by the Present Day English Group of Modern Language Association and committee appointed.
1929 (January). Independently proposed by delegate of Linguistic Society of America to the American Council of Learned Societies.
1929 (February). Meeting at Cleveland of MLA committee and representative of ACLS.
1929 (August). Conference at Yale University of fifty scholars; committee appointed.
1930 (January). ACLS endorsed in principle the plan of the committee for a Linguistic Atlas of the United States and Canada and recommended experimental work in limited area.
1931 (January). ACLS approved plan of committee for a Linguistic Atlas of New England and made appropriation for expenses; appropriation later augmented by Yale University, Brown University, and University of Vermont.
1931 (July). Atlas staff under Hans Kurath, director, and Miles L. Hanley, associate director, met for six weeks' training in New York City. Prof. Jakob Jud (Zürich) and Dr. Paul Sheuermeier (Bern), linguistic geographers with experience in Switzerland and Italy, attended as advisors.
1931 (Summer). Marcus L. Hansen made study of history of population of New England.
1931–33. Field work in New England.
1933–36, 1945–48. Field work in South Atlantic states.
1935–57. Collateral field work in Louisiana.

some questionnaires had been circulated[5] and numerous word lists collected, articles written, and personal observations made.

But with analysis of the great quantities of carefully selected data gathered by the *Atlas*, speech boundaries or isoglosses[6] could be defined accurately. Since the *Linguistic Atlas of New England* was the earliest portion of the *Atlas* to be published (1939–1943), it was first possible to locate a boundary between Eastern speech and that of the remainder of the country. Instead of beginning with the Hudson River or the New York-Connecticut line and extending north through Lake Champlain, as it had been thought to do, this boundary[7] was found more accurately to follow up the Connecticut River and thence northward along the summits of the Green Mountains of Vermont.[8]

The foregoing represents the situation as to the usual names and the general extent allotted to the great speech regions of America up to the time of the publication of Kurath's *A Word Geography of the Eastern States*. This book furnished systematic lexical confirmation of the existence of a region in the

---

1939. Publication of Volume I, *Linguistic Atlas of New England* (Brown University Press).

1939. Publication of *Handbook of Linguistic Geography of New England* (Brown University Press).

1938–49. Field work in Middle Atlantic states.

1938–40, 1948. Collateral field work in North Central states—Michigan, Wisconsin, Ohio, Indiana, Illinois, Kentucky, and in southwest Ontario.

1941. Publication of Volume II, *Linguistic Atlas of New England.*

1943. Publication of Volume III, *Linguistic Atlas of New England.*

1946. Headquarters of Atlas moved from Brown University to University of Michigan.

1947. Collateral field work in Upper Middle states—Minnesota, North Dakota, South Dakota, Iowa, Nebraska, Missouri.

1949. Publication of Kurath's *A Word Geography of the Eastern United States* (University of Michigan Press).

1950–53. Collateral field work in Colorado, Hawaii.

1952. Collateral field work in California.

1953. Publication of E. Bagby Atwood's *Eastern Verb Geography* (University of Michigan Press).

In summary, as of this date, the Atlas organization has collected the New England data, edited it, and published the eight books listed above; it has collected Atlantic coast data, including data on the inland or nearly inland states of West Virginia, Pennsylvania and New York; and it has done a wide-meshed survey of considerable detail of the territory north of the Ohio River. Other related survey projects almost cover the remainder of the United States and some of Canada.

[5] E.g., that of C. H. Grandgent, who collected data on words spelled with *oo* as early as 1895; cf. his "English in America," in *Die Neueren Sprachen*, 1895, 2, p. 857. Cf. also *From Franklin to Lowell*, PMLA, 1899, 7, p. 217, for his study of the "New England Short *o*."

[6] Isogloss, from Gk. *isos* (the same) and *glossos* (tongue). Cf. *isotherm, isobar, isometric*, etc. An isogloss may be based on pronunciation, vocabulary, inflection, syntax or any desired feature of speech. For this book, naturally, the basis should be pronunciation.

[7] Determined by important lexical and pronunciation features.

[8] Hans Kurath, *Handbook of the Linguistic Atlas of New England*, p. 29–34, charts 7, 8, 9, 12, 16. For the more recent tendency to regard this boundary as a secondary one, and to group some of the area west of it with New England areas, see p. 174.

east-central states which had already been tentatively designated the Midland.[9] Having traced the isoglosses which define the northern and southern boundaries of the Midland, Kurath adopted for the area to the north and east the name the North, and for that south and west, the name the South. Kurath thus established for his book three area-names for the eastern states, only one of which, the South, conformed to the traditional names. Figure 3 of *Word Geography* is a map of the east coast and Appalachian country from Maine to South Carolina, with the boundaries separating North, Midland, and South drawn upon it, and with a tabulation of the eighteen sub-areas which make up the three larger areas, as follows:

THE SPEECH AREAS OF THE EASTERN STATES

The North

1. Northeastern New England
2. Southeastern New England
3. Southwestern New England
4. Upstate New York and west Vermont
5. The Hudson Valley
6. Metropolitan New York

The Midland

7. The Delaware Valley (Philadelphia Area)
8. The Susquehanna Valley
9. The Upper Potomac and Shenandoah Valley
10. The Upper Ohio Valley (Pittsburgh Area)
11. Northern West Virginia
12. Southern West Virginia
13. Western North and South Carolina

The South

14. Delmarva (Eastern Shore of Maryland and Virginia, and southern Delaware)
15. The Virginia Piedmont
16. Northeastern North Carolina (Albemarle Sound and Neuse Valley)
17. The Cape Fear and Peedee Valley
18. South Carolina.

This new plan of division of Kurath's has the effect of adding to what had been called the East the whole of New York State, the northeastern half of New Jersey, and the northern third of Pennsylvania. This addition necessitated the subordination of the Connecticut River-Green Mountains line to that between the Midland and the North (see page 173). Metropolitan New York,

---

[9] C. K. Thomas, *Phonetics of American English* (New York: The Ronald Press, 1947), map on pp. 142–144, and Fig. 5, p. 145.

with its encircling commuter area in New Jersey, the New York mainland, Connecticut, and Long Island, is included as sub-area 6 of the North.[10]

The plan had the further effect of taking away from the South the whole southern Appalachian area, including a portion of the Blue Ridge piedmont from Lynchburg southwest, and adding it to the Midland. The South gained, on the other hand, over half of Maryland and Delaware.

Evidence is accumulating that a projection of these North and Midland lexical areas can be traced westward, perhaps even across the Mississippi River. It is to be expected that the boundaries will become increasingly blurred the farther west they are traced,[11] for the more nearly level plains from the Alleghenies west, even before railroads, promoted mobility of population, and many river courses cut across the lines of westward migration, diverting the movement locally both northward and southward.

Space is too limited here to review the findings of *Word Geography*. For a single example, however, Figure 4 finds the North characterized by the use of *whiffletree* and *whippletree* for what is in other areas called *swingletree, singletree*; it finds the Midland characterized by the use of *sook* as a call to cows; and it finds the South characterized by the use of *light-wood* [ˈlaɪtəd, ˈlaɪtɚd] for *kindling*. The 163 full-page charts of the book give many comparable variations of characteristic vocabulary. The student should study these charts.

A brief overview of the causes leading to the existence of boundaries between the vocabulary areas called North, Midland, and South is in order.[12] That part of the North which is west of New England was settled, after the Revolution,

---

[10] It is possible, very roughly and largely speculatively, to group here also the maritime provinces of Canada, viz., New Brunswick, Nova Scotia and Prince Edward Island, and even Newfoundland, for the speech of these provinces has some features in common with New England. In certain cases, the speech is actually transplanted New England speech, carried northward by loyalists who migrated from the New England colonies at the time of the American Revolution. But Quebec and parts of eastern Ontario, where the speech is predominantly French, cannot, of course, be included.

[11] Cf. Raven I. McDavid, Jr., "Midland and Canadian Words in Upstate New York," *American Speech*, December, 1951, pp. 248–256; Alva L. Davis and Raven I. McDavid, Jr., "Northwestern Ohio: A Transition Area," *Language*, April–June, 1950, pp. 264–273; Albert H. Marckwardt, "Middle English *Wa* in the Speech of the Great Lakes Region," *American Speech*, December 1942, pp. 226–234; F. G. Cassidy, "Some New England Words in Wisconsin," *Language*, October-December, 1941, pp. 324–339.

[12] See Kurath, *Word Geography*, pp. 2–7.

Various writers have undertaken to trace American regional dialectal features back to British dialect areas:

George Philip Krapp, *The English Language in America*, 2 vols. (New York: Century, 1925).

Hans Kurath, "The Origin of Dialectal Differences in Spoken American English," *Modern Philology*, XXV, pp. 385–395.

Cleanth Brooks, *The Relation of the Alabama-Georgia Dialect to the Provincial Dialects of Great Britain* (Baton Rouge: Louisiana State University Press, 1935).

William Cabell Greet, "Southern Speech," *Culture in the South*, ed. by W. T. Couch, (Chapel Hill: University of North Carolina Press, 1934, pp. 594–615), refers to the theo-

mainly by people from western New England, hence its homogeneity with the strip of New England west of the Connecticut River-Green Mountains line.

The Midland could almost be called by some name derived from the word Pennsylvania. For it was descendants of colonial Pennsylvanians, augmented by people from southern and western New Jersey and some New Englanders, who migrated after the Revolution directly west toward Ohio, and southwest down the Ohio River Valley. And it was Pennsylvanians, augmented by Palatine Germans and Scotch Irish[13] who came to Delaware Bay and Pennsylvania after 1720, who streamed southward across the western panhandle of Maryland into the Shenandoah valley of Virginia. Thence the migrants moved out on the southern end of the Blue Ridge piedmont, where their progress was slowed down by the fact that westward-moving southerners had already taken up much of the land. The mingling of the southerners and the Pennsylvanians here produced the characteristic mixed speech in the piedmont area southwest of Lynchburg, in the piedmont of the two Carolinas, and in northern Georgia, as well as throughout the whole southern Appalachian area.

Later the Pennsylvanians pushed through the mountain gaps into eastern Kentucky and Tennessee, whence they turned north into southern Ohio and Indiana, meeting the settlers who, as already noted, were descending the Ohio valley. As an eddy between these two major streams of people there was a smaller group who had found their way over the mountains from Pennsylvania and the northern Shenandoah Valley into the Kanawha Valley of West Virginia. Thus the primary migration for this area was complete, though of course other native Americans and other immigrants were to follow as time went on.

It is unfortunate for present purposes that data on pronunciation for the eastern states (outside New England) has not yet been published paralleling

---

ries of British regional origin for American regional speech, but calls attention to its lack of accurate basic information. He says: "It is the custom to say that the speech of the Atlantic seaboard, with the exception of New Jersey, and the speech of the lowlands of the South, is similar in type to that of the east of England; and that the speech of the eastern mountain regions, both in the North and the South, and the speech of the Middle West is like the speech of the north of England. There is some evidence that the migration to coastal New England was particularly heavy from the east coast of England. The great influx of Scots and groups from Ireland came after the middle of the eighteenth century and pushed west to the hills for land. When New York and Western Reserve were settled and the speech more or less fixed, it was the hill or Northern British type that dominated the new country. The Scots, Irish and northern Englishmen made a common speech which we now call the middle western [G. A.] type.

"W. D. Rockwell believes that the speech of the New England coast reflects the southwest of England as well as East Anglia. There is evidence in Wright's Dialect Grammar to support this contention. He groups hill country (Appalachian and Ozark) and cattle country (referring particularly to Texas) together, as contrasting with the cotton country. He traces many resemblances between N. W. coastal and S. speech."

[13] Ulster Scots whose Presbyterian ancestors had been sent by James I to colonize the northern part of Catholic Ireland.

the data on word distribution, for it is difficult to predict how far vocabulary boundaries and pronunciation boundaries will coincide. Considering the separate origins of the westerly migrating groups, it seems reasonable to think that they would have continued pronouncing differently as they moved westward— assuming, of course, that western New England and Pennsylvania pronounced their words with significant differences in the beginning. Kurath has said that he believes the lexical and phonetic isoglosses will substantially coincide in this case.[14] Correspondence from and conversation with other *Atlas* workers indicate that they believe so too. Studies now under way may, when published, confirm their belief. If so, the situation will, pending still further extension of *Atlas* surveys and the processing of further data, rest thus:

1. For the Atlantic Coast and the Appalachian area, the terms North, Midland, and South can be used.

2. The projection of these areas toward the Mississippi can be anticipated.

3. Projection of the areas for some distance across the Mississippi can be conjectured, and perhaps in time, and in some degree, realized.

4. There may be some name devised for the area from, say, Missouri and Iowa west, to supplant the term General American; possibly the terms of the East may be extended westward, perhaps with some qualifications for the far West.

The carrying on and interpretation of research in these matters will be eagerly awaited. Meanwhile, it is to be expected that both sets of terms, (1) North, Midland, and South, and (2) Eastern, Southern, and General American will be used, according to the needs (and biases) of given individuals and publications. Works dealing with the eastern seaboard and mountain states can use the North-Midland-South designations easily for lexical purposes, and, if they care to anticipate published evidence, for phonetic purposes as well, venturing that the phonological and lexical isoglosses will agree. Works dealing with the whole country cannot risk using terms for the Middle and West that have not been confirmed by research.

This book, which deals with the country as a whole, undertakes to make as much use as possible of the conclusions of *Word Geography of the Eastern States.* It adopts, as a major example, the southern boundary of the Midland as the boundary between the South and the rest of the country so far as the isoglosses have been traced. And it recognizes that the homogeneity of the vocabulary in northern New Jersey and Pennsylvania and in New York State with that in western New England, when coupled with a body of known evidence on pro-

---

[14] In an address to a section meeting of the Speech Association of America, New York City, December, 1950.

nunciation,[15] links the two areas together. If, thereupon, the line separating eastern and western New England is accepted as a secondary boundary, then all of New England, all of New York, and the northern parts of New Jersey and Pennsylvania may be grouped into one area (designated by Kurath's term, North).

Boundaries of the speech regions of the United States. If it is wished to separate what has been called the East proper (meaning central and eastern New England) from the rest of the country, the Connecticut River-Green Mountains line serves as a good approximation. If it is desired to separate Kurath's "North" from the rest of the country, the line begins a little south of center on the New Jersey coast, ranges northwestward to Pennsylvania, and proceeds across that state in a northwesterly and westerly fashion, dividing it so as to place about one-third of it north of the line. The line leaves Pennsylvania at a point a few miles south of where the Pennsylvania-Ohio state line enters Lake Erie, and stops in extreme northeastern Ohio, awaiting data for tracing it further.

The boundary between the southern speech area and the rest of the country begins on Delaware Bay at very nearly the latitude of Dover and swings in an approximate semicircle north of Baltimore and then southwestward to cross the Potomac a little below Harper's Ferry. Thence it follows the Blue Ridge to the latitude of Lynchburg, where it turns southeastward and again southwestward on the Piedmont of Virginia and the two Carolinas. At the extremity of the Blue Ridge, it swings westward. Here the data of the *Atlas* breaks off, pending further field work, and for the time the line has to be projected speculatively on the basis of non-statistical data.

Since it is known that the cotton-growing southerners of Virginia and the Carolinas expanded their operations around the southern end of the Appalachians and into the cotton lands west of the mountains, it may be postulated that the boundary we have been tracing will be found to continue around the tip of the Appalachians and to run northerly across central Tennessee and Kentucky between the hill country and the cotton country until it intersects the Ohio River somewhere in the neighborhood of Louisville and Cincinnati.

The line may then be considered as going thence down the Ohio to the Mississippi; thence across the southeast corner of Missouri and southward through Arkansas in such a way as to divide the lowland cotton country from the upland hill country; thence southward, then westward, and then northwestward in Louisiana, again dividing the cotton country from the hill country, and intersecting the Louisiana-Texas line near Shreveport; thence across the southeast corner of Texas to the Gulf of Mexico in such a way as to place what

---

[15] Cf. O. F. Emerson, "The Ithaca Dialect," *Dialect Notes*, 1891; the several installments of C. K. Thomas, "Pronunciation in Upstate New York," *American Speech*, April, 1935, *et seq.*; and *The Linguistic Atlas of New England*.

s called east Texas, as well as the cities of Beaumont, Galveston, and Houston,
n the southern area.

The nature of speech boundaries. Unless the division between speech
areas is a natural barrier, say a body of water, like that between England and
Ireland, the differences between the speech of adjacent areas are not sharp and
definite in all aspects. The boundary itself between contiguous areas is never
a line, but rather a band or strip of territory, within which the speech features
are mixed, partaking of features from both sides.[16]

Let us now consider the border strip lying along the arbitrary line just traced.
We shall be able to use the information supplied by the *Atlas* to make interpretations regarding the eastern end; but for the remaining distance we shall
have to make temporary judgments on scattered data. When the Atlas work
has spread to the central Mississippi valley, these judgments can be amended.

To begin with, there is the Delmarva (Delaware-Maryland-Virginia) Peninsula
and the remainder of Maryland. These were all slave-holding areas, though like
the other slave-holding border areas, West Virginia, Kentucky, Missouri, they
did not secede (excluding the tip belonging to Virginia). We place nearly all of
Delmarva-Maryland in the South, but there are enough non-Southern features
to make the speech a mixed speech. Washington, D. C., with its extensive
suburban commuting areas on both sides of the Potomac in Maryland and
Virginia, is highly cosmopolitan and contains large numbers of General American
and some Eastern speakers. Then, as we have pointed out, the whole southern
Appalachian highland has some Southern features. The "strip," then, is now
a huge southern bulge.[17] On the north side of the Ohio, the strip is probably

---

[16] Chas. H. Grandgent, *Modern Language Notes*, Vol. VIII, No. 5, p. 274. "Whatever
the quality of the speech we are examining, we must not expect distinct geographical
boundaries: the most we can do is to establish, roughly, for the different parts of the
country, the relations which certain conflicting types of pronunciation bear to each other
in the class of society we are studying."

[17] J. Wesley Hatcher, "Appalachian America," *Culture in the South,* ed. W. T. Couch
(University of North Carolina Press, 1934), pp. 374–402, defines the Appalachian area
somewhat more inclusively at the southern end than the speech data now at hand would
justify.

Boundaries: West border of Pennsylvania at Ohio River, down Ohio to Maysville,
Kentucky; thence to Tullahoma, Tennessee, Decatur, Alabama, Birmingham; on North,
follows Pennsylvania boundary to Eastern boundary of Frederick County, Maryland;
thence to Lynchburg, Virginia to Spartanburg, South Carolina, Cartersville, Georgia,
ending at S. boundary of Cousa County, Alabama:

Length—650 mi.; width, 170 mi.

Area—British Isles or New York and New England.

Includes—West Virginia, 4 western counties of Maryland, Blue Ridge Valley, Allegheny
counties of Virginia, Eastern end of Kentucky, Eastern Tennessee, Western North
Carolina, 4 northwest counties of South Carolina, North Georgia, and Northeast Alabama.

"The people are of Scotch, Scotch-Irish, and Roundhead English descent, with a
group of Germans here and there with whom the German edition of Presbyterianism—the
Reformed Church—prevailed, with a sprinkling of French Huguenots, who are Calvinistic
in doctrine." Presbyterianism dominates.

more strip-like once more, but is probably rather wide, with many South Midland features.

Now it is known that the Ozark highland area was populated to a considerable extent by Appalachian highlanders. Obviously, then, beginning a little north of where the Missouri-Arkansas line intersects the Mississippi River, and sweeping southward to include all the Ozark area and the contiguous hill area in southern Arkansas and northern Louisiana, there is another area of mixed speech which will constitute another huge bulge.

From there onward, pending Atlas surveys, it is anybody's guess as to how the strip should be drawn. One thing we may venture: it will be very wide. Since much of Oklahoma and Texas was settled suddenly, as it were, by large migrant groups, many of whom came from central and southern mountain areas, many from the central states and many from the "deep" South, we can expect broad areas of mixed speech. Though both Oklahoma and most of Texas are more Western than Southern in many ways, and though we can say that their speech is General American, yet there are Southern features, usually at the substandard level, scattered far and wide, sometimes as far as the panhandle of Oklahoma and the panhandle of Texas. The bulges in the strip here are undoubtedly very extensive.

The future of American speech. The question is often asked as to what will be the ultimate nature of American speech—will it blend into a single dialect, and if so, which one? If we were to judge by the several regional dialects of England, with the very numerous county and intra-county dialects, we should have to say our American dialects would remain distinct. But America is now suddenly an almost completely mobile country, with nearly everybody traveling nearly everywhere and finding employment in every part. In such a situation, numbers count heavily. What has been called the General American dialect will presumably have the advantage. Some of the explanations for this advantage follow:

1. General American speech has, at the present time, a large numerical preponderance over the other two dialects.

2. Modern ease of transportation will tend to make this preponderance effective in modifying the speech of the smaller areas.

3. Radio speech, whether that of announcers, actors, or casual speakers, is already predominantly General American and can hardly fail to affect the speech of all listeners.

4. Similarly, speech in the motion pictures and in television is largely General American, except where plays or other programs demand specific dialects.

On the other hand, it is observable that some dialect features of the less numerous groups are spreading. The Southern *pin*-for-*pen* type of pronunciation, for example, has been observed spreading northward and westward. Perhaps, then we may venture the prediction that the future American speech will be a blend of all three of our dialects, with General American predominating.

Within the three great speech regions we have several sub-dialects. Within the East there are New York speech and French-Canadian. Within the South there are Negro speech and Louisiana French-English. Within the General American there are Pennsylvania German, the Appalachian and Ozark mountain speech, and the southwestern Mexican-English. On the basis of a few prominent features, such as *hog* [hɑg], *audience* [ˈɑdɪənts], etc., we could perhaps designate a Rocky Mountain dialect in the Utah-Southern Idaho-Southwestern Wyoming area. There are dialects of limited area, like those, say, of Charleston, South Carolina, and of St. Louis. We sometimes speak of urban dialect and coastal dialect – matters which should be studied.

Some of the more important of the American sub-dialects will be taken up in the latter part of this book. The three great regional dialects will be taken up in the ensuing three chapters.

Southern speech will be defined as the speech of the area designated as the South in *Word Geography*, together with such additional territory as is tentatively included within the boundaries described earlier in this chapter (pages 178–179).

Eastern speech will be defined as the speech of the area designated in *Word Geography* as the North, which, awaiting further study, will tentatively be considered as extending as far west as northeastern Ohio. The approaching chapter on Eastern speech will treat in greatest detail the speech of the area east of the Connecticut River and the Green Mountains.

General American speech will be defined as the speech of the area including the country described as Midland in *Word Geography*, together, tentatively, with the remainder of the United States toward the west, northwest, and southwest not included in the South. Very roughly, the speech of as yet undefined portions of Canada from Montreal west may be found to resemble in some features the speech of adjacent parts of the United States.

CHAPTER 7

General American English
Standard and Substandard

Taking the three great regional dialects of the United States in the order of their size, we now proceed to examine their characteristics. General American English is distinguishable from the speech of other regions by certain characteristics of intonation and pronunciation.

Despite valuable work on intonation by many authors, from John Hart,[1] 1569, to Kenneth L. Pike,[2] 1945, no simple and highly efficient system of symbolization or notation for intonation has ever been designed.[3] To understand the "tune" of a dialect, it is necessary to hear it. Fortunately, now that it is easy to make sound recordings, it is possible to hear a given dialect almost at will.

Pronunciation, on the other hand, can be recorded quite satisfactorily in phonetic symbols. This chapter undertakes to present the identifying characteristics of the speech of that great area of the United States and Canada called the General American area.

In describing General American speech, and later in describing the speech of other divisions of the English language, only those characteristics will be enumerated which are peculiar to the speech of the area, or which contrast with the corresponding characteristics of other areas. Conversely, characteristics which are common to all the English-speaking areas under consideration will be omitted as unnecessary for English-speaking readers.

---

[1] John Hart, *An Orthographie, Conteyning the Due Order and Reason, Howe to Write or Paint the Image of Mannes Voice, Most Like to Life or Nature* (London: Wm. Seres, 1559).

[2] Kenneth L. Pike, *The Intonation of American English* (Ann Arbor, University of Michigan Press, 1945). See pp. 3–11 for survey of the works of many English and American authors touching upon intonation.

[3] This is not to say that indications of relative pitch and loudness are not helpful, for they are. Cf. Pike, *op. cit.*, sec. 4.3.3., p. 71:

Tommie   come   here!
⁰2:–3/   4:–   ⁰2:–3:/; or Trager and Smith (*op. cit.*, sec. 2.12, p. 57) ⁻|/ ²têyk + ³hə́hr¹ ‡.

But they are the most helpful to those who know the language or dialect best, and can supply the proper degrees of pitch and loudness from memory. They are least helpful when applied to a language or dialect unfamiliar to the reader.

182

In recording the three great regional dialects of America, both standard and substandard forms will be set down—standard being defined, as before, in terms of what is believed to be cultivated and generally acceptable speech, and substandard as less cultivated and less acceptable speech.

Standard General American English

Stressed Vowels and Diphthongs

a = [æ] in the so-called "broad *a*" words, most of which are spelled with *a* preceding [f] ([v] in some plurals), [s], [θ] ([ð] in some plurals and isolated words), and [n] + a consonant, as in *half* [hæf], *fast* [fæst], *bath* [bæθ], *rather* [ˈræðɚ], and *can't* [kænt]. (These words are pronounced with [ɑ] in southern British English and in some Eastern American speech. See definition of "broad *a*," page 222.)

> *Transcribe with* [æ]: calf, calves, path, paths, aghast, latter, repast, cant, implant, enchant, example, transferable, advantage, command, franchise.

a = [ɑ] in *water* [wɑtɚ] and *watch* [wɑtʃ], and [ɔ] in *wash* [wɔʃ], *want* [wɔnt], and *walk* [wɔk]. That is to say, in this miscellaneous list of familiar, frequently used "wa" words, these pronunciations are probably the most frequently heard. But the vowels of these and several other words containing *a* preceded by initial [w] alone or by [w] in an initial consonant cluster (spelled with *qu*) are notably unstable and vacillate in pronunciation between [ɑ], [ɔ]. In Iowa, available evidence[4] shows [ˈwɑtɚ], [wɑtʃ], and [wɔʃ] in the lead. The same is true in Missouri. It is a question why the rounding effect which might be expected from [w] preceding the vowel in these words has not uniformly rounded [ɑ] to [ɔ] as it has in words like *quart*, *warm*, and *wall*, where *a* is preceded by the sound of [w] and followed orthographically by *r* or *l*.

> *Transcribe in G. A.*, but use your own pronunciation of *a*: Bayswater, watchtower, Washington, unwanted, boardwalk, waspish, wanderer, quarterstaff, quantity, quality, was, what, squalor, swapped, qualify.

a = [ɔ], or [ɑ], with [ɔ] probably predominating, in "wa" words where *a* is followed by *r* plus a vowel, as in *warrant* [ˈwɔrənt, ˈwɑrənt]; *Warren* [ˈwɔrən, ˈwɑrən]; *quarantine* [ˈkwɔrənˌtin, ˈkwɑrənˌtin].[5]

> *Transcribe in G. A.*, but use your own pronunciation of *a*: quarries, quarrelsome, quarrier, warranty, warrantee, warranter, warrener.

a = [ɔ] without exception in words beginning with the sound [w] plus orthographic *a* and followed by final [r] or [r] beginning a consonant cluster in the same syllable, as in *war* [wɔr], *warmth* [wɔrmpθ], *quart* [kwɔrt], *ward* [wɔrd], *wart* [wɔrt]. This pronunciation is, of course, the same in all standard dialects

---

[4] Sarah T. Barrows, "Watch, Water, and Wash," *American Speech*, April, 1929.
[5] See discussion of "short *o*" = [ɑ], p. 186.

of English,but differs from those of some Irish and Scotch speakers, who will in at least some of these words, use [ɑ].

> *Transcribe in G. A.*: quarter, wardrobe, warmer, warp, warm, Warsaw, quartile, quarto, quartz, quartet.

Au, aw, and *a* before *l* or *ll* = [ɔ] in such words as *gaunt* [gɔnt], *haunt* [hɔnt], *laundry* [ˈlɔndrɪ], *jaunt* [dʒɔnt], *sauce* [sɔs], *sausage* [ˈsɔsɪdʒ], *daughter* [ˈdɔtɚ], *author* [ˈɔθɚ], *audience* [ˈɔdɪənts], *Maude* [mɔd], *hawk* [hɔk], *talk* [tɔk]. All these words may occasionally be heard with [ɑ]. But *aunt* is [ænt].

> *Transcribe*: shawl, fraught, audiometer, hall, Claude, Laurel, ball, daunt, walk, caller, balk, calk, wall, bald, Laughton, fall, saurian, haunch, paucity, fawn, saunter, vaunt, faucet, gaudy, tawdry, haul, lawyer, Lawson, caudal, maul, nauseate, all, nautical, Paul, raw, raucous, saw, salt, Walter, caterwaul, vault, fraught, taught, saw.

a, ai, and sometimes *ea*, with occasional *ae* and *ay* = [æ] or [ɛ] in words of the type of *pare* [pær, pɛr], *pair* [pær, pɛr], *pear* [pær, pɛr], *carry* [ˈkærɪ, ˈkɛrɪ], *aeroplane* [ˈæroˌpleɪn, ˈɛroˌpleɪn], *prayer* [prær, prɛr], where the vowel is followed by *r* in the same syllable or by *rr* plus a vowel. [æ] probably predominates in the General American area at large. But individuals and communities lean to the one or to the other, or are inexplicably inconsistent. Historical considerations are largely obliterated. Both [æ] and [ɛ] are regarded as standard. Indeed, such is the influence of the [r]-coloring on the preceding vowels (see page 101), so likely is it that the [æ] involved is a raised [æ] and the [ɛ] a lowered [ɛ], and so frequently are both pronunciations heard, that commonly only a sensitive ear will detect the difference. We may therefore have *beware* [bɪˈwær, bɪˈwɛr], *care* [kær, kɛr], *dare* [dær, dɛr].

> *Transcribe*: hair, hare, airy, heiress, Harry, swear, bearing, farewell, fairer, chair, mare, aeronaut, prayerful, blare, wearing, repair, charity.

a, ai, ay, ea, ei, and *ey* = [eɪ] in monosyllables and stressed syllables in such words as *ate* [eɪt], *afraid* [əˈfreɪd], *stay* [steɪ], *break* [breɪk], *neighbor* [ˈneɪbɚ], *prey* [preɪ]. This is equivalent to saying that the normal pronunciation of the foregoing spellings in General American English monosyllables and stressed syllables is the diphthongal [eɪ],[6] rather than the pure [e]. This is in contrast to the pure [e] of, e.g., Scotch dialect, and to that of most foreign languages. Any change from [eɪ] to [e] in syllables of primary or secondary stress in English is dialectal but non-significant; in lightly stressed syllables, [e] is regular.

---

[6] This is of course, a generalization. Individual pronunciations vary widely, as close transcriptions show. See G. E. Peterson and M. S. Coxe, "The Vowels [e] and [o] in American Speech," *The Quarterly Journal of Speech*, Vol. 39, No. 1 (February), 1953, pp. 33–41. Using the evidence of the Sound Spectrograph, the authors determine their pronunciation of this diphthong to be approximately [ɛɪ] or [ɛe].

Transcribe: amiable, bracing, raised, eighty-eight, Grey, prey, repatriate, ingratiate, apparatus, data, strata, separate, amentia, atypical.

-ear, *-er*, *-ir*, *-or*, *-ur*, and *-yr* = [ɝ] in a group of words of the class of *learn* [lɝn], *herd* [hɝd], *bird* [bɝd], *word* [wɝd], *burn* [bɝn], *myrtle* [ˈmɝtl̩]. The same sound occurs in *hurry* [ˈhɝɪ], *worry* [ˈwɝɪ]. (Compare with Southern [ˈhʌrɪ, ˈwʌrɪ]).

Transcribe: merciful, hurtle, wormwood, firmament, rehearsal, journalistic, myrrh, curry, furry, thoroughly, furrow, burrow.

o, *oa*, *oe*, *ou*, and *ow* = [oʊ] in stressed syllables in words like *go* [goʊ], *goal* [goʊl], *soul* [soʊl], *toe* [toʊ], *below* [bɪˈloʊ]. This is equivalent to saying that the normal nucleus of the foregoing stressed syllables in General American is the diphthong [oʊ],[7] in contrast to the [ɜʊ] of standard southern British with its variants [ɛʊ] and [ʌʊ], and to the pure [o] of most other languages. This applies to syllables of primary stress, as in *oval* [ˈoʊvəl]; and to syllables of secondary stress, as in *isotope* [ˈaɪsəˌtoʊp]. In lightly stressed syllables, [o] is regular.

Transcribe: ocean, oceanic, odoriferous, roaming, hoeing, mouldy, rowboat, blow, crow, omit, alto, canto, obey, potato, tomato, window, fellow, solo, yellow, hollow, Chevrolet.

o = [ɔ] usually, [ɑ] occasionally, in stressed syllables spelled with *or* or *orr* followed by a vowel, as in *coral* [ˈkɔrəl], *horror* [ˈhɔrɚ]. Exceptions: words in *-orrow*, such as *sorrow* [ˈsaro], *tomorrow*, *borrow*.

Transcribe: Florida, Morris, corridor, horrid, moral, Morrell, oranges, forested, torrential, orifice, orotund, orator, oratory, Gorrell, horrible, sorrel.

o = [ɔ] predominantly, [ɑ] sporadically, in monosyllables and other stressed syllables spelled with *og*, as in *dog* [dɔg], *foggy* [ˈfɔgɪ]. Frequent exceptions: *cog* [kɑg], *jog* [dʒɑg], *eggnog* [ˈɛgˌnɑg], *clog* [klɑg], *togs* [tɑgz], *toggle* [ˈtɑgəl].

Transcribe: boggy, catalog, analog, toboggan, frog, hog, sawlog, groggy.

o before *r* = [ɔ] in words like *corn* [kɔrn], *order* [ˈɔrdɚ], *horse* [hɔrs].

Transcribe, lordship, orderly, corded, chords, reborn, adornment, reform, misfortune, remorse, mortal, forked, fortunately, fortifications, pitchfork, horsemanship, northerly, torchlight, scorch, disgorge, for.

o = [ɔ] or [oʊ] in *coarse* [kɔrs, koʊrs], *more* [mɔr, moʊr], *course* [kɔrs, koʊrs], and *hoarse* [hɔrs, hoʊrs].

Transcribe: deplore, chore, tore, four, doorway, hoarfrost, courtly, forcible, hoarsely, resourceful, henceforth, report, swordplay, sport.

---

[7] Peterson and Coxe, *loc. cit.*, determine their diphthong to be [ɔo], [ʌo], or [ou].

"Short *o*" and sometimes *a* after [w] = [ɑ], as in *not* [nɑt], *got* [gɑt], *possible* [ˈpɑsəb]̩], *water* [ˈwɑtɚ], *quality* [ˈkwɑlətɪ].

> *Transcribe:* bottle, cotton, crop, lot, opposite, wasn̩'t, optimist, copper, jolly, following, stopper, operate, watch, what, quantity, quadratic.

u, eu and *ew* = [u], [ju] after [d], [t], and [n], as in *duty* [ˈdutɪ, ˈdjutɪ]; *tune* [tun, tjun]; *neutral* [ˈnutrəl, ˈnjutrəl], *new* [nu, nju]. In the vast majority of cases, [u] is used, but there is some educational pressure and a strong radio pressure toward [ju]. As a variant of [ju], we may find [ɪu], as in [ˈdɪutɪ].

> *Transcribe:* pneumatic, Tudor, pneumonia, Studebaker, Newcastle, Purdue, duplicity, stupid, adduce, numeration, neutrality.

u = [u] after [l], [θ], [s], and [z], as in *absolute* [ˈæbsəˌlut], *enthusiasm* [ɪnˈθuzɪˌæzəm], *pursuit* [pɚˈsut], and *presume* [prɪˈzum].

> *Transcribe:* lute, resume, consume, suitable, lucid, enthusiastic, subsume, insuperable, elucidate, Susan, Zulu.

aw, a before *ll, au, ou* = a low mid-back [ɔ], and not the higher member of the phoneme which suggests [o], as in British and some New York City and urban New England speech.

> *Transcribe and pronounce:* law–low, call–coal, ball–bole, saw–sew, bought–boat, wrought–rote, caught–coat, saw–sow, ought–oat, Paul–pole, maul–mole, haul–hole, thought, all, fall–foal, daughter–doter, gall–goal, jaw–Joe, daw, caw, maw–mow (to cut), gnaw–no, paw–Poe, raw–roe, haw–hoe, tall–toll.

[ʌ] = a very nearly mid-central vowel, being only a little farther back than [ə], which it resembles except in tenseness and duration. This sound does not suggest [ɑ], as in British and some Eastern speech.

> *Transcribe and pronounce:* buddy–body, bum–balm, come–calm, lull–loll, mull–moll, one–wan, puppy–poppy, buck–bock, cup–cop, hut–hot, jut–jot, nut–not, govern, must, just, muddle, love, lunch, bunch.

Unstressed Vowels

It has been noted that pure [e] and [o] appear as weakly stressed sounds in their respective phonemes. This, though a normal form of unstressing in many foreign languages, is exceptional in English.

Aside from the relatively uncommon instances of [e] and [o], English vowels unstress nearly always to [ə] or [ɪ] (exceptions are noted later). In General American, the tendency is heavily toward [ə], which appears predominantly in many contexts where [ɪ] predominates in Eastern, Southern, and British. The paragraphs following present some of the more common contexts and indicate the unstressings found in General American.

In nearly all unstressed suffixes, the vowels unstress to [ə]. In contrast with Southern, Eastern, and British speech, [ə] appears predominantly in the particular suffixes -ace, -ad, -ase, -ate, -ed, -es, -ess, -et, -ice, -id, -ip, -ite, -op, -ous, -uce, -up, and -us, as in *palace* [ˈpæləs], *salad* [ˈsæləd], *purchase* [ˈpɝtʃəs], *palate* [ˈpælət], *wanted* [ˈwɔntəd], *churches* [ˈtʃɝtʃəz], *fearless* [ˈfɪrləs], *pocket* [ˈpakət], *Alice* [ˈæləs], *solid* [ˈsaləd], *Philip* [ˈfɪləp], *opposite* [ˈapəzət], *wallop* [ˈwaləp], *lettuce* [ˈlɛtəs], *syrup* [ˈsɪrəp], *fetus* [ˈfitəs]. While [ɪ] is known in words of these types, it is much less frequent than [ə].

> *Transcribe:* malice, wicket, limpid, thicket, passes, duchess, primate, necklace, ballad, jaundice, gallop, opposite, callus, callous.

e, i, y, medially = [ə], as in *telegraph* [ˈtɛləˌgræf], *intimate* [ˈɪntəmət].

> *Transcribe:* teletype, calibrate, telephone, alligator, allegation, fascinate, Philippines, Filipino, paralysis.

But medial *e* and *i* = [ɪ] before a vowel, as in *react* [rɪˈækt].

> *Transcribe:* palliate, roseate, oriole, appreciate, vitiate, Simeon.

a = [e] in syllables of weak stress, as in *orate* [ˈoʊret].

> *Transcribe:* chaotically, amentia,

-ar, -er, -ir, -or, -our, -ur, and *-yr* unstressed = [ɚ], as in *attar* [ˈætɚ], *mother* [ˈmʌðɚ], *tapir* [ˈteɪpɚ], *neighbor* [ˈneɪbɚ], *neighbour* (Can.) [ˈneɪbɚ], *murmur* [ˈmɝmɚ], *pasture* [ˈpæstʃɚ], *satyr* [ˈseɪtɚ].

> *Transcribe:* pillar, feeler, elixir, favor, favour (Br. and Can.), stupor, anchor, lemur, nature, zephyr, center, centre.

o and *ow* = pure [o] in weakly stressed syllables, as in *opinion* [oˈpɪnjən], *window* [ˈwɪndo], *tomato* [təˈmeɪto]. In very informal speech, but still within the probable limits of standard General American speech, this [o] may be further unstressed to [ʊ] or to [ə], as in *disobedience* [ˌdɪsʊˈbidɪənts] or [ˈdɪsəˈbidɪənts], *potato* [pəˈteɪtʊ] or [pəˈteɪtə], *tomato* [təˈmeɪtʊ] or [təˈmeɪtə], *pillow* [ˈpɪlʊ] or [ˈpɪlə].

> *Transcribe:* obeisance, omission, obese, marshmallow, mellow, hallow, oasis.

-ile = [l̩] in such words as *fertile* [ˈfɝtl̩], *reptile* [ˈrɛptl̩]. *Senile* vacillates between [ˈsinl̩, ˈsiˌnaɪl], and *juvenile* between [ˈdʒuvənl̩, ˈdʒuvəˌnaɪl].

Consonants

wh = [ʍ] as in *while* [ʍaɪl], *wheat* [ʍit], *whistle* [ˈʍɪsl̩] *why* [ʍaɪ].But the expletive *why*, as distinguished from the interrogative adverb *why*, if spoken rapidly, is [waɪ]. Exceptions: *whole* [hoʊl], *who* [hu], and a very few other words.

Transcribe: when, while, where, which, whether, whither, wheel, whistle, wheat, whack, whim.

l = dark or back [ł]. The degree of darkness varies with the vowel – front vowels, especially high front vowels, forcing the preceding [l] somewhat toward the front and making it clearer, as in *lead* [lid], *lay* [leɪ]. But compared with the clear [l]'s of Southern, Eastern, and British, or of the Romance languages, General American *l*'s are dark even before front vowels. Before back vowels and finally, there is, of course, no competitive influence to neutralize their dark quality.

Transcribe: loyal, leak, player, blade, feeling, steely, equally, lore, layer, flare, fleece, spleen, explode.

r = [r] and is always pronounced. It varies slightly according to context, ranging from the non-fricative [r] of *roam* [roʊm] and *clear* [klɪr] through the fricative [ɹ] of *dry* [dɹaɪ] to the voiceless fricative of *try* [tɹ̥aɪ]. But it is never silent and never becomes [ə] as in other English dialects. It does admittedly become silent by dissimilation in the speech of some, in words like *surprise* and *governor* where [səˈpraɪz] and [ˈgʌvənɚ] may be heard. But so infrequent are the words where this is possible, and so strong is the influence of the invariably pronounced *r*'s of all other words, that to obey the phonetic tendency of dissimilation here is usually regarded with disfavor.

r never occurs in the same syllable following [i], [eɪ], or [u]. Where these might be expected in *clear*, *they're*, and *boor*, they have been lowered by the influence of the succeeding *r*'s so that the words are pronounced [klɪr], [ðɛr], and [bʊr].

Transcribe and pronounce: real, preen, dream, trail, every, oriole, mortal, chore, choir, accord, roar, rear, share.

Special words

either and *neither* = [ˈiðɚ] and [ˈniðɚ].

holiday is pronounced with secondary accent [ˈhɑləˌdei], but *yesterday, Monday, Tuesday*, etc. are [ˈjɛstɚdɪ], [ˈmʌndɪ], [ˈt(j)uzdɪ], etc.

again = [əˈgɛn]. Similarly, *against* [əˈgɛnst].

Stress

Polysyllabic words in *-ary, -ery, -ory*, as well as some other polysyllabic words, have both primary and secondary stress, as in *dictionary* [ˈdɪkʃənˌɛrɪ], *confectionery* [kənˈfɛkʃənˌɛrɪ], *territory* [ˈtɛrəˌtoʊrɪ], *advertisement* [ˌædvɚˈtaɪzmənt].

Transcribe: necessary, adversary, obituary, eleemosynary. fiduciary, actuary, cautionary, mortuary, tertiary, lapidary, sanitary, capillary, mercenary, oratory, missionary, stationary, stationery, Canterbury, observatory, obligatory, library, cemetery, laboratory, auditory, solitary, dormitory, secondary, declamatory, customary, arbitrary, ordinary, extraordinary, ceremony, military, itinerary, remunerative, salutary, nominative, melancholy, preparatory, tributary.

Transcription in Standard General American

ɪf aɪ wɚ æskt ən əpɪnjən, aɪ wəd kɔl ðɪs ən ʌngrəmætɪkəl neɪʃən. ðɛr ɪz noʊ sʌtʃ θɪŋ əz ə pɚfɪkt græmɚ ənd aɪ doʊnt ɔlwɪz spik gʊd græmɚ məsɛlf, bʌt aɪ əv bɪn fourgæðɚɪŋ fɚ ðə pæst fju deɪz wɪð prəfɛsɚz əv əmɛrəkən junəvɚsətɪz ən aɪv hɚd ðəm ɔl seɪ θɪŋz laɪk ðɪs: "hi wʊd hæv laɪkt tə hæv dʌn ət." jul kætʃ səm ɛdʒəkeɪtəd əmɛrəkənz seɪɪŋ ðæt. ʍɛn ðiz mɛn teɪk pɛn ɪn hænd, ðeɪ raɪt wɪð əz gʊd græmɚ əz ɛni; bʌt ðə moʊmənt ðeɪ θroʊ ðə pɛn əsaɪd, ðeɪ θroʊ grəmætɪkəl mɔrəlz əsaɪd wɪð ət.

tu ɪləstreɪt ðə dɪzaɪrəbɪləti əv kʌnsəntreɪʃən, aɪ məst:ɛl ju ə stoʊrɪ əv maɪ sɪks-jɪr-oʊld dɔtɚ. ðə gʌvɚnəs əd bɪn tɪtʃɪŋ ɚ əbaʊt ðə reɪndɪr, ænd, əz ðə kʌstəm wɑz, ʃi ritoʊld ət tə ðə fæməlɪ. ʃi rɪd(j)ust ðə hɪstərɪ əv ðæt reɪndɪr tə tu ɚ θri sɛntəntsəz, ʍɛn ðə gʌvɚnəs kʊd nɑt əv pʊt ət ɪntu ə peɪdʒ. ʃi sɛd: "ðə reɪndɪr ɪz ə vɛrɪ swɪft ænəməl. ə reɪndɪr wʌnts dru ə slɛd four hʌndrəd maɪlz ɪn tu aʊrz." ʃi əpɛndəd ðə kɑmɛnt, "ðɪs wəz rəgɑrdəd æz ɪkstrɔrdṇɛrɪ," ænd kənkludəd, "ʍɛn ðæt reɪndɪr wəz drɔɪŋ ðæt slɛd four hʌndrəd maɪlz ɪn tu aʊrz, ɪt daɪd."

əz ə faɪnəl ɪnstənts əv ðə fɔurs əv lɪməteɪʃənz ɪn ðə dəvɛləpmənt əv kʌnsəntreɪʃən, aɪ məst mɛntʃən ðæt bjutɪfəl krɪtʃɚ hɛlən kɛlɚ, hum aɪ hæv noʊn fɚ ðiz mɛnɪ jɪrz. aɪ æm fɪld wɪð:ə wʌndɚ əv ɚ nɑlɪdʒ əkwaɪrd bɪkɔz ʃʌt aʊt frəm ɔl dɪstrækʃən. ɪf aɪ kəd əv bɪn dɛf, dʌm ənd blaɪnd, aɪ ɔlso maɪt əv əraɪvd ət sʌmpθɪŋ.

Mark Twain

Transcribe in standard General American: one page of any textbook material.

Deviations from Standard General American Speech

Since the standard speech of any region has been defined as the cultivated speech of that region, substandard speech may be defined as uncultivated. More accurately, the term substandard applies to specific pronunciations that do not measure up to standard, rather than to an individual's speech as a whole. Actually, the speech of a given individual may be in large measure at the standard level, with only a few words or classes of words pronounced in a substandard way. This is true of the General American speech, where the substandard form is so nearly up to the standard level that the difference between the two is slight. Such differences as there are will be found distributed between intonation, which is not represented in this book, and phonetic characteristics, which will presently be recorded.

As in all substandard speech, there are some characteristic pronunciations in substandard General American which are to be explained by the lack of education of the speaker. Since faulty grammar is often concomitant with faulty pronunciation, many of the pronunciations may appertain to non-standard verb-forms, such as *heared, throwed,* and *had showed*; or noun-forms, such as *sheeps*; or adjective forms, such as *more better* and *badder*. These are hardly phonetic errors, since the sounds are simply misplaced by analogy with such words as *feared, rowed, heaps, more evil,* and *sadder*. The analogical regularizing of irregular verbs is especially frequent among children and uneducated adults. (Compare *see – seed* with *free – freed*); likewise the giving of strong forms to weak verbs (compare *fight – fit* with *bite – bit*). These deviations and their correction are mainly problems for the grammarian. But if *borrow* is pronounced *borry*, the change is phonetic and lies within the province of the phonetician. Most of the pronunciations recorded as substandard in this book will be of the latter type, though grammatical shifts having phonetic aspects may be included occasionally.

[ɔr] or [ɔɪ] for [ɔ] in orthographic *-osh, -ash* after [w], and other spellings pronounced [ɔʃ]. Thus [wɔrʃ] or [wɔɪʃ] for *wash* [wɔʃ], [bɔrʃ] or [bɔɪʃ] for *bosh* [bɔʃ], [ˈkɔrʃəs] or [ˈkɔɪʃəs] for *cautious* [ˈkɔʃəs]. (Some speakers use [ɑ] in these words. In such cases, the likelihood of the appearance of an intrusive sound is reduced; but occasionally [r] may be found, as in [gɑrʃ] for *gosh* [gɑʃ].)

> *Transcribe with* [ɔ] *or* [ɑ], *according to your own dialect, and pronounce carefully:*
> Washington, washes, washing, washed, Oshkosh, squash, quash, precaution, Joshua, bosh.

[ur] or [uɪ] for [u] in *-ush* pronounced [uʃ]. Thus [purʃ] or [puɪʃ] for *push* [puʃ].

> *Transcribe and pronounce:* bush, cushion, bushel, bushing, bushman, Cushing, bush-master, bush-ranger, bush-whacker.

[ɝ] or [ʌɪ] for [ʌ] in *-ush* and other spellings pronounced [ʌʃ]. Thus [hɝʃ] or [hʌɪʃ] for *hush* [hʌʃ].

> *Transcribe and pronounce:* mush, flush, lush, mushroom, mushy, rush, Russia, Russian.

[ɚ] for [o] in words ending in unstressed *o* or *ow*. Thus, [pəˈteɪtɚ] for *potato* [pəˈteɪto], [ˈwɪndɚ] for *window* [ˈwɪndo].

> *Transcribe and pronounce:* tomato, tomorrow, fellow, mellow, bellow, hollow, follow, shallow, callow, marshmallow, wallow, sallow, billow, willow, fallow, tallow, pillow, following, piano, yellow.

[ʏ] for [u] in words in *-ould* and in *-oo* which are pronounced with [u]. Thus, gʊd] for *good* [gʊd], [ʃʊd] for *should* [ʃud]. The substandard sound here is an unrounded [ʊ], the symbol for which in close transcription is [ʊ].

Transcribe: could, would, book, took, look, hook, shook, cook, wood, hood.

Anticipatory raising of vowels through the influence of adjacent consonants accounts for a considerable number of substandard pronunciations. Thus, *can* > kɪn] because the tongue, anticipating the necessary rise for the [n], rises prematurely so that [ɪ], not [æ], is produced. It is possible also to explain this shift as the result of unstressing [æ] to [ɪ] and subsequently restressing the [ɪ]. In any event, the process happened long ago in the history of the language, of course, and many individuals say [kɪn] in imitation of their elders. But with other individuals, the mutation is currently in progress. Other words whose history, earlier or later, is similar are *get* [gɛt] > [gɪt], *catch* [kætʃ] > [kɛtʃ], *radish* ['rædɪʃ] > ['rɛdɪʃ] (here a folk etymology involving a fancied relation of the word *radish* to the word *red* may also be in operation), *itch* [ɪtʃ] > [itʃ], *drain* [dreɪn] > [drin]. The type of shift whereby *men* [mɛn] > [mɪn] and *sense* ['sɛnts] > [sɪnts], which is mentioned elsewhere as a mark of the Southern-General American border, belongs in the category here being discussed and, as stated, occasionally, though rarely, develops independently at points distant from the border.

The dark [l], i.e., [ł], of General American speech becomes exaggerated through abnormal duration, until it forms an extra syllable. In such cases, [ə] intrudes to augment the syllable; thus, *fool* [ful] > ['fuəl]. Usually unrounding and lowering accompanies syllabication. Thus, *mule* [mjul] > ['mjuəl] or even ['mjuwəl], *school* [skul] > ['skuəl].

In addition to subtle intonation, the drawl of General American speech, popularly called the "Western drawl," has for one of its characteristics a disyllabication of single syllables. Examples have already been given in the discussion of dark [l]. Thus, *pool* [pul] > ['puəl]. Similarly *good* [gʊd] > ['gʊəd] or ['gʊəd], as already noted. This disyllabication is relatively infrequent.

[r] > "burred r," i.e., an excessively retroflex, exaggerated [ɽ] in final and preconsonantal positions; *car* [kar] > [kaɽ], *barn* [barn] > [baɽn], *corn* [kɔrn] > [kɔɽn].

[ɚ] as the value of unstressed *-ar, -er, -ir, -or, -ur*, as in *tartar* ['tartɚ], *bitter* ['bɪtɚ], *elixir* [i'lɪksɚ], *color* ['kʌlɚ], *murmur* ['mɝmɚ], is subject to excessive exaggeration also, which may best be expressed with the lengthening sign—thus, *mother* ['mʌðɚ:].

[ɝ], when exaggerated, is regarded as substandard. We ordinarily use a lengthening sign to represent the exaggeration, thus, [bɝ:d]. In the pronunciation of some individuals, the sound is additionally rounded. This effect may be represented in close transcription by [ɝ].

[ɛ] > [ɝ] in a limited number of words, particularly *American* [ə'mɛrəkən], *very* [ˈvɛrɪ], and *terrible* [ˈtɛrəbəl], which are heard as [əˈmɜɹəkən], [ˈvɜrɪ], and [ˈtɜɹəbəl].

Southern-General American Border Substandard Pronunciations

Along the wide border between the Southern and General American areas there is, naturally, a mixed speech. Cultivated speakers use a combination of standard General American and standard Southern, and other speakers a combination of substandard speech from both areas. The border substandard General American sometimes borrows a Southern substandard characteristic bodily, as in upland Arkansas, southeast Texas, and elsewhere where the Southern recessive stress on dissyllables and occasional trisyllables shows up in speech predominantly General American. Thus, dissyllables and trisyllables normally stressed on the second syllable are stressed on the first, as [ˈriˌleɪt] for *relate* [rɪˈleɪt], [ˈdiˌmænd] for *demand* [dɪˈmænd], [ˈɪnˌʃurənts] for *insurance* [ɪnˈʃurənts].[8]

In other instances, as on the extreme southwest borders of Louisiana, near Texas, there is an interesting superimposing of Southern and General American characteristics:

[ar] > [ɔr] in accented syllables spelled with *ar* final or plus a consonant and not preceded by the sound of [w]. This is the [a] > [ɔ] shift of the deep South, with the normal General American [r] added. Thus, *card* [kard] > [kɔrd], *hard* [hard] > [hɔrd], *heart* [hart] > [hɔrt], *garden* [ˈgardn̩] > [ˈgɔrdn̩].

> *Transcribe and pronounce:* Marshall, martial, farce, partial, arsenal, pharmacy, tar, larceny, spar, char, charm, carnival, marked.

[r] is inserted by analogy in a limited number of words like *Chicago* [ʃəˈkago] > [ʃəˈkargo]. This superfluous [r] is not related to the excrescent linking [r] well known in substandard Eastern, British, and (occasionally) Southern speech. It may be rationalized as follows: the border General American speaker is continually having to translate the silent final and preconsonantal *r*'s of his southern neighbors into vocality. Thus, when he hears [ka:] for *car*, he himself says [kar]. If, as an individual, he is not too literate, analogy may lead him to suspect *r*'s where there are none, and so change *Chicago* [ʃəˈkago] to [ʃəˈkargo]. *Dog* [dɔg] > [dɔrg] may have the same history. So may *good 'ern* [gud ɚn] for *good 'un* (i.e., *good one*), *youerns* [ˈjuɚnz] for *you-uns* (equivalent of Southern *you-all* and *y'all*, or of the standard plural, *you*), and *lighterd* [ˈlaɪtɚd] for *light 'ood*, i.e., *light wood* (pine knots for kindling).

But *ought* [ɔt] > [ɔrt], while probably having the same analogical origin, is found far "inland" away from southern borders, and so must have sprung from Eastern-General American contacts as well, or even from the clashing r-silent and r-pronouncing dialects in England.

---

[8] It should be added that this manner of stressing is known to some extent throughout rural America, especially on such words as *recess*, *Detroit*, and *cement*.

[ɛ] > [ɪ] before nasals, of which [n] is the most frequent. Thus *pen* [pɛn] > [pɪn], *again* [əˈgɛn] > [əˈgɪn], *cents* [sɛnts] > [sɪnts]. The vowel preceding [n] is affected by the premature rise of the tongue to the [n]-position. This pronunciation is also found in very limited degree "inland" in the General American area, probably having arisen in the same fashion as in the South.

Transcribe and pronounce: immense, resentful, forensic, agenda, lemon, Mengel, eminent, essential, torrential, clemency, venturesome, endocrine, kennel, calendula, rent, gently, offender, splendid.

[ɪ] > [ɛ] in a few words, such as *been* [bɪn] > [bɛn], *since* [sɪnts] > [sɛnts].

Transcribe and pronounce: minimum, tinder, flinders, flimsy, fling, flint, winsome, window, windrow, mimic, pantomimic, kindred, cling, clinical, crinoline, squint, quinsy, plinth, swim.

Urban Substandard Speech

Cities tend to develop an argot of their own, regardless of the rural section in which they lie. Cities in all regions tend to resemble each other in their gamin and underworld talk. The items listed here, except [ɑr > ɔr], are unknown in General American speech outside the large cities.

[ð] > [d]. Thus, *this* [ðɪs] > [dɪs], *that* [ðæt] > [dæt], *with* [wɪð] > [wɪd], *brother* [ˈbrʌðɚ] > [ˈbrʌdɚ].

[θ] > [t]. Thus *thing* [θɪŋ] > [tɪŋ], *with* [wɪθ] > [wɪt], *nothing* [ˈnʌθɪŋ] > [ˈnʌtn̩].

[ɑ] > [ɔ] in words spelled *ar*[9] final or preconsonantal in stressed syllables. Thus, *car* [kɑr] > [kɔr], *hard* [hɑrd] > [hɔrd]. (See also page 192.)

[ʍ] > [w] as in *which* [ʍɪtʃ] > [wɪtʃ], *when* [ʍɛn] > [wɛn], *whistle* [ˈʍɪsl̩] > [ˈwɪsl̩]. (See also page 187.)

Deviations from Standard General American, Southern, and Eastern Speech

The deviations in the following paragraphs are common to all three of the American regional dialects, General American, Southern, and Eastern. They should be studied as a part of the preceding section on General American, and of the later sections on Southern and Eastern.

Relic pronunciations. All the regional dialects contain certain old or archaic pronunciations, many of which were once a part of the standard speech, but

---

[9] This observation was made in St. Louis. The shift is the equivalent of the identical substandard General American pronunciation on the southern border. It seems also to run down the Atlantic Coast from New York City through Philadelphia, Baltimore, Washington, and Norfolk.

have been superseded by other pronunciations in the normal evolution o.
the language. When such historical sound features are retained after obso-
lescence, they come to be regarded as substandard. Thus, *afeared* [əˈfɪrd, əˈfɪəd]
for *afraid* [əˈfreɪd], *air* [ær, ɛr, ˈæə, ˈɛə] for *are* [ɑr, ɑ], *et* [ɛt][10] for *ate* [eɪt], *ile*
[aɪl] for *oil* [ɔɪl], *shear* [ʃɪr, ˈʃɪə] for *share* [ʃær, ʃɛr, ˈʃæə, ˈʃɛə], *sartain* [ˈsɑrtn̩, ˈsatɪ
for *certain* [ˈsɜtn̩, ˈsɜtn̩], *deef* [dif] for *deaf* [dɛf], *larn* [lɑrn, lɑn] for *learn* [lɜn,
lən], *'tarnal* [ˈtɑrnəl, ˈtɑnəl] for *eternal* [iˈtɜnəl, iˈtɜnəl], [ˈfɜdɚ, ˈfɜdə] for *further*
and *farther* [ˈfɜðɚ, ˈfɜðə, ˈfɑrðɚ, ˈfɑðə], [fɜ] for *far* [fɑr, fɑ], *hant* [hænt] for
haunt [hɔnt], *yarb* [jɑrb, jɑb] for *herb* [(h)ɜb, (h)əb], *theirn* [ðɛrn, ˈðɛən] for
theirs [ðɛrz, ˈðɛəz], *sass* [sæs] for *sauce* [sɔs], *pa'm* [pæm] for *palm* [pɑm], [gum]
for *gum* [gʌm], [joʊ] for *ewe* [ju].

> *Transcribe and pronounce:* care, careful, carelessly, chair, cheer, chairman,
> rocking chair, afraid, shared, sheared, sheer, boil, join, point, poison, spoil,
> pint, joist, joint, roil, coil, nearer, gaunt, jaunt, daunt, launch, calm, psalm,
> balm, yours, hers, his, yours, scarce, saucy, saucer, oblige, yonder, parcel,
> sarsaparilla, drain, pert.

Spelling pronunciation. The following are not pronounced as spelled. In
other words, the spelling pronunciations are not the standard ones. If you do
not know the standard pronunciation, use a good dictionary.

> *Transcribe and pronounce:* alms, calm, almond, garage, chassis, often, Green-
> wich, toward, towards, worsted, Worcester, victuals, exhibit, Connecticut.

A convenient source of words whose pronunciation disagrees radically with
their spelling is British proper names.

> *Here are a few for transcription and pronunciation:* Leicester, Norwich, Edin-
> burgh, Warwick, Woolwich, Gloucester.

Folk etymology. In the effort to recognize a familiar word or syllable in a
strange word, the folk often change the sound of the word to agree with the
imagined etymology. This is folk etymology. (See page 166.)

> Try to discover the standard word corresponding to each of the following.
> (If you fail on any word you will find the standard form in the succeeding
> paragraph.) After making identifications, *transcribe:* cartoon, cow buckle,
> diptheria, dipthong, empire (in baseball), loom, mad axe, mushmelon, mushrat,
> overhauls, redish, selphur, world serious, steeple (a double-pointed nail),
> plowsheer, drugs, job, stock [stɔk], pinchers (a tool), study, Westminister,
> wrench. A cartoon of eggs, a cow buckle on his arm, the empire called a strike,
> the soil is a black loom, dig with a mad axe, blue denim overhauls, eat a redish,
> his plowsheer was sharp, coffee drugs, job him, livestock, the world serious,
> fasten the wire with a steeple, hold it study, wrench the clothes.
> Insert the following words in the proper places above before transcribing:
> overalls, rinse, series, diphtheria, muskmelon, loam, radish, sulphur, umpire,

---

[10] Still acceptable in England.

staple, diphthong, mattock, steady, carton, carbuncle, plowshare, dregs, jab, stock [stɑk, stɒk], pincers, Westminster.

Hyperurbanism. The folk sometimes apply mistaken corrective processes to words that seem to them to resemble words actually needing correction. Thus, *mornin'*, properly corrected, becomes *morning*; *mountain*, similarly "corrected," becomes *mounting*. This is hyperurbanism. (See page 166.)

Transcribe and pronounce:
Indian loan-words properly ending in *i* [ɪ], not *a* [ə]
   Missouri, Miami
Latin loan-word properly ending in *i* [ɪ], not *a* [ə]
   Cincinnati
Italian loan-words properly ending in *i* [ɪ], not *a* [ə]
   confetti, spaghetti, macaroni
English words properly pronounced with [ən], not [ɪŋ]
   kitchen, chicken, often, Edinburg, Allen, Johnson, linen

Colloquial assimilations. (See definition of assimilation, page 153.)

Restore the spelling of the following, *transcribe, and pronounce:* clo'es, gimme, lemme, gonna go, mont's, winner (for winter), wanna go, idn't (isn't), wadn't, gib 'em up, cenner (center), [ðætǀduzwɛlzɛnɪweɪ].

Metathesis. (See definition, page 165.)

Change the spellings in the following to restore the exchanged sounds to their normal order, *transcribe, and pronounce:* aporn, calvary (soldiers on horseback), ax (to inquire), axes, axed, bronical, childern, hunderd, larnyx, pharnyx, modren, pattren, prespiration, preform, perdiction, purty.

Analogy. The first word of each of the following pairs is often pronounced by analogy with either the second word or some word like it, as when *colyumn* [ˈkɑljəm] is used for *column* [ˈkɑləm] by analogy with *volume* [ˈvɑljəm]. (See page 166.)

Transcribe each pair and pronounce, making clear that the second word in each does not borrow from the first. (The critical spellings are italicized.)

Jan*u*ary	Feb*r*uary
ev*er*	ev*er*y
*ea*rth	h*ea*rth
f*u*ss	c*u*rse
physi*o*logy	gen*ea*logy
b*u*st	b*u*rst
form*u*late	perc*o*late
f*oo*t	r*oo*t
b*u*t	p*u*t
*ga*ther	to*ge*ther
to*ge*ther	*ga*ther
dr*o*ve	d*o*ve (from dive)
z*oo*	z*oo*logy

stimulate	substantiate
simulate	similar
religious	sacrilegious
thickish	licorice
furnish	punish

Certain weak verbs acquire past tense forms on the analogy of strong verbs. For instance, on the analogy of sweep–swept, keep–kept, we have leap–leaped [lɛpt], reap–reaped [rɛpt], lean–leaned [lɛnt].

Syncope. (See definition, page 164.) Example: *acc'rate* [ˈækrət] for *accurate* [ˈækjurət, ˈækjərət]. In the transcription list below, the standard number of syllables is indicated by the numbers in parentheses after each word.

> *Transcribe and pronounce:* regular (3), family (3), company (3), adjective (3), geography (4), tolerable (4), battery (3), veteran (3), every (3), opera (3), buttery (3), physiology (5), history (3).

Syllabic syncope is also found in [kjuˈrɑsətɪ] for *curiosity* [ˌkjurɪˈɑsətɪ], [ˌluzɪˈænə] for *Louisiana* [ˌluɪzɪˈænə].

> *Transcribe and pronounce,* taking care not to omit any syllable: territorial, pictorial, experience, realize, quarreled, positive, serial, cereal, Ariel, miserable, Pierot, Pierrette, furiously.

Anaptyxis. (See complete definition, page 162.) The propagation of a super-fluous syllable is called anaptyxis. It occurs in a limited number of words like *athaletic* [ˌæθəˈlɛtɪk] for *athletic* [ˌæθˈlɛtɪk].

> *Restore the spelling in the list below, transcribe, and pronounce (the correct number of syllables is indicated by the number in parentheses after each word):* athalete (2), ellum (1), fillum (1), world serious (2), perairie (2), pullease (1), Henery (2), grievious (2), mischievious (3), umberella (3). Such pronunciations as *grievious, mischievious* are possibly on the analogy of *delirious.*

Retracted stress. Current editions of dictionaries, contrary to earlier ones, recognize the pronunciation of the following words with stress on the initial syllable as secondary choice. It is still a mark of standard pronunciation to place the stress on the final syllable.

> *Transcribe and pronounce:* address, adult, ally, allies, defect, research, recess. The following are recognized as standard only when stressed on the second syllable. *Transcribe and pronounce:* cement, Detroit, Des Moines, Supreme (Court), United (States), United (Nations).

Restressing. It will be remembered from page 160 that many frequently used words are most often pronounced in their unstressed forms and that there is a strong tendency, therefore, to pronounce them when stressed with the vowels of the unstressed forms. Thus:

Word	Stressed pronunciation	Regularly unstressed as	Colloquially restressed as	Standard restressing
for	fɔr, fɔ	fɚ, fə	fɝ, fɜ	fɔr, fɔ
of	ɑv	əv, ə	ʌv	ɑv
have	hæv	əv, ə	ʌv, ɑv	hæv
from	frɑm	frəm	frʌm	frɑm
was	wɑz, wɒz	wəz	wʌz	wɑz, wɒz
what	ʌʌat, wɒt	ʌʌət, wət	ʌʌʌt, wʌt	ʌʌat, wɒt
and	ænd	ən, n̩	æn	ænd
than	ðæn	n̩	æn	ðæn

Note that since *of* and *have* are both unstressed to [əv], they may become confused in the restressing of, e.g., *I would 've* [əv] *gone* as *I would of* [ɑv] *gone*. Likewise since *and* and *than* are both unstressed to [n̩], they may be confused in the substandard restressing of *more 'n'* [n̩] *that* as *more and* [ænd] *that*.

> *Transcribe and pronounce* the following, distinguishing carefully between stressed and unstressed forms: What for? Not *for* me; *from* me. Of the people, by the people, for the people. Was he here? He was. Two for a quarter. Greater than he. I have it. I should have seen it. Three of a kind. I know what he saw. What?

Intrusive sounds. (See page 190 for discussion of the propagation of intrusive sounds.)

> Write out the normal spellings of the following, *transcribe and pronounce:* chimley,[11] fambly, [puɪʃ], *wash* [wɔɪʃ] (see also page 190).

Voicing unvoiced consonants. (See page 156.) Consonants are often colloquially voiced by the assimilative influence of a vowel on either side, as in *nodice* [ˈnoʊdəs, ˈnoʊdɪs] for *notice* [ˈnoʊtəs, ˈnoʊtɪs] and *Babdist* [ˈbæbdɪst] for *Baptist* [ˈbæptɪst]; or of a preceding voiced consonant, as in *abzurd* [ˌæbˈzɝd, ˌæbˈzɜd] for *absurd* [ˌæbˈsɝd, ˌæbˈsɜd].

> Restore the spelling of the following, transcribe, and pronounce: abzorb, abzurdity, babdize, addic, hosbital, liddle, prodestant, sadisfaction, signivigant, lugzhury. *Transcribe and pronounce*, taking care not to voice any voiceless consonants: water, latter, Patty, Dakota, Lottie, pretty, catty, cattle, kettle, victuals, luxurious.

Unvoicing voiced consonants. It is sometimes speculated that the assimilative effect of silence after a word may cause the unvoicing of a voiced final consonant. At any rate, most of the common words so affected are often found at the end of the utterance, as in [kɛtʃ əˈhoʊlt] for *catch hold* [kætʃ ˈhoʊld] (see page 157).

---

[11] Note here that [n] has been assimilated to [m], but that the tongue position of [n], held through the pronunciation of [m], has been modified by depression laterally to produce [l].

Restore the spelling, transcribe, and pronounce: secont, hunnert, he was kilt, helt.

Some words have, by unvoicing, acquired doublets which have been accepted: spilled–spilt, smelled–smelt, burned–burnt, spelled–spelt. See also uncultivated *allus* for *always*, *bellus* for *bellows*, *gallus* for *gallows* (whence *galluses* for *suspenders*).

Fronting (sometimes accompanied by raising) of [ʌ] before front consonants. Example: [ʤɛst, ʤɪst] for *just* [ʤʌst].[12]

> *Transcribe and pronounce* the standard forms below:
> brush, not [brɛʃ]; cover, not [ˈkɪvɚ, ˈkɪvə]; discover, not [dɪsˈkɪvɚ, dɪsˈkɪvə]; hush, not [hɛʃ]; judge, not [ʤɛʤ]; judgement, not [ˈʤɛʤmənt]; shut- (ter), not [ʃɛt(ə, ɚ)]; touch, not [tɛtʃ].

Centralized vowels. (See page 158.) In a small group of words, the stressed front vowel, usually [ɛ], [æ] or [ɪ], has become centralized and may be represented by [ʌ]. Sometimes this transcription is quite accurate, as when *trestle* [ˈtrɛsl̩] is pronounced *trustle* [ˈtrʌsl̩] and *rather* [ˈræðɚ, ˈræðə, ˈraðə] is [ˈrʌðə], but only approximate when *minister* [ˈmɪnəstɚ, ˈmɪnəstə] is transcribed [ˈmʌnəstɚ, ˈmʌnəstə]. (The symbol [ɨ], i.e., the centralized [ɪ], would perhaps be more accurate here. See footnote 12).

Frequently *yr*, *ir* are pronounced [ɝ] as in *syrup* [ˈsɝəp] for [ˈsɪrəp], *stirrup* [ˈstɝəp] for [ˈstɪrəp]. Similarly *er* may be pronounced [ɝ], as in *America* [əˈmɝəkə] for [əˈmɛrəkə].

The *oo* of *-ook* (and of *oo* *-oot* in the one word *soot*) is in a few words pronounced [ʌ], as in [tʌk] for *took*.

> *Transcribe and pronounce:* seminary, cemetery, centenary, leather, West-minster, ministerial, president, senator, sinister, sinistrality, simple, whip, very, terrible, serenade, Cherokee, sheriff, shook, soot.

Raising: [ɪ], [ɛ], [æ] *raised before front consonants*. Examples: [kənˈdiʃən] for *condition* [kənˈdɪʃən], [gɪt] for *get* [gɛt], [kɛtʃ] for *catch* [kætʃ], [kɪn] for *can* [kæn], [ˈlit l̩] for *little* [ˈlɪt l̩].

> *Transcribe and pronounce:* edition, ambition, superstition, additional, fishes, sufficiently, wishful, again, kettle, steady, instead, yesterday, chest, forget, have, has, had, catching, gather, inch, itch, district, yet, chair. (See also page 191.)

Lowering: [i] > [ɪ] as in *creek* [krɪk], *sleek* [slɪk] (referring to coats of animals). [ɪ] > [ɛ], as in *spirit* > [ˈspɛrət].

> *Transcribe and pronounce:* hinder, been, stint, pith, rid, rinse, since, miracle.

[eɪ] > [æ], as in [næp] for *nape*, [slæk] for *slake* (of lime), [ˈægɚ] for *ague*, [plæt] for *pleat* [pleɪt, plit] (meaning *braid*).

---

[12] One pronunciation of *just*, [ʤɪst], contains what some linguists now regard as one of the vowel phonemes of English, viz., /ɨ/.

Palatalization of [g] **and** [k] **before** [æ] **and** [au], **accompanying raising or raising and nasalization of** [æ]. Example: [kjæ⁺ʊ] for *cow* [kaʊ], [gjæ̃⁺ũn] for *gown* [gaʊn], [kjæ⁺t] for *cat* [kæt], and [gjæ⁺s] for *gas* [gæs]. (Note that in addition to the palatalization of [k] and [g], [aʊ] shifts to [æ̃⁺ũ], especially before nasal consonants. See page 215.)

> *Transcribe and pronounce* without [j], without nasalizing [æ], and without raising [æ]. (To insure lack of raising [æ], let the tongue lie on the floor of the mouth, completely out of contact with the upper molars. It is the contact of the sides of the tongue with the teeth that constitutes the kinesthetic evidence of raising.): count, can, county, calla, gather, gouge, Gowdy, gallows, gap, cant, canter.

Palatalization of [d] **before** [u, ju]: *juberous* for *dubious*, *tremenjous* [tri-ˈmɛnʤəs] for *tremendous*.

Nasality. Nasality is known in almost every dialect of English. In some dialects, it is limited to the pronunciation of individuals; in others it is more general. The nasality of General American speech differs from the adenoidal whine of Cockney, the dry twang of New England, and the high shrillness of Southern American women. It is relatively low pitched, and in men, often almost mellow. It is in some individuals a general nasality spread over all the speech sounds, including most consonants; in others it is limited to vowels adjacent to, particularly preceding, [m], [n], [ŋ], where the velum drops too soon and allows the preceding vowel to become nasal. In yet other speakers it strikes a middle ground and affects vowels preceding nasal consonants, the vowel [æ] in any position, and the diphthong [aʊ] in any position, without affecting other sounds.

Nasality, as a defect of English speech, may be defined as undue nasal resonance on speech sounds other than [m], [n], and [ŋ]. The word "undue" is used here in recognition of the experimentally demonstrated fact that the velum may drop enough to permit a slight nasal exit of air on almost any vowel or continuant consonant without damage to the acoustic quality of the sound.[13] In song, indeed, a degree of deliberate nasality of this sort is often taught as a desirable resonance characteristic, even though such improved resonant quality has been demonstrated to be achieved at the expense of carrying power.[14] We speak of nasality as a defect only when it becomes noticeable and unpleasant acoustically.

Nasality in American speech is especially criticized by Englishmen, who associate it inaccurately with lower class speech, such as Cockney; it is spoken of disparagingly by all other Europeans. It is regarded in Europe as the outstanding characteristic of American English.

---

[13] Joseph P. Kelly, "Studies in Nasality," *Archives of Speech*, January, 1934; and G. O. Russell, *Speech and Voice* (New York: The Macmillan Co., 1931), p. 42.
[14] C. M. Wise, "Chest Resonance," *Quarterly Journal of Speech*, June, 1932.

Example of general nasality: *I don't know what you mean.* [aĩ dʌn: õũ ʍatʃə mĩn].

Example of nasality before nasal consonants: *then* [ðɛ̃n], *man* [mæ̃n], *moon* [mũn].

Examples of nasality on [æ] and [aʊ]. [æ] > [æ̆ᵗ]; that is, [æ] is raised, by elevation of the whole body of the tongue back of the tip, to a kind of fricative [ɛ]. This raising appears to promote nasality, perhaps because the restriction of the air passage through the mouth seems to increase the temptation to drop the velum for freer discharge of the breath stream. Thus, *that* [ðæt] > [ðæ̆ᵗt], *bad* [bæd] > [bæ̃ĩd]. The [a] of the diphthong [aʊ] tends to become [æ], after which it may proceed to [æᵗ] and [æ̆ᵗ]. Thus, *down* [daʊn] > [dæ̆ᵗũn], *sound* [saʊnd] > [sæ̆ᵗũnd]. After [g] or [k] the diphthong [aʊ] tends to become three sounds beginning with [j]. Thus, *gown* [gaʊn] > [gjæ̆ᵗũn], *gouge* [gaʊdʒ] > [gjæ̆ᵗʊdʒ], *cow* [kaʊ] > [kjæ̆ᵗũ], *county* [ˈkaʊntɪ] > [ˈkjæ̆ᵗũntɪ]. In these instances, [g] and [k] are fronted, and in a closer transcription would be written [ɟ] and [c]; *gown* and *cow* would, then, be [ɟjæ̆ᵗũn] and [cjæ̆ᵗũ]. Since the changes affecting [æ] and [aʊ] are found independent from contexts containing [g] and [k], it may be assumed that the fronting of these consonants to [ɟ] and [c] results from the raising of [æ] and [aʊ] rather than vice versa. The [j] creeps in as a palatal glide, induced by the high-front sounds before and after it, and particularly by the quasi-palatal-fricative quality which the vowel takes on. As indicated on page 101, the normal American [æ] is made with the tongue lying flat in the mouth, entirely without contact with the upper molars, whereas the [æᵗ] is made with the tongue in bilateral contact with the upper molars, much as for [i, ɪ, e, ɛ].

Superfluous [t] **and** [əd]. In words of the type of *acrost* [əˈkrɔst] for [əˈkrɔs], the tongue has been allowed to rise into alveolar contact after [s], so that [t] is produced excrescently. In words of the type of *drownded* [ˈdraʊndəd] for *drowned* [draʊnd], a superfluous past tense ending has been added.

> *Transcribe and pronounce* the standard forms here following: *closer*, not [ˈkloʊstɚ, ˈkloʊstə]; *close* (adj.), not [kloʊst]; *dose*, not [doʊst]; *attacked*, not [əˈtæktəd].

[w] **for** [ʍ]. In the General American and Southern speech regions, the opinion is generally held that [ʍ] should be used in nearly all words beginning with *wh* except *who*, *whole*, and their derivatives. Actually [w] for *wh* is seldom heard in these regions except occasionally in cities. In the Eastern region, there is difference of opinion as to whether [w] may be used instead of [ʍ]. The transcription below is intended either for those who prefer [ʍ], as in *white* [ʍaɪt], or for those who prefer [w], as in *w'ite* [waɪt].

> *Transcribe and pronounce:* which, when, why, whisper, whistle, whither, whether, wheel, wheat, whirr, whirl, what, whale, wharf, whelp, overwhelm,

whence, where, whey, Whig, while, whim, whimper, whip, whisk, Whitman, Whitney, Whittier.

Loss of [h] **from** [hj] **in certain words with stressed initial** *hu*. Thus, [ˈjumən] for *human* [ˈhjumən].[15]

Transcribe with [h] *and pronounce:* Hugh, hue, humanity, huge, Hubert, Hewson, Houston, Hume, Hugo, humane, humerus, humidity, humiliation, humor, humus. ([h] is used initially in *haint*, doublet of *ain't*. Since *haint* = *have not*, as well as *am not*, the [h] may be a residue of *have*.)

Loss of [t] **from** [spt]. Thus, *crisp'* [krɪsp] for *crisped* [krɪspt].

Transcribe and pronounce: clasped, grasped, rasped.

Loss of [s] **or** [ts] **from** [sts]. Thus, *roas'* [roʊs:] or *roast'* [roʊst] for *roasts* [roʊsts]. Note that in the case of [roʊs:], the loss of the consonants has been compensated for by the lengthening of the [s].

Transcribe and pronounce: boasts, beasts, costs, casts, cysts, boosts, dusts, ghosts, fasts, mists, interests, twists, lists, consists, insists, resists, persists, wrists, wastes, waists, fists, jousts, frosts, yeasts, roosts.

Loss of [k] **or** [t] **from** [skt]. Thus, *ris'ed* [rɪst] or *risk'* [rɪsk] for *risked* [rɪskt].

Transcribe and pronounce: basked, masked, asked, tasked.

Loss of [ps] **or** [s] **from** [sps]. Thus, *wis'* [wɪs:] or *wisp'* [wɪsp] for *wisps* [wɪsps]. (Note that in the case of [wɪs:] the loss of the consonants is compensated for by the lengthening of the [s].)

Transcribe and pronounce: asps, clasps, hasps, grasps, crisps, cusps, rasps, wasps.

Loss of [s] **or** [sk] **from** [sks]. Thus, *ris'* [rɪs:] or *risk'* [rɪsk] for *risks* [rɪsks]. (Note that in [rɪs:] the [s] is lengthened to compensate for the loss of the other consonants. Here is one of the rare instances where duration is significant in English. The length of the [s] in *casks* [kæs:] distinguishes this substandardism from *Cass* [kæs].)

Transcribe and pronounce: Basques, basks, casques, casks, bisques, flasks, masks, masques, musks, casks, rusks.

Loss of [t] **final in syllable.** [t] is omitted when final in a consonant cluster at the end of a syllable, particularly before [l], as in *mos'ly* for *mostly*, *cos'ly* for *costly*, *direc'ly* for *directly*, *exac'ly* for *exactly*, *sof'ly* for *softly*, *jus'ly* for *justly*, *bankrup'* for *bankrupt*, *musn'* for *musn't*, *didn'* for *didn't*, *shouldn'* for *shouldn't*, *wouldn'* for *wouldn't*, *oughtn'* for *oughtn't*.

---

[15] If a word beginning like *human* is spoken tensely and breathily, the result is [ˈçumən]. The sound [ç] is identical with the *Ichlaut* of German (see p. 381).

Loss of [t] **from** [pt] **of past tense of verbs.** Thus, *swep'* [swɛp] for *swept* [swɛpt].[16]

Transcribe and pronounce: kept, slept, crept, wept.

Loss of [d] **from** [nd], [ndz], **and** [ld]. Thus, *win's* [wɪnz] for *winds* [wɪndz]. [d] is lost from [ld] in [ˈskæfəl] for *scaffold*.

Transcribe and pronounce: lends, binds, sends, wounds, sounds, lands, hands, brands, bounds, kinds, mounds, pounds, cold, held, fold.

[t] **for** [k] **and** [d] **for** [g] **before** [l]. Thus, *tlass* [tlæs] for *class* [klæs], *dlass* [dlæs] for *glass* [glæs]. (See page 126.)

Transcribe with [k] *and* [g] *and pronounce:* clean, glean, climb, glow, clever, glad, cloud, gleam, glide, clock, close, glimmer.

[k] **for** [t], **as in turkle for turtle,** [ˈbrɪkəl] **for brittle.**

[n] **for** [ŋ] **in two special words.** Thus, *stren'th* [strɛnθ] for *strength* [strɛŋkθ]. *Len'th* and *stren'th* are used only by the aged or unlettered in most of the United States. In the South, and to a lesser degree in the East, this pronunciation is more widespread. Note that *length* is derived by umlaut (see page 155) from *long*, and *strength* from *strong*; the [ŋ] is properly retained in the derivatives.

Transcribe and pronounce: long-length, strong-strength, lengthy, lengths, strengths, lengthier. Note also that when [ŋ] is retained, it is usually preserved by the insertion of the glide [k], while [n] may be preserved by the glide [t]. The following scheme illustrates this:

$$\text{lɛŋθ} > \begin{bmatrix} \text{lɛŋkθ} \\ \\ \text{lɛntθ} \end{bmatrix}$$

[n] **for** [ŋ] **in endings in -ing.** Thus, *eatin'* for *eating*. This is popularly called "g-dropping." It is not, since phonetically [ˈæskɪŋ] contains no [g]. If a student believes that he has dropped a [g], he may try to replace it by saying [ˈæskɪŋg]. The change is actually the substitution of [n] for [ŋ].

Transcribe and pronounce: morning, evening, walking, talking, coming, going, something, nothing, reading, writing, singing, laughing.

[ɔ] **for** [æ] **in -amp, etc.** Thus, *stomp* [stɔmp] for *stamp* [stæmp], *pamper* > [ˈpɔmpɚ].

Transcribe and pronounce: tramps, champs(v.), tassel.

[ʊ] **for** [u]. Lying between words invariably pronounced with [u], such as *boon, boot, boost, moon, cool, loose*, etc., and words invariably pronounced with [ʊ], such as *book, good, look, wood, hook, cook, look, wool*, etc., is a list of words

---

[16] See p. 218 for analogous loss of consonants in substandard Southern speech.

in which the practice varies between [u] and [ʊ]. Thus, *room* [rum, rʊm].¹⁷
When the two pronunciations prevail, it appears that the one with [u] is usually
in better standing. Exception, *soot* [sʊt, sut].

> *Transcribe and pronounce:* roof, hoof, broom, spoon, soon, coop.

[eɪ] or [æ] for [ɛ] before [g] or [dʒ] and [eɪ] for [ɛ] before [ʒ]. The sound
[ɛ] is notably unstable, shifting upward or downward before [g], and upward
before [ʒ]. Thus, [eɪg] or [æg] for *egg* [ɛg], [ˈmeɪʒɚ, ˈmeɪʒə] for *measure* [ˈmɛʒɚ,
ˈmɛʒə].

> *Transcribe and pronounce:* leg, lag, keg, beg, bag, edge, age, sedge, sage,
> wedge, wage, kedge, cage, cadge, nutmeg, pleasure.

Loss of [l] **from** [lj], [lr], [l] **plus vowel or** [w]. Thus, [ˈmɪjən] for *million*
[ˈmɪljən].

> *Transcribe and pronounce:* billion, trillion, William, trillium, volume; already,
> all right, tolerable, college, collar, dollar, color, always, stallion, alien.

[ə] **for** [ju, jə] **in unstressed medial syllables containing u.** Thus,
[əˈkjuməˌleɪt] for *accumulate* [əˈkjumjuˌleɪt]. Cf. [ˈfigə, ˈfigɚ] for *figure* [ˈfigjə,
ˈfigjɚ].

> *Transcribe and pronounce:* regulate, regular, accurate, calculate, reputation,
> strangulate, formulate.

[ɪ] **for** [ʊ, ə] **in you** [ju, jə]. Example: *I see ye* [ˌaɪ ˈsi jɪ] for *I see you* [ˌaɪ ˈsi ju, jə].

> *Transcribe and pronounce:* Do you hear? Can you come? I know you. Where
> are you? Confound you!

[ɪ] **for** [ə] **in words with unstressed a, final in a word or syllable.** Thus,
sofy [ˈsoʊfɪ] for *sofa* [ˈsoʊfə].

> *Transcribe and pronounce:* soda, china, Bertha, California, opera, Oklahoma,
> America, Alabama, Russia, banana, calla, Nebraska, Arizona, Ida, Idaho,
> Georgia, Minnesota, Laura, Ada, Nita, Cora, Dora, Hannah, Norma, Myra,
> Vera, Omaha. (In close acoustic resemblance to the words above is the
> substandard pronunciation of *alcohol* as [ˈælkɪˌhɔl].)

[o] **for** [ə] **in words with unstressed la, final in a word or syllable.** Thus
cupola [ˈkjupəlo], *fistula* [ˈfɪstjulo], *scrofula* [ˈskrɔfjulo] for [ˈkjupələ], etc.

[ə] **for** [ɪ] **in unstressed form of him, etc.** The usual unstressed form of
him, i.e., [ɪm], is sometimes changed to [əm], practically exclusively in cities.
Thus, [aɪ si əm] may displace the normal *I see him* [aɪ si ɪm]. In some cases,
[aɪ si əm] may even be used for *I see her, I see it.* For *I see them*, [aɪ si əm] is
the normal unstressed form.

> *Transcribe and pronounce:* I heard him. We know him. You saw her. He got
> it. Have you seen him? Has he met him?

---

¹⁷ See C. H. Grandgent, "English in America," *Die Neueren Sprachen* (New York:
Stechert, 1895), Vol. II, p. 257.

Yes is modified in many ways, as seen in [jɛ, ˈjɛə, jɛp].

[ŋ] is substituted for prepositions in [aʊtŋ] for *out of*, and [ɔfŋ] for *off of* and *off from*.

[k] is lost from [sk], as in [æs:] for *ask*.

The prefix *un* is pronounced [ɔn], as in *unhappy* [ɔnˈhæpɪ].

Transcribe and pronounce: untied, unnecessary, uneasy, unsure.

[ʃ] > [s] before [r] as in *s'red, s'rivel*.

Transcribe and pronounce: shrink, shrive, shrove, Shreveport, shrimp.

[s] is prefixed superfluously in *cringe* [skrɪndʒ], *crouch* [skraʊtʃ], *plunge* [splʌndʒ]. [splʌndʒ].

[s] may appear excrescently in *nowheres, anywheres, somewheres*.

Miscellaneous substandard pronunciations. Use a good dictionary as necessary to ascertain the standard pronunciation of the words below.

Transcribe and pronounce the standard forms:

arrow, not [ˈɑro, ˈærɪ, ˈɑrɪ]	daren't, not [ˈdæsn̩t]
barrow, not [ˈbɑro]	yeast, not [ist]
because, not [bɪˈkʌz]	partner, not [ˈpɑrdnɚ, ˈpɑːdnə]
been, not [bɛn]	curse, not [kʌs]
borrow, not [ˈbɑrɪ]	burst, not [bʌst]
chew, not [tʃɔ]	bundle, not [ˈbʌnl̩]
every, not [ˈɛvɚ, ˈɛvə]	rather, not [ˈrʌðɚ]
far, not [fɚ, fɜ]	bulge, not [bʊldʒ]
forward, not [ˈfaʊwɚd, ˈfaʊwəd]	bulk, not [bʊlk]
guarantee, not [ˌgɑrənˈti]	cud, not [kʊd]
harrow, not [ˈhɑro, ˈhærɪ, ˈhɑrɪ]	shook, not [ʃʌk]
learn, not [lɑrn, lɑn]	took, not [tʌk]
narrow, not [ˈnɑro, ˈnærɪ, ˈnɑrɪ]	soot, not [sʌt]
parents, not [ˈpeɪrənts]	spirit, not [ˈspɛrət]
quarry, not [ˈkweɪrɪ]	sure, not [ʃoʊr, ʃoʊ]
seven, not [ˈsɛbm̩]	yellow, not [ˈjælɚ, ˈjælə]
eleven, not [ˈlɛbm̩]	yonder, not [ˈjændɚ, ˈjændə]
pretty, not [ˈpɚtɪ]	your, not [joʊr, joʊ]
audacious, not [aʊˈdeɪʃəs]	ear, not [jɪr, ˈjɪə]

CHAPTER 8

Southern American English
Standard and Substandard

The speech of the South, like any other regional speech, is characterized by many subtle nuances of duration, pitch, tempo, and rhythm, which defy easy symbolization. These shadings must be heard to be appreciated. Such characteristics are not regarded as violations of standard Southern practice, so long as they remain relatively small. If such small differences are disregarded in the three major American dialects, it will be seen that standard Southern speech bears a close kinship with standard Eastern American speech in respect to the treatment of unstressing, and in the use of /r/ and its realted vowels and of the combination *o* plus *r* plus vowel, as in *horror*. In respect to the distribution of many of the other English phonemes, it bears a close relation to General American speech.

But these statements apply well only to the standard forms of regional speech. As soon as substandard forms are compared, it will be seen that the /r/-systems of the Southern and Eastern areas diverge considerably, and that the distribution and use of the other phonemes in Southern and General American diverge very greatly indeed.

Standard Southern Speech

Stressed Vowels and Diphthongs

a = [ɔ] or [ɑ] in *water, watch, wash*. Prevailingly, these words are pronounced ['wɔtə], [waʧ], [waʃ]; some individuals say ['watə], [wɔʧ], [wɔʃ].

> *Transcribe:* watershed, watchful, washday.

a = [ɑ] in *was* [waz] and *what* [ʍat].

> *Transcribe:* Was he here? He was. Whatever, somewhat. What for? For what?

a = [æ] in all "broad-*a*" words, largely encompassed in the combinations *a* before [f-(v)], [s], [θ-(ð)], and [n] plus consonant, as in the words *laughter* ['læftə], *class* [klæs], *bath* [bæθ], *rather* ['ræðə], *calves* [kævz], *shan't* [ʃænt], etc. As the

205

exception, some speakers in tidewater Virginia, and occasionally further down the coast, use [ɑ]. (See page 240 on "broad *a*.")

> *Transcribe:* surpass, implant, transfer, chaff, looking-glass, enchant, halves, rafter, lancet.

a = [ɑ] or [ɔ] in [w]*a* words where [w]*a* is followed by [r] plus a vowel, as in *warrant* [ˈwɑrənt, ˈwɔrənt]; *Warren* [ˈwɑrən, ˈwɔrən]; *quarantine* [ˈkwɑrənˌtin, ˈkwɔrənˌtin]: Cf. also *o* + *r* (*r*) + vowel, as in *orange* [ˈɑrɪndʒ, ˈɔrɪndʒ].

> *Transcribe:* quarrying, quarreling, warrant-officer, forest, Florida, torrid.

o = [ɔ] predominantly in the words with *og*, as in *analog* [ˈænəˌlɔg]. In some words, [ɑ] is used alternatively, as *log* [lɔg, lɑg]. In Louisiana, of 380 instances, 316 yielded [ɔ], 64 yielded [ɑ]. The sound [ɑ] appeared most often in *fog*, least often in *log* and *dog*. *Cog* was preponderantly pronounced with [ɑ].[1]

> *Transcribe:* befog, frog, cog, jog, bog, boggy, foggy, catalog, dog, hog.

[ʌ] = a central vowel, very like [ə] except a little lower and farther back, and acoustically very close except for greater duration. It contrasts with British [ʌ], which is still lower and farther back, suggesting [ɑ] to American ears.

> *Transcribe and pronounce:* cut–cart–cot, butter–barter, hut–heart–hot, love, wonderful, roughly, stuff, above, upper, under, udder, other, cud, muster, mustard, cuffed, sullen.

a before *r* and *rr*, and *ai*, *ea*, and *ei* before *r* = [æ] prevailingly in *hare* [ˈhæə], *carry* [ˈkærɪ], *fair* [ˈfæə], *wear* [ˈwæə], *heir* [ˈæə], etc. A few speakers use [ɛ] in this class of words.

> *Transcribe:* hairy, marry, marriage, bear, swear, share, heiress, Harry, fairy, bare, carriage, square, chairman.

au, *aw*, and *al* = [ɔ] as in *haunt* [hɔnt], *daughter* [ˈdɔtə], *audience* [ˈɔdɪənts], *hawk* [hɔk], *talk* [tɔk]. This is in contrast with the [ɑ] of Scots dialect and the [ɔ˔, o] of New York and British speech.

> *Transcribe:* walk, stalk, gaunt, shawl, pshaw, Shaw, jaunt, auditory, audio-meter, taught, law, saw, raucous, chalk, mawkish, maul, paw, caught.

-ear, *-er*, *-ir*, *-or*, *-our*, *-ur*, and *-yr* stressed = [ɜ] in words like *heard* [hɜd], *fern* [fɜn], *shirt* [ʃɜt], *work* [wɜk], *journey* [ˈdʒɜnɪ], *urn* [ɜn], *myrrh* [mɜ]. But the related sound before *rr* in *hurry*, *worry*, etc., is [ʌ]; thus [ˈhʌrɪ, ˈwʌrɪ]. [ɝ] may also be heard in all the foregoing words.

> *Transcribe:* overheard, mercy, whirler, overwork, worded, inurn, shirr, her, hers, herd, Turkey, Myrtle, flourish, furry, journalistic, curry, quirt, squirt, hurry, wordy, shirring, shirk.

---

[1] Albert Donald George, *Some Louisiana Isoglosses* (Unpublished M. A. thesis, Louisiana State University, 1951).

"Short *o*" = [ɑ], as in *rob* [rɑb]. The spelling of this sound is typically *o* plus consonant in a monosyllable, as in *rob*, or *o* plus a doubled consonant, as in *robbing* [ˈrɑbɪŋ]. Two consonants of identical sound serve equally well to insure the use of [ɑ], as in *rock* [rɑk], *rocking* [ˈrɑkɪŋ]. The addition of a final *e* changes [ɑ] to [ou], as in *rob* [rɑb]—*robe* [roub]. Often, but not invariably, a single medial consonant has the same effect, as in *robbing* [ˈrɑbɪŋ]—*robing* [ˈroubɪŋ]. A few words spelled with *a* after [w] fall into this category, such as *was* [wɑz], *what* [ʍɑt], *quality* [ˈkwɑlətɪ].

> *Transcribe:* top, crop, cropped, follow, hod, hop, drop, dropper, chock, lock, locked, operate, optimum, obviate, soluble, moderate, copper, copula, shot, sot, lot, hotter, gotten, blotter, obstinate, optimist, clot, squat, whatever, holly, jot.

a or *ai* = [eɪ] as well as [ɛ] in a number of words where *a* or *ai* precedes *r* in stressed syllables followed by a vowel, as in *various* [ˈveɪrɪəs, ˈvɛrɪəs], *dairy* [ˈdeɪrɪ, ˈdɛrɪ].

> *Transcribe:* vary, Mary, gregarious, variable, variance, variant, variation, varicolored, varicose, variegate, variorum, variole, variform, Marius.

a = [ɑ] in monosyllables and stressed syllables containing *ar* final or preconsonantal and not preceded by the sound of [w], as in *bar* [bɑ], *bard* [bɑd].

> *Transcribe:* cartel, Margaret, farcical, argumentative, cardiac, horsecar, hardy, shipyard, spark, remark, hearken, parley, cart–cot,[2] card–cod.

In tidewater Virginia *ou* and *ow*, when followed by voiceless consonants, are pronounced [ɜu], as in *out* [ɜut], *about* [əˈbɜut], *doubt* [dɜut], *rout* [rɜut]; but when final or followed by voiced consonants, are [au] (or substandard [æu]) as in *down* [daun], *cow* [kau], *how* [hau], *houses* [ˈhauzɪz].

o plus *r* final or followed by a consonant = [ɔ] or [ɔə] as in *cord* [kɔd, ˈkɔed], *organize* [ˈɔgəˌnaɪz, ˈɔəgəˌnaɪz], *remorse* [rɪˈmɔs, rɪˈmɔəs]. [r] may also be heard in these and all other words containing postvocalic *r*.

> *Transcribe:* seahorse, Orkneys, border, forswear, cork, torque, mortality, or, for.

o plus *re* = [ˈoə] (not [ˈouə]) as in *more* [ˈmoə], *bore* [ˈboə], *sore* [ˈsoə].

> *Transcribe:* shore, store, tore, chore, lore, core, gore, spore, galore, wore.

oa, *oo*, and *ou* plus *r*; also *o* plus *rt* and *rd* = [ˈoə] as in *coarse* [ˈkoəs], *floor*

---

[2] Although duration is not significant in English as a general rule, it is occasionally so in standard Southern. Such pairs as *cart–cot* cannot be transcribed or pronounced [kɑt–kɑt] without ambiguity. It is necessary, therefore, to transcribe and pronounce the pair as [kɑ:t–kɑt]. Obviously, length, here, is significant. Ambiguity between *cart* and *cot* could not arise in General American [kɑrt–kɑt], in Eastern [kat, kɑt–kɒt], nor in British [kɑt–kɒt]; it is a characteristic of Southern only. (See discussion of this function of length, page 162, footnote 25.)

[ˈfloə], *course* [ˈkoəs], *four* [ˈfoə], *fort* [ˈfoət], *ford* [ˈfoəd], *sport* [ˈspoət]. Exception: *forty* [ˈfɔtɪ].

> *Transcribe:* court, boar, door, hoarse, fourth.

u, eu, and *ew* = [ju] after [d], [t], and [n], as in *due* [dju], *tulip* [ˈtjulɪp], *neutral* [ˈnjutrəl], *knew* [nju]. [u] is occasionally heard here.

> *Transcribe:* tupelo, Newfoundland, pneumatic, duplicate, duplicity, tumor, pneumonic, gnu, dewberry.

u = [u] after [l], [θ], [s], and [z], as in *lute* [lut], *enthusiastic* [ɪnˌθuzɪˈæstɪk], *suit* [sut], *resume* [rɪˈzum].

> *Transcribe:* presume, assume, suitable, enthusiasm, suture, lawsuit.

-ar, -er, -ir, -or, -our (Br. and Can.), *-ur(e),* and *-yr* as unstressed suffixes = [ə] as in *tartar* [ˈtɑːtə], *feather* [ˈfɛðə], *elixir* [ɪˈlɪksə], *labor* [ˈleɪbə], *labour* [ˈleɪbə], *murmur* [ˈmɜmə], *nature* [ˈneɪtʃə], *satyr* [ˈseɪtə]. [ɚ] may also be heard in these words.

> *Transcribe:* Ophir, batter, tutor, corridor, pasture, pallor, vapour (Br. and Can.), cheddar, collar, cedar, doctor.

-ile = [l̩] or [əl] in such words as *futile* [ˈfjutl̩] and *reptile* [ˈrɛptəl]. Words like *juvenile* admit also the pronunciation [-aɪl], so that we have [ˈdʒuvənl̩, ˈdʒuvənˌaɪl]. Other words of less frequent usage, such as *quartile* and *sextile,* are uniformly pronounced with [-aɪl].

> *Transcribe:* subtile, profile. (Use list on page 242.)

In the following unstressed suffixes, the vowels nearly always unstress to [ɪ]: *-ace, -ad, -as, -ase, -ate, -ed, -en, -es, -ess, -et, -ice, -id, -in, -ip, -is, -ist, -it, -ite, -op, -uce, -ute.* Thus, *solace* [ˈsɑlɪs], *salad* [ˈsælɪd], *purchase* [ˈpɜtʃɪs], *palate* [ˈpælɪt], *hunted* [ˈhʌntɪd], *boxes* [ˈbɑksɪz], *kitchen* [ˈkɪtʃɪn], *ruthless* [ˈruθlɪs], *locket* [ˈlɑkɪt], *chalice* [ˈtʃælɪs], *palid* [ˈpælɪd], *puffin* [ˈpʌfɪn], *crisis* [ˈkraɪsɪs], *artist* [ˈɑtɪst], *profit* [ˈprɑfɪt], *lettuce* [ˈlɛtɪs], *circus* [ˈsɜkɪs]. [ə] is known in words of this type, but less frequently than [ɪ].

> *Transcribe:* Use list on page 187.

e and *i* and *y* medially usually = [ə] as in *telegram* [ˈtɛləˌgræm], *participate* [pəˈtɪsəˌpeɪt], *analysis* [əˈnæləsɪs]. But before a vowel, *i* = [ɪ] always, as in *associate* [əˈsoʊs(ʃ)ɪˌeɪt], *oriole* [ˈoʊrɪˌoʊl].

> *Transcribe:* permeate, appetite, telegraph, initiate, ominous, paralysis, calibrate, repetition, cultivation, cauliflower, roseate.

Consonants

l usually = clear [l] before stressed front vowels, as in *leader* [ˈlidə], and especially intervocalically with front vowels, as in *filling* [ˈfɪlɪŋ].

Transcribe and pronounce: lean, litter, chilling, filly, saline, least, gleamings, cleaner, freely, spilling.

l = dark [ɫ] before back vowels as in *load* [ɫoud], finally as in *fill* [fɪɫ] and *gold* [gouɫd], and in intermediate positions after stressed back vowels, as in *pulley* [ˈpuɫɪ].

Transcribe: churl, poll, eel, coal, haul, cannibal, thistle, long, lock, holy, valley.

wh = [ʍ] as in *which* [ʍɪtʃ], *wheel* [ʍil], *whittle* [ˈʍɪtɫ]. Some speakers in New Orleans and perhaps other metropolitan areas use [w] as well as [ʍ]. Thus, [wɪtʃ], [wil], and [ˈwɪtɫ]. The expletive *why* is always [waɪ].

Transcribe: witch, whistle, whale, wharf, wheat, while, whelp, where, when, whiff, whet, whip, wheeze, whisper, whortleberry, whorl. Note exceptions *who*, *whole*, and derivatives.

r = [r] intervocalically (a) medially in a word, as in *carry* [ˈkærɪ], *very* [ˈvɛrɪ], and (b) at the end of a word followed by another word beginning with a vowel, as in *there is* [ðɛrˈɪz] and *where are you* [ˌʍɛr ˈɑ ju]. This intervocalic [r] is the so-called linking [r], used in liaison. Only a limited number of very careful speakers use it at the end of a word followed by another word beginning with a vowel. But cultivated speakers use it within a word always.

Transcribe: Larry, Geraldine, more and more, merry, marry, Mary, carry, query, peering, fair and warmer, wear it, as sure as fate, the bar is down, fear of failure.

r is silent finally and preconsonantally after [ɑ], [ɜ], and [ə], as in *car* [kɑ], *harm* [hɑm], *turn* [tɜn], *buttered* [ˈbʌtəd]. When *r* is silent in a stressed syllable, its time value is given to the preceding vowel. However, in this book, no symbol is used for added length, except to prevent ambiguity.

Non-statistical evidence appears to show that in many parts of the South, especially in urban centers, the pronunciation of *r* as [r] in final and preconsonantal positions is increasing.

Syllabication in Southern, Eastern, and British speech. It seems necessary to interpolate here a commentary on syllabication. The pronunciation of final *r* as [ə] in many words in Southern, Eastern, and British speech raises the question of whether an orthographic combination comprising one syllable in General American should be considered two syllables in the other dialects. For example, should *bore* [bour], which is a monosyllable in General American, be considered a dissyllable when pronounced [ˈboə] in Southern? The following analogies may throw light on the matter:

Since *boa* is considered a dissyllable, thus [ˈbo-ə], then *bore*, where pronounced [ˈbo-ə], exactly like the first word, is also a dissyllable.

In the same way, we may examine *koa*. It is a dissyllable, [ˈko-ə]. Therefore *core*, when pronounced [ˈko-ə], is also a dissyllable.

It seems reasonable, consequently, to regard as dissyllables *bore, core* and many analogous words, such as *fire, our, poor, pure, there, fear*, etc., when pronounced in Southern, Eastern, or British.[3]

r = [ə] finally and preconsonantally in unstressed syllables after [ɪ], [ɛ], [æ], [o], [ʊ], [aʊ], [aɪ]. Thus, *here* [ˈhɪə], *beer* [ˈbɪə], *beard* [ˈbɪəd], *where* [ˈʍɛə], *fair* [ˈfæə], *dared* [ˈdæəd], *wear* [ˈwæə], *doors* [ˈdoəz], *four* [ˈfoə], *sure* [ˈʃʊə], *poor* [ˈpʊə], *flour* [ˈflaʊə], *flowers* [ˈflaʊəz], *tired* [ˈtaɪəd], *friar* [ˈfraɪə], *lyre* [ˈlaɪə].

The following diagram summarizes the treatment of final and preconsonantal *r* in Southern American English in unstressed syllables after the various vowels.

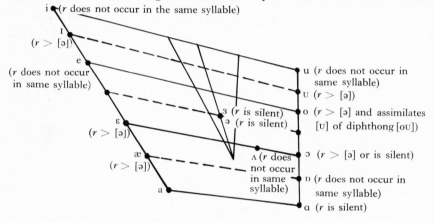

The same information, plus analogous information on *r* after diphthongs, can be stated in tabular form as follows:

r does not occur in the same syllable after	*r* is silent after	*r* = [ə] after
i	ɑ	ɪ
e	ɔ*	ɛ
u	ɜ	æ
ʌ	ə	ɔ
ɔɪ		o
eɪ		ʊ
		aɪ
		aʊ

* But see also next column.

---

[3] This would seem to argue that there is no such thing in English as a diphthong wherein the second element is schwa.

Note that in every case where [i], [e], or [u] historically preceded *r*, Modern English now has [ɪ], [ɛ], and [ʊ], as in *cheer* [ˈtʃɪə], *they're* [ˈðɛə], *poor* [ˈpʊə]. The sounds [i], [e], and [u] were lowered through the influence of *r* (before it was lost) to [ɪ], [ɛ], and [ʊ].

Stress

Polysyllabic words in *-ary*, *-ery*, *-ory*, as well as some other polysyllabic words, have both primary and secondary stress, as in *ordinary* [ˈɔdn̩ˌɛrɪ], *circumstance* [ˈsɜkəmˌstænts], *advertisement* [ˌædvəˈtaɪzmənt].

Transcribe: Use list on page 243.

Special Words

Either and *neither* = [ˈiðə, ˈniðə].
Holiday has secondary stress. Thus [ˈhɑləˌdeɪ]. Likewise *yesterday* [ˈjɛstəˌdeɪ].
But the days of the week are usually *Monday* [ˈmʌndɪ], *Tuesday* [ˈtjuzdɪ], etc.
Again and *against* = [əˈgeɪn, əˈgeɪnst] most often, and [əˈgɛn, əˈgɛnst] less frequently.

Standard Southern Speech

THE MARSHES OF GLYNN

glumz əv ðə laɪv oʊk bjutɪfəl breɪdɪd
    ənd woʊvən
wɪð ɪntrɪkɪt ʃeɪdz əv:aɪnz ðət mɪrɪəd-kloʊvən
    klæmbə ðə fɔks əv ðə mʌltəfɔm baʊz;
    ɛmərəld twaɪlaɪts,
    vɜdʒənəl ʃaɪ laɪts,
rɔt əv ðə livz tu əluə tə ðə
    ʍɪspər əv:aʊz.
ʍɛn lʌvəz peɪs tɪmɪdlɪ daʊn θru
    ðə grin kɑləneɪdz
əʌ ðə dɪm swit wʊdz, əv ðə
    dɪə dɑ:k wʊdz,
əv ðə hɛvənlɪ wʊdz ən gleɪdz
ðət rʌn tə ðə reɪdɪənt mɑdʒənəl
    sændbɪtʃ wɪðɪn
ðə waɪd si mɑʃɪz əv glɪn;
bjutɪfəl glumz, sɔft dʌsks ɪn ðə
    nundeɪ faɪə,
waɪldwʊd praɪvəsɪz, klɑzɪts əv
    loʊn dɪzaɪə,

ʧeɪmbə frəm ʧeɪmbə pɑːtɪd
wɪð weɪvərɪŋ ærɪs əv livz,
sɛlz fə ðə pæʃənɪt plɛʒər əv
præə tə ðə soʊl ðət grivz,
pjuə wɪð ə sɛnts əv ðə pæsɪŋ əv
seɪnts θru ðə wʊd,
kul fə ðə djutɪfəl weɪɪŋ əv ivəl wɪð gʊd;
oʊ breɪdɪd dʌsks əv ðɪ oʊk ənd
woʊvən ʃeɪdz əv ðə vaɪn
ʍaɪl ðə raɪətəs nundeɪ sʌn əv
ðə ʤun deɪ lɔŋ dɪd ʃaɪn
ji hɛld mi fæst ɪn juə hɑːt ənd aɪ
hɛld ju fæst ɪn maɪn.

SIDNEY LANIER

Transcribe: A page of any textbook material.

Deviations from Standard Southern American Speech

NOTE: It will be well for the reader to peruse again the first two paragraphs under the heading "Deviations from Standard General American Speech" (page 189) in order to learn the point of view of what follows here. Study also "Deviations from Standard General American, Southern, and Eastern Speech" (Chapter 7, page 193).

The Southern Drawl

A great many of the substandard pronunciations of Southern speech are related to the southern drawl. Hence it seems reasonable to begin with a discussion of the drawl and to follow with other phenomena which are related to it.

The southern drawl is popularly thought of as consisting of an excessive slowness in speech. This concept is erroneous. Southern speech ordinarily is no slower than General American speech and probably not so slow as rural Eastern speech or dialectal mountain speech. Motion picture directors have often required particularly ridiculous renditions of Southern speech in films by slowing the rate down unreasonably. The actual phenomena which characterize the southern drawl are two in number: (a) intonational characteristics; and (b) diphthongization and other forms of the multiplication of sounds.

As repeatedly stated in this book, intonational characteristics are difficult to represent symbolically, since they consist of pitch changes. In drawling Southern speech, the voice pitch shifts liltingly over a very wide range, producing patterns quite different in character and meaning from the corresponding patterns of General American and Eastern speech. Whatever may develop in the symbolization of intonation, it will probably remain that the best way to learn Southern intonation is to hear it, either in the actual speech of people or in the now easily procurable phonograph records of the speech of this region.

Diphthongization, on the other hand, can be completely represented. It should be recalled here that in nearly all English speech regions, diphthongization is a dominant and conspicuous characteristic. It is very nearly true that there are no pure long vowels in English comparable to those of the Romance languages. Even vowels not commonly represented by diphthongal symbolization have off-glides consisting of other vowels or of other forms of the main vowel itself, with differing degrees of pitch and muscular tension. Thus the vowel [i] as in *seed*, when spoken by nearly any English-speaking person, will seem distinctly diphthongal to speakers of many other languages. This diphthongization is so persistent and aggressive that throughout this book we have transcribed the English rendition corresponding to [e] and [o] as [eɪ] and [oʊ] respectively.

Now the southerner goes further than the speakers of many other regions in the process of diphthongizing and otherwise multiplying sounds. Without retarding his speech to a slowness in excess of other regional speech, he manages within the duration of a given vowel to produce two, three, or four perceptible sounds. Obviously, the changes of pitch contribute to the ease of this process, as will appear below. When the vowels are thus broken into several sounds, it may be observed that [j] develops medially after front vowels, and [w] after back vowels. Theoretically this may happen to any stressed vowel. Actually it happens only to certain ones, most of these being lax vowels. A schema of the possible development follows:

[ɪ]   becomes [ˈɪjə], as in *sit* [ˈsɪjət].

[ɛ]   becomes [ˈɛjə, ˈɛɪjə], as in *less* [ˈlɛjəs, ˈlɛɪjəs]. The [ɛ] may even be raised and diphthongized to [eɪ], so that [ˈleɪjəs] results.

[æ]   becomes [ˈæjə, ˈæɪjə], as in *class* [ˈklæjəs, ˈklæɪjəs].

[ɔ]   becomes [ˈɔwə], as in *cord* [ˈkɔwəd].

[oʊ] becomes [ˈoʊwə], as in *board* [ˈboʊwəd].

[ʊ]   becomes [ˈʊwə], as in *good* [ˈgʊwəd].

[ɜ]   being central, does not develop [j] or [w], but becomes [ɜɪ], as in *burn* [bɜɪn].

Now it cannot be truthfully said that a majority of southerners, even those who use substandard speech, multiply their sounds to the extent indicated above. But a sufficient number do to make people say loosely that the drawl, that is the use of two, three, or four sounds for one, is typical of the South. The truth is that drawling, or any other characteristic called typical, is not something found in the speech of the majority; so-called typical Southern speech is speech *found only in the South*, and it will still be called typical, regardless of whether large numbers use it.

Of a nature related to the phenomena discussed above are the following:

Changing Vowels to Diphthongs

Stressed -*ear*, -*er*, -*ir*, -*our*, -*or*, -*ur*, -*yr*, followed by a consonant, in words normally containing the vowel [ɜ], exhibit the dialectal diphthongizing of [ɜ] to [ɜɪ]. Thus *heard* [hɜd] > [hɜɪd], *herd* [hɜd] > [hɜɪd], *bird* [bɜd] > [bɜɪd], *worth* [wɜθ] > [wɜɪθ], *journal* [ˈʤɜnəl] > [ˈʤɜɪnəl], *hurt* [hɜt] > [hɜɪt], *myrtle* [ˈmɜtl̩] > [ˈmɜɪtl̩].

Words of the class just discussed are occasionally, though rarely, pronounced with [ɔɪ] in New Orleans and perhaps other cities. Thus, *Herman* [ˈhɜmən] > [ˈhɔɪmən], *turn* [tɜn] > [tɔɪn].

Transcribe: Use list on page 185.

[æ] > [æɪ] in many words, especially where [d], [t], [n] or [ʃ] follows the vowel, any of these alveolar or palatal consonants tending to induce the tongue to rise through the [ɪ]-position on the way to the consonant position. Thus *mad* [mæd] > [mæɪd], *dance* [dænts] > [dæɪnts], *man* [mæn] > [mæɪn], *crash* [kræʃ] > [kræɪʃ]. This [æ] may develop further to [æjə] or [æɪjə], as indicated in the discussion on page 213.

Transcribe: last, asters, splash, bandanna, canna, cadmium, adulate, scatter, flash, mash, fan, stands, dash, handle, candle.

[ɛ] > [eɪ] before [d], and sometimes [s] as in *head* [hɛd] > [heɪd], *yes* [jɛs] > [jeɪs]. Here [ɛ] deviates from its normal tendency to migrate to the nearest lax vowel, as in *ten* [tɛn] > [tɪn], and goes to the nearest tense vowel above, [e(ɪ)]. It may be speculated that the tension of [d] and [s] may have something to do with this shift. This [ɛ] may develop further to [ɛjə] or [ɛɪjə], as indicated in the discussion on page 213. It may also develop into [ejə] or [eɪjə].

Transcribe: headship, red, bed, yes, led, fed, dread, bread, shed, mess, dress.

[æ] > [eɪ] in *can't*, which is pronounced [keɪnt].

Transcribe and pronounce: Can't you see? No, I can't. I can't hear, either.

[ɔ] > [ɔo] or [ɔʊ]. Thus *walk* [wɔk] > [wɔok], *hawk* [hɔk] > [hɔok], *log* [lɔg] > [lɔog], *coffee* [ˈkɔfɪ] > [ˈkɔofɪ]. Sometimes we have even [ɔ] > [aʊ], as in *walk* [wɔk] > [waʊk], *talk* [tɔk] > [taʊk].

Transcribe and pronounce: fall, all, ball, cauldron, cough, offset, strongly, furlong, squawk, chalk, awkward, moth-eaten, squall, mawkish, allspice, Walter, vault, talkative.

[ɔ] > [oʊ] in a limited number of words, notably *on* [ɔn] > [oʊn], *want* [wɔnt] > [woʊnt], *gone* [gɔn] > [goʊn]. This diphthong may possibly be explained as having followed the sequence [ɔ > ɔo > o > oʊ], where [ɔ] is lost, whereupon [o] develops its own customary off-glide, [ʊ]. Another possible explanation would, as in British English, follow the sequence [ɔ > ɔ˖ > o˕ > o > ou], where [ɔ] is raised to [o], after which it develops the off-glide [ʊ].

Transcribe and pronounce: upon, whereupon, thereupon, onset, fore-gone, all gone, begone, wanted, wants, wanting.

Intrusive [j] and [ɪ]

[j] intrudes between [k] or [g]. Thus *car* [kɑ] > [kjɑ], *guard* [gɑ:d] > [gjɑ:d]. It is evident that the [g] and [k] here are the front members of their phonemes, even before back vowels. The insertion of [j] before back vowels is a custom particularly noticeable in Virginia.

Transcribe: cart, garner, garter, Carter of Cartersville, garment.

oo [u] > [ɪu] after [t], [d], and [n]. Thus *too* [tu] > [tɪu], *do* [du] > [dɪu], [nun] > [nɪun]. This is obviously analogous to the pronunciation of *u* after [d], [t], and [n], and is promoted by the same linguistic influence that causes this *u* to be pronounced [ju].

Transcribe and pronounce: ado, noonday, doomsday, noodle, tool-chest, toot, doom.

Changing Diphthongs to Pure Vowels

It is frequently noticeable in the study of sound-change that a tendency in any direction is likely to be balanced by a compensatory opposite tendency. Thus the diphthongizing just noted has its counterpart in the reduction of diphthongs to pure, i.e., single, vowels.

[aɪ] > [a] or, much more rarely, > [ɑ], as in *I* [aɪ] > [a], *my* [maɪ] > [ma], *high* [haɪ] > [ha]. This change occurs oftenest before voiced consonants and finally, but may occur before voiceless consonants.[4]

When speakers say [ɑ] for [aɪ], they most frequently do so in the pronouns *I* and *my*, which become [ɑ] and [mɑ]; however, *blind* has been heard as *blond* [blɑnd]. Both [a] and [ɑ] as renderings of [aɪ] are spelled *ah* by dialect writers.

Transcribe and pronounce: kindly, wise, winding, wild, sine, biennial, Bible, child, China, fine, file, guise, guile, guide, hide, height, giant, gyroscope, live (adj), align, mine, thine, whine, wine.

[aɪ] > [ɑ] before [r], as in [tɑ] for *tire* [ˈtaɪə].

Transcribe: wire, hired, tired, iron, fire, wired, hire, squire, spire.

[eɪ] > [ɛ] in a few words, as in [mɛk] for *make* [meɪk].

Transcribe: snake, naked, afraid, take.

---

[4] C. M. Wise, W. Scott Nobles, and Herbert Metz, "The Southern American Diphthong [aɪ]," *The Southern Speech Journal*, Vol. 19, No. 4 (May, 1954), pp. 304–312.

[ɔɪ] > [ɔ] before *l*, as in *oil* [ɔɪl] > [ɔl], *spoil* [spɔɪl] > [spɔl]. This is a more general tendency than the one explained immediately below.

Transcribe and pronounce: boil, coil, foil, roil, recoil, soil, toil.

[ɔɪ] > [ɝ] before consonant, as *spoil* [spɔɪl] > [spɝl]. This change is found on rare occasions in New Orleans and, still less often, in other cities.

Transcribe and pronounce: oyster, Boylston, hoist, parboil, purloin, anoint, appoint, goiter, moisture, Croyden, quoin, pointed, choice, joist, rejoice, hoist.

[oə] > [o], as in *door* [ˈdoə] > [do], *floor* [ˈfloə] > [flo]. Variations of this change are *your* [ˈjuə] > [jo], *poor* [ˈpuə] > [po].

Transcribe and pronounce: doorway, poorhouse, yourselves, four-by-fours four-teen feet long, store, more, pour, pore, core, sure.

Centralizing

[aɪ] > [ɜɪ] before voiceless consonants in tidewater Virginia and sometimes elsewhere on the South's Atlantic coast, as in [mɜɪt][5] for *might* [maɪt].

Transcribe: white, wife, ice, mice, nice, tight, sight, site, cite, plight, bite, fight, wipe, like.

Lowering

[ɛ] > [æ] in the two words [ˈʌæə] and [ˈðæə] for *where* [ˈʌɛə] and *there* [ˈðɛə].

Raising of Vowels

In substandard Southern speech, certain vowels and the initial elements of certain diphthongs are habitually raised, notably [æ] and the [a] of [aʊ]. Thus *sat* [sæt] > [sæᵗt], which is very close to [sɛt]. This shift comes about through keeping the tongue in bilateral contact with the upper molars during the phonation of [æ], whereas the tongue should break all upper dental contact and lie on the floor of the mouth. The same thing happens in the diphthong [aʊ], which becomes successively [æʊ] and [æᵗʊ].

This raising is accompanied by excessive diphthongizing (see page 213), by the instrusion of [j] after [k] and [g] (see page 215), and by nasality. Sometimes it affects not merely [æ] and [aʊ], but most of the whole vowel system. It is another of the characteristics of substandard Southern speech which people call, with negative implication, typical.

a before *r* > [ɔ] in monosyllables and stressed syllables, final or pre-consonantal, but not preceded by [w]. Thus *yard* [jɑd] > [jɔd]. Homo-nyms are produced by this process: e.g., *hark* [hɔk]–*hawk* [hɔk], *stark* [stɔk]–

---

[5] E. W. Shewmake, "Laws of Pronunciation in Virginia," *Modern Language Notes,* December, 1925, pp. 489–492. Also in *English Pronunciation in Virginia* (Davidson, N. C.: Davidson, 1927), pp. 23–24.

stalk [stɔk], *ardor* [ˈɔdə]–*order* [ˈɔdə], *far* [fɔ]–*for* [fɔ], *jar* [ʤɔ] – *jaw* [ʤɔ], *are* [ɔ] – *or* [ˈɔə]. But in at least some of these words, the tendency toward homonymity is checked by the change from [ɔ] to [ɔo, ɔʊ] in the second word of the pair, so that *hark – hawk*, for instance, becomes not [hɔk–hɔk], but [hɔk–hɔok, hɔʊk].

> Transcribe and pronounce: car–caw, dawn–darn, par–paw, tar–taw, Arthur–
> author, bark–balk, marl–maul, mar–maw, art–ought, stark–stalk, farmer–
> former, tart–tort, farm–form, card–cord, lard–Lord, Carl–call, card–cawed,
> hearty–haughty, cart–caught, yarn–yawn.

[ɛ] > [ɪ] before [n], and sometimes before [m] and [ŋ], as in *benefit* [ˈbɛnəfɪt] > [ˈbɪnəfɪt], *hen* [hɛn] > [hɪn], *lemon* [ˈlɛmən] > [ˈlɪmən], *when* [ʍɛn] > [ʍɪn], *contempt* [kənˈtɛmpt] > [kənˈtɪmpt], *strength* [strɛŋkθ] > [strɪŋkθ], *against* [əˈgɛnst] > [əˈgɪnst], *length* [lɛŋkθ] > [lɪŋkθ], *bench* [bɛntʃ] > [bɪntʃ]—but see *strength* [strɛnθ], *length* [lɛnθ], page 202.

> Transcribe: send–sinned, pen–pin, tender–tinder, hem–him, tent–tint,
> gem–Jim, meant–mint, Ben–bin, cents–since, tense–tints, ten–tin, friend, con-
> demned, again, end, splendid, apprehend, spent, fence, contend, comprehen-
> sion, attend, extend, adventure, mend, plenty, enemy, twenty, anything, sens-
> ible, rent, went, general, anyone, amend, drenched, invention, appendix, at-
> tempt, trenches, envious, torments, anybody, any, many.

See again [ɔ] > [oʊ], [æ] > [eɪ], etc., in discussion of diphthongizing.

It has been noted (page 215) that a shift in one direction may be balanced by a shift in the opposite direction.[6] The shift of [ɛ] to [ɪ] just noted, of which *men* [mɛn] > [mɪn] is typical, is balanced by a shift of [ɪ] to [ɛ], of which *interest* [ˈɪntərɪst] > [ˈɛntərɪst] is typical. The words following often illustrate the latter shift.

> Transcribe and pronounce: Minden, since, simple, thing, import, been, fin,
> in, mint, sing, tin, limb, whim, sinful, Timothy, finical, trim, nimble, bring,
> jingle, tingle.

Nasality

It will be well here to reread the material on nasality in the section on General American speech. In Southern speech, as noted above, nasality is particularly likely to occur with [æ] and the substandard form of [aʊ], which is [æʊ]. Nasality easily combines with the raising of the tongue, with excessive diphthongizing, and with the intrusion of [j] after [k] and [g]. Collecting all these features into two words, we have *cat* [kæt] > [ˈkjæ̃ˈɪ̃jət], *cow* [kaʊ] > [kjæ̃ˈũ]. Nasality is, of course, even more conspicuous in words where the stressed vowel is followed by a nasal, as in *county* [ˈkaʊntɪ] > [ˈkjæ̃ũntɪ].

---

6 C. M. Wise, "Militarism and Pacificism Among Phonemes," in *Proceedings of the Third International Congress on Phonetic Sciences*, Ghent, 1938.

Dissimilation

Dissimilation, as indicated on page 157, is the loss or replacement of one of two (a) duplicate sounds or (b) duplicate syllables (haplology) within a word. Examples: Dissimilation of [ɪs]—*Mississippi* [ˌmɪsɪˈsɪpɪ] > [ˌmɪsˈsɪpɪ]. (Note the compensatory lengthening of [s] in [ˌmɪsˈsɪpɪ].)

Note that the term "haplology" may apply to the foregoing change in *Mississippi*, since there is dissimilation of a reduplicative syllable.

Dissimilation of [n]—*government* [ˈgʌvənmənt] > [ˈgʌvəmənt].
Dissimilation of [d]—*candidate* [ˈkændəˌdeɪt] > [ˈkænəˌdeɪt].
Dissimilation of [r]—*library* [ˈlaɪˌbrɛrɪ] > [ˈlaɪˌbɛrɪ].
Dissimilation of one of two velars—*recognize* [ˈrɛkəgˌnaɪz] [ˈrɛkəˌnaɪz].

Loss of Consonants

[l] from words spelled with with *el*, *il* plus consonant, and vowel plus medial [l], as in *self* [sɛlf] > [sɛf], *help* [hɛlp] > [hɛp], *twelve* [twɛlv] > [twɛv], *film* [fɪlm] > [fɪm], *college* [ˈkɑlɪʤ] > [ˈkɑɪʤ].

Transcribe and pronounce: myself, yourself, yourselves, ourselves, himself, herself, themselves, itself, shelf, twelves, whelp, yelp, gulf, million, William, helm, helpful, helpless, self-help.

[t] from words in final [ft], [st], [kt], [pt], as in *left* [lɛft] > [lɛf], *first* [fɜst] > [fɜɪs] (note diphthongization, also), *last* [læst] > [læs] or [ˈlæɪjəs], *next* [nɛkst] > [nɛks].

Transcribe and pronounce: priest, least, worst, cost, most, chest, stuffed, boost, fist, missed, roost, post, baked, lift, swift, draft, rift, loosed, feast, faced, traced, east, west, must, coast, toast, paste, hoped, capped, lapped.

[d] from [ld], [nd], as in *cold* [koʊld] > [koʊl], *find* [faɪnd] > [fan].

Transcribe and pronounce: hold, old, sold, mould, wild, sealed, failed, wold, held, swelled, felled, fold, bold, scold, told, gold, behind, kind, blind.

Linking [r] is dropped (a) medially as in *very* [ˈvɛrɪ] > [ˈvɛɪ], *carry* [ˈkærɪ] > [ˈkæɪ], etc.; (b) at the end of a word followed without pause by another word beginning with a vowel, as in *far away* [fɑr əˈweɪ] > [fɑ əˈweɪ], *our own* [aʊr ˈoʊn] > [aʊ ˈoʊn] or [aˈoʊn]. (Note that the glottal stop may develop in either of these instances, and a medial glide [w] in the second instance.)

Transcribe and pronounce: over and over, her own, marry, marriage, ferry, wherein, whereon, thereon, whereof, thereof, forever, her enemies, sore eyes, poor Ann, bear it, fear it, there are a few, share a little, peer around.

Intrusive [r]

Instrusive linking [r] occurs, as in *Chinar and Japan* [ˈtʃaɪnər ən dʒəˈpæn] for *China and Japan* [ˈtʃaɪnə ən dʒəˈpæn]. (See discussion, page 233.)

Transcribe: Martha and I, Louisiana[7] and Alabama, Alabama and Georgia, Georgia and Florida, Florida and North Carolina, soda and salt, sofa and chair, the idea of democracy, Hannah is here.

Substitutions

[t] for [θ], as in *thing* [θɪŋ] > [tɪŋ], *with* [wɪθ] > [wɪt]. In the final position, *th* is often [f], as in *both* [boʊθ] > [boʊf].

Transcribe and pronounce: nothing, Ethel, truth, fifth, sixth, fourth.

[d] for [ð], as in *this* [ðɪs] > [dɪs], *that* [ðæt] > [dæt], *the* [ðə] > [də], *with* [wɪð] > [wɪd], and other short, frequently used words. Both [ð] and [θ] are pronounced freely in longer, less common words.

Transcribe and pronounce: they, them, these, those, themselves, the, there, father, mother, brother, farther, further, either, neither.

[l] > [ə], [ʊ], [o] in context vowel plus *l* plus zero or plosive consonant, as in [ˈmɪək, ˈmɪʊk, ˈmɪok] for *milk* [mɪlk].

Transcribe: felt, melt, silk, silt, built, build, fill, kill, mill, bill, hill, will, chill, Jill, gill, pill.

Displaced Stress

Retracted stress: In a dissyllable normally stressed on the second syllable, the stress goes back to the first syllable, with accompanying restressing, as in *police* [pəˈlis] > [ˈpoʊˌlis], *Monroe* [mənˈroʊ] > [ˈmʌnro], *pecan* [pɪˈkɑn] or [pəˈkɑn] >[ˈpʌkˌɔn], *event* [ɪˈvɛnt] > [ˈiˌvɛnt]. Sometimes the stress in trisyllables becomes recessive in the same way, as in *insurance* [ɪnˈʃʊrənts] > [ˈɪnˌʃʊrənts], *afternoon* [ˌæftəˈnun] > [ˈæftəˌnun].

Transcribe and pronounce: replace, erect, return, cigar, cigarette, report, inspire, reflect, relate, select, escape, express, reply, review.

Advanced stress: In apparent compensation for retraction of stress in some words, certain other words show advancing of stress. Examples: *locate* [ˈloʊˌkeɪt] > [loˈkeɪt].

Transcribe and pronounce: rotate, gyrate.

---

[7] Not [lə ˈwizɪ ˌænə], since *Louisiana* is derived from *Louis*, not *Louise*.
The intrusive link may become permanently attached to a word, as *Ellar* for *Ella*, *Melbar* for *Melba*, *Alabamar* for *Alabama*, *Selmar* for *Selma*.

Miscellaneous Substandard Pronunciations

[ˈtʃuən, tʃɜn] for *children* [ˈtʃɪldrən]

[rɑp] for *wrap* [ræp]

[dræp] for *drop* [drɑp]

[ʍup, ʍʌp, ʍup] for *whip* [ʍɪp]

[ˈnɪgrə, ˈnɪgə] for *Negro* [ˈniˌgrou]

[gwaɪn] for *going* [ˈgouɪŋ]

[ˈhaŋgrɪ, ˈhɔŋgrɪ] for *hungry* [ˈhʌŋgrɪ]

[hɪt] for *it*.

Substandard Southern Speech

From *First Person, Singular* *
I Cant Make Up My Mind
(Note unique stress patterns.)

ˈou ˈju ˈsleɪ ˈmi. ˈæbˈsouˈlutlɪ ˈsleɪ mɪ. ˈdɪə ˈou ˈdɪə. al ˈda ˈˈlæɪjəfɪn. ˈpazəˈtɪvlɪ ... ˈnat ˈsɪnts a wəz ˈboon, hæˑv a ˈsin ˈɪnɪθɛŋ ˈwʌn ˈhæɪjəf ˈsou ˈhɛvənlɪ ... ɔ wʌn ˈkwɔːːodə ... av bɛn ˈoun ma ˈfit sɪnts ˈdɔowən ... ˈɛvə sɪnts ˈnan ə ˈtɪn ðɪs ˈmɔonɪn.

ˈsʌmˈtamz a ˈˈlæɪjəf ən ˈˈlæɪjəf ... a ˈdʒɪs ˈkeɪnt ˈstap ˈˈlæɪjəfɪn; æn ˈsʌmˈtamz a ˈdæɪnts ən ˈdæɪnts. ˈou jə ˈθɛŋk a ˈdu? ˈwɛl ˈðæɪjəts ˈæbˈsouˈlutlɪ əˈdoəbəl ʌv jə tə ˈseɪ ˈðæɪjət, bɪˈkɔoz əv ˈkous a nou ˈɔl əˈbæut ˈdæɪntsɪn. ˈsʌmˈtamz a θɛŋk al ˈdu ˈðæɪjət ɪnˈstɪd əv ˈgou tə ˈka-ɪdʒ. əv ˈkous a ˈnou ɪts ˈfraɪtfəlɪ ˈdɪfə-kʌlt tə gɪt ˈstɔdɪd, bət ma ˈdrɛsmeɪkə ... ˈɪnɪweɪ, ʃi ˈhæˑz ə ˈsɪstə hu ˈnouz ə ˈgɜɪl huz ɪn ə ˈnjuˈjok ˈrivju ... a ˈdount ˈdʒɪs rɪˈmɪmbə hə ˈneɪm, bət a ˈnou ʃi ˈkeɪnt ˈjivən ˈsɪŋ, ˈnou, nə ˈdæɪnts ˈɪðə. ʃiz ˈgat ə ˈbæɪk, ən ˈleɪgz, əv ˈkous.

ˈou ɪz ˈðæt jou ˈkɔ ˈæut ˈðæə? ˈnat ðə ˈroudstə wɪðːə ˈtɜɪn ˈdæun ˈtap ən ˈwa ˈʍilz. ɪt ˈɪjəz? ˈou ˈɪzn̩t ɪt ˈsʌmplɪ ˈgɔodʒəs? wud a ˈˈlaɪktə ˈrad ɪn ɪt? ˈwa, ˈaːd ˈˈlʌəv ɪt.

Florence Ryerson

CHAPTER 9

Eastern American English

Standard and Substandard

The older a speech area is, the harder it is to discover any single system of pronunciation in it. Thus England has any number of traditional systems of pronunciation, each one of honorable history in its own county. Only the political, commercial, literary, and social power of a London could have caused southern British speech to be preferred over all the rest, and even then the score or so of other dialects persisted among the folk, so that educated country dwellers were forced to become essentially bilingual.

The General American area, at the other extreme, is nearly homogeneous for the precise reason of its youth and its lack of local traditions. Without the retarding influence of precedents for pronunciation, it is a fairly easy task for teachers, textbooks, and dictionaries to keep pronunciation relatively standardized.

Next to the General American area, the South is the least hampered by tradition, but, as we have seen, there are old cultural areas like Virginia and the Carolinas where local traditions have to be considered in determining what is the Southern pronunciation. The Virginia [ə'baʊt] is spoken by so many people of education, and is withal so musical to the ears of those who have been conditioned to the sound [ɜʊ] as a common substitute for [aʊ], that we are constrained to say merely that it is one of the correct ways of pronouncing *about* in the South.

Now New England is much like England herself in that her localities have become crystalized and dignified by age and tradition. But Boston and her environs, including Cambridge and Concord with all their history of literary culture, hardly constitute a dominant linguistic center in New England. It is very hard, therefore, to select from among the many pronunciations in honorable service in New England one set that shall be said to be *the* Eastern pronunciation. Very often we shall have to admit coordinate pronunciations. And certain of the pronunciations called dialectal will undoubtedly be used by some who will stoutly deny that they are dialectal. The data following comprise a synthesis of pronunciation found in various parts of New England and the area to the westward subject to New England influences, viz., New York state, northern Penn-

221

sylvania and northern New Jersey. They will inevitably seem generalized and arbitrary. Those applying to extreme Eastern standard speech are selected more from eastern New England than from farther west and more from the cities than from the countryside. Every such item has been checked against the *Linguistic Atlas of New England*.[1]

Standard Eastern Speech

Vowels and Diphthongs

a = [æ], [a], or [ɑ] in many words before [f] ([v] in plurals), [s], [θ] ([ð] in plurals), and [n] plus a consonant. Thus, e.g., *calf* [kæf, kaf, kɑf], *class* [klæs, klas, klɑs], *bath* [bæθ, baθ, bɑθ], *rather* [ˈræðə, ˈraðə, ˈrɑðə], *chance* [tʃænts, tʃants, tʃɑnts]. This is the much discussed "broad *a*." In this book, the term "broad *a*" is applied only to the sound [ɑ] as a pronunciation of the spellings just indicated. That is to say, the [ɑ] in words like *father* [ˈfɑðə] and *far* [fɑ]—the vowels of which are pronounced nearly identically in all standard dialects—is not thought of as a "broad *a*"; but the [ɑ] in *ask* [ɑsk], which is used only in occasional Eastern speech and in southern British, and which contrasts sharply with the [æ] of *ask* [æsk] in General American and Southern speech, comes properly under the name "broad *a*."

It will be noted that the sounds succeeding [ɑ] in the list at the beginning of the preceding paragraph are all expressed with phonetic symbols. The spellings vary. For example, [f] is spelled with *f* in *after* [ˈɑftə], but with *gh* in *laugh* [lɑf]; [s] is spelled with *s* when followed by a consonant in *blast* [blɑst] and *castle* [ˈkɑsl̩], but with *ss* when final in a syllable, as in *glass* [glɑs] and *brass* [brɑs]. Practically every spelling which yields the "broad *a*" includes exceptions. That is, many words spelled in ways parallel to the "broad *a*" words are pronounced with [æ]. For example, *mass* is pronounced [mæs], despite its orthographic parallelism with *pass* [pɑs]; *cant* is [kænt], despite its close orthographic resemblance to *can't* [kɑnt]. Words in *-and* present special complication. Although it is said that *a* followed by *n* plus a consonant is pronounced [ɑ], as in *plant* [plɑnt], it is evident that most *-and* words constitute exceptions, since *and, hand, stand*, etc., are all pronounced with [æ]. Immediately an exception to the exception presents itself in the form of the considerable list of words derived from the Latin root, *mandare*. Thus we have *command* [kəˈmɑnd], *demand* [dɪˈmɑnd], *reprimand* [ˈrɛprɪˌmɑnd], *countermand* [ˌkaʊntəˈmɑnd], etc. Then, as an exception to the exception to the exception, the word *mandate* is pronounced with [æ]. *Fancy*, often pronounced [ˈfɑnsɪ] as a joke, is regularly pronounced [ˈfænsɪ].

---

[1] Hans Kurath, *The Linguistic Atlas of New England* (Providence: Brown University Press, 1939). Referred to hereafter as *Atlas*.

There seem to be no exceptions to words in -*alf* and -*augh*, as in *half* [hɑf] and *draught* [drɑft]. When [f] changes to [v] in plurals and derivatives, as in *halves* [hɑvz] and *halving* [ˈhɑvɪŋ], the vowel sound remains the same. The same is true when [θ] changes to [ð] in plurals, as in *bath* [bɑθ] > [bɑðz]. *Rather* is [ˈrɑðə] also. Some "broad *a*" words do not fit into the orthographic classification listed above; e. g., *aunt* [ɑnt], *rather* [ˈrɑðə], *example* [ɪɡˈzɑmpl̩].

Actually, only a minority of speakers in the East use the "broad *a*." The great majority in rural communities, particularly toward the west and northwest, use [æ] in all these combinations, just as in the General American area and in the South. Between these two extremes, the "compromise" vowel [a] is flourishing, giving *grass* [gras], *calf* [kaf], etc. It is a situation where, on the evidence of counting educated speakers, we should have to say that *a* in *can't* is pronounced in three standard ways: [ɑ], [a], and [æ]. Despite the practice of the majority who use [æ] and the many who use [a], the pressure of Cambridge and Back Bay, of the stage, and of the admiration for England is strong enough to induce a few urban and coastal people in the East to affirm that the type vowel in this context is [ɑ].

"The 'broad *a*' appears with some regularity around Boston (within thirty-five miles of the city) and again in Maine from Portland eastward. Elsewhere its occurrence is haphazard, sometimes as a survival, sometimes as a recent fashionable pronunciation. In western New England it is exceedingly rare."[2]

The use of [a] in the "broad *a*" words in New England is spread widely over eastern and central New England, sporadically elsewhere. In west central and western communities [æ] prevails, and even in eastern New England it is to be found plentifully.

In New York City the "broad *a*" is used by only a minority, few of whom come by it through family use; those who do use it have usually acquired it for pedantic or stage or fashionable purposes. In its place [æ] is used mainly, [a] somewhat.

Transcribe and pronounce according to your own dialect, or in pursuance of your current purpose, with [ɑ, a, æ][3]: aft, after, alas, ask, asp, aghast, alabaster, advance, aunt, aspen, advantage, behalf, bath, baths, bass, brass, blaspheme, bask, basket, blast, blanch, Blanche, branch, calf, calves, chaff, craft, class, crass, cask, casket, cast, caste, contrast, castle, castor, command, chance, can't, chant, daft, draft, draught, disaster, dance, enhance, enchant, example, fast, flask, France, Francis, Frances, photograph, grasp, graft, glass, grass, gasp, grasp, ghastly, glance, grant, half, halve, hasp, halves, haft, hasp, laugh, laughter,

[2] Hans Kurath, *Handbook of the Linguistic Geography of New England* (Providence: Brown University Press, 1939), Chart 15, p. 34. Note: Hereafter this book will be referred to as *Handbook*.
[3] For authoritative reference on "broad *a*" words, refer to Daniel Jones, *An English Pronouncing Dictionary* (New York: E. P. Dutton and Co., Inc., 1947). Ordinary dictionaries are of little value in identifying these words.

last, lass, lance, lancer, lath, laths, mask, mast, master, mastiff, nasty, past, path, paths, passage, passenger, pastime, pastor, pasture, plant, plaster, prance, raft, rafter, rasp, repast, remand, reprimand, shaft, shan't, slant, stanch, telegraph, task, transfer, vast, waft.

a = [a] or [ɑ] in stressed *ar* final or plus a consonant but not preceded by the sound of [w], as in *charge* [tʃadʒ, tʃadʒ]. *ar* pronounced [a] runs to the west and through the Mohawk Valley and Erie canal route at least as far as the south shore of Lake Erie in the Western Reserve of northeastern Ohio. Throughout New England the use of [a] in this category is very frequent. Incidentally, New England furnishes the only instances of the use of [a] in isolation (i. e., not in a diphthong) in a standard American English dialect.

Transcribe: Harvard, farthest, barn,[4] barbed wire,[5] car,[6] cartridge,[7] far,[8] far off,[9] garbage,[10] guardian,[11] harmonics,[12] harness,[13] hearth,[14] largest,[15] marsh,[16] park.

a = [ɔ], [ɒ] and [ɑ] in *wash* and *watch*[17]: [wɒʃ, wɒtʃ] mainly along the Atlantic coast, and [waʃ, watʃ] mainly west of the Connecticut River. In upstate New York evidence shows *swath* [swɑθ], *swallows* ['swɑloz], *swans* [swɑnz], *wander* ['wɑndɚ], *want* [wɑnt] (a New England trace which fades out farther west). *Wash* [waʃ], *wasp* [wasp], and *squalid* ['skwɑlɪd] lead over pronunciations with [ɔ]. But ['wɔtɚ] leads over ['watɚ] in upstate New York.[18]

a = [ɒ] and [ɑ] in *was*[19] [wɒz, waz], *what*[20] [ʌɒt, ʌat], [wɒt, wat].

a = [ɑ], [a] before *lm* as in *calm* [kɑm, kam], *psalm* [sɑm, sam], *balm* [bɑm, bam].

Transcribe: balmy, palm, psalmist, psalmody, calmly, Palmer.

a = [ɑ], [ɔ], [ɒ] in words containing [w] plus *a* plus [r] plus a vowel as in *quarry* ['kwɑrɪ, 'kwɔrɪ, 'kwɒrɪ], *warrant* ['warənt, 'wɔrənt, 'wɒrənt]. The preferred form is [ɑ]. Statistics show it to be used 40 per cent of the time in New England as a whole. In eastern and central New England, [ɑ] predominates; in western New England, [ɔ].[21]

Transcribe: Use list on page 206.

---

[4] *Atlas*, 1, p. 101.
[5] *Atlas*, 1, p. 116.
[6] *Atlas*, 1, p. 184.
[7] *Atlas*, 1, p. 167.
[8] *Atlas*, 1, p. 47.
[9] *Atlas*, 1, p. 48.
[10] *Atlas*, 1, p. 135.

[11] *Atlas*, 2, p. 391.
[12] *Atlas*, 1, p. 176.
[13] *Atlas*, 2, p. 329.
[14] *Atlas*, 2, p. 27.
[15] *Atlas*, 1, p. 31.
[16] *Atlas*, 3, p. 546.

[17] John Samuel Kenyon and Thomas Knott, *A Pronouncing Dictionary of American English* (Springfield, Mass.: G. and C. Merriam Co., 1944), p. 470.

[18] C. K. Thomas, "Pronunciation in Upstate New York," I, *American Speech*, April, 1935; and II, *American Speech*, October, 1935.

[19] *Atlas*, 3, p. 604.

[20] *Atlas*, 2, p. 329.

[21] C. K. Thomas, 1944, "The Dialectical Significance of the Non-Phonemic Low-Back Vowel Variants Before R," *Studies in Speech and Drama in Honor of Alexander M. Drummond* (Ithaca, N. Y.: Cornell University Press, 1944), p. 249.

a = [ɔ] without exception in stressed syllables beginning with [w] or [kw] plus *a* plus final *r*, or *r* followed by consonant, as in *war* [wɔ], *quarter* [ˈkwɔtə], *warmth* [wɔmpθ]. This is standard in all the regional dialects of America. It differs, however, from some dialectal pronunciations, such as Irish. *au*, particularly in *-aun* = [ɑ] or [ɔ] in most words like *daunt* [dɑnt] or [dɔnt], *gaunt* [gɑnt, gɔnt] *launch* [lɑntʃ, lɔntʃ]. *Laundry* is pronounced [ˈlɔndrɪ, ˈlɑndrɪ]. But *aunt* remains separate from other words in *-aun*, since it is never pronounced with [ɔ]. It may be considered a member of the "broad *a*" category, being pronounced [ɑnt] as well as [ant] and [ænt]. It is pronounced with [ɑ] by people who rarely go beyond [a] with other "broad *a*" words.

[æ] and [ε], with [æ] predominating, occur in a considerable list of words spelled with *-air, -are, -arr, -ear*, as in *chair*[22] [ˈtʃæə, ˈtʃεə], *care*[23] [ˈkæə, ˈkεə], *marry*[24] [ˈmærɪ, ˈmεrɪ]. [ε] is also heard in upstate New York, and in those areas generally whose settlers came from New England.

Transcribe: harrow,[25] wheelbarrow,[26] parents,[27] bear, bare, square,[28] fair, fare, parry, pare, pear, pair, fairy, carry, lare, flare, mare, lair, hair, hare, dare, glare, rare, tare, tear, wear.

o = [ou] when stressed, as in *open* [ˈoupən]. On rare occasions, usually as an acquired form derived from the British, it is pronounced [ɜu], as in *smoke* [smɜuk].

Transcribe: bone, Constantinople, Oberlin, boracic, almost, cone, cove, cobra, zone, coal, adobe, abode, scroll, foal, broken, Moses, sober, soapstone.

o before *r* plus a vowel in such stressed syllables as the following = [ɑ], [ɔ], or [ɒ] as in *Florida*[29] [ˈflɑrɪdə], [ˈflɔrɪdə], [ˈflɒrɪdə]; *forest* [ˈfɑrɪst], [ˈfɔrɪst], [ˈfɒrɪst]; *horrid* [ˈhɑrɪd], [ˈhɔrɪd], [ˈhɒrɪd]; *orange*[30] [ˈɑrɪndʒ], [ˈɔrɪndʒ], [ˈɒrɪndʒ]; *quarry* [ˈkwɑrɪ], [ˈkwɔrɪ], [ˈkwɒrɪ]; *torrent* [ˈtɑrənt], [ˈtɔrənt], [ˈtɒrənt]. In eastern and central New England, [ɑ] predominates; in western New England, [ɔ, ɒ].[31]

Transcribe: sorry, horrid, horrible, foreign, authority, corridor, tomorrow[32] ([ɑ] only occasionally), torrential.

o in *-og* = [ɑ], [ɒ], [ɔ], as in *fog* [fɑg], [fɒg], [fɔg]; *grog* [grɑg], [grɒg], [grɔg]; *log* [lɑg], [lɒg], [lɔg]; but *dog* is [dɔg], [dɒg], and only very seldom [dɑg]. The general preference is for [ɑ], except in *dog*,[33] [ɑ] being found predominantly in southern, western, and central New England.

---

[22] *Atlas*, 2, p. 27.
[23] *Atlas*, 2, p. 396.
[24] *Atlas*, 2, p. 408.
[25] *Atlas*, 1, p. 167.
[26] *Atlas*, 1, p. 163.
[27] *Atlas*, 2, p. 373.
[28] *Atlas*, ɜ, p. 546.
[29] *Atlas*, 1, p. 15.
[30] *Atlas*, 1, p. 273.
[31] Thomas, "Dialectal Significance," *loc. cit.*, pp. 244–254.
[32] *Atlas*, 1, p. 72.
[33] *Atlas*, 1, p. 211.

"Short *o*" = [ɒ] and [ɑ], as in *oxen* [ˈɒksən, ˈaksən]; *crop*[34] [krɒp, krɑp]; *cot* [kɒt, kɑt], *college*[35] [ˈkɒlɪʤ, ˈkɑlɪʤ], *cottage*[36] [ˈkɒtɪʤ, ˈkɑtɪʤ], *foxes*[37] [ˈfɒksɪz, ˈfaksɪz], *not*[38] [nɒt, nɑt], *rods*[39] [rɒdz, rɑdz], *tot*[40] [tɒt, tɑt].

Transcribe: A list of your own making, containing twenty-five words of the order of *frog, cog, jog, catalog(ue), decalog(ue), boggy.*

o before final or preconsonantal *r* = [ɔ], [ɔə] as in *corn*[41] [ˈkɔən, kɔn], *horse*[42] [ˈhɔəs, hɔs], *orchard*[43] [ˈɔətʃəd, ˈɔtʃəd]. The sound [ɒ] is found as a variant among words of this class. And if such words begin with a labiodental, or with a bilabial or alveolar plosive, [ɔə] appears as a predominant pronunciation. Thus *ford* may be [ˈfoəd]; *port*, [ˈpoət]; *porch*,[44] [ˈpoətʃ]; *torn*,[45] [ˈtoən].

o plus *r* or *re*; and *oa, oo,* or *ou* plus *r* = [oə] or [ɔə], as in such words as *chore*[46] [ˈtʃoə, ˈtʃɔə], *four*[47] [ˈfoə, ˈfɔə], *boar* [ˈboə, ˈbɔə], *floor* [ˈfloə, ˈflɔə].

Transcribe: border,[48] clapboards,[49] bore, cord, core,[50] door,[51] gourd, hoard, sore, more, tore, hoary, Cora, Flora, explore.

/ɔ/ in New England varies greatly within its phonemic limits, appearing high, medium and low, thus [ɔˑ, ɔ, ɔˑ]. Moreover, an /ɔ/-word may sporadically appear with a substituted higher vowel, [o], outside the /ɔ/-phoneme, or a lower vowel, [ɒ] or [ɑ]. On the average, we find [ɔ] or [ɔˑ], as in *cork*[52] [kɔk], [kɔˑk].

Transcribe: frost,[53] cough,[54] hornet,[55] loft,[56] saw,[57] raw, ought, law, call, haughty, naughty.

[ɔ] not followed by *r*, in New York City, is high, sounding like [o] to listeners from elsewhere. Thus *call* [kɔˑl] or [kol], *law* [lɔˑ, lo], *ought* [ɔˑt, ot].

Transcribe: caught, sought, bought, naught, saw, all, fall, ball, Paul, wrought, wall, hall, haul, awkward, hawk, talk, walk, balk, cause, because.

u, eu, and *ew* = [u], [ju] after [d], [t], [n][58] as in *dew* [du], [dju], *tune* [tun, tjun],

---

[34] *Atlas*, 1, p. 124.
[35] *Atlas*, 3, p. 537.
[36] *Atlas*, 2, p. 299.
[37] *Atlas*, 1, p. 128.
[42] *Atlas*, 1, p. 196; 1, p. 199 (horseshoes); 1, p. 109 (horsestable).
[43] *Atlas*, 2, p. 246.
[44] *Atlas*, 2, p. 397.
[45] *Atlas*, 3, p. 665.
[46] *Atlas*, 1, p. 217.
[47] *Atlas*, 1, p. 000.
[48] *Atlas*, 1, p. 271.
[49] *Atlas*, 2, p. 250.
[50] *Atlas*, 2, p. 271.
[38] *Atlas*, 3, p. 674.
[39] *Atlas*, 1, p. 45.
[40] *Atlas*, 2, p. 379.
[41] *Atlas*, 1, p. 106.
[51] *Atlas*, 2, p. 347.
[52] *Atlas*, 1, p. 144.
[53] *Atlas*, 1, p. 98.
[54] *Atlas*, 3, p. 500.
[55] *Atlas*, 1, pp. 240–241.
[56] *Atlas*, 1, p. 102.
[57] *Atlas*, 3, p. 659.
[58] *Handbook*, Chart 17, p. 35, "For eastern New England, the simple vowel [u, uu] predominates in words of this (tube, new) type."

and *neutral* ['nutrəl, 'njutrəl]. Rural communities use [u] almost exclusively. When [ju] is used, it is alternated with its prototype [ɪu], as in *tune* [tɪun]. Urban New England uses [ju] in these contexts often.

Educated city dwellers sometimes use [ju] also where the letter *u* occurs after [s], [z], and [θ], as in *assume* [ə'sjum], *resume* [rɪ'zjum], and *enthusiastic* [ɪn₁θuzɪ-'æstɪk]. In rare cases, [ju] is used after *l* as in *absolutely* [₁æbsə'ljutlɪ], and *resolution* [₁rɛzə'lju∫ən].

> *Transcribe:* dues,[59] new,[60] student,[61] Tuesday,[62] lute, presume, suit,[63] pursuit,
> suitable, pneumonia, renew, tube, consume, enthusiasm.

[ʌ] is lowered or lowered and backed in the British fashion in the speech of some New Englanders, particularly in north and central New England. This sound, [ʌʴ], to listeners from elsewhere sounds like [ɑ], so that New England *such* [sʌʴt∫] suggests [sɑt∫]. In the word *pluck*, a raised [ɑ], i. e., [ɑᵗ], is common, thus, [plɑᵗk]; but [plʌʴk] and [plʌʴk] are found sporadically, with [plʌk] actually the most frequent.

> *Transcribe:* luck, love, above, upper, cupful, bulk,[64] bulge,[65] cup,[66] gully,[67]
> lugged,[68] mumps,[69] mumble, tumble, stumble, grumble, crumble, fun, funny,
> come, comfortable, lovable, son, sun, gun, gum, shut,[70] tucked.[71]

oo = [u] or [ʊ], as in all English dialects, but the East uses [ʊ] much more than do the Southern and General American regions. *Pool* is always [pul], and *book* is always [bʊk]; but *broom, coop, Cooper, hoof, hoop, nook, proof, roof,*[72] *rook, room, rooster, root, soot, spook, woof,* are pronounced with both [u] and [ʊ].[73] However, [u] is often regarded as preferable in case of controversy.

-ar, -er, -ir, -or, -ur(e) and *-yr* as unstressed suffixes = [ə], as in *mortar* ['mɔtə], *upper* ['ʌpə], *tapir* ['teɪpə], *pallor* ['pælə], *murmur* ['mɜmə], *nurture* ['nɜt∫ə] and *martyr* ['mɑːtə].

> *Transcribe:* Use list on page 208.

-ile = [l̩], as in *fertile*[74] ['fɜtl̩], *futile* ['fjutl̩].[75] Some words of this class are pronounced with both [l̩] and [aɪl], as in *senile* ['sinl̩, 'si₁naɪl], *juvenile* ['dʒuvənl̩,

---

[59] *Atlas*, 3, p. 563.
[60] *Atlas*, 2, p. 361a.
[61] *Atlas*, 2, p. 445.
[62] *Atlas*, 1, p. 67.
[63] *Atlas*, 2, p. 361a.
[64] *Atlas*, 3, p. 55.
[65] *Atlas*, 2, p. 362.
[66] *Atlas*, 1, p. 133.
[67] *Atlas*, 1, p. 37.
[68] *Atlas*, 1, p. 165.
[69] *Atlas*, 3, p. 508.
[70] *Atlas*, 2, p. 347.
[71] *Atlas*, 2, p. 481.
[72] *Atlas*, 2, p. 348.
[73] C. H. Grandgent, "English in America," *Die Neueren Sprachen* (New York: G. E Stechert and Co., 1895), Vol. II, p. 457. Contains list of words in *oo*.
[74] Kenyon and Knott, *op. cit.*, p. 118.
[75] *Ibid.*, p. 178.

ˈʤuvəˌnaɪl]. Words of less frequent usage, such as *percentile, quartile* are uniformly pronounced with [aɪl].

Transcribe: Use list on page 242.

e and *i* = [ɪ] or [ə] in most unstressed initial syllables in consonant plus *e* or *i*, as in *refused*[76] [rɪˈfjuzd, rəˈfjuzd], *divide* [dɪˈvaɪd, dəˈvaɪd].

Transcribe: reflect, report, deflect, division, select, deduce, digress, desert, revile, Detroit, debate, digest, deportment, divine.

In the following unstressed suffixes, the vowels are unstressed to [ɪ] usually, [ə] occasionally: *-ace, -ain, -ad, -as, -ase, -ate, -ed, -en, -es, -ess, -est, -et, -ice, -id, -in* (if the stressed syllable contains a front vowel), *-ip, -is, -ist, -ite, -uce, -us, -ute,* as in *solace* [ˈsɑlɪs -əs], *salad*[77] [ˈsælɪd -əd], *mountain*[78] [ˈmaʊntɪn -ən], *Texas* [ˈtɛksɪs -əs], *purchase* [ˈpətʃɪs -əs], *Pilate* [ˈpaɪlɪt -ət], *daunted* [ˈdɔntɪd -əd], *chicken*[79] [ˈtʃɪkɪn -ən], *foxes*[80] [ˈfaksɪz -əz], *fearless* [ˈfɪəlɪs -əs], *farthest* [ˈfɑðɪst -əst], *jacket* [ˈʤækɪt -ət], *Alice* [ˈælɪs -əs], *solid* [ˈsɑlɪd -əd], *coffin*[81] [ˈkɔfɪn -ən], *Philip* [ˈfɪlɪp -əp], *Griffin* [ˈɡrɪfɪn -ən], *tennis* [ˈtɛnɪs -əs], *tourist*[82] [ˈtʊrɪst, ˈtʊrəst], *vomit*[83] [ˈvɑmɪt - ət], *opposite* [ˈɒpəzɪt -ət], *lettuce*[84] [ˈlɛtɪs -əs], *minute* [ˈmɪnɪt -ət].

The foregoing holds for most words in this category. In an occasional word, such as *salad,* [ə] prevails. The use of [ə] in this class is most frequent in southwest and northwest New England, and in the neighborhood of Boston.

Transcribe: obstinate,[85] exhausted,[86] actress,[87] basket,[88] jaundice,[89] appendicitis.[89]

Medial *e, i,* and *y* = [ə] or [ɪ] in *ability* [əˈbɪlətɪ, əˈbɪlɪtɪ], *telegram* [ˈtɛləˌɡræm, ˈtɛlɪˌɡræm], *Connecticut* [kəˈnɛtəkət, kəˈnɛtɪkət], *paralysis* [pəˈræləsəs, pəˈrælɪsɪs]. The pronoun *it,* unstressed, is [ɪt], as in *Find it* [ˈfaɪnd ɪt]. (When *e* or *i* is followed by a vowel, it is pronounced [ɪ] in all dialects, as in *permeate* [ˈpəmɪˌeɪt], *palliate* [ˈpælɪˌeɪt].)

Transcribe: American,[90] cemetery,[91] tenement,[92] seminary, lapidary, elephant, electrolysis, oligarchy, teletype.

o = [o], i.e., the pure vowel as distinguished from the diphthongal [oʊ], in certain syllables of light stress, as in *quotation* [kwoˈteɪʃən]. Such words must be distinguished from words with final unstressed *o* or *ow,* which are rendered

[76] *Atlas,* 2, p. 407a.
[77] *Atlas,* 2, p. 309.
[78] *Atlas,* 1, p. 39.
[79] *Atlas,* 1, p. 214.
[80] *Atlas,* 1, p. 228.
[81] *Atlas,* 3, p. 524.
[82] *Atlas,* 2, p. 449.
[83] *Atlas,* 3, p. 504.
[84] *Atlas,* 2, p. 254.

[85] *Atlas,* 2, p. 471.
[86] *Atlas,* 2, p. 482.
[87] *Atlas,* 2, p. 488.
[88] *Atlas,* 3, p. 511.
[89] *Atlas,* 3, p. 509.
[90] *Atlas,* 2, p. 451.
[91] *Atlas,* 3, p. 525.
[92] *Atlas,* 2, p. 355.

both with [o] and with the colloquial [ə], as in *tomato* [toˈmeɪto, təˈmeɪtə], *mellow* [ˈmɛlo, ˈmɛlə]. Words containing secondary stress are pronounced with [ou], as in *solo* [ˈsouˌlou], *alto* [ˈælˌtou].

Transcribe: rotation, rotunda, romance, window, barrow, sorrow, arrow, potato, tomorrow, omission.

a = [e], i.e., the pure vowel, as distinguished from the diphthongal [eɪ], when lightly stressed, as in *chaotic* [keˈɒtɪk , keˈɑtɪk].

R, consonant and vowel, in Eastern speech, in both stressed and unstressed syllables.

In all the dialects of American English, orthographic *r* intervocalic, i.e., linking *r*, is pronounced *r* (sometimes [ɾ] in Eastern), as in *fury* [ˈfjʊrɪ, ˈfjʊɾɪ], *for always* [fɔr ˈɔlwɪz, fɔɾˈɔlwɪz].

Transcribe: See list page 209. Use [r] or [ɾ] as needed.

In both the Southern and Eastern dialects, orthographic final and preconsonantal *r* appears to be emerging from its obscurity as a silent letter, or as having the value of [ə], and to be increasingly pronounced as [r].

The situation in New England when the data for the material for *Linguistic Atlas of the United States and Canada* were gathered in 1931–1933 was summarized as follows:

In western New England and in New Brunswick the [final and preconsonantal] *r* is regularly pronounced, in most of eastern New England it is dropped (or appears as [ə]), while the Connecticut valley is mixed and unstable in practice.[93]

But for the present decades, probably for the active lifetime of this book, the rendering of final and postvocalic *r* by silence or [ə] in New England and New York City will probably be regarded as typical, and will be so described herein. The various uses of the final and preconsonantal *r*, and of the intervocalic (or linking) *r* follow.

[ɜ] appears in many monosyllables and stressed syllables spelled with -*ear*, -*er*, -*ir*, -*or*, -*our*, -*ur*, -*yr*, where *r* is final or preconsonantal in the syllable. Thus, *heard* [hɜd], *herd* [hɜd], *birch* [bɜtʃ], *word* [wɜd], *journal* [ˈdʒɜnl̩], *curl* [kɜl], *myrtle* [ˈmɜtl̩]. [ɝ] may also be heard in these words.

Transcribe: See list page 242.

[ɜ] and [ʌ] are used interchangeably in certain words spelled with *e*, *i*, *o* or *u* plus *r* or *rr* plus vowel, as in *furrow*[94] [ˈfɜro, ˈfʌro], *borough* [ˈbɜro, ˈbʌro], *worry*[95] [ˈwɜrɪ, ˈwʌrɪ], *deferring* [dɪˈfɜrɪŋ, dɪˈfʌrɪŋ].

Transcribe: thorough, curry, hurry, burrow, blurry, thoroughfare, Murray, surrey, blurring, hurrying, stirring, whirring, conferring, concurring.

---

[93] *Handbook*, Chart 16, p. 34.
[94] *Atlas*, 1, p. 123.
[95] *Atlas*, 3, p. 498.

[ə] is used to express the complete acoustic value of unstressed syllables spelled with -ar, -er, -ir, -or, -our, -ur(e), -yr, as in mortar ['mɔtə], helper ['hɛlpə] tapir ['teɪpə], favor ['feɪvə], favour (Canadian spelling) ['feɪvə], sulphur ['sʌlfə], martyr ['mɑtə]. [ɚ] is also heard in these words.

Transcribe: Use list page 208.

[ə] is used in monosyllables containing [r] preceded by [ɪ], [ɛ], [æ], [o], [ʊ], [aɪ], [aʊ], as in the following (see diagram, page 210):
After

    [ɪ] *fear* ['fɪə], *mere* ['mɪə], *peer* ['pɪə]

    [ɛ] *there* ['ðɛə]

    [æ] *pair* ['pæə, 'pɛə], *pare* ['pæə, 'pɛə], *pear* ['pæə, 'pɛə]

    [o] *fort* ['foət], *hoard* ['hoəd] (See p. 226 for [ɔ, 'ɔə] in these words. See also page 207 for discussion of ['oʊə > 'oə])

    [ʊ] *sure* ['ʃʊə]

    [aɪ] *fire* ['faɪə]

    [aʊ] *flour* ['flaʊə]

[r] is also heard instead of [ə] in these words.

Transcribe: See list page 242.

r = either [ə] or silence in monosyllables and stressed syllables where *r* is preceded by [ɔ], as in *for* ['fɔə, fɔ], *record* [rɪ'kɔəd, rɪ'kɔd]. [r] is also to be heard in these words.

Transcribe: horse, chord, border, cork, cord, form, mortal, coral, order, organ, mortify, Lord, sort, dormer, hortatory, north, born.

r is silent after [ɑ, a] and [ɜ], as in *cart* [kɑːt,[96] kat], *earn* [ɜn]. [r] is also to be heard in these words.

Transcribe: hardy, chard, charred, part–pot, tart–tot, card–cod, guard–god, hard–hod, heart–hot.

r never occurs following [i], [eɪ], or [u] in the same syllable. Where these might be expected, as in *cheer, they're* and *poor,* they have been lowered to [ɪ], [ɛ], [ʊ] respectively, so that we have ['tʃɪə], ['ðɛə], ['pʊə].

Transcribe: where, dispair, chairman, sure, pure, appear, deer, clear.

wh = [w] or [ʍ] in nearly all words with initial *wh* except *who, whole* and their derivatives. Thus, *white* [waɪt, ʍaɪt].

---

[96] Here the lengthening sign is necessary to prevent the ambiguity which would result from transcribing both *cart* and *cot* as [kat]. For people whose pronunciation of *cot* is [kɒt], there would be, of course, no ambiguity.

Transcribe: when, while,[97] wheel, whet, what,[98] wheat,[99] wheelbarrow,[100] whip, whinny,[101] whale, whelk, whizz, Whig, whey, wheeze, wherefore, whicker, whipstock.

l = clear [l], i. e., [l] made in the front of the mouth, symbol [l̡], with considerable regularity before front vowels, as in *lease, lick*, [l̡is], [l̡ık]. It is especially clear *between* front vowels, as in *Billy* [ˈbɪl̡ɪ].

Transcribe: lane,[102] feeling,[103] Nelly,[104] milling, silly, hilly, least, leaning, live, spleen, plead, clean, cleave, Cleveland, clip, clay.

l = is dark [l], symbol [ł], before back vowels, in final clusters, and finally in syllables, as in *law* [łɔ], *milk* [mɪłk], *hill* [hɪł].

Transcribe: lawful, hale, salary, poll, panel, cavalry, palfrey, filbert, wail, squall, luck, chapel, fallacy, cabal, bulk, bilge, bulge.

Special Words

Either and *neither* = [ˈaɪðə] and [ˈnaɪðə], but [ˈiðə] and [ˈniðə] are well known and considerably used.

Stress

Polysyllabic words ending in -ary, -ery, -ory, as well as some other polysyllabic words, are often spoken without secondary stress. Thus, *dictionary* [ˈdɪkʃənərɪ, ˈdɪkʃənəɾɪ], *confectionery* [kənˈfɛkʃənərɪ, kənˈfɛkʃənəɾɪ], *territory* [ˈtɛrətərɪ, ˈtɛrɪtəɾɪ]. But [ˈdɪkʃəˌnɛrɪ], etc., are also used.

Transcribe: See list page 243.
See Kenyon, 4th Ed., 1924, pp. 160–164, for long list of these words.

Standard Eastern Speech
(Urban type)
From *The Question of Our Speech* *

aı æm ɔfəd ðı ɒpətjunɪtɪ əv ədrɛsɪŋ ju ə fju ɒbzəveɪʃənz ɔn ə sʌbʤɪkt ðət ʃud kəntɛnt ɪtsɛlf, tə maɪ θɪŋkɪŋ, wɪð nou sɛkəndəɾɪ pleɪs əmʌŋ ðouz ʤʌstlɪ kəmɛndɪd tə juɾ ətɛntʃən ɔn sʌtʃ ə deɪ əz ðɪs, ənd ðət jɛt wɪl nɒt, aɪ dɛə seɪ, həv bɪn tritɪd bɪfɔə ju, vɛɾɪ ɔfən, əz ə mætəɾ əspɛʃəlɪ ɪnvaɪtɪŋ ðæt ətɛntʃən. ju wɪl əv bɪn əpild tu, ət ðɪsːizən, ɪn prɛpəɾeɪʃən fə ðɪs əkeɪʒən, wɪð ædməɾəbəl pəsweɪʒən ənd ædməɾəbəl əfɛkt, aɪ meɪk nou daʊt, ɔn bɪhaf əv mɛnɪ əv ðɪ ɪntəɾɪsts ənd aɪdɪəlz, skɒləlɪ, mɔɾəl, souʃəl, ju hæv hɪə so hæpɪlɪ pəsjud. mɛnɪ əv ðə djutɪz, rɪspɒnsɪbɪlɪtɪz, ɒpətjunɪtɪz ju həv lənd, ɪn ðiz bjutɪfəl kəndɪʃənz, ət ðə θrɛʃhould əv

97 *Atlas*, 3, p. 727.
98 *Atlas*, 3, p. 561.
99 *Atlas*, 2, p. 281.
100 *Atlas*, 1, p. 163.
101 *Atlas*, 1, p. 178.
102 *Atlas*, 1, p. 44.
103 *Atlas*, 3, p. 493.
104 *Atlas*, 2, p. 433.

232 EASTERN AMERICAN ENGLISH

laɪf, tə si oupən aut təgɛðə, wɪl həv bɔən, əsɛntʃəlɪ, əpɒn ðə kwɛstʃən əv kʌltʃə,
əz juv ɪkspɛktɪd tə kənsidəɾ ənd tʃɛɾɪʃ ɪt; ənd sʌm əv ðəm, næʧəɾəlɪ, wɪl əv prɛst
ɒn ðə haɪə, ðɪ ədvɑntst dɪvɛləpmənt əv ðæt kwɛstʃən, ðouz ðət ɑ fɔɾɛvə flauɾɪŋ
əbʌv auə hɛdz ənd weɪvɪŋ ənd rʌslɪŋ ðɛə brɑntʃɪz ɪn ðə blu vɑst əv hjumən θɒt.

<h2 style="text-align:center">Standard Eastern Speech
(Less extreme type)</h2>

ʌðəz, minʍaɪl, wɪl əv lɪŋgəd ouvə fʌndəmɛntəlz, əz wi meɪ kɔl ðəm, ðə sɒlɪd,
sɛt|d, sitɪd ɛləmənts əv ɛʤəkeɪʃən, ðə θɪŋz əv ʍɪtʃ ɪt ɪz hɛld, ɪn ʤɛnərəl, ðət
auə nid əv biɪŋ rɪmaɪndɪd əv ðɛm məst rɪəlɪ bi əlaud tə bɪkʌm ə dɛspərɪt ər ə
fivərɪʃ nid. ðiz ʌndəlaɪɪŋ θɪŋz, truðz əv trədɪʃən, əv æspəreɪʃən, əv dɪsəplɪn,
əv treɪnɪŋ kɒnsɪkreɪtɪd baɪ ɪkspɪrɪənts, ɑr ʌndəstud əz prɛzənt ɪn ɛnɪ lɪbərəl
kɔs əv stʌdɪ ɔ skim əv kærɪktə. jɛt ðeɪ pəmɪt əv ə sɔtən rinjud rɛfərənts ən slaɪtlɪ
sɛrəmounɪəl ɪnsɪstənts, pəhæps, ɒn haɪ deɪz ənd hɒlədeɪz; wɪðaut ðə fɪə, ɒn ðə
pɑ:t əv ɛnɪwʌn kənsɔnd, əv ðɛə fɔlɪŋ tu mʌtʃ ɪntə ðə kætəgɔrɪ əv ðə kɒmənpleɪs.
aɪ rɪpit, hauɛvə, ðət ðɛr ɪz ə praɪm pɑ:t əv ɛʤəkeɪʃən, ən ɛləmənt əv ðə beɪsɪs
ɪtself, ɪn rɪgɑd tə ʍɪtʃ aɪ prɒbəblɪ rɪmeɪn wɪðɪn ðə baundz əv seɪftɪ ɪn dɪklærɪŋ
ðət nou ɪksplɪsɪt, nou sɛpərɪt, nou ædəkwɪt pli wɪl bi laɪklɪ tu əv reɪnʤd ɪtself
ʌndər ɛnɪ wʌn əv juə kʌstəmɛrɪ hɛdz əv kəmɛməreɪʃən.

HENRY JAMES

<h2 style="text-align:center">Standard Eastern Speech
(Urban type)
From Men, Women and Goats*</h2>

Warden: aɪ ɑsk ju wʌnts mɔə, ɔlkət, wɒts ðə jus? wɛn aɪ tuk ðɪs ʤɒb ɪt wəz
wɪð:ə θɒt ðət prɪzənəz wə stɪl hjumən biɪŋz ņ mɛn ņ wəd bi trɪtɪd əz sʌtʃ, n:ɒt
kɪkt əz ɪf ðeɪ wə sou mʌtʃ skʌm.

Guard: wɛl, ju sɔtņlɪ əv bɪn gud tə ðəm ņd aɪ θɪŋk ðeɪ ɔl əprɪʃɪeɪt ɪt.

Warden: ņd jɛt ju stænd ðɛɾ ənd tɛl mi ðət dæn məkaθɪ wɔkt aut θru ðə meɪn
geɪt əv ðɪs ʤeɪl waɪl ju brɪljənt ņ breɪv jʌŋ dɪfɛndəz stud ɒn gɑ:d.

Guard: jɛs, sɔ, bʌt —

Warden: ðɛə wə nou "bʌts" ɪn bɛn bʌtləz ɑmi — ən ðæts nɒt səpouzd tə bi
ə ʤouk aɪðə. sou ɪt tuk ju θri deɪz tə faɪnd məkaθɪ?

Guard: jɛs, sɔ, ðæt ɪz . . . hi keɪm bæk baɪ ɪmsɛlf ænd . . .

Warden: ðæts wʌndəfəl. hi faɪndz ɪt əz izɪ tə gɛt ɪntə ðɪs ʤeɪl əz i dɪd tə gɛt
aut əv ɪt. mavələs gɑ:dz. . . . ju fɛloz . . . izɪ tə pɑs ɪn aɪðə dɪrɛkʃən . . . nou
kwɛstʃənz ɑskt.

Guard: bət məkaθɪ . . .

Warden: aɪ hæv profaund rɪspɛkt fə mɪstə məkaθɪ . . . hi nouz stjupɪdɪtɪ wɛn
I siz ɪt. kæn ju si ðə hɛdlaɪnz ɪn hɪgɪnbɒtəmz peɪpə tənaɪt, ɪf ðɪs gɛts aut? "prɪzənə

wɔks past ɑmd gɑːdz n̩ kwɪts ðə d͡ʒeɪl wɪðaʊt ə wɜd əv θæŋks tə ðə hjumeɪn wɔdn̩." aʊə hoʊl ədmɪnɪstreɪʃən wɪl bi hɛld ʌp tə rɪdɪkjul — ɔ wɜs.

CHARLES O'BRIEN KENNEDY

Deviations from Standard Eastern Speech

a = [æ] in words or syllables containing *ar* finally or preconsonantally and not preceded by [w]. Thus, [pæk] for *park* [pɑk, pak], [tæt] for *tart*[105] [tɑːt, tat], [ˈkætrɪd͡ʒ] for *cartridge* [ˈkɑtrɪd͡ʒ, ˈkatrɪd͡ʒ].

Transcribe: mart-mat, marred-mad, card-cad, hard-had, heart-hat, lard-lad, cart-cat, larder-ladder, part-pat, marred-mad, bard-bad, lark-lack, tart-tat.

o = [ɵ] in a limited list of words, of which *whole* [hoʊl], *home* [hoʊm], *stone* [stoʊn] and *only* [ˈoʊnlɪ] are the most common, with *boat* [boʊt] *coat* [koʊt], and a few other words following closely in frequency. The vowel here resembles [ʌ] sufficiently to induce dialect writers to use *hum, stun,* etc., but it is really a centralized unrounded [ɵ], considerably higher than [ʌ]. Thus, [hɵl], [hɵm], [stɵn], [ˈɵnlɪ], [bɵt], [kɵt]. This sound is called the "New England short *o*."[106] It is found rurally in most of New England, but dwindles in central and western Massachusetts and Connecticut, and in western Vermont.

Transcribe: polka, folks, most, Polk, Holmes, colt, short, bloat, stony, homely.

-ure = [ə] in rustic speech (also [ɚ] in western and northern New England). Thus, *paster* [ˈpæstə, ˈpæstɚ] for *pasture* [ˈpæstʃə, ˈpæstʃɚ] and *figger* [ˈfɪgə, ˈfɪgɚ] for figure [ˈfɪgjə, ˈfɪgjɚ]. Related to this pronunciation is the pronunciation of *contribute* [kənˈtrɪbjət], *regulate* [ˈrɛgjəˌleɪt], *particular* [pəˈtɪkjələ] as [kənˈtrɪbɪt], [ˈrɛgəˌleɪt], [pəˈtɪklə].

oy, oi = [aɪ] rustically as in [ɪnˈd͡ʒaɪ] for *enjoy* [ɪnˈd͡ʒɔɪ], *point* [paɪnt].

A word ending in a vowel sound, when followed by another word beginning with a vowel, often takes on an excrescent *r*, also called the intrusive *r* or the false linking *r*. Thus, *soda and milk* [ˈsoʊdɚ ən ˌmɪlk], *law and order* [ˌlɔr ənd ˈɔdə]. The fact that many words have two pronunciations as the result of the use of the legitimate link promotes this insertion. When we compare [ðə wɔ bɪgæn, ə ˌwɔr ɪz ˈhɪə] with [ðə ˌlɔ bɪˈgæn, ðə ˌlɔr ɪz ˈhɪə] we can see the principle at work. The relationship here may be expressed thus: [wɔ] is to [wɔr] as [lɔ] is to [lɔr]. Sometimes the excrescent *r* develops analogously when a word ending in a vowel sound takes on a suffix beginning with a vowel sound, as in *drawing* [ˈdrɔrɪŋ]. When a word to which the excrescent *r* has become attached is lifted out of

---

[105] The lengthening sign is used to prevent ambiguity with *tot* on the part of those who pronounce it [tat]. For those who pronounce it [tɒt], there will be no ambiguity.

[106] C. H. Grandgent, "From Franklin to Lowell," PMLA, 1899, 7, p. 217. This article lists a number of words of this class. Cf. also *Handbook*, Chart 1, p. 26.

context and used in isolation or preceding a consonant, the *r* often clings to it. Thus, *Hannah* ['hænə], *Maria* [mə'raɪə], *idea* [aɪ'dɪə].

> *Transcribe and pronounce:* China, China and Japan; soda, sofa, sofa and chair; raw, raw oysters; Augusta is in Maine; follow, following; Arizona, Arizona and New Mexico; Nevada, Nevada and Utah; Clorinda, Ada, Juanita, Eva, Ella.

oo = [ʊ] in some words where only [u] is used in standard Eastern. Thus, [sʊn] for *soon* [sun], [spʊn] for *spoon* [spun].

> *Transcribe:* school, Tuesday,[107] tube,[108] noon, Reuben, boon, Boone.

[aɪ] = [ɜɪ] as in [mɜɪs] for *mice* [maɪs], [flɜɪz] for *flies* [flaɪz], [wɜɪf] for *wife* [waɪf]. This is a survival of an old British pronunciation brought to New England by the colonists. Ellis[109] records it as normal in England even as late as 1874, and Franklin, who was born in Boston, records it in the phonetic alphabet he invented in 1768[110]. When heard nowadays, it is usually in the speech of elderly rural and village people of such regions as southeast Massachusetts (particularly Cape Cod) and Rhode Island.

o and *ow* final = [ə] rustically in western and northern New England, where final and preconsonantal *r* are pronounced. Thus, *taller* ['tælə] for *tallow* ['tælo], *potater* [pə'teɪtə] for *potato* [po'teɪto].

> *Transcribe:* tomato, mellow, fellow, shadow, pillow, hollow, fallow, bellow, swallow, mosquito.

[ɜ] > [ʌ] in certain words, such as *wuth* [wʌθ] for *worth* [wɜθ], *fust* [fʌst] for *first* [fɜst], *wust* [wʌst] for *worst* [wɜst], *wuss* [wʌs] for *worse* [wɜs], *nuss* [nʌs] for *nurse* [nɜs].

[æ] > [æⁱ] as in *that* [ðæⁱt]. Dialect writers spell this pronunciation with *e*, as in *thet* for *that*. Probably the transcription [ðɛt] would not be much exaggerated.

> *Transcribe:* have, had, has, etc.

[aʊ] > [æʊ] or [jæʊ] as in *out* [æʊt] and *cow* [kjæʊ], *gown* [gjæʊn]. Both [æ] and [æʊ] above are highly subject to nasalization. In many individuals the nasalization spreads over the whole vocal picture. (See page 109 for discussion of nasalization.)

oi = ['oə], in words spelled with *-oil*, as in ['boəl] for boil [bɔɪl]. The pronunciation ['boəl] is found principally in the Long Island Sound coastal region of New

---

[107] *Atlas*, 1, p. 67.   [108] *Atlas*, 2, p. 186.

[109] A. J. Ellis, "Early English Pronunciation, etc." *Early English Text Society*, Extra Series, No. 24 (London: Trübner), 1874, p. 1100, Part 4.

[110] Jared Sparks, Ed., *The Works of Benjamin Franklin* (Boston: Tappan and Whittemore, 1838), 6, pp. 293–303.

England. The use of [aɪ] as in [baɪl] for these and related words is widely distributed rustically. (See page 194 for discussion.)

Transcribe: oil,[111] toil, soil, spoil, roil, coil, foil.

Labialization. There is in New England a tendency toward excessive lip-rounding (labialization) on stressed back vowels, as in [ˈeɪˌgjy̠] for *ague*[112] [ˈeɪˌgju], [ˈbɔ̠stən] for *Boston* [ˈbɔstən].

Transcribe: boys, boil,[113] crib[114] (exceptional in view of the front vowel), goal,[115] down,[116] humor,[117] loose,[118] music,[119] new,[120] oats,[121] school.[122]

Miscellaneous. [gumz] for *gums* [gʌmz], [wæl, wal] for *well* [wɛl], [ˈfæsɪt] for *faucet* [ˈfɔsɪt, ˈfɔsət], [trɔθ] for *trough* [trɔf].

Substandard Eastern Speech

From *The Revolt of Mother*

ə wɑntə si jɪ ʤɛst ə mɪnɪt, faðə. ə wɑntə noʊ ʍʌt ju ə bɪldɪn ðɛt nu ban fɔ. bi jɪ goʊɪn tə baɪ moə kæʊz? ə noʊ jɪ bi, əz wɛl əz ə wɑntə. næʊ, faðə, lʊk hɪə. aɪm goʊɪn tə tɔk rɪəl pleɪn tə ju. ə nɛvə hɛv sɛnts ə mɛrɪd:ʒɪ. bət əm goʊɪntə næʊ. jɪ si ðɪs rʊm hɪə, faðə; ju lʊk æt ɪt wɛl. jɪ si ðɛr eɪnt noʊ kapɪt ɔn ðə floə, ən jɪ si ðə peɪpər ɪz ɔl dɔtɪ ən drɔpɪn ɔf ðə wɔlz. wi eɪnt hɛd noʊ nu peɪpər ɔn ɪt fə tɛn jɪə, ən ðɛn ə pʊt ɪt ɔn məsɛlf ən ɪt dɪdn̩t kɔst bət naɪnpənts ə roʊl. jə si ðɪs rʊm, faðə? ɪts ɔl ðə wʌn aɪv hɛd tə wɜk ɪn, ən ɪt ɪn, ən sɛt ɪn sɛnts wi wəz mɛrɪd. ðɛr eɪnt ənʌðə wʊmən ɪn ðə hɔl tæʊn huz hʌzbənd eɪnt gɒt haf ðə minz ju hɛv bət ʍʌts gɒt bɛtə. ɪts ɔl ðə rʊm ænəz gɒt tə hɛv ə kʌmpnɪ ɪn, ən ðɛr eɪnt wʌn əv ə meɪts bət ʍʌts gɒt bɛtə, ən ðɛə faðəz nɒt soʊ eɪbəl əz hɜz ɪz. ɪts ɔl ðə rʊm ʃɪl hɛv tə bɪ mɛrɪd ɪn. ʍʌt wəd ju əv θɔt, faðə, if wi əd hɛd æʊə wedn̩ ɪn ə rʊm noʊ bɛtə ðən ðɪs? aɪ wəz mɛrɪd ɪn mə mʌðəz palə wɪð ə kapɪt ɔn ðə floə, ən stʌft fənɪtʃər ən ə məhɔgənɪ kad teɪbəl, ən ðɪs ɪz ɔl ðə rʊm ænər əl hɛv tə bi mɛrɪd ɪn.

MARY E. WILKINS FREEMAN

Urban Substandardisms

The following is based on the speech of New York City and its immediate commuting area. (See Chapter 14 for more complete treatment.) Parts apply to the speech of other cities, in the East as well as elsewhere. Some of the sounds originate in foreign accent.

[111] *Atlas*, 1, p. 187.
[112] *Atlas*, 3, p. 505.
[113] *Atlas*, 3, p. 512.
[114] [kwɪb] *Atlas*, 1, p. 106.
[115] [guwl], *Atlas*, 3, p. 585.
[116] *Atlas*, 3, p. 494.
[117] *Atlas*, 2, p. 469.
[118] *Atlas*, 3, p. 555.
[119] *Atlas*, 2, p. 412.
[120] *Atlas*, 2, p. 361 A.
[121] [oˑwts], *Atlas*, 1, p. 128.
[122] [skuwl], *Atlas*, 2, p. 444.

Substitution of [ɪ] for [i] in monosyllables and stressed syllables ending in a consonant, as in [kɪp] for *keep* [kip], [əˈslɪp] for *asleep* [əˈslip].

> *Transcribe:* beat, creep, deep, feed, heap, keen, keel, leap, meat, need, peel, reel, seed, weed.

Substitution of [ɛ] or [ˈɛə] for [æ] in monosyllables and stressed syllables, as in the following: [bɛt, ˈbɛət] for *bat* [bæt], [ˈpɛsɪŋ, ˈpɛəsɪŋ] for *passing* [ˈpæsɪŋ].

> *Transcribe:* bass, class, dash, fad, fashion, gallon, hack, Jack, lack, mad, nab, pack, sad.

Substitution of [ɛi] or [ei] for [i] in monosyllables and stressed final syllables ending in [i], as in the following: [əˈgrɛi, əˈgrei] for *agree* [əˈgri], [mɛi, mei] for *me* [mi].

> *Transcribe:* bee, debris, degree, fee, he, key, knee, Lee, pea, plea, quay, sea, tea, we.

Substitution of [ɔ] for [ɑ] in monosyllables and stressed syllables spelled with *ar* final or followed by a consonant but not preceded by [w], as in [kɔ] for *car* [kɑ], [ˈfɔmə] for *farmer* [ˈfɑmə]. ([r] is often pronounced in such words.)

> *Transcribe:* art, arbor, bark, cart, card, dark, hark, lard, lark, mar, marble, mark, martyr, park, star.

Substitution of [ˈoə] and [ˈɔə] for [ɔ] in monosyllables and stressed syllables spelled with *a* + [l] or *aw* final, and *a* + [l], *augh*, *aw*, or *ough* plus one or more consonants, as in [ˈkoəl, ˈkɔəl] for *call* [kɔl], [əˈpoəl, əˈpɔəl] for *appall* [əˈpɔl].

> *Transcribe:* all, bought, caught, daughter, fought, haughty, law, naughty, ought, Paul, raw, saw, taught, thought, wall, walled, wrought.

Substitution of [ɑ] for [ʌ] as in [sɑm] for *some* [sʌm], [ɑp] for *up* [ʌp].

> *Transcribe:* bun, done, fun, gum, jump, just, love, run, son, sun, won, company, country, comfortable.

Substitution of [ɒɪ, ɑɪ] for [aɪ], as in [ɒɪ, ɑɪ] for *I* [aɪ], [mɒɪ, mɑɪ] for *my* [maɪ].

> *Transcribe:* buy, die, dye, dyke, fight, fly, guide, hide, high, cider, kind, lie, live, mine, night, pike, pine, quiet, ripe, rise, side, sigh, size, tie, tide, tile, time, vine, wide.

Substitution of [ɜɪ, ɔɪ] for [ɜ] in words spelled with *ear, er, ir, or, our, ur, yr*, plus consonant, in words such as the following: [bɜɪd, bɔɪd] for *bird* [bɜd], [ˈsɜɪtn̩, ˈsɔɪtn̩] for *certain* [ˈsɜtn̩].

> *Transcribe:* burn, burst, burly, circle, curl, dermis, dirt, fern, firm, flirt, further, germ, Germany, girl, girder, girdle, heard, herd, hurl, Herkimer, jerk, journal, journey, Kirk, kirtle, learn, Lerner, mirth, murder, myrtle, pearl, serve, serge, sermon, skirt, turn, urn, verge, Virgil, word, work, worth, purple, third, thirty.

Substitution of [ɜɪ], [ɜ˞] for [ɔɪ] in words spelled with *oi* or *oy* plus consonant. Examples: [bɜɪl, bɜ˞l] for *boil* [bɔɪl], [ˈpɜɪzn̩, ˈpɜ˞zn̩] for *poison* [ˈpɔɪzn̩].

Transcribe: coil, Coit, Doyle, foil, goiter, hoist, hoyden, join, joint, joist, loin, moist, oil, ointment, oyster, point, soil, spoil, toil, void.

Substitution of [ɪu, ɛu] for [u] in words or stressed syllables ending in [u], as in [dɪu, dɛu] for *do* [du], [trɪu, trɛu] for *true* [tru].

Transcribe: clue, crew, flue, too, two, shrew.

Substitution of [əm] for [ɪm], [ə], [ɪt], in the unstressed words *him, her, it*, as in [ˌaɪ ˈkoət əm] for *I caught him* [ˌaɪ ˈkoət ɪm], [aɪ koət əm] for *I caught her* [ˌaɪ ˈkɔt ə], [ˌaɪ ˈkoət əm] for *I caught it* [ˌaɪ ˈkɔt ɪt].

Unvoicing final voiced consonants. Substitution of [t] for [d], as in [ˈbɛət] for *bad* [bæd], [saɪt] for *side* [saɪd].

Transcribe: bed, bid, cede, died, goad, head, hide, hoed, killed, lad, led, mowed, neighed, paid, piled, posed, stayed, wade.

Substitution of [f] for [v], as in [ˈhɛəf] for *have* [hæv], [lɪf] for *live* (v.) [lɪv].

Transcribe: brave, cave, drove, eve, gave, give, heave, hive, live (adj.), love, move, prove, strive, strove, verve, weave, wove.

Substitution of [s] for [z], as in [gos] for *goes* [goʊz], [ɪs] for *is* [ɪz].

Transcribe: bays, bees, boys, days, dies, doze, flays, flees, flies, froze, gaze, goes, haze, hose, jays, Joe's, Jews, keys, knows, lies, mows, news, nose, pays, peas, peruse, pose, rose, says, sews, ways.

Substitution of [p] for [b], as in [rop] for *robe* [roʊb], [rɪp] for *rib* [rɪb].

Transcribe: cab, daub, ebb, gab, hub, job, lobe, Mab, nab, probe, rub, stab.

Substitution of [t] for [θ], and [d] for [ð]. These are evidences of foreign accent, or of street gamin talk. An immigrant may make the substitution in any words spelled with *th*, but the street gamin will do so only with a limited number of frequently used words, such as in [də, dɪ] for *the* [ðə, ðɪ], [dɪs] for *this* [ðɪs], [ˈdɛət] for *that* [ðæt], [diz] for *these* [ðiz], [doʊz] for *those* [ðoʊz], [tɪŋ] for *thing* [θɪŋ], [ˈnʌtn̩] for *nothing* [ˈnʌθɪŋ].

Transcribe: bath, bathroom, both, bother, brother, death, father, mother, other, than, thick, thin, think, thumb, tooth, whether.

Affrication. Substitution of [ts] and [dz] for initial [t] and [d], as in [tsul] for *tool* [tul], [dzoʊm] for *dome* [doʊm].

Transcribe: tale, tame, teal, tide, told, dame, deal, dime, door, doom.

Intrusion of [g] or [k] after [ŋ]. Use of [ŋg] or [ŋk] instead of [ŋ] alone in most words spelled with *ng*—as in [ˌlɔŋˈgaɪlənd] for *Long Island* [ˌlɔŋ ˈaɪlənd], [ˈnatɪŋk] for *nothing* [ˈnʌθɪŋ].

Transcribe: bringing, calling, coming, darling, evening, flinging, going, hoisting, imagining, jumping, longing, morning, nursing, opening, playing, ringing, singing, thronging, working.

Exceptions: finger ['fɪŋgə], and words such as those in the first exercise below. Omission of [g]. Use of [ŋ] alone, instead of [ŋg], as in ['ɪŋlɪʃ] for *English* ['ɪŋglɪʃ], ['fɪŋə] for *finger* ['fɪŋgə].

> *Transcribe:* bangle, Bangor, dangle, jangle, jingle, jungle, langor, linger, tangle, tingle, wrangle.

The glottal stop. The glottal stop is not phonemic in English. It is substituted for [t] and occasionally [k], as in ['kɛə ʔl̩] for *cattle* ['kætl̩], [lɪ ʔl̩] for *little* ['lɪtl̩], ['beɪʔn̩] for *bacon* ['beɪkən].

> *Transcribe:* battle, bottle, chatter, doctor, fattest, fiddle, fittest, gentle, hottest, latter, middle, patter, sitter, tattle, water, written.

Substitution of [v] for [r], as in [pvi'sid] for *precede* [pri'sid].

> *Transcribe:* previous, promise, brown, bramble, precedent, president, provident, prove.

Voicing of final [s], where the word or syllable following [s] begins with a vowel or a voiced consonant: ['beɪz₁bɔl] for *baseball* ['beɪs₁bɔl], ['gɛəz₁mɛəsk] for *gas mask* ['gæs₁mæsk].

> *Transcribe:* bass voice, case of samples, face down, lace gloves, loose ends, nice baby, piece goods, this man.

Substitution of [ʃ] for [stʃ], as in ['kwɛʃən] for *question* ['kwɛstʃən].

> *Transcribe:* bastion, digestion, indigestion, ingestion, questionable, suggestion.

Omission of [h] from [hj] in the pronunciation of words spelled with *h* plus *ew, u, ue,* as in [ju] for *Hugh* [hju].

> *Transcribe:* Hume, humid, hue, hew, Hudibras, Huguenot. See additional words of this class, page 201.

Substitution of [tʃ] for [dʒ], as in ['kulɪtʃ] for *Coolidge* ['kulɪdʒ], [tʃemps] for *James* [dʒeɪmz].

> *Transcribe:* age, bridge, budge, cabbage, cottage, college, courage, dirge, edge, gem, gist, Hodges, jail, jelly, Jim, joke, Jukes, Madge, passage, porridge, rage, ridge, sage, sedge, sludge, wedge.

CHAPTER 10

Standard Southern British

"Stage Speech"

Standard southern British speech (cultivated London speech) is used in the professional and semi-professional theater (college, university, and civic theater) for a wide variety of plays in which the several native dialects of the usual company of actors would produce an irrational dialectal hodge-podge instead of the consistency and homogeneity of dialect required. Some types of plays requiring stage speech are listed below.

It will be understood that this standard stage speech is used only by such actors as are by the nature of their parts required to speak cultivated, grammatical English. Other actors, required by the nature of their parts to use uncultivated dialects of English, regional or local dialects of English, or broken foreign-English dialects, will need to study and use the dialects appropriate to the characters they represent.

Plays Requiring or Permitting Stage Speech for the Grammatically Accurate Portions

Shakespearean and other Elizabethan plays.
British plays of later date, especially modern British plays.
Classic non-English plays in translation.
Modern foreign plays in translation.
Plays written on a foreign background and reading as if translated from a foreign language.
American, Canadian, and other non-British English language plays if written without specified locale, setting, or flavor requiring special dialect.

NOTE. It is possible to play any of the types named above, from the third onward, in any standard dialect, provided only that all the actors speak it. If they do not and therefore have to agree arbitrarily on some one dialect, they had as well use southern British, since it is the commonest of all stage dialects.

(When, as implied above, other dialects become necessary for any of these plays, they will likely be found in the latter portion of this book, which is given over to dialects. As will be developed later, plays written completely in a special dialect, such as the Irish of Robinson, Synge, and Lady Gregory, or the general American of Elmer Conkle, must of necessity be played in the intended dialect—certainly not southern British.)

High school playing groups and dialectally untrained community playing groups had best use the standard speech of their own communities as their basic dialect, to which special dialects required by a given play can be added.

Sound System of Southern British (Stage) Speech

[ɪ] generally in the unstressed suffixes *ace, ain, ate, ed, en* (if the stem contains a front vowel), *es, ess, et, ice, id, in, ip, is, ist, it, ite, uce, ute*, as in *necklace* [ˈnɛklɪs], *mountain* [ˈmaʊntɪn], *pirate* [ˈpaɪrɪt], *pointed* [ˈpɔɪntɪd], *chicken* [ˈtʃɪkɪn] *coaches* [ˈkoʊtʃɪz], *actress* [ˈæktrɪs], *packet* [ˈpækɪt], *Alice* [ˈælɪs], *solid* [ˈsɒlɪd], *puffin* [ˈpʌˑfɪn], *fillip* [ˈfɪlɪp], *basis* [ˈbeɪsɪs], *artist* [ˈɑtɪst], *limit* [ˈlɪmɪt], *definite* [ˈdɛfɪnɪt], *lettuce* [ˈlɛtɪs], *minute* [ˈmɪnɪt].

> *Transcribe:* solace, palace, pinnace, curtain, mountain, batted, blotted, patches, leeches, bridges, botches, Jewess, mistress, seamstress, locket, picket, chalice, stolid, pallid, muffin, Phillip, stasis, purist, habit, infinite.

[ɪ] generally in unstressed medial syllables spelled with *e, i,* and *y,* as in *celebrate* [ˈsɛlɪˌbreɪt], *president* [ˈprɛzɪdənt], *analysis* [əˈnælɪsɪs]. With medial *y,* [ə] is used alternatively with [ɪ] as in *paralysis* [pəˈræləsɪs, pəˈrælɪsɪs].

> *Transcribe:* ability, polyglot, felicity, Halifax, dandelion, handicap, polygon, palliate, insanity.

[ɛ] in numerous words spelled with *air, are, ear,* as in *pair* [ˈpɛə], *pare* [ˈpɛə], *pear* [ˈpɛə]. But words in *ar* and *arr* plus a vowel other than *e* are pronounced with [æ], as in *paramount* [ˈpærəˌmaʊnt], *carry* [ˈkærɪ].

> *Transcribe:* Barry, fair, spare, lair, airy, mare, tare, tear, wear, share, flair, chair, bear, bare, tarry, hare, swear, blare, Clare, parallel, charity, glare, rare, affair, dispair, declare.

[ɑ] in "broad *a*" words, i.e., words which are, in most cases, spelled with *a* plus [f] ([v] in some plurals), [s], [θ] ([ð] in some plurals), and *n* plus a consonant, as in *half* [hɑf], *halves* [hɑvz], *last* [lɑst], *bath* [bɑθ], *baths* [bɑðz], *dance* [dɑns]. Certain "broad *a*" words do not fall precisely into the foregoing categories, e.g., *aunt, banana, example, rather.* Note that words in *and* are not "broad *a*" words, except *command* [kəˈmɑnd], *demand* [dɪˈmɑnd], and most other derivatives of Latin *mandare.*

> *Transcribe:* abaft, advance, after, answer, ask, aunt, bath, behalf, blast, branch, brass, can't, cask, cast, caste, castle, chance, chant, clasp, class, com-

mander, craft, dance, demanded, fast, flask, France, glance, glass, grass, lance, lasting, laughter, mask, mast, master, nasty, pastor, pasture, pass, past, path, remand, repast, reprimand, shaft, shan't, staff, task, telegraph, vast.

[ɔ] in many words spelled with *all, aul,* or *aw* final in the syllable, or with *al, augh, aul, aw,* or *ough* plus one or more consonants, is pronounced with the tongue higher in the mouth than for the same words in American English, and likewise higher than for [ɔ] followed by *r* in British English. This [ɔˑ] suggests [o] to most Americans. Examples: *ball* [bɔˑl], *Paul* [pɔˑl], *saw* [sɔˑ]; *talk* [tɔˑk], *caught* [kɔˑt], *baulk* [bɔˑk], *hawk* [hɔˑk], *ought* [ɔˑt].

> *Transcribe:* bought, distraught, call, draw, raw, caught, caul, dawn, drawn, slaughter, slaw, daughter, fall, yawl, hall, haul, naughty, haughty, law, nought, Saul, sought, shawl, tall, maul, taught, wall, wrought.

[ɔ] in many words in *oar, oor, ore, our,* as in *hoard* [hɔd], *floor* [flɔ], *sore* [sɔ], *four* [fɔ]. As an alternate for [ɔ], [ɔə] is used, but [ɔ] is most frequently found.

> *Transcribe:* soar, hoarse, shore, pore, pour, core, coarse, course, mourn, fourteen, hoard, roar, board, gore, lore, chore, deplore, wore, tore, adore, explore, door.

[ɒ] in all "short *o*" words, and in some words spelled with *wa, wha,* and *qua,* as in *got* [gɒt], *not* [nɒt], *bottle* [ˈbɒtəl], *wad* [wɒd], *what* [wɒt], *squad* [skwɒd].

> *Transcribe:* totter, pottage, lot, quantity, bob, hod, pop, odd, sod, squabble, cot, waddle, quadruped, hominy, squalid, knob, knot, swallow, slop, shop, swan, trod, wallop, fodder, otter, plod.

[ou] or [ɜu] in monosyllables and stressed syllables where only [ou] would be used in most American English. Only [ou] is found in Jones,[1] but it is likely that [ɜu] is used much oftener than [ou] in southern British and on the British stage. Examples: *boast* [bɜust], *grow* [grɜu], *oh* [ɜu].

> *Transcribe:* toast, sole, soul, dose, load, ghost, roam, Rome, no, smoke, host, whole, roll, cold, boat, bode, mode, most, holy, bestow, low, wrote, don't, old, sew, dome, soldier.

[ʌ] in southern British is lower and farther back than in most American speech. It sounds nearly like [ɑ] to Americans. Example, *just* [dʒʌˑˑst].

> *Transcribe:* love, run, judge, lunch, pluck, done, become, up, fun, couple, one, tumble, brunt, clutch, much, Dutch, rut, trudge, buzz.

[ɜ] in all monosyllables and stressed syllables containing the vowel of *bird* [bɜd]. The usual spellings are *ear, er, ir, or, our, ur,* and *yr,* as in *heard* [hɜd], *fern* [fɜn],

---

[1] Daniel Jones, *An English Pronouncing Dictionary* (New York: E. P. Dutton, 1937). Note: This dictionary should be used exclusively for stage speech. Ordinary dictionaries are of little use for this purpose.

kirk [kɜk], *worst* [wɜst], *journal* [ˈdʒɜnl̩], *curl* [kɜl], *myrrh* [mɜ]. Exceptions: In words in which an unstressed vowel follows *r* or *rr*, the spellings *or, orr, our, ur, urr* are pronounced with [ʌ], as in *borough* [ˈbʌɾə], *worry* [ˈwʌɾɪ], *courage* [ˈkʌɾɪdʒ], *surrey* [ˈsʌɾɪ]. This variation does not apply to similarly spelled words derived from a root pronounced with [ɜ], as in *furry* [ˈfɜɾɪ], derived from *fur* [fɜ].

> *Transcribe:* fur, first, worm, worth, her, church, curl, murky, nervous, tern, hearse, early, furl, burned, adjourn, purse, journey, lurch, hurdle, worth, twirl, serve, earl, earnest, firm, fir, jerk, earthy, dirt, curry, currish, hurry, furrow, encouraging, vermin, wordy, spurn, myrtle, worldly.

[ə] in unstressed syllables ending in *ar, er, ir, or, our, ur, yr*, as in *mortar* [ˈmɔtə], *further* [ˈfɜðə], *tapir* [ˈteɪpə], *odor* [ˈoʊdə], *favour* (British and Canadian spelling) [ˈfeɪvə], *murmur* [ˈmɜmə], *satyr* [ˈsætə].

> *Transcribe:* Tartar, over, actor, upper, vapor, fakir, rumor, martyr, luster, reaper, Astor, muster, neighbor, upper, searcher, cooler, color, pallor, plaster, attar, pillar.

[ə] as the pronunciation of *r* when a monosyllable or stressed syllable ends in *r* after [ɪ], [ɛ], [ʊ], [aɪ], [aʊ], as in *clear* [ˈklɪə], *where* [ˈwɛə], *sure* [ˈʃʊə], *fire* [ˈfaɪə], *flour* [ˈflaʊə] (see diagram, page 210).

> *Transcribe:* cheer, Lear, appear, hour, pyre, fear, dire, veer, everywhere, therefore, rear, peer, sour, Windermere, nearly, revere, spire, acquire.

[ə] or silence is used where *r* appears after [ɔ] in monosyllables and stressed syllables. Silence is the more frequent. Examples: *lore* [lɔ, ˈlɔə], *hoarse* [hɔs, ˈhɔəs], *course* [kɔs, ˈkɔəs], *door* [dɔ, ˈdɔə].

> *Transcribe:* cord, gourd, ignore, border, short. Note: *r* does not appear following [i], [eɪ], [u], [ʌ] in the same syllable.

[ɾ] in the intervocalic position within a word and at the end of a word before another word beginning with a vowel, as in *merry* [ˈmɛɾɪ], *far away* [ˌfɑɾəˈweɪ].

> *Transcribe:* marry, fairy, hurry (use [ʌ]), furnish, glory, curry, sorry, nearing, orate, starring, carry, very, there are two, here it is, her intention, bearing, forest, pouring, tourist, tarry, bury, berry, fury, foray, coronation.

[t] medially is aspirate, as in *pretty* [ˈprɪtˤɪ],[2] not weakened to [ɾ] or [d] as in [ˈprɪɾɪ, ˈprɪdɪ].

> *Transcribe:* city, ditty, pity, jetty, netted, little, battle, kitten, cotton, pattern, flutter, rotting, witty, British, trotted, Saturday, settle, kettle, fatten.

[aɪl] in the suffix *ile* as in *futile* [ˈfjuˌtaɪl].

> *Transcribe:* reptile, volatile, puerile, versatile, senile, fertile, juvenile, prehensile.

---

[2] The sign [ˤ] indicates strong aspiration.

[l] before front vowels is clear (front, dental) as in *least* [list], *chilly* [ˈtʃɪlɪ]. When necessary, the special symbol [l̪] may be used. Dark [l] (special symbol [ɫ]) is used in other positions than before front vowels.

> *Transcribe:* relate, lazy, Blake, leader, letter, listen, living, literal, legion, blame, bleach, cleave.

[ju] in words spelled with *eu*, *ew*, or *u* after [d], [t], [n], [θ], [s], [z] and in some cases [l]. Examples: *dew* [dju], *duty* [ˈdjutɪ], *tulip* [ˈtjulɪp], *neural* [ˈnjurəl], *knew* [nju], *nutrition* [njuˈtrɪʃən], *thews* [θjuz], *enthusiastic* [ɪnˌθjuzɪˈæstɪk], *assume* əˈsjum], *resume* [rɪˈzjum], *absolute* [ˈæbsəˌljut].

> *Transcribe:* constitute, endue, dutiful, absolution, newsprint, neutral, pursuant, pneumonia, suit, presume, enthusiasm, neuro-muscular, pursuit.

[w] in words spelled with *wh* (frequently used exceptions are *who, whole*, and their derivatives), as in *which* [wɪtʃ], *wheel* [wil]. [ʍ] is also used, but less frequently, as in [ʍɪtʃ], [ʍil].

> *Transcribe:* when, why, whether, whither, whisk, wheat, white, wharf, what, wheeze, whelp, where, whet, whey, whiff, Whig, while, whim, whip, whirl, whiskey, whisper, whistle, whit, whopper.

[sj] is preferred to [ʃ] in *issue* [ˈɪsju], *tissue* [ˈtɪsju].

The archaic pronunciation of *e* before *r*, preserved in America in the word *sergeant* [ˈsɑdʒənt, ˈsɑrdʒənt], is found in words like *clerk* [klɑːk].

> *Transcribe:* derby, Berkeley, Herford, Hertford, Herts, Hervey.

Polysyllables have secondary accent less frequently than in American English, especially polysyllables in *ary, ery, ory*, as in *ordinary*, [ˈɔdn̩ərɪ].

> *Transcribe:* secretary, library, necessary, territory, stationery, advertisement, administrative, communicative, sanctuary, promontory, accumulative, repository, purgatory, predatory, cemetery, solitary, voluntary, January, adversary, military, mercenary.

Miscellaneous pronunciations: *ate* [ɛt], *again(st)* [əˈgeɪn(st)], *been* [bin], *either* [ˈaɪðə], *neither* [ˈnaɪðə], *nephew* [ˈnɛvju], *tomato* [təˈmɑto], *record* (n.) [ˈrɛkˌɔd], *lieutenant* (army) [lɛfˈtɛnənt], *schedule* [ˈʃɛdˌjul], *pajamas* [pəˈdʒɑməz].

Transcription in Southern British or
Stage Pronunciation

NOTE: An alternate transcription in southern British would follow Jones in using [ou] instead of [ɜu] in stressed syllables, and [o] instead of [ɜu] in unstressed syllables. In practical stage speech, an acceptable substitute for [ʌˑr] is [ɑ]; for [ɔˑ], [oˑ]; and for [ns] as in *chance* [tʃɑns], [nts] as in [tʃɑnts].

tə bi ɔ nɒt tə bi; ðæt ɪz ðə kwɛstʃən; wɛðə tɪz nɜublər ɪn ðə maɪnd tə sʌˑrfə ðə slɪŋz ənd ærɜuz əv autreɪdʒəs fɔtʃən, ɔ tə teɪk ɑmz əgeɪnst ə si əv trʌˑrbl̩z,

n̩ baɪ əpɜʊzɪŋ ɛnd ðəm? tə daɪ; tə slip; nɛʊ mɔ; æn baɪ ə slip tə seɪ wi ɛnd ðə
haːteɪk n̩ ðə θaʊzənd nætʃərəl ʃɒks ðət fleʃ ɪz ɛə tu, tɪz ə kɒnsəmeɪʃən dɪvaʊtl
tə bi wɪʃt. tə daɪ; tə slip; tə slip; pətʃans tə drim; aɪ, ðɛəz ðə rʌˑˑb; fɔɾ ɪn ðæ
slip əv dɛθ wɒt drimz meɪ kʌˑˑm wɛn wi əv ʃʌˑˑf|d ɔˑf ðɪs mɔtəl kɔɪl, məst gɪv ə
pɔˑz; ðɛəz ðə rɪspɛkt ðət meɪks kəlæmɪtɪ əv sɜʊ lɔŋ laɪf; fɔ hu wəd bɛə ðə wɪp
n̩ skɔnz əv taɪm, ðɪ əprɛsəz rɔŋ, ðə praʊd mænz kɒntjumlɪ, ðə pæŋz əv dɪspaɪzə
lʌˑˑv, ðə lɔˑz dɪleɪ, ðɪ ɪnsəln̩s əv ɒfɪs, ən ðə spɜnz ðət peɪʃənt mɛɾɪt əv ð
ʌˑˑnwɜðɪ teɪks, wɛn hi hɪmsɛlf maɪt ɪz kwaɪɪtəs meɪk wɪð ə ˈbɛə bɒdkɪn? hʊ
wəd fadl̩z bɛə, tə grʌˑˑnt n̩ swɛt ʌˑˑndəɾ ə wɪəɾɪ laɪf, bət ðət ðə drɛd əv sʌˑˑmθɪɾ
aftə dɛθ, ðɪ ʌˑˑndɪskʌˑˑvəd kʌˑˑntrɪ frəm huz bɔn nɜʊ trævələ riˈtɜnz, pʌˑˑz|ə
ðə wɪl, n̩ meɪks əs raðə bɛə ðɜʊz ɪlz wi hæv ðən flaɪ tu ʌˑˑðəz ðət wi nɜʊ nɒt ɒv
ðʌˑˑs kɒnʃəns dʌˑˑz meɪk kaʊədz əv əs ɔˑl; n̩ ðʌˑˑs ðə neɪtɪv hju əv rɛzəljuʃəɾ
ɪz sɪklɪd ɔ wɪðːə peɪl kʌst əv θɔˑt, ənd ɛntəpraɪzɪz əv greɪt pɪtʃ n̩ mɜʊmən
wɪðːɪs rɪgad ðɛə kʌɾənts tɜn əɾaɪ, n̩ luz ðə neɪm ʌ ækʃən. sɒft ju naʊ. ðə
fɛəɾ ɜʊfiljə. nɪmf, ɪn ðaɪ ɔrɪzənz bi ɔˑl maɪ sɪnz rɪmɛmbəd.

Transcribe: Speak the speech, I pray you, as I pronounced it to you, trippingly on the tongue: but if you mouth it, as many of your players do, I had as lief the town-crier spoke my lines. Nor do not saw the air too much with your hand, thus; but use all gently; for in the very torrent, tempest, and, as I may say, whirlwind of your passion, you must acquire and beget a temperance that may give it smoothness. O, it offends me to the soul to hear a robustious periwig-pated fellow tear a passion to tatters, to very rags, to split the ears of the groundlings, who for the most part are capable of nothing but inexplicable dumb-shows and noise: I would have such a fellow whipped for o'erdoing Termagant; it out-herods Herod: pray you, avoid it. Be not too tame neither, but let your own discretion be your tutor: suit the action to the word, the word to the action; with this special observance, that you o'erstep not the modesty of nature; for anything so overdone is from the purpose of playing, whose end, both at the first and now, was and is, to hold, as 'twere, the mirror up to nature; to show virtue her own feature, scorn her own image, and the very age and body of the time his form and pressure. Now this overdone, or come tardy off, though it make the unskilful laugh, cannot but make the judicious grieve; the censure of which one must in your allowance o'erweigh a whole theater of others. O, there be players that I have seen play, and heard others praise, and that highly, not to speak it profanely, that neither having the accent of Christians nor the gait of Christian, pagan, nor man, have so strutted and bellowed, that I have thought some of nature's journeymen had made men and not made them well, they imitated humanity so abominably. O, reform it altogether. And let those that play your clowns speak no more than is set down for them: for there be of them that will themselves laugh, to set on some quantity of barren spectators to laugh too, though in the meantime some necessary question of the play be then to be considered: that's villainous, and shows a most pitiful ambition in the fool that uses it. Go, make you ready.

PART THREE

CHAPTER 11

Cockney

The Cockney[1] dialect is the dialect spoken by the less educated people of London. There is an old tradition that one must be born within the sound of Bow bells[2] to be a true Cockney, and it is true that the dialect is especially prevalent in that part of London called the East End; but for the purpose of this discussion, the speech of any person whose pronunciation agrees with the common concept of Cockney will be called Cockney, no matter what the origin of the speaker.

The origin of Cockney. Reference to literary history reveals the existence of Cockney at least as far back as the 16th century. Matthews[3] regards Shakespeare's Dogberry, Verges, Mrs. Quickly, *et al.*, as being Cockney characters, along with corresponding characters in the plays of Beaumont and Fletcher, Dekker, Heywood, Ben Jonson, and Middleton. Zachrisson,[4] in discussing the popular English belief that Cockney stems from the eastern British dialect (e.g., Essex and Norfolk), concedes that "in early new English times the London pronunciation was strongly influenced by the Eastern dialects." But he thinks it possible that there has been a reciprocal Cockney influence on these dialects themselves, which confuses the issue. Zachrisson believes that Cockney owes its origin to the drastic changes which occurred as a result of the Industrial Revolution. Up until that time, while the language of the Court was taken as a model, there was no definite standard of speech. The margin of correctness was much wider than it is now. The correspondence of the people of high social position, such as Lady Wentworth, and even of Queen Elizabeth I herself, reveals pronunciations that grammarians of the period stigmatized as vulgar or incorrect.

But with the increase of wealth in the middle classes, a "rage for grandeur and

---

[1] The Middle English form of the word was *cokenay* or *coke ney*, probably derived from French *coquin*, knave, rogue, rascal.

[2] Bow bells, the bells of Bow Church, or the Church of St. Mary-le-Bow, near the center of present-day London.

[3] William Matthews, *Cockney Past and Present* (New York: Sutton, 1938), Chapters 1 and 2.

[4] R. E. Zachrisson, "Notes on the Essex Dialect and the Origin of Vulgar London Speech," in *Englische Studien*, V. 59, no. 3, p. 359.

gentility among the rich middle class people" caused them to become "jealous guardians of a correct standard of pronunciation which put an end to the easy tolerance that had characterized the polite speech of an earlier period."[5] Compilation of pronouncing dictionaries became a lucrative business. This became a very effective means by which pronunciation was stabilized. The children of the poorer classes, not having the advantages of school, pronouncing dictionaries, or an environment of careful speech, grew up adhering to the older and looser system of pronunciation and at the same time using new forms of their own which did not extend into the ranks of conservative speakers. "What characterizes Cockney as distinct from Standard English is therefore the retention of old-fashioned, irregular and dialectal forms, on the one hand, and the adoption of new and advanced forms of pronunciation, on the other."[6] The old and dialectal forms referred to are, very likely, the features which the Cockney of today exhibits in common with the eastern dialects.

Cockney in the 19th century. By the 19th century, Cockney had become an invaluable literary medium in the hands of writers. Thackeray burlesqued Cockney by means of the letters of Jeems Yellowplush in the *Yellowplush Papers* and Dickens reveled in a long list of Cockney characters, at the top of which most surely, we should place Sam Weller. There is no doubt that the writers of this period mingled with their representations of true Cockney a good deal of sheer imitation of each other. Perhaps they seldom introduced a pronunciation feature that cannot be confirmed in the naive spellings of diarists, letter-writers, parish clerks, and the like; but they undoubtedly exaggerated some of these features, such as prefixing of *h* to words beginning with vowels, as in Jeems Yellowplush's *Halfred*, and the exchanging of *v* and *w*, as in Sam Weller's *vether* and *wery*, which illustrate the *v-w* reversal. This latter feature has practically disappeared from modern Cockney, and it probably would not have done so if it had been as frequently used as the literature indicates. The prefixed *h* is believed to be of much less frequent occurrence in actual speech than in literature, and to be losing ground orally.

Present-day Cockney. Matthews[7] believes that present-day Cockney had come into well-developed form by 1880. Bernard Shaw[8] agrees with him. Writing of his use of Cockney dialect in the speech of Drinkwater in *Captain Brassbound's Conversion* (1899), Shaw says that he intends Drinkwater as an illustration of Cockney "for the benefit of the mass of readers outside London who still form their notions of Cockney dialect on Sam Weller." Comparison of Shaw's Cockney with that to be heard in London today would seem to prove that

---

[5] Zachrisson, p. 357.
[6] Zachrisson, p. 358.
[7] Matthews, Chapter 3.
[8] Bernard Shaw, in notes to "Captain Brassbound's Conversion" in *The Collected Works of Bernard Shaw* (Wm. H. Wise and Co., 1930), Vol. IX, p. 305.

there has been no basic change in the dialect in the last fifty to seventy-five years. If this assumption is true, the following comment of Zachrisson (1925), made in view of the widening gulf between Cockney and Standard British after the Industrial Revolution, and in view of the inability of the elementary and secondary schools of London to narrow the breach, is probably still a fair estimate of the situation:

> The present vulgar speech of London is a caricature of early Standard English. It is the language of the splendid Stuart period seen through the splinter of glass of which we read in one of Andersen's Fairy Tales; the wicked splinter which distorts the picture and makes it assume fantastic and grotesque shapes. The broad tolerance which characterized early standard speech has in Vulgar English deteriorated into a total lack of fixed rules and forms. At the same time the conservative forces which operate through oral tradition have been broken down and the way paved to a whole host of innovations, especially in the province of pronunciation. It is this mixture of new and old, resulting in a confusion worse confounded, that is the most typical mark of vulgar as opposed to standard speech.[9]

Tone and intonation of Cockney. The tone of Cockney is prominently nasal. The nasality, taking the form of a drawling whine as contrasted with the twang of a good number of American speakers, arrests attention even more sharply than the more vital substandard American. This nasality may be localized on the vowels adjacent to nasal consonants, but it often spreads over the whole vocal picture.

Matthews[10] says, "Cockneys avoid movement of the lips and jaw as far as possible, preserving a roughly half-open position of the lips. This habit causes a slight but very noticeable nasalization and leads to a slight rounding of the vowel sounds which need a full opening of the lips for their correct articulation. As a further tendency of the dialect is to centralize back vowels and diphthongs, many sounds which are widely separated in Standard speech come closer to one another in Cockney. . . . The general effect of these tendencies is to make the dialect rather confused and flabby, an effect which is increased by the habit of many Londoners to drag out an accented syllable (e. g., whisk . . . ers, pota . . . to). . . . Other Cockneys, costermongers in particular, overcome the defect by a loud utterance which transforms the dialect into a speech which is vigorous and confident, although ugly and raucous."

The intonation of Cockney, like that of any other dialect, is an important characteristic, but it cannot be successfully recorded on paper. Certain broad intonation characteristics of southern British speech in general, such as the falling voice at the end of questions capable of being answered by yes or no, can be learned by contrast with the characteristic rising inflection on such questions in American English. But in the main no amount of attention to vowel

---

[9] Zachrisson, pp. 358–359.
[10] Matthews, p. 77.

and consonant changes is likely to be truly effective unless the reader has heard Cockney speech and has captured the nuances of tempo, timbre, and pitch, which cannot be represented in a phonetic transcription. The reader should avail himself of the opportunity of hearing Cockney speech from the speakers themselves, in motion pictures, by radio, and through the medium of phonograph records.[11]

The interpretation of authors' spellings of Cockney. As in dealing with all dialects, authors are handicapped in spelling Cockney by the impossibility of representing certain sounds without a phonetic alphabet. Fortunately, since this is a phonetic book, the features difficult to represent in spelling will be clarified in the pages following.

Authors are further handicapped by a subconscious tendency to spell in terms of their own pronunciation. Since Cockney literature is nearly all produced by British writers, there is need to be forewarned concerning certain British conventions of spelling which they are prone to employ. These are perfectly intelligible to British readers, but American readers are in danger of misinterpreting them. A good example is the effort to represent on paper the drawl which so frequently accompanies the Cockney nasality. Dialect writers often try to indicate the drawl by using *h* as a diacritic denoting length, as in *abaht* [əbɑ::t] for *about*. Other writers use *r* in the same diacritic sense, as in *abart* [əˈbɑ::t] for *about* and *blarst it* [blɑ::st ɪt] for *blast it*. The orthographic *r* used in the diacritic sense is especially likely to prove misleading to General American speakers and to others who pronounce postvocalic *r*. These will think [əˈbɑrt] and [blɑrst] are intended. *Half* spelled *arf* and *off* spelled *orf* are, of course, intended by the writer to be pronounced [ɑ::f] and [ɔ˔::f], but they may be mistaken by many readers for [ɑrf] and [ɔrf]. Obviously, the only writers who would use *r* as a lengthening sign are English writers or those from the southern or eastern United States, and the only readers who would misunderstand their efforts are the General American speakers and others referred to above. But the misunderstanding of the authors' intention is sufficiently frequent that the reader should always take into careful consideration the form of English spoken by the writer whom he is interpreting. Correlatively, the reader should be conscious of his own native speech inclinations and should be on guard not to allow them to lead him into a misinterpretation of a writer who uses a different pronunciation.

Actors, interpretative readers, and other readers, if they take the precautions implied in the preceding, will usually be able to determine from the author's pseudo-phonetic spellings approximately what his intentions are. If it appears that the author meant to present a character using only a degree of Cockney speech, the reader had best give Cockney pronunciation only to the words in

---

[11] Dialect records may be obtained from The British Drama League, 9 Fitzroy Square, London, W. I.

which the author has modified the spelling. The remaining words should be pronounced, not in the reader's habitual speech, especially if it is so far removed from British Speech as the General American, but instead in the Standard British of London. If, on the other hand, it appears that the author intended to represent an extreme Cockney character, the reader had best pronounce in a Cockney fashion even those words in which the author has not modified the spelling. It must be remembered that an author, being deprived of a phonetic alphabet, often not merely cannot find a spelling which will express the Cockney pronunciation, but has to beware of burdening his page with so many deviations from ordinary spelling as to make the matter partially illegible and unintelligible to the lay reader. Still further, the ear of the author may be sensitized to only a certain number of the characteristic Cockney variants. To do complete justice to the author's script, the reader must add the remaining Cockney characteristics. Whether the characteristics be represented as a moderate or an extreme Cockney, the reader will be justified in falling back upon the Standard British pronunciations at any point where the author's suggestions or the suggestions of these pages do not cover the situation.

Some Important Pronunciation Features of Cockney Vowels

[i] ∽[12] [əi] as in *me* [məi], *see* [səi]. The [ə] in [əi] must be pronounced as an on-glide to the principal sound [i], so that the stress of the sound combination remains on [i], much as if the on-glide were not present.

[ɪə] ∽ [ˈijə], as in *fear* [ˈfijə], *clear* [ˈklijə]. An extreme development of this sound combination is [ˈɪɪjə], as in *peer* [ˈpɪɪjə].[13]

[eɪ] ∽ [aɪ] as in *maid* [maɪd], *train* [traɪn]. A variant of this pronunciation, thought by some to represent the true Cockney more accurately, is [ʌɪ], as in *day* [dʌɪ]. When the diphthong occurs before a final *l*, it is modified to [æə], as in *pail* [ˈpæəl].[14]

[æ] ∽ [ɛ], as in *ham* [ɛm], *back* [bɛk]. This pronunciation must not be attributed to Cockney alone. Though much opposed, it appears in standard southern British, as in *majesty* [ˈmɛdʒɪstɪ].

[aɪ] ∽ [ɑɪ], as in *fine* [fɑɪn], *time* [tɑɪm]. Probably a closer transcription such as [ʌˑɪ] is more nearly exact, but the acoustic difference would not be great. Since [ʌˑɪ] and [ɑɪ] cannot be represented in ordinary print, this pronunciation is generally conventionalized in literature as *oi*, as in *roide* [rɔɪd] for *ride*. This pronunciation actually appears at times, but is less frequent than [ɑɪ]. Other

---

[12] Here, as elsewhere in this book, the symbol (∽) means "corresponds to." [i] ∽ [əi] should be read "the Standard English [i] corresponds to the Cockney [əi]."

[13] Ida C. Ward, *The Phonetics of English* (Cambridge: Heffer and Sons, Ltd., 1929), p. 104.

[14] Ward, p. 98.

variants are [ɑːɪ][15] and [ɒɪ]. Under social pressure, the Cockney will use [æɪ] as a *"refined"* [rɪˈfæɪnd] pronunciation.[16]

[aʊ] ~ [ɑː], as in *down* [dɑːn], *out* [ɑːt]. One may also hear [ɛʊ] as in *round* [rɛʊnd].[17] The sound [æʊ], as in *found* [fæʊnd], occurs as a "refined" pronunciation.

[a] ~ [ɒː], as in *ask* [ɒːsk] and other "broad-*a*" words. In print, this sound is usually represented with *aw*, a spelling which promotes the sound [ɔ]; actually [ɔ] is very satisfactory for stage use in representing extreme Cockney speech. However, many Cockneys simply use the [ɑ] of Standard Southern British, as in *half* [ɑf].

[a] ~ [ɔ] or [ɒː] occasionally, both at present and as early as the 17th century,[18] in stressed syllables in *ar*, as in *charm* [tʃɔm], *Charles* [tʃɔlz]. However, the standard [ɑ] appears to be more common.

[ɔɪ] ~ [ɔː], as *spoil* [spɔːl],[19] *noise* [nɔːz]. This pronunciation is rather extreme. In many instances a normal [ɔɪ] is used, as in *oil* [ɔɪl].

[oʊ] ~ [ʌʊ, aʊ], as in *rode* [rʌʊd, raʊd]. Of these two pronunciations, Matthews[20] regards the former as more exact. However, because of the simplicity of printing the sound with *ow*, as in *now* [naʊ] for *no*, the pronunciation [aʊ] is well established in this connection and is probably the most satisfactory for stage use.

[oə] ~ [ˈowə], as in *sore* [ˈsowə], *four* [ˈfowə].[21]

[u] ~ [əʉ, ɪu], as in *do* [dəʉ, dɪu]. Of these two pronunciations, the second is the easier to pronounce, representing, as it does, an approach to [ju], as in *dew* [dju]. Jones and Ward both record this sound as [ʉ].[22]

[u] before dark *l* ~ [oː], as in *cool* [koːɫ].[23]

[ʌ] ~ [ɑ], as in *up* [ɑp], *mother* [ˈmɑðə]. Before dark *l* [ʌ] ~ [ɔ], as *bulk* [bɔɫk], *multiple* [ˈmɔɫtɪpəl].[24]

Some Important Pronunciation Features of Cockney Consonants

[p] initially ~ [pˤ], as *put* [pˤut]. This is simply an over-aspiration of [p].

[p] medially ~ [ʔ], as in *paper* [ˈpaɪʔə].

[t] initially ~ [ts], as in *time* [tsaɪm]. This is a type of over-aspiration of [t] which results in the production of the affricate [ts].

[t] medially ~ [ɾ], as in *better* [ˈbɛɾə]. See also [t] ~ [ʔ], page 253.

---

[15] As of 1899, Shaw interpreted the sound as [ɔːɪ]. Shaw, *op. cit.*, p. 305.
[16] Ward, p. 101.
[17] Jones, *The Pronunciation of English* (New York: Cambridge University Press, 1950), p. 60.
[18] Matthews, p. 167.
[19] Shaw, *Pygmalion*, the character Eliza.
[20] Matthews, p. 79.
[21] Jones, *The Pronunciation of English*, p. 64. Also Ward, p. 83.
[22] Jones, p. 42. Ward, pp. 86–87.
[23] Ward, p. 87.
[24] Ward, p. 88.

[t] medially and finally ∼ [ʔ], as in *better* [ˈbɛʔə], *little* [ˈlɪʔl̩], *cattle* [ˈkɛʔl̩], *bottle* [ˈbɒʔl̩], *battle* [ˈbɛʔl̩], *got* [gɒʔ].

[t] is added excrescently after [s] final, as in [wɒnst] for *once* and [klaʊst] for *close*.

[d] is added excrescently after final *n* and *r*, as [gɑnd, gæʊnd] for *gown*, [ˈskɒləd] for *scholar*.

[k] initially ∼ [kx] as in *cut* [kxɑt]. This is a type of over-aspiration which results in the production of the affricate [kx].

[k] medially and finally ∼ [ʔ], as in *bacon* [ˈbaɪʔn̩], *talk* [tɔʔ].

[dj] ∼ [dʒ], as in *duke* [dʒuk], *immediately* [ɪˈməidʒɪtlɪ].

[l], as in Standard Southern British, is clear before front vowels and dark before back vowels and finally; but by comparison, Cockney dark *l* is excessively dark, with a resonance of [ɔ] or [o], instead of the standard [ʊ]. As indicated in the next paragraph, the quality of [ɔ] or [o] may replace [l] entirely.

[l] ∼ [o, ɔ], as in *Bill* [ˈbɪo, ˈbɪɔ], *sell* [sɛo, sɛɔ], *milk* [ˈmɪok, ˈmɪɔk]. For stage purposes, this sound is most simply represented by [o].

[r] appears in an excrescent or supernumerary fashion: (1) between words where the first ends with a vowel and the second begins with a vowel, as in "idear of it"; (2) within words where a syllable ending in a vowel is followed by a syllable beginning with a vowel, as in "jawring"; and (3) at the end of a word spelled with a final vowel, as in "Louisar." The last instance may be regarded as a residue from contexts such as (1) above; that is, "Louisar," in *Her name is Louisar*, may be taken as a development from "Louisar and John."

[n] ∼ [m] in rapid speech after [p] and [b] by assimilation, as in *heaven* [ˈɛbm̩], *halfpenny* [ˈaɪpmɪ]. (See note under [v].)

[n] ∼ [ŋ] by over-correction (hyperurbanism), as in *garden* [ˈgɑːdɪŋ], *kitchen* [ˈkɪtʃɪŋ].

[ŋ] ∼ [ŋk], as in compounds of *-thing*, such as *nothing* [ˈnafɪŋk], *something* [ˈsamfɪŋk].

[ŋ] ∼ [n], as in all dialects, in words such as *happening* [ˈɛpnɪn], *blooming* [ˈblɪumɪn], *going* [ˈgaʊɪn].

[θ] ∼ [f], as in *thing* [fɪn], *three* [frəi], *thirst* [fɜst].

[ð] ∼ [v], as in *feather* [ˈfɛvə], *those* [vaʊz]. This is an extreme feature.

[v] in final unstressed *-ven* ∼ [b], as in *seven* [ˈsɛbm̩], *heaven* [ˈɛbm̩]. NOTE: Here the labio-dental [v] has become bilabial, after which, by progressive assimilation, it has labialized the [n].

[h] ∼ zero in initial positions, as in *hold* [aʊld], *hook* [ʊk]. The corresponding addition of [h] to words beginning with a stressed vowel, such as *Everett* [ˈhɛvrɪt] is believed to be disappearing.

[ə] appears by anaptyxis between *r* and a preceding consonant, as in *Henry* [ˈɛnərɪ], *surprised* [səpəˈraɪzd], *umbrella* [ˌʌmbəˈrɛlə], *proprietor* [ˌprɒpəˈraɪətə]. This feature, well known (as in Dickens) in the 18th and 19th centuries, is thought to be waning.[25]

---

[25] Matthews, p. 173.

Characteristics of Standard Southern British Speech Peculiarly Necessary to the Pronunciation of Cockney

It has already been recommended that where the foregoing specific features of Cockney do not cover the ground, the reader of Cockney dialect should complete the pronunciation system by drawing upon Standard Southern British as outlined in Chapter 10. The following are particularly necessary features, some of which might not occur to an American reader. (Some of these are not recognized as standard pronunciations, yet they are frequently used by educated speakers.)

1. [jə] or [jʌ] for [ɪə], as in *here* [hjə, hjʌ], etc.
2. [ɑ] for [ə], as in *butter* [ˈbɑtɑ].
3. [ɔ] rather than [ˈɔə], as in *four* [fɔ], *more* [mɔ], *floor* [flɔ].
4. [ɔ] for [ʊ] or [ˈʊə], as in *pure* [pjɔ], *sure* [ʃɔ], *curious* [ˈkjɔɾɪəs], *furious* [ˈfjɔɾɪəs].
5. Intrusive or excrescent *r*, as in *soda and milk* [ˌsoʊdəɾənˈmɪlk], *Pandora* [pænˈdɔɾər].
6. Clear *l* before front vowels, as in *place* [pl̥eɪs].
7. [ɔ] is raised to a point close to [o] in the spellings *all*, *au*, and *aw*, as in *fall* [fɔˋl], *Paul* [pɔˋl], *law* [lɔˋ].

Illustrative Transcription of Cockney

From *Pygmalion*

(Transcription shows extreme Cockney, rather more detailed than Shaw's spelling justifies.)

GIRL. nɑː vɛn, frɛdɪ, luʔ wə jə gaʊɪn, dɪjɑ.

FREDDY. sɒɾɪ.

GIRL. ðejəz mɛnəz fjə. tɪu bantʃɪz ə vaɪlɪts trɒd ɪntə ðə mad.

THE MOTHER. haʊ dʊ ju nɜʊ ðət maɪ sanz neɪm ɪz frɛdɪ, preɪ?

GIRL. aʊ, iʒ jɪuɑ san, ɪz i? wɛo, fjud dan jə dʒɪutɪ bamz ə mavə ʃud, id naʊ bɛtə n tə spɒl ə pɔ gɛəlz flɑːz, vɛn ran əwaɪ əvɑːt paɪjɪn. wɪo jɪu paɪ mɪ fə ðm̩? . . aɪ kŋ gɪv jə tʃaɪndʒ f ə tɛnə, kaˈɪnd laɪdɪ. θɛŋk jə kaˈɪndlɪ, laɪdɪ.

G. B. SHAW

Fragments from *The Admirable Crichton* *

luʔ wɒʔ aɪ fɑːnd. ðeɪ graʊz ɔn traɪz. aɪ θɔˋʔ əz aʊ ðeɪ grɪu ɪn ə raʊ ɔn tɒp ə lɪʔl stɪks ——— aɪm ful ə valgə wɜdz n̩ waɪz, n̩ ðaʊ ə maɪ kəɪp m̩ ɪn ðɛɾ aʊlz wɛn juə baɪ, əz sɪun əz aɪm baɪ məsɛof, at ðeɪ kamz ɪn ə raʃ laik bəɪʔlz wɛn ði as ɪz dak. aɪ sɛz əm glaʊʔn̩-laik ɪn mɪ ɛd. "blɪumɪn," aɪ sɛz, "ɛu məɪ aɪ," aɪ sɛz, n̩ "dʒɪndʒə," n̩ "nafɪŋk." n̩ ɔˋl ðə taɪm wɪ wəz bəɪən rɛkt, aɪ wəz praɪən tə məsɛof, pləɪz ðə lɔˋd, ɪt maɪʔ bəɪ ə naɪlənd əz ɑ ɪts nɛtʃəɾəl tə bəɪ valgəɾ ɔn.

JAMES M. BARRIE

To be transcribed in Cockney dialect:
Drinkwater in *Captain Brassbound's Conversion*
(Note that Shaw's spelling appears to indicate the [aɪ] ∽ [ɔ])

"Wot abaht them! Waw, they're eah. Lannid aht of a steam yacht in Mogador awbor not twenty minnits agow. Gorn to the British consul's. E'll send em orn to you: e ynt got naowheres to put em. Sor em awr a Harab an two Krooboys to kerry their laggige. Thort awd cam an teoll yer.

"Downt mention it, gavner. Lor bless yer, wawnt it you as converted me? Wot was aw wen aw cam eah but a pore lorst sinner? Downt aw owe y'u a turn fer thet? Besawds, gavner, this Lidy Sisly Winefleet mawt wornt to tike a walk, crost Morocker—a rawd inter the mahntns or sech lawk. Weoll, as you knaow, gavner, thet cawnt be done eah withaht a hescort."

G. B. SHAW

The Cockney Tongue[26]

Vere was a bloke goin' dahn tah'r Bridge Road, an' ve Decima Stree' click se' abaht 'im. Vey dropped 'im one, wen' froo 'is chain and lockets, 'alf inched 'is splosh and lef' 'im barmy. Arter a bi' came along a parson, 'oo fought 'e was blindo an' steered righ' rahnd 'im. Arter anover li'l bi' one of ve club yobos came along, 'ad a dekko a' 'im an' said, "Ere, I ain' goin' to be mixed up in a rough 'ahse, my name's drippin!" so 'e 'opped it too. Bimeby came along a Jew boy, 'oo 'ad a peep a' 'im, an' felt real sorry for ve poor bloke. So 'e picked 'im aht of ve gu'er, fahnd 'is 'at and pu' it on 'is napper, an' took 'im to ve doss 'ahse, where 'e kipped 'imself. In ve morning, 'e said to ve boss, "Look 'ere, guvnor, this poor bloke ain' 'alf 'ad a kybosh, you look arter 'im an' I'll see you Sa'urday night." Nah ven, which of vose free blokes was a real Chrischen? . . . ve Jew Boy? No' 'alf 'e weren't.

W. McEAGER

Bibliography

Cockney

Books
Matthews, William, *Cockney Past and Present* (New York: E. P. Dutton and Co., 1938).
Shaw, G. B., *Notes to "Captain Brassbound's Conversion"* in *The Collected Works of Bernard Shaw* (New York: Wm. H. Wise and Co., 1930).
Ward, Ida C., *The Phonetics of English* (Cambridge: Heffer and Sons, Ltd., 1929).

Periodicals
Zachrisson, R. E., "Notes on the Essex Dialect and the Origin of Vulgar London Speech," in *Englische Studien*, vol. 59, no. 3, 1925.

---

[26] In *Contemporary Review*, September, 1922, p. 370.

CHAPTER 12

Scottish

Strictly speaking, it is not proper to say "Scots dialect"; instead it is "Scots dialects," for there is no other area in the English-speaking world as small as Scotland which has so many dialects. Where in England we speak of the dialect of a given county, in Scotland we must speak of the dialect of a given valley, or village, or other tiny homogeneous area.[1] Scotland is essentially a rural area, despite its three good-sized cities; and the Scots agriculturists do not travel frequently or far, for the rugged nature of the country discourages travel. The age-long limitations in transit have resulted in an isloation even as great as that in Ireland. The result of this isolation is not one dialect but a system of dialects, whose differences are exceedingly sharp and contrasting; where the man on the street in Edinburgh says *do* [du] and the gardener in the suburbs says *dae* [de], the native of Buchan in Aberdeenshire says *tee* [ti].[2] Or even more surprisingly, we may find *what* [ʍɒt] varying toward Northern Scotland through [xʍɒt] to [fɒt][3] (Northern Scots).

And yet, all these widely divergent dialects possess a degree of similarity. It is this similarity to which one customarily refers when one speaks of Scottish

---

[1] Ellis (*Early English Pronunciation*, V., p. 681) divides Scotland into four divisions: south, mid, north, and insular-lowland. The counties assigned to these four divisions are as follows:

South: The South Lowland—Selkirk, Roxburgh, East and Central Dumfries.

Mid: (1) Eastern Mid-Lowland—Peebles, Berwick, Haddington, Edinburgh, Linlithgow, Mid- and East Sterling, Clackmannan, Kinrose, all Fife, except North-west; (2) Western Mid-Lowland—Lanark, North Ayr, Renfrew, Dumbarton, Argyle (near Dunoon), most of Bute; (3) Southern Mid-Lowland—East Perth, North-west Fife, and West Forfar.

North: (1) Southern North Lowland—East Forfar, Kincardine, (except the extreme northern portion); (2) Mid-North Lowland—Aberdeen, most of Banff, Elgin, and Nairn, East Cromarty; (3) Northern North Lowland—Northeast of Caithness.

Insular-Lowland: (1) Southern Insular—Orkney; (2) Northern Insular—Shetland. From Alex. Warrack in *A Scots Dialect Dictionary*, p. lx.

[2] Eugen Dieth, *A Grammar of the Buchan Dialect* (Cambridge: W. Heffer and Sons, Ltd., 1932), p. 8.

[3] William Grant, *The Pronunciation of English in Scotland* (Cambridge: Cambridge University Press, 1913), p. 38.

dialect. The data which follow undertake to record certain of these similarities There is no attempt here to describe all the dialects of Scotland. There is, indeed, a definite effort not to be drawn into lengthy description of the dialect of any single small area. Instead, a kind of composite dialect is indicated, not precisely true for any one part of Scotland, but being generalized for most of the country, aside from isolated or distant parts, such as Caithness or the Orkney and Shetland Islands. Such generalization is, incidentally, in keeping with the practice of many Scottish writers, including, notably, Robert Louis Stevenson.[4]

This composite or synthetic dialect will, however, answer the purposes of actors, interpretative readers, stage directors, and others who wish to use a Scots suggestive of the reality but not too detailed or "thick" to be unintelligible to a non-Scots audience. Applied to the problem of pronouncing the writings of a good writer of Scottish dialect literature, the result will be satisfactory to most audiences, perhaps even in Scotland itself, for the data are not intended to supply vocabulary or syntax (the author will do that), but only the pronunciation of material already provided.

The sources of information whence the following is derived are themselves so various as to point toward a composite result. They consist of (1) travel in Scotland, during which phonetic transcriptions of pronunciation were continually recorded; (2) the examination of dialect literature for the sifting out of characteristic pronunciations; and (3) the writings of phoneticians and other linguists. Each item has been checked against the findings of such authorities as Warrack,[5] Ellis,[6] Dieth,[7] Jones,[8] Ward,[9] Grant and Dixon,[10] and Murray.[11]

The material here included consists of (1) a summary of the standard dialects of Scotland, as spoken by educated people; and (2) selected features of folk pronunciation, regarded as deviations from the standard.

---

[4] William Grant and James Main Dixon, *Manual of Modern Scots* (Cambridge: Cambridge University Press, 1921), p. 20. At the present time, Scottish dialect varies from one district to another all over the lowland area, in pronunciation, idiom, vocabulary, and intonation. Most of our Scottish writers, however, have refused to bind themselves to any local form of dialect. They aim to be understood by the nation, and not merely by the parish or county. "I simply wrote my Scots as I was able," remarks Stevenson, "not caring if it hailed from Lauderdale or Angus, Mearns or Galloway; if I had ever heard a good word, I used it without shame, and when Scots was lacking or a rhyme jibbed I was glad, like my betters, to fall back on English."

[5] Alexander Warrack, *A Scots Dialect Dictionary* (London and Edinburgh: W. and R. Chambers, Ltd., 1911).

[6] A. J. Ellis, *Early English Pronunciation* (New York: Oxford University Press, 1869).

[7] *op. cit.*

[8] Daniel Jones, *The Pronunciation of English* (London, Cambridge University Press, 1950).

[9] Ida C. Ward, *The Phonetics of English* (Cambridge: Cambridge University Press, 1929).

[10] *op. cit.*

[11] James A. H. Murray, *The Dialect of the Southern Counties of Scotland* (London: Asher, 1873).

It must be understood that in this brief treatment of Scots little attempt is made to provide an exhaustive list of words used in the dialect or to indicate the modification of words by way of dropping sounds. Data on these characteristics can be omitted here because the dialect literature which the users of this book will be reading (plays, poetry, novels, etc.) will show word choice and the dropping of sounds in context.

The intention here is to provide a reasonably reliable guide for the pronunciation of the words that appear in literature, rather than to categorize the features themselves extensively on the basis of word-selection or spelling.

Some Characteristics of Standard Scottish Pronunciation

[eɪ] ∼ [e],[12] as in *fade* [fed], *way* [we]. This is the pure vowel [e], as contrasted with the dipthongal [eɪ].

[oʊ] ∼ [o], as in *rode* [rod], *low* [lo]. This is the pure vowel [o], as contrasted with the diphthongal [oʊ]. [i] and [u] are single sounds pronounced without perceptible change of pitch and without the addition of off-glides, as in the [iɪ] and [uʊ] of many dialects of English. Thus: [si] instead of [siɪ] for *see*, [du] instead of [duʊ] for *do*.

[ɪr, ɪə] ∼ [ir],[13] as in *beer* [bir], *dear* [dir]. (Note that [r] is trilled.)

Transcribe: fear, clear, seer, sear, sere, mere, cheer, peer, appear, queer.

[ε, æ] ∼ [e] in a class of words spelled with *are, air, arr, ear, eir*, such as *fair* [fer], *care* [ker], *bear* [ber], *heir* [er], *chair* [tʃer], *marry* [ˈmerɪ].

Transcribe: fare, rare, dare, hare, hair, stair, pair, pare, pear, wear, carry, Harry, hairy, fairy, bare, bear, square, share, mare, rarely, swear.

[æ] ∼ [a] in all "short *a*" spellings as in *man* [man], *bat* [bat].

Transcribe: at, that, acts, amity, altitude, family, battery, scatter.

The "broad *a*" [ɑ] ∼ [a, ɑ], as in *ask* [ask, ɑsk], *path* [paθ, pɑθ]. This is the familiar category spelled most often with *a* plus [f] ([v] in plurals), [s], [θ] ([ð] in plurals), and [n] plus a consonant (see p. 222). According to Grant,[14] [ɑ] is preferred in some words and [a] in others; but apparently either may be used in nearly any "broad *a*" word. In general, [a] is more frequently used.

Transcribe: laughing, aftermath, last, half, halves, past, bath, baths, branch, chance.

---

[12] Here, as elsewhere in this book, the symbol (∼) means "corresponds to." The entry above should be read: Standard English diphthongal [eɪ] corresponds to the Scottish pure vowel [e].

[13] As will be indicated later, all *r*'s in Scots are to be pronounced with the tongue-point trill.

[14] Grant, *op. cit.,* p. 95.

[ɑ, ɒ] ~ [ɒ], as in most "short *o*" words, such as *got* [gɒt], *operate* [ˈɒpəˈret]. Certain words spelled with *wa*, *wha*, are pronounced in the same way, as in *was* [wɒz], *watch* [wɒtʃ], *what* [ʌɒt].

[o] is used in words spelled with *oar*, *ore*, *oor*, *our*, as in *boar* [bor], *board* [bord].

> *Transcribe:* bore, coarse, core, course, courtier, door, floor, fore, four, gore, hoarse, hoary, more, mourn, oar, pour, story, more.

[o] is also used in a number of words spelled with *or* plus a consonant, such as *afford*, *ford*, *horde*, *sworn*, *fort*, *port*, *sport*, *forth*, *divorce*, *force*, *borne*, *torn*, *worn*, *forge*, *port*. *Sworn*, *torn*, *worn*, *pork*, and *sword* are also pronounced with [ɔ]. *Transcribe the foregoing.* Most other words with *or* or *or* plus *u* plus consonant, such as *cord*, are pronounced with [ɔ]. *Forty*, despite its relation to *four*, and *fortify* and *fortification*, despite their relation to *fort*, are pronounced with [ɔ].

[ʊ] ~ [u], as in *full* [ful], *good* [gud]. The [u] used here is somewhat briefer in duration than that in *fool* and *food*, but otherwise differs from it very slightly if at all. In an occasional word, such as *woman* [ˈwʊmən], the earlier sound [u] has given way to [ʊ], and in general it may be said that, in recent years, most words which are pronounced with [ʊ] in southern British or in American English are gradually coming to be pronounced with [ʊ] in Scottish also. After [d], [t], and [n], the spellings *eu*, *ew*, *u*, and *ue* are pronounced [ju], as in *deuce* [djus], *due* [dju], *duty* [ˈdjutɪ], *due* [dju], *Teutonic* [tjuˈtɒnɪk], *tutor* [ˈtjutər], *Tuesday* [ˈtjuzdɪ], *pneumatic* [njuˈmatɪk] *knew* [nju], *numeral* [ˈnjumərəl].

> *Transcribe:* Deuteronomy, dewy, duly, duke, tune, neutral, neutron, newt, nude, nuisance.

The Scottish sounds corresponding to [з] and [ɝ]: 1. [з, ɝ] ~ [ʌr] in words spelled with *ur*, *or*, and *our* in the stressed syllables, as in *turn* [tʌrn], *work* [wʌrk], *nourish* [ˈnʌrɪʃ].

> *Transcribe:* worse, worst, worms, world, journey, churn, hurt, hurl, fur, curve, flourish, curt, burst, curse, Burke, urn, journal.

2. [з, ɝ] ~ [ɛr] in words spelled with *er* and *ear* in the stressed syllables, as in *defer* [dɪˈfɛr] (and other compounds of *fer*), *heard* [hɛrd], *tern* [tɛrn].

> *Transcribe:* earn, early, discern, earnest, Ernest, learn, fern, yearn, prefer, aver, were, certain.

3. [з, ɝ] ~ [зr] in words spelled with *ir* in the stressed syllable, as in *bird* [bзrd], *sir* [sзr]. In this usage [зr] must not be considered the equivalent of [ɝ] where the sound of [з] and the [r] are integrated into a single sound. In [зr], on the other hand, the two sounds are in sequence, with no more integration than is implied when any two sounds are in close juncture. In addition, the [r] is, of course, trilled.

> *Transcribe:* firm, first, third, twirl, squirm, fir, gird, squirt, swirl, quirk.

[ə, ɚ] ~ [ər] in words spelled with unstressed *ar, er, ir, or, our, ur, yr*, as in *mortar* [ˈmɔrtər], *worker* [ˈwʌrkər], *tapir* [ˈtepər], *rector* [ˈrɛktər], *savour* (Br. and Can.) [ˈsevər], *murmur* [ˈmʌrmər], *martyr* [ˈmartər]. [ər] has, of course, the trilled [r].

Transcribe: Lascar, Madagascar, blister, roaster, fakir, sector, vector, labor, labour, satyr.

[aɪ] ~ [ɜɪ, aɪ]. Some speakers use [aɪ] all the time and some [ɜɪ] all the time. Others use both, sometimes according to rather complicated rules, as indicated in footnotes 15 and 16. It is very difficult to make a statement as to when the one diphthong or the other is used. For purposes of drama or interpretative reading it is probably best to use [ɜɪ] before voiceless consonants, as in *wife* [wɜɪf], *bite* [bɜɪt], and [aɪ] in all other cases, as in *item* [ˈaɪtəm], *inspiring* [ɪnˈspaɪrɪŋ], *dry* [draɪ]. See comments by Grant[15] and Jones[16] below.

[aʊ] ~ [ɜʊ, aʊ], (sometimes [ɑʊ] or [ʌʊ]).Some speakers use [aʊ] all the time,[17] some [ɜʊ] all the time, and some both, according to somewhat involved rules.[18] The simplest of these rules specifies that [ɜʊ] be used before voiceless consonants, as in *out* [ɜʊt], *mouse* [mɜʊs], and [aʊ] everywhere else, as in *bough* [baʊ], *cloud* [klaʊd].

Either and *neither* are pronounced [ˈiðər] and [ˈniðər];[ˈaɪðər] and [ˈnaɪðər] are also known. See substandard pronunciation, page 268.

[l] ~ [ł], i.e., "dark *l*." Authorities differ on the question of "dark *l*" and "clear *l*" in Standard Scottish speech. Grant[19] believes that "clear *l*" is more common than "dark *l*" initially before front vowels, while Jones[20] states unequivocally that all Scottish *l*'s are dark.

---

[15] Grant, p. 63. "[a] is generally the first element in the diphthong [aɪ], heard in *high, rise*, etc. ... Many good speakers use [aɪ] wherever this diphthong occurs, but the majority of Scottish speakers use a distinct variant. ...

"This [ɜɪ] (Grant's rendering) is allowable except when the diphthong ends the syllable or stands before [r, z, v, ð]. ... Note that an inflectional ending does not alter the sound, e. g. *sigh* [saɪ], *sighed* [saɪd]. It sometimes happens also that people who observe the rule of [aɪ] and [ɜɪ] are occasionally influenced by analogy, e. g., they will say [wɜɪvz] instead of [waɪvz], because of the singular [wɜɪf]."

[16] Jones, p. 57. "Some use it [ɜɪ] everywhere. ... They pronounce *fly* and *time* as [flɜɪ] and [tɜɪm]. Some make an exception of final positions and of words with the inflectional ending *d* and *z*. They pronounce *time, ride, prize* as [tɜɪm, rɜɪd, prɜɪz], but *try, tried, tries* as [traɪ, traɪd, traɪz] ... Probably the commonest of all in Scotland, is to pronounce [ɜɪ] before breathed [voiceless] consonants but [aɪ] in all other positions."

[17] Grant, p. 53.

[18] Jones, p. 60. "Some use it [ɜʊ] (Jones's rendering = [ɜʊ]) everywhere. ... They pronounce *how, town, out* as [hɜʊ], [tɜʊn], [ɜʊt]. Some use a variety of [aʊ] finally and before the inflectional endings [z] and [d], but [ɜʊ] elsewhere, thus [haʊ], [braʊ], (brow) [braʊz] (brows), but [tɜʊn], [ɜʊt], [brɜʊz] (browse). But probably the most frequent pronunciation in Scotland is to use [ɜʊ] before breathed [voiceless] consonants and [aʊ] in all other positions. ..."

[19] Grant, p. 33.

[20] Jones, p. 89.

[r] ~ "trilled *r*" [ř]. This is the tongue-point trill. In initial and medial contexts, where the trill is difficult, a retroflex fricative or non-fricative *r* is often used. It is regarded as correct, however, to trill every orthographic *r*.

NOTE: In final and preconsonantal positions, the trill may be weakened to a single tap; thus, *for* [fɔɾ], *ford* [fɔɾd], instead of [fɔr] and [ford]. Under the influence of British speech, this [r] may lose the trill entirely[21] (but without becoming silent) and be pronounced like a General American *r*.

NOTE: In words ending in [tər] it seems nearly impossible not to introduce an off-glide in the form of [θ] between the [t] proper and the trilled *r*; thus *better* [ˈbɛtər] is almost inevitably pronounced [ˈbɛtθər].

[tʃ] ~ [tj], as in *pasture* [ˈpastjər], *question* [ˈkwɛstjən].

[dʒ] ~ [dj], as in *verdure* [ˈvɛrdjər], *educate* [ˈɛdjuˌket].

These pronunciations represent a conservative attitude which appears to be yielding to the use of [tʃ] and [dʒ].

Transcribe: nature, feature, nurture, furniture, investiture, literature, adulation, modulate.

[ð] ~ [θ] in *though* [θo], *thence* [θɛnts], *thither* [ˈθɪðər], *with* [wɪθ]. The voiced [ð] is also used in these words.

[x] is used for the spelling *ch* after back vowels in some Gaelic words, especially place names such as *Loch Lomond* [ˌlɔx ˈlomənd]. Further use of this sound is considered substandard. (See page 269.)

See also substandard use of [ç], page 269.

wh [ʍ] is used in nearly all words spelled with *wh* except *who*, *whole*, and their derivatives. Examples: *which* [ʍɪtʃ], *when* [ʍɛn].

Transcribe: where, wheel, whistle, wheat, whir, whiskey, whether, wither, whence, why, what, whip.

Stress

Polysyllables ending in *ary*, *ery*, *ory*, and certain other polysyllables which have both primary and secondary stress in American English, have only primary stress in Standard Scottish. The stress system appears to agree with that of Standard Southern British. Examples: *dictionary* [ˈdɪkʃənərɪ], *antiquary* [ˈantɪkwərɪ]. Final unstressed syllables ending in a consonant generally use [ə] rather than [ɪ], as in *blanket* [ˈblaŋkət], a pattern essentially parallel with that of General American English. (See pages 187 ff.) Medial unstressed syllables spelled with *e*, *i*, and *y* are generally [ɪ], instead of [ə] as in *civilized* [ˈsivɪˌlaɪzd], essentially according to the pattern of Standard Southern British. (See pages 240 ff.)

---

[21] Grant, p. 35.

Deviations from Standard Scottish

The following are some of the pronunciations that characterize a generalized or composite Scots dialect at levels below that of the educated middle class. In reading dialect literature of this level, the reader or actor should fall back (1) upon the pronunciations of Standard Scottish as given above, (2) upon general English language pronunciation for all points not covered in this book.

The reader must not expect entire consistency. The same word is often pronounced in two or more different ways, and may be used herein to illustrate as many characteristic sounds.

Some Dialectal Features Evident in Spelling

In a brief account such as this, it is economical to omit detailed discussion of dialectal features whose nature and acoustic effect are evident in the spelling of dialect writers. A number of these orthographically evident features are briefly listed here.

Metathesis. Metathesis is an exchange of the positions of sounds. It is common in all languages, but particularly prevalent in Scots. Compare *gerse, gerss, girse,* (grass); *corse* (cross); *kirsen* (christen); *warsle* (wrestle); *brunt* (burnt); *crub* (curb); *rhubrub* (rhubarb); *provribs* (proverbs); *wrat* (wort); *girn* (grin); *thretteen* (thirteen); *thretty* (thirty); *girsie, gersy* (grassy); *girstle* (gristle); *girst* (grist); *girt* (great); *wordle* (world); *thred* (third).

Anaptyxis. Anaptyxis is the intrusion of a vowel adjacent to a vowel-like consonant, as in *shiriek* (shriek), *spelay* (splay), *sherill* (shrill), *gurrul* (girl), *warrum* (worm).

b does not appear after [m] in such words as ~~nummer, nimmer~~ (number), ~~thummle~~ (thimble), *chamer* (chamber), *skemmel* (shamble).

d is dropped after [n] from such words as *winner* (wonder), *yon'er* (yonder).

t is dropped after [k], [p], [x-ç] in such words as *affec', inflic', direc', swep', kep', emp'y, brichen* [ˈbrɪçən] (brighten), *lichnin* [ˈlɪçnən] (lightning), *bochen* [ˈbɔxən] (boughten).

Certain nouns ending in [f] are pluralized without changing the [f] to [v]. Examples: *halfs, laifs* (loaves), *elfs, shelfs, wifes, lifes, thiefs, knifes, leafs.*

[f] and [v] are omitted medially and finally in some words: *del'* (delve), *doo* (dove), *e'en* (even), *gie* (give), *lo'e* (love), *lea'e* (leave), *o'er* (over), *pree* (prove), *lee-lane* (livelong), *sel'* (self and derivatives), *ser'* (serve), *siller* (silver), *twal'* (twelve), *shuil, shool, shule* (shovel).

[f] is used in the Northeast for initial [θ], as in *fresh* (thresh).

[v] is used in the Northeast for initial silent *w* and for some final *w*'s, as in *vrang* [vraŋ] (wrong), *snauve* [snɑv] (snow).

[θ] is sometimes used for [xt, çt] in the North, as in *micht* [mɪθ] (might), *dochter, dother* [ˈdoθər] (daughter).

[d] ∼ [ð] medially before *er*, as in *lether* (ladder), *shoother* (shoulder). This pronunciation is sporadic, and should be used only when the spelling indicates it.

[θ] and [ð] finally are often omitted, as in *mou'* (mouth), *wi'* (with), *quo'* (quoth).

[ʃ] ∼ [s] in a number of words, such as *buss*, *bus'* [bʌs] (bush), *sal* [sɑl] (shall), *sud* [sʌd, səd, sud] (should), *wuss* [wʌs] (wish).

ol, *oll* and a variety of other original English spellings ∼ [ʌu] (except in S. Sc., where it is [ɔu]), as in *gold* (gowd, goud) [gʌud], *poll* (pow) [pʌu]. The dialect spellings are *ou*, *ow*, *owe*. Compare *tow*, *tollbooth* [ˈtʌubyθ], *fowks* (folks), *bowe* (boll), *rowe* (roll), *loup* (leap—cf. E. *lope*), *bow*, *cowt* (colt), *grow*, *houp* (hope), *row*, *fower* (four), *ower* (over).

[s] ∼ [ʃ] in numerous words. The spelling may appear as *sh* or *sch*, or it may remain *s*. Examples: *schui* [ʃy] (she), *sune* [ʃun] (soon), *says* [ʃɛz], *said* [ʃɛd], *suit* [ʃyt, ʃut], *shoo* [ʃu] (sir), *schir* [ʃɜr] (sir), *offishers* (officers), *veshel* (vessel), *notis* [ˈnotɪʃ] (notice), *rinsh* [rɪnʃ] (rinse). For [y], pronounce [i] with lips rounded.

[ʤ] ∼ [ʧ] finally in unstressed syllables as in *foggage* [ˈfɒgɪʧ] (forage), *pairritch* [ˈparɪʧ] (porridge), *marriage* [ˈmarɪʧ]. The spelling is inconsistent, sometimes showing the pronunciation, sometimes not.

[ʧ] ∼ [ʃ] sporadically, as in [ʃiz] for *cheese*.

[ʃ] ∼ [ʧ] sporadically, as in *chop* for *shop*, *chingle* for *shingle*.

[d] and [t] ∼ [ʤ] in a few words, as in *jouk* [ʤuk] (duck), *jow* [ʤʌu] (toll).

[j] appears before a vowel in certain words. It is usually spelled with *y*, but sometimes it is not indicated. Examples: *yerl* (earl), *yerth*, *yird* (earth), *yin* (ane, one), *ae* [je, e] (one).

eu or *iu* before a back consonant or [r] is pronounced [ju], as in *eneuch* [əˈnjux] (enough), *beuk*, *biuk* [bjuk] (book).

[w] is often lost before vowels, especially *u*, as in *oo* [u] (wool), *ook* [uk] (week), *athoot* [əˈθut] (without), *soom* [sum] (swim).

[h] is sometimes retained in an emphatic *it*, spelled *hit* and pronounced [hɪˈt, hʌt]. In some few instances, the dialectal omission and insertion of *h* is to be observed, as in *hus* for *us*.

Vowels

For the most part, the illustrative words used in this discussion are spelled in the conventional way. Dialect writers undertake to suggest the pronunciations by various respellings of very inconsistent nature. Occasionally some of these will be listed.

The sound [i] is used in Scots dialect in the place of a remarkable number of sounds, as will be seen below. The dialect writers spell the sound with *ee*, *ea*, *e* (+ *consonant* + *e*), *ea*, *e'e*, *ei*, and no doubt other ways:

[ɛ] ∼ [i] spelled *ee*, *e* + *consonant* + *e*, *ei*, *ea*, as in *devil* (deevil, deil) [ˈdivəl, dil], *friends* (freends) [frindz], *dead* (dede, deid) [did]. Compare also *press* (prees, preise, prease), *farewell* (fareweel), *next* (neist, neisht) [nist, niʃt], *seven* (seeven), *head* (heid), *well* (weel).

[aɪ] ∼ [i], spelled *ee, ei, e'e, ie* as in *oblige* (obleedge, *obleish*, obleege) [əˈbliʤ, əˈbliʃ] (and other analogous Romance words), *die* (dee) [di], *lyin'* (leein') [ˈliən]. Compare also *precise* (preceese), *fly* (flee), *baptise* (bapteese, bapteeze) [babˈtis, babˈtiz], *thigh* (thee, theigh) [θi, θiç], *high* (hie, heich) [hi, hiç], *sly* (slee), *child* (chield), *highland* (hielan', hieland, hielant), *eye* (e'e), *Irish* (Eerish).

[u] ∼ [i], particularly in Aberdeen. The spelling is *o, oo*. Examples: *proof* (preef, prief) [prif], *moon* (meen) [min]. Compare also *prove* (preeve, pree'), *forenoon* (foreneen), *moonlight* (meenlicht).

[eɪ] ∼ [i], as in *neighbours* (neebours, neibours) [ˈnibərz], *gave* (gied, from gie—give) [gid], *Jamie* [ˈʤimɪ].

[ɪ] ∼ [i], as in *civil* (ceevil) [ˈsivəl], *pity* (peety) [ˈpitɛ]. Compare also *privilege* (preevilege), *position* (poseetion), *consider* (conseeder), *William* (Weeliam), *minute* (meenit, meenute, meenont), *give* (gie) [gi], *given* (gi'en) [ˈgiən], *breeches* (breeks) [briks], *original* (oreeginal), *opinion* (opeenion), *predicament* (predeecament).

[ɑ, ɔ] ∼ [i], as in *washed* (weesh'd, weeshen) [wiʃt, ˈwiʃən].

[ɪ] ∼ [i] in stressed open syllables as in *condition* (sometimes spelled *condeetion*) [kənˈdiʃən]. Compare also *addition, position, admission, revision, division*. Words of this class are regularly pronounced with [i], even when the spelling does not show it.

[ɪ] ∼ [ɛ] in unstressed final syllables, as in *pity* [ˈpitɛ], *spirit* [ˈspirɛt]. Compare also *city, ruby, folly, hilly, gully*. The word *very* is customarily spelled *verra* and pronounced [ˈvɛrə].

[ɪ] ∼ [ɛˆ, ɪˠ] or [ʌ]. Before *l*, dialect writers often write *e* or *u*, as in *hell* and *hull* for *hill*, *Wull* and *Wullie* for *Will* and *Willie*, *fifty* and *fufty* for *fifty*. In other contexts, writers do not change the spelling from *i*, but they expect it to be pronounced with a lowered [ɪˠ], which often seems nearer to [ɛ] than to [ɪ]. Thus *did* [dɪˠd], *him* [hɪˠm] may closely approach [dɛd], [hɛm]. Examples: *spin* [spɪˠn], *busy* [ˈbˠɪzɛ]. Compare *silly, chilly, sit, business, is, doesn't* (disna), *till, think, put* (pit), *wasn't* (wisna), *which* (whilk).

[ɪ] ∼ [ɑ] in the word *sixpence* (saxpence) [ˈsɑkspənts]. Compare also *six* (sax), *sixty* (saxty).

[ɪ] ∼ [ʌ] in a number of words spelled with *whi* and *wi*, as *whistle* [ˈʍʌsl], *witch* (wutch) [wʌtʃ], *whiskey* [ˈʍʌskɪ], *will* (wull) [wʌl]. (See also above for other pronunciations of some of these words.) Compare also *ditch, fish, little, million* (mullion).

The sound [ɪ] represents a wide variety of standard sounds. When it appears instead of [i], [ʌ], or [ɛ], it is less likely to be lowered to [ɪˠ] than when it appears in its own right. However, it is possible to find any [ɪ] lowered.[22] Though *i* is

---

[22] Grant and Dixon, *op. cit.*, p. 42.

much used to indicate these pronunciations, the spelling is not consistent.

[i] ~ [ɪ] in *fever* (fivver) [ˈfɪvər], *creature* (critter) [ˈkrɪtər].

[ɛ] ~ [ɪ], as in *chest* (kist) [kɪst], *kettle* (kittle) [ˈkɪtl], *together* (thegither) [təˈgɪðər, θəˈgɪðər], *never* (niver) [ˈnɪvər], *ever* (iver) [ˈɪvər], *seven* (siven) [ˈsɪvən], *friend* (frind) [frɪnd], *yesterday* (yisterday).

[æ] ~ [ɪ] in *hang* (hing) [hɪŋ].

[ʌ] ~ [ɪ], as in *brother* (brither) [ˈbrɪðər], *summer* (simmer) [ˈsɪmər]. Compare also *mother, hussy* [ˈhɪzɪ], *nut, wonder* [ˈwɪnər], *supper, other, son, stubble, another, such* (sic), *running* (rinnin'), *honey, the other* [ˈtɪðər], *putting* [ˈpɪtn̩], *sun, dun, sundry* [ˈsɪnərɛ], *touch* (tich).

[aɪ] ~ [ɪ], as in *find* [fɪˈnd], *night* [nɪˈçt]. Compare also *light, bright, sight, might, slight, sleight, fright, blight, knight, style, trifle.*

[ɪ, i] ~ [i] in the word *been* [bin].

The sound [ɛ] represents a considerable number of sounds in a variety of spellings:

[æ] ~ [ɛ] in a number of words, such as *brass* (bress) [brɛs], *Glasgow* (Gleskie) [ˈglɛskɪˈ], *glass* (gless), *saddle* (saiddle), *ask* (esk), *Jack* (Jeck), *cap* (kep), *path* (peth).

[3, ɝ] ~ [rɛ] by metathesis in *thirty* (thretty) [ˈθrɛtɪˈ], *thirteen* (thretteen) [ˈθrɛt:in].

[eɪ] ~ [ɛ] in a few words in *ai*, such as *paint* (pent) [pɛnt], *acquaint* (acquent) [əˈkwɛnt].

The sound [e] corresponds to a large number of other standard English sounds. Dialect writers commonly represent [e] by *ai, ae, a* (+consonant+*e*) and *ay*:

[ɪ] ~ [e] as in *smear* [smer], *beard* [berd].

[ɛ, eɪ] ~ [e] in the words *again* [əˈgen] and *against*.

[æ] ~ [e], as in *have* (hae) [he].

[ɑ] ~ [e] in many words spelled with *ar* stressed, as in *part* [pert], *art* [ert]. Compare also *charge* (chairge), *garden* (gairden), *smart* (smairt), *argue* (airgy), *farm, large, cart, arms.* Not all words of this orthographic class are pronounced with [e]; some retain the standard [ɑ]. The spelling usually indicates the author's intention.

[ɑ] ~ [ɛ] often in words spelled with *ar* in the stressed syllables, as in *arm* (airm) [ɛrm], *artless* (airtless) [ˈɛrtləs]. Compare *heart* (hairt), *starch* (stairch), *charge* (chairge), *cart* (cairt), *start* (stert), *yard* (yerd), *harvest* (hervest) [ˈhɛrvəst]. Many words of this class are pronounced with [ɑ] as in standard English dialects. Examples: *Marget, barley, barber, park.* It appears safest for the reader to pronounce words of this class with [ɑ] unless a different pronunciation is indicated by the author's respelling.

[ɔ] ~ [e] as in *straw* [stre], *broad* [bred], *gone* [gen].

[u] ~ [e], as in *blue* [ble].[23]

---

[23] Grant and Dixon, p. 43.

[ʌ] ~ [e], as in *one* (ae, ane) [e, en], *nothing* (naething) [ˈneθiŋ], *once* (ance) [ents].

[aɪ] ~ [e], as in *quiet* [kwet], *binder* [ˈbendər], *writing* [ˈreʔn̩].

[oʊ] ~ [e] in *home* (hame) [hem], *more* (mair) [mer], *toe* [te]. Compare also *load* (lade), *both* (baith), *lone* (lane), *lonely* (lanely), *woe* (wae), *those* (thae) [ðe], *go* (gae), *sore* (sair), *oath* (aith), *foe* (fae), *groan* (grane), *no* (nae), *stone* (stane), *almost* (amaist), *so* (sae), *going* (gaen) [ˈgeən], *own* (ain), *moan* (mane), *brimstone* (brumstane), *clothes* (claes) [klez, kleʃ], *holy* (haily), *ghost* (ghaist), *toad* (tade), *sloes* (slaes), *floor* (flaer).

[æ] ~ [a] in all "short *a*" words, as in *man* [man], *that* [ðat, θat]. Compare also *sack, jagged* (jagget), *grandmother* (-mither), *had, thanks, angry, black, dad, prattlin', drop* (drap), *anticipate, admonition, command, lad, lassie, strappin', bashfu', candle, canna, clapped(t), back, magpie, trampin', mad, black, answered(t), password*.

[ɑ, ɒ] ~ [ʌ] in a few words in some districts. Examples: *bonnet* (bunnet) [ˈbʌnət], *bother* (buther) [ˈbʌðər], *Robert* (Rubbert) [ˈrʌbərt], *many* (mony>muny [ˈmʌnɪ]),[24] *body* (buddy) [ˈbʌdɪ] instead of the more common [ˈbodɪ].

[ɔ] ~ [ɑ] in most words where standard English dialects have [ɔ] except in spellings with *or, ought, aught.* Exceptions such as *braid* [bred] for *broad,* are usually made obvious by the spellings of the dialect writer. Dialect writers use a wide variety of spellings for this [ɑ], viz., *a, al, a', au, aw.* Readers must be on guard not to pronounce any of these spellings [ɔ] as in analogous English contexts; likewise *au* must not be pronounced [au] as in German. Examples: *scald* (scaud) [skɑd], *all* [ɑ], *walk* [wɑk], *hawk* [hɑk], *false* (fa'se) [fɑs]. Compare *wrong* (wrang), *long* (lang), *off* (aff), *awful* (awfu'), *belong* (belang), *shaw, talk, fall* (fa'), *wall* (wa'), *warm, warder, warrant, warrior, warp, warm, water, hall* (ha'), *Walter* (Wattie).

[o] ~ [ə] in unstressed final *ow*, as *morrow* [ˈmɒrə], *borrow* [ˈbɒrə].

O adjacent to a labial ~ generally to [ɑ]. Dialect writers usually use *a* in the spelling. Examples: *drap* [drɑp] (drop), *saft* [sɑft] (soft), *Rab* [rɑb] (Rob). When words of this class are not spelled with *a* by the dialect writer, the reader may well fall back on [ɒ] for the pronunciation.

[ʊ] ~ [ʌ] in a few words, such as *woman* (wumman) [ˈwʌmən], *pushing* [ˈpʌʃən].

[ʊ] ~ [u], as in *book* [buk], *cook* [kuk], *look* [luk].

[u] ~ [ʉ] in Gaelic-speaking western communities and near Glasgow.[25] Examples: *true* [trʉ], *good* (gude, guid) [gʉd]. Compare also *fool, cool, fool, cow* (coo), *moon.* This [ʉ] is pronounced by advancing the tongue halfway from [u] to [y]. (See page 263.) In generalized Scots the simpler, frequently used [u] may be freely chosen instead.

---

[24] Grant and Dixon, p. 51.
[25] Grant and Dixon, pp. 48–49.

[ʊ] ∼ [ʉ], as in pull (pu') [pʉ], full (fu') [fʉ]. See note on [u] ∼ [ʉ] above.

[u] ∼ [ʏ], particularly in mid-lowland areas, before all consonants except [r] and the voiced fricatives.[26] This [ʏ] is a lip-rounded [ɪ], as in the German *fünf* [fʏnf]. The spellings are usually *ui, u* (+consonant+*e*), *oo*, as in *tomb* (tuim) [tʏm], *moon* (mune) [mʏn], *shoes* (schoon) [ʃʏn]. Compare also *fruit, blood* (bluid), *just* (juist), *use* (n.). In northeast Scots [i] is used instead of [ʏ]. In generalized Scots [u] may be freely used. Compare *good* (gude, guid), *booth, done* (dune), *food, fool* (fule), *poor* (puir), *tuneful* (tunefu').

[ʌ] ∼ [u], as in *blood* (blude) [blud], *done* (dune) [dun], *above* (aboon) [ə'bun]. Compare also *just, love* (luve, lo'e) [luv, lu], *cud, done* (doo) [du]. In some Gaelic-speaking areas, this [u] is rendered [ʉ].

[eɪ, ɛ] sometimes ∼ [ɑ], as in *spade* [spɑd], *shaking* ['ʃɑkən], *makes* [mɑks], *breakfast* ['brɑkfəst], *came* (cam') [kɑm]. Sometimes authors make an attempt to indicate this pronunciation by the spelling, as in *mak'* for *make*.

[aɪ] ∼ [ɑ] in the pronoun *I* [ɑ].

[aʊ] ∼ [u], as in *town* [tun], *out* [ut], *hour* [ur], *cow* [ku]. Cf. *doubt, found, south, round, sound, gown*, etc.

[oʊ] ∼ [ʌʊ] when respelled dialectally with *ow*, as in *truth* (trowth) [trʌʊθ], *woe* (wow) [wʌʊ], *poll* (pow) [pʌʊ], *pony* (pownie) ['pʌʊnɪ'], *over* (owre) [ʌʊr], *folks* (fowks) [fʌʊks]. Sometimes an original spelling with *ow* is pronounced in the same way, as in *grown* [grʌʊn]. Occasionally other spellings, difficult of classification, yield the pronunciation [ʌʊ], as in *four* [fʌʊr], and *our* [ʌʊr]. Compare *gold* (gowd), *golden* (gowden).

The sound [ʌʊ] is also found in southern Scots instead of final [u], as *you* [jʌʊ]. The best advice to the reader seems in general to be to use [ʌʊ] only when a word is respelled with *ow*. In many cases, this will represent the historical situation where older English had *ow* or *o(l)*, which has given [oʊ] in Modern English. If the words are respelled in some other way, the pronunciation should follow such spellings. If there is no deviation from standard English spelling, it is best to fall back upon standard English pronunciation.

[ɜ] ∼ [ɑr] in several words spelled with *or*, such as *world* (warld) [wɑrld], *work* (wark) [wɑrk], *worse* (waur) [wɑr].

[ø] appears finally and before voiced fricatives and [r], in words spelled with *o, oe, oo, ou, ui* and *u* + consonant + *e*. Examples: *do* [dø], *too* [tø], *cousin* ['køzən], *shoe* [ʃø], *poor* (puir) [pør], *use* [jøz]. Compare *refuse, excuse, moor* (muir), *ford* (fuird), *sure, used* [jøst], *usual* ['jøzwə].

In Scots, which is not too "broad," *do* is pronounced *dae* [de], while most other words in the class are either pronounced with [y] or in the ordinary English fashion, according to the author's indication in the spelling.

Miscellaneous: *Father* (faither) ['feðər], *master* (maister) ['mestər], *twenty*

---

[26] Grant and Dixon, p. 45.

(twunty) [ˈtwʌntɪˠ], *among* (amang) [əˈmaŋ], *bald* (beld) [bɛld], *spoke* (spake >
spak) [spɑk]. *Any* (ony) and *many* (mony) are pronounced [ˈonɛ] and [ˈmonɛ].
Body is pronounced with [o], thus [ˈbodɛ]; *John* is [dʒon], *Robin* is [ˈrobɪn]; *either*,
neither are often [ˈeðər, ˈneðər].

The prefix *un* is frequently respelled *on* [ɒn], as in *until* (ontil) [ɒnˈtɪˠl]. Compare
ongainly, onhappy, ongentle, onripe.

Consonants

[d] ~ [t] following *p, t, k, b, d, g*, in adjectival and verb endings.[27] The *ed* of
many words like *carried*, which in standard dialects is pronounced as a part of
the preceding syllable, is in Scots folk speech often pronounced as a separate
syllable. This is a variable feature. An author's spelling will usually give a clew
to whether he intends the syllable to be a separate one. Examples: *dogged* (doggit)
[ˈdɔgət], *rugged* (ruggit) [ˈrʌgət], *carried* (carriet) [ˈkariət], *happened* (happnet)
[ˈhapnət], *guarded* (gairdit) [ˈgerdət], *rubbed* (rubbit) [ˈrʌbət], *turned* [ˈtʌrnət],
dumbfounded [ˌdʌmˈfunərt], *intended* [ɪnˈtɛndət], *twirled* [twɜrlt], *listened* [ˈlɪstn̩t],
ribboned [ˈrɪbənt], *spared* (spert). Cf. *looked* (lookit), *kept* (keepit, keppit), *helped*
(helpit), *selected* (seleckit), *condemned* (condemt), *risked* (riskit), *rotted* (rottit),
begged (begget), *heaped* (heapit). The spelling does not always indicate the
dialectal pronunciation. Compare *expected* [ɪkˈspɛk(t)ət], *talked* [ˈtɑkət].

Medial and often final [t], sometimes [k], sometimes [ð], and, on rare occasions,
[p] ~ [ʔ], as in *gutter* [ˈgʌʔər], *within* [wɪˈʔɪn], *breakfast* [ˈbrɛʔfəst], *keep your hand in*
[kɪʔ jər hand ɪn], *the lot of it* [ðə lɒʔ əv ɪˠt]. Compare also *Thackeray, bottle,
battle, cutter, batter, bitter, don't like.*

Silent *k* and *g* ~ [k] and (occasionally, as in Buchan) [g] respectively, as in
kneel [knil], *gnash* [gnaʃ]. Compare *knead, knee, gnaw, gnarl, gnome, knight,
knot, knob, knock, knack, knave, knell.*

"In Forfar and East Perth,"[28] [t] is used in place of [k] in words like those
above, as in *kneel* (tneel) [tnil]. Compare Barrie's *Tnowhead*.[29] Analogously, we
have [t] in *quilt* (twult) [twʌlt].

[ɪŋ], as a verbal termination, ~ [ən] as in *guttering* [ˈgʌtərən] (in Glasgow dialect,
[ˈgʌʔərən]), *walking* [ˈwɑkən, ˈwaʔən]. The Scots dialect writers do not show this
feature by the dropping of the *g* as consistently as do writers in other dialects.

[ŋ] ~ [n] in the two words *length* [lɛnθ] and *strength* [strɛnθ].

[n] ~ [ŋ] in *opinion* [əˈpɪŋjən].[30]

[ŋ] ~ [ŋg] in the north and west highlands, as in *sing* [siŋg], *sang* [saŋg].
Compare also *bring, singer, swinger, song, rung.*

[27] Grant and Dixon, p. 8.
[28] *Ibid.*
[29] J. M. Barrie, *A Window in Thrums.*
[30] Grant, p. 32.

[ŋg] ~ [ŋ], as in *longer* (langer) [ˈlaŋər], *finger* [ˈfiŋər]. Compare also, *linger, single, mingle, jingle, wrangle, jungle, tingle, hungry.*

[l] ~ [j] sometimes, as in *bew* [bju] (blue). The spelling does not always indicate the pronunciation. Compare *ploo* [plju].

[θ] before [r] ~ [x] in the Mid-areas. Examples, *three* [xri], *throo* [xru]. The spelling does not indicate this pronunciation.

[r] ~ [ʀ] occasionally, not in sections of the country, but in the usage of individuals, as in *row* [ʀo], *draw* [dʀɑ]. [ʀ] is the uvular trill. See page 377.

[ð] ~ [θ] in the English of Gaelic speakers, as in *the* [θi], *that* [θat], *truths* [truθs]. Compare also *laths, baths, seethe, farther, weather, there, other, feather, wither, mother, brother.*[31] In general in Scots dialect, [θ] is regularly used in a few words, particularly *though* [θo], *thence* [θɛnts], *thither* [ˈθɪθər], *with* [wɪθ].[32]

[z] ~ [s] in the pronunciation of Gaelic speakers, as in *his* [hɪs], *zest* [sɛst], Compare also *sins, bones, is, was, goes, zinc, plays, raise.*[33]

[ʍ] ~ [f] in north Scots, as in *what* (fat) [fat], *who* (fa) [fɑ].

[x] (allophone [ç] after front vowels) is used for spellings which were pronounced [x, ç] historically, as in *light* (licht) [liçt], *enough* (eneuch) [əˈnjux]. These are the *Achlaut* and *Ichlaut* of German. Compare also the *jota* of Spanish. See pages 367, 466. Compare also *bright, night, sought, brought, nought, ought, tight, fought, thought, right, sight, Almighty, sough, laugh* (lauch), *straight* (straicht), *fight* (fecht), *bought.* When the spelling undertakes to indicate this pronunciation, *ch* is commonly used.

Transcription in generalized Scottish dialect
from *The Little Minister* *

ɪˈts tum — dɪˈnə θɪˈŋk ɑ nid tə fɪˈl ət ðɪˈs marnən. am rɪˈçt aŋrɪˈ ət məsɛl fɔr biən se ɔngretfə laɪk.

a ʌmblɪˈ spir jər fərgivnəs, sɜr, ən ji mɪˈçt baɪd d͡ʒɪˈst ə wi jɛt. av bin rɛdɪˈ tə gaŋ ðis twa urz, bət nu ðət ðə məʃin ɪz ət ðə geʔ, a dɪˈnə kɛn hu ɪˈt ɪˈz, bət am tɛrɪbəl swir tə kʌm əwa. o, miˈstər dɪˈshart, iˈts rɪˈçt:ru ʍat ðə dɒktər ʃɛz əbut ðə — ðə ples, bət a kanə d͡ʒɪˈst:ak ɪˈt ɪˈn. am — am ge ʌud.

ɪˈt wəz forpənts ðə jir, ən:at lɛs ʍɛn wi bɔxt ɪˈt ət saml̩ karz, ai, bət ɪˈt həz bin tʌrnd saks taɪmz sɪˈnts saɪn.

saml̩z bernt dun wɪ skarlət fɪvər n̩ laɪk tə di, ən hɪˈm biən ə wɪˈdə man hi həz gen jusləs. ji manə blem ðə waɪvz ɪˈn ðə tɛnəmənts fɔr hʌudn̩ bak. ðer flid tə smɪˈt ðer en lɪˈʔl̩ ənz; and əz ɪˈt hapənz, saml̩z frinz ɪˈz a af tə ðə glɛn. wil, hi ran gritən tə ðə mants fər mɪˈstər dɪˈshart, and ðə ledɪˈ hɛrd ɪˈm kraɪən ðrux

[31] Grant, p. 40.
[32] Grant, p. 41.
[33] Grant, p. 42.

ðə dor ənd ʍɑt dəz ʃi de bət gaŋ strɑuxt:ə ðə tɛnəmənts wɪ samḷ. hɛr gudnəs had natərəlɪˑ pɪˑt ðə fʌuk ɔn hɛr saɪd əgenst ðə minɪstər.

ʃiz ɪˑz ɪˑntɛndət. aɪ, ju nidnə stert. ʃi əz kʌm a ðə rod fre glɛskɪˑ tə tʃalənʤ ɪˑm əbut ðə ʤɪˑpsɪˑ. ðə pɪˑʔɪfəl ðɪˑŋ ɪˑz ðət mɪsɪz dɪˑshɑrt lɑxt əwɑ hər firz, ənd nu ðer beθ wetən fər ɪz rɪtʌrn, əz hapɪˑ əz ɪgnərənts ken mɑk ðəm.

jər sɪˑnz a ðə ɛrθ tə jɪ, bət maɪ ɛldərʃɪˑps əz mʌkḷ tə mi. sɑks n̩ twʌntɪˑ jirz he a bɪn ən ɛldər, ən nu a mɑn gi ət ʌp.

JAMES M. BARRIE

Transcription in generalized Scots dialect

From *Reminiscences of Scottish Life and Character*

ɪˑn lɑnɑrkʃər ðer lɪˑvd ə smɑ lerd nempt hamɪltən ʍa wəz notət fər ɪz ɛksɛntrisɪtɪˑ. ɔn ən əkeʒən, ə nibər wetət ɔn ɪˑm, ənd rɪkwestət ɪz nem əz ən əkɒmədeʃən tə ə bɪˑʔ bɪˑl fər twʌntɪˑ punz ət ðri mʌnts det ʍʌtʃ lɛd tə ðə fɒloɪŋ karɪktəristɪk ən trulɪˑ skɒtɪʃ kɒləkwɪˑ.

"nɑ nɑ, a kanə de ðat."

"ʍat fɔr, lerd, ji he dun ðə sem ðɪˑŋ fər ɪðərz."

"aɪ, aɪ, tɑməs, bət ðerz ʍilz wɪʔɪn ʍilz ji ken neðɪˑŋ əbut; a kanə dut."

"əts ə ʃem əfer tə rɪfjuz mɪ, lerd."

"wil, dji si, tɑməs, ɪˑf a wəz tə pɪˑʔ mə nem tɪˑlt, ji wad gɛʔ ðə sɪˑlər fre ðə baŋk, ən ʍɛn ðə taɪm kem rund ji wadnə bi rɛdɪˑ, ən a wad he tə pet; se ðɛn ju n̩ mi wad kwarəl, se wi me ʤɪst əz wil kwarəl ðə nu, əz laŋz ðə sɪˑlərz ɪn mə putʃ."

E. M. RAMSEN

Transcribe:

WHAT TO SAY TO THE NEW MUNE

New mune, true mune,
   Tell unto me,
If my ane true love
   He will marry me.
If he marry me in haste,
Let me see his bonny face;
If he marry me betide,
Let me see his bonnie side.
If he marry me ava'
Turn his back and gae awa'.

POUSSIE BAUDRONS

Poussie, Poussie Baudrons,
Where hae ye been?

I've been at London,
Seeing the Queen.

Poussie, Poussie Baudrons,
What got ye there?
I got a guid fat mousikie,
Rinning up a stair.

Poussie, Poussie Baudrons,
What did ye do wi't?
I put it in my meal-poke,
To eat it to my bread.

Transcribe:

From *The Antiquary*

"I wud be baith a grievance and a disgrace to your fine servants, my leddy, and I have never been a disgrace to onybody yet that I ken of."

"It respects yoursel, and it is in your power, and I maun come out wi' it—ye are a bonny young leddy, and a gud ane, and maybe a well-tochered ane—but dinna ye sneer awa the lad Lovell, as I saw ye baith, and heard ye, too, though ye saw nae me. Be canny wi' the lad, for he lo'es ye weel, and it's to him and no to onything I could have done for you, that Sir Arthur and you wan ower, yestreen."

SIR WALTER SCOTT

Transcribe:

From *Scottish Life and Character*

Lord dibble thou the kail seed of thy grace into our hearts and if we grow not up good kail, mak' us good sprouts at least.

Oh, Lord, we're aye gangin' an' we're aye gettin', we s'oud aye be comin' to Thee, but we're aye forgettin'.

Toot, havers, ye needna ha'e been in sic a hurry wi' the bits o' coppers; I could ha'e gotten them frae ye ony time. Oh, but it was nae trouble ava', for there was naebody at the plate and I juist slippit in without onything.

A lad was on one occasion accused of stealing some articles from a doctor's shop. The judge was much struck with his personal appearance, and asked him why he was guilty of such a contemptible act. "Weel, ye see," replied the prisoner, "I had a bit o' a pain in ma side, and my mither tauld me to gang to the doctor's and tak' something." "Ho, yes," said the judge; "but surely she didn't tell you to go and take an eight-day clock." The prisoner was evidently nonplussed, but it was only for a moment. Turning to the judge, a bright smile of humour stealing over his countenance, he replied, "There's an auld proverb that says, 'Time an' the doctor cure a' diseases,' an' sae I thoucht ————."

WILLIAM HARVEY

Transcribe:

From The Bishopshire and Its People

"Helpin' Tam Broon." — A neighbouring laird in the estate of Kinneston on one occasion called out to one of his young lads, who was passing somewhat smartly, "Whaur noo, Jock?"

"Od, maister, I'm gaun to my supper; it's sax o'clock, isn't it?"

"Maybe it is, Jock," says the laird, "but what hae ye been daein' the day?"

"O," says Jock, "I was helpin' Tam Broon."

"Just so," says the laird, "but what was Tam Broon daein'?"

"Weel," says Jock, "he was daein' naething."

It is to this day a proverb in the district to say of anyone who is lazy and doing little, that he has been "helpin' Tam Broon."

DAVID BEATH

Bibliography

Scots

Books

Dieth, Eugen, *A Grammar of the Buchan Dialect* (Cambridge: W. Heffer and Sons, Ltd., 1932).

Grant, William, *The Pronunciation of English in Scotland* (London: Cambridge University Press, 1913).

Grant, William, and James Main Dixon, *Manual of Modern Scots* (London: Cambridge University Press, 1921).

Jones, Daniel, *The Pronunciation of English* (London: Cambridge University Press, 1950).

Murray, James A. H., *The Dialect of the Southern Counties of Scotland* (London: Asher and Co., 1873).

Ward, Ida C., *The Phonetics of English* (London: W. Heffer and Sons, Ltd., 1929).

Warrack, Alexander, *A Scots Dialect Dictionary* (London and Edinburgh: W. R. Chambers, Ltd., 1911).

CHAPTER 13

Irish

The Irish dialect is one of the most delightful and entertaining of all the regional dialects of English. It takes its unique quality from the fact that underneath the English lies a substratum of Celtic language influence. For although the native Celtic, or Irish Gaelic, is spoken as a home language by only a small part of the population, the Gaelic intonations and rhythms have never been lost. Now that all but the six northern counties of the island of Ireland constitutes a separate commonwealth called Eire, within which Gaelic is taught with varying emphasis in the schools and used in the Dail, or Parliament, the Gaelic flavor may be expected to maintain itself in the English language spoken by the people.

America once received almost uncounted thousands of Irish immigrants each year. Even under the quota system now in vogue, more people are admitted from the British Isles than from most countries. Accordingly, the Irish dialect remains well known throughout the United States. The same is true of Canada. Moreover, there is an abundant literature—poetry, song, drama, and novel—which features Irish. It becomes therefore both imperative and rewarding to study the dialect formally.

As in Scotland, there is no one dialect which we may call Irish. For south, west, central and north, as one may listen to the speech of Cork, Killarney, Dublin, and Belfast, there are undeniable regional differences. This book does not try meticulously to separate the regional features—that is not necessary, save perhaps in Ireland itself; but the dialect of Cork weighs heavily in this account, perhaps the more because the author's notebooks are heavily loaded with features gathered from that area.

[i] ~ [e] in words spelled with *ea*, as in *easily* [ˈezɪlɪ], *clean* [klen]. The rare spelling *oe* in Greek words is also pronounced [e], as in *Phoenix* [ˈfenɪks].

The Irish learned to pronounce words in *ea* with [e] at a time when the English were so pronouncing them. It is a truism that English poetry, as in the case of Pope, rhymed such words as *day* and *sea*. In the course of time, the vowels of all of these words changed from [e] to [i], except in a few instances, such as may be noted in *steak*, *break*, *great*, *yea*, and various proper names.

It appears likely that the Irish were confused by this transition and had some tendency to pronounce with [e] other English words than those spelled with *ea*. In 1874 Ellis[1] records *daicent* ['desṇt] for *decent, fraiquent* for *frequent, aiquel* for *equal, skaim* for *scheme, saicret* for *secret, aither* for *either, laizhir* for *leisure*.[2] This confusion of *ea* words with words spelled with *e, ee, ei* and *ie*, as in *scheme, meet, neither, priest*, still obtains to some extent; but observations made by the writer in the Cork and the Killarney areas in 1935 indicated that those elderly and less literate people who still used [e] in words such as *meat* would seldom or never do so in words such as *meet*.

[ɪ] ~ [i] before *r*, as in *peer* [pir], *year* [jir].

[ɪ] ~ [ə] in final unstressed positions in the word *sorry* [sɑrə] and possibly a few others. Compare Scots *very* [vɛrə].

[əi] ~ [j] in certain unstressed syllables such as *villain* ['vɪljən], *Victoria* [vɪk'torjə], *glorious* ['glorjəs]. Related to these are *minute* ['mɪnjət] and *column* ['kaljəm].

[ɛ] ~ [ɪ] before nasals, especially [n], as in *send* [sɪnd], *intend* [ɪn'tɪnd], *spent* [spɪnt], *contempt* [kən'tɪmpt], *attempt* [ə'tɪmpt], *Jenkins* ['dʒɪŋkənz], *again(st)* [ə'gɪn(st)], *engine* ['ɪndʒən].

[ɛ] ~ [ɪ] if followed by *v*, as in *every* ['ɪvrɪ], *ever* ['ɪvər], *never* ['nɪvər], *seven* ['sɪvən], *heaven* ['hɪvən], *devil* ['dɪvəl], *clever* ['klɪvər], *reverence* ['rɪvərənts].

[ɛ] ~ [ɪ] if followed by *l*, as in *self* [sɪlf] and its compounds (such as *myself* [mɪ'sɪlf], *selfish* ['sɪlfɪʃ], *himself* [hɪm'sɪlf], etc.), *else* [ɪls], *elegant* ['ɪlɪgənt].

[ɛ] ~ [ɪ] before *t* in the words *get* [gɪt], *yet* [jɪt].

[ɛ] ~ [ɪ] before *s*, as in *yesterday* ['jɪstərdɪ], *chest* [tʃɪst].

[ɛ] ~ [ɪ] before [k] in *next* [nɪkst].

[ɛ] ~ [a] in the two words *many* ['manɪ] and *any* ['anɪ] and the derivatives of the latter (*anything* ['anɪˌθɪŋ], *anyone* ['anɪˌwan], etc.).

[æ] ~ [a], as in *grandstand* ['grandˌstand], *travel* ['travəl], *ham* [ham], *bag* [bag], *Catholic* ['kaθəlɪk], *mass* [mas].

[ɑ] when representing the "broad *a*" of British ~ [a], as in *half* [haf], *castle* ['kasɫ].

[ɑ] ~ [a] before *r*, as in *part* [part], *warm* [warm], *derbies* [ˌdarbɪz], *garden* ['gjardṇ], *are* [ar], *tar* [tar], *far* [far], *mark* [mark]. This [a] is frequently raised to [æ], as in *park* [park, pærk].

[ɑ, ɒ] ~ [a] in "short *o*" words, as in *soft* [saft], *top* [tap], *stop* [stap] (but see [ɑ, ɒ] ~ [ɑ], below). Ellis recounts many examples of this pronunciation in 1874,[3] but it is believed largely to have died out.

[ɑ, ɒ] ~ [ɑ] in "short *o*" words, such as *stop* [stɑp], *clock* [klɑk], *shock* [ʃɑk],

[1] Alexander J. Ellis, *Early English Pronunciation*, Part IV, pp. 1235–36.

[2] Ellis transcribes all of these with "*ee*" and "*ee*", which signify the then current vowels of *ailing* and *Mary* respectively. He intends here to indicate that [e] followed by *r* differs from [e] in other contexts by some slight degree of *r*-coloration.

[3] Ellis, Part IV, p. 1238.

hot [hɑt]. A few words spelled with *a* after *w*, *wh*, belong in this category, such as *was* [wɑz], *watch* [wɑtʃ], *what* [ʍɑt, ɸɑt].[4]

[ɔ] ~ [ɑ], as in *off* [ɑf], *across* [əˈkrɑs], *George* [dʒɑrdʒ], *haw* [hɑ], *August* [ˈɑgəst], *offices* [ˈɑfəsəz], *walls* [ˈwɑlz], *all* [ɑl], *warm* [wɑrm], *quarter* [ˈkwɑrtər].

[o, ə] ~ [ɪ] in words spelled with unstressed final *o*, *ow*, as in *tobacco* [təˈbakɪ], *window* [ˈwɪndɪ], *potato* [ˈpretɪ].

[ʊ] ~ [u], in some words spelled with *oo*, such as *cooked* [kukt].

[ʊ] ~ [ʌ], in a few words, such as *put* [pʌt], *foot* [fʌt], *took* [tʌk], *shook* [ʃʌk], *stood* [stʌd], *would* [wʌd], *could* [kʌd].

[ʌ] ~ [a] in the word *one* [wan] and its derivatives, such as *once* [wanst], *everyone* [ˈɪvrɪˌwan].

[ʌ] ~ [ɔ] in the prefix *un-*, as in *uncommon* [ˌɔnˈkamən]. Compare *uneducated, undeniable, uneasy, unjust, unmanly, unpleasant, unwell, unpaid.*

[ʌ] ~ [ʊ], as in *rub* [rʊb], *tub* [tʊb], *recumbent* [rɪˈkʊmbənt], *bust* [bʊst].

[ɜ, ɝ] ~ [ɑr] in certain words with *er* and *ear* spellings which retain archaic pronunciations, such as *learn* [lɑrn], *servant* [ˈsɑrvənt], *nervous* [ˈnɑrvəs], *eternal* [iˈtɑrnəl], *certain* [ˈsɑrtn̩], *search* [sɑrtʃ], *determined* [dɪˈtɑrmənd], *concern* [kənˈsɑrn], *divert* [dɪˈvɑrt], *deserve* [dɪˈzɑrv], *deserts* [dɪˈzɑrts].

[ɜ, ɝ] ~ [ʌr] in words spelled with *ir*, *ur*, *or*, as in *bird* [bʌrd], *burn* [bʌrn], *work* [wʌrk]. (Words spelled with *er* and *ear* that are not included above fall into this class.)

[ə] ~ [ɪ] in final unstressed syllables spelled with *a*, as in *America* [əˈmɛrɪkɪ], *Russia* [ˈruʃɪ], *China* [ˈtʃaɪnɪ]. (See page 203.)

[ə] appears between *l* and *m* by anaptyxis to make disyllables of the following: *elm* [ˈɛləm], *helm* [ˈhɛləm], *realm* [ˈrɛləm], *(over)whelm* [ˈʍɛləm], *film* [ˈfɪləm], etc.

[eɪ] ~ [e], as in *place* [ples], *eight* [et], *late* [let], *patience* [ˈpeʃənts], *baked* [bekt], *days* [dez].

[aɪ] ~ [ɪ] in *my* unstressed, as in *my hat* [mɪ ˈhat].

[aɪ] ~ [ɔɪ], as *time* [tɔɪm], *five* [fɔɪv], *tine* [tɔɪn]. This pronunciation characterizes individuals and communities and, being easy to imitate, is widely used on the stage. But the next paragraph shows an alternative and widely used pronunciation.

[aɪ] ~ [ʌɪ], as in *night* [nʌɪt], *Ireland* [ˈʌɪrlənd], *spider* [ˈʃpʌɪdər], *five* [fʌɪv], *died* [dʌɪd], *time* [tʌɪm], *ninety* [ˈnʌɪntɪ], *style* [stʌɪl], *nicer* [ˈnʌɪsər], *buy* [bʌɪ], *July* [dʒuˈlʌɪ], *mile* [mʌɪl], *I* [ʌɪ].

[aʊ] ~ [ʌo], as in *about* [əˈbʌot], *out* [ʌot], *towels* [tʌolz], *down* [dʌon], *thousand* [ˈθʌozənd], *house* [hʌos], *town* [tʌon], *doubt* [dʌot].

[ɔɪ] ~ [aɪ] before *l*, *nt*, *st*, as in *point* [paɪnt], *oil* [aɪl], *boil* [baɪl], *toilet* [ˈtaɪlət], *joist* [dʒaɪst].

[ju] ~ [ɪ] in unstressed medial and final syllables, as in *impudent* [ˈɪmpɪdənt],

---

4 The sound [ɸ] is a bilabial spirant, made by blowing through tensely rounded lips, as in extinguishing a candle.

argue [ˈargɪ], *manufacture* [ˌmanɪˈfaktər]. Related to the foregoing is *educate* [ˈɛdɪˌket].

[oʊ] ∼ [o], as in *pony* [ˈponɪ].

[oʊr, oə, ɔr, ɔ] ∼ [u] before *r* in words spelled with *oa, oo, ou*, as in *course* [kurs], *court* [kurt], *door* [dur], *floor* [flur], *board* [burd], *sport* [spurt]. The sound [u] can also be heard in *book* [buk], but this pronunciation is dying out.[5]

[oʊ] ∼ [ʌo, aʊ] when followed by *l*, as in *bold* [bʌold, baʊld], *cold* [kʌold, kaʊld]. Compare *hold, colt, bolt, jolt, old, mole, pole, roll, scold, sold, told.*

[t] ∼ [t̪] frequently but not universally, as in *twenty* [ˈt̪wɛnt̪ɪ], *straight* [st̪ret̪], *cattle* [ˈkat̪əl], *mountains* [ˈmʌont̪n̪z].

[t] is excrescent finally in *once* [wanst], *twice* [twʌɪst], *close* [klost], *sudden* [ˈsʌdn̪t], *darling* [ˈdarlɪnt], *orphan* [ˈarfɪnt], *attack* [əˈtakt]. (See page 200.)

[t] is omitted from final *pt*, as in *crept* [krɛp], *kept* [kɛp], *slept* [ʃlɛp]. (See page 202.)

[d, dj] ∼ [dʒ], as in *tremendous* [triˈmɪndʒəs], *endure* [ɪnˈdʒur].

[k] ∼ [kj] before *ar*, as in *car* [kjar], *cart* [kjart]. Compare *carpet, carpenter, cargo, cardinal, carve, carcass.*

[g] ∼ [gj] before *ar*, as in *garden* [ˈgjardən], *garter* [ˈgjartər]. Compare *garlic, garment, cigar, disregard.*

[ɪŋ] ∼ [ən] in present participial endings and in a few other instances, as in *singing* [ˈsɪŋən], *evening* [ˈivnən], *something* [ˈsʌmpən].

[ŋ] ∼ [n] in *length* [lɛnθ], *strength* [strɛnθ].

[r] ∼ [ř], i.e., it is trilled, in all positions, as in *right* [řʌɪt], *car* [kjař], *card* [kjařd], *heard* [hʌřd], *carry* [kařɪ]. No special symbol will be used elsewhere in this chapter for the trilled *r*, but *r* must be consistently trilled.

NOTE: In the attempts of dialect writers to spell the trilled *r* after *t* and *d*, such spellings as *thry, wather* occur. These are subject to misinterpretation and sometimes pronounced [θrʌɪ], [ˈwaθər]. This misunderstanding is to be avoided and the words should be pronounced (with trilled *r*, of course), as [trʌɪ], [ˈwatər].

There is no doubt in these instances that [t] is dental and may, therefore, suggest [θ] to the ear, somewhat as the spellings *thry* and *wather* suggest it to the eye. But the pronunciation should maintain the sequence of plosive plus trill, as indicated above. The same dentality is inevitably present in the combination *dr*, as in *dry, rider*, which dialect writers sometimes represent as *dhry* and *ridher*. Again, the sequence plosive plus trill must be maintained in the pronunciation.

Another attempt to indicate the trill by means of spelling appears in words such as *gurrul, wurruk*. It is likely that the effect of making a monosyllable into a disyllable is not intended.

[5] Jeremiah J. Hogan, *The English Language in Ireland* (Dublin: The Educational Company of Ireland, 1927), p. 66.

[θ] ~ [t] sporadically, as in *thousand* [ˈtʌozn̩d], *thick* [tɪk], *thirteen* [ˌtʌrtˈtin], *cathedral* [kaˈtidrəl].

[ð] ~ [d̪] sporadically, as in *this* [d̪ɪs], *there* [d̪ɛr], *the* [d̪ə], *they* [d̪e], *that* [d̪at]. This [d] retains the dental position of [ð].

[s] ~ [ʃ] in initial clusters before *p* and *t*, as in *speak* [ʃpek], *steal* [ʃtel].[6] Sometimes it appears in other analogous combinations, as *snob* [ʃnab], *sky* [ʃkʌɪ]. Historically, [ʃ] appears for [s] in almost any position as in *cease* [ʃiʃ], *face* [feʃ], but these extremes are seldom if ever found nowadays.

[ʃ] ~ [s] as in *shrink* [srɪŋk], *shrill* [srɪl]. Compare *shrub, shrine, shrew, shrewd, shrug, shrank, shred, shrivel, shroud, shrunk.*

[ʍ] ~ [ɸ] with speakers who also speak Gaelic. Example *what* [ɸat, ɸʌt]. This sound is often written *ph, f, fw,* thus: *phat, fat, fwat,* all intended to be pronounced alike, viz., [ɸat]. The sound [ɸ] is made simply by blowing through the pursed lips.

There is some unvoicing of final voiced consonants, as in *drive* [drʌɪf], *twelve* [twɛlf], *hundred* [ˈhʊndərt], *bells* [bɛls], *beans* [bins], *strangers* [ˈstrend͡ʒərs]. This unvoicing is a relic feature representing substratum Celtic speech influence. Hogan illustrates with such words as *payte* [pet], for *paid, Irelant* for *Ireland,* *hant* for *hand, delightet* for *delighted.* He states that the *n* in such words is unvoiced also.[7]

Palatalization: [t, d] before [u] are palatalized in many words (where standard speech admits only of [tj, dj]), as in *tune* [t͡ʃun], *Tuesday* [ˈt͡ʃuzdɪ], *reduce* [riˈd͡ʒus], *duke* [d͡ʒuk]. Similar palatalizations take place before [ɪ, ə], as in *Indian* [ˈɪnd͡ʒɪən] and *tremendous* [trɪˈmɪnd͡ʒəs].

Metathesis. The following words are typical examples of the inversion called metathesis: *afraid* [əˈfɪrd], *pretty* [ˈpʌrtɪ], *scruff* [skʌrf], *curd* [krʌd], *asking* [ˈaksən], *massacre* [ˈmasəˌkri].

Miscellaneous. Following is a list of words whose pronunciation in Irish dialect does not fall into any of the foregoing categories: *potato* [pɪˈtetɪ, ˈpjetɪ, ˈpretɪ], *chimney* [ˈt͡ʃɪmblɪ], *supple* [ˈsupəl], *catch* [kɛt͡ʃ], *by* [bɪ], *sir* [sɔr], *boy* [bwɔɪ, bɔɪ, bwʌɪ, bʌɪ] (compare the spelling *bhoy*), *flannel* [ˈflanɪn], *children* [ˈt͡ʃɪldər], *was* [wʌz] (by restressing, more common in Irish dialect than in most others), *terrier* [ˈtarɪər], *spirit* and *miracle* [ˈspɛrət, ˈmɛrəkəl] (see page 198), *lilac* [ˈlelak] (by folk etymology), *quote* [kot], *to him* [tʊ əm] (see page 203), *cartridges* [ˈkatrɪd͡ʒɪz] (see page 224).

From *The Playboy of the Western World** *

Michael: ɪts ðə wɪl ə gad, ʌɪm θɪŋkən, θət al ʃəd wɪn ən ezɪ ər ə kruəl ɪnd, ənd əts ðə wɪl ə gad ðət al ʃəd rɪr ʊp lɛnθɪ famblɪz fər ðə nʌrt͡ʃər əv ðɪ arθ.

6 Hogan, p. 66.
7 Hogan, pp. 72–73.

ʤats ə sɪŋgəl man, ʌɪ ask jɪ, etən ɪn wan hʌos, n̩ drɪŋkən ə sʊp ɪn ənʌðər an hi wɪðʌot no ples əv ɪz ʌon lʌɪk n̩ ʌold brejən ʤakas. ɪts manɪ wʌd bi ɪn drɛd tə brɪŋ jər lʌɪks ɪntə ðər hʌos fər tʊ ɪnd ðɪm, mebɪ wɪð ə sʌdənt ɪnd, bət ʌɪm ə desn̩t man əv ʌɪrlənd ənd ʌɪd lifər fes ðə grev ənd ʌɪ siən ə skor ə gransʌnz groən ʊp ɪntə galənt lɪtəl swarərz, ðən go piplən mɪ bɛdsʌɪd wɪd pjunɪ widz ðə lʌɪk ə ʤat jid ɪvər brid, ʌɪm θɪŋkən, ʌot ə ʃanin kiox. ə darən fɛlə ɪz ðə ʤuəl əv ðə wʌrld, so me gɑd ənd merɪ ənd sent patrɪk blɛs jɪ, ənd ɪnkres jɪ frəm ðɪs mɑrtəl de.

J. M. Sʏɴɢᴇ

An Old Woman Outside the Abbey Theatre

ɪn ðɪs θiˈetər ðe haz plez
an ʌs ənd hʌɪ-ʊp pipəl kʊmz
ənd pez tə si θɪŋz pleən hɪr
ðed rʌn lʌɪk hɛl frʌm ɪn ðə ʃlʊmz.

— L. A. G. Sᴛʀᴏɴɢ

Transcribe:

Tʜᴇ Aᴍᴇʀɪᴄᴀɴ Sᴛᴀɢᴇ

From *Mr. Dooley's Philosophy*

"I've niver been much iv a hand f'r th' theaytre," said Mr. Dooley. "Whin I was a young man an' Crosby's Opry house was r-runnin' I used to go down wanst in a while an' see Jawn Dillon throwin' things around f'r th' amusemint iv th' popylace an' whin Shakespere was played I often had a seat in th' gal'ry, not because I liked th' actin', d'ye mind, but because I'd heerd me frind Hogan speak iv Shakespere. He was a good man, that Shakespere, but his pieces is full iv th' ol' gags that I heerd whin I was a boy. Th' trouble with me about goin' to plays is that no matther wher I set I cud see some hired man in his shirt sleeves argyin' with wan iv his frinds about a dog fight while Romeo was makin' th' kind iv love ye wuddent want ye'er daughter to hear to Juliet in the little burrd cage they calls a balcony. It must've ben because I wanst knowed a man be the name iv Gallagher that was a scene painter that I cud niver get misilf to th' pint iv concedin' that th' mountains that other people agreed was manny miles in the distance was in no danger iv bein' rubbed off th' map be th' coattails iv wan iv th' principal characters. An' I always had me watch out to time th' moon whin 'twas shoved acrost th' sky an' record th' breakin' iv day in th' robbers' cave where th' robbers don't dare f'r to shtep on the rock f'r fear they'll stave it in. If day iver broke on th' level th' way it does on the stage twud tear th' bastin' threads out iv what Hogan calls th' firmymint. Hogan says I haven't th' dhramatic delusion an' he must be r-right f'r ye can't make me believe that twinty years has elapsed whin I know that I've jist had time to pass th' time iv day with th' bartinder nex dure.

"Plays is upside down, Hinnisy, an' inside out. They begin with a full statement iv what's goin' to happen an' how it's goin' to come out an' thin ye're asked to forget what ye heerd an' be surprised be th' outcome. I always feel like goin' to th' office an' gettin' me money or me lithograph pass back afther th' first act."   FINLEY PETER DUNNE

Transcribe:

THE LEGEND OF THE LITTLE WEAVER OF DULEEK GATE

From *The Irish Fairy Book*

You see, there was a waiver lived wanst upon a time in Duleek here, hard by the gate, and a very honest, industherous man he was by all accounts. Well, it was one mornin' that his housekeeper called to him, and he sitting very busy throwin' the shuttle, and says she, "Your brekquest is ready!" "Lave me alone," says he; "I'm busy with a patthern here that is brakin' my heart, and until I complate and masther it intirely I wont quit."

"Oh, think o' the iligant stirabout that'll be spylte intirely."

"To the divil with the stirabout!" says he.

"God forgive you," says she, "for cursin' your good brekquest."

Well, he left the loom at last and wint over to the stirabout, and what would you think, but whin he looked at it, it was as black as a crow; for you see, it was in the hoighth o' summer, and the flies lit upon it to that degree that the stirabout was fairly covered with them.

"Why, thin, bad luck to your impidence," says the waiver; "would no place sarve you but that? And is it spyling my brekquest yiz are, you dirty bastes?" And with that, bein' altogether cruked tempered at the time, he lifted his hand, and he made one great slam at the dish.

                                                        GRAVES

Bibliography

Irish

Books

Darrow, Anne, *Phonetic Studies in Folk Speech and Broken English* (Boston: Expression Co., 1937).

Ellis, Alexander J., "Irish Pronunciation of English" in *Early English Pronunciation*, Part IV (London: Asher and Co. and Trübner and Co., 1874).

Hogan, Jeremiah J., *The English Language in Ireland* (Dublin: The Educational Company of Ireland, 1927).

CHAPTER 14

Speech of New York City

Standard and Substandard

As explained earlier in this book, the speech of New York City is herein regarded as a metropolitan sub-form of Eastern Speech.[1] As noted, this classification of New York City speech is not in accord with the opinions of some authorities, who regard it as sufficiently *sui generis* to constitute a regional speech in its own right. Nevertheless the inclusion of New York speech with Eastern speech has many lexical and phonetic justifications and a considerable measure of practical convenience.

The New York City speech area, incidentally, includes not merely Manhattan and much of Long Island, but also a large environmental area in nearby eastern New Jersey, the lower Hudson River valley, and southeastern Connecticut.

Since standard New York speech, often euphemistically called "cultivated New York speech," admittedly has some features which are not found in New England in exactly the same form and degree, this chapter will give attention (1) to certain selected representatives of these features and (2) to such substandard or "uncultivated" pronunciations as may be thought to be useful to persons concerned with play-production, interpretative reading, and the like, where a knowledge of substandardisms may be needed. In dealing with the substandard dialect, it is intended that the reader fall back upon the standard New York speech at any point where there is no prevalent substandardism; in turn, at any point where the standard New York features fail, he may fall back upon Standard Eastern speech, as earlier outlined (pages 221–235).

Hubbell, who has studied the use of [ɑə, ɑ] more closely than anyone else, finds that, though rules may be established for the use of the one sound or the other, it is nearly always possible to find many violations of such rules.[2]

---

[1] Hans Kurath, in *Word Geography of the Eastern United States*, q.v., p. 175, includes New York City speech with New England speech in what he designates as Northern speech.

[2] Allan Forbes Hubbell, *The Pronunciation of English in New York City* (New York: Columbia University Press, 1950), p. 82.

The actual situation, then, is one of great irregularity in all of the spellings related to these pronunciations, e.g., stressed *ar* as in *far*, "short *o*" as in *cod*, and *o* before *r* as in *tomorrow*. It should be borne in mind that [ɑə, ɑ] are used in New York City both in standard and substandard speech in a great many words where [ɔ] is found either regularly or in alternation with [ɑ] in other dialects. Among these words are *Omaha*, *Utah*, *bog*, *log*, *fog*, and a good many other words with *og*; *authority*, *foreign*, *forest*, *horrid*, *quarry*, *warrant*, and a good many other words with stressed *o* plus *r* plus unstressed syllable, or stressed *a* plus *r* plus unstressed syllable.

It must be added that in both standard and substandard New York speech there is a noticeable, though inconsistent, use of [ɒ] in the "short *o*" words, as in *got* [gɒt].

In almost all the instances where [ɔr, ɔ, ɔə] prevail in other standard American dialects, New York speech uses [ɔə]. In addition, the differences between *for-four*, *horse-hoarse*, and *morning-mourning* are leveled in favor of [ɔə], so that these pairs are homonyms. Words similar to any of them, such as *course-coarse*, *border-boarder*, are pronounced with [ɔə].

So also are words pronounced with [oʊ] in the Southern and General American dialects, such as *pore*, *pour*, *sore*, *source*, *worn*, *choral*, *sport*, *door*. [ɔr] is also common in the word-types in this paragraph.

Exception is made in the instance of certain words ending in *ong*, which are pronounced with [ɑ]. Examples: *ding-dong*, *gong*, *prong*, *throng*, *tongs*, etc. *Honk* is usually [hɑŋk].[3]

[ɑ, a] ∼ [ɑ, ˈɑə, a, ˈaə] in words spelled with *ar* in the stressed syllable, such as *mark* [mɑːk, ˈmɑək, mak, ˈmaək]. (It will be noted that in the use of [a] in these words New York speech parallels New England speech.) The monophthongs [ɑ] and [a] are most frequently found before intervocalic consonants, as in *carting* [ˈkɑtɪŋ, ˈkatɪŋ], but may be found in any position. The off-glide [ə], when it occurs at all, is usually light and inconspicuous.[4] [r] is also common here.

[ɑ, a, æ] ∼ [ɑə, ɑ, a, aə, æ] in the "broad *a*" words, as in *last* [ˈlɑəst, lɑst, last, ˈlaəst, læst]. (Note that all these pronunciations agree with pronunciations found in New England, the main difference being that the off-glide [ə] is less common in New England.)

Deviations from Standard New York Speech

Vowels

[ɔ] ∼ [ˈɔ̝̼˔ə] in words spelled with *al*, *au*, *aw*, *aught*, *ought*, as in *all*, *fault*, *law*, *taught*, *thought*. The complicated symbolization [ˈɔ̝̼˔ə] represents a sound

[3] Hubbell, *op. cit.*, p. 84, and C. K. Thomas, *An Introduction to the Phonetics of American English* (New York: The Ronald Press Co., 1947), p. 157.

[4] Hubbell, *op. cit.*, p. 77.

which is acoustically very close to [ˈoə], since the [ɔ] is raised and the lips rounded (and often protruded) as for [o]. The fact that the tongue is retracted, and especially the fact that the glossal muscles are tense, also gives the hearer an impression of [o], since [o-ɔ] are commonly thought of as a tense-lax pair. For purposes of this book, the sound will be transcribed with the simplified combination [ɔˑə]. But it must be borne in mind that the acoustic approach to [ˈoə] is often very close indeed. We may then transcribe the words above as [ˈɔˑəl], [ˈfɔˑəlt], [ˈlɔˑə], [ˈtɔˑət], [ˈθɔˑət].

The sound [ɔˑ] is a frequently occurring variant of [ˈɔˑə], especially before intervocalic consonants, as in *awful* [ˈɔˑfəl], but not finally before a pause,[5] as in *it is the law* [ɪt ɪz ðə lɔˑə]. Such an allophonic [ɔˑ] continues to be acoustically close to [o], as indicated above.

> Examples utilizing [ɔˑə, ɔˑ]: law, door, your, chalk, salt, talk, paw, launder, sought, maul, almost (a'most), always (a'ways), Austria, August, author, auto, because, bought, caught, daub, daunt, false, faucet, haunt, launch, laundry, to Laura, laurel, gaunt, sauce, saunter, sausage, small, walnut, Walter, waltz, hall, Galton, haul, wall, want, tall, Paul, pall, Saul, wrought, caw, raw, balk, stalk, straw, malt, caulk, sauce, laud.

[ɑ, ɔ] ∼ [ˈɔˑə] in the word *chocolate* [ˈtʃɔˑək(ə)lət-lɪt]. Here again, [ɔˑ] is very nearly [o].

[ɑ, a] ∼ [aˑ, ˈaˑə] in words spelled with *ar* in stressed syllables. This sound is sometimes represented as [ɒ][6] which, when lengthened, as it often is, represents a sound acoustically very close to [ɔ]. Since we have used [ɔ] for a corresponding sound in substandard Southern speech (page 216) and since the New York pronunciation here agrees closely with the Southern pronunciation, we shall use [ɔ] here. Example *hart* [hɔt, ˈhɔət]. Compare *card, mark, marble*. In a few words this sound is spelled *ea*, as in *heart, hearth*. [r] is heard also in these words.

[ɪ] ∼ [ɨ] in most words of the type *bit* [bɨt], *quick* [kwɨk], etc. [ɨ] is pronounced with the tongue retracted so that the tongue-arch is near the center of the mouth. In words containing [ɨ] before [l], the retraction is more pronounced, so that the vowel [ɨ] approaches [ʊ] acoustically, and words like *Billy-bully* sound considerably alike. Compare *rid, mitt, limb, silly, chilly*. This vowel shift is promoted especially by frequent use of the blade-articulated [l]. (See page 288.)

[ɛr, ær, ˈɛə, ˈæə] ∼ [ɛː] in words spelled with *er, ear, eir, are, air*, before a pause, as in *there* [ðɛː], *bear* [bɛː], *their* [ðɛː], *care* [kɛː], *hair* [hɛː]. Compare *where, wear, fare, fair, bare, heir*.

[eɪ] ∼ [ˈɛə] in certain words containing vowel plus [l], such as *sale* [ˈsɛəl], *sailing* [ˈsɛəlɪŋ].[7] Compare *gale, fail, bail, daily*. Before an intervocalic consonant, [ˈɛə] may be reduced to [ɛ], as in *sailor* [ˈsɛlə].

---

[5] Hubbell, p. 82.
[6] *Manual for Speech I and Speech II* (Brooklyn College Press, 1939–40), p. 32.
[7] Hubbell, p. 75.

[æ] ~ [ˈɛə] in most words spelled with what has customarily been called "short *a*"; a few such words adhere to the pronunciation with [æ]. The conditions according to which the two sounds [ɛə] and [æ] maintain a rather unstable degree of distinction from one another have been subjected to careful phonemic and phonetic scrutiny over a long period of time, the best work on the subject having been done by George L. Trager[8] and Allan Forbes Hubbell.[9] The rules which have been deduced by these authors, while entirely sound, are subject to exception and violation to so great a degree as to be impractical for the use of any but the most exacting actor, interpretative reader, or dramatic director. Such a person can settle any moot question by reference to the works cited in footnotes 2 and 8. Regarding the complications of following the uncertain New York pattern for the separation of [ɛə] and [æ], Hubbell says:

> Many New Yorkers—and this is perhaps the commonest pattern of all . . . pronounce [ɛə], [ɛ·], [æə], [æ·], in words like *glad, stand, jazz* in an extremely haphazard fashion, often they will pronounce the higher and lower varieties in successive utterances of the same word. . . .[10]

Both Hubbell and Thomas[11] suggest that the unpopularity of using [ɛə] for [æ] which has been generated in the New York City school system may have resulted in attempts to avoid [ɛə] by many speakers who are successful in doing so only a part of the time. In any case, the casual student of substandard New York speech is passably safe in rendering almost any "short *a*" as [ˈɛə]. The three words quoted above—*glad, stand, jazz*—are, then, [ˈglɛəd, ˈstɛənd, ˈdʒɛəz]. Compare *cab, mad, flag, badge, taffy, lath, pass, lash, davenport, razz, clam, pan.*

NOTE: It may be mentioned in passing that the raising process whereby [æ] has been displaced by [ɛ] has by no means stopped at [ɛ]. In Boston, in street gamin talk, the word *stand* may be heard as [stɪnd, ˈstɪənd] any day, in the speech of the children who recite a memorized rigamarole concerning Bunker Hill Monument in the hope of eliciting tips from sight-seers. [ˈstɪənd] may, indeed, be heard in New York.

[ʌ] ~ [ɑ] in words beginning with stressed *con, com,* as in *comfortable* [ˈkʌmfətəbəl], *constable* [ˈkɑnstəbəl]. This is believed to be a spelling pronunciation analogus to *constant* [ˈkɑnstənt], *comparable* [ˈkɑmpɚəbəl]. Related to these are words such as *some* [sɑm], *come* [kɑm]. Compare *become, color, something, comfort, monger, government.* Also related acoustically to the words above are words

---

[8] George L. Trager "The Pronunciation of 'Short-a' in American Standard English," *American Speech*, June, 1930, pp. 396–400.

——, "What Conditions Limit Variance of a Phoneme," *American Speech*, September, 1934, pp. 313–15.

——, "One Phonemic Entity Becomes Two: The Case of 'Short-a," *American Speech*, October, 1940, pp. 255–58.

[9] Hubbell, pp. 75–78.

[10] Hubbell, p. 78.

[11] C. K. Thomas, "Pronunciation in Downstate New York (I)" *American Speech*, February, 1942, p. 32.

containing [ʌ] spelled in other ways, such as *cup* [kɑp], *upper* [ˈʌpə], *love* [lʌv]; such pronunciations originate in foreign dialect. (See page 236.) Compare *subway, stuff, rough, bump, above, son, sun.*

[ɝ, ɜ] ~ [ʌ] in final positions, as in *fur* [fʌ], *fir* [fʌ]. Compare *her, whirr, blur, purr, stir, cur, burr.* (In standard dialects, [ʌ] is ordinarily not used finally.)

[i] ~ [ɪi, əi],[12] [iˑ ɪ],[13] [ɛɪ, eɪ],[14] for [i] final before pause. Of these transcriptions [ɛi] and [əi] seem acoustically very close to the pronunciation as heard. We may, then, transcribe *see, degree* as [sɛi, səi; dəˈgrɛi, dəˈgrəi].

[ɔɪ] ~ [oɪ] in final open syllables and in stressed syllables before a vowel, as in *boy* [boɪ], *royal* [ˈroɪəl].[15] This classification ordinarily includes derivatives of words containing the diphthong finally, such as *boyish* [ˈboɪɪʃ]. The [o] of the diphthong [oɪ] is very retracted and tense, and is often pronounced with the lips protruding. Compare *employ, destroy, joy, toy, annoy, deploy, destroys, employable, employer, coy, soy, Foy, loyal, Roy, envoy.*

[ɔɪ] ~ [ɜɪ, ɝ] in words where the diphthong is followed by a consonant, as in *loin* [lɜɪn, lɝn], *oil* [ɔɪl, ɝl]. In most cases the syllable containing the diphthong is a closed syllable, but there are some exceptions, as in *goiter* [ˈgɜɪtə]. (See footnote 15 below.) Compare *boil, choice, oyster, ointment, point, poison, spoil, joint, rejoice.* In words of this class, the sound [ɝ], while it is well known, does not occur as frequently as the comic paper would imply. This statement applies equally to [ɔɪ] in the paragraph immediately following.

[ɝ, ɜ] ~ [ɜɪ, ɔɪ], in all words where [ɝ, ɜ] occurs in standard dialects, except in final positions. Examples: *learn* [lɜɪn, lɔɪn], *earl* [ɜɪl, ɔɪl], *earnest* [ˈɜɪnɪst, ˈɔɪnɪst]. Compare *burn, burst, curve, dirt, fern, girl, heard, hearse, jerk, lurk, Myrtle, nurse, nervous, purple, purse, person, service, circle, skirt, turn, turtle, thirty-third, thirsty, verse, worse, word, work.* It will be seen that if the General American pronunciation is applied to words in this category, the sounds become identical with one of the substandard pronunciations indicated in the paragraph above, and certain pairs of words become homonyms. Examples: *loin* [lɝn], *learn* [lɝn]; *oil* [ɝl], *earl* [ɝl]; *coil* [kɝl], *curl* [kɝl]. (See footnote 15 below.)

[aʊ] ~ [æʊ], very frequently nasalized to [æ̃ʊ̃], as in *now* [næʊ, næ̃ʊ̃]. Compare *count, round, town, owl, about, bounce, bound, drouth.* Exceptions: *our, ours,* which are [ˈɑə, ˈɑəz].[16]

---

[12] C. K. Thomas's transcription in "Pronunciation in Downstate New York (I)," *American Speech*, February, 1942, p. 31.

[13] Hubbell's description, p. 64.

[14] M. S. Coxe's transcription in letter to author.

[15] This statement is highly generalized and quite practical but does not cover every instance. For an exceedingly close and authoritative study of the sounds in this and the immediately succeeding paragraph, see Hubbell, "Curl and Coil in New York City," *American Speech*, December, 1940, pp. 372–76.

[16] Hubbell, p. 71.

[oʊ] ∼ [ɛʊ, eʊ], as in *note* [nɛʊt, neʊt].[17] Compare *oh, go, old, cold, goat, open.* This pronunciation is extreme. In the form [ɜʊ], it is thought to be an imitation of southern British speech.[18] The almost universal [oʊ] of other American dialects is much used also.

[aɪ] ∼ [ɒɪ], as in *mind* [mɒɪnd], *time* [tɒɪm], *find* [fɒɪnd].

[aɪ] ∼ [ɑ] in the pronoun *I* [ɑ], and more strikingly in *I'll* [ɑl], *I'm* [ɑm], *I've* [ɑv], and *I'd* [ɑd].

Omission and intrusion of [ə]. [ə] is omitted from certain unstressed syllables in such a way as to reduce the number of syllables in the words by one, as in *giant* [dʒɒɪnt], *really* ['rilɪ, 'rɪlɪ]. Compare *champion* [ˌtʃɛəm'pin], *manual* ['mɛən-jəl], *diary* ['dɒɪrɪ], *real* [ril], *cruel* [krul], *towel* [tæul], *ev'ry, jew'lry, poem* [poʊm], *voy'ge, loy'lty, roy'lty, fam'ly.* [ə] is intruded by anaptyxis in words such as ['ɛləm] for *elm,* ['fɪləm] for *film,* ['ɛəθəˌlit] for *athlete.*

Consonants

[b] is sometimes lost by assimilation as in [ˌsaməˈrin] for *submarine,* and a syllable may be lost by syllabic dissimilation (haplology), as in ['prɑblɪ] for *probably.* This word may be further reduced by elision to ['prɑlɪ].

[t] ∼ [d] where [t] occurs between vowels or between a vowel and [l] as in *batter* ['bɛədə], *exhibiting* [ɪgˈzɪbədɪn], *rattle* ['reədl].[19] Though this voicing of [t] is known throughout the country, it appears to be more prominent in New York than elsewhere. It occurs not merely within words, but within phrases, as in *get it over* [ˌgɪdədˈɛʊvə], *let her be* [ˌlɛdəˈbəɪ]. Compare *better, notice, scuttle, kitty, right over here, see that he does it, put it on, felted, seventy, settle, kettle, battle.* The one tap trill [ɾ] may, as in all other American dialects, appear instead of [d] in examples such as those above. Paradoxically, an over-aspirated [tˈ] is also common with the words above. (See page 286.)

The imploded (unreleased) [t] and [d] are often omitted from consonant clusters before other plosives, as in *stuffed crabs* [ˌstʌf ˈkreəbz], *boiled beef* [bɜɪl, ˌbɜl ˈbif]; [t] is also omitted from consonant clusters consisting of consonant plus [ts], as *expects* [ɪkˈspɛks]; *gifts* [gɪfs], *interrupts* [ˌɪnəˈrʌps].

[d] is omitted from the medial consonant cluster [nd] as in *wonderful* ['wanəfəl], *sending* ['sɛnːɪŋ]. Compare *bundle, Sunday school, fundamental, trundle.*

[tθ] final ∼ [θ] in *eighth* [eɪθ]. Compare one pronunciation of *height* [haɪtθ, haɪθ].

[dθ] final ∼ [θ] in *width* [wɪθ]. Compare *breadth.*

Initial [t] in a stressed syllable (including [t] in the cluster [tr]) and final [t]

---

[17] C. K. Thomas, "Jewish Dialect and New York Dialect," *American Speech,* June, 1932, p. 324.

[18] Hubbell, p. 71.

[19] See p. 286 for [t] ∼ [ʔ].

if exploded before a pause may be affricated to produce a pronunciation which may be roughly indicated as [ts], as in *Times Square* [tsɒɪmz skwɛ:], *put him out* [pʊdəmˈæuts]. Compare *tall, take, train, troops, It's a hit.* This [ts] is not usually tongue-point but may more properly be described as a "heavily affricated blade alveolar."[20] The point of the tongue may touch the upper teeth, but in nearly all cases rests behind the lower teeth.

Initial [d] in a stressed syllable and final [d] before a pause may be rendered as [dz], as *dial* [dzɒɪl], *it's too wide* [əts tsu ˈwɒɪdz]. This [dz] is not usually tongue-point alveolar but may be more properly described as a blade–articulated alveolar affricate,[21] since the tip of the tongue usually rests behind the lower teeth. Compare *doll, daily, dame, that's bad.*

[t] initial in a medial or final unstressed syllable is frequently over-aspirated, as if it were initial in a stressed syllable. In fluent conversation in American English, when no unusual precision is intended, such a [t] is actually a one-tap trill and may be expressed by the symbol [ɾ], as in *city* [ˈsɪɾɪ]. In substandard New York speech the pronunciation is [ˈsɪtʻɪ], which in fluent conversation gives the effect of over-precision where casualness is to be desired. This aspirated [t] may also be used in fluent conversation where a nasally exploded [t] is expected, as in [ˈboʊltʻən] for *Bolton* [ˈboʊltn̩]. The substandard New York pronunciation of this word is [ˈbɛʊltʻsən]. Note that in this context the [t] is affricated even though it is not in a stressed syllable. Affrication may also take place where [s] precedes the syllable containing [t], as in *Boston* [ˈbɒstʻsən]. Compare *laughter, beautiful, writer, hunted, cultivated, faculty, pretty, kitty, twenty, British, scatter, setter, jointed.* Note that many of these words may be pronounced with [d] (see page 285) or [ʔ] in substandard New York speech.

[t] ~ [ʔ] in medial positions, most frequently where the context in standard speech is [tl] or [tn̩], as *settle* [ˈsɛʔl̩], *mutton* [ˈmɑʔn̩]. With considerable frequency, final [t] in a word preceding a vowel will be displaced by the glottal stop, as in *not ever* [nɑʔˈɛəvə]. When there is a simultaneous lingua-alveolar stop alongside the glottal stop in words of the type of *Benton*, i.e., where *t* is preceded by [n] and followed by [n̩], the pronunciation is hardly regarded as substandard; but if the glottal stop appears elsewhere, and as a substitute for a consonant, it is so regarded. Compare *glottal, vital, gentleman, mitten, kitten, button, bitten, little, kettle, bottle, battle, rotten, mortal, cattle, metal, fundamental, title, fatten, batten, turtle.* Note that many of the words may be pronounced with the over-aspirated [t] (see above) or with [d] (see page 285) in substandard New York speech.

Theoretically the glottal stop may be substituted (though often with simultaneous oral articulation) for any plosive medial or final in a word, as indeed

[20] Hubbell, p. 26.
[21] Hubbell, p. 28.

often happens in Cockney and Scottish. Such pronunciations as [ˈdɒʔə] for *doctor* and [ðɛʔ ˈmɛən] for *that man* have been noted in New York speech, but the contexts indicated above are the ones which most frequently yield this substitution.

[k] is dropped from the combination [ks] in words of the class *accelerate* [əˈsɛləˌreɪt]. Compare *eccentric, accessory, accessible.*

Vowel plus [n] ~ nasalized vowel in both stressed and unstressed words and syllables, but most often in stressed elements before unstressed ones, as in *contact* [ˈkã̠ˌtɛk], *on guard* [ˌõˈgɔəd], *on top* [ˌõˈtɒp]. It should be recognized that nasalization of vowels such as those above is common throughout the United States; but usually the nasal consonant is retained as well, as in *contact* [ˈkã̠nˌtækt]. The complete absorption of the nasal consonant into the vowel is characteristic of the New York form of nasalization. A by-product of this nasalization is the loss of the glide [t], as in *conscience* [ˈkɑntʃənts > ˈkã̠ʃənts]. Compare *compact, contents, influence, conduct, conciousness, conversation, ancient, enthusiastic, instead, mention, engage, one time, when reading, science, length and strength* (from [lɛnθ, strɛnθ], q. v., page 202). In certain words spelled with *im* from historical *in*, the same phenomenon of nasalization can be noted, as in *impact, import, implication.*

[m] plus front consonant may correspond to [mp] plus front consonant, as *he came to see me* [hi ˌkeɪmptə ˈsi mi].[22] This is analogous to well-known examples, such as OE *emti* > MnE *empty.* (See page 164.)

[ð] ~ approximately to [d] in such familiar, frequently used words as *the* [də], *this* [dɪs], *that* [ˌdɛət], *those* [dɛʊz], *with* [wɪd], *mother* [ˈmɑdə], *brother* [ˈbrɑdə], *other* [ˈɑdə]. Speakers who use this [d] and the [t] of the words in the following section are almost always capable of pronouncing [ð] and [θ], but do not do so in certain common words, simply because at their educational and social level it is not customary. This pronunciation begins at the street gamin level and dwindles out somewhere near the middle of the rising social scale.

Hubbell,[23] who has studied this pronunciation scrutinizingly, believes that, while [d] may occur here, a dental affricate, [dð], is often actually used. But for purposes of plays and interpretative reading, it is justifiable to use [d].

[θ] ~ approximately to [t] in such familiar, frequently used words as *thread* [ˈtrɛəd], *Catholic* [ˈkɛətlɪk], *truth* [trʊt], *sixth* [sɪkst], *thirty* [ˈtɜɪtɪ, ˈtɔɪtɪ]. Hubbell[24] believes that, while an unmistakable [t] may occur instead of [θ], more frequently a blade-articulated [t], made with the tongue against the posterior surfaces of the lower front teeth, is used instead. However, for purposes of representing substandard New York speech in plays and readings, it is probably best, at least

---

[22] Hubbell, p. 55.
[23] Hubbell, pp. 36–37.
[24] Hubbell, pp. 35–36.

for the non-New Yorker, to use the ordinary, even if somewhat inaccurate, alveolar [t]. Compare *theory, with, nothing, fifteenth, third, through, Ethel, fifth.*

[ðz] ∼ [θs] in the plurals of words ending in [θ], as in *mouths* [mæuθs], *baths* [ˈbɛəθs]. Compare *booths, laths, truths, moths, paths, oaths.*

[ŋ] ∼ [ŋg] intervocalically in many words and phrases, as in *singer* [ˈsɪŋgə], *Long Island* [ˌlɔŋˈgɒɪlən]. Compare *bringing up, stinger, longing, ringing, wringer, long ago, sing it, coming up, something old, ring out the old, ring in the new.* Occasionally, instead of [ŋg], we may find [ŋk]; also occasionally an excrescent [g] or [k] may appear finally after [ŋ]. Compare *believing anything wrong.*

[ŋg] ∼ [ŋ] in words of the class of *finger* [ˈfɪŋə], *single* [ˈsɪŋl̩]. Compare *linger, angry, angle, English, England, language, lingual, jingle, younger, hungry.* It is believed that pronunciations both of the [ˌlɔŋˈgɒɪlən] and [ˈsɪŋl̩] types, when found in the speech of New Yorkers, stem from foreign influence. The confusion of foreigners over such perverse English pronunciations as *singer-linger* and the presence among foreigners of such pronunciations as German *finger* [ˈfɪŋər] and Italian *banco* [ˈbaŋko] complicates the pronunciations greatly and induces mistaken attempts at correction which may readily be carried over to native New Yorkers, especially the younger ones.

[t, d, n, s, z] ∼ [t̪, d̪, n̪, s̪, z̪]. The dentalization may be accomplished with the tip of the tongue against the posterior surfaces of the upper front teeth, but it is also often achieved with the tongue against the inner surfaces of the lower teeth. The latter tongue position forces a blade articulation of the consonant and so produces consonants of appreciably different quality from those produced by tongue-point articulation. A blade-articulated [t] has a suggestion of [θ] at the end; [d] has [ð]; [n] faintly suggests [ŋ]; while [s] and [z], being produced through a wider aperture than tongue-point [s] and [z], have a rougher sound, possibly of lower pitch than tongue-point [s] and [z].[25] In some instances [ʃ, ʒ, tʃ, dʒ, l] are also pronounced with blade articulation and with the point of the tongue behind the lower teeth. So articulated, [l] somewhat resembles [λ]. It must be admitted that the pronunciation of these sounds with blade articulation is awkward for those not accustomed to it. It should therefore be considered permissible for actors and interpretative readers to use the simpler tongue-point-upper teeth dentality in reproducing this aspect of substandard New York speech.

It must be remembered that the dentality just discussed may occur alone or in combination with affrication in stressed syllables beginning with [t] or [d]. Compare *tame* [t̪(s)eɪm], *dame* [d̪(z)eɪm], *tile, dial, ninth, sale, sight, zoo, zodiac.*

[hj] ∼ [j] in words spelled with initial *hu* pronounced [hju] in standard dialect. Examples: *human* [ˈjumən], *Hugh* [ju]. Compare *hue, humor, Hubert, Hughes, humane, humid, humility, humidor.*

---

[25] Hubbell, pp. 38–40.

[tʃ] ~ [ʃ] in some instances in -tion, -ture, and analogous suffixes after [s, p, k]. Examples: *picture* [ˈpɪkʃə], *question* [ˈkwəʃən]. Compare *capture, structure, suggestion, digestion, lecture, actually, actuate.*

[dʒ] ~ [tʃ] finally, as in *cottage* [ˈkɑtɪtʃ]. An intermediate of the shift [dʒ] ~ [tʃ] is [dʃ]. The unvoicing of [dʒ] final is believed to be the result of foreign language influence. Compare *college, cabbage, garbage, spinach, privilege, marriage.*

Excessive lip-rounding may be observed in the pronunciation of [ʃ, ʒ, tʃ, dʒ, r], as in *sure* [tˈʃʊə], *pleasure* [ˈpleɪʒə], *chew* [tʃu], *Joe* [dʒou], *right* [rɒɪt].

[r] occurs intrusively where a word ending in a vowel is followed without pause by another word or syllable beginning with a vowel, as in *drawing* [ˈdrɔrɪŋ], *Asia and Africa* [ˌeɪʒərənˈɛəfrɪkə], *Africa and Asia* [ˌɛəfrɪkərənˈeɪʒə]. There is the possibility, as indicated earlier (page 233), of reasoning by analogy to explain the intrusive *r*, viz., if *war* has two pronunciations in [ˌwɔr ənd ˈpis] and [ˈtoutəl ˌwɔə], it is analogously (if speciously) reasonable that *law* should have two pronunciations in [ˌlɔr əv ˈɪŋglənd] and [ˈkɒmənˌlɔə]. (Exception: in words ending in vowel plus *r* plus vowel, such as *Laura and May*, dissimilative influences inhibit the introduction of another [r].)[26] In frequently used words, the intrusive *r* may be carried along as an integral part of the word or syllable, even when it is not followed by another word or syllable beginning with a vowel. Thus we may have both *the idear of it* and *the very idear.* Compare *Clarinda is in Iowa, Ava and Rita, Manila envelope, sofa and chair, soda and salt, jawing, Jamaica Avenue.*

[l] ~ [ł] when pronounced with blade articulation. This [l] is dark in any context and, when final, often has no lingua-alveolar contact. Without such alveolar contact the [l] becomes [ʊ] or [o], as in the sequence [fił > fiʊ > fio] for *feel.*

[ʍ] ~ [w] generally in most words spelled with *wh*, except *who, whole* and their derivatives, as in *which* [wɪtʃ], *when* [ˈwɛən]. Compare *what, where, whale, whether, whim, why, whistle, wheedle.*

The unstressed syllable [əm] is used, not merely for *them*, as in all parts of the country, but for *him*, and even for *her* and *it*. Example: *I heard him, her, it, them* [ɒɪ ˈhɜɪd əm].

[s] ~ [z], usually by way of regressive assimilation, in certain locutions such as *gas meter* [ˈgɛəzˌmitə], *baseball* [ˈbeɪzˌbɔl]. Compare *iceman, this boy, classmate, last night, must be.* In extreme cases the voicing of the [s] will carry over into isolated positions where there is no assimilative influence. Compare *at last, turn on the gas, first base.* This pronunciation is quite possibly of foreign origin, but it has been widely adopted by native speakers.

After [t, d, n], the vowel [u] is used almost consistently in substandard speech, contrasting with the mixed use of [u, ju] in standard speech, as in *tune* [tun],

---

[26] Hubbell, p. 45.

due [du], *knew* [nu]. This is not to say that [u] in these contexts is substandard, for it is found to a greater or lesser extent in standard speech throughout the country. Nevertheless, it helps identify substandard speech, since it is used there to the exclusion of [ju]. Compare *neutral, newspaper, tube, tumor, duke, dual.*

Substandard New York speech contains many of the features common to the substandard speech of the country at large. (See pages 193–204.) These are often indicated in dialect writing, but it is perhaps worth while to mention some of them here, to guard against oversight. The pronunciations of *catch* as [kɛtʃ], *get* as [gɪt], and *just* as [dʒɪst] are as common in New York as anywhere else. The same may be said of the substitution of [n] for [ŋ], as in *coming* [ˈkʌmɪn]. It is possible that omissions from complicated consonant clusters are more common in New York than in some other places. Examples: *gif's* for *gifts*, *erup's* for *erupts*, *contrac's* for *contracts*, *insis's* for *insists.*

Miscellaneous pronunciation: [ˈrædɪo] for *radio*, [ˈrædɪˌeɪdə] for *radiator*, [ˈpɛrəˌmɑnt] for *paramount*, [bɪˈkoəs] for *because*, [ˈfaˌhɛd] for *forehead*, [wʊnt] for *won't*, [ˌθiˈeɪdə] for *theater*, [juz] (unstressed [jəz]) for *you* (sing. and pl.), [ˈhanət] for *hundred*, [ˈpɒkəˌbʊk] for *pocketbook*, [wʊnt] for *wouldn't*, [ʃʊnt] for *shouldn't*, [kʊnt] for *couldn't*, [dɪnt] for *didn't.*

Extreme Substandard New York Speech

From *Dead End* *

Tommy: hlɜu, eɪndʒəl, hlɜu, dzɪpɪ.

Zippy: ʃaɾəp, wɪljə, spɪts.

Spit: rɒɪt ɪnə bɛlɪ bʌʔn̩.

Tommy: leɪ əəf əm, wɒɪ dɛuntʃə?

Spit: dɪ nɒk əm ɪnəz dɪ.

Tommy: wɑsə mɛədə? jə ə wɒɪz gɒɪ ərə bɒɪ skæut? kəmɑn ɪn, dzɪpɪ.

Angel: hæuzə wɔədə, tsɒmɪ?

Tommy: bɒɪ! də nʌts!

Spit: dʒiz, greɪt!

Angel: kɜuld?

Tommy: nɑ. swɛəl, dʒɪs rɒɪt.

T. B.: dɛə wəz ə gɒɪ ət rɪfɔəm skuəl wʌnst justə smɛuk mɛrɪwanə. jə nɛu wɔt dɛət ɪz? dɛup. əts lɒɪk dɛup. əts dɜup. ət gɪvz jə drimz.

Angel: dɪdʒə trɒɪ ət?

T. B.: nɑ. dɪ kɛənt smɛuk ən əkæunə mə ti bi. ɪt gɪts mi. dɪ kɔf lɒɪk ɛənɪtɪŋ.

Sidney Kingsley

ɑɪ sɪn ə fə hɛrɪnz ɪn ʃi ɛəs fə waɪt fɪʃ, stupɪd gɜɪl. seɪm t̬ɪŋ wɪˈn ɑɪ sɪn ə fə bɜld hɛːəm. ʃi gɪt⁽ᵈ⁾s vədʒɪnjə hɛːəm. ɑɪ nɪvə sɔr sʌtʃ ə dʌm gɜɪl ɪn ɔl mɑɪ laıf. ʃi meı bi maı dɔrdə bəd ə gɛs ʃi ın hɛrıts hə breınz frɱ ər oʊl mɛən. jɛə. wıl, aıl teık ɖə hɛrınz n̩ ɱ sari tə həv baɖəd jə.

Transcription by John B. Newman, Queens College.

Transcribe:

From *Having Wonderful Time* *

Rosalind: Don't worry about Fay, Teddy. She's prolly looking all over camp for you. Dijja see that evening gown? It was beaudyful.

Lois: That must cost a good ninedy semny-five wholesale.

Fay: Teddy, dolling!

Teddy: Hello, Fay.

Fay: I din know till just this minute.

Eli: Guess he's been examining the new arrivals.

Hi: Well, Casanova, dijja see what landed?

Barney: Yeah. Not bad.

Hi: Not bad!

Schmutz: Dincha see their faces? At lease with a pretty dame . . . .

Tobias: A check fa this, a check fa that. What'm I made of, fourteen-karat gold, fa heaven's sakes?

Itchy: Hoddeya like that? The Master of Cemeteries gets the razzberry! Comes the revolution I'll get razzberries with crimm!

Fay: What'd I tell you? Some sense a yewma!

Itchy: Seriously, folks, I wanna extend in the name of Mr. Tobias a welcome to the newcomers who are new to this camp. To the old–timers I wanna say that Camp Kare-Free's still got the old carefree spirit and—well, we wanna get your cooperation to keep the camp spirit as such.

Fay: He talks a very nice grammar.

Rosalind. He's got a sister who's a liberrian.

ARTHUR KOBER

Criticism: This is, of course, very light dialect writing. Kober has depended quite heavily on consonant omissions as in his "prolly" for "probably," and "lease" for "least." In several places he seems to have confused Yiddish with New Yorkese, as in "crimm" for "cream."

Transcribe:

From *Dead End*

Spit: Hey, should we go tuh Schultzie's 'n' see if we kin snitch sumpm?

Tommy: Nah, Schultzie's wise tuh us.

Angel: We could try some udduh staws.

Tommy: Nah, dey're all wise tuh us. Duh minute we walk in 'ey asks u, wadda we want. If we had some dough, while one uv us wuz buyin sumpm de udduh guys could swipe some stuff, see? I got faw cents but 'at ain' enough. Anybody got any dough heah? Hey, yew, Angel yuh got some?

Martin: Say, maybe yuh changed, huh? Maybe yuh become a rat. Maybe yuh'd like tuh git dat faw grand 'at's up fuh me . . . .

Gimpty: You know better.

Martin: I'm not so sure. Fawty-two hundred bucks is pretty big dough fer a joik like yew.

SIDNEY KINGSLEY

Bibliography

New York Speech

Books

Hubbell, Allan Forbes, *The Pronunciation of English in New York City* (New York: Columbia University Press, 1950).

Manual for Speech I and Speech II (New York: Brooklyn College Press, 1939–40).

Thomas, C. K., *An Introduction to the Phonetics of American English* (New York: The Ronald Press Co., 1947).

Periodicals

Hubbell, Allan Forbes, "Curl and Coil in New York City," *American Speech*, December, 1940.

Thomas, C. K., "Jewish Dialect and New York Dialect," *American Speech*, June, 1932.

CHAPTER 15

Substandard Southern Negro Speech

It is a principle which may be confirmed by observation that small details of dialectal difference tend to lose themselves in the surrounding language. Accordingly, where the discussion of a dialect does not appear to cover a given case, one is safe to fall back upon the language of the section in which the dialect is found. The principle is strikingly illustrated in the case of the two French-American dialects, French-Canadian and Creole, where in the first case that part of the sound system used which is not French is English, of either the Eastern or the General American type, and in the second case, English of the Southern type. The principle is nowhere more noticeable than in the case of substandard Negro dialect, where any feature of pronunciation not belonging specifically to Negro speech is to be found in the surrounding substandard Southern speech.

Offhand, one would say that substandard Negro speech is of all dialects the most strikingly different from the cultivated English spoken by educated Southerners, both Negro and white. In a sense this is true, but very many of the differences are not differences of pronunciation proper, and are therefore not easily reducible to phonetic terms. These differences are, instead, somewhat as follows:

a. Those of vocabulary, including a considerable number of words used frequently by uneducated Negroes and seldom or never by educated Southerners, either white or Negro. Among these are (1) a few words of African origin,[1] (2) certain archaic English words, (3) garbled modern English words. Examples:

1. *goober* [ˈgubə] (peanut), *pinder* [ˈpɪndə] (peanut), *buckra* [ˈbʌkrə] (white man), *gumbo* [ˈgʌmbo] (okra).
2. *sont* (sent), *holp* [houp] (help).
3. *madaxe* (mattock), *cowbuckle* (carbuncle).

---

[1] Lorenzo D. Turner, *Africanisms in the Gullah Dialect* (Chicago: University of Chicago Press, 1949), p. 43 ff.

293

b. Of conjugation, as in the ungrammatical (and by no means universally or consistently used) forms below:

ah	has		we	
you			we's	
yo'	} has		we-all	} has
			us	
			y'all	has
he	has		dey	has
	(elegant) *have*			

c. Of declension, as

	Nom.	*man*	*mens*
	Gen.	*man's*	*mens's*
and			

	ah	*we*
Nom.		*we's*
		we-all
		us

	mah	*ouah, ouahs*
Gen.	*mine*	*we-all's*
		us's

| | *me* | *we-all* |
| Acc. | | *us* |

d. Of intonation, which is baffling to record on paper (despite excellent work on it by noted phoneticians), but which is one of the outstanding characteristics of Negro speech.

e. Of voice quality. Contrary to some casual opinion, Negro voice quality does not result from any peculiar physical formation of Negro resonance cavities. Northern Negroes, who have been reared among a majority of whites, have nothing of this so-called Negro voice quality. When in relatively complete isolation from large numbers of their race who are either fresh from the South or have preserved their southern voice quality in large urban speech islands, these northern Negroes cannot be distinguished from white people through any characteristic of voice.

Southern Negro voice quality appears with many speakers to come from a consistent elevation of the blade of the tongue in the direction of the hard palate or of the juncture between the hard and soft palates. All vowels are consequently something less than open and free. Some front vowels tend to take on a kind of [e]-resonance; [æ] and [ε] do so especially.

Substandard Negro enunciation tends to be lax and blurred. Many consonants are omitted entirely. A certain Negro bricklayer regularly says [nɔˈɱm] for *no, sir.* In Evangeline Parish in Louisiana, it is often necessary to move very close to a group of Negro conversationalists to make sure whether the burbling stream of their vocables is intended for English or French—or a mixture of the two.

It is continually necessary, then, for those who would reproduce the dialectal speech, to hear it from persons or recordings, and to catch its intonations and qualities at first hand. Having done this, they can, by observing the spellings of a given author and the pronunciations indicated herein, make a satisfactory approach to the task; for the Negro intonation patterns and tone qualities are among the easiest in all languages to imitate successfully, perhaps for the very reason of their great difference from those of standard speech.

The speech of the Virginia Negroes is considerably different, and of the Carolina Negroes somewhat different, from that of Negroes in the rest of the South.[2] Not that the rest of the South has homogeneous Negro speech, but in the rest of the South it is sufficiently homogeneous for general treatment. This book, accordingly, deals with Negro speech in the South at large.

A word is in order about dialect spelling, not merely of Negro dialect, but of all dialects. Authors cannot be expected to be phoneticians, and consequently their spellings are often imperfect and inconsistent. Some sounds cannot be represented by means of the ordinary letters of the alphabet, and of course the phonetic alphabet is not available for use in the usual books and magazines. Moreover, writers must follow conventional spellings to a considerable degree, in order not to be annoying and unintelligible to the average reader. These spellings have to be interpreted by the actor or interpretative reader in the light of the probable intention of the authors. Southern authors, particularly, are inconsistent about the handling of *r's*. They will very likely indicate a silent *r* in *dah*, because that pronunciation is so radically different from their own *there* [ˈðɛə] that they feel as if something ought to be done about it; but since the Negro's pronunciation of *butter* is not likely to be different from a writer's own [ˈbʌtə], it does not occur to the writer that to write it *butter* will be misleading to every reader in the General American speech area. The reader simply has to understand that all the *r's* he encounters should be treated as southern *r's* are customarily treated in the given contexts. So with all other features; the actor or interpreter using Negro dialect or any other dialect has as his first duty the task of "reworking" the text to give the pronunciation completeness and consistency.

---

[2] Gullah speech, as spoken typically on the "sea islands" of the South Atlantic coast, is quite unlike any other southern speech. It is a relic speech, carried down from early days almost without later contamination with the speech of white people.

The following statement of hypothesis, concerning the persistence of Negro dialect and the reciprocal action of white and Negro speech upon each other in the South, may partially answer the persistent question as to the relationship of white and Negro speech.

In the beginning, Negroes arriving from Africa learned their speech from their white owners, male and female; that is to say, the adult Negroes did. The children, prohibited from any great freedom of the white houses, and often prohibited from playing with white children, had to learn from their elders, who, of course, spoke a very broken English, with sound substitutions and intonations retained from the African home-languages. The children of these children learned from their own parents and so on even to the present time, so that the faulty Afro-English of the first slaves has repeated itself generation after generation with only such modifications as the following may suggest.

It is true, as is often said, that the speech of the dominant group has a strong influence on the speech of the population as a whole. The operation of this principle in the South is considerably interfered with by the fact that on a plantation there may be only one white family and anywhere from ten to fifty Negro families, so that the numerical preponderance of speakers of broken English is very great. Then, too, in the past only a few Negroes, principally female domestics, had much opportunity to hear the conversational English of white people. Negro men heard very little consecutive white speech indeed, except from foremen, whose own speech, influenced by constant association with workers, often came to resemble the workers' speech. As Negroes become increasingly educated, some of the principles just explained gradually cease to operate.

It may be interesting to consider for the moment how white speech has been influenced by Negro speech. In infancy, nearly every southern white person in the higher economic brackets is cared for by a Negro servant and first learns to talk partly from her. Such early learning, achieved while neuro-muscular patterns are becoming established, inevitably has some permanence. After the child leaves the nurse's hands, the impacts of Negro speech on his own decrease sharply in frequency.

In general, one may say that up to recent times in the South, white speech has affected Negro speech very little indeed, and that Negro speech has affected white speech very little after the childhood of the white speaker. But economic and educational evolution is tending to increase the frequency of the impacts of the two dialects upon each other.

Many of the pronunciations which characterize substandard Negro speech are, in the nature of the case, paralleled in substandard Southern speech. (See pages 212–220.) Others parallel substandard speech of the country as a whole. (See pages 193–204.) But, as implied earlier, some Negro pronunciations are, even aside from their intonation characteristics, the specific property of Negro-

English. Following are three lists of phonetic features, in the order suggested above. As sta~~~ ~~~~~~ ~~~er these lists fail to cover a given problem, the reader may ~~~ ~~~~ ~~ ~~~~~~~~~~ Southern speech. (See pages 212–220.) The following ~~~~ ~~~ ~~~~~ ~~~~ ~~~~ ~~ the substandard Negro speech of Louisiana than ~~~~ ~~~~ ~~ ~~~~~ ~~~~~~~ ~~ of the country, where, as already noted, there are ~~~~~~~~~~~ ~~~~~~~~~~~. ~~~~alization, which Stanley[3] finds very marked in Texas, ~~ ~~~ ~~ ~~~~~~~~~~~ ~~ ~~egro speech in Louisiana as it is in the speech of ~~~~~ ~~~~~~~.

~~~~~~~~ ~~ ~~~~~~~~~~ Negro Speech Held in Common with ~~~~~~~~~~ ~~~~~~~~~ American Speech in General

~~~~ ~~~ ~~ ~ ~~~ ~~~~~, ~~~~ as *egg* [eɪg], *leg* [leɪg], *edge* [eɪdʒ]. (See pages ~~~ ~~~ ~~~.)

~~~ ~ ~~~ ~~ ~~~~ ~~~~~ ~~ *touch* [tɛtʃ], *brush* [brɛʃ], *shut* [ʃɛt], *just* [dʒɛs]. ~~~~ ~~~~ ~~~.)

~~~ ~ ~~~ ~~ ~~~~~ such as *haunt* [hænt]. (See page 194.)

[aʊ] ∼ [æʊ], as in *out* [æʊt]. (See page 200.)

[k, g] ∼ [kj, gj] with low or mid vowels, as in *car* [kja, kjɔ], *garden* [ˈgjadn̩, ˈgjɔdn̩], *kind* [kjan], *count* [kjæʊnt], *corner* [ˈkjɔnə, ˈkjɔɔnə]. This pronunciation is less conspicuous in Louisiana than in Virginia and the Carolinas. Similar palatalization before high vowels occurs,[4] but is much less common than before the lower vowels. (See pages 200, 215.)

Final [t] is dropped from the consonant clusters [kst, st, ft], as in *next* [nɛks], *best* [bɛs], *soft* [sɔf]. (See page 201.)

[t] is dropped from [sts], as in *posts* [poʊs:] (*postes* [ˈpoʊstəz] is also common). (See page 201.)

One or more members is dropped from each of the consonant clusters [sks, skt], as in *asks* [æs:, æsk], *asked* [æsk, æst, æs:]. (See page 201.)

One member is dropped from each of the consonant clusters [sps, spt], as in *wasps* [wɔs:], *clasped* [klæsp]. (See page 201.)

Hyperurbanisms are very common, as in *chicken* [ˈtʃɪkɪŋ], perhaps more so than in other dialects. (See page 166.)

Folk etymologies (see page 166) are perhaps more common than in any other dialect. E.g., *flatform* for *platform*, *broom sage* for *broom sedge*.

[ʊ, o] ∼ [ʌ] in *shook* [ʃʌk], *took* [tʌk], *put* [pʌt], *woke* [wʌk], *broke* [brʌk]. (See page 204.)

---

[3] Oma Stanley, "Negro Speech of East Texas," *American Speech*, February, 1941, p. 3.
[4] Stanley, p. 16.

[s] finally ∼ [st], [ʃ] finally ∼ [ʃt], as in *once* [wʌnst], *wish* [wɪʃt]. (See page 200.)

Features of Substandard Negro Speech Held in Common with Substandard Southern White Speech

Stressed *ar*, final or preconsonantal, and not preceded by [w] ∼ [ɔ], as in *hard* [hɔ:d]. (See page 216.) This shift from [ɑ] to [ɔ] does not occur as frequently in Negro speech as in white speech of the same area.

[aɪ] ∼ [a, ɑ], as in *I* [ɑ, a], *like* [lak]. (See page 215.)

[æ, a, ɑ] ∼ [eɪ] in a few words, such as *can't* [keɪnt], *aunt* [eɪnt], *man* [meɪn]. (See page 215.)

[ɔɪ] before *l*, *s*, *n* ∼ [aɪ], as in *oil* [aɪl], *join* [dʒaɪn], *poison* ['paɪzən]. (See page 194).

[ɔɪ] before *l* ∼ [ɔ] as in *boil* [bɔl], *oil* [ɔl]. (See page 216).

[eɪ] before [k] ∼ [ɛ], in a few words, such as *snake* [snɛk], *take* [tɛk], *naked* ['nɛkɪd]. (See page 215.)

[ɝ, ɜ] ∼ [ɜ, ʌ, ɜɪ][5] in all words of the class of *bird* [bɜd, bʌd, bɜɪd]. (See page 214.) Even in sections where white people use [ɜɪ], [ʌ, ɵ] are the more common in substandard Negro speech.

Linking *r* is omitted both within a word and between words, as in *carry* ['kæɪ], *far away* [ˌfɑ'weɪ]. (See page 218.)

It [ɪt] ∼ *hit* [hɪt], usually in stressed positions. (See page 313.)

[l] is omitted before [f], [v] and [j] in words such as *self* [sɛf], *shelf* [ʃɛf], *twelve* [twɛv], *million* ['mɪjən].

[ɫ] is omitted before [m] as in *film* [fɪm] (but [ə] may be propagated by anaptyxis to produce ['fɪləm]).

[l] before [k] ∼ [ə, ʊ, o], as in *milk* ['mɪək, 'mɪʊk, 'mɪok]. (See page 219.)

Final [d] is dropped from the clusters [md, nd, ŋd, bd, zd, ld, vd, dʒd], as in *gummed* [gʌm], *hand* [hæn], *ringed* [rɪŋ], *rubbed* [rʌb], *raised* [reɪz], *world* [wɜl, wɜɪl], *lived* [lɪv], *judged* [dʒɛdʒ]. (See page 218.) It is evident that many of the foregoing are verb forms in the past tense and it is probably debatable whether the [d] is actually dropped or whether the speaker merely uses the present for the past. Since, however, past participial forms, as in *mix' pickles* and *boil' crabs*, give the impression of having lost the final [d], it may be argued that the [d] has been similarly lost from past tense forms.

[ɛ] before nasals ∼ [ɪ], as in *general* ['dʒɪnrəl, 'dʒɪnəl], *cemetery* ['sɪməˌtɛrɪ, 'sɪmɪˌtɛɪ], *strength* [strɪŋkθ] (also [strɪnθ, strɛnθ]). (See pages 193 and 217.)

[ə] ∼ [ɪ], in final unstressed syllables spelled with *a*, as in *Georgia* ['dʒɔʊdʒɪ], *sofa* ['soʊfɪ]. (See page 203.)

---

[5] [ɵ] equals [ɜ] with strong lip rounding.

Dialectal secondary stress occurs as in *argument* [ˈagəˌmɪnt, ˈɔgəˌmɪnt], *accident* [ˈæksəˌdɪnt], *president* [ˈprɛzəˌdɪnt].

Specific Features of Substandard Southern Negro Speech[6]

[our, oə; ɔ, ɔə] ~ [o] in words (and derivatives) spelled *ore, oor, our*, as in *store* [sto], *door* [do], *four* [fo]. (See page 216.) [ou] is also used.

[ur, uə] ~ [o] in words spelled *our, ure*, such as *your* [jo], *sure* [ʃo]. [ou] is also known. Both of the two foregoing pronunciations are to be found in substandard white speech (see page 216), but they are believed to be more prevalent in substandard Negro speech.

[ʌ] ~ [ɑ] in *hungry* [ˈhaŋgrɪ]. (See page 312.)

[ʌ] spelled with *o* before *v* ~ [ɪ], as in *cover* [ˈkɪvə], *discover* [dɪsˈkɪvə]. This pronunciation is found also in mountain speech. (See page 200.)

[θ, ð] ~ [t, d] respectively, as in *thing* [tɪŋ], *this* [dɪs], *that, these, those, them, they, with,* and in a few other familiar words. (See page 237.) The speakers can pronounce [θ, ð] and do so in most words; but they retain the [t] and [d] of the native languages of their forebears (there being no [θ] and [ð] in most African languages), which, being little opposed by education until recently, have persisted down through the generations. Compare *thin, thought, there, father, mother, brother, other, think.*

Final [θ, ð] frequently ~ [f, v] respectively, as in *both* [bouf], *breathe* [briv]. Compare *breath, mouth, truth, with, death, earth, south, smooth.*

The prefix *un* ~ [ɔn], as in *unhappy* [ɔnˈhæpɪ], *until* [ɔnˈtɛl].

[ɛ] before [d] ~ [eɪ], as in *head* [heɪd]. Compare *dead, bed, red, bread, spread.* (See page 214.)

[ɛ] before [r] ~ [æ], as in *there* [dæ(ə)], *where* [ʍæ(ə)], *terrapin* [ˈtæ(ə)pɪn], *terrible* [ˈtæ(ə)bəl]. *There* is also [dɑ:], and *where* [ʍɑ:, ʍʌ].

[ɔ] in *orn* spellings ~ [ou], as *born* [boun]. Compare *corn, morning, horn, torn, worn.* (Also [tou], [wou]; it is possible that *tore* and *wore* are intended here.)

[aɪ] before [r] ~ [ɑ], as in *fire(d)* [fɑ], *tire* [tɑ:]. Compare *hire(d), iron(ed), tired, wire(d), mire(d), acquire, desire.* (See page 213.) These words are also pronounced with [a].

Yes and *no* come in for particular consideration. Either one, standing alone, may be perfectly normal or may take on any of the modifications known the country over; but they may also take the special pronunciations [jeɪs] and [nɔ]. The combinations *yes sir* and *yes ma'am* are likely to be heard [ˈjæs:ə, ˈjɔsə], [ˈjæsəm, ˈjɔsəm]. *No sir* and *no ma'am* are likely to be heard as [ˈnɔ:sə] and [noum].

---

[6] Most of these features can undoubtedly be found in other substandard dialects; but on non-statistical evidence they are believed to be more prominent, percentage-wise, in this dialect than in others.

[n] finally ~ [m] in a number of words where it cannot be accounted for by assimilation, as in *rosin* ['rɔzəm], *telephone* ['tɛlə₁foʊm], *turpentine* ['tɜpm̩₁taɪm]. The last two can be accounted for by folk etymology, but not the first.

[r] is lost from the initial clusters [θr, pr], as *throw* [θo, θoʊ], *present* [pə'zɪnt, pə'zɛnt]. Compare *throat, through, preserve, prefer, promote, produce.*

Lost word elements. The lack of visual word images on the part of illiterate speakers, the former lack of any feeling of need for accuracy, and the uncorrected mishearing of words pronounced by other people have resulted in the loss of many of the syllables of words in standard pronunciation. Following are various forms of syllable loss:

The loss of initial syllables, such as *about* [bæʊt], *behind* [ha:n], *elect* [lɛk], *peculiar* ['kjuljə], *respond* [span], *depends* [pɪnz], *considerable* ['sɪdəbl̩], *molasses* ['læsəz], *oblige* [blɪdʒ], *potatoes* ['teɪdəz], *imagine* ['mædʒɪn].

The loss of medial syllables or parts of syllables. Almost any medial syllable faces the likelihood of being dropped or contracted to [ə] or to a component consonant. Apparently the only retarding factors are the necessity for retaining the intelligibility of the word and for keeping the reduced word in a form convenient for pronunciation. Examples: *aggravate* ['ægə₁veɪt], *arguing* ['agɪn, 'ɔgɪn], *argument* ['agɪ₁mɪnt, 'ɔgə₁mɪnt], *battery* ['bætrɪ], *actual* ['ækʃəl], *comfortable* ['kʌmfəbl̩], *curiosity* [₁kju'rasətɪ], *burying* ['bejɪn], *dangerous* ['deɪndʒəs], *difference* ['dɪfənts], *considerable* ['sɪdəbl̩], *electricity* [₁lɛk'trɪstɪ], *gallery* ['gjælrɪ], *generally* ['dʒɪnəlɪ], *interest* ['ɪntrəs], *miserable* ['mɪzəbl̩], *positive* ['pɑztɪv], *regular* ['rɛglə], *Saturday* ['sæ:dɪ], *tolerable* ['taləbl̩].[7]

The omission of final syllables is mainly limited to certain words ending in *ow*, such as *barrow pit* ['ba:pɪt], *barrow* [ba:], *furrow* [fɜ:], *harrow* [ha:], *sparrow* [spa:], *tomorrow* [tə'ma:], *wheelbarrow* ['ʍil₁ba:]. Some other final syllables are reduced, with accompanying assimilation, to syllabic [m, n, ŋ], as in *eleven* ['lɛbm̩], *even* ['ibm̩], *heaven* ['hɛbm̩], *open* ['oʊpm̩], *seven* ['sɛbm̩], *bacon* ['beɪkn̩], *reckon* ['rɛkn̩], *grabbing* ['græbm̩].

The combining of syllables. Syllables are combined by dropping the vowel of a syllable and incorporating the consonant or consonants into the succeeding syllable, as in *below* [bloʊ], *believe,* [bliv], *belong* [blɔŋ], *directly* ['drɛklɪ], *correctly* ['krɛklɪ], *surprise* [spraɪz], *suppose* [spoʊz], *surrender* ['srɛndə].

The combining of words through loss of consonants. In fluent speech, the initial consonant of a word is very often lost in the process of coalescing the word with the previous word, as in *in the house* [ɪnə'hæʊs], *is that you* [ɪ₁zæt'ju], *is this it* [ɪ₁zɪs'ɪt], *get that there thing* ['gɪt₁æt₁æə₁tɪŋ].

Miscellaneous instances of raising before front consonants: *deaf* [dɛf] ~ [dif], *get* [gɛt] ~ [gɪt], *catch* [kætʃ] ~ [kɛtʃ], *can* [kæn] ~ [kɪn], *instead* [ɪn'stɛd] ~ [stɪd], *bedstead* ['bɛd₁stɛd] ~ ['beɪd₁stɪd].

---

[7] Adapted from list in Stanley, p. 9.

Miscellaneous words: *rather* ~ [ˈrʌðə, ˈrʌdə], *hear* ~ [ˈhjɛə, hjɑ], *ear* ~ [ˈjɪə, ˈjɛə], *whip* ~ [ʍup, ʍʌp], *ate* ~ [ɛt], *wrap* ~ [rɑp], *drop* ~ [dræp], *crop* ~ [kræp], *stamp* (v.) ~ [stɔmp], *tramp* ~ [trɔmp], *tassel* ~ [ˈtɔsəl], *going* ~ [gwaɪn], *bundle* ~ [ˈbʌnḷ], *saucy* ~ [ˈsæsɪ], *sausage* ~ [ˈsæsɪdʒ], *doctor* ~ [ˈdɔktə].

Transcription from *In Abraham's Bosom* *

Goldie: muv josɛf, mʌ:, lɛmɪ hæŋ ʌp dɪʃ:it.

Muh Mack: lɛmɪ loʊn. keɪnt slip, rɛs—nʌθɪn.

Goldie: gjitn̩ njɛə bæut deɪ-dæun, mʌ:; tam tə stɑ:t sʌpə.

Muh Mack: jɛ:, jɛə, ɪt ɪz n̩ a gʌtə gɪt ɪt, a rɛkŋ.

Goldie: jɛ: mɪz djuk gɑtə hæəv ə kloʊz təmɑ:, a dʌn sɛd.

Muh Mack: o mi ma! ma leɪg dʌn gɔon əslip. jo wɑdə ɔl gwaɪn baɪl we.

Goldie: gɪmɪ hjʌ.

Muh Mack: ʍʌt a gwaɪn kʊk?

Goldie: mɛk səm kɔəm breɪd, n̩ deɪz ə lɪdḷ pis ə bɔltəmo mit ɪnə tʃɪs.

Muh Mack: hjɛə dɛm oʊl bʊks ə eɪbz, pal rat hjʌ ɪnə weɪ, man tə bʌn əm ʌp. ɔləs ʍa deɪ eɪn gʌt noʊ bɪznəs.

Goldie: jɛ:, jɛ: . . .

Muh Mack: hʌ, lʊk ət dɪs, wɪljə? eɪn mon:ʌf tə fɪl ma oʊl hɑlə tuf. keɪnt əs gɪt sʌmpm̩ ɛls fə sʌpə? a ɛt dæt oʊl mit n̩ kɔəmbreɪd tɛl hɪt mɛk mɪ hiv tə lʊk æt ɪt.

Goldie: dæt ɔl de ɪz.

Muh Mack: dæt wõ mɛk ə mæuf:ʊl fə eɪb. ʍʌt wi gwaɪn it?

Goldie: eɪb woʊn ɪt ɪt noʊhæu, n̩ a dõ wɔnt nʌfɪn. ju n̩ dʌglɪs kən it ɪt.

Muh Mack: boʊf ə ju gwaɪn da ɛf ju doʊn it. dæt eɪb:ɪn lɪvɪn ɔfən kɔofɪ n̩ breɪd tu wiks næu. noʊ wʌndə i lʊk lak ə ʃædə n̩ keɪnt hæəf du iz wʌk.

Goldie: keɪnt it ʍɪn jə eɪn gʌt ɪt.

Muh Mack: wɛəl, stɑ:vɪn eɪnt gwaɪn gɪv jə strenθ tə gɪt no mo. hæu jə gwaɪn kip wɔʃɪn fə foʊks n̩ jə doʊn it?

Goldie: oʊ lɔ:d gɑd ɪn hɛbm̩, a dõno.

Transcribe:

Lige: Lawd, Bud, you sho' led us a race dis mawning on dem dere boxes. Musta sweat a peck er mo'.

Bud: Race? Hunh, wait till fo' o'clock dis evening, you gwine call foh de ca'f rope, sho 'nough. And po' Puny, de monkey have rid him to deaf.

Puny: Ain't no monkey rid me, I tells you. Little but loud. Be right dere when de hawn blows.

Bud: Mought, and you stubbering yo' work. I cawners my boxes lak de Colonel calls fah. You des' gi' 'em a lick and a promise. Ain't it so, Lige?

Lige: Dunno, dunno. He do all right, reckon.

Puny: Put us in de cotton patch, and I kin kill you off de way a king snake do a lizard.

Bud: Picking cotton! Dat 'oman and chillun's job. No reg'lar man mess wid dat. Turpentiming's de stuff.

Lige: Whyn't Abe come on? Time's he eating.

Bud: Let him rair. 'On't hurt hisself a-cutting. Getting to be de no-'countest hand I ever see.

Lige: Useter could cut boxes lak a house afiah.

Puny: And hack! Lawd, dat nigger could hack.

Lige: De champeen o' de woods and de swamps.

Puny: Bedder'n Bud, bedder'n all. Knowed him to dip eight barrels many day.

Bud: Cain't he'p whut has been. Ain't wuth my ol' hat now. Colonel Mack say so too. And I heahd Mr. Lonnie talking rough to him over at de weaving house day fo' yestiday 'bout his gitting trifling heah lately.

PAUL GREEN

Bibliography

Books

Turner, Lorenzo D., *Africanisms in the Gullah Dialects* (Chicago: University of Chicago Press, 1949).

Periodicals

McDavid, Raven I., and Virginia Glenn McDavid, "The Relationship of the Speech of American Negroes to the Speech of Whites," *American Speech*, February, 1951.

Patten, Nathan van, "The Vocabulary of the American Negro as Set Forth in Contemporary Literature," *American Speech*, October, 1931.

Stanley, Oma, "Negro Speech of East Texas," *American Speech*, February, 1941.

Turner, Lorenzo D., "Notes on the Sounds and Vocabulary of Gullah," a publication of the American Dialect Society, May, 1945.

CHAPTER 16

Mountain Speech

As used here, the term Mountain speech is intended to designate the folk speech of the Ozarks and the Appalachians,[1] where the English of the pioneer period has been relatively isolated from that of the rest of the country and has retained its phonological characteristics along with its balladry and folklore. So far as the area south of Pennsylvania is concerned, the speech is, in terms of *Word Geography*, Midland speech, which in this book is classified as a part of General American. The Ozark speech resembles it fairly closely. In the southern part of the Appalachians, both piedmont and highland, there is an admixture of Southern speech features.

Mountain speech, taken in all its aspects, including the stylistic, has a richness of quality not to be equaled in any other variety of American speech. "It is forceful speech. It can clothe the most extraordinary incident with matter-of-fact colors of reality and it can give to casual bits of everyday life the most delicate shadings of romance."[2] Perry[3] comments in the same vein:

Mountain speech is usually brief, vivid, expressive and very often exhibits real poetic qualities . . . . "Hit cried till it couldn't," remarked the mother of a baby that had almost cried itself to death. "He's right good help, a man workin' with him," explained the employer of a mediocre "hired hand." These would seem to epitomize both brevity and expressiveness . . . . To illustrate the poetic qualities of the dialect these bits may be quoted: "They ain't nothin' purtier than just growin' corn," or "They say when you leave the hills you miss 'em. In these level lands you look an' look hopin' to see a mountain, but you can't see ary one."

As is the case with any older or more isolated speech, the unique characteristics of mountain speech tend to run to quaint idiom and unusual diction as well as to variant pronunciation. Usually there is little difficulty whatever in pronouncing the idiom or the strange word, once an author brings it to us. *Boughten*

---

[1] The Rocky Mountains have been settled too late and by too mobile a population to develop a dialect different enough from the general American speech to warrant attention.
[2] Charles Morrow Wilson, "Beefsteak When I'm Hungry," *The Virginia Quarterly Review*, April, 1940, p. 240.
[3] Louise S. Perry, *A Study of the Pronoun Hit in Grassy Branch, North Carolina* (Unpublished Master's thesis, Louisiana State University, June, 1940), pp. 2–3.

and *bounden* are entirely clear in *boughten tobaccer* and *bounden duty*. The *filth* (meaning weeds) in the flower beds, the *ramption* of rats in the barn, the *poke* of meal or candy, the swain who is *talkin' to* (courting) the maiden of his choice, the squash that is called *candy-roast* or *candy-roaster*, the sun-dried green beans called *leather britches*—these are interesting in the extreme, and definitely of mountain quality, but they present no pronunciation problem. But many unique pronunciation items can be isolated, and these will follow.

Little effort is made in this work to distinguish among the dialectal characteristics of the areas just named. There is a sufficient degree of homogeneity throughout the whole mountain area to make this unnecessary for most people who wish to use Mountain speech in plays and readings. Reference to Hall, Crumb, Randolph, Berrey,[4] *et al.*, will narrow the areas of prevalence of a given feature for those who need specificity in these matters.

It will be remembered from the discussion of the principal speech regions of America (pages 171 ff.) that the Appalachian area was populated largely by people who migrated from the Pennsylvania country southward through the valleys and along the piedmont, where they mingled to some degree with lowland southern immigrants coming in from the east and farther south. These people were by origin Scotch-Irish, Palatine Germans, Swiss, Scots, and Englishmen,[5] some immediately from overseas, some already established as colonials. The English language prevailed among them. Later, many groups from this blended Appalachian population migrated westward to the Ozarks.

This mingling of colonial populations established the previously indicated relationship between Mountain speech and Southern on the one hand and between Mountain speech and General American on the other. The resultant large contribution of General American to the speech of the area makes it necessary either to duplicate a listing of certain general American features or to indicate their prevalence by cross-reference. To a lesser degree, it seems necessary to indicate the relation of Mountain speech to Southern speech, and even, in certain rare instances, to Eastern speech. In order to give a reasonably complete picture of Mountain speech, it seems best to combine the two methods, i.e.,

[4] Joseph Sargent Hall, "The Phonetics of Great Smoky Mountain Speech," *American Speech Reprints and Monographs*, No. 4, April, 1942 (New York: King's Crown Press, 1942), p. 65.

D. S. Crumb, "The Dialect of Southeastern Missouri," *Dialect Notes*, vol. 2 (1903), pp. 304–337.

Vance Randolph and Anna A. Ingleman, "Pronunciation in the Ozark Dialect," *American Speech*, III, 5 (1927–28), pp. 401–407.

Lester V. Berrey, "Southern Mountain Dialect," *American Speech*, XV (1940), pp. 45–50.

[5] Hans Kurath, *A Word Geography of the Eastern United States* (Ann Arbor: University of Michigan Press, 1949), pp. 2–4.

Carl Bridenbaugh, *Myths and Realities: Societies of the Colonial South* (Baton Rouge: Louisiana State University Press, 1952), Chapter III.

to indicate the presence in mountain speech of features common to other dialects by brief, duplicative mentions accompanied by cross-references. Since a great many of the characterizing features of Mountain speech are identical with substandard features common to all three major regional dialects, the first division of the discussion immediately following will be devoted to these.

Features of Mountain Speech Held in Common with Substandard General American, Southern, and Eastern Speech: Vowels

[i] ~ [ɪ] in [ˈstɪljəˑd] for *steelyard*, [slɪk] for *sleek* (referring to coats of animals, not to surfaces in general), [krɪk] (also [kreɪk]) for *creek* [krik]. (See page 198.)

[ɪ] ~ [i] in [ˈlit̮l] for *little*, [it͡ʃ] for *itch*, [int͡ʃ] for *inch*, [ˈidɪət] for *idiot*, [slik] for *slick* (referring to slippery surfaces), [ˈbrit͡ʃəz] for *breeches* [ˈbrɪt͡ʃəz] (possibly a retention of the original pronunciation or, alternately, a return to it), [ˈdistrɪk(t)] for *district*. (See page 198.)

[ɪ] ~ [ɛ] as in [pɛθ] for *pith*, [ˈspɛrət] for *spirit*, [ˈhɛndəˑ] for *hinder*, [stɛnt] for *stint*, [ɛf] for *if*, [bɛn] for *been* [bɪn], [rɛd] for *rid*, [rɛnts] or *wrench* [rɛnt͡ʃ] for *rinse*. (*Wrench* is possibly a folk-etymology suggested by the twisting or wrenching motion in wringing clothes dry after the rinsing process.) The vowel shift in all these words seems to arise from the confusion created by the assimilative rise of [ɛ] to [ɪ] before front consonants (particularly [t] and [n]), as in [sɪnts] for *cents* and [gɪt] for *get*. *Hender*, etc., may represent a reaction against the [ɛ] > [ɪ] tendency.

[ɪ] ~ [æ] as in [rær] for *rear*.

[ɪ] ~ [aɪ] in [ˌaɪˈtæljən] for *Italian*, [ˌdaɪˈd͡ʒɛst] for *digest*, [ˌdaɪˈrɛk] for *direct*. There appears to be here a spelling pronunciation of the letter *i*, accompanied by, or perhaps preceded by, the addition of secondary stress to the initial syllable. In most words so affected the original primary stress on the second syllable remains undiminished.

[ɪ] is inserted before *ous*, as in *nervious* for *nervous*, *barbarious* for *barbarous*, *stupendious* for *stupendous*, *heinious* for *heinous*, *mountaneous* [ˌmaʊnˈteɪnɪəs] for *mountainous*, *mischievious* for *mischievous*. This insertion is possibly on the analogy of *laborious*, etc. In some words, such as *mischievious*, *barbarious*, the addition promotes a shift of stress to the syllable just preceding the inserted vowel.

[ɛ] ~ [i], as in *deef* for *deaf*. (See page 194.)

[ɛ] ~ [ɪ], by assimilative raising toward the position of the front consonants [t, n], as in [ˈkɪt̮l] for *kettle*, *chist* for *chest*, *git* for *get*, *yit* for *yet*, *min* for *men*, *agin(st)* for *again(st)*, [ˈɪnɪ] for *any*, [ˈmɪnɪ] for *many*, *giner'ly* for *generally*.

[ɛ, æ] ~ [ɪ] in [t͡ʃɪr] for *chair* [t͡ʃer, t͡ʃær], [kɪr] for *care*, [skɪrs(lɪ)] for *scarce(ly)*, [ʃɪr] for *share*, [ˈplaʊˌʃɪr] for *plowshare*. (See page 194.) [ˈplaʊˌʃɪr] is possibly arrived at by a folk-etymology based on the word *shear*, to cut.

[ɛ] ~ [æ] as in [θræʃ] for *thresh*, [ˈræsl] for *wrestle*, *kag* for *keg*, *lag* for *leg*, *agg* for *egg*, *yaller* for *yellow*. (See page 203.)

[ɛ] ~ [ʌ] (by analogy with the noun *drugs* as a pharmaceutical term) in *drugs* for *dregs*. (See page 194.)

[ɛ] ~ [eɪ] before [g, d] in [leɪg] for *leg* [lɛg], [eɪg] for *egg* [ɛg], *broom sage* [ˈbrʊm ˌseɪʤ] for *broom sedge* [ˈbrʊm ˌsɛʤ], [eɪʤ] for *edge* [ɛʤ], [heɪd] for *head* [hɛd]. (See page 203.)

[æ] ~ [ɪ] as *tabernickle* for *tabernacle* (by folk etymology), [ˈɔlməˌnɪk] for *almanac*.

[æ] ~ [ɛ] in *gether* for *gather*, (by analogy with *together*), [ˈrɛðɚ] for *rather*, *ketch* for *catch*, *thet* for *that* (by assimilative raising before a front consonant). (See page 194.)

[æ] ~ [ɑ] before [b], as in [ʤɑb] for *jab*, [stɑb] for *stab*. (See page 194.)

[æ, ɛ] ~ [ɑ] in [ˈgɑr(ə)nˌti] for *guarantee*. (See page 204.)

[æ] ~ [ɔ] before [m], as in *tromp* for *tramp*, *stomp* for *stamp*, *pomper* for *pamper*. (See page 202.)

[æ] ~ [ʌ] in *ruther* [ˈrʌðɚ] for *rather*. (See page 204.)

[ɑ] ~ [æ] as in [kæm] for *calm*, [bæm] for *balm*, [sæm] for *psalm*, [ˈjændɚ] for *yonder*. (See page 194.)

[ɑ(r)] ~ [æ] in [ˈkætrɪʤ] for *cartridge*, [ˈpætrɪʤ] for *partridge*, *passel* for *parcel*, [ˈsæsəpəˌrɪlə] for *sarsaparilla*, *air* for *are* (See page 233.)

[ɑ] ~ [ɔ] in [stɔk] for *stock* [stɑk]. (See page 194.)

[ʌ] ~ [ɔ] in the prefix *un*, as [ˌɔnˈtɛl] for *until*, [ˌɔnˈhæpɪ] for *unhappy*. (See page 204.) This prefix may be accompanied by a suffix *less*, producing the effect of a double negative, as in *ungodless*.

[ɔ] ~ [ʌ] in [əˈpʌn] for *upon*.

[ɔ] ~ [æ] in *sassy* for *saucy*, [gænt] for *gaunt*. (See page 194.)

[ɔ] ~ [aʊ] in [ˌaʊˈdeɪʃəs] for *audacious* [ˌɔˈdeɪʃəs].

[ʊ] ~ [ʌ] in [sʌt] for *soot* [sʊt], [hʌf] (occasionally) for *hoof*, [pʌt] for *put*, [ʃʌk] for *shook* [ʃʊk], [tʌk] for *took* [tʊk]. (See page 204.)

[ʊ] ~ [oʊ] in [ʃoʊr] for *sure*, [pjoʊr] for *pure*, [poʊr] for *poor*. (See page 216.)

[u] is omitted medially from [ˈgræʤəl] for *gradual*, [ˈækʃəl] for *actual*. (See p age 203.)

[ʌ] ~ [ɛ] in [brɛʃ] for *brush*, *jedge* for *judge*, *tetch* for *touch*, *shet* for *shut*. (See page 198.)

[ʌ] ~ [ʊ] in [bʊlʤ] for *bulge* [bʌlʤ], [bʊlk] for *bulk*, [bʌlk], [kʊd] for *cud* [kʌd]. (See page 204.)

[ɜ, ɝ] ~ [ɪr], as in [pɪrt] for *pert*.

[ə] ~ [ɪ] unstressed medially, as in [ˈaɪdɪˌhoʊ] for *Idaho*, [ˈoʊmɪˌhɔ] for *Omaha*, [ˈælkɪˌhɔl] for *alcohol*, [ˈdaɪnɪˌmaɪt] for *dynamite*.

[ə, jə] ~ [ɪ, jɪ] spelled *a, ea, ia* finally, as in [ˈsoʊdɪ] for *soda*, [ˈaɪdɪ] for *Ida*, [ˌælˈfælfɪ] for *alfalfa*, [ˈɛkstrɪ] for *extra*, [ˈaɪdɪ] for *idea* (emphatic [ˌaɪˈdi]), [ˌnuˈmoʊnjɪ] for *pneumonia*, [məˈlɛrɪ] for *malaria*. (See page 203.)

[ə] (spelled with *a* after l) ∼ [oʊ] in [ˈkjupəˌloʊ] for *cupola* [ˈkjupələ], [ˈfɪstəˌloʊ] for *fistula* [ˈfɪstjulə], [ˈskrɑfəˌloʊ] for *scrofula* [ˈskrɑfjulə]. (See page 203.) The vowel shift carries with it the change of the final unstressed syllable to secondary stress.

[ə] ∼ [ʌ], by restressing, in [ʍʌt] from [ʍət] (unstressed form of *what*), [wʌz] from [wəz] (unstressed form of *was*), [frʌm] from [frəm] (unstressed form of *from*). (See page 197.)

[ə, ɚ] ∼ [ɝ], by restressing, in [fɝ] for [fɚ] (unstressed form of *for*). (See page 197.)

[ə] appears through anaptyxis, as in *umberel'* for *umbrella*. The loss of final [ə] in *umbrella* appears to be an isolated instance in Mountain speech, paralleled only by the *Alabam'* of jocular speech. (See page 162.)

[eɪ] ∼ [i] in [drin] for *drain*.

[eɪ] ∼ [ɛ] in archaic *et* for *ate*.

[eɪ] ∼ [æ], as in the archaic [ˈæntʃənt] for *ancient* [ˈeɪntʃənt], [plæt] for *plait* [pleɪt] (to braid), [ˈægɚ] for *ague* [ˈeɪˌgju], [næp] for *nape*, [slæk] for *slake* (of lime). (See page 198.)

[aʊ] ∼ [æʊ], frequently nasalized, as in [tæ̃ũn] for *town*. (See page 199.)

[ɔɪ] ∼ [aɪ], as in [laɪn] for *loin*, [paɪnt] for *point* (and so with other words in *oin, oint*), [raɪl(ɪ)] for *roil(y)*, [kwaɪl] for *coil* (and so with other words ending in *oil*), [ˈpaɪzn̩] for *poison*. (See page 194.)

[oʊz] ∼ [əs], by unstressing, as in [ˈbɛləs] for *bellows*, [ˈgæləsɪz] (pl., from *gallows*, sing.). (See page 199.)

[ju, jə] ∼ [ə] (in unstressed position) in [əkˈjuməˌleɪt] for *accumulate* [əˈkjumjuˌleɪt], [ˈækərət] for *accurate* [ˈækjurət], [ˈæmbələnts] for *ambulance* [ˈæmbjulənts], [ˈkælkəˌleɪt] for *calculate* [ˈkælkjuˌleɪt], [ˈrɛgəˌleɪt] for *regulate* [ˈrɛgjuˌleɪt]. [ˈakəˌpaɪ] for *occupy*, [ˈdɛpətɪ] for *deputy*. (See page 196.)

[ju] ∼ [joʊ] in archaic [joʊ] for *ewe* [ju].

Of, from ∼ *en* in *outen* for *out of, offen* for *off from*. (Compare *'bouten* for *about*, probably on the analogy of *outen*.)

Yes suffers the usual modifications found in most dialects, appearing most frequently as *yeah* [ˈjɛə] and *yep* [jɛp]. (See page 299.)

Consonants

[p] ∼ [b] in *babtist* for *baptist, babtize* for *baptize*. (See "Voicing," page 156.) The voicing of [p] is possibly a manifestation of progressive assimilation induced by the initial [b].

[b] appears as an intrusive glide generated by [m] in [ˈfæmblɪ] for *family*, [ˈtʃɪmblɪ] for *chimney*. (See page 164. See also page 197 for [l] in *chimley*.)

[t] ∼ [d] intervocalically as in *nodice* for *notice, sadisfy* for *satisfy*. (See "Voicing," page 156.)

[t] ∼ [k] in *brickle* for *brittle, vomick* for *vomit, turkle* for *turtle*. (See page 202.)

[t] ~ [ʧ] by palatalization in [ˈʧuzdɪ] for *Tuesday* and [ʧun] for *tune*. (See page 159.)

[t] ~ [θ] in [haɪθ] for *height* [haɪt], by analogy with *length, width*. (See page 166.)

[t] is inserted, as a spelling pronunciation, in [ˈɔftən] for *often*. (See page 166.)

[t] is excrescent after [f, s, ʃ, n], as in *clift* for *cliff*, *skift* for *skiff*, *troft* [trɔft] for *trough*, *wunst* for *once*, [twaɪst] for *twice*, *acrost* for *across*, [doʊst] for *dose*, *wisht* for *wish* (v.), *suddent* for *sudden*, *varmint* (from *vermin*). (See page 163.)

[t] is dropped from final [ft, kt, pt, st], as *drif'* for *drift*, *ac'* for *act*, *'cep'* for *except*, *feis'* [faɪs] for *feist*. (See page 201.)

[t] is omitted from final [nt] as the contraction of *not*, as in *mus'n'* for *mustn't* *shouldn'* for *shouldn't*, *wouldn'* for *wouldn't*, *oughtn'* for *oughtn't*. (See page 163.)

[t] is omitted from *let's* [lɛs]. (See page 162.)

[d] ~ [t] in *helt* for *held*, *holt* for *hold*, *aholt* for *a hold*. (See page 157.) (For the proclitic *a*, see page 316.)

[dj] ~ [ʤ] in *juberous* for *dubious* (see page 199), [ʤuk] meaning *stoop*.

[d] is intrusive in [ˈnɪrdɚ] for *nearer*.

[d] is omitted from the final consonant clusters [ld, nd, ndz], as [ˈskæfəl] for *scaffold*, [əˈraʊn] for *around*, [maʊn] for *mound*, *groun'* for *ground*, [faɪn] for *find*, [graɪn] for *grind*, [bræn:(j)u] for *brand new*, [stænz] for *stands*, *ol'* for *old*, *gol'* for *gold*, *sol'* for *sold*. It must be borne in mind that these omissions do not take place in every instance of the spellings named. Most of them seldom occur in a word which is final in a sentence, except in the case of [ndz], but in contexts such as *gol' watch, san' pile, lan' sakes, groun' corn*, etc. (See page 202.)

[kʧ] >[6] [kʃ], through assimilation of [t] > [k] in [ˈlɛkʃɚ] for *lecture*, [ˈækʃəl] for *actual*. (See page 155.)

[kʧ] > [ʧ], through assimilation of [k] > [t] in [ˈpɪʧɚ] for *picture*.

[k] or [t] is dropped from *skt*, as in [æsk] or [æst] for *asked*. (See page 200.)

[n] is retained in the archaic disjunctives of certain pronouns, as in *hern* for *hers, theirn* for *theirs, ourn* for *ours, his'n* for *his*. (See page 194.)

[ŋ] ~ [n] in [lɛnθ] for *length*, [strɛnθ] for *strength*. (See page 202.)

[rənt] ~ [sn̩t] in [ˈdæsn̩t] for *daren't = dare(s) not*.

[ɝ, ɜ] ~ [ʌ] in certain words, such as *bust* for *burst, cuss* for *curse, nuss* for *nurse, fust* for *first*, [ˈpʌsɪ] for *pursy*. (See page 158.)

[ð] ~ [d] in [ˈfɝdɚ] for *further*. (See page 194.)

[s] ~ [ʧ] by folk etymology in *pinchers* for *pincers*. (See page 166.)

[sk] ~ [ks] by metathesis, as in [æks] for *ask*. (See page 165.)

[s] ~ [z] by assimilation in *abzorb* for *absorb, abzurd* for *absurd*. (See page 153.)

[s] ~ [ʃ] (presumably by analogy with such words as *sweetish*) in *lik'rish* [ˈlɪkrɪʃ] for *licorice*. (See page 166.)

---

[6] The symbol > means "becomes," "goes to," "changes to," "to." Conversely < means "comes from," "from."

[sk] ~ [ʃ], as in *mushrat* (also *mus'rat*) for *muskrat, mushmelon* for *muskmelon*, *tush* for *tusk*. (See page 166.)

[s] is prefixed to certain words, such as [skraʊtʃ] from *crouch*, [skrɪnʤ] for *cringe, splunge* for *plunge*. The effect of this addition is apparently an intensification of the meaning of the root word. *Splunge* is possibly a blend of *splash* and *plunge*. (See page 166.)

[z] appears excrescently in the adverbs *nowheres* for *nowhere, somewheres* [ˈsʌmɚz] for *somewhere, anywheres* for *anywhere, ever'wheres* for *everywhere*. It is an inheritance from an old genitive used adverbially.

[s] or [k] is dropped from *sk*, as in [æs:, æsk] for *asks*. (See page 201.)

[z] ~ [s] in *allus* [ˈɔləs] for *always* and [ˈbɛləs] for *bellows*, [ˈgæləs] for *gallows* (hence *galluses* [ˈgæləsəz] for *suspenders*). (See page 199.)

[ʃ] ~ [s] before [r],[7] as in [srɛd] for *shred* [ʃrɛd], [srʌg] for *shrug*, [srɪmp] for *shrimp*, [srɪŋk] for *shrink*, [srik] for *shriek*.

[h] is used initially in *haint*, doublet of *ain't*.

[j] is prefixed in [jɪr] for *ear* (of grain or an animal), [ˈroʊsn̩ ˌjɪrz] for *roasting ears*.

[j] is omitted in [ˈfigɚ] for *figure*. (See page 203.)

As indicated at the beginning of the section immediately preceding, the migration from the direction of Pennsylvania, flowing southward through the mountain valleys of the Appalachians, joined with considerable migrations from the South and East. As a result, there are noticeable contributions of lowland Southern speech to Mountain speech. The further migration of mixed Appalachian and Southern people into the Ozarks, augmented by some additions from directly south of the Ozarks, promoted a similar admixture of Southern elements into the Mountain speech of Missouri and Arkansas.

The magnitude of the Southern contribution is sufficient to have given rise to the designation "southern highland speech" for the speech of the whole southern Appalachian-Ozark area. It is likely that the location of this whole area within former slave territory has had much to do with referring to Mountain speech as "southern highland speech"; but the fact remains that there are notable Southern components among the essentially General American features of the dialect.

Features of Mountain Speech Held in Common with Substandard Southern Speech: Vowels

[ɪ] ~ [ˈɛjə, ˈɪjə] sporadically in stressed syllables, as in *Bill* [ˈbɛjəl, ˈbɪjəl], *pin* [ˈpɛjən, ˈpɪjən]. This is the regular Southern pattern of breaking vowels into two, three, or four sounds. According to the operation of this phenomenon,

---

[7] This can happen easily, since there is no opposition; i.e., there are no words in English beginning with *sr*.

which is a form of the Southern drawl, front vowels develop [j] centrally in the cluster and back vowels [w]. (See page 212.)

[ɪ] in the single word *whip* is subject to an unusual number of variations, as in [ʍʌp, ʍʊp, ʍup, ʍoʊp, ʍɜp]. (See page 220.)

[ɑ] ∼ [ɔ] in stressed syllables spelled with *ar*, as in [ˈkɔrbəˌreɪtɚ] for *carburetor* and [ˈhɔrnəs] for *harness*.

[ɜ] ∼ [æ] in [ˈhærɪˌkeɪn] for *hurricane*.

[eɪ] ∼ [ɛ] as in [ˈnɛkɪd] for *naked*, [əˈfrɛd] for *afraid*. (See page 215.)

[aɪ] ∼ [a] sporadically, particularly in areas adjacent to the southern lowlands, as in [fan] for *fine*. (See page 215.)

[aɪ] ∼ [a, ɑ] in the two words *I* [a, ɑ] and *my* [ma, mɑ]. (See page 215.) The fact that the only orthographic resources of dialect writers are *ah* and *mah* tends to exaggerate the prevalence of this pronunciation.

[oʊ, ʊ] ∼ [o] in a few words, particularly [jo] for *your*, [ʃo] for *sure*. Other words, such as [flo] for *floor*, [mo] for *more*, are affected less frequently, depending on the proximity of the lowland border and the migration of lowland people into the mountains. In the case of *your* and *sure* (less frequently *poor*), the evolution of the pronunciation is probably [ʊr > our > o], thus precipitating these words into the class of *floor*, *more*, etc. The diphthongal [oʊ] appears alongside [o]. (See page 216.)

[oʊ] ∼ [u] in [lum] for *loam*. (See page 194.)

[ɔ] ∼ [ɔo, ɔoʊ] as in *song* [sɔoŋ, sɔoʊŋ], *cloth* [klɔoθ, klɔoʊθ]. (See page 214.)

[k] and [g] ∼ [kj] and [gj] by palatalization, especially before [ɑ] and [aʊ > æʊ] —as in [kjɑrd] for *card*, [ˈgjɑrdn̩] for *garden*, [kjæʊ] for *cow*. (See page 215.) The combination [kj] for [k] before [ɑ] is regarded as particularly prevalent in tidewater and piedmont Virginia, and in the corresponding areas extending southward down the Atlantic Coast; whereas [kj] before [aʊ, æʊ] is to be found throughout the South and in the mountains.

[l] is dropped before labials, as in *se'f* for *self*, *he'p* for *help*. *twe've* for *twelve*, *fi'm* [fɪːm] for *film*, *bu'b* [bʌːb] for *bulb*. (See page 218.) It is possible that *bulb* is affected by the analogy of *bub* (*brother*). (See page 166.)

[r] is dropped and the vowel shifted in *ar*, *or*, *ur* spellings, as in *passel* for *parcel*, *futher* for *further*, [wʌs(t)] for *worse(t)*. Parallels for these are found in both Southern and New England speech. (See page 195.)

r is dropped from a few words, after the Southern fashion, as in [nɔθ] for *north*, [kɔn] for *corn*, [hɔs] for *horse*, [ˈfoʊməst] for *foremost*.

Pronunciation Features Regarded as Peculiar to Mountain Speech

In the section following, the pronunciation characteristics listed are regarded as belonging particularly to Mountain speech. It must not be assumed that they cannot be found elsewhere. Instead, it must be understood that they are allocated to Mountain 'speech by reason of belief that they are more prominent in the mountains than elsewhere. It is obvious that in the regions from which the mountains were colonized and in other regions to which the mountain people have subsequently migrated, these characteristics will be found, sometimes quite frequently. The items following are, then, gathered into a single list as a matter of convenience for users of Mountain speech in drama, public speaking, radio, television, and the like.

Vowels and Consonants

[i] ~ [æ] in [blæt] for *bleat*.

[i] ~ [eɪ] in [reɪl(ɪ)] for *real(ly)*, [ʤeɪnz] for *jeans*, [bleɪt] for *bleat*.

[ɪ] ~ [ɛ] in [ˈɔnˈtɛl] for *until*, [rɛsk] for *risk*, [lɛd] for *lid*, [mɛlk] for *milk*, [klɛr] for *clear*, [ˈmɛrəkəl] for *miracle*.

[ɪ] ~ [æ] in [ˈmærəkəl] (also [ˈmɛrəkəl]) for *miracle*. (See page 198.)

[ɪ] ~ [ɛ, æ] before [n, ŋ] as in [klɛntʃ] for *clinch*, [θɛŋ, θæŋ] for *thing*, [drɛŋk, dræŋk] for *drink*. [æ] appears to be used only before [ŋ].

[ɪ] ~ [æ, ɑ] in [kwær, kwɑr] for *queer*, [klær, klɑr] for *clear*, [rær, rɑr] for *rear* (v.), [hjɑr] for *here*.

[ɪ] is omitted medially before a vowel, as in *mater'al* for *material*, *cur'osity* for *curiosity*, *memor'al* for *memorial*, [ˈbɛrəl] for *burial*, *exper'ence* for *experience*, *carr'n* [kjɑrn] for *carrion*, *jov'al* for *jovial*, [ˈsɪrəl] for *serial*, *scorp'on* for *scorpion*, [ˈsɪrəslɪ] for *seriously*.[8] (See page 196.)

[ɪ] is omitted in final unstressed positions provided the succeeding sound is identical or homorganic with the sound preceeding [ɪ],[9] as in *might'nigh*, *might'tall*, *twent'nine*, *an'time* [ˈɪnˌtaɪm] for *anytime*.

[ɛ] ~ [ɪ] sporadically in [ˈɪvənz] for *Evans* and [ˌrɪkəˈlɛkt] (also [ˌrikəˈlɛkt]) for *recollect*.

[ɛ] ~ [ɝ] (by analogy with words such as *verdant* [ˈvɝdn̩t]), as in [ˈvɝɪ] for *very*, [ˈtɝəbəl] for *terrible* [ˈtɛrəbəl], [ˌsɝəˈneɪd] for *serenade* [ˌsɛrəˈneɪd], [ˈtʃɝəˌki] for *Cherokee* [ˈtʃɛrəˌki], [ˈʃɝəf] for *Sheriff* [ˈʃɛrəf], [ˈʃɝədn̩] for *Sheridan* [ˈʃɛrədn̩]. (See page 191.)

[æ] ~ [ɑ] in [rɑp] for *rap, wrap*.

[ɑ] ~ [æ] in [ˈgægəl] for *gargle*, [kræp] for *crop*.

[ɑ(r), ɔ(r)] ~ [ɝ] in [fɝ] for *far*, [ˈʤɝdn̩] for *Jordan*. (See G. A., page 204.)

[ɑ] ~ [ɔɪ] in [wɔɪʃ] for [wɑʃ, wɔʃ], [skwɔɪʃ] for [skwɑʃ, skwɔʃ]. (See page 190.)

[ɔ, ɔɪ] ~ [ɔr] (possibly by the analogy of words like *wart*), as in [wɔrʃ] for

[8] Hall, Joseph Sargent, "The Phonetics of Great Smoky Mountain Speech" *American Speech Reprints and Monographs*, No. 4, April, 1942 (New York: King's Crown Press, 1942), p. 65.

[9] Hall, p. 79.

wash, [ˈdɔrtɚ] for *daughter*, [ˈwɔrtɚ] for *water*, [ˈtɔrlɪt] for *toilet*, [ɔrl] for *oil*, [ˈɔrtə] for *ought to*, [skwɔrʃ] for *squash*. (See G. A., page 190.)

[o] is dropped from words ending in final *row*, as in *narrow* [nar:], *arrow* [ar:], *barrow* [bar:], and the like. The sequence is probably [naro > narɚ > nar:].

[ʌ] ∼ [ɑ] as in [ˈhaŋgrɪ] for *hungry*. (See page 299.)

[ʌ] ∼ [u] in *goom* for *gum*.

[ʌ] ∼ [ɝ] in [fɝs] for *fuss*, [mɝʃ] for *mush*, [ɝs] for *us*, [nɝf] for *enough*, [pɝp] for *pup*. (See also G. A., page 190.)

[ɜ, ɝ] ∼ [ɪr] in [pɪrtʃ] for *perch*.

[ɜ, ɝ] ∼ [æ] in [ˈmæsɪ] for *mercy*.

[ɜ, ɝ] ∼ [ɛr, ær] as in [ɛrθ, ærθ] for *earth*.

[ɜ, ɝ] ∼ [ɑr] as in [twɑrnt] for *'tweren't* (it were not), [kənˈsɑrn] for *concern*.

[ə, ɪ] ∼ [ɝ] in the word *ruin* [ˈruɚn] and its derivatives (*ruined* [ˈruɚnt], etc.); also [uə, uɪ] ∼ [ɝ], as in [rɝn] for *ruin* and [rɝnt] for *ruined*.

[ə, o] ∼ [ɚ] finally, as in *feller* [ˈfɛlɚ] for *fellow*, *piller* [ˈpɪlɚ] for *pillow*, *potater* [pəˈteɪtɚ] for *potato*, *winder* [ˈwɪndɚ] for *window*, *tobaccer* [təˈbækɚ] for *tobacco*, *narrer* [ˈnarɚ] for *narrow*, *holler* [ˈhalɚ] for *hollow*, *tomorrer* [təˈmarɚ] for *tomorrow*, *waller* [ˈwalɚ] for *wallow*, *banjer* [ˈbændʒɚ] for *banjo*. (See also G. A., page 190.)

[ə] ∼ [ɚ] finally as in *bananer* [bəˈnænɚ] for *banana*, *Mariar* [məˈraɪɚ] for *Maria*, *Hannar* [ˈhænɚ] for *Hannah*. (See also E., page 233.)

[ə] ∼ [ɚ] intrusively, as in [ˈhiðɚn] for *heathen*, [ˌmægɚˈzin] for *magazine*, [ˈwʊmɚn] for *woman*, [ˌjuɚnˈmi] for *you and me*, [ˈwɪmɚn] for *women*, [ˈgɪlɪɚd] for *Gilead*, [ˈɪŋɚn, ˈɛŋɚn] for *onion*.

[ɚ] ∼ [r + vowel] through metathesis, as in [prɪˈfɔrm] for *perform*, [prɪˈkʌʃən] for *percussion*, [ˌprɛspəˈreɪʃən] for *perspiration*. (See page 165.)

[eɪ] ∼ [ɪ] in [grɪt] for *grate* (v.).

[aɪ] ∼ [ɑ] in [fɑr] for *fire*, [ɑrn] for *iron*, [war] for *wire*, [har] for *hire*, [ɑrʃ] for *Irish*, [kwar] for *choir*.

[aɪ] ∼ [aʊ] in [maʊt] for *might* and [faʊt] for *fight*.

[ɔr] ∼ [ɝ] in [ˈfɝən(ɚ)] for *foreign(er)*.

[ju] ∼ [jɪ] in the word *you*, singular and plural. (See G. A., page 203.)

An from the archaic *if and* survives as *en* in *iffen* for modern *if*.

[p] is omitted from [sp], as in [wɔs] for *wasp*, etc. (See page 201.)

[d] ∼ [t], by unvoicing in final positions, as in *sallit* for *salad*, *ballit* for *ballad*, *kilt* for *killed*, *errant* for *errand*, [skɪrt] for *scared*, [lɑrnt] for *learned*, [ɑrnt] for *earned*, *diamint* for *diamond*, [ˈruɚnt, rɝnt] for *ruined*.

[d] appears as an intrusive glide in [ˈkɔrndɚ] for *corner*, [ˈɛndɪŋ] for *inning*. (See also folk etymology, page 166.)

[d] appears as a glide in [maldz] for *miles*.

[d] is omitted for the cluster [ndl], in [ˈhænl̩] for *handle*, [ˈkænl̩] for *candle*, *dwin'le* for *dwindle*, *bun'le* for *bundle*.

[d] is omitted from [ˈʧulɚn] for *children*, [wɪθ] for *width*.

[k] ∼ [t], by dissimilation, in [stɑrt ˈnɛkɪd] for *stark naked*. This dissimilation is facilitated by the presence of [n] in [ˈnɛkɪd], which is homorganic with [t]. In consideration of this factor, it could be said that we have here, not a dissimilation of [k] to [t], but an assimilation of [k] to [t] under the influence of [n].

[k] ∼ [kj], through palatalization, in [skjɑr] for *scar*, [kjɑrn] for *carrion*, [kjɪl] for [kɪl]. (See page 215.)

[kt] > [k] to avoid two stops in [ˈkrɛklɪ] for *correctly*, [ˈdrɛklɪ] for *directly*, [ˈpɚfɪklɪ] for *perfectly*.

[ʧ] ∼ [t], archaically, as in [ˈneɪtɚ] for *nature*, [ˈskrɪptɚ] for *scripture*, [ˈpæstɚ] for *pasture*. (See E., page 233.)

[l] ∼ [r], by dissimilation in *frail* for *flail*.

[l] ∼ [r] in [ˈwarˌnʌt] for *walnut*.

[l] is omitted in [əˈrɛdɪ] for *already*, [əˈmoʊs] for *almost*.

[r + vowel] ∼ [ɚ], through metathesis, as in [ˌɪntɚˈdjus] for *introduce*, [ˈhʌndɚd] for *hundred*, [ˈeɪpɚn] for *apron*, [ˈʧuldɚn, ˈʧɪlɚn] for *children*, [ˈbɛtɚn] for *better than*, [pɚˈdjus] for *produce*, [ˌægɚˈvaɪt] for *aggravate*, [pɚˈtɛnd] for *pretend*, [pɚˈfɚ] for *prefer*, [ˈwɪlfɚd] for *Wilfred*, [ˈælfɚd] for *Alfred*, [ˈʃɛɚf] for *sheriff*, [ˈkæθɚn] for *Catherine*.[10] In the single word [ˈpɚtɪ] for *pretty*, this particular methathesis affects a stressed syllable. (See G. A., page 195.)

[r] is intrusive as in [ˈsɔrdɚ] for *solder*, [ˈkɔrkəs] for *caucus*, [ˈpɔrpɚ] for *pauper*.[11]

[r] appears intrusively in [ˈɔrgəst] for *August*, [sɚˈpɚb] for *superb*, [ˈpɑrmɚ][12] for *Palmer*.

[r] is omitted irregularly in [klɑ(r)k] for *clerk* [klɚk].[13]

[r] is dropped from the cluster [θr], as in [θoʊt] for *throat*, [θoʊ] for *throw*. (See page 300.)

[f] is omitted in the word *after* [ˈætɚ].

[θ] ∼ [t] in [fɪft] for *fifth*, [sɪkst] for *sixth*, [twɛlft] for *twelfth*. (See page 162.)

[ð] is eliminated by dissimilation in [ˌðætˈlɑr] for [ˌðæt ˈðɑr < ˌðæt ˈðɛr].

[s] ∼ [k] by dissimilation in [ˈsæsɪˌfræk] for *sassafras*.

[s] ∼ [ʃ], finally, as in *nervish* for *nervous*, *glimpsh* for *glimpse*.

[h] appears archaically in *hit* for *it*, most often in stressed positions (especially initially); but it is found with noticeable frequency in unstressed positions,

---

10 Josiah H. Combs, "The Language of the Southern Highlanders," *Publications of the Modern Language Association*, Vol. 46 (1931), p. 17.

11 Hall, "The Phonetics of the Great Smoky Mountain Speech," p. 106.

12 Hall, p. 106.

13 John P. Fruit, "Kentucky Words" in *Dialect Notes*, V. 1 (*Norwood, Mass*: J. S. Cushing and Co., 1896, p. 229.)

possibly by overcorrection as the result of an attempt at carefulness or precision of utterance, possibly in conformity with certain rhythmic patterns of Mountain speech.[14]

[j] ~ [ʤ] in the word *onion*, pronounced ['ʌnʤən].

[j] is prefixed [jɑrθ, jɛrθ, jærθ] for *earth*, [jɜn] for *earn*, [jɜb, jɛrb, jɑrb] for *herb*.

[j] is intrusive in ['vɪljən] for *villain*, on the analogy of *million*, etc.

[w] is omitted in ['ikəl] for *equal*, ['ɔləs] for *always*.

Pronunciation Features Classified According to Certain Linguistic Formulae

In the foregoing material it has been possible to classify features of Mountain speech according to the vowels or consonants affected. The following are a number of entries which are difficult to classify among either vowels or consonants. They are therefore treated as manifestations of one or another commonly recognized linguistic formula or phenomenon.

Folk etymology: ['ræfəl] for *rifle*; ['laɪˌbɪl] for *libel*; *kiverlid*, ['kɪvɚˌlɛd] for *coverlet*; ['ɛndɪŋ] for *inning*; [ˌtɑr'pouljən] for *tarpaulin*; *steeple* for *staple*; *kindly* for *kinda* = *kind of*; *sobby* for *soggy*; *panter*, *painter* for *panther*. It is possible to assume here that the last two syllables of the word *Napoleon* may have an analogic influence on *tarpaulin*. (See page 166.)

Hyperurbanism (or overcorrection): *mounting* for *mountain*, *eleving* for *eleven*, *seving* for *seven*, *kitching* for *kitchen*. (See page 166.)

Miscellaneous assimilations: *sumpin*, *sump'm* for *something*, *pime blank* for *point blank*, *epitap* for *epitaph*, *flatform* for *platform*, ['ʌbm̩] for *of them*, ['ibm̩] for *even*, ['ʧænʧ] for *chance*. (It is extremely likely that, in addition to the assimilative influence operative in *epitap* and *flatform*, there is some degree of folk etymology involved, as suggested by the words *tap* and *flat*.)

Syncopy of medial syllables, many containing [r, ɚ]: [kən'sɪdəbl̩] for *considerable*, [kə'laɪnə] for *Carolina*, ['kʌmpftəbl̩] for *comfortable*, ['ʤɛnəlɪ] for *generally*, [ˌrɛk'lɛk] for *recollect*, [ˌæksɪ'dɛntlɪ] for *accidentally*, ['faɪnlɪ] for *finally*, ['kʌmpnɪ] for *company*, ['hɪkrɪ] for *hickory*, ['hɪstrɪ] for *history*, ['sælrɪ] for *salary*, ['mɛmrɪ] for *memory*, ['ɪgnɚnt] for *ignorant*.

Syncopy of [w] from *ward(s)*; ['bækɚd(z)] for *backward(s)*, ['ɔkɚd] for *awkward*, ['ɛdɚd] for *Edward*, ['ɪnɚd(z)] for *inward(s)*, ['ʌpɚd(z)] for *upward(s)*, ['fɔrɚd(z)] for *forward(s)*.

Syncopy of vowel from initial unstressed syllable: [krin] for *careen*,[15] [krɛkt] for *correct*, ['krɛklɪ] for *correctly*, ['drɛklɪ] for *directly*.

---

[14] Perry *op. cit.*, for a searching account of this word.
[15] Wilson, p. 41.

Dropping [ə] from final unstressed [ɪə] and [jə]: [dɪsˈpɛpsɪ] for *dyspepsia*, [məˈlɛrɪ] for *malaria*, [njuˈmoʊnɪ] for *pneumonia*. These endings are analogous to, but not of identical origin with, those of [ˈsoʊdɪ], [ˈsoʊfɪ], etc.; [ˈaɪdɪ] for *idea* is a closely related pronunciation, having presumably gone through the intermediate pronunciation [ˈaɪdɪə].

Omission by aphesis of initial syllables: *'crost* for *across*, *'count* for *account*, [ˈkɔrdn̩] for *according*, [pɪrz] for *appears*, *'most* for *almost*, *'spect* for *expect*, [ˈtɑrnəl] for *eternal*, [keɪz, kɔz] for *because*, *'spise* for *despise*, *'bout* for *about*, *'low* for *allow*, *'fraid* for *afraid*.

Stressing and Unstressing

Primary stress shifted to first syllable of a disyllable or trisyllable: [ˈsiˌgɑr] for *cigar*, [ˈgɪtˌtɑr] for *guitar*, [ˈɪnˌfɜmərɪ] for *infimary*, [ˈɪnˌspɛktɚ] for *inspector*, [ˈɪnˌʃurənts] for *insurance*, [ˈtɪnəˌsi] for [ˌtɛnəˈsi], [ˈdiˌsɛmbɚ] for *December*, [ˈkriˌeɪt] for *create*, [ˈspiˌdɑmətɚ] for *speedometer*. It will be noted that the stress never completely abandons the originally stressed syllable, but remains there as secondary stress. It will be remembered that the shifting of stress to the initial syllable is a characteristic of substandard Southern speech (see page 219). In all likelihood, it appears in Mountain speech through the influence of Southern migration into the mountains; but in many instances the vocabulary is peculiar to Mountain speech, as, for example, the use of *settlement* for *neighborhood* or *community* (see below).

Secondary stress imposed upon an originally unstressed syllable: [ˈpʊlˌpɪt] for *pulpit*, [ˈprɛzəˌdɛnt] for *president*, [ˈsɛtlˌmɛnt] for *settlement*, [ˈɛvəˌdɛnts] for *evidence*. Although the foregoing words have been transcribed with secondary stress, it must be recognized that in sentences where the words must be spoken with rising inflection, as in *Is this the pulpit?*, the two stressed syllables will bear approximately equal stress and the word may therefore be said to have level stress. The syllable *ent* (as in *president*) is also pronounced [ɪnt] in some communities, presumably under the influence of lowland Southern speech.

One ∼ [n̩, ən] (also [ɚn]), by unstressing, in certain pronoun and adjective-pronoun complexes: [ˈðætn̩] for *that one*, [ˈʍɪtʃən, ˈʍɪtʃn̩] for *which one*, [ˈbɪgən, ˈbɪgɚn] for *big one*, [əˈnʌðɚn] for *another one*, [ˈðɪsn̩] for *this one*, [ˈgʊdn̩, gʊdɚn] for *good one*. The foregoing may of course be found outside the mountain area, though perhaps they may not occur so frequently elsewhere.

The expressions following, while known in a limited degree outside the mountains, are peculiarly characteristic of Mountain speech. While the word *one* is undoubtedly represented vestigially in each of these expressions, the meaning of *one* scarcely survives in the minds of the speakers to the extent that it does in an expression such as *that one*. Instead, the speaker has in mind only the grammatical plural, which, to be sure, is a plural in the same redundant sense as *you all*. Incidentally, *you all* is in the process of replacing the second person form based on *one*.[16] The speech of the mountains still contains, however, [ˈjuənz] for *you* plural, and [ˈwiənz] for *we*. *You-uns* is occasionally used in the possessive form as *you-uns's*. As above, the second elements appear sporadically as [ɚn], as in [ˈbɪgɚnz, ˈjuɚnz].

The proclitic particle *a* appears with present and past participles of verbs and with some nouns and adjectives, such as *a-comin'*, *a-seein'*, *a-skeered* for *a-scared*, *a-purpose*.[17]

Dialectal strong verb construction: This phenomenon appears in various manifestations, viz., (1) the supplying of a strong preterite for a weak verb, (2) the substitution of an analogical strong preterite for a strong verb, (3) the supplying of a weak preterite for a strong verb, (4) the use of preterites for perfect participles, and (5) the use of perfect participles for preterites. Examples of (1): *div, dove* for *dived*; *skun* for *skinned*; *het* for *heated*; *clim, clumb, clomb* (archaic) for *climbed*; *holp* [hoʊp] (archaic) for *helped* (also used for present infinitive as in *"Let me holp you"*); *fotch* for *fetched* (also used for present infinitive); *retch* for *reached*; *sont* [sɑnt] for *sent*; *drug* for *dragged*. Examples of (2): [wɑr] for *were*, *shuck* for *shook*, *tuk* for *took*, *driv* for *drove*, *fit* for *fought*, *friz* for *froze*, *bruk* for *broke*, *rid* for *rode*, *sot* for *sat*. Examples of (3): *knowed* for *knew*, *drawed* for *drew*, *drinked* for *drank*, *ketched* for *caught*, *blowed* for *blew*, *seed* for *saw*, *throwed* for *threw*. Almost invariably the forms above can be used also for perfect participles. Examples of (4): *broke* for *broken*, *did* for *done*, *wrote* or [rɪt] for *written*, *tuck* [tʌk] for *taken*, *shuck* [ʃʌk] for *shaken*, *rode* for *ridden*, *knew* or *knowed* for *known*, *saw* for *seen*. Examples of (5): *done* for *did*, *seen* for *saw*, *drunk* for *drank*, *swum* for *swam*, *taken* for *took*.

Analogous weak verb constructions: [i] ~ [ɛ], by analogy with such irregular weak verbs as *sleep, slept, slept*, as in [lɛpt] for *leaped*, [lɛnt] for *leaned*, [rɛpt] for *reaped*.

Analogous present tense endings (cf. *trudges*, etc.): *costes* for *costs*, [ˈteɪstəz] for *tastes*, [ˈweɪstəz] for *wastes*, *rustes* for *rusts*.

Analogous plurals (cf. *horses*, etc.): *nestes* for *nests*, *postes* for *posts*, *beastes* for *beast*, *jistes* [ˈdʒaɪstəz] for *joists*, *ghostes* for *ghosts*, *fistes, fisties* for *fists*, *locuses* for *locusts*, *waspes* for *wasps*.

Illustrative Transcription

Mountain Speech

Peggy

Herman: gɪt ʌp, kɪt, ʍoʊ, hjɑ.

Mag: gɪt æutn̩ maɪ weɪ n̩ gɪt oʊvər ðɑr ɪn ðə kɔrnər. goʊ gɪt mi ə tɜn ə wʊd,

16 Hall, p. 39.
17 Hall, p. 52.

ņ dountʃı teık ɔl deı əbæut ət, niðər. (Enter Jed.) aı θɔt ji wəz wıl, ʤed. sin ɛnıθıŋ ə pɛg? hıts əgıtņ maıtı haı taım ʃız bæk hjɑr.

Jed: ðæts ʍʌt ə kʌm tə si jı əbæut, mæg.

Mag: eınt nʌθən hæpənd, ær ðe, ʤed?

Jed: nʌθən tə gıt skırt əbæut, bʌt oʊl mæn məkdɑnəldz bɔı kʌm ın frəm wʌn ə ðɛm ær kalıʤəz ðı ʌðər deı, æn aı ʤɛs sin pɛg dæʊn jændər ətɔkən tʊ ım æn əlʊkən æt ım maıtı switlaık. teınt ðə fʌst:aım, niðər.

Mag: soʊ ðæts ʍʌts bɛn əkipən ɚ?

Jed: jɛə, æn ıf ji doʊnt watʃ æʊt, mæg, ðəz ə teıl goən tə gıt æʊt, æn oʊl mæn məkdɑnəld l̩ draıv ju ɔfņ ðə pleıs.

Mag: joʊr:aıt, ʤed. ʤes weıtl̩ mi ņ ər pɔ gıts θru wıð ɚ.

Jed: næʊ doʊnt goʊ ņ tɛl ɚ aı toʊld ji.

Mag: ju nidņ bi skırt. aı bın əθıŋkən əz mʌtʃ məsɛlf. ʃiz bın pæʊrflı ʌpətı leıtlı. hər pɔ ɔlɚz sɛd ðæt pırt feıs ə hɚn əd ruɚn ər.

HAROLD WILLIAMSON

Transcribe: From *Trees of Heaven* *

Yes ye did, Mom. Ye done all ye could. I kin recollect once when school wuz a-goin' on five miles down the road, I wuz too little to walk it. In the mornings Mom used to tote me most of the way. I ain't fergot, Mom. I never will.

"Jest lucky," says Anse, "that I got that polecat off'n my farm on the second trial. I listened to Lawyer Waddell Burton. I didn't lose my head. I bit my lips to endure the trial. It was a sight the lies they swore on me."

"It's all over now, Pa," says Tarvin, "I was over there when Sheriff Bradley put Boliver off'n the place. I never felt so sorry fer a man in my life. Boliver was out there drunk as a biled owl. 'I won't go nary step. I won't leave this land.' There was a washpan laying there. Boliver grabbed it and seized it with his teeth. The galvanize flew off in tiny flakes. Then he jumped and grabbed a barb war in the barnlot fence with his teeth. We couldn't git 'im loose without jerkin a lot of teeth out'n his mouth . . ."

"Jest to think," says Tarvin, "Boliver was hauled to Greenwood with his fam'ly and put out in the middle of the street. Think he finally found a house jest because of the condition of his wife and his daughter. Pa, this is awful. They air human bein's same as we air."

"Son, since we have that den of thieves off'n our place," Anse reminds Tarvin, "we'll have both terbacker crops to handle. We'd better go around yander to that patch of dead chestnuts in the woods pasture and start cuttin tier poles fer the terbacker barn this mornin."

"Jest as you say, Pa," says Tarvin.

"Aint bad mules to run away" says Anse, "but I jest want to be shore they

* Copyright, 1940, by Jesse Stuart. Published by E. P. Dutton & Company, Inc.

don't run off when we start cuttin these tier poles. Mules air powerful bad to skeer at fallin trees."

"You air doin' right, Pa" says Tarvin. "I'll be tickled to death that you air lettin' Boliver move back to the shack. He'll be at home thar. He ought to be thar instid of town. He aint happy cooped up like a turkey in town."

"Lawsuits never settled anything in Greenwood," says Anse. "When the suit is over the fight is jest beginnin'. After the suit is over, the guns begin to crack. Our trouble won't be over with the Tussies, but I aint afeared now. I know that I aint treated 'em right and if I treat 'em right then it won't be long until they'll be goin all the way with me. It took Anse Bushman so long to find out how to live. Now he has larned how to live on earth, when he is about ready to kick the bucket and go to the next world to meet his loved ones gone on before."

JESSE STUART

Transcribe:

ELECTIONEERIN' ON BIG INJUN MOUNTING *

"An' ef ye'll believe me, he hev hed the face an' grace ter come a-prowlin' up hyar on Big Injun Mounting, electioneerin' fur votes, an' a-shakin' hands with every darned critter on it."

"Waal, they tell me ez he made a powerful good 'torney-general las' time. An' it 'pears ter me ez the mounting folks oughter vote fur him agin them town cusses, 'kase he war born an' raised right down hyar on the slope of Big Injun Mounting. He never lef' thar till he war twenty year old, when he went ter live yonder at Carrick Court House, an' after a while tuk ter studyin' of law."

"Ye're a darned fool ter be braggin' that Rufus Chadd air a mounting boy!. . . He hev hed the insurance ter git ez thick ez he kin with them town folks down thar at Ephesus, an' he hev made ez hard speeches agin everybody that war tuk ter jail from Big Injun ez ef he had never laid eyes on 'em till that minit; an' arter all that the mounting folks hev done fur him too! 'Twar thar vote that put up that thar Taylor man, what nobody knowed nuthin' about an' jes' dispised; an' the t'other candidates wouldn't agree ter the convention, but jes' went before the people ennyhow, an' the vote war so split that Big Injun kerried Rufe Chadd in, an' what do he do? Ef it hedn't hev been fur his term a-givin' out he would hev jailed the whole mounting arter a while."

"I hev hearn tell that the kin-folks of some of them convicts, what he made sech hard speeches agin, hev swore ter git even with him yit. Rufe Chadd hev been shot at twice in the woods sense he kem up on Big Injun Mounting. I seen him yestiddy, an' he tol' me so; an' he showed me his hat whar a rifle ball hed done gone through. An' I axed him ef he warnt afeared of all them men what hed sech a grudge agin him. 'Mister Stubbs,' he say, sorta soft,—ye

* From *In the Tennessee Mountains* (1904). Published by Harper & Brothers.

know them's the ways he hev larned in Ephesus an' Colbury an' sech, an' he
had, afore he ever left Big Injun Mounting, the sassiest tongue that ever wagged.—
'Mister Stubbs,' Rufe say, mighty perlite, 'foolin' with me is like makin' faces
at a rattlesnake: it may be satisfying to the feelin's but 'taint safe.' That's what
Rufe tole ter me."

"'T would pleasure me some ter see Rufe Chadd agin," said the driver of the
slide. "Me an' him air jes' the same age—thirty-three year. We used ter go
huntin' together some. They tells me ez he hev appinted ter speak termorrer
at the Settlemint along of them t'other fine candidates what air a-runnin agin
him. I likes ter hear him speak; he knocks things up somehow."

Mary N. Murfree

Transcribe:

From Nancy Hanks, Bondwoman

Sarah: Nancy—Nancy?
Nancy: Yes'm, Miss Enloe . . .?
Mrs. Enloe: I thought you . . . Who was that come in?
Nancy: Hit was Lemmer.
Sarah: Ah . . . Nancy, I do wish't ye'd come in to this fire when ye draw
            a breath. Hit's the wu'st coggled-up fire I ever laid eyes on.
Nancy: In one more list. I'll fotch a little kindlin' . . .
Lemmer: Mornin', Mis' Enloe. Ye're lookin' pearter'n common, jedgemati-
            cally.
Sarah: Mornin', Lemmer, can't confidence my looks. Hit's the hurtin' in
            my chist, an' the shivers, I reckon, that keeps me a-bidden' it.
Lemmer: An' ye've shore had a spell of it, if'n I ever seen one. This spell's
            kept ye a-bidden' hit fer nigh onto four months, haint hit?
Nancy: Yer fire's goin' right good now. I'd better git to hit. The shivers'll
            set in if'n I don't.
Lemmer: Well, an' how is Mis' Enloe this mornin', do you think?
Nancy: Well as common.
Lemmer: As good a womern as ever lived. The Lord only knows where
            we-uns would a-been 'thout'n her. Now take yourself, when your
            ol' pappy was a-layin' in the Rutherford County jail, an' your pore
            ol' ma had nothin' to do but hire you-uns out. Mis' Ensloe didn't
            specially need a young-un, but she took you in, and they've been
            good to ye. Course they've been good to me, too, but ye've got
            a right good eddication. Ye read the Bible in meetin' an' they've
            larned ye to back letters.
Tom: Howdy.
Sarah: Howdy, Tom Lincoln.

Tom: I was a-wantin' to have a few words with Mister Abraham. Is he about?

Sarah: He went to Soco this mornin', but I'm lookin' fer him now. Won't ye set?

Tom: Well, I'm in right smart of a hurry. I reckon I'll walk on up the road apiece an' meet him. You say he ought to be back?

Sarah: Hit's long after time fer him. Set if ye will.

Lemmer: I reckon he's doin' right well over thar in Kaintucky, a-grindin' for you-uns.

Sarah: Looks like it might be a hard winter. Reckon you-uns in Kaintucky are fixed.

Tom: A-h-h, I reckon. Folks in thar've been smarter'n common with their crops. Sure got a chanct o' hawg-meat laid by. Killed hawgs day a-fore I started.

Abraham: . . . Ain't courtin' none over thar, are ye?

Tom: Wimmern's is scaircer'n hen's teeth in them parts, an' what's thar is uglier'n a meat-ax! Courtin'!

Abraham: Tom, aint ye aimin' to marry?

Tom: I reckon not, Mr. Abraham. Reckon women-folks is too much of an undertakin' fer me. They're allus a-ailin', an I aint aimin' to have no passel of young-uns traipsin' behin' me.

                                                        JANIE M. BRITT

                                    From *Swappin' Fever* *

Phronie: Bill, ye ort to be ashamed o' yersef wastin' yer time like that when the garden needs hoein'. I seen some 'tater bugs on the 'taters while ago. They ort to be got off, 'fore they git a start.

Bill: Let 'em git their bellies full first. I hate to kill anything when its hongry. I'll knock 'em off before dinner.

Phronie: Ye won't do no sich of a thing. All ye'll do all day'll be to fool with that old contraption that aint worth a settin' o' rotten aigs.

Bill: Now that's whar you're wrong. Soon as I git the churnin' part put on, ye can churn an' fan yourself all at the same time by jes' workin' the pedal with yer foot.

Charley: You ought to like it. Your land won't raise more'n tin bushels o' wheat to the acre.

Bill: That's right, 'taint near as fer-tile as that two-thousand-acre farm I had when I was farmin' up in Bolton County. The clover growed so high on that place that I had to stand on a fince post to find the cows in it! And them cows didn't give a drop o' mick while they was pasturin' in it. No sir, nairy a drop!

                                                        L. N. JONES

Bibliography

Mountain

Books

Hall, Joseph Sargent, *The Phonetics of Great Smoky Mountain Speech* (New York: King's Crown Press, 1942; *American Speech* Reprints and Monographs, No. 4, April, 1942).

Hatcher, J. Wesley, "Appalachian America" in *Culture in the South*, W. T. Couch, ed. (University of North Carolina Press, 1934).

Perry, Louise S., *A Study of the Pronoun Hit in Grassy Branch, N. C.* (Louisiana State University: unpublished M. A. thesis, 1940).

Periodicals

Berrey, Lester V., "Southern Mountain Dialect," *American Speech*, XV (1940), 45–50.

Carpenter, Charles, "Variations in the Southern Mountain Dialect," *American Speech*, February, 1933.

Crumb, D. S., "The Dialect of Southeastern Missouri," *Dialect Notes*, vol. 2 (1903), pp. 304–337.

Farr, T. J., "The Language of the Tennessee Mountain Regions," *American Speech*, April, 1939.

Fruit, John P., "Kentucky Words," in *Dialect Notes*, vol. 1, 1896.

Harris, Jesse W., "The Dialect of Appalachia in Southern Illinois," *American Speech*, April, 1946.

Matthias, Virginia Park, "Folk Speech of Pine Mountain, Kentucky," *American Speech*, October, 1946.

Owens, Bess Alice, "Folk Speech of the Cumberlands," *American Speech*, December, 1931.

Randolph, Vance, and Anna A. Ingleman, "Pronunciation in the Ozark Dialect," *American Speech*, June, 1928.

Randolph, Vance, and Patti Sankee, "Dialect Survivals in the Ozarks, I," *American Speech*, February, 1930.

———, "Dialect Survivals in the Ozarks, II," *American Speech*, April, 1930.

———, "Dialect Survivals in the Ozarks," *American Speech*, June, 1930.

Randolph, Vance, "A Third Ozark Word-List," *American Speech*, October, 1929.

———, "A Fourth Ozark Word-List," *American Speech*, February, 1933.

———, "A Possible Source of Some Ozark Neologisms," *American Speech*, December, 1928.

Tresidder, Argus, "Speech of the Shenandoah Valley," *American Speech*, December, 1937.

Warner, James H., "Southern Arkansas Word List," *American Speech*, February, 1938.

PART FOUR

French

Including Louisiana French and French-Canadian

The French in North America: Their language. The French people were early colonial adventurers and settlers in America. The centers of their concentration were Maryland, the provinces of Quebec and Nova Scotia (earlier called Acadia), Louisiana, and Missouri. Because of their ready assimilability, they were soon lost in the engulfing English-speaking population in Maryland and Missouri,[1] and to a lesser degree in Louisiana. Because of the large areas settled almost exclusively by people of French blood in Louisiana and Canada, and because in both areas the French-speaking people are also in large part English-speaking, there is, and for a long time will be, a great deal of dialectal French-English in America.

As in the case of every other immigrant group which once contributed heavily to the population of the United States, the number of French immigrants was so much reduced by the establishment of the quota system in 1921–24 that French dialect as spoken by people from France has become almost negligible. However, the dialect continues to appear in literature, and, coupled with the somewhat different French-Canadian and Louisiana French dialects already mentioned, constitutes ample reason for a study of its underlying principles and acoustic characteristics.

Following are (1) a chart of the sounds of French in order, with directions for pronunciation; (2) a quantity of general information on the French language; (3) an outline of the spelling of the French phonemes; and (4) a discussion of (a) the dialect of French people from France, (b) of the French-Canadian dialect, and (c) of the Louisiana French-English dialect.

---

[1] However, at this date (1957), a very few people in Ste. Genevieve and its environs speak a much leveled French patois as a home language.

The Sounds of French

Vowels

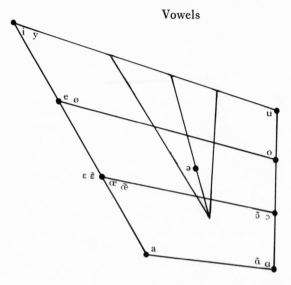

Consonants

	Bi-labial	Labio-dental	Dental	Alve-olar	Palato-Alveolar	Palatal	Velar	Uvular
Plosive	p b		t d				k g	
Nasal	m		n			ɲ		
Lateral			l					
Trilled				r				R
Fricative		f v		s z	ʃ ʒ	j		
Frictionless Continuant	w ɥ					j (ɥ)	(w)	

Notes on Pronouncing French Sounds

Vowels

1. [e] is a simple, or "pure," sound, not a diphthong as in English. Pronounce:

English	French
day [deɪ]	des [ḍe]
lay [leɪ]	les [ḷe]
may [meɪ]	mes [me]

2. [o] is a simple, or "pure," sound, not a diphthong as in English. Pronounce:

English	French
low [loʊ]	*l'eau* [lo]
oh [oʊ]	*oh* [o]
mow [moʊ]	*mot* [mo]

3. Before *r*, [ɛ] is lower than English [ɛ]; e.g., in *père* [pʼɛːr] it is very close to [æ]. Before other consonants, as in *cette* [sɛt], *est* [ɛ], French [ɛ] approximates English [ɛ].

4. [a] is equivalent to the English [a] which is used as the first element in [aɪ] or [aʊ], as in *ice* [aɪs], *owl* [aʊl]. To make [a] in isolation, first pronounce the the pronoun *I* with considerable duration, thus: [aːːːːɪ]. Then repeat, stopping without pronouncing [ɪ]. The result will be [a]. Use this sound in French.

5. [y] is made by pronouncing [i] with the lips rounded. Pronounce in pairs for comparison:

English	French
(unrounded [i])	(rounded [y])
e'en [in]	*une* [yn̩]
eat [it]	*ut* [yt̪]
bees [biz]	*buse* [byːz][2]

6. [ø] is made by pronouncing [e] with the lips rounded. Pronounce in pairs for comparison. Do not make the French vowels diphthongal.

English	French
(unrounded [e])	(rounded [ø])
bay [beɪ]	*boeufs* [bø]
aye [eɪ]	*oeufs* [ø]
fay [feɪ]	*feu* [fø]

7. [œ] is made by pronouncing [ɛ] with the lips rounded. Pronounce in pairs for comparison:

English	French
(unrounded [ɛ])	(rounded [œ])
sell [sɛl]	*seul* [sœl]
Neff [nɛf]	*neuf* [n̩œf]

8. [ɑ̃] and [ɔ̃] are made by nasalizing [ɑ] and [ɔ] respectively; i.e., air is emitted from the nose and mouth simultaneously while pronouncing the vowels. Pronounce for comparison. Do not use a final [m] or [n] in the French words.

---

[2] Length is not a separate phoneme in French. However, lengthened sounds do occur in certain contexts, and less regularly as a stylistic effect. See Language Monograph No. 24, "Structural Sketches 1, French," by Robert Hall, Jr., p. 10, § 1.131 and p. 14, § 1.521. It is beside the purpose of this book to explain the details of French vowel length, but length signs will be arbitrarily included where customary.

English (non-nasal)	French (nasalized)
calm [kɑm]	camp [kɑ̃]
dawn [dɔn]	don [d̪ɔ̃]

9. [ɛ̃] is made by nasalizing the low French [ɛ] (actually very nearly [æ]); that is, the vowel is pronounced while the breath stream is passing out through the nose and mouth simultaneously. Pronounce for comparison. Do not use a final [m] or [n] in the French words.

English (non-nasal [æ])	French (nasalized [ɛ̃])
fan [fæn]	faim [fɛ̃]
pan [pæn]	pain [p'ɛ̃]

10. [œ̃] is made by nasalizing the French [œ]. To arrive at the correct sound, proceed by the following three steps: (a) pronounce English [ɛ], (b) round the lips and pronounce French [œ], (c) drop the velum and pronounce [œ̃]. The tongue will remain in the same position throughout all three steps. Pronounce successively:

[ɛ]	[œ]	[œ̃]
reine [ɾɛn]	seul [sœl̪]	un [œ̃]

Consonants

1. [p], [t], and [k] are unaspirate. That is, they have a much weaker explosion than in English. Accordingly, they suggest [b], [d], [g] to the speaker of English. Pronounce in pairs for comparison:

English	French
pat [p'æt]³	patte [p'at]³
too [t'u]	tout [t'u]
car [k'ɑ(r)]	car [k'a:ɾ]

2. [t], [d] and [n] are dental in French. That is, they are made with the tip of the tongue touching the inside surfaces of the upper front teeth. Pronounce in pairs for comparison:

English	French
two [t'u]	tout [t̪'u]
dough [doʊ]	dos [d̪o]
no [noʊ]	nos [n̪o]

3. [l] is clear, symbolized as [l̪]. It is made with the tip of the tongue touching the inside surfaces of the upper front teeth. Pronounce for comparison:

English	French
cell [sɛl]	celle [sɛl̪]
belle [bɛl]	belle [bɛl̪]

³ The signs ['] and ['] signify aspiration and unaspiration respectively.

4. French contains both the tongue-point trilled [ř], and the uvular trill [ʀ]. The uvular [ʀ] is made by vibrating the uvula, the pendulous tip of the soft palate. Beginners can try a snoring sound to experience the kinesthesia or "feel" of uvular vibration. Snoring is produced by inspired breath. By reversing the breath stream so as to send it outward, at the same time continuing to let it vibrate the uvula, the sound of [R] can be achieved. Pronounce:

role [řo:l] [Ro:l]
rose [řo:z] [Ro:z]
sur [sy:ř] [sy:R]

[ɲ] is made with the tip of the tongue placed behind the lower front teeth. Acoustically, the resulting sound is very similar to English [nj] in *onion* [ˈʌnjən]. Placing the tongue in the proper position, pronounce the corresponding French word *oignon* [ɔˈɲɔ̃]. Pronounce *digne* [diɲ], *champagne* [ʃɑ̃ˈpaɲ].

[ɥ], called "tense *w*," is made by starting from the position of [y] (lips round, tongue in position for [i]), and gliding rapidly to the succeeding vowel. The muscles involved are, as the name suggests, tenser than for [w].

COMPARISON OF [w] AND [ɥ]

Starting Point	Condition of muscles	Resulting Sound	as in
[u]	lax	[w]	*Louis* [lwi]
[y]	tense	[ɥ]	*lui* [lɥi]

[j] has two values in French: (1) non-fricative [j] as in *nation* [naˈsjɔ̃], resembling [j] in English *yes* [jɛs]; (2) fricative [j] as in *fille* [fij]. To make the fricative [j], place the tongue in the position for the English [j] as in *yes* [jɛs], then raise it to form a vertically narrow aperture between the blade of the tongue and the hard palate and, with muscles tense, force the air out with buzzing, fricative sound.

Dialects in France; Standard French; [r] and [ʀ]. That there are many dialects in France itself can readily be noted by travel there, or by a glance at the *Linguistic Atlas of France*.[4] Sometimes these dialects are exceedingly divergent, as in the case of the French spoken in Brittany, where it is influenced by Breton, a Celtic language used as a home language by many of the inhabitants; in Alsace-Lorraine, where it is influenced by the German; in Navarre, where it is influenced by Basque, a primitive non-Indo-European language structurally unrelated to French or to any other western European language; or in Languedoc, Provence, etc. For purposes of this book it seems unwise to attempt regional distinctions, either for France itself or for Belgium, Switzerland, Luxembourg, Canada, or such distant areas as Algeria, Haiti, Indo-China,

---

[4] J. Guilliéron, *Atlas Linguistique de la France* (Paris: H. Champion, 1902–10).

Madagascar, New Caledonia, Syria, etc., where French is spoken by larger or smaller numbers of the population, and with greater or lesser degrees of creolization.

One difference of pronunciation does require to be mentioned. That is the alternation of the tongue-point trilled [r̃], and the uvular [R]. Both are widely used. The difference between them is non-significant, i.e., they are not in phonemic contrast. Regionally, [R] is most prevalent in Paris and the surrounding Ile de France, with [r̃] being common elsewhere throughout the country. But the dialect of the Ile de France is regarded as setting the standard for spoken French, and so [R] has the advantage of being designated as a standard by the Dictionary of the French Academy.[5] It is, moreover, more fashionable than [r̃]. But [r̃] has a large majority among the total number of speakers.

A fairly well established custom in using the French dialect of English in drama is to allocate [R]'s to Parisian socialites, to officials and the like, and [r̃] to people from other areas and to the common people.

Since it is cumbersome to include both [R] and [r̃] in the transcription of every word containing [r], this book will follow the usual custom of using [r] solely. It is to be understood that [R] can be substituted whenever the speech of a person who uses it in French, or who carries it over into his pronunciation of English, is to be presented.

NOTE: From this point on, the symbols [l, ‸, '] will also not be used. Their values will be understood to apply automatically to [l, t, d, n, p, k] as explained earlier.

Stress in French. It is a characteristic of French utterance that all syllables (including monosyllables) except those containing [ə] and syllabic [l] and [r] are of very nearly equal stress. But there is appreciably greater stress on the final syllable (with the exceptions noted) of each polysyllable. Since the peculiar non-English rhythm of this stressing system carries over into the Frenchman's speaking of English, it is necessary to understand its nature.

Stress in French is characterized by differences in intensity (loudness); that is, any increase in stress implies an increase in intensity. As a feature of individual syllables, stress lacks phonemic significance in French, but unusually heavy stress may be used for emphasis.[6]

Degrees of stress in French. Contrary to the foregoing expression of opinion as to the near-levelness of stress in French, French phoneticians measure stress in three degrees of strength. They recognize syllables of primary (strong, tonic) stress, syllables of secondary (moderately strong, paratonic) stress, and unstressed (weak, atonic) syllables. These factors of strength maintain certain constant relationships to one another in words in isolation, and somewhat different relationships in words in context.

---

[5] *Le Dictionnaire de l'Académie Française* (Paris: J. B. Coignard, 1694).

[6] Robert A. Hall, Jr., "French," in *Language Monograph No. 24* (Baltimore: Linguistic Society of America, July–Sept., 1948), p. 15.

In this book, only primary stress will be marked, since the syllables of secondary stress distinguish themselves automatically from weakly stressed [ə, l̩, r̩], which are usually described simply as unstressed.

Primary stress in words in isolation. In words in isolation, primary stress in a polysyllable falls on the last pronounced syllable, except in words ending in syllabic [l̩] or [r̩], and in words in oratory, poetry, song, and serious drama, where ordinarily silent final *e*'s are pronounced [ə].[7] In such exceptional words, the stress is on the syllable before the last.

A monosyllable in isolation is thought of as carrying primary stress except when its vowel is [ə].

EXAMPLES

Words Stressed on the Last Pronounced Syllable

voisin [vwa'zɛ̃]	*écrire* [e'kri:r]
capitaine [kapi'tɛn]	*liberté* [libɛr'te]
perdu [pɛr'dy]	*persuader* [pɛrsɥa'de]
secouer [sə'kwe]	*parfaitement* [parfɛt'mɑ̃]
disputaient [dispy'tɛ]	*occasion* [ɔkɑ'zjɔ̃]
	faisait [fə'zɛ]

Words Stressed on Next to the Last Syllable

théâtre [te'ɑtr]	*table* ['tabl]
descendre [de'sɑ̃:dr]	*impossible* [ɛ̃pɔ'sibl]

espèce [ɛs'pɛs(ə)] ([ə] in poetry, song, and, decreasingly, in classic tragedy)

Monosyllables

Stressed	Unstressed
car [kar]	*le* [lə]
leur [lœr]	*se* [sə]
dos [do]	*de* [də]

Silent Letters in French

The Vowel *e*

Final *e* is silent in prose unless marked with either the grave accent mark (è) or the acute accent mark (é). Compare *militaire* [mili'tɛ:r], *famine* [fa'min], *sabre* ['sabr], *fable* ['fɑ:bl]. Such a final *e* may in poetry and song be pronounced

---

[7] Hall, p. 7, §§ 0.111, 0.112, 0,113, distinguishes three types of pronunciation, viz., archaic, slow colloquial and fast colloquial. He distinguishes archaic pronunciation as that used formally in oratory, declamation and singing, and serving "as a basis for conventional orthography and classical versification." It retains [ə] finally and in some other places "where it has been lost in everyday speech since the sixteenth century." He distinguishes slow colloquial pronunciation as that retaining [ə] only "after initial consonants and before or after certain clusters of consonants in the interior of words and phrases." He distinguishes fast colloquial pronunciation as that which loses [ə] "after initial consonants and before or after clusters of consonants containing [l] or [r], with simplification of resultant clusters; and by loss of phonemic contrast between [ɑ] and [a], [e] and [ɛ], and [ø] and [œ]."

[ə] wherever the scansion or the musical notation requires it. In serious drama it may be similarly pronounced.

Between *g* and a back vowel letter, *e* is also silent, serving only to "soften" the *g*, i.e., to cause it to be pronounced [ʒ], not [g].

Consonants

Final consonants are generally silent, excepting *c, f, l, r*, as in *avec* [aˈvɛk], *soif* [swaf], *fil* [fil], *sur* [sy:r].

Exceptions:

r in the ending *er* of infinitives, as in *laisser* [lɛˈse].

r in *er* and *ers* in certain nouns, adjectives, and adverbs, as in *acquiers* [aˈkje], *ouvrier(s)* [uvriˈe], *premier(s)* [prəˈmje], *volontiers* [vɔlɔ̃ˈtje].

See also under [k] for *c*, under [f], and under [l].

Final silent *e* restores an otherwise silent preceding final consonant to its regular sound. This occurs, e.g., in the feminine of adjectives, such as *vert* [vɛ:r], *verte* [vɛrt]. Analogously, *e* prevents an immediately preceding consonant from being silent. Example, *base* [bɑ:z].

Verb endings which are silent: in the present tense, third person, plural—first conj., *ils trouvent* [il truv], *ils donnent* [il dɔn]—in second conj., *ils finissent* [il fiˈnis]—third conj. *ils vendent* [il vɑ̃d]; in the past descriptive, *aient* is [ɛ], as in *ils trouvaient, ils finissaient, ils vendaient, ils avaient*. Silent endings also occur in the third person plural of the present subjunctive.

The consonant *h* is silent whether initial or final in a syllable, as in *habit* [aˈbi], *ah* [ɑ]. (See under [ʃ] for orthographic *ch*.)

Exception: Certain words spelled with *h* retain vestiges of historical [h] in one of two or three residual forms. (1) A vowel preceding such a word is not slurred into the vowel of the word itself; rather, the word begins with "renewed syllable onset,"[8] possibly accompanied by some narrowing of the glottis. Moreover, such words do not permit of liaison or elision; e.g., whereas words outside this group, such as *hôpital* [ɔpiˈtal], when used with the article *le*, will be written *l'hôpital* [lɔpiˈtal], a member of the group, such as *hamac* [aˈmak], when used with the article, will be written *le hamac* [lə aˈmak]. (2) In oratory or other emphatic utterance, the syllable onset may take the form of a glottal stop, as in *honte* [ʔɔ̃:t]. (3) In free alteration with [ʔ] in emphatic style, [h] itself may occur. In fact, a few words, regularly emphatic by nature, are often pronounced with [h], as in *haha* [ɑˈhɑ], *hahe* [aˈhe], *hare* [ha:r] (halloo). This pronounced [h], with its allophone [ʔ] and syllable onset (syllable onset, it must be remembered, is not necessarily accompanied by either the glottal stop or [h]), is variously called aspirate *h*, emphatic *h*, and preventive *h* ("preventive" referring to the

---

[8] Hall, p. 10, § 1.13.

FRENCH 333

prevention of liaison and/or elision). Words containing this *h* are not ordinarily identifield by rules, though some rules can be established; e.g., the *h* of words from the Greek beginning *hy* is not preventive, as in *hydrate* [iˡdrat]; it is customary to refer to dictionaries, where the preventive *h* is identified variously with dagger, apostrophe, or asterisk.

Elision

The vowel is dropped from *ce, de, je, la, le, me, ne, que* and certain of its compounds, *se,* and *le* before a word beginning with an orthographic vowel, a "non-preventive" *h,* or *y,* as in *l'occasion* [lɔkɑˡzjɔ̃], *l'abbé* [laˡbe], *j'abonne* [ʒaˡbɔn], *s'abonner* [sabɔˡne], *d'abord* [daˡbɔ:r], *n'était* [neˡtɛ], *m'y voilà* [mi vwaˡla], *qu'elle* [kɛl], *c'était* [seˡtɛ], *l'yeuse* [ljø:z].

The vowel is dropped from *si* before *il(s)*: thus *s'il(s)* [sil].

There is no elision before preventive *h, onze, oui, uhlan,* as in *le héraut* [lə eˡro], *le onze Juin* [lə ɔ̃z ˡʒɥɛ̃].

There is no elision when one of the monosyllables above is written with a preceding verb as a hyphenated word, as in *présentez-le à Jean* [prezɑ̃ˡte-lə a ʒɑ̃].

Liaison

Liaison or linking in French is the pronouncing of an ordinarily silent final orthographic consonant before a closely related word beginning with an orthographic vowel, a "non-preventive" *h,* or *y.* In such liaison, *d* is pronounced [t], *g* is pronounced [k], *s* and *x* are pronounced [z], and *n* as a nasalizing agent for a preceding vowel is pronounced [n], the vowel being denasalized.[9] Liaison is not invariable in all possible contexts. Ordinarily it occurs:

1. When an article is followed by a noun, as in *les herbes* [leˡzɛrb], *aux observateurs* [ozɔpsɛrvaˡtœ:r].

2. When an adjective is followed by a noun or *vice versa,* as in *deux hommes* [døzˡɔm], *grand amour* [grɑ̃taˡmu:r], *banc illégal* [bɑ̃kileˡgal], *fait accompli* [fɛtakɔ̃ˡpli].

3. When a pronoun is followed by a verb, as in *nous allons* [nuzaˡlɔ̃].

4. When a plural noun is followed by an adjective, as in *portes ouvertes* [pɔrtzuˡvɛ:rt].

5. When a verb is followed by a hyphenated pronoun or adverb, as in *dit-elle* [ˡditɛl], *mangez-en* [mɑ̃ˡʒezɑ̃].

6. When an adverb is followed by an adjective or participle, as in *fort*[10] *apprécié* [fɔrtapreˡsje], *bien ambitieux* [bjɛnɑ̃biˡsjø].

---

[9] This pattern of denasalization is said to be of decreasing frequency in recent times.
[10] [fɔr apreˡsje] is now increasingly common.

7. When a preposition is followed by a substantive or one of its modifiers, as in *dans un moment* [dɑ̃z œ̃ moˈmɑ̃].

8. Often when an auxiliary verb is followed by a vowel, as in *je suis arrivé* [ʒəsɥizariˈve], *il est agité* [ilɛtaʒiˈte].

NOTE: The *t* of *et* never effects a liaison; it is always silent. The *s* of *pas*, on the other hand, is used in liaison.

"Open" and "Close" Vowels; "Open" and "Closed" Syllables

In the study of French the terms "open" and "close" as referring to vowels and "open" and "closed" as referring to syllables are common nomenclature. The terms are by no means as useful in determining French pronunciation as in determining Spanish pronunciation (q.v., pages 454–56). In Spanish, open vowels are found uniformly in closed syllables and close vowels in open syllables. In French there is some tendency to follow this pattern. The amount of conformity is sufficient to render the understanding of the nomenclature involved moderately useful. But contrary to Spanish, where all consonants which may end syllables are invariably pronounced, there is in French great irregularity in the pronunciation of consonants, some being sounded and others being silent. Parallel spellings in French do not always have parallel pronunciations: Compare *clef* [kle] and *chef* [ʃɛf]. Even consonants in the same word are not always pronounced the same way; cf. *neuf heures* [nœˈvœːr] and *neuf filles* [nœˈfiːj]. As a result of the irregularity in sounding or not sounding an orthographic consonant, the recognition of a closed or an open syllable in French is hindered by our uncertainty in knowing whether to regard only phonetic (that is, pronounced) consonants as functional in closing syllables, or both phonetic consonants and orthographic (but silent) consonants.[11] Actually, syllables are closed in both ways, as will be seen. Moreover, close vowels are sometimes paradoxically found in closed syllables, as in *sur* [syːr], and open vowels in open syllables, as in *essai* [eˈsɛ].

Notwithstanding the confusion implied in all these contingencies, we are retaining the terms open-close and open and closed, for what value may be derived from them. Open and close are terms attaching to vowels and referring to the relative height of the tongue in the mouth in pronouncing open-close pairs. The vowel of a pair which is pronounced with the tongue the higher in the mouth is a close vowel; the other member of the pair, pronounced with the tongue the lower in the mouth, is an open vowel. The close-open pairs are as follows:

Close	i	y	e	ø	a	o	u
Open	—	—	ɛ	œ	ɑ	ɔ	—

[11] Historical study shows that the loss of consonants in situations like this has phonemicized what was originally only allophonic variation of the vowels involved.

It should be noted that [i], [y] and [u] are regarded as close vowels in French despite the fact that their open counterparts [ɪ], [Y] and [ʊ] do not occur in the language. Furthermore it should be noted that, paradoxically enough, a given close vowel may actually be more open than a given open vowel. For example, [a], though called close, is pronounced with the tongue lower than [ɛ], which is called open. Evidently close and open are terms applicable only to vowels in pairs, and not to vowels as a class. Still further, in regarding [a] - [ɑ] as a close-open pair, it must be recalled that many vowel diagrams in many publications place [a] and [ɑ] on a horizontal line, rather than on a line slanting downward from left to right and so more nearly representing the true physiological situation where [a] is higher than [ɑ].

In language in general, an open syllable is a syllable ending in a pronounced vowel. In French, the vowel is sometimes merely orthographic, sometimes phonetic. In language in general, a closed syllable is a syllable ending in a pronounced consonant (including fricative [j]). In French, the consonant is sometimes merely orthographic, sometimes phonetic.

The Sounds of French

The Principal Ways in Which the Sounds Are Orthographically Represented

The Vowels

NOTE: Students who wish to go directly to a consideration of the French dialect of English without a study of French orthography may reserve the material immediately following for reference and turn at once to page 349.

[i]

1. *i* in general, as in *vie* [vi], *plier* [pliˈe], *criard* [kriˈaːr]. NOTE: See exceptions under [j], page 348; [ɛ̃], page 340; [w], page 348.

2. *ï*, as in *haïr* [aˈiːr].

3. *î*, as in *gîte* [ʒit]. NOTE: See exception under [w], page 348; [ɛ̃], page 340.

4. *y*, as in *type* [tip], *y* [i], *payions* [pɛiˈjõ], *pays* [peˈi], *abbaye* [abeˈi]. (NOTE: *Pays* and *abbaye* are also pronounced [peˈji] and [abeˈji], [i] being the second element of the combination [ji], which constitutes the pronunciation here of *y*).

5. *y*, as in *fuyant* [fɥiˈjã], where [i] is the first element of the combination [ij], which constitutes the pronunciation of *y*. NOTE: See exceptions under [j], page 348, and [ɛ̃], page 340.

[e]

1. *e* in general before a final silent consonant or consonant cluster, except *t*, as in *passer* [pɑˈse], *volontiers* [vɔlõˈtje], *des* [de], *pieds* [pje]. NOTE: Here *e* appears in phonetically open (though orthographically closed) syllables.

2. *e* as an exception before *t*, as in *et* [e].

3. *e* in all words beginning *eff*; as in *effort* [eˈfɔːr], *effleurer* [eflœˈre], *efficace* [efiˈkas]; in the following words (with their derivatives) beginning *ess*, viz., *essence* [eˈsãːs], *essai* [eˈsɛ], *essorer* [esɔˈre], *essui* [eˈsɥi], *essoucher* [esuˈʃe], *essoufler* [esuˈfle]; and in certain learned words, such as *ecclésiastique* [eklezjasˈtik].

4. *e* in *ex* followed by a vowel or *h*, as in *exemple* [egˈzãːpl], *exhalaison* [egzalɛˈzɔ̃].

5. *é*, as in *été* [eˈte], *établir* [etaˈbliːr]. NOTE: *é* is almost invariably pronounced [e], but see rare exception with *je*, etc., under [ɛ].

6. *e* in all words beginning *desc*, as in *descente* [deˈsãːt], *description* [deskripˈsjɔ̃]; in a few words beginning *dess*, as in *dessert* [deˈsɛːr]; in *ressui* [reˈsɥi] and *ressusciter* [resysiˈte]. (In all other words beginning *ress*, *e* = [ə], except in *ressac* [rɛˈsak].)

7. *a*, as in the word *abbaye* [abeˈi, abeˈji], and in the word *pays* [peˈi, peˈji] and its derivatives.

8. *ai* finally (hence in open syllables) in verb endings, as in *écouterai* [ekuˈtre]; in *donnai* [dɔˈne], and in the words *gai* [ge] and *geai* [ʒe].

9. *ai* exceptionally when not final in the present of *aller* and *savoir*, viz., *vais* [ve], *sais* [se], *sait* [se].

10. *ay* rarely, as in the word *ray-grass* [reˈgrɑːs].

11. œ initially in occasional Greek borrowings, such as *Œdipe* [eˈdip].

12. *ai* in *aiguille* [eˈgɥiːj] and derivatives.

[ɛ]

1. *e* in general in phonetically closed syllables, as in *cette* [sɛt], *ennemi* [ɛnˈmi], *elle* [ɛl], *esquif* [ɛsˈkif], *essor* [ɛˈsɔːr] (and in nearly all words where *es*—but not its derivative *é*—has been prefixed by prothesis to Latin roots or loanwords beginning with *s*), *est* [ɛst] (east).

2. *e* in *ex* followed by a consonant (except *h*), as in *expert* [ɛksˈpɛːr]. NOTE: This is, of course, a special case of *e* in a closed syllable.

3. *e* in a syllable orthographically closed by silent *t* (alone or in an orthographic consonant cluster), as in *œillet* [œˈjɛ], *canivet* [kaniˈvɛ], *aspect* [asˈpɛ], *est* [ɛ] (is). NOTE: See exceptional case of *et* under [e] above.

4. *e* at the end of a syllable before *y*, as in *grasseyer* [grasɛˈje].

5. *e* in cases where [ɛ] has been denasalized, as in *bien abrégé* [bjɛnabreˈʒe] —recent practice often [bjẽabrɛˈʒe].

6. *é* exceptionally before *je*, as in *arrivé-je* [ariˈvɛʒ], and in a few words like *abréger* [abrɛˈʒe] and its derivatives. NOTE: Here the almost infallible rule that *é* is pronounced [e] is broken.

7. *ë* in the word *Noël* [nɔˈɛl].

8. *è* (unfailingly), as in *mère* [mɛːr], *dès* [dɛ]. Note that *è* occurs only in a syllable orthographically, and, generally, phonetically closed.

9. *ê* (unfailingly), as in *fête* [fɛt]. Note that *ê* occurs only in a phonetically closed syllable.

10. *ai* in general, except when final in tense endings (see under [e], page 336), as in *commençais* [kɔmɑ̃ˈsɛ], *commençaient* [kɔmɑ̃ˈsɛ] (see exceptions for present of *aller* and *savoir* under [e], page 336), *ordinaire* [ɔrdiˈnɛːr], *aimable* [ɛˈmabl], *mais* [mɛ], *essai* [eˈsɛ]. NOTE: (1) The examples include syllables both open and closed orthographically. (2) See exceptions for *-ail* and *-aille* under [ɑ], page 338; [a], page 337; [j], page 348. (3) See rare exception of *ai* in *faisance* and other derivatives of *faire*, under [ə], page 339.

11. *a* before *y* as in *payer* [pɛˈje]. NOTE: See exceptions for *abbaye*, *pays*, etc., under [e], page 336.

12. *aie* in the word *baie* [bɛ].

13. *aî* as in *faîte* [fɛːt], *maître* [mɛːtr].

14. *ay* in general, as in *payer* [pɛˈje]. (See exception under [e], page 336.)

15. *aye* in the word *payement* [pɛˈmɑ̃].

16. *ei* as in *reine* [rɛːn], *peine* [pɛːn], *sommeil* [sɔˈmɛːj], *bouteille* [buˈtɛːj]. NOTE: Where *ei* is followed by *l*, it may be open to question whether the [ɛ] is a pronunciation of *e* alone or of *ei*, and conversely, whether the [j] is a pronunciation of *l* or *il*.

[a]

1. *a* in general followed by a consonant or consonant cluster, phonetic or orthographic; as in *animal* [aniˈmal], *retard* [rəˈtaːr], *Paris* [paˈri], *basin* [baˈzɛ̃], *casanier* [kazaˈnje], *nation* [naˈsjɔ̃] (*a* in *ation* may also be pronounced [ɑ]). NOTE: See exceptions under [ɑ], page 338.

2. *a* finally, as in *mangea* [mɑ̃ˈʒa], *la* [la].

3. *a* in *aill(e)*, *ail*, as in *taillir* [taˈjiːr], *bataille* [baˈtaːj], *travail* [traˈvaːj] (see also under [ɑ], page 338), *bataillon* [bataˈjɔ̃].

4. *à*, as in *là* [la], *déjà* [deˈʒa].

5. *â* in the first and second person plural, past definite endings, and in the third person singular imperfect subjunctive, of the first conjugation and certain irregular verbs, as in *donnâmes* [dɔˈnam], *donnâtes* [dɔˈnat], *allâmes* [aˈlam] (from *aller*), *allâtes* [aˈlat], *donnât* [dɔˈna], *allât* [aˈla]. NOTE: See other cases of *â* under [ɑ], page 338.

6. *e* before *mm* in adverbs in *-emment*, as in *récemment* [resaˈmɑ̃]; before *nn*, as in *hennir* [aˈniːr]; and in the word *femme* [fam].

7. *oe* (the second phonetic element of [wa]), as in *moelle* [mwal].

8. *oê* (the second phonetic element of [wa]), as in *poêle* [pwaːl] (also [pwɑːl]).

9. *oi* (the second phonetic element of [wa]), as in *doit* [dwa], *poil* [pwal], *doigt* [dwa], *moi* [mwa]. NOTE: See exceptions under [ɔ], page 338; [wɑ], page 348; and [wɛ̃], page 348.

10. *oî* (the second phonetic element of [wa]) in general, as in *boîte* [bwat]. NOTE: See exception under [wɑ], page 348.

11. *oy* (the second phonetic element of [wa]), as in *doyen* [dwaˈjɛ̃], *moyen* [mwaˈjɛ̃].

338 FRENCH

[ɑ]

1. *a* in *asse*, as in *classe* [klɑ:s].

2. *a* before *s* final, as in *bras* [brɑ], *pas* [pɑ], *bas* [bɑ].

3. *a* before final *se*, as in *base* [bɑ:z], *vase* [vɑ:z], *phrase* [frɑ:z].

4. *a* before *s* followed by a pronounced vowel in many words, as in *baser* [bɑˡze], *basique* [bɑˡzik], *braser* [brɑˡze], *bazane* [bɑˡzan], *brasure* [brɑˡzyr]. NOTE: See exception for some of this category under [a], page 337.

5. *a* in *ation*, as in *nation* [nɑˡsjɔ̃] (also pronounced [naˡsjɔ̃]).

6. *a* in *ail*, *aill(e)*, as in *travail* [traˡvɑ:j], *bataille* [bɑˡtɑ:j], *taillis* [tɑˡji]. NOTE: See also under [a], page 337.

7. *a* in a few exceptional words, including *ah* [ɑ], *bascule* [bɑsˡkyl], *damner* [dɑˡne], *espace* [ɛsˡpɑ:s], *cadre* [kɑdr].

8. *a* denasalized before *n* in liaison, as in *en avant* [ɑnaˡvɑ̃]—also [ɑ̃naˡvɑ̃].

9. *â*, as in *grâce* [grɑs], *bâton* [bɑˡtɔ̃], *âme* [ɑ:m], *bâiller* [bɑˡje]. NOTE: See under [a] the pronunciation of certain verb endings in *â*.

10. *oi* (second phonetic element of [wɑ]) following *r*, as in *roi* [rwɑ], *croix* [krwɑ], and in a few exceptional words, including *bois* [bwɑ], *loi* [lwɑ].

11. *oî* (second phonetic element of [wɑ]) following *r*, as in *croît* [krwɑ].

12. *oê* (second phonetic element of [wɑ]), as in *poêle* [pwɑ:l] (also [pwa:l]).

[ɔ]

1. *o* generally, as in *coq* [kɔk], *votre* [vɔtr], *sotte* [sɔt], *social* [sɔˡsjal], *monopole* [monoˡpɔl], *possibilité* [pɔsibiliˡte]. NOTE: See exceptions under [o].

2. *o* in the combination *oi* in *oignon* [ɔˡɲɔ̃].

3. *o* before an *n* which is pronounced only in liaison, as in *mon ami* [monaˡmi] —also [mɔ̃naˡmi].

4. *o* before *s* followed by a pronounced vowel in a few words such as *mosaique* [mozaˡik], *mosette* [moˡzɛt], *losange* [loˡzɑ̃:ʒ].

5. *ô* in the words *hôpital* [ɔpiˡtal] and *hôtel* [ɔˡtɛl].

6. *au* before *r*, as in *Laure* [lɔ:r], *aura* [ɔˡra], *j'aurai* [ʒoˡre]; and *au* in a few other words, including *Paul* [ˡpɔl].

7. *u* before *m* finally in words of Latin derivation, as in *calcium* [kalˡsjɔm].

[o]

1. *o* finally in a word, as in *numéro* [nymeˡro].

2. *o* before a final, silent consonant, as in *trop* [tro], *nos* [no], *mot* [mo].

3. *o* before *s* or *m* followed by an orthographic vowel, as in *prose* [pro:z], *rose* [ro:z], *position* [poziˡsjɔ̃], *gnome* [gno:m]. NOTE: See exceptions under [ɔ], page 338.

4. *o* at the beginning in *-otion*, as in *potion* [poˡsjɔ̃].

5. *ô*, as in *tôt* [to], *ôter* [oˡte], *dôme* [do:m]. NOTE: See exceptions under [ɔ].

6. *au*, except before *r*, as in *faux* [fo], *animaux* [aniˈmo], *autre* [otr], *cause* [koz], *aucun* [oˈkœ̃]. NOTE: See exception under [ɔ], page 338.

7. *eau*, as in *tableau* [taˈblo], *gâteau* [gɑˈto], *beau* [bo].

[u]

1. *ou* before a consonant sound or as the last sound of a word, as in *amour* [aˈmuːr], *poudre* [pudr], *bouche* [buʃ], *bouillon* [buˈjɔ̃], *chou* [ʃu], *nous* [nu], *bout* [bu], *moue* [mu], *noue* [nu].

2. *ou* after *l* or *r*, as in *clouer* [kluˈe], *prouesse* [pruˈɛs], *brouette* [bruˈɛt]. NOTE: This constitutes an exception to the rule that *ou* before a pronounced vowel is pronounced [w].

3. *oû*, as in *dégoût* [deˈgu], *goûter* [guˈte], *août* [aˈu, u].

4. *où* in the word *où* [u].

5. *ou* before *ill*, as in *bouillon* [buˈjɔ̃]. NOTE: Here also is an exception to the rule that *ou* before a pronounced vowel letter is [w].

[ə]

1. *e* is pronounced [ə] when it is the vowel of any unstressed syllable, as in *venir* [vəˈniːr], *devant* [dəˈvã], *cheval* [ʃəˈval], *recevoir* [rəsəˈvwaːr]. NOTE: The word *unstressed* is used arbitrarily here to refer to the very light tertiary stress of a word or syllable as distinguished from primary or secondary stress. In *religion* [rəˌliˈʒjɔ̃], [ʒjɔ̃] has primary stress, [li] has secondary stress, [rə] has tertiary stress and is customarily called unstressed.

2. The following monosyllabic articles, prepositions, adverbs, and pronouns are regularly pronounced with [ə]: *le, de, je, me, te, se, ce, ne, que.*

3. In context in slow colloquial speech (upon which the examples in this book are based—see page 331, footnote 7), [ə] is dropped under the following described conditions:

a. When dropping it does not produce a consonant combination impossible in French. Examples: *contenir* [kɔ̃tˈniːr], *appeller* [aˈple].

b. In a succession of words containing [ə], the [ə] of the second word is usually dropped and alternate [ə]'s dropped thereafter. Example: *je ne te le donne pas* [ʒən təl dɔn pɑ]. However, the combination *ce que* is pronounced [skə].

As indicated earlier (page 331), in poetry and song an otherwise silent *e* is pronounced where needed in the scansion, and often at the ends of lines. In drama (especially classic tragedy) the same custom is followed. This is a characteristic of archaic speech. (See page 331, footnote 7.)

4. Exceptionally, *ai* is pronounced [ə] in *bien faisance* [bjɛ̃fəˈzɑ̃ːs] and related words derived from *faire*.

5. Exceptionally, *on* is pronounced [ə] in *monsieur* [məˈsjø].

[y]

1. *u* as in *rude* [ryd], *écu* [e'ky], *une* [yn]. NOTE: See *u* followed by *m* or *n* under [œ̃], page 341.

2. *û*, as in *mûrir* [my'ri:r], *dû* [dy].

3. *ue* final in a syllable, except after *g* or *q*, as in *revue* [rə'vy].

4. *üe*, as in *aigüe* [ɛ'gy].

5. *eu* in the various forms of *avoir*, such as *eu* [y], *eut* [y], *eussent* [ys].

6. *eû* in the following forms of *avoir*: *eûmes* [ym], *eûtes* [yt], *eût* [y].

[ø]

1. *eu* before *s* or *x* followed by a vowel letter, as in *creuser* [krø'ze], *deuxieme* [dø'zjɛm], *creuse* [krøz].

2. *eu* before *-ill* followed by a phonetic vowel, as in *feuillage* [fø'ja:ʒ].

3. *eu* before pronounced *t*, as in *feutre* [fø:tr], *neutre* [nø:tr], *meute* [mø:t].

4. *eu* before a vowel as in *bleuâtre* [blø'ɑ:tr].

5. *eu* as the last sound of a word (finally, or before a final silent consonant), as in *peu* [pø], *feu* [fø], *creux* [krø].

6. *eû* as in *jeûne* [ʒø:n]. NOTE: See exception under [y], page 340, for the past absolute forms of *avoir*.

7. *œu* finally or before a final silent consonant or consonant cluster, as in *vœu* [vø], *nœud* [nø], *œufs* [ø], *bœufs* [bø]. NOTE: Phonetically speaking, these are, of course, open syllables.

[œ]

1. *eu* before a pronounced consonant, except *s* [z], *x* [z], or *t*. Thus: *fleur* [flœ:r], *neuf* [nœf], *seul* [sœl].

2. *eu* before *-il* [j] or *-ill* [j] final, as in *deuil* [dœ:j], *feuille* [fœ:j].

3. *œ* before *-il* [j] or *-ill* [j], as in *œil* [œ:j], *œillade* [œ'jad].

4. *œu* before a pronounced consonant, i.e., in a closed syllable, as in *œuf* [œf], *bœuf* [bœf], *cœur* [kœr], *œuvre* [œvr].

5. *ue* before *-il* or *-ill*, as in *cercueil* [sɛr'kœj], *recueillir* [rəkœ'jir].

[ɛ̃]

1. *aim* or *ain*, as in *faim* [fɛ̃], *vain* [vɛ̃].

2. *en* following *e*, *i*, or *y*, as in *européen* [œrɔpe'ɛ̃], *bien* [bjɛ̃], *moyen* [mwa'jɛ̃].

3. *em* in a few exceptional words, including *sempiternel* [sɛ̃pitɛr'nɛl].

4. *eim* or *ein*, as in *Reims* [rɛ̃s], *plein* [plɛ̃].

5. *im* or *in*, as in *impossible* [ɛ̃pɔ'sibl], *fin* [fɛ̃], *Chopin* [ʃo'pɛ̃].

6. *în*, as in *vînmes* [vɛ̃m].

7. *ym* or *yn*, as in *sympathie* [sɛ̃pa'ti], *syntaxe* [sɛ̃'taks].

[ɑ̃]

1. *am* or *an*, as in *lampe* [lɑ̃:p], *grand* [grɑ̃].

2. *em* or *en*, except after *e*, *i* or *y*, as in *tempête* [tã¹pɛ:t], *dent* [dã], *en* [ã].

3. *aon*, as in *paon* [pã], *taon* [tã].

[ɔ̃]

1. *om* or *on*, as in *tomber* [tɔ̃¹be], *mon* [mɔ̃]. Exception: the word *monsieur* [mə¹sjø]. NOTE: In liaison [ɔ̃] is denasalized to [ɔ], as in *mon ami* [mɔna¹mi]—also [mɔ̃na¹mi] (see page 333, footnote 9). See exceptions under [ɔ], page 338, *calcium* [kal¹sjɔm], *album* [al¹bɔm], etc.

[œ̃]

1. *eun*, as in *jeun* [ʒœ̃].

2. *um* or *un*, as in *parfum* [par¹fœ̃], *chacun* [ʃa¹kœ̃].

Consonants

[b]

1. *b* initially in a syllable, as in *bal* [bal], *cabinet* [kabi¹nɛ].

2. *b* finally in any syllable except the last syllable of a word, if not followed by another syllable beginning with *s* or *t*. Thus, *object* [ɔb¹ʒɛ]. NOTE: See below under [p].

3. *b* followed by *e(s)* finally in a syllable, as in *jambe* [ʒã:b], *jambes* [ʒã:b], *gabegie* [gab¹ʒi]. NOTE: *b* at the end of a word, either alone, or in the consonant cluster *bs*, is silent, as in *plomb* [plɔ̃], *aplombs* [a¹plɔ̃].

4. *bb*, as in *abbé* [a¹be].

[p]

1. *p* initially in a syllable, as in *patte* [pat], *psaume* [pso:m], *épeler* [e¹ple].

2. *p* finally in any syllable except the last syllable of a word. Thus *aptitude* [apti¹tyd]. Exceptions: *compter* [kɔ̃¹te], *dompter* [dɔ̃¹te], *sculpter* [skyl¹te], *baptême* [ba¹tɛm] and related words and derivatives.

3. *p* alone or in a consonant cluster, followed by *e* or *es* finally in a syllable, as in *cape(s)* [kap], *dépenailler* [depna¹je], *inepte* [i¹nɛpt]. NOTE: *p* in the absolute final position in a word is silent, as in *loup* [lu]. Exceptions: *cap* [kap], *cep* [sɛp]. Also in the consonant clusters *ps* and *pt* finally in a word, *p* is silent. Thus: *loups* [lu], *corps* [kɔr], *exempt* [eg¹zã], *prompt* [prɔ̃], *sept* [sɛt], *temps* [tã], and verb forms like *romps* [rɔ̃] and *rompt* [rɔ̃]. After a nasal, *p* in such a cluster is silent even when followed by *e*, as in *compte* [kɔ̃t].

4. *pp*, as in *appétit* [ape¹ti].

5. *p* in liaison, as in *un loup acrimonieux* [œ̃ lupakrimɔn¹jø].

6. *b* finally in a syllable followed by another syllable beginning with *s* or *t*, as in *obscure* [ɔps¹ky:r], *obtenir* [ɔptə¹ni:r]. (See also above.)

[d]

1. *d* initially in a syllable, as in *dos* [do], *radis* [ra¹di]

2. *d* finally in a syllable except the last syllable of a word, as in *cadmium* [kad¹mjɔm]. NOTE: *d* at the end of a word, either in the absolute final position or followed by *s*, is silent. Thus: *regard* [rə¹ga:r], *pied* [pje], *pieds* [pje], *poids* [pwɑ], *assieds* [a¹sje] and analogous verb forms. Exception: *sud* [syd].

3. *d* followed by *e* finally in a syllable, as in *façade* [fa¹sad], *cadenas* [kad¹na]. NOTE: *d* in liaison is pronounced [t], as in *un grand objet* [ɶ̃ grɑ̃t ɔb¹ʒɛ].

4. *dd* as in *addition* [adi¹sjɔ̃].

[t]

1. *t* initially in a syllable, as in *tenir* [tə¹ni:r], *atome* [a¹tom], *modestie* [mɔdɛs¹ti], *question* [kɛs¹tjɔ̃], *inimitié* [inimi¹tje], *chrétien* [kre¹tjɛ̃], *héritier* [eri¹tje], *volontiers* [vɔlɔ̃¹tje], *huitieme* [ɥi¹tjɛm], *portiez* [pɔr¹tje] (note that the *t* is part of the verb stem).

2. *t* followed by *e* final in a syllable, as in *tête* [tɛ:t], *note* [nɔt], *serte* [sɛrt].

3. *t* in the consonant cluster *ct*, as in *impact* [ɛ̃¹pakt].

4. *t* in the consonant cluster *st* in certain words, including *ouest* [wɛst], *est* [ɛst] (east), *zest* [zɛst].

5. *t* in the consonant cluster *pt* in the single word *sept* [sɛt] and its derivatives (but when modifying a noun beginning with a consonant, *sept* may be [sɛ]).

6. *t* in the word *huit* [ɥit], except when modifying a noun beginning with a consonant, as in *huit coqs* [ɥi kɔk].

7. *t* in certain exceptional words including *chut* [ʃyt], *dot* [dɔt], *fat* [fat], *lut* [lyt], *mat* [mat], *net* [nɛt], and *soit* [swat] when used as an adverb.

8. *t* in liaison, as in *est-il* [ɛ¹til]. NOTE: Final *t* in most other cases is silent, as in *béret* [be¹rɛ]. This includes *t* in the consonant cluster *ts*, as in *bérets* [be¹rɛ] and in such verb forms as *bats* [ba] (from *battre*), *mets* [mɛ] (from *mettre*), *vêts* [vɛ] (from *vêtir*).

9. *tt*, as in *attention* [atɑ̃¹sjɔ̃], *cette* [sɛt].

10. *th* in certain words mainly from the Greek, as in *thermal* [tɛr¹mal]. Exceptions: *th* is silent in the words *asthme* [asm], and *isthme* [ism], with their derivatives.

11. *d* in liaison, as in *un grand objet* [ɶ̃ grɑ̃t ɔb¹ʒɛ]. (See also above.)

[g]

1. *g* initially in a syllable, before *a*, *o* or *u*, as in *gable* [¹gabl], *guttural* [gyty¹ral], *agonie* [agɔ¹ni], *guise* [gi:z], *guerre* [gɛ:r]. NOTE: When *u* is inserted before *e* or *i* it is to make the *g* "hard," that is, [g].

2. *g* initially before a consonant in a syllable, as in *agréable* [agre¹abl], *église* [e¹gli:z], *gnome* [gno:m]. NOTE: Standard French words with initial *gn* pronounced [gn] in the root syllable come from the Greek.

3. *g* finally in any syllable except the last syllable of a word, as in *augment* [ɔg¹mɑ̃], *ignition* [igni¹sjɔ̃] (but observe that final *g* is [g] before *n* only in a few

late borrowings from the Latin, the *gn* in words which have come through old French having by reciprocal assimilation evolved into [ɲ], as in *ignoble* [iˈɲɔbl]). NOTE: *g* finally in a word, either alone or followed by *s*, *t* or *ts* is silent. Thus, *rang(s)* [rɑ̃], *doigt(s)* [dwa], *vingt* [vɛ̃]. NOTE: See exception for *g* in liaison under [k] below.

4. *gg*, as in *agglomerer* [aglɔmeˈre]. NOTE: See exception for *gg* before *e* under [ʒ], page 348.

5. *x* (first consonantal phonetic element in the prefix *ex* before a vowel), as in *exister* [egzisˈte].

6. *c* in the words *second* [səˈgɔ̃, zgɔ̃], and *anecdote* [anɛgˈdɔt], and their derivatives. (Here we have assimilative voicing of [k] to [g].)

[k]

1. *c* initially in a syllable, either alone or preceded by *s*, before *a*, *o*, *u*, or a consonant, as in *cadre* [kɑ:dr], *col* [kɔl], *culotte* [kyˈlɔt], *craindre* [krɛ̃:dr], *scalpe* [skalp].

2. *c* finally, either alone or in the consonant cluster *ct*. Thus, *avec* [aˈvɛk], *circonspect* [sirkɔ̃ˈspɛkt] and the combination *cric crac* [krik:rak]. Exceptions: certain words including *accroc* [aˈkro], *clerc* [klɛ:r], *caoutchouc* [kauˈtʃu], *cric* [kri], *croc* [kro], *escroc* [ɛsˈkro], *estomac* [ɛstɔˈma], *marc* [mar], *tabac* [taˈba], *aspect* [asˈpɛ], *respect* [rɛsˈpɛ]; *c* or *ct* after *n*, as in *franc* [frɑ̃], *instinct* [ɛ̃stɛ̃]. (*Donc* [dɔ̃] is changed to [dɔk] when it begins a clause.)

3. *cc* before *a*, *o*, *u* or a consonant, as *accabler* [akɑˈble], *accomoder* [akɔmɔˈde], *accusation* [akyzɑˈsjɔ̃], *accréditer* [akrediˈte].

4. *cc* (the first element of the cluster [ks]), before *e* or *i*, (as in *accent* [akˈsɑ̃], *succinct* [sykˈsɛ̃]).

5. *ch* before *a*, *o*, *u* or a consonant in words of Greek derivation, as *chaos* [kaˈo], *catéchuménat* [katekymeˈna], *chronologie* [krɔnɔlɔˈʒi].

6. *ch* before *e*, *i*, or *y* in a few such exceptional words from the Greek as *chélidoine* [keliˈdwan], *chiasme* [kiˈasm], *tachygraphe* [takiˈgraf].

7. *cqu* as in *acquitter* [akiˈte].

8. *q* finally in a few words, as *coq* [kɔk].

9. *qu* initially in a syllable, before *a*, *o*, *e*, or *i*, as in *quart* [ka:r], *quotepart* [kɔtˈpa:r], *question* [kɛsˈtjɔ̃], *qui* [ki].

10. *q* before *uoi*, as in *quoi* [kwa], and before *ua* in a few exceptional words, as *équation* [ekwaˈsjɔ̃].

11. *que* finally in a syllable, as in *piqueter* [pikˈte], *clique* [klik].

12. *x* (the first phonetic element of [ks]), initially in a syllable in some words from Greek, as in *xylème* [ksiˈlɛm].

13. *x* (the first phonetic element of [ks]), finally in a syllable, as in *axis* [akˈsis], *axonge* [akˈsɔ̃:ʒ], *toxicologie* [tɔksikɔlɔˈʒi], *excitation* [ɛksitɑˈsjɔ̃], *sextant* [sɛksˈtɑ̃].

NOTE: In the case of initial *ex* the pronunciation [ks] occurs only before a consonant. (See exception for *ex* before a vowel under [g], page 342.)

14. *x* (the first phonetic element of [ks]) followed by *e* or a consonant plus *e*, at the end of a word, as in *sexe* [sɛks], *texte* [tɛkst], also final in a few words such as *index* [ẽˈdɛks], *codex* [kɔˈdɛks]. NOTE: *x* in the absolute final position of a word is usually silent, as in *roux* [ru]. NOTE: See exceptions under [s] and [z].

15. *k* in relatively small group of words of late borrowing, as *kérosène* [keroˈzɛːn], *krach* [kraʃ], *lakiste* [laˈkist]. NOTE: Strictly speaking, *k* is not a part of the native French alphabet.

16. *g* in liaison, as in *long object* [lɔ̃kɔbˈʒɛ] (see page 343).

[m]

1. *m* preceding an orthographic vowel, as in *mons* [mɔ̃], *même* [mɛm], *chemin* [ʃəˈmẽ].

2. *m* preceding *n*, as in *somnambule* [sɔmnãˈbyl]. Exceptions: *automne* [oˈtɔn], and *damner* [dɑˈne]. NOTE: *m* before any other orthographic consonant than *n*, or finally in a word, is silent, its sole function being that of promoting nasality in the preceding vowel. Thus: *romps* [rɔ̃], *nom* [nɔ̃].

3. *mm*, as in *comme* [kɔm], *immense* [iˈmãːs], *imminence* [imiˈnãːs].

[n]

1. *n* preceding any orthographic vowel, as in *nature* [naˈtyːr], *scène* [sɛːn]. (Here, as is regular in French, the final *e* serves to prevent the preceding consonant from being silent.) NOTE: *n* before most orthographic consonants or at the end of a word is silent, serving merely to nasalize the preceding vowel. Thus: *monter* [mɔ̃ˈte], *son* [sɔ̃].

2. *nn*, as in *sonner* [sɔˈne], *annal* [aˈnal].

[ɲ]

1. *gn*, as in *bagne* [baɲ], *soigner* [swaˈɲe]. NOTE: In late borrowings from the Latin, *gn* is [gn], as in *ignition* [igniˈsjɔ̃] (see page 342). The same is true of roots from the Greek containing initial *gn*, like *gnome* [gnom] (see page 342).

[l]

1. *l* in general (initial, medial, final) and in consonant clusters, as in *livre* [liːvr], *celui* [səˈlɥi], *humble* [œ̃ːbl], *il* [il], *poil* [pwal], *plume* [plym]. Exceptions: (1) In the following words, derived from Latin words with a single *l*, final *l* is silent: *cul* [ky], *grésil* [greˈzi], *mil* (millet) [mi], *soul* [su], *gentil* [ʒãˈti], *surcil* [syrˈsi], etc., and *fils* [fis], *pouls* [pu]; (2) *l* is silent finally in the combination *il* after a vowel (except *o*), as in *conseil* [kɔ̃ˈsɛːj].

2. (a) *ll* after any vowel except *i* as referred to in note after (d) below, as in *allège* [aˈlɛːʒ], *bulle* [byl], *quelle* [kɛl], *balle* [bal]. Also, even after *i*, in *ville* [vil]

and its derivatives, and in numeral adjectives, such as *mille* [mil], *billion* [bi'ljɔ̃].

(b) After *i* in the initial combination *ill*—as in *illustration* [ilystra'sjɔ̃], *illicite* [il:i'sit]. (Here, since *il* preceding a stem beginning with *l* means "not," the *ll* is often pronounced [l:]; but [ili'sit] is also known.)

(c) After *i* in the combination *-ill-* followed by *i* plus a vowel (in which case *i* is pronounced [j]), as in *millier* [mi'lje].

(d) In a few exceptional words in which *-ille* follows a consonant, including *gille* [ʒil], *millénaire* [mile'nɛ:r], *pillage* [pi'la:ʒ] ([pi'ja:ʒ] is also known), *tranquille* [trã'kil]. Note that the *ll*'s in *mille, ville, village,* etc., represent Latin *ll*'s. NOTE: For *ll* in the combination *ill* following an orthographic vowel, and *ill* in general after a consonant, see under [j], page 348.

[r, R]

NOTE: As indicated earlier (p. 329), [r] and [R] are both regularly used in French, and may both be regarded as standard. However, [R] is prevalent in Paris and vicinity, and is therefore preferred by many. Throughout this book, the symbol [r] is used, but [R] may be substituted for it at any point. Let it be remembered, as explained on page 329, that in French [r] is a tongue-point trill and [R] is a uvular trill.

1. *r* initially in a syllable, alone or in a cluster, as in *reste* [rɛst], *bride* [brid]; and final in a syllable, alone or in a cluster, after *a, i, o, u,* as in *sur* [sy:r], *car* [kar], *mourir* [mu'ri:r], *mort* [mɔr], *impur* [ɛ̃'py:r]. NOTE: Final *r* is silent in *monsieur* [mə'sjø], *messieurs* [me'sjø], and in polysyllables ending in *er* and *ers*, as in *pencher* [pã'ʃe] and all infinitives in *er*, *merciers* [mɛr'sje], and most polysyllabic nouns in *-er*.

2. *r* in exceptional words, such as *amer* [a'mɛ:r], *cuiller* [kɥi'jɛ:r], *enfer* [ã'fɛ:r], *éther* [e'tɛ:r], *hiver* [i've:r], *fier* [fjɛ:r], *hier* [jɛ:r].

3. *rr*, as in *erreur* [ɛ'rœ:r], *irrationel* [irasjɔ'nɛl].

4. *rh* and *rrh*, as in *rhétorique* [retɔ'rik], *myrrhe* [mi:r].

[v]

1. *v* wherever it occurs, as in *verre* [vɛ:r], *avec* [a'vɛk], *verve* [vɛ:rv], *vivre* [vi:vr].

2. *f* in the word *neuf* when it occurs in liaison with the words *heures* and *ans*. Thus: *neuf heures* [nœ'vœ:r] and *neuf ans* [nœ'vã].

[f]

1. *f*, as in *fou* [fu], *refuser* [rəfy'ze], *clef* [klɛf] (in music), *soif* [swaf]. Exceptions: Final *f* is silent in *cerf* [sɛ:r], *nerf* [nɛ:r], *clef* [kle] (a key or wrench), *bœufs* [bø], *œufs* [ø], *chef-d'œuvre* [ʃe'dœ:vr], and *neuf* [nœ] preceding a noun beginning with a consonant, as in *neuf poupées* [nœpu'pe]; final *f* is pronounced [v] in the phrases *neuf ans* [nœ'vã] and *neuf heures* [nœ'vœr], as seen above.

2. *ff*, as in *effacer* [efa'se].

3. *ph*, as in *phrase* [frɑ:z].

[z]

1. *z* initially in a syllable, as in *zénith* [ze'nit], *dizain* [di'zɛ̃].

2. *z* finally in liaison, as in *nez et bouche* [neze'buʃ]. NOTE: Final *z* not in liaison is silent, as in *avez* [a've].

3. *s* intervocalically, as in *casette* [ka'zɛt]. NOTE: See exception for compounds under [s], below.

4. *s* in syllables ending in vowel plus *s* plus *e* or *es*, as in *fraise* [frɛ:z], *chaises* [ʃɛ:z].

5. *s* in the prefix *trans-* before a vowel, as in *transalpin* [trɑ̃zal'pɛ̃]. NOTE: See exception for *trans-* before the root of a word beginning with [s], page 347.

6. *s* before *b* as in *asbeste* [az'bɛst], *esbroufe* [ɛz'bruf].

7. *s* in the word *balsamier* [balza'mje], and its derivatives.

8. *s* in liaison, as in *les hommes* [le'zɔm].

9. *x* in the polysyllabic numerals *deuxième* [dø'zjɛm], *sixième* [si'zjɛm], *dixième* [di'zjɛm], *dix-huit* [di'zɥit], *dix-neuf* [diz'nœf], *sixain* [si'zɛ̃].

10. *x* in liaison, as in *deux anges* [dø'zɑ̃:ʒ].

11. *x* (the second phonetic element of [gz]) in the prefix *ex-* before a vowel, as in *exister* [egzis'te]. NOTE: Authority may be found for pronouncing *x* as [gz], as well as [ks], in prefixes *hex-*, *sex-* before vowel.

[s]

1. *s* initially in a word, as in *salle* [sal].

2. *s* initially in a syllable preceded by syllable ending in a consonant, as in *ensemble* [ɑ̃'sɑ̃:bl]. NOTE: This *s* is thus distinguished from intervocalic *s*. See under [z].

3. *s* initially in the second element of a compound word, as in *antisémite* [ɑ̃tise'mit]. NOTE: This *s* is in contrast with intervocalic [z], but can, since it is initial in a semantic element, be predicted from the spelling if the meaning and etymology are understood. In this case, since it belongs to the root word, it is considered initial, not intervocalic, and is therefore pronounced [s].

4. *s* finally in an exceptional group of words, including: *axis* [ak'sis], *aloès* [alɔ'ɛ:s], *as* [as], *atlas* [at'lɑ:s], *bis* (the adverb) [bi:s], *cassis* [ka'sis], *cens* [sɑ̃:s], *ès* [ɛs], *fils* [fis], *hélas* [e'lɑ:s], *ibis* [i'bi:s], *iris* [i'ri:s], *jadis* [ʒa'di:s], *lapis* [la'pi:s], *laps* [laps], *lis* [lis] (except in the combination *fleur-de-lis* [flœrdə'li]), *maïs* [ma'is], *mars* [mars], *métis* [me'ti:s], *mœurs* [mœrs] (sometimes [mœr]), *oasis* [oa'zi:s], *os* (the singular) [ɔs] or [o:s], *ours* [urs], *pathos* [pa'tɔ:s], *plus* [plys] (emphatic, or meaning "plus," or included in *en plus* [ɑ̃'plys] or *plus-que-parfait* [plyskəpar'fɛ]), *relaps* [rə'laps], *rhinocéros* [rinɔse'rɔ:s], *sens* [sɑ̃:ns] (except in the combination *sens commun* [sɑ̃kɔ'mœ̃]), *tous* [tu:s] (when emphatic, or a pronoun, or not

followed immediately by noun).[12] NOTE: *s* finally in plural nouns, pronouns, adjectives, and verbs is silent. Thus: *livres* [liːvr], *mes* [me] (even in the combinations *mesdames* [meˈdam], *mesdemoiselles* [medmwaˈzɛl]), *les* [le] (even in the combination *lesquel* [leˈkɛl]), *petites* [pəˈtit], *dos* [do], *gris* [gri], *sors* [sɔr], *donnons* [dɔˈnõ].

5. *s* finally in a syllable before a syllable beginning with a consonant, as in *disputer* [dispyˈte].

6. *s* in the suffix *-isme*, as in *égoisme* [egɔˈism].

7. *s* in the prefix *trans-* before a consonant; when attached to the root of a word beginning with *s*, as in *transept* [trãˈsɛ], *transylvain* [trãsilˈvẽ]; and in the word *transir* [trãˈsir].

8. *ss*, as in *masse* [mas], *massage* [maˈsaːʒ].

9. *sc* before *e*, *i*, or *y*, as in *sceptre* [sɛptr], *science* [sjãːs], *scythe* [sit].

10. *c* followed by *e*, *i*, or *y*, as in *précéder* [preseˈde], *service* [sɛrˈvis], *précis* [preˈsi], *cycle* [sikl].

11. *ç* as in *français* [frãˈsɛ].

12. *t* in *-tie* preceded by a consonant in certain words, including *ineptie* [inɛpˈsi], *inertie* [inɛrˈsi], *autocratie* [ɔtɔkraˈsi].

13. *t* in *-tion* not preceded by *s* or *x*, as in *action* [akˈsjõ]. NOTE: *t* in *-tion* preceded by *s* or *x* is pronounced [t], as in *question* [kɛsˈtjõ]. (See page 342.)

14. *t* in certain words ending in *-tier*, including *balbutier* [balbyˈsje], *différentier* [diferãˈsje], *initier* [iniˈsje], *transsubstantier* [trãsːypstãˈsje].

15. *x* in the three words *soixante* [swaˈsãt], *six* [sis], *dix* [dis]. NOTE: When *six* or *dix* modifies a noun beginning in a consonant, the *x* is silent, as in *dix francs* [diˈfrã]. For these words in liaison, see under [z].

16. *x* in *excavateur* [ɛskavaˈtœːr], *excavation* [ɛskavaˈsjõ]—also [ɛks] in these words.

17. *x* (the second phonetic element of [ks]), initially in a syllable, as in *xiphias* [ksiˈfjas].

18. *x* (the second phonetic element of [ks]), in the prefixes *ex*, *hex* and *sex*, when followed by a consonant, as in *exitation* [ɛksitɑˈsjõ], *exposer* [ɛkspoˈze], *sextant* [sɛksˈtã], *hexagonal* [eksagɔˈnal]. Exceptions: *excavateur* [ɛskavaˈtœr], *excavation* [ɛskavaˈsjõ].

19. *x* (the second phonetic element of [ks]), following *a* or *o*, as in *axis* [akˈsis], *axonge* [akˈsõːʒ], *toxicologie* [tɔksikɔlɔˈʒi].

20. *x* (the second phonetic element of [ks]), followed by *e*, or a consonant plus *e*, at the end of a word, as in *axe* [aks], *sexe* [sɛks], *texte* [tɛkst]. NOTE: *x* in the absolute final position is generally silent, as in *roux* [ru].

---

[12] Also *sus* [sys], according to some authorities, when used in the phrase *en sus* [ãsys]; and *us* [yːs] in the single expression *un savant en us* [œ̃saˈvɑ̃tãˈnyːs] (a man learned in Latin).

21. *x* (the second phonetic element of [ks]), final in certain Latin words, such as *index* [ɛ̃ˈdɛks], *codex* [kɔˈdɛks].

[ʒ]

1. *j*, as in *jolie* [ʒɔˈli], *jeune* [ʒœn].

2. *g* before *e*, *i*, and *y*, as in *général* [ʒeneˈral], *geôle* [ʒo:l], *ouvrage* [uvˈra:ʒ], *gilet* [ʒiˈlɛ], *gymnastique* [ʒimnɑsˈtik].

3. *gg* (the second *g*) before *e*, as in *suggestion* [sygʒɛsˈtjɔ̃].

[ʃ]

1. *ch* as in *chaise* [ʃɛ:z], *crêche* [krɛ:ʃ], *chirurgie* [ʃiryrˈʒi], *chyme* [ʃim]. NOTE: See exception for words of Greek derivation containing *ch* before *a*, *o*, *u*, or a consonant, and in a few words before *e*, *i*, or *y*, under [k].

2. *sch* as in *schéma* [ʃeˈma].

[w]

1. *ou* before a pronounced vowel, as in *rouage* [rwa:ʒ], *ouest* [wɛst], *fouir* [fwi:r]. NOTE: See exceptions under [u], page 339.

2. *u* in the combination *ua* after *g* or *q*, as in *lingual* [lɛ̃ˈgwal], *quadrupède* [kwadryˈpɛd].

3. *oi, oî, oe, oê, oy* (the first phonetic element of [wa], [wɑ], or [wɛ̃]) as follows:

a. *doit* [dwa], *roi* [rwɑ], *poing* [pwɛ̃]. NOTE: See exception for *oignon* under [ɔ].

b. *boîte* [bwat], *croît* [krwɑ].

c. *oe* (the first phonetic element of [wa]), in the word *moelle* [mwal] and its derivatives.

d. *poêle* [pwɑl] or [pwal].

e. *soyer* [swaˈje].

[ɥ]

1. *u* before a pronounced vowel in the same syllable, except after *q* and *g*. Thus: *lui* [lɥi], *ruade* [rɥad], *nuage* [nɥa:ʒ], *remuer* [rəˈmɥe], *puy* [pɥi]. NOTE: For *qu* and *gu*, see under [k] and [w]. *Aiguille* [eˈgɥi:j], however, contains [ɥ].

[j]

1. *y* before any vowel except *i*, as in *yacht* [jɔt], *yeux* [jø], *fuyant* [fɥiˈjɑ̃], *voyer* [vwaˈje]. In *fuyant*, *y* = [ij].

2. *i* before a vowel, except when preceded by a consonant cluster ending in *l* or *r*, as in *bien* [bjɛ̃], *nation* [naˈsjɔ̃], *deuxième* [døˈzjɛm], *faience* [faˈjɑ̃:s], *iambe* [jɑ̃b]. NOTE: For *i* after clusters ending in *l* or *r*, see [i], page 335.

3. *i* as the second *i* of *ii*, as in *priions* [priˈjɔ̃].

4. *il* finally and *ill* in the combination *ille* after a vowel (except *o*), as in *conseil* [kɔ̃ˈsɛ:j], *travail* [traˈva:j], *retaille* [rəˈta:j]. NOTE: Any final [j] is fricative.

5. Medial *ill* following a vowel, *bataillon* [bataˈjɔ̃].

6. *ll* in *ill* following a consonant, as in *billet* [biljɛ]. NOTE: See exceptions under [l].

This is the appropriate place to do transcription exercises in French. Use any French text or word list.

Sounds of French Not in English

(These are the sounds which one learning French must master.)

Vowels   [y, ø, œ, ɛ̃, œ̃, ɑ̃, ɔ̃]

Consonants   [ɲ, ɥ, ŕ, R]

English Sounds Not in French

It is these sounds for which the French speaker of English is likely to make substitutions.

Vowels

[ɪ]   [ʒ]
[eɪ] (The corresponding French sound   [ɝ]
is the pure [e], not the dipthongal [eɪ].)   [ɚ]
[æ]   [aʊ]
[ɒ]   [ɔɪ]
[ʌ]   [aɪ] French has
[oʊ] (The corresponding French sound   no diphthongs.
is the pure [o], not the dipthongal [oʊ].)

Consonants

[θ]   [tʃ] French has both [t] and [ʃ], but not
[ð]   in the combination [tʃ].
[ŋ]   [dʒ] French has both [d] and [ʒ], but not
[h]   in the combination [dʒ].
[ʍ]

French Dialectal Substitutions for the Sounds Listed Above

Vowels

[ɪ] > [i], as in *bit* [bit].
[eɪ] > [e], as in *day* [de].
[æ] > [a], as in *am* [am].
[ɒ] > [ɑ], as in *lot* [lɑt].
[ʌ] > [ɑ] or [ɔ], as in *must* [mɑst], [mɔst].
[oʊ] > [o], as in *vote* [vot].
[ʒ] and [ɝ] > [ɛr], as in *kirk* [kɛrk].

[ɝ] > [ɛr], as in *summer* [ˈsɑˌmɛr].
[aʊ] > [au], as in *sound* [saund].
[ɔɪ] > [ɔi], as in *soil* [sɔil].
[aɪ] > [a], [ai] or [aj], as in *ice* [as], [ais] or [ajs].

Consonants

[θ] > [s] or [t], as in *think* [siŋk, tiŋk].
[ð] > [z] or [d], as in *them* [zɛm, dɛm].
[ŋ] may, until learned, be suggested by nasalizing
   the preceeding vowel, as in *sink* [sĩk].
[h] will be omitted, as in *had* [ad].
[ʧ] may be [ʃ], as in *child* [ʃaild].
[ʤ] may be [ʒ], as in *Jim* [ʒim].
[ʍ] > [w], as in *when* [wɛn].

Sounds Common to English and French, but with Variants in the Two Languages

English	French
Aspirated [pʿ, tʿ, kʿ]	Unaspirated [pʼ, tʼ, kʼ]
Alveolar [t, d, n]	Dental [t̪, d̪, n̪]
Dark [ł] (where used)	Clear [l̡]
Frictionless [r]	Trilled [r̃] or uvular [R]
[ɛ]	Lowered [ɛᵀ] before [r], which will suggest [æ].

French-English Dialects

French-English As Spoken by Speakers from France

As mentioned earlier (page 329), it is conventional, though not completely defensible, to characterize the English speech of most Parisians, and of upper rank French people generally, by the use of the uvular [R], and by the substitution of [s] for [θ] and [z] for [ð]. Contrariwise, the speech of most people of lower rank is conventionally characterized by the use of the trilled [r̃], and by the use of dental [t̪] for [θ] and dental [d̪] for [ð].

French Dialect—As Spoken by a Person Directly from France
From *Fashion*

Millinette: Oui, you mean wat espèce, what kind of personnes are Monsieur et Madame Tiffany. Ah, Monsieur ees not de same ting as Madame—not at all ... Monsieur is a man of business, Madame is lady of fashion. Monsieur make de money, Madame she spend it. Monsieur ees nobody at all, Madame everybody altogether. Ah, de money is all dat is necessaire in dis country to make one lady of fashion.   ANNA CORA MOWATT

You remember, my friend, dat a voyage you took
Wiz dat Frenchman distingué, le Capitaine Shook.
How to him a snuff box more superbe you present,
Because he speak French wiz such parfait accent.
Dey have actors, and poets, and musicien here,
And wan tip-topographical grand Engineer.

Exercise: Read aloud.

ju rimɛmbɛr, ma fren, dat ə vwajaːʒ ju tuk
wiz dat frɛnʃman distẽge, lə kapitɛn ʃuk.
au tu im ə snɑfbɑks mɔr supɛrb ju prizɛnt,
bikɔz i spik frɛnʃ wiz saʃ parfɛ aksɛnt.
de av aktɛrz an poɛts an myzisjɑ̃ ir,
an wan tiptɑpografikal grɑt ɑ̃ʒẽnir.

Exercise: Continue the transcription. Read aloud.

Wid de song and de dance de saloon shall resound,
And de jest, and the brandy smash too, shall abound.
Toujours you shall laugh, while on board here you are.
So mash—sacre bleu,—you get some sleep nevaire.
And de table! mon Dieu! mon Prince—nevaire, no nevaire
Shall a man eat so much as he has to eat here:
Four times each day is de table serve up.
To breakfast, to dinner, to tea, and to sup;
Four times each day you shall eat four times more
Than ever you eat in four days on de shore.

Ah, Paris! Your triomphes de table dey few is,
When compare with the table on the St. Louis:
Der is fowl, der is flesh and magnifique becasse,
Which the man who don't eat shall be set down an ass.
Der is fish which will fill de soul full delight,
And wild duck wiz his sauce dat will fill you up quite;
Den de beds of repose; dey are quite soft enough,
As Maccabess say to—"Lay on MacDuff";
And de julip de menthe, so delicious is he—
Jove his nectar would leave, and his ambroisie.
Oh, my friend, if once more you should see l'Amerique,
Introduce yourself straight to le Capitaine Floyd,
You will be, as Jean Bull say, too happy—be gar.
Mais adieu, I most stop, tho' I've much more to say,
Mais because he await me.

JEAN BON ST. ANDRÉ

French-Canadian

The French-Canadian dialect takes its color from the English abutting a given section of French Canada. In the East it is the Eastern American which in Maine and in the Maritime Provinces affects the French-Canadian. The thousands of French-Canadian people who have poured into New England to work in textile mills and other industries have particularly had their dialect modified by that of New England, in this case mainly by that of Massachusetts, Rhode Island, and Connecticut. Farther west, where the French area joins Vermont, New York, and eastern Ontario, much of the English is the General American, and the French-Canadian is affected accordingly.

The fact that in Quebec the schools are in French keeps the French component in Canadian French nearer to European French than the French of any other American area.

From *Belle Elmire*

Venez ici, mon cher ami, an' sit down by me—so
An' I will tole you story of old tam long ago—
W'en ev'ryt'ing is happy—w'en all de bird is sing
An' me!—I'm young an' strong lak moose an' not afraid no t'ing.
O dem was pleasure day for sure, dem day of long ago
W'en I was play wit' all de boy, an' all de girl also;
An' many tam w'en I'm alone an' t'ink of day gone by
An' pull latire an' spark de girl, I cry upon my eye.
Wall! we leev happy on de farm for nearly fifty year,
Till wan day on de summer tam—she die—ma belle Elmire.

Exercise: Read aloud.

vənez isi, mɔ̃ ʃɛr ami, an sid:aun ba mi, so,
an a wil tol ju stori av di ol tam lɔŋ əgo
wɛn ɛvritiŋ iz api, an ɔl də bɛrdz iz siŋ,
an mi, am jɔŋ an strɔŋ lak mus, an nɑt afrəd nɔtiŋ.
o: dɛm wɑz plɛʒər de fɔr ʃur dɛm de av lɔŋ əgo
wɛn a wɑz ple wɪt ɔl də bɔi, an ɔl də gɛrl ɔlso;
an ˈmɛni tam wɛn am alon an tiŋk av de gɔn bai,
an pul latir an spark də gɛrl, a krai ɑpɔn ma ai.
wɛl, wi liv api ɔn də fɑrm fɔr nirli fifti jir
til wan de ɔn də sɑmɛr tam,
ʃi dai, ma bɛl ɛlmir.

From *The Wreck of the Julie Plante*

A Legend of Lac-St. Pierre

On wan dark night on Lac St. Pierre,
De win' she blow, blow, blow,

An' de crew of de wood scow "Julie Plante"
Got scar't an' run below—
For de win' she blow lak hurricane,
Bimeby she blow some more,
An' de scow bus' up on Lac St. Pierre
Wan arpent from de shore.

Exercise: Read aloud.

ɔn wɑn dark nat ɔn lak sɛ̃ pjɛr,
də win ʃi blo, blo, blo.
an də kru ɑv də wud skau, "ʒuˡli plɑ̃t"
gɑt skɛrt an rɑn bilo—
fɔr də win ʃi blo lak ɑriken,
bamba ʃi blo sɑmːor,
an də skau bɑs ɑp ɔn lak sɛ̃ pjɛːr,
wɑn ɑrpɑ̃ frɑm də ʃor.

De captinne walk on de front deck,
An' walk de hin' deck too—
He call de crew from up de hole,
He call de cook also.
De cook she's name was Rosie,
She come from Montreal,
Was chambre maid on lumber barge,
On de Grande Lachine Canal.

Exercise: Read Aloud.

di kaptɛn wɔk ɔn də frɔ̃ dɛk,
an wɔk di ain dɛk tu.
i kɔl di kru ɑp frɑm de ol,
i kɔl di kuk ɔlso.
di kuk ʃiz nem wɑz rozi
ʃi kam frɑm mɔ̃real,
wɑz ʃɑ̃br med ɔn lambɛr barʒ,
ɔn di grɑ̃d laʃin kanal.

De win' she blow from nort-eas'-wes'—
De sout' win' she blow too,
W'en Rosie cry "Mon cher captinne,
Mon cher, w'at I shall do?"
Den de captinne t'row de big ankerre,
But still the scow she dreef,
De crew he can't pass on de shore,
Becos' he los' hees skeef.

Exercise: Read aloud.

> də win ʃi blo frɑm nort-is-wɛs,
> də saut win ʃi blo tu,
> wɛn rozi krai, "mɔ̃ ʃɛːr kaptɛn,
> mɔ̃ ʃɛːr, wɑt ʃal a du?"
> dɛn də kaptɛn tro də big ãkɛr,
> bɑt stil də skau ʃi drif,
> də kru i kant pas ɔn də ʃor,
> bikɔz i lɔs iz skif.

Exercise:

> De night was dark lak' wan black cat,
> De wave run high an' fas',
> W'en de captinne tak' de Rosie girl
> An' tie her to de mas'.
> Den he also tak' de life preserve,
> An' jomp off on de lak',
> An' say, "Good-bye, ma Rosie dear,
> I go drown for your sak'."
>
> Nex' morning very early
> About ha'f-pas' two—t'ree-four—
> De captinne—scow—an' de poor Rosie
> Was corpses on de shore,
> For de win' she blow lak' hurricane,
> Bimeby she blow some more,
> An' de scow bus' upon Lac St. Pierre,
> Wan arpent from de shore.

Moral

> Now all good wood scow sailor man
> Tak' warning by dat storm,
> An' go an' marry some nice French girl,
> An' leev on wan beeg farm.
> De win' can blow lak' hurricane
> An' s'pose she blow some more,
> You can't get drown on Lac St. Pierre
> So long you stay on shore.

WILLIAM HENRY DRUMMOND

Louisiana French-English

Louisiana French-English is sometimes called Creole, but more often "Cajan" or "Cajun." It is primarily the dialect of the French people who were transported by the British from Nova Scotia, or "Acadia," the word "Cajun" being a corruption of "Acadian." "Cajun" is not in good standing among the Louisiana French, because it has a peasant connotation and is used in a condescending or derogatory sense by other Louisianians, particularly other French people whose ancestors came directly from France.

The Acadians have lived in large numbers along the bayous and on the prairies of Louisiana and have spoken the French language for the greater part of two centuries. They still speak French today—a curiously leveled patois, in which the difficult French verb has lost intricacy until a Parisian cannot follow it, and in which even *je* and *tu* become often *mo* (from *moi*) and *to* (from *toi*) with the less educated speakers, including the Negroes who are descended from the slaves of French families.

It has been an interesting experiment—the isolation of a language from its mother sources, without a literature or an educational system of any great consequence, and with the surroundings essentially rustic. It is a situation comparable to that of the English language in the time of the Norman ascendancy, when in the hands of peasants it also lost inflection and leveled much—but not enough—of its irregularity.

French is still the home language of these folk, but nearly all of them, except some elderly and middle-aged people, speak English also. Naturally, their English is affected by the intrusion of French sound-patterns into English contexts. The resultant Creole dialect is very like that of the French-Canadians or of French immigrants. The main difference lies in the fact that the dialect, so far as it is English, is Southern American English, whereas French-Canadian is, as previously mentioned, based on English more like Eastern or General American English. Consequently, there are mingled with the trilled *r*'s of the French language the silent or softened *r*'s of the South, and with the pure French vowels, the diphthongs and melodic patterns of Southern colloquial speech. Since those who speak the most broken and typical French dialect tend to be the least educated of the French population, on the average it follows that their association is with the less educated non-French population. Hence they acquire the substandard Southern American English more readily than they acquire the polish and finish of educated Southern speech.

The characteristics of Southern speech, both standard and substandard, have been outlined in Chapter III. The following outline will therefore undertake to record only the characteristic deviations from that speech.

1. The silent final and pre-consonantal *r* of Southern speech often shows in Louisiana French dialect, despite the prevalence of the tongue-point trilled [r] (the uvular [ʀ] is practically unknown in Louisiana) in the French spoken in the family circle. Thus we may hear *fire* pronounced [faɪə], *her*, [hɜ], etc.

2. The prevalence of English is so great, it being the language of Louisiana

schools, that many English vowels not in French, such as [ɪ], [æ], [ɜ], [ʊ], etc., may appear in dialectal French English. Thus *sister*, pronounced [ˈsɪstə], may appear side by side with *sit* pronounced [sit].

3. The [ɑ > ɔ] substitution of the South readily finds lodgement in Louisiana French. Thus a *car* may readily be called a [kɔ], a *yard* a [jɔd], etc.

4. The [ɜ] > [ɜɪ] shift also appears often. Thus *heard* [hɜd] may be pronounced [hɜɪd].

5. As is true of French-Canadian English, the English [h] often intrudes where no [h] is needed, so that *up* [ʌp] may appear as [hɑp] or [hɔp].

6. Certain French contexts, when paralleled in English, may produce substitution:

a. In liaison, final [f] becomes [v] in the frequently used expression *neuf heures* [nœ ˈvœr]. This may induce a change in such contexts as *my wife had* [maɪ waɪv ad].

b. Similarly, *s* is so frequently [z] in French contexts that it very commonly becomes [z] in analogous English contexts, *viz.*:

In liaison, as in *mes amis* [mezaˈmi], *s* becomes [z] before a word beginning with a vowel. Hence *this arm* is likely to become [ziz ɑrm, diz ɑrm] and *nice apple* may become [naɪz apəl].

In *trans* before a vowel-letter, as in *transatlantique* [trɑ̃zatlɑ̃ˈtik], *s* becomes [z]. Hence *transalpine* may become [tranzalˈpaɪn].

s between a vowel and a voiced consonant becomes [z], as in *asbeste* [azˈbɛst]. Hence *asbestos* may become [azˈbɛstos], and *nice boy* may become [naɪz bɔɪ]. (See No. 5 above.)

c. *h* is normally not pronounced in French, and so words beginning with *h* in English are likely to be pronounced without it, as *hope* [op], *home* [om]. On the other hand, in the effort to conform to English pronunciation of *h*, the Frenchmen often uses the sound initially where it does not belong, as in [ˈhoˌvɛr] for *over*.

d. Since the plural sign *s* is not pronounced in French, *ami* and *amis*, for example, being alike [aˈmi], there is strong inclination not to pronounce the plural sign in English. Hence *boys* [bɔɪ], *strawberries* [ˈstrɔˌbɛrɪ], *leaves* [liv], etc.

e. Since *m* and *n* in French are so frequently "checked," i.e., serving only to produce nasalization of preceding vowels, they are likely to be so regarded in English. Hence *grandfather* [ˈgrɑ̃fɑˌdɛr].

7. French is spoken with tenser lips, more active tongue, and in general more vigorous and definite movement of the whole musculature than English. Every syllable is given individual and careful attention, and there is no unstressing of vowels, except mute *e*, which is itself more of a vowel entity than the unstressed [ə] of English. While individual words have little stress, French sentences

fall into phrases or breath-groups which themselves sound like very long words, with a definite rise or fall of the voice at the end of each. This gives to English ears a kind of lurching, staggering effect to French conversation. The rises and falls of voice are wider than in English, extending frequently to an entire octave. Thus the last syllable of a breath-group may be very high, or may drop entirely to a whisper, according to sense.[13] These qualities, especially that of careful, definite, vigorous syllabication, tend to carry over into French-English speech.

Dialect writers, not always accurately, but sometimes merely conventionally, use deviations not emphasized in the preceding outline. One such is *lak* for *like*, showing the omission of the second element of the diphthong. These often indicate individual idiosyncracies or hearing-impressions, and as such are valid. Dialect spelling will usually serve at least as clews, provided the symbol values are spoken as indicated above. The reader may often have to correct the writer, who is seldom a phonetician.

The following transcriptions will undertake to show the slight differences that distinguish the English of a Louisiana-French speaker:

From *Mayor of Bayou Pom Pom*

Alcide Exonerates Mayor

"Telesfore, maybe you forget dat meetin' we done had tonight on top of firehouse, hein? Well, an'way me, I make excuse fo' you. I see you in de bank w'en I pass by to de meetin' an' w'en you don'd show hup I tell dem you wo'k on beeg problem fo' de bank."

"Ah, mon ami, 'tis not de bank w'at mak' dat problem," said the mayor, who was now in a talkative mood, "'tis dat confoun' real estate wish mak' me all capsize. De real estate done inhale ma bank.

"Real estate, ma frien', is a business w'at an'one can enter in five mineet bot it tak' five year fo' git out off it. Especial, wen you drain off lan' an' loose in dose wide crack mak' by de drain, some off you hog an' cow, wat venture too far out. Yas andeed, den fo' mak' planty sale so as fo' catch back, you sell dat lan' on wat you call de "Axcitement plan," fo' a lil beat cash an' de balance wen day catch you. Yas, Alcide, dass how dat expression of "I got hees goat" come to be, cause only goat can eat dose paper note, I tell you dat.

"Tak' heah on de Bayou. W'en a man loose hees good job, he go into one off two business, Insurance or Real Estate. If he can read an' write he go into de Insurance business. Das why os in de bayou got so many people in Real Estate."

Alcide Exonerates Mayor
(Note mixture of French and Southern stress patterns.)

talɛsfor, mebi ju fɔrgat dat mitṇ wi dɔn ad ɔn tɑp ɑv fairaus, ɛ̃? wal, anwe,

[13] William A. Nitze, Ernest H. Wilkins and Clarence E. Parmenter, *A Handbook of French Phonetics* (New York: Holt, 1929), p. 68.

mi, a mek akskjus fo ju. a si ju in də baŋk wɛn a pas ba tu də mitn̩, an wɛn ju dond ʃo hɑp a tæl dɛm ju wɜik ɔn big prɔbˈlɛm fo də baŋk.

ɑ, mɔnaˈmi, tiz nɑt də baŋk wɑt mek dat prɔbˈlɛm, sɛd ðə meɪə, hu wəz naʊ ɪn ə tɔkətɪv mud, tiz dat ˈkɑnfaʊn ril ˈɛstet wiʃ mek mi ɔl kapˈsaiz. də ril ˈɛstet dɔn inˈhel ma baŋk.

ril ˈɛstet, ma fræn, iz ə bizˈnɛs wɑt ˈaniwɑn kan ɛnˈtær in fav miˈnit, bɑt tek fav jir fo gɪt aʊt ɔf it, aspæʃəl, wɛn ju dren ɔf lan, an luz in doz wad krak mek ba də dren, sɑm ɔf ju hɔg an kau, wɑt vantʃər tu fɑr aut, jæs ændid. dæn fo mek planti sel, so az fo katʃ bak, ju sæl dat lan ɔn wɑt ju kɔl di akˈsaitˈmɑ̃ plan, fo ə lɪl bit kaʃ an də balɑ̃s wɛn de katʃ ju. jæs, alsid, dæs hau dat ækspræsjɔ̃ ɔf ai gɑt iz got kɑm tu bi, kɔz onli got kan it doz pepər not, ai tæl ju dat.

tek iə ɔn də baiˈju wæn ə man lus iz gud dʒɔb, i go intu wan ɔf tu bizˈnɛs, ˈinʃurɑ̃s ɔr ril ˈɛstet. if i kan rid an rait, i go intu di ˈinʃurɑ̃s bizˈnɛs, an das waɪ ɔs in də baiˈju gɑt so mænɪ pipl̩ in ril ˈɛstet.

WALTER COQUILLE

From The Cajun

Exercise: *Transcribe and read aloud.*

Pierre: Julie ... Julie, my love.

Julie: Pierre, what has happen? Pierre—

Armide: Where is license, my son? Let me see.

Pierre: We ... Tante Armide, we must go out of state, Julie and me, for get marry.

Armide: Out of state! ... What you mean?

Pierre: Tante Armide ... I ... when I get to town I find the law make object for us to get marry, Julie and me. I go to the court, and the court say no! ... Two month ago—a law she was pass ... in the state. The judge he say he try to get word to the father, through all the parish ... but the road was so bad he can't reach us.

Armide: But the law, the law! What kind of law?

Pierre: The law—wait, I try make you explain. The law it say first cousin can't marry. Can't get license. They call it the First Cousin Law—

Julie: But we must to get marry. Our ... bann, she been read. I—I feel marry already.

Armide: What law is this, my son? What a way to treat good Catholic citizen —make law to say who they must marry! And how come they wait to pass law like that 'til you and Julie fall in love! ... Bah! What they think!

  . . . . . .

Listen, chère. This cross—This must I say, before you make marry; for the time is come when in the sight of God it is well to speak of such thing, of such sacred thing. When, after long time, I find another

little one is coming to me . . . . my mama, your grand-mama—up
there—what was Pierre' grand-mama too . . . she give this to me. She
say this was bless' by the Pope. And she say to me, "Take it and
wear it—and peace will be yours."

ADA JACK CARVER

Exercise: *Transcribe and read aloud.*

A *jeu d'esprit*, from the *Journal of the Louisiana Teachers' Association*, 1933.

Quartee,
Nouvelle Orleans.

Ma Good Fren:

Eet was good yes to see Quartee once more en read all about de school news
of de beeg ceetee; but doan you ceetee peepel t'ink for one momen' dat you
are so far ahead of de bayou, cuz I wan' tell you dat all durin' de summer our
school board was meetin' too, to balance de budget weech nobodee on de bayou
hear from befo dees year, no, ma fren, not even de school board.

Firs' place Jean Marie Landry, presiden' of de board, propose one budget
wid leetle salary reduction for de two teachair en doin way wid whole lot of
teeng dat de bayou school got een de las few years.

Jean Marie teenk dat seence de bayou now got two, tree radio, de cheeldren
doan need music appreciation een de school cuz dey leesten to song wat dey
doan understand noways; but wat you teenk, ma good fren? Theophile Martin,
wat own de beeg store in de parish seat en sell de phonograph record for de
school, he objec' en cuz hees brodair mak de assessbens, de school board teenk
maybe music ees a good teeng, so de presiden' he lose out on dat part of hees
budget plan.

Now, ma good fren, Jean Marie he doan wan cut no salary for de teechair,
cuz dey board buy his brodair house en it take almos' all de salary now to pay
de beel, so Jean Marie sugges' dat to geet de monaiy dey need de school board
charge de public for catching crawfeesh from de bank of the bayou on de
school groun'; but tree membair of de board wat weel run for re-election before
crawfeesh season end get fraid de public woan like dat, so Jean Marie he lose
again en de poor fellair say he got no more chance wid de board den wen he
get in one argumen' wid hees wife at home, yes.

Well, ma fren, de fight she go long time wid de board trying to save dees
en save dat, but dey can't save noways; no, ma fren, en de only place lef was
de payroll. Firs' dey wan' cut de man teacher from $73.65 to $64.80 en de ladee
from $70 to $60 en de publeek dey doan say notheeng; no, ma fren. Well de
board wait about tree week before dey pass final on de budget.

De teachair dey both come to de las meetin' and say someteeng about scienteefic salary-making base' on leeving wage, but de board say not even Nouvelle Orleans got nothing like dat, ma fren.

But de ladee, she owe de wife of one membair of de board tree dollair for making her one dress een de summair, en dat membair he agree wid her in private to fight to make her pay $63 eef she weel pay for de dress when she get firs' pay check, en you might be surprize', but de board agree to dat.

De man teachair tell de board he mus' have living wage too en eff dey make he's pay one dollair more den de $64.80 he weel cut de wood fo' de fire in de schoolhouse; but Auguste Landry always get dat job en he keeck, so de teachair lose.

Aftair all de budget she feex wid everybody satisfied excep' de teachair. De board tell dem to make up for de cut dey weel get more holiday dees year wid one week more vacation while de crawfeesh ees givin', extra time for Creesmus, en one week for Easter, so de teachair dey get satisfied too, ma fren.

But now, ma good fren, my wife she call for me to hol' de baby nose while she geev heem castor oil, so I mus' say au revoir.

Your good fren,
Jean Jacques Boudreaux
(H. W. Bierhorst)

Exercise: *Transcribe and read aloud.*

Coulée Croche, La.
le 6 mars, 1935

Chère Josephine Bobine:

I was in New Orlean' fo' de Mardi Gras wid ma sista wot work fo' de Relief. We stay to de Hotel Monteleon. Das a fine place, yas! Two kin hav de room an de bath (lak dey say) or dey can give you de bath by youself fo' 4 dollas an' ring up on de fone an' all lak dat. You can receive company eef you want an' go rock youself on de secon' flo' in de pawlaw, an dey don' neva tell yu nuttin'. It's don' make no different eef you tak' yo' self two bath, one in de mo'nin' and one at nite, an' you can use de fone all you want to. On de contrary, I don' neva see Mr. Monteleon. 'E leave you do jus' lak you want.

Ma parole d'honneur, it's a beeg crowd peeple dey got in de city! Ah neva knew to be so many. De parade dey pass an' pass, teel me, crazy fool dat ah am, ah don' know who's one mardigras from de odder. You walk an' walk an' git so ti'ed you don' see whare you goin'. As fo' me, ah sit on de sidewalk in front Maison Blanche to res' masalf an ah took off ma new shoe. Ma feet swole so much ah cooden' put dem back, so wat you t'ink? Ah go back to de hotel barefoot. Ah, chère, dat felt fine, yas! Ah tie ma shoestring an t'ro' de shoe across ma shoulda an use ma helbow an poosh troo de crowd an' den ah don' haf to go back to de hotel now, 'cause now ah can las' all day walkin' troo de street. Its

mo' fine de Mardi Gras here den to Coulée Croche. You mus' come an see
fo' yousalf one of dese days. Eh, bien, ah got to go feed ma chicken, so au revoir.
Come pass de day wid me Sonday. We gon' have gombo.

You fran,
Clothilde Cleopule

Humpie Starts the Game

Exercise: *Transcribe and read aloud.*

All this talk about the world's series between the St. Louis Cardinals and
the New York Yankees has penetrated at last to Bayou Pom Pom. It has done
more than penetrate. It has started emulation.

"Hey! Alcide, you jus' de man I wand fo' see," called Telesfore Boudreaux
to his friend, Alcide Lamazou, as he alighted from his horse to enter Papa
Felicien's General Merchandise Store.

"Because you got 'sperience as fiel' han'," continued Telesfore, "I wand you
to play in de center off de fiel' on h'our baseball team wat us jus' h'organize
an' wat us call de 'Bayous.'"

"Sh, ma frien', talk 'bout dat game we call 'Pitchin' de horse's shoe' an'
'croquet', hein, bot de game call baseball got dose two beat to piece.

"Las' Sonday, de 'Bayous' play de 'La Villes,' an' de game bust h'op wen
Gaby Trezemont mak' run home. Anyway, leave me start at de commencement.
Fo' play baseball each side mus' have nine mans in case you don't know. Each
mans got nam' fo' fit de position wat he play. For h'instant, de one wat pitch
an' de one wat ketch, day call Messeur Pitch an' Messeur Ketch an' dose wat
stan' on de tree sack, lak' us have on de levee at high water, day give dem nam'
off Messeur First, Second an' T'ird Base an' day select tall mans lak' you fo' de
fiel', fo' ketch high ball, an' nam' dem Messeur Right Fiel', Lef' Fiel' an'
Center Fiel', an' de shortes' mans on each side, day stan' heem in de back off
Messeur Pitch an' call heem Messeur Short Stop. Den day have one humpback
man wat don'd belong to eider side an' day nam' heem 'Humpie.' Hee's position
ees fo' keep bot' team mad all de time.

"In case day trow de baton or ball at heem, he don'd git hurt, fo' hees well
protect. He wear boid cage on hees haid an' beeg pad on hees chest an' laig.

"He start de game by trowin' de baton h'at one off de player, who ketch eet,
mad lak' an' dan a player from de opposite side wrassle wit' dat mans fo' de
possession off de baton, wat got nam' like dat night boid, leave me see wat dey
call, oh, yas, de bat. De side wat gain de bat, have wat you call, first h'innin'.
From wat I see las' Sonday de objec' off de gam', ees fo' Messeur Pitch fo'
strike down de mans wat hol' de bat, wat dey nam' de badder. W'en de ball
come hees way, he swing madly at eet, an' eef he hit eet, maybe he strike down
Messeur Pitch or any off hees man. Eef he miss, Messeur Ketch, wat crouch

behin' de badder, immeddiat'l return de ball to Messeur Pitch fo' annudder chanct. Eef by h'axiden' de badder strike de ball, like Alphonse Malonaise, he do, h'our firs' mans h'op, you mus' keep h'on runnin' ontil you touch wit' you foot dose tree sack which ees ver' far part. Whoever ketch de ball ees suppose' fo' hit you wit' eet, lak "Crackerbounce," bot not so long as you stay on dose sack.

"Dat Humpie git h'all ma peop'l mad, yas, wen he keep say' 'One strike,' wen Malonaise was not struck an' 'Two ball' wen we know you can'd play baseball wit' bot one ball, an' one time he call Malonaise a 'Foul,' nam' lak' chicken.

"An'way, Malonaise heet dat ball so strong dat he mak' t'ird base befo' eet was foun'.

"'Boobootz' Trosclair, secon' mans h'op, he speet on hees han' good. Dat ball pass queek, befo' he strike. 'One strike!' dat Humpie holler. 'Boobootz' look at heem, mad like an' poosh hees han' deep in de dust, fo' ketch one good hold on dat bat. He stan' h'op dare, brave like, an' tak' good aim. 'Bam!' he heet dat ball. Hot dog, dat ball she travel way h'op in de air till you cand see her no mo' fo' lil while an' she final' come down behin' de fence. By dat time 'Boobootz' walk almos' to secon' bag.

"Gaby Trezemont, t'ird mans h'op, wat was fanned by de ball wat pass so close by heem; de t'ird time he swing so hard dat he spin 'round lak' one top an' let slip from hees han' de bat, wat strike dat Humpie on de boid cage so hard dat Etienne Le Blanc, de tinsmit', spend one hour for cot de cage from off hees haid, off dat Humpie.

"W'en dat happen, some one holler 'One man's h'out.'

"W'en Messeur Humpie came to, he mak' bee line for Trezemont, who was not dare, so de game bus' h'op on 'count us was short one mans wat mak' wat day call in baseball 'Run Home.'"

WALTER COQUILLE

Bibliography

French

Books

Broussard, J. F., *Elements of French Pronunciation* (New York: Scribner's, 1918).

———, *Louisiana Creole Dialect* (Baton Rouge: Louisiana State University Press, 1942).

Guilléron, J., *Atlas Linguistique de la France* (Paris: H. Champion, 1902–10).

Nitze, W. A., Ernest H. Wilkins and Clarence E. Parmenter, *A Handbook of French Phonetics* (New York: Henry Holt and Co., 1929).

Nitze, W. A., and Ernest H. Wilkins, *The French Verb* (Chicago: University of Chicago Press, 1914).

Read, William A., *Louisiana-French* (Baton Rouge: Louisiana State University Press, University Studies, No. 5, 1931).

Periodicals

Carrière, J. M., "Creole Dialect of Missouri," *American Speech*, April, 1939.

Hall, Robert A., Jr., "French," Language Monograph No. 24, Structural Sketches 1, *Supplement to Language*, July-September, 1948.

Haden, Ernest F., "French Fricative Consonants," *American Speech*, October, 1937.

Lane, George S., "Notes on Louisiana French," *Language*, March, 1935.

CHAPTER 18

German

Until about the second quarter of the present century, German dialect was one of the commonest forms of broken English in America. German immigrants were scattered over the length and breadth of the land. In some areas they were concentrated in populous groups, as in Pennsylvania, south central Texas, St. Louis, Milwaukee, Iowa, and the north central states generally. As a result, the drama, poetry, and fiction of the century ending with the First World War became well sprinkled with German dialect, and a large fund of anecdote using the dialect floated continuously about. Nearly everyone in the United States and Canada heard German dialect often, and many people, especially those who retailed the anecdotes, could imitate it well. More often than not, actors and interpretative readers could imitate the dialect as a matter of course.

With the establishment of the quota system in 1921–24 as a means of controlling the flow of immigration into the United States, the stream of incoming Germans was abruptly checked. Immediately the volume of German dialect speech began to decrease rapidly. This rapid decrease was in some degree the result of attitudes growing out of the First World War, with its brief but sharp wave of anti-German prejudice. In a much larger measure, it was the result of the quota system itself, coupled with the extreme assimilability of the German people. The western European habits of the German immigrants, their customs and tastes, their fair complexions (an important item in a country unhappily conditioned against dark skins by its history of Negro slavery), and their varied occupations fitted them readily into the American scene. Their willingness to take up rural life promoted the distribution of most of them among the already Americanized population, and thus largely obviated such urban speech islands as those into which transplanted nationals from southern and central Europe congregated. Partly to avoid ridicule from their non-German fellows, and partly

364

in eagerness to seem completely American, most German children, except in areas of thickly settled immigrant population, insisted on speaking only English. As a result, the German language died in a single generation in most families, and the German dialect of English all but disappeared from the United States.

The Second World War hardly affected the situation as just described, except to interrupt still further the influx of German immigrants. There was no new rise of prejudice against the German language—rather the opposite, since the United States adopted during the war a national policy of studying all pertinent languages, both of enemies and of allies.

The situation nowadays indicates a new period in the history of German dialect in America. We still have our inheritance of dialect literature; we have a residue of anecdotal tradition; we have Pennsylvania German and Milwaukee German, two analogous dialectal forms containing a substratum of German idiom and syntax, often in the form of more or less literal translation, such as "The bread is all but the buns are yet." Though speakers of these dialects sound as if they could speak German, and though they may use a number of actual German words and phrases, often they can speak no German at all—only their somewhat oblique English. Their speech illustrates what happens when the concentration of an immigrant population is so great as partially to overpower the local English influence; lacking sufficiently frequent opportunity to compare their English with pure native English, the speakers tend to develop a distinctive type of English that is underlaid with a substratum of foreign characteristics.

In addition to the residues of the once ubiquitous German dialect just mentioned, there will always be, of course, the speech of such German immigrants as may still be permitted to come to America. All these instances of the existence of German dialect constitute sufficient reason for a continuance of its study. The persistence of German dialect literature, particularly, and the development of radio as a method of international communication, contribute also to this end.

The material following is designed to make the study of German dialect orderly and relatively accurate. Data are included to demonstrate why broken German-English takes on its identifying characteristics. Other data are added which, taken with the purely dialectal data, will aid speech correctionists in teaching German-speaking students to improve their English; and still further data are included to help speakers of English toward a better pronunciation of the German language.

The diagrams on the following page will serve to introduce the sounds of German.

CONSONANTS	Bi-labial	Labio-dental	Den-tal	Alve-olar	Palato-Alveolar	Palatal	Velar	Uvu-lar	Glot-tal
Plosive	p b		t d				k g		ʔ
Nasal	m		n				ŋ		
Lateral Non-fricative			l						
Trilled				r				R	
Fricative	ϕ^1 β^1	f v F¹		s z	ʃ³	ç	x γ¹		h
Frictionless Continuant		ʋ				j			
VOWELS	(y) (u) (Y) (ʊ) (ø) (o) (œ) (ɔ)					iy u ıY U eø o ə ε³œ³ ɔ³ a² ɑ³			

DIPHTHONGS:

   [ɑi];   variants, [aı, ɑy].

   [ɑu];   variant, [aʊ].

   [ɔi];   variants, [ɔı, ɔy].

Non-English Sounds in German

The strictly non-English sounds in German are [ϕ, β, F, ʋ, ç, x, γ, y, Y, ø, œ]. Of these, [y, ø, œ] have been described in the chapter on French, and need be mentioned only briefly here.

[ϕ] and [β], commonly referred to as *phi* and *beta* respectively, are a voiceless-voiced bilabial pair of consonants. [ϕ] is made by the simple blowing of air through tensely rounded lips; [β] is a buzzing sound made in the same way, with the addition of voice.

[F, ʋ] known as lax *f* and lax *v* respectively, are a voiceless-voiced pair of labiodental consonants, differing from ordinary [f] and [v] by being made with only very light contact of the lower lip and upper front teeth, or even with only a lax gesture toward such contact, with no actual touching of lip and teeth.

---

[1] Sounds generally regarded as non-standard, used in various parts of Germany. See explanatory notes on pages following. (The status of [β] and [γ] is debatable. Some authorities accept them as a standard form, but not for the stage.)

[2] The sound [a] does not appear in isolation in standard German, but is used by many individuals in the diphthongs [aı] and [aʊ]. See discussion later.

[3] The sounds [ʒ, ε̃, œ̃, ɑ̃, ɔ̃] sometimes appear with tables of German sounds alongside [ʃ, ε, œ, ɑ, ɔ] respectively, as aids in pronouncing French loan-words.

[ç], called the *ichlaut* [ˈɪçlɑut], is a voiceless fricative palatal consonant, made with the tip of the tongue down and the blade of the tongue arched upward toward the hard palate at a point just back of the alveolar ridge. The friction of the breath stream through the narrow horizontal slit between the tongue blade and the palate produces the sound. The sound [ç] is to be found in English as an allophone of /h/ when *h* occurs before *u* as in *hue*. If the pronunciation is performed with tense musculature, the result is [çu], rather than the lax [hju]. In German, [ç] is found before and after front vowels, as in *mich* [mɪç], and after *l* and *r*, as in *durch* [durç] and *Kelch* [kɛlç]. The voiced counterpart of [ç] is the fricative [j], as in French *travail* [traˈva:j].

[x] and [γ], called the *achlaut* [ˈɑxlɑut] and *gamma* respectively, are a voiceless-voiced pair of consonants. [x] is made by the friction of the breath stream between the velum and the arched rear portion of the dorsum of the tongue; [γ] by the same action, plus voice. [x] can be derived from [ç] by substituting a back vowel for a front vowel, as in *dich* [dɪç] > *Dach* [dɑx]. [γ] can then be arrived at by voicing [x].

The consonant [ʀ], called the uvular *r*, is made by the vibration of the uvula, plus voice, as in French.

The vowel [y] is made by pronouncing [i] as modified by having the lips rounded, as described in the chapter on French.

[Y] is made by pronouncing [ɪ] as modified by having the lips rounded.

[ø] is made by pronouncing [e] as modified by having the lips rounded, as described in the chapter on French.

[œ] is made by pronouncing [ɛ] as modified by having the lips rounded, as described in the chapter on French.

The Spelling of German Sounds

(NOTE: Students who wish to go directly to the consideration of the German dialect of English without a study of German orthography may reserve the material immediately following for reference and turn to page 393.)

An understanding of the way German sounds are spelled in German goes far toward explaining the defects of a literate German's English. His knowledge of the appearance of English on the page becomes actually a temporary handicap to him, since it tempts him to pronounce the English words in the German fashion. Often it is possible to determine whether a given error arises from hearing the English word or from seeing it. For example, a German hearing the word *up* [ʌp] is likely to repeat it with the substitution of some vowel near-by, saying [ɔp] or, more likely, [ɑp]; but if he sees *up* on the page, the German value of the *u* may assert itself in his mind, suggesting to him the pronunciation [up].

The following summary of the orthographic equivalents of the sounds of

German speech deals mainly with the spellings which are of Germanic origin. Except for names, German has borrowed much less than other languages, even from Greek and Latin, and so such a procedure is the appropriate one for a study of this kind. In the instance of certain Greek derivatives which have actually been assimilated into German, such as *Telegraph* [ˌteleˈɡrɑːf] and *Chronometer* [ˌkroːnoˈmeːtər], the Greek spellings have become a part of the German, and are so noted here. Latin words in German attract less attention orthographically than do Greek words, since the Latin and German values of corresponding symbols are so nearly identical. Compare Lat. *immoralitas* [ˌɪmoˈrɑːlɪtɑs], Ger. *Immoralität* [ˌɪmorɑliˈteːt].[4]

In the case of borrowings from modern languages, there has been a strong tendency to transplant with the foreign orthographies many of their foreign sound values. Compare *clown* [klɑun] for English [klaʊn], *Chef* [ʃɛf] for French [ʃɛf], *Cicerone* [ˌtʃitʃəˈroːnə] for Italian [ˌtʃitʃeˈrone]. These loan-words usually have little Germanization, and often none at all; as with loan-words in other languages, they are pronounced with a close approximation of their original native sound-values. The lesser used types of these will usually be omitted here, and when any are recorded, they will be distinguished from Germanic words.

The outstanding violations of the German sound-values for the letters of the alphabet in loan-words appear in words beginning with *c*, *ch* or *v*. *C* does not occur alone in German, but only in the clusters *sch*, *chs*, *ch* and *ck*. Since *ch* does not occur initially in Germanic roots, borrowing a foreign word beginning with *ch* requires either that the foreign sound-values be borrowed also, or that some German value be substituted. The same thing is true for an isolated *c*. As stated previously, the tendency is to approximate the foreign values, as in French *charge* [ʃɑrʒ]. But sometimes German values are substituted, as in *Citrone* [tsiˈtroːnə] for Castilian [θiˈtrɔn] or colonial Spanish [siˈtrɔn]. On the other hand, though *v* is always pronounced [f] in Germanic words, in borrowed words it is often pronounced [v], as in *Viper* [ˈviːpər], *vital* [viˈtɑːl].

It must be borne in mind that there are many dialects of German, each with its characteristic variations from the pronunciation of other dialects. Some of these variations will be noted, especially those that can be shown to affect the German's speaking of English.

The basic sound system here following will, however, consist principally of the sounds of High German (i.e., high*land* German, as contrasted with low*land* German), with considerable attention to stage pronunciation.

A word is necessary about stage pronunciation. As far back as 1896, conversations took place looking towards standardizing the pronunciations in serious drama, which was sometimes defined as classic and historical drama, and

---

[4] See p. 388 for discussion of the variant pronunciation of *ä* as [ɛː].

sometimes negatively and more inclusively as plays or parts of plays not requiring local or provincial dialect for characterization purposes or for comic effect. German phoneticians, linguists, and theatre people went into conference, and by 1898 had produced a systematic, uniform arrangement of the pronunciations of the various vowels, consonants, and combinations thereof which make up German spelling.[5] Though the pronunciations thus agreed upon have become the basis for the standard pronouncing dictionaries (cf. Viëtor's, mentioned in footnote 5 below, and Heath's German-English, English-German Dictionary[6]), these pronunciations have not all come to be used by the majority of the educated part of the population, even of the High German area. In the pages following, the stage pronunciations are usually set down as the accepted pronunciations; sometimes an alternate pronunciation is used instead, with comments.

Consonants

[p]

1. p wherever encountered in Germanic words, as in Psalm [psɑlm], Paar [pɑ:r], Kopf [kɔpf], Oper ['o:pər].

NOTES: (a) Exception must be made of p in the ph of words of Greek origin, as in Philosoph [ˌfiloˈzo:f].

(b) The p in pf is often labio-dental, under the assimilative influence of the f, as in Kopf. The cluster pf, initial as in Pfahl [pfɑ:l], or after m as in Kampf [kɑmpf], is often colloquially pronounced [f] in the North and Middle.[7]

2. pp wherever encountered, as in Mappe ['mɑpə], Krupp [krʊp].

3. b finally in words or syllables, alone or in a consonant cluster, as in Grab [grɑ:p], Herbst [hɛrpst], abhängen [ˈbˈapˌhɛŋən], Liebchen [ˈli:pçən], Erbse [ˈbˈɛrpsə], Trübsal [ˈtry:pˌzɑ:l].

NOTES: (a) Syllabication. In German syllabication a single intervocalic consonant, not a part of a separate word-building element, as in abändern [ˈapˌʔɛndərn], regularly goes with the following vowel, so that b in an inflectional form, such as Grabes [ˈgrɑ:bəs],

---

[5] Cf. Theodor Siebs, Deutsche Bühnenaussprache (Berlin, Köln und Leipzig: Albert Ahn, 1905), pp. 1–30; and Wilhelm Viëtor, Deutsches Aussprache-Wörterbuch (Leipzig: O. R. Reisland, 1915), pp. V–XI. The principal linguists and phoneticians concerned were Theodor Siebs (native of Bremen), Edward Sievers (native of Hesse), Karl Luick (native of Austria), Joseph Seemüller (native of Austria), and Wilhelm Viëtor (native of Nassau). Among the theater people concerned were men from Berlin, Brandenburg, Silesia and Austria. Thus all the principal parts of German-speaking Europe were represented.

[6] Karl Breul, Heath's New German and English Dictionary (Boston: Heath, 1939).

[7] Georg Hempl, German Orthography and Phonology (New York: Ginn, 1897.)

is not final in the syllable. In such cases it is therefore pronounced [b].[8]

(b) *Aspiration.* The voiceless [p], as in English, is more strongly
aspirated than its voiced opposite, [b]. That is to say, initial
[p] is more strongly aspirated than initial [b], and medial
[p] than medial [b].

In stage speech, it is enjoined that all [p]'s be aspirated.[9]
This injunction must be interpreted to mean that the aspiration be stronger than that of [b] in corresponding positions;
included is final [p] from *b*, as in *ob* [ʔɔpˤ], *taub* [taupˤ],[10]
which should be more strongly aspirated than a mere voiceless
(and, of course, lenis) [b]; i.e., on the stage, final [b̥] =
[pˤ], as in *Dieb* [diːpˤ].

(c) In normalized High German for general use, [p] is aspirated
when initial or final in a stressed syllable, or when medial and
spelled *pp*, as in *Pfannkuchen* [ˈpˤfanˌkuːxən], *Pabst* [pˤɑpst],
starb [ʃtarpˤ], *rappeln* [ˈrapˤəln].[11]

Exception can be made in the instance of medial [p] spelled
with a single *p*, as in *tapferig* [ˈtaːpfərɪç], which is even
weaker than English [p], as in *ripen.* In unstressed syllables,
as in *obgleich* [ɔpˈglaiç], *Palast* [paˈlast], [p] is regularly unaspirated.[12] Let it be emphasized that this unaspiration is
relative, being less than for an aspirated [p], but more than
for [b].

(d) *Some Dialectal Deviations.* In South and Middle Germany
the voiceless lenis [b], i.e., [b̥], is in many cases used for [p].[13]
Though this sound serves well enough for [p] in respect to
voicelessness, the lack of aspiration makes it possible for the
English ear to confuse it with [b]. Accordingly, German *platt*

---

[8] In addition to the convenience of drawing upon the arbitrary German rule for syllabication to explain the voicing here, we shall do well to remember that as a general
rule in language, an intervocalic consonant tends to become voiced. The same principle
will reappear presently in the discussion of *d* and *g*, which, though voiceless finally, remain
voiced intervocalically.

[9] Siebs, p. 74.

[10] The symbol for aspiration, [ˤ], will occasionally be used where it is desired to make
emphatic the contrast between aspirated and unaspirated sounds.

[11] Edward Prokosch, *Sounds and History of the German Language* (New York: Holt,
1916), p. 18, includes only "initial *p*, and *pp*." Wilhelm Viëtor, *German Pronunciation*
(Heilbronn: Henninger Bros., 1885), includes "initial [p], preceding an accented vowel, or
final [p] following one." In *Elemente der Phonetik* (Heilbronn: Gebr. Henninger, 1884),
p. 147, Viëtor says, "Neben starkbetontem Vokal tritt (zunächst im An- und Auslaut)
Aspiration des *p* ein."

[12] Prokosch, *Sounds and History,* p. 14.

[13] Viëtor, *Elemente,* p. 147; Viëtor, *German Pronunciation,* p. 37.

[pˤlɑt], if pronounced [b̥lɑt], may sound like *Blatt* [blɑt]. In the same way, a south or middle German, speaking English, may pronounce *pack* so that it will be heard by English ears as *back*. See reference to this deviation in the section later on German-English dialect.

(e) *pf*, as in *Pferd* [pfeːrt], is sometimes dialectally pronounced simply [f] in North and Central Germany.[14]

[b]

1. *b* wherever encountered, except finally in words or syllables, alone or in consonant clusters. Thus *Bibel* [ˈbiːbəl].

2. *bb* wherever encountered, as in Low German words and loan-words. Thus *Ebbe* [ˈɛbə], *sabbatlich* [ˈzabatlıç].

NOTES: (a) The generalization is often made that there are no voiced plosives in South and Middle Germany.[15] There initial *b* is pronounced with the voiceless lenis [b], i.e., [b̥]. In that [b̥] is unaspirate, it resembles [b], but in that it is voiceless, it resembles [p], so that *Blatt* [blɑt], pronounced as [b̥lɑt] may be confused with *platt* [plɑt]. This has a bearing on the pronunciation of English by a South or Middle German, in that his rendition of *bay* with [b̥] may, despite the lack of aspiration, be heard as *pay*.

(b) Intervocalically, *b* in South and Middle Germany is likewise often not a plosive, but the bilabial spirant [β]. Thus *aber* [ˈaːβər], *über* [ˈyːβər].[16] The sound [β] is, of course, not in English. English-speaking listeners usually hear it as [w] or [v].

[t]

1. *t* wherever encountered in Germanic words, as in *Tat* [tɑːt], *Knecht* [knɛçt], *Tante* [ˈtantə].

2. *tt* wherever encountered, as in *bitten* [ˈbɪtn̩], *schnitt* [ʃnɪt].

3. *dt* wherever encountered, as in *Stadt* [ʃtat].

4. *th* in certain Germanic words written or printed before 1901, such as *Thal* [tɑːl], now *Tal; Rathszimmer* [ˈrɑːtsˌtsɪmər], now *Ratszimmer*.

5. *th* also currently in words of foreign, usually Greek, origin, such as *Thema* [ˈteːmɑ], *Theologie* [ˌteoloˈgiː], *Theater* [teˈaːtər].

6. *d* finally in words or syllables, as in *Bad* [bɑːt], *todmüde* [ˈtoːtˌmyːdə].

7. As the first sound in the voiceless affricate [ts], spelled *z, tz*, as in *Zimmer* [ˈtsɪmər], *Graz* [grɑts], *Satz* [zɑts]. [ts] also occurs in Romance derivatives in

---

[14] Siebs, p. 58; Hempl, p. 145.
[15] Prokosch, p. 15; Viëtor, *Elemente*, p. 147.
[16] Prokosch, p. 16.

-tial, -tion, -tient, etc., as in *Aspiration* [ˌɑspirɑtsɪˈoːn]; it is also spelled with initial *c* before *e* or *i*, as in *Ces* [tsɛs].

NOTES: (a) As in the case of *b*, p. 369, in the syllabication of inflectional forms, like *Bades* [ˈbɑːdəs] (from *Bad*), the *d* goes with the vowel following, thus ceases to be final, and is thereupon voiced, like other initial consonants in German, and like intervocalic consonants in language in general.

(b) *Aspiration.* The voiceless [t], as in English, is more strongly aspirated than its voiced opposite [d]. That is, initial [t] is more strongly aspirated than initial [d], and medial [t] than medial [d].

In stage speech, it is urged that all [t]'s be aspirated.[17] This must be taken to mean that the aspiration should be stronger than that of [d] in corresponding positions; this would include final [t] from [d], as in *Rad* [rɑːtˀ], which should in stage speech be more strongly aspirated than a voiceless lenis [d], i.e., [d̥].

(c) In normalized High German for general use, [t] is aspirated when initial or final in a stressed syllable, or when medial and spelled with *tt*, as in *Tat* [tˀɑːtˀ], *Ritter* [ˈrɪtˀər].[18] It is possible to except a single medial *t* as in *deutet* [ˈdɔitət]. In unstressed syllables, as in *entschliessen* [ɛntˈʃliːsən], *lautet* [ˈlautət], [t] is regularly unaspirated. So with [d̥] = [t], as in *Rad* [rɑːt].[19] Such unaspiration is, of course, relative; it is less than that for an aspirated [t], and more than for [d].

(d) *Some dialectal substitutions.* In South and Middle Germany there is, as a general thing, no [d], but instead a substituted voiceless [d], i.e., [d̥].[20] This [d], so far as its unaspiration identifies it, serves for [d]; but since it is voiceless, it resembles [t], so that *Dahl* [dɑːl] may be mistaken by the hearer for *Tal* [tɑːl].

It follows that a South or Middle German, pronouncing English *dime* with [d̥], may be thought by English-speaking hearers to have said *time*. See reference to this deviation in the section later on German-English dialect.

[17] Siebs, p. 74.

[18] Prokosch, p. 19, "Initial *t* and medial *tt* are aspirated fortes"; Viëtor, *Elemente*, p. 145, "Vor oder im Auslaut nach starkbetontem Vokal tritt Aspiration ein."

[19] Prokosch, p. 19. "Many Germans, especially in the North, do distinguish these sounds."

[20] Viëtor, *Elemente*, p. 145, "In Süd- und Mitteldeutschland gilt für *d* stimmloses *d*, welches .... auch in das Gebiet des *t* übergreift"; Prokosch, p. 19, "South and Middle Germans substitute their voiceless lenis [d̥] for voiced [d]."

(e) *Dentality*. The sound [t] is farther front in German than in English. Though German [t] is not always made with the tongue completely against the teeth, the tongue is closer to the teeth (postdental or pre-alveolar, as contrasted with the English alvoelar [t]).[21] We may generalize by saying that German [t] can be roughly designated as dental, that it is indubitably more nearly so than in English, but that it is less aggressively so than in the Romance languages. When it is desired to emphasize dentality, the symbol [.] can be used; thus [t̪]. (Statements corresponding to those in this paragraph can be made for German [d] and [n]. See references under these two symbols later.)

[d]

1. *d* wherever encountered, except finally in words or syllables, alone or in a consonant cluster. Thus *Dame* [ˈdaːmə], *reden* [ˈreːdn̩].

2. *dd* wherever encountered, usually in words of Low German origin, such as *Kladde* [ˈkladə].

NOTES: (a) *Dentality*. German [d] is more nearly dental than English [d], less aggressively so than Romance [d]. (See discussion in Note (e) under [t] above.) When it is desired to emphasize dentality, the symbol [.] may be used; thus [d̪].

(b) *Some dialectal deviations*. South and Middle Germans have, in general, no voiced plosives, hence no [d]. They use instead, the voiceless lenis [d], i. e.,[d̥].[22] Since [d̥] is voiceless, it may, notwithstanding its lack of aspiration, become confused with [t], so that *Dahl*, pronounced with [d̥], may be mistaken for *Tal*.

Similarly a South or Middle German, speaking English, may pronounce *dole* with [d̥], so that the English-speaking hearer may mistake it for *toll*. See references to this matter in the section later on German-English dialect.

[k]

1. *k* wherever encountered, as in *Knabe* [ˈknaːbə], *Kirche* [ˈkɪrçə].
2. *ck* wherever encountered, as in *Backstein* [ˈbak̩ʃtain].
3. Initial *ch* before back vowels or consonants in Greek derivatives, as in *Character* [kaˈraktər], *Chor* [koːr], *christlich* [ˈkrɪstlɪç], *chromatisch* [kroˈmaːtɪʃ].
4. The first sound in [ks] (spelled *x*), as in *existieren* [ˌɛksɪsˈtiːrən].
5. *ch* in the cluster *chs*, as in *wachsen* [ˈvaksən], *Ochs* [ɔks], *wechseln* [ˈvɛksəln].
6. *q* in the cluster *qu*, as in *Quelle* [ˈkvɛlə], *Quadrat* [kvadˈraːt].

21 Prokosch, p. 18; Siebs, p. 74; Viëtor, *Kleine Phonetik*, p. 144; *Elemente*, 67.
22 Prokosch, p. 19; Viëtor, *Elemente*, p. 145.

7. c (occasionally cc) before a, o, u, or a consonant in a variety of foreign loan-words, such as Café [ka¹fe:], Clique [kli:k], Accord [a¹kɔrt], etc., most of which have been respelled; cf. Kaffee, Akkord.

8. In stage speech, g final, alone or in a consonant cluster, after any vowel but i, and even after i if lich follows.[23] Thus Tag [tɑ:k], Weg [ve:k], Krieg [kri:k], Herzog [¹hɛr₁tso:k], Zug [tsu:k], Augsburg [¹ɑuks₁burk], Berg [bɛrk], königlich [¹kø:nɪklɪç], fragte [¹frɑ:ktə].

NOTES: (a) The voiceless [k], like English [k], is more strongly aspirated than its voiced counterpart, [g]. That is, initial [k] is more strongly aspirated than initial [g], and medial [k] more than medial [g].

In stage speech the instructions are to aspirate all [k]'s.[24] This must be interpreted to mean that the aspiration is stronger than that of [g] in corresponding positions; this interpretation would apply also to final [k] from g, which should be more strongly aspirated than a voiceless lenis [g], i.e., [g̊].

(b) In normalized High German for general use, [k] is aspirated when initial or final with a stressed vowel, or when medial and spelled with ck (= [k]), as in Koch [kʻɔx], Röcke [¹rœkʻə], Bock [bɔkʻ].[25] In unstressed syllables, as in exakt [ɛks¹ʔɑkt], Erika [ɛ¹ri:kɑ], [k] is relatively unaspirated; that is, it is less aspirated than an initial [k], more aspirated than a [g].

(c) Some dialectal deviations. In South and Middle Germany, the people do not aspirate k before consonants.[26] That is, they use the lenis voiceless [g] = [g̊] instead. Thus Kraus closely resembles Graus. Some (e.g., in Saxony and Thuringia) use [g̊] for [k] even before vowels, so that Kaiser may sound like Geiser, and Kaffee like [gɑ¹fe:].

It follows that South or Middle Germans, in speaking English, may not aspirate [k] in crew and thus may be understood by English-speaking hearers to have said grew. Similarly, cold may sound like gold, and coast like ghost. This matter will be referred to in the section on German-English dialect.

[g]

1. g wherever encountered, except finally (alone or in a consonant cluster).

[23] Siebs, pp. 75–76; Hempl, p. 130; Prokosch, p. 28.
[24] Siebs, p. 75.
[25] Prokosch, p. 28; Viëtor, Kleine Phonetik, p. 65. Prokosch disagrees with Viëtor in respect to [k] final in stressed syllables; he states that it is unaspirated.
[26] Prokosch, p. 29; Viëtor, Elemente, p. 142.

Thus, *gelten* [ˈgɛltn̩], *Gipfel* [ˈgɪpfəl], *Aufgabe* [ˈaufˌgaːbə], *Gläubiger* [ˈglɔibɪgər], *Tage* [ˈtaːgə], *Gnom* [gnoːm].

2. *gg* wherever encountered, usually in words originally Low German, such as *Dogger* [ˈdɔgər], *Egge* [ˈɛgə], *Flagge* [ˈflagə].

NOTES: *Dialectal variations.* (a) In North Germany intervocalic *g* after a back vowel is frequently pronounced [ɣ] (variant [x]), as in [ˈtaːɣə].[27] In Berlin even initial *g* may be pronounced [ɣ].[28] Intervocalically in the endings *ige, iges,* etc., *g* is pronounced [j] in North Germany. Thus, *Könige* [ˈkøːnɪjə], *wichtige* [ˈvɪçtɪjə].[29] These pronounciations, although regional, are not regarded as precisely substandard for daily use, but are forbidden on the stage.[30]

(b) In Central and South Germany, *g* is very frequently voiceless and thus sounds like [k], even though lacking the aspiration of [k].[31] *Graus* may accordingly sound like *Kraus*, *Gram* like *Kram*, and *Geiser* like *Kaiser*.

It follows that when a Central or South German is pronouncing English, his *grime* may sound like *crime*, *grow* like *crow*, *gale* like *kale*, etc.

[ʔ]

[ʔ] is the glottal stop or voiceless plosive made by closing the glottis, building up air pressure below it, and suddenly opening it to permit an out-going puff of the breath.

The glottal stop, [ʔ], occurs before a stressed initial syllable beginning with a vowel. Thus, *meine eigene Heimat* [mainə ʔaigənə ˈhaimat]. A vowel is regarded as initial when preceded by the separable prefix of a verb, as in *verehren* [fɛrˈʔeːrən], or when in any instance of a stressed syllable beginning with a vowel it appears in a compound, the parts of which are felt to have a separate existence, as in *Verein* [fɛrˈʔain].

NOTES: (a) The glottal stop is not strictly a phoneme of the same order as the sounds of which words are composed. It is rather a boundary-marker—the type of phoneme called juncture. Specifically, it is an allophone of the plus juncture phoneme, viz., [+].

---

[27] Viëtor, *Elemente,* p. 105.
[28] Viëtor, *German Pronunciation,* p. 52. See pp. 50–56 for a large number of regional variations of the velar consonants.
[29] Prokosch, p. 30.
[30] Siebs, pp. 69–70.
[31] Viëtor, *Elemente,* p. 142.

(b) The glottal stop is convenient to prevent ambiguity in both German and English. It helps distinguish *der Igel* [de:r ˡʔiːgəl] from *der Riegel* [deːrːiːgəl], just as it helps distinguish *slim Anne* [slɪm ʔæn] from *slim man* [slɪmːæn]. (The long consonants [rː] and [mː], whose added length is also an allophone of the plus juncture phoneme, can distinguish minimal pairs without [ʔ], thus: / de·ri·gəl – de·r + rigəl /, / slɪm æn – slɪm + mæn / .) South Germans use the glottal stop seldom or not at all.

[m]

1. *m* wherever encountered, as in *Memel* [ˡmeːməl], *Strom* [ʃtroːm].
2. *mm* wherever encountered, as in *Stimme* [ˡʃtɪmə], *Stamm* [ʃtɑm].

NOTE: German [m] is always short and abrupt.

[n]

1. *n* wherever encountered (except in the clusters *ng, nk*), as in *nun* [nuːn], *ohne* [ˡoːnə]. (*n* may, of course, be pronounced *m* by assimilation, as in *leben* [ˡleːbən > ˡleːbm̩].)
2. *nn* wherever encountered, as in *brennen* [ˡbrɛnən], *dünn* [dʏn].

NOTES: (a) German [n] is farther front than English [n], but (see notes *ante* on [t] and [d]) less conspicuously dental than in the Romance languages. When it is desired to emphasize dentality, the sign [ˌ] can be used.
(b) German [n] is always short and abrupt.

[ŋ]

1. *ng* wherever encountered in Germanic words, as in *Finger* [ˡfɪŋər], *Singer* [ˡzɪŋər], *Entwicklung* [entˡvɪklʊŋ].
2. *n* before *k*, as in *Finke* [ˡfɪŋkə].

NOTE: *ng* is dialectally pronounced [ŋk], as in *Ring* [rɪŋk], and even [ŋg], as in *ringen* [ˡrɪŋgən], by some speakers in parts of Germany, particularly in the Northwest.[32] This accounts for [ŋk], [ŋg] in German-English dialect, as will be seen later.

[l]

1. *l* wherever encountered, as in *lassen* [ˡlɑsən], *viele* [ˡfiːlə], *kühl* [kyːl].
2. *ll* wherever encountered, as in *bellen* [ˡbɛlən], *hell* [hɛl].

NOTE: German [l] tends, on the average, to be more nearly front or

[32] Viëtor, *German Pronunciation*, p. 32; Prokosch, p. 29.

clear than English [l], but varies greatly among individuals, dialectal regions and phonetic contexts. As to the last, the presence of front vowels induces front [l], especially in the case of [l] followed by a high front vowel. But it is not as conspicuously front as the [l] of Romance languages. Accordingly, it can seldom be called dental; but it is far enough front to be called pre-alveolar. When a symbol for clear [l] is needed, [ļ] can be used.

[r]

[r] is the tongue-point trill, made with the vibration of the tip of the tongue against the alveolar ridge. The velum closes the nasal passages.

1. *r* wherever encountered, as in *Reuter* ['rɔitər], *Garn* [gɑrn].
2. *rr* wherever encountered, as in *irren* ['ɪrən], *Pfarrer* ['pfɑrər].

NOTES: (a) No special symbol for trilling is consistently used in this book, it being understood that in most languages, aside from English, [r] is trilled.

(b) The tongue point trill is obligatory on the stage.[33] It is used in everyday speech throughout Germany, except in cities and elsewhere where the uvular variety, i.e., [R], has displaced it.

(c) In cities and among individuals elsewhere, postvocalic [r] often weakens to a very reduced trill, or to [ə], which in turn may be exaggerated (e.g., in Berlin) to [ɑ], as in [ve:r, ve:ə, ve:ɑ] for *wer* [ve:r]. After stressed [ɑ], postvocalic [r] may even become silent, as in ['vɑ:hait] for *Wahrheit* ['vɑ:rhait].[34]

[R]

[R] is the uvular trill. It is made with the tongue lying flat except at the back, where it rises toward the uvula, permitting the latter to touch the tongue or to lie in the median raphe or furrow of the tongue. Here, actuated by the outgoing breath, the uvula vibrates and produces the sound [R]. The velum closes the nasal passages.

1. *r* wherever encountered, as in *rot* [Ro:t], *Prall* [pRɑl], *Diener* ['di:nəR], *Führer* ['fy:RəR].
2. *rr* wherever encountered, as in *klirren* ['klɪRən].

---

[33] Siebs, pp. 56–55.
[34] Viëtor, *Elemente*, p. 129, "Im Auslaut tritt für -r, -er vielfach ein a- oder auch a-Laut ein, die jedoch keinen Ausspruch auf orthoepische Anerkennung machen können." Apparently Viëtor is groping for a value to assign to this reduced *r*. In general, [ə] is doubtless a reasonable choice, though some value of [ɑ] is sometimes clearly present. Viëtor himself (pp. 41 and 104) mentions [ə]. He adds (p. 29) that tongue-point [r] may also weaken to the same [ə]-like sound, or even (p. 105) become entirely silent. "In Wiesbaden höre ich in der Sprache des untern Mittelstandes keinen Unterschied zwischen *ja* und *Jahr, hat* und *hart*." See also Siebs, pp. 55–56.

NOTES: (a) [R] is forbidden on the stage in serious drama.

(b) [ʀ] in rapid speech, and with some speakers in all speech, weakens to the so-called uvular scrape (symbol [ʁ]), which is made with a weak fluttering of the uvula, rather than a clear trill. Postvocalically, the sound is often further weakened to a mere friction of the airstream passing between the back of the tongue and the soft palate at the point of the uvula, and sounding like a fricative, retracted [ə]. Often this [ə] evolves into a frictionless [ə], as in English *fear* [fɪə], or (particularly in Berlin) into an [ɑ]. Thus *der* may be heard as [deːʁ], [deːə], or (in Berlin) [deːɑ]. After [ɑ], *r* has been known, e.g., in Wiesbaden, to disappear, as in [bɑːt] for *Bart* [bɑːʁt].

The weak [ʁ] is said to evolve at times before *t* into [x], as in [ˈtsɑːxtən] for *zarten* [ˈtsɑːʁtən].[35]

(c) Many German scholars oppose [R] and [ʁ] violently for use in serious drama, and actually for all purposes. They regard it as unpleasant to the ear, lacking in precision and intelligibility, and liable to confusion with [x–γ]. They scorn it as having been borrowed from the French in an attitude of social-climbing snobbery. Prokosch[36] says, "The stage pronunciation and the majority of phonetic authorities unconditionally require the dental *r*." Siebs is equally emphatic,[37] and Trautmann is aggressively satiric concerning "das Zäpfchen-r," i.e., the uvular [R].[38]

[ɸ]

[ɸ] is the voiceless bilabial spirant. It is made by almost closing the lips and blowing out the breath. It corresponds to the voiced bilabial spirant [β]. The velum closes the nasal passages.

1. *w* and *u* (in *qu*) in dialectal Middle and South German; quite frequently in the combinations *qu*, *zw*, and *schw*, where it is not particularly condemned; but it is known even as a substitute initial *w*,[39] where it is not well regarded.

[35] Siebs, pp. 55–56.
[36] *Op. cit.*, p. 31.
[37] *Op. cit.*, p. 55, "Es ist in allen Fällen durchaus gerolltes Zungenspitzen-r zu fordern."
[38] Moritz Trautmann, *Kleine Lautlehre des Deutschen, Französischen und Englischen* (Bonn: C. Georgi's Buchdruckerei, 1903), pp. 97 ff. "Das Zäpfchen-r ist kein ursprünglich deustcher Laut, sondern ist vor wenig mehr als 150 Jahren aus Frankreich eingeschleppt worden. Dies wird am meisten durch die Tatsache bewiesen, dass die Zäpfchen-r-Laute hauptsächlich bei den Gebildeten und in den Städten zu Hause sind . . . . Die Verbreitung und Verteilung von Zungen- und Zäpfchen-r war bis vor Kurzem und ist in der Hauptsache noch heute keine örtliche, sondern wesentlich eine gesellschaftliche. Und hierin liegt der Beweis, dass das Zäpfchen-r aus Frankreich zu uns gekommen ist. In diesem Lande ward bald nach 1650 das Zäpfchen-r-Sprechen aufgebracht, und es kam im Laufe der Zeit in der feinen französischen Gesellschaft immer mehr in Auf-

Thus, *Quartier* [kɸarˈtiːr], *Zweig* [tsɸaiç], *Schwert* [ʃɸeːrt], *wandeln* [ˈɸandəln], for stage [kvarˈtiːr], [tsvaik], [ʃveːrt], [ˈvandəln], and standard High German [kʋarˈtiːr], [tsʋaiç], [ʃʋeːrt], [ˈvandəln]. In *qua*, *zw*, and *schw*, North Germans also use [ɸ], as above.[40]

NOTES: (a) Stage speech demands [v] in all the spellings above.[41]

(b) Standard High German uses [v] also, but permits [ʋ] (i.e., the lax [v], q. v.) in *qu*, *zw*, and *schw*.[42]

[β]

This is the voiced bilabial spirant. It is made by almost closing the lips and forcing the voiced breath stream through the resulting opening. The velum closes the nasal passages.

1. *w* and *u* (in *qu*) in regional pronunciation in Middle and South Germany, as in *Willen* [ˈβɪlən], *schwingen* [ˈʃβɪŋən], *Zwielicht* [ˈtsβiːlıçt], *Quantität* [ˌkβantiˈteːt] for [ˈvɪlən], [ˈʃʋɪŋən], [ˈtsʋiːlıçt], [ˌkʋantiˈteːt].[43] Though prohibited for the stage in serious drama, it is reasonably well regarded for daily use. In North Germany, [β] is used[44] in *qu*, *schw*, *zw*, as in *Qual* [kβaːl], *Schwalben* [ˈʃβalbən], *Zwieback* [ˈtsβiːbak], for stage [kvaːl], [ˈʃvalbən], [ˈtsviːbak], and for general High German [kʋaːl], [ˈʃʋalbən], [ˈtsʋiːbak]. It is not, however, used for *w* in other contexts.

[F]

[F] is the voiceless opposite of the lax [ʋ]. [F] is made with the upper front teeth barely touching, or almost touching, the lower lip, usually at the inner surface.

1. *u* (in *qu*) as a non-significant variant of [ʋ] (q.v. below), as in [kFeːr], [kFarts] for *quer* [kʋeːr], *Quartz* [kʋarts].

2. *w* in *schw*, *zw*, as a non-significant variant of [ʋ], as in [tsFɛk], [ˈtsFantsıç] for *Zweck* [tsʋɛk], *zwanzig* [ˈtsʋantsıç].

nahme. Um 1650 und noch hundert Jahre länger schlief das Selbstgefühl des deutschen Volkes einen totähnlichen Schlummer; der gebildete Deutsche kannte kein höheres Ziel als zu denken und zu tun wie der Franzose; ... wie jede französische Mode getreulich von ihr nachgeahmt wurde, so musste auch geschnarrt werden, wie man in Paris schnarrt. Liessen sich nun jene trefflichen Deutschen herbei, ihre Muttersprache zu reden, so übertragen sie natürlich die 'feinen' französischen Laute auch in diese, und so kam das Deutsche zum Zäpfchen-r."

[39] Viëtor, *German Pronunciation*, pp. 39–40; *Kleine Phonetik*, p. 60–61; Hempl, p. 156.
[40] Prokosch, p. 16; Hempl, p. 156.
[41] Siebs, p. 59.
[42] Prokosch, p. 17.
[43] Hempl, p. 156; Viëtor, *Kleine Phonetik*, pp. 60–61, *German Pronunciation*, pp. 39–40; Prokosch, p. 16.
[44] Hempl, p. 156; Prokosch, p. 16.

[ʋ]

[ʋ] is the lax [v]. It is made with the upper front teeth touching, or almost touching, the lower lip, usually at the inner edge.

1. *u* (in *qu*), as in *bequem* [bəˈkʋe:m], *qualitativ* [ˌkʋalitaˈti:f].
2. *w* in *schw*, *zw*, as in *schwer* [ʃʋe:r], *zwar* [tsʋɑ:r].

NOTE: [ʋ] is accepted in general High German, but [v] is required for the stage.

[f]

1. *f* wherever encountered, as in *faul* [faul], *Zipf* [tsɪpf].
2. *ff* wherever encountered, as in *Schiffe* [ˈʃɪfə].
3. *ph* in words of Greek origin, such as *Phonologie* [fonoloˈgi:].
4. *v* wherever encountered in Germanic words, as in *viel* [fi:l], in completely Germanized foreign words and finally, as in *Vaterland* [ˈfɑ:tərlɑnt], *Vitrine* [fiˈtri:nə], *Vitriol* [fitriˈo:l], *genitiv* [geniˈti:f].

NOTES: (a) North Germans tend to pronounce *v* in foreign words as [v] except when it is final.[45]

(b) Middle and South Germans tend to pronounce *v* in foreign words as [β], except when final.[46]

[v]

1. *w* wherever encountered in stage speech, as in *Wasser* [ˈvasər], *Löwe* [ˈlø:ve].
2. *v* in certain foreign loan-words not completely Germanized, such as *Ventilator* [ˌvɛntiˈla:tor], *Vatikan* [ˌvatiˈka:n], *Universität* [ˌunivɛrziˈte:t], and in Low German names such as *Ravensberg* [ˈra:vənsˌbɛrç].
3. *u* (in *qu*) in stage speech, as in *quadratisch* [kvadˈra:tɪʃ].

NOTES: (a) In much standard High German, *w* and *u* in *schw*, *zw*, and *qu* are pronounced [ʋ], as in *Schwanz* [ʃʋants], *Zweifel* [ˈtsʋaifəl], *quadratisch* [kʋadˈra:tɪʃ].

(b) South and Middle dialectally substitute [β] and even [ɸ] for [v],[47] and North Germans for [ʋ] in *schw*, *zw*, *qu*.[48]

[s]

1. *s* in the absolute final position in words and syllables, and in final consonant clusters (excepting *sch* [ʃ]), as in *das* [das], *Palast* [paˈlast], *Maske* [ˈmaskə], *ebenfalls* [ˈe:bənˌfals], *Rätsel* [ˈre:tsəl], *Fuchs* [fuks].

---

[45] Hempl, p. 155.

[46] Hempl, p. 155.

[47] Hempl, p. 156; Viëtor, *Kleine Phonetik*, pp. 60–61, *German Pronunciation*, pp. 39–40.

[48] Hempl, p. 156.

2. *ss* and *ß* (called *Ess-tset*), wherever encountered, as in *bloß* [blo:s], *essen* [ˈɛsən], *ißt* [ɪst], *Fuß* [fu:s], *Füße* [ˈfy:sə], *Kuß* [kʊs], *Küsse* [ˈkʏsə].

[z]

1. *s* initially and intervocalically, as in *Seele* [ˈze:lə], *Rose* [ˈro:zə]. (Initial *s* is still considered initial even when preceded by a word or syllable in compounding and word building, as in *langsam* [ˈlaŋza:m], *desselbe* [dɛsˈzɛlbə].)

2. *s* after *m*, *l*, *n* is [z], as in *Gemse* [ˈgɛmzə], *Elsa* [ˈɛlza:], *Gänse* [ˈgɛnzə]. But *s* is not pronounced [z] when initial in the consonant cluster *sch*, as in *schon* [ʃo:n], nor in the clusters *sp* and *st* used initially in words and syllables, as in *sprechen* [ˈʃprɛçən], *stehen* [ˈʃte:ən], *Gestalt* [gəˈʃtalt].

NOTE: In Middle and South Germany, as a general thing, [z] is not used; [s] is used instead.

[ʃ]

1. *sch* wherever encountered, as in *Schlacht* [ʃlaxt], *waschen* [ˈvaʃən], *deutsch* [dɔitʃ].

2. *s* initially in words and syllables before *p* and *t*, as in *spielen* [ˈʃpi:lən], *stand* [ʃtant], *gestanden* [gəˈʃtandən].

3. *ch* in French loan words, such as *Chenille* [ʃəˈnɪljə].[49]

NOTE: The voiced sound corresponding to [ʃ], i. e., [ʒ], is also to be found in French loan-words, such as *Charge* [ˈʃarʒə], *chargieren* [ʃarˈʒi:-rən].

[ç]

1. *ch* in Germanic words before or after a front vowel in the same syllable, and after *r* or *l* in the same syllable, as in *riechen* [ˈri:çən], *Licht* [lɪçt], *Reich* [raiç], *euch* [ɔiç], *Fechter* [ˈfɛçtər], *Veilchen* [ˈfailçən], *Bücher* [ˈby:çər], *höchlich* [ˈhø:çlɪç], *horchsam* [ˈhɔrçza:m], *Kelch* [kɛlç].

NOTE: The diminutive suffix *chen* is always [çən], as in *Kindchen* [ˈkɪntçən], but must be distinguished from similar spellings, as in *machen* [ˈmaxən], where *ch* is [x], under the influence of the preceding back vowel.

2. *ch* before vowels in many words of foreign origin, such as *chemisch* [ˈçe:mɪʃ], *Chirurg* [çiˈrurç], *China* [ˈçi:na:], *Charkow* [ˈçarkɔf], *Cheops* [ˈçe:ɔps].

3. *g* finally after front vowels, as in *Weg* [ve:ç], *Krieg* [kri:ç], *traurig* [ˈtraurɪç].

NOTES: (a) But in stage speech only *g* after *i* remains [ç], *g* after *e* and after back vowels being pronounced [k], as in *Weg* [ve:k], *Krieg* [kri:k], *Tag* [ta:k].

---

[49] Prokosch, p. 30.

(b) Final *g* is still regarded as final even if other words follow in compounding. Thus *wegnehmen* [ˈvɛçˌneːmən, ˈvɛkˌneːmən]. It is pronounced [ç, k], i.e., it is voiceless, when followed by a suffix beginning with a consonant, as in *täglich* [ˈteːçlɪç, ˈteːklɪç], but becomes [g] before a suffix beginning with a vowel, as in *Tagen* [ˈtaːgən], since it is then intervocalic.

[j]

1. *j* wherever encountered, as in *jedermann* [ˈjeːdərˌman].
2. Often unstressed *i* plus vowel after *l*, as in *Familie* [faˈmiːljə] (variant faˈmiːlɪə]).

NOTE: *g* in *ige* in North Germany is pronounced [j],[50] as in [ˈkøːnɪjə] for *Könige* [ˈkøːnɪgə]. Though regional, and though forbidden on the stage, it is regarded as acceptable in everyday speech.

[x]

1. *ch* in Germanic words after back vowels (but not in the combinations *chs* or *sch*), as in *Schlacht* [ʃlaxt], *Loch* [lɔx], *Fluch* [fluːx].
2. *g* finally after back vowels, as in *Tag* [taːx], *Herzog* [ˈhɛrtsoːx], *Zug* [tsuːx].

NOTE: But in stage speech, *g* final, alone or preconsonantal, after any vowel except *i*, is pronounced [k].

[ɣ]

g intervocalically (except in *ige*) in North Germany, as in *Tages* [ˈtaːɣəs], *Auge* [ˈauɣə], *Bogen* [ˈboːɣən].[51] Though this sound is regional, and though it is forbidden on the stage, it is fairly well regarded, at least locally.

[h]

1. *h* initially in words or syllables, as in *halten* [ˈhaltən], *gehabt* [gəˈhapt]. Orthographic *h* is silent after vowels in the same syllable, being used mainly to indicate that [i, y, e, ø, aː, o, u] are intended instead of [ɪ, ʏ, ɛ, œ, a, ɔ, ʊ], in words like *Ihnen* [ˈiːnən], *Bühne* [ˈbyːnə], *sehnen* [ˈzeːnən], *fröhlich* [ˈfrøːlɪç], *fahren* [ˈfaːrən],[52] *Ohr* [oːr], *Ruhr* [ruːr]. Other orthographic *h*'s are used in

---

[50] Prokosch, p. 30.
[51] Prokosch, p. 30.
[52] We have here the genuinely long vowel, [aː], which in this discussion has to be distinguished from the genuinely short vowel [a]. Compare *fahren* [ˈfaːrən], *Farren* [ˈfarən]. In this pair, length, that is, actual duration, is the differentiating factor. In the remaining pairs, while difference of length may exist, the outstanding differentiating factor is a true change in vowel quality, as seen in *Ihnen* [ˈiːnən], *schnitten* [ˈʃnɪtn̩]; *sehen* [ˈzeːən], *dessen* [ˈdɛsən]; *Bühne* [ˈbyːnə], *dünn* [dʏn].

consonant clusters without individual sound or significance, since a complete cluster is required to symbolize a single sound: thus *ch* = [ç], [x], [k], or [ʃ], in *ich* [ɪç], *ach* [ax], *Psychologie* [psyçolo¹gi:], *chassieren* [ʃa¹si:rən]; *sch* [ʃ], as in *schwartz* [ʃʋarts]; and *ph* = [f] in words of Greek origin, such as *Phrase* [¹fra:zə].

Some Sounds Peculiarly German in Their Position or Combination

[ts]

1. *t* in the suffixes *tion*, *tient*, *tial*, and in the combining suffix *ti*. Thus, *Nation* [natsɪ¹o:n], *Patient* [patsɪ¹ɛnt], *partial* [partsɪ¹a:l], *differentiirt* [ˌdɪfərɛntsɪ¹i:rt].

2. *tz* wherever encountered, as in *blitzen* [¹blɪtsən].

3. *z* wherever encountered, as in *Zeit* [tsait].

4. *c* before front vowels in a few Latin and Romance loan-words such as *Cicero* [¹tsitsəro], *Citrone* [tsi¹tro:nə], *Ceder* [¹tse:dər], *Cid* [tsi:t]. Some of these words have been Germanized in more recent publications, as in the case of *Zeder, Zitrone*. See introduction to this section.

NOTE: In *Zitrone*, *i* is pronounced [i], despite being followed by two consonants.

[ks]

1. *chs* in the same syllable, as in *Fuchs* [fuks]. Possessives are excepted, as in *Bachs Werke* [baxs ¹vɛrkə]; alsò contractions, such as *durchs* [durçs] for *durch das*.

2. *x* as in *xylophon* [ˌksylo¹fo:n].

[pf]

1. *pf* as in *Pferd* [pfe:rt], *Pflanze* [¹pflantsə], *Kopf* [kɔpf].

NOTE: In North and Central Germany, [pf] often weakens to [f].[53]

[ps]

1. *ps* initially in words of Greek origin, such as *Psychologie* [psyçolo¹gi:].

[tʃ]

1. *tsch* as in *Klatsch* [klatʃ].

2. *c* before *e* and *i* in Italian loan-words, as in *vivace* [vi¹va:tʃe:]. See introduction to this section.

[gn]

gn initially, as in *Gnade* [¹gna:də].

---

53 Hempl, p. 145; Siebs, p. 58.

[kn]

kn initially, as in *Knecht* [knɛçt].

[kʋ]

qu as in *Qualität* [kʋaliˈteːt], *quer* [kʋeːr].

[ʦʋ]

zw as in *zwei* [ʦʋai], *zwanzig* [ˈʦʋanʦɪç].

[ʃʋ]

schw as in *Schweiz* [ʃʋaiʦ].

Vowels

[i]

1. *i* followed by a single medial consonant in stressed syllables and in syllables immediately preceding stressed syllables, as in *Igel* [ˈiːgəl], *wider* [ˈviːdər], *Idee* [iˈdeː], *Minute* [miˈnuːtə], *Kapital* [kapiˈtaːl], *Kritik* [kriˈtiːk].

2. *ie* in *rief* [riːf], *viel* [fiːl], *Vieh* [fiː].

NOTES: (a) *h* after a vowel in the same syllable is not pronounced.
     (b) See rare exceptions *viertel* [ˈfɪrtəl], etc., under [ɪ]. See also *i* and *e* in adjacent syllables, as in *Sobrietät* [ˌzobrieˈteːt], *Kolonien* [koloˈniːən].

3. *ih* as in *ihr* [iːr], *ihm* [iːm].

NOTE: Silent *h* after *i* may be regarded as having the effect of a diacritic indicating that the preceding sound is [i], not [ɪ].

4. *i* followed by *r* in monosyllables and stressed syllables, as in *mir* [miːr], *dir* [diːr].

5. *i* in a number of final stressed syllables, mostly in foreign words, consisting of *i* plus a single consonant, as in *ik, im, in, ip, it, iv, iz*. Thus, Gk. *Physik* [fyˈziːk], Lat. *sublim* [zuˈbliːm], Slav. *Berlin* [bɛrˈliːn], Lat. *Prinzip* [prɪnˈʦiːp], *Appetit* [ˌapəˈtiːt], *Akkusativ* [aˌkuzaˈtiːf], *Notiz* [noˈtiːʦ].

6. *i* in unstressed syllables before a single consonant internally in Latin words, such as *Spiritualismus* [ˌspirituaˈlɪsmʊs], *Indikator* [ɪndiˈkaːtɔr].

7. Final *i* as in *Juni* [ˈjuːni], *Juli* [ˈjuːli].

NOTE: There are many minute details and some exceptions applying to [i] in proper nouns, foreign loan-words, and some common words, which are omitted here. When these occur, Siebs' *Deutsche Bühnen-*

*aussprache*⁵⁴ and Hempl's *German Orthography and Phonology*⁵⁵ will prove valuable for classifications, and Viëtor's *Deutsches Aussprachewörterbuch* (*German Pronouncing Dictionary*) or *Heath's Dictionary*⁵⁶ for pronunciations in phonetic symbols.

NOTE: Verbs in *ieren* retain the sound [i] despite loss of the *e* in inflection, as in *isolieren, isolirt* [ˌizoˈliːrən, ˌizoˈliːrt].

[ɪ]

1. *i* when followed by doubled consonants (including *ß* only when it is final), as in *Schritt* [ʃrɪt], *drinnen* [ˈdrɪnən], *Zimmer* [ˈtsɪmər], *gewiß* [gəˈvɪs], *gewissen* [gəˈvɪsən].

2. *i* followed by two or more different consonants.

NOTES: (a) In this context *ch*, *sch* and *ng* are regarded as consisting of more than one consonant each, despite the fact that each combination represents only one sound, viz., [ç] (or [x]), [ʃ] and [ŋ] respectively.

(b) In general, the two or more consonants referred to in No. 2 may be in the same syllable or in adjacent syllables. Thus, *frisch* [frɪʃ], *Blick* [blɪk], *Zirkel* [ˈtsɪrkəl], *Dinge* [ˈdɪŋə], *bilden* [ˈbɪldən], *Schrift* [ʃrɪft], *Irrtümer* [ˈɪrˌtyːmər], *sicher* [ˈzɪçər], *Himbeere* [ˈhɪmˌbeːrə].

3. *i* in monosyllables and unstressed syllables when followed by a single phonetic consonant (*r* excluded), as in *bis* [bɪs], *bin* [bɪn], *in* [ɪn], *im* [ɪm], *ich* [ɪç], *Fisch* [fɪʃ], *mit* [mɪt] *Finsternis* [ˈfɪnstərnɪs], *freilich* [ˈfrailɪç], *dreckig* [ˈdrɛkɪç], *Lehrerin* [ˈleːrərɪn], *Ethik* [ˈeːtɪk], *Grammatik* [graˈmaːtɪk].

4. *ie* exceptionally in certain derivatives of *vier* [fiːr], as *vierzehn* [ˈfɪrˌtseːn], *Viertel* [ˈfɪrtəl] (but not in *Vierteil* [ˈfiːrˌtail]).

5. *i* unstressed before a vowel in Latin words in *tion, tial, ium, io*, such as *Konversation* [ˌkɔnvɛrzatsɪˈoːn], *partial* [partsɪˈaːl], *Radium* [ˈraːdɪum], *Radioaktivität* [raːdɪoʔaktiviˈtɛːt]. Similarly, unstressed *i* before a vowel in a succeeding syllable, as in *Komitien* [koˈmiːtsɪən].

NOTE: For minutiae regarding additional proper nouns, foreign loanwords, and exceptional cases, see Siebs,⁵⁷ Hempl,⁵⁸ Viëtor,⁵⁹ and Cassel,⁶⁰ as referred to under [i].

⁵⁴ Pp. 44–46.
⁵⁵ Pp. 135–137.
⁵⁶ Viëtor, *op. cit.*; Heath, *op. cit.*
⁵⁷ Pp. 44–46.
⁵⁸ Pp. 135–137.
⁵⁹ Aussprachewörterbuch.
⁶⁰ Dictionary.

[y]

1. *ü* followed by a single consonant or by a "genuine" *β*,[61] as in *Tür* [ty:r] *grüßen* ['gry:sən], *süß* [zy:s], *Füße* ['fy:sə], *für* [fy:r].

NOTE: This class includes contractions like *übrig* ['y:brɪç], *Lügner* ['ly:gnər], from *über* ['y:bər] and *lügen* ['ly:gən]; [y] is retained despite the multiplication of consonants.

2. *üh* as in *Gebühr* [gə'by:r]. When *h* follows *ü* in the same syllable, it is acoustically silent, and merely indicates that the sound of *ü* is [y], not [ʏ].
3. *ü* before *st*, in some words, such as *wüst* [vy:st], *Düster* ['dy:stər].
4. *y* in certain words of Greek origin, as in *Lyrik* ['ly:rɪk], *Zylinder* [tsy'lɪndər], *Zyklometrie* [tsy̩klome'tri:].

NOTE: Foreign words in general exhibit considerable irregularity. Consult Siebs,[62] Hempl,[63] Viëtor,[64] and Cassell.[65]

[Y]

1. *ü* before doubled consonants ("genuine" *β* excepted), as in *müssen* ['mʏsən], *Hütte* ['hʏtə].

---

[61] Ess-tset, i.e., *β*, is used indiscriminately in German Gothic type for double-*s* at the end of a word, singly or in a compound, with or without a following *t*. It is also used medially (alone, i.e., without any following consonant) to indicate that the preceding vowel is long. "Long," in this connection, means primarily long in duration, but it also means long in the loose, inaccurate sense of a related but different vowel. In the case of [ɑ:] and [ɛ:] in the following list, "long" means only duration; in the case of the remaining vowels, "long" means both duration and a related different vowel. For present purposes, only the latter meaning is significant. Specifically, the presence of medial *β* indicates that the preceding vowel will be either [i], [y], [e], [ø], [ɛ:] (as a variant pronunciation of long *ä*), [o], [ɑ:], or [u].

If, instead of *β*, *ss* is used, it is indicated that the preceding vowel is [ɪ], [ʏ], [ɛ], [œ], [ɔ], [a], or [ʊ].

For purposes of this discussion, the *β* which does not change to *ss* in inflectional forms is referred to as a "genuine" ess-tset.

The only way to be sure whether *β* at the end of a given word or element of a compound has the power to indicate phonemes as just explained, and is not a mere typographic device to end a syllable, is to find the word in Gothic type with an inflectional ending beginning with a vowel. If the type uses *β* there, it is "genuine," and the preceding vowel is from the list beginning with [i]. Thus in *Füße* we have *β* intervocalically, which is proof that the vowel is [y] rather than [ʏ], as in *küssen* ['kʏsən], where the vowel is followed by *ss*. Having thus located an authentic *β* (which is regarded as a single orthographic consonant, not a doubled one), we know that it is likewise the same sort of *β* in all other forms of the same word. Other *β*'s are only final *ss*'s and the vowels preceding them are from the list previous of "short" vowels, beginning with [ɪ].

[62] Pp. 52–53.
[63] Pp. 154–155.
[64] Aussprachewörterbuch.
[65] Dictionary.

2. *u* in general before two or more unlike consonants, as in *stützen* ['ʃtʏtsən], *fünfzig* ['fʏnftsɪç], *flüstern* ['flʏstərn].

NOTE: See under [y] for instances where *u* before *st* is [y].

3. *y* in certain words of Greek origin, such as *Satyr* ['zɑːtʏr], *Symbol* [zʏm'boːl], *Symmetrie* [zʏme'triː].

NOTES: (a) Foreign words in general show irregularity. See references under [y].
(b) Where type-fonts do not contain *ü*, *ue* is used, as in *gruen*.

[e]⁶⁶

NOTE: German [e] is the pure, undiphthongized [e], in contrast with the diphthongal [eɪ] of English. Compare German *Feder* ['feːdər] with English *fading* ['feɪdɪŋ].

1. *e* usually in a stressed open syllable, i.e., a syllable ending in a vowel, as in *je* [jeː], *Rede* ['reː-də], *gewesen* [gə've:-zən], *pflegen* ['pfle:-gən], *edel* ['eː-dəl].

NOTE: The addition of consonants through inflection, vowel omission, and compounding does not ordinarily change the value of [e]. Thus *pflegt* [pfleːçt], *pflegst* [pfleːçst].

2. *e* usually in stressed syllables when followed by a single consonant in the same syllable, as in *regnen* ['reː-ç-nən], *schwer* [ʃveːr], *bequem* [bə'kveːm], *der* [deːr], *dem* [deːm], *den* [deːn], *wem* [veːm], *wen* [veːn], *quer* [kveːr], *Dresden* ['dreːs-dən], *Schleswig* ['ʃleːs-vɪç].

NOTES: (a) The vowels of the pronouns and articles in the list above, especially *der*, often weaken in fluent speech to [ɛ] and [ə], as in [dɛr], [dər].
(b) The list in No. 2 above does not include *des* [dɛs], *wes* [vɛs], or *es* [ɛs].
(c) It is convenient here to call attention to a principle sometimes cited, viz., that the true value of vowel is to be found in the inflected form of a word. *Bequem* illustrates this principle, since the comparative form, *bequemer*, shows the stressed *e* in an open syllable, thus [bə'kveː-mər].

3. *e* usually in stressed syllables before *rd, rt, rst, bs, bst, ts*, as in *Pferd* [pfeːrt], *wert* [veːrt], *erst* [eːrst], *Krebs* [kreːps], *nebst* [neːpst], *stets* [ʃteːts].

---

⁶⁶ For special cases where the history of a word causes it to violate modern rules for pronunciation, or where modern rules cause it to violate its history, see Hempl, p. 95; 125–126.

4. *ee*, as in *See* [ze:], *Seele* [ˈze:lə], *Heer* [he:r].

5. *eh*, as in *nehmen* [ˈne:mən], *Fehler* [ˈfe:lər].

6. *ä* followed in the same stressed syllable by a single consonant, or by an *β*[67] which does not represent a final *ss*, as in *Bär* [be:r],[68] *Mädchen* [ˈme:tçən], *spät* [ʃpe:t], *Käse* [ˈke:zə], *regelmäßig* [ˈre:gəlˌme:sɪç], *Gespräch* [gəˈʃpre:ç] (derived from *sprachen*, which has a long [ɑ]), *Gefäße* [gəˈfe:sə], *erklärt* [ɛrˈkle:rt] (from *erklaren*).

7. *äh*, as in *ähnlich* [ˈe:nlɪç].

NOTE: There is considerable irregularity in the choice of [e] and [ɛ] in proper names and foreign words. It is best to refer to a good pronouncing dictionary (e.g., Viëtor or Heath) for these.

[ɛ][69]

1. *e* followed by a doubled consonant (including *β* when it represents final *ss*), as in *nett* [nɛt], *Messer* [ˈmɛsər], *Heß* [hɛs], *Herr* [hɛr].

2. *e* followed by two or more different consonants in the same syllable, as in *Held* [hɛlt], *decken* [ˈdɛkən], *deckst* [dɛkst], *schlecht* [ʃlɛçt], *Vers* [fɛrs].

NOTE: The prefixes *er*, *ver*, *zer*, even though unstressed, employ [ɛ], not [ə]. Thus *Ersatz* [ɛrˈzats], *verstehen* [fɛrˈʃte:ən], *zerbrechen* [tsɛrˈbrɛçən].

3. *e* in certain monosyllables even when followed by a single consonant (except *r*, *m*, *n*), as in *wes* [vɛs], *es* [ɛs], *des* [dɛs], *weg* [vɛç] (adv.).

---

[67] See note on *β* under [y].

[68] There is controversy over the pronunciation of *ä* of long duration, the question being whether it should be pronounced [e:] or [ɛ:]. The history of the two sounds in their various spellings is a confused chapter in German linguistics, and there is no doubt that both pronunciations are widely used today. The Conference on stage speech favored in majority the use of [ɛ:], and it was so ordered (Siebs, pp. 40–44). Viëtor followed the decision of the Conference and used [ɛ:] in his *Aussprachewörterbuch*, and other dictionaries (Muret-Sanders, Berlin-Schöneberg, Langenscheidtsche Verlagsbuchlandlung, 1910; Heath, K. Breul, ed., N. Y., 1939; etc.) followed Siebs and Viëtor. But Viëtor, Prokosch, and others yield with reluctance. Prokosch states (p. 40):

"Long *ä*, *äh* (gäbe, nähme) is generally pronounced opener than [e:], nearly low-front, as in English *care*. Still, there is good authority for using the sound in *gäbe* and *gebe*, *nähme* and *nehme*, *Säle* and *Seele*, namely mid-front narrow. In teaching German, it is certainly to be recommended."

Viëtor (*Kleine Phonetik*, p. I.) predicts the ultimate predominance of [e] and appears to wish to hasten that outcome.

"Wer der ziemlich sicheren Entwicklung der Dinge voraneilen will, mag für dieses auch in meinem Wörterbuch durchgeführte [ɛ:] überall den 'geschlossenen' Laut [e:] sprechen."*

* Die weite Verbreitung dieses [e:] in Norddeutschland wird von Fräulein Taubner zu obiger bestätigt.

[69] For special cases where the history of words makes them appear to violate modern rules, or where modern spelling causes them to violate their etymological history, see Hempl, pp. 95, 126–128.

4. *ä* followed by a doubled consonant (or *ß* representing final *ss*), as in *Blätter* [ˈblɛtər], *läßt* [lɛst], *Gäßchen* [ˈgɛsçən].

5. *ä* followed by two or more different consonants, except where the multiplication of consonants results from inflection, syncope or word compounding, and excepting most instances of *rd, rt, rst, bs, bst, ts*, as noted in No. 3 under [e]. Thus *Bächlein* [ˈbɛçlɑin] (from *Bach*, which contains a short *a*), *hält* [hɛlt], *wränge* [ˈvrɛŋə], *Äste* [ˈɛstə], *Hände* [ˈhɛndə], *älter* [ˈɛltər], *Ärmel* [ˈɛrməl], *Wäsche* [ˈvɛʃə].

NOTES: (a) For names of foreign persons and places, and for other foreign loan-words, it is often safest to use a good pronouncing dictionary, such as Viëtor or Cassell.

(b) Where type fonts do not contain *ä*, *ae* is used. Names often use *ae*, as in *Baer*.

[ø]

1. *ö* in stressed open syllables, and in stressed syllables when followed by a single consonant (including *ß* when not representing final *ss*) in the same syllable, as in *hören* [ˈhøːrən], *größer* [ˈgrøːsər], *Öl* [øːl], *Röslein* [ˈrøːslɑin], *schön* [ʃøːn].

NOTE: Adding consonants by inflection does not change the vowel. Compare *hörst* [ˈhøːrst], *hört* [høːrt].

2. *ö* in *Österreich* [ˈøːstərˌrɑiç], despite [œ] in *östlich* [ˈœstlɪç]. *Ost* itself varies between [oːst] and [ɔst], hence the variation in its derivatives.[70]

3. *öh* wherever encountered, as in *Öhren* [ˈøːrən], *Böhme* [ˈbøːmə].

NOTES: (a) Where type fonts do not contain *ö*, *oe* is used. Names often use *oe*, as in *Goethe* [ˈgøːtə], *Roehmer* [ˈrøːmər].

(b) For foreign names and other loan-words, it is best to use a pronouncing dictionary, such as Viëtor or Heath.

[œ][71]

1. *ö* followed by a doubled consonant (including *ß* when it represents final *ss*),[72] as in *Götter* [ˈgœtər], *können* [ˈkœnən], *Rößchen* [ˈrœsçən] (here *ß* = final *ss*).

2. *ö* followed by two or more different consonants (including *ch* when the uninflected form contains [ɔ]) in the same syllable, as in *Glöcklein* [ˈglœklɑin], *Dörfer* [ˈdœrfər], *Köche* [ˈkœçə], *Frösche* [ˈfrœʃə], *Körbe* [ˈkœrbə], *Mönch* [mœnç].

---

[70] See Hempl, pp. 95, 144–145, for problems arising from the history of the duration of vowels. See Siebs, p. 49, for a special list of words in *öft, ögt, örd, ösch, öst*, pronounced with [ø].

[71] See Hempl, pp. 95, 144–145; Siebs, pp. 49–50 for special cases, special lists, and historical explanations of irregularities.

[72] See note on *ß* under [y].

NOTE: For foreign loan-words and names see a pronouncing dictionary, such as Viëtor or Heath.

[ɑ]⁷³

NOTE: The following represents a non-exhaustive break-down for [ɑ:] and [ɑ], similar to that for the other vowels.

Long [ɑ:]

1. *a* final or followed by single consonant or by *ß* when it does not represent *ss*,⁷⁴ as in *ja* [jɑ:], *Plan* [plɑ:n], *Name* [ˈnɑ:mə], *maßen* [ˈmɑ:sən], *nach* [nɑ:x] (vowel long because related to [ɑ:] in *nahe*).

NOTE: As elsewhere, inflection and other word-building processes do not change vowel length. Thus *fragen* [ˈfrɑ:gən], *fragte* [ˈfrɑ:xtə] both have long [ɑ], notwithstanding the multiplication of consonants.

2. *aa*, as in *Haar* [hɑ:r], *Saar* [zɑ:r].
3. *ah*, as in *Kahn* [kɑ:n], *Bahnhof* [ˈbɑ:nho:f].

Short [ɑ]

1. *a* followed by a double consonant (including *ß* when it represents *ss*),⁷⁴ as in *dann* [dɑn], *lassen* [ˈlɑsən], *daß* [dɑs].

2. *a* followed by two different consonants, as in *backen* [ˈbɑkən], *schwach* [ʃvɑx] (short *a* because not derived from a form containing long *a*).

3. Exceptions to No. 1 above are many, consisting largely of familiar words and syllables, such as *ab* [ɑp], *das* [dɑs], *am* [ɑm], *an* [ɑn], *man* [mɑn], *hat*, [hɑt], *Monat* [ˈmo:nɑt].⁷⁴

[o]⁷⁵

NOTE: [o] is a pure vowel, not diphthongal as in English. Compare German *Not* [no:t] with English *note* [nout].

1. *o* in open syllables, as in *wo* [vo:], *also* [ˈɑlzo:], *oben* [ˈo:bən], *Hoboe* [hoˈbo:ə], *Kola* [ˈko:lɑ:].

2. *o* plus a single consonant or *ß* when it does not represent *ss*,⁷⁷ as in *rot* [ro:t], *los* [lo:s], *vor* [fo:r], *groß* [gro:s].⁷⁶

Some words in *ch*, as in *hoch* [ho:x], belong in this category. Whenever an

---

⁷³ For details on foreign words and names, see Siebs, pp. 35–37.

⁷⁴ For detailed consideration of vowel quantity, see Hempl, pp. 92–96.

⁷⁵ For excellent list of foreign words with rules (e.g., *oe* and *oi* = [o] in Low German; *oi*, *oy* = [oa] in French, etc.), see Siebs, pp. 47–49. Regarding length, see Hempl, pp. 92–96.

⁷⁶ See note on *ß* under [y].

inflected form of a word in *oß* or *och* has [o] or [ø], then the vowel of the uninflected form is [o].

Some words that contradict the rule that *o* + a single consonant = [o], and
o plus more than one consonant = [ɔ], are *Obst* [o:pst], *Mond* [mo:nt], *Montag*
[ˈmo:ntɑx], *Kloster* [ˈklo:stər], *Trost* [tro:st], *Ost* [o:st] (also [ɔst]).

3. *oo*, as in *Moos* [mo:s], *Boot* [bo:t].

4. *oh*, as in *Bohne* [ˈbo:nə], *wohnen* [ˈvo:nən], *Lohn* [lo:n].

$$[ɔ]^{77}$$

1. *o* plus a doubled consonant (including final *ß* when it represents *ss*), as
in *Bonn* [bɔn], *Gott* [gɔt], *Sonne* [ˈzɔnə], *Roß* [rɔs], *offen* [ˈɔfən].

2. *o* plus two or more different consonants, as in *Bock* [bɔk], *Loch* [lɔx],
Morgen [ˈmɔrgən], *fordern* [ˈfɔrdərn], *Horn* [hɔrn].

3. Some exceptional words with [ɔ] ending in only one consonant are *ob*
[ɔp], *von* [fɔn], *vom* [fɔm].

4. In some foreign words it is the rule that final syllables containing *o* before
a single consonant, but unstressed, are pronounced with [ɔ], if stressed, with
[o], thus, *Lexikon* [ˈlɛksikɔn], *Doktor* [ˈdɔktɔr], *Motor* [ˈmo:tɔr], *Professor* [proˈfɛsɔr].

NOTE: *Doktoren* [dɔkˈto:rən], *Professoren* [profɛˈso:rən], etc., when the stress
shifts.)

$$[u]^{78}$$

1. *u* in open syllables, as in *du* [du:], *nu* [nu:], *Stube* [ˈʃtu:bə], *Student* [ʃtuˈdɛnt].

2. *u* followed by a single consonant or *ß* when it does not represent *ss*,[79]
as in *Fuß* [fu:s], *Blut* [blu:t], *Mut* [mu:t], *Zug* [tsu:x], *nun* [nu:n], *nur* [nu:r],
Buch [bu:x], *Besuch* [bəˈzu:x]. (Words in *ch* are pronounced with [u] if the
inflected forms contain [u] or [y], as in *Bücher* [ˈby:çər], *Besuche* [bəˈzu:xə]),
zur [tsur]—unless unstressed.)

3. *uh*, as in *ruhen* [ru:ən], *Stuhl* [ʃtu:l].

4. Some special words in [u] are *flugs* [flu:xs] (from *Fluges* [ˈflu:gəs]), *Geburt*
[gəˈbu:rt], *Urgrossvater* [ˈu:rgro:sˌfa:tər] (and other compounds of *ur*, excepting
Urteil [ˈurˌtail]), *Schuster* [ˈʃu:stər] (from *Schuh* [ʃu:]), *Wust* [vu:st] (and several
other words in *ust*), *Knutschen* [ˈknu:tʃən], *duzen* [ˈdu:tsən], *Luther* [ˈlu:tər].

$$[ʊ]^{80}$$

1. *u* followed by a doubled consonant (including *ß* when it represents *ss*),[81]

---

77 For helpful discussions on length, see Hempl, pp. 92–96; on foreign words in *o*,
Siebs, pp. 49–50.

78 For discussion of length, see Hempl, pp. 92–95. For a useful classification of foreign
loan-words, see Siebs, pp. 51–52.

79 See note on *ß* under [y].

80 For discussion of length, see Hempl, pp. 92–96. For an extensive list of foreign words
pronounced with [ʊ], see Siebs, pp. 51–52.

81 See footnote under [y].

as in *Futter* [ˈfʊtər], *Krumm* [krʊm], *Bummel* [ˈbʊməl], *muß* [mʊs].

2. *u* followed by two or more different consonants, as in *unser* [ˈʊnzər], *unter* [ˈʊntər], *Urteil* [ˈʊrˌtail], *Brust* [brʊst], *Bruch* [brʊx] (from *brechen*, which has short [ε], hence, the short [ʊ]), *Bucht* [bʊxt].

3. Some exceptional words having [ʊ] for *u* followed by only one consonant are *zur* [tsʊr] (when unstressed), *zum*, [tsʊm] (always unstressed).

[ə]

1. *e* unstressed, as *Knabe* [ˈknɑːbə], *Katze* [ˈkatsə], *geehrt* [gəˈʔeːrt], *binden* [ˈbɪndən], *Gelegenheit* [gəˈleːgənhait], *neues* [ˈnɔiəs]. *Der, den, dem,* etc., if very greatly unstressed, may appear with [ə], thus, [dər, dən, dəm], etc.

2. *o* greatly unstressed in *von* [fən].

> NOTE: The prefixes *er, ver, zer* are pronounced with [ε], even though always unstressed. Thus *erzählen* [εrˈtseːlən], *verzeien* [fεrˈtsaiən], *vereinigen* [fεrˈʔainɪgən].

[au]

1. *au* as in *aus* [aus], *Haus* [haus].

> NOTE: This diphthong is variously interpreted as [aʊ], [ɑʊ], [ɑu], [ao] by different phoneticians and in different dialects.

[ɔi]

1. *eu* as in *euch* [ɔiç], *Feuer* [ˈfɔiər].
2. *äu* as in *Häuser* [ˈhɔizər], *Bäume* [ˈbɔimə].

> NOTE: This diphthong is variously interpreted as [ɔi], [ɔɪ], [ɔY], [oY], etc. by different phoneticians, and in different dialects. A substandard version of it is [ai].

[ai]

1. *ai* as in *Maid* [mait], *Mai* [mai].
2. *ei* as in *sein* [zain], *Allerlei* [ˈalərˌlai].
3. *ay* as in *Mayer* [ˈmaiər].
4. *ey* as in *Meyer* [ˈmaiər].

> NOTE: This diphthong is variously interpreted as [aɪ], [ɑɪ], [εi], [εɪ], [ae], by different phoneticians and in different dialects.

Transcription in German

Some classes or individual students will wish to apply the preceding information to the transcription of German into phonetic symbols. This is the proper point for such practice. Select material from any German book and transcribe a sufficient quantity to ensure encountering the various spellings of the several phonemes.

Comparison of German and English Sounds

A comparison of the sounds of German as just discussed, with the sounds of English (page 46), shows at once that certain sounds appear in English which do not appear in German. German speakers may, and often do, learn these sounds, but while the learning process is still incomplete they will substitute German sounds for the unfamiliar English elements. Some never learn the correct English sounds, but continue to make substitutions throughout their lives. The English sounds not common to German follow:

ENGLISH SOUNDS THAT DO NOT OCCUR IN GERMAN

Consonants

[θ]	thin	[θɪn]	
[ð]	this	[ðɪs]	
[ʍ]	wheat	[ʍit]	voiceless as contrasted to the voiced [w] in *wish* [wɪʃ].
[ʒ]	casual	[ˈkæʒuəl]	appears only in borrowed words (usually French) in German.
[w]	wish	[wɪʃ]	

Vowels

[æ]	hat	[hæt]	
[ʌ]	cup	[kʌp]	
[ɝ]	heard	[hɝd]	General American pronunciation.
[ɜ]	heard	[hɜ:d]	Southern and Eastern American and British pronunciation.
[ɒ]	hot	[hɒt]	British and Eastern American pronunciation.
[ɚ]	butter	[ˈbʌtɚ]	General American pronunciation.

Diphthongs

| [ou] | note | [nout] | |
| [eɪ] | late | [leɪt] | |

As substitutes for the unfamiliar English sounds, the German will draw not merely upon the sounds common to the two languages, but upon some of the German sounds which do not appear in English. These latter sounds are listed below for particular attention.

GERMAN SOUNDS THAT DO NOT OCCUR IN ENGLISH[82]

Consonants

| [ʀ] | reden | [ˈʀe:dn̩] | in sections where the uvular *r* is used. |

---

[82] It is these sounds which the speaker of English must learn in order to speak German without objectional accent.

[ɸ]	Pferd	[ɸeːrt]	in North and Middle German.
[β]	Wasser	[ˈβasər]	in sections where the spirant *b* is used.
[ç]	durch	[dʊrç]	
[x]	Buch	[buːx]	
[ɣ]	Wagen	[ˈβaːɣən]	in sections where the spirant *g* is used.
[ʋ]	Quelle	[ˈkʋɛlə]	in *qu, schw,* and *zw* spellings.
[ꜰ]	Quelle	[ˈkꜰɛlə]	as a variant of [ʋ].

Vowels

[y]	kühn	[kyːn]	
[ʏ]	hübsch	[hʏpʃ]	
[ø]	schön	[ʃøːn]	
[œ]	Körper	[ˈkœrpər]	
[e]	ewig	[ˈeːvɪç]	rather than the English diphthongal [eɪ].
[o]	Sohn	[zoːn]	rather than the English diphthongal [oʊ].

German Substitutions in English

Even where the German and English phonemes coincide in a general way, there are differences in the choice of the allophones of phonemes, in the choice as between pure vowels and diphthongs, in degrees of aspiration, etc., which make for many substitutions by a German struggling to speak English. In the discussion following, the substitutions of approximately corresponding sounds are discussed separately from the substitutions of entirely different phonemes. These approximate substitutions will be seen to consist of three classes:

1. Those resulting from the fact that German [e] and [o] are relatively pure, i.e., monophthongal, as compared with the diphthongal English [eɪ] and [oʊ].

2. Those resulting from the fact that German plosives, especially in certain dialects, have aspiration and voicing patterns which are essentially reversed from those of English, even in initial syllables. That is, [p, t, k] in Middle and South Germany are unaspirate, instead of aspirate, as in English, and thus sound much like [b, d, g], while [b, d, g] are voiceless, and hence sound like [p, t, k].

3. Those resulting from the fact that certain vowels, though belonging to analogous phonemes in the two languages, are at higher or lower levels in German, when compared with English vowels. E.g., German [ʊ] is higher, German [ɛ] lower.

Other substitutions, as implied above, are actually from different phonemes. These are sometimes promoted by the physical nearness of the phonemes, as when [t] is substituted for [θ]; and sometimes by pronunciation habits inherent in the German language, such as the invariable unvoicing of final plosive and fricative consonants. Since German *Tod* is [toːt], the German speaker is strongly tempted to pronounce English *Toad* [toʊd] as [tot]; and English final [z], as in *is* [ɪz], will almost invariably be pronounced [s].

Still another form of substitution is promoted by orthography. Thus, since *j* is [j] in German, English *joke* [ʤoʊk] may be pronounced *yoke* [jok] because of its spelling.

The following-named German sounds will be substituted for the approximately corresponding sounds in English:

[e] for [ei]. Thus *ale* [eɪl] > [el].

[ɛˀ] for English [ɛ]. German [ɛˀ] is lower than English [ɛ] and may suggest [æ]. The German [ɛˀ] is so nearly on the boundary between the English [ɛ] and [æ]-phonemes that *lettuce* [ˈlɛtəs] will sound like *lattice* [ˈlætəs], *medicine* [ˈmɛdəsən] like *Madison* [ˈmædəsən], and vice versa.

[ʊˑ] for English [ʊ]. German [ʊˑ] is closer than English [ʊ] and may sound like [u]. Thus, *look* [lʊk] > [luˑk], which suggests [luk].

[o] for English [oʊ]. German [o] is relatively pure and may suggest [ɔ]. Thus *oatmeal* [ˌoʊtˈmil] > [ˌotˈmil], which suggests [ˌɔtˈmil].

[tˀ] for English [tˈ]. Middle and South German [tˀ] is unaspirated[83] and may very strongly suggest [d], especially in the initial positions. Thus *tale* [tˀel] may sound like *dale* [deɪl].

[d̥] for English [d]. The Middle and South German [d] is in some dialects voiceless, and may easily be mistaken for English [t]. Thus, *dale* [d̥el] may sound like *tale* [teɪl].

[pˀ] for English [pˈ]. Middle and South German [pˀ] is uanspirated, and often may be easily mistaken for [b]. Thus, *petting* [ˈpˀɛtɪŋ] may sound like *betting* [ˈbɛtɪŋ]. Combining the unaspirate effect with the lowered [ɛ], we may find the word mistaken for *batting* [ˈbætɪŋ].

[b̥] for English [b]. Middle and South German [b] is frequently voiceless, and may easily be mistaken for [p]. Thus, *betting* [ˈb̥ɛtɪŋ] may sound like [ˈpɛtɪŋ]. Combining the voiceless effect with the lowered [ɛ], we may find the word mistaken for *patting* [ˈpætɪŋ].

[kˀ] for English [kˈ]. Middle and South German [k] is frequently so unaspirated as to be easily confounded with [g]. Thus, *coat* [kˀot] may sound like *goat* [goʊt].

[g̊] for English [g]. German [g] is frequently voiceless, so that it may be confounded with English [k]. Thus, *goat* [g̊ot] may sound like *coat* [koʊt].

Trilled [ř] or [ʀ] or [ʁ] for English [r]. The German trilled [ř] readily becomes reduced to the English "smooth" [r]. But the uvular, in either the scrape [ʁ] or trilled [ʀ] form, changes toward English [r] much less readily. It is easily mistaken for [w] or [l] according to whether the labial or the lingual part of the articulation is stressed. *Cigarette* [ˌsigəˈʀɛt] is therefore heard as [ˌsigəˈwɛt] or [ˌsigəˈlɛt].

---

[83] The degree of unaspiration of [p], [t], and [k] varies greatly with the different German dialects. The same is true of the unvoicing of non-final [d], [b], and [g]. In some dialects these effects, which are arranged exactly opposite to those in English, are so strong as to give the English-speaking hearer the impression that the German is exactly reversing the use of [p, t, k] and [b, d, g].

The [β] of North, Middle, and South German (the bi-labial spirant), for both English [v] and [w]. This sound, being essentially a [v] in respect to fricative quality, and a [w] in respect to rounding, suggests to English ears both [v] and [w]. Accordingly, when it is used for [v], English-speaking people will hear it as [w], and when it is used for [w], it will be heard as [v]. *West* will sound like *vest*, and vice versa, though in both cases the German has said [βɛst].

Numerous other German sounds are not quite equal to the corresponding English sounds, as in the case of [ʃ], which is more rounded and forceful in the German than the English, but the differences are too slight to have noticeable dialectal effect.

The following-named English sounds which do not appear in German have to be replaced by German sounds which are noticeably unsuitable:

[æ], which will be replaced by the German low [ɛˑ]. It suggests both [æ] and [ɛ], being apparently practically on the boundary between the English [æ] and [ɛ] phonemes, so that *latter* [ˈlætər] will sound like *letter* [ˈlɛtɚ], and *Madison* [ˈmædəsən] like *medicine* [ˈmɛdəsən], and vice versa. When the spellings of [æ] suggest familiar spellings of [ɑ] in German, then [ɑ] is likely to be substituted, especially by Germans who read a great deal of English early in their experience with the language. Such speakers will say *last* [lɑst], *branch* [brɑntʃ], *calf* [kɑf], etc.

[ʌ], which will be substituted for variously by Germans of different dialects, and by an individual speaker according to the phonetic context in a given word or breath group. [ɔ] is the most obvious substitute, it being more open in German than in English, and indeed often very close to [ʌ], as in *von* [fɔn], *Sonne* [ˈzɔnə]. [ɑ] is another possibility, as in *enough* [ɪˈnɑf]. But [u] or [ʊ] are by far the most common substitutes, *up* becoming [up], *just* becoming [jʊst], etc. Probably the spelling aids this selection of substitute.

[ɜ] and [ɝ] have no obvious substitute. Some Germans use [ɛ], some [œ]. The latter is quite close, and if the German drops [f̆] or [ʀ] or [ʁ] and acquires an English [r], his substitution may attract but little attention. The selection of substitutes also varies with English spelling; *word*, following the German *Wort*, will appear as [vɔrt], but *herd* as [hɛrt].

[ð], which will usually be replaced by [d], as in *this* [dɪs], *that* [dɛˑt]. The latter will sound very much like [dæt]. Spelling may influence pronunciation so as to produce [dɑt] here; i.e., since *a* is [ɑ] in German, the speaker may expect it to be [ɑ] in English. A few Germans, usually the more educated ones, will substitute [z] for [ð] and say [zɪs].

[θ], which will be replaced by [t], as in *thing* [tɪŋ]. A few Germans, usually the more educated ones, will substitute [s] for [θ] and say [sɪŋ].

[ʤ], which will be replaced by [tʃ] or [j], as in *jump* [tʃʊmp, jʊmp].

[w] and [ʍ], which will be replaced by [v], as in *wish* [vɪʃ], *quick* [kvɪk],[84] *when* [vɛn], *why* [vai].

Following are some German contexts likely to affect German-English: The German consonants b, d, g, and v-w, whenever they are placed in a final position, become voiceless, their counterparts being [p], [t], [ç, x, k], and [f]. Thus, *gab* [gap], *Tod* [toːt], *fertig* [ˈfɛrtɪç], *Tag* [tax, tak], *Kiev-Kiew* [kiˈɛf]. Following his native habit, the German tends to unvoice final English voiced sounds, as in *dead* [dɛt], *rob* [rap], *dog* [dɔk], *leave* [lif].

There is likewise no final voiced affricate [ʤ] or fricative [z] in German. Hence such sounds in English become voiceless in the German dialect. Thus *trudge* becomes [traʧ], *his* becomes [hɪs], etc.

st and *sp* initially in German are pronounced [ʃt] and [ʃp]. Germans tend to carry this practice into English. Thus, *stole* [ʃtol], *spoke* [ʃpok]. Likewise, in words in initial *sl*, *sm*, *sn*, *sw*, where corresponding German words are spelled with *sch*, [ʃ] is to be expected, as in *slay* [ʃle], *small* [ʃmal], *snore* [ʃnor], *swing* [ʃvɪŋ].

Various spellings with *a* will suggest [a] for [ɔ] to the German who is undertaking to speak English, because of the familiar corresponding spellings in his native tongue. He may err, even though [ɔ] is a common sound in German. Thus, he may say *ball* [bal], *call* [kal], *back* [bak], *hack* [hak], etc.

Some of the Problems of Foreign Dialect in English

German dialect, or any other foreign dialect of English, presents a number of problems which have to be met and solved—often by compromise. Some of these problems follow.

Intonation. This book deals very little with intonation. Despite much work on the subject, no simple notation has been devised for the economical representation of intonation (but see page 182). Until such a notation is available, it is best to rely on phonograph records or the living speech of suitable informants to suggest all but the broadest aspects of the intonation (lilt, melody, pitch variation) of a foreigner's rendition of English speech. This will apply to all the dialects considered in this book, German among the rest.

The speaker's degree of literacy. In rendering the dialect of a given individual, the degree of literacy of such individual must be taken into account. The more educated the speaker, the more likely he will be to have studied English in a formal way and to be aware of the problems of speaking the language. The reference earlier to the variant renderings of [θ] and [ð] is a case in point; the

---

[84] Also [kʊɪk]. However, the difference between [v] and [ʊ] will hardly be noticed by the English ear.

more educated German speakers will likely have learned how these sounds are made, and will be less likely than other people to substitute [t] and [d].

Visual errors and auditory errors. Related to the previous paragraph is the problem of whether a given dialectal speaker is basing his mispronunciations of English on having seen the English words on the page, or having heard them from English speakers. If the former, he is likely to pronounce words spelled in a given fashion as suggested by the instance where English spelling resembles the spelling in the speaker's native language. Thus a German, seeing English *fall*, may pronounce it [fɑl]. If the latter, the foreign speaker of English will substitute his native version of any phoneme he hears. Thus a German hearing English *rate*, will say [ret].

The foreigner's dialect of his own language. It is obvious that the speech patterns of a foreigner's home dialect will affect his speaking of English. For a specific instance, a South German, who says *wissen* [ˈβɪsən] will probably be understood to say *which* [wɪtʃ] in English, while a North German, who says *wissen* [ˈvɪsən], will be heard to say [vɪtʃ]. Within his own country, these variations are important, and they are conceivably important in special cases elsewhere. But at a distance, and in general, these variations are to be disregarded, and the dialect can be generalized without offence or particular damage to the enjoyment of a play or reading.

To illustrate, in plays of World War II, a Nazi officer was usually represented as using the uvular [R] except finally, where [ə] or [ɑ] may be used, as in German *Roemer* [ˈRømə] or English *raider* [ˈRedə]. This practice was probably intended to suggest Berlin pronounciation, which, in this special case was thought to be appropriate to such a character. But in general, German characters used the tongue-point trill for *r*, no matter what their native region in Germany.

For all the dialects treated in this book, the plan of generalizing will usually be followed, as being on the one hand convenient, and on the other hand entirely satisfactory to hearers in the large majority of cases.

The length of time the speaker has been speaking English. It goes without saying that the longer an individual speaks English, the better he should do. Some of the errors he makes early in his experience will disappear in time. Illustrating from German, we may say that the speaker who at first says *sale* [zel], will later say [sel], not retaining the initial [z] for *s* at all, or only in especially German-like words, such as *so* [zo]. Using such a generalized plan, transcribe the lists below.

Exercises in German Dialect

Suggestions:

1. Use either [r] or [R]; let it be understood in either case that the sound is a trill without the use of a diacritic to indicate it.

2. Write the dental signs under [d, t, n], at least at first, to emphasize dentality.

3. Use the symbol [ł], at least at first, to emphasize the clearness of [l].

4. For practice, transcribe as if the speakers made all the possible errors. Later, in actual practice in plays, readings, radio programs, etc., omit extreme characteristics as the exigencies of the occasion may demand.

5. Since the de-aspiration of [p, t, k] and the unvoicing of [b, d, g] give the effect of exchanging these consonants, they may be so exchanged in the following transcription. For greater accuracy, the closer transcriptions [p', t', k'] and [b̥, d̥, g̊] may be used later as needed.

6. Do not disturb [p, t, k, s] final. Any such change would violate the principle of the German language that final plosives and fricatives are voiceless.

tale, tame, tattle, toll, totter, tatter, task, tent, attend, time, too, attached.

dame, dangle, dole, daughter, dime, do, due, doddering, dozen, did.

pale, play, paddle, pole, pattered, patter, pent, pine, pool, apply, plop.

bale, blame, battle, boll, batter, bask, bend, blent, blind, blue.

kale, came, kind, can, can't, back, canned, could, account, acoustics, acacia.

gale, game, guile, gold, ghost, aggravate, aghast, gander, gag.

rail, raid, error, fear, care, rear, roarer, rider, here, hearer, clearer.

add, ask, alley, valley, fact, action, addle, demand, cattle, matter, mad.

under, truck, buck, upper, adjust, fun, son, love, does, tough, tug, lug, mull.

earl, furl, journal, spurt, tern, quirt, squirrel, worker, wordy, myrrh.

this, that, these, those, them, than, with, wither, writhe, soothe, seethe, booths, soothes, smooths, whether, weather, truths, rather, father.

thing, thimble, withe, forsooth, truth, Ruth, thistle, throttle, thermostat, thermometer, thrash, thrush, three, thirteen, thirty.

jail, June, July, judgment, George, fudge, gill (¼ pint), James, gem, general, jostle, jumped, juggled, jangles, gyrate.

sad, sod, sag, log, tab, Job, lobe, robe, rag, trade, drugs, tags, buzz, raise, adz.

stay, stool, stand, spade, spoil, spool, smack, smock, smile, snags, sneeze, snivels, switched, swamp, swage, assuage.

wail, whale, whistle, wild, wall, want, what, was, wade, wag, wagon, whine, whey, whimper, whist, wisp.

The German rhythm and stress are much more nearly like English than are the corresponding characteristics of any of the Romance languages. Nevertheless, except in the cases of the unstressing of *e* to [ə], German unstressing goes by no means so far in obliterating the identity of vowels as does English unstressing. Vowels retain their identity—a fact which indicates more painstaking pronunciation of syllables than in English. This carefulness is likely to carry over into English and affect the dialect.

The following tabulation summarizes the most important items of the foregoing. The illustrative single words are in close transcription, the sentences are broad transcription, representing not so much what the German actually says, as what the English speaker thinks he hears the German say.

[ɛˑ] for [æ]. Thus, [mɛˑt], suggesting [mɛt] for *mat* [mæt]. *On the mat in Madison.* [ɔn də mɛt ɪn mɛtəsən].

[uˑ] for [ʊ]. Thus, [fuˑ]], suggesting [fu]] for *full* [fʊl]. *The book is full of footnotes. Look!* [də puk ɪs fu], əf futnots.]uk!].

[t'] for [t]. Thus, [t'em], suggesting [dem] for *tame* [teɪm]. *It's time to talk to him.* [ɪts daɪm du dɔk du hɪm].

[d̬] for [d]. Thus, [d̬em], suggesting [tem] for *dame* [deɪm]. *Do or die.* [tu ɔr taɪ].

[p'] for [p]. Thus, [p'e], suggesting [be] for *pay* [peɪ]. *Pay the piper.* [be də baipər].

[b̬] for [b]. Thus, [b̬e], suggesting [pe] for *bay* [beɪ]. *Bay the moon, Beppo.* [pe də mun, pɛbo].

[k'] for [k]. Thus, [k'em], suggesting [gem] for *came* [keɪm]. *Call Kate.* [gɔ], get].

[g̬] for [g]. Thus, [g̬em], suggesting [kem] for *game* [geɪm]. *Go on, Jack, get into the game.* [ko ɔn, tʃɛk, kɛt ɪndʊ də kem].

[ʀ] for [r]. Thus, [ʀo], suggesting [wo] for *row* [roʊ]. *Row, brothers, row, 'round the lake.* [wo, bradərs, wo, wɑunt də]ek].

NOTE: This is an effect not to be overworked. Better, actually use [ʀ] — [ʀo, ʀɑunt]. But use sparingly, and only when the German regional dialect demands it.

Trilled [r] for [r]. Thus, [rɪŋ] with trill for [rɪŋ]. *Ring, rang, rung* [rɪŋ, rɛŋ, rɑŋ].

[ʁ > ə] for [r]. Thus, [fɪʁ] > [fɪə] for *fear* G. A. [fɪr], S. and E. [fɪə]. *Here they brew beer.* [hɪə de pru pɪə].

[β] for [w]. Thus, [βɛst], suggesting [vɛst], for *west* [wɛst]. *Mr. West, are you going westward?* [mɪstər vɛst, ɑr ju koiŋ vɛstvərt?]. Probably it is better actually to use [β] — [βɛst, ˈβɛstβərt]. But use sparingly, and only when the regional German dialect demands it.

[β] for [v]. Thus, [βɛst], suggesting [wɛst], for *vest* [vɛst]. *Mr. Vest, play your valuable violin.* [mɪstər wɛst, b]e jur wɛ]juəbəl waio]ɪn]. Do not put this dialectal variation and the one imediately above into the same individual's dialect.

[u, ɔ, ɑ] for [ʌ]. Thus, [up, ɔp, ɑp] for *up* [ʌp]. *Up, up, run for the cup.* [ɑp, ɑp, rɑn fɔr də gɑp], or [up, up, rɑn fɔr də gup].

[ɛə, ɛ, œ] for S. and E. [ɜ]. Thus, [bɛətʃ, bɛʁtʃ, bœtʃ] for *birch* [bɜːtʃ].

[ɛr, ɛ, œr] for G. A., [ɝ]. Thus [fɛr, fɛʁ, fœr] for *fur* [fɝ].

[d] for [ð]. Thus, [doz] for *those* [ðoʊz]. *This, that, these and those are the other pronouns* [dɪs, dɛt, dis, ənt dos ɑr di adə bronɑuns].

[t] for [θ]. Thus, [tɪn] for *thin* [θɪn]. *Things thickly thrust Thatcher athwart the throng* [tɪŋs tɪklɪ trɑst tɛtʃər ətvɑrt də trɔŋ].

[tʃ, j] for [dʒ]. Thus, [tʃok, jok] for *joke* [dʒoʊk]. *Judge James Jones* [tʃatʃ tʃems tʃons].

[z] for [s] in initial positions. Thus, [zo] for *so* [soʊ]. *So he saw the sail* [zo hi zɔ də zeḷ].

[s] for [z] in final positions. Thus, [hɪs] for *his* [hɪz]. *The rose that froze is his.* [də ros dɛt fros ɪs hɪs].

[t] for [d] in final positions. Thus, [rot, ʀot] for *road* [roʊd]. *Sing the ode on the lonely road to his sad abode* [zɪŋ dɪ ot ɔn də lonlɪ rot dʊ hɪs zɛt əbot].

[k] for [g] in final positions. Thus, [p'lak] for *plug* [plʌg]. *Lug the jug to the rug* [lak də tʃak dʊ də rak].

[ʃ] for [ʒ]. Thus, [ˈpᵊlɛʃər] for *pleasure*, G. A. [ˈplɛʒɚr], E., S. and Br. [ˈplɛʒə]. *Leisure is a measure of our pleasure* [ḷiʃər ɪs ə mɛʃər af aʊr bḷɛʃər].

[f] for [v] in final positions. Thus, [gɪf] for *give* [gɪv]. *Love and live, wive and shrive* [laf ənt ḷɪf, vaɪf ənt ʃraɪf].

With the foregoing examples in mind, transcribe the following from Zangwill's *The Melting Pot*. Note that the author has suggested some of the broken English pronunciations, but by no means all of them. As in every such case, the phonetician must complete what the author has suggested—even correct him if, as often happens, he has made the speaker say what such a speaker would not or could not say, or has tried to spell something in ordinary type which can be expressed only in phonetic symbols.

From *The Melting Pot* *

(Enter Herr Pappelmeister, a burly German figure.—His English, as roughly indicated in the text, is extremely Teutonic.)

Pappelmeister—I haf not de honour. But, if you brefer, I will gut out from my brogrammes all de Chewish composers. Was?

Pappel.—Blay it? Am I an orchestra? I blay it in my brain.—So!

Pappel.—In Germany! Germany has nodings to teach him. He has to teach Germany.

Pappel.—I should be proud to indroduce it to de vorld.

Pappel.—I see von Finale scratched out and anoder not quite completed. But anyhow, ve couldn't broduce it before Saturday fortnight?

Pappel.—Somedings must be sagrificed.

Pappel.—Ja, my own band. Ven I left dat comic opera millionaire, dey all shtick to me almost to von man.

Pappel.—All egsept de Christian—he vas de von man. He shtick to de millionaire. So I lose my brincipal first violin.

Pappel.—Vat on earth does one go to a beer-hall for? Ha! Ha! Ha! For vater! —Ven I hear you blay, I dink mit myself—if my blans succeed and I get Carnegie

Hall for Saturday Symphony Concerts, dat boy shall be one of my first violins. Was?

Pappel.—And zo are my congratulations!

Pappel.—But you must come and speak to all de people in America who undershtand music.

Pappel.—De dird vampire says it is a great vork greatly performed.

Pappel.—Nein. Ven critics disagree—I agree mit mineself.—A great vork dat vill be even better performed next time.—Ten dousand congratulations.

Pappel.—I knew your nerves would be all shnapping like fiddlestrings. Oh you cheniuses! You like neider de clappings nor de criticisms,—was?

ISRAEL ZANGWILL

Bibliography

German

Books

Ekwall, Eilert, *Historische neuenglische Laut- und Formenlehre* (Berlin and Leipzig: Walter de Gruyter and Co., 1922).

Hempl, George, *German Orthography and Phonology* (New York: Ginn and Co., 1897).

Prokosch, Edward, *A Comparative German Grammar* (Philadelphia: Linguistic Society of America, University of Pennsylvania, 1939).

———, *An Outline of German Historical Grammar* (New York: Oxford University Press, 1933).

———, *Sounds and History of the German Language* (New York: Henry Holt and Sons, 1916).

Siebs, Theodor, *Deutsche Bühnenaussprache* (Berlin, Köln and Leipzig: Albert Ahn, 1905).

Trautmann, Moritz, *Kleine Lautlehre des Deutschen, Französischen und Englischen* (Bonn: C. Georgi's Universitäts Buchdruckerei, 1903).

Viëtor, Wilhelm, *Deutsches Aussprache-Wörterbuch* (Leipzig: O. R. Reisland, 1915).

———, *Elemente der Phonetik* (Heilbronn: Henninger Bros., 1884).

———, *German Pronunciation* (Heilbronn: Henninger Bros., 1885).

CHAPTER 19

Pennsylvania German
("Pennsylvania Dutch")

One of the most picturesque and delightful of English dialects is the Pennsylvania German-English dialect. Although this dialect is thought of as being limited principally to the counties of Northampton, Lehigh, Berks, Lebanon, Lancaster, York, Schuylkill, and Dauphin in southeastern Pennsylvania, it is spoken to some extent in adjacent parts of Maryland, Virginia, and West Virginia. Despite the circumscribed area in which this dialect is used naturally, so to speak, it is widely known throughout the United States as an attractive medium for the writing of verses, short stories, songs, plays, and some novels.

The Pennsylvania German dialect of English is the English spoken by people of German extraction in the areas indicated above. Many of them use Pennsylvania German itself as a home language. However, considerable numbers of people who do not speak the local dialect of German nevertheless sound as if they ought to be able to do so, since they have had little opportunity to learn any other English than that underlaid by a noticeable substratum of dialectal pronunciation, diction, syntax, and intonation.

The German spoken by the Pennsylvania German people has been cut off from Germany for a very long time, since the main period of German colonization in Pennsylvania took place between 1683 and 1734 and was largely completed by 1750. Most of the people came from Württemberg, the Palatinate, the neighborhood of Darmstadt, and the area north of Cologne in Germany, and from Zürich, Bern, and Schaffhausen in Switzerland. The dialects which the immigrants spoke in Europe are known to differ from standard High German (though not nearly so much as the Low German of the North) and, to some extent, from each other. However, on arriving in Pennsylvania, the people were irrevocably separated from Germany and Switzerland both by distance and by the attitudes of the relatively small religious groups (Dunkers, Mennonites, and Amish) to which many of them belonged, and so their dialects fused together into a single dialect in which distinguishing features of the original components were soon practically lost. As it exists now, Pennsylvania German possesses no rounded front sounds such as High German possesses; contains no aspirate plosives, i.e., no aspirate [p, t, k], except initially before a vowel; contains no voiced plosives at all, i.e., no [b, d, g]; and has no voiced fricatives except [γ], and [β], so that there is no [v] (except as a member of the [β] phoneme), and no consistent use of [z]. As will be seen, these same conditions as to aspiration and voicing apply, with reasonable uniformity, to the speaking of English by the Pennsylvania German people.

As is to be expected when a language exists as an island surrounded by another language, Pennsylvania German contains a long list of English loan words, most of which have been acclimated to the German phonological framework in which they are now found, so that they retain only a modicum of their English character, being pronounced, instead, very much as if they were German words. M. B. Lambert, in his *Dictionary*[1], lists 517 such words, "wholly or partly of English origin compiled to illustrate (1) the retention of English sounds, (2) the changes which English sounds and words have undergone in the process of adoption, (3) the addition of German prefixes, suffixes, and endings to English words, (4) the formation of hybrid compounds." Some such words are *beind* [b̥aɪn̮d̥] (pine), *fackdri* [ˈfag̊dri] (factory), *gardien* [g̊arˈd̥in] (guardian), *intchein* [ˈɪn̩d̥ʃaɪn] (engine), *redder* [ˈrɛd̥ər] (rather), *warnish* [ˈwarnɪʃ] (varnish).[2]

It is natural to expect that these loan words, when restored to English context, will retain something of their Germanized pronunciation. The evidence appears to show that though they do retain certain features, any German word-building elements which an English word may have acquired when being borrowed will be stripped away. Thus *uffborde* (to board up) will lose the local dialectal prefix *uff*—and the dialectal infinitive ending—*e*, so as to return to the English language in approximately its original English orthographic form, *board up*. On the other hand, purely phonetic German elements are retained, so that the word will be pronounced [ˌb̥ɔəd̥ ˈap], [ˌb̥ord̥ ˈap], or [ˌb̥ɔn̮d̥ ˈap]. Likewise, *Tschulei* (July) continues to be pronounced [ɪd̥ʃuˈlaɪ], even after being returned to the context of the English language. The reader can usually be guided in respect to words of this sort by the spellings of the dialect writer. For further guidance, he can refer to the Lambert list mentioned above or to the more accessible derivative lists in Borchers and Wise, *Modern Speech*.[3]

When the people speak English, the linguistic habits of the Pennsylvania German tend to affect also those English words which have never been adopted

---

[1] Marcus Bachman Lambert, *A Dictionary of the Non-English Words of the Pennsylvania-German Dialect* (Lancaster, Pa.: Pennsylvania-German Society, Lancaster Press, Inc., 1924), pp. 189–193.

[2] The voiceless sign [̥] or [°] is used here with [b, d, g] to represent the unaspiration of [p, t, k]. Thus [b̥] = [p'], [d̥] = t'], and [g̊] = [k']. All [r]'s are tongue-point trilled.

[3] Gladys Borchers and C. M. Wise, *Modern Speech* (New York: Harcourt, Brace, 1947), pp. 478–488.

as loan words in the German dialect itself. The resultant dialect, consisting thus of recaptured loan words from the German, other similarly modified English words, and, as may be expected, some German loan words reciprocally borrowed into English, make up what we have referred to as the Pennsylvania German Dialect of English.

Perhaps this is the proper place to mention that the word *Dutch* < Pa. Ger. Deitsch [d̥aɪd̥ʃ] < High German *Deutsch* [dɔɪtʃ] (German) is popularly used to designate both the German dialect and the English dialect spoken in the area under discussion. This book uses *German* instead of *Dutch* in view of the fact that Dutch is more accurately used to designate the language and people of Holland. Accordingly, *Pennsylvania German* is here used instead of *Pennsylvania Dutch* for the local dialect of German, and the *Pennsylvania German Dialect of English* is used instead of *Pennsylvania Dutch* for the dialectal English spoken.

The discussion following undertakes to indicate the main features in which the Pennsylvania German Dialect of English differs from standard English. These features, in the main, are chosen as for the less educated members of the population.[4]

[i] is used in the words *itch* [id̥ʃ] and *deaf* [d̥if], following the local English vernacular. It is also used in some words ending in [ə] spelled with *a*, as *extra* [ˈɛksd̥ri],[5]

[ɑ] in the spelling *ar*, stressed ∼ [æ], as in *car* [kæɒ], *carpet* [ˈkæɒb̥əd̥].[6]

[ʌ] ∼ [ɑ:] irregularly in some words, *nothing* [ˈnɑ:θɪŋ], *comfortable* [ˈkɑ:mfətəbəl], and *country* [ˈkɑ:ntrɪ].[7] Other words similarly affected are *tongue, among, above, love, cover, oven.*

[ʌ] ∼ [ɔ] in the prefix *un*, following the English vernacular, in words such as *unhappy* [ˌɔnˈhæb̥ɪ], and in a few other words, such as *cup* [g̊ɔb̥]. Other words in which [ɔ] is similarly used are *undertake, untie, unpleasant, unfasten, unkind,* etc.[8]

[ə], [ə], spelled *er, ur*, etc., ∼ [ɚ, ər, ɒ] indifferently, as in *leather* [ˈlɛð̣ɚ, ˈlɛðər, lɛɒ̣], *caterpillar* [ˈkæd̥ɚˌb̥ɪlɚ, ˈkæd̥ərˌb̥ɪlər, ˈkæd̥ɒˌb̥ɪlɒ].

---

[4] Four levels of speech are recognized in the Pennsylvania German area, viz., (1) Pennsylvania German itself; (2) Pennsylvania German Dialect of English as spoken by less literate people; (3) English affected little in pronunciation, but containing numbers of unconsciously inserted German idioms; (4) Standard General American English, containing no noticeable German pronunciation features, and no German idioms except as consciously used by way of quasi-quotation.

[5] J. William Frey, "The English of the Pennsylvania Germans of York County, Pennsylvania," *Morning Call*, Allentown, Pa., May 18, 1940.

[6] J. William Frey, "The Phonemics of English Loan Words in Eastern York County Pennsylvania Dutch," *American Speech*, April, 1942, p. 94.

[7] George G. Struble, "English of the Pennsylvania Germans," *American Speech*, October, 1935, p. 165.

[8] R. Whitney Tucker, "Linguistic Substrata in Pennsylvania and Elsewhere," *Language*, March, 1934, p. 2.

[r] postvocalic ∼ [ə, r, ɒ] indifferently, as in *board* [b̥oəd̥, b̥ourd̥, b̥oɒd̥], *four* [foə, four, foɒ].

[ɔɪ] ∼ [aɪ] as in *joint* [d̥ʃaɪnd̥], *boil* [b̥aɪl]. Cf. *boiler, joist, hoist*, etc.

[p] ∼ [b̥] as in *plenty* ['b̥lɛnd̥ɪ], *upper* [ab̥ɒ], *profit* ['b̥rafɪd̥], *whip* [wɪb̥], but not in such words as *pole* [poʊl], where the initial plosive is followed by a vowel and remains aspirate. However, the very frequently used [b̥ɔɪ] for *pie* begins with the voiceless unaspirate [b̥]. It is thought that this word, like a few others (*cf.* [b̥aɪnd̥]), was borrowed in very early colonial times. Later English borrowings seem to retain the aspiration on initial *p* before a vowel.[9]

[t] ∼ [d̥] as *try* [d̥raɪ], *better* ['b̥ɛd̥ɒ], *trot* [d̥rɑd̥], but not in such words as *tie* [taɪ], where the initial plosive is followed by a vowel and remains aspirate.

[k] ∼ [g̊] as in *creek* [g̊rɪg̊], *racket* ['ræg̊əd̥], *crime* [g̊raɪm], *close* [g̊los], etc., but not as in *kill* [kɪl], where the initial plosive is followed by a vowel and remains aspirate.

[d̠ʒ] ∼ [d̥ʃ] as in *Jake* [d̥ʃeɪg̊], *engine* ['ɪnˌd̥ʃaɪn], *judge* [d̥ʃɑːd̥ʃ]. Other words similarly affected are *James, George, jump*.

[n] ∼ [ən] as in *own* ['oʊən], *strewn* ['ʃd̥ruən], *prune* ['b̥ruən]. Other words similarly affected are *known, shown, thrown, blown, hewn*.[10]

[ŋg] ∼ [ŋ] in such words as *finger* ['fɪŋɚ], *longer* ['lɔŋɚ]. Other words similarly affected are *hungry, angry, linger, stronger, English*, etc.

[v] ∼ [v, β] intervocalically as in *ever* ['ɛvər, 'ɛβər].

[v] ∼ [w, β] initially as in *vinegar* ['wɪnəg̊ɚ, 'βɪnəg̊ɚ], *veal* [wil, βil]. Other words similarly affected are *varnish, vow, vicar*. Even in the case of words such as *view*, where the use of initial [w] would require the awkward [wju], [β] is sometimes used. But speakers from the town of Valley View are widely known for their pronunciation ['wali 'wju]. [v] final is unchanged and remains [v], as in *give* [g̊ɪv]. ([β] is the bilabial spirant, made by placing the lips as for blowing out a candle and expelling the breath with voicing.)

[θ] ∼ [s] irregularly as in *south* [sɑːs], *north* [nɔrs].

[s] ∼ [ʃ] in initial *st* and *sp*, as in *stop* [ʃd̥ab̥], *spoil* [ʃb̥aɪl].

[z] ∼ [s] irregularly in final positions, as in *has* [hæs], *was* [wɑs], *is* [ɪs]. That this unvoicing of [z] does not occur regularly in final positions as when speakers of Standard High German use English, doubtless results from the fact that in the more than 200 years of residence in an English-speaking country, English language patterns have intruded themselves among the German patterns.

[aʊ] ∼ [av] intervocalically, as in *coward* ['kɑːvərd̥],[11] *our* ['avər], *sour* ['savər].

[w] ∼ [v] as in *wiles* [vaɪls]. Other words similarly affected are *wake, wall*. The confusion between [v] and [w] obviously begins with the fact that in the Pennsylvania German the bilabial spirant [β] is used for both sounds. Speakers

---

[9] Frey, "Phonemics of English Loan Words," *American Speech*, April, 1942, p. 94.
[10] Tucker, p. 2.
[11] Frey, "The English of the Pennsylvania Germans of York County, Pennsylvania."

of English hearing [β] almost invariably hear it as [v] if it is intended for [w] and as [w] if it is intended for [v]. It must be assumed that as Pennsylvania Germans perfect their English, they begin to hear [β] somewhat as other speakers of English do. Since they learn to pronounce both [v] and [w] in school, they can use both readily, but they remain confused as to which is required in a given case.

In matters of diction and syntax the literature of this dialect supplies the variations from standard English without effort on the part of the reader, but the printed page does not ordinarily supply information on intonation. In questions and in some declarative sentences, in the intonation of the Pennsylvania German English dialect, the voice rises on the stressed word or syllable preceding the word or last syllable. Examples: Where's your fáther gòing? He's in the grócery stòre. Frey illustrates another type of intonation in what he calls "the backward question."[12] He says, "In this type of question, the finite verb is in initial position and takes the principal accent, the rest of the sentence 'sloping down,' as it were; sometimes another word near the end of the question will take a kind of secondary accent, for example: 'Are you goin' down town?' or 'Is he gonna go?'" Frey also mentions an "odd lengthening of vowels which come at the end of a sentence . . . elongated into a singsong effect which approaches the vowel sounds found in Swedish." Example: When are you gonna go-a ['goə]?

The following transcriptions are made by permission from phonograph records by Professor J. W. Frey of Franklin and Marshall College, Lancaster, Pa.[13] It is recommended that students secure these and similar records, particularly for the study of intonation characteristics.

DAUGHTER, WILL YOU MARRY?

wɛl, naʊ, hɪrz sʊsɪ, ðə d̪ʌd̪ʃ farmɚs d̪ədər, æn paḅ hi wɔnd̪s tə mærɪ hɚ ɔf. ɪd̪s əḅaʊd̪:aɪm; ʃi ɪz ˌsɪg̊sd̪in sɪnd̪s læs d̪ʃun ərɛd̪ɪ, pɚd̪ɪ əz ðeɪ kʌm, æn ə raɪd̪ ʃmɑᴅd̪ med̪ḷ; ḅət ʃiz g̊ad̪ ə hɛd̪ əv ɛ oʊn, sʊsi d̪ʌs. wɪð al paḅs aɪd̪ɪs ḅad̪ ᴧᴧd̪ fɚ mæn ʃɪ ʃəl hæv, βaɪ hɪr ʃi g̊oʊz n̩ rʌnz ɔf βɪð:æt ˌnɪg̊s nʊsɪç g̊ud̪ fᴅ nɑðɪŋ fɪd̪ˌlᴅ.

d̪ədər, βɪl jʊ mærɪ? jeɪ, fad̪ᴅ, jeɪ.

n̩ βɪl jə mærɪ ə farmɚ? neɪ, fad̪ᴅ, neɪ.

aɪl mærɪ nʌn ə ðə farmɚs:ɔrd̪;

sd̪eɪḅəl g̊lɪnɪŋ ɪz nad̪ maɪ fɔrd̪. neɪ, faðə, neɪ.

d̪əd̪ɚ, βɪl jʊ mærɪ? jeɪ, fad̪ᴅ, jeɪ. wɪl jə mærɪ ə ḅrɪd̪ʃɚ? neɪ, faðɚ, neɪ. mærɪ ə ḅrɪtʃɚ? oʊ, noʊ, d̪ɪr. aɪd̪ ḅi rag̊ŋ ə g̊reɪd̪əl ɛvrɪ jɪr. neɪ, fad̪ᴅ, neɪ.

---

12 Frey, "The English of the Pennsylvania Germans of York County, Pennsylvania."

13 J. W. Frey, Folksongs of the Pennsylvania Dutch, Nelson Cornell Custom Records, Inc., Distributed by the Pennsylvania Dutch Folklore Society, Lancaster, Pa.

d̦od̦ɚ, βɪl jʊ mærɪ? jeɪ, faðɚ, jeɪ. wɪl jə mærɪ ə d̦og̦dər? neɪ, faðɚ, neɪ. ə d̦og̦ɚdz waɪf aɪ βɪl nat b̦i; pɔɪznɪŋ pib̦əl ɪz nad̦ fɚ mi. neɪ, faðɚ, neɪ.

d̦od̦ɚ, vɪl jʊ mærɪ? jeɪ, faðɚ, jeɪ. wɪl jʊ mærɪ ə lɔjɚ? neɪ, faðɚ, neɪ. aɪl nad̦:eɪg̦ ə lɔjɚ ət ɛnɪ b̦raɪs; d̦ʃid̦ɪŋ pɪb̦əl d̦ʃʌsd̦ eɪn:aɪs. neɪ, faðɚ, neɪ.

d̦od̦ɚ, vɪl jʊ mæri? jeɪ, faðɚ, jei. wɪl jə mærɪ ə fɪd̦lɚ? jeɪ, faðɚ, jeɪ. aɪ βɔnd̦tə b̦i ə fɪd̦lə z waɪf; tʊ sɪŋ n̦ tʊ d̦ænd̦s ɪz ə d̦ʃɔɪ tə maɪ laɪf. jeɪ, faðɚ, jeɪ.

Dear Henry (Leever Heindrich)

ðeɪ tɔg̦ sd̦ɪl əb̦ad̦ ðə d̦am d̦ʌd̦ʃ. wl̦ əf ju sɛd̦ d̦ʃɔad̦ʃ wəz d̦amən̦ haɪnrɪç, aɪd̦ g̦ɪv jə ra:ɪd̦. βaɪ d̦ʃɔad̦ʃ ɪz d̦aməɒn̦ d̦ʃeɪg̦ βeɪd̦s b̦ʊl jɛd̦. hɪ rʌn ɪn ðə g̦rɪg̦ tə g̦ɪd̦ a:t ðə re:n. ja, g̦əvɪs, ðæd̦s fɔ ʃʊɚ! ðə b̦ɔɪs ɚ hævɪŋ ə lɪd̦l̦ hard̦ saɪd̦ɒ—ɪf ɪd̦ aɪnd̦ dænd̦ɪlaɪən βaɪn—n̦ dam d̦ʃɔad̦ʃ hɪ g̦əmb̦leɪnz ðæd̦ ðə d̦ʃʌg̦ hæz ə hoʊl ɪn əd̦. his:oʊ d̦ʌd̦ʃ hi kænt tʃɪst hɪz taŋ ərand̦:ɪ ɪŋlɪs jɛd̦, b̦əd̦ haɪnrɪç ænsɚz ɪm pɚd̦ɪ ʃnæb̦ɪ jɛd̦ ɪn hoxɪŋlɪʃ—haɪ ɪŋlɪʃ—ʊn wɛn haɪnrɪç g̦ɛd̦s mad̦ βʌnd̦s ɪd̦ riəlɪ meɪg̦s.

naʊ maɪnd̦ aɪ tɛl jə.

d̦ʃʌg̦ hæz ə hoʊl ɪn id̦? βɛl jə d̦am ðɪŋ, ðɛn b̦lʌg̦ əd̦ ʌb̦.

b̦lʌg̦ əd̦ ʌb̦, jɪ d̦am e:səl? βaɪ βɪθ ə ʃd̦rɔ:

tu lɔŋ? wə ðɛn jə d̦ʃʌs d̦ʃab̦ ɪd̦ ɔ:f. βaɪ jə d̦ʃab̦ əd̦ ɔf, ji d̦am ðɪŋ, βɪθ ðə hæd̦ʃɪd̦. ðə hæd̦ʃɪd̦s tu d̦ʌəl? vaɪ ðɛn jə meɪg̦ ɪd̦ ʃaɚb̦.

wəd̦ ʃəl jə meɪg̦ əd̦ ʃarb̦ ɔn? ʊn sɛləm ʃd̦e:n—ɔn ðæd̦ stoʊn.

oʊ, ju d̦am e:zəl! naʊ jə seɪ ðə sd̦oʊns tu d̦raɪ. wə ðɛn jə d̦ʃʌs meɪg̦ əd̦ ved̦. meɪg̦ ɪd̦ ved̦? βaɪ d̦ʃʌs βɪθ ˈwɔəd̦ɒ. wʌd̦ ʃəl jə kærɪ ðə wɔd̦ər ɪn? βaɪ ju d̦am ðɪŋ, βaɪ ɪn ðæd̦ d̦ʃʌg̦, ə koʊrs.

naʊ aɪ sɛd̦ d̦βaɪs ərɛd̦ɪ, b̦lʌg̦ ɪt ʌb̦.

jə noʊ βi du hæf səm fʌnɪ kʌsd̦əmz. βaɪ ðə læst fɛlə aʊd̦ə b̦ed̦ ɔn fɔs nɔxt d̦eɪ—n̦ ðæts ðə d̦eɪ b̦ifoʊr æʃ βɛnzd̦ɪ—ɪs kɔld̦ ðə fɔs nɔxt. æn̦ ðə neg̦s d̦eɪ, ðə læs fɛlə aʊd̦ə b̦ed̦ ɪn ðə haʊs ɪs kɔld̦ ðɪ ɛʃəpud̦əl. æn ðə d̦eɪ æfd̦ɚ ðæd̦, ɪf i g̦ɛd̦s ʌb̦ ðə læst wʌn, βaɪ ðɛn hɪs kɔld̦ ðə ʃb̦ɪlumb̦asug̦lɒ. æn ɔn fraɪd̦ɪ əv ðæd̦ β̦ig̦, vi d̦ʃʌs kɔl ɪm ðə ki:ʃβand̦s—ðɪ oʊl kaʊs d̦eɪl.

oʊ aɪ wɪʃd̦ aɪ vʌz ə farmɚ ʊnd̦ hæd̦ ə hoʊmʃd̦ed̦ farm, βɪθ hɔrsəs g̦rɪn n̦ jɛlə kaʊs n̦ ə βaɪf tə kɪb̦ mi βɔrm.

> aɪ βɪʃ aɪ hæd̦ ə hoʊmʃd̦ed̦ farm
> ɔn ðə kanəʃd̦oʊg̦əz b̦aŋg̦s.
> aid̦ b̦id̦ ðə b̦ʌg̦s ɪn ə ʃud̦ɪŋ mæd̦ʃ
> ɪn ðə sβid̦ pəd̦ed̦ə ræŋg̦s.

> βɪθ kæd̦ɒb̦ɪlɒz ɔn ðə βid̦s,
> ðə d̦ʃig̦ənz fʊl ə fliz,
> ðə kæb̦ɪd̦ʃ βɚm ɔn ðə hɪg̦rɪ nʌd̦s,
> ɛn laɪs əpɔn ðə d̦riz.

ðis:ɪŋz mʌsd ɔl b̥ɪg̊ɪn tə g̊rɔl,
ɪf aɪd̥ ə farmɚ b̥i.
βɪθ pærɪs grin n̥ ə b̥lʌnd̥ɚb̥ʌs
aɪd̥ ʃb̥reɪ ðɛm βɛl, ju si.

aɪd̥ ʃd̥art raɪd̥ hɪr ə fæʃən nu:
ɪn βɪnd̥ɒ aɪd̥ meɪg̊ heɪ;
n̥ βɛn ɪd̥s had̥ aɪd̥ d̥ʃʌs kib̥ kul
n̥ rɛsd̥ ðə lɪvlɔŋ d̥eɪ.

aɪd̥ g̊ɛt maɪsɛlf ə g̊rim d̥ʃiz kaʊ,
ə flag̊ ə g̊ɪnɪ hɛns,
ə maɪd̥ɪ haɪ g̊ud̥ rɛd̥ b̥id̥:ri
n̥ ə pæd̥n̥d̥ lɛðɒ fɛnd̥s.

aɪd̥ kib̥ ðə d̥ʃɪg̊ənz ɪn ðə haʊs,
ðə pɪg̊ pɛn b̥aɪ ðə d̥ɒa.
βɪθ koʊd̥ n̥ pænd̥s əv kæləg̊o,
n̥ peɪb̥ɒ kalɒs foə̥.

aɪd̥ b̥ɪld̥ əb̥ɔn maɪ hoʊmʃd̥ɛd̥ farm
ə haʊs ɔl peɪnd̥əd̥ vaɪd̥,
suraʊnd̥ɪd̥ βɪθ maɪ βalnʌd̥:riz,
ɪd̥ rɪlɪ b̥i ə saɪd̥.

ɑx, ɪf aɪ βas ə farmɪŋ mæn,
n̥ hæd̥ ə hoʊmʃd̥ɛd̥ farm,
n̥ hæd̥ ə vaɪf so b̥ɪg̊ n̥ fæd̥
tə kib̥ ðɪs farmɚ βɔrm.

Transcribe in Pennsylvania German-English Dialect:

I will write a few lines to you about the work. Why I can't go so far like Kutztown to work? Why, I can't come their. Why, its to far walk and I don't have a machine to go there for to work, and knowbody out here that I can get along out. Please be so good and kind and give work nearer at my place where I live—maybe that chop (job) come up near Driebellis, where I work this winter. Their I can walk to for work; that's not so far that—about 4 or 5 miles from me. I am every hours to work. But not so far off. I can't come their. I have no machine, to go. If its not so far, I can walk to work.

If you have that chop up near Driebellis station, let me come there to work. Or another chop nearer my home so that can come their to work. Why, I must walk. We have no machine.[14]

---

[14] Letter at the semi-literate level, Eugene R. Page, "English in the Pennsylvania German Area," in *American Speech*, Oct., 1937, p. 206.

Bibliography

Pennsylvania-German

Books

Lambert, Marcus Bachman, *A Dictionary of the Non-English Words of the Pennsylvania-German Dialect* (Lancaster, Pa.: Lancaster Press, pub. by the Pennsylvania-German Society, 1924).

Oswald, V. O. *The Phonemes of a Lehigh County Dialect of Pennsylvania-German* (Columbia University: Ph. D. dissertation, 1949, composed on varitype and privately issued, 1949).

Reed, Carroll E., *The Pennsylvania German Dialect Spoken in the Counties of Lehigh and Berks* (Seattle: University of Washington Press, 1949).

Periodicals

Bickel, Paul J., "Notes on Pennsylvania German," *American Speech*, April, 1930.

Buffington, Albert F., "Pennsylvania German; Its Relation to Other German Dialects," *American Speech*, December, 1939.

Follin, Maynard D., "Pennsylvania Dutch," *American Speech*, August, 1928.

Frey, J. William, "The English of the Pennsylvania Germans of York County, Pa.," *The Morning Call*, Allentown, Pa., May 18, 1940.

————, "Notes on the Diphthong *oi* in Pennsylvania Dutch," *American Speech*, April, 1943.

————, "The Phonemics of English Loan Words in Eastern York County Pennsylvania Dutch," *American Speech*, April, 1942.

Page, Eugene R., "Pennsylvania German English," (so indexed: actual title: "English in the Pennsylvania German Area"), *American Speech*, October, 1937.

Reed, Carroll E., "The Gender of English Loan Words in Pennsylvania German," *American Speech*, February, 1942.

Struble, George G., "English of the Pennsylvania Germans," *American Speech*, October, 1935.

Tucker, R. Whitney, "Linguistic Substrata in Pennsylvania and Elsewhere," *Language*, March, 1934.

Werner, William L., "English Words in the Pennsylvania-German Dialect," *American Speech*, December, 1930.

————, "Pennsylvania-German, 1927–37," *American Speech*, April, 1938.

CHAPTER 20

Yiddish

The term "Yiddish Dialect," as used herein, is to be defined as the substandard English speech used by less-educated Jews in New York City. The Jewish dialect of other cities is not identical with that of New York, but is sufficiently like it to make the selection of the New York City version as the norm a practical one. Conversely, the word Yiddish[1] will not be used in this book to refer to the dialects of German spoken by Jewish immigrants from Germany, Czechoslovakia, Poland, Hungary, Roumania, Russia, etc. For these dialects, the term Judeo-German will be used.

The features included here as Yiddish features are basically drawn from the speech of second-to-fourth generation New York Jews, but it reaches back, to a considerable extent, to the speech of immigrant Jews.

As an English dialect, Yiddish is obviously based on substandard New York speech. In the following pages it is intended that whenever no specific pronunciation is indicated as being characteristically Yiddish, substandard New York speech is to be used. For convenience, some of the features of New York speech which are most frequently used in Yiddish are here included with the features more specifically Yiddish.

Dentality of [t, d, n, l, s, z, ʧ, ʤ]. This dentality is least conspicuous on [n, l], has the effect of a lisp on [s, z], and is accompanied by over-energized explosiveness on [t, d],[2] especially of [t] after [n] and [l]. Although these features are found generally in New York City, the dentalization of [t, d, n] and the over-aspiration of [t] after [n, l] seem to be especially prominent features of Yiddish.[3]

[ŋ] ~ [ŋg, ŋk]. The latter is more frequent in Yiddish than in New York speech proper, but both are common, as in *singer* [ˈsɪŋgə], *coming* [ˈkɑmɪŋk]. (See page 288.) Conversely, the omission of [g] from [ŋg] is common, as in *longer* [ˈlɔŋə]. (See page 288.)

---

[1] The word "Yiddish" means, simply, "Jewish." The German noun *Jude* (Jew) yields the adjective *jüdisch* (Jewish), whence *Yiddish*.

[2] C. K. Thomas, "Jewish Dialect and New York Dialect," *American Speech*, June, 1932, p. 323.

[3] Phyllis Betts Arlt, *A Phonological Study of the English Dialect of New York City Jews*. Cornell University, unpublished M. A. thesis, 1939, pp. 33–34. The author states that 95 per cent of the New York Jews surveyed had these characteristics.

The use of [ʔ], as in *little* [ˈlɪʔl̩]. (See page 283.)

[æ] ∼ [ɛə], as in *dance* [d̪ẓɛənt̪s̪]. (See page 283.) (Lengthened, overtense [æ̃, æ̃ə̃] may be found.)

[ʍ] ∼ [w], as in *when* [wɛn]. (See page 286.)

[ɜ] ∼ [ɜɪ], rarely [ɔɪ], as in *curl* [kɜɪl, kɔɪl]. (See page 284.)

[ɜ] ∼ [ʌ], finally, as in *stir* [stʌ].

[ɔɪ] ∼ [ɜɪ], rarely [ɝ], as in *coil* [kɜɪl, kɜ l]. (See page 284.)

[ɔɪ] finally ∼ [oɪ] as in *boy* [boɪ].

[θ, ð] ∼ [t̪, d̪] as in *thin* [t̪ɪn], *this* [d̪ɪs].

Affrication of [t, d], as in *two* [t̪s̪u], *do* [d̪ẓu].

Instrusive [r], as in *idea* [ɒɪˈd̪ɪər].

[ɑ] ∼ [ɔ], as in *farm* [fɔ:m].[4]

[au] ∼ [æʊ], as in *now* [næʊ].

[ou] ∼ [ɛʊ, eʊ], as in *note* [nɛʊt̪, neʊt̪].[5]

[aɪ] ∼ [ɒɪ], as in substandard New York speech, but is frequently heard as [ɑɪ] and even [ɔɪ], as in *time* [t̪s̪ɒɪm, t̪s̪ɑɪm, t̪s̪ɔɪm].

Final [s] before voiced consonant is voiced, as in *ice box* [ˈɒɪzbɑks].

Final [z] is frequently unvoiced, as in *raise* [reɪs], *because* [bəˈkɔs].[6]

Intervocalic [t] is voiced, as in *ladder* for *letter*.

[r] ∼ trilled *r* [r̃], [ʀ] mainly with first generation Jews. Example: *ride* [r̃ɒɪd̪ẓ, ʀɒɪd̪ẓ]. Choice between tongue-point trilled *r* and uvular *r* appears to lie with the individual and to depend on which one of the *r*'s is used in the Judeo-German he speaks. Compare *ring, bringer, fire, rat, burning.*

[eɪ, oʊ] ∼ [e, o], as in *day* [d̪e], *go* [go].

Initial [r] ∼ [vr], as in *right* [vrɒɪt̪s̪]. This is not a universal feature, but it frequently appears.

[s] ∼ sometimes [l̥, θ, ʃ]. Such features are of irregular distribution and are found less frequently among the Jews of New York City than elsewhere.[7] Example: *see* [l̥i, θi, ʃi]. These pronunciations are to be used with some discretion. Since not one of them is universal, in a given piece of literature it is probably best to depend on the orthographic or descriptive clues. Compare *eastside, song, sale, Sunday.*

Models for Yiddish Speech

As in the reproduction of all dialects, those who wish to reproduce Yiddish dialect with fidelity of voice quality and intonation should by all means find opportunity to hear speakers to whom it is a normal mode of specch. Such

---

[4] Arlt, p. 36.
[5] Thomas, p. 324.
[6] Arlt, p. 36.
[7] Thomas, p. 324.

speakers are, naturally, much better models than actors or other performers who are themselves imitating the original speech. Listening to phonograph records is nearly as good for this purpose as listening to the speakers themselves. Besides, records have the advantage of being readily available.

Certain general characteristics of timbre and intonation may well be borne in mind. Many speakers of Yiddish sound guttural, with the related qualities of hoarseness and coarseness of voice. The drawl, which Yiddish has in common with New York speech (as evidenced in such diphthongs as [ɛə]) is a conspicuous characteristic. Nasalization is very common, both of the positive kind, which is high and strident, and of the negative variety, which is dull and muffled. Positive nasality is accentuated by the habit of many people of speaking with the mouth almost closed, even on low vowel sounds. Some sounds are over-labialized, lengthened, and over-tense, with a corresponding modification of timbre, as in the case of some pronunciations of [ɔ]. These qualities are found both in substandard New York speech proper and in Yiddish. It is a debatable question as to which is the true source.

Yiddish as It Is Written

Certain usable characteristics of Yiddish dialect at the immigrant level can best be approached through the works of competent writers, such as Milt Gross and Leonard Q. Ross. In Gross' *Dunt Esk*,[8] *Nize Baby*,[9] and *Hiawatta Witt No Odder Poems*,[10] and in Ross' *The Education of Hyman Kaplan*[11] may be observed certain conventionalizations and justifiable exaggerations which can be applied with great effectiveness in drama and in platform reading. The most important of these follow:

[ɛ] and [æ]. Both Gross and Ross assume that the immigrant speaker has an almost unfailing facility for exchanging the sounds [ɛ] and [æ]. According to this assumption, a phrase such as *imagine yet* will be pronounced [ɪˈmɛtʃən jæt]. Any explanation pointing out the possibility of confusion over the relative height of Judeo-German and English vowels is beside the point, considering the effective humorousness of simply exchanging [ɛ] and [æ] in most words where it is possible to do so. Following are some of Milt Gross' spellings:

[ɛ]-words — *badder* for *better*, *sad* for *said*, *himsalf* for *himself*, *spagatty* for *spaghetti*.

[æ]-words — *esk* for *ask*, *dregon* for *dragon*, *jeckel* for *jackal*.

Ross' spellings:

[ɛ]-words — *prazident* for *president*, *mat* for *met*, *Amerson* for *Emerson*.

---

8 Doran, 1926.
9 Doran, 1926.
10 Doran, 1926.
11 Harcourt, Brace, 1937.

[æ]-words — *pents* for *pants*, *eskink* for *asking*, *netcheral* for *natural*.

[i] and [ɪ]. In precisely the same way and for the same reasons, these writers assume the exchange of [i] and [ɪ] (except in final positions). Here are Gross' spellings:

[i]-words — *binns* for *beans*, *list* for *least*, *itch* for *each*, *liff* for *leaf*.

[ɪ]-words — *beezness* for *business*, *feenished* for *finished*, *breengin'* for *bringing*. Ross' spellings:

[i]-words — *minnick* for *meaning*, *ticher* for *teacher*, *strit* for *street*, *dip* for *deep*.

[ɪ]-words — *Pockheel* for *Parkhill*, *green* for *grin*, *feesh* for *fish*. Ross does not use many instances of [i] for [ɪ], but is very prolific in instances of [ɪ] for [i].

[w] and [v]. Here Gross and Ross disagree in practice. Gross uses [w] for [w, ʍ, v], as in *wow* for *vow*, *rewench* for *revenge*, *wot* for *what*. However, he does not use [v] for [w]. Ross, on the contrary, uses [v] for [w, ʍ], as in *vife* for *wife*, *vy* for *why*, *vould* for *would*; but he does not use [w] for [v].

[ɑ] and [aʊ]. Gross' spellings:

[ɑ]-words—*astoundished* for *astonished*, *countasts* for *contests*, *mounstrous* for *monstrous*.

[aʊ]-words—*Sprotts* for *sprouts*, *sond* for *sound*, *montain* for *mountain*. Ross' spellings:

[aʊ]-words—*abot* for *about*, *clons* for *clowns*, *ott* for *out*. Ross does not use [aʊ] for [ɑ].

[ɑ] for [ʌ]. Gross' spellings:

[ʌ]-words—*honter* for *hunter*, *opp* for *up*, *roshed* for *rushed*, *hogly* for *ugly*. Ross' spellings:

[ʌ]-words—*bos* for *bus*, *brodder* for *brother*, *som* for *some*.

[ʌ] for [oʊ]. Gross' spellings: *brukken* for *broken*, *grussery-sturr* for *grocery-store*, *sturrs* for *stores*, *assussiation* for *association*, *uppen* for *open*, *nuts* for *notes*.

Gross does not use this shift uniformly. Since [ʌ] never appears finally in English, he does not use it finally, and he does not use it in words spelled with *old*. With other spellings of [ʌ], he does not follow a uniform practice. Ross does not use [ʌ] for [oʊ].

[ɑ] for [ʌ]. Gross' spellings:

sobway for *subway*, *sotch* for *such*, *cot-opps* for *cut-ups*.

Ross' spellings:

collars for *colors*, *somting* for *something*.

[ʌ] for [ɔ]. Gross' spellings:

suds for *swords, shut* for *short, bot* for *but, assuttment* for *assortment, gudgeous* for *gorgeous, cuss* for *course* [kɔs].

Ross' spellings:

Velley Fudge for *Valley Forge.*

[ɔ] for [ou].

sauce for *source, aupen* for *open, haukay* for *okey.*

Both Gross and Ross introduce excrescent initial [h] very frequently:

hoats for *oats, hout* for *out, hentered* for *entered, howl* for *owl, haxclimation* for *exclamation.*

Unvoicing of final voiced consonants. As may be expected in consideration of the fact that the family speech of Jewish immigrants is a dialect of German, the final voiced plosives and fricatives of English are unvoiced in Yiddish according to the German pattern. In many cases the German influence is supported by that of a second language. The speech of Russian Jews, for example, will be influenced by the fact that in Russian also the final voiced plosives and fricatives are unvoiced.

Examples from Gross and Ross:

Rache for *rage, tiffs* for *thieves, potatoss* for *potatoes, rewench* for *revenge, becauss* for *because, peckitch* for *package, jop* for *job.*

Another carry-over from German is the pronunciation of initial *c* as [ts]. German does not use *c* in isolation except in loan words, such as *citron* [tsɪˈtroːn]. It is reasonable, accordingly, that *civil* would be pronounced [ˈtsɪvəl] or [ˈtsivəl], *Cincinnati* as [ˌtsɪntsɪˈnɛtɪ].

By analogy, words beginning with *s* may also be pronounced as *ts*, as in *tsingle, tsimple, tsyllable.* This pattern is not uniformly used in dialect writing and should not be used in reading unless the dialectal respelling justifies it.

The customary weak medial [t], pronounced [ɾ] in American English, is sometimes recognized in dialect writing by using *r* in the spelling, as in *beauriful* for *beautiful, parron* for *pardon, kirro* for *kiddo.*

The shortening of long vowels in Yiddish is recognized in various ways in dialect writing, usually by the doubling of consonants or by the respelling of the words with a different vowel, which is put into a context requiring a short vowel in English. Examples: *dippotted* for *deported, sputt* for *sport, cuss* for *course, pipple* for *people, betwinn* for *between, sutts* for *sorts, intrikking* for *intriguing, concill de rill fillings* for *conceal the real feelings, wukking* for *walking, stoss* for *stars, pukk* for *poke, chifful* for *cheerful, skimm* for *scheme, shopp* for *sharp, gutt* for *goat, smot* for *smart.*

It is possible to speculate that the vowel shifts which accompany many of these shortenings are the result of the shortening itself, and not necessarily a carry-over of vowels from other languages.

(Extreme Accent)
From *Dunt Esk* *

ʤulaɪ sikst—spænt manɪŋk ɪn mənɛtʃərɪ. ɪt əraɪft gadn̩ sɪts fram kaŋgrɪsmən. wæntʃr ə tʌtl̩ lʌs; wæʤətəbl̩ dɪlə rɪfjuzəs tə baɪ gadn̩ sɪts. stadɪt haʊt aɪ ʃut bi ə gleʃə. hop wat holt ledɪ wʊdn̩t mis glɛs fram piktʃərs ɪn palə. prɛktɪst wɪt ɪzədors haɪglɛsəs aɪ ʃut pʊt ɪn n̩ tek haʊt windo pens. ɪs grɛtʃuəl nat so bɛt. lɔɪnt wɔrts fram "wələntʃɪə." ɪzədor fɛl dʌnstɛs. holt mæn flaɪs hʌf fram hɛndl̩. sno jus, aɪl hɛvtə gæt mɛrɪt.

MILT GROSS

(Less Extreme Accent)
From *The Education of Hyman Kaplan* †

ʌfkɔs ɪz ɔl kɒɪn halədes ɪn ju ɛs e. halədes fɔr palətɪk, fɔr rɪlɪtʃəs, ən plen halədes. ɪn fæbrærɪ, vi gat tʃatʃ vaʃɪŋtəns bɔɪtde, ə fɒɪn halədə, also ebræm lɪŋkoəns. ɪn me vi gat mɛmorəbəl de fɔr dæd solʤərs. ɪn tʃulɒɪ kams, nɛtʃərəl, fɔrt tʃulɒɪ. also vi hɛf lebər de, dɛŋksgɪvɪŋk, fɔr də pilgrəms, ən fɔr də finɪʃ fram də vɔɪlt vɔr, armɪstrəs de.

bʌt ərant dis tɒɪm jir vi hɛv ə difərənts kɒɪn halədə, ə spæʃəl, mavələs tɒɪm. dæts kɔlt krɪsməs. ɔl hovər də vɔɪlt ɪz pɪpl̩ sɛləbrekɪŋ dis vandərful tɒɪm. bɪkɔs fɔr sɒm pɪpl̩ ɪs pæsovər, ɔr tʃanuka, bætər, də most fɒɪn, də most bjurɪfəl, də most sikrət halədə fram də hol bantʃ.

LEONARD Q. ROSS.

(Overheard on the corner of East 4th St. and Ave. C, N. Y. C.)

ʌv kʌs akṭoubə fʌɪsṭ jə sɪpʌusṭə muv; dɛṭs wɛn ḍeɪ gɪv ḍi nu lɪsts fə rʊms ɪn əpaṭmn̩ts.

jə ʃəḍ si mai nu rʊms. haḍ wʌḍər ʌːl deɪ jɪnːaiṭ; krʌs væn̩ːt̩leɪʃn̩; wɪnɪʃn blaɪn̩ds; pakɛṭ flʌːs, ɪn ʌːl ḍi leɪṭɪsṭ imprʊvmən̩ːṭs. ʌn̩ḷi ṭʌɪḍzi fʌː dalɪz ə mʌnt.

Transcribe:

From *Nize-Baby* *

Bomplesealskin

Pot I

Oohoo, nize baby, itt opp all de crembarry suss so momma'll gonna tell you a ferry tale from Bomplesealskin. Wance oppon a time was a werry, werry poor fommer wot he dicited wot he'll gonna go witt a weesit to de Keeng. So in horder he should make a imprassion on de Keeng wot he was a somebody so he cocknocted a skim witt a bloff wot he sad, he hed it a dudder, wot she could speen straw in a speening-whill it should come out gold. Of cuss, she didn't rilly could, it was jost a hux on de pot from de fommer. (Nize baby, take anodder spoon crembarry suss.)

Pot II

So de Keeng was all agrog from excitamment wot it stodded in to hitch by heem de palm. (He was a werry griddy micer.) So he lad her in a room wot it was full from straw, so he sad, "Noo, speen!" Und he locked de door und went away.

So de poor dudder was full from griff wot she deedn't know ivvin how to monopolate a speening-whill. So she was seeting witt tears in de heyes, so all from a sodden it stood in de front from her a leedle Dwuff, witt beeg wheeskers, wot he sad?

"Why you wipping, leedle goil?"

So she explained heem de rizzon, so he sad, "Hm! Und soppose wot I do dees for you, wot you'll gonna geeve me?"

So she sad: "Mine ganuine poil nacklaze from hunbreakable poils."

So he sad: "Is a boggain!!" So he set don, so in fife meenits he sponn de whole straw wot it was a room full from 14 kerrot gold!!

Pot III

So de naxt monnink de Keeng was extrimmingly jubilious, wot he robbed gliffully de hends. Bot instat he should be setisfite, dot apparitious crichure, he lad her in de grend ballroom wot it was feeled witt straw, witt hay, witt hoats yat, so he sad: "Eef you'll gonna speen all dees stoff it should be gold, so to-morrow, we'll gat gredually married wot you'll be de Quinn... Eef no— Hm, you gatting pale, ha? So take hidd!!!!"

MILT GROSS.

From *The Education of Hyman Kaplan* *

Transcribe:

Wen we walkink don de stritt an' is snow on de floor an' all kinds tarrible cold! Ven ve see in de windows trees mit rad an' grin laktric lights boinink! Ven is de time for tellink de fancy-tales abot Sandy Claws commink fromm Naut Pole on rainenimals, an' climbink don de jiminies mit *stockings* for all de leetle kits! Ven ve hearink abot de beauriful toughts of de Tree Vise Guys who were follerink a star fromm de dasert! Ven pipple sayink, "Oh, Mary Chrissmas! Oh, Heppy Noo Yiss! Oh, bast regotts!" Den ve all got a varm fillink in de heart for all humanity vich should be brodders!

LEONARD Q. ROSS.

Bibliography

Yiddish

Books

Arlt, Phyllis Betts, *A Phonological Study of the English Dialect of New York City Jews* (Cornell University: unpublished M. A. thesis, 1939).

Gross, Milt, *Dunt Esk* (New York: Doran and Co., 1926).

————, *Nize Baby* (New York: Doran and Co., 1926).

Ross, Leonard Q., *The Education of Hyman Kaplan* (New York: Harcourt, Brace, 1937).

Periodicals

Rothenberg, Julius G., "Some American Idioms from the Yiddish," *American Speech,* February, 1943.

Thomas, C. K., "Jewish Dialect and New York Dialect," *American Speech,* June, 1932.

CHAPTER 21

Norwegian

Of the two Scandinavian dialects most prevalent in America, Norwegian and Swedish,[1] Norwegian has been selected for inclusion in this book as being the most generally useful. The selected features given here for the Norwegian pronunciation of English have so much in common with those characteristic of the Swedish pronunciation of English that they will be found very helpful in dealing with the Swedish. Actually, outside the areas where both of these Scandinavian dialects are intimately known, the Norwegian dialect can be used with little modification to represent Swedish without disturbing the sensibilities of the average lay hearer.

It has been mentioned earlier that immigrants who are thinly scattered through the native American population generally lose all dialectal speech in the second or, at most, in the third generation. Norwegian dialect does not fall completely into this pattern of early obliteration. Nearly a million Norwegians emigrated to America during the 1800's and some of the communities in which they settled were so solidly Norwegian that they constituted effective speech islands in which the broken English dialect persisted and, to some extent, still persists. These Norwegian communities are mainly to be found in Illinois, Iowa, North and South Dakota, Minnesota, and Wisconsin. In the century and a quarter of the sojourn of Norwegians in America, a considerable body of literature, and a voluminous body of anecdote using the characteristic Norwegian English have been built up.

A knowledge of the sounds of Norwegian will aid in the understanding of the sound substitutions made by the Norwegians speaking English. Here follows a list of the sounds of Norwegian based on the Dano-Norwegian Riksmål or Bokmål, which is the language of greatest literary and social usage in Norway.

---

[1] Danish, despite its relation to Norwegian and Swedish as a fellow member of the North Germanic group of languages, cannot be placed with them as giving rise to a similar dialect of English. Actually, since the Danish language lacks the musical intonation (see p. 407) of Norwegian and Swedish, and since, like the German, it has the glottal stop ([ʔ]), the uvular r ([R]), and the unaspirated voiceless plosives ([p', t', k']), it gives rise to a dialect of English which is in many ways similar to the German dialect of English (see Chapter 18).

It is also the language of greatest written usage among the Norwegian immigrants to the United States, whose Norwegian language newspapers, magazines, and fiction follow it closely.[2] The sounds of the various spoken dialects to which the various groups of immigrants are native are not sufficiently different from those of the Riksmål to be of concern for the purposes of this chapter.

Intonation

A very important feature of the pronunciation of Norwegian is its characteristic intonation or speech melody. The melody of Norwegian (which is not unlike that of Swedish) differs from that of English in two respects. The stressed syllables in a word or sentence have either a low or a falling tone where English has a high tone. One of these two forms of intonation or pitch-change characterizes every word spoken.

The low tone goes with what is often called "simple"[3] intonation, which begins on the stressed syllable of a short sentence, or of a phrase in a longer sentence, and rises to the end of the sentence or phrase, thus: (⌣́). In greater detail, what takes place may be described as follows: The pitch begins at a low level on the stressed syllable and rises as much as six or seven tones before the next stress or the end of the utterance. All monosyllables have simple intonation.

The falling tone goes with "compound"[3] intonation. The difference between "simple" and "compound" intonation distinguishes otherwise identical words. Compound intonation begins with a relatively high pitch just before the stress, falls to the stressed syllable, and then rises to the end of the sentence or phrase, thus: (⌢⌣́). (Substitution of a falling tone at the end seems to be a meaningful stylistic variant, associated with an attitude of finality or lack of interest.) In compound intonation, the pitch begins above the mean level, falls five or six tones, and then rises six or seven tones. Polysyllables in Norwegian may have either simple or compound intonation, depending on whether they have originated from monosyllables or polysyllables respectively in Old Norse. In either case, the rise of pitch begins in the stressed syllables and continues through any remaining portion of the word. It may be surmised that the presence of long consonants in Norwegian, as in *komme* [ˈkomːə], adds yet further to the strikingly different melodic effect produced on English-speaking hearers by Norwegian intonation. Long consonants occur when an orthographic consonant is doubled; often when one of two consonants in a cluster is omitted, as in *blind* [blinː]; with certain single final consonants, as in *hvem* [vemː], *hjem* [jemː], *hvis* [visː]; etc.

---

[2] The Landsmål or Nynorsk of Ivar Aasen, a written language based on native dialects of Norway which were relatively untouched by Danish influence during the four hundred years of union with Denmark under Danish monarchs (1397–1814), has had less currency in America.

[3] Einar I. Haugen, *Beginning Norwegian* (New York: Crofts, 1937), p. 19.

It is natural that such a strongly grounded feature of Norwegian would continue as a substratum characteristic in the English spoken by Norwegians. Here again, monosyllables will have the simple rising intonation. Polysyllables, such as *Unitarianism*, are, since the speaker can have no "feel" for their etymologic origin, likely to take also the simple low-rising intonation; Norwegians generally use the simple tone on foreign words. Of course, recognizable compounds, such as *radio station*, will be given the compound intonation.

All the statements in the foregoing, as applied to both Norwegian and English, are best exemplified when words are spoken in isolation. In sentences, the intonation characteristics of unstressed words are obscured; conversely, intonation characteristics are most conspicuous on words bearing sentence stress.

Anyone attempting to imitate these intonation characteristics of Norwegian English should by all means listen to Norwegian speakers, either in person or by recordings. Intelligent listening to the speaking of the Norwegian language itself will be beneficial—only less so than hearing Norwegian immigrants speak English.

It is exceedingly important that the intonation features be observed to a reasonable degree. Norwegian-English dialect without the characteristic fall and rise of Scandinavian speech melody would be very disappointing indeed.

For the purposes of this book, a complete view of the spellings of the Norwegian sounds is not included; but a few brief comments concerning some of the sounds are in order.

Sounds of Norwegian

Vowels[4]

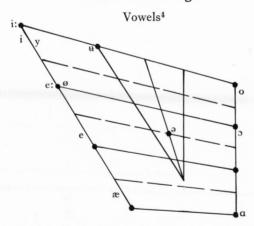

---

[4] The whole system of rounded vowels is shifted in Norwegian from the positions common to other Germanic languages such as English and German. [ɑ], not a rounded vowel in English, is rounded or backed (or both) in Norwegian until it has [ɒ]-quality; Norwegian [ɔ] is raised nearly to the position of English [o]; Norwegian [o] is over-rounded and raised nearly to English [u]; Norwegian [u] is fronted to a precentral [ʉ], very close to German [y]; Norwegian [y] is unrounded nearly to English [i]. Only [ø] remains substantially like German [ø].

Diphthongs

ei

øi

æu

Consonants

	Bi-labial	Labio-dental	Dental	Alve-olar	Palato-Alveolar	Palatal	Velar	Uvu-lar	Glot-tal
Plosive	p b		t d				k g		
Nasal	m		n				ŋ		
Lateral			l						
Trilled				r				ʀ	
Fricative		f v		s	ʃ	ç			h
Frictionless Continuant						j			

NOTE: Students who wish to go directly to a consideration of the Norwegian dialect of English without a study of Norwegian orthography may reserve the material immediately following for reference and turn at once to page 427.

Vowels

[i:]

The long[5] sound [i:] is spelled with the letter *i*, as in *ski* [ʃi:], *hvit* [vi:t]. [i:] is distinguished from [i] typically by being final or followed by a single consonant.[6]

[i]

The short sound [i] is spelled with *i*, as in *kikke* [¹çik:ə], *blind* [blin:] and with *e*, as in *de* [di]. It is briefer and more lax than [i:], and consequently lower;

---

[5] A long vowel has about twice the duration of a short vowel. A Norwegian long vowel has about the length of an English stressed vowel; short Norwegian vowels are shorter than any analogous English vowels. Vowels are usually shortened before two or more consonants.

[6] Haugen, p. 11. "In the present spelling of Norwegian (adopted 1917) *long vowels in accented syllables are regularly followed by one consonant or none, short vowels by two or more.* In unaccented syllables, practically all vowels are short.

"The principal exceptions are: (1) *m* is never doubled when final (*lam, dum*; but *lammene, dumme*); (2) *rn* is always and *rd* frequently preceded by a long vowel; (3) the ending *-t* following a stem consonant does not always cause shortening of the preceding vowel (*dyrt, pent*)."

but it is still somewhat too high to be equated with English [ɪ]. [i] is found typically before two consonants, consisting either of a consonant orthographically doubled, as *kk* above, or of two different consonants, as *nd* above.

[e:]

The long sound [e:] is a pure vowel, not the diphthong [eɪ] as in English. An acoustically similar diphthong [ei] occurs, but it is usually recognizable by the spelling *ei*. [e:] is ordinarily spelled with *e*, but also with the orthographic symbol *æ* when it is not followed by *r*. Examples: *det* [de:], *klæ* [kle:].

[e]

The short sound [e] is spelled with the letter *e*, as in *venn* [ven]. [e] is briefer and more lax, and therefore lower, than [e:]; but it is still somewhat too high to be equated with English [ɛ].

[æ:, æ]

Norwegian is one of the few languages besides English containing the sound [æ]. It is spelled with the orthographic symbol *æ* followed by *r* and sometimes with *e* followed by *r*, as in *værelse* [ˈvæːrəlsə], *her* [hæ:r], *herr* [hær:]. The sound [æ] is also spelled with *a* in the diphthong *au* [æu]. The difference of length between [æ:] and [æ] does not materially affect timbre as in the case of [i:, i] and [e:, e].

[y:, y]

The sound [y] (see page 327) is a front vowel, pronounced with tongue in the position for [i] and with the lips somewhat rounded, but much less so than in German and French. Its sound is between German [y] and English [i], strongly suggesting [i] to English ears. It is spelled with the orthographic symbol *y*, as in *dyp* [dy:p], *dryppe* [ˈdryp:ə]. The difference of length between [y:] and [y] does not materially affect timbre.

[ø:, ø]

The sound [ø] (see page 327) is a rounded front vowel, as in German and French, pronounced with the tongue in position for [e] and with the lips rounded. It is spelled with the orthographic symbol *ø*, as in *død* [dø:], *føtter* [ˈføt:ər]. The difference in length between [ø:] and [ø] does not materially affect timbre.

[a:, a]

The sound [a], is spelled with *a*, as in *betale* [bəˈta:lə], *blandt* [blant]. It is farther back and more round than the English [a], suggesting [ɒ] (= [aˈ]), where the symbol [ɒ], as in the *Atlas* (see Chapter V), is used for an extreme low back vowel. The difference in length between [a:] and [a] does not materially affect timbre.

[o:, o]

The sound [o] is a pure vowel, not the diphthong [ou] as in English. There is no corresponding diphthong in Norwegian. Norwegian [o] (= [oᐩ]) is between English [o] and English [u]. Compared with English [o], it is over-rounded and suggests [u]. It is spelled with the orthographic symbols o and u, as in onkel [ˈoŋkəl], bok [bo:k], lukke [ˈlok:ə]. The difference in length between [o:] and [o] does not materially affect timbre.

[ɔ:, ɔ]

The sound [ɔ] is spelled both with o and with the special symbol å. Before 1917, when å came into general use, the spelling aa was used. Books printed before that date and some proper names even yet use aa. The Norwegian [ɔ] (= [ɔᐩ]) is higher then the English [ɔ], and therefore more nearly approaches [o]. Examples: fortelle [fɔrˈtel:ə], gråt [grɔ:t], forstå [fɔrˈstɔ:], bånd [bɔn:], som [sɔm]. The difference in length between [ɔ:] and [ɔ] does not materially affect timbre.

[ʉ:, ʉ]

The sound [ʉ] is spelled with u, as in gult [gʉ:lt], hund [hʉn:]. It is sharply fronted (= [uᐩᐩ] or [ʉᐩ]) even past center, and is likely to be interpreted as [y] by those who know [y] in German and French. The difference in length between [ʉ:] and [ʉ] does not materially affect timbre.

[ə]

The sound [ə] is spelled, as in German, with e in unstressed syllables, as in lette [ˈlet:ə].

Diphthongs

[ei]

The diphthong [ei] is spelled ei, as in pleie [ˈpleiə], and with eg in egn, as in regne [ˈreinə].

[øi]

The diphthong [øi] is spelled øi and øy, as in oine [ˈøinə].

[æʉ]

The diphthong [æʉ] is spelled au, as in tau [tæʉ].

Consonants

[p]

The sound [p] is spelled with p, as in pike [ˈpi:kə], and b before s, as in absolutt [ɑpsoˈlʉt:], Ibsen [ˈipsən].

[b]

The sound [b], spelled *b*, has the approximate value of English [b], as in *arbeide* ['ar₁beidə].

NOTE: See [p] above for *b* pronounced [p] before *s*.

[t]

The sound [t] is spelled with *t* or *dt* as in *femti* ['femti], *blandt* [blɑnt]. It approximates the English [t], except that Norwegian [t] is perceptibly dental, thus, [t̪].

NOTE: Orthographic *t* is silent in the definite ending of the neuter noun, as in *barnet* ['bɑrnə].

[d]

The sound [d] is spelled with *d* as in *dårlig* ['dɔ:rli].

NOTE: The letter *d* is usually silent after *l, n, r* and frequently after a long vowel, as in *kveld* [kvel:], *blind* [blin:], *gjerde* ['jæ:rə], *bred* [bre:]. It is unvoiced before *t, s*, as in *godt* [gɔt:], *guds* [gʉts].
Norwegian [d] is dental, thus, [d̪].

[k]

The sound [k] is spelled with *k* as in *kort* [kɔrt], and with *g* before *t, s*, as in *bragt* [brɑkt], *dags* [dɑks]. The letter *k*, initially, as in German, is pronounced before *n*, as in *kne* [kne].

NOTE: See under [ʃ], page 426, for *k* in *sk, skj*.

[g]

The sound [g] is spelled with *g* before *a, o, u, l, r*, as in *ga* [gɑ:], *god* [go:], *gult* [gʉlt], *glad* [glɑ:], *grei* [grei]. Initially, as in German, *g* is pronounced [g] before *n*, as in *gnage* ['gnɑgə].

NOTE: The letter *g* is silent in the adjectival ending *-ig*, in the words *og* [ɔ], *jeg* [jei], and irregularly in some other words. Examples: *modig* ['mo:di], *lykkelig* ['lyk:əli], *fugl* [fʉ:l]. In non-initial *gn*, *g* is either pronounced [ŋ], as in *sogn* [sɔŋn], or is [i] or silent, as in *regn* [rein].

NOTE: See under [k], above, for *g* pronounced [k] before *s, t*.

[m]

The sound [m] is spelled *m*, as in *melk* [melk].

[n]

The sound [n] is spelled *n*, as in *nei* [nei]. Norwegian [n] is dental, thus, [n̪].

[ŋ]

The sound [ŋ] is spelled *ng*, as in English and German, but must never be pronounced [ŋg]. Example: *lang* [lɑŋ]. In non-initial *gn* it is also spelled simply *g*, as in *sogn* [sɔŋn]. (But see *egn* under [ei].)

[l]

The sound [l] is spelled *l*, as in *lyst* [ly:st]. It is consistently more nearly a clear [l], even before back vowels, than in English.

[r̠]

The standard Norwegian [r] is a tongue-point trill, as in *rotte* [ˈr̠ɔt:ə]. In some sections, as in Bergen and Stavanger, it is the uvular *r* [R], as in *rette* [ˈRɛt:ə].

NOTE: "Before *l*, *n*, *t*, and sometimes *d* . . . *r* loses its vibration and becomes somewhat like an American *r*. . . . [It] also combines with a following *s* into a sound very much like [ʃ]."[7] Compare *kort* [kɔr̠t, kɔrt], *norsk* [nɔr̠sk, nɔʃk]. See under [ʃ] below.

[f]

The sound [f] is spelled *f*, as in *fred* [fre:d], and *v* before *s* and *t*, as in *stivt* [sti:ft], *havs* [hɑfs].

[v]

The sound [v] is spelled with *v*, as in *varm* [vɑrm].

NOTES: (a) The letter *v* is silent after *l* in the words *selv* [sel], *halv* [hɑl], *tolv* [tɔl:], *sølv* [søl].

(b) See under [f] above for *v* pronounced [f] before *s*, *t*.

[s]

The sound [s] is spelled *s*, as in *som* [sɔm].

NOTE: See under [ʃ] below for the orthographic clusters *sj*, *skj*, and *sk*, which spell [ʃ] before *i*, *y*, *e*, *æ*, and *ø*.

[ʃ]

The sound [ʃ] is spelled *sj*, *skj*, and *sk* before *i*, *y*, *e*, *æ* and *ø*, as in *sjø* [ʃø], *skjære* [ˈʃæ:rə], *ski* [ʃi:], *sky* [ʃy:].

NOTE: Sometimes the spelling *rs* suggests [ʃ], as in *første* [ˈførstə], [ˈføʃtə].

[ç]

The sound [ç] is spelled with *kj*, and *k* before *y* and *i*, as in *kjerring* [ˈçær:iŋ], *kyss* [çys:], *kinn* [çin:].

---

7 Haugen, p. 16.

[h]

The letter *h* is silent before *j* and *v*, as in *hjørne* [ˈjøːrnə], *hviske* [ˈviskə]. Otherwise it is much like English *h*, as in *hånd* [hɔn:].

[j]

The sound [j] is spelled with *j*, *g* followed by *i* and *y*, and with *gj*, *hj*, *lj*, as in *ja* [jɑ], *fjerde* [ˈfjæːrə], *gift* [jift], *gyte* [ˈjyːtə], *gjerne* [ˈjæːrnə], *hjem* [jem].

NOTE: See under [ʃ], page 426, for *j* in the orthographic clusters *sj* and *skj*.

Transcription in Norwgeian

This is the appropriate point to do transcription in Norwegian. Use any Norwegian text or word list.

Sounds of English Not Found in Norwegian, with Probable Norwegian Substitutions

English Sounds Entirely Different from Norwegian Sounds				English Sounds Partially Different from Norwegian Sounds			
English Vowels	Norwe-gian Sub-stitution	English Conso-nants	Norwe-gian Sub-stitutions	English Vowels	Norwe-gian Sub-stitutions	English Conso-nants	Norwe-gian Sub-stitution
		z	s	æ	e (>E. [ɛ])	r	ɾ, ʀ
u	ʉ	ʒ	ʃ	ɛ	e, æ		
ʊ	ʉ, ɔˑ	θ	t	ɪ	i		
ʌ	ɔˑ, ɑ,	ð	d	ɔ	ɔˑ		
	ʉ, ø, ɔˑ	w	v	eɪ	e, ei		
ɜ, ɝ	ər, ør	ʍ	v	oʊ	ɔˑ		
ɚ	ər, ør	ʤ	j, dj	aɪ	ei		
		ʧ	ç, tç	aʊ	æʉ		

From the preceding table, it can be largely determined what substitutions or other changes the Norwegian speaker is likely to make when speaking English. Here following is a brief supplementary discussion.

1. Norwegian sounds, when something like English sounds, will be substituted for as follows:

Vowels

[e] for English [eɪ]. The Norwegian sound is pure, while the English sound is the diphthongal [eɪ]. Example, *dale* [del], for [deɪl]. But [ei] may be used here.

[ɔˑ] for English [ou]. Example, *dole* [dɔˑl].

[ʉ] for English [u]. Example, *you* [jʉ], for [ju]; *food* [fʉd], for [fud].

[ɚ], [ø̆r] for English [ɚ, ə].[8] Example, *sister* [ˈsɪstɚ], [ˈsistø̆r] for [ˈsɪstɚ, ˈsɪstə].

[i] for English [ɪ]. Example, *sing* [siŋ] for [sɪŋ].

Diphthongs

[æʉ] for English [au]. Example, *cow* [kæʉ] for [kau].

Norwegian contains [ɔ] and [i], hence the Norwegian speaker is likely to have no great trouble with [ɔi].

Consonants

[t̪] for English [t]. Example, *ten* [t̪æn], for [tɛn].

[d̪] for English [d]. Example, *den* [d̪æn], for [dɛn].

[n̪] for English [n]. Example, *name* [n̪em], for [neɪm].

Clear [l̪] for English dark [l]. Example, *fell* [fæl̪], for [fɛɫ].

Trilled [r̆] for English "smooth" [r]. Uvular [R] is heard sometimes but is rarely used. Example, *rest* [r̆æst] or [Ræst], for [rɛst].

2. English sounds not in Norwegian, with their substitutes.

Vowels

For [ɜ, ɝ] substitute [er, ør]. Example, *heard* [herd, hørd], for [hɜd, hɝd].

For [ʌ] substitute [ʉ, a, ø, ɔˑ]. Example, *up* [ʉp, ap, øp, ɔˑp], for [ʌp]; *but* [bʉt, bat, bøt, bɔˑt] for [bʌt].

In the case of English [æ] and [ɛ], the Norwegian speaker is often confused. He has the sounds [æ] and the lowered [e] of Norwegian, but may exchange them in practice, so as to say [fleg: > flɛg:] for *flag* [flæg], and [bleŋk > blɛŋk] for *blank* [blæŋk]; but [tæl:] for *tell*, [hælp] for *help*.[9]

For [aɪ] substitute [ei]. Example, *I* [ei], for [aɪ]; *fine* [fein], for [faɪn].

NOTE: Norwegian contains [ɑ] and [i], from which an acceptable substitute, [ɑi], for [aɪ] is often made; e.g., in *pie* [pɑi].

---

[8] This applies only to such [ə]'s as are equivalent in S., E., Br. to [ɚ].

[9] When a Norwegian pronounces English *e* in *let*, he places it too high (*i.e.*, [eˑ]) or mistakes it for his [æ], which is too low. Before two consonants, as in *blank*, and often before a single final consonant (which he lengthens), he shortens the vowel according to the regular Norwegian pattern. If in his dialect of Norwegian there is no short [æ] (and of course he cannot use a long [æ] before two consonants or a long consonant), the Norwegian is compelled to use [eˑ]. Since [eˑ] suggests [ɛ] to English ears, his [bleˑŋk], fleˑg:] will be heard as [blɛŋk, flɛg:].

On the other hand, a dialect which contains a short [æ] will likely have no short [e], so that *tell* and *help* will have to be pronounced [tæl:] and [hælp]. Short [e] and [æ] became confused as far back as Old Norse times, when *i*-umlauted [ɑ], [= æ], and [e] fell together.

Consonants

For [θ] substitute [t]. Example, *thing* [tiŋ].
For [ð] substitute [d]. Example, *this* [dis].
For [z] substitute [s]. Example, *eyes* [ais].
For [ʒ] substitute [ʃ]. Example, *measure* [ˈmɛʃər].
For [ʤ] substitute [j, dj, tj > ʧ].
Example, *general* [ˈjenərəl, ˈdjenərəl, ˈʧenərəl].
For [ʧ] substitute [ʃ]. Example, *chill* [ʃil].
For [ʌ] substitute [v]. Example, *what* [vɑt].
For [w] substitute [v]. Example, *we* [vi].

A characteristic confusion occurs among Norwegians who have been corrected
in their spelling pronunciation of *jump, Jim*, etc., as [jʌmp], [jim]. These speakers
appear to become afraid of being wrong on any word beginning with a [j]-sound,
and will pronounce *union* as [ˈʤʉnjən], *use* as [ʤʉs], *Yale* as [ʤel].[10]
It must be expected that the Norwegian speaker will have difficulty when
he encounters English spellings which would have special significance for him
if they were in Norwegian. Since Norwegian *d* is silent after *n, l, r* and long
vowels, he will have a tendency to think the *d*'s are silent in similar contexts
in English; since *sk* before *i* and *y* are pronounced [ʃ] in Norwegian, there will
be a tendency to pronounce them so in English; and since *g* and *k* are [j] and
[ç] respectively before *i* in Norwegian, there will be a tendency to pronounce
them so in English. Such pronunciations will vary greatly with the amount of
reading done by the speaker in either language, and with the length of time he
has been speaking English. There is never complete consistency in the use of
any dialect.

Norwegian Dialect

(Close Transcription)

From *I Remember Mama* *

UNCLE CHRIS—gæʈ æuʈ! ei d̪oˑn̪ʈ vɔˑn̪ʈ jʉ hiŕ! d̪æʈ is væŕ ei vɔˑn̪ʈ jʉ—ɔˑn̪ d̪ə
poˑŕʈç.

hæʉ is d̪ə kn̪i? kæn̪ ɑŕn̪ə vɔˑŕk gʉd̪? kæn̪ hi ŕɑn̪?

ei ʈæl̪ jʉ ɔˑl̪ ʈʉ gæʈ æuʈ! æksæpʈ mɑrʈɑ! æn̪d̪ kɑʈŕin̪! kɑʈŕin̪ æn̪d̪ ei hæv ə
sikŕəʈ. jʉ ŕimembəŕ, kɑʈŕin̪?

vi kæn̪ɑʈ veisʈ vɑʈ is l̪æfʈ in d̪ə bɑʈəl̪ jʉ d̪ʉ n̪ɑʈ d̪ŕiŋk iʈ. hʉ vil̪ d̪ŕiŋk iʈ ven̪
ei æm gɔˑn̪? vɑʈ hɑŕm kæn̪ iʈ d̪ʉ n̪æʉ? ei d̪ei en̪ivei. jʉ giv iʈ ʈʉ mi.

(Broader Transcription)

mɑrtɑ, ei hæv nɛvər med ə vɪl. dær vɑs nɛvər inɑf moni. bɑt jʉ sæl dɪs rænʧ.

---

[10] Anne Simley, "A Study of Norwegian Dialect in Minnesota," *Dialect Notes*, April,
1930.

ɪt vɪl nɑt brɪŋ mɑtʃ. ei hæv nɑt hæd ɪt lɔŋ inɑf. bɪg mɔrgɪtʃ. bɑt ɪt vɪl liv ə lɪtəl, mebi tʉ tri hɑndrəd dɑlərs. jʉ gɪv ɪt tə jɛsɪ.

Transcribe:

UNCLE CHRIS—Yessie Brown. My housekeeper. No, vy I call her dat to you? You understand. She is my voman. Tvelve years she has been my voman. My vife, only I cannot marry her. She has a husband alive somevere. She vas a trained nurse, but she get sick and I bring her to de country to get vell again. Dere vill be no money for you, Marta. Alvays I vanted dere should be money to make Nels a doctor. But dere vere odder t'ings ... qvick t'ings. And now dere is no time to make more. Dere is no money, but you make Nels a doctor, all de same. You like dat?

De greatest t'ing in the vorld is to have a little of God in you. Alvays I vanted to be a doctor myself. It is de only t'ing I have ever vanted. Nels must do it for me.

Good! You are de good one. I am glad you come, *Lille Ven.*

You do not mind if she is here?

You call her. I like you both to be here. Katrin, your Mama says you drink coffee now? Katrin, who vill be writer ... You are not frightened of me now?

One day maybe you vill write a story about Uncle Chris. If you remember.

I like you both stay vit me ... now ... I t'ink best maybe now Katrin go avay. Good-by, Katrin. Farvell, Katrin.

KATRIN—Good-by, Uncle Chris.

UNCLE CHRIS—You say it in Norvegian, as I do.

KATRIN—Farvell, Onkel Chris.

JOHN VAN DRUTEN

Bibliography

Norwegian

Books

Einar Haugen, *Beginning Norwegian* (New York: Crofts), 1937.

———, "Phonological Shifting in American Norwegian," *Language*, April-June, 1938.

———, "Intonation Patterns in American Norwegian," *Language*, January-March, 1941.

———, *Spoken Norwegian* (New York: Holt), 1946.

———, *The Norwegian Language in America; A Study in Bilingual Behavior* (Philadelphia: University of Pennsylvania Press), 1953.

CHAPTER 22

Italian

The history of the Italian dialect in America differs sharply from that of the German and French dialects. The French people had a strong early colonial foothold, with a greatly diminishing immigration rate thereafter. Except where the concentration of population spread over large areas, rural as well as urban, the French language gave way rapidly to the English, largely because of the ready assimilability of the people into the enveloping English-speaking population. The Germans for the most part arrived later than the English, and except for large concentrations, as in the Pennsylvania and the Milwaukee areas, were even more fully absorbed, people and language, into the English population and language.

But the main body of the Italian immigration arrived still later. The Italians have never been explorers, notwithstanding the early example of Columbus. Neither have they been settlers. Not until the mid-eighteen hundreds, after Garibaldi, Mazzini, and Cavour, did Italy consist of a unified single nation which could readily acquire colonies. Unlike France, and more than Germany, Italy has consistently produced a population far too numerous for the living space in her limited area. When during the late nineteenth century and early twentieth century the teeming millions of Italians overflowed their narrow peninsula, they sought the United States more eagerly than any other place. The reckless stories of easily acquired wealth which found their way across the Atlantic filled the steerages of ocean liners with crowds of eager comers.

Unfortunately for the complete success of America as the great melting pot, the newcomers did not prove as assimilable as the Germans and French. There were a number of reasons for this. Though largely agricultural at home, relatively few Italians became agriculturists in America. Nearly any foreign group, sprinkled scatteringly through an English-speaking population, will presently lose its foreign identity. But the Italians sought cities, secured industrial jobs, and clung together in speech islands—our metropolitan Little Italy's. They were not solely to blame for this action, of course. The steamship companies and the industrialists who wanted cheap labor had conspired to bring them and plant them in proximity to the factories which employed them. Like all people who feel strange or lonely or only partially welcome in a foreign land, they kept mainly to the cities where they might have the companionship of their own countrymen.

These conditions have contributed to the development and persistence of a distinct Italian dialect. Isolated peoples learn their speech from each other. Italian immigrants spoke dialectal English, if any English, as a matter of course. Their children learned a certain amount of dialectal speech from their elders; and their children learned from them. Unlike the descendants of more thinly scattered immigrants and of those more completely assimilated, these people were shut off from hearing a sufficient amount of undialectal English to allow them to perfect their own English speech. Hearing for the most part only each other, mingling continually, until the passage of the quota laws restricting immigration, with immigrants fresh from Italy, and, moreover, continuing often to use the Italian language itself for a family speech, they perpetuated some characteristics of dialectal pronunciation, and many of intonation, so that Italian dialect is a common thing in cities and industrial suburbs to this day.

Some Important Pronunciation Features of the Italian Language

Dentals. In Italian, [d, t, n] are dental. The word *dentality*, as used here, refers to the definite contact of the tip of the tongue against the inner surfaces of the upper teeth. This definition does not include the contact of the tongue with the gum ridge back of the teeth, for which the contrasting term at this point would be alveolar.

Laterals. Italian [l] is clear. Since the tip of the tongue usually makes contact with the inner surfaces of the upper teeth, it is possible to use the term dental with [l] as well as with [t, d, n]. The acoustic effect of clearness or dentality is, naturally, greater when [l] precedes front vowels than when it precedes back vowels. Since [l] is seldom final, the likelihood of the occurrence of dark [l] in Italian is greatly reduced, as compared with other languages.

The sound [λ] is a front sound as well, by reason of being made, typically, with the tip of the tongue behind the lower teeth. The blade of the tongue simultaneously makes contact with the palate over a rather broad surface, extending from the hard palate proper in a forward direction across the alveolar ridge and as far front as is physically possible. Contrary to the distribution patterns of English which forbid the use of [lj] initially in a word, Italian [λ] may be so used, as in *gli* [λi]. Italian [λ] is acoustically very close to the English [lj], as in *million* ['mɪljən]; however [lj], whether considered as two sounds in succession or as the single sound [ḽ], is a palatalized sound, in contrast with which [λ] is palatal.

The distinction lies in the fact that with [lj] the tongue tip starts from a position against the alveolar ridge and glides to a position behind the lower teeth, the contact of the tongue tip against the alveolar ridge being replaced by contact of the blade of the tongue against the hard palate. With [ʎ], the position of the tongue tip behind the lower teeth and the contact of the blade of the tongue with the hard palate obtain throughout the utterance of the sound, from the beginning as well as at the end.

Nasals. The sound [m], since it is made by simple bilabial closure, tends to remain stable in most languages. However, there is in Italian the non-significant [ɱ],[1] which, being made labiodentally, by contact of the lower lip and upper teeth, resembles [m] both visually and acoustically. It occurs in the spellings *nf* and *nv*, as in *inverno* [iɱˈvɛrno] and *inferiore* [iɱferˈjore].

[ŋ]. As stated in another connection, [ŋ] in Italian is an allophone of the phoneme /n/, occurring when *n* is followed by [k] or [g], as in *banco* [ˈbaŋko] and *lungo* [ˈluŋgo]. This book will use the symbol [ŋ] wherever the sound occurs, despite its allophonic relation to /n/. This is necessary for English speaking readers, to whom /n/ and /ŋ/ are separate phonemes. Such readers would attempt to read [ˈbanko] with the [n] of English *ban* rather than the [ŋ] of English *bank*.

[ɲ]. The sound [ɲ], as in Italian *segno* [ˈseɲo], is acoustically very close to the [nj] of English *pinion* [ˈpinjən]. However, the Italian [ɲ] is made with the tip of the tongue behind the lower teeth and the blade of the tongue in contact with the hard palate. Thus [ɲ] is definitely a palatal sound, while [nj], whether considered as two sounds in succession or as the single sound [ɲ], is instead a palatalized sound. The distribution of [ɲ] in Italian differs from that of [nj] in English in that Italian [ɲ] may be used initially in a word, as in *gnocchi* [ˈɲɔk:i], while English [nj] is used only intervocalically.

Trills. The typical Italian [r] is a clear tongue-point trill. Non-significant variation occurs in the speech of individuals or groups. None of these (apical, retroflex, flapped, etc.) is of any particular difficulty, except, perhaps, the rare uvular [ʀ], conspicuous by its resemblance to the French [ʀ], of which it is considered an imitation.[2] In this chapter the symbol [r] will be used consistently, with no diacritic indicating the trill; the reader must therefore bear in mind that all Italian [r]'s are tongue-point trills.

Long Consonants

1. As a general principle, the orthographic doubling of a consonant, as in *cello* [ˈtʃɛl:o], or *giammai* [dʒamˈmai],[3] results in a long consonant in pronunci-

---

[1] Although English [ɱ] probably can be proved to be an allophone of /m/, with accompanying morphophonemic alternation with n, Italian [ɱ] is an allophone of /n/.

[2] Robert A. Hall, Jr., *Descriptive Italian Grammar* (Ithaca, N. Y., Cornell University Press and Linguistic Society of America, 1948), p. 9, footnote 4.

[3] [mm] is used here instead of [m:] in order to be able to place the stress mark where it logically belongs.

ation. It will be recalled (see pages 121, 127) that in the case of a continuant, as with [l:] and [mm] above, lengthening means precisely what the word implies, increase of duration. In the case of a plosive, there is also increased duration, coupled with the peculiar circumstance that after the first position for the plosive is assumed by the organs used in speech, the plosion is delayed for the desired length of time; thus, *gatto* ['gat:o]. In the case of affricates, the increased duration is coupled with the still more complicated circumstance that the organs of speech take the position of the first element of the affricate, after which there is a period of delay followed by a plosion through the aperture characteristic of the second element of the affricate; thus, *maggio* ['maddʒo]. In words containing lengthened consonants between two syllables, the second of which is stressed; the symbolization raises a special problem as to where to place the stress mark, since it is necessary, according to Italian syllabification (q. v.), to show that the first part of the lengthened consonant belongs to the first syllable and the second part to the succeeding syllable. It is possible to show this as in the following: *conduttore* [kondut'tɔre], *viaggiare* [vjad'dʒare], *ammettere* [am'met:ere]. Problems such as the foregoing lend color to the habit of many phoneticians of doubling with phonetic symbols instead of using a lengthening sign [:] for long consonants. Since this can be misleading when affricates are doubled, as with [tʃtʃ, dʒdʒ], this book will write lengthened affricates [ttʃ, ddʒ, tts], in its transcriptions of Italian, to avoid the difficulty. Non-affricate consonants, when lengthened, will be written, e.g., [t:], as in *gatto* ['gat:o], or, if a medial stress mark intrudes, [m'm], as in *giammai* [dʒam'mai].

2. When a word ends in a stressed vowel and is followed by another word beginning with a consonant, the context has the effect of lengthening the initial consonant of the second word, as in *a campo* [ak'kampo].

Silent Letters

1. *h.* The historical *h* as in the present indicative of *avere* [a'vere], *ho* [ɔ], *hai* [ai], *ha* [a], *hanno* ['an:o].

The letter *h* used as a diacritic after *c* and *g* before *e* and *i* to preserve the "hard" sounds of [k] and [g], as in *che* [ke], *recchi* ['rɛk:i], *ghiro* ['giro], *ghetto* ['gɛt:o].

2. *i.* The letter *i* after *c* and *g* before *a, o, u* to preserve the "soft" sounds of [tʃ] and [dʒ], as in *ciaba* ['tʃaba], *coccia* ['kɔttʃa], *cio* [tʃɔ], *ciuco* ['tʃuko], *gia* [dʒa], *foggia* ['fɔddʒa], *Giovanni* [dʒo'van:i], *giu* [dʒu]. A special case of the foregoing is the use of *i* after *sc* before *a, o, u* to preserve the "soft" sound [ʃ], as in *sciamo* ['ʃamo]. Silent *i* is retained in *scienza* ['ʃɛntsa], from the Latin *scientia*.

Syllabification. In Italian nearly all syllables end in vowels, as in *co-me*, *ve-do*. As many as three consonants may precede a vowel, as in *scri-ve-re*. Double consonants and groups of consonants consisting of *l, n,* or *r* followed by another consonant are divided, as *set-ti-mo, sal-va-re, pre-sen-ta-re, par-la-re, par-te.*

Stress. Exceptions to any rules which may be given for stress are numerous. However, in general, the majority of Italian words are stressed on the penult, as in *zatta* [ˈdzatːa] and *cosa* [ˈkɔsa]. Words stressed on the last syllable are so marked by a grave accent, as in *legò* [leˈgɔ] and *facoltà* [fakolˈta]. Words of more than two syllables are frequently stressed on the antepenult, as in *porgere* [ˈpɔrdʒere], *albero* [ˈalbero]. A lesser number of words are stressed on the syllable preceding the antepenult, as in *illuminano* [ilˈluminano]. Most of these later are third person plural forms of verbs with more than four syllables in the infinitive. The further operation of this rule is too complicated for inclusion here. For details see Phelps, page 16.[4] As has been stated, these rules admit of many exceptions. Stress should be learned along with the. word itself, and a dictionary used whenever there is doubt.

The Sounds of Italian

Consonants

	Bi-labial	Labio-Dental	Dental	Alveolar	Palato-alveolar	Palatal	Velar
Plosive	p b		t d				k g
Nasal	m	(ɱ)*	n			ɲ	(ŋ)*
Lateral Non-fricative				l		ʎ	
Trilled				r			
Fricative		f v		s z	ʃ (ʒ)*		
Frictionless Continuants	w					j	(w)

*[ɱ] and [ŋ] are allophones of /m/ and [n] respectively; [ʒ] is the second element of [dʒ].

Affricates:	*Diphthongs:*
dz	ei
ts	ɛi
tʃ	ai
dʒ	au
	ɔi
	oi

4 Ruth Shepard Phelps, *An Italian Grammar* (New York: Ginn & Co., 1907).

Vowels

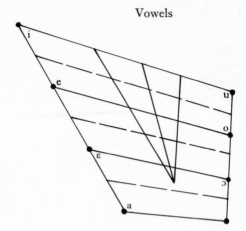

NOTE: Students who wish to go directly to a consideration of the Italian dialect of English without a study of Italian orthography may reserve the material immediately following for reference and turn at once to page 447.

To understand Italian dialect fully, however, it is necessary to know the spelling of the sounds of Italian. Such knowledge is likewise indispensable to a study of the language itself. For both these purposes, a summary of Italian spelling is here included, classified according to the Italian sounds represented.

The Sounds of Italian

The Principal Ways in Which the Sounds Are
Orthographically Represented

[i]

1. *i* generally, whether stressed or unstressed, as in *gli* [λi], *vino* [ˈvino], *rimani* [riˈmani], *stipite* [ˈstipite].[5]

NOTE: All stressed vowels in free (open) non-final syllables are pronounced longer than elsewhere.

Exceptions: See *i* before vowel under [j], page 441.

See also *sci* followed by *a, o, u* under [ʃ], page 445; see *ci* followed by *a, o, u*

---

[5] It is the practice of some phoneticians to indicate added length to the vowel of a syllable of primary stress in Italian when the vowel is followed by a single orthographic consonant. This agrees with the pronunciation of central and southern Italy, but not usually with that of northern Italy. (Cf. Hall, p. 13.) Examples: With lengthening sign, *vino* [ˈviːno], *rimani* [riˈmaːni], *stipite* [ˈstiːpite], *cacio* [ˈkaːtʃo]; without lengthening sign, [ˈvino], [riˈmani], [ˈstipite], [ˈkatʃo]. Since vowel length is, in such instances, non-significant, and since with native speakers of English as well as of Italian, there is a tendency to lengthen vowels in these positions automatically, the lengthening sign will not be used with such vowels in the following pages.

under [tʃ] page 447; see *gi* followed by *a, o, u* under [ʤ], page 447; see *gli* under [ʎ], page 444.

2. *ii*, normally, when unstressed and final in a word, as in *studii* [ˈstudi].

3. *y* in borrowed, words, as in *Harry* [ˈari]. The letter *y* is extremely infrequent in the Italian alpabet.

[e, ɛ]

The pronunciation of orthographic *e* presents one of the two most baffling problems in Italian phonology, the other being the pronunciation of *o*. Since this book is intended for use by students many of whom have not studied either vulgar Latin or classic Latin, there can be no help drawn from the history of the Italian language—not even from such simple facts as that *e* existed in both "short" and "long" forms in classic Latin. Moreover, in attempting to describe contexts in which [e] and [ɛ] are found in Italian, it seems impossible to avoid the listing of environmental sounds as if they were causal factors governing the incidence of [e] or [ɛ], when in reality they often are not. As a matter of fact, only a few rules for distinguishing between [e] and [ɛ] can be stated which are of sufficiently frequent application to make them useful.

The focus of difficulty resides in the pronunciation of *e* in stressed syllables. Here, any number of rules of limited application can be devised, but these presently become so numerous and so beset by exceptions that it is easier to look up individual words in a good dictionary and memorize the pronunciations than to try to apply the rules. In deriving most of the following statements on stressed *e*, a sampling has been taken consisting of pages 1, 11, 21, etc., of *A Short Italian Dictionary*,[6] to which were added samplings from pages having a high incidence of *e* in stressed syllables, nearly one-fifth of the dictionary being so analyzed. Such statements below as are derived from these samplings, can, of course, be taken only as showing trends.

The entries immediately following are not based on the samplings referred to above. They are generalizations which are either incontrovertible, or which hold true with some degree of consistency.

Orthographic *e* pronounced as:

[e]	[ɛ]
(the pure [e], not the diphthong [eɪ] as in English).	
1. *e* in unstressed syllables, as in *come* [ˈkɔme], *cadere* [kaˈdere], *fedele* [feˈdele], *tenere* [teˈnere].	1. *e* when pronounced [ɛ] is always in a stressed syllable. (But this statement must not be taken to

[6] Alfred Hoare, *A Short Italian Dictionary* (London: Cambridge University Press, 1943, V. I).

Note: Hall[7] holds that *e* unstressed and preceding a nasal, a lateral, or a trill is pronounced [ɛ] as in *menare* [mɛ'nare]. He adds that "most discussions of the point deny the occurrence of [ɛ, ɔ] in unstressed syllables." The present discussion adheres to the conventional view that unstressed *e* is [e], not [ɛ].

imply that *e* in stressed syllables is always pronounced [ɛ]; instead we may have either [ɛ] or [e] with greater or lesser consistency of phonological context, as will appear below.)

2. *é* wherever found, as where the acute accent mark distinguishes between words like *sé* [se] and *se* [sɛ].

2. *è* as in *perchè* [per'kɛ], *mercè* [mer'ʧɛ].
Note: Concerning oxytones (dissyllables stressed on the second syllable], such as those above, some writers hold that *è* is pronounced [e].[8]

3. *e* in verbs: whenever stressed in the infinitive as in *sedere* [se'dere]; past descriptive as in *vendevo* [ven'devo];[9] future as in *sarete* [sa'rete]; past absolute as in *fondesti* [fon'desti]; and past subjunctive as in *ridessi* [ri'des:i]; in the second plural of the present indicative and imperative as in *avete* [a'vete]; in the second singular of the past future as in *troveresti* [trove'resti], and in the first and second plural of the past future as in *troveremmo* [trove'rem:o]; in the past absolutes as in *piacesti* [pja'ʧesti], *desti* ['desti]; and in past participles in *-esi* ['esi] and *-eso-a* ['eso-a], (except *chiesi* ['kjɛsi] and its compounds). Examples: *offesi* [of'fesi]; *acceso-a* [at'ʧeso-a].

3. *e* in verbs as follows: in past absolutes in *-etti* ['ɛt:i], as in *credetti* [kre'dɛt:i]; in past participles in *-ento* ['ɛnto] and *-etto* ['ɛt:o], as in *redento* [re'dɛnto] and *protetto* [pro'tɛt:o]; in present participles in *-endo* ['ɛndo] and *-ente* ['ɛnte], as in *volendo* [vo'lɛndo] and *dicente* [di'ʧɛnte]; in the first and third singular and third plural of the past future, as in *troverei* [trove'rɛi], *troverebbe* [trove'rɛb:e], and *troverebbero* [trove'rɛb:ero] respectively.

---

[7] Hall, p. 12, footnote 8. In a letter to the author of later date than the book (Nov. 6, 1952), Hall rephrases his view as follows: "The difference between [e] and [ɛ] is significant only in stressed syllables. Elsewhere, the vowel sound may vary over a continuous range from [e] to [ɛ], with a statistical predominance of the more open types before nasals, laterals or trills. Likewise for [o] and [ɔ]. Phonemically, the way to take care of the situation is by recognizing only two vowel phonemes in the mid range, /e/ and /o/, with a contrast of close vs. open applying only when the vowels are stressed."

[8] Phelps, p. 3.

[9] As a phenomenon of close juncture, sibilants, nasals, laterals, and trills are slightly lengthened when final in a syllable before a consonant. Thus [ven·'devo], [fon·'des·ti], [trove'res·ti], [re'den·to], [vo'lɛn·do].

4. *e* when preceded by *i* or when *i*
has been dropped from before it,
as in *cieco* ['tʃɛko], *sete* (for *siete*)
['sɛte].

Following are some observations for distinguishing *e* as [e] or [ɛ] in stressed
syllables, according to the samplings previously referred to. It would appear
that stressed *e* is predominantly pronounced [ɛ]. But there are some notable
instances where it is pronounced [e], as follows:

1. *e* in the endings *-etto-a-e* (except in verbs), *-eso-a-e*, *-mento-a*, and in
the medial combination *-endi-*;
2. *e* followed by *pp*, *cc* [k:], *ga*, *go*, *v*, *zz*, *ci*, *cci*, *mb*, *np*, *gn*, *gli* and *l*
plus consonant.

It would appear further that it is difficult to state whether stressed *e* is pronounced
[e] or [ɛ] in a number of instances as follows:

1. *e* followed by *bb* (except in some verb endings), *ta*, *to*, *tt* (except in some
verb endings), *cch* [k:], *sc* [ʃ], *gge*, *ggi*, *mm*, *nn*. With words spelled with
the foregoing combinations, there seems little to do but check each word
by the dictionary.

[a-ɑ]

Hall says, "The low vowel /a/ is indifferent as to front or back tongue-position."[10] This may be interpreted as meaning that *a* may be pronounced [a] or
[ɑ] interchangeably. Since with many speakers the acoustic effect is fairly consistently [a], this pronunciation only will be indicated in this book.

1. *a* stressed and unstressed, as in *canto* ['kanto], *ombra* ['ombra], *abito*
[a'bito], *fame* ['fame], *mai* [mai].

[o, ɔ]

The sounds [o] (the pure [o], not the diphthong [oʊ], as in English) and [ɔ],
represented by orthographic *o*, are somewhat more stable than the sounds of *e*.
Certain general rules may be formulated which will hold with some consistency.
(See footnote 7, page 438.)

[o]	[ɔ]
1. *o* in unstressed syllables, as in *cieco* ['tʃɛko], *spirito* ['spirito].	1. *o* when pronounced [ɔ] is always in a stressed syllable. (But this statement must not be taken to imply that *o* in stressed syllables is always pronounced [ɔ]; instead, it may be either [ɔ] or [o], with greater or lesser consistent relationship to the phonological context, as will appear below.)

---

[10] Hall, p. 7.

2. *ó*, as in *tósco* ['tosko].

2. *ò*, as in *ciò* [tʃɔ], *andò* [an'dɔ], *farò* [fa'rɔ].

3. *o* final in the monosyllable *lo* [lo].

3. *o* final in monosyllables, as in *Po* [pɔ], *do* [dɔ], *no* [nɔ].

4. *o* when followed by a vowel in the endings *-oio-a* and in a few words such as *noi* [noi] and *voi* [voi].

4. *o* when followed by an orthographic vowel, as in *noia* ['nɔja], *poi* [pɔi], *noioso* ['nɔjoso], *poero* ['pɔero].

5. *o* in past absolutes and past participles in *-osi*, *-osso*, *-osto*, *-otte*, as in *posi* ['posi], *rosso* ['ros:o], *oposto* [o'posto], *rotte* ['rot:e].

5. *o* in past absolutes in *-ossi*, *-olsi-e*, as in *mossi* ['mɔs:i], *colsi* ['kɔlsi], *sciolse* ['ʃɔlse].

6. *o* in *uo*, as in *cuore* ['kwɔre], *uopo* ['wɔpo], *nuovo* ['nwɔvo].

Tabulation of samplings taken, consisting of pages, 3, 13, 23, etc., of Hoare's *A Short Italian Dictionary*, to which were added samplings from pages having a high incidence of *o* in stressed syllables, the whole totaling nearly one-fifth of the dictionary, adduce the following generalizations concerning the occurrence of [o] and [ɔ] in stressed syllables.

It would appear that stressed *o* is predominantly pronounced [ɔ] except in a few notable instances where it is pronounced [o]. Note [o], as follows:

1. In the endings *-ona-e-i*, *-ore*;
2. *o* followed by *pp* when *o* is in the stressed antepenult; by *bl, s, ce* and *m* when *o* is in the stressed penult: by *mb, mp, mm, n* plus a consonant (except *nto*), *gna, rb, rm*.

It would appear further that it is difficult to state whether stressed *o* is pronounced [o] or [ɔ] in a number of instances as follows:

1. *o* followed by *sc, ss, ll, ra, r* plus consonant, *rr*. With words so spelled, there seems little to do except check by the dictionary.

[u]

u = [u] wherever found except when followed by another vowel in the same syllable (see under [w], page 441), as in *una* ['una], *tutto* ['tut:o], *truppe* ['trup:e], *punire* [pu'nire], *unito* [u'nito], *causa* ['kauza].

Diphthongs

The following are analogous to the common English diphthongs.

[ai]

ai as in *mai* [mai].

[au]

au as in *flautino* [flauˈtino]

[ei, εi]

ei as in *pei* [pei].
ei as in *lei* [lεi].

[oi, ɔi]

oi as in *noi* [noi].
oi as in *poi* [pɔi].

The following are also designated as diphthongs in Italian grammars, because they are spelled with adjacent vowel letters and are not separated in word-division at the end of a line; but they actually form separate syllables.

[ae]

ae as in *paesano* [paeˈzano].

[εo]

eo as in *ebreo* [eˈbrεo].

[εu]

eu as in *europa* [εuˈrɔpa]

[ɔa]

oa as in *Balboa* [balˈbɔa].

The following are called diphthongs in traditional Italian grammar because they are spelled with two vowel letters; they consist of [j], spelled *i*, or [w], spelled *u*, plus vowel, and have an acoustic effect similar to that of the English consonants [j] or [w] plus vowel.

[j] plus vowel

[ja]

ia as in *piazza* [ˈpjattsa]

[je]

ie as in *grazie* [ˈgratsje].

[jε]

ie as in *piena* [ˈpjεna]

[ju]

iu as in *piu* [pju].

[w] plus vowel

[wa]

ua as in *guanto* [ˈgwanto].

[we]

ue as in *questo* [ˈkwesto].

[wɛ]

ue as in *guerra* [ˈgwɛr:a]

[wi]

ui as in *guida* [ˈgwida].

[wɔ]

uo as in *fuoco* [ˈfwɔko].

Triphthongs

So-called triphthongs, in Italian, spelled with three vowel letters, actually consist of the consonant [j] or the consonant [w] plus a diphthong. Examples: *miei* [mjɛi], *suoi* [swɔi], *rinunziai* [rinunˈtsjai].

Consonants

[p]

p and *pp* as in *pagato* [paˈgato], *pupilla* [puˈpil:a], *impero* [imˈpɛro], *gruppa* [ˈgrup:a], *zoppo* [ˈtsɔp:o].

[b]

b and *bb* as in *bastone* [basˈtone], *abbia* [ˈab:ja], *sbarco* [ˈzbarko], *debbo* [ˈdɛb:o].

[t]

The sound [t] is dental in Italian.

t and *tt*, as in *tutti* [ˈtut:i], *costare* [kosˈtare], *potere* [poˈtere], *città* [ʧitˈta]. *c* and *cc*, when pronounced [ʧ], [tʧ], include [t] as the first element of [ʧ], [tʧ] (see [ʧ], page 447).

z and *zz*, pronounced [ts], [t:ts] and include [t] as the first element of [ts] [tts] (see [ts], page 446).

[d]

The sound [d] is dental in Italian.

d and *dd* in such words as *divano* [diˈvano], *dove* [ˈdove], *addure* [adˈdur:e], *addirsi* [adˈdirsi], *dita* [ˈdita].

g and *gg*, when pronounced [ʤ], [dʤ] (see [ʤ], page 447), include [d] as the first element of [ʤ].

z and *zz*, when pronounced [dz], [ddz], include [d] as the first element of [dz, ddz] (see [z], page 446).

[k]

The sound [k] is pre-velar before front vowels and medio-velar elsewhere.[11]

c or *cc* followed by *a, o, u*, as in *capello* [kaˈpel:o], *conforto* [komˈfɔrto], *cultura* [kulˈtura], *cioccolata* [ʧɔk:oˈlata], *ricco* [ˈrik:o].

cq, q or *qq* followed by unstressed *u* plus vowel as in *dunque* [ˈduŋkwe], *acquerello* [ak:weˈrɛl:o], *quasi* [ˈkwasi], *soqquadro* [sokˈkwadro].

---

[11] Hall, p. 8.

ch or *cch*, as in *benchè* [beŋˈkɛ], *che* [ke], *pacchetto* [pakˈket:o], *macchina* [makˈkina] *c* before *l* and *r*, as in *acre* [ˈakre], *classe* [ˈklas:e], *credere* [ˈkredere], *recluta* [reˈkluta].

k in borrowed words, as in *krak* [krak]. The letter *k* occurs very infrequently in the Italian alphabet.

[g]

g or *gg*, followed by *a, o, u* or a phonetic consonant ([w], from *u*), as in *rigato* [riˈgato], *prego* [ˈprɛgo], *singulto* [siŋˈgulto], *agguantare* [ag:wanˈtare], *tragga* [ˈtrag:a], *allegro* [alˈlegro], *gloria* [ˈglorja], *grido* [ˈgrido].

gh or *ggh*, as in *mughetto* [muˈget:o], *ghiaccio* [ˈgjatʃo], *sogghignare* [sog:iˈɲare]. Exceptions: *gli* and *glie* plus vowel are excluded from the foregoing (see [λ], page 444) except in the instance of such words as the Greek derivative *ganglio* [ˈgaŋglio], which retains the original consonantal values.

[m]

m or *mm*, as in *primavera* [primaˈvɛra], *ammalato* [am:aˈllato], *colomba* [koˈlomba], *giammai* [dʒamˈmai].

n by morphophonemic alternation, in close juncture before [p, b, m], as in *un barco* [umˈbarko], where the dental [n] is assimilated into homorganic agreement with the bilabial [b].

[ɱ]

n followed by *f* and *v*, as in *infatti* [iɱˈfat:i], *invasione* [iɱvaˈzjone]. This labio-dental nasal is an allophone of /m/.

[n]

The sound [n] is dental in Italian.

n or *nn* (except in such consonant clusters as *gn* [ɲ], *ng* [ŋg], *nc* [ŋk], *nch*, [ŋk], *nqu* [ŋkw]), as in *vano* [ˈvano], *gente* [ˈdʒɛnte], *nonno* [ˈnɔn:o], *sonnetto* [sonˈnet:o].

NOTE: [n] has the allophone [ŋ] before [g] and [k], (see below), and the allophone [ɱ] when followed by *f, v*. (See [ɱ] above.)[12]

[ɲ]

gn as in *bisogna* [biˈzoɲa], *insegnare* [inseˈɲare], *Signori* [siˈɲɔri], *campagna* [kamˈpaɲa].

[ŋ]

n before [g] and [k], as in *francobolli* [fraŋkoˈbol:i], *affinche* [afˈfiŋke], *qualunque* [kwaˈluŋkwe], *vengo* [ˈvɛŋgo], *cinque* [ˈtʃiŋkwe], *anche* [ˈaŋke], *pongo* [ˈpoŋgo], *stanco* [ˈstaŋko]. [ŋ] is an allophone of /n/.

---

12 See Hall, p. 9.

[l]

Italian [l] is clear and dental. It may be represented by the symbol [ḷ], which designates it as a front [l].

l or *ll* (except in the consonant cluster *gl* when pronounced [ʎ]), as in *solo* ['solo], *quale* ['kwale], *maledetto* [male'det:o], *alluso* [al'luzo], *illudere* [il'ludere], *allora* [al'lora].

[ʎ]

gl, as in *gli* [ʎi], *egli* ['eʎi], *eglino* [e'ʎino].

NOTE: *gl* is pronounced [gl] initially in a number of words, such as *glaciale*, *glandula*, *glastro*, *gleba*, *globo*, *gloria*, *glossa*, *glottide*, *glutine* and their derivatives. It is also found internally in certain Greek derivatives, such as *ganglio* ['ganglio].

gli before a vowel, as in *bagaglio* [ba'gaʎo], *foglia* ['fɔʎa], *paglia* ['paʎa], *Pagliacci* [pa'ʎattʃi], *glie* [ʎe], *gliene* [ˌʎɛne].

[r]

This sound is a tongue-point trill [r] in Italian. It may be represented by the symbol [ř]. When followed by another consonant in the same syllable, it may be lengthened to [r·] or [r:]; *rr* is also long, thus [r:]. The uvular [ʀ] occurs occasionally, primarily as an urban phenomenon, usually considered a Gallicism.[12]

r or *rr* as in *patriota* [patri'ɔta], *parente* [pa'rɛnte], *tirare* [ti'rare], *torre* ['tor:e], *condurre* [kon'dur:e].

[f]

f or *ff* as in *difilato* [difi'lato], *fiume* ['fjume], *offrire* [of'frire].

[v]

v or *vv* as in *salvare* [sal'vare], *scrivere* [skri'vere], *avverto* [av'verto], *avventarsi* [av:en'tarsi].

w in borrowed words, as in *water* ['vater]. The letter *w* occurs very infreqently in Italian.

[s]

s initial before a vowel, as in *sola* ['sola], *sette* ['sɛt:e], *se* [se].

ss, as in *fosse* ['fos:e], *patisse* [pa'tis:e].

s followed by *c* before *a, o, u* as in *scarpe* ['skarpe], *scopo* ['skɔpo], *scudo* ['skudo], *scranna* ['skran:a], or *s* before a voiceless consonant, as in *sfacciato* [sfat'tʃato], *rispondere* [rispon'dere], *squilla* ['skwil:a], *stare* ['stare], *scherzo* ['skerʦo].

s in a few words ending in *-eso-a-e-i* [eso-a-e-i] or in *-oso-a-e-i* [oso-a-e-i] (when *e* and *o* of these endings are [e] and [o]), as in *appeso* [ap'peso], *difesa* [di'fesa] *inglese* [in'glese], *scesi* ['ʃesi]; *faticoso* [fati'koso], *rosa* ['rosa], *ariose* [ari'ose], *rosi* ['rosi].

---

13 Hall, p. 9.

s intervocalic by virtue of a prefix ending in a vowel, as in *prosapia* [proˡsapja], *trentasei* [trentaˡsei], *diserrare* [diserˡrare].

s intervocalically in roots (see treatment of prefixes and suffixes above), as in *fuso* [ˡfuso], *rimasi* [riˡmasi], *cosi* [ˡkosi], *casa* [ˡkasa], *asino* [aˡsino], *Pisa* [ˡpisa], *raso* [ˡraso], *susina* [suˡsina]. It must be noted that intervocalic *s* is pronounced [s] with relative consistency only in southern Italy; in northern Italy [z] is found with relative consistency; in central Italy, both [s] and [z] are used with great inconsistency.[14]

z and *zz*, when pronounced [ts], [tts], include [s] as the final element of [ts, tts].

[z]

s intervocalically in roots (see treatment of prefixes and suffixes under [s]), as in *asilo* [aˡzilo], *fuso* [fuzo], *casa* [kaza], *cosi* [ˡkozi], *asino* [aˡzino]. (See note on interchangeability of intervocalic [s] and [z] under [s] above.)

s when followed by a voiced consonant (*b*, *d*, *g*, *l*, *m*, *n*, *r*, or *v*), as in *sbarcare* [zbarˡkare], *sdrucire* [zdruˡtʃire], *sgonfio* [ˡzgɔnfjo], *slittare* [zlitˡtare], *sverre* [ˡzvɛr:e].

z and *zz*, when pronounced [dz], [ddz]; include [z] as the final element of [dz, ddz]. (See [dz], page 446). Both [dz] and [ddz] are found intervocalically in such words as *bizantino* [bidzanˡtino], *ozono* [odzɔno], and [dz] is found initially in such words as *zonzo* [ˡdzondzo], *zenzero* [dzɛnˡdzero], *zizzania* [dzidˡdzanja].

zz is found in infinitives of four syllables ending in *-izzare* [idˡdzare], as in *particolarizzare* [partikolaridˡdzare], *rattizzare* [rat:idˡdzare]. It also is found intervocalically in a few words such as *azzimo* [ˡaddzimo], *bizza* [ˡbiddza], *gazza* [ˡgaddza], *lazzo* [ˡladdzo], *rezzo* [ˡreddzo], *sizza* [ˡsiddza].

[ʃ]

sc followed by *e* or *i* plus consonant, or in *sce* final in a word, as in *scegliere* [ʃeˡʎere], *fascisti* [faˡʃisti], *rincresce* [rinˡkreʃe].

sci before a vowel, as in *sciopero* [ʃɔˡpero], *sciupo* [ˡʃupo], *lasciare* [laˡʃare], *sciente* [ˡʃɛnte].

NOTE: *i* after *sc* before *a*, *o*, *u* is silent, serving only to indicate that the preceding *sc* is pronounced [ʃ].

It may be noted that we have in *scie* one of the few superfluities in Italian spelling; *sce* would be [ʃe] without the intervention of the silent *i*. The *i* is, of course, retained historically.

c and *cc*, when pronounced [tʃ], [ttʃ], include [ʃ] as the second element of [tʃ, ttʃ].

---

[14] Hall, p. 9, especially footnote 3.

[ʒ]

g and *gg*, when pronounced [ʤ], [dʤ] include [ʒ] as the final element of [ʤ, dʤ].

The sound [ʒ] is not used separately in Italian, except as an allophone of /ʤ/ in central Italy, where *agio* [ˈaʤo] may be heard as [ˈaʒo].[15]

h

h is always silent in Italian, as in *ho* [ɔ], *vaghezza* [vaˈgettsa], *macchia* [ˈmakːja], *hanno* [ˈanːo].

NOTE: *h* is used after *c, sc, g* before *e* or *i* to indicate that the pronunciation is [k], [sk], [g], respectively, as in *rechero* [reˈkero], *pochi* [ˈpɔki], *rischio* [ˈriskjo], *schioppo* [ˈskjɔpːo], *mughetto* [muˈgetːo]. In the words such as *ho, hai, ha,* and *hanno,* the orthographic *h* is a historical survival from Latin *habere.*

[ts]

z and *zz* followed by *ia, ie, io,* as in *essenziale* [esːenˈtsjale], *grazie* [ˈgratsje], *ambizioso* [ambiˈtsjoso], *polizia* [poˈlitsja], *impaziente* [impaˈtsjɛnte], *condizione* [kondiˈtsjone].

z initially except in about forty root words (see [dz] below). Examples: *zaffo* [ˈtsafːo], *zana* [ˈtsana], *zio* [ˈtsio], *zolfo* [ˈtsolfo], *zoppo* [ˈtsɔpːo], *zuffa* [ˈtsufːa], *zitto* [ˈtsitːo].

zz in certain pairs of words spelled alike, the other member of which is pronounced with [ddz]. Examples: *bozzo* [ˈbɔttso] (sketch), *mezzo* [ˈmettso] (wet), *mozzo* [ˈmottso] (cabin boy), *razza* [ˈrattsa] (race), (see also under [dz] below).

z and *zz* intervocalically in all except about a hundred words (see under [dz] below). Examples: *bellezza* [belˈlettsa], *carezza* [kaˈrettsa], *lunghezza* [luŋˈgettsa] *spezzare* [spetˈtsare].[16]

[dz]

z initially in about forty root words, most of which are relatively uncommon. Examples: *zaffiro* [dzafˈfiro], *zannata* [dzanˈnata], *zanzara* [dzanˈdzara], *zotico* [ˈdzɔtiko].

zz in certain pairs of words spelled alike, the other member of which is pronounced with [tts]. Examples: *bozzo* [ˈbɔddzo] (pool), *mezzo* [ˈmɛddzo] (half), *mozzo* [ˈmɔddzo] (hub), *razza* [ˈraddza] (a ray-fish). (See also under [ts] above).

z and *zz* intervocalically in about a hundred words,[17] including numerous

---

[15] Hall, p. 9, footnote 2.
[16] Phelps, pp. 13, 14.
[17] For list see Phelps, pp. 13–14.

long words from Greek, Hebrew, and Arabic. (These words do not include those where *z*, *zz* is followed by *ia*, *io*, *iu*; (see [ts], page 434.) Examples: *protozoi* [proto'dzɔi], *azzurro* [ad'dzur:o], *zenit* ['dzenit], *Lazzaro* [lad'dzaro], *zanzara* [dzan'dzara].

zz in infinitives of four syllables or more ending in *-izzare* [id'dzare], as in *polverizzare* [polverid'dzare], *magnetizzare* [magnetid'dzare], *notomizzare* [noto-mid'dzare], *realizzare* [realid'dzare].

[ʧ]

c or *cc* followed by *e* or *i*, as in *uccello* [ut'ʧɛl:o], *tredici* [tre'diʧi], *vicino* [vi'ʧino], *capace* [ka'paʧe], *cucire* [ku'ʧire].

NOTE: *i* following *c* before *a*, *o*, *u*, *e* is silent, serving only to indicate that the preceding *c* is pronounced [ʧ], as in *ciarpetta* [ʧar'pet:a], *cioccolata* [ʧok:o'lata], *ciuco* ['ʧuko], *cieco* ['ʧɛko]. Note that *i* in *cieco* is superfluous, since *c* before *e* would be [ʧ] without it.

[ʤ]

g or *gg* followed by *e* or *i*, as in *agire* [a'ʤire], *bigio* [bi'ʤo], *costaggiu* [kostad-'ʤu], *eleggere* [e'lɛdʤere], *genere* ['ʤɛnere], *porgere* ['pɔrʤere], *valigia* [va'liʤa], *giunto* ['ʤunto].

NOTE: *i* following *g* before *a*, *o*, *u* is silent, serving only to indicate that the preceding *g* is pronounced [ʤ], as in *Giacomo* ['ʤakomo], *Giovanni* [ʤo'van:i], *Giuseppe* [ʤu'zɛp:e], *maggiore* [mad'ʤore].

[ks]

x in the neolatinism *uxoricida* [uksori'ʧida], from the single Latin root *-uxor-*[18] but see original derivative *ussoricida* [us:ori'ʧida].

Transcription in Italian

It is appropriate at this point to do transcription exercises in Italian. Use any Italian text or word list.

Some Characteristics of Italian Contexts and Their
Effects on English Pronunciation

The supernumerary final vowel. Almost every word in Italian ends in a vowel. As a result, the Italian develops a subconscious need for a vowel with which to complete any English word ending with a consonant. Accordingly,

---

[18] Hall, p. 210.

he uses the sound [a] (which in time reduces itself to [ə]) as a kind of stop-gap at the close of many words, especially words stressed within a breath-group. Dialect writers usually spell this supernumerary final vowel with *a*, as in *maka* [ˈmeka], *wanta* [ˈwanta], etc.

The excrescent [k] and [g] after [ŋ]. Strictly speaking, Italian has no /ŋ/ phoneme. In Italian, [ŋ] belongs to the /n/ phoneme, as it doubtless would do in English if it occurred only in words like *bank* [bæŋk] and *single* [ˈsiŋgəl], or if there were no words like *sing*. Italian has only the *bank – single* type of words containing [ŋ], as *banco* [ˈbaŋko], *venga* [ˈvɛ̃ŋga]. This being the case, [ŋ] fixes itself in the Italian mind as simply one kind of /n/, a kind which, moreover, is invariably followed by [k] or [g]. Accordingly, whenever [ŋ] occurs in English, there arises the temptation to add [k] or [g]—indeed many Italians at first find it impossible to àvoid doing so. Thus: *sing* [sɪŋ] > [siŋg], or less regularly, [siŋk].

The mistaken value of z. Anyone reading a strange language is likely at first to insert the sound values of his native language where symbols common to both occur in the foreign language. The Italian is subject to this tendency in respect to *z*, sometimes pronouncing it [ts] or [dz]. Thus: *Arizona* [ariˈdzona], *zone* [ˈtsone].

Reading errors like that just discussed may happen, of course, with any letter of the alphabet that is pronounced differently in Italian and English. Thus, *c* before *e*, or *g* before *e* or *i*, may be pronounced [tʃ] as in *cell* [tʃɛl], [dʒ] as in *giggle* [ˈdʒigɛl], etc. The fact that [ʒ] occurs in Italian only in the affricate [dʒ] makes the sound awkward in isolation.

From the foregoing, it can be readily seen that the English sounds not found in Italian, and therefore demanding the attention of Italians learning English, are as follows:

Vowels	Consonants
ɪ	Entirely different
eɪ regularly instead of [e]	θ
æ	ð
ɑ (but Italian [a] is often retracted to approximate [ɑ])	ʍ
oʊ regularly instead of [o]	Different in certain features
ɜ	t, d, n, alveolar, not dental
ɝ	ł as explained p. 131
ə	r retroflex, not trilled
ɚ	ʒ as a separate phoneme
ʌ	

Conversely, the sounds of Italian not in English, and therefore demanding attention from English-speaking learners are as follows:

Vowels	*Consonants*
e always pure, not diphthongal	Entirely different
a in isolation as well as in diph- thongs	ɲ (but acoustically close to [nj]) ʎ (but acoustically close to [lj])
o always pure, not diphthongal	Different in certain features
	t, d, n, dental, not alveolar
	l always clear
	r tongue-point trilled
	ts, ʤ independent phonemes

From the paragraphs immediately following charts A and B above, it can be seen that the Italian is likely to make substitutions for unfamiliar English sounds somewhat as follows:

English Sounds	*Italian Substitutions*
ɪ	i
eɪ	e
æ	a
ɑ	a
oʊ	o
ʊ	u
ɝ, ɜ	ɛr
ɚ, ə (spelled with vowel plus *r*)	ɛr
ə (when not spelled with vowel plus *r*)	a
ʌ	ɑ, u
θ	t̪
ð	d̪
ʍ	w
t, d, n	t̪, d̪, n̪
ł	l̪
r	ŕ

In addition to these substitutions, the Italian, especially if a beginner in English or a relatively illiterate person, is likely *to add* a vowel ([a] at first, later [ə]) to many English words ending in a consonant, as in *gotta* [ˈgata, ˈgatə]. This is in accordance with the fact that indigenous Italian words nearly always end in vowels. Conversely, in trying to correct this tendency to add superfluous vowels, the Italian will sometimes leave off final vowels from English words, as in *mon'* for *money.*

Transcription in Italian Dialect

(Close Transcription)

DA GREATA BASABALL *

o greta gem iz besabɔl
fɔr jɔŋg amɛrikan;

---

* From *Selected Poems of T. A. Daly.* Copyright, 1936, by T. A. Daly. Published by Harcourt, Brace.

bat o ma frɛn, iz nat at ɔl
    da tiŋk fɔr dego man.

o lisɛn, plis, ai tɛl tu ju
    abaut wan gem wi ple
wɛn gras iz grin, an
    skai iz blu
an it iz ɔlide.

spagɛt:i se, wi tek a trip
    fɔr ple da bɔl, an si
witʃ said iz win da tʃampaʃip
    fɔr litla itali.

([ə] used instead of [a])

so ɔf:ɔr polo graun wi go
wit besəbɔl an bat
an start də gretə gem, bat, o
it iz nat finiʃ jɛt.

spolatro iz də bɔs fɔr said
dat wet fər katʃ də bɔl;
spagɛt:i nain iz fɛrst dat traid
fɔr nak it over wɔl.

an so spagɛt:i kam fɔr bat.
aha də gretə man!
də hanz hi gat; so big, so fat,
iz laik tu bantʃ banan.

spolatro pitʃ də bɔl, an dɛr
spagɛt:iz bat iz swiŋ,
an kwik də bɔl ap in di ɛr
iz flai laik ɛnitiŋ.

ju no in disə gem iz man
dats kɔl də lɛftə fil.
wɛl, dis wan kip pinatə stan
an laik fɔr sitin stil.

an do dis bɔl spagɛt:i it
is pasə bai iz we,

i dɔntə kɛrə litlə bit
if it iz gɔn ɔl de.

də sɛntrə fildə man, ju no,
dats nɛkst tu im—i kɔl:
"ai! wai ju dontə ʤampə,
       ʤo,
an ran ən gɛt də bɔl?"

bat ʤo i ʤustə sitə stil
til bɔl iz autə sait.
dis mek so mad də sɛntrə fil
i iz begin tə fait.

dɛn kamz ənadər man—ju si,
ai dontə no iz nem,
or au ju kɔl dis man,
bat i iz big man in də gem,

i iz də man dat mek də rul
for ple də gemə rait,
an so i go for doz tu ful
aut in də fil dat fait.

i puʃ də sɛntrə fild əwe,
an sutʃə nemz i kɔl!
an dɛn i grabə ʤo an se,
"kɔm, ran an gɛt də bɔl."

bat ʤo i graul an taɛl im, "no.
iz nat for mi at ɔl
spagɛt:i it də bɔl, an so
spagɛt:i gɛt də bɔl."

o gretə gem iz besəbɔl
for jɔŋg əmɛrikan
bat o mai frɛn, iz nat at ɔl
də tiŋ for dego man.

T. A. DALY

MIA CARLOTTA *

ʤuzɛp:i də barbɛr iz gretə for maʃ.
i gatə də bigə, də blakə mustaʃ,

* From *Selected Poems of T. A. Daly*. Copyright, 1936, by T. A. Daly. Published by Harcourt, Brace.

gud kloz an gud stailə an plɛntə gud kaʃ.
wɛnɛvrə ʤuzɛpːi is wɔk ɔn də strit,
də piplə de tɔkə, au nabi, au nit;
au sɔftə di andə, au smɔlə də fit.

MIA CARLOTTA (continued)

Exercise for Transcription

He raisa hees hat an' he shaka hees curls,
An smila weeth teetha so shiny like pearls;
O! many da heart of da seely young girls
   He gotta.
     Yes, playnta he gotta—
     But notta
     Carlotta!

Giuseppe, da barber, he maka da eye,
An' like da steam engine puffa an' sigh,
For catcha Carlotta w'en she ees go by.
Carlotta she walka weeth nose in da air,
And look through Guiseppe weeth far-away stare,
As eef she no see dere ees som'body dere.

Giuseppe, da barber, he gotta da cash,
He gotta da clo'es an' da bigga mustache,
He gotta da seely young girls for da "mash,"
     But notta—
     You bat my life, notta—
     Carlotta.
     I gotta!

                              T. A. DALY

Transcribe:

From *They Knew What They Wanted* *

Tony: W'en I'm young, I got nothing. I'm broke all the time, you remember?
I got no money for havin' wife. I don't want no wife for mak' her work
all da time. Da's no good, dat. Da's mak' her no more young, no more
prett'. Evrabody say, Tony is crazy for no havin' wife. I say Tony is
no dam' fool. What is happen? Pro'ibish is com. Wat I'm doin? I'm
keep the grape, eh? I say, "I come in dees country for growin' da grape!
God mak' dees country for growin' da grape! Ees not for pro'ibish God

* Copyright, 1925, by Sidney Howard.

mak' dees country. Ees for growin' da grape, ees true? Sure ees true! And w'at happen! Before pro'ibish I sell ma grape for 10 mebbe 12 littla dollar da ton. Now I sell my grape sometime 100 dollar da ton. Pro'ibish is mak' me verra rich. I gotta fine house. I got one Ford car. I got all I want, evrathing, except only wife. Now I'm goin' have wife. Verra nice an' young an' fat. Not for work, no. For sit and holdin' da hands. Da's fine for God and evrabody! I tell you Padre, Tony know w'at he want.

SIDNEY HOWARD

Bibliography

Italian

Books

Hall, Robert A., Jr., *Descriptive Italian Grammar* (Ithaca, N. Y.: Cornell University Press and Linguistic Society of America, 1948).

Pei, Mario A., *The Italian Language* (New York: Columbia University Press, 1941).

Phelps, Ruth Shepard, *An Italian Grammar* (New York: Ginn and Co., 1907).

CHAPTER 23

Spanish

Including Mexican

The Spanish language in North America had a promising beginning. Spanish occupation of the American continent focused in the Southwest and in Florida, Louisiana, and St. Louis. But because of the early transfer of the last-named three areas to other European countries and ultimately to the United States, Spanish-language influence there practically faded out almost a century ago. Some slight influence remains in St. Augustine and in Louisiana. But in the latter place whatever flavor Spanish contributes to the dialect of such centers as New Iberia and New Orleans has been lost in stronger French-language influence prevalent in the central and southern parts of the state.

For Spanish-English dialect in America, then, we must go to the Southwest. Here there remains some residue of the Spanish language, planted there by the conquistadores and the missionary padres. But for the most part, the Spanish now found in that part of the United States is spoken by Mexican immigrants and their descendants. Among these the Mexican Spanish is largely retained as a family language, even though each child learns English as soon as he goes to school. Conditions like these are conducive to a long continuance of broken Spanish-English dialect.

For the better understanding of Spanish-English dialect, as well as for the more intelligent handling of the Spanish language itself, a study of the Spanish sound system is indicated.

In dealing with Spanish pronunciation, it is necessary to understand a linguistic concept important in all Romance languages, that of open and closed syllables. An open syllable is a syllable ending in a vowel or diphthong. A closed syllable is a syllable ending in a consonant. But the clarity of these two statements is vastly clouded by the complex rules of Spanish syllabication, which often makes any decision as to whether a syllable ends in a vowel or consonant a difficult one. A resumé of these rules for syllabication is inserted here.

The behavior of consonants in syllabication. Consonants begin syllables phonetically, and usually, but not always, orthographically, as follows:

1. A single consonant between two vowels, as in *hora*[1] [ˈo-ra], *niño* [ˈni-ɲo], *rojo* [ˈro-xo].

2. *ch* [ʧ], *ll* [λ, j],[2] *rr* [r:], as in *muchacho* [mu-ˈʧa-ʧo], *silla* [ˈsi-λa, ˈsi-ja], *guerra* [ˈgɛ-r:a].

3. Any consonant plus *l* or *r* (except *rl*, *sl*, *tl*, *sr*), as in *siglo* [ˈsi-glo], *madre* [ˈma-ɖre, ˈma-ðre],[3] *abrigar* [a-βri-ˈɣar]. (In *abrigar* the phonetic syllabication violates the orthographic syllabication, *ab-ri-gar*, which does not permit the breaking up of a prefix.)

Consonant clusters other than consonant plus *l* or *r* are broken up in syllabication as follows:

1. With *rl*, *sl*, *tl*, *sr*, and any other two consonants not covered under (2) and (3) above, the first goes with the preceding syllable, the second with the succeeding, as in *corlar* [kɔr-ˈlar], *eslovaco* [ɛs-lo-ˈβa-ko], *alto* [ˈal-to], *Israel* [is-ra-ˈel], *arbol* [ar-ˈβɔl], *Calderón* [kɑl-de-ˈrɔn], *cantar* [kan-ˈtar].

2. With clusters of more than two consonants, only the last, or the last two if inseparable, begin the succeeding syllable. Thus, *inspirar* [ins-pi-ˈrar], *hombre* [ˈɔm-bre], *ingles* [iŋ-ˈgles].

The behavior of vowels in syllabication. 1. When two strong vowels (*a, e, o*) are adjacent, they fall into separate syllables, as in *leer* [le-ˈɛr], *caer* [ka-ˈɛr], *pasear* [pa-se-ˈar], *peón* [pe-ˈon].

2. A strongly stressed vowel plus a weakly stressed vowel (*i, u,* sometimes *y*) form a single so-called diphthongal syllable. Thus, *baile* [ˈbai-le], *causa* [ˈkɑu-sa], *ahoy* [a-ˈɔi], *rey* [rɛi], *hay* [ai], *deuda* [ˈdeu-ɖa, ˈdeu-ða]. (Note that Spanish diphthongs differ in character from English diphthongs, in that the two elements are more widely spaced, as will be discussed later.)

3. A weak vowel followed by any other vowel becomes consonantal; i.e., *i* becomes [j], and *u* becomes [w], as in *ciudad* [θju-ˈɖaɖ, sju-ˈðað] (see footnote 11), *siempre* [ˈsjempre], *cuadro* [ˈkwa-ɖro, ˈkwa-ðro]. Any irregularity in syllabication (and stress) of vowels adjacent to each other is indicated by the acute accent mark, as in *país* [pa-ˈis].

Syllabication in breath groups. A consonant at the end of a word followed by another word beginning with a vowel in a breath-group is regarded as intervocalic, and is considered phonetically as beginning the first syllable of the succeeding word. Thus, *los hermanos* [lo-sɛr-ˈma-nɔs], *las animas* [la-ˈsa-ni-mas], *con otros amigos* [ko-ˈno-tro-sa-ˈmi-ɣɔs]. This is liaison or linking.

It is evident that the Spanish manner of syllabication in breath-groups disturbs the pronunciation applicable to words in isolation. In the examples above, for

---

[1] Orthographic *h* is always silent in Spanish.
[2] Both the Castilian [λ] (see page 463) and the colonial [j] are given throughout this chapter.
[3] Both the Castilian [ɖ] (see page 465) and the colonial [ð] are given throughout this chapter.

instance, the article *los*, which, standing alone, is a closed syllable pronounced [lɔs], becomes an open syllable in [lo-sɛr-ˈma-nɔs], and is pronounced [lo]. The change from closed to open syllable induces a change of vowel value, from [ɔ] to [o]. In the same manner the pronunciation of a vowel may change as a singular becomes plural, by reason of the change of a syllable from open to closed, as in *niño* [ˈni-ɲo], *niños* [ˈni-ɲɔs].

Very frequently the explanation of an erroneous pronunciation made in English by a speaker of Spanish lies in the speaker's attempt to apply Spanish patterns of syllabication to English speech.

Sounds of Spanish

Vowels

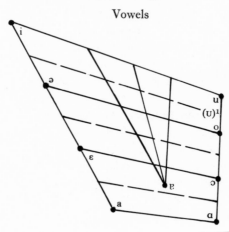

Diphthongs: αu
              αi
              ɛi
              ɔi
              ɛu
              ou (rare)

---

[1] Allophone of /u/, heard irregularly in closed syllables and before [r:] and [x].

Consonants

	Bi-Labial	Labio-dental	Dental	Alveolar	Palato-alveolar	Palatal	Velar
Plosive	p b		t d				k g
Nasal	m	(ɱ)²	n			ɲ	(ŋ)²
Lateral non-fricative			l			λ	
Trilled				r			
Fricative	(φ)³ β	f (v)⁴	s (z)⁵	θ⁶ ð đ (đ̥⁷)	(ʃ)⁸ (ʒ)⁹		x γ
Frictionless Consonants	w					j	(w)

Affricates: ʧ
ʤ (dialectal substitute for initial [j])

NOTE: Students who wish to go directly to a consideration of the Spanish dialect of English without a study of Spanish orthography may reserve the material immediately following for reference and turn at once to page 467.

Vowels

[i]

The sound [i] is uniformly spelled in Spanish with *i* and *y*. In fact, *i* and *y* in Spanish may be said to have no other pronunciation, except when they become [j], by reason of being followed by another vowel. But the Spanish phoneme /i/ includes four variants, semi-close [i], semi-open [i] or [ɪ], the unstressed [i] or [ⁱ], and the centralized [i] or [ɨ] used in diphthongs. All of these [i]'s lie between English [i] and English [ɪ].

1. Close [i], spelled with *i*, is a little lower and a little more lax than English [i]. (See page 334, in the chapter on French, for explanation of close and open vowels.) In conformity with the rules of syllabication previously detailed, it is

---

² Allophones of /m/ and /n/ respectively.
³ Voiceless variant of [β].
⁴ Dialectal pronunciation of *b* and *v*.
⁵ Voiced variant of [s] before a voiced consonant.
⁶ Castilian pronunciation of *z* and of *c* before *e*, *i*, and *y*.
⁷ Voiceless variant of [đ].
⁸ Second element of [ʧ].
⁹ Second element of [ʤ].

found in most stressed open syllables and in some unstressed open syllables if slowly pronounced, as in

a-pli-car	[a-pli-ˈkar]
a-pri-sa	[a-ˈpri-sa]
ab-ri-gar	[aβ-ri-ˈɣar]
ni-ño	[ˈni-ɲo]
si-lla	[ˈsi-ʎa, ˈsi-ja]
bi-cho	[ˈbi-t͡ʃo]
bi-rre-ta	[bi-ˈr:e-ta]

NOTE: Primary stress in Spanish polysyllables occurs as follows:

a. On a final syllable ending in a consonant (other than *n*, *s*, or *z*), as in *tomar* [toˈmar].

b. On the syllable immediately preceding a final syllable ending in a vowel or *n*, *s*, or *z*, as in *declive* [de-ˈkli-βe], *orden* [ˈɔr-đen, ˈɔr-ðen] *crestas* [ˈkres-tas], *dejadez* [de-ˈxa-đeθ, de-ˈxa-ðes].

c. Where indicated by the acute accent mark, as in *cupón* [ku-ˈpɔn].

2. Open [ɪ] spelled *i*, is found in stressed closed syllables, and in certain open syllables where the vowel is preceded or followed by [r],[10] or where it is followed by [x], as in *morir* [mo-ˈrɪr], *afirmar* [a-fɪr-ˈmar], *cortijo* [kɔr-ˈtɪ-xo], *rica* [ˈr:ɪ-ka]. (The symbol [ɪ] will not be further used.)

3. Unstressed [i] or [ⁱ], spelled *i*, is found in those definitely unstressed syllables which fall between syllables of stronger stress, either primary or secondary, as in *solido* [ˈso-lⁱ-đo, ˈso-lⁱ-ðo], *edificio* [e-đⁱ-ˈfi-θjo, e-ðⁱ-ˈfi-sjo].[11] Spelled *y* (the conjunction), it is found between consonants, as in *pan y mantiquilla* [pan-ⁱ-man-tⁱ-ˈki-ʎa, pan-ⁱ-man-tⁱ-ˈki-ja]. (The elevated [ⁱ] of close transcription which is used for demonstration here is not used elsewhere in this book.)

4. Centralized [i̥], or [ɨ], spelled *i* or *y*, is found as the second element of the diphthongs spelled *ai, ay, oi, oy, ei, ey*. Thus, *baile* [ˈbai̥-le], *hay* [ai̥], *oiga* [ˈɔi̥-ga], *soy* [sɔi̥], *aceite* [a-ˈθɛi̥-te, a-ˈsɛi̥-te], *ley* [lɛi̥]. Spelled *y* (the conjunction) it is found between a vowel and a consonant, as in *rico y pobre* [ri-ko-i̥-ˈpo-βre]. (The barred [ɨ] of close transcription which is used here for demonstration is not used elsewhere in this chapter.)

[e]

The sound [e], spelled with *e*, is a pure vowel, as contrasted with the diphthongal English [eɪ]. It exists in two forms, the stressed [e] and the lax or unstressed [ᵉ].

---

[10] [r̄:], i.e., long trilled [r], as distinguished from [r̄] the short trilled [r], is found, as later to be discussed, when *r* is initial, double, or after *l*, *n*, or *s*.

[11] Both the Castilian [θ] and the colonial [s] are given throughout this chapter.

a. Stressed [e] is a little less tense than French [e] in *été*, but otherwise resembles it greatly. It is found (except when adjacent to multiple trilled *r* [r̄:]): (a) in open syllables, as in *pero* [ˈpe-ro], *señor* [se-ˈɲɔr], *cena* [ˈθe-na, ˈse-na]; (b) in closed syllables before *m, n, s, d,* and *z,* and before *x* (pronounced [s]) plus a consonant, as in *siempre* [ˈsjem-pr^e], *penitente* [pe-ni-ˈten-t^e], *desde* [ˈdez-đ^e, ˈdez-ð^e],[12] *pared* [pa-ˈred, pa-ˈreð], *vez* [beθ, bes], *expedir* [es-pe-ˈdir, es-pe-ˈðir].

b. Unstressed *e* or [^e] occurs between more strongly stressed syllables, either primary or secondary. It occurs also finally before a pause. It is a true [e], not to be confused with such English unstressed vowels as [ɪ] or [ə], but it is very brief and slight. Thus, *numero* [ˈnu-m^e-ro], *noche* [ˈno-tʃ^e]. (The elevated [^e] used here for demonstration is not used elsewhere in this book; [e] is used instead.)

$$[\varepsilon]$$

Open *e* or [ε] occurs:

1. In closed syllables except those closed by *d, m, n, s, z,* or *x* (pronounced [s]). Thus, *mantel* [man-ˈtεl], *dirección* [di-rεy-ˈθjon, di-rεk-ˈsjon].

2. In open syllables, if in contact with multiple trilled *r* [r̄:], as in *regla* [ˈr̄:ε-γla], *perro* [ˈpε-r̄:o].

3. In open syllables before the sound [x], as in *lejos* [ˈlε-xɔs], *Méjico* [ˈmε-xi-ko], *Tejas* [ˈtε-xɑs].

4. In the diphthongs [εi] and [εu] as in *rey* [r̄:εi], *reina* [ˈr̄:εi-na], *reuma* [ˈr̄:εu-ma].

$$[a]$$

The pronunciation of *a* in Spanish is in general [a]. But the [a] of Spanish is a little farther back, i.e., more centralized than the [a] of French, or of English. It varies considerably according to the sounds with which it is in contact, tending to be farther back when back sounds are adjacent. In a limited number of cases, it is far enough back to be written [ɑ]. (See below.)

1. [a] occurs as the pronunciation of the *a*-spelling everywhere except in those cases listed under [ɑ] below. Thus *carta* [ˈkar-ta], *lado* [ˈla-đo, ˈla-ðo], *padre* [ˈpa-đre, ˈpa-ðre].

2. When *a* precedes *ch, ll, ñ,* and *y,* it is perceptibly farther back than in the average case, but not far enough back to warrant the use of the symbol [ɑ]. In close transcription, [a˅] might be used, as in *muchacha* [mu-ˈtʃa˅-tʃa], *calle* [ˈka˅-ʎe, ˈka˅-je], *baño* [ˈba˅-ɲo], *vaya* [ˈba˅-ja].

[ɐ], spelled *a,* the unstressed form of [a], occurs in definitely unstressed positions, medial and final, as in *casa* [ˈka-sɐ], *caballero* [ka-βɐ-ˈʎe-ro, ka-βɐ-ˈje-ro].

---

[12] Orthographic *s,* nearly always pronounced [s], when followed immediately by a voiced consonant becomes voiced by assimilation and is pronounced [z], as in *desde* above. This voicing appears to be more frequent in Castilian than in colonial Spanish.

It is acoustically intermediate between English [a] and [ə]. (The close transcription [ɐ], used here for demonstration, will not be used elsewhere in this book; [a] will be used instead.)

[ɑ]

[ɑ], spelled *a*, occurs as follows:

1. In the diphthongs [ɑi], as in *baile* [ˈbɑi-le], and [ɑu], as in *flauta* [ˈflɑu-ta].

2. Immediately before *o*, as in *carabao* [ka-ra-ˈβa-o].

3. In contact with [γ] or [x], as in *rogar* [ro-ˈγar], *bajo* [ˈbɑ-xo].

4. Before *l* final in a syllable, as in *maldad* [mɑl-ˈdad, mɑl-ˈdað].

[o]

1. Spanish [o], spelled *o*, is pure, i.e., not diphthongal like the English [ou]. It is a little lower than English *o* and occurs in open syllables, as in *osos* [ˈo-sɔs], *como* [ˈko-mo].

2. Relaxed or unstressed [°], spelled *o*, occurs in definitely unstressed positions, either medially between stressed syllables as in *automovil* [ɑu-t°-ˈmo-βil], or finally as in *bajo* [ˈbɑ-x°]. (The close transcription [°], used here for demonstration, is not used elsewhere in this book; [o] is used instead.)

[ɔ]

Spanish [ɔ], spelled *o*, is higher than English [ɔ], and therefore nearer [o]. [ɔ] occurs:

1. In closed syllables, as *donde* [ˈdɔn-de], *dos* [dɔs].

2. Adjacent to a long trilled r [r:], as in *correr* [kɔ-ˈr:ɛr].

3. Preceding the sound [x], as in *rojo* [ˈrɔ-xo].

4. In the diphthongs *oi* and *oy*, as in *soy* [sɔi], *heroico* [e-ˈrɔi-ko].

5. Stressed and between *a* and *l* or *r*, as in *la olive* [lɑ-ɔ-ˈli-βe], *la oración* [lɑ-ɔ-ra-ˈθjɔn, lɑ-ɔ-ra-ˈsjɔn].

[u]

Spanish [ʊ], spelled *u*, is a little higher than English [ʊ] with the result that Spanish [u] and [ʊ] are very close together. [ʊ] occurs:

1. In closed syllables, as in *culpa* [ˈkʊl-pa].

2. Before long-trilled *r*, as in *burro* [ˈbʊ-r:o].

3. Before the sound [x], as in *mujer* [mʊ-ˈxɛr].

(In some colonial speech, [ʊ] is seldom heard. In most Spanish, it is safe to use [u] for *u* always, since [ʊ] is a non-distinctive allophone of /u/.

[u]

1. [u], spelled *u*, in Spanish is a little lower than English [u]. It occurs in open syllables, as in *musica* [ˈmu-si-ka], *uno* [ˈu-no].

2. [u], spelled *u*, occurs in relaxed and unstressed positions, as in *capitulo* [ka-ˈpi-tu-lo], *tengo un libro* [teŋ-go-un-ˈli-βro].

3. The centralized [ʉ] occurs in the diphthongs [aʉ, ɛʉ, oʉ], as in *flauta* [ˈflaʉ-ta], *reuma* [ˈr:ɛʉ-ma], *bou* [boʉ]. (The symbol [ʉ] will not be further used.)

Diphthongs

The Spanish diphthongs have been touched upon in the preceding paragraphs. Spanish phoneticians divide them into what are sometimes called decreasing or falling diphthongs, i.e., diphthongs in which the first element receives the stress, and increasing or rising diphthongs, i.e., diphthongs in which the second element receives the stress.

1. The so-called decreasing diphthongs are *ai* or *ay* [ai], *au* [au], *ei* or *ey* [ɛi], *oi* or *oy* [ɔi], *eu* [ɛu], *ou* [ou]. Thus, *baile* [ˈbai-le], *causar* [kau-ˈsar], *estoy* [es-ˈtɔi], *heroica* [eˈrɔi-ka] *rey*, [r:ɛi], *reina* [ˈr:ɛi-na], *reuma* [ˈr:ɛu-ma], *bou* [bou].

2. The so-called increasing diphthongs of Spanish are actually vowels preceded by [j] or [w]. They are *ia*, *ie*, *io*, *iu*; *ua*, *ue*, *ui*, *uo*, as in *lluvia* [ˈʎu-βja, ˈju-βja], *pies* [pjes], *patio* [ˈpa-tjo], *cuidad* [θju-ˈdad, sju-ˈðað], *agua* [ˈa-ɣwa], *puede* [ˈpwe-de, ˈpwe-ðe], *cuita* [ˈkwi-ta], *cuota* [ˈkwo-ta].

Triphthongs

The so-called triphthongs of Spanish, are, in fact, diphthongs introduced by [j] or [w]. They are as follows:

1. *iai* [jai], as in *estudiáis* [es-tud-ˈjais, es-tuð-ˈjais].
2. *iei* [jɛi], as in *cambiéis* [kam-ˈbjɛis].
3. *uay* or *uai* [wai], as in *Uruguay* [u-ru-ˈɣwai], *aguáis* [a-ˈɣwais].
4. *uei* or *uey* [wɛi], as in *continuéis* [kɔn-tin-ˈwɛis], *buey* [bwɛi]. (This [w] may, if spoken slowly, sound to English speakers like [uw].)

Consonants

[p]

[p] is spelled p, as in *poner* [poˈnɛr], *concepción* [kɔnθɛpˈθjɔn, kɔnsɛpˈsjɔn]. [p] in Spanish is unaspirated, even in initial positions.

NOTE: Henceforth in this book the division of syllables will not be indicated. Exceptions:

1. In rapid or careless speech, *p* before *c* or *s* may become [β]. Thus *concepción* [kɔnθɛβˈθjɔn, kɔnsɛβˈsjɔn]. In substandard speech this *p* may be entirely silent.
2. *p* is silent in the initial *ps* of words from the Greek. Thus, *psicopata* [sikoˈpata].
3. *p* is silent in rapid or informal conversation in words from the Latin containing *pc*, as in *inscripción* [inskriˈθjɔn, inskriˈsjɔn].

4. *p* is silent in rapid speech, even of the rank of standard, in words from the Latin containing *pt*, as *Septiembre* [sɛltjembre].

[b]

[b] is spelled *b* or *v*. It occurs in the following-named positions:

1. Initial in a breath group (the absolute initial position), as in *baile* [ˈbɑile], *vaso* [ˈbaso].

2. After a nasal, within a word or by juxtaposition of words. Thus, *hombre* [ˈɔmbre], *un beso* [um ˈbeso], *invitar* [imbiˈtar], *un vaso* [um ˈbaso].

[t]

[t] is spelled *t* as in *tio* [tio], *tortilla* [tɔrˈtiʎa, tɔrˈtija]. Exception: Final *t* in a syllable in informal speech. Here [t] becomes [d̪] or [ð], as in *atleta* [ad̪ˈleta, aðˈleta].

[t] in Spanish is unaspirated, even in initial positions. It is also dental.

[d]

[d], spelled *d*, occurs as follows:

1. *d* initial in a breath group (the absolute initial position), as in *dia* [dia].

2. *d* after *l* or *n*, as in *maldad* [malˈdad̪, malˈdað], *mandolina* [mandoˈlina].

[d] in Spanish is dental.

[k]

[k] is spelled as follows:

1. *c* before *a*, *o*, *u*, or a consonant. Thus, *calle* [ˈkaʎe, ˈkaje], *cosa* [ˈkosa], *cuatro* [ˈkwatro], *cuita* [ˈkwita], *cuenta* [ˈkwenta], *clavo* [ˈklaβo].

NOTE: *u* is used before *e* and *i* to "harden" the *c*, i.e., to make it [k] rather than [θ] or [s].

2. *qu* as in *que* [ke], *queso* [ˈkeso], *quita* [ˈkita].

3. *k* in loan words, as in *kaiser* [ˈkaisɛr], *kilogram* [kiloˈgram], *doktor* [dɔkˈtɔr]. Strictly speaking, the Spanish alphabet does not contain the letter *k*.

4. *x* (first element) in stilted speech, as in *exclamación* [ɛksklamaˈθjɔn, ɛksklamaˈsjɔn]. This [k] becomes silent in colloquial Spanish.

[k] in Spanish is unaspirated, even in initial positions.

[g]

[g] is spelled as follows:

1. *g* initially in a breath group (the absolute initial position) before *a*, *o*, *u*, or a consonant, as in *gallina* [gaˈʎina, gaˈjina], *goma* [ˈgoma], *Guadalupe* [gwadaˈlupe, gwaðaˈlupe], *guerra* [ˈgɛr:a], *guisar* [giˈsar] *grasa* [ˈgrasa].

NOTE: *u* is used before *e* and *i* to "harden" the *g*, i.e., to make it [g] rather than [x].

2. [g] after *n* before *a, o, u,* or a consonant, within a word or by juxtaposition of words, as in *tengo* [ˈteŋgo], *venga* [ˈbeŋga], *con gracias* [kɔŋˈgraθjas, kɔŋˈgrasjas].

[m]

[m] is spelled as follows:
1. *m* wherever found, as in *madre* [ˈmadre, ˈmaðre].
2. *n* by morpho-phonemic alternation before *b, v* [b], *p,* or *m,* either within a word or between words. Thus, *un bolso* [um ˈbɔlso], *invierno* [imˈbjɛrno], *un vaso* [um ˈbaso], *un peso* [um ˈpeso], *con madre* [kɔmˈmadre, kɔmˈmaðre].

[ɱ]

[ɱ] is spelled *n* before *f,* as *enfasis* [eɱfaˈsis], *un frijol* [uɱ friˈxɔl].
[ɱ] is a labio-dental nasal (see page 433).

[n]

[n] is spelled as follows:
1. *n* initial, as in *niño* [ˈniɲo].
2. *n* between vowels or finally when not followed by *b, v, p,* or *m,* and not spelled *ñ.* Thus *poner* [poˈnɛr], *con* [kɔn].
[n] in Spanish is dental.

[ɲ]

[ɲ] is spelled *ñ,* as in *mañana* [maˈɲana]
[ɲ] is a palatal nasal (see page 433).

[ŋ]

[ŋ] is spelled *n* before *g* or [k], as in *tengo* [ˈteŋgo], *cinco* [ˈθiŋko, ˈsiŋko].

[l]

[l] is spelled *l* wherever found, as in *lagrima* [ˈlaɣrima]. [l] is clear except when a context of adjacent back sounds tends to draw the tongue back. Even then, Spanish [l] is clearer, that is, made with tongue farther front, than the corresponding English sound.

[ʎ]

[ʎ] is spelled *ll* in Castilian. (It does not occur frequently in most colonial Spanish dialects.) Thus *llamar* [ʎaˈmar], *caballo* [kaˈβaʎo].
[ʎ] is a lateral palatal (see page 432).

[r̄:] (multiple trill)

1. [r̄:] is spelled *r* initially in a word or after *n, l, s.* Thus, *rosa* [ˈr̄:osa], *malrotar* [malr̄:oˈtar], *enrojar* [enr̄:oˈxar], *desreputación* [desr̄:eputaˈθjon, desr̄:eputaˈsjon].
2. *rr* wherever encountered, as in *carro* [ˈkar̄:o], *perro* [ˈper̄:o].

[r̃] (simple trill)

[r̃] is spelled *r* in all positions not covered by [r̃:] above, i.e., not preceded by *l*, *n*, or *s*, not initial and not doubled. Thus *pero* ['pero].

NOTE: No trill sign is used with [r] in this book, except where it is desired to call especial attention to the trill. It is understood that Spanish [r] has the tongue-point trill with only infrequent exception, as later indicated under the fricative [ɹ].

[ɹ]

Any Spanish *r*, but especially the intervocalic and final *r*, may weaken to [ɹ] in familiar speech. [ɹ] is a retroflex fricative, much as in English dry [dɹaɪ]. Often it is unvoiced toward the end, as in *ir* [iɹɹ̥].

[β]

[β] is a voiced bilabial spirant (see page 379). It is spelled as follows:

1. *b* and *v* wherever not absolutely initial, and not after *m* or *n*; i.e., *b* between vowels, as in *la boca* [la 'βoka]; between a vowel and a consonant, as in *pobre* [po'βre]; between a consonant and a vowel, as in *las bocas* [laz 'βokas]; between two consonants *el brazo* [ɛl 'βraθo, ɛl 'βraso], and final in a word, as in *Jacob* [xa'kɔβ].

2. *p* before *e* or *s* in rapid speech as in *concepción* [kɔnθɛβ'θjɔn, kɔnsɛβ'sjɔn].

b ([β]) before a voiceless consonant in rapid conversation may become voiceless [ɸ] by assimilation, as in *objeción* [ɔɸxɛk'θjɔn, ɔɸxɛk'sjɔn]. [ɸ] is a voiceless bilabial spirant. (See page 378.)

[f]

[f] is spelled *f* wherever encountered, as in *facil* [fa'θil, fa'sil].

[v]

v and occasionally *b* are pronounced [v] in some colonial Spanish, as in *centavo* [sɛn'tavo], *abierto* [a'vjɛrto]. Strictly speaking, the sound [v] is not a regular Spanish sound.

[θ]

[θ] is primarily a Castilian sound. It is spelled as follows:

1. *c* before *e* or *i*, as in *cinco* ['θiŋko], *centavo* [θen'taβo]. (Note the colonial pronunciation of this *c* under [s].)

2. *z* (except before voiced consonants in rapid conversation), as in *diez* [djeθ]. (Colonial pronunciation, [s].)

3. *d* final in some provincial and colonial speech, as in *virtud* [bir'tuθ].

4. *d* before a voiceless fricative in some provincial speech, as in *adjetivo* [aθxe'tiβo].

SPANISH 465

[ɖ] (Castilian affricate [dð])

[ɖ] is spelled as follows:

1. *d* intervocalic, as in *nada* [ˈnaɖa].
2. *d* between a vowel and a consonant, as *padre* [ˈpaɖre].
3. *d* between a non-nasal or lateral consonant and a vowel as in *desde* [ˈdezɖe].
4. *d* finally, as in *bondad* [bɔnˈdaɖ].

NOTE: (a) Another way of explaining the incidence of [ɖ] is as follows: wherever the spelling *d* occurs in Castilian except after a pause (the absolute initial position), and after *l* or *n*.
(b) In the ending *ado*, the [ɖ] tends to drop out, except in the most careful speech. Thus, *estado* [esˈtɑo].

[ð]

As in the instance of Castilian [ɖ], colonial [ð] occurs wherever the spelling *d* occurs, except after a pause (the absolute initial position) and after *l* or *n*, as in *nada* [ˈnaða], *Trinidad* [triniˈðað].

z before a voiced consonant in Castilian, as in *en vez de* [em beð de]. (In colonial Spanish, *z* is pronounced [s], but may change to [z] when followed by a voiced consonant.

[s]

[s] is spelled as follows:

1. *s*, as in *cosa* [ˈkosa], *adios* [aɖˈjɔs, aðˈjɔs]. Exception: *s* (irregularly, but the more frequently in Castilian) before a voiced consonant, as in *mismo* [ˈmizmo], *las bocas* [laz ˈβokas]. The sound [z] does not occur phonemically in Spanish: here it is an allophone of /s/.
2. *x* as in *extremidad* [estremiˈdaɖ, estremiˈðað].

NOTE: In very careful and emphatic speech this *x* equals [ks], as in [ekstremiˈdaɖ].
3. *c* before *e* and *i* in most colonial speech; as in *cinco* [ˈsiŋko], *centavo* [senˈtaβo].
4. *z* in most colonial speech, as in *voz* [bɔs].

[j]

[j] is spelled as follows:

1. *i* as the first element of a so-called increasing diphthong, as in *piedra* [ˈpjeɖra, ˈpjeðra], *pronunciación* [pronunθjaˈθjɔn, pronunsjaˈsjɔn], *hierro* [ˈjɛr:o].
2. *y* (conjunction) between consonant and vowel, as in *liberdad y humanidad* [liβɛrˈdaɖ jumaniˈdaɖ, liβɛrˈðað jumaniˈðað].
3. *y* initial in a syllable followed by a vowel, as in *yo* [jo], *blanco y hermoso* [ˈblaŋko jɛrˈmoso].
4. *ll* in colonial Spanish, as in *calle* [ˈkaje].

[tʃ]

[tʃ] is spelled *ch*, as in *Chile* [ˈtʃile].

NOTE: The [ʃ] in this affricate is briefer than in the English [tʃ].

[ʤ]

NOTE: This sound is not always precisely [ʤ], the voiced analog of [ʧ], but it resembles it very closely. [ʤ] is an alternative for [j], occurring sporadically in both Castilian and colonial speech.

[ʤ] is spelled as follows:

1. *y* initial in a syllable preceded by *l* or *n*, as in *el yerro* [ɛl ˈʤɛr:o], *con yeso* [kɔn ˈʤeso].

2. *hi* initial in a syllable when preceded by *l* or *n*, as in *con hielo* [kɔn ˈʤelo], *el hierro* [ɛl ˈʤɛr:o].

3. *y* in other contexts in the dialect of some individuals and communities, as in *yo* [ʤo].

[x]

[x] is spelled as follows:

1. *j*, as in *jota* [ˈxota].

2. *g* before *e* and *i*, as in *gente* [ˈxente], *gitano* [xiˈtano]. (Before *e* and *i* [x] tends towards [ç], but is never as far front as the corresponding German sound.)

[x] is a voiceless velar spirant (see page 367).

[γ]

[γ] is spelled as follows:

1. *g* before *a, o, u* when not absolutely initial (initial after a pause) in a word, and not preceded by *n*, as in *pegar* [peˈγar], *hago* [ˈaγo], *agua* [ˈaγwa].

2. *cc* (first element), as in *lección* [lɛγˈθjɔn, lɛγˈsjɔn].

3. *c* in the consonant cluster *cn*, in familiar speech, as in *tecnología* [tɛγnoloˈxia].

[γ] is a voiced back velar spirant. It is the voiced sound corresponding to the voiceless [x]. (See page 367.)

[w]

[w] is spelled *u* (or *hu, h* being silent) immediately before a vowel in the same syllable, as in *bueno* [ˈbweno], *huevo* [ˈweβo], *jaguar* [xaˈγwar], *perro u oso* [pɛr:o woso].

NOTE: *u* after *q*, and *u* after *g* before *e* and *i* are exceptions and are silent. The *u* after *g* before *e* and *i* serves to "harden" the *g*, i.e., to cause it to be pronounced [g], not [x]. Thus, *que* [ke], *qui* [ki], *guisar* [giˈsar], *guerra* [ˈgɛr:a].

Transcription in Spanish

It is appropriate at this point to do transcription exercises in Spanish. Use any Spanish text or word list.

Reduction

Syneresis: When vowels which belong to different syllables come together within a word they combine as follows:

(a) Two identical vowels form a single vowel.

(b) Two different vowels form a diphthong.

Synalepha: When vowels which belong to different words come together, the effect is the same.

1. Spanish Sounds That Do Not Appear in English. Consonants: [ŋ], [ɲ], [ʎ], [đ], [ɣ], [x], [r̄:], [β]. It is these sounds which the speaker of English must learn in order to improve his Spanish.

2. English Sounds That Do Not Appear in Spanish. Consonants: [h], [ʃ] (appears in Spanish only in the combination [tʃ]), [ʒ] (appears sporadically in dialectal [ʤ]), [v] (appears sporadically in colonial dialects), [ʍ].

Vowels: [ɪ], [æ], [ə], [ʌ], [ɜ], [ɝ], [ɚ], [ɒ]. It is these sounds which the speaker of Spanish will find difficult in speaking English. He will make substitutions somewhat as indicated in the following discussions.

Spanish Dialect

1. Sounds of Spanish which are similar to English sounds and which will be substituted for the corresponding English sounds.:

a. [e] for [eɪ]. Spanish [e] is pure, not diphthongal as in English. It will suggest [ɛ] to English ears.

b. [o] for [oʊ]. Spanish [o] is pure, not diphthongal as in English. It will suggest [ɔ] to English ears.

c. Unaspirated [t̪'] for English aspirated [tˤ]. The Spanish sound, moreover, is dental, spoken with the tongue against the upper teeth, rather than against the gum ridge. Since it is unaspirated, it will suggest [d].

d. Clear [l̥] for the English dark [ł].

e. Unaspirated [k'] for English aspirated [kˤ]. It will suggest [g] to English ears.

f. Unaspirated [p'] for English aspirated [pˤ]. The Spanish [p'] very frequently may suggest [b].

g. [r̄] for English [r]. The Spanish [r̄] is trilled more often than not. When final, it may modulate into voiceless [r r̥], and so resemble something like the English [r] plus [ç], thus [rç], as in *ir* [irç].

2. English sounds which do not occur in Spanish:

a. [ɪ], which may be replaced by [i],[13] as in *it is this* [it is 'ðis]. Though the Spanish has a low [i] which is close to English [ɪ], it is still a combinative variant of the phoneme /i/, and is to the speaker of Spanish non-distinctive, and unlikely to be used consistently for English [ɪ]. The student's aim must be re-defined so as to make him conscious of the low, lax character of English [ɪ].

---

[13] What the speaker of Spanish often does is to pronounce for both English [i] and [ɪ] his own close [i], which is only a little higher than half-way between the two. The English-speaking hearer feels, accordingly, that he hears an [i] that is somewhat like [ɪ], and an [ɪ] that is very like an [i].

b. [æ], which may be replaced by the Spanish [a], as in *at that house* [at ðat aus].

c. [ʊ], which may be replaced by [u] or by the Spanish *u abierta*, or open *u*, a sound very close to the *u cerrada*, or close *u*, and too high, close, and generally like [u] to serve for [ʊ]. Thus, *pull* [pul].[14]

NOTE: Even when the Spanish open [u] (sometimes written [ʊ]) is used, it is still an allophone of /u/, and unlikely to be chosen consistently for English [ʊ]. The student must be made conscious of the low, lax character of English [ʊ], so that he can use that sound overtly.

d. [ʌ], which is replaced by any low back vowel, usually [ɑ]. Thus, *cut* [kɑt].

e. [ɝ], [ɚ] (when a pronunciation of vowel plus *r*, as in *summer*), [ɜ], and [ə], for which the substitution is very uncertain. The English spellings of these sounds are of such wide variety that speakers who read English are likely to make substitutions suggested by the orthography. Those who try to imitate the sound as heard are likely to use [ɛr], with, of course, the trilled [r]. Thus, *girl* [gɛř l], *summer* [ˈsɑmˌɛř].

f. [ð], which occurs in Spanish, but not initially, so that in *this*, *that*, etc., it is often replaced by [d], producing [dis], [dat].

g. [θ] does not occur in Mexican or most other colonial Spanish. It is usually replaced by [s]. Thus, Spanish *centavo* [senˈtaβo], English *thing* [siŋg]. It may also be replaced by [t]. Thus *thank* [taŋk].

h. [h], which may be replaced by [x], or left silent, as it would be in Spanish. Thus, *how much* [xɑu ˈmatʃ], [au ˈmatʃ].

i. [ʃ], which may be replaced by [s], but which is usually so quickly learned as not to appear in dialect writing. The fact that [ʃ] occurs in the Spanish affricate [tʃ] facilitates its being separately learned. However, [ʃ] may be confused with [tʃ] and replaced by it, as in [tʃi] for *she*.

j. [ʒ], which may be replaced by [ʃ] or [tʃ], as in [ruʃ] or [rutʃ] for *rouge*.

k. [ʤ], which may be replaced by [tʃ]. Thus, *jump* [tʃamp].

l. [ʍ], which may be replaced by [w], as in *whistle* [ˈwisl].

3. Special contexts of Spanish, which, when they occur in English, will produce un-English sounds:

a. [ŋ] occurs in Spanish, but always as a member of the phoneme /n/, when *n* is followed by [k] or [g]. Thus, *cinco* [ˈθiŋko, ˈsiŋko], *venga* [ˈbeŋga]. The native speaker of Spanish therefore tends to pronounce [g] or, less frequently, [k], after English [ŋ], as in *sing* [siŋg], *something* [ˈsamsiŋk].

b. *b* is occlusive in Spanish, i.e., like the English [b], only initially after a

---

[14] Here the phenomenon described for [i-ɪ] is sometimes repeated. Though the Spanish [u] is properly close and round, individuals may lower it until there is little difference between their own *u cerrada* and *u abierta*. This sound they use for both [u] and [ʊ] in English. The sound is somewhat too [ʊ]-like for [u], and much too [u]-like for [ʊ].

pause, or in the interior of a word preceded by a nasal. Everywhere else[15] in Spanish, *b* is the fricative [β]. The Spaniard will accordingly incline, especially when first learning English, to use this fricative [β] in *sober* ['soβɛr], *able* ['eβɛl], *arbor* ['arβɔr], *Albright* [ɔl'βrait], *abnegate* ['aβniget], *obsess* ['ɔβsɛs], *crib* [kriβ].

c. *v* is treated exactly like *b*. Initially after a pause, or preceded by a nasal, it is [b]. Elsewhere it is [β]. It confuses Spanish-speaking students especially in the two positions first named, thus:

x. *Very* ['bɛri], *Virginia* [bir'tʃinja], *valley* ['bali].

y. *Invite* [im'bait], *environment* [ɛm'bairɔnmɛnt].

d. Final *m* is sometimes [n] in Spanish, as in *álbum* ['alβun], and may, in rare cases, tend to be so in Spanish-English.

NOTE: This final [n], as in words spelled with *n*, may be assimilated to [m] or [ŋ], as in *álbum blanco* [album 'blaŋko], *álbum con pinturas* [albuŋ kɔm pin'turas].

e. *s* before a voiced consonant becomes [z] in Spanish, despite the fact that there is no [z]-phoneme in the language. This [z] is an allophone of the phoneme /s/; it acquires its voicing by assimilation from the voiced consonant following. Thus *rasgar* [raz'ɣar], *desde* ['dezde, 'dezðe], *los bolsos* [lɔz 'βolsɔs]. In a similar way, [s] may become [z] in *nice boy*, making it [naiz 'bɔi] or [naiz 'βɔi].

f. *d* initial after a pause or preceded by *n* or *l* is pronounced *d*. Elsewhere[16] it is fricative, i.e., [d] in Castilian and [ð] in colonial Spanish. In final positions it may become unvoiced to [d̥] and [θ] respectively. All of these pronunciations may sometimes, though rarely, affect [d] in English.

g. *g* before a consonant, or before *a*, *o*, or *u*, when initial after a pause or preceded by *n*, is pronounced [g]. Elsewhere,[17] except before *e* or *i*, it is the fricative [ɣ]. It follows that the speaker of Spanish may use [ɣ] in English where *g* is not initial or preceded by a nasal. Thus *dragging* ['draɣiŋg].

4. Of Spanish intonation, rhythm, etc., little can be said in a hurried generalization. Spanish treats breath-groups somewhat as does French, but there is less of running on in a monotone between the extremities of the group than in French; Spanish stress gives variation within the group, where French, almost without stress, has little. The lurching effect of French, if toned down

---

[15] Specifically, according to Navarro Tomás, *Pronunciación Española* (pp. 82–83), as follows:
   a. Inicial de sílaba entre vocales: *lobo* ['loβo].
   b. Inicial de sílaba entre vocal y consonante: *pobreza* [po'βreθa].
   c. Inicial de sílaba entre consonante y vocal: *alba* ['alβa].
   d. Inicial de sílaba entre consonantes: *albricias* [al'βriθjas].
   e. Final de sílaba ante consonante sonora: *abdicar* [aβ'dikar].
   f. Final de sílaba ante consonante sorda: *obsesión* [ɔβse'sjɔn].
   g. Final de palabra: *Jacob* [xa'kɔβ].
[16] See Tomás, pp. 98–100.
[17] *Ibid.*, pp. 135–136.

to a point halfway between it and the almost lawless rhythm of English, will approximate the Spanish.[18]

5. More can be said of syllable treatment. Every syllable is carefully spoken, with an individual attention which, if the consonants were not so languid, would produce almost a staccato effect. There is some unstressing of vowels in unaccented syllables, but even so, each vowel retains its identity. This quality is the one sure to carry over into the English of every speaker of Spanish—and this quality must be observed by those who would be proficient in reproducing Spanish dialect.

6. Latin words beginning with *sc, sp,* or *st* took on an initial *e* in Spanish by prothesis (see page 162). Ex., *schola > escuela, spiritus > espiritu, status > estado.* By the same principle, the speaker of Spanish will prefix *e* to English words, thus: *scold > escold, speak > espeak, stand > estand.*

Illustrative Close Transcription of Spanish Dialect

Castilian Dialect Version of "To Celia," by Ben Jonson.

NOTE: Bear in mind that [t, d, n, l] are *dental* in Spanish, and that [p, t, k] are unaspirated. Bear in mind also that [r] is trilled.

drիŋk tu mi ɔnli wiθ ᵭain ais,
and ai wil plɛʧ wiθ main;
ɔr liβ a kiz βat in ᵭa kap,
and ail nat ask fɔr wain.
ᵭa tɛrst ᵭat fram ᵭa sɔl ᵭaᵭ rais
ᵭaᵭ ask a driŋk diβain;
bat mait ai af ʧɔfs nɛγtar sip,
ai wuᵭ nat ʧenʧ fɔr ᵭain.
ai sɛnt ᵭi let a rosi riθ,
nat so maʧ anriŋg ᵭi,
as giβiŋg it ᵭa ɔp ᵭat ᵭɛr
it wuᵭ nat wiᵭɛrᵭ βi.
bat ᵭau ᵭɛrɔn didst ɔnli βriᵭ
and sɛntst it βak tu mi,
sints wɛn it βlums and smɛls, ai swɛr,
nat af itsɛlf βat ᵭi.

The following illustrates Spanish influence in the English speech of a student from Puerto Rico at the end of two years in the United States. (The student had studied English in four years of high school in Puerto Rico.)

Broad Transcription. Paragraph designed to observe: [ʃ], [ʒ], [n], [v], [h], [ð],

---

[18] Navarro Tomás, *op. cit.,* has an accurate organization of this subject with diagrams and exercises, p. 250, *et seq.*

[ɪ], [æ], [oʊ], [ɔɪ], [eɪ], [aɪ], [aʊ], [ɝ], [ɜ], [ɚ]. (Note that the speaker has learned many English sounds, but not all of them.)

She didn't know which way she should go,   so she counted her cash in
ʃi   didn̥   noʊ   ʌitʃ   we   ʃi   ʃud   goʊ, so ʃi   kaʊntəd   ɛr   kaʃ   in

casual fashion, and boarded the very next   car for Johnson Street. Her brother
kasʊl   faʃən,   an   bɔrdəd   ði   vɛrɪ   nɛkst kar fɔr ʤansɔn ɛstrit.   hɛr brʌdər

John said they had been waiting there where she could see them when she
ʤon   sɛd   ðeɪ   had   bin   weɪtɪŋ   ðɛr   ʌɛr   ʃi   kud   si   ðɛm   wɛn   ʃi

arrived. She gave the boy a tip and some candy.
araɪvd.   ʃi   geɪf   ɖi   bɔi   e ðip an   sum   kanɖi.

The following is an illustration of Spanish influence in the speech of a young woman from Cuba after several years in the United States.

Broad Transcription. (Paragraph designed to observe [ʃ], [ʒ], [ʌ], [v], [h], [ð] [ɪ], [æ], [oʊ], [ɔɪ], [eɪ], [aɪ], [aʊ], [ɝ], [ɜ], [ɚ].)

She didn't know which way she should go so she counted her cash in casual
ʃi   didn̥   no   wɪtʃ   weɪ ʃi   ʃud   go so ʃi   kaʊntəd hɝ kaʃ   in kaʃʊl

fashion and boarded the very next   car for Johnson Street. Her brother John
faʃʊn   an   bɔrdɪd   ði   vɛrɪ   nɛkst kar fɔr ʤansən ɛstrit.   hɝ   brudər   ʤɔn

said they had been waiting there where she could see them when she arrived.
seɪ   deɪ   had   bin   weɪtɪŋ   ðɛr   wɛr   ʃi   kud   si   ðɛm   wɛn   ʃi   araɪvd.

She gave the boy a tip and some candy.
ʃi   geɪv   ði   bɔi   e tip an   sʊm   kanɖi.

AFRAID OF THE DARK
Broad Transcription

Juan Castaniegos—a young Mexican.

Help me to leave from thees place.
ɛlp   mi tu liv   fram ðis   ples.

But, Señor Capitan, me—I 'av do notheeng.
bat, se'ɲɔr 'kapitan, mi—ai av du 'naθiŋ.

Notheeng, Señor Capitan . . . To them I   am say I   know not of what they
'naθiŋ,   se'ɲɔr 'kapitan . . . tu ðɛm   ai am se   ai no   nat av wat   ðe

speak.
spik.

They are currse me an' say a foreigner ees keel a white lady.They whip
ðe   ɑr kɛȑs   mi an se   e ˈfɔrɛnɛr is   kil   e wɑit ˈledi. ðe   wip

me until my eyes cannot see, and my legs they cannot stand.
mi ɑnˈtil mɑi ɑis ˈkɑnɑt si, an   mɑi lɛgs de   ˈkɑnɑt ɛsˈtand.

And me—I 'av done notheeng to anybody.
an   mi—ɑi av dɑn ˈnɑθiŋ   tu ɛnibɑdi.

I am no sure. I 'ave expect to die, surely—but not so soon.
ɑi am no ʃur. ɑi av   ɛkˈspɛk tu dɑi, ˈʃurli —bɑt nɑt so sun.

That ees it, Señor Capitan. That ees it ... thee darkness on thee other side
ðat   is it, seˈɲɔr ˈkapitan. ðat is   it ... ði ˈdarknɛs ɔn ði   aðɛr said

of life.
ɑv lɑif.

Transcribe:

Eef I die like thees—thee death of a criminal—will I go to ... thee hell?

Please, Padre, I 'ave no words to say.

Padre mio, ees eet that I am to be forgiven for sometheeng I 'ave not do?

No, no, Padre. Eet ees not me who should 'ave thee forgiveness. Eet ees thee
men who say I am to die. Thee men who send me to thees place ... thee men
who take me to thees chair ... those men keel me. .... You pray for those men,
no, Padre?

I am crazy because I speak thee truth?

Padre mio, thee heart of me is full of theengs to say, but only of one theeng
would I speak to you.

The lady they say I 'ave keeled, I 'ave never seen her ... when she is alive
... or when she ees dead.
Thee good God weel understand.
I 'ave pray all thee night long.
I go to meet heem.
Eet ees permitted me that I speak weeth my friends?

WILLIAM E. CALLAHAN

SPANISH

THE BAD MAN

PANCHO LOPEZ – a Mexican bandit

Lucia. Ees putty name. Come 'ere. Come 'ere! I would see more of you. Not bad. 'Ow you like to go wiz me to Mexico?

Certamente. You capture ze prisoner. You 'ave no jail to put 'im in. You cannot pack him around wiz you. If you let 'im go, 'e come back to fight you again. So you kill him. Sabe?

It is because you 'ave never really lived. Because you 'ave been always protect by ozzers. I kill only men. And only evil men. And when I kill evil men, it makes me very 'appy. For I 'ave did a good deed.

Oh! I see I do business wiz business men. Wise business men. Bueno. Now here we are togezzer, three wise business men. Suppose I shall show you where ze oil she is. What zen?

Ze little paper. You both want so bad. Bueno. You shall both 'ave chance, for we will, 'ow you say, 'old ze little hauction.

Si. And to him who bids ze 'ighest, shall go ze little paper and he shall come wiz me while I show 'im where ze oil she is 'iding. To him what does not bid ze 'ighest, he shall stay 'ere wiz Pedro until eight o'clock tonight.

Ze idea, my friend, is zis. I am not interes' in pieces of paper. I do not accep' checks. Also I am no dam' fool. You sink I sink you go away and bring back two 'onderd sousand dollars? Two 'ondred sousand soldier, mebbe. But two 'ondred sousand dollar! Pah!

PORTER EMERSON BROWN

Transcription of the Speech of an Arizona Child of Mexican Parentage. Age 12.

NOTE: Children of this type do not know either Spanish or English well. They can read only English. Their speech patterns show an inconsistent mixture of the two languages. An unusual pronunciation found in their speech is [ˈguman] for *woman*.

Transcription by Dr. Klonda Lynn, University of Arizona.

Carmen and Joe are two children who live in a small town. They like to
kærmɪn n̥ tʃo ar tʊ tʃɪldrɪn hu lɪf in e smɔl taʊn. ðeɪ laɪk tu

stop at the house of their teacher because she always gives them a peach or
stɑp ɛt də haʊs əf ðɛr tɪtʃɚ bɪkɔs ʃɪ ɔlwes gɪf ðɛm e pɪʃ ɔr

a piece of chicken to eat.
e pis əf tʃɪtʃɪn tʊ it.

Their teacher loves animals. She has a dog, a cat, a puppy and a cow. The
ðɛr tɪtʃɚ lʌfs ɛnɪməls. ʃɪ hæs e dɔk, e kɛt, e pɑpɪ ɛn e kaʊ. də

dog has large white teeth and makes a noise with his mouth.
dɔk hæs larʒ ʍaɪt tɪθ æn meks e nos wiθ hɪs mauθ.

One day the cow found the onion patch. They threw sticks and stones at
ʍʌn de ðə kau faun di anjən pɛʃ. deɪ tru stɪks ɛn stons ɛt

her, but she would not budge.
hɜ, bət ʧɪ wut nət bʌʒ.

The little puppy is always playing and running about the yard. He likes to
də lɪtəl papɪ ɪs ɔlweɪs pleɪɪn ɛn rʌnɪn əbaut dɪ jard. hɪ laɪks tu

catch the stick which Joe pushes before him in the dirt.
kæʃ ðə stɪk ʍɪʃ ʧo puʃɪs bifor him in də dɜt.

After school they climb trees and run about on the grass. Sometimes they
ɛftɜ skul ðe klaɪm tris ɛn ran əbat ɔn di græs. samtaɪm ðeɪ

help their father get a truck load of wood to burn in the stove.
hɛlp ðɛr faðɜ gɛt e trak lot əf wud tə bɜn in di stɔf.

One day before very many years pass away, I hope that you will have the
wən de βifo βɛrɪ mɛnɪ jɪr pæs əwe, a hop ðɛt ju wil hæf di

joy and pleasure of a visit to the home of Carmen and Joe.
ʧo ə plɛʒur af ə bizɪt tu di haus əf karmɪn ɛn ʧo.

Bibliography

Spanish

Books

Lynn, Klonda, *A Phonetic Analysis of the English Spoken by Mexican Children in the Elementary Schools of Arizona* (Louisiana State University, Baton Rouge, La., un-published dissertation, 1940).

Tomás, T. Navarro, *Manual de Pronunciación Española* (Madrid: Revista de Filología Española, 1926).

CHAPTER 24

Russian

English-speaking students studying Russian encounter certain standard difficulties in the pronunciation of the language. Russian students studying English encounter corresponding difficulties in pronouncing English. The following pages undertake to simplify some of these difficulties from the point of view of both types of students. They indicate also some of the characteristics of the Russian dialect of English.

The main difficulties of the English-speaking student approaching Russian may be enumerated as follows:

1. The pronunciation of non-English sounds in Russian.
2. The two "aspects" of Russian verbs, viz., the imperfective and the perfective.
3. The arbitrary gender of nouns.
4. The six cases of Russian substantives and adjectives, with endings for masculine, feminine, and neuter, singular and plural.
5. The duplication of the functions of the endings through the use of prepositions, much as in Latin, Greek, and German.
6. The lack of any large number of Latin derivatives in Russian, such as prove so helpful in learning Romance languages; and the lack of any large number of easily recognizable words which are cognate with English by reason of common Indo-European ancestors for the Slavic and Germanic roots.
7. Irregular stress.

The first of these items will be taken up in this chapter.

The main difficulties of the Russian student approaching English may be enumerated as follows:

1. The pronunciation of non-Russian sounds in English.
2. The inconsistent English spellings.
3. The six English tenses, each with its two to three simple, progressive, and emphatic forms.

4. The difficulty of distinguishing parts of speech without the aid of identifying endings.
5. The high incidence of idioms in English.
6. Irregular stress.

The first of these items will be taken up in this chapter.

A word about modern Russian. Of the sixteen republics which compose Russia, only three speak Russian with any degree of exclusiveness. These are Russia proper, comprising the northernmost and largest section of Russia in Europe, together with contiguous territory in Asia, where the regional dialect is Great Russian; White Russia, a smaller area adjoining Poland, where the regional dialect is White Russian; and the Ukraine, lying along the Black Sea, south of White Russia and Russia proper, where the regional dialect is Ukrainian. Great Russian is spoken by about 100 million people; White Russian, by about 5 million; and Ukrainian, by about 28 million. In the other republics, Great Russian is known through officials and emigrants, but the native language of each republic is official alongside Great Russian. A Russian three-ruble banknote, for instance, has the words "Three Rubles" in Great Russian, White Russian, Ukrainian, Armenian, and the languages of three other republics. Stalin himself is said to have spoken Great Russian with a slight accent, for he was a Georgian, i.e., a native of Georgia, a small republic in the Caucasus, north of the tiny Armenian Republic and touching the east end of the Black Sea.

While the three Russian regional dialects are mutually intelligible, they do not, unfortunately, use identical alphabets. All three alphabets are derived from church Slavonic, or Old Bulgarian, whose ninth-century adaptor, Cyril of Thessalia, took its symbols principally from the Greek, but partly from the Latin. These alphabets differed somewhat among themselves even before the Revolution; but afterwards, when Great Russian discarded two symbols, changed another, and limited the so-called hard sign to a very few instances, White Russian and Ukrainian, which did not follow in these changes, became more conspicuously different to the eye, though there was no added change to the ear.

This discussion is limited to the Moscow dialect of Great Russian. Being thus limited, it does not agree in every particular with existing treatments of Russian,[1] but the deviations are not great, and are matters of detail, not of basic significance. The treatment herein is, naturally, considering the purpose of this chapter, a phonetic treatment, rather than a phonemic treatment.

---

[1] Cf. M. V. Trofimov and Daniel Jones, *The Pronunciation of Russian* (Cambridge University Press, 1923); L. Scerba, *Court exposé de la prononciation russe*, (London: Trinity College, l'Association Phonétique Internationale, 1911); George L. Trager, "The Phonemes of Russian," in *Language*, Vol. X, No. 4, December, 1934, p. 334.

The English and Russian Sound Systems

(References for use with Tables I, II, and III)

I. Palatalizing ("soft") vowels: я [ja], e [(j)ɛ], и [(j)i], ё [jɔ], ю [ju].

II. Palatal ("soft") consonants:

    1. ч [tʃ], щ [ʃtʃ], ь [j]. ([j] is the usual value of the "soft" sign[2] ь, when ь follows a consonant; but it never appears alone, and its value is merged with that of the consonant, as in ть, which equals [t̯]. [j] is also implicit in a palatalizing vowel, and attaches itself to and merges with a preceding consonant—except those in no. 3 below—as in те [t̯ɛ], тю [t̯u] тя [t̯a].)

    2. Consonants followed by the "soft" sign ь.

    3. Any other consonant (except ж [ʒ], ш [ʃ], ц [ts], and those followed by the "hard" sign ъ), if followed (a) by a palatalizing vowel; or (b) by one of the palatal consonants; or (c) by the "soft" sign ь; or (d) by an already palatalized consonant. (See note, page 482, on к [k], г [g], х [x], which, when followed by a palatalizing vowel, are fronted, and behave very much like palatal consonants.)

III. Non-palatalizing ("hard") vowels: a, э, ы, о, у. ("Hard," or "non-palatalizing," as applied to vowels, means that there is no [j] implicit in the vowel, as explained in II above. Compare та [ta], то [tɔ].)

IV. Non-palatal ("hard") consonants:

    1. ж [ʒ], ш [ʃ], ц [ts], (these three always "hard"),[3] and those followed by the "hard" sign ъ.

    NOTE: When the "hard" sign is between a consonant and e, ё, or я, the consonant is, of course, non-palatal, and the [j] implicit in the vowel is pronounced before it, thus, [jɛ, jɔ, ja], as in съел [sjɛl] (ate up).

    2. Any other consonant not followed (a) by a palatalizing vowel, or (b) by the "soft" sign ь, or (c) by a consonant already palatal according to 2 and 3 under II above.

---

[2] After final ж, ч, ш, and щ, ь has no phonetic value, serving instead grammatically, e.g., to indicate to which declension a word belongs. After other consonants and before и, e, ё, ю, or я, ь indicates a fricative [j], which is followed by a second [j] implicit in the vowel, as in вьюга ['vjugə] (snowstorm). See Trofimov and Jones, *Pronunciation of Russian*, pages 113 and 143, for discussion of the palatal quality of ч [tʃ] and щ [ʃtʃ] respectively.

[3] Here we have the doubtful expedient of equating "non-palatal" with the Russian term "hard." English [ʃ] and [ʒ] are, of course, palatal, but the Russian [ʃ] and [ʒ] are by comparison much farther back, and could well be transcribed [ʃˠ] and [ʒˠ]. In its backed position, [ʃˠ], for example, does not end with a [j]-like effect, as does English [ʃ]. (Compare the beginning student's transcription of *shoot* as [ʃjut].) Hence Russian [ʃ] is called "hard," and since it is made at the very back of the hard palate, if not actually behind it, we may, with some show of justice, agree that it is also "non-palatal."

V. Stress:

In these tables the Russian nomenclature for degrees of stress is used, in order to prepare the learner to use grammars, dictionaries, and other works on the Russian language. The Russian terms, with their approximate English equivalents, are as follows:

Tonic syllable =

a syllable of primary stress, such as маль ['maļ] in мальчик ['maļʧɪk] (boy), or *child* [ʧaɪld] in *childish* ['ʧaɪldɪʃ]. A monosyllable is considered as having primary stress, as in лук [luk] (onion); however a short particle, such as не (not), без (without), из (from) до (as far as), is absorbed into the stress system of whatever word follows, and is pronounced as if it were a pretonic or atonic syllable of that word.

Pretonic syllable =

a syllable immediately before a tonic syllable, bearing a degree of stress roughly comparable to secondary stress in English, such as ки [ki] in кисель [ki' şeļ] (jelly), or *ab* [æb] in *abject* [ˌæb'ʤɛkt]. Pretonic stress is recognized by the position of the syllable, and requires no stress mark.

Atonic syllable =

any syllable not tonic or pretonic, such as бо [bə] and ня [ņə] in богадельня [bəga'deļņə] (almshouse), or *li* [lə] and *tion* [ʃən] in *application* [ˌæplə'keɪʃən].

VI. Assimilation:

Many of the entries following must be interpreted in the light of the fact that regressive assimilation operates in Russian as follows:

1. A voiceless plosive or fricative followed by any voiced plosive or fricative, except в [v], will become voiced.
2. A voiced plosive or fricative followed by any voiceless plosive or fricative becomes voiceless.

Pronouncing Russian Vowels

It is convenient to separate out from the paired lists in Table I the sounds of Russian which are in any way problem-sounds to the English-speaking learner.

[ɨ]

Of all these, the sound [ɨ] is the most difficult for the speaker of English. It is centralized [i], and does not frequently occur in English. Two purely mechanical devices for learning to say it are (1) to clench the teeth and try to say [i], and (2) to thrust the lower jaw forward and try to say [i]. A somewhat more scientific plan is to learn how to centralize the highest part of the tongue arch without the foregoing somewhat face-contorting tricks, as follows:

1. Pronounce [i] before a mirror, being sure that the lips are completely unround, i. e., in a smiling position.

2. With the lips held in the unround position and not permitted to change in the slightest degree, try to say [u]. The tongue will draw back in the mouth and the resultant sound will be the unround [u], the symbol of which is [ɯ]. Now shuttle the tongue backward and forward (with the lips still unround), pronouncing [i—ɯ, i—ɯ, i—ɯ] many times. Finally, begin with [i] and slowly draw the tongue backward a little past half-way. The result should be the Russian [ɨ]. Now pronounce ты [tɨ] (thou), сыр [sɨř] (cheese), дым [d̦ɨm] (smoke).

When preceded by a bilabial or labiodental, [ɨ] has a tendency to acquire an on-glide [w], this despite the fact that [w] does not exist as a phoneme in Russian. Thus мыло [ˈm(w)ɨɫə] (soap), мы [m(w)ɨ] (we), быть [b(w)ɨț] (to be), вы [v(w)ɨ] (you).

[ʉ]

The sound ʉ, like [ɨ], is central, but unlike [ɨ], is rounded. The steps in learning it are as follows:

1. Pronounce [u], with careful lip-rounding.

2. With the lips still in the position for [u], move the tongue forward to the position of [i]. The sound pronounced in this position will be [y], as in German and French.

3. Maintaining continuous phonation, shuttle the tongue backward and forward between [y] and [u], then draw the tongue back from [y] to a position half-way between [y] and [u]. The sound pronounced in this position will be [ʉ], as in люди [ˈlʉd̦ɪ] (people).

[e]

The sound [e] is a pure or non-diphthongal sound, familiar to students of Romance languages as a common pronunciation of e, as in Fr. été [eˈte] (summer), Sp. vez [beθ] (time), It. credo [ˈkřed̦o] (I believe). It is also found in English in certain unstressed syllables, as in chaotic [keˈɑtɪk]. It contrasts with the diphthong [eɪ], as in day [deɪ]. The English speaker must avoid the diphthong by simply omitting the sound [ɪ], holding the tongue and jaw steadily in the position for [e] throughout the length of the vowel. Example: весь [ye̦ș] (all), день [d̦en̦] (day). It appears in stressed interpalatal contexts.

[ɔ]

The sound [ɔ] presents no difficulties in most words, such as он [ɔn̦] (he) город [ˈgɔrəț] (city). But after [k], it is rounded so much more than English [ɔ] that it gives the acoustic effect of having an on-glide [w], despite the fact, as indicated earlier, that phonemic [w] does not exist in Russian. Examples: кофи ['k(w)ɔ(i)fɪ] (coffee), коцка ['k(w)ɔ(i)ʃkə] (cat). Also, [ɔ] before palatal (palatalized consonant or palatal consonant or affricate) develops an off-glide [i]. Examples: бровь [br̥ɔ(i)f] (brow), дочь [dɔ(i)ʧ] (daughter). (See also the two examples above.) Occasionally, there is a suggestion of [w] between [g] and [ɔ]. But in the Moscow dialect, it is not conspicuous enough for transcription, unless, perhaps, by a diacritic indicating a very round [ɔ]: thus, [ǫ].

[a]

The sound [a] is common in English as the first element of the diphthong [aɪ] and of the diphthong [aʊ], but it is less common in isolation. Southern Americans can find examples of [a] alone in the substandard pronounciations [a] and [ha] for *I* and *high*. Easterners can find it in their common alternative pronunciation of *car* and *card* as [ka] and [kad]. Those who know the Romance languages can isolate the vowel of Fr. *la* [la], Sp. *casa* ['kasa], or It. *vaso* ['vazo]. Those who have none of these resources, but whose pronounciation of *I* is [aɪ], can simply leave off the [ɪ] of the diphthong. Those whose *I* is [ɑɪ] will have to practice making [a] with the tongue as low in the mouth as possible, and as far front as possible. Examples in Russian: да [da] (yes), рука [r̥u'ka] (hand, arm).

Before an approaching front vowel, as [i], [a] often diphthongizes to [ai]. Example: the [a] бумага [bu'magə] (paper) becomes [ai] in бумаги [bu'maigɪ] (papers).

Diphthongs

The fact that the diphthongs [ei], [ai], [æi], [ɔi], and [ui] end in [i] rather than the customary English [ɪ] should offer no real difficulty beyond that of giving overt attention to the rendering of the final element of each diphthong as [i]. Examples: всей [fşei] (of all—f. gen. plu.), трамвай [tr̥am'vai] (tramway), прощаите [pr̥a'ʃʧæiţɪ] (goodbye), троица ['tr̥ɔitsə] (trinity), дорогой [dər̥a'gɔi] (expensive), поцелуй [pətsɛ'lui] (kiss).

Of the diphthongs [ii], [ii], [ʉi] and [əi], the only ones that present any difficulty are [ii] and [ʉi], which begin with the unusual [i] and[ʉ], discussed a few paragraphs earlier. Examples: тихий ['ţixii] (quiet, slow); выйти ['v(w)iiţɪ] (to cry), скорый ['skɔr̥əi] (quick), начуй [na'ʧʉi] (spend the night).

The sound [ɛ] becomes quasi-diphthongal by developing an off-glide [ə], in stressed final positions. Examples: где [gdɛ(ə)] (here), на столе [nə sta'lɛ(ə)] (on the table).

Variant Vowels According to Context

It is possible to recognize centralized [u], or [ʉ], and a centralized [ɔ], or [ɔˑ]. The [ʉ] and [ɔˑ] appear between palatals. There are many analogous shadings of vowel value, such as the apparent shift of [ɔ] to [ɛ] in сколько [ˈskwɔḷkə > ˈskwɛḷkə] (how much). Most of these are forms of assimilation, and most of them, fortunately, take place automatically by reason of the neighboring sounds in the vocal context.

Pronouncing Russian Consonants

Separating out the Russian consonants which offer the major difficulties to English speakers, we have the following:

ḅ	m̦	f̦	ʃʳ	ʃʧ	ɟ
p̦	n̦	r	ȝʳ	ʦ	
ț	ŋ̦	f̦	x	ʥ	
ţ	ḷ	ɣ	ç̦	kj	
ḍ	ḷ	ș	ɣ	c	
d̦	f̦	z̦	ʧ	gj	

[t̪], [d̪], [n̪]

The sounds [t̪], [d̪], and [n̪] are, as the diacritics show, dental. That is, they are made with the tongue definitely against the back surface of the upper teeth. Those who know other languages can find these sounds in Fr. *tout* [t̪u] (all), *dos* [d̪o] (back); *nous* [n̪u] (we); Sp. *tomar* [t̪oˈmar̪] (to take), *dos* [d̪os] (two), *no* [n̪o] (no, not); It. *tutti* [ˈt̪ut̪ːi] (all), *dove* [ˈd̪ove] (where), *non* [n̪on̪] (no). Examples in Russian: там [t̪am] (there); друг [d̪r̪uk], (friend); нож [n̪ɔʃʳ] (knife).

[ḅ], [p̦], [ț], [d̦], [m̦], [n̦], [ḷ], [r̦], [f̦], [ɣ], [ș], [z̦]

The sounds [ḅ], [p̦], [ț], [d̦], [m̦], [n̦], [ḷ], [r̦], [f̦], [ɣ], [ș], and [z̦] can be handled in a group. They are the most homogeneous of Russian palatalized or "soft" consonants. As a general proposition, they can be said to consist of the ordinary consonants as indicated by their respective symbols, each of which terminates in a closely integrated [j]. When the palatalized consonant is final in a syllable, or before a vowel, the [j] is so intimately blended with the consonant proper that it may be said actually to comprise the latter part of it. This [j] varies a great deal in duration, according to the dialect being spoken. In the Moscow dialect, it is very prominent, for example, in final [ț]. In this instance, the final [ț] is so far front that the ear of the speaker of English may easily report having heard [t̪s]; in other dialects the effect of [j] in [ț] is briefer and less audible. In some dialects, the tongue may seem to make only the gesture of producing [j], without any audible fricative sound. But even so, the Russian ear detects a significant difference between such a palatalized or "soft" [ț] and a non-palatalized or "hard" [t̪]. A striking instance of the Russian insistence on the difference between "soft" and "hard" consonants appears when a consonant capable of palatalization appears before another palatalized consonant, as in сегодня [ṣɛˈvɔ(i)dɳə] (today)—also [ṣɪˈvɔ(i)dɳə]. The palatalization of the [d] seems to the English ear no more than theoretic, yet the Russian feels sure the [d] is "soft."

When the palatalized consonant precedes a vowel, the glide effect of [j] is usually prominent in all dialects. As will be seen in the examples presently, the pronunciation of, e.g., [p̡] followed by a vowel is not far removed acoustically from the analogous English pronunciation in a word like *pure* [pjʊr, pjʊə], where the [j] is a conspicuous glide from the [p] to the [u].

Palatalization, as noted earlier, is effected in Russian by the presence of any of the orthographic symbols и, е, ё, я, ю, whose basic sounds are [(j)i], [(j)ɛ], [jɔ], [ja], and [ju], or by the presence of the so-called "soft sign" ь, following any of the consonants under discussion. These sounds, together with the soft sign, which may be thought of as [j] or as being only a diacritic having no sound of its own, may be referred to as palatalizing agents.

While the effect of the palatalizing agents is in general to give a terminal [j]-effect, as has been described, which may be expanded into a glide to the following vowel, there are cases where the effect is either actually or acoustically different. Some of these are as follows:

1. [l̡] final in a syllable is usually heard as a very clear (front, dental) sound; thus, [l̡], as in рубль [rubl̡] (ruble)]. It is also often heard as the fronted [l̡] when it precedes [i], as in лицо [l̡iˈtsɔ] (face).

2. [r̡] before [i] and finally is rather generally heard as a dental trill, as in рис [r̡is] (rice), царь [tsar̡ > tsar̡] (Tsar).

3. [d] before [v] and [m] is sometimes heard as [dz], as in дверь [dyɛr̡ > ʣyɛr̡] (door); седьмой [ṣɪdˈmɔi > ṣɪʣˈmɔi] (seventh).

4. All of the palatalized consonants tend to lose the acoustic effect of palatalization in unstressed syllables and, as already mentioned, before other consonants in the same syllable, at least to the ear of the speaker of English. But no doubt the Russian speaker often puts his tongue inaudibly through the motions of palatalization, even in such contexts.

Examples of palatalized consonants: обед [aˈb̡ɛt] (dinner); песня [ˈp̡ɛṣɳə] (song); тело [ˈt̡ɛlə] (body); мать [mat̡] (mother); дерево [ˈd̡er̡ɪvə] (tree); место [ˈm̡ɛst̡ə] (place), семь [ṣɛm̡] (seven); небо [ˈn̡ɛbə] (sky); день [d̡ɛn̡] (day); лето [ˈl̡ɛt̡ə] (summer); сколько [ˈsk(w)ɔl̡kə] (how many, how much)— often heard as [ˈsk(w)ɛl̡kə]; рюмка [ˈr̡umkə] (wine glass); река [r̡ɛˈka] (often heard as [r̡iˈka]) (river); дверь [dyɛr̡] (often heard as [ʣyɛr̡]) (door); ферма [ˈf̡ɛrmə] (farm); бровь [br̡ɔ(i)f] (brow); семя [ˈṣɛm̡ə] (seed); семья [ṣɪm̡ˈja] (family); весь [yɛṣ] (all, the whole); зять [zæt̡] (son-in-law).

In addition to the regular palatalized consonants, the sounds [x], [k], and [g], if followed by a vowel which is a palatalizing agent (q. v.), behave much like palatalized consonants. Though they are sometimes said to be in these cases only the fronted members ([ç], [c], and [ɟ]) of their respective phonemes, the acoustic effect is very much like that of palatalized sounds. Examples: кем [cɛm] or [kɛm] (instrumental case of кто [kt̬ɔ] (who)), кит [cit̬] or [kit̬] (whale), легенда [l̬ɪˈɟɛn̬d̬ə] or [l̬ɪˈgɛn̬d̬ə] (legend); химик [ˈxim̬ik] or [ˈçim̬ɪk] (chemist).

[r̥]

The sound [r̥], when not palatalized at the end of a syllable, is very positively and definitely a vigorous tongue-point trill. The substitution of any English [r] is highly unacceptable. Examples: дорога [d̬aˈr̥ɔgə] (road), рот [r̥ɔt] (mouth).

See earlier discussion of [ɽ] and [r̥], page 482.

[ʃˤ]

The Russian sound corresponding to English [ʃ] in *she* [ʃi] is retracted. Even with front vowels, it is made with the tongue as far back as in *shawl* [ʃˤɔl]. Example: шест [ʃˤɛst] (perch). With back vowels, the sound is even farther back. Example: штука [ˈʃˤtukə] (trick).

[ʒˤ]

The discussion of [ʃˤ] applies to [ʒˤ]. Examples: житель [ˈʒˤit̬ɪl̬] (inhabitant), жёлтый [ˈʒˤɔltəi] (yellow).

[ʧ]

The affricate [ʧ], like the English [ʧ], varies between a more frontal or a more retracted articulation according to the vowel which follows. Note the variation in English *cheese* [ʧiz], *chalk* [ʧɔk], and in the following examples: учитель [uˈʧit̬ɪl̬] (teacher), чёрный [ˈʧɔrnəi] (black—masc. sing.). But in either case, ч is palatal.

In some words, [ʧ] often degenerates to merely [ʃˤ]. Example: что [ʧt̬ɔ > ʃˤtɔ] (what—interrog., that—rel.).

[ʃʧ]

The discussions above as to fronting and retraction apply to [ʃʧ]. Examples: щи [ʃʧi] (cabbage soup), щётка [ˈʃʧɔtkə] (brush.)

In some words, [ʃʧ] degenerates merely to [ʃ]. Example: товарищ [t̬aˈvar̥ɪʃʧ > t̬aˈvar̥ɪʃ] (comrade). But щ is always palatal.

[x]—Variant [ç]

The sound [x] is a voiceless lingua-velar fricative, identical with what in German is called the *Achlaut* [ˈɑxlaut] and in Spanish *jota* [ˈxota]. To pronounce it the tongue is elevated at the back so as to make a narrow horizontal passage between the tongue and the soft palate, through which the air is forced (the nasal passages being closed at the back by the velum) so as to produce a rough, breathy sound. A speaker of English as yet unfamiliar with [x] may conveniently start with the *Ichlaut* [ˈɪçlaut], [ç], which occurs in English as a member of the /h/-phoneme.

Pronounce *huge* tensely and breathily. The result should be not ᴊhe theoretically normal [hjuʤ], but [çuʤ], which many speakers of English actually use most of the time. Practice also *Hugh* [çu], *human* [ˈçumən], *Hubert* [ˈçubət, ˈçubət]. Now place the vowel [ɪ] before [çuʤ] and pronounce [ɪçuʤ]. Next, leave off [udʒ] and pronounce German *ich* [ɪç] (I). Substitute [ɑ] for ⌊ɪ⌋. The sound [x] will automatically displace [ç] and the result will be German *ach* [ɑx] (oh). Finally, place [x] in the initial position, as in Russian [xan] (Khan). It will now be possible to pronounce Russian words containing [x] correctly, whether the sound is initial or final in the syllable. When this sound appears in Russian before front vowels, it automatically becomes [ç]. The Russian [ç] is usually not as far front as the German or English [ç]. Sometimes it is referred to as a fronted variety of [x]. Examples in Russian: холм [xɔlm] (hill), химик [ˈçimɪk] (chemist), хлеб [çʲlɛp] (bread), хула [xuˈlɑ] (blame).

The sound [x] sometimes appears as a voiceless counterpart of [g], as in ʙоɪ [bɔx] (God), which is spelled with a final г.

[ɣ]

The sound [ɣ] is a voiced velar fricative, the voiced analog of [x], made with the same positions of vocal organs. It occurs only seldom. Examples: Ꮟога [ˈbɔɣə] (God—gen.), благо [ˈblaɣə] (good, welfare).

[ʦ]

The cluster [ʦ] occurs non-phonemically in English, as in *eats* [its]. But it is always final in the syllable in English, whereas in Russian it is either initial or final. English speakers sometimes have to strive rather hard to use it in the unfamiliar initial position. Those who know German will have met initial [ʦ] already, as in *Zeit* [ʦait] (time). Examples in Russian: царь [ʦarʲ] (Tsar or Czar), отец [aˈʦɛʦ] (father).

Two or three statements touching on orthography may be made, together with some related statements on stress.

1. Of Russian *a* pronounced in stressed syllables [a] and [ɑ], [a] is the basic sound. The variant [ɑ] occurs before the back consonants г [g], к [k], and especially dark л [ɫ]. Examples: бумага [buˈmɑgə] (paper), собака [saˈbakə] (dog), бал [baɫ] (ball), балкон [baɫˈkɔn] (balcony). (Note:—Most discussions of Russian recognize [ɑ] only before [ɫ]. In the other parts of this chapter, [ɑ] is used only before [ɫ].)

2. As in English, stress is largely unpredictable, according to present knowledge. In both languages, better definitions of the many subtle guides for stressing, for which native speakers have a "feel," await formulation. Nevertheless, in Russian, the pronunciation of most orthographic vowel symbols depends on the stress. As indicated earlier, Russian recognizes three degrees of stressed

syllables: tonic syllables, pretonic syllables, and atonic syllables. A tonic syllable is a heavily stressed syllable; a pretonic syllable is a syllable immediately preceding a tonic syllable, and it has secondary stress; an atonic syllable is any other syllable. Some orthographic vowels have three sounds for the three degrees of stressing, some fewer. The orthographic vowel *o*, whose basic sound is [ɔ]—(never [o] nor [ou] in the Moscow dialect of Russian), is the classic instance. In the example following, each of the three vowels is orthographically *o*; yet each has a different pronunciation, [ɔ] in the tonic syllable, [a] in the pretonic syllable, [ə] in the atonic syllable. Thus, хорошо [xəra'ʃˤɔ] (well).

3. Closely related to stress is, naturally, intonation. It has been studied and described,[4] but should be heard to be appreciated.[5] It is characterized by interesting rises of pitch in the earlier parts of many clauses, with (to English ears) startling drops at the end below the initial pitch.

4. Regressive assimilation is a very active factor in Russian pronunciation. A normally voiced plosive or fricative preceding a voiceless one becomes voiceless. The sounds [b], [d], [g], [v], [ɣ], [z], and [ʒ] behave in this manner. Example: вчера [ftʃɛ'ra] (yesterday), where the pronunciation [f] is used for the orthographic symbol в, normally pronounced [v].

Likewise a voiceless plosive or fricative preceding a voiced one (except в [v]) becomes voiced. Example: к даске [g das'kjɛ(ə)] (to the blackboard), where the [g] is spelled with the orthographic symbol к, normally pronounced [k].

5. The sounds [b], [d], [g], [ɣ], [z], [v], and [ʒ] become voiceless when final; i. e., [b] becomes [p], [d] becomes [t], [g] becomes [k], [ɣ] becomes [x], [z] becomes [s], [v] becomes [f], and [ʒ] becomes [ʃ]. Examples:

мужа ['muʒə] (husband's)—муж [muʃ] (husband)
лошади ['lɔʃɪdɪ] (horses)—лошадь ['lɔʃɪt] (horse)
Чехова ['tʃɛxəvə] (Chekhov's)—Чехов ['tʃɛxəf] (Chekhov)
сада ['sadə] (of the garden)—сад [sat] (garden)
глаза [glaz'a] (of the eye)—глаз [glas] (eye)
Богу ['bɔɣu] (God–dat. sing.)—Бог [bɔx] (God)
слогу ['slɔgu] (syllable–dat.)—слог [slɔk] (syllable)
хлеба ['xlɛbə] or ['çlɛbə] (of bread)—хлеб [xlɛp] or [çlɛp] (bread)

---

[4] See M. V. Trofimov and Daniel Jones, *The Pronunciation of Russian*. (London: Trinity College, Cambridge University Press, 1923), Ch. XXII.
[5] The Linguaphone Company, Rockefeller Center, New York 20, New York, has a set of lessons on phonograph records.

TABLE 1—VOWELS

English Sounds	Russian		Stress and context in Russian
	Frequent Spellings	Sounds	
i	и	i	Tonic: (1) between palatal and non-palatal, as in книга [ˈkn̯igə] (book) NOTE: See illustration, page 482, of possible transcription with fronted [k], i.e., [c], as in [ˈcn̯igə]
			(2) interpalatal, as in бить [b̯it̯] (to beat)
			(3) final after palatal, as in щи [ʃtʃi] (cabbage soup), три [t̯r̯i] (three)
			(4) initial, as in искра [ˈiskrə] (sparkle)
			Pretonic: between palatal and non-palatal, as in лицо [l̯iˈtsɔ] (face)
	й	i	In diphthongs [ɪi, ei, æi, ai, ɔi, ui, ʉi, əi] (see pages 480, 491-492)
ɨ	ы	ɨ	Tonic: after non-palatal, as in мыло [ˈm(w)ɨlə] (soap)
			Pretonic: after non-palatal, as in дыра [dɨˈra] (hole)
			In diphthong [ɨi] (page 480)
	и	ɨ	Tonic or pretonic: (1) after ш [ʃˠ], as in шире [ˈʃɨr̯ɪ] (width)
			(2) after ж [ʒˠ], as in жизнь [ˈʒɨz̯n̯] (life)
			(3) after ц [ts], as in циклист [tsɨˈkl̯ist] (cyclist)
I	я	I	Pretonic: interpalatal, as in рябить [r̯Iˈb̯it̯] (ripple)
			Atonic: interpalatal: пятидесятый [p̯Ɪt̯Idɪˈs̯atəi] (fiftieth)
	e	I	Pretonic: interpalatal, as in семья [s̯Im̯ˈja] (family)
			Atonic: (1) between palatal and non-palatal, as in седоватый [s̯Ɪdaˈvatəi] (grayish)

English Sounds	Russian		Stress and context in Russian
	Frequent Spellings	Sounds	
ɪ	е	ɪ	(2) interpalatal, as in семьдесят [ˈşem̢d̢ɪşət] (seventy) (3) final after palatal, as in море [ˈmɔɽɪ] (sea)
	и	ɪ	Atonic: (1) between palatal and non-palatal, as in чистаган [t̢ʃɪstaˈgan] (cash) (2) interpalatal, as in синева [şɪn̢ɛˈva] (blueness) (3) final after palatal, as in если [ˈjeşļɪ] (if) In diphthong [ɪi] (see page 480)
	ий	ɪ	Atonic: final after non-palatal, as in маленький [ˈmaļɪn̢kɪ] (little)
e	е	e	Tonic: interpalatal, as in речь [ɽet̢ʃ] (speech) In diphthong [ei] (see page 480)
ɛ	э	ɛ	Tonic: initial, as in этот [ˈɛtət] (it, this, that)
		ɛ	Pretonic: initial in foreign words, as in экспорт [ɛksˈpɔrt] (export)
		ɛ	Atonic: initial in foreign words, as in the transliteration этикет [ɛt̢ɪˈkɛt] (etiquette).
		ɛ	In transliterations generally, as in дуэт [duˈɛt] (duet)
	е	ɛ	Tonic: (1) after non-palatal, as in концерт [kanˈtsɛrt] (concert) (2) between palatal and non-palatal, as in нет [n̢ɛt] (no), ест [jɛst] (eats), приезд [pɽiˈjɛst] (arrival)
		ɛ	Pretonic: (1) after non-palatal, as in цена [tsɛˈna] (price) (2) between palatal and non-palatal, as in сезон [şɛˈzɔn] (season)—also [şɪˈzɔn]

English Sounds	Russian Frequent Spellings	Russian Sounds	Stress and context in Russian
ɛ	e	ɛ	Tonic: after ъ, as in съел [sjɛl] (ate up)
	e	ɛ	Tonic: after ь, as in в статье [f stat̡ʲjɛ(ə)] (in the article)
a	a	a	Tonic: (1) after non-palatal, as in карта [ˈkartə] (card)
			(2) between palatal and non-palatal, as in час [ʧas] (hour)
			Pretonic: (1) after non-palatal, as in картель [karˈt̡el̡] (cartel)
			(2) between palatal and non-palatal, as in часы [ʧaˈsɨ] (clock)
			In diphthong [ai] (see page 480)
	я	a	Tonic: between palatal and non-palatal, as in яма [ˈjamə] (ditch)
			Pretonic: between palatal and non-palatal, as in пята [p̡aˈta] (heel)
	o	a	Pretonic: after non-palatal, as in тоска [tasˈka] (pain)
ɑ	a	ɑ	Tonic: in closed syllable before the back non-palatal [ł], as in балка [ˈbɑłka] (beam)
			Pretonic: in closed syllable before the same back non-palatal, as in балкон [bɑłˈkɔn] (balcony)
æ	a	æ	Tonic: (1) interpalatal, as in кончать [kanˈʧæt̡] (to end)
			In diphthong [æi] (see page 480)
	я	æ	Tonic: interpalatal, as in пять [p̡æt̡] (five)
			In diphthong [æi] (see page 480)
ɔ	o	ɔ	Tonic: (1) after non-palatal, as in Бог [bɔx] (God)
			(2) between palatal and non-palatal, as in чорт [ʧɔrt] (devil)

English Sounds	Russian		Stress and context in Russian
	Frequent Spellings	Sounds	
ɔ	o	ɔ	In diphthong [ɔi] (see page 480)
	ё	ɔ	Tonic: (1) after non-palatal, as in шёлк [ʃɔlk] (silk)
			(2) between palatal and non-palatal, as in лёт [l̯ɔt] (flight), ёлка [ˈjɔlkə] (spruce), заём [zaˈjɔm] (loan), подъём [padˈjɔm] (ascent), пьёт [p̯ɔt] (drinks—3rd sing.)
	a	ɔ	Tonic: exceptionally, as in платишь [ˈplɔtɪʃ] (pay—imp.)
	я	ɔ	Tonic: exceptionally, as in запряг [zaˈpr̯ɔk] (yoked)
	ё	øˑ	Tonic: interpalatal, as in тётя [ˈt̯øˑt̯ə] (aunt)
u	y	u	Tonic: (1) after non-palatal, as in кус [kus] (morsel)
			(2) between palatal and non-palatal, as in чуб [tʃup] (boundary)
			In diphthong [ui] (see page 480)
		u	Pretonic: (1) after non-palatal, as in рука [ruˈka] (hand, arm)
			(2) between palatal and non-palatal, as in чума [tʃuˈma] (pest)
	ю	(j)u	Tonic: between palatal and non-palatal, as in любо [ˈl̯ubə] (agreeably), юнга [ˈjungə] (cabin boy)
			Pretonic: between palatal and non-palatal, as in любовник [l̯uˈbɔvnɪk] (lover)
	y	ʉ	Tonic: interpalatal, as in чуть [tʃʉt̯] (almost)
			Pretonic: interpalatal, as in чутьё [tʃʉt̯ˈjɔ] (instinct —of animals)

English Sounds	Russian		Stress and context in Russian
	Frequent Spellings	Sounds	
	у	ʉ	In diphthong [ʉi] (see page 480)
	ю	ʉ	Tonic: interpalatal, as in люди [ˈl̡ʉd̡ɪ] (people)
			Pretonic: interpalatal, as in любить [l̡ʉˈb̡it̡] (to love)
U	у	U	Atonic: (1) after non-palatal, as in зубоскал [zʊbaˈskɑɫ] (scoffer)
			(2) between palatal and non-palatal, as in чужеземец [tʃʊʒɛˈz̡em̡ɪts] (foreigner)
			(3) interpalatal, as in чудеса [tʃʊd̡ɛˈsa] (miracle)—also [tʃʊd̡ɪˈsa]
			(4) final after palatal, as in врачу [ˈvratʃʊ] (doctor's)
ʌ	а	ʌ	Pretonic: variant of pretonic [a], as in сарай [sʌˈrai] (shed)
	о	ʌ	Pretonic: variant of pretonic [a], as in собака [sʌˈbakə] (dog)
	ю	U	Atonic: (1) between palatal and non-palatal, as in любоваться [l̡ʊbaˈvats̡ə] (to admire)
			(2) interpalatal, as in тюфячок [t̡ʊf̡ɪˈtʃɔk] (mattress)
			(3) final after palatal, as in няню [ˈn̡æn̡ʊ] (nurse—acc.)
ə	а	ə	Atonic: (1) after non-palatal, as in комната [ˈkɔmnətə] (room)
			(2) between palatal and non-palatal, as in частокол [tʃəstaˈkɔl] (stockade)
			(3) final after palatal, as in борща [ˈbɔrʃtʃə] (of beet soup)

English Sounds	Russian		Stress and context in Russian
	Frequent Spellings	Sounds	
ə	я	ə	Atonic: (1) between palatal and non-palatal, as in явнобрачный [jəvnaˈbratʃnəɪ] (pertaining to a seed plant)
			(2) final after palatal, as in категория [kətɛˈgorɪjə] (category)
	е	ə	Atonic: (1) after non-palatal, as in целовать [tsalaˈvat] (to kiss)
			(2) final after palatal, as in ·уверение [ʊʝɪˈreṇɪjə] (certainly)
	о	ə	Atonic: after non-palatal, as in холодок [xəlaˈdɔk] (coolness)
ɝ			
ɚ			

TABLE II—DIPHTHONGS

English Sounds	Russian		Stress and context in Russian
	Frequent Spellings	Sounds	
	ий	ɪi	Atonic: after palatal, as in линий [ˈḷiṇɪi] (line—gen.)
	ей		Atonic: after palatal, as in мыслей [ˈm(w)i̥s̪ḷɪi] (of thoughts—gen. plu.)
	ай		Atonic: after palatal, as in обычай [aˈbi̥tʃɪi] (custom)
	ый	ɨi	Tonic: as in выйти [ˈv(w)i̥iṭɪ] (to go out)
eɪ	ей	ei	Tonic: after palatal, as in дверей [d̪ʝɪˈɽei] (of trees—gen. plu.)

English Sounds	Russian		Stress and context in Russian
	Frequent Spellings	Sounds	
aɪ	ай	ai	Tonic: after non-palatal, as in дайте [ˈdaiṭɪ] (give —imp. plu.)
			Pretonic: after non-palatal, as in гайдук [gaiˈduk] (servant)
æɪ	ай	æi	Tonic: after palatal, as in чай [ʧæi] (tea)
	яй	æi	Tonic: after palatal, as in лентяй [l̩ɪn̩ˈṭæi] (idler)
ɔɪ	ой	ɔi	Tonic: as in отбой [adˈbɔi] (retreat)
aʊ	ау	au	In transliteration, as in пауза [ˈpauzə] (pause)— hardly to be regarded as a true Russian diphthong
	уй	ui	Tonic: after non-palatal, as in буйный [ˈbuinəi] (boisterous)
			Pretonic: as in уйти [uiˈṭi] (to go out)
	уй	ʉi	Tonic: after palatal, ночуй [naˈʧʉi] (spend the night)
	ае	əi	Atonic: as in делается [ˈd̪ɛləitʂə] (is becoming)
	ай		Atonic: as in делайте [ˈd̪ɛləɪṭɪ] (do—imp. plu.)
	ый		Atonic: final, as in новый [ˈnɔvəi] (new)

TABLE III—CONSONANTS

English Sounds	Russian		Stress and context in Russian
	Frequent Spellings	Sounds	
p	п	p	Before a non-palatalizing vowel, as in потом [paˈtɔm] (afterwards)

English Sounds	Russian Frequent Spellings	Russian Sounds	Stress and context in Russian
p	п	p	Before non-palatal consonants excluding voiced plosives and fricatives except в [v] (See note on assimilation, page 485), as in прок [prɔk] (profit)
		p	Final, as in поп [pɔp] (priest)
	б	p	Before a voiceless non-palatal fricative or plosive as in обход [ap¹xɔt] (tour)
		p	Final, as in зуб [zup] (tooth)
pj	пь	p̜	Wherever it occurs, except before voiced plosives and fricatives, not including в [v], as in копь [kɔp̜] (a mine)
	п	p̜	Before a palatalizing vowel, as in певец [p̜ɪ¹γɛts] (singer)
		p̜	Before palatal consonants, excluding all voiced plosives and fricatives except в [v], as in плющ [p̜ᶥuʃʧ] (ivy)
	б	p̜	Before a voiceless palatal consonant, as in обчесть [ap̜¹ʧest̜] (miscalculation)
	бь	p̜	Final, as in скорбь [skɔrp̜] (affliction)
b	б	b	Before a non-palatalizing vowel, as in боль [bɔl̜] (pain).
		b	Before a voiced non-palatal consonant, as in брат [brat] (brother)
	бъ	b	As in объяснить [əbja¹sn̜it̜] (to explain)
	п	b	Before voiced non-palatal plosives and fricatives except в [v], as in труп друга [ˌtrub ¹drugə] (corpse of a friend)
bj	бь	ḅ	Non-final, as in бью [ḅju] (I beat)—(Note: the first of the two [j]'s in contexts like [ḅju] is fricative

English Sounds	Russian		Stress and context in Russian
	Frequent Spellings	Sounds	
bj	б	b̦	Before a palatalizing vowel, as in бюст [b̦ust] (bust)
		b̦	Before a voiced palatal consonant, as in блеск [b̦l̦ɛsk] (gleam)
	п	b̦	Before a voiced palatal plosive or fricative, except в [v], as in этот поп деликатный [ˌɛtət pɔb̦ d̦ɪl̦iˈkatnəɪ] (This priest is delicate)
t	т	t	Before a non-palatalizing vowel, as in статья [statˡja] (chapter)
		t	Before non-palatal consonants, excluding all voiced plosives and fricatives except в [v], as in твой [tvɔi] (they)
		silent	In the clusters стн, стл, as in известный [ɪzˈɣɛs-nəɪ] (famous)
		t	Final, as in этот [ˈɛtət] (this)
	д	t	Before voiceless non-palatal fricatives or plosives, as in подходнть [pətxaˡd̦iț] (to approach)
		t	~~Final, as in сад [sat] (garden)~~
tj	ть	ț	Wherever it occurs, except before voiced plosives and fricatives, not including в [v], as in тьма [țma] (darkness)
	т	ț	Before a palatalizing vowel, as in стена [sțɛˡna] (wall)
		ț	Before palatal consonants, excluding voiced plosives and fricatives except в [v], as in стремя [ˡsțr̦emə] (stirrup)
	д	ț	Before a voiceless palatal fricative or plosive, as in подснежник [pațˡsn̦ɛʒn̦ɪk] (snowdrop)
	дь	ț	Final, as in грудь [gruț] (chest)

English Sounds	Russian		Stress and context in Russian
	Frequent Spellings	Sounds	
d	д	d	Before a non-palatalizing vowel, as in дом [dɔm] (house)
		d	Before a voiced non-palatal consonant, as in след золота [slɛd ˈzɔlətə] (a trace of gold)
	дъ	d	As in подъезд [padˈjɛst] (entrance)
	т	d	Before non-palatal plosives and fricatives, except в [v], as in отбор [adˈbɔr] (choice)
	д	silent	In the word сердце [ˈsɛrt͜sə] (heart) and in the cluster здн, as in поздно [ˈpɔznə] (late)
dj	дь	d̡	Non-final and not followed by a voiceless consonant, as in усадьба [uˈsad̡bə] (farm), ладья [lad̡ˈja] (boat)
	д	d̡	Before a palatalizing vowel, as in дюйм [d̡uim] (inch)
		d̡	Before a voiced palatal consonant, as in дрек [d̡r̡ɛk] (grapnel)
	ть	d̡	Before a voiced plosive or fricative, except в [v], as in молотьба [məlad̡ˈba] (threshing)
	т	d̡	Before a voiced palatal plosive or fricative, except в [v], as in вот зебра [vɔd̡ ˈz̡ɛbrə] (there is a zebra)
k	к	k	Before a non-palatalizing vowel, as in камыш [kaˈmiʃ] (cane)
		k	Before non-palatal consonants, excluding voiced plosives and fricatives, except в [v], as in кнут [knut] (whip)
	к	k	Final as in клык [klɨk] (tusk)
	г	k	Before a voiceless fricative or plosive, as in улёгся [uˈlɔks̡ə] (he lay)
		k	Final, as in друг [druk] (friend)

English Sounds	Russian		Stress and context in Russian
	Frequent Spellings	Sounds	
c (= k')	к	c (= k')- usually tran- scribed k	Before a palatalizing vowel, as in кедр [cɛdr] (cedar)
		c	Before a palatal consonant, excluding voiced plosives and fricatives except в [v], as in клевер ['cl̢eɣɪr] (clover)
	г	c	Before a voiceless palatal fricative or plosive, as in мой друг в театре [mɔi druk ʃ t̢ɛ'at̢ɪ] (my friend in the theater), лягте ['l̢akt̢ɪ] (lie down—imp.), almost ['l̢ækt̢ɪ], in view of the quasi-interpalatal position of the stressed vowel
g	г	g	Before a non-palatalizing vowel, as in гость [gɔst̢] (guest)
		g	Before a voiced non-palatal consonant, as in громкий ['grɔmkɪ] (loud)
	к	g	Before voiced non-palatal plosives and fricatives, except в [v], as in к дому [g 'dɔmʊ] (to the house)
ɟ (= g')	г	ɟ (= g')- usually tran- scribed g	Before a palatalizing vowel, as in генерал [ɟɪn̢ɛ'raɫ] (general)
		ɟ	Before voiced palatal consonant, as in где [ɟdɛ(ə)].
	к	ɟ	Before a voiced palatal plosive or fricative, except в [v], as in к денница [ɟ d̢ɪn̢'n̢it̢sə] (by daybreak)
m	м	m	Before non-palatalizing vowel, as in мальчик ['maɫtʃɪk] (boy)
		m	Before non-palatal consonant, as in темнота [t̢ɪmna'ta] (darkness)
		m	Final, as in там [tam] (there)

English Sounds	Russian		Stress and context in Russian
	Frequent Spellings	Sounds	
mj	мь	m̦	Wherever found, as in семь [ˈșem̦] (seven)
	м	m̦	Before a palatalizing vowel, as in смерть [șm̦erț] (death)
		m̦	Before a palatal consonant, as in мне [m̦n̦ɛ(ə)] (to me)
n	н	n	Before a non-palatalizing vowel, as in нух [nux] (ghost)
		n	Before a non-palatal consonant, as in нрав [nraf] (disposition)
		n	Final, as in сын [sin] (son)
nj	нь	n̦	Wherever found, as in день [d̦en̦] (day)
	н	n̦	Before a palatalizing vowel, as in нёбо [ˈn̦ɔbə] (palate)
		n̦	Before a palatal consonant, as in сентябрь [șɪn̦-ˈțab̦r̦] (September)
l	л	l	Before a non-palatalizing vowel, as in лошадь [ˈlɔʃəț] (horse)
		l	Before a non-palatal consonant, as in полночь [ˈpɔlnətʃ] (midnight)
		l	Final, as in пол [pɔl] (floor)
		silent	In the word солнце [ˈsɔntsɪ] (sun)
lj	ль	l̦	Wherever found, as in мысль [m(w)ișl̦] (thought)
	л	l̦	Before a palatalizing vowel, as in лестница [ˈl̦eștn̦ɪtsə] (staircase)
		l̦	Before a palatal consonant, as in полдня [pal̦-ˈd̦n̦a] (half a day)
r	р	r	Before a non-palatalizing vowel, as in раз [ras] (once, a time)

English Sounds	Russian		Stress and context in Russian
	Frequent Spellings	Sounds	
r	р	r	Before a non-palatal consonant, as in сорт [sɔrt] (sort, kind)
		r	Final, as in север [ˈs̯eɣɪr] (north)
rj	рь	ŗ	Wherever found, as in дверь [dɣeŗ] (door)
	р	ŗ	Before a palatalizing vowel, as in река [ŗɛˈka] (river)—also [ŗɪˈka]
		ŗ	Before a palatal consonant, as in скатерть [ˈskaṭɪŗṭ] (table-cloth)
f	ф	f	Before a non-palatal vowel, as in фонарь [faˈnaŗ] (street lamp)
		f	Before a non-palatal consonant, excluding voiced plosives and fricatives except в [v], as in француз [franˈtsus] (Frenchman)
		f	Final, as in граф [graf] (count)
	в	f	Before a voiceless non-palatal fricative or plosive, as in в саду [f saˈdu] (in the garden)
		f	Final, as in против [ˈprɔṭɪf] (opposite)
fj	фь	ʃ	Wherever found, except before voiced plosives and fricatives, except в [v], as in верфь [ɣeŗʃ] (dock-yard)
	ф	ʃ	Before a palatalizing vowel, as in февраль [ʃɛvˈral] (February)
		ʃ	Before a palatal consonant, excluding voiced plosives and fricatives except в [v], as in флёр [ʃḷɔr] (gauze)
	в	ʃ	Before a voiceless palatal fricative or plosive, as in всегда [ʃsɛgˈda]—also [ʃsɛɣˈda, ʃsɪgˈda] (always). (Colloquially [ʃsɪgəˈda].)
	вь	ʃ	Final, as in ветвь [ɣeṭʃ] (bough)

English Sounds	Russian		Stress and context in Russian
	Frequent Spellings	Sounds	
v	в	v	Before a non-palatalizing vowel, as in вымыть [ˈv(w)i̜mət] (to wash)
		v	Before a voiced non-palatal consonant, as in в доме [v ˈdɔmɪ] (in the house)
	въ	v	Non-final, and not before voiceless plosives and fricatives, except в [v], as in въезжать [vɛʒˈʒat] (to drive in)
	ф	v	Before a voiced non-palatal plosive or fricative, except в [v], as in этот риф долгий [ɛtət r̥iv ˈdɔlgɪ] (This reef is long)
	г	v	In эго [jɛˈvɔ] (his, its) and analogous genitives, such as этого [ˈɛtəvə] from этот [ˈɛtət] (this), того [taˈvɔ] from то [tɔ] (that), всего [f̜s̜ɛˈvɔ] from весь [ɣes̜] (all), большого [baļˈʃovə] from большой [baļˈʃɔi] (large). Note especially сегодня [s̜ɛˈvɔ(ɪ)dnə]—also [s̜ɪˈvɔ(ɪ)dnə] (to-day)
vj	вь	ɣ	Non-final, and not before voiceless plosives or fricatives, except в [v], as in навьючивать [naɣˈjutʃɪvət] (to load)
	в	ɣ	Before a palatalizing vowel, as in верх [ɣɛrx] (top)
		ɣ	Before a voiced palatal consonant, as in взвивать [ɣzɣiˈvat] (to bring up)
		ɣ	Before a voiced palatal plosive or fricative, except в [v], as in этот риф белый [ɛtət r̥iɣ ˈb̜ɛləi] (This reef is white)
θ			
ð			

English Sounds	Russian		Stress and context in Russian
	Frequent Spellings	Sounds	
s	c	s	Before a non-palatalizing vowel, as in сорок ['sɔrək] (forty)
		s	Before a non-palatal consonant, excluding voiced plosives and fricatives, except в [v], as in скальп [ska̦p] (scalp)
		s	Final, as in час [t͡ʃas] (hour)
	з	s	Before a voiceless non-palatal plosive or fricative, as in из комнаты [is 'kɔmnətə, 'kɔmnəti] (out of the room)
		s	Final, as in раз [ras] (time)
sj	сь	ş	As in весь [ɣeş] (all)
	c	ş	Before a palatalizing vowel, as in село [şɛ'lɔ] (village—with a church)—also [şɪ'lɔ]
		ş	Before a palatal consonant, excluding voiced plosives and fricatives, except в [v], as in свет [şɣɛt] (light)
	з	ş	Before a voiceless palatal fricative or plosive, as in без четверти [b̦iş' t͡ʃetɣɪɽțɪ] (a quater to)
	зь	ş	Final, as in грязь [gɽaş] (mud)
z	з	z	Before a non-palatalizing vowel, as in завтра ['zaftrə] (tomorrow)
		z	Before a voiced non-palatal consonant, as in звон [zvɔn] (ringing of bells)
	зъ	z	Wherever it occurs, except before voiceless plosives and fricatives, or final, as in изъян [iz'jan] (defect)
	c	z	Before voiced non-palatal plosives and fricatives, except в [v], as in с дуру [z 'durʊ] (foolishly)

English Sounds	Russian		Stress and context in Russian
	Frequent Spellings	Sounds	
zj	зь	ẓ	Non-final, and not before voiceless plosives or fricatives, except в [v], as in грязьи ['gṛæẓɪ] (of mud—gen.)
	з	ẓ	Before a palatalizing vowel, as in земец ['ẓem̗ɪts] (peasant)
		ẓ	Before a voiced palatal consonant, as in змея [ẓm̗ɪ'ja] (snake)
	с	ẓ	Before a voiced palatal plosive or fricative, as in сделать ['ẓd̗ɛlət̗] (to do)
ʃ	ш	ʃ	Wherever found, except before voiced plosives or fricatives, not including в [v], as in мышь [m(w)i̗ʃ] (mouse)
		ʃ	Before a vowel, as in шакал [ʃa'kaɫ] (jackal); шёлк [ʃɔlk] (silk)
		ʃ	Before a consonant, excluding voiced plosives and fricatives, except в [v], as in шлак [ʃlak] (slag)
	ш	ʃ	Final, as in ваш [vaʃ] (your)
	ж	ʃ	Before a voiceless consonant, as in ложка ['lɔʃkə] (spoon)
	жь	ʃ	Final, as in ложь [lɔʃ] (falsehood)
	ж	ʃ	Final, as in муж [muʃ] (husband)
	с	ʃ	Before [ʃ], as in с шара [ʃ 'ʃarə] (from the globe)
	ч	ʃ	Occasionally, by contraction of [tʃ] to [ʃ], as in что [ʃtɔ] (for [tʃtɔ]) (what), конечно [ka'n̗eʃnə] (to be sure)
ʒ	ж	ʒ	Before a vowel, as in жало ['ʒalə] (sting); жила ['ʒilə] (vein)
		ʒ	Before a voiced consonant, as in жбан [ʒban] (wooden jug)

English Sounds	Russian		Stress and context in Russian
	Frequent Spellings	Sounds	
ʒ	ш	ʒ	Before a voiced plosive or fricative, except в [v], as in ваш брат [vaʒ ˈbrat] (your brother)
	с	ʒ	Before ж [ʒ], as in с жёлоба [ʒ ˈʒɔləbə] (from the spout)
	з	ʒ	Before [ʒ], as in из жилище [iʒ ˈʒiḷɪʃʧɪ] (out of the dwelling)
	х	x	Before a non-palatalizing vowel, as in холод [ˈxɔlət] (cold)
		x	Before a non-palatal consonant, excluding voiced plosives and fricatives, except в [v], as in хвалить [xvaˈliṭ] (to praise)
		x	Final, as in трах [trax] (bang!)
	г	x	Before a voiceless plosive or fricative, as in легко [ḷɛxˈkɔ] (easily), ногти [ˈnɔxṭɪ] (nails)
		x (usually k)	Final in rare instances, as in Бог [bɔx] (God)
	х	ç (= xʲ) (usually written x)	Before a palatalizing vowel, as in хинин [çiˈn̦in] (quinine)
		ç	Before a palatal consonant, excluding voiced plosives and fricatives, except в [v], as in хлеб [çḷɛp] (bread)
	г	ɣ	Intervocalic in rare instances, as in Богу [ˈbɔɣu] (God—dat.)
	х	ɣ	Before a voiced plosive or fricative, as in мох зелёный [mɔɣ z̦ɪˈḷɔnəi] (green moss)
h			

English Sounds	Russian		Stress and context in Russian
	Frequent Spellings	Sounds	
w	y	w	Unstressed in rapid speech, as in пожалуйста [pa'ʒɑɫwɪstə] (please)
		w	Non-significant glide between 1. к and о plus ш [ʃ] in a stressed syllable, as in кошка ['k(w)ɔ(ɪ)ʃkə] (cat) 2. б and ы, as in быль [b(w)ɨl] (true tale) 3. м and ы, as in мы [m(w)ɨ] (we) 4. в and ы, as in вы [v(w)ɨ] (you—plu.)
tʃ	ч	tʃ	Initially, medially, or finally (but not when contracted to [ʃ]—See under [ʃ], page 000—or followed by a voiced plosive or fricative, excluding в [v]), as in ничего [nɪtʃɛ'vɔ] (nothing)—also [nɪtʃɪ'vɔ]
	чь	tʃ	As in ночь [nɔ(ɪ)tʃ] (night)
ʤ	ч	ʤ	Before a voiced plosive or fricative, except в [v], as in клич дедушки [klʲiʤ 'dʲeduʃkɪ] (the shout of a child)
	чь	ʤ	Before a voiced plosive or fricative, (except в [v], as in эта печь большая [ɛtə pʲeʤ balʲ'ʃajə] (This oven is large)
	щ	ʃtʃ	In all positions, as in щит [ʃtʃit] (shield)
ts	ц	ts	In all positions, except before voiced plosives or fricatives (aside from в [v]), as in самец [sa'mʲɛts] (male)
dz	ц	dz	Before a voiced plosive or fricative, except в [v], as in отец грустный [aʦɛdz 'grustnəi] (Father is sad)

Russian Pronunciation of English Vowels

Of the English vowels, the following present problems to the Russian:

ɪ	o	ʊ	ɜ	ɝ
æ	ou	ʌ	ɚ	

[ɪ]

It seems surprising that the Russians, having [ɪ] in their own language, should have difficulty with the English [ɪ]. But they do have very great difficulty, their fault being the substitution of [i], so that *ship*, for example, becomes *sheep*. The explanation is that many instances of the English [ɪ] occur in monosyllables and the stressed syllables of polysyllabic words, whereas in Russian, [ɪ] never occurs except in an unstressed syllable. Moreover, the Russian [ɪ] belongs to the [i]-phoneme. This is another way of saying that Russian [ɪ] is an allophonic variant of [i], not a separate phoneme, as in English, and when the Russian thinks of the sound, even in an unstressed syllable, he is thinking of [i]. Accordingly, when he attempts to reproduce it in isolation, he almost inevitably pronounces [i].

Nevertheless, it helps the Russian learner to have [ɪ] pointed out to him in his own language, as in маленький ['maļɪncɪ] or ['maļɪnkɪ] (little—masc. sing.) or учитель [u'tʃiţɪļ] (teacher). It helps also to point out that [ɪ] is made with tongue muscles lax, while [i] is made with tongue muscles tense. The difference can be demonstrated by placing the student's thumb and forefinger under the teacher's lower jaw, so that the shift of the musculature from tense to lax can be felt as the teacher pronounces [i-ɪ], *seat* [sit]—*sit* [sɪt], *bead* [bid]—*bid* [bɪd], etc. In fact, there is no better way for the student himself to "split" [i] and [ɪ] apart than to pronounce pairs like the following:

eat [it] – it [ɪt]	fit [fɪt] – feat [fit]
meal [mil] – mill [mɪl]	bit [bɪt] – beat [bit]
he's [hiz] – his [hɪz]	knit [nɪt] – neat [nit]
mead [mid] – mid [mɪd]	hit [hɪt] – heat [hit]
peat [pit] – pit [pɪt]	rid [rɪd] – read [rid]
keel [kił] – kill [kɪł]	hill [hɪł] – heel [hił]

[æ]

The sound [æ] likewise occurs in Russian, always between palatalized consonants. But it is a member of the [a]-phoneme, and as such is subject to some of the same difficulties as [ɪ]. Fortunately, however, it occurs in stressed syllables in Russian, and so lends itself to being pronounced in isolation. Examples: пять [p̡æt̡] (five), дядя ['d̡æd̡ə] (uncle), няня ['n̡æn̡ə] (nurse). It is effective to begin by pairing the Russian words with similar-sounding English words, thus:

[p̡æt̡] – pat [pæt]
['d̡æd̡ə] – daddy ['dædɪ]
['n̡æn̡ə] – Nancy ['næntsɪ]

After [æ] is established, the following list may be used for practice:

add [æd]	at [æt]	apt [æpt]	act [ækt]	am [æm]
bad [bæd]	bat [bæt]	cap [kæp]	fact [fækt]	Sam [sæm]
lad [læd]	fat [fæt]	nap [næp]	tract [trækt]	lamb [læm]
sad [sæd]	sat [sæt]	lap [læp]	cracked [krækt]	tram [træm]

[o, ou]

Most Russians learn [o] quite rapidly by beginning with [ɔ], which is their normal pronunciation of orthographic *o*, and rounding the lips more positively. Undiphthongized [o] is infrequent in English, but is generally used in the following, which can be used for practice:

obey [o'beɪ]   oration [o'reɪʃən]
omit [o'mɪt]   cooperate [ko'ɑpə,reɪt, ko'ɒpə,reɪt]

For [ou], the student had best learn [ʊ] in the next paragraph, and then put [o] and [ʊ] together to produce [ou]. If he has difficulty, he may be allowed to use [ou] at first, [u] being more familiar to him. Word list: *old* [ould], *coat* [kout], *most* [moust], *hose* [houz].

[ʊ]

Because [ʊ] belongs to the [u]-phoneme in Russian, and is used only in unstressed syllables, it is difficult for the Russian to produce it in stressed syllables or in isolation. His tendency is, of course, to produce [u]. But it aids him to have [ʊ] pointed out in Russian words such as август ['avgʊst] (August). It is well also to demonstrate that whereas [u] is tense, [ʊ] is lax. By the same process as for [i-ɪ], this can be demonstrated. Then [u] and [ʊ] can be "split" apart by pronouncing paired words, such as the following:

boom [bum] – book [bʊk]
boot [but] – put [pʊt]
fool [fuł] – foot [fʊt]
cool [kuł] – cook [kʊk]
tomb [tum] – took [tʊk]
who [hu] – hook [hʊk]

[ʌ]

British phoneticians[6] are able to find the equivalent of the low-back, [ɑ]-like British [ʌ] in certain pretonic syllables where the orthographic vowel is *a*, such as the word for work, работа, which they interpret as [rʌ'bɔtə], but which Ameri-

---

6 Trofimov and Jones, *op. cit.*, p. 180.

cans hear as [ra'bɔtə]. Since the American [ʌ] is very nearly a central vowel, resembling [ə] except for being of longer duration and completely unround, it is best to base its pronunciation on [ə], a sound very familiar to Russians. Therefore, select a word containing [ə], such as это ['ɛtə] (this, that—nom. sing. neut.). Pronounce the word with the [ə] greatly lengthened, thus: [ɛtə:::::]. Repeat with the lips completely unrounded. The result should be a fair approximation of [ʌ]. Caution the student against using [ɑ], which appears to be his most common substitute. To "split" [ʌ] and [ɑ] apart, have him practice the following pairs:

up [ʌp] – Opp [ɑp, ɒp]
cup [kʌp] – cop [kɑp, kɒp]
cub [kʌb] – cob [kɑb, kɒb]
love [lʌv] – lot [lɑt, lɒt]
above [ə'bʌv] – abolish [ə'bɑlɪʃ, ə'bɒlɪʃ]
son [sʌn] – solve [sɑlv, sɒlv]
judge [ʤʌʤ] – job [ʤɑb, ʤɒb]

[ɜ]

The learning of the E., S., Br., [ɜ] may also be based on [ə]. Again have the student pronounce это ['ɛtə:::::]. Let him repeat with the lips slightly rounded. The result should be a fair approximation of [ɜ]. Caution the student against substituting [ɛɾ]. The following will serve for practice:

her [hɜ], not [hɛɾ][7]
bird [bɜd], not [bɛɾd]
fern [fɜn], not [fɛɾn]

Since [ɔ] and [ɔɾ] are also sometimes substituted, the following practice list may be used:

thirty ['θɜtɪ], not ['θɔtɪ] or ['θɔrtɪ]
word [wɜd], not [wɔd] or [wɔɾd]

[ɝ]

The General American [ɝ] is in some ways easier for Russians to learn than [ɜ]. That is, it is practically automatic for a Russian to use some value of *r* wherever *r* appears in the English spelling. But of course, the Russian's *r* is the tongue-point trill, vigorous and prominent. Along with teaching him the value of the vowel [ɝ], must go the suppression of the trill. It has proved reasonably successful for the teacher to draw diagrams of the tongue with the point elevated toward, but not touching, the middle of the hard palate, and to demonstrate this tongue position with his own tongue. When the student adds to the vowel [ɜ], as described above, the quality arising from the elevated tongue

[7] Throughout these exercises, only one error at a time is considered. Actually the Russian is likely to pronounce *her* as [çɛɾ].

position, a passable [ɝ] should result. But [ɜ] and [ɝ], like most central vowels, are difficult for foreigners to learn. Much patience and repetition is necessary. Since [ɛɾ] and [ɔɾ] are common substitutes, the following will serve for drill.

> concern [kən'sɝn], not [kən'sɛɾn] nor [kən'sɔɾn]
> pearl [pɝɫ], not [pɛɾl] nor [pɔɾl]
> whirl [ʍɝɫ], not [ʍɛɾl] nor [ʍɔɾl]
> work [wɝk], not [wɛɾk] nor [wɔɾk]
> journal ['ʤɝnəɫ], not ['ʤɛrnəl] nor ['ʤɔrnəl]

[ɚ]

Once having learned [ɝ], the Russian can often achieve a passable [ɚ] by shortening and relaxing [ɝ]. Or he can apply to his well known [ə] the elevated tongue position described above for [ɝ]. The most frequent substitution is [ɛɾ]. Words for practice:

> reader ['ridɚ], not ['ɾidɛɾ]
> border ['bɔrdɚ], not ['bɔrdɛɾ]

Russian Pronunciation of English Consonants

Of the English consonants, the following present problems to the Russians:

t	ŋ	ð	h	ʧ
d	r	ʃ	w	ʤ
n	θ	ʒ	ʍ	

[t], [d], [n]

The sounds [t], [d], and [n] are alveolar in English, not dental, as in Russian. The student must be taught by diagram and personal demonstration to place the tip of his tongue on the alveolar ridge, back of the upper front teeth, not against the teeth themselves. Words for practice:

> net [nɛt], not [n̪ɛt̪]
> den [dɛn], not [d̪ɛn̪]
> gnaw [nɔ], not [n̪ɔ]
> dawn [dɔn], not [d̪ɔn̪]

[ʃ], [ʒ]

The sounds [ʃ] and [ʒ] are made with the tongue farther front in the mouth than in Russian. Students will need to practice words like the following:

> she [ʃi], not [ʃˠi]
> leisure ['liʒɚ, 'liʒə], not ['liʒˠɚ, 'liʒˠə]

[ʤ]

The sound [ʤ] requires special notice here. Despite the fact that it is found in Russian, it is so infrequent there that Russians seem unfamiliar with it.

Accordingly, as seen above, they substitute [ʧ], [ʒ] or [ʤ] for it. A phrase like дочь да сын [dͻ(i)ʤ də ˈsiṇ] (daughter and son), where the [ʧ] of [dͻ(i)ʧ] (daughter) has been voiced by the succeeding voiced consonant [d], may aid the student; or he may find success in voicing [ʧ] outright; or he may place together his wellknown [d] and [ʒ] to make [ʤ]; or he may know the loan-words бюджет [bu̥ˈʤɛt] (budget) or джут [ʤut] (jute). The common substitutions are [ʧ] and [ʒ]. The following will serve for practice:

> John [ʤɑn, ʤɒn], not [ʧɑn, ʒɑn]
> James [ʤeɪmz], not [ʧeɪmz, ʒeɪmz]
> budge [bʌʤ], not [bʌʧ, bʌʒ]
> judge [ʤʌʤ], not [ʧʌʧ, ʒʌʒ]
> bridge [brɪʤ], not [brɪʧ, brɪʒ]

[ŋ]

The sound [ŋ] does not occur in Russian. The student readily understands diagrams and demonstrations showing that the back of the tongue is raised to touch the soft palate, the latter being dropped so as to leave the nasal passages open, and he makes the sound equally readily. But he experiences difficulty in stopping it without adding [g] or [k]. A good corrective device is to have the student pronounce sustained [m], [n], and [ŋ] in succession, thus: [m::::], [n::::], [ŋ::::]. The fact that he can pronounce [m] and [n] without plosives, since he is used to them, will help him with the [ŋ]. Pronouncing paired [ŋg, ŋ]-words will help "split" [ŋg] and [ŋ] apart.

> finger [ˈfɪŋgɚ, ˈfɪŋgə] – singer [ˈsɪŋɚ, ˈsɪŋə]
> tingle [ˈtɪŋgəł] – bringing [ˈbrɪŋɪŋ]
> mingle [ˈmɪŋgəł] – clinging [ˈklɪŋɪŋ]
> tangle [ˈtæŋgəł] – wronging [ˈrͻŋɪŋ]
> jungle [ˈʤʌŋgəł] – flinging [ˈflɪŋɪŋ]
> English [ˈɪŋglɪʃ] – song [sͻŋ]
> longest [ˈlͻŋgəst, ˈlͻŋgɪst] – long [lͻŋ]

[r]

The sound [ɹ] has already been discussed. A shortened form of it serves passably for the consonantal [r] as in *roll* [rouł]. The tongue points toward the middle of the roof of the mouth, as before. The trill must be suppressed—a difficult assignment for the Russian. Word list:

> ring [rɪŋ], not [ɼɪŋ]
> ride [raɪd], not [ɼaɪd]
> wrote [rout], not [ɼout]

[θ], [ð]

The sounds [θ] and [ð] do not occur in Russian. The prevalent substitutions are [s] and [z] or [t] and [d]. The best way to teach the two sounds seems to be to demonstrate them at first as interdentals, made with the tongue visibly protruding between the teeth. Later, as articulatory speed develops, the tongue will come no farther forward than the back surface of the upper teeth, which is the normal position with English speaking people. Word list:

> this [ðɪs], not [zɪs] nor [dɪs]
> that [ðæt], not [zæt] nor [dæt]
> those [ðoʊz], not [zoʊz] nor [doʊz]
> thing [θɪŋ], not [sɪŋ] nor [tɪŋ]
> three [θri], not [sri] nor [tri]
> throw [θroʊ], not [sroʊ] nor [troʊ]

[h]

The sound [h] does not occur in Russian. The student will substitute [x]. He must be shown that [h] is not made in the back of the mouth, as is [x], but in the larynx. Demonstrations of panting sounds seem to convey the idea of [h]. Much patient, repetitive practice is needed. Word list:

> how [haʊ], not [xaʊ]
> hide [haɪd], not [xaɪd]
> hoe [hoʊ], not [xoʊ]
> who [hu], not [xu]
> have [hæv], not [xæv]

[w]

The sound [w] occurs in Russian as a labial glide, as in кофи [ˈkwɔ(i)fɪ] (coffee), or as a variant of [u] in [ui], as in пожалуиста [paˈʒaɫwɪstə] < [paˈʒaɫuistə] (please). But the sound is not significant and does not "register" as [w] with the Russian speaker. Moreover, Russian newspapers and books transliterate English [w] as [v]. For instance, *Washington* is transliterated вашингтон, indicating the pronunciation [ˈvaʃˈɪŋgtən]. Accordingly, the speaker tends to pronounce *w* as [v]. It is valuable to point out the [w]'s in Russian pronunciation, as above. But better still is to explain that [w] is based on [u]—that the "leaping point" of the [w]-glide is [u]. *We* can therefore be transcribed and at first pronounced as [u-i], *wall* as [u-ɔɫ], etc. Soon the speed of pronouncing the [u] can be quickened, so that [wi] and [wɔɫ] eventuate. List:

> weal [wiɫ], not veal [viɫ]
> wine [waɪn], not vine [vaɪn]
> wide [waɪd], not vied [vaɪd]

[ʌ]

The sound [ʌ] does not occur in Russian. The best approach to it is to put together [h] and [u] for a beginning. *When* can then be transcribed and pronounced as [hu-ɛn], *while* as [hu-aɪl], etc. Soon [hu] can be quickened, and the friction-producing stricture changed from the glottis to the interior of the mouth and the lips, so as to produce [ʌ]. The Russian substitution is [v]. List:

> why [ʌaɪ], not vie [vaɪ]
> wheel [ʌil], not veal [vil]
> what [ʌɑt, ʌɒt]
> when [ʌɛn]
> which [ʌɪtʃ]
> whether ['ʌɛðɚ, 'ʌɛðə]

Certain habits of the Russian tend to persist in the Russian's rendition of English:

1. The unvoicing of final [b, d, g, ʒ]. List:

> tab [tæb], not tap [tæp]
> bad [bæd], not bat [bæt]
> tag [tæg], not tack [tæk]
> rouge [ruʒ], not [ruʃ]

2. Voicing and unvoicing by regressive assimilation persists in English. List:

> fish bait [fɪʃ beɪt], not [fɪʒ beɪt]
> this boy [ðɪs bɔɪ], not [ðɪz bɔɪ]
> back down [bæk daʊn], not [bæg daʊn]
> rag tag [ræg tæg], not [ræk tæg]
> write back [raɪt bæk], not [raɪd bæk]

3. The palatalization of consonants followed by [e], [ɛ], [i], [ɪ] persists in English. List:

> fate [feɪt], not [f̡eɪt]
> nest [nɛst], not [ņɛst]
> see [si], not [ș̡i]
> tin [tɪn], not [ţɪn]

A passage of uncorrected Russian dialect: xaf ju ţɛņ fiņgjɛřs?

ņɔ ai ḑu ņɑţ xaf ţɛņ fiņgjɛřs, ai xaf et fiņgjɛřs ɛņţ ţu ţams. vaɪ is iḑ zaţ ņipļ ɔlves xaf kaʊņţəţ sɔ impɛřfɪkţlɪ? oņ itʃʳ fuţ ai xaf faɪf fiņgjɛřs—ţɛn ɔļţʊgjezɛř, baḑ zɛř ař nɔ ţams.

Transcribe in a Russian dialect of English:

The Lower Depths, Maxim Gorky (excerpt).

NATASHA. Thieves?

LUKA. Exactly! Thieves creeping in! I took my gun—I went out. I looked and saw two of them opening a window—and so busy that they didn't even see me. I yell: "Hey there—get out of here!" And they turn on me with their axes—I warn them to stand back, or I'd shoot—and as I speak, I keep on covering them with my gun, first the one, then the other—they go down on their knees, as if to implore me for mercy. And by that time I was furious—because of those axes, you see—and so I say to them: "I was chasing you, you scoundrels—and you didn't go. Now you go and break off some stout branches!"—and they did so—and I say: "Now—one of you lie down and let the other one flog him!" So they obey me and flog each other—and then they begin to implore me again. "Grandfather," they say, "for God's sake give us some bread! We're hungry!" There's thieves for you, my dear!

Bibliography

Birkett, G. A., *A Modern Russian Course* (London: Methuen and Company, 1942).

Bondar, *Bondar's Simplified Russian Method* (New York: Pitman Publishing Corporation, no date).

Potapova, Nina, *Russian* (Moscow: Foreign Languages Publishing House, 1945).

Semeonoff, Anna H., *A New Russian Grammar* (New York: E. P. Dutton and Company, Inc., 1943).

Scerba, L., *Court exposé de la prononciation russe* (London: Trinity College, l'Association Phonétique Internationale, 1911).

Trager, George L., "The Phonemes of Russian," in *Language*, Vol. X, No. 4, December, 1934, pages 334–344.

Trofimov, M. V., and Daniel Jones, *The Pronunciation of Russian* (Cambridge: Cambridge University Press, 1923).

Brazilian Portuguese Dialect

The Sounds of Brazilian Portuguese; the Brazilian Dialect of English

Brazilian Portuguese, like American English, has come to have more than provincial status; the speech of educated Brazilians has taken its place as a standard Portuguese dialect. Like American English, Brazilian Portuguese is made up of various component dialects, prominent among which are those of Rio de Janeiro (the Carioca dialect) and of São Paulo (the Paulista dialect).

Of the areas where Portuguese is spoken, in addition to Portugal herself and Brazil, we may name the Azores; the Madeira Islands; the Cape Verde Islands; parts of West Africa, of India, of the Malay Peninsula, and of Hawaii; and communities of the Pacific and Atlantic coasts of the United States, particularly in Massachusetts, Rhode Island, and New Jersey.[1] Whereas in Portugal, where about seven million of the some 57 million Portuguese-speaking people of the world live,[2] the dialect between and including Lisbon and Coimbra is regarded as standard, in Brazil, where, out of a total of over 48 million people, about 44 million Portuguese-speaking people live, there is a considerable tendency to regard the Carioca of Rio de Janeiro as a kind of standard Brazilian. The government designates it as the model for schools, and the stage and radio use it.[3] These pages deal principally with Carioca; but occasional comparisons are made with Paulista and other Brazilian dialects, and there is added a brief section on differences between Brazilian Portuguese and European Portuguese.

The spellings used herein take cognizance of the reformed spelling, the *nova ortografia*, first formulated in 1911 and officially adopted in 1916 by the Portuguese government. This reformed spelling has been subsequently slightly

---

[1] Leo Pap, *Portuguese-American Speech* (New York: King's Crown Press, Columbia University, 1948), pp. 1–15.

[2] E. B. Williams, *From Latin to Portuguese* (Philadelphia: University of Pennsylvania Press, 1938), p. 17.

[3] Christopher Stavrou, *Brazilian-Portuguese Pronunciation* (Philadelphia: David McKay Co., 1947), p. 3.

altered, especially by the "Acordo Ortografico Luso-Brazileiro," on the basis
of which the *nova ortografia* was adopted by Brazil in 1931.

As in analogous chapters earlier in this book, the treatment of the sounds of
Brazilian Portuguese, as given in these pages, is phonetic rather than phonemic.
Following the explanation of the sounds, there is a section touching upon the
speaking of English by Brazilians.

The Vowels of Brazilian Portuguese

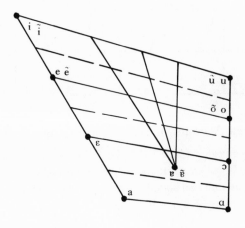

The Diphthongs of Brazilian Portuguese

iu	ai	ẽĭ
eu	ɑu	ɐ̃ĭ
ei	oi	õĭ
ɛu	ɔi	ũĭ
ɛi		ɐ̃ũ

The Consonants of Brazilian Portuguese

	Bi-labial	Labio-Dental	Dental	Alveolar	Palatal	Velar
Plosive	p b		t d			k g
Nasal	m	ɱ	n		ɲ	ŋ
Lateral			l	ɫ	λ	
Trilled				ɾ (r)[4]		
Fricative		f v		s z ʃˑ ʃ ʒˑ ʒ		x
Frictionless Continuant	w				j	(w)

Detailed Account of Brazilian Portuguese Sounds

As previously indicated (page 512), the following is primarily a discussion of the sounds of Brazilian Portuguese, principally as found in the dialect of Rio de Janeiro. The differing sounds as found in standard European Portuguese (of the Lisbon-Coimbra area) are listed at the end.

Vowels

[i]

The Portuguese [i] resembles the French [i], but is less tense. The various spellings are as follows:

1. *i* stressed wherever found (except before a nasal), as in *princípio* [pɾĩˈsipiu],[5] *invisível* [iɱviˈzivɛɫ], *incrível* [iŋˈkrivɛɫ], *jesuíta* [ʒezuˈitɐ],[6] *isso* [ˈisu], *mira* [ˈmiɾɐ], *visita* [viˈzitɐ], *si* [si], *fila* [ˈfilɐ], *sitio* [ˈsitiu], *ir* [ix], *digno* [ˈdiginu], *dia* [diɐ],[7] *tio* [tiu].

2. *i* unstressed wherever found (except where alternatively pronounced [j]

---

[4] This [r] is a tongue-point trill, used by many Paulistas where Cariocas use [x], a slightly retroflex velar spirant, closely akin to the [x] of German. It is optional in song, oratory, and radio; is freely understood by speakers of all dialects; and is used by some speakers alternatively with [x].

[5] See p. 528 for alternate transcription of *i* in unstressed *i* + vowel as [j]. See also Stavrou, pp. 9, 59 *passim*.

[6] Stavrou, p. 42, prefers [a] for unstressed *a* in final syllables.

[7] See p. 528 for alternate transcription of stressed *i* before vowel as [ij], thus, *dia* [ˈdijɐ]. See also Stavrou, p. 8.

before a vowel), as in *pimenta* [piˈmẽntu],[8] *pretérito* [preˈteɾitu], *sitio* [ˈsitiu], *radio* [ˈxadiu], *serie* [ˈsɛɾii], *infancia* [ĩɱˈfẽsiɐ], *militar* [miliˈtax], *nacional* [nasiõˈnał], *adiar* [adiˈax], *hiato* [iˈatu], *juri* [ˈʒuɾi].

NOTE: Colloquially, [i] is inserted to break up the consonant clusters *bs*, *bz*, *bj* [bʒ], *dj* [dʒ], as in *absoluto* [abisoˈlutu], *objeto* [ɔbiˈʒɛtu], *adjetivo* [adiʒɛˈtivu]. This insertion is, however, considered a "vice" ("vício de linguagem") by grammarians.[9]

3. *i* in the diphthongs [oi], [ɔi], and [ui], as in *boiar* [boiˈjax], *pois* [ˈpoiʃˈ], *oiro* [ˈoiɾu]; *heroico* [eˈɾɔiku], *faróis* [faˈɾoiʃˈ], *fui* [fui], *azuis* [aˈzuiʃˈ].

4. *e* in the diphthong [ui], as in *conclue* [kõŋˈklui], *azues* [aˈzuiʃˈ].

5. *e* [i], the conjunction *and*, when unstressed; also *e* in other unstressed monosyllables such as *me* [mi], *te* [ti], *lhe* [λi], *se* [si], *que* [ki] (interrogative *who*).

6. *e* in final unstressed syllables, as in *gente* [ˈʒẽntʃˈi] ([e] for final [i] in Paulista), *bule* [ˈbuli], *este* [ˈeʃˈtʃˈi], *arte* [ˈaxtʃˈi], *morre* [ˈmoxi], *arvores* [ˈaxvoɾiʃˈ].

NOTE: Final unstressed [i] is very frequently unvoiced, as are final unstressed syllables generally. This variation between voicing and voicelessness is non-significant.

7. *e* in *ex*, *es*, *des* + consonant, *el*, etc., before a stressed syllable and not followed by [ʃ, ʒ] (as distinguished from [ʃˈ, ʒˈ] – see pages 527, 528), [ɲ] or [λ], as in *exclusivo* [iʃˈkluˈzivu], *esperto* [iʃˈˈpɛxtu], *despejar* [diʃˈpeˈʒax], *eletrico* [iˈlɛtɾiku],[10] *esmolas* [iʒˈˈmɔlɐʃˈ].

8. *e* before stressed vowel, as in *cear* [siˈax],[11] *ceei* [siˈei].

NOTE: Paulista does not reduce unstressed *e* to [i] in such words as *cear* but uses [e] instead.

9. *e* (not nasalized) in a syllable immediately preceding a stressed syllable containing *e* or *i* as in *devi* [diˈvi], *feliz* [fiˈliʃˈ], *pepino* [piˈpinu].

NOTES: (a) See exceptions, page 516, for learned words.
(b) Some dialects pronounce any unstressed *e* as [i].

10. *e* post-tonic and followed by a final vowel, as in *férreo* [ˈfɛxiu], *fêmea* [ˈfẽmiɐ].[12]

11. *e* irregularly in *paletó* [paliˈtɔ], *pequeno* [piˈkẽnu], *segundo* [siˈgũndu], *senhor* [sĭˈɲox], *senhora* [sĭˈɲɔɾa].

---

[8] It is a debatable question whether, phonetically considered, the *n* of *pimento* retains an individual existence after nasalizing the *e*. The view followed here is that the homorganic [t] tends to preserve it. See under nasal vowels, pp. 521 ff., and under [n], p. 525. For *n* preserved as [ŋ] before [k, g], see p. 521. For *n*, *m* preserved as [m] before [p, b], see p. 521. For *n* preserved as [ɱ], the labio-dental [ɱ], before [f, v], see p. 521. For all such instances, see Stavrou, pp. 59 *passim*.

[9] Eduardo Carlos Pereira, *Gramática Expositiva*. (São Paulo: Companhia Editora Nacional, 1901), p. 268.

[10] Stavrou prefers [e].

[11] Stavrou, p. 16.

[12] Stavrou, p. 14, holds that unstressed *e* in words like these is pronounced [j].

[e]

The Brazilian [e] is similar to French [e], but not so tense.

1. *e* stressed, as in *mesa* [ˈmezɐ], *cedo* [ˈsedu], *terço* [ˈtexsu], *seda* [ˈsedɐ].

NOTE: Stressed *e* is also pronounced [ɛ]. (See under [ɛ] below.) There are few dependable rules for distinguishing the pronunciation of stressed *e* as [e] or [ɛ]. The correct sound, generally speaking, must be learned with the word. However, in cases where the location of the stress is exceptional, diacritics are used to mark the stress, and these distinguish [e] from [ɛ]. Thus *ê* = [e] and *é* = [ɛ].

2. *e* unstressed except when final, nasalized, or in initial *ex, es, des* in certain contexts (see page 515), as in *refletir* [xefleˈtix], *reconhecer* [xekuɲeˈsex], *fechar* [feˈʃax], *telephone* [teleˈfõni].

3. *e* in *ei, eu*, as in *lei* [lei], *rei* [xei], *leu* [leu], *meu* [meu]. The spelling *eu* invariably yields [e]. (But *éu* = [ɛu], as in *chapéu* [ʃaˈpɛu].

4. *e* in certain learned words despite the fact that the vowel of the succeeding syllable is [i] (see page 515), as in *periodico* [peɾiˈɔdiku, peɾiˈɔdʒˑiku], *dedicar* [dediˈkax, dedʒˑiˈkax], *reciproco* [xeˈsipɾoku]).[13]

5. *e* in certain learned words despite immediately succeeding vowels, as in *deísmo* [deˈiʒˑmu], *preocupar* [pɾeokuˈpax], *veículo* [veˈikulu].

6. *ê* as in *vê* [ve], *sêlo* [ˈselu], *bêbedo* [ˈbebedu], *crê* [kɾe]. This spelling is invariably pronounced [e].

NOTE: Umlaut is a characteristic feature of Portuguese words and influences the use of [e, ɛ] and [o, ɔ] in cognates. Open stressed radical *e* [ɛ] and *o* [ɔ] frequently become [e] and [o] in derivative or inflectional forms ending in *o* [u], as in *pega-apêgo* [pɛgɐ-aˈpegu], *roda-rôdo* [xɔdɐ-ˈxodu]. However, historical considerations of Portuguese are beyond the scope of this work, and no attempt will be made here to formulate rules for the use of [ɛ-e], [ɔ-o] on this basis. For discussion of the principles involved, see William J. Entwistle, *The Spanish Language* (London: Faber and Faber, Ltd., 1936, page 284); Pereira, page 127; Stavrou, pages 44–49 ff. Stavrou has developed rules for numerous verb-forms and cognate noun-forms.

7. *e* in *que* [ke] (what).

8. *ei* as in *peito* [ˈpetu], *peixe* [ˈpeʃi], *Brasileiro* [bɾaziˈleɾu].

NOTE: *ei* is also pronounced as the diphthong [ei] by some speakers.

[ɛ]

1. *e* stressed as in *sete* [ˈsɛtʃˑi], *bebe* [ˈbɛbi]. (But see note under [e], No. 1 above.)

---

[13] Some non-final unstressed *o*'s are at times pronounced [u], thus: [xeˈsipɾuku].

2. *é* as in *é* [ɛ], *sé* [sɛ], *pé* [pɛ], *crédito* [ˈkɾɛditu], *réis* [ˈxɛiʃˀ], *chapéu* [ʃaˈpɛu], *século* [ˈsɛkulu]. This spelling is invariably pronounced [ɛ].

3. *e* unstressed before *l* or *r* final in a syllable, as in *amavel* [ɐ̆ˈmavɛɫ], *delgado* [dɛɫˈgadu], *caráter* [kaˈɾatɛx], *éter* [ˈɛtɛx]. These spellings are invariably pronounced [ɛ].

4. *è*, as in *lèpidamente* [lɛpidaˈmẽntʃˀi].

[a]

In Brazilian [a] varies from a low front to a low central position.

1. *a* stressed or unstressed when not final, nasalized nor followed by *l* or *u*. Cf. *casado* [kaˈzadu], *atuar* [atuˈax].

2. *á*, as in *amável* [ɐ̆ˈmavɛɫ], *análise* [ɐ̆ˈnalizi]; *à* (the contraction of preposition plus feminine article), as in *à casa* [ˈakazɐ].

[ɑ]

1. *a* before *l* final or before *u*, as in *mal* [mɑɫ], *mau* [mɑu].
2. *á* before *u*, as in *Áustria* [ˈɑuʃˀtɾiɐ].

[ɐ]

1. *a* in unstressed final syllables, as in *casada* [kaˈzadɐ], *alta* [ˈaɫtɐ].

NOTE: It is a debatable question whether to transcribe final unstressed *a* as [a] or [ɐ].[14] There is a similar problem with the final unstressed *a* in Spanish and Italian, where in this book [a] has been chosen for the relatively broad transcription used. But since in Brazilian the nasalized [ɐ̃] must necessarily be used, and since the unstressed final *a* sounds much like a denasalized [ɐ̃], i.e., [ɐ], it seems reasonable to use [ɐ] as in No. 1 above.

NOTE: [ɐ] is used in European Portuguese in certain stressed syllables (see page 529);[15] the corresponding sounds in Brazilian Portuguese are [a] or, before nasals, [ɐ̃] (see page 522).

[ɔ]

1. *o* stressed (not followed by a nasal consonant, and not in *oi* or *ou*), as in *nova* [ˈnɔvɐ], *pobre* [ˈpɔbɾi], *volta* [ˈvɔltɐ], *solo* [ˈsɔlu].

NOTE: Stressed *o* is also pronounced [o]. (See under [o] below.) There are few dependable rules for the pronunciation of stressed *o* as [ɔ] or [o]. The correct sound must, generally speaking, be learned with the word. But, in cases where the stress is exceptional, diacritics are used to mark the stress, and these diacritics also distinguish [o] from [ɔ]. Thus *ô* = [o] and *ó* = [ɔ], as in *avô*

---

[14] Stavrou, p. 42, expresses the opinion that [ɐ] does not exist in Brazil.
[15] Laudelimo Feire, *Grammatica Expositiva, Curso Superior* (Sao Paulo: Companhia Editora Nacional, 1941), p. 26.

[aˈvo] (*grandfather*), *avó* [aˈvɔ] (*grandmother*). See note on umlaut relative to [e, ɛ], page 516; the situation for [o, ɔ] is a parallel one.

2. *ó* as in *pó* [pɔ], *petróleo* [peˈtrɔlɪu], *móbil* [ˈmɔbił], *sólido* [ˈsɔlidu]. The pronunciation of this spelling is invariable.

3. Pretonic *o* before [ks], as in *oxítono* [ɔkˈsɪtõnu], *occipital* [ɔksipiˈtał]. (Pretonic here means in any syllable previous to the tonic or stressed syllable. Ordinarily, pretonic means immediately before the stressed syllable.)

[o]

The Brazilian [o] is the "pure" [o], not the diphthong [oʊ] as in English. It is comparable to German [o] in *froh* [fro:], French *eau* [o].

1. *o* stressed, as in *todo* [ˈtodu], *ovo* [ˈovu].

NOTE: Stressed *o* is also pronounced [ɔ]. (See under [ɔ] above.) There are few reliable rules for the pronunciation of *o* as [o] or [ɔ]. The correct sound must, generally speaking, be learned with the word. (See note on umlaut, page 516. But see also note on diacritics under [ɔ] above.)

2. *ô* as in *pôs* [ˈpoʃ], *lôbrego* [ˈlobɾegu]. The pronunciation of this spelling is invariable.

3. *o* unstressed and not final (in careful speech), especially in Sao Paulo and rather generally outside Rio de Janeiro, as in *colocar* [koloˈkax], *recíproco* [reˈsipɾoku]. In general, even in the capital, it is seldom that the pronunciation of unstressed non-final *o* as [o] will attract criticism, unless with certain words (see list under [u], page 519). Paulistas pronounce even final unstressed *o* as [o] (see under [u], page 519). In a polysyllable (except *porque* [puxˈke]), the *o* in *por* appears almost invariably to be pronounced [o], as in *portador* [poxtaˈdɔx]. (But see *portanto* [puxˈtẽntu], *Portugal* [puxtuˈgał], etc.) The same may nearly always be said of *o* in a closed syllable immediately preceding a stressed syllable, as in *olfato* [ołˈfatu], *objeto* [obˈʒɛtu], *voltar* [vołˈtax]; but a considerable number of words of this class are pronounced with [u] (see list page 519). However, in quite formal speech, [o] may be restored, even with these.

4. *ou* as in *soubesse* [soˈbɛsi], *toucador* [tokaˈdox], *louça* [ˈlosɐ], *ouro* [ˈoɾu], *louco* [ˈloku], *louro* [ˈloɾu].

NOTE: *ou* in stressed syllables is pronounced [oʊ] by some speakers. But [ɔ] never occurs with this spelling.

5. *o* in *oi*, as in *noivo* [ˈnoivu].

6. *o* post-tonic plus vowel in careful speech, as in *névoa* [ˈnevoɐ], *pascoa* [ˈpaskoɐ]. (In rapid speech this *o* is pronounced [w]. See page 529. Learned words also retain this [o], as in *álcool* [ˈałkoɔł].)

[u]

In Brazilian, [u] is not so tense nor so high as the French *ou* [u].

1. *u, ú*, stressed or unstressed (except as below), as in *subir* [su'bix], *culpa* ['kulpɐ], *tribu* ['tribu], *pacú* [pa'ku], *Xingú* [ʃĩŋ'gu], *recuar* [xeku'ax], *saúde* [sa'udʒ'i].

NOTES: (a) See page 518 under [o] for *u* in *ou* [o].

(b) See page 522 under [ũ] for *u* before a nasal.

The letter *u* is not pronounced in the syllables *que, qui*—neither in monosyllables nor in polysyllables. Cf. *quilo* ['kilu], *quer* [kɛx].

The letter *u*, unpronounced, serves as a diacritic to preserve the "hard" [g] before *e* and *i* in the syllables *gui, gue*, as in *guia* ['giɐ], *guerra* ['gɛxɐ].

See page 528 for *u* pronounced [w] before a vowel in *qua, gua*.

2. *u* even though unstressed, as in two verbs, *argüir* [ɑxgu'ix], *redargüido* [xedaxgu'idu].

NOTE: Other instances of *ü* are pronounced [w].

3. *u* in the diphthongs *eu, au*, as in *seu* [seu], *autor* [ɑu'tox].

4. *o* in monosyllables when unstressed in context, as in *o* [u]; *os* [uʃ'] before voiceless consonants ([uʒ'] before voiced consonants, [uz] before vowels in rapid speech); *por* [pux], *do* [du], *no* [nu].

5. *o* final, unstressed, or in unstressed *os*, as in *porco* ['poxku], *colo* ['kɔlu], *novo* ['novu], *passos* ['pasuʃ'], *mato* ['matu], *portos* ['pɔxtuʃ']. (Final *o* remains [o] in the dialect of São Paulo, as noted above.)

6. *o* non-nasalized, unstressed but not final, may, it appears, except in the few instances where it is pronounced [ɔ] (compare [ɔ], page 517), be pronounced [o] in careful speech, especially outside Rio de Janeiro; but there is little doubt that, especially within Rio de Janeiro, such pronunciation is, with certain words, regarded as pedantic, the popular pronunciation being [u]. Following are some instances where [u] is used:

a. *o* post-tonic but not final, as in *método* ['metudu], *recíproco* [xe'sipruku], *fósforo* ['fɔʃ'furu]. But see *período* [pe'riodu].

b. *o* pretonic in a few words, as in *coberto* [ku'bɛxtu]. Some words particularly likely to be pronounced with [u] pretonically in informal speech are *colher* [ku'ʎɛx], *sotaque* [su'taki], *político* [pu'litiku], *português* [puxtu'geʃ'], *tostão* [tuʃ'-'tɐ̃ũ], *colega* [ku'lɛgɐ], *possível* [pu'sivɛł], *almoçar* [ałmu'sax], *gordura* [gux'durɐ], *portanto* [pux'tɐ̃ntu].[16]

c. *o* pretonic before a vowel with which it does not form a diphthong, as in *doente* [du'ẽntʃ'i], *poeta* [pu'ɛtɐ].

7. *u* before *e, o*, or *a* post-tonically (according to some authorities), as in *tênue* ['tẽnui], *inócuo* [i'nɔkuu], *mutua* ['mutuɐ].

Diphthongs

[iu]

1. *iu*, finally, as in *viu* [viu], *partiu* [pax'tiu].
2. *io*, finally, as in *rio* [xiu], *tio* [tiu].

NOTE: Final *io* may also be pronounced as a dissyllable, with [j] inserted, thus: ['xiju], ['tiju].

[ei]

ei, as in *lei* [lei], *Brasileiro* [bɾazi'leiɾu], *feito* ['feitu].

NOTE: Many speakers reduce [ei] to [e] (see page 516).

[eu]

eu as in *meu* [meu], *deu* [deu].

[ɛu]

éu as in *chapéu* [ʃa'pɛu], *céu* [sɛu].

[ɛi]

ei, stressed and unstressed, as in *reis* [xɛiʃˑ], *hotéis* [o'tɛiʃˑ].

[ai]

ai, stressed and unstressed, as in *pai* [pai], *mais* [maiʃˑ], *pairar* [pai'ɾax].

NOTE: Some speakers pronounce [ai] before [ʃˑ] as [a]. On the other hand, they may pronounce *a* as [ai] before *s*, *z*, as in *alias* [ali'aiʃˑ], *rapaz* [xa'paiʃˑ] for [ali'aʃˑ], [xa'paʃˑ].

[au]

1. *au*, stressed and unstressed. Examples: *mau* [mau], *causar* [kau'zax].
2. *ao* in unstressed *ao* (*to the*) [au].

NOTE: *aú* is not a diphthong. Compare *baú* [ba'u].[17]

[oi]

1. *oi*, as in *coisa* ['koizɐ], *noite* ['noitʃˑi], *foi* [foi].

[ɔi]

1. *ói*, as in *faróis* [fa'ɾɔiʃˑ].

[ui]

1. *ui*, as in *fui* [fui], *uivar* [ui'vax].
2. *ue*, as in *azues* [a'zuiʃˑ].

---

[17] E. B. Williams, *First Brazilian Grammar* (New York: Crofts, 1944), p. 7. Stavrou, p. 18.

Nasal Vowels and Diphthongs

Nasal vowels and diphthongs are characteristic of Portuguese. Nasality in "pure" vowels occurs frequently in French, but the nasal diphthongs of Portuguese are unique among the principal European languages.[18] Nasalization is indicated in several ways. The vowel of the last syllable of a word may by marked with a tilde (Port. *til*) placed over an *a* or an *o*, as in *lã* [lɐ̃], *põe* [põĩ]. In a diphthong the tilde is placed over the stressed element, but the nasality extends to both the elements, as in *tão* [tɐ̃ũ]. Final *m* indicates nasalization of the preceding sound, as in *bom* [bõ]. Within a word, *n*, *m*, or *nh* will nasalize a preceding vowel, though with unstressed vowel plus nasal plus stressed vowel, the nasalization may or may not occur, as in *camada* [kɐ̃ˈmadɐ, kaˈmadɐ], *binario* [bĩˈnaɾiu, biˈnaɾiu], *nacional* [nasiõˈnaɫ, nasioˈnaɫ], *fumar* [fũˈmax, fuˈmax].

The problem of what becomes of the nasal consonant phonetically, once it has nasalized the preceding vowel, is a complex one. Here follow some of the various outcomes.

1. *m* and *n*, when intervocalic, continue to exist in their own right, as in *Dona* [ˈdõnɐ], *drama* [ˈdɾɐ̃mɐ].

2. *nh* [ɲ], being always intervocalic, continues to exist in its own right, as in *banho* [ˈbɐ̃ɲu].

3. *n* before *t*, *d* maintains an existence as [n], often very slight, and possible to disregard in transcription, as in *conde* [ˈkõ(n)dʒˈi], *conta* [ˈkõ(n)tɐ]; before [k, g], as [ŋ], as in *incluir* [ĩ(ŋ)kluˈix], *inglês* [ĩ(ŋ)ˈgleʃˈ]; before [f, v], as [ɱ],[19] as in *infantil* [ĩ(ɱ)fɐ̃ˈtiɫ], *invadir* [ĩ(ɱ)vaˈdix]. In each of these cases, it will be noted that the residual nasal is of the same order homorganically as the consonant following; thus, [n, t, d], [ŋ, k, g], [ɱ, f, v].

4. In liaison, *m* behaves in a similar fashion, persisting as [m], often a light [m], before [p, b], as in *bem preparado* [bẽĩ(m) prepaˈxadu], *be(m) banhado* [bẽĩm bɐ̃ˈɲadu]; as [ŋ], before [k, g]; and as [ɱ], before [f, v].

5. *m* may even assert itself as [ɲ] in liaison intervocalically, as in *vem o trem* [vẽĩɲuˈtɾẽĩ].

6. [ɐ̃], even, may develop [m, n, ŋ] in liaison, as in *lã tinta* [lɐ̃nˈtĩntɐ], *lã branca* [lɐ̃mˈbɾɐ̃ŋkɐ], *vão cantar* [vɐ̃ũŋkɐ̃nˈtax].

7. But both within words and in liaison, [m] and [n] before any consonant except [p, b, t, d, k, g, f, v] lose identity as such, merely nasalizing the preceding vowel, as in *bem suportado* [bẽĩ supoxˈtadu], *consulta* [kõˈsuɫtɐ].

---

[18] Gonçalves Viana, *Vocabulário Ortographico e Ortoépico*, p. 15.

[19] A sound related acoustically to [m], but made with the upper teeth resting lightly on the lower lip, as for [f] and [v].

Nasal Vowels

[ĭ]

1. *îm, în,* as in *índole* ['ĭndoli], *altímetro* [al'tĭmetɾu].

2. *in, im, inh,* as in *tinta* ['tĭntɐ], *vim* [vĭ], *inseto* [ĭ'sɛtu], *Coimbra* [ko'ĭmbɾe], *capim* [ka'pĭ], *ninho* ['nĭɲu], *invadir* [ĭɲva'dix].

NOTE: Final [ĭ] is always spelled *im,* the *m* not being pronounced, unless in liaison (see page 521).

3. *e* before nasal (typically *n*—followed by *i*), as in *menino* [mĭ'nĭnu].

4. *en, em* unstressed before a consonant, as in *empurrar* [ĭmpu'xax], *ensinar* [ĭsi'nax].

5. *i* in open syllable before nasal may be [ĭ] or [i], as in *binario* [bĭ'naɾiu, bi'naɾiu].

[ẽ]

êm, ên, as in *fêmea* ['fẽmiɐ], *agência* [a'ʒẽsiɐ].

en, em, enh, as in *doenca* [do'ẽsɐ], *embelecer* [ẽmbɛle'sex], *vento* ['vẽntu], *endereço* [ẽnde'ɾesu], *desenha* [de'zẽɲɐ].

NOTE: Final [ẽ] is always spelled *em,* the *m* not being pronounced, unless in liaison.

NOTE: Stressed *an* before *d, t,* pronounced [ẽ], has been noted in Rio de Janeiró, as in *grande* [grẽdʒʼi], *imigrante* [ĭmi'grẽtʃʼi].[20]

[ɐ̃]

1. *an, am, âm,* as in *ansiedade* [ɐ̃sie'dadʒʼi], *banco* ['bɐ̃ŋku], *romance* [xo'mɐ̃si], *pranto* ['pɾɐ̃ntu], *Tupan* [tu'pɐ̃], *mancho* ['mɐ̃ʃu], *camara* ['kɐ̃maɾa], *canhão* [kɐ̃'ɲɐ̃u].

NOTE: *am* final is never pronounced [ɐ̃] alone, but always [ɐ̃u] (see page 523).

2. *ã,* as in *lã* [lɐ̃], *irmã* [ix'mɐ̃].

NOTE: Final [ɐ̃] is usually spelled *ã,* but occasionally *an.*

3. *ãm, ãn,* as in *camera* ['kɐ̃maɾɐ], *ânsia* ['ɐ̃siɐ].

[õ]

1. *ô,* as in *fenômeno* [fe'nõmẽnu], *quilómetro* [ki'lõmetɾu].

2. *on, om, onh,* stressed, as in *onça* ['õsɐ], *honra* ['õxɐ], *quilombo* [ki'lõmbu], *bomba* ['bõmbɐ], *bom* [bõ], *Dom* [dõ], *vergonha* [vɛx'gõɲɐ].

NOTE: Final [õ] is always spelled *om,* the *m* not being pronounced, unless in liaison.

[ũ]

1. *un, um,* as in *mundo* [mũndu], *chumbo* ['ʃũmbu], *algum* [aɫ'gũ], *um* [ũ].

---

[20] Stavrou, p. 7.

NOTE: Final [ũ] is always spelled *um*, the *m* not being pronounced, unless in liaison.

2. *ûm, ûn*, as in *núncio* [ˈnũsiu], *húmido* [ˈũmidu].

3. *om, onh*, pretonic, as in *comêço* [kũˈmesu], *conhecer* [kũɲeˈsex].

NOTE: This pronunciation of *o* is not regarded as standard.

Nasal Diphthongs

[ẽĩ]

1. *em* final, stressed, as in *bem* [bẽĩ], *tem* [tẽĩ], *vem* [vẽĩ]; unstressed, as in *vivem* [ˈvivẽĩ], *devem* [ˈdɛvẽĩ], *viagem* [viˈaʒẽĩ], *lêem* [ˈleẽĩ], *crêem* [ˈkɾeẽĩ], *pôem* [ˈpõẽĩ].

2. *ém* final, as in *Belém* [beˈlẽĩ].

3. *en* in final *ens*, as in *trens* [tɾẽĩʃ], *viagens* [viˈaʒẽĩʃ], *contens* [kõnˈtẽĩʃ].

4. *êm* final in the words *têm* and *vêm* may have a doubling of this diphthong in the pronunciations [tẽĩẽi] and vẽiẽi], but is sometimes shortened to [tẽĩ] and [vẽĩ].

NOTE: The older spelling of these words was *teem* and *veem*.

5. *en, enh*, non-final in some words, as *enviar* [ẽĩŋviˈax], *nenhum* [nẽĩɲũ] or [nẽĩũ] (stress on either syllable according to context).

[ẽ̆ĩ]

1. *ãe*, as in *mãe* [mẽ̆ĩ], *pães* [pẽ̆ĩʃ].

[ẽ̆ũ]

1. *ão*, as in *órfão* [ˈɔxfẽ̆ũ], *pão* [pẽ̆ũ], *mão* [mẽ̆ũ].

2. *am*, as in *falam* [ˈfalẽ̆ũ], *vôam* [ˈvoẽ̆ũ].

[õĩ]

1. *õe*, as in *põe* [põĩ].

[ũĩ]

1. *ui* in the words *mui* [mũĩ] and *muito* [mũˈĩntu].

NOTE: Observe that there is no tilde. Note also the supernumerary [n] pronounced in [mũˈĩntu].

Consonants

[p]

The sound [p] is unaspirated in Brazilian.

p, as in *limpo* [ˈlĩmpu], *peço* [ˈpesu].

[b]

b wherever found, as in *bôca* [ˈbokɐ], *bater* [baˈtex], *câmbio* [ˈkãmbiu], *ambos* [ˈẽmbuʃ].

[t]

The sound [t] is dental and unaspirated.

t wherever found (except before unstressed final *e*), as in *tema* [ˈtemɐ], *peito* [ˈpeitu], *penetrar* [pĕneˈtɾax].

[d]

The sound [d] is dental.

d wherever found (except before unstressed final *e*), as in *diga* [ˈdigɐ], *dia* [diɐ], *mando* [ˈmĕndu].

[k]

1. *c* before *a*, *o*, *u*, or before a consonant (except *h*), as in *cada* [ˈkadɐ], *côco* [ˈkoku], *curso* [ˈkuxsu], *classe* [ˈklasi], *cruz* [kɾuʃˑ], *fricção* [fɾikˈsĕũ].

2. *q* (always followed by *u*), as in *quinto* [ˈkĩntu], *quer* [kɛx], *qual* [kwaɫ], *freqüente* [fɾeˈkwĕntʃ ˑi].

NOTE: In *qu*, the *u* is generally silent except before *a*, and when marked with a grave accent, (ù), or the dieresis, (ü); this *u* has the value of [w].

3. The single letter *x* contains the sound of [k] in the cluster [ks] between vowels in a few words, as in *taxi* [ˈtaksi], *sexo* [ˈseksu]; also sometimes finally as in *ônix* [ˈõniks], *torax* [ˈtoɾaks].

[g]

g, before *a*, *o*, *u*, or a consonant, as in *gas* [gaʃˑ], *algo* [ˈaɫgu], *algum* [aɫˈgũ], *grupo* [ˈgɾupu]. This includes *g* before *ue* and *ui*, as in *guerrra* [ˈgɛxɐ], *guia* [ˈgiɐ], *agüentar* [agwĕnˈtax].

NOTE: Here the unmarked *u* is silent and merely indicates the value of *g* as [g]. If marked with the grave accent or the dieresis, *u* has the value of [w] (see page 528).

[m]

1. *m* initial in a syllable, as in *mil* [miɫ], *motor* [moˈtox], *alma* [ˈaɫmɐ].

2. *m* intervocalic, as in *amar* [ɐˈmax], *como* [ˈkõmu]. Note that [m] persists, even after nasalizing the preceding vowel.

3. *m* before *p* or *b*, as in *cumprir* [kũmˈprix], *câmbio* [ˈkĕmbiu]. Note that, after nasalizing the preceding vowel, [m] persists under the assimilative influence of the following bilabial [p] or [b].

NOTE: *m* final or followed by a nonplosive consonant nasalizes the preceding vowel but does not maintain an existence in its own right. (But see no. 4.)

4. *m* final in a few foreign words, as in *totem* [ˈtɔtĕm].

[ɱ]

1. *n* before [f, v], as in *infantil* [ĩɱfĕnˈtiɫ], *invadir* [ĩɱvaˈdix].

[n]

Brazilian [n] is dental.

1. *n* initially in a word or syllable, as in *nada* [ˈnadɐ], *terno* [ˈtɛxnu].
2. *n* intervocalically, as in *Dona* [ˈdõnɐ].
3. *n* followed by *t* or *d* as in *tinta* [ˈtĩntɐ], *bando* [ˈbẽndu].

NOTES: (a) Some authorities deny the persistence of [n] before the homorganic [t, d], asserting that it merely nasalizes the preceding vowel.[21]

(b) See under [ŋ] for pronunciation of *n* before [k, g], and under [ɲ] for *nh*.

4. [n] appears in a manner related to its appearance in No. 3 above, when *ã* or *ão* precedes a word beginning with *t* or *d*, as in *lã tinta* [lẽn ˈtĩntɐ], *mão direito* [mẽũn diˈɾetu].

5. *m* final in liaison before *t* or *d* is pronounced [n] by assimilation, as in *bem tratado* [bẽĩn tɾaˈtadu], *sem dúvida* [sẽĩn ˈduvidɐ].

6. *n* final, as in *pólen* [ˈpolẽn], *regimen* [xeˈʒimẽn], *cânon* [ˈkẽnõn].

[ɲ]

nh as in *ganhar* [gẽˈɲax], *banha* [ˈbẽɲɐ], *piranha* [piˈɾẽɲɐ].

NOTES: (a) In Rio de Janeiro, *n* before *i* in substandard speech is sometimes pronounced [ɲ], as in *menino* [miˈɲinu].[22]

(b) Some Brazilians pronounce *nh* as [j], as in *fronha* [ˈfɾõjẽ]. The nasalization continues through the [j].

[ŋ]

1. *n* before *k* or *g*, as in *banco* [ˈbẽŋku], *manga* [ˈmẽŋgɐ].

NOTE: There is a difference of opinion as to whether [ŋ] persists here before the homorganic [k, g].

2. *m* final in liaison before *k* or *g*, as in *de vez em quando* [ʤˈi vez ẽĩŋˈkwẽndu], *bem governado* [bẽĩŋ govɛxˈnadu].

[l]

The symbol [l] is used herein for clear *l*, as contrasted with dark *l* [ł], *q.v.* below.

l initial, intervocalic, or after a consonant, as in *leve* [ˈlɛvi], *selim* [seˈlĩ], *claro* [ˈklaɾu].

NOTE: In substandard speech in Rio de Janeiro, *l* before *i* is sometimes pronounced [λ], as in *livro* [ˈλivɾu].

[ł]

This is the dark *l*, which in Brazilian Portuguese is not only alveolar, as in English, but labialized as well.

---

[21] Stavrou, p. 28.
[22] Stavrou, p. 27.

NOTES: (a) Finally in a word [ł > u] colloquially, as in *mal* [mɑu], *Brasil* [bɾeziu]; [ł] is dropped colloquially by some speakers, as in *animal* [ẽnĩˈmɑ].

(b) Rural Paulistas often change medial [ł] to an Eng. [r], as in *falso* [ˈfɑrsũ].

l final in a word, or when followed by a consonant within a word; in other words, final in a syllable. Thus: *Brasil* [bɾɑˈził], *mal* [mɑł], *balcão* [bɑłˈkẽũ], *caldo* [ˈkɑłdu], *calças* [ˈkɑłsɐʃ].

NOTE: For the sound of *l* in the diagraph *lh*, see [ʎ] below.

[ʎ]

The sound [ʎ] is analogous to English [lj] in *million* [ˈmiljən], but is made by placing the tongue-tip against the lower front teeth and elevating the blade of the tongue. In bilateral exit of the air, and in acoustic effect, the English and the Brazilian sounds are much alike.

lh, as in *mulher* [muˈʎɛx], *milho* [ˈmiʎu], *lhe* [ʎi].

NOTE: Some substandard speakers use [l:] or [j] for [ʎ], as in *colhe* [kulˈlɛ, kuˈjɛ].

[ɾ]

This is the one-tap trill or flapped *r*.

1. *r* intervocalically, as in *caro* [ˈkaɾu].

2. *r* after a consonant which is intial in a word or syllable, as in *brando* [ˈbɾẽndu], *abrir* [aˈbɾix], *tratar* [tɾaˈtax], *frio* [ˈfɾiu].

[x]

This is a voiceless velar spirant, usually with the fore part of the tongue sufficiently high to add a slight retroflex color. The sound contrasts with the [x] of German, being farther back, less fricative, as well as with slight retroflexion. In rapid speech, the sound more nearly approximates the German sound.

1. *r* initially in a word, as in *rabo* [ˈxabu], *rio* [xiu].

2. *r* initially in a syllable after *n* or *l*, as in *honra* [ˈõxɐ], *milreis* [milˈxeiʃ].

3. *r* initial in a root preceded by a prefix ending in a consonant, as in *abrogar* [abxoˈgax], *subrogar* [sub(i)xoˈgax]. But this *r* is probably more often pronounced [ɾ], as in No. 2 under [ɾ].

4. *r* before a consonant, as in *porto* [ˈpoxtu], *arco* [ˈaxku], *garfo* [ˈgaxfu].

5. *r* final, as in *amar* [aˈmax], *viver* [viˈvex].

6. *rr*, as in *carro* [ˈkaxu], *erro* [ˈexu], *erre* [ˈexi] (the name of the letter *r*).

NOTES: (a) Initial *r* is pronounced as a lengthened tongue-point trill in some radio and stage speech.

(b) In the interior of Brazil, *r* is often pronounced as in General American speech.

(c) Instead of [x], some speakers in Rio de Janeiro pronounce [h] (non-final), others the uvular trill [R].[23]

---

[23] Stavrou, p. 30.

[f]

[f] as in *tarefa* [taˈɾɛfɐ], *fujo* [ˈfuʒu].

[v]

v as in *vaca* [ˈvakɐ], *uva* [ˈuvɐ].

[s]

1. *s* initial, as in *sexto* [ˈseʃˈtu].
2. *s* after a consonant usually, as in *senso* [ˈsẽsu]. But see exceptions under [z] below.
3. *s* before a word beginning with [s] as in *os selêncios* [us siˈlẽsiuʃˈ], *as cenas* [asˈsẽnɐʃˈ].
4. *sc* before *e* or *i*, as in *descer* [deˈsex], *nascido* [naˈsidu].
5. *ss*, as in *sessenta* [seˈsẽntɐ].
6. *c* before *e* or *i*, as in *céu* [sɛu], *ciciar* [sisiˈax]; also in *cc* [ks], as in *seccionar* [seksioˈnax].
7. *ç*, as in *nação* [naˈsɐ̃ũ]; also in *cç* [ks], as in *secção* [sekˈsɐ̃ũ].
8. *xc* before *e* or *i*, as in *excesso* [eˈsɛsu], *excitar* [esiˈtax].
9. In *x* [ks] sometimes intervocalically, as in *fixo* [ˈfiksu].
10. In *x* [ks] in *ex* plus vowel in Greek words, as in *exegese* [ekseˈʒɛsi]; also sometimes initial, as in *xeroftalmia* [kseɾofˈtɑɫmiɐ].
11. *x* intervocalically, often, especially before *i*, as in *maximo* [ˈmasimu].

[z]

1. *z* non-final, as in *zona* [ˈzõnɐ], *vazio* [vaˈziu, vaˈziju].
2. *z* final if before a vowel, as in *luz aquela* [luz aˈkɛlɐ].
3. Often *s* intervocalic, as in *riso* [ˈxizu], *as operas* [az ˈɔpeɾɐʃˈ].
4. *s* in *obséquio* [obˈzɛkiu] and in *trans-* before a vowel, as in *transatlantico* [tɾẽzatˈlẽntiku].
5. *s* before a word beginning with *z*, as in *as zebras* [az ˈzebɾɐʃˈ].
6. *x* in *ex* before a vowel, as in *exito* [ˈezitu], *exemplo* [eˈzẽmplu].

NOTE: This constitutes an exception to *x* often pronounced [ks] intervocalically (see 11 above).

[ʃˈ]

1. *s* finally before a pause, as in *matos* [ˈmatuʃˈ].
2. *s* before a word beginning with a voiceless consonant (except [s]) as in *as crianças* [aʃˈkɾiˈẽsɐʃˈ], *meus pais* [meuʃˈ ˈpaiʃˈ].
3. *s* within a word before a voiceless consonant (except [s]), as in *questão* [ˈkeʃˈtɐ̃ũ].
4. *z* finally before a pause, as in *rapaz* [xaˈpaʃˈ].
5. *z* before a word beginning with a voiceless consonant (except [s]), as in *rapaz que* [xaˈpaʃˈ ki].

6. *x* finally before a pause, as in *Félix* [ˈfɛliʃˆ].

7. *x* before a word beginning with a voiceless consonant (except [s]), as in *fênix que* [ˈfẽniʃˆ ki].

8. *x* within a word before a voiceless consonant (except [s]), as in *expedir* [iʃˆpiˈdix].

[ʃ]

1. *x* intervocalically, often, as in *roxo* [ˈxoʃu].

2. *ch*, as in *chino* [ˈʃinu], *macho* [ˈmaʃu].

3. *x* initially, as in *xicara* [ˈʃikaɾe].

4. *x* after a consonant *enxada* [ĩˈʃadɐ].

5. *x* after a diphthong, as in *caixa* [ˈkaiʃɐ].

[ʒˆ]

1. *s* within a word before a voiced consonant (except [z]), as in *desde* [ˈdeʒˆʤˆi].

2. *s* before a word beginning with a voiced consonant, (except [z]), as in *as vistas* [aʒˆ ˈviʃˆteʃˆ], *os dias* [uʒˆ ˈdieʃˆ].

3. *z* before a word beginning with a voiced consonant, as in *luz verde* [luʒˆ ˈvexʤˆi].

4. *x* before a word beginning with a voiced consonant, as in *fênix grande* [feniʒˆ ˈgɾẽnʤˆi].

[ʒ]

1. *j*, as in *justa* [ˈʒuʃˆtɐ], *feijão* [feiˈʒẽũ].

2. *g* before *e* or *i*, as in *gente* [ˈʒẽntʃˆi], *girar* [ˈʒiɾax].

[j]

1. *i* unstressed before an unstressed vowel (according to some authorities), as in *Julia* [ˈʒuljɐ] for [ˈʒuliɐ], *labio* [ˈlabju] for [ˈlabiu].

2. As an off-glide of [i], as in *tio* [ˈtiju] (according to some authorities).

3. *e* unstressed before an unstressed vowel (according to some authorities), as in *contemporaneo* [kõntẽmpoˈɾẽnju].

4. *y* in proper names, as in *Yolanda* [joˈlẽndɐ].

[w]

1. *u* in *qua, quo, gua*, as in *quadro* [ˈkwadɾu], *quota* [ˈkwotɐ], *guarda* [ˈgwaxdɐ].

2. *u* as an on-glide (according to some authorities) to another vowel when both are unstressed, as in *fátua* [ˈfatwɐ], *tênue* [ˈtẽnwi], *inócuo* [iˈnɔkwu].

NOTE: See page 519 for this *u* pronounced [u].

3. *ü* in *qüi, qüe, güi, güa*, as in *tranqüilo* [tɾẽˈkwilu], *freqüente* [freˈkwẽntʃˆi], *bilingue* [biˈlĩŋgwi], *agüentar* [agwẽnˈtax].

4. *o* post-tonic followed by a vowel, as in *páscoa* [ˈpaskwɐ], except in careful speech, where it remains [u].

5. Irregularly as an off-glide of stressed [o], as in *boa* [ˈbowɐ].

6. *au, ou, eu,* plus vowel may develop [w], as in *Mauá* [mauˈwa].

[tʃˑ]

1. *t* before unstressed final *e*, as in *arte* [ˈaxtʃˑi], *leite* [ˈleitʃˑi].

2. *t* before [i] non-final by some speakers in Rio de Janeiro, even when the [i] is stressed, as in *tio* [tʃˑiu], *ultimo* [ˈuɫtʃˑimu].

[ʤˑ]

1. *d* before unstressed final *e*, as in *cidade* [siˈdaʤˑi], *rede* [ˈxeʤˑi], *Rio de Janeiro* [xiu ʤˑi ʒaˈneiɾu]. Note exception of *d* after *s*, as in *desde* [ˈdeʒdi].

2. *d* in *de* unstressed has been noted as [ʤˑ]; thus, [ʤˑi].

3. *d* even in stressed syllables, such as *dia*, has been noted as [ʤˑ]; thus, *dia* [ˈʤˑiɐ].

Some Differences Between Brazilian Portuguese and European Portuguese.

Consonants

Brazilian	European
Intervocalic [b]	[β]
Intervocalic [d]	[ð]
Intervocalic [g]	[γ]
Final *r* = [x]	[r] (Trill; [ə] often added)
Initial *r* and medial *rr* = [x]	[r:] (trill)
Before [p] and [b], light [m] or none	Prominent [m]
Before [t] and [d], light [n] or none	Prominent [n]
Moderate palatalization of *s* and *z* to [ʃˑ] and [ʒˑ]	Strong palatalization

Vowels

Unstressed *a* may be pronounced [a] or, if final or in an article, [ɐ]	
a before intervocalic nasal = [ɐ̃]	[ɐ]
Stressed close *e* = [e]	[ɐ] except optionally [e] before a palatal
e followed by intervocalic nasal = [ẽ]	[e]
Unstressed non-final *e* = [e]	[ə] except before palatals, where it is [i]

Unstressed final e = [i]	Usually dropped; may be retained as [ə]
e in ex- = [i]	Often [ɐi]
e initial, unstressed, before non-palatal = [e]	[i]
o followed by intervocalic nasal = [õ]	[o]
o unstressed, usually [o] unless final, when it is [u]	Nearly always [u]; final o often dropped
ei = [ei] or [e]	Usually [ɐi], optionally [ei]
em final = [ẽĩ]	[ɐ̃ĩ]

The foregoing are outstanding differences. For some additional differences, see Stavrou, pages 41–44.

Today, the Portuguese centers of the United States are composed chiefly of American-born people whose English speech shows little influence of the Portuguese language. It follows, then, that our contact with Portuguese-speaking people is chiefly with those from Brazil. Our growing cultural and business intercourse with that country has given a new importance to the Portuguese language. Enrollment of Brazilian students in American colleges and universities has increased considerably and teachers frequently have the problem of communication with these students. There are few serious difficulties involved in teaching the sounds of English to Brazilian-speaking people, inasmuch as most of the sounds of English occur in Portuguese. The problem of the English-speaking student learning Brazilian Portuguese is somewhat more complex, as there are a number of sounds in the Portuguese language which are not found in English.

The following paragraphs will outline briefly the sounds which are not common to the two languages.

Brazilian Portuguese Sounds Not in English

1. [ɐ], acoustically similar to [ə].
2. The nasal vowels and diphthongs, some of which occur in substandard English. These are [ĩ, ẽ, ɐ̃, õ, ũ; ẽĩ, ɐ̃ĩ, õĩ, ũĩ, ẽũ].
3. The voiced palatal nasal [ɲ].
4. The voiced palatal lateral [ʎ].
5. The velar fricative [x].
6. The labio-dental [ɱ].

English Sounds Not in Brazilian Portuguese

1. [ɪ], [æ], [ʊ].
2. The centralized vowels [ʌ, ɝ, ɜ, ɚ, ə].
3. The interdentals [ð, θ].

4. The non-trilled [r].
5. [ʍ].
6. [h].

The sound substitutions which may be expected from a Brazilian speaker learning English pronunciation are those which, by and large, are common to speakers of Romance languages in their experiences with the English tongue.

Vowels

There is a strong tendency to substitute [i] for [ɪ], especially in stressed positions.

The sound [æ] of English does not appear in Brazilian Portuguese and most Brazilian speakers in pronouncing English tend to substitute a vowel varying from [a] to [ɑ]. Variation in the other direction, that is, toward [ɛ], also occurs. However, the sound seems to offer no enduring difficulty.

For [ʊ] there is a strong tendency to substitute [u], especially in stressed positions.

For the centralized vowel [ʌ], the substitution is [ɑ], [ɔ], and sometimes the spelling-induced use of [u]; however, there is usually little difficulty with this sound.

Similarly, the centralized "r-colored" vowels [ɝ, ɚ] present little difficulty, although there is some tendency for the substitution of [ɛr, ɚr] ([r] trilled). Some substitution of [e] for [eɪ] and of [o] for [oʊ] will occur.

Two carry-overs from Portuguese language habits may be noticed in the English speech of Brazilian Portuguese speakers. They are (1) the unvoicing of final vowels and (2) the addition of a final vowel (usually [ɐ] or [i]) to English words ending in consonants other than those in which Portuguese words may end, viz., *l, r, s, z*, and occasionally *n, x*. Examples: *Ruth* [ˈxutʃˈi], *club* [ˈklubi], *bull dog* [buɫˈdɔgi], *film* [ˈfiɫmi].

Consonants

Dentality of [t, d, n] will be frequent.

The affricates [tʃ] and [dʒ] occur as modifications of [t] and [d] before [i] in the Brazilian Portuguese language. As a matter of fact, however, there is frequent substitution of [ʃ] and [ʒ] respectively, as in *church* [ˈʃexʃi], *jump* [ʒump]. When [t, d] are followed by [i] in English, anticipation of the vowel results in a palatal release of the plosive, ranging from [tj, dj] to [tʃ, dʒ]. Examples are *ordinal* [oxdʒˈiˈnaɫ], *tide* [ˈtʃˈidʒˈi]. The writer has heard from Brazilians the substitution of [tʃ] for [dʒ], as in *judge* [tʃatʃ].

The postdentals of English offer some difficulties to a person natively speaking Portuguese. The substitutions [s] and [t] for [θ] and [d] and [ð] occur, the latter being more frequent.

English consonantal [r] tends to be replaced with [x] except intervocalically and post-consonantally.

In reading, the Brazilian speaker frequently makes a syllable of the English finals -ed, -e, -es in contexts where they are not syllabic in English, as in *checked* [ˈʃɛkəd], *make* [ˈmeki], *takes* [ˈtekəs].

It has been noted elsewhere (page 515) that even in their own language Brazilians have great difficulty with certain consonant clusters, viz., *bs*, *ps*, *gn*, *pt*, etc., and insert vowels to break them up. Examples: *absoluto* [abisoˈlutu], *psikologia* [pisikoloˈʒi(j)ɐ], *indignar* [ĩdigiˈnax], *optar* [opiˈtax], *Edmundo* [ediˈmũdu]. Similar difficulty in English may be expected.

Portuguese words do not begin with *sc* [sk], *sp* or *st*, hence the prefixing of a vowel, as in *sport* [iʃˈˠpɔɾtʃˠi], *stock* [iʃˈˠtɔki]. All such words which have been borrowed by the Brazilian Portuguese language have been respelled, as *sport–esporte*, *stock–estoque*. Transition forms used by Brazilians learning English are [ɛsˈpɔɾt], [ɛsˈtɔk].

Brazilian Dialect of English

zi ˈunaitəd istets xas ə ˈdɛmokɾəsi wiʃ is nat laik zi ˈdɛmokɾəsi af mani saus amɛɾıkən kantɾis. in mos af zis kantɾis zə wumən das nat xaf zə vot. anazər faktɐx is zə lak af xiəl univɛxsał ɛdukeʃən in sam af zis kantɾis. maʃ af zi pIpəl xas bin onli in ˈpɾaiməɾi ɪskuł. zis kips zɛm fɾam ʃuziŋ waizli. if pipəl kan:at xid an xait, ai dʊ nat ziŋk ze ʃuəd vot. af kuxs, ai am nat ə ʒaʃ, an mai opinjən is nat joxs, mebi, bat zis is wat ai siŋk.

Exercise

Transcribe one page of any reading material in Brazilian dialect.

Bibliography

Agard, Frederick B., Hélio Lobo, and Raymond S. Willis, *Brazilian Portuguese From Thought to Word* (Princeton University Press, 1944).

Hills, E. C., J. D. M. Ford, and Ja. de Siqueira Coutinho, *Portuguese Grammar* (Chicago: D. C. Heath, 1925). Revised by L. G. Moffat, 1944.

Jucá, Cândido (Falho), *A Pronúncia Brasíléira* (Rio do Janeiro: Coeditora Brasilica, 1939).

Pap, Leo, *Portuguese-American Speech* (New York: King's Crown Press, Columbia University, 1949).

Pereira, Eduardo Carlos, *Gramática Expositiva* (Rio de Janeiro: Companhia Editora Nacional, 1941).

Stavrou, Christopher, *Brazilian-Portuguese Pronunciation* (Philadelphia: David McKay Co., 1947).

de Vasconcellos, J. Leite, *Mappa Dialectologico do Continente Português* (Lisbon: Guellard, Ailland & Co., 1897).

Williams, Edwin B., *First Brazilian Grammar* (New York: F. S. Crofts, 1944).

——————————, *From Latin to Portuguese* (University of Pennsylvania Press, 1938).

Index

A

[a], 23, 102, 103; as a "compromise" vowel, 101, 102; in Brazilian Portuguese, 517; in French, 337; in Italian, 439; in Russian, 480, 488; in Spanish, 459, 460
Aasen, Ivar, cited, 420n
Advanced stress, in Southern speech, 219
[ae], in Italian, 441
Affricates, 62
Affrication, in Yiddish, 412
[aɪ], 23, 103, 104
[ai], in Brazilian Portuguese, 520; in Italian, 441; in Russian, 492
Alveolars, 48
American Council of Learned Societies, cited, 172n
Analogy, 166, 195
Anaptyxis, 162, 196; in Scottish, 262
An, used by error before pronounced *h,* 112; used by error before words beginning with *u,* 112n
Aphesis, 162, 163
Apocope, 165
Areas where Russian is spoken, 476
Arlt, Phyllis Betts, cited, 411n, 412n
Aspirates, 64
Aspiration, 64; in German, 370
Assimilation, complete (equalization), 155, 156; distant (incontiguous, dilated), 155; in Russian, 478; partial (accommodation), 155; progressive, 153; progressive-regressive (reciprocal), 154; regressive, 153; regressive, in Russian, 485
Assimilations, colloquial, 195
Atlas of New England, Linguistic, 222, 222n; *Linguistic, of the United States and Canada,* quoted, 229
Atonic stress, in Russian, 478
Atwood, E. Bagby, cited, 173n
[au], in Italian, 441; in Russian, 492

[aʊ], 23, 104
[ɒ], 22, 104, 106
[ĕ], in Brazilian Portuguese, 522
[ĕi], In Brazilian Portuguese, 523
[ĕũ], in Brazilian Portuguese, 523
[æ], 11, 101, 102; English,pron unciation by Russians, 504, 505; for [ɛ], 203; in Norwegian, 423
[æ:], in Norwegian, 423
[æi], in Russian, 492
[æu], in Norwegian, 424
ä, controversy over pronunciation of, in German, 388n
[ɑ], 12, 22, 23, 104, 106; in Brazilian Portuguese, 517; in French, 338; in German, 390; in Italian, 439; in Norwegian, 423; in Russian, 488; in Spanish, 460
[ɑ:], in German, 390; in Norwegian, 423
[ɑ̃], in French, 340, 341
[ɑi], in German, 392; in Spanish, 461
[ɑu], in Brazilian Portuguese, 520; in German, 392; in Spanish, 461

B

[b], 122; in Brazilian Portuguese, 523; in French, 341; in German, 371; in Italian, 442; in Norwegian, 425; in Russian, 493; in Spanish, 462
[b̥], in Russian, 481, 493, 494
[β], in German, 379; in Spanish, 464
Backing, 157
Back vowels, 87
Barnhart, Clarence L., cited, 89, 89n
Barrie, J. M., cited, 268
Barrows, Sarah T., cited, 182n
Baugh, Albert C., cited, 171n
Beaumont, Francis, cited, 247
Behavior, of consonants in syllabication in Spanish, 454, 455; of vowels in syllabication in Spanish, 455

Bell, Alexander Graham, cited, 7

Bell, Alexander Melville, cited, 7, 150

Berrey, Lester V., cited, 304, 304n

Bilabials, 48

Blend-words (portmanteau words, contamination), 166

Bloch, Bernard, cited, 77n; (and George L. Trager), cited, 13n, 74n, 77n, 95n, 97n

Bloomfield, Leonard, cited, 70n, 97n, 148n, 151, 153, 164n, 168

Borchers, Gladys (and C. M. Wise), cited, 404, 404n

Border substandardisms of General American speech, 192

Boundaries, of speech regions, 172, 178; speech, nature of, 179

Brazilian Portuguese, consonants, compared with European Portuguese consonants, 529; discussion, 523, 529; consonants of, 514; dialects of, 512, 532; dialect, transcription, 532; diphthongs, discussion, 520; diphthongs of, 513; nasal diphthongs in, 523; nasal vowels in, 522, 523; sounds not in English, 530; sounds of, 513, 514; vowels, 513; vowels, compared with European Portuguese consonants, 529, 530; vowels, discussion, 514–523

Bridenbaugh, Carl, 304n

Broad Romic, 8, 150

"Broad a," in Eastern speech, 222, 223n, 224; in Cockney, 252

Brooks, Cleanth, cited, 175n

Buchanan, James, cited, 8n; 150

Bullokar, William, cited, 8n; 150

Burgess, Gelett, cited, 168

Butler, Charles, cited, 8n

C

[c], in Russian, 496

[c], symbol front [k], 125

[c], in German, 381, 382; in Norwegian, 426; in Russian, 483, 484

Caffee, N. M. (and T. A. Kirby), cited, 108n

Cardinal vowels, 84–87

Carroll, Lewis, cited, 167

Cassidy, F. G., cited, 175

Causes of sound change, physiological, 150; psychological, 151; sociological, 151

Cavity resonance, 53, 54

Celtic language, features of, in the English of Ireland, 273

Central vowels, 87

Centralization, 158; of [aɪ] to [ɜ], 216

Centralized vowels, 198

Chaucer, Geoffrey, quoted, 165

Church Slavonic or Old Bulgarian, 476

Close juncture, excrescent plosives in, after nasals, 164; in French, 334

Closed syllables, in French, 334; in Spanish, 454

Cockney, 235; interpretation of spelling of, 250; origin of, 247; pronunciation features of consonants in, 252; Southern British characteristics in, 254; spelling of, 250; transcription of, 254; use of "Broad a," 252; vowels, pronunciation features of, 251

Colloquial assimilations, 195

Combining, of syllables in Substandard Negro speech, 300; of words in Substandard Negro speech, 300, 301

Committee on stage pronunciation in German, 369n

Comparison of English and German sounds, 393

Compensatory lengthening, tabulation of, 161

Complementary distribution, defined, 77n

Complete assimilation (equalization), 155, 156

Combs, Josiah H., cited, 313

Connotation, 168

Consonant, clusters, simplification of, 162; definition, 74; distinguished from vowel, 65–73; r, in Eastern speech, 229

Consonants, Brazilian, discussion, 523–529; Brazilian Portuguese, 514; English, not in French, 349; English, pronunciation by Brazilian Portuguese speakers, 531, 532; French, 341–349; French, chart, 326; French, not in English, 349; German, discussion, 369–384; in Scottish dialect, 268, 269; in Substandard New York speech, 285–290; Italian, discussion, 442–447; loss of in Southern speech, 218; non-palatal ("hard") in Russian, 477; Norwegian, chart, 422; Norwegian, discussed, 424–427; pronunciation features of in Cockney, 252; pronunciation of, in General American speech, 187, 188; Russian, palatal ("soft") 477; Russian, pronunciation according to context, 492–503; Russian, pronunciation of, 481–485; silent, in French, 332; Spanish, chart, 45.'; Spanish, discussion, 466

Contamination (blend-words, portmanteau words), 166

Context, as a basis for separating vowels and consonants, 68–73

Continuants, 64

Corti, organ of, 49

Courtenay, Badouin de, cited 74n

Coxe, M. S., cited, 284; (and G. E. Peterson) cited, 184n, 185n

Crumb, D. S., cited, 304n

D

[d], 124, 125; English, pronunciation by Russians, 507; for [g], before [l], 202; in Brazilian Portuguese, 524; in French, 341, 342; in German, 373; in Italian, 442; in Norwegian, 425; in Russian, 493;' in Spanish, 462; loss of, from [nd], [ndz], 202

[d], in Russian, 495

[d], in Castilian Spanish, 465

[ð], 19; English, pronunciation by Russians, 508, 509; in Spanish, 465

Daggett, Windsor P., cited, 172n

Danish, relation to Norwegian, 419

Davis, Alva L., cited 175n

Degeneration (pejoration), 168

Degrees of stress, in French, 330

Dekker, Thomas, cited, 247

Delmarva Peninsula, 179

Dentality, in Yiddish, 411

Dentals, 48; in Italian, 432

Displaced stress, in Southern speech, 219

Dissimilation, 157, 218

Distant assimilation (incontiguous, dilated), 155

Distribution, Spanish-speaking people in the United States, 454

Dixon, James Main (and William Grant), cited, 257n, 266n, 267n, 268n

Drawl, Southern, 212, 213

Dunn, H. K., cited, 84n

Duration, of stressed vowels, 117, 118

Dyche, Thomas, cited, 150

[dz], in Italian, 446

[dʒ], Brazilian Portuguese, 529; English, pronunciation by Russians, 507, 508; Italian, 447; Spanish, 466; phonemic indivisibility of, 20

Deviations, from Standard Eastern speech, 233; from Standard General American, Southern, and Eastern speech, 193–204; from Standard General American speech, 189–204; from Standard New York speech, 283–292; from Standard Scottish, 262

Dialectal features of Scottish, spelling of, 262; strong verb construction in Mountain speech, 316

Dialect, Brazilian Portuguese, transcription, 532

Dialects, of Brazilian Portuguese, 512; Russian, regional, 476; Spanish, 467–474

Dictionaries, phonetic, 89; uses of in transcription 89

Dieth, Eugen, cited, 256n, 257, 257n

Diphthongization, 159

Diphthongs, 63; Brazilian, discussion, 520; Brazilian Portuguese, 513; English, 95–98; German, 366; Italian, discussion, 440–442; nasal, in Brazilian Portuguese, 523; Norwegian, 422; Norwegian, discussed, 424; Russian, pronunciation according to stress and context, 491, 492; Russian, pronunciation of, 480; Spanish, 456, 461; stressed, 182; stressed and unstressed, 111

E

[e], 17, 98–100; in Brazilian Portuguese, 516; in French, 335; in German, 387, 388; in Italian, 437–439; in Norwegian, 423; in Russian, 479; in Spanish, 478, 479

e, silent in French, when, 331

[e:], in Norwegian, 423

[ẽ], in Brazilian Portuguese, 522

[ə], 12, 19, 22, 115–117; compared with [ɜ], 118, 119; for [ju] or [jə], 203; for [ɪ], 203; in French, 339; in German, 392; in Norwegian, 424; in Russian, 490, 491

[ɚ], 22, 119, 120, 135, 136; as the first sound in a word or syllable, 120; English, pronunciation by Russians, 507
[əɪ], 15
Eastern speech, 172; extent of, 221, 222; stress in, 231
Effect, of experience on German speaker's use of English, 398; of German speaker's own dialect on his English, 398; of literacy in German-English dialect, 398
[ẽi], in Brazilian Portuguese, 520; in Italian, 441; in Norwegian, 424; in Russian, 491
[ei], in Brazilian Portuguese, 523
[eɪ], 98–100, for [ɛ], 203
Ekwall, Eilert, cited, 107n
Elevation (amelioration), 168
Elision, in French, 333
Ellis, Alexander J., cited, 7n, 150, 150n, 234, 257, 257n, 274n
English and German sounds compared, 393
English and Russian sound systems, 477
English consonants, not in French, 349; pronunciation by Brazilian Portuguese speakers, 531, 532; pronunciation by Russians, 507–510
English diphthongs, 95–98
English sounds, not in Brazilian Portuguese, 530; not in French, 349; not in Norwegian, chart, 427; not in Spanish, 467
English vowels, pronunciation by Brazilian Portuguese speakers, 531; not in French, 249
Emerson, O. F., cited, 178n
Ess-tset, [β], use of. in German spelling 386n
[eu], in Brazilian Portuguese, 520
Excrescent [k] and [g] after [ŋ] in the pronunciation of English by Italians, 448; plosives, in close juncture after nasals, 164; sounds, 163, 164
Exercises, in German dialect, 398, 399–401
Experience, effect of, on German speaker's English, 398
[ɛ], 11, 100–101; in Brazilian Portuguese, 516, 517; in French, 336; in German, 388, 389; in Italian, 437–439; in Russian, 487, 488; in Spanish, 459
[ɛi], in Brazilian Portuguese, 520; in Italian, 441; in Spanish, 461

[ɛo], in Italian, 441
[ɛu], in Brazilian Portuguese, 520; in Italian, 441
[ɛ̃], in French, 340
[ə], 21, 118
[ɝ], 21, 119, 120; English, pronunciation by Russian, 506, 507

                    F

[f], 133; in Brazilian Portuguese, 527; in French, 345, 346; in German, 380; in Italian, 444; in Norwegian, 426; in Russian, 498; in Spanish, 464
[f̡], in Russian, 498
[F], in German, 379
Falsetto, definition, 36; production of, 65
Features of Mountain speech, held in common with Substandard General American, Southern, and Eastern speech, 305–309; held in common with Substandard Southern speech, 309, 310
Feire, Laudelimo, cited, 517n
Fletcher, John, cited, 247
Folk etymology, 166, 194
Fortis and lenis, 65
Franklin, Benjamin, cited, 8n, 150
French-Canadian, 352–354
French, closed syllables in, 334; consonants not in English, 349; consonants, chart, 326; consonants of, 335–349; consonants, substituted for English consonants, 350; degrees of stress in, 330; dialectal substitutions for English sounds, 349, 350; elision in, 333; in North America, 325; liaison in, 333, 334; open syllables in, 334; open vowels in, 334; orthographic representation of, 335–349; primary stress in, in words in isolation, 331; silent letters in, 331, 332; sounds of, charts, 326; sounds of, not in English, 349; stress in, 330; vowels not in English, 349; vowels of, 335–341; vowels of, charts, 326; vowels, substituted for English vowels, 349, 350
French-English dialect, 350–363; as spoken by speakers from France, 350, 351; Louisiana, 354–363; transcription, 351
Frey, J. William, cited, 405n, 406n, 407n
Fronting, 157; of [ʌ], 198

Front vowels, 87
Fruit, John P., cited, 313
Fundamental tone, 50
Future of American speech, 180, 181

G

[g], 126, 127; excrescent after [ŋ] in pronunciation of English by Italians, 448; in Brazilian Portuguese, 524; in French, 342, 343; in German, 175, 374; in Italian, 443; in Norwegian, 425; in Russian, 496; in Spanish, 462, 463
[ɟ], in Russian, 496
General American speech, 172; predominance of, 180; standard, transcription of, 189; unstressed vowels in, 186
German, 364–402; and English sounds, compared, 393; consonants, discussion, 369–384, dialect, exercises in 399–401; diphthongs, 366; immigrants in the United States, 364, 365; intonation in English, 397; non-English sounds in, 366, 367; sounds of, chart, 366; speaker's own dialect, effect of in his English, 398; sounds, spelling of, 367–392; stage pronunciation in, 368, 369; substitutions in English, 394–397; vowels, discussion, 384–392; sounds which are not in English, 393
George, Albert Donald, cited, 206n
Gill, Alexander, cited, 8n
Gleason, H. A., cited, 13n
Glides, 45
Glossotype, 8n
Glottals, 48
Glottal stop, 127, 128
[gn], in German, 383
"Grade," in Indo-European linguistics, 14n
Grandgent, C. H., cited, 109n, 173n, 179n, 203, 227, 233n
Gray, Giles W. (and Claude M. Wise), cited, 58n, 148n, 167n, 168
Gray, Louis H., cited, 151, 152
Greet, William Cabell, cited, 175n
Grimm, Jakob, cited, 147, 168
Grimm's law, 168
Gross, Milt, quoted, 412–417
Gullah speech, 295n
Gutterals, 65

[ʏ], in German, 382, 386, 387; in Spanish, 466; in Russian, 484
Grant, William, cited, 256n; quoted, 260n; (and James Main Dixon), cited, 257n, 265n, 266n, 267n, 268n

H

[h], 139; English, pronunciation by Russians, 509; in German, 382, 383; in Norwegian, 427; loss of, from [hj], 201; voiced, 139
Hall, Robert A., Jr., cited 95n, 327n; the three types of pronunciation in French, 331n; quoted, 331n; cited, 436n, 439n, 442n, 444n, 445n, 446n, 447n
Hall, Joseph Sargent, cited, 304n, 311n, 313
Hansen, Marcus L., cited, 172
Hanley, Miles L., cited, 172n
Haplology, 165, 166
Harmonic theory of voice production, 42n
Hart, John, cited, 8n, 150, 182, 182n
Harris, Zellig S., cited, 156n
Hatcher, J. Wesley, cited, 179
Haugen, Einar, cited, 167, 420n, 422n, 426n
Heffner, R-M. S., quoted, 74n; cited, 82n, 121, 135n, 139n
Hempl, George, cited, 369n, 379n, 380n, 383n, 388n, 389n, 390n, 391n, 393
Heywood, John, cited, 247
High vowels, 87
Hoare, Alfred, cited, 437n
Hogan, Jeremiah J., cited, 276n, 277n
Homorganic sounds, 91, 92
Hubbell, Allan F., cited, 91n, 280, 280n, 281n, 282, 282n, 284n, 285n, 286n, 287n, 288n, 289n
Hultzén, Lee S., cited, 112n
Hyperbole, 168
Hyperurbanism, 195
Hyperurbanism (over-correction), 166

I

[i], 9, 90–92; in Brazilian Portuguese, 514, 515, 522; in French, 335; in German, 384, 385; in Italian, 436, 437; in Norwegian, 422, 423; in Russian, 486; in Spanish, 457, 458

[i:], in Norwegian, 422
[ɨ], in Russian, 478, 479
[iu], in Brazilian Portuguese, 520
[ɪ], 9, 91, 92; English, pronunciation by Russians, 504; for [ʊ], [ə], 203; in German, 385; regarded as a phoneme, 198; in Russian, 486, 487
Indo-European languages, table, 148, 149
Influence of Italian contexts on pronunciation of English by Italians, 447, 448
Ingleman, Anna H. (and Vance Randolph), cited, 304, 304n
Interpretation of spelling of Cockney, 250
Intonation, German, in English, 397; Norwegian, 420, 421; symbolization of, 182, 182n
Intrusive, [r] in Southern speech, 219; sounds, 197
Invention of words, 166, 167
International Phonetic Alphabet, 150; relation to Broad Romic, 8
International Phonetic Association, founding of, 8
Immigrants, German, in the United States, 364, 365; Italian, distribution of, 431, 432; Norwegian, distribution of, 419
Immigration, Italian, 432
Irish dialect, 273–279
Italian, 431–453; consonants, discussion, 442–447; contexts, influence of, on the pronunciation of English by Italians, 447, 448; dialect, transcription, 449–452; diphthongs, discussion, 440–442; immigrants, distribution of, 431, 432; immigration, 431, 432; pronunciation features, 432–436; sounds, charts, 435, 436; sounds, discussion, 436; vowels, discussed, 436–440

J

[j], 23, 139–144; in Brazilian Portuguese, 528; in German, 382; in French, 348, 349; in Norwegian, 426; in Spanish, 465
[ja], in Italian, 441
[je], in Italian, 441
[jɛ], in Italian, 441
[ju], in Italian, 441
Jones, Daniel, cited, 70n, 82n, 89, 89n, 223, 241, 252n, 257, 257n, 260n; quoted, 75n; (and M. V. Trofimov) cited, 476n, 485n, 505n; (and V. Trofimov) quoted, 75n
Jonson, Ben, cited, 150, 247
Joos, Martin, cited, 45n; quoted, 84n
Jud, Jakob, cited, 172
Junggrammatiker, 147n

K

[k], 125; excrescent after [ŋ] in pronunciation of English by Italians, 448; for [t], 202; in Brazilian Portuguese, 524; in French, 343, 344; in German, 373, 374; in Italian, 442, 443; in Norwegian, 425; in Russian, 495, 496; in Spanish, 462; loss of from [skt], 201
Kelly, Joseph P., cited, 199
Kenyon, J. S., cited, 70n, 112n, 172; (and Thos. A. Knott), 89, 89n, 91n, 97n, 224n, 227n
Key words, 24–30
Kirby, T. A. (and N. M. Caffee), cited, 108n
[kn], in German, 384
Knott, Thos. A. (and J. S. Kenyon), 89, 89n, 91n, 97n, 224n, 227n
Krapp, George Philip, quoted, 172n, 175n
[ks], in German, 383; in Italian, 447
[kʊ], in German, 384
Kurath, Hans, cited, 1n, 222n, 223n, 280n, 304n; quoted, 171n, 172n; cited, 173, 173n, 174, 175n

L

[l], 131, 132; in Brazilian Portuguese, 525; in French, 344, 345; in German, 376, 377; in Italian, 444; loss of, from [lj], [lr], [l] + vowel or [w], 203; in Norwegian, 426; in Russian, 497; in Spanish, 463
[l̥], in Russian, 497
[ɫ], in Brazilian Portuguese, 525, 526
[ʎ], in Brazilian Portuguese, 526; in Italian, 444; in Spanish, 463
Labiodentals, 48
Laguaite, Jeannette, cited, 137n
Lambert, Marcus Bachman, cited, 404, 404n
Landsmål, 420
Language substrata, 167

Laterals, 45; in Italian, 432, 433

Lautgesetze, 147n

Lax vowels, 61

Le Maître Phonétique, 8

Length, phonemic status of, in French, 326

Lengthening, compensatory, 161, 162; tabulation of, 161

Liaison, in French, 333, 334

Level stress, 17

Linguistic Atlas of New England, 222, 222n

Linguistic Atlas of the United States and Canada, cited, 172; history of, 172n, 173n; quoted, 229

Linking *r*, 21

Liquids, 65

Literacy, effect of, in German-English dialect, 397, 398

Litotes, 168

Long consonants, in Italian, 433, 434

Long vowels, in Norwegian, 422

Loss, of consonants, in Southern speech, 218; of medial syllables in Substandard Negro speech, 300

Lost word elements, in Substandard Negro speech, 300

Lowering, 158; of [ɛ] to [æ], 216; of [i], 198

Low vowels, 87

Luick, Karl, cited, 369

Louisiana French-English, 354–363; transcription, 357–358

Lynn, Klonda, cited, 473

M

[m], 129, 130; in Brazilian Portuguese, 524; in French, 344; in German, 376; in Italian, 443; in Norwegian, 425; in Russian, 496; in Spanish, 463

[m̥], in Brazilian Portuguese, 524; in Italian, 443; in Spanish, 463

[m̥], in Russian, 497

Marcquardt, Albert H., cited, 153, 165, 175

Matthews, William, cited, 247, 247n; quoted, 249; cited, 249n, 253n

Metaphor, 168

McDavid, Raven I., cited, 175n

Metathesis, 158n, 165, 195; in Irish dialect, 277; in Scottish, 262

Metonymy, 168

Middleton, Thomas, cited, 247

Midland speech area of the Eastern United States, 174–177

Midwestern speech, inappropriateness of name, 171

Mid vowels, 87

Migration into Appalachians from Pennsylvania, 309

Miscellaneous, substandard pronunciations, 204; Substandard Southern pronunciations, 220

Models for Yiddish speech, 411–417

Modern Language Association, cited, 172n

Monophthongization, 159

Monosyllables, unstressed in word groups, 112–115

Morphophonemics, 156n

Motors, for vocal vibration, 37

Mountain Speech, 303–322; features held in common with General American, Southern and Eastern speech, 305–309; features held in common with Substandard Southern speech, 309; features peculiar to, 310–314; stressing in, 315; transcription in, 217; unstressing in, 315; weak verb construction in 316

Mountain people, origin of, 304

Mudd, Charles, cited, 58n

Murray, James A. H., cited, 257, 257n

N

[n], 130; assimilative influence of on preceding vowels, 130; English, pronunciation by Russians, 507; for [ŋ], in *-ing*, 202; for [ŋ], in *length, strength*, 202; in Brazilian Portuguese, 525; in French, 344; in German, 376; in Italian, 443; in Norwegian, 425; in Russian, 497; in Spanish, 463

[n̥], in Russian, 497

[ɲ], in Brazilian Portuguese, 525; in French, 344; in Italian, 443; in Spanish, 463

[ŋ], 19, 131; in Brazilian Portuguese, 525; English, pronunciation by Russians, 598; in German, 376; in Italian, 443; in Norwegian, 426; in Spanish, 463

Narrowing (specialization), 168

Narrow Romic, 8

Nasal, diphthongs, in Brazilian Portuguese, 521–523; vowels, in Brazilian Portuguese, 522, 523

Nasality, 88, 199; in Southern speech, 217; in Cockney, 250

Nasals, 45; consonantal, 128, 129; in Italian, 433; syllabic, 128, 129

Nature of speech boundaries, 179

Negus, V. E., cited, 33n, 34n, 35n

Negro speech, Southern, Substandard, 293–302; Substandard, combining of syllables, 300; Substandard, combining of words through the loss of consonants, 300, 301; Substandard, features held in common with Southern white speech 298, 299; Substandard, features held in common with Substandard American speech in general, 297, 298; Substandard, specific features of, 299–301; Substandard, transcription of, 301

Neurograms, fading of, 151

New York City, speech, 280–292

Nitze, William A. (and Ernest H. Wilkins and Clarence E. Parmenter), cited, 357n

Noise, 61

Non-English sounds in German, 366, 367

Non-palatal ("hard") consonants, Russian, 477

Non-palatalizing ("hard") vowels, Russian, 477

Non-speech sounds, varieties of, 35

North-and-West, 171

Northern speech, inappropriateness of name, 171; area (of the Eastern United States), 174–177

Norwegian, 419–430; consonants, chart, 422; consonants, discussed, 424–427; consonants, substituted in English, discussion, 428, 429; dialect, transcription in, 429, 430; diphthongs, 422; diphthongs discussed, 424; diphthong, substituted in English, 428; immigrants, 419; intonation, 420, 421; sounds of, 421–427; substitutions for English sounds, chart, 427; vowels, chart, 421; vowels discussed, 422–424; vowels, substituted in English, discussion, 427, 428

Nynorsk, 420

O

[o], 17, 19, 107, 108; English, pronunciation by Russians, 505; for [ə], 203; in Brazilian Portuguese, 518; in French 338, 339; in German, 390; in Italian, 439, 440; in Norwegian, 424; in Spanish, 460

[o:], in Norwegian, 424

[õ], in Brazilian Portuguese, 522, 523

[oa], in Italian, 441

Oertel, Hans, cited, 164n

[oi], in Brazilian Portuguese, 520; in Italian, 441

[õi], in Brazilian Portuguese, 523

[ɔɪ], 23, 107

[ɔ], 12, 106, 107; for [æ], 202; in Brazilian Portuguese, 518, 519; in French, 338; in German, 391; in Italian, 439; 440; in Norwegian, 424; in Russian, 479, 480; in Spanish, 460

[ɔ:], in Norwegian, 424

[ɔ̃], in French, 341

[ɔɪ], 107

[ɔi], in Brazilian Portuguese, 520; in Italian, 441

[ø], 275n; in French, 340; in German, 379; in Norwegian, 423

[ø:], in Norwegian, 423

[øi], In Norwegian, 424

[œ], in French, 340; in German, 389, 390

[œ̃], in French, 341

Old Bulgarian or Church Slavonic, 476

Orm (Orme, Ormmin), cited, 7n, 150, 150n

One-tap trill, 21, 45, 132, 133

Open, syllables, in French, 334; in Spanish, 454; vowels, in French, 334

Organ of Corti, 49

Origin of Cockney, 247

Orthographic representation, of French, 335–349

Ossicular chain, 49

[oʊ], 15, 107, 108; English, pronunciation by Russians, 505

Over-correction (hyperurbanism), 166

Overtones, 50; importance of, 52

P

[p], 120; in Brazilian Portuguese, 529; in French, 341; in German, 369; in Italian,

442; in Russian, 492, 493; in Norwegian, 424; in Spanish, 461, 462

[ɲ], in Russian, 493

Page, Eugene R., cited, 409

Palato-alveolars, 48

Palatalization, 159, 160; in Irish dialect, 277; of consonants, persistence of, in Russian pronunciation of English, 510; of [d], 199; of [g] and [k], 199

Palatalizing vowels, Russian, 477

Palatals, 48

Palatal (soft) consonants, Russian, 477

Paleotype, 8n

Parmenter, Clarence E., cited, 84n; (with William A. Nitze and Ernest H. Wilkins) cited, 357n

Pap, Leo, cited, 512n

Papillon, T. L., cited, 153

Partial assimilation (accommodation), 155

Partials, 50

Pattern congruity, definition, 77n

Paul, Hermann, cited, 151

Pennsylvania German, 403–408; characteristics of, 404–407; four levels of, 405n; origin of, 403; transcription, 407, 409

Pennsylvania migration into Appalachians, 309

Perception indeterminacy, 45

Pereira, Edwardo Carlos, cited, 515n

Perry, Louise S., quoted, 303n

Peterson, Gordon E., cited, 84; quoted, 42n; (and M. S. Coxe) cited, 184n, 185n

[pf], in German, 383

Phelps, Ruth Shepard, cited, 435n

Phoneme, definitions, 77; indispensability of concept of, 74

Phonemic similarity, 77n

Phonetic Alphabet, International, 131; need for, 5; dictionaries, 89

Phonetics, definition, 7

Pike, Kenneth L., cited, 36n, 59n, 67n, 73, 73n, 82n, 139n, 182, 182n; quoted, 78n

Pitch, as related to resonating cavities, 52; as the identifying characteristic of a sound, 52; phonemes of, 36n; normal, above and below normal, 36

Pitman, Isaac, cited, 8n

Pleonasm (redundancy), 168

Plosives, stop-compression, 44; voiced and voiceless, ways of distinguishing, 123; excrescent, in close juncture after nasals, 164

Plays, requiring or permitting "stage speech", 239

Portmanteau words (blend-words, contamination), 166

Portuguese (European) consonants, compared with Brazilian Portuguese consonants, 529; (European) vowels, compared with Brazilian Portuguese vowels, 529, 530; Language, distribution of, 512

Pretonic stress, in Russian, 478

Primary stress, in French words in isolation, 331

Progressive assimilation, 153

Progressive-regressive (reciprocal) assimilation, 154

Prokosch, Edward, cited, 147n, 168, 370n, 371n, 372n, 374n, 375n, 379n, 381n, 382n; quoted, 388, 388n

Pronounceability, as a basis for separating vowels and consonants, 66

Pronouncing Russian consonants, 481-485

Pronunciation features, Italian, 432–436; features of Mountain speech, classified according to linguistic formulae, 314, 315; of Russian diphthongs, 480; of Russian vowels, 478–480; peculiar to Mountain speech, 310–314

Prothesis, 162

[ps], in German, 383; loss of, from [sps], 201

Puff theory of voice production, 42n

R

[r], 132, 133; consonantal, in Eastern speech, 229; English, pronunciation by Russians, 508; fricative, 132; in French, 345; in German, 377; in Italian, 444; intrusive, in Southern speech, 219

[ř], in Norwegian, 426; in Russian, 483; in Spanish, 463

[ɽ], in Russian, 498

[r:], in Spanish, 463

[ɹ], in Spanish, 464

[ɾ], 21; in Brazilian Portuguese, 526; in Eastern speech, 229; in Southern British speech, 242

[R], in German, 377, 378; in French, 345

Raising, 158; of [ɪ], [ɛ], [æ], 198; of vowels in Southern speech, 216, 217

Randolph, Vance, (and Anna A. Ingleman), cited, 304, 304n

Reduction in Spanish, 466, 467

Regional dialects, Russian, 476

"Registers," 58

Regressive assimilation, 153, 154; in Russian, 485; persistence of, in English pronunciation by Russians, 510

Relic pronunciations, 193

Relocation of stress, 161

Resonance, definition, 52; in whispering, 59

Resonators, cavities and sounding boards, 52; Helmholtz, 52; open-tube and closed-tube, 56

Restressing, 160, 196; tabulation of, 160

Retracted stress, 196; in Southern speech, 219

Retroflex sounds, 45

Rockwell, W. D., cited, 176n

Romic, 8; broad, 150

Ross, Leonard Q., quoted, 412–417

Rounded vowels, shift in Norwegian, 421n

r, vowel, in Eastern speech, 229

Russell, G. Oscar, cited, 84n, 88, 199

Russian, 475–511; assimilation in, 478; consonants, non-palatal ("hard"), 477; consonants, palatal, ("soft"), 477; consonants, pronunciation according to context, 492–503; consonants, pronunciation of, 480–485; dialect of, transcription, 510; diphthongs, pronunciation according to stress and context, 491, 492; diphthongs, pronunciation of, 480; pronunciation of English consonants, 507–510; pronunciation of English vowels, 504–507; regional dialects, 476; regressive assimilation in, 485; stress, atonic, 478; stress in, 478; stress, pretonic, 478; tonic stress, 478; varieties, areas where spoken, 476; vowels, pronunciation according to stress and context, 486–491; vowels, non-palatalizing ("hard"), 477; vowels, palatalizing, 477; vowels, pronunciation of, 478–480; vowels, variation according to stress, 484, 485; vowels, variation in pronunciation according to context, 480

S

[s], 135, 136; in Brazilian Portuguese, 527; in French, 346–348; in German, 380, 381; in Italian, 444, 445; in Norwegian, 426; in Russian, 500; in Spanish, 465; loss of, from [sps], [sk], [sks], 201

[s̪], in Russian, 500

[sk], loss of from [sks], 201

[ʃ], 20, 136, 137; in Brazilian Portuguese, 528; English, pronunciation by Russians, 507; in French, 348; in Italian, 445; in Norwegian, 426; in Russian, 501

[ʃ'], in Brazilian Portuguese, 527, 528

[ʃʲ], in Russian, 483

[ʃtʃ], in Russian, 483

[ʃʊ], in German, 384

Salesbury, William, cited, 150

Saussure, Ferdinand de, cited, 74n

Scerba, L., cited, 476n

Scheuermeier, Paul, cited, 172

Schlauch, Margaret, cited, 157

Schwa, source of word, 12

Scottish, 256–270; dialect, transcription, 269, 270; standard, 258–261n

Secondary stress, 17

Semantic changes, 168

Shaw, G. B., cited, 252n

Sheridan, Thomas, cited, 150

Shift of rounded vowels in Norwegian, 421n

"Short o," i.e., [ɵ], in Standard Eastern speech, 226

Short vowels in Norwegian, 422

Sibilants, 65

Siebs, Theodor, cited, 369n, 370n, 371n, 372, 374n, 375n, 377n, 378n, 379n, 388n, 389n, 390n, 391n

Sievers, Edward, cited, 369

Silent, consonants, in French, 332; letters, in French, 331, 332; letters, in Italian, 434

Simplification of consonant clusters, 162

Smear, 45

Smith, Henry Lee (and George L. Trager), cited, 74n, 139n; quoted, 182n

Smith, Sir Thomas, cited, 8n, 150

"Soft," (palatalizing) vowels, Russian, 477

Sonority, 61; as a basis for separating vowels and consonants, 67

Sound change, non-systemic, 146; systemic, 146–148; specific, 151

Sound, definition, 49; system of Southern British (stage) speech, 240–244; waves, speed of, 49

Sounding boards, 58

Sounds, Brazilian Portuguese, 513, 514; not in English, 530, 531

Sounds, common to English and French, but varying from each other, 350; complex, 50, 51; English, not in Brazilian Portuguese, 530, 531; English, not in French, 249; English, not in Norwegian, 427; English, not in Spanish, 467; English, tabulated, 46, 47; excrescent, 163, 164; French, charts, 326; French, not in English, 349; German, chart, 366; Italian, charts, 435, 436; Italian, discussion, 436–447; lax, 61; Norwegian, 421–427; retroflex, 45; Spanish, charts, 456–457; Spanish, not in English, 467; speech and non-speech, 35; tense, 61; voiced, 62; voiceless, 62

Southern British, characteristics of, in Cockney, 254; speech sound system of, 240–244; (stage) speech, transcription of, 243, 244

Southern dawl, 212, 213

Southern-General American Border substandard pronunciations, 192, 193

Southern Negro speech, substandard, 293–302; pronunciations, miscellaneous substandard, 220

Southern speech, 172; area of the Eastern United States, 174–177; characteristics of, 205; standard, 205–212; substandard, transcription, 220

Spanish, 454–474; behavior of consonants in syllabication in, 454, 455; behavior of vowels in syllabication in, 455; closed syllables in, 454; consonants, chart, 457; consonants, discussion, 461–466; dialect, 467–474; dialect, transcription, 470–472; diphthongs, 456; diphthongs, discussion, 461; open syllables in, 454; sounds of, charts, 456, 457; sounds not in English, 467; speaking peoples, distribution of, in the United States, 454; syllabication in breath groups in, 455; "triphthongs,"

461; vowels, chart, 456; vowels, discussion, 457–461

Sparks, Jared, cited, 8n, 150n, 234

Specific features of substandard Southern Negro speech, 299–301

Spectrograph, use of, 71n

Speech, areas of the Eastern States, 174–177; as an overlaid function, 33; boundaries, nature of, 179; regions, boundaries, 172; regions, extent, 172; sounds, varieties of, 35

Spelling of German sounds, 367–392; pronunciation, 166, 194

Spirants, 64

Stage pronunciation, in Germany, 368, 369; Committee on, 369n

"Stage speech," 239–244

Standard Eastern speech, 222–233; deviations from, 233; transcription, 231–233

Standard General American speech, deviations from, 189ff.; transcription of, 189

Standard, New York speech, deviations from, 283–292; Scottish, 258; Southern British speech, 239–244; Southern speech, 205–212

Stanley, Oma, cited, 297n, 300n

Stavrou, Christopher, cited, 512n, 515n, 517n, 519n, 522n, 525n, 526n

Stetson, R. H., cited, 73n

Stops, 44

Stress, advanced, in Southern speech, 219; atonic, in Russian, 478; definition, 12; degrees of, 13; degrees of, in French, 330; displaced, in Southern speech, 219; in diphthongs, 11; in Eastern speech, 231; in French, 330; in General American speech, 188, 189; in Italian, 435

Stress, in Russian, 478; in Southern speech, 211; level, 17, 18; marking of, 18; phonemes, 10n; Phonemes, 13n; pretonic, in Russian, 478; primary and secondary, primary and weak, primary, secondary and weak, 111; primary, in French words in isolation, 331; relocation of, 161; retracted, 196; retracted, in Southern speech, 219; Russian, irregularity of, 484; secondary, 17, 18; tonic, in Russian, 478; weak, 18

Stressed diphthongs, 182; vowels, 183; vowels, duration in English, 117, 118

Stressing, 13; and unstressing, in pairs of vowels, 115; in Mountain speech, 315

Strictures, 44

Strong verb construction, dialectal, in Mountain speech, 316

Struble, George G., cited, 405n

Stuart, T. P. A., cited, 33n

Substandard, Eastern speech, transcription, 235; Negro speech features held in common with Substandard Southern white speech, 298, 299; Negro Speech, features in common with Substandard American speech in general 297, 298; New York speech, consonants 285–290; New York speech, transcription, 290–291; New York speech, vowels, 281–285; pronunciations, miscellaneous, 204; Southern Negro speech, 293–302; Southern pronunciations, miscellaneous, 220; Southern speech, transcription, 220

Substandardisms, urban, 233

Substrata, language, 167

Substratum, of Celtic language features in the English of Ireland, 273

Substitutions, French consonants for English consonants, 350; French sounds for English words, 349, 350; French vowels for English vowels, 349, 350; German, in English, 394–397; in Southern speech, 219; made by Italians in pronouncing English, 448, 449; Norwegian for English, chart, 427

Supernumerary final vowel, in pronunciation of English by Italians, 447, 448

Swadesh, Morris, cited, 77n

Swedish, relation to Norwegian, 419

Sweet, Henry, cited, 7n, 150, 150n

Syllabic, [ḷ], 91; [m̩], 91, 92; [n̩], 91, 92; [ŋ̩], 91, 92

Syllabication, in breath groups in Spanish, 455; in German, 369, 370; in Italian, 434, 435; in S., E., and Br. speech, 209

Synalepha in Spanish, 467

Syncope, 164, 165, 196

Synecdoche, 168

Syneresis in Spanish, 466

T

[t], 124; and [əd], used superfluously, 200; English, pronunciation by Russians, 507; for [k], before [l], 202; in Brazilian Portuguese, 524; in French, 342; in German, 371, 372; in Italian, 442; in Norwegian, 425; in Russian, 494; in Spanish, 462; loss of from [spt], 202; loss of from end of syllable, 201; loss of, from [skt], 201

[ʔ], in German, 375, 376

[ts], in German, 383; in Italian, 446

[ts], loss of, from [sts], 201

[t̯s], in Russian, 484

[tsu], in German, 384

[tʃ], 20; phonemic indivisibility of, 20n; in German, 383; in Italian, 447; in Russian, 483; in Spanish, 465

[t̯ʃˑ], in Brazilian Portuguese, 529

[t̯], in Russian, 494

[θ], 19, 134, 233; English, pronunciation by Russians, 508, 509; in Spanish, 464

Tabulation of compensatory lengthenings, 161; of restressings, 160

Tense vowels, 61

Tests, for voicelessness and voicing, 63, 64

Thomas, C. K., cited, 91n, 174n, 178n, 224n, 225n, 281, 283, 283n, 284n, 285n, 411n, 412n

Tomás, Navarro, cited, 469, 470

Tone, 61

Tonic stress, in Russian, 478

Trager, George L., cited, 75, 283, 476n; quoted, 77n; (and Bernard Bloch), cited, 13n, 74n, 77n, 97n; (and Bernard Bloch), quoted, 95n; (and Henry Lee Smith), cited, 74n, 139n; (and Henry Lee Smith), quoted, 182n

Transcription, Brazilian Portuguese dialect, 532; Cockney, 254; French-Canadian, 352–354; Italian dialect, 449–452; Irish dialect, 277, 278; Louisiana French English, 357–358; Mountain speech, 317; Norwegian dialect, 429, 430; Pennsylvania German, 407–409; Russian dialect, 510; Scottish dialect, 269, 270; Southern British (stage) speech, 243, 244; Spanish dialect, 470–472; speech of Mexican child in Arizona, 473, 474; Standard Eastern speech, 231, 235; Standard General American speech, 189; Standard Southern speech, 211; Substandard

Negro speech, 301; Substandard New York speech, 290–291; Substandard Southern speech, 220; Yiddish, 416
Trautman, Moritz, quoted, 378, 379
Treviño, S. N., cited, 84n
Trill, 132; in Italian, 433; one-tap, 45, 132
"Triphthongs," in Italian, 442; Spanish, 461
Trofimov, M. V. (and Daniel Jones), cited, 476n, 485n, 505n; quoted, 75n
Trubetzskoy, N. S., cited, 140n
Tucker, R. Whitney, cited, 405
Turner, Lorenzo D., cited, 293
Twaddell, W. Freeman, cited, 74n
Twain, Mark, quoted in phonetic transcription, 189
Tympanic membrane, 49

U

[u], 12; in Brazilian Portuguese, 518, 519; in French, 339; in German, 391; in Italian, 440; in Russian, 489; in Spanish, 460, 461
[ʉ], in Russian, 479, 490
[ʉ:], in Norwegian, 424
[ũ], in Brazilian Portuguese, 522
[ui], in Brazilian Portuguese, 520
[ũi], in Brazilian Portuguese, 523
[ʊ], 12, 109, 110; English, pronunciation by Russians, 505; for [u], 202; in German, 391, 392; in Spanish, 460; in Russian, 490
[ʌ], 12, 115–117; English, pronunciation by Russians, 505, 506; in Russian, 490
Ukranian, 476
Unrounding, 158
Unstressed vowels, "correctness" of, 14; in General American speech, 186; pronunciation of, 14
Unstressing, 13, 160; in Indo-European, 13n; in Mountain speech, 315; in sentences, 110, 111; in word groups, 111; of monosyllables in word groups, 112–115
Unvoicing, 157, 197; of English final [b, d, g, z] by Russians, 510
Urban, substandard speech, 193; substandardisms, 235–238

V

[v], 133, 134; in Brazilian Portuguese, 527; in French, 345; in German, 380; 391; in Italian, 444; in Norwegian, 426; in Russian, 499; in Spanish, 464
[ɣ], in Russian, 499
[ʋ], in German, 380
Valves, 44
Velars, 48
Vendryes, J., cited, 153
Verner, Karl Adolph, cited, 147n, 168
Verner's law, 168
Viana, Goncalves, cited, 521
Vibration, motive power for, 36; vocal, motors for, 37
Vibrator, for whispered sounds, 42; for voiceless sounds, 43
Vibrators, kinds for different musical instruments, 36; vocal, 37
Vietor, Wilhelm, cited, 370n, 371n, 372n, 373n, 374n, 375n, 376n; quoted, 377n, cited 379n, 380n, 385n; quoted, 388n
Visible Speech, 7, 8, 150
Voiced and voiceless plosives, ways of distinguishing, 123
Voiced consonants vocal component of, 123; [h], 139; sounds, 62
Voicelessness, tests for, 63, 64
Voiceless sounds, 62; vibrator for, 43
Voicing, 197; tests for, 64
Vowel, definition, 73; diagram, developed by the spectrograph, 83; diagram, developed by X-ray, 82; diagram, evolution of, 82, 83; distinguished from consonants, 65–73; [ḷ], 91; [ɱ], 91, 92; [n̩], 91, 92; [ŋ̩], 91, 92
Vowelization, 158
Vowel, definition, 73
Vowels, back, 87; Brazilian Portuguese, 513; Brazilian Portuguese, discussion, 514–523; central, 87; centralized, 198; duration of, when stressed, 117, 118; English, not in French, 249; English, pronunciation by Brazilian Portuguese speakers, 531; English, pronunciation by Russians, 505–507; French, 335–341; French, chart, 326; French, not in English, 349; front, 87; German, discussion, 384–392; high, 87; Italian, discussion, 436–440; long, in

Norwegian, 422; low, 87; mid, 87; nasal, in Brazilian Portuguese, 522, 523; Norwegian, chart, 421; Norwegian discussed, 422–424; open, in French, 334; palatalizing ("soft"), Russian, 477; *r*, in Eastern speech, 229; Russian, pronunciation according to stress and context, 486–491; Russian, pronunciation of, 478–480; Russian, variation in pronunciation according to context, 480, 481; Scottish dialect, 263–268; short, in Norwegian, 422; Spanish, chart, 456; Spanish, discussion, 457–461; stressed, 182; Substandard New York speech, 281–285; unstressed, in General American speech, 186

W

[w], 144, 145, 200; in Brazilian Portuguese, 528, 529; English, pronunciation in Russian, 509; in French, 348; in Italian, 441, 442; in Russian, 509; in Spanish, 466
[ʍ], 145, 200; English, pronunciation in Russian, 509, 510
[wa], in Italian, 441
Wallis, John, cited, 150
Ward, Ida C., cited, 82n, 251, 252n
Warrack, Alexander, cited, 257, 257n
[we], in Italian, 441
Weak, stress, 18; verb construction in Mountain speech, 316
Western speech, inappropriateness of, 171
[wɛ], in Italian, 442
Whispered sounds, vibrator for, 42
Whispering, 36
White Russian, 476
[wi], in Italian, 442
Widening (generalization), 168
Wilkins, Ernest H. (with William A. Nitze and Clarence E. Parmenter), cited, 357n
Williams, E. B., cited, 512n, 520n

Wilkins, John cited, 8n, 150
Wilson, Charles Morrow, cited, 303n
Wise, C. M., cited, 8n, 58n, 129n, 150n, 199n, 217n; (and Giles W. Gray) cited, 58n, 148n, 167, 168; (and Gladys Borchers), cited, 404, 404n
Wise, H. S., cited, 33n
Worcester, Joseph Emerson, cited, 66n
Word, elements, lost in substandard Negro speech, 300; shrinkage, 165
[wɔ], in Italian, 442

X

[x], in Brazilian Portuguese, 526; in German, 381; in Spanish, 466; in Russian, 483, 484

Y

[y], 131; in French, 340, 348; in German, 386; in Norwegian, 423
[y:], in Norwegian, 423
Yiddish, 411–418; affrication in, 412; as written, 413–417; dentality in, 411; homelands of speakers, 411; models for, 411–417; origin of word, 411n; transcription in, 416
y, unstressed, 91

Z

[z], 136; in Brazilian Portuguese, 527; in French, 346; in German, 381; in Italian, 445; in Russian, 500
[z̦], in Russian, 501
Zachrisson, R. E., cited, 247, 247n, 249, 249n
Zeemuller, Joseph, cited, 369
[ʒ], 20, 137, 138; in Brazilian Portuguese, 528; English, pronunciation by Russians, 506, 507; in French, 348; in Italian, 446; in Russian, 483

In the Beginning

Decked out for the hunt, King Assurbanipal of Assyria pursues his quarry, as depicted in a bas-relief from the seventh century B.C.

In the Beginning
An Introduction to Archaeology

BRIAN M. FAGAN

University of California, Santa Barbara

Little, Brown and Company   Boston

Library of Congress Catalog Card No. 74–183044

Second Printing

Published simultaneously in Canada
by Little, Brown & Company (Canada) Limited

Printed in the United States of America

Credits for Illustrations

Cover photo: Altamira prehistoric cave painting from Editorial Photocolor Archives

The sources for the text figures appear below, except for those given with the illustrations. The artwork has, for the most part, been redrawn; the artists are Richard H. Sanderson and New England Illustrators, Inc. The author wishes to thank the publishers, authors, photographers, and illustrators involved for their courtesy in granting permission to use their material. The figures without specified credits have been drawn specially for this book.

FRONTISPIECE: Hirmer Fotoarchiv, Munich, Germany. Courtesy of the Trustees of the British Museum, London. Used in *Crade of Civilization,* p. 63, © 1967 Time Inc.
CHAPTER 2: *2.2* (after Oakley) and *2.3* Redrawn from John Alexander, *The Directing of Archaeological Excavations,* Figs. 16a and 36; London: John Baker Publishers Limited, 1970. New York: Humanities Press, Inc. *2.4* and *2.10* After J. G. D. Clark, *Starr Carr,* Figs. 78 and 27b; London: Cambridge University Press, 1954. *2.6* After F. Clark Howell. Redrawn by permission of the American Anthropological Association from *American Anthropologist,* "Observations on the Earlier Phases of the European Lower Paleolithic," Vol. 68, No. 2, Pt. 2, 1966, Fig. 16. *2.7* After I. W. Cornwall, *Bones for the Archaeologist,* Fig. 22; London: Phoenix House, 1956. Redrawn by permission of Winant Towers, Ltd., London. *2.8* and *2.9* Adapted from Kenneth P. Oakley, *Frameworks for Dating Fossil Man* (Chicago: Aldine Publishing Company: London: Weidenfeld and Nicolson, 1964), Figs. 22 and 7; copyright © 1964 by Kenneth P. Oakley. *2.11* Redrawn from *Prehistoric Europe: The Economic Basis* by J. G. D. Clark, Fig. 145, with the permission of the publishers, Stanford University Press. Copyright © 1952 by J. G. D. Clark; London: Methuen and Company, Ltd. *2.12* Redrawn from F. E. Zeuner, *Dating the Past,* Fig. 3; London: Methuen and Company, Ltd., 1958. *2.13* After Hans E. Suess, "Secular Variations of the Cosmic-Ray-Produced Carbon 14 in the Atmosphere and Their Interpretations," *Journal of Geophysical Research,* 70:23, 1965, Fig. 4.
CHAPTER 3: *3.1* Sir Mortimer Wheeler and the Society of Antiquaries of London.
CHAPTER 4: *4.1* From *Gentleman's Magazine,* 1852, p. 569. *4.2, 4.3,* and *4.10* Sir Mortimer Wheeler and the Society of Antiquaries of London. *4.6* and *4.8* After Ivor Noël Hume, *Historical Archaeology,* Figs. 10 and 23; New York: Alfred A. Knopf, Inc., 1968. Redrawn by permission of the author, the publisher, and Curtis Brown, Ltd. Copyright © 1968 by Ivor Noël Hume. *4.9* Brian M. Fagan.
CHAPTER 5: *5.1* J. Desmond Clark. *5.2* After Richard G. Klein, *Man and Culture in the Late Pleistocene,* Fig. 50; San Francisco: Chandler Publishing Co., 1969. *5.3* J. Desmond Clark. Used in *Early Man,* p. 70, © 1965 Time, Inc. *5.4* After J. G. D. Clark, *Star Carr,* Fig. 4; London: Cambridge University Press, 1954. *5.5* and *5.6* After Charles B. M. McBurney, *The Haua Fteah (Cyrenaica),* Pl. I.2(a), and Fig. I.3; London: Cambridge University Press, 1967, *5.7* From *Early Man,* p. 165, photograph by Robert Morton, © 1965 Time Inc. *5.10, 5.20, 5.21,* and *5.32* Redrawn from John Alexander, *The Directing of Archaeological Excavations,* Figs. 33, 25, 34, 58; London: John Baker Publishers Limited, 1970; New York: Humanities Press, Inc. *5.11* and *5.23* Copyright reserved: Winchester Excavations Committee. *5.12* Redrawn from *Prehistoric Europe: The Economic Basis* by J. G. D. Clark, Fig. 66, with the permission of the publishers, Stanford University Press. Copyright © 1952 by J. G. D. Clark; London: Methuen and Company Ltd. *5.14, 5.15,* and *5.30* Brian M. Fagan. *5.16* After Sir Mortimer Wheeler, *Archaeology from the Earth,* Fig. 16;

Oxford: Clarendon Press, 1954. *5.17* and *5.18* Adapted from Stuart Piggott, *Ancient Europe* (Chicago: Aldine Publishing Company, 1965), Figs. 21 and 67; copyright © Stuart Piggott, 1965. Edinburgh: Edinburgh University Press. *5.19* Sir Mortimer Wheeler and the Society of Antiquaries of London. *5.22* and *5.33* After Sir Mortimer Wheeler in John Alexander, *The Directing of Archaeological Excavations*, Figs. 50 and 60; London: John Baker Publishers Limited, 1970; New York: Humanities Press, Inc. *5.25, 5.26, 5.29,* and *5.31* Sir Mortimer Wheeler (*5.29* and *5.31* copyright Society of Antiquaries of London). *5.27* Patricia M. Christie. *5.34* After Ivor Noël Hume, *Historical Archaeology*, Fig. 15; New York: Alfred A. Knopf, Inc., 1968. Redrawn by permission of the author, the publisher, and Curtis Brown, Ltd. Copyright © 1968 by Ivor Noël Hume. *5.35* Wilfred Shawcross.

CHAPTER 6: *6.1* After Charles B. M. McBurney, *The Haua Fteah (Cyrenaica)*, Fig. II.6; London: Cambridge University Press, 1967. *6.2* and *6.5* After J. G. D. Clark, *Star Carr*, Figs. 8 and 73; London: Cambridge University Press, 1954. *6.3* and *6.17* After Sonia Cole, *The Neolithic Revolution*, Figs. 25 and 6; London, 1959. By permission of the Trustees of the British Museum (Natural History). *6.8* Redrawn from M. L. Ryder, *Animal Bones in Archaeology*, 1969, Figs. 5 and 6; Oxford: Blackwell Scientific Publications Ltd. *6.9* and *6.18* Copyright reserved: University Museum of Archaeology and Ethnology, Cambridge, England. *6.10* After S. von Heberstain, *Rerum Moscoviti carum commentarii*, Berlin (1549). *6.11* After Sir Arthur Evans, *The Palace of Minos at Knossos*, London, 1921, by permission of Agathon Press Inc., New York. *6.12* Courtesy of The Oriental Institute of the University of Chicago. Used in *Cradle of Civilization*, p. 89, © 1967 Time Inc. *6.13* After N. de G. Davies, *The Rock Tombs of El Armarna*—V, London, 1908. *6.16* and *6.26* After J. G. D. Clark, *Aspects of Prehistory*, Figs. 12 and 9, Berkeley, 1970. Originally published by the University of California Press; redrawn by permission of The Regents of the University of California. *6.19, 6.21,* and *6.25* Redrawn from *Prehistoric Europe: The Economic Basis* by J. G. D. Clark, Figs. 44, 17, and 11, with the permission of the publishers, Stanford University Press. Copyright © 1952 by J. G. D. Clark. London: Methuen and Company Ltd. *6.20* and *6.22* Brian M. Fagan. *6.23 South African Archaeological Bulletin*, Vol. V, No. 18, June 1950, cover design. *6.24* Patricia Vinnecombe, "A Fishing Scene from the Tsoelike River, South-Eastern Basutoland," *South African Archaeological Bulletin*, Vol. 15, No. 57, March 1960, p. 15, Fig. 1.

CHAPTER 7: *7.1* From *Early Man*, p. 163, drawing by Jay H. Matternes, © 1965 Time Inc. *7.2, 7.4, 7.5,* and *7.12* Redrawn from *Early Man*, pp. 105, 110, and 111, drawings by Lowell Hess, © 1965 Time Inc. *7.6* After Derek Roe, *Prehistory*, Figs. 10 and 11, © 1970 by Derek Roe. Originally published by the University of California Press; redrawn by permission of The Regents of the University of California and Macmillan London and Basingstoke. Based on Fig. 7, No. 9, and Fig. 26, No. 3, in *The Swanscombe Skull, A Survey of Research on a Pleistocene Site*, Royal Anthropological Institute, *Occasional Paper, No. 20. 7.7* Derek Roe. Copyright Pitt Rivers Museum, University of Oxford. *7.8* After J. M. Coles and E. S. Higgs, *The Archaeology of Early Man*, Fig. 81; London: Faber and Faber Ltd., 1968; New York: Praeger Publishers, Inc. *7.9, 7.10* and *7.11* After F. Bordes, *The Old Stone Age*, Figs. 34, 54, and 55; London: Weidenfeld & Nicolson Ltd., 1968. *7.13* After G. H. S. Bushnell, *The First Americans*, Fig. 2; copyright © 1968 Thames and Hudson Ltd., London. *7.14* After J. G. D. Clark, *Star Carr*, Fig. 35; London: Cambridge University Press, 1954. *7.15* Olmec jade ceremonial axe, 9th–4th c. B.C., courtesy of the Trustees of the British Museum, London, photograph by Derek Bayes. From *Ancient America*, p. 32, © 1967 Time Inc. *7.16* After J. G. D. Clark, *Aspects of Prehistory*, Fig. 6, Berkeley, 1970. Originally published by the University of California Press; redrawn by permission of The Regents of the University of California. *7.17, 7.23, 7.26, 7.27,* and *7.30* Brian M. Fagan. *7.18* Kenneth MacLeish. Used in *Early Man*, p. 59, © 1965 Time Inc. *7.19* J. Vertut. *7.20* and *7.24* Redrawn from Gordon R. Willey, *An Introduction to Archaeology*, Volume One: *North and Middle America*, © 1966, Figs. 7–11, 7–12, and 3–98, by permission of Prentice-Hall, Inc., Englewood Cliffs, N.J. *7.29* Adapted from Stuart Piggott, *Ancient Europe* (Chicago: Aldine Publishing Company, 1965), Fig. 66; copyright © Stuart Piggott, 1965. Edinburgh: Edinburgh University Press. *7.31* After Kenneth P. Oakley, *Man the Toolmaker*, Fig. 12; London, 1949. By permission of the Trustees of the British Museum (Natural History). *7.32* From *Invitation to Archaeology* by James Deetz, Fig. 9. Copyright © 1967 by James Deetz. Redrawn by permission of the author and Doubleday & Company, Inc.

CHAPTER 8: *8.1* After Sir John Evans from J. G. D. Clark, *Archaeology and Society*, Fig. 18; London: Methuen and Company Ltd., 1939; reprinted by Barnes and Noble, New York. *8.2* After Derek Roe, *Prehistory*, Fig. 99, © 1970 by Derek Roe. Originally published by the University of California Press; redrawn by permission of The Regents of the University of California and Macmillan London and Basingstoke. Also originally published in the *Proceedings of the Prehistoric Society*, 1963, 29:258–325, and the *Guide Catalogue of the Neolithic and Bronze Age Collections in Devizes Museum*, p. 130. *8.3* After James A. Ford, technical manual 1, *A Quantitative Method for Deriving Cultural Chronology*, Fig. 8, Pan American Union, published by the Organization of American States, Washington, D.C., 1962. *8.4, 8.5,* and *8.6* From *Invitation to Archaeology*

For Judy
with love—and not least
because of Catticus

Preface

This introduction to archaeology approaches the subject both from the historical angle and from the perspective of the latest scientific methods. Its aim is to provide a comprehensive summary of the methods and techniques of archaeology for beginning students and interested persons who have not encountered the prehistoric past before.

In the Beginning summarizes the early development of archaeology, chronological methods, site survey and excavation, and analysis of prehistoric economies and artifacts. A major section of the book traces the history of archaeological theory from the Age of Romance to the 1970s, putting the latest advances in the subject into a wider perspective.

Archaeology has witnessed a knowledge explosion in the past decade and we face a major shift in research objectives in which both sophisticated systems models and quantitative methods will play an increasingly important part. Future archaeologists will undoubtedly need a grounding in scientific method and explanation,[1] as well as statistical techniques—these topics, while discussed, are not treated exhaustively here.

Included are a glossary of technical terms and a bibliography that

[1] For a brief synthesis of explanation in archaeology, see Patty Jo Watson, Steven A. LeBlanc, and Charles L. Redman, *Explanation in Archaeology*, New York, 1971.

Some reading in the works of philosophers of science belonging to the logical, positivist school is desirable for professionally oriented students. Two basic references are: Carl G. Hempel, *Philosophy of Natural Science* (New York, 1966), and Ernst Nagel, *The Structure of Science: Problems in the Logic of Scientific Explanation* (New York, 1966).

lists books covering the prehistoric archaeology of different areas of the world; these works could be read in conjunction with this volume. Each chapter is supplemented with notes at the back of the book, which can be used to base further discussion or to suggest more exhaustive reading on particular topics. The notes and bibliography offer greater flexibility in learning than serried rows of uncritically presented references.

This book has been written from predominantly English language sources for a number of reasons. The recent spate of archaeological literature has been enormous and my reading has been necessarily selective and predominantly in English. Readers are directed toward English language sources as much as possible as this is, in most cases, their mother tongue. Those interested in a more detailed knowledge of a particular topic are strongly advised to consult a specialist before wading into archaeological literature in other languages. Inevitably, this volume has some bias toward the achievements and writings of English-speaking archaeologists, an emphasis that evolved from linguistic abilities and time, rather than nationalistic propensities. The horsemen of Pazyryk and the Shang tombs are as much part of archaeology as Cahokia and medieval Winchester.

I am very grateful to all those colleagues and students who have commented on this book in draft form, especially Drs. Ralph M. Rowlett, Albert Spaulding, and Barbara Voorhies. I am deeply indebted to Dr. Elvin Hatch for his constant advice and criticism of Chapters 10 and 11. Valuable contributions were also made by Michael Bisson and my wife. Mrs. Linda Cordell was of the greatest assistance with Part Three, and her advice has been invaluable. Mrs. Phyllis Frezin shouldered the unenviable task of typing my complicated arabesques. Miss Freda Alexander was an able and efficient editor in Boston. This book would never have been written without Milton Johnson at the other end of the telephone—I have enjoyed both his encouragement and his lunches.

Contents

Part One
Digging up the Past   1

Chapter 1
Introduction   3

THE FIRST ARCHAEOLOGISTS   4

THE ANTIQUITY OF MAN   9

ARCHAEOLOGY IN THE NEW WORLD   16

ARCHAEOLOGY   19

HISTORY AND ARCHAEOLOGY   22

Chapter 2
Time   26

THE THREE AGES   27

RELATIVE AND ABSOLUTE CHRONOLOGY   29

STRATIGRAPHY AND SUPERPOSITION   33

PLEISTOCENE GEOCHRONOLOGY   36

POLLEN ANALYSIS   43

ABSOLUTE CHRONOLOGY   48

OBJECTS OF KNOWN AGE   49

DENDROCHRONOLOGY   51

THERMOLUMINESCENCE   54

RADIOCARBON DATING   55

POTASSIUM ARGON DATING   56

Chapter 3
Preservation and Discovery   59
PRESERVATION   59
FINDING ARCHAEOLOGICAL SITES   66
AERIAL PHOTOGRAPHY   68
ACCIDENTAL DISCOVERIES   70
ARCHAEOLOGICAL SURVEY   74

Chapter 4
Excavation   77
EXCAVATION METHODS   81
TYPES OF EXCAVATION   84
SAMPLING   89
HOW DO YOU DIG?   91
RECORDING   92
ORGANIZATION OF AN EXCAVATION   94

Chapter 5
Excavation Problems   98
OPEN HUNTING CAMPS   98
CAVES AND ROCKSHELTERS   102
STRUCTURES AND DWELLINGS   107
VILLAGES AND TOWNS   116
MOUND SITES   122
BARROWS, OR SMALL BURIAL MOUNDS   125
CEMETERIES AND SKELETONS   129
FORTIFIED SETTLEMENTS AND EARTHWORKS   131
SHELL MIDDENS   136

Part Two
Analysis of the Past   139

Chapter 6
Environment and Subsistence   141
RECONSTRUCTING ANCIENT ENVIRONMENTS   142
PALYNOLOGY   145
SUBSISTENCE   146
ANIMAL BONES   150
VEGETAL REMAINS   164
AGRICULTURE AND DOMESTIC AND WILD ANIMALS   171
BIRDS, FISH, AND MOLLUSCA   174
ROCK ART   180

PREHISTORIC DIET   182

TRADE   184

Chapter 7

Technology and Artifacts   187

STONE TECHNOLOGY   188

WOOD   203

BONE   204

CLAY   208

METALLURGY: IRON AND COPPER   215

CLASSIFICATION OF ARTIFACTS   222

CLASSIFICATION IN ARCHAEOLOGY   223

Chapter 8

Ordering and Interpretation   229

ARTIFACTS AND TIME   229

ARTIFACTS IN SPACE   235

ARCHAEOLOGICAL UNITS   236

ARCHAEOLOGICAL CULTURES   238

CULTURE CHANGE: INVENTION, MIGRATION, AND DIFFUSION   239

SOCIAL ORGANIZATION   246

RELIGION AND RITUAL   248

ANALOGY IN ARCHAEOLOGY   248

Chapter 9

Settlement Archaeology   257

STRUCTURES   260

COMMUNITIES   263

POPULATION DISTRIBUTIONS   268

SUMMARY   270

Part Three

Frameworks for the Past   273

Chapter 10

Intellectual Frameworks:
Mercati to Durkheim   275

RATIONALISM, SCEPTICISM, AND A NATURALISTIC PHILOSOPHY
OF EVENTS   276

DEGENERATION AND PROGRESS   279

EVOLUTION   282

DIFFUSION AND RELATIVISM   289

EMIL DURKHEIM AND FUNCTIONALISM   291

Chapter 11
Toward Explanation: 1900 to the 1970s   294

FRANZ BOAS AND ARCHAEOLOGY   294

V. GORDON CHILDE   298

NEW WORLD ARCHAEOLOGY: 1920–1950   301

ECOLOGICAL APPROACHES TO ARCHAEOLOGY   303

EXPLANATION AND VERIFICATION   306

SYSTEMS THEORY   309

Chapter 12
Conclusion   316

Notes   320
Bibliography of Area Archaeologies   341
Glossary   345
Index   349

In the Beginning

Part One
Digging up the Past

A mere hole in the ground, which of all sights is perhaps the least vivid and dramatic, is enough to grip their attention for hours at a time.

P. G. Wodehouse, *A Damsel in Distress*

Chapter 1
Introduction

"And God said, 'Let us make man in our image, after our likeness: and let them have dominion over the fish of the sea, and over the fowl of the air, and over the cattle, and over all the earth, and over every creeping thing that creepeth upon the earth.' " Thus the first chapter of Genesis, a majestic panorama of the story of the Creation, gives an account of man's origins familiar to centuries of scholars and worshippers. Indeed, man has probably always been curious about his origins, and sought justification for his presence on this planet. This intellectual curiosity about his antecedents has led man to historical inquiry and to development of archaeology as a serious discipline for studying prehistoric culture, as well as to historiography which is a major concern of twentieth-century scholars. Lively speculation about the past reflects man's attempts to create theoretical models of his ancestry, either based on philosophical models or, more recently, on scientific fact.

To many people, the past is featureless, without any memorable events to partition it or bring it into focus. Their perspective covers only several generations of family history or, conceivably, a few centuries of written history dealing with the deeds of kings and politicians. To most Americans, the history of the American Indian involves them little emotionally, for their identification with the New World is a provincial one, bounded by the frontiers of their own society and its limited history. The written history of American Indians, on the other hand, hardly exists, but their ancestry extends many thousands of years back into a still imperfectly known past. Many

3

black Africans are conscious that their societies have existed for centuries, and retain a lively curiosity about tribal history, listening eagerly to the accounts which tribal historians have handed down orally from generation to generation. Only in recent years have oral historians and archaeologists begun to recover Africa's unwritten past, thus giving its new nations a longer perspective and greater national identity.

Studying archaeology is one of the primary ways in which mankind's featureless past can be put into correct philosophical perspective. Yet the researches of archaeologists remain surprisingly unfamiliar to the public, which pictures the archaeologist as a grey-bearded treasure hunter, perpetually digging around pyramids. Nothing could be further from the truth. Archaeological research has become meticulous, laborious, and complicated, with many startling achievements to its credit. Man's origins have been traced back over 5 million years. Human settlement in the New World has been dated to over 20,000 years ago, while farming villages in the Near East have been excavated and dated to nearly 8000 B.C. Major changes in human culture have been traced through millennia of prehistoric time, while increasingly accurate methods of dating the past have been developed and applied to archaeological sites all over the world. The archaeologist's work is transforming featureless prehistory into a fascinating landscape of hominid evolution, cultural change, and technological advance—reflecting man's increased control over his natural environment. The first steps toward a world prehistory have been taken, giving new perspectives of time and human history, as well as exciting theoretical models of man's past.

THE FIRST ARCHAEOLOGISTS

The intellectual curiosity of early scholars about their past was the first stage in developing archaeology as a serious scientific discipline. Although, in the sixth century B.C., the Babylonian king Nabonidus did engage in some antiquarian research and made excavations at Ur-of-the-Chaldees, he was hardly an archaeologist. Greek writers like Herodotus travelled widely, and came into contact with barbarian peoples living on the fringes of the Ancient World, who were still living in prehistory. Herodotus left valuable, if picturesque, descriptions of the Scythians and their material culture, confirmed by excavations in modern times, but no one set out to make a systematic study of European or Saharan tribes. Although neither the Greeks nor Romans excavated for the past, the former began to reach the stage of rational reflection about man's origins, a necessary stage before the impetus to study the past systematically. Their reflections probably arose from their concern with the relationship between primitive peoples and their own comfortable civilization. One philosophical model of early man was that of Hesiod,[1] * who wrote a book entitled *Works and Days* in the eighth century B.C. He visualized man's past as five distinct stages. An age of Gold and the Immortals was comprised of people who "dwelt in ease and peace upon their lands with many good things, rich in flocks and loved by the blessed gods." An age of Silver found man infinitely less respectable. An age of Bronze arrived when man originated from "a brazen race sprung from ash trees, who delighted in war." These men were the first to eat animal food and to use bronze for their armor and houses, as well as their implements—iron was not yet in use. The last two ages included that of the Epic Heroes, who were a distinct improvement on their predecessors, and the age of Iron, one of terrible sorrow when man never ceased laboring during the day and perished by night. Hesiod's speculations are typical of ancient scholars, who approached the unknown past with a philosophy tempered with inherited knowledge of recent prehistory, a familiarity with Homer, and a wide geographic background. A similar concept of ages, this time of stone, bronze, and iron, is that of a Chinese writer in A.D. 52, perhaps derived from a folk memory of prehistoric achievement.

Archaeology really developed in the last two hundred years, but has its roots in a heightened intellectual curiosity about the past some centuries earlier.[2] At the end of the Middle Ages and during the Renaissance there was a revival of interest in the Classical world. Renewed study of Greek and Roman literature revealed fascinating accounts of hitherto unknown peoples who were living in much of Central and Northern Europe during Classical times, so an additional chapter of man's past was suddenly added to the comfortable world of the Middle Ages. Sixteenth-century scholars and travelers began to study the archaeological remains of the Greek and Roman civilizations.

During succeeding centuries the discovery of Classical antiquities led to a dramatic increase in interest in the past. Men of leisure and wealth traveled widely in Italy and Greece studying antiquities and acquiring many examples of Classical sculpture and statuary. These visible remains of the past turned men's minds toward their own origins. Frustrated Classical antiquarians and other scholars who remained at home began to speculate about ancient British and European history, too; they acquired an active interest in the conspicuous ar-

* See pages 320–321 for notes to Chapter 1.

chaeological sites which dotted the European landscape. In England, monuments such as Stonehenge and Avebury were examined; burial mounds were found scattered throughout the rolling grasslands of Wessex. Taking the first steps in the rediscovery of prehistory, local antiquarians and topographers traveled widely throughout Europe examining antiquities and describing them; they speculated on their origins, liberally using legends and folklore. These gentlemen did not excavate the sites they discovered, they merely described them. (Figures 1.1–1.6 show the locations of most sites mentioned in the text.)

One famous antiquarian was William Camden (1551–1623),[3] who was successively a schoolmaster and then an authority on heraldry. Camden traveled extensively in Great Britain, studying its antiquities and describing archaeological sites. He was a meticulous observer and even recorded crop marks—a phenomenon widely used today in archaeological reconnaissance from the air—for he observed the streets of the Roman town of Silchester from the differential growth marks in the corn fields growing on the site. In 1586 Camden published a volume entitled *Britannia,* the first complete directory to the antiquities of Britain. His purpose was clearly set out: "to renew the memory of what was old, illustrate what was obscure, and settle what was doubtful, and recover some certainty in our affairs." The great geographer Abraham Ortelius begged him to "acquaint the world with Britain, that ancient island; that is to restore Britain to its Antiquities and its Antiquities to Britain."

Two other celebrated antiquarians were John Aubrey (1626–1697), a Wiltshire squire, and William Stukeley (1687–1765),[4] both of whom carried on the tradition so ably started by Camden. John Aubrey and his contemporaries were much influenced by the romantic accounts of primitive peoples described by explorers and voyagers to the New World, Africa, and Asia. The cartographer John Speed published vivid accounts of the strange customs of American Indians, who, with other strange peoples, were described as living in a vague kind of romantic savagery. The concept of the "Noble Savage" came into fashion, and inevitably affected antiquarian writing and interpretation (see Figure 10.1). Sober antiquarian observation combined with fanciful speculation and classical allusion to bring the past to life. John Aubrey writing at his best typifies such seventeenth-century expression:

> Let us imagine then what kind of countrie this was in the time of the Ancient Britons. By the nature of the soil, which is a sour woodsere land, very natural for the production of akes especially, one may conclude that

Fig. 1.1 Archaeological sites in the United States and Mesoamerica. The Virú Valley in Peru does not appear on the map.

this North Division was a shady dismal wood; and the inhabitants almost as savage as the Beasts whose skins were their only rayment. The language British, which for the honour of it was spoken from the Orcades to Italie and Spain. The Boats of the Avon (which signifies River) were basketts of twigges covered with an oxe skin; which the poore people in Wales use

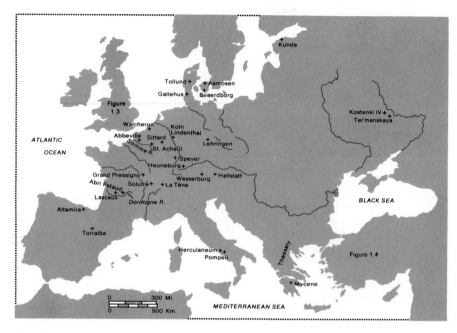

Fig. 1.2   Archaeological sites in Europe.

to this day. They call them curricles. Within this Shire I believe that there
were several Reguli which often made war upon another; and the great
ditches which run on the Plaines and elsewhere so many miles (not unlikely) their boundaries; and withal served for defense against the in-
cursions of their enemies, as the Pict's wall, Offa's Ditch; and that in
China, to compare things small to great. Their religion is at large described by Caesar. Their priests were Druids some of their temples I
pretend to have restored, as Avebury, Stonehenge, etc. as also British
sepulchres. Their way of fighting is lively sett down by Caesar. Their
camps with their way of meeting I have sett down in another place. They
knew the use of iron. . . . They were two or three degrees I suppose less
savage than the Americans. . . . The Romans subdued and civilized them.[5]

Aubrey and Stukeley, the latter remembered above all for his
preoccupation with the ancient British cult of the Druids, described
by Caesar, were at a loss to interpret the numerous sites they described.
In the end they were forced to interpret their finds in terms of their
only available historical source, the Classical past. But the seventeenth-century antiquarian was beginning to recognize that there was
a long period of prehistoric time preceding the Roman occupation
of Europe. It began to seem that archaeology was the best prospect
for uncovering earlier times.

Fig. 1.3   Archaeological sites in the United Kingdom.

THE ANTIQUITY OF MAN

One problem that antiquarians of the seventeenth and eighteenth centuries faced was a complete lack of information on how long man had been living on the earth. The prehistoric past was confusing, for archaeologists had no means of dating prehistory, nor had they any chronological depth for their finds. Until these two requirements

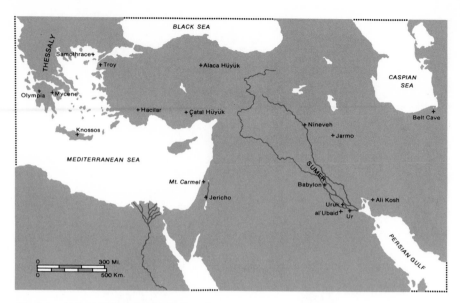

Fig. 1.4   Archaeological sites in the Near East.

were satisfied, archaeologists could not introduce order into the incredible jumble of antiquities beginning to crowd the collectors' cabinets and the pages of antiquarian topographies.

One problem was the dogma of the Christian church. The first chapter of Genesis stated that God created the world and man in six days. The story of Adam and Eve provided an entirely consistent explanation for the Creation of Man and the world's population. The Bible's early chapters are full of complicated genealogical tables for the early families who populated the earth. Men attempted to use the tables for calculating the date of the Flood and the Creation. In 1650 Archbishop James Ussher used the genealogies in the Old Testament to calculate that the world was created in 4004 B.C. This was refined by Dr. John Lightfoot of Cambridge who published a monograph in 1642 in which he declared that man was created at 9 A.M. on October 23, 4004 B.C.[6] These calculations and theories received almost universal acceptance and became a dogmatic canon defended with almost fanatical frenzy in the nineteenth century. It was a comfortable theory which allowed approximately 4,000 years for all prehistoric time. All kinds of romantic legends were concocted to fill these 4,000 years, in order to produce some explanation for the chaotic jumble of antiquities found both by surface discovery and, increasingly during the eighteenth century, by excavations.

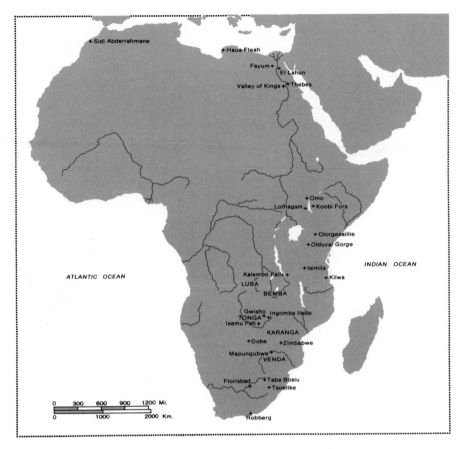

Fig. 1.5   Archaeological sites in Africa.

Excavation became popular with those unable to afford the expense of a grand tour to the Mediterranean. Local squires began to excavate the burial mounds and other antiquities on their property. One was English landowner Sir Richard Colt-Hoare, who dug no less than 379 burial mounds in the early nineteenth century, not only recording his observations with care, but also distinguishing between different types of burial, as well as original and later interments. He published his archaeological sites in detail, as part of a history of Wiltshire county, dealing specifically with the archaeological record as opposed to folklore and family histories. But, after ten years' work, he was forced to confess total ignorance as to the builders of these burial mounds: "We have evidence of the very high antiquity of our Wiltshire barrows but none respecting the tribes to whom they appertain, that

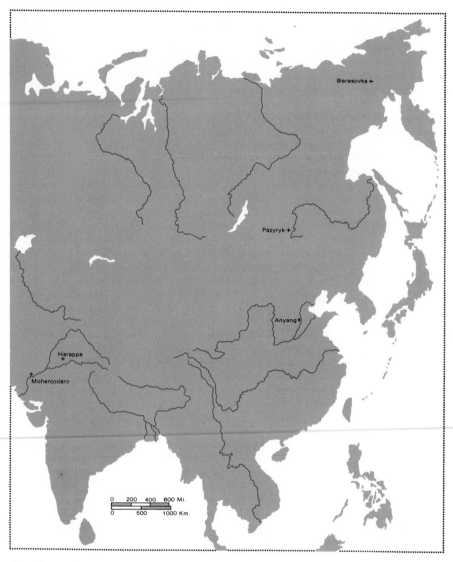

Fig. 1.6   Archaeological sites in Asia. Galatea Bay, Auckland, New Zealand, does not appear on the map.

can rest on solid foundations."[7] So he ascribed the prehistoric sites of Wiltshire to the Ancient Britons. No one had as yet found a way of putting in order the 4,000 years of prehistory alleged to exist by Biblical scholars.

Discoveries were beginning to come to light, however, which threw serious doubt on Ussher's dating. Ever since the sixteenth century, discoveries had been made both of extinct animals' bones and also of stone tools whose shapes differed so from natural rocks that it was difficult to explain them away. A number of authorities interpreted such rocks as thunderbolts, or meteorites. Others, however, such as the sixteenth-century scholar, Mercati, disagreed and called them weapons used by peoples ignorant of the use of iron.[8] Seventeenth-century antiquarians like Sir William Dugdale and Dr. Robert Plot believed that these stone tools were weapons used by the Ancient Britons before metallurgy was known. In the same century, Isaac de la Peyrère described the so-called thunderbolts as the tools of men who dated before the time of Adam; his book was burned in public. These finds, mainly of isolated tools, were attracting attention among scholars interested in the past, but no one as yet recognized them as evidence for man's high antiquity.

Then people began to find the bones of monstrous extinct animals such as the elephant and hippopotamus in European river gravel beds, in direct association with the very stones described by the antiquarians as the tools of ancient man. In 1715 John Bagford reported the discovery of a stone axe and elephant bones found in London gravel beds by a man called Conyers. The finder described the tool as that of an ancient Briton who did not know how to use metal, but Bagford said the elephant was Roman.

A far more significant discovery was made by a country squire in Suffolk named John Frere. On June 22, 1797, Frere wrote to the Secretary of the Society of Antiquaries describing and enclosing some stone implements found in a gravel pit at Hoxne. His letter and finds were published in the Society's journal. The tools consisted of a series of what are now known as Acheulian hand axes which were found 3.7 meters (12 feet) below the surface in direct association with the bones of extinct animals. Frere described them: "They are, I think, evidently weapons of war fabricated and used by a people who had not the use of metals. . . . The situation in which these weapons were found may tempt us to refer them to a very remote period indeed, even beyond that of the present world."[9]

John Frere's remarks were noted but forgotten. By this time people were familiar with stone implements but they were not ready to accept the idea that they came from a remote past beyond that of the comfortable world described by Sir Thomas Browne in 1635: "Time we may comprehend 'tis but five days elder than ourselves and hath the same Horoscope with the World." The Biblical story of the Creation still had a great hold on scientists of the time. In the early nineteenth century, people were still vociferously supporting Archbishop Ussher's chronology for the Creation. Typically, William Paley wrote his *Natural*

Theology in 1802, in which he endeavored to prove that man had inhabited the world for 6,000 years and that it "teemed with delighted existence"—a beautiful world inhabited by beautiful people.[10] By the late eighteenth century, a serious anomaly between the archaeological record and theological canon was increasingly apparent. The antiquarians were confused by a lack of time depth, and had no means of classifying the past, and were mystified by the increasing frequency with which stone tools were being found in contexts that, theologically speaking, were impossible. They lacked a chronology for the period between written history and 4004 B.C., and failed to realize that cultural reconstruction was possible in prehistory. Man's high antiquity had to be proven and a means of measuring prehistoric time devised before archaeology came into its own as a serious, scientific discipline.

The events which led up to the recognition of the antiquity of man resulted from a number of basic discoveries in biology, geology, and paleontology.[11] Vertebrate paleontology was not studied much until the eighteenth century, when a remarkable Frenchman, Jacques Cuvier (1769–1832) began a lifetime's work on fossil mammals. The first great paleontologist, Cuvier studied the fossil records of rocks and the geological history of the world by using his animals as type indicators for different strata, distinguishing periods when particular species such as dinosaurs had been dominant. In so doing he denied stoutly that man also existed in the fossil record. Instead, his interpretation of the earth's history was based on the theory that there had been a series of great catastrophes which had resulted in the destruction of one fauna and the creation of another. The Biblical Flood was the latest catastrophic event in a long series of cataclysms. But at the same time, William "Strata" Smith (1769–1839), a geologist, was beginning to study the stratification of the earth. He recognized that the geological processes of erosion, accumulation, weathering, and tectonic movement, which were still occurring in his time, were far more likely agents of geological change than successive catastrophes. Smith produced a complicated table of geological time in which he identified a large number of different fossil animal types. He stressed that the rocks of the earth had formed as a result of continuous natural geological processes without the catastrophic changes proposed by Cuvier and others. In 1785, James Hutton (1726–1797) published his *Theory of the Earth*, in which he supported Smith's findings and proposed that the earth was formed by natural processes. This theory became known as the doctrine of uniformitarianism, and caused immediate controversy, dividing geologists into two distinct camps: one accepted the new doctrine, but the other was made up of ardent catastrophists, the most famous of whom was Dean William Buckland (1784–1856). His *Geology and Mineralogy Considered in Relation to Natural Theology* appeared in 1836 and became a best-seller. It set out to prove that the geological record was confirmation of the "power, wisdom and goodness of God as manifested in creation." The issue came to a head in the 1830s as a result of the publication of Sir Charles Lyell's *Principles of Geology*, produced in three volumes between 1830–1833. Lyell synthesized the latest data from geological sources and accepted the new theories in general terms; his book reached a popular audience and, gradually, uniformitarianism achieved much wider acceptance.[12]

The theory of uniformitarianism suggested that there was no reason at all why man should not have been living on the earth for far longer than the six thousand years of Ussher's chronology. This meant that one could readily accept the contemporaneity of man and extinct animals, an association of which many scientists were now finding increasingly numerous examples in different localities. But not until nearly twenty years after the publication of Lyell's volumes was the antiquity of man finally accepted by the scientific world.

Lyell's work also had a profound effect on Charles Darwin who published *The Origin of Species* in 1859.[13] Charles Lyell used the philosophy of gradual change in his geological textbook when he described the different types of fossils found in the successive strata of the earth. His conclusions assisted Darwin in his formulation of the theories of evolution and natural selection. The latter was able to demonstrate that life and animal forms could change as the result of natural selection through the survival of the fittest. This was a far more logical explanation than that of the paleontological catastrophists.

In the 1820s some excavations in English caves led to further discoveries of man and extinct animals. Father J. MacEnery excavated at Kent's Cavern near Torquay in Devon in 1824–1829. He found the remains of extinct animals associated with stone implements; the layer in which they were found was sealed by a zone of stalagmite, a cave deposit having the consistency of cement, which takes a long time to form. MacEnery discussed his finds with Dean Buckland, who refused to accept the contemporaneity of the bones and stones and insisted that Ancient Britons had made ovens in the stalagmite, thereby introducing their implements into the older, lower levels.

While MacEnery did not publish his results for fear of ridicule, a Frenchman named Jacques Boucher de Perthes was not afraid to do so.[14] In 1837, de Perthes, who was a customs officer at Abbeville in northwestern France, began collecting stone implements and fossils from the gravels of the Somme River. Immediately, he began to find hand axes and the bones of extinct animals in the same sealed gravel beds in such numbers that he was convinced that he had found pre-Flood man. He insisted that human beings had lived before the last catastrophic cataclysm to overwhelm the world, before the start of Ussherian time. De Perthes's findings were ridiculed when he published them in 1847, but he persisted in his investigations until word of his discoveries came to the ears of two eminent English scientists John Evans and Joseph Prestwich, who decided to visit Boucher de Perthes at Abbeville in 1859. They examined his findings and his sites and published papers upon their return to England which fully supported de Perthes's findings. In June, 1859, Evans spoke to the Society of Antiquaries in London; his paper contained this statement: "This much appears established beyond doubt, that in a period of antiquity remote beyond any of which we have hitherto found traces, this portion of the globe was peopled by man."[15]

In 1858 and 1859 a schoolmaster, William Pengelly, excavated at Kent's Cavern again, this time on behalf of a committee of the British Association for the Advancement of Science. He dug in a cave near the neighboring town of Brixham and discovered flint tools in association with the bones of lion, cave bear, mammoth, rhinoceros, and reindeer. Pengelly's findings, supporting those of de Perthes, finally dispersed the remaining confusion. There followed a rapid and fairly general acceptance of the idea, as a scientific fact, that man had been living on this earth longer than 4004 B.C., the date compounded by Archbishop Ussher and his successors. The new, potentially long chronology for man was made easier by the publication of Darwin's theory of natural selection, itself widely accepted by his fellow scientists soon after publication. Darwin himself was cautious in *The Origin of Species:* "Light will be thrown on the origin of man and his history." But Thomas Huxley, Darwin's most ardent supporter, went even further. Acceptance of Darwin's views, he said, "will extend by long epochs the most liberal estimate that has yet been made of the Antiquity of Man."[16] Apart from the religious controversies, however, people began to realize that the past before the advent of written records was knowable, and that it was possible to measure the enormous time scales going back to when man lived at the same time as extinct animals.

ARCHAEOLOGY IN THE NEW WORLD

With the widespread acceptance of the antiquity of man, archaeology spread its frontiers rapidly. The history of New World archaeology is intimately bound up with the development of prehistoric research in

Europe.[17] Speculation about the inhabitants of the New World was rife from the days of the earliest European settlement, a time when the perspectives of Western civilization were being widened rapidly. The Americas were inhabited by strange races whose civilizations were in some respects similar to, yet in others very different from, those of the Old World. John Speed's romantic visions of the Red Indian were one reason for the flourishing antiquarian tradition of eighteenth-century Europe. Others speculated as to the origins of these remarkable people; Ethiopians, Canaanites, Celts, Chinese, and Phoenicians were some of the peoples thought to have been the American natives' ancestors. A theory with a particularly long life considered the American Indians the descendents of the Ten Lost Tribes of Israel.

By the early nineteenth century, field research and museum work began to replace the wild speculations of earlier scholars. Site descriptions and excavations became more common, having their roots in the surveys of important sites by Spanish authorities in Central America and culminating in John Lloyd Stephens's and Frederick Catherwood's outstanding reports on Maya sites published in 1841–1843.[18] Some sober accounts of Indian mounds in North America began to appear. Thomas Jefferson excavated an Indian mound in Virginia in 1784, and made careful notes on his observations, which included some interpretation of occupation layers.[19] Caleb Atwater studied mounds and earthworks in Ohio in the early nineteenth century,[20] while E. G. Squier and E. H. Davis surveyed and dug others in the Ohio and Mississippi valleys, described in their important monograph *Ancient Monuments of the Mississippi Valley* in 1848. By the mid-nineteenth century, an era of factual description was beginning, which had its roots in a number of events. One was a long synthesis of American archaeology, written by Samuel Haven, called *Archaeology of the United States* and published by the newly established Smithsonian Institution in 1856. Haven's comprehensive essay reviews all the published speculations about the origins of the pre-Columbian Indians, most of which he dismissed as pure fantasy. After a review of historical linguistics and a survey of the racial characteristics of the American Indian, Haven describes the archaeology of North America, largely that of the mounds and earthworks of the eastern states containing artifacts of known historic Indian origin. In contrast, Caleb Atwater and other pioneers had regarded the Ohio mounds as the work of civilized ancients who were quite distinct from the modern Indian population. Samuel Haven agreed with other physical anthropologists that the American Indians were a distinct race with some Mongolian affinities, designating the earliest inhabitants of the New World as northeastern Asiatics who migrated into North America at an unknown date. He was careful not to embroil himself in the theological controversies between the catastrophists and the newer uniformitarian school, merely seeking enough time for the physical and linguistic diversity of the different American Indian tribes to be established.

Yet Haven's essay did reflect the new and more systematic approach to archaeology both in Europe and the New World, a symptom of an era of tremendous scientific advance on many fronts. Darwin's researches, the new geology, and Boucher de Perthes's discoveries, as well as the development of the Three-Age system in Scandinavia (described in Chapter 2), gave a new lease on life to a scientific approach to the problem of man's origins in the New World, with a search for Paleolithic man in North America and for the ancestors of the Indian tribes, whose ethnography was a subject of absorbing interest to nineteenth-century scholars. Mexican and Central American archaeology flourished, many scholars being attracted by the richness of the archaeological records and the native literature.

More important than the overoptimistic searchers for Paleolithic Man in the New World were the late nineteenth-century demonstrations that the Ohio mound builders were the ancestors of modern Indian populations, whose ethnography had long and largely unknown roots in the cultures of the past. Cyrus Thomas worked back from the ethnographic present to the archaeological past to prove the ownership of the mounds, publishing his results in an article entitled "Who Were the Mound Builders?" in 1884.[21] This approach to the American past became known in a more refined form as the "direct-historical approach," and was developed to a fine art in an expedition to the southwestern United States, which sought the prehistoric forebears of the Zuñi tribe. F. H. Cushing described the pottery of the Pueblo Indians in 1890,[22] and carried out much primary research in which anthropology and archaeology were combined to produce an effective approach to Zuñi history. Thus, the close marriage between archaeology and anthropology in New World archaeology stemmed directly from the field problem in North America, that of relating an indigenous population to spectacular prehistoric sites. Unlike European prehistorians, New World archaeologists had little or no identity with those they studied; they were concerned with the Indian tribe as a living and prehistoric entity whose culture, society, and identity had evolved through an unknown period of time. In contrast, one senses in the nineteenth-century European archaeologist a greater identity with the more recent prehistoric past and an intense nationalism resulting in a distinct motivation to write the prehistoric past of Europe as background to the great racial movements of more recent times and to justify major philological theories of the day. Archaeology was regarded as one of a battery of techniques used to study the history of European mankind. This dichotomy between New and Old World archaeology occurs early in the development of the subject, and is due almost entirely to historical circumstances.

ARCHAEOLOGY

The preceding include some of the major events leading to the development of archaeology as a scientific discipline, even if the direction of the subject and research in it have diversified over the years. Originally, in the nineteenth century, *archaeology* embraced the study of ancient history, but the word was gradually narrowed in meaning: in today's sense, it is the study of history or ancient cultures by the use of archaeological techniques. The label *prehistory* was first employed by a French scholar named Tournal in 1833, but came into widespread use in the middle of the nineteenth century to refer to the archaeology of the periods before literate history—which is the meaning used herein. Archaeology straddles many well established areas of academic inquiry, including anthropology, history, philosophy, and the natural sciences.[23] We have talked of archaeology as a "discipline," a label deliberately chosen as it fits well. The methods of archaeological research imply discipline—accurate recording, precise excavation, use of scientific method, and detailed analysis in the laboratory. In the academic world, too, the term refers to a subject that requires disciplined observation, deduction, and testing if it is to be successfully pursued. Everyone agrees that prehistoric archaeology involves the systematic study of archaeological sites and the artifacts found in them as a means of reconstructing life in the past. One studies the material remains of man in the past, whether from within the framework of anthropology, history, or other disciplines, but archaeology itself is really a distinct discipline, a combination of a wide battery of field, laboratory, and quantitative research methods oriented toward the study of man in the past, using interpretative techniques and theoretical concepts specially designed for this task.

To understand what archaeology involves necessitates some comprehension of the nature of archaeological evidence.[24] Archaeologists study those material remains of prehistoric man that have survived the ravages of time. As shown in Chapter 3, some raw materials preserve much more readily than others. Stone and clay vessels are virtually indestructible while wood, skin, metals, and bone are much more friable. Thus, in most archaeological sites only the most durable remains of human material culture are preserved for the archaeologist to study. Any picture of the prehistoric past obtained from archaeological investigations is likely to give a very one-sided picture of that life. As a result, the unfortunate archaeologist is like a detective fitting together a complicated series of clues to give a generalized impression, and explanation, of prehistoric culture and society. Much effort has gone into developing sophisticated methods for studying the prehistoric past. Often it is somewhat like taking a handful of miscellaneous objects—say two spark plugs, a fragmentary china cup, a needle, a grindstone, and a candle holder—and trying to reconstruct the culture of the makers of these diverse objects on the basis of the collection alone. Archaeologists have begun to develop sophisticated theoretical approaches to the material remains they study, making increasing use of hypothesis-testing and other attributes of scientific method to build testable propositions about the prehistoric past. Man's artifacts are seen as part of a system of interrelated phenomena in which culture is only one element.[25]

Most archaeologists would agree that there are three basic objectives in archaeological research—reconstruction of culture history, reconstruction of past lifeways, and the study of cultural process.[26] The first two objectives have been the subject of inquiry for many years, and some methods used and results obtained are summarized in this volume. How were stone implements made? What smelting processes resulted in the production of early copper tools? What was the significance of ivory to the prehistoric Eskimo? How did early man make his living? These are examples of questions which may confront the excavator. The tendency until recently has been to concentrate on description of the past and on the classification of archaeological cultures and artifacts. But the third objective, that of explaining cultural process in the past, is assuming increasing importance and becoming a paramount concern of many scholars. New heuristic methods such as Systems Theory and the use of Scientific Method are becoming more commonplace in archaeology,[27] and are discussed in Chapter 11. More and more archaeologists are using new theoretical approaches to the past in order to overcome the serious limitations of archaeological evidence itself when considered in isolation from other aspects of cultural systems.

There is a great diversity of archaeologists. Some study the living floors of early man and have a pressing concern with stone technologies and Pleistocene geology. Many archaeologists study the prehistory of early food production in the New and Old Worlds, developing new techniques for the study of prehistoric food residues and early domestic animals. Others study the origins of urban civilization or Mesoamerican states. Archaeologists examine the material remains of Colonial American settlements, medieval cities, or even early factories of the Industrial Revolution. Many Classical archaeologists are predominantly art historians or experts on hieroglyphics, while others will play an active role in the writing of national histories for new nations, where archaeology is a primary source of historical information.

The diversity of approaches to archaeology and its problems, as well as to the differing historical perspectives of the subject result in contrasting definitions and attitudes toward archaeology. In the United States, we have noted that archaeology is regarded as the concern of a special type of anthropologist.[28] Anthropology in the American context is the study of man in a very broad sense. It includes his culture, his psychology, and his physical anthropology, as well as the interrelationships between various aspects of man's being. American scholars regard archaeologists as anthropologists who usually excavate the material remains of man in the past, giving anthropology a time dimension. Thus, many of their objectives go beyond the basic description of artifacts and archaeological cultures to the explanation of cultural change, process, and evolution in prehistory. An impressive array of methods and theoretical approaches has been developed to study prehistoric social organization, settlement patterns, and economy, but the ultimate aim of New World archaeologists is not only description of the past but also determination of the nature of cultural societies at different stages in man's evolution in all parts of the world. The American archaeologist is thus particularly concerned with the development of testable propositions relating to man's past which are supported, modified, or rejected on the basis of excavated and analyzed archaeological data.

While American archaeology owes its approaches to the close marriage between anthropology and the study of the past, European archaeologists are much more forthright in their definition of archaeology as a part of history.[29] In the Old World, the arts of excavation have been developed to a high pitch by a historical tradition which began with A. H. L. Fox Pitt Rivers and continued with Sir Mortimer Wheeler and many postwar archaeologists. Both British and Continental prehistorians have placed great emphasis on the recovery of data from the ground, on the tracing of settlement patterns and structures, on economic reconstruction, and on the detailed analysis of artifact types and complicated typologies. Many archaeologists have acquired international reputations on the basis of their skill as excavators or museum men. The archaeologist is seen as a craftsman with diverse skills, not the least of which is the effective writing of history, both to amplify the written record and also to create a historical story, albeit incomplete, for periods when no archives exist to throw light on the deeds of chiefs or the attitudes of individuals.

One can argue in circles forever as to the correct definition and disciplinary place of archaeology. The subject itself is basically a battery of methods and techniques for the study of man in the past. Whether the discipline is a science, an art, or a part of anthropology or history, is perhaps irrelevant, for its basic concern, like that of much anthropology or all of history, is the understanding of man in the past.

HISTORY AND ARCHAEOLOGY

Although both historians and archaeologists study man in the past, there is a sharp distinction between the types of evidence which they employ.[30] Historians rely on written records such as government archives, private papers, and other documentary sources for primary evidence for the reconstruction of man's history since the beginnings of writing. The historical record extends back to about 3000 B.C. in the Near East, even if the earlier portions of this 5,000-year period are illuminated but little by documentary history. Continuous written history in Britain, on the other hand, begins with the Roman conquest some 2,000 years ago, while written records in the New World commenced with Christopher Columbus, even if the Maya had a script and a form of calendar. Some parts of the world did not come into contact with literate peoples until much more recently. The pastoral Khoi Khoi of the Cape of Good Hope emerged from prehistory in 1652 and were first known to the outside world when Bartholomew Diaz met them in the late fifteenth century. The tribes of the Central African interior had their first contact with David Livingstone in 1855. Continuous government records of this area did not begin until the late nineteenth century, while parts of New Guinea and the Amazon basin are still emerging from their prehistoric past. But, according to the latest researches, man has been living on this planet for at least 5 million years. Written history describes less than one-tenth of one percent of that enormous time. So archaeology remains the primary source of information on most of man's enormously long history since he was an Australopithecine on the East African savannah.

There is a sharp contrast between documentary history and a view of man's past reconstructed from the archaeological record. In the first place, the historian works with accurate chronologies. He can date an event certainly to within a year, possibly even as closely as a minute or second. Secondly, his history is that of individuals, groups, governments, and even several nations interacting with each other, reacting to events and struggling for power. He is able to glimpse the subtle interplay of human intellects, for his principal players have often recorded their impressions or deeds on paper. But there tend to be gaps in the record. Details of political events are likely to be far more complete than those of day-to-day existence or the trivia of village life. These were often of little consequence to contemporary observers, perhaps because they had experienced such commonplace things in the same way as we are used to driving in a car. Such minor details of past human behavior absorb students of ancient society, especially archaeologists interested in broad patterns of human change and early cultures, and it is here that the archaeologist may be useful to the historian. More and more excavations are being conducted on historical sites. The redoubtable King Henry VIII built a great palace at Nonsuch, south of London, in 1538, which was demolished 149 years later.[31] The ground plan was lost, despite a wealth of documentary information about the palace's history, until archaeologists uncovered the foundations of what was once one of the greatest buildings of Tudor England. They found not only the Banqueting Hall but also the wine cellar, and many fragments of the elaborate carved stone and molded plaster stucco, decoration from the fronts and inner courtyard of the building, which had made Nonsuch the talk of European society. The vast scheme of ornamentation was completely lost when seventeenth-century demolition contractors razed the palace.

On prehistoric sites, however, the archaeologist can at best only obtain a generalized and blurred impression of the period when a particular site was occupied. He is dealing with periods of human development and with broad patterns of human cultural change and behavior. His chronologies are less precise and the dates of occupation and abandonment of prehistoric settlements can rarely be established within such precise limits as a decade, let alone a year. The artifacts found in the excavations of the archaeologist represent the results of human behavior. They are anonymous, and rarely reveal the names of their owners. Man's achievements have become anonymous and no longer reflect the deeds of known individuals who have recorded their feelings for later generations to assess and discuss. Human behavior is reflected in many different ways in the archaeological record. It may be represented by large structures such as long houses, or monumental structures in stone too massive to be moved or studied outside their natural environment. Portable objects are the result of human behavior, too: stone implements, clay vessels, stone bowls, iron swords, or an infinite variety of ornaments, all of which can be removed from their archaeological context and studied in the laboratory. Equally well, the results of human behavior are seen in the fragmentary animal bones found with the tools of man, such as those discovered on early living floors in Africa, or in the sea shells found in the middens of California Indians. Sometimes special finds will throw detailed light on life in the past. A burial found in a cave dating to 12,000 B.C. in southwestern France is the result of human behavior. So is the imported faience bead of Mediterranean origin discovered in a northern European farming site, carried there along well-established trading routes. The archaeological record is formed from multiple types of evidence which reflect the infinite variability of human behavior. The archaeologist is thrown back on material objects which give the anonymous past which he reconstructs an immediate technological bias. Much of archaeology is traditionally concerned with inference and with analogy from artifacts, leading to an imaginative reconstruction of prehistory within the limitations of the archaeological evidence available.[32]

Archaeology can acquire a new dimension when used in conjunction with oral tradition. In many parts of the world where documentary history began with colonial rule in the late nineteenth century, where there were strongly centralized political organizations and kingships in prehistoric times, long genealogies and oral records of important political events and personalities may survive as important unwritten historical archives. These have been handed down from generation to generation and may extend back as far as 400 to 500 years into the past when circumstances for their preservation are favorable. Oral histories have been particularly well studied in parts of sub-Saharan Africa where scholars such as Jan Vansina[33] and others have worked hard to recover the lost history of the Bantu-speaking peoples of the tropical savannah regions of Central Africa. This type of research is an important primary historical source for the study of later prehistoric times. Archaeologists are beginning to cooperate with oral historians, adding valuable information on daily life among such groups to the traditional histories. The actual settlements attributed to ancient chiefs mentioned in the oral histories can be excavated, making the historical account a fuller one. The combination of two distinct types of historical discipline results in a much more complete picture of recent prehistoric society.

So the archaeologist must be a man of many parts. Aside from being a careful student of technology and material culture, he must have a thorough grounding in the identification, classification, and statistical treatment of artifacts, as well as in the principles of anthropology. He must be a skillful excavator and be able to apply the scientific method to his subject rigorously. Above all, he must be able to recognize the limitations of his evidence and of archaeology as a whole, and to comprehend the aims of historians and others who have no concern with archaeology. The reconstruction of prehistoric societies depends on research in many other fields, especially the natural sciences. Botanists provide identification of plants, while zoologists study the changing paleontological record found in early prehistoric sites. Chemists will process radiocarbon dates; soil scientists may provide critical information on the formation of occupation levels in ancient villages. These and many other related disciplines are all important to the archaeologist who must employ many differing scientific techniques in order to research some of the major events of human history. More and more multidisciplinary research teams are going into the field, ensuring effective cooperation between several disciplines such as archaeology, geology, pedology, and paleontology on the excavation itself.

What was the settlement pattern and way of life of the earliest hominids? How did man first "come down from the trees"? When did man first begin to make tools? When, where, and how did man first cultivate crops or domesticate animals? What is the early history of, and how revolutionary were the effects of, metallurgy on the history of mankind? When was the New World first populated by hunter-gatherers? These—historical events which were in their time as earth-shaking as the atomic bomb—and many other questions rely on the spade of the archaeologist for resolution. An understanding of the cultural processes involved in these events gives us a better perspective of our own culture and society.

Chapter 2

Time

A sense of time depth and chronology is something which we all possess to some degree. Indeed, man's innate curiosity about his past stems in part from his sense of time perspective as regards his own life and experience. Early antiquarians and theologians wrestled with the enigma of the Biblical legend of the Creation and the finds of fossil animals and human artifacts. Since the establishment of a high antiquity for man in 1859, however, the measurement of time has become one of the principal preoccupations of those who study the prehistoric past. How does one classify the past and measure the age of the great events of prehistory? The time dimension of archaeology is a vital element in our description and interpretation of prehistory.

The boundaries of our world are infinite. At one end of the time scale, the paleontologist and archaeologist are finding traces of early humans, dated by radioactive techniques to over 5.5 million years old. Today, we are reaching out into space with its incredible distances and toward other worlds, where, perhaps, human experience has been paralleled. Yet, our own perspectives of time and philosophies of life have taken little account of these vast new chronological horizons.

Consider for a moment how you view time. What is the earliest date you can remember? Mine is my third birthday—I have a vague memory of balloons and lots of people. My continuous memory of people as individuals and of day-to-day events begins at age 8. Most adults have a somewhat similar span of recollection, and a chronological perspective on their lives which extends back into early childhood. But our sense of personal involvement in human history only extends over the period of our lifetimes. We have an indirect involvement with the lives of our parents, relatives, or other friends, some of whom may have been alive 50 to 70 years before we were born. Perhaps our profoundest involvement with time occurs toward the end of our lives, with a period covering the lives of our immediate family. But we also have a marginal sense of longer chronologies and a perspective on events within them—our family ancestry, the history of our community, of our nation—and in these days of ardent internationalism, with the world as well. Few people have a sense of perspective for the whole span of human experience. Some still believe the Ussherian legend. We must look for a moment at the ways in which the vast new time scales of prehistory were established.

THE THREE AGES

In Chapter 1, we saw how the classification of the past was a major problem for early excavators, confronted with a jumble of artifacts from burial mounds or settlements. They had no means of subdividing or measuring the past. Until the nineteenth century, the world had been comfortably secure. Man had speculated freely about his origins, but within the narrow horizons of the Biblical account of the Creation. What happened before the Creation was a blank. Christians had contemplated eternity, but it was the shadowless, changeless eternity of God. Ussher's 6,000 years sufficed for all prehistory, even if subdividing the six millennia presented a problem. The story of archaeology is that of classifying and measuring time, a process given impetus by the apparently limitless frontiers of the prehistoric past opened up by Boucher de Perthes and Charles Darwin.

Scandinavian archaeologists were the first to develop a framework into which the bewildering mixture of artifacts from their excavations could be fitted. At the end of the eighteenth century, they were writing about ages of stone, copper, and iron, which flourished in prehistoric times. But as late as 1806, Professor Rasmus Nyerup of the University of Copenhagen complained that "everything which has come down to us from heathendom is wrapped in a thick fog; it belongs to a space of time which we cannot measure."[1]* Nyerup and others were responsible for the setting up of a Danish National Museum which housed a confusing collection of artifacts from bogs, burial chambers, and shell middens. The first curator of the Museum, Christian Jurgensen Thomsen (1788–1865), was appointed in 1816. Thomsen put the

---

* See pages 321–323 for notes to Chapter 2.

Museum collections in order by classifying them into three groups, representing ages of Stone, Bronze, and Iron, using sealed finds in graves as a basis for his classification. He claimed that his Three Ages were chronologically ranked.[2] Thomsen's bold classification was taken up by another Dane, J. J. A. Worsaae, who proved the basic stratigraphic validity of the system, and by studying archaeological finds from all over Europe demonstrated the widespread validity of what became known as the Three-Age System. Worsaae was a remarkable man, the first professional archaeologist to publish an exposition on excavation and classification of the past; this work which formed the foundation of most European archaeology[3] was printed in 1843, fifteen years before *The Origin of Species* was on the presses.

The Three-Age System was a technological subdivision of the prehistoric past, which gave the archaeologist a broad context within which his own finds could be placed. Thomsen, Worsaae, and others not only developed a museum classification system but also proved it by excavation. Worsaae admitted that he had been influenced by ethnographic accounts of stone-using Australians and Pacific islanders in postulating a Stone Age in the past. The close relationship of archaeology and anthropology was already clear. Thomsen's Three Ages were a first attempt at a chronology of relationship for the prehistoric past and were widely adopted as a basis for classifying prehistoric sites in the Old World. The establishment of a chronology for world prehistory thus began with Thomsen and Worsaae; the Three-Age scheme's validity was confirmed by excavations both in river gravels where the early flaked axes of Boucher de Perthes were found, and also in caves such as those excavated by Lartet and Christy in the Dordogne area of France which yielded different implements.[4] These in turn differed from those found in excavations in Swiss lakes where record low levels in 1853–1854 had exposed remains of prehistoric farming villages.[5] By the 1900s, scientists thought in terms of a Paleolithic or Old Stone Age to which the implements found in river gravels and the French caves belonged, a Neolithic, or Later Stone Age, when polished (as opposed to flaked) stone implements were in fashion, and Bronze and Iron Ages.[6] This framework for Old World prehistory, in a modified form, survives today (Table 2.1).

The Three-Age System of the Scandinavians was not adopted in North America. Systematic archaeological research flourished in the New World after 1859, but early attempts to find Paleolithic man were unsuccessful. The complicated geological strata of the European rivers with their rich storehouses of hand axes did not exist, but the relationships between the Indian population and the finds of the archaeologist were soon established. Stratigraphic observations and

Table 2.1   Some Nomenclature of Old World Archaeology

Approximate age in years	Geological era	Three-Age terminology	Important events
3000 B.C.	Holocene	Iron Age Bronze Age Neolithic	Writing in the Near East Origins of food production
7800 B.C.		Mesolithic	
35,000 B.C.		Upper Paleolithic	Origins of blade technology
70,000 B.C. 400,000 B.C.	Pleistocene (Quaternary)	Middle Paleolithic	Hand axes in widespread use
1.75 million B.C. ±5 million B.C.		Lower Paleolithic	
	Pliocene		Origins of toolmaking

local cultural sequences did not preoccupy American archaeologists, unlike the European, and few researchers bothered to apply meticulous excavation techniques to later New World archaeological sites, in which, in any case, almost no metals were found. Not until 1914 did chronology and detailed stratigraphic observations of the past become important in American archaeology, when N. C. Nelson[7] and later A. V. Kidder began to use potsherds in southwestern sites as stratigraphic indicators; Kidder's classic excavations at the Pecos Pueblo[8] brought about a conference there in 1927 which delineated eight sequential stages of Pueblo culture. The foundations of accurate stratigraphic and chronological studies in American archaeology were soundly laid in the classic archaeological laboratory of the Southwest. We summarize some salient features of American archaeology in Table 2.2 and of human evolution in Figure 2.1, but it should be emphasized that both diagrams are so simplified as to be almost theoretical in impact.

RELATIVE AND ABSOLUTE CHRONOLOGY

As already observed, we all have a sense of time, indeed our lives are governed by appointments, airline schedules, and tax deadlines. We unconsciously add a sense of historical time to our daily round. When a radio station plays a tune first popular in 1958, the announcer may mention associations of that year, and jumbled events contemporary with the song fill our minds. People's birthdays, dates of elections, or space shots are all part of our sense of history, which is most strongly developed around our own lifetimes. Learning history is part of our school experience, a process that considerably extends

Table 2.2 General Outline of New World Archaeology[a]

Dates	South America	Mesoamerica	North America — Southwest	North America — Plains	North America — East
A.D. 1500	Inca Empire	Aztecs and other Toltecs	Pueblo I–IV	Plains Village Period	Temple Mound Period
A.D. 1000	Tiahuanaco-Huari expansion	Classic Period (Maya) Teotihuacán	Basketmaker I and II	Woodland Period	Burial Mound Period
0	Mochica, Nasca, Tiahuanaco Paracas	Pre-Classic Period			
500 B.C.	Chavín				
1000 B.C.	First ceremonial centers Maize grown		Cochise Period	Archaic Period	Archaic Period
2000 B.C.	Incipient cultivation and food collecting	Incipient cultivation and food collecting			
3000 B.C.					
5000 B.C.					
7000 B.C.	Early hunters and gatherers	Paleo-Indian Period	Paleo-Indian Period	Paleo-Indian Period	Paleo-Indian Period
10,000 B.C.					
20,000 B.C.					
±40,000 B.C.					

[a] This is a gross simplification for vocabulary purposes, and many major cultural areas are omitted.

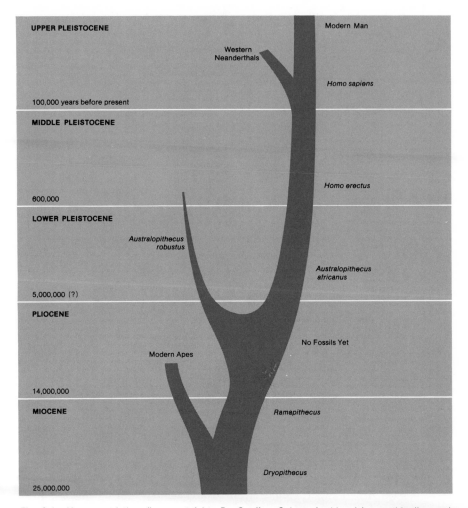

Fig. 2.1 Human evolution. (I am grateful to Dr. Geoffrey Gaherty for his advice on this diagram.)

our time perspective. Diverse histories are ordered into centuries, years, hours, and even minutes. George Washington's life story and his dates are known to most, because the events of his presidency are abundantly documented in school textbooks, archives, and historical records. Time is such an integral part of our lives that we tend to take it for granted, as well as the chronological subdivisions of our more recent history.

Studying documentary history revolves around people and events, political maneuvers and social change. A kaleidoscope of happenings threatens to engulf the person researching a rapidly deepening political crisis or field campaign. The exact chronological order of the contributing events has to be established as a preliminary to any serious research. At what exact moment on June 18, 1815, did Emperor Napoleon order his Imperial Guard to charge the British squares at Waterloo? At what point during the battle of Mobile Bay in 1864 did David Glasgow Farragut make his famous remark about torpedoes? These are details of consuming importance to the historian with his need for extreme accuracy.

Prehistoric chronologies cover far longer periods of time, millennia and centuries, as opposed to days or even minutes. Some idea of the scale of prehistoric time can be gained by piling up a hundred quarters. If the whole pile represents the time that man and his culture have been on earth, the length of time covered by historical records would equal considerably less than the thickness of one quarter. In fact, 99.9 per cent of man's history lies within prehistoric times. Prehistoric time scales are staggering and difficult to measure because cultural change has proceeded slowly for most of man's existence—the humdrum tempo of cultural evolution only accelerating in recent millennia. Without comparatively accurate chronologies, the landscape of prehistory is featureless, and we face the same problem as the early antiquarians.

Julius Caesar landed in Britain in 55 B.C.; Washington, D.C., was founded in A.D. 1800. These are dates in years, and immediately give us a sense of the *absolute date* of both events. The current absolute dates for the earliest hominids range around 5 million years ago—nothing like the preciseness of Caesar's—but are expressed in years and can be directly related to those of the Roman general who ended Britain's prehistoric isolation. In other words, the dating standards of the historian are being applied, albeit crudely, to the prehistoric past. Much experimental effort in archaeology during the last fifty years has attempted to devise accurate methods of absolute dating.[9] Archaeologists draw widely on the techniques used by geologists and invented by physicists and chemists, as well as in addition to inventing many ingenious devices for dating the past which enjoy momentary popularity before sinking into dignified obscurity. Absolute chronologies are so important that the enormous expenditure of time on devising methods of dating sites or objects is entirely justified.[10] Not only are dates important, but so are the interrelationships between one prehistoric society and another that are revealed by them. Are two neighboring prehistoric peoples within a limited area contemporary, or are they separated by a considerable time span? What effect did they have on one another? Is one derived from the other? What was the rate of cultural change or technological innovation? The solution of these problems depends upon accurate and reliable absolute chronologies, for neither technological advance nor cultural change proceeds at the same rate everywhere, even within limited geographic areas.

Relationships in time are simpler to establish. If I place a book on the table, and then pile another one on top of it, clearly the upper one of the two was placed on the table after, and at a later moment in time than, the original volume. The second book became part of the pile after the first, but how long afterward we have no means of telling. This example illustrates the principle of superposition, one of the cornerstones of archaeological research and *relative chronology*, that is, correlating prehistoric sites or cultures with one another by their relative age.

STRATIGRAPHY AND SUPERPOSITION

Stratigraphical observations and the principle of superposition are two foundations for effective study of man's past. The use of stratigraphy in archaeology came from the studies of geologists such as William Smith, Sir Charles Lyell, and others, in the late eighteenth and nineteenth centuries. The finding of stone implements in Pleistocene deposits like river gravels led to an intimate marriage between Stone Age archaeology and geology, and from there it was a logical step to the confines of an archaeological site. Relative chronology in archaeology has its basis in large- or small-scale stratigraphic observations in archaeological sites of all ages. As the eminent British archaeologist Sir Mortimer Wheeler has cogently argued, the basis of scientific excavation is the accurately observed and carefully recorded stratigraphic profile.[11]

The basic principle in most stratigraphic observation is a simple one: the geological layers of the earth are superimposed one upon another almost like the layers of a cake. Easily viewed examples are cliffs by the seashore or in quarries which show a series of geological levels. Obviously, any object found in the lowermost levels was deposited before the upper horizons were accumulated. In other words, the lower levels are *relatively earlier* than the upper strata. The superposition of a series of occupation levels or geological strata in order can be achieved by many different processes; wind erosion, water action, earthquakes, and glacial action have all played their part in the accumulation of the earth's strata. At times man's artifacts have been found in settlement sites contemporary with major geological events in situations where the stratigraphy of the geologist is in direct association with the prehistorian's findings.

Superposition is fundamental to studying archaeological sites, for many settlements, such as Near Eastern mounds, or Indian villages in the Ohio Valley, or cave sites, contain multilevel occupations whose decipherment is the key to their relative chronology. Sir Mortimer Wheeler has ably described the processes of human occupation as applied to stratigraphy:

> The human occupation of a site normally results in the accumulation of material of one kind or another on and about the area occupied. Objects are lost or discarded and become imbedded in the earth. Floors are re-newed and old ones buried. Buildings crumble and new ones are built on the ruins. A flood may destroy a building or a town and deposit a layer of alluvium on its debris and later, when the flood has subsided, the level site may be reoccupied. Sometimes, the process is in the reverse direc-tion. Evidences of occupation may be removed as in the deepening of an unsurfaced street by traffic, or the digging of a pit for the disposal of rubbish or for burial . . . in one way or another the surface of an ancient town or village is constantly altering in response to human effort or neglect; and it is by interpreting rightly these evidences of alteration that we may hope to reconstruct something of the vicissitudes of the site and its occupants.[12]

Although we shall touch on the observation of stratigraphic profiles later on, Figures 2.2 and 2.3 present examples of sections illustrating the significance of stratigraphy in the archaeological record.[13]

Fig. 2.2   *An idealized section through an Upper and Middle Paleolithic cave in France. The four archaeological culture layers are separated by sterile layers, the Mousterian being earlier than the Aurignacian, and so on. Most stratigraphic sequences are, of course, much more complicated than this hypothetical example. (After Oakley.)*

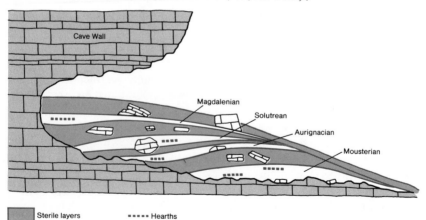

Cave Wall

Magdalenian

Solutrean

Aurignacian

Mousterian

Sterile layers   ▪ ▪ ▪ ▪ ▪ Hearths

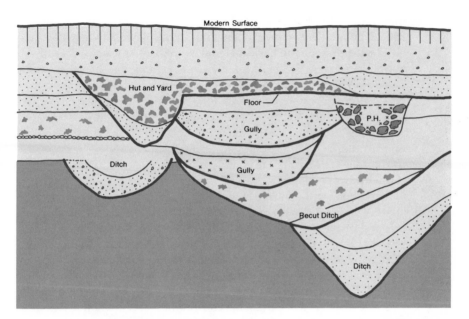

Fig. 2.3   *A stratigraphic section through a town site in Cambridge, England, showing profiles of pre-*
historic and Roman enclosures and huts with a post hole (P.H.), gullies, and ditches. The
complex stratigraphy is interpreted by correlating the various features with their horizontal
layers. (One thirty-second actual size.)

Stratigraphy as applied to archaeological sites is on a much smaller scale than that of geology, but often correspondingly more complicated. Most archaeological relative chronology employs careful observations of sequences of occupation levels and the correlation of these with cultural sequences at other sites in the same area. Successive occupation levels can be found at the same spot, such as in a cave, fort, or mound site, where many generations of settlers lived within a circumscribed or restricted area. In other cases, however, the chronological sequence can be horizontal. Such a situation arises when economic or political conditions dictate a regular movement of villages when fields are exhausted or residence rules modified. In this case a cultural sequence may be scattered through a series of single-level occupation sites over a large area, and can only be put together by judicious survey work and careful analysis of the artifacts found in the different sites.

Occupation levels and other strata are useless if observed in isolation, for the artifacts, food bones, or other finds recovered from the layers of a site are as critical as the stratigraphy itself. Each level in a settlement, however massive or small, has its associated artifacts, the objects that the archaeologist uses as his indicators of cultural and economic change. Indeed, the finds in each layer and their associations often provide the basic material for relative chronology. Furthermore, the relative dating of many sites is complicated by other questions. Has the site been occupied continuously? Do stratigraphic profiles reflect a continuous occupation over a long period of time, or a sequence which has been interrupted several times by warfare, or simple abandonment of the site? Such problems can be resolved by careful examination of excavated profiles.

Another factor which may affect the interpretation of stratigraphy is the breaks or disruptions in the layering caused by human activity. Later occupants of a village may dig rubbish pits or graves into earlier strata. Cattle may be kept on the site, their hooves removing the soil and disturbing the upper levels of the underlying horizons; this process also may be caused by later people cultivating the rich soils of an abandoned village site. Building activities may cause foundation trenches and even stone walls to be sunk into earlier levels. The inhabitants' technological level has a direct bearing on their ability to destroy evidence of earlier and contemporary occupation. Obviously the inhabitants of a Near Eastern city are more likely to have destroyed evidence of earlier occupation with constant rebuilding than are a group of farmers without metal tools, who merely reoccupy earlier village sites with minimal disturbance of the underlying levels. Burrowing animals, too, enjoy archaeological sites, worming their way through the soft, organic soils of caves or village sites and disrupting stratigraphic observations over large areas of the settlement. Moles, gophers, and rabbits are foes of gardener and archaeologist alike.

PLEISTOCENE GEOCHRONOLOGY

For over 90 per cent of his existence on earth, man was a stone toolmaker. Most of his early history lies within the last major geological epoch, that of the Pleistocene, which began more than 2 million years ago and ended, by conventional definition, 8,000 years before Christ.[14] The Pleistocene was characterized by major fluctuations of climate, from extreme cold to tropical heat. Geologists consider the Pleistocene to be one of the most complicated of all field problems, for many of its deposits have local origin and incredible complexity. In extreme cases, the effects of glaciation and permafrost conditions might be combined with those of water action and extensive tectonic movement within the narrow confines of a single stratigraphic profile. From the archaeological point of view the attraction of the Pleistocene is in the direct association of human living sites with Quaternary deposits, because the major climatic events of the last two million years provide an admirable framework for a relative chronology of human culture. The science of geochronology, or geological dating, is a complex, multidisciplinary approach to dating early man, and involves the study of the Pleistocene geological record in many temperate and tropical areas.

Glaciations

Climatic changes during past millennia are preserved in numerous different types of deposit. Huge ice sheets covered much of northern Europe, North America, and the Alpine areas of France, Italy, and Switzerland. At least four times, arctic conditions prevailed over the Northern hemisphere, reflected in extensive deposits of glacial moraines and other related geological phenomena. These periods of extreme cold alternated with prolonged interglacial phases when the European climate was considerably warmer than today's. During the longest interglacial, tropical animals like the hippopotamus flourished in Western Europe. In the Old World, where man's prehistory extends back at least five million years, these glacial advances and retreats have been correlated with stages of human culture. European geologists have distinguished at least four glacial periods in the Alps, known as Gunz, Mindel, Riss, and Würm,[15] although there may have been other periods of intense cold (Table 2.3). Except in the closing millennia of the Pleistocene, there are few direct associations of human culture with deposits of the Ice Age glaciers. Numerous associated deposits, however, were laid down in periglacial areas which are associated directly with evidence of human occupation. These include river gravels affected by permafrost conditions and also extensive deposits of a windblown sand, called "loess," deposited over much of Central Europe by chilly Arctic winds blowing a detritus of fine dust from the ice sheets.[16]

High Sea Levels

High sea levels are another phenomenon extensively used to correlate archaeological remains with interglacial periods.[17] The study of sea levels is controversial, particularly in areas where extensive earth movement may have affected the elevation of ancient beach levels above the modern level. The study and correlation of raised beaches is based on the theory of Glacial Eustasy: during periods of intense cold when the Polar and Alpine ice sheets reached their maximum extent, a general fall in ocean levels resulted because moisture was incorporated into these ice sheets. With the shrinkage of ice sheets during the interglacials, the sea level rose and, in addition, the earth's

Table 2.3   Geological Events and Glaciations in Europe during the Pleistocene

Years	Alpine glaciation	Scandin-avian glaciation	Loess	Sea level	Inter-glacial	Pollen species	Fossil animals	Key archaeological sites
8,000 B.C. to present	Postglacial	Weathering		Versilian		Temperate	Modern fauna	Mesolithic and later
8,000–70,000 (?) B.C.	Würm III, II, I	Weichsel	Younger Loess I–III				Elephas primigenius	Middle and Upper Paleolithic
		Weathering		Monastirian 15–18 M	Eemian	No Azolla	Elephas antiquus	Levalloisian technology
	Riss II, I	Warthe Saale	Older Loess I–II					
270,000 (?) B.C.		Weathering		Tyrrhenian 30–45 M	Hoxnian	Azolla filiculoides (water fern)	Elephas antiquus	Hoxne, Swanscombe, Clacton
400,000 (?) (avg.) B.C.	Mindel II, I	Elster ?	Oldest Loess					Olduvai Gorge
	(Climatic changes uncertain earlier than Mindel)			Sicilian I 100 M	Cromerian	Azolla a.ff. filiculoides (water fern)	Archidiskodon ? Machairodus	Olduvai Gorge
	Gunz	?	?					
				Calabrian 200 M	Tiglian	Azolla tege-lensis (water fern)	Villafranchian[a]	
	Donau	?	?					

[a] Base of a Villafranchian faunal bed in Southern Europe dated to 3.0 million years; Upper Villafranchian faunal beds in East Africa dated to 1.75 million years.

crust gradually readjusted to compensate for the release of the extra weight of the glacial sheets. Major geographical changes resulted. For example, until 4000 or 5000 B.C., Britain was joined to the Continent by a strip of marsh; it covered what is now the North Sea and part of the English Channel. Similar, major sea-level changes have taken place in the New World, the Mediterranean area, and also Scandinavia (Figure 2.4).

Raised beaches are found in the geological record as a series of terraces along the fringes of modern coastal plains. They are widely distributed on the East Coast of the United States and especially in the Mediterranean, where they have been intensively studied by French and Italian geologists. In many parts of the world, modern beaches are dotted with shell middens which represent the occupations of recent prehistoric strandlooping peoples who lived on fish and shellfish. Many sites like this are found near Southern California beaches and on the southeastern and southwestern coasts of South Africa, yielding numerous fishbones and freshwater shells. Cave sites near the edge of the modern seashore were often occupied by prehistoric peoples with a similar dietary pattern. The cave at Robberg in the Cape Province of South Africa, which has been skillfully excavated by R. R. Inskeep,[18] furnished a wealth of information on ancient

Fig. 2.4   *Great Britain and Scandinavia at the end of the Pleistocene, showing sea levels* ca. *7000* B.C.

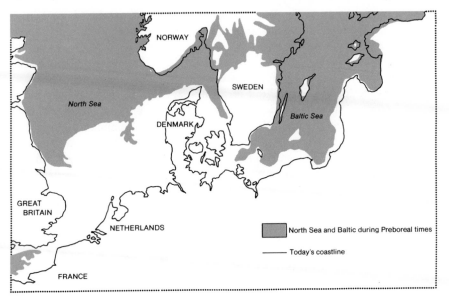

economic practices and fishing habits in a coastal region about the
first millennium B.C., when the sea was slightly lower than it is now.
The high-level beaches of the Mediterranean and Northwest Africa
occasionally yield traces of earlier Stone Age occupation. One famous
site is the raised beach at Sidi Abderrahmane[19] in Morocco. Here
an early Pleistocene sea level was covered by a deposit of consolidated
sand dune which not only sealed the beach but also a deposit of
early stone artifacts. A subsequent higher sea level, belonging to the
Mindel-Riss interglacial, cut a cave into this consolidated dune, in
which man lived during the succeeding low sea level period, i.e., during
the Riss glaciation. Hand axes, animal bones, and some fragments
of the men who made the implements, *Homo erectus,* were found in
the cave. The human fossil is securely relative-dated by its proximity
to the high sea level of the preceding interglacial. Numerous other
examples exist but, unfortunately, many archaeological sites found
on high sea levels are extensively disturbed by later geological action
and have, perhaps, a rather more marginal interest to the archaeologist
than sites in less disturbed localities.

Lakes and Rivers

Lake beds and river gravels are some of the most important Pleistocene
deposits used in relative dating. Small lakes and other permanent
bodies of water were attractive habitats to early hunters. The Australopithecines at Olduvai Gorge were found on their living floors
at the edge of a large shallow lake, their settlements subsequently
buried by softly deposited water-lain sediments which did not disturb
the abandoned artifacts and bones. Another famous example is John
Frere's lake-bed site at Hoxne in England (Figure 2.5),[20] where the
remains of a small interglacial lake are sealed between two glacial
moraines of widely differing age.

The great river valleys of Europe and Africa have yielded a rich
crop of stone tools dating from all Pleistocene periods. Early man
favored the great floodplains of the Thames, Somme, Zambezi, and
other large rivers,[21] for they furnished abundant game and vegetable
foods as well as permanent water supplies and fish. Their hunting
camps by the river banks were buried by alluvium or scattered by
floodwater; the artifacts, and sometimes the bones of their quarry,
became part of the Pleistocene gravels which form the sides of the
modern river valley. The world's great rivers have become smaller
since Pleistocene times, and have documented their history as a result
of falling sea levels, crustal movement, or erosion. A series of stable
periods or downcutting have formed terraces on the edge of the river
valleys as the rivers became smaller. Quarries and natural exposures

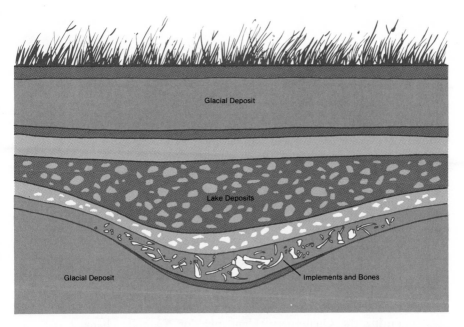

Fig. 2.5   A much simplified stratigraphic profile from the Hoxne site, England, showing the association of implements and fossil bones with lake-bed deposits sealed by two layers of glacial origin. (Not to scale.)

in the terraces yield stone tools to the archaeologist, which can be relatively dated. A famous example is the Swanscombe skull site in the Thames Valley where a human cranium was found in association with stone hand axes; it was dated to the Mindel-Riss interglacial (Figure 2.6).[22] River gravels are not, however, the most satisfactory forms of archaeological deposit to analyze. Unlike lake beds, where actual living floors are often preserved, the rough-and-tumble of water action has often jumbled artifacts, transporting many some distance from the living floor where they were used. The chances of finding undisturbed living sites in river gravels is thus correspondingly lower.

Animal Bones

Another type of geochronology comes from the study of vertebrate fauna found in Pleistocene sites. Stone Age man killed a wide range of large and small mammals for food, whose broken bones are often preserved in river gravels, living floors, and other sites. The animals hunted often were species now extinct, such as the giant pigs and buffalo found at Olduvai Gorge in Tanzania by Dr. Louis Leakey.[23] Paleontologists have classified Pleistocene faunas from many localities,

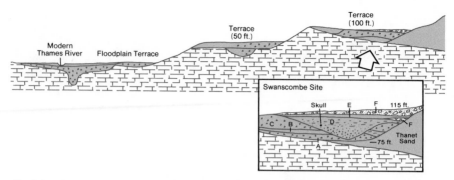

Fig. 2.6   A schematic diagram of the Thames terraces at Swanscombe, England, with a small inset
of the Swanscombe site, showing the complex sequence of layers. Stone artifacts were
found with the skull and were profuse in layers A, C, D, and F, with B and E sealing the
culture layers. (North/south cross section; not to scale.)

often using the remains of animals hunted by man, and have tried
to build up a very simple relative chronology of mammal types through
the Pleistocene. The evolution of the large mammals proceeded rapidly
during the Quaternary. Elephants, for example, changed radically
during each European interglacial. The evolving species can be distinguished by the distinctive cusp patterns of their teeth (Figures 2.7 and
2.8).[24] In the Gunz-Mindel interglacial, an early form of *Palaeoloxodon
antiquus* lived on the plains of Central Europe. During the Mindel-Riss
or Great Interglacial, some quarter of a million years later, he was
succeeded by a more developed form of the same species. Different
elephants flourished during the colder spells. During the last glaciation,
the mammoth, *Mammuthus primigenius*, a hairy elephant with large
tusks, lived in Central Europe. A fairly reliable relative date can be
assigned to a site where elephants occur merely by examining the
teeth.

Unfortunately, however, the use of vertebrate fauna is severely
limited by the difficulty of identifying different mammal species.
Certain animals are more sensitive to climatic change than others.
Some are tolerant of both cold and warm climates, although others
prefer warm weather but can stand perversely low temperatures with
remarkable resilience. Furthermore, so many environmental factors
affect the distribution of mammals and the extinction of one species
at the expense of another that it is very difficult to be sure that one
is dealing with a chronological, as opposed to an environmental,
difference. But, with Lower or Middle Pleistocene sites, the uses of
animal bones as chronological indicators are magnified simply because
enormous time scales are involved and minor details are obscured.

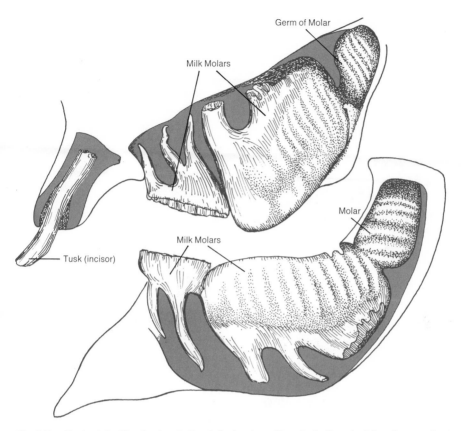

Germ of Molar

Milk Molars

Molar

Milk Molars

Tusk (incisor)

Fig. 2.7   Elephant dentition in place in the skull, showing milk molar teeth and adult molars erupting. (After Cornwall.)

POLLEN ANALYSIS

Vegetation is one of the best indicators of ecological change, for it depends on climate and soil for survival and is a sensitive barometer of climatic alteration. Pollen analysis, or palynology, is a comprehensive way of studying ancient vegetation; it was developed in 1916 by a Swede, Lennart van Post, who used forest trees, and subsequently this analysis extended to all pollen-liberating vegetation. The principle of pollen analysis is simple.[25] Large numbers of pollen grains are suspended in the atmosphere and have remarkable preservative properties if deposited in an unaerated geological horizon. The pollen spores can be identified microscopically (Figure 2.9) with great accuracy and used to reconstruct the vegetation which grew near the spot

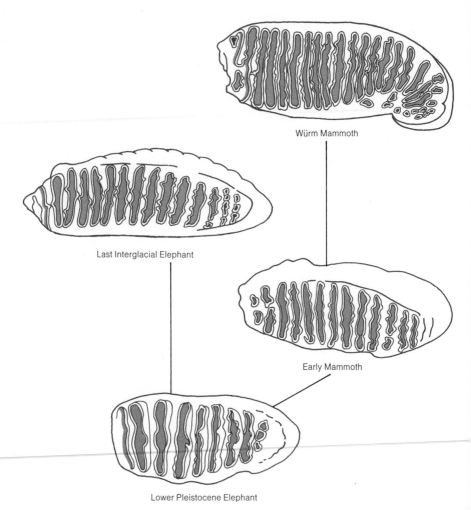

Würm Mammoth

Last Interglacial Elephant

Early Mammoth

Lower Pleistocene Elephant

Fig. 2.8   Grinding surfaces of third upper molars of four types of Pleistocene elephant, illustrating the differences in enamel patterns from earlier (bottom) to later (upper) types. (One-fifth actual size.) (After Oakley.)

where they are found. Palynology has been widely employed by bota-nists from many countries. Though the method has been especially used on peat-bog deposits and clays, it has also been applied to clay cores from Central African lakes, to samples obtained by dredging from the bed of the sea, and even to cave deposits and to lenses of organic material in the middle of river terraces.

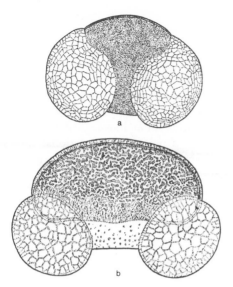

Fig. 2.9   Pollen spores. (a) Spruce. (b) Silver Fir. (Both 340 times actual size.) (After Oakley.)

Pollen spores are normally only identifiable under a very powerful microscope. Samples are taken through stratigraphic sections at close intervals and subjected to identification and statistical treatment. The grains of each genus or species present are counted, and the percentage of frequencies calculated. The counts are then correlated stratigraphically with one another to provide a sequence of vegetational change. When sufficient sections have been analyzed, the palynologist is able to zonate the vegetation according to distinct vegetational periods and to use such zones, and the characteristic pollen diagrams associated with them, as evidence for assigning a particular deposit to a place within a relative, chronological framework worked out at a series of type localities.

Palynology has obvious applications to prehistory, for sites are often found in swampy deposits where pollen is preserved, especially fishing or fowling camps and settlements near water. Isolated artifacts or even human corpses (such as that of Tollund man found in a Danish bog) are also discovered in these deposits; sometimes pollen is obtained from small peat lumps adhering to crevices in such finds. Thus the botanists can assign relative dates to even isolated finds which otherwise would remain undated. The palynologists have worked out a long sequence of vegetational history for Northern Europe, which begins about 13,000 B.C. with Arctic tundra covering much of Western Europe.[26] After a number of fluctuations, this gives way to birch and pine forest and later to mixed oak forest, characteristic of a temperate climate. A summary of the vegetational history of that area appears in Table 2.4. Pollen diagrams for earlier Pleistocene interglacials have also been obtained from many localities, sometimes in association with human artifacts. Obviously, an archaeological site with a pollen graph coinciding with that of a particular vegetational zone belongs within that period, an admirable method of relative chronology—an example appears in Figure 2.10.

Table 2.4   Postglacial Vegetational Zones in Northern Europe[a]

Approximate dates in years	Blytt and Sernander climatic periods	Zone numbers	Vegetation	Archaeology
600 B.C.	Sub-Atlantic (wetter and colder)	IX	Beech increase. Extensive clearance	Historic and Iron Age
3000 B.C.	Sub-Boreal (warm, dry, continental)	VIII	Decrease of mixed oak forest—more pine. Extensive forest clearance by man	Bronze Age "Neolithic"
5500 B.C.	Atlantic (warm maximum, moist and oceanic)	VII	Oak, elm, lime, alder (mixed oak forest)	"Neolithic" Mesolithic
7700 B.C.	Boreal (rising temperatures, dry, continental)	VI	Hazel, less pine, start of mixed oak forest	Mesolithic
8300 B.C.	Pre-Boreal (rising temperatures, cool)	V/IV	Birch, beech, pine	Mesolithic
8800 B.C.	Younger Dryas (cold)	III	Tundra	Late Glacial
10,000 B.C.	Allerod Oscillation (warmer interval)	II	Birch and oak, tundra	Hunting cultures
ca. 15,000 B.C.	Older Dryas (Arctic cold)	I	Arctic tundra	
	(end of Würm maximum)			

[a] Amended from Jane Gray and Watson Smith, "Fossil Pollen and Archaeology," Archaeology, 1962, 15 (1):16–26.

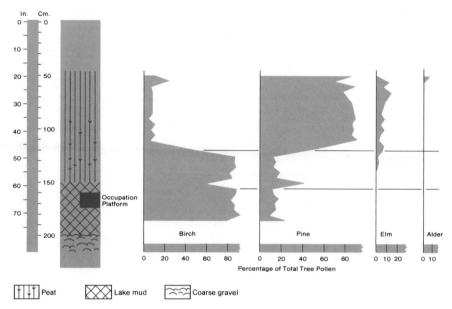

Fig. 2.10 The pollen diagram from the hunting camp at Star Carr, England. The occupation platform was in use when birch was common near the site.

Ordering of Artifacts

Another method of relative chronology uses artifacts found in sealed stratigraphic contexts. Fashions change, and the forms of artifacts do, too; particular styles enjoy fleeting popularity for varying periods of time before going out of favor. The celebrated Egyptologist Sir Flinders Petrie was among the first to use artifacts for chronological ordering, and developed a method of relative dating Pre-Dynastic Egyptian graves through stylistic changes in strap-handled vases.[27] Subsequently, many archaeologists have used pottery and other artifacts for similar research, basing their work on the assumption that "each type of artifact orginates at a given time at a given place, is made in gradually increasing numbers as time goes on, then decreases in popularity until it becomes forgotten, never to reoccur in an identical form." [28] Each chronological period has its own unique assemblage of artifacts and frequencies of different tool types. The presence or absence and relative abundance of artifacts are data which one can order through time, using the technique of seriation, described more fully in Chapter 8. But the principle of seriation is that of popularity, the basic assumption being that sites with the greatest agreement either in the occurrence of artifacts or in their frequencies will lie closest in time.

ABSOLUTE CHRONOLOGY

More effort has been devoted toward inventing methods of absolute dating in archaeology than to almost any other aspect of the subject. It is hardly surprising, for fundamental questions about the past are involved. How old is this tool? How long ago was that site occupied? Are these villages contemporary? These are probably the first questions asked by anyone curious about an artifact or a prehistoric village, as well as by the archaeologist himself. They remain some of the most difficult questions to answer.

An impressive array of chronological techniques has been developed to date the past. Some have become well established reliable methods of dating. Others, after a brief vogue, have been ejected into academic oblivion upon the discovery of some fatal flaw. In practice, the huge span of human cultural history is dated by a number of scientific methods; the chronological span is shown in Table 2.3. Potassium argon dating provides a somewhat generalized chronology for the first two-thirds of man's history, its recent limits reaching up to some 400,000 years ago. The other major radioactive technique, radiocarbon dating, covers a period from approximately 55,000 years ago up to as recently as A.D. 1500, when the standard errors are too large compared with the small time spans involved. (See Table 2.5.) No one has yet developed a dating method to cover the 350,000 years or so between the outer limits of radiocarbon dating and the beginnings of potassium argon chronology.[29]

Historical documents provide a fairly accurate chronology for kings and political events for over 5,000 years in the Near East and for shorter periods elsewhere in the world. Prehistoric chronology in the New World ends with white settlement of the Americas from the fifteenth century on. These more recent periods, frequently times when archaeology can be used in conjunction with historical documents or oral records, are covered by many other dating methods, including imported objects of known historical date and dendrochronology. Dates in years not only tell how old a site is, but also illuminate the relationships between different communities, cultures, or larger

Table 2.5   Radiocarbon Dates—Accuracy Shown by an Example

Sample radiocarbon date = 3,621 ± 180 years (plus or minus factor)
1 standard deviation = 3,441 or 3,801 years
With 1 deviation, it is 68% certain that the date span is correct.
2 standard deviations = 3,261 or 3,981 years
With 2 deviations, chances are 19/20 that the date span is correct.

geographic or social units. Were the inhabitants of a hill fort occupied in the first century b.c. in southern Britain contemporary with the people living on a similar site 150 miles away? Were two broadly similar prehistoric cultures, whose distributions overlap, contemporary, or was one earlier than the other? Did food production originate first in the Near East or in Southeast Asia? Was Patagonia settled by early man before Peru? Such questions, sometimes trivial, sometimes of major significance in the study of human history, can only be answered by absolute chronologies of acceptable accuracy and reliability.

OBJECTS OF KNOWN AGE

The most reliable dates are those derived from historical documentation of archaeological sites. We know, for example, the year when King Henry VIII began to build his palace at Nonsuch, England, as well as the chronology of Plimoth Plantation in Massachusetts, from contemporary records, and our primary interest lies in discovering details of settlement layout or day-to-day life. Many later sites yield easily dated artifacts, such as coins dropped by the inhabitants on the floors of buildings or elsewhere in the settlement's strata. Such objects can provide accurate dates for the earliest age of the archaeological sites being investigated.

Trade diffused similar, well dated objects from areas of advanced technological achievement to less fortunate regions of Europe, Africa, and Asia. Technological innovation flourished with the advent of urban civilization, with more advanced materials being used to create a wide range of luxury objects or ornaments. Chinese porcelain, Roman glass vessels, faience or glass beads, cotton and flax fabrics, bronze daggers, and Greek wine amphorae were luxuries diffused widely through the Ancient World, often to the barbarian tribes on the fringe of the unknown. The dates of styles of Chinese porcelain or Greek vases, changing according to the fashion's dictates, are firmly established in historical records. Such objects are found hundreds and even thousands of miles from the source of manufacture in undated prehistoric camps or trading centers. Since the date of the import is known at its source, the settlement in which it is found can be dated to a period at least as early as the exotic object of known age. This dating method is known as "cross-dating."[30]

Imports have proved of inestimable use in dating many sites far from the centers of ancient civilization. Chinese Nankin porcelain has been found in the far interior of southeast Africa, where the great trading confederacy of the hereditary chief Monomotapa flourished 500 years ago.[31] African minerals, ivory, and slaves were coveted by the Indian Ocean traders, who established well-trodden trade and barter routes into the African interior. They exchanged such exotic luxuries as seashells, Indian cloth and glass beads, and Chinese porcelain for copper, gold, iron, and ivory collected or mined by the chiefs of the African plateau. Zimbabwe was one of the greatest commercial and religious centers of the interior, a great complex of stone enclosures and spectacular walls, and for many centuries a headquarters of the Karanga kingdom. The nineteenth-century explorers who found Zimbabwe deep in the African savannah far from any known civilization were amazed and bemused; they described it as the lost kingdom of the Phoenicians and the Queen of Sheba. How else, they argued, could the great stone walls of Zimbabwe have been erected, for the local people had no knowledge of such activity. Theodore Bent, Richard Hall, and other investigators dated Zimbabwe to the pre-Christian era, and spoke of a lost civilization in the African bush. Then Randall MacIver came along, a pupil of the Egyptologist, Flinders Petrie, and trained in scientific excavation techniques. He realized the value of the Nankin china and Arab glass fragments found by diggers in the ruins, and sent them to experts in the British Museum in London. They reported that the imports dated to the thirteenth or fourteenth centuries A.D., so MacIver was able to demonstrate a medieval date for Zimbabwe and the southeast African gold trade, a dramatic example of how imports can date an archaeological site far from centers of literate civilization.

Imported luxuries are of considerable use for dating if their dates of manufacture in their homelands are known within fine limits, as well as their stratigraphic associations. Exotic imports were rare in most remoter areas, undoubtedly prized by their owners and sometimes kept as heirlooms. The Venda people of the Northern Transvaal, South Africa, still possess strings of ancestral glass beads which have been carefully preserved for generations.[32] Many originated as barter items in the prehistoric gold trade of earlier centuries. Similar cases are known from other parts of the world, complicating the dating of prehistoric settlements.

European prehistoric sites contain various small trade artifacts primarily of Mediterranean origin. The date, for example, of Egyptian faience beads in the Mediterranean basin has been established at about 1400 B.C.[33] Such ornaments are found in Europe as far north as Great Britain and Scandinavia, and provided a useful chronological horizon for sites containing them before the advent of radiocarbon dating (Figure 2.11). Although imports have a chronological range of several thousand years B.C., they are useless for dating the earlier millennia of prehistory.

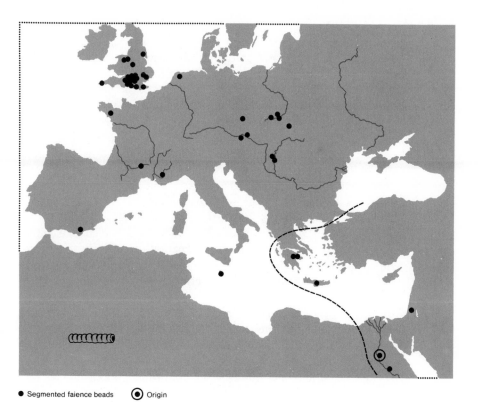

● Segmented faience beads   ◉ Origin

Fig. 2.11 The distribution of segmented faience beads in Europe. Those within the broken line come from the Mycenaean, Cretan, and Egyptian distribution area. (After Clark.)

Cross-dating can, of course, be used with horizon markers of unknown absolute age, as well as with those of a known age in a historic context. Such relative dating horizon markers as particular forms of decorated potsherd or house types whose stratigraphic horizon is firmly and precisely established in one area can be used for the purpose of stratigraphic cross-correlations with other regions. This method is often employed in later European prehistory, but has been less frequently applied in the New World.

DENDROCHRONOLOGY

Dendrochronology, or tree-ring dating, was developed in Arizona by Dr. A. E. Douglass about 1913.[34] However, the idea of using tree rings as a method of dating archaeological sites is much older. As early as 1788, the Reverend Manasseh Cutler was counting the rings on trees growing on archaeological sites near Marietta, Ohio, and suggested that the site he was studying was about a thousand years old. But the prehistoric time scale established from tree rings goes back considerably further into the past, especially in the Southwest where it has been applied successfully to wooden beams in ancient Pueblos, preserved by the dry, desertic conditions. Both the slow-growing *Sequoia* and California bristlecone pine (*Pinus aristata*) provide long tree-ring sequences, the latter providing a continuous tree-ring chronology of 7,100 years. One pine tree 4,900 years old has been reported.

Everyone is familiar with tree rings, a concentric series of circles, each representing annual growth, visible on the cross section of a felled trunk. These rings are formed on most trees, but especially in areas where there is a marked seasonal weather change, either a wet and dry season, or marked alternation of summer and winter temperatures. As a rule, trees produce one growth ring a year, which is formed by the cambium lying between the wood and the bark. When the growing season starts, sets of large cells are added to the wood. These cells become thicker-walled and smaller as the growing season progresses—by the end of the growth season, cell production has ceased altogether. This process occurs every growing year; a distinct line is formed between the wood of the previous season and its small cells, and the wood of the following period and its new large cells. The thickness of each ring may vary according to the tree's age and annual climatic variations, thick rings being characteristic of good growth years.

Weather variations within a circumscribed area tend to run in cycles. A decade of wet years may be followed by five dry ones. One season may bring a forty-year rainfall record. These cycles of climate are reflected in patterns of thicker or thinner rings, which are repeated from tree to tree within a limited area. Dendrochronologists have developed sophisticated methods of correlating sets of rings from different trees so that they build up long sequences of rings from a number of trunks which may extend over many centuries (Figure 2.12). By using modern trees whose date of felling is known, they are able to reconstruct accurate dating as far back as 4,000 years ago. Actual applications to archaeological wood are much harder, but archaeological chronology for the American Southwest now goes back to the first century B.C.

The disadvantage of the method is the limited number of areas where it can be applied. In a climate which is generally humid or cold, or in an area where trees enjoy a constant water supply, the

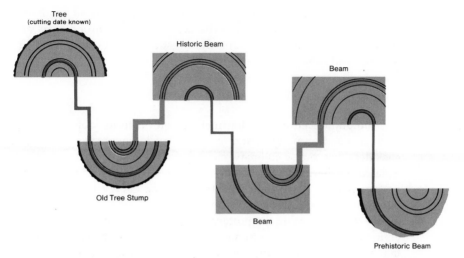

Tree
(cutting date known)

Historic Beam

Beam

Old Tree Stump

Beam

Prehistoric Beam

Fig. 2.12 Schematic drawings of a series of timbers, showing how a chronological sequence is built up.

difference in annual growth rings is either blurred or insignificant. Dendrochronology cannot be used under these circumstances. In addition to the Southwest, however, the method has been applied in the Missouri Valley, Canada, Scandinavia, England, and Germany. The results of such work are still experimental but a beginning has been made in establishing chronological sequences for such buildings as medieval churches, ancient town halls, and other structures.

The extremely accurate chronology for Southwestern sites has been achieved by correlating a master tree-ring sequence from felled trees and dated structures with beams from Indian pueblos. The beams in many such structures have been used again and again, so some are very much older than the houses which they were used to support. Such beams were found to link prehistoric dwelling sites and modern times. The earliest tree rings obtained from such settlements date to the first century B.C., but most timbers were in use between A.D. 1000 and historic times. There are some disadvantages to tree-ring dates, for readings from archaeological sites are affected by numerous factors. Many house beams are trimmed or reused several times, the outside surface of the log being removed in the process. The felling date cannot be established accurately without carefully observing the context and archaeological association of the beam.

Dendrochronology has a limited time span, but its accuracy is precise; its application has great importance, especially in semi-arid areas like the Southwest where the archaeologists' chronologies are envied by less fortunate scholars who wrestle with radiocarbon dating, imports, and other less accurate methods.

THERMOLUMINESCENCE

Thermoluminescence, a dating method with a formidable sounding name, is used on pottery, and is in the development stage.[35] It holds considerable promise and may one day provide absolute dating of even isolated potsherds. The principle is simple. The materials from which pottery is made have the property of storing energy by trapping of electrons as atomic defects or impurity sites. This stored energy can be released by heating the pottery, at which time visible light rays are emitted, known as thermoluminescence. All pottery and ceramics contain some radioactive impurities to a concentration of several parts per million. These materials emit alpha particles at a known rate, depending how densely concentrated they are in the sample. When an alpha particle is absorbed by the pottery minerals around the radioactive impurities, it causes mineral atoms to ionize. Electrons are then released from their binding to the nuclei and settle later at a metastable state of higher energy. This energy is stored unless the parent material is heated—for example, during the firing of a pot—when the trapped electrons are released and thermoluminescence occurs. Since the pot was fired, alpha particles are again absorbed by the material, and the thermoluminescence increases with time if the pot is heated again. Thus, to date a clay vessel involves measuring the thermoluminescence of the sample, as well as its alpha-radioactivity and its potential susceptibility to the production of thermoluminescence. In the laboratory, the trapped electrons are released from a powdered pottery fragment by sudden and violent heating under controlled conditions.

The method is still being developed, and there are numerous factors that affect its accuracy. Like other dating methods, results have been obtained initially from vessels of known age; because of these results, several investigators claim accuracies of plus or minus 5 per cent for prehistoric dates. Other proponents of the method are more cautious, however, and the potential of thermoluminescence will not fully be assessed for some time. But its future use could be unlimited for later prehistory, for pottery is one of the commonest archaeological finds.

At this point, though not described here, several other potential dating methods should be mentioned; these include archaeomagnetism, obsidian dating, and the Fission Track technique.[36]

RADIOCARBON DATING

Until recently no one had been able to date most archaeological sites at all precisely. Then, in 1949, J. R. Arnold and W. F. Libby published a paper in *Science* describing the dating of samples from objects of known age by their radiocarbon content.[37] The paper caused an archaeological furore, and once checked out was soon applied to organic materials from prehistoric sites, hitherto undated by any reliable chronometric method. Over twenty years have elapsed since the radiocarbon dating method became a regular part of the archaeologist's tool kit. For the first time a world chronology for prehistory has begun to emerge, based almost entirely on dates obtained from Libby's great discovery.

The radiocarbon dating method is based on the fact that cosmic radiation produces neutron particles in the upper atmosphere of the earth. Some particles hit atoms of ordinary nitrogen with an atomic weight of 14. These are captured by a nucleus which gives off a proton of atomic weight 1 thereby changing to carbon 14. Carbon 14, which is radioactive and by losing an electron reverts to nitrogen, is an isotope of ordinary carbon, which has an atomic weight of 12. It is believed to behave exactly like ordinary carbon from a chemical standpoint, and enters, together with ordinary carbon, into the carbon dioxide of the atmosphere, in which a constant amount of carbon 14 is to be found. The tempo of the process corresponds to the rates of supply and disintegration. Since living vegetation builds up its own organic matter by photosynthesis and by using atmospheric carbon dioxide, the proportion of radiocarbon present in it equals that in the atmosphere, neglecting the very short lifetime of individual plants compared with the half life of radiocarbon. As soon as an organism dies, no further radiocarbon is incorporated. The radiocarbon present in the dead organism will immediately begin to disintegrate slowly so that after 5,568 years[38] only half the original amount will be left, after about 11,400 years only a quarter, and so on. Thus, if you measure the ratio of carbon 14 to carbon 12, you can obtain an idea of the age of the specimen being measured. The initial amount of radiocarbon in a particular sample is low, so the limit of detectability is soon reached. Samples earlier than 50,000–60,000 years old contain insufficient quantities of carbon 14—the method is most effective on more recent sites.

Radiocarbon dates can be taken from samples of a wide range of organic material. About a handful of charcoal, burnt bone, shell, hair, skin, wood, or other organic substance is needed for the laboratory. The samples themselves are collected with meticulous care during excavation from impeccable stratigraphical contexts so that an exact location, specific structure, or even hearth is dated. Several dates should be taken from each level, as one sample may have been contaminated by a variety of causes. Modern rootlets, disturbances in the stratigraphy, and even packing with cotton wool or in newspapers can introduce younger carbon into an ancient sample, although some more obvious contaminations are eliminated by careful laboratory treatment.

The date arrives from the laboratory with a plus-or-minus factor attached to it, which is explained in Table 2.5. Thus a radiocarbon date is never the exact age of a sample, merely the statistically most likely *radiocarbon age.*[39] No one has yet been able to establish the exact relationship between a radiocarbon age and the true age of a sample, although calibrations with tree-ring dates will eventually provide an accurate true chronology for the past 4,000 years (Figure 2.13). Earlier dates will remain "radiocarbon ages" and, as such, are of unknown accuracy as there is as yet no means of extending dendrochronology further back into the past. "Before present," a term used with radiocarbon dates, means "before A.D. 1950"—by international agreement.

POTASSIUM ARGON DATING

The earliest sites dated by the radiocarbon method are about 55,000 years old, leaving an enormous span of human history still to be dated. Until recently, only relative dates were available for the earlier periods of the Stone Age, despite attempts to use solar radiation fluctuations as a basis for dating the recent geological past. But the geologists have recently developed a battery of radioactive and other counting techniques for dating the earth's age, one of which, the potassium argon method can be used to date geological strata as recent as 400,000 years old.[40] This method measures the ratio of potassium 40 (K40) to gas argon (A40), both elements which occur in many minerals. Radioactive K40 decays at a fixed rate to form A40. By measuring the ratio of K40 to A40 in a spectrometer, one can calculate the age of volcanic rocks like lava. Fortunately, many early human settlements in the Old World are found in volcanic areas, where such deposits as lava flows and tuffs are found in profusion.

The first and one of the most dramatic archaeological dates to be obtained from this method came from Olduvai Gorge, Tanzania, where Dr. and Mrs. Louis Leakey have found a long sequence of human culture extending over much of the Lower and Middle Pleistocene, associated with human fossils. Olduvai, a jagged slash in the

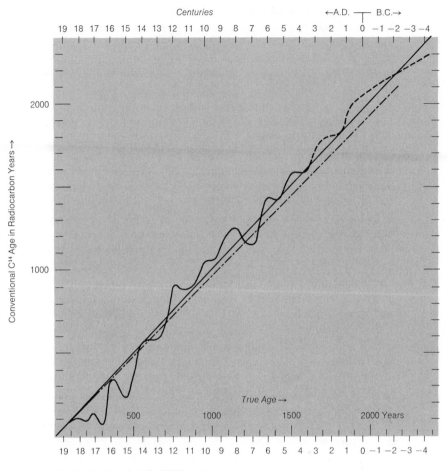

Fig. 2.13 *This diagram was compiled by the La Jolla Radiocarbon Laboratory to show the approximate empirical relationship between radiocarbon dates and dendochronologically determined wood ages.*

Serengeti Plains, was formed by earth movement which has exposed the beds of a long-forgotten Pleistocene lake overlying a layer of volcanic tuff. Early man camped around the shores of the lake; his living floors are preserved in the sides of the gorge, and his implements and broken animal bones lie on them where they were dropped by their owners, and were preserved under layers of fine lake silt. The remains of Australopithecines have been found on the living floors, associated with the tools and bones, together with lumps of lava either deposited naturally by the lake or brought to the site by early man. Some lava on the floors have been dated by the potassium argon technique, and samples from a living floor where the first cranium of *Australopithecus robustus* was discovered were dated to about 1.75 million years.[41] At the time, these and other nearly contemporary dates were a sensation, for most people had imagined that the Pleistocene began about a million years ago. At one step, man had almost doubled his antiquity. Even earlier dates have come from the Omo Valley in southern Ethiopia, where American, French, and Kenyan expeditions have investigated extensive Lower Pleistocene deposits long-known for their rich fossil beds. Fragmentary Australopithecines were found at several localities, but no traces of tools, potassium argon dates giving readings between 2 and 4 million for deposits yielding hominid fossils. Tools were found in levels between two dates of 2 and 2.5 million years. Chopper tools of undoubted human manufacture have come from Koobi Fora in Northern Kenya, dated to about 2.61 million years, at the time of writing the earliest known date for human artifacts.[42]

Unfortunately, the potassium argon method is comparatively inaccurate, with large statistical margins, amounting to as much as a quarter of a million years on Olduvai dates, and can only be used on a limited range of rocks, so that only those sites in volcanic areas can be dated by this method. This and other absolute dating methods have expanded the time scale of human evolution dramatically and revolutionized our ideas about the tempo of human evolution—gradual at first, with the pace of physical and cultural development accelerating rapidly from about 50,000 years ago to the present almost frenetic quest for change in human culture. Archaeological chronologies primarily aim to set up the time framework for our perception of the magnitude of human achievement.

Chapter 3
Preservation and Discovery

PRESERVATION

"After the exertion of entering into such a place, through a passage of . . . perhaps six hundred yards, nearly overcome, I sought a resting place, found one, and continued to sit; but when my weight bore on the body of an Egyptian, it crushed it like a band-box."[1]* Tomb robber Giovanni Belzoni wrote this in 1820 as he pillaged the mausolea of Egypt. How many times have we read that such and such a find was "crumbled to dust" upon discovery, or that exposure to the open air caused the finds to "dissolve before our very eyes." Modern archaeologists have developed a battery of methods to recover fragile objects from the soil, for preservation is a key factor both in the discovery of archaeological sites and in our reconstruction of the past. Whatever the theoretical approach one uses, a serious limiting factor to scientific investigation in archaeology is the degree to which sites and the artifacts preserved in them have survived many centuries in the inhospitable soil.

Preservation conditions depend largely on the soil and the general climatic regimen in the area of a site. Under favorable conditions, a wide range of artifactual materials are preserved, including such perishable items as leather containers, basketry, wooden arrowheads, or furniture. But under normal circumstances, usually only the most durable artifacts survive.

In general terms, the objects found in archaeological sites can be

* See pages 323–325 for notes to Chapter 3.

divided into two broad categories: inorganic finds and organic materials. Inorganic objects include stone implements made from a variety of rocks including flint, quartzite, and quartz, although these can weather quite severely, resulting in surface coating or patination. Gold, silver, bronze, copper, and lead, also inorganic substances, preserve well, but iron rusts easily and frequently only survives as a discoloration in the soil. Clay pots are among the most durable of human artifacts, especially if they are well fired, although the clay surfaces may be somewhat altered. Masonry and bricks fired in kilns survive well but have a rather limited role in the interpretation of the past, being confined to those prehistoric sites where substantial brick or stone structures are found. Sun-dried bricks or mud hut floors or walls have less durable characteristics, for they tend to become constituent elements of the archaeological deposits as a result of wind and weather. But they are often of critical use to stratigraphers or students of architectural styles in Near Eastern mounds or African villages.

An enormous range of organic substances were used by prehistoric man, whether a hunter or agriculturalist. Bones and antlers were vital raw materials to the Upper Paleolithic hunters of southwestern France 12,000 years before Christ; the Pueblo dwellers of the American Southwest used several types of fiber to make sophisticated baskets. Prehistoric Bushmen at the Gwisho hunting camps in central Zambia were making wooden digging sticks and fine arrowheads 4,000 years ago, which are perfectly preserved in the deposits of a hot spring.[2] The Acheulian hunter-gatherers of the Kalambo Falls lake basin in Central Africa were using wooden implements, including possibly a club, as early as 55,000 years ago,[3] and a yew spearpoint was found in the Middle Pleistocene deposits of the Clacton Channel in eastern England, a relic of a Pleistocene hunt (see Figure 7.16). Bone, ivory, hair, skin, and vegetal remains are other examples of organic materials utilized by prehistoric man. Alas, they only rarely survive in the archaeological record.

Waterlogged or peat-bog conditions are particularly favorable for preserving wood or vegetal remains, whether the climate is subtropical or temperate. While tropical rain forests such as those of the Amazon basin or the Congo are far from kind to wooden artifacts, many archaeological sites are found near springs or in marshes where the water table is high, and where perennial waterlogging of occupation layers has occurred since they were abandoned. Danish bogs have yielded a rich harvest of wooden hafted weapons, clothing, ornaments, traps, and even complete corpses, such as that of Tollund man.[4] This unfortunate individual's body was found by two peat cutters in 1950, lying on its side in a brown peat bed in a crouched position, a severe expression on the face and eyes lightly closed. Tollund man wore a pointed skin cap and a hide belt—nothing else. He had been hanged, the cord which was the cause of his death knotted tightly around his neck. The Tollund corpse has been shown to be about 2,000 years old and to belong to the Danish Iron Age. So perfect were preservation conditions that much of his skin still survived, and his peaceful portrait has been included in many archaeological volumes. A formidable team of medical experts examined his cadaver, among them a paleobotanist who established that Tollund man's last meal consisted of a gruel made from barley, linseed, and several wild grasses and weeds, eaten some twelve to twenty-four hours before his death. He is thought to have been a sacrificial victim of a fertility cult, hanged to ensure the success of crops and the continuation of life.

Most finds in waterlogged contexts are less spectacular, but often highly revealing, like Star Carr in northeast England (see Figure 2.10). Waterlogged deposits there preserved a wide range of organic materials, including a platform of birch saplings through which the reeds had grown later. Rolls of birch bark, a canoe paddle, numerous barbed spearheads, and a series of stag antler frontlets made into headdresses came from the platform area; chipping debris from the manufacture of numerous stone arrow barbs and scrapers littered the settlement. The excellent conditions preserved much organic material of the hunters' culture. As a result, Grahame Clark could paint vividly that the hunters' life style was oriented toward the red deer whose antlers provided so much of their tool kit, as well as other forest animals like the elk.

Before Star Carr was discovered, the only finds of this period in England had been some isolated bone or antler spearheads and scatters of the small stone tools used by hunters. Such limited discoveries are typical of unfavorable preservation conditions in temperate climates—the contrast with Star Carr is dramatic. Yet most archaeological sites are located in areas where soil or climatic conditions destroy all inorganic materials. Our total knowledge of the Middle Stone Age of Central Africa, for example, is confined to drawer after drawer of stone tools which, at best, can only tell us something about their makers' technological abilities.

Very arid environments, like those of the American Southwest or the Nile Valley, are even better than waterlogged localities. Undoubtedly one of the most famous of all archaeological discoveries is the amazing tomb of Tutankhamen (*ca.* 1345 B.C.), unearthed by Lord Carnarvon and Howard Carter in 1922,[5] where dry conditions were still damp enough to cause some deterioration of organic finds. The undisturbed burial chamber was opened, revealing the grave furniture exactly in the state in which it had been laid out by the king's mourners. Gilded wood chests, cloth, ivory caskets, models of chariots and boats, and mummies were all perfectly preserved, together with a bewildering array of jewelry and wall frescoes shining as brightly as the day they were painted, even showing the somewhat hasty execution accorded them by the artist. Tutankhamen's sepulchre provides as vivid a glimpse of the past as we are ever likely to obtain. Papyrus texts have been preserved by the dry Egyptian conditions in many Nile Valley cemeteries, too, giving an unrivalled picture of the Ancient Egyptian world.[6]

The American West is rich in organic finds. Arid levels at Danger Cave in Utah contained wooden arrows, knife handles, trap springs, and other wood tools,[7] and fiber sandals, string aprons, and baskets have come from Anasazi culture Basketmaker II sites, dating to between A.D. 46 and 330. As important as these artifacts are the caches of domesticated plant remains. Caves near the Talus Slope Village site in the northern San Juan region, near Durango, Colorado,[8] contained maize cobs and traces of squashes; wild foods included sunflower seeds, amaranth, and tansy mustard seeds. Other sites contained feathered ornaments, textiles, and netting. A series of burials from Coastal Peruvian Inca and pre-Inca sites have been recovered in a desiccated state, too, so much so that traces of tattooing and feathered headdresses have been recovered by the archaeologists.[9]

The dry conditions of Southwestern sites are highly conducive to the survival of vegetal remains, and archaeologists and botanists have been able to describe the evolution of maize and other domestic crops. The maize from the Durango sites is genetically more advanced than the earliest Mogollan maize from Bat Cave and Tularosa Cave.[10] MacNeish and others have similarly traced the history of domestic crops in Central America where dry conditions have also preserved cobs of early corn.[11] In contrast, the development of prehistoric agriculture in the Near East is less well known, owing to less favorable site conditions.

Arctic sites, too, are excellent for the preservation of man's past. The circumpolar regions of Siberia and the New World have acted like a giant refrigerator, where the processes of decay have been held in check for thousands of years. Close to the Arctic Sea, the carcasses of mammoths have survived thousands of winters in a state of perennial refrigeration. The Beresovka mammoth from Siberia was studied in 1901 by a Soviet expedition whose dogs ate the flesh of the Pleistocene beast as it was being dismembered.[12] The hair was perfectly preserved, and the remains of its last meal were found on its tongue and in its stomach.

Russian archaeologist Sergei Rudenko was responsible for some remarkable excavations at the Pazyryk burial mounds in Siberia, not far from the Chinese and Mongolian borders. The Pazyryk mounds lie in an area where summers are short and winters intensely cold, and have been dated by radiocarbon and cross-dating techniques to around 400 B.C. They are thought to be associated with the Yue-Chi peoples of southern Siberia. Although the mounds are south of the permafrost zones of Siberia, the sites themselves are permanently refrigerated, a special microclimate being formed inside them by the heat conducting properties of the stone cairn forming each mound's core. The mounds themselves covered burial shafts filled with logs and rocks; log chambers containing the burials lay under this filling. The roofs of the chambers were covered with birchbark strips and the flooring was often planked. The bodies were deposited in log coffins, invariably lying in an extended position with their heads facing east. They were usually partly clothed and accompanied by wooden pillows and tables with dishes of food—cheese and fluid residues in them. A wealth of small objects came from the burials, including a Chinese mirror, beads, seashells, lacquer, gold pins, and the remains of clothing. Horses were buried with their masters, having been dispatched with a pole axe and placed in the burial shafts. Seven to nine or more horses were usually thrust into the shafts, their heads often facing east. Bridles, saddles, and head decorations accompanied the horses. Solid-wheeled wooden trolleys were found in each barrow; one contained a four-wheeled carriage with draught pole. The horse carcasses were so well preserved in the refrigerated conditions that their hides could be studied: none had their winter coats. The horses were rather emaciated, as if they had survived a hard winter and had been slaughtered in early summer. Furthermore, the flowers of white-yellow scabious, which blooms between the end of June and early July, were found in the moss-packing of one burial chamber. Thus it was deduced that Pazyryk burials were interred in the early summer months.

The refrigerated conditions of the mounds preserved not only an array of wooden artifacts, horse harnesses, carpets, and even felt wall-coverings and canopies with elaborate naturalistic motifs, but also the clothes and flesh of the individuals buried there. Linen shirts adorned with braid, caftans decorated with leather and gold discs, and headdresses of felt and leather came from the coffins, as did women's bootees, aprons, and stockings. Much of the clothing was elaborately decorated, whereas the individuals' hair was shaved. In addition to small ornaments, several bodies bore remarkable and elaborate tattooing. One chief's body showed a lively picture of a monster like a lion-griffin or some other imaginary creature. Deer, birds, and carnivores also adorned his body, with tattooing over the heart and arms and also on the legs. Presumably the figures had some magical significance as well as a decorative intent.

The Pazyryk finds are so extensive that describing even a small proportion of them is impossible here.[13] Among the fascinating details is the fact that the horses bore ownership marks, their elaborate harnesses having analogy with Scythian practice; a lively and unusual animal art tradition is associated with the harness, art that is both exuberant and distorted to fit the twisted shapes of bridle and saddle fittings. The remarkable discoveries at Pazyryk have a local importance because they show the long cultural ancestry of the modern pastoral tribes of south Siberia. But to archaeology as a whole they reveal the potential richness of archaeological sites under the preservation conditions sometimes found in the Arctic.

Eskimo archaeology has benefitted enormously from the Arctic cold, where permafrost, especially in Greenland and the more northern parts of Arctic territory, has refrigerated wooden objects, bone and ivory artifacts, and the remains of animals hunted by the artifact makers. Sometimes summer thaws have softened the upper layers of Eskimo middens which resulted in some destruction of material, so only the lower horizons with their better refrigeration furnish a complete range of prehistoric artifacts. The Bering Straits area of Alaska is famous for some remarkable Eskimo settlements which have provided rich archaeological treasures. Miyowagh on St. Lawrence Island is a midden site belonging within the Northern Maritime subtradition, as much as two meters deep in some places; a seaside settlement, it is now over one-half mile from the ocean because of successive building of beach lines since the camp was occupied about 2,000 years ago. The earliest houses at Miyowagh were built on the shore, and covered by a rich, black midden of animal bones, baleen, and artifact waste. The houses were rectangular and had been floored with stone slabs; driftwood and whalebone walls were laid horizontally and held in place by upright posts and boulders; the roofs were probably made of timbers and whalebones. The entries to the huts were large passages. So many sea mammal bones were used in Miyo-wagh home construction that the pursuit of such beasts must have been a primary activity of the inhabitants. The ivory, wood, and bone components of the harpoons used in the chase are some of the most frequent finds in Arctic sites. Thanks to excellent preservation conditions, archaeologists can use the minor technical and stylistic changes in the harpoon to delineate landmarks in the Arctic cultural sequence. Ivory is so well preserved in Northern Maritime sites that Collins and other scholars have been able to describe the distinctive art of the Old Bering Sea phase with its characteristic linear and circle and dot motifs, used to adorn harpoon heads, needle cases, and other prosaic domestic objects.[14]

Another remarkable site is the Ipiutak settlement near Point Hope on the Chukchi Sea, dated to the first few centuries A.D.[15] Over 60 semi-subterranean dwellings were excavated out of an estimated 600–700 on the site. The floor level of the Ipiutak houses was about 50 centimeters (19 inches) below the ground, with the squarish floor between 3 and 7 meters (10 and 23 feet) in diameter. A central fireplace lay on the floor of packed gravel or logs, while sleeping benches of gravel and earth lined three walls. Vertical logs or poles, caulked with finer timbers, formed the walls; the whole structure, including the wooden roof, was covered with arctic moss. In a nearby cemetery, wooden coffins containing a single burial were built in small pits, most of them at least a half-meter (19 inches) deep. Few grave goods were associated with these burials in contrast to a series of skeletons deposited only a few centimeters below the surface. The bodies when discovered were partially disarticulated, lying in a deposit of wood fragments, which included some flamboyant ivory carvings, and midden soil. The excavators inferred that the dead had been deposited on the ground, enclosed in a wooden frame or a pile of logs. Elaborate ivory carvings were invariably associated with the surface burials at Ipiutak, preserved by the cold conditions which have pertained at the site since its abandonment. Ipiutak art is dominated by small sculptures of bears, walruses, and other animals, while composite masks and delicate spiral ornaments were probably fastened to the grave coverings. It is sobering to realize that under temperate conditions only stone artifacts and the outlines of the Ipiutak houses and bed platforms would have survived the 2,000 years since the settlement was occupied.

The deposit in which antiquities are found has an important bearing on their preservation, just as the association of one artifact with another within the soil has. Classic examples are the Roman cities of Herculaneum and Pompeii, overwhelmed by a sea of ash or lava in A.D. 79 by an eruption of Vesuvius graphically described by the elder Pliny. Pompeii has been excavated from the lava to reveal a Roman town in which life stopped at an instant in time. Bodies of people fleeing from the molten lava, dog corpses, and complete buildings came to light, giving a clear but pathetic picture of the doomed city in its last moments.

Geological deposits, such as oil-bearing layers in Poland or tar beds in the New World, have supplied many fossil remains of large mammals trapped in the treacherous deposits thousands of years ago. A dog corpse from a Basketmaker site in the Southwest survived so well in dry soil that the flies which fed on the putrefying corpse were found with the skeleton. Viking ships are preserved in the acid soils of temperate climates by the stones, clay, and peat packed around them by their owners. Even the wine of Roman times has come down to us. In 1867 a bottle of wine dating from the third century A.D. was found in a Roman sarcophagus at Speyer; the bottle was still full, and the liquid was analyzed to be wine mixed with honey. A thick layer of olive oil covered the wine, poured into the bottle by the original bottler to preserve the contents; this had become resinated, preventing the wine from evaporating.[16]

In spite of these exceptional instances, most soils tend to be destructive. Acid soils destroy inorganic objects rapidly, but the dark discolorations of postholes and hut foundations often remain, and challenge the archaeologist to reconstruct structures whose actual substance has vanished. The granitic soils of subtropical regions tend to be highly destructive, while the chalk deposits of Europe preserve animal bones, burials, and metals moderately well. The great loess belts of Central Europe have mantled many Upper Paleolithic settlements, preserving the floor plans of the mammoth hunters' camps, some of the earliest human structures ever recovered.[17]

The archaeologist who chances on a site where the conditions of preservation allow him a glance at the more perishable aspects of prehistoric man's material culture and economy is lucky. Small wonder that the most famous archaeological sites are those where climate, soil, or geology have been kind to the artifacts of prehistoric man.

FINDING ARCHAEOLOGICAL SITES

For the early antiquarians, sites were discovered by locating burial mounds, stone structures, hillforts, and other conspicuous traces of prehistoric man's impact on the European landscape. The "tells" of the Near East, occupied by generation after generation of city dwellers, were easily recognized by early travelers, and the temples and monuments of Ancient Egypt have attracted antiquarian and plunderer alike for many centuries. New World archaeological sites were described by some of the first conquistadores—later, Copán, the ruined Maya city, was studied by Garcia de Palacio in 1576. Maya sites were vividly cataloged by John Lloyd Stephens and Frederick Catherwood in the mid-nineteenth century, and the wonders of Mesoamerican civilization laboriously recovered from the rain forest that engulfed them.

But many prehistoric settlements are inconspicuous or even invisible to the naked eye, forgotten by the present inhabitants of the area where they are found. It is safe to say that many of the world's most conspicuous and spectacular archaeological sites are known, even if they have not been excavated. Today's archaeologist is often concerned with the location of large numbers of small sites within a well-circumscribed region as part of prehistoric settlement pattern study. His techniques of site location are many and ingenious, but still stem from perceptive observation in the field. Field archaeology, in the sense of site surveys conducted without recourse to excavation, has a respectable ancestry in the travels of William Camden and the generations of antiquarians who followed him. Camden himself was a perceptive field observer, who spoke with peasants and squires and observed the ways in which natural phenomena could be used to help the archaeologist. He visited the former Roman town at Richborough in Kent: "But now age has erased the very tracks of it; and to teach us that cities dye as well as men, it is at this day a cornfield, wherein when the corn is grown up, one may observe the draughts of the streets crossing one another (for where they have gone the corn is thinner)."[18]

Site survey became a serious part of archaeology when field archaeologists began to realize that man had enacted his life against the background of a contemporary landscape, and that all they would find would be what Francis Bacon defined as "some remnants of history which have casually escaped the shipwreck of time." The early twentieth century was a great time for field archaeology in Europe. J. P. Williams Freeman and O. G. S. Crawford, among others, traced Roman roads and ancient field systems, walking and bicycling over the countryside in search of known and unknown sites, while in Bolivia and Peru, Max Uhle, a German, was among those who pioneered systematic field survey in the New World. The techniques developed by these scholars form the basis for much archaeological fieldwork today.[19]

Before we examine some ways in which archaeological sites are located, we should define "field archaeology." Field survey is concerned with archaeological sites in space: prehistoric settlements are located, their surface features plotted and carefully reported, and their relationship to other sites recorded on detailed maps. Extensive surface collections are an important part of the survey process, for the artifacts found on a site, either exposed by natural factors or in animal burrows, give a general impression of its inhabitants. In the classical sense field archaeology involves no excavations, no studies of stratigraphic profiles from trenches, and no radiocarbon dating from excavated samples of charcoal; it is merely surface survey. Beyond the actual mechanics of site location, the information obtained from a field survey is concerned with the relationship—in space—of one site to another, and of coherent groups of sites with each other. Each settlement had an individual ecological niche, and a group of sites as a whole may have a complex relationship with a variety of soil types, water supplies, and vegetational covers, all of which may have varied in importance through time. Iron Age villages in southern Britain, for example, were often associated with complex agricultural systems, surviving in the archaeological record as field boundaries. The relationship between homesteads and fields was a critical factor in the residential stability, land-tenure systems, and society of the inhabitants of the area. Relationship in space is such an important part of prehistory that field archaeology has become an important handmaiden of those who study man's complex and ever-changing relationship with his environment.

AERIAL PHOTOGRAPHY

O. G. S. Crawford, best known as the founder of the celebrated archaeological journal *Antiquity*, was a brilliant exponent of field archaeology. A perceptive countryman, he soon became aware of the value of an overhead view of the countryside. Crawford had read Camden's accounts of Richborough and Roman Silchester, where the street plans were exposed in the growing corn, and had observed the rolling landscape of rural Britain from church towers and hills, a low sun or snow emphasizing the relief of prehistoric earthworks or field systems. Then, during World War I, Crawford flew as an observer on the Western Front, taking aerial photographs for reconnaissance purposes, and immediately realized the potential of air photography for the location and planning of all types of archaeological sites, even those invisible to the surface observer. The Germans even photographed deserted cities in the northern Sinai Desert during the war. Fields, streets, buildings, and other features showed up with astonishing clarity; Dr. Theodore Wiegand, who published the photographs, hailed a new era in archaeological reconnaissance. Thanks to these pioneer war surveys and the vigorous efforts of Crawford and other former airmen, aerial survey has become a formidable tool.[20] Thousands of hitherto unknown sites have been plotted on maps for the first time, whole field systems and roadways have been incorporated into panoramas of prehistoric or Roman landscapes in Italy and North Africa, and well-known sites like Stonehenge or Mesoamerican temples have been photographed in the context of their landscapes (Figure 3.1).

Aerial photography gives an unrivalled overhead view of the past.

Fig. 3.1   An aerial photograph of the earthworks at Maiden Castle, Dorset, England.

Sites can be photographed from oblique or vertical angles, at different
seasons or times of day, and from many directions. Numerous sites
which have left almost no surface traces on the ground have come
to light through the all-embracing eye of the air photograph. Many
earthworks or other complex structures have been levelled by plough
or erosion, but their reduced topography clearly shows up from the
air. The rising or setting sun can set off long shadows which emphasize
the relief of almost vanished banks or ditches, so the features of the
site stand out in the oblique light. Such phenomena are sometimes
called "shadow sites." More important are crop and soil marks, found
in areas where the subsoil is suitable to detect differences in soil
color and in the richness of crop growth on a particular soil. Such
marks cannot be detected easily on the surface, but can be clearly
seen under favorable circumstances from the air. The principle upon
which the crop mark is based is the fact that the growth and color
of a crop are greatly determined by the amount of moisture the plant
can derive from the soil and subsoil. If the soil depth has increased
by digging features such as pits and ditches and then filling them

69

in, or by heaping up additional earth to form artificial banks or mounds, the crops growing over such abandoned structures are high and well nourished. The converse is also true in areas where soil has been removed and the infertile subsoil is near the surface, or where there are impenetrable surfaces such as paved streets below ground level and crops are stunted. Thus a dark crop mark can be taken for a ditch or pit, while a lighter line will define a more substantial structure. Soil marks result from ploughing soil from such features as banks, which show up as a lighter color, in contrast to the darker deeper soil around them. Crop marks are very useful in chalk country, where the subsoil is a brilliant white. Infrared photography is now being used to locate field systems for the first time.[21]

Much of the world has been covered by military photographers, normally from an altitude of around 24,000 feet. These mosaics are most often used by expeditions to remote areas who want to survey a large tract of country at minimum expense. A classic example of air photograph usage was provided by Gordon Willey who used a standard Peruvian Air Force mosaic of the cultivated valley bottoms and margins of the Virú Valley in northern coastal Peru to survey changing settlement patterns there.[22] Willey employed these photographs as the basis for a master site map for the Valley, and was able to plot many different archaeological features. Three hundred and fifteen sites in the Virú Valley were located, many of them stone buildings, walls, or terraces which showed up quite well on the mosaics. Some much less conspicuous sites were also spotted, among them midden heaps without stone walls, refuse mounds which appeared as low hillocks on the photographs, and small pyramidal mounds of insignificant proportions. Adobe houses did not show up as clearly as stone structures. An enormous amount of time was saved, time which otherwise would have been spent walking over rough countryside. The aerial photographs enabled Willey and his team to pinpoint many sites before going out in the field. The finds were later investigated on the spot. The result was the fascinating story of shifting settlement patterns in Virú over many thousands of years, which has become a classic study of its kind.

ACCIDENTAL DISCOVERIES

The ingenious gentlemen who calculate such things estimate that something like a quarter of all archaeological sites have been discovered because of nature's or humans' activity. Whole chapters of man's past have emerged through accidental discoveries of sites, spectacular artifacts, or skeletons. A famous and flamboyant archaeological discovery was made by a girl named Kirsten Svendsdatter at Gallehus, Denmark, in August, 1639.[23] She stumbled over a root and found a curved golden horn, over two and a half feet long and elaborately embossed with decoration in high relief. The horn found its way into the royal treasury and was almost forgotten until, ninety-five years later, a smallholder named Erik Lassen found a second, incomplete but slightly heavier horn of the same metal. It joined its companion in the royal library in Copenhagen, where the horns remained on exhibition for sixty-eight years. In 1802, tragically, they were stolen and melted down before the thief was apprehended; this left notes and drawings as our only record of them, from which silver gilt copies were made in 1861. The Gallehus horns bear runic inscriptions and decoration which date them to the period A.D. 400–450, an unsettled time in Western European history. One horn bears the runic inscription: "I Laegaest son of Holte made the horn," and they are thought to be of ceremonial origin.

The Gallehus horns are one of many discoveries of cached weapons, coins, smiths' tools, and sacrificial objects found in the fields of the Western world. Ploughing, peat cutting, road-making, and other day-to-day activities have been a fruitful source of archaeological discoveries. Industrial activity, highway construction, airport expansion, and other destructive pastimes of twentieth-century man have unearthed countless archaeological sites, many of which have to be investigated hurriedly before the bulldozers remove all traces of the site. Deep ploughing, freeway construction, and urban renewal are bitter enemies of the past. Yet dramatic discoveries have resulted from man's despoiling of his environment. Some states require highway contractors to allocate a proportion of their contract budgets for the investigation of any archaeological sites found in the path of their freeways—this at least permits some investigation of accidentally discovered settlements. But many construction programs pay little heed to the pleas of the archaeologist and bulldoze away the past with minimal concern.

An example of a startling accidental discovery was that made on a ridge named Ingombe Ilede in the Middle Zambezi Valley, Central Africa, in 1960.[24] A water storage tank and pump house was to be built there to supply water to the many villages in the vicinity. In digging the foundations of the water tank bones were discovered. Fortunately, a local government officer happened to pass by and collected the finds, including some copper ingots and gold beads. Due to his urgent telephoning, archaeologists launched a rescue excavation on the site and recovered a series of eleven richly decorated burials from the summit of Ingombe Ilede. The skeletons, probably buried in the fifteenth century A.D., bore ornaments of copper, gold, and iron, as well as glass beads, remains of clothing, and necklaces of seashells imported from the East African coast over 400 miles away. Without the government officer's action, a major chapter in African history would never have been written, and we would know almost nothing of early commerce in south-central Africa before the Portuguese arrived at the mouth of the Zambezi River in the late fifteenth century.

Hydroelectric schemes in developing countries are a major source of site destruction, and yet have stimulated much intensive survey. The Aswan Dam scheme in Nubia provided a rare opportunity for intensive investigation of Pleistocene geology and Stone Age sites in the areas now flooded by the Nile waters.[25] Kariba dam and lake in Central Africa inundated a vast tract of the Zambezi Valley which could only be surveyed in haste months before the Valley was flooded. In both these areas, as well as with Ghana's Upper Volta scheme, much archaeological information has been lost forever.

Nature itself sometimes uncovers sites for us, which are located by a sharp-eyed archaeologist looking for natural exposures of likely geological strata. Erosion, flooding, tidal waves, low lake levels, earthquakes, and wind action can all lead to the exposure of archaeological sites. A most famous site is Olduvai Gorge in Tanzania,[26] a great gash in the Serengeti Plains, where nature, through earth movement, has sliced through hundreds of meters of Pleistocene lake bed to expose numerous living floors of early man. Fossil animal bones were found in the Gorge's exposed strata by Professor Kattwinkel as early as 1911, which led to a fossil-hunting expedition under Professor Hans Reck, and ultimately to Dr. and Mrs. Leakey's long and patient investigations in the Gorge. The results of their excavations are spectacular—a series of living floors stratified one above another upon which hominid fossils, broken animal bones, stone implements, and even traces of possible structures have been found and dated to ages ranging from 400,000 for *Homo erectus* to 1,750,000 years before the present for living floors in the earliest bed of the Gorge.

Most finds exposed by nature are not so spectacular. For example, in 1641 a great storm ravaged the coasts of the Low Countries, and laid bare the long buried shrine of a Roman goddess, Nehalennia, on the island of Walcheren, now once again covered by the North Sea.[27] Inland, the forces of nature have exposed a multitude of archaeological sites. The great river valleys of Europe, Africa, and Asia are filled with extensive deposits of water-laid alluvium and gravel, exposed when the vegetation is low in the dry season or uncovered by erosion and commercial work. Boucher de Perthes found his hand axes in the Somme River quarries; for many years the relative chronology of African prehistory and the European Lower Paleolithic rested on cultural sequences derived from the terraces of the Somme, Thames, Nile, Zambezi, and other rivers. Erosion gullies and sand dunes are also likely geological contexts for the field archaeologist to examine; these are particularly common in subtropical areas where erosion is often uncontrolled and results in the rapid destruction of valuable agricultural land. In 1951, a schoolmaster named MacLennan was driving from Nairobi to Johannesburg along the Great North Road which winds over thousands of miles from Capetown to East Africa. He noticed a series of large erosion gullies to the east of the road at Isimila near the small town of Iringa, central Tanzania, and stopped to explore the sandy deposits left standing by centuries of water erosion. MacLennan returned to his car with twenty-six beautiful Acheulian hand axes which he had picked up on the gully slopes. Fortunately he reported his finds to a South African archaeologist who published them. Six years later a team of University of Chicago archaeologists under F. Clark Howell excavated at Isimila, exposing a series of well-preserved Acheulian living floors in the walls of the eroded ravines. Such occupation areas have been found only at a handful of sites in Africa, Europe, and the Near East, most of which will be referred to in this book. At Isimila, surface erosion made a major contribution to prehistoric research.[28]

In late 1957, another remarkable discovery was made, this time in the semiarid country in southeastern Colorado.[29] Wind erosion exposed what appeared to be five separate piles of bison bones in an arroyo near Kit Carson. Some projectile points were also found with the bones. The bone bed at what became known as the Olsen-Chubbuck site lay in a filled buffalo trail, of a type which crisscrossed the plains in early frontier days. The bones were carefully excavated, and shown to come from *Bison occidentalis*, an extinct species. Separate piles, made up of different bone types such as limb bones, pelvic girdles, etc., gave a clue to the hunters' butchery techniques. They had cut up the carcasses systematically, piling the detached members in the arroyo in separate heaps, dismembering several bison at a time. The remains of nearly 200 bison came from the arroyo, but only a proportion was fully dismembered. Clearly the arroyo was a trap into which the beasts had been stampeded. (They have a keen sense of smell, but poor vision; a lumbering herd of these gregarious beasts can be readily stampeded into an abrupt declivity, and the leaders have no option but to plunge into the gully and be immobilized or disabled by the weight of those behind them.) So vivid a reconstruction of the Paleo-Indians' hunt could be made that the excavators were even able to guess at the direction of the wind on the day of the stampede. The vivid traces of this hunt of 6500 B.C. were buried in the arroyo by nature, and exposed again eight thousand years later, to be discovered by the vigilant eye of an amateur archaeologist.

ARCHAEOLOGICAL SURVEY

Most sites are found by skillful survey and thorough examination of the countryside for both conspicuous and inconspicuous traces of the past. The first stage in an archaeological survey involves work in the laboratory. Geology, soils, water supplies, and vegetation have all played their part in determining prehistoric settlement patterns and the location of ancient settlements. Maps and air photographs are assembled; the scientific literature on the region is perused. After some days, one goes into the field armed with an intimate knowledge of the survey area, its topography, geology, soils, vegetation, hydrology, and population. The result is a minimum of wasted time, for many areas—as discovered in the laboratory—may be quite unsuitable for prehistoric settlement.

An example of a find through such survey lies in southern Zambia, where the Southern Province of the country extends from the Kafue River in the north to the Zambezi in the south, a distance of some three hundred miles (Figure 3.2).[30] Most of the province is undulating plateau covered with savannah woodland, with an average altitude of 4,000 feet (1,220 meters). The savannah woodland of the highlands is dotted with prehistoric farming sites, many of which were occupied for several hundred years. Soils are moderately fertile, grazing grass is abundant, and the environment abounds in wild vegetable foods and game for the hunter. But both sides of the plateau are bounded by belts of country inhospitable to the farmer. The eastern borders of the highlands abut a steep escarpment of dry, stony hills, which plunges over 2,000 feet (610 meters) to the floor of the Zambezi Valley, 1,200 feet (365 meters) above sea level. Water supplies among the hills are minimal except in one or two deep valleys, and human settlement is a horrendous undertaking for subsistence farmers. Our survey area was thus delimited to the east by natural topographic features, while the western boundary was marked by a band of infertile agricultural country where a *mopane* (evergreen woodland) flourished on a deep, hard, clayey soil which is infertile to prehistoric farmers with only limited bush-clearing equipment and a simple agricultural technology. Thus our search for archaeological sites in southern Zambia was largely limited to the highland areas of the plateau and to the Kafue and Zambezi valleys. We were able to eliminate much of southern Zambia from intensive survey attention by dint of careful

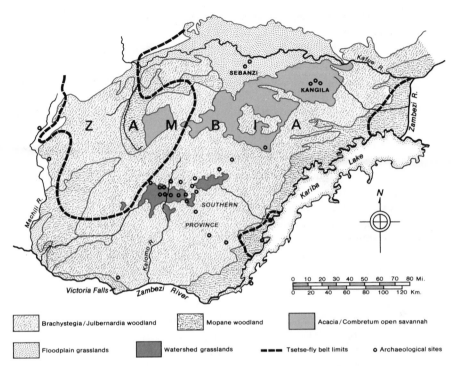

Fig. 3.2 Southern Zambia, showing vegetational zones, some archaeological sites, and areas of settlement.

laboratory research beforehand. The highland areas themselves have yielded over thirty large farming villages built on low ridges on the woodland and occupied intermittently over many generations by farmers equipped with simple iron tools. They kept cattle, small stock, and dogs and cultivated cereal crops; they lived in small mud-and-stick huts with thatched roofs, which were built on traditional village sites near good grazing areas in the savannah woodland. The thirty sites already known are but a fraction of the settlements that await discovery.

Field surveys are always conducted systematically, with careful reference to the preparatory work in the laboratory. The chosen country is traversed by automobile, on horseback or camel, by bicycle, or, most effectively, on foot. Most famous field archaeologists of this century have been avid walkers. In fact, one well known archaeologist used to boast that he had walked off the feet of certain colleagues in pursuit of the past. Footwork is important, for it enables the archaeologist to develop an eye for topography and the relationships of human settlement to the landscape. He watches for the soil colors underfoot in modern farming villages—is the grey organic soil underfoot likely to have formed in prehistoric settlements? Are abandoned recent village sites characterized by a certain vegetational cover which may also be found on the surface of much older sites? Ploughed fields may display telltale traces of ash, artifacts, or hut foundations. Vegetation may grow more lushly on areas where the subsoil has been disturbed or the nitrogen content of the soil is greater.[31] Soil discolorations in ploughed land or exposures of eroded soil may yield broken bones, stone implements, potsherds, or other evidences of prehistoric occupation. The local inhabitants, too, may provide information about places where "ancient bones" or traces of old settlements have been found. Every area has its folklore of "warriors' bones" or spectacular artifacts found during ploughing or digging house foundations. Some are founded on fact. Observation is the key to finding archaeological sites. Heinrich Schliemann's discoveries at Troy and those of Arthur Evans at Knossos in Crete resulted from judicious use of historical sources and careful observation. The prehistorian has less conspicuous signs to guide him. Grey soil from a rabbit hole, a handful of humanly fractured flints in river gravel, a blurred mark in a ploughed field— these are the signs of antiquity which he seeks. In doing this, he is following in a tradition of archaeological field survey with roots in the travels of Camden and the curiosity of medieval scholars.

Chapter 4

Excavation

A romantic atmosphere with images of elderly men in sun helmets, sweating natives, great pyramids, and buried treasure surrounds the popular view of archaeological excavation. Yet, though the image may remain, the techniques of modern excavation are rigorous and demanding, requiring long training in practical field techniques. We cannot compare archaeological digging with clearing a drainage ditch or digging up an acre of potatoes, although regrettably some excavations of my acquaintance bear such a resemblance. Archaeological excavation has certainly come a long way since the eighteenth century when it first became a serious tool of students of the past. Most early excavators were little more than treasure hunters ardently searching for antiquities for their cabinets—archetypes for the helmeted archaeologist of cartoon and popular legend. Many nineteenth-century excavations were almost carnivals, where several burial mounds would be opened in the course of a day while the supervisors of the excavations would "continue to pass our time, at intervals between digging and pic-nicing, in games of various descriptions—not exactly such as those which the builders of the mound celebrated when they laid the deceased on his funeral pile" (Figure 4.1). The antiquarian Thomas Wright, who wrote these words, and his colleagues of the 1840s led strenuous lives, as his description of an 1844 burial excavation reveals:

> Between 9 and 10 o'clock, the members assembled on the Breach Downs to be present at the opening of some barrows under the superintendence of the noble President. The workmen employed had previously

Fig. 4.1   Nineteenth-century barrow excavation.

excavated the barrows to within a foot of the place of a presumed deposit. Eight barrows were examined ... most of them contained skeletons, more or less entire, with the remains of weapons in iron, bosses of shields, urns, beads, fibulae, armlets, bones of more animals, and occasionally more vessels. ... After the examination of these barrows, the whole party visited the mansion of the noble President, at Bourne, and having inspected his lordship's interesting collection of antiquities, and partaken of a substantial repast, attended the excavation of two barrows in his lordship's paddock, forming part of the group of which some had been recently opened. . . .[1]*

At the same time, the great civilizations of the Near East and Egypt were being unearthed from millennia of oblivion, with Henry Layard, Auguste Mariette, Heinrich Schliemann, and others hastily uncovering and removing literally tons of antiquities from their proper archaeological context. "Nothing was done with any uniform plan," complained Sir Flinders Petrie, doyen of early Egyptologists, of Mariette's work in the Nile Valley in 1883, "It is sickening to see the rate at which everything is being destroyed, and the little regard paid to preservation."[2]

But a century before, Thomas Jefferson, third President of the United States and author of the Declaration of Independence, had spent some time investigating burial mounds in Virginia. He excavated one such mound, and wrote a careful description of the layers and burials in it, drawing conclusions from his finds and noting their relationship to local theories about the mounds. Jefferson's perceptive observations and the lighthearted adventures of Victorian antiquarians together represent a polarity of curiosity about the past which forms one of the roots of archaeological scholarship.

The foundations of modern excavation lie in many beginnings. They have roots in the enthusiasm of Heinrich Schliemann, discoverer and excavator of prehistoric Troy, in the dedication of Sir Flinders Petrie, who brought order to Egyptian archaeology, and especially in the work of European archaeologists. In 1873, the Austrians under Alexander Conze began excavating at the Sanctuary of the Great Gods on the island of Samothrace. The dig lasted two years; the team of scientists included a photographer and two architects—and a man-of-war. The report was beautifully illustrated and full of accurate plans, one of the first modern archaeological monographs. The German Ernst Curtius began digging at Olympia in 1875, and worked there for six seasons. His excavations were conducted with Teutonic thoroughness, with careful planning of the architecture and detailed studies of the stratigraphy. New methods of digging and recording were developed, soon to be disseminated by Curtius's colleagues, among them Wilhelm Dorpfeld who turned Schliemann's excavations at Troy from "digging to dissection" of a complicated sequence of stratified layers.[2]

The sense of purpose and discipline the Germans and Austrians inculcated into the digging process was also practiced by a military gentleman in Britain. General Lane Fox retired from active duty in 1880 and succeeded to the Rivers estate in southern England, changing his name to Pitt Rivers. The General was a man of many parts, who had already studied the evolution of firearms and other artifacts and gained wide anthropological interests. He devoted the last twenty years of his life to a detailed exploration of the archaeological sites on or near his estate with a scientific thoroughness that had firm roots in his military training. Pitt Rivers' methods were elaborate and pains-taking; he recorded every object found in his trenches in such a manner that its exact find spot could be identified in the future, with reference to sections and plans of the dig. Three-dimensional recording was a cornerstone of his excavations, as were accurate stratigraphic profiles with the finds recorded on them, a large and competent staff, and prompt and meticulous publication of his results. The General is a colossus in the history of archaeology—the labor involved in producing the elegant blue and gold monographs describing his excavations must have been enormous.[4]

The lessons learned from the Pitt Rivers campaigns fell on many deaf ears, but were heeded by other pioneers. Pitt Rivers, the Germans, and Egyptologist Sir Flinders Petrie led a revolution in Old World archaeology that gradually steered the discipline away from treasure hunting to the study of people, their artifacts, and environment. But the early years of the twentieth century saw little progress, with wholesale digging of precious sites on both sides of the Atlantic and scant regard for stratigraphy or accurate record. New World archae-ology had entered a "descriptive-historic" period with the beginnings of potsherd stratigraphy and the excavations by Kidder at Pecos.[5] But excavation techniques were still primitive, and often hair-raising by modern standards. In the 1930s, however, scientific excavation again became a serious concern. Sir Cyril Fox and Sir Mortimer Wheeler excavated a series of important sites in Britain, basing their methods on those of Pitt Rivers and the Germans. Gerard Bersu in Germany, Howard Carter in the Valley of the Kings, and Sir Leonard Woolley in Iraq, all played their part in the development of modern excavation in the Old World, while W. S. Webb in the southeastern United States and Glenn A. Black in the Midwest helped advance scientific digging in the New World. The excavators of the 1930s changed the face of archaeological digging. The sweating graduate student digging for cultural sequences in the Peruvian rain forest inevitably applies many basic recording techniques developed by Pitt Rivers and his successors. In like manner, the excavator of Colonial Williamsburg or a Paleolithic cave in the Near East records his stratigraphic profiles and small finds according to principles enumerated by the remarkable General and refined thirty years ago.

A great exponent of the art of excavation has been Sir Mortimer Wheeler, whose short monograph *Archaeology from the Earth,* is an elegant and lively part of any archaeologist's library. Wheeler's digs were organized on basically military lines. The techniques of Pitt Rivers and his successors were refined and applied with consistent energy; the central emphasis in excavation shifted from finding objects to developing a strategy for an excavation campaign oriented toward the solution of archaeological problems, rather than discovery for discovery's sake. Wheeler's forthright denunciation of shoddy methods in archaeological fieldwork rubbed off on a generation of students who dug with him on the chalk downs of England or in India, and then applied his methods in remote parts of the British Empire, as well as at home. The past decade has seen great refinement of Wheeler's methods both in Great Britain and on the Continent, where particular attention has been paid to urban archaeology. Martin Biddle in medieval Winchester and Barrie Cunliffe at Fishborne, England, are among the excavators who have improved Sir Mortimer Wheeler's recording and digging methods. In the United States, Ivor Noël Hume has used meticulous excavation methods in his study of Colonial Williamsburg. The following section on excavation owes much to Wheeler and those who have followed him.

EXCAVATION METHODS

The last century has seen a transformation from treasure hunting to scientific investigation with a battery of well-disciplined methods, from curiosity to problem-oriented excavation. Archaeologists are digging up the past at a ferocious rate in all corners of the world. Dr. and Mrs. Leakey are exploring Olduvai Gorge in Tanzania with its rich storehouse of early living floors and hominid fossils. Professor Jelinek of the University of Arizona is reexcavating a Paleolithic cave at Mount Carmel in Israel. Martin Biddle is working with a large team of volunteers on the archaeology of medieval Winchester in England. Summer archaeology field schools are being conducted all over the United States, and American expeditions are working in Guatemala, Kenya, and Peru. All this activity will result in publications, reports, analyses, and descriptions of a multitude of different archaeological sites, prehistoric peoples, and research problems. But most professional archaeologists now understand the responsibilities and basic principles of excavation—guidelines developed in over two hundred years of archaeological exploration.[7]

The first lesson that any budding excavator learns is that his work is potentially destructive. Excavation is destruction—the archaeological deposits so carefully dissected during any dig are destroyed forever, and their contents removed. Here, again, there is a radical difference from history and other subjects. A scientist can readily recreate the conditions for a basic experiment; the historian can return to his archives for a reevaluation of the complex events in a politician's life. All that remains after an excavation is the finds from the trenches, the untouched portions of the site, and the photographs, notes, and drawings that record the excavator's observations for posterity. Thus, accurate recording and observation play an overwhelmingly vital role in the day-to-day work of an archaeologist, not only for the sake of the accuracy of his own research, but because he is creating an archive of archaeological information which may be consulted by others. Most of the basic handbooks on excavation refer to this need for discipline and meticulous recording during the unavoidable de-struction of a chosen site.[8] Good excavators generally do not dig an entire site, but deliberately leave part of it for workers who come along later with new ideas and methods. Numberless different sites have been excavated during the past fifty years in every extreme of environment and with a bewildering array of research problems or preservation conditions that confronted the investigators. Yet all sites have fundamentally similar recording problems, whatever the reason they were excavated. The finds from any site are useless unless considered with reference to their context. *Context* means stratigraphy, chronology, and association—the three basic attributes of any find. Apart from the basic motions of uncovering a site, the crux of serious excavation is in the observation and ongoing interpretation of the significance of the layers being dissected by shovel, pick, and trowel.

Belzoni, Mariette, and those nineteenth-century barrow diggers were looking for archaeological treasure. But Thomas Jefferson spent some summer days in 1784 excavating for information about the inhabitants of Virginian burial mounds. Today, we follow in Jefferson's footsteps and search for the past in the widest sense, excavation being but one method at our disposal, even if it is a vital one. Archaeological research, like any scientific inquiry, is concerned with problems, models, and hypotheses that are constantly tested against new and existing evidence. Thus, any excavation is planned around a set of problems, and the objectives and strategy of the dig depend to a great extent on the dictates of the wider research project.

The research plan can be a simple one, and can involve simple propositions to be tested against excavated evidence. How old is that burial mound? Who occupied that shell midden, when, and what did they live on? What is the cultural sequence at Olduvai Gorge? Or, most fundamental of all—what is that site? What can we find out about its inhabitants? Such questions are normally asked during the first stages of a field campaign when a site has been located but no trenches sunk into it. As investigations proceed, stratigraphy is established, and dates obtained, then the research objectives may change and become highly specific and extremely complex.

The end products of even a month's excavation on a moderately productive site are a daunting prospect. Box upon box of potsherds, stone tools, bones, and other finds are stacked in the laboratory, the contents to be cleaned, sorted, marked, and studied. Hundreds of slides and photographs await processing and cataloging. Rolls of drawings, compiled with care in the field, contain important stratigraphic data without which the finds are meaningless. Cartons of soil and pollen samples, burials, radiocarbon samples, and other sources of information are piled up for eventual dispatch to specialists who will evaluate them. One expert excavator once told me that he estimated that a month's fieldwork meant a minimum of six months' laboratory work. My own experience suggests he cannot be far wrong. Excavation costs are such that problem-oriented digging is now the rule rather than the exception, with the laboratory work forming part of the ongoing evaluation of the research problem. The large piles of finds and records accumulated at the end of even a small field season contain a bewildering array of interdigitating facts which the researcher has to evaluate and reevaluate as his inquiry proceeds. He is constantly arranging his propositions and hypotheses, correlating his observations, and reevaluating his interpretations of the archaeological evidence. His boxes and plans are the basis of his research strategy and affect his fieldwork plans for the future. The days when a site was excavated because it "looked good," or because sheer lack of imagination precluded the development of a research strategy, have been replaced by a process of constant reevaluation of research objectives.

An early example of archaeological strategy was the discovery of the Minoan civilization. Sir Arthur Evans, son of the John Evans who was a central figure in the establishment of man's antiquity, was one of the greatest archaeologists of all time, combining organizing genius with scholarly integrity and brilliant insights, the latter perhaps the most important quality for any archaeologist.[9] In 1894 he visited Crete, determined to dig at Knossos, legendary site of ancient Cretan civilization. For many years, he had been interested in Mycenaean gems and had become interested in the origins of writing, convinced that a picture script was a precursor of literacy. His researches on gems led him to Crete, where he found that others had been stopped from digging at Knossos, although finds from it were in antique dealers' stores. After protracted negotiations, lengthened by uprisings and civil turmoil, he began digging on March 23, 1899. By April 13 he had discovered Linear B tablets, the mysterious Minoan script that was not deciphered until more than fifty years later, and was on his way to the unearthing of Minoan civilization, almost forgotten since Bronze Age times. Throughout the five years of excavation which followed, he issued annual summary reports, realizing in 1905 that a major study of the finds was necessary. Unlike many other spectacular excavations, the Palace at Knossos was fully published, with a minute attention to detail remarkable for the time. The *Palace of Minos* began to appear in 1921, the last volume in 1935, when Arthur Evans was seventy-nine years old. It is a magisterial work, the culmination of forty years of Cretan research which was pursued with relentless rigor and meticulous care. The result—a new civilization described for science through rudimentary research strategy, even if Knossos sits at the center of numerous other localities whose significance has not been coordinated with the finds from the great Palace itself. Although the descriptive genius of the Minoan discoverer excites the layman, the sound research tactics shine through the great work.[10]

One's research strategy depends considerably on the facilities available, the time at one's disposal, and the nature of the research problem. The only general rule is: no excavation is carried out without a strategy behind it and without attention to day-to-day tactics. To quote Sir Mortimer Wheeler again: "The excavator without an intelligent policy may be described as an archaeological food-gatherer, master of a skill, perhaps, but not creative in the wider terms of constructive science."[11]

TYPES OF EXCAVATION

Thus, strategy and problem-solving are two factors that determine the dig's layout. While the size and character of the site also play their part, and sampling techniques, if used, will affect digging plans, I have always mentally made two fundamental distinctions as far as trench layout is concerned, for excavations can be either selective or total. Since the settlements of prehistoric man are frequently sizable, complete excavation is a rarity, even if a considerable area of the site is investigated. Selective investigation is commonplace. Trenches are limited, the dig's objectives are often limited to stratigraphic and chronological considerations, or the solution of specific research problems to amplify larger digs elsewhere. A cross section of pottery, stone tools, and animal bones from a site are obtained from a selective dig, perhaps as a lead-in for future investigations, or as a trial strati-graphic sequence to test against other sites where similar types of excavation are planned. Surface features can be tested by selective trenching in advance of a major dig.

The layout of small digs is determined by the surface topography, density of finds, sampling factors, electronic survey,[12] or visible features on the site. Selective excavation has the advantage that it is much cheaper than larger-scale digging. If the excavation is planned carefully many complex problems can be solved with a minimum expenditure of time and money. In a world where fieldwork costs are escalating rapidly, this is an important consideration; the days of larger excava-tions are probably behind us except under exceptional circumstances. The high cost of excavation means careful planning and coordinated strategy so that no trench is wasted and the maximum information obtained. But, with a possibility that large-scale excavation will take place later, trenches must be carefully sited to avoid hindering any such future excavation.

Some of the world's most important sites have been excavated selectively, using the concept of *vertical excavation* where limited areas are excavated for specific information (Figure 4.2). Selective excavation has also become a powerful technique often widely used when "res-cue" digs are carried out in advance of construction work when there is no time to carry out large-scale operations.

Area excavation is on a much larger scale and is naturally far more expensive. An area dig implies *horizontality*—covering large areas to recover building plans or the layouts of entire settlements (Figure 4.3). While stratigraphy and chronology are still vital, the primary concern of area excavation is either settlement pattern, houses and other structures, or horizontal relationships. The only sites that are almost invariably totally excavated are very small hunting camps, isolated huts, and burial mounds. The problems with horizontal digs are exactly the same as those with any excavation, those of stratigraphic control and accurate measurement. Figures 4.4 and 4.5 show three-dimensional recording and ways in which archaeologists measure their sites and record their field data. In a horizontal excavation, hundreds of meters of ground are removed to expose large complexes of struc-tures like, for example, the rooms of a pueblo. The former palace at Nonsuch in southeastern England is a famous example, where the ground plan of the entire palace, which had been lost, was recovered by horizontal excavation, adding a new portrait to the already glittering history of Henry VIII's reign.[13]

Area excavations imply the exposure of large open areas of ground to a depth of several meters. A complex network of walls or post

Fig. 4.2   A vertical excavation at Maiden Castle, Dorset, England.

holes may lie within the area to be investigated. Each feature relates to other structures, a relationship which must be carefully recorded to interpret the site correctly, especially if several periods of occupation are involved. If the entire area is uncovered, it is obviously difficult to measure the position of the structures in the middle of the trench, far from the walls at the excavation's edge. To achieve better control of measurement and record, it is better to use a system that gives a network of vertical stratigraphic sections across the area to be excavated. This is normally done by laying out a grid of square or rectangular trenches with walls several centimeters thick between each square (Figure 4.6). Such areas may average 3.7 meters (12 feet) square in size, or larger. As Figure 4.6 shows, this system allows

Fig. 4.3   A horizontal, grid-type excavation at Maiden Castle.

Fig. 4.4   A site grid. Every spot within the grid, which is usually extended over the entire site, can be measured in two directions. The trenches are laid out with reference to the grid, and the finds in them can be assigned exact, three-dimensional measurements—two giving an object's spot within the site and the third giving its depth.

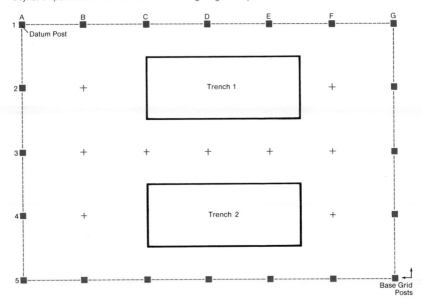

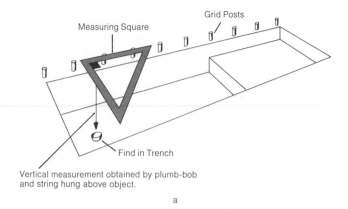

Grid Posts

Measuring Square

Find in Trench

Vertical measurement obtained by plumb-bob
and string hung above object.

a

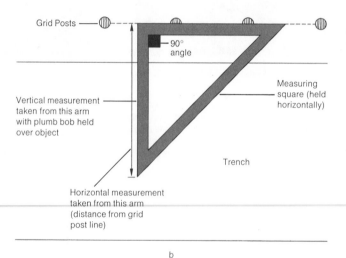

Grid Posts

90°
angle

Vertical measurement
taken from this arm
with plumb bob held
over object

Measuring
square (held
horizontally)

Trench

Horizontal measurement
taken from this arm
(distance from grid
post line)

b

*Fig. 4.5   Three-dimensional recording. (a) The use of a measuring square. (b) A close view of the
square from above. The horizontal measurement is taken along the edge, perpendicular to
the grid post line, and the vertical measurement from that arm with a plumb bob.*

stratigraphic control of considerable areas, and ground does not have
to be removed except in areas where the finds are especially important.
Large-scale excavation with grids is extremely expensive and time-
consuming and is difficult to use in areas with irregular ground, but
it has been employed with great success at many excavations, being
used to uncover structures, town plans, and fortifications.

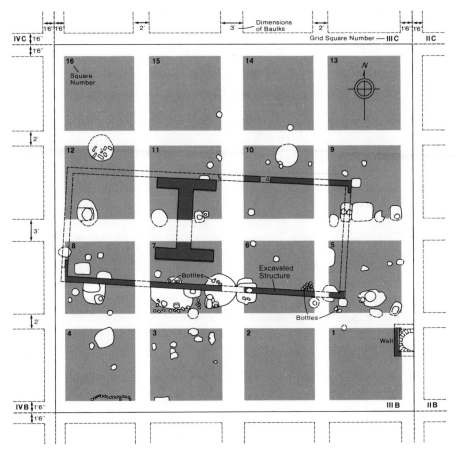

Fig. 4.6   A horizontal grid excavation, showing the layout of squares relative to an excavated structure at Colonial Williamsburg.

SAMPLING

Some archaeologists are beginning to use sampling techniques, too. They argue that, since we are relying more and more on statistical approaches to archaeological data in the reconstruction of prehistoric lifeways, the effects of uncontrolled bias in excavation are more noticeable. For example, if we are interested in past adaptations to environmental conditions, we must sample different types of sites in each environmental zone, and not merely those that "look important" or could yield spectacular finds. Unfortunately, resources are limited, and we obviously cannot dig all the sites in an area where hundreds may occur. Thus, these archaeologists argue, we must use sampling techniques to ensure a statistically reliable basis of excavated data from which we can make generalizations about our research problem.

Sampling has been defined as the "science of controlling and measuring the reliability of information through the theory of probability."[14] American archaeologist Lewis Binford has explored this subject, and in several articles argues against conscious or unconscious bias in selecting which site, or part of a site, should be excavated. Bias might consist of logistical convenience, destruction of the site, close proximity of a base camp, or a multitude of unconscious but pervasive factors. Yet we cannot assume that the sites which our bias leads us to select are the same as those which we did not select. Thus, Binford suggests, if the "universe" we seek to study—perhaps a region, a site, or a "culture"—represents similar kinds of archaeological unit and is "homogeneous," then we can use sampling techniques to choose our units of study free of selective bias.

This is achieved by assigning numbers to all units being studied, deciding how many can be dug with the resources available, and then selecting that many units from a published list of *random* numbers. Such a technique can be used only if all units are homogeneous, and in cases in which each possible sampling unit has an equal probability of being selected for excavation by random methods. If the "universe" is not homogeneous, perhaps consisting of ceremonial sites, villages, and burial grounds, or of sites of widely differing size, or of settlements in different ecological zones, then "stratified sampling" is employed. Each category of site or unit is treated as a separate homogeneous universe, which is selected randomly, with care taken that the numerically less common universes are proportionately adequately represented among the excavated units.

Sound sampling procedures, it is argued, permit generalizations about archaeological units to be made with confidence. Valid generalizations are not possible if all sites excavated, for example, came from areas chosen because they were near paved roads—that case is only generalizing on the basis of chosen bias. With random sampling, sites near the road are no different from those away from tarmac, and some activities are not represented in a site, not by accident but because they did not take place. And with sound sampling procedures, statistical tests can evaluate the confidence to be placed in generalizations made.

Sampling technique is new to archaeology, and as this methodology is developed and applied more widely, excavation methods will change, especially on sites which lend themselves to quantitative investigation, such as shell middens, living floors, caves, or town sites.

HOW DO YOU DIG?

What tools does the archaeologist use?[15] The traditional archaeological
symbol is the spade, which has a flat back and straight edge, and
is used for cleaning walls. Shovels, with their scoop-like shape, are
used for piling up earth in a trench preparatory to its being sorted,
and have innumerable applications in cleaning straight edges and
tidying trenches; shovels are the principal working tool of the archaeologist under conditions where much ground has to be uncovered.

The principal tools for loosening soil are the pick, the mattock,
and the fork. The pick and the mattock may be considered together
because they are variants on the same type of tool; when used with
care, they are a delicate gauge of soil texture, an indication much
used in larger sites. But the most common archaeological tool is the
diamond-shaped trowel, its straight edges and tip having innumerable
uses: soil can be eased from a delicate specimen; the edges can scrape
a feature in sandy soil into higher relief; and as weapons of stratigraphic recording, they can trace a scarcely visible stratum line or
barely discernible feature. In addition, they are used for clearing postholes and other minor work, so much so that they are rarely out
of a digger's hand on smaller sites.

Another important small tool is the brush, which of course has
its greatest application on dry sites. The most commonly used brush
is the household type with fairly coarse bristles; it can be held by
the handle or the bristles and, wielded with short strokes, effectively
cleans objects found in dry and preferably hard soil. The excavator
uses various paintbrushes for more delicate jobs. The one-inch or
one-half-inch domestic paintbrush has wide application in the cleaning
of animal bones and more coarse specimens. Fine, camel's hair artist's
brushes are best for most delicate bones, beads, and fragile ironwork.
Many other small implements, some improvised on the site, aid in
brush work. Six-inch nails may be filed to a point and used for delicate
clearing jobs on bones and other fragile artifacts. The needle is another
tool to clear soil from such delicate parts of skeletons as the eye
sockets and cheekbones. One of the most useful digging tools is the
dental pick, available in a bewildering variety of shapes. Often, dental
picks can be obtained without charge through dentists, who discard
them as soon as they show signs of wear. Continental European
archaeologists have used a small, hooked digging tool, called a *crochet*,
for many years; this is widely used for those excavations where a
trowel is too big but where smaller tools are too slow and inefficient.
The screen is another important tool because many finds, such as
coins, glass beads, shells, small tacks, nails, and other small artifacts

are miniscule. Most deposit from sites where small artifacts are likely to occur is laboriously sifted through fine screens, of one-half to one-eighth-inch size.

The archaeologist's surveying instruments normally include linen or metal tapes, plumb bobs, string, spirit levels, drawing boards, drawing instruments, a plane table, and a surveyor's level and compass—all essential for accurate recording of site plans and sections, and for setting up the archaeological archive.

RECORDING

As noted earlier, excavation is destruction, and an artifact's context is as important as its typological features.[16] Detailed records and accurate measurement are the foundation of sound, scientific excavation, and some understanding of site records is as important as a grasp of the principle of superposition—indeed the director of an excavation spends more time writing and drawing than he does digging. He maintains a number of different notebooks throughout the excavation, including the site diary or day book. This large notebook records all events at the site—the amount of work done, the daily schedule, the number of people on the digging team, and any labor problems that may arise. Dimensions of all sites and trenches are recorded. Any interpretations or ideas on the interpretations, even those considered and then discarded, are meticulously recorded in this book. Important finds and significant stratigraphic details are also noted carefully, as is much apparently insignificant information, which may, however, prove to be vital in the laboratory. The site diary purports to be a complete record of the procedures and proceedings of the excavation. The site diary is more than an aid to the fallible memory of the excavator; it is a permanent record of the dig for future generations of scientists who may return to the same site to amplify the original findings. Site diaries can be a most important tool in the hands of later researchers—for instance, the Knossos site diaries kept by Sir Arthur Evans as he uncovered Minoan Civilization for the first time, which have been used again and again by later investigators in Crete.[17]

A "small-finds" register is important in the records on any dig. But in many cases, while some artifacts such as pottery or stone implements may be very common, others, such as iron tools or beads, will be extremely rare and have special significance. So a "small-finds register" is maintained. Each "small find" is given a special number and labelled with its level, trench number, and depth below surface; additional information relating to the layer in which the object was found is also noted. This procedure provides a permanent record of significant artifacts that must be described individually in the final report and whose preservation is important. The researcher also lists the bags of finds made during the excavation in the same book. Each bag, especially of common artifacts like pottery, animal bones, and stone implements, receives a serial number and is recorded in a list in the back of the small-finds register.

The recording methods mentioned so far are basic ones used by archaeologists during excavation. But the recording both of the site plan and of its structures, as well as of stratigraphic sections, is just as important. The site plan may vary from a simple contour plan for a burial mound or occupation midden (Figure 4.7), to a complex plan of an entire prehistoric town or of a complicated series of structures.[18] Accurate plans are important, for they provide a record of the measurement and recording grid, set up before excavation to provide a metrical framework for the trenching (Figure 4.6).

Drawing stratigraphic profiles is a complex process and requires not only skill in recording but considerable interpretative ability. The difficulty of recording a section varies with the site's complexity and with its stratigraphic conditions. In many cases, the different occupation levels or geological events are clearly delineated in the section and it is easy to record the limits of particular levels with light lines drawn with a trowel. On other sites, however, the sedimentary record may be much more complex and less visible, particularly in drier climates where the soil's aridity has tended to leach out colors (Figure 4.8).[19] The recording method varies according to the profile's complexity. With smaller and more simple sections, it normally is possible to set up a horizontal datum string on the wall, the depth of which is measured carefully below the datum point for the entire site. All features on the profiles and the depths on the cutting are carefully recorded with reference to vertical measurements taken from the datum line. The whole of the section is therefore automatically measured relative to datum. On larger sites, where the stratigraphy is complex and on a large scale, a surveyor's level may be used for greater accuracy. Photography is extensively used in stratigraphic interpretation (Figures 4.9 and 4.10). Stratigraphic profiles present a most critical operation in archaeology, rivalled only by the necessity for accurate and dispassionate observation of the excavated evidence.

Three-dimensional recording of major features or important artifacts is another vital part of the excavation process. Many huts, pits, or burial groups are important merely because of their association with other features or artifacts. Such information can only be recovered by three-dimensional measurement, where the feature's horizontal and vertical coordinates are recorded with reference to the site grid.

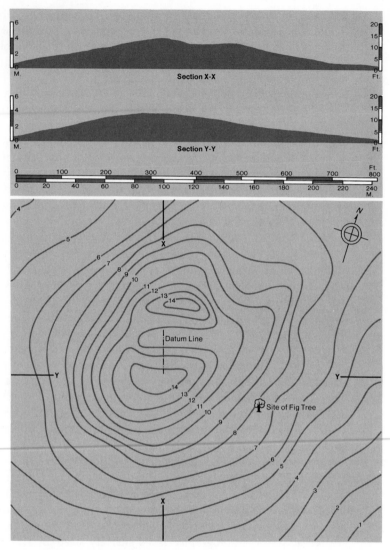

Fig. 4.7   A simple contour plan of a large village mound at Kalomo, Zambia.

ORGANIZATION OF AN EXCAVATION

The director of an archaeological field expedition needs skills in addition to those of a competent archaeologist. He has to be an accountant, politician, doctor, mechanic, personnel manager, and even a cook. On a large dig, though manual labor may not be his respon-

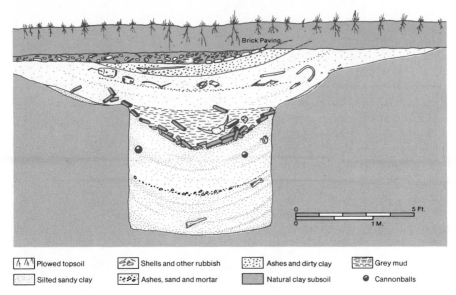

Brick Paving

5 Ft.

1 M.

Plowed topsoil	Shells and other rubbish	Ashes and dirty clay	Grey mud
Silted sandy clay	Ashes, sand and mortar	Natural clay subsoil	Cannonballs

Fig. 4.8   A section through a seventeenth-century ice-house pit at Colonial Williamsburg, showing the way in which the strata settled. The figure illustrates the complexity of archaeological stratigraphy.

sibility, his logistic problems are compounded and he will head a staff of site supervisors, artists, photographers, and numerous minor functionaries who form the excavation team on a city dig or a field school.[20]

In these days of rising costs and financial stringencies, most excavations are on a comparatively small scale, a team of students or laborers under the overall supervision of the director and perhaps one or two assistants; the assistants may be graduate students with some technical training in archaeological fieldwork and can take some of the routine tasks from the director's shoulders, allowing him to concentrate on general supervision and interpretative problems. But in many cases the director will not only be in charge of the research and the arrangements for the excavation, he will also personally supervise all trenches excavated on the site. On him, therefore, devolve the tasks of recording, photography, drawing, measurement, and labor supervision. He may also take his turn at the recovery of fragile burials and other delicate objects that he cannot entrust to his students or workmen; he is also responsible for maintaining the excavation diaries and find notebooks, the storage and marking of artifacts, and the logistics of packing finds and shipping them to the laboratory. So varied are

Fig. 4.9   A stratigraphic profile from Kalundu mound, Zambia. The scale is in feet, and the labels denote excavated layers.

the skills of the excavator that much of a professional archaeologist's training in the field is obtained as a graduate student working at routine tasks and gaining experience in the methods of excavation and site-survey under experienced supervision. For the director, such students provide not only useful supervisory labor but also an admirable hone upon which they can try out their favorite theories and discuss in ruthless detail the interpretation of the site. Many an

Fig. 4.10   A stratigraphic profile through a ditch at Maiden Castle.

elaborate and much cherished theoretical model has been demolished over a disputed profile or an evening camp fire! Opportunities to gain excavation experience are always open, and notices of digs can be found on many college and university bulletin boards. The comradery and happiness of a well-run, student-oriented excavation is one of the more worthwhile experiences of archaeology.

Chapter 5

Excavation Problems

OPEN HUNTING CAMPS

The remains of temporary hunting camps should, theoretically, be the most common archaeological sites, but undisturbed examples are rare and consequently assume great importance. Land surfaces occupied by hunting bands are the most useful source of information on the life of early man. Living-floor archaeology has become a most important type of excavation in recent years, revolutionizing our ideas on early human cultural evolution. Until recently most evidence for the early stages of cultural evolution existed in isolated artifacts found in river gravel beds and alluvia associated with a jumble of fractured animal bones and other artifacts. The picture has changed in recent years, with greater emphasis being placed on the excavation of living-floor sites found in lake-bed deposits, undisturbed since their occupation in the Lower or Middle Pleistocene.[1]* Hunting camps come from later contexts, as well. The Star Carr encampment has been mentioned in earlier chapters,[2] while extensive Upper Paleolithic mammoth-hunting sites have been discovered in Czechoslovakia and eastern Russia.[3] Numerous examples of kill sites come from the New World.[4] All are open-air sites, which are particularly difficult to locate because their occupants left few traces of their presence during their short stay and had few material possessions. The thickness of the occupation deposit may not be more than a few centimeters, and

* See pages 326–328 for notes to Chapter 5.

Fig. 5.1 Olduvai Gorge, Tanzania.

several settlements may be placed one above another, representing different visits to the same locality over a period of years. Most sites were occupied for a short period and the localities were chosen for pragmatic reasons—the butchering of a large mammal, availability of water or vegetation, or an abundance of tool-making stone.[5] A few important open-air hunting sites were occupied again and again, and were often situated in areas of particular richness in game or vegetable foods.[6]

Olduvai Gorge in Tanzania contains many early hunting sites which have been excavated over many years by the Leakey family (Figure 5.1).[7] The living floors are buried under tons of overburden which has to be removed before the last few centimeters of deposit above the occupation level are carefully removed with trowel and brush. A grid network is laid out over the floor, so that each artifact, bone fragment, or natural stone can be plotted in position on a master plan before removal. Thus, the associations of each object on the floor are carefully recorded for posterity.

The results of the Olduvai excavations have been spectacular. The remains of both a robust and a gracile form of Australopithecine have been found on living surfaces in Bed I at Olduvai,[8] in direct association with stone chopping tools and broken bones of small animals. A cranium of *Homo erectus* has been found in overlying Bed II, in levels potassium argon dated to *ca.* 400,000 years ago, where stone hand axes and large mammal bones have been found.[9] Early hunting camps have also been found at Olorgesaillie in Kenya,[10] Kalambo Falls in Zambia,[11] in northern Malawi,[12] at Isimila in Tanzania[13] as well as in Syria[14] and Torralba, Spain.[15] In all these sites the tools of early man were uncovered in direct association with the remains of the game he hunted. Stratigraphic information, dating samples, and a settlement pattern were obtained by careful area excavation, the tools being plotted in position and photographed carefully before being lifted for further study in the laboratory. Figure 5.2 shows the complexity of such sites.

In the New World, horizontal excavation has also yielded significant results, especially where the kills of early man, mammoth-hunters in particular, are concerned.[16] A primary objective here has been to study the association between early man's tools and the extinct animals he hunted. Area excavation has been particularly used for this purpose; an example is the bison-kill site in Colorado excavated by Joe Ben Wheat, who found that a narrow arroyo was used as a death trap for a herd of bison (see Chapter 3).[17]

Living-floor excavations are normally on a large scale (Figure 5.3), and frequently involve the services of a Pleistocene geologist. Hunting-camp excavations aim at uncovering settlement patterns and structures as well as the dating or stratigraphy of sites. Concentrations of dismembered animal carcasses,[18] sleeping places, hearths, the remains of windbreaks,[19] or piles of flaked stone debris[20] are all elements of a settlement pattern on a living floor that should be considered in relation to one another. The potential for complete reconstruction of the environment and subsistence patterns of hunting-camp inhabitants is excellent, especially if preservation conditions are good, as they were, for instance, in the case of Star Carr (Figure 5.4) or the second millennium B.C. Stone Age hunting camps at Gwisho hot springs in Zambia. The latter were sited in the middle of a hot springs complex, overlooking the floodplain of the Kafue River. Wooden digging sticks and arrowheads, as well as thousands of animal bones and seeds, were found in association with traces of a windbreak and other structures, and some detailed analogies with modern Bushman subsistence

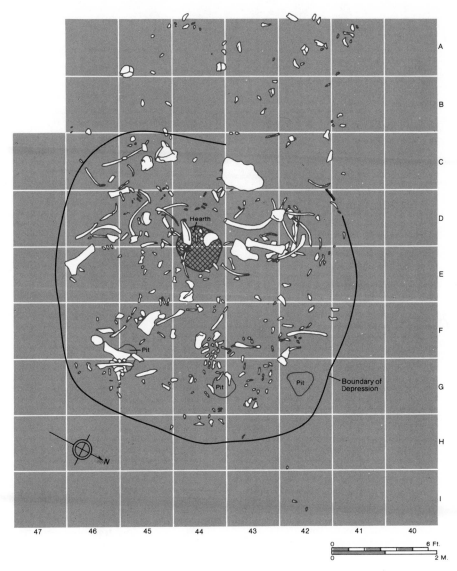

Fig. 5.2   *A plan of a living horizon at the Paleolithic site of Tel'manskaya, USSR, showing the scattering of debris and a structure. The letters and figures at the edges of the drawing refer to the grid squares laid over the site. For example, the hearth is found in square 44DE.*

patterns were made,[21] for the ancestry of the modern hunting population of southern Africa is known to lie with the Bushmen.[22] Recent intensive investigations of the !Kung Bushmen of the Kalahari Desert

Fig. 5.3   Visiting scientists inspecting the excavations in Olduvai Gorge, Bed I, with Dr. Leakey (right).

have focused on their ecology, subsistence, and settlement patterns to such an extent that an archaeologist accompanied the anthropologists in the field to study modern abandoned Bushman hunting camps from the archaeological standpoint.[23] Research like this has obvious application to the archaeology of open hunting camps.

CAVES AND ROCKSHELTERS

The mouth of a cave or a rockshelter overhang was a favorite home of prehistoric man. Both give shelter from the elements and shade on hot days. Caves and rockshelters are common where geological conditions—especially granite or limestone outcrops—permit. The river valleys of the Dordogne in southwestern France are lined by great rockshelters and deep caves in the high forested cliffs overlooking

Worked flints

18 + per square yard   36 + per square yard   90 + per square yard

Fig. 5.4 Densities of artifacts on living floors are frequently plotted square by square. This plan shows the distribution of worked flint on the Star Carr site in England.

lush floodplains.[24] Prehistoric hunters lived in the Dordogne rockshelters for over 40,000 years, leaving behind dense layers of occupation. The dolomitic limestone of Mount Carmel in Israel formed caves that were Middle and Upper Paleolithic man's home for thousands of years, and his burials in the caves have been uncovered to add a new chapter to the story of human evolution.[25] Rockshelters and caves in the New World have also yielded key cultural sequences. Danger Cave on the western edge of Great Salt Lake Desert in western Utah was occupied by prehistoric man from about 9000 B.C. until recent times.[26] The cave mouth was choked with 3.9 meters (13 feet) of occupation debris, representing five periods of use over thousands of years. Lovelock Cave is another important site, where caches of tools for fishing and duck-hunting were found, dating to about 2500 B.C.[27] Weasel, skunk, mink, antelope, and other mammal bones were discovered, and in addition, the dry conditions at Lovelock preserved many grasses and vegetable foods.

Cave and rockshelter excavations are some of the most common digs, and certainly some of the hardest to carry through successfully. The ground below the cliff overhang at the cave mouth usually consists of ash and other debris piled up through successive human occupation, intercalated with sterile layers where geological phenomena have added to the deposits (Figure 5.5). A few millennia of hard frosts and hot summers, or cold rain, will cause cliff fragments to split off in angular chunks and fall to the ground, perhaps forming a sterile layer of debris. Layers of windblown sand sometimes seal off human occupation levels, both assisting and complicating stratigraphic observations.

Excavation of caves or rockshelters is slow and meticulous work. The size of trenches is normally constricted by the dimensions of the site, and digs tend to be selective rather than area-oriented, except at the largest rockshelters where there is room to move and the occupation has been concentrated under different parts of the overhang. The stratigraphy is often compressed or made up of a series of fine hearth lines, abandoned camp fires of visiting hunting bands. Figure 5.6 shows a stratigraphic profile from Haua Fteah Cave in Libya, a large site where the stratigraphy is level but still extremely complicated.[28]

Cave and rockshelter excavations are normally oriented toward chronological and stratigraphic problems. Accurate digging and meticulous recording of data are essential, and are based on small-scale grids. In caves where stone implements are rare and it is important to obtain stratigraphic evidence for them, the position of each artifact may be measured exactly. The Upper Paleolithic hunters of Britain were few and are imperfectly known from rockshelter excavations, most of which were conducted in the late nineteenth century. Compared with the rich French rockshelters of the Dordogne, most British caves yielded a scatter of tools and some fossil animal bones, enough to give a shadowy picture of a hunting culture known as the Creswellian, named after a cave in Derbyshire. Some years ago, C. B. M. McBurney excavated several caves in South Wales that contained Upper Paleolithic implements in very small numbers, but associated with important geological evidence, and fractured animal bones.[29] So little was known of the stratigraphic associations of the Creswellian that McBurney and his team recorded the exact position of every flint chip or stone implement found in the deposits of the Cat Hole and other rockshelters he excavated. The result—a better definition of the Creswellian and its geological and chronological associations.

Fig. 5.5   Haua Fteah Cave, Libya.

An interesting example of a large-scale rockshelter excavation is the work of Professor H. L. Movius of Harvard University at the Abri Pataud in Les Eyzies, France, the Mecca of Stone Age archaeologists.[30] Abri Pataud is being excavated on a coordinated, master-plan basis, involving not only archaeologists, but also geologists, botanists, chemists, paleontologists, and numerous other specialists. Over 6 meters (20 feet) of deposit have already been meticulously removed, occupation layer by occupation layer, using a lateral excavation method developed by the Chinese archaeologist Kwang-Chih Chang. Every hearth, major find, and artifact has precise recorded coordinates and is carefully described on a card index. Excavation is slow work. Trowels, crochets, dental picks, and brushes are used to ease the dirt away; a constant record is being kept of soil color, texture, and the slopes of natural layers in the deposit. The Abri Pataud has already yielded six layers of Upper Paleolithic occupation (9,000–40,000 years ago), including both Perigordian (Gravettian) and Aurignacian horizons,

105

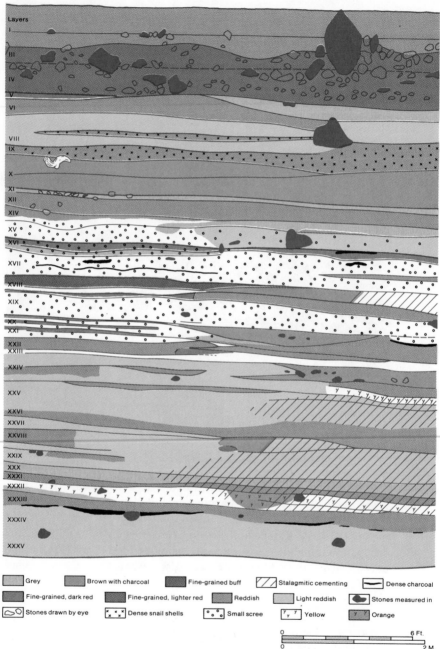

Grey   Brown with charcoal   Fine-grained buff   Stalagmitic cementing   Dense charcoal

Fine-grained, dark red   Fine-grained, lighter red   Reddish   Light reddish   Stones measured in

Stones drawn by eye   Dense snail shells   Small scree   Yellow   Orange

0   6 Ft.
0   2 M.

Fig. 5.6   A stratigraphic section through the deposits of the Upper- and Post-Pleistocene cave of Haua Fteah. The drawing shows a complex sequence of layers and lenses, most of them associated with cultural material; the key gives the colors of the earth.

Fig. 5.7   Abri Pataud rockshelter, Les Eyzies, France.

through which the archaeologists have traced minute changes in tool
types, excavating to a far higher standard and resulting in more basic
information than ever before obtained (Figure 5.7).

STRUCTURES AND DWELLINGS

For much of his history, man lived in simple windbreaks, skin tents,
or portable structures that leave little trace in the archaeological record.
But, with the advent of food production and more permanent settlement, his housing became more permanent and is more frequently
discovered in excavations. Dwellings may vary from a simple round
hut with pole walls and a thatched roof (Figure 5.8)[31] or a mud house
with a flat roof and an entrance through the roof[32] (Figure 5.9), to
an elaborate stone farmhouse or a palace[33] (Figure 5.10). In the larger
house, the normal household activities—living, sleeping, cooking,
storage—took place in separate rooms, but in a smaller one, these
activities, reflected both in artifacts like cooking utensils and in features like hearths or sleeping platforms, occurred within a single area.
Discovering the relationship between different rooms and separate

107

Fig. 5.8   A pole and mud hut, typical of the Zambezi Valley, Zambia.

Fig. 5.9   A schematic reconstruction of houses and shrines from Level VI at Çatal Hüyük, Turkey, showing flat-roof architecture and roof entrances. (After James Mellaart, Çatal Hüyük, Fig. 12. Copyright © 1967, Thames and Hudson Ltd. Used with permission of McGraw-Hill Book Company; London: Thames and Hudson Ltd.)

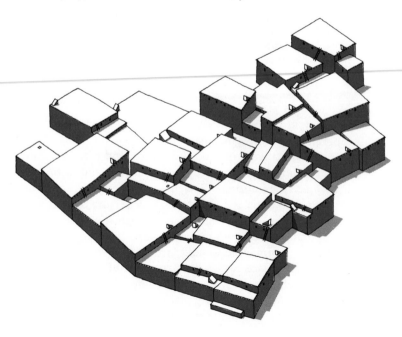

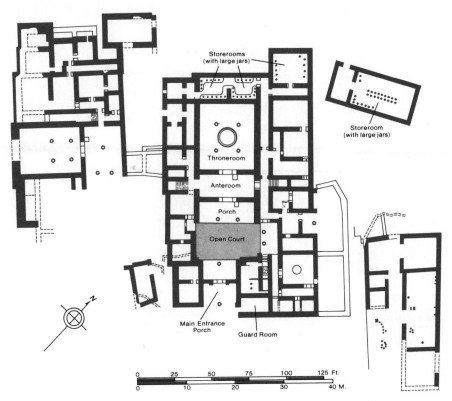

Fig. 5.10 A plan of a Bronze Age palace.

activities is as important in the excavation of a house as establishing its dating and the method of construction.

Grid excavations are normally used to uncover structures of any size (Figure 5.11).[34] These allow stratigraphic control over the building site, and especially the study of successive occupation stages. In many cases, the structures may have been built of perishable materials like wood or matting. Wooden houses are normally recognized through the post holes of the wall timbers and sometimes foundation trenches (Figure 5.12). Clay walls collapse into a pile when a hut is burnt or falls down (Figures 5.13–5.15); the wall clay may bear impressions of matting, sticks, or thatch. Stone structures are often better preserved, especially if mortar was used, although sometimes the stone has been removed by later builders and only foundation trenches remain (Figure 5.16). Stratigraphic cross sections across walls given an insight into the structure's history. The dating of most stone structures is compli-

Fig. 5.11   Horizontal excavations at the site of the Old Minster, Winchester Cathedral, England.

cated, especially when successive rebuilding or occupation of the building is involved.[35] Obviously, excavating a stone structure by following the walls around its perimeter is a mistake (Figure 5.16) because this destroys the complicated history of the building and the vicissitudes through which it has passed. For example, this would ruin the means of telling who the original builders were, when the structure was destroyed, and when it was rebuilt. Careful stratigraphic control through horizontal excavation is essential to gain these insights.

The dating or cultural setting of any building is based ideally on three categories of objects.[36] The first are those that come from the levels accumulated before the building was constructed; the second are contemporary with the structure; and the third are the finds made in the levels that overlie the structure and perhaps bury it. All these finds have a chronological relationship to the building: the first are

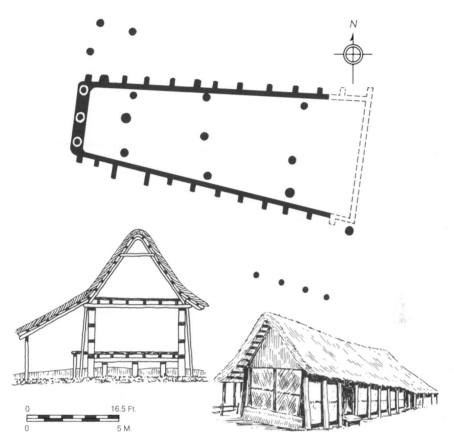

Fig. 5.12 The plan and reconstruction of a trapeze-shaped Neolithic house in Deiringsen-Ruploh, Germany. (After Buttler.)

earlier, the last are later, and those in the middle are contemporary with the building. The object of excavating stone structures is not merely to trace a building's outline, and then to reconstruct its plans, but also to reconstruct its history, understand its architecture, and establish how it was built.

Some of the most spectacular structures include those that have left few traces on the surface. European archaeologists have scored many notable triumphs in recovering timber structures from sandy soils where only traces of post holes and house foundations remain. At Koln-Lindenthal in Germany, an early farming village of at least twenty-one households was discovered which had been successively rebuilt some seven times.[37] The early farming communities that oc-

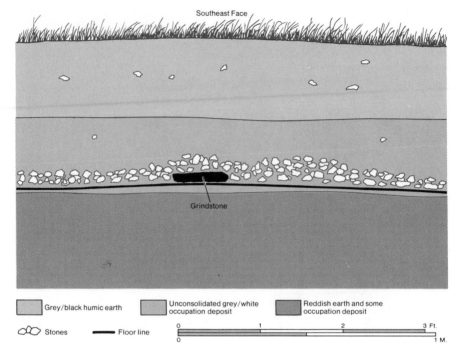

Southeast Face

Grindstone

| | Grey/black humic earth | | Unconsolidated grey/white occupation deposit | | Reddish earth and some occupation deposit |

⌀ Stones   ▬ Floor line

0   1   2   3 Ft.
0   1 M.

Fig. 5.13   The collapsed remains of a pole and mud hut, overlaid with occupation deposit, in Kangila site, Zambia.

cupied Koln-Lindenthal and other similar sites in the fifth millennium B.C. lived in huge long houses with massive timber framing; they measured up to 30.5 meters (100 feet) long and 7.6 meters (25 feet) wide, and had clay daubed walls. These remarkably standardized dwellings are known to us almost entirely from the post holes and bedding-trenches found in the sandy soils which the inhabitants favored for settlement and agriculture. The plan of an early farming settlement at Sittard in the Netherlands shows the complexity of such a constantly reoccupied longhouse settlement (Figure 5.17). Many farming villages of timber houses are known from prehistoric Europe. The timber-built settlement at the Wasserburg in southern Germany[38] dates to the twelfth to ninth centuries B.C.; an island settlement with timber palisades, its first phase contained thirty-eight small rectangular houses, replaced later on by nine big houses with a hall, wings, and associated byres. One such structure had six rooms and a main hall.

Wagon burials are found in Czechoslovakia and the Upper Danube, dating from 700 B.C.[39] The dead were deposited in wooden mortuary

Fig. 5.14 Pole and mud houses and grain bins—from the Middle Zambezi Valley, Zambia. (Compare with Figure 5.15.)

Fig. 5.15 A clay floor overlaid by wall rubble in a village mound at Isamu Pati, Zambia, showing the archaeological evidence for houses of the general type in Figure 5.14.

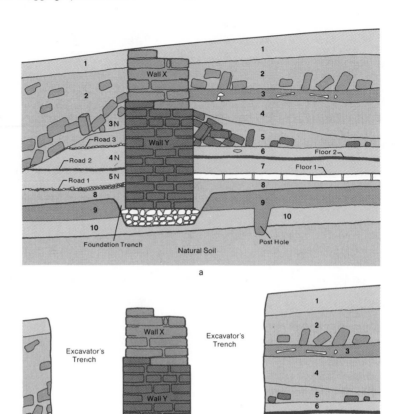

Fig. 5.16   The stratigraphy of walling showing the foundation trench and the relationship of the archaeological strata to the wall. (a) A stratigraphic cross section from use of correct excavating methods. (b) The same section, showing how much information is destroyed through excavation by following the wall.

houses, often sunk in the ground and buried under earth mounds (Figure 5.18). A spoked four-wheeled vehicle, sometimes used as a hearse, commonly accompanied the body. The horses were not buried with the wagon, but their harnesses and yokes were laid in the grave—often two sets, one for the cart horses and one for the warrior's own steed. Skillful excavation, allied with excellent preservation con-

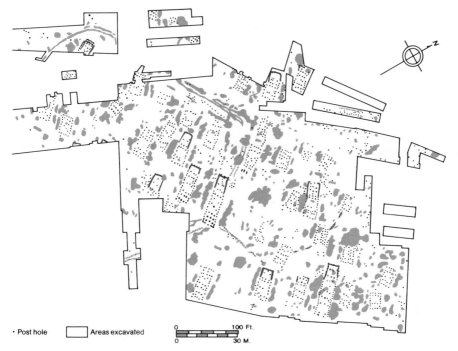

· Post hole   ☐ Areas excavated   0   100 Ft.   0   30 M.

Fig. 5.17 Ground plans of longhouses at Sittard, Netherlands, built by Danubian people.

ditions, has permitted the reconstruction not only of the funerary wagons but also of the horse harnesses, as well as the armament and ornamentation of the wagon's owner. Impeccable plans of the various artifacts' positions and of the wagon components were necessary before the burials were lifted. The great tombs of the Shang civilization of northern China are another example of complex tombs where able excavation recorded many features that would otherwise have been lost. The shaft, axle, and lower parts of the chariot wheels are visible as discolored areas in the ground, which were excavated to recover the dimensions and character of the chariots in which the charioteers were buried to accompany their masters; these chariots were found at the entrance ramps of the great Shang tombs.

Storage pits are commonly found on prehistoric farming sites, and many reach several meters in depth (Figure 5.19).[40] Their contents furnish important information on dietary habits gleaned from food residues or caches of seeds. Trash pits are even more informative (Figure 5.20). Garbage pits and privies at Colonial Williamsburg have yielded a host of esoteric finds, including wax seals from documents

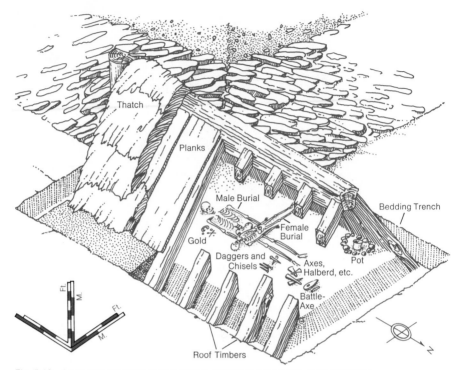

Fig. 5.18   A wooden mortuary house from a barrow at Leubingen, East Germany.

used as toilet tissue.[41] Some historic pits can be dated from military buttons and other finds.

VILLAGES AND TOWNS

Prehistoric communities may vary in size from a cluster of buildings (Figure 5.21) to a complete medieval or Colonial town. Horizontal grid excavation combined with trial excavation is the only approach to settlement problems of this type, for problems of relationship over large areas of ground are involved and accurate stratigraphic control is again essential. Obviously, total excavation is out of the question on the largest sites; instead, archaeologists try to excavate examples of all existing varieties of structure or groups of buildings (Figure 5.22). One town or village can include not only dwelling units, but also markets, reception halls, palaces, shops, government offices, workshops, law courts, and drainage systems.[42] The main excavation

Fig. 5.19 A double pit at Maiden Castle, Dorset, England, which is cut into chalk subsoil.

problem revolves around disentangling different periods of each successive occupation in situations where the stratigraphy has been complicated by extensive disturbance of underlying strata by later and modern activity (Figure 5.23).[43] Urban archaeology has become increasingly important in recent years as many long-established cities like England's Colchester, Winchester, and London have been rebuilt after World War II, or as early Colonial buildings destroyed by industrial activity in the eastern United States are traced. A remarkable example of this type of archaeology came from Winchester, where the history of a row of cottages, eleven houses, and two churches

117

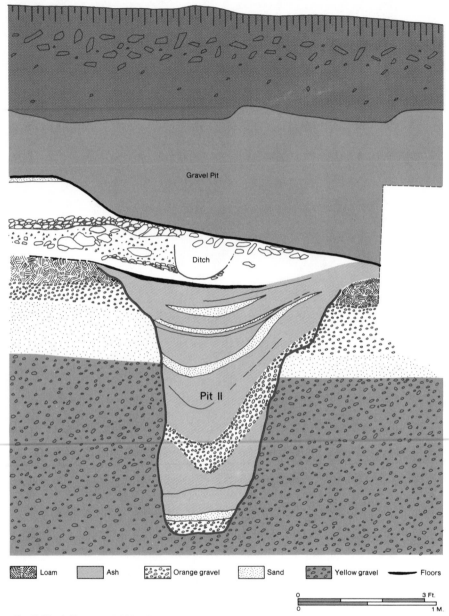

Fig. 5.20 A Roman rubbish pit overlaid by house floors found at Storey's Paddock, Cambridge, England.

was recreated from documents and archaeological research.[44] The Brooks area of Winchester was formerly a cloth-working area where dyeing and fulling took place. The Brooks houses had workrooms

Now plowed   Cemetery   Areas of excavation   0   200 Ft.
                                                                    0   60 M.

*Fig. 5.21   A plan of the deserted medieval village at Clopton, England, showing that limited excavations
(black areas) have established many main features.*

and shops facing the street with the water channels for the dyeing
process penetrating the front walls; working and living quarters were
behind or on top of the shop. A title deed to one house shows that
by 1366 it was owned by Richard Bosynton, a leading fuller of his
day, who became City Cofferer (treasurer) in 1380/81. Bosynton
appears as a strong character, who was fined sixpence in 1390 for
polluting the stream that ran by the Brooks houses with dyer's waste.
He sold part of his house in 1407 when he retired, and the surviving
deed describes the house in detail at the time. Another house was

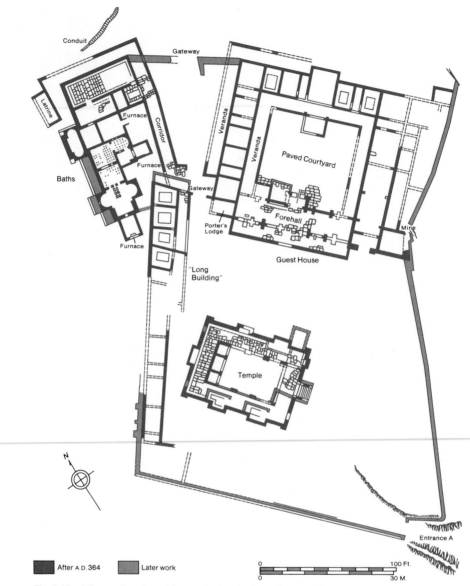

Fig. 5.22   A Roman temple and its precincts at Lydney, England. Consider how you would excavate
this site to obtain information about the different structures involved.

owned by William Bolt, a vigorous business man, who evicted a
feckless tenant named John Shovelar from it in 1402 as a result of
a complex law case. Shovelar had been in trouble with the courts
for, among other offenses, erecting a public urinal on his property—urine was a vital ingredient in the fulling process, acting as a

Fig. 5.23   Views of Brooks site, Winchester, England: above, the outlines of the thirteenth-century cottage walls and of small rooms are clear, as is the small lane in front of the houses; below, a vertical view of three-dimensional recording of features of the thirteenth-century cottages. The circle of stones is a nineteenth-century well. Note the baulks and the use of the recording grid.

type of soap. In this and other instances at Winchester, documents and excavations were linked to provide a remarkably graphic picture of life in a medieval town.

MOUND SITES

Mounds of varying size or shape are among the most common archaeological sites. Burial mounds, sometimes called barrows or tumuli (especially in Europe), are the first type that comes to mind when such sites are mentioned. But many mounds are habitation sites, or tells; others, especially in America, comprise the foundations of temples; still others have accumulated due to refuse-dumping or shellfish-collecting. Excavation methods for dissecting these mounds radically differ according to the size and character of the site.

Many human settlements have occupied the same site for centuries or even millennia, with successive generations living on top of earlier occupation levels. In other cases, the same site may be used by different peoples who may have no knowledge of each other, or instead who have succeeded each other because of battle or political action; the later change is reflected in differing material culture, architecture, or economic practices.

Settlement sites occupied over long periods of time often form mounds of occupation debris and subsoil, often deliberately accumulated by the inhabitants to raise the level of their settlement. Traditional village sites are occupied again and again for many reasons. The low ridges formed by earlier occupation may serve to elevate the new settlement above floodwaters, or provide a better drained or cooler dwelling place. The low hill formed by an earlier settlement may have strategic advantages in flat country. The site may lie near one of the few permanent water supplies for many miles, so that the inhabitants move from the settlement only when their grazing grounds or gardens are exhausted. Whatever the reason, mound sites are commonly discovered and investigated largely because they frequently yield stratigraphic information, valuable especially for establishing local cultural sequences in little-known areas. Although Indian mounds in the Ohio Valley received attention from early nineteenth-century archaeologists, the most famous settlement mounds are probably the tells of the Near East, a favorite target of nineteenth-century antiquarians who plundered them unmercifully. Sir Henry Layard made spectacular finds at Nineveh in the mid-nineteenth century, uncovering the marvels of a long-abandoned city.[45] In more recent times, the Indus civilizations have been uncovered from the mounds at Harappa and Mohenjodaro in Pakistan, while the origins of food production and urban life in the Near East have been wrested from the deposits of such tells as Jericho, Jarmo, and Ubaid.[46]

The logistics of excavating mound sites can be enormous, especially where the settlement extends over many acres as it often does in the Near East. The depth of the mound can vary greatly as well. Mound sites from central Zambia range between 1.1 meters (3.5 feet) and 5.5 meters (18 feet) in depth, the latter presenting considerable excavation problems.[47] The truncated pyramidal mounds of the Mississippian peoples of North America were part of huge religious complexes; they center around the rich floodplains of the St. Louis, Missouri, and Natchez, Mississippi, areas.[48] Clusters of mounds were arranged around a plaza, some consisting of eight to ten construction phases with mud and thatch temples built on top. The mounds were enlarged by destroying the temple on top, and encasing the mound in another layer of earth. The largest known is that at Cahokia, Illinois, near St. Louis; 30.5 meters (100 feet) high, it covers an area of sixteen acres. A height of 15.2 meters (50 feet) is common at lesser sites, creating formidable problems even for the determined excavator. Some clay, stone, and stucco pyramids and mounds of Mexico also reach impressive size.

Clearly, with sites of these great dimensions, only a sampling of the deposits and stratigraphy can be made without prohibitive expense. Some idea of the general layout of the settlement can be obtained from a careful plot of the exposed surface features and air photographs of the site, but excavations are inevitably expensive and extremely difficult. Although both vertical and horizontal excavations have been applied to mound sites with success, the most important objective is a clear understanding of a mound's stratigraphy.

Many archaeologists glibly describe mound excavation as the process of stripping successive layers from a cake. This simplistic analogy is partly true, but many factors are at work in the formation of a tell. The inhabitants may first pile up a small hill of subsoil before living on their new site. Alternatively, they may live there and build it up systematically at the same time; this will result in artificial expansion of the culture layers, which are thickened by sterile subsoil. Such an instance occurred with two large mounds in central Zambia, occupied by subsistence farmers and ironworkers over a millennium ago, where it was estimated that the mound's height had been increased by a third during the occupation by deliberate accumulation of subsoil. The result—a lower density of finds and a chronological time span in 5.5 meters (18 feet) similar to that found in 10 feet of mound deposit in neighboring areas.

Mound stratigraphy is rarely simple, for both man and animals complicate it. Burrowing mammals stroll through the soft soil of the occupation levels, disturbing burials, huts, and the complex layering of consuming interest to the excavator. Rubbish, burial, and storage pits are dug into lower levels; drains, new street levels, and house foundations disturb natural accumulations. As Braidwood and Howe, the excavators of the early farming village at Jarmo in the Near East remarked: "The . . . strata of the archaeological sites may pitch and toss in ways their surface contours seldom suggest. . . ."[49]

Mounds are accumulated by many natural and artificial processes still imperfectly understood. The tells of the Near East reach great heights mostly because of the decay of mud-brick houses. In the warm climates of the Mediterranean and Near East, prehistoric and indeed modern peoples extensively use sun-dried mud and poles to build their houses, as have many Africans within the past two thousand years. The houses are abandoned, often the poles are removed to be used again in other structures, the gaunt walls eventually collapse and form piles of mud, upon which, perhaps, a later generation builds. Whole cities were constructed in this way and over many generations, with the need for defensive walls and increased shortage of agricultural land, people continued to live in the same place as their ancestors. Thus, the mound villages that litter the plains of the Near East today were formed. Mounds in other parts of the world probably developed by similar processes, even though deliberate accumulation and other factors may have contributed more to their height.[50]

A mound excavation is normally carried out in three ways. A vertical trench or series of cuttings may be made to establish the stratigraphy and sequence of a site's cultural layers. This technique requires meticulous observation of the layering, especially if there are disturbances of the soil. The stratigraphy has to be studied three-dimensionally to establish the orientation and slope of the strata. Furthermore, as Figure 5.24 shows, there is no guarantee that a trench has penetrated the mound's core and sampled the earliest occupation. The logistics of digging small cuttings at great depth are also formidable, so much so that most excavations on large mounds, short of tunnelling, must be on a fairly large scale.

A trench may be sunk against a vertical face, starting the excavation of a level at the edge of the mound, and then removing it horizontally across the site before starting the underlying stratum. The end result of a vertical face dig is normally a large stepped trench with a gradually diminishing area size for the lower strata. Ideally, the technique should be combined with vertical test-trenching so the strata can be studied on a small scale and structures or major changes in the stratigraphy can be anticipated.

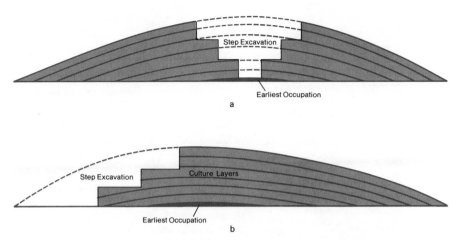

Fig. 5.24   *Some approaches to mound trenching (not to scale). (a) A stepped trench from the summit exposes a small amount of the original occupation, if this is at the mound's center. All earth must be lifted out. (b) A stepped cutting at the mound's edge may miss the core occupation, but soil is easily disposed of. In both (a) and (b), stepping of the walls prevents collapse.*

Another way of excavating mounds is to carry out a conventional grid or horizontal excavation, stripping large areas of the mound down to bedrock. This is enormously expensive, but useful when major settlement patterns or large areas of houses are to be studied. Wheeler has used this technique with success in Pakistan, where he was able to recover a vivid picture of the Indus civilization.[51] Much of Wheeler's success was due to his penchant for carefully selecting significant areas of the city for excavation by surface observation. At Harappa and Mohenjodaro, great citadels and ceremonial centers dominate extensive cities laid out on a grid pattern; some houses still stand to the first-floor level (Figures 5.25 and 5.26).

BARROWS, OR SMALL BURIAL MOUNDS

Burial mounds, or barrows, are found throughout the world in an infinite variety of forms.[52] The so-called round barrow of Europe may be up to 36 meters (120 feet) across and about 4–5 meters (15 feet) deep. A long type, up to 90 meters (300 feet) in length, has a basically rectangular ground plan.[53] Some mounds contain one interment; others, several deposited at different times; and some, numerous burials such as occur in the frequently used Megalithic tombs of Western Europe.[54]

In the nineteenth century and, alas, upon many occasions in the twentieth, the dead were removed from barrows by means of a hastily dug pit or trench (Figure 4.1). But now excavators realize that the

Fig. 5.25 A portion of the mud-brick defenses at Harappa, Pakistan.

burial itself is only part of a burial place's history, for the graves form an integral part of the structure and have a definite relationship to the barrow's stratigraphy. The objectives of burial-mound excavation include obtaining details on sepulchral customs, dating the burials, and recovering as much information as possible on climatic conditions, vegetational cover, and the soil chemistry of the mound.

A common way of digging a round barrow is by the "quadrant"

Fig. 5.26 *A brick revetment of the defenses at Kaushambi, India.*

system.[55] The mound is dissected like a large cake (Figure 5.27); vertical profiles are left along both axes of the barrow to establish the mound's stratigraphy, and the associations of the burials. The original ground surface under the barrow is carefully uncovered, and pollen samples taken from the base as well as from the body of the mound. Palynology determines the flora present on the site when the mound was built, locates the old land surface under the barrow, and if possible sheds light on the materials from which the mound was constructed. By no means are all mounds conducive to the survival of pollen spore—in many cases the grains are leached out by acid soils. There is the

Fig. 5.27 A quadrant excavation on a round barrow from Wiltshire, England, photographed from
above.

danger of differential destruction of pollen grains, too, so the results
must be interpreted with care.

A 2.4 meter-high burial mound (8 feet) near Portesham in southern
England was excavated in 1955, and found to have a core of turfs,
about 13.7 meters (45 feet) in diameter.[56] Although no traces of a
main interment were found, the excavator recovered four cremation
urns of Late Bronze Age form, all secondary burials. Pollen samples
were taken through the mound, both from the surface under the
barrow and the turf core, as well as from the upper levels. Geoffrey
Dimbleby, who analyzed the samples, found that an early period of
oak, lime, and birch forest had given way to more open country where

bracken, grass, and cultivation weeds were frequent—the change obviously the result of agriculture. Ivy was also common; he found that
this species was common in the turf levels, as if the turfs had been
cut near the mound.

As noted above, burial mounds vary widely in shape, size, and
mode of construction. Not every barrow is totally excavated, but
enough has been learned to demonstrate how important stratigraphic
profiles and processes of mound-building are in studying these conspicuous sepulchral monuments.

CEMETERIES AND SKELETONS

Burial grounds are a specialized form of site, dug for specific purposes—to obtain information on burial customs and population statistics[57] from large numbers of skeletons, or to recover pots, weapons, and
other tools from sealed graves for typological purposes.[58] The best
way to excavate a cemetery is on a grid pattern, with stratigraphic
control over the whole site, to establish whether the cemetery was
used at different times, the relative ages of the skeletons found there,
and the relative positions of the burials. If a skeleton projects into
a baulk between two trenches, it can still be recovered by removing
the wall when the recording process has been completed. Accurate
three-dimensional recording is essential if the grave goods and bodies
are to be recorded for posterity. Some idea of the problem's complexity
can be gained by looking at Figure 5.28 which shows a series of
richly decorated burials from a Zambian trading village.

The unearthing and recording of human burials is considered by
the layman to be one of the most romantic aspects of the archaeologist's job. No doubt this is true when the skeletons are adorned
with an array of rich grave goods. But, in fact, the excavation of burials
is a difficult and routine task which must be performed with care
because of the delicacy and often bad state of the bones. The record
of the bones' position, and the placement of the grave goods and
the body ornaments is as important as the association of the burial,
for the objective is reconstructing burial customs as much as establishing chronology.[59] Skeletons are normally buried in grave pits, coffins,
or sometimes more elaborate structures. Most commonly, however,
in prehistoric times, human burials were deposited in shallow pits
dug into underlying strata. The position of the bones and grave goods
is recorded as well as the burial's stratigraphic position relative to
the strata around it. In multilevel occupation sites, later burials may
be dug into underlying horizons, confusing the stratigraphic picture.
All too often, this particular aspect of a burial has been ignored in

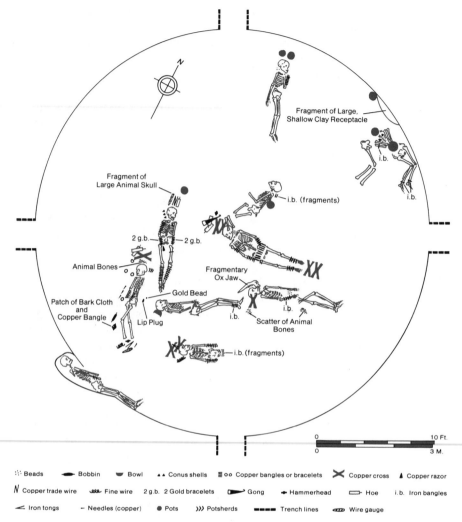

Fig. 5.28 A plan of a series of richly decorated burials at Ingombe Ilede, Zambia, showing the association of grave goods and bodies.

excavation reports, making it difficult to date a skeleton with any degree of accuracy.[60]

A burial is normally located from a surface feature such as a gravestone or pile of stones, or from an accidental discovery during excavation. Once the grave outline has been found, the skeleton is carefully exposed from above. The first part of the skeleton to be identified will probably be the skull or one of the limb bones, and the main outline of the burial is traced before the backbone, ribs, feet, and finger bones are uncovered (Figures 5.29 and 5.30). The greatest care is taken not to displace the bones, or any ornaments or grave goods that surround them. In many cases the burial is in a delicate state and the bones may be soft, so the bones are exposed gradually, giving them time to dry before they are coated with a suitable chemical such as polyvinyl acetate or bedacryl. The hardened bones can then be removed to the safety of the laboratory.[61] Normally, the undersurfaces of the bones are left in the soil so that the skeleton may be recorded photographically before removal. The photography of skeletons requires careful use of the camera to avoid parallax errors and a scale so that the scale of the photograph may be apparent to the viewer. The burial is either removed bone by bone, or is surrounded with a cocoon of plaster of paris and metal strip, the inside of which is packed with earth; the whole structure is then transported to the laboratory where it is cleaned at leisure. This technique is expensive in time and labor and is normally only used when a skeleton is of outstanding scientific importance or to be displayed in a museum. Normally, however, the bones are carefully removed, one by one, hardened with chemicals and then packed in cardboard cartons or wooden boxes with cotton, wool, and straw for transport to the laboratory.

FORTIFIED SETTLEMENTS AND EARTHWORKS

Fortified settlements and earthworks still conspicuous in the landscape today form an important category of archaeological site. Their excavation is invariably a large-scale operation, requiring sophisticated planning and a careful blend of horizontal and vertical trenching. Few have been excavated adequately. Earthworks are a common feature of the Early and Middle Woodland Adena and Hopewell cultures of the eastern United States.[62] The Hopewell Adena heartland is in the central Ohio Valley where many sites are characterized by vast high narrow ridges of earth that enclose large "fields." The enclosures can be circular, square, or pentagonal; their earthworks often border cliffs or promontories along rivers and creeks. Burial mounds are found inside these enclosures, and Adena funerary customs are well known. The Adena people are estimated to have been living from about 1000 B.C. to A.D. 200. They were less sophisticated culturally than their Hopewell contemporaries, and their economy was based on collecting and on maize agriculture. Unfortunately, the significance of their earthworks is still unknown, for no one has yet carried out large-scale excavations on them—a potentially expensive project but one worthy of long-term research.

Fig. 5.29 An Iron Age war casualty from Maiden Castle, holding the remains of a leg of lamb in his hand.

Fig. 5.30 An infant burial at Ingombe, Ilede, Zambia, dating from the seventh century A.D., or later. (The scale is in inches.)

Fig. 5.31   An Iron Age earthwork at Maiden Castle.

The serried ditches and banks of Maiden Castle in southern England[63] (Figure 5.31) or of the Heuneburg in Germany,[64] required a combination of vertical and area excavation to establish the stratigraphy and chronology of the earthworks and also the layout of the houses and wooden palisades at the entrance to the settlements. Sir Mortimer Wheeler's description of the battle that led to the sack of Maiden Castle is a classic of archaeology; the story of a desperate defense of the town is preserved in the strata of the site's entrance, which disclosed a series of hastily buried war casualties and burnt houses.[65] "Causewayed camps" in southern England, the huge ditch-enclosed settlements of early farmers in southern Italy, or the standardized square ramparts of Roman legionary forts (Figure 5.32) dot the European landscape and provide a fruitful source of inquiry for the student of earthworks.[66] The dating of earthworks, their use and mode of construction, and the history of the site itself are primary concerns in such excavations. Careful cross-sectioning of banks and ditches is an effective way of dating many earthworks.[67] When a deep

133

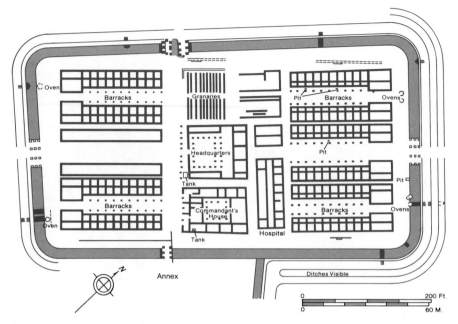

Fig. 5.32   A plan of a Roman fort at Fendoch, Scotland.

ditch is dug, its bottom is clean and regular, but very soon some natural silting of the walls takes place, as a result of rainstorms, wind, and other climatic or human factors. Such silt can normally be identified at the bottom of the stratigraphic section of a ditch and is known as "primary silting" (see Figure 4.10). Obviously, any artifact, like a potsherd, found in this layer provides a date *after which* the ditch cannot have been built. This primary silting is overlain by the secondary filling which, of course, is later than the date of construction and primary silting. Unless the ditch has been filled deliberately, this silting is entirely natural and gives a clue as to the later history of the settlement. A cross section of ramparts may also yield dating evidence, for accurately dateable artifacts, like imported pottery, coins, or charcoal which can be radiocarbon dated, can occur in the silt layers (Figures 5.33 and 5.34).

Earthworks and forts often have buildings with them that require area excavation.[68] Barrack blocks, houses, roadways, and guard huts, as well as refuse pits, are only a few of the structures that may await investigation. Some idea of the problem can be gained from an examination of Figure 5.32. Here, obviously, the location of the roadways is important, with selective excavation of each type of structure located

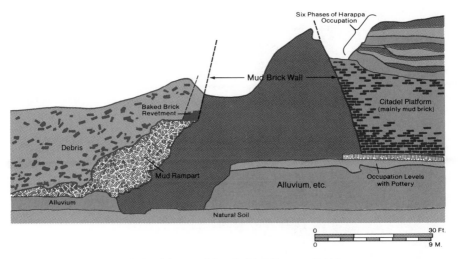

Fig. 5.33   A section through the defenses of the citadel at Harappa, Pakistan.

Fig. 5.34   Dating the construction and the destruction of a building by its associated artifacts—at Colonial Williamsburg.

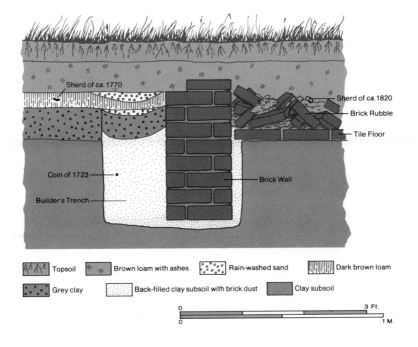

Fig. 5.35   Excavations on the Galatea Bay midden. North Island, New Zealand.

inside the fort. Aerial photographs or electronic survey may be useful in establishing the interior layout, too.

SHELL MIDDENS

Shell middens are common in coastal areas, especially in the southeastern United States, California, New Zealand, and South Africa.[69] The kitchen middens of Denmark were already being investigated on a large scale in the nineteenth century, and were vividly described by Sir John Lubbock in his *Prehistoric Times,* surely one of the best books on prehistory written in the nineteenth century. Remarkable results have been obtained from shell-midden excavations, especially in the reconstruction of diet, which is referred to in future chapters. The excavation problem is not so much one of identifying features as one of obtaining statistically reliable samples of the food and occupation residues in the body of the midden. E. W. Gifford calculated the relative proportions of various elements in some California shell middens many years ago and obtained the following figures:[70]

Fish remains	0.031%	Charcoal	0.220%
Shell	52.070%	Stone	7.500%
Ash	12.270%	Bones of vertebrates	0.055%
Soil	27.840%		

The figures indicate the types of finds in such sites, for adequate samples of the various constituents of the mound are needed for detailed analysis in the laboratory. Apart from the sampling question, concentrations of artifacts or food residues may provide evidence of specialized economic activity or insight into the settlement pattern of the users of the midden. Although some shell midden digs are designed purely to sample the deposits, many shell midden investigations in recent times have been horizontal digs, either laid out on a grid pattern, as for example at Galatea Bay in New Zealand (Figure 5.35),[71] or by systematically removing the midden, square by square, as has been practiced at Robberg Cave in South Africa.[72] Another classic shell midden excavation was carried out by Clement Meighan on Catalina Island off Los Angeles.[73] Sites like these, found on many shores, can give a good picture of riverine and seaside strandlooping economies like those also recorded in historical descriptions of prehistoric peoples in South Africa, California, and elsewhere.[74]

Stratigraphy and settlement patterns, chronologies and cultural sequences, strategy and careful survey—again and again we come back to the principles of excavation so carefully enumerated by Pitt Rivers, Wheeler, and other leading excavators over the past eighty years. Though individual methods may vary from site to site and from area to area, and their effective application depends on the archaeologist's ability, no one denies that the fundamental purpose of excavation is recovery of information and the solution of specific research problems.

Part Two
Analysis of the Past

Like earnest mastodons petrified in the forests of their own apparatus the archaeologists come and go, each with his pocket Odyssey and his lack of modern Greek.
Diligently working upon the refuse-heaps of some township for a number of years
they erect on the basis of a few sherds or a piece of dramatic drainage, a sickly
and enfeebled portrait of a way of life. How true it is we cannot say; but if an Eskimo
were asked to describe our way of life, deducing all his evidence from a search
in a contemporary refuse dump, his picture might lack certain formidable essentials.

Lawrence Durrell, *Prospero's Cell*

Chapter 6

Environment and Subsistence

Ever since the early hominids camped by African lakes, human societies have been vehicles whereby man has adapted himself to his
ecosystem. Modern societies function within an environment to which
they have adapted their culture and which they exploit to the limits
of their day-to-day requirements and technological competence.

The anthropologist studies the societies within their environment,
evaluates the adaptations they have made, and identifies the factors
that act on them. Animal societies fit into their respective ecosystems
in a simple manner.[1]* They maintain an equilibrium with other animals
and plants in the system, an equilibrium which is, however, subject
to constant readjustment as all elements in the system change. Human
societies also live in ecosystems, as animals do, but the instinctive
reactions of the latter are, in the case of man, modified by the inherited
behavior of preceding generations. We eat with a knife and fork,
use iron tools, or undergo complicated initiation rites at puberty—all
these culture traits are inherited from earlier generations.

Cultural inheritance has become an increasingly powerful factor
in human history. The earliest Australopithecines lived in small bands
and enjoyed the simplest of cultures;[2] their inherited cultural heritage
was small. As speech, art, and writing were developed, however,
human society was increasingly shaped by inheritance, and culture
became more effectively disseminated and transmitted to a growing
world population.

* See pages 328–331 for notes to Chapter 6.

Our relationship to our ecosystem is determined by our culture. Through the millennia of human history, our control over the environment has increased to the extent that today we completely dominate it and are destroying it. Our culture now shapes our ecosystem, for all aspects of it react to the diverse changes that we impose. Thus, studying man's history is, to a considerable degree, the examination of ecosystems within which human culture has flourished and of the increasing control exercised by man over his environment. We learn not only about cultural process in the past, but also about the conditions under which prehistoric peoples developed their culture and utilized their environment.

Understanding paleoecology is vital not only to the understanding of cultural process but also in the finding of archaeological sites in the field, where preservation conditions also play an important part. Before finding our sites, we must establish something about their ancient environmental setting, even if the finer details of the picture must await excavation.

RECONSTRUCTING ANCIENT ENVIRONMENTS

The glacials and interglacials provide us with a broad canvas of climatic phases and broad environmental generalizations for the Pleistocene. We know, for instance, that Western Europe had an Arctic climate in 33,000 b.c. and that a warmer regimen existed in Central Europe 100,000 years ago. Such broad categories of climate are adequate for geologists but too imprecise for archaeologists concerned with the minutiae of human adaptations within a limited area around a prehistoric hunting camp over a very short period of time. Some broad indications on environment can be obtained from animal bones. Many southwestern French caves were occupied 15,000 years before Christ by reindeer hunters, who also pursued mammoths, woolly rhinoceros, and wild horses. They were obviously living in an Arctic, tundra type of environment, whereas the hunters of Swanscombe in the Thames Valley during the Mindel-Riss Interglacial were living off animals that favored warm climates, such as the rhinoceros and various deer. Such major climatic subdivisions are readily identified, especially in glaciated areas, where the geological record shows much contrast and traces of glacial activity. Animal bones are far harder to use in Mediterranean or tropical areas where the major climatic changes of the Pleistocene were reflected in rainfall and temperature changes rather than the advance of ice sheets. Many animals taken by Paleolithic hunters were comparatively tolerant of temperature change, and even of increasing aridity, making environmental reconstruction more difficult.

The Haua Fteah Cave east of Benghazi on the coast of Libya is an excellent example of how animal bones are used to study paleoecology.[3] Charles McBurney, who excavated the Haua, found a huge sequence of Stone Age cultures, beginning with Middle Paleolithic levels at the base estimated to date to about 90,000 B.C., and passing through the Upper Paleolithic to agricultural peoples and the remains of historical occupation. Enormous numbers of broken animal bones were found in the levels of Haua Fteah, and a simplified graph of the finds shows major fluctuations (Figure 6.1). There are three main food animals in the Haua collections. The gazelle, a small antelope, requires little water and would be more common when desert conditions encroached near the cave. Barbary sheep, another important quarry, tolerates widely ranging conditions, and could endure a wide range of climates. In contrast, large bovines such as wild cattle cannot flourish without perennial water supplies, and are highly sensitive to climatic change. Haua Fteah has an annual rainfall of 500–550 millimeters (20–22 inches), and lies within a narrow coastal belt of bush country with pine trees. This gives way south of the site to cypress and more high country, abruptly changing from bush to desert steppe some 40 kilometers inland, and to stony desert in another 40 kilometers. Today, cattle are kept within the coastal bush country, sheep and camels live in the desert steppe, and gazelle are common eating on the desert fringes. Because cattle, sheep, and gazelle bones are all found in Haua Fteah, and major fluctuations in the Saharan climate are known to have occurred during the Pleistocene, it is believed that proportions of game animal bones in the cave fluctuated with climatic change, as the vegetational zones shifted with changes in rainfall. Hunting preferences cannot be regarded as a reason for the fluctuations because changes in animal counts do not coincide with cultural changes. Furthermore, it is unlikely that the Haua Fteah hunters would have neglected such readily available quarry as the wild ox if it lived in the area.

The graph of the game animals shows that wild bovines were abundant in the Middle and in the early part of the Upper Paleolithic. About 30,000 B.C., however, the hunters took more and more wild sheep and increased numbers of gazelle and horses, a trend that lasted into historic times; the increased cattle values in the late Upper Paleolithic reflect some minor increase in rainfall. Gazelle were very important in the early part of the sequence but decreased in significance sometime before 80,000 B.C. Haua Fteah is so close to the sea that fluctuations in the Mediterranean's temperature, measured accurately by use of deep sea cores, can be extrapolated against the radiocarbon-dated cultural sequence in the cave. The periods of warmer seawater temperature coincide with times when the large bovines were common,

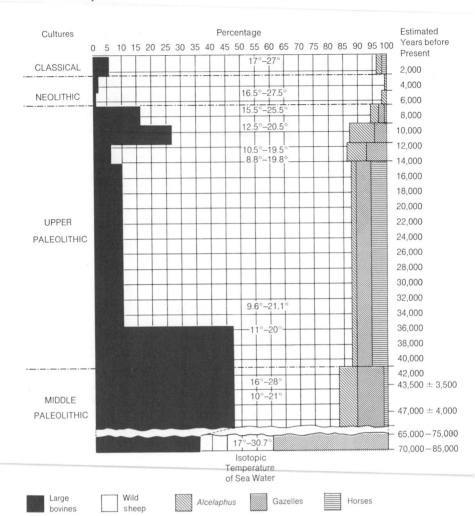

Fig. 6.1   *The main mammals at Haua Fteah, Libya, plotted against a radiocarbon time-scale, and isotopic temperature readings from deep-sea cores in the Mediterranean. The earliest dates are little better than estimates.*

whereas the colder ocean temperatures pertained when the hunters were not taking wild cattle. Thus, bovines were common at Haua Fteah in periods of warmer, drier conditions, probably moving southward, away from the coastal belt, into the present desert steppe areas when the climate became colder and wetter, times when standing water may have been available in the Sahara for much of the year. Such generalized reconstructions of ancient environment are based on diverse evidence in addition to the animal bones. The climate and vegetation pattern at the present day is projected into the past, with calculations as to the probable effects of a major increase or decrease in rainfall. The ecological niches of the animals, even small rodents, whose remains are found in the sites, are carefully studied; their needs, such as dependence on regular water supplies, are taken into account. If possible, geological or related data, as with the sea cores at the Haua, is related to the human occupation.

But the character of the vegetation is left to intelligent guesswork for projections of present floral conditions. This is through no fault of the excavators, who rely on the evidence from the deposits available to them. In some caves or other sites, remains of nuts, berries, or even wood are found, and can be used to identify a few tree species in the area at the time of occupation.[4] The evidence is frequently sparse and reflects only those species collected by the inhabitants, rather than giving a complete picture of the microenvironment around the cave. Fortunately, however, the technique of palynology has led to tracing the vegetational history for much of Europe and North America from pollen grains found in bogs, clays, and other similar deposits.

PALYNOLOGY

The basic principles of pollen analysis are described in Chapter 2. Palynology has obvious applications to paleoecology, and can supply a vivid picture of the environs of a prehistoric settlement, especially if combined with other evidence. While man had little effect on the natural vegetation until he began forest clearance and food production, pollen analysis can measure such effects and date the appearance of agriculture and forest clearance.[5]

The Stone Age hunting camp at Star Carr, England, is a classic example of pollen analysis being applied to date and reconstruct the ecology.[6] This small prehistoric settlement consisted of little more than a platform of birch brush sited in some reeds at the edge of a small lake, and was occupied in the eighth millennium B.C. The deposits were peaty, and pollens as well as wood were preserved in the deposits. Star Carr's pollen diagram is illustrated in Figure 2.9, with the occupation level indicated (see page 47). At the time the camp was occupied, birch trees were common around the site, with some pine and willow. Elm, oak, and hazel were almost nonexistent. The stratigraphic profile from Star Carr clearly shows the sloping edge of the lake, with the occupation deposits spreading out into deeper water. Traces of reeds in the deposit were common, evidence that the platform was thrown down in the reed swamp at the lake's edge (Figure 6.2) and probably lay within the reeds and at the edge of the forest, resting on a muddy gravel. Water plants, as well as fungi, were found in the occupation levels, together with abundant remains of forest game animals like the red deer. We shall return to Star Carr later in this volume.

Pollen analysis is also used for environmental reconstruction in less temperate areas of the world. A famous instance is the Kalambo Falls prehistoric site on the border of Zambia and Tanzania in East Africa.[7] J. Desmond Clark found a long sequence of Stone Age occupation sites flooded by silts and gravels from a Pleistocene lake which formerly flourished in a shallow valley behind the 665 meter-high Kalambo Falls (726 feet). Hand-axe makers, whose living floors are more than 55,000 years old, were the first known occupants of the lake shore, to be followed during subsequent millennia by later hunters and gatherers as well as farmers. The Acheulian people who lived at Kalambo settled in temporary hunting camps on the lake's edge. The horizons in which their living floors are found were partly waterlogged, which preserved a large quantity of organic materials including tree trunks, leaves, twigs, and lumps of organic deposit from which numerous pollen samples were taken. The spore counts showed that the area, now under savannah woodland, had had a denser rain forest cover when Early Stone Age hunters lived there. Unfortunately, examples like Kalambo Falls and Star Carr are rare, and our picture of prehistoric ecology is almost always incomplete and inadequate. But more and more attention is being paid to palynology in prehistoric research.

SUBSISTENCE

The ways in which man has obtained his food since the Lower Pleistocene have affected not only his survival, but nearly every aspect of the society and culture in which he lives. Man's long history covers a period of over four million years of food-getting, beginning in the earliest times with simple gathering and hunting economies that evolved to more specialized subsistence patterns of the same type, and later, more rapidly developed to food production by highly advanced methods of agriculture and stock-raising. The prehistory of man is the story of his diverse adaptations to world environments and of his increasing control over the same, to the extent that today we have caused a serious ecological crisis.

But in Stone Age times, when man was a hunter and gatherer, his subsistence patterns were intimately tied to his environment. The

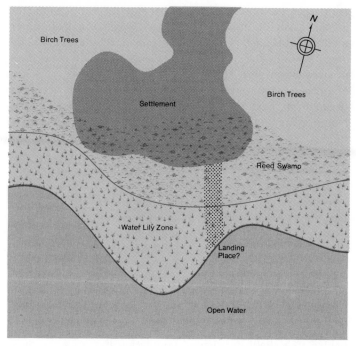

Fig. 6.2 A reconstruction of the vegetational surroundings of the Star Carr site in England.

migrations of game, the seasons of vegetable foods, and the availability of permanent water supplies during dry periods of the year—even salmon runs—vitally affected how hunters obtained their food, influenced their weapon design, and were reflected in their settlement patterns, architecture, and material culture. Nevertheless, while the availability of food supplies and water, as well as climate and soils, did set broad limits on how prehistoric peoples could make their living, a wide range of choices was still available to those living in a particular environment. These choices in turn were limited by the societal constraints of the community. Furthermore, the development of prehistoric economies and of new techniques of making one's living depended not only on changes in the natural environment and in the people's habitats, but also on the creation of more effective means of obtaining food, especially in producing it rather than merely gathering it. Both social evolution and density of population bear a direct relationship to the effectiveness of hunting or subsistence agriculture.

We considered paleoecology briefly in Chapter 3, and will now look at the methods developed for studying subsistence activities.

Although nineteenth-century archaeologists examined the bones from French caves or Indian mounds and eager scientists described the mollusca in Danish shell middens, only in recent years has the archaeology of subsistence become a major field of research. A natural preoccupation with chronology and classification was characteristic of archaeology until the 1940s, when pioneers such as Grahame Clark began to emphasize the ecological approach to prehistoric archaeology.[8] No one disputed that man has either been a hunter-gatherer, a pastoralist, or a farmer during his early history. Many scholars felt that such broad categories of subsistence activity were quite adequate, and that there were higher priorities in research than the minutiae of animal bones or vegetal remains.[9]

A greater understanding of ecology and its implications to archaeology led people to view man and his culture as merely one element in a complex ecosystem.[10] Immediately, detailed information on subsistence activities within an individual site or culture assumes great importance, for we have to view the inhabitants' relationship with their ecosystem, and study not only their subsistence activities, but their environment as well. Many fundamental questions require answers. The following are merely a selection: What was the role of domestic animals in a mixed farming economy? How important was fishing to a shellfish-oriented population living by the sea? Was the site occupied seasonally when the inhabitants engaged in a specialized economic activity? Did old habits of hunting and gathering persist as a new economy based on food production was introduced? What systems of agriculture were used and how was the land cultivated? What species of domestic animals were present and what plants were grown? Were domestic stock kept for breeding, meat, or draught purposes? What effect did the subsistence pattern have on permanency of settlement? This chapter reviews some ways in which the answers to questions such as these are sought.

The tangible evidence for prehistoric subsistence consists not only of artifacts, but also of food residues left by prehistoric populations, as well as contemporary drawings or paintings of economic life.[11] How much survives is dependent on the soil and climatic conditions. All too often the evidence is incomplete, one-sided, or trivial rather than important. The picture of human subsistence yielded by artifacts is necessarily limited. Flint axes, pressure-flaked arrowheads, iron hoes, or digging-stick weights may indicate the outlines of the picture, but hardly clothe it with substance and intricate detail (Figure 6.3). So many critical artifacts used in the chase or garden were made from perishable materials such as basketry, wood, or fiber that few details of economic life can be obtained from man's more durable achieve-

Fig. 6.3   A reconstructed Neolithic chert axe with a wooden handle of ash wood (approximate length, 30 inches). The handle is a copy of an example found in a Danish bog; only the stone is original, which illustrates how little of an artifact survives under normal conditions.

ments in stone or metal (Figure 6.4). Food residues from prehistoric sites also survive unevenly and differ widely, their abundance being a direct reflection of the preservation conditions. Mammal bones, the

Fig. 6.4   Some iron arrowheads from a thousand-year-old farming village in Central Africa (one-half actual size).

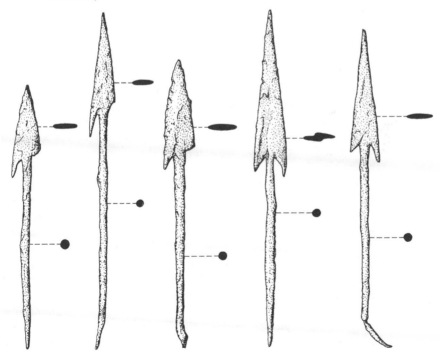

remains of animals butchered for food or ritual purposes, are the most common economic data, while bird and fish bones and the remains of invertebrates like beetles or frogs are not uncommon. Carbonized seeds occur in many hearths or cooking pots and provide a momentary insight into collecting or agricultural habits, while dry or wet sites may yield large collections of vegetal remains in a fresh state. Human feces and palynology are other sources of economic evidence, as are fresh or seawater mollusca and the stomach contents of bog corpses. Rock paintings can give a pictorial representation of subsistence activity, another source of evidence about prehistoric economy.

ANIMAL BONES

Sorting and Identification

Broken food bones are probably the most tangible remains of human subsistence patterns to survive from the past. Bone is one of the more durable raw materials and survives in various environments either in a fossilized or fresh form. Most people think skeletal remains occur in a more or less complete state, but rarely does an animal obligingly lie down and die in an archaeological site. Indeed, about the only mammals to do so are small rodents[12] who have died in their burrows or domestic animals like dogs that were not normally eaten.

All other faunal remains are usually fragmentary, coming from dismembered carcasses butchered either at the archaeological site or at the hunting grounds. To some degree, how much of the carcass is carried back to camp depends on the animal's size. Small deer may be taken back whole, slung from a pole carried by two hunters. A hunting band may sometimes camp at the site of the kill of a large animal, both eating their fill and drying parts of the carcass for later use. Almost invariably, however, the bones found in occupation sites have literally been sliced to ribbons. Every piece of usable meat is stripped from the bones: sinews are made into thongs, and the skin becomes clothing, or containers, or sometimes housing. Even the entrails are eaten. Limb bones are split for their delicious marrow: some bones are transformed into tools like harpoon heads, arrow tips, or leather working tools (Figure 6.5). The fragmentary bones found in an archaeological deposit represent the byproducts of many subsistence and cultural activities that can only be inferred from a detailed study of the bones. The archaeologist's job is attempting to conjure up a picture of the animal that was hunted or kept by the site's inhabitants from the fragmentary bone they dropped into

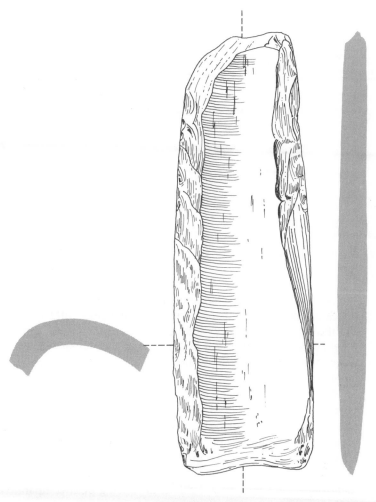

Fig. 6.5   A leather-working tool from Star Carr, made of wild ox bone (two-thirds actual size).

their occupation layer. But he also has to envisage the role that mammal played in the economy and culture of those who killed it—a difficult problem for the difference between the "actual animal" slaughtered by prehistoric man and the "archaeological animal" found, identified, and studied by the archaeologist is considerable.[13]

Animal bones are rarely found in articulation in an occupation level, unless one is excavating a kill site or finds some extremities of a fore or hind limb detached from the long bones in one piece. The fragments occur throughout the deposit, at some places in signifi-

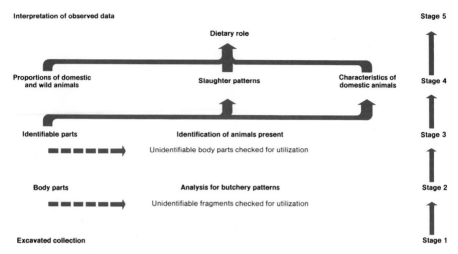

Fig. 6.6   Animal bone analysis.

cant concentrations, at others merely scattered over a living area. Bone distributions are carefully plotted on living floor sites to show any significant associations of body parts with artifacts, windbreaks, or other structures. But unless a living floor is definitely identified, the fragments are normally handled in bulk and bagged carefully for laboratory study.

The study of animal bones is traditionally regarded by archaeologists as the preserve of the zoologist and osteologist. But, in fact, this particular aspect of archaeology is by no means difficult; methods of day-to-day identification and analysis can readily be learned by anyone with a bent for examining osteological remains. Zoologists, indeed, are often so busy that more and more archaeologists are identifying their own faunal collections, using both comparative collections and numerous excellent osteological manuals that have appeared in recent years.[14] But mammalogists are always glad to assist with difficult identification problems and to discuss the implications of findings from the taxonomic or ecological viewpoint.

The first step in analysis is the cleaning and basic sorting of the collection (Figure 6.6). All fragments are examined; those that can be assigned to a body part are put on one side for further examination and counting. The unidentifiable fragments are counted, checked for signs of use as tools, and then discarded or put on one side.[15] This leaves a much smaller collection to handle, and the body part counts can be entered on a suitable form for more detailed analysis of butchery practices at a later stage. Some skeleton parts can positively

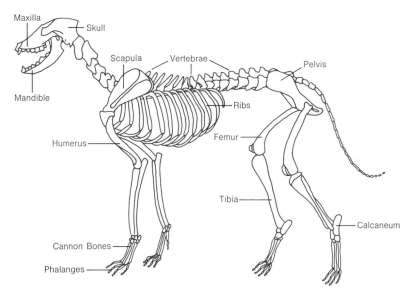

Fig. 6.7   A dog skeleton showing the most important body parts from the osteological viewpoint.

identify the animal to which they belonged, but only a small proportion of the body parts in a collection are sufficiently characteristic for this purpose. As an example, only 2,128 fragments of a collection of 195,415 from a Stone Age hunting camp in Zambia could be identified;[16] a further 9,207 could be assigned to a particular body part. The remainder of the collection had been smashed into small pieces by hunters in search of marrow, sinew, or meat. The skeleton of a dog in Figure 6.7 illustrates a typical mammal skeleton. Small skull fragments, vertebrae, ribs, scapulae, and pelvic bones are normally of little use to identify a domestic as opposed to a wild animal, or to differentiate one species of antelope from another. Upper and lower jaws and their dentition, individual teeth, the bony cores of horns, and sometimes the articular surfaces of long bones are susceptible to identification.[17] Teeth are identified by comparing the cusp patterns on their surfaces with those on comparative collections carefully collected from the site area (Figure 6.8). This task is made harder by the fragmentary nature of the material, for often individual teeth are relied on to identify an entire animal. In some parts of the world, the articular ends of long bones can be used as well, especially in regions like the Near East or parts of North America where the indigenous mammalian fauna is somewhat restricted.[18] It is even possible to distinguish the fragmentary long bones of domestic stock from

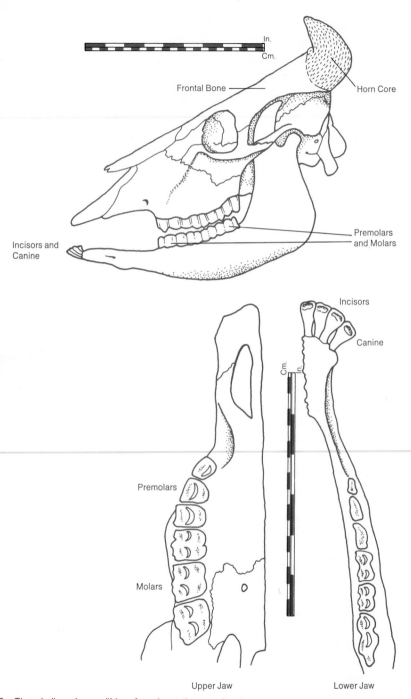

Fig. 6.8 The skull and mandible of a domestic ox, showing important osteological features (one-fourth actual size).

those of wild animals of the same size in the Near East, provided that the collections are large enough and the comparative material sufficiently complete and representative of all ages of individual and of variations in size from male to female individuals. But in other areas, such as sub-Saharan Africa, for example, the indigenous fauna is so rich and varied, with such small variations in skeletal geography, that only horn cores or teeth can distinguish between different species of antelope and separate domestic stock from game animals. Even the dentition is confusing, for the cusp patterns of buffalo and domestic cattle are remarkably similar, often only distinguishable by the smaller size of the latter.[19]

Most bone identification is by direct comparison, and is a fairly simple process, easily learned by anyone with sharp eyes. Statistical techniques are being used more frequently for comparing long bones as well as teeth, especially where fine distinctions between individual species are involved, or male/female size differences are a problem.[20] The identification stage of a bone analysis is the most important of all, for several fundamental questions need answering: Are domestic and wild species present? If so, what are the proportions of each group? What types of domestic stock were kept by the inhabitants? Did they have any hunting preferences that are reflected in the proportions of game animals found in the occupation levels? Are any wild species characteristic of vegetational associations no longer found in the area today?

The first stage in attacking these problems is a complete listing of the animals in the collection and a count of identifiable fragments of each represented. Although these can be counted and expressed as a percentage of all identified bones, such figures are meaningless. We have to equate the "archaeological animal" as represented by the bones with the game animal or domestic beast killed by the man who dropped the remains of his meal. No one has yet succeeded in developing a technique for overcoming this problem.[21]

Game Animals

Though the listing of game animals and their habits gives an insight into hunting practices, in many cases the content of the faunal list gains particular significance when we seek to explain why the hunters concentrated on certain species and apparently ignored others.

The dominance of a particular game species can result from economic necessity, convenience, or a matter of cultural preference. Many societies restrict the hunting of particular animals or the consumption of certain game meat to one or the other sex. The !Kung Bushmen of the Dobe area of Botswana have a complicated series of personal, age specific, and sex specific taboos in eating mammals.[22] No one can eat all twenty-nine game animals regularly taken by the Bushmen; indeed no two individuals will have the same set of taboos. Some mammals are eaten by everyone, but with restrictions on what part they may eat. Ritual curers will set personal dietary restrictions on other animals, although no one eats primates and some carnivores. Such complicated taboos are repeated with innumerable variations in other hunting and agricultural societies, and have undoubtedly affected the proportions of game animals found in archaeological sites.

Examples of specialized hunting are common, even if the reasons for the attention given to one or more species are rarely explained. Upper Paleolithic hunters of Solutré in southwest France concentrated on wild horses, apparently driving them over cliffs in large herds.[23] At the eighth millennium B.C. hunting camp of Star Carr in northeast England, Grahame Clark found the remains of a minimum of eighty red deer in the occupation levels, while roe deer, thirty-three individuals, was the next most common game.[24] The Archaic Riverton culture peoples of the central Wabash Valley, Illinois,[25] hunted the white-tailed deer as the basic meat staple in their diet, to the extent that the remains of this mammal were more numerous than those of any other species in the sites, including in most cases birds, fish, and turtles as well. The specialized big game hunting economies of the Plains Indians are well known, reflected in the archaeological record by spectacular bison-kill sites in Colorado, at Plainview, Texas, and at Folsom, New Mexico.[26]

Another factor is overhunting, or the gradual extinction of a favorite species. One well known example is the history of the North American bison, a major food source for all Plains tribes until its near extinction in the late nineteenth century.[27] *Bos primigenius*, the European aurochs or wild ox, was a major quarry of Upper Paleolithic hunters in Western Europe, and was still hunted in Post Glacial times and after the advent of food production (Figure 6.9).[28] The last aurochs died in a Polish park in 1627, and we know from illustrations and contemporary descriptions what these massive animals looked like. The bulls were large, up to six and a half feet at the shoulder, and often wore very long horns. The male coat was black with a white stripe along the back and white curly hair between the horns. Professor Lutz Heck of Berlin has tried to reconstitute the aurochs, by crossing breeds of cattle that exhibit certain characteristics of the wild ancestor. Heck's experiments were most successful, forty "reconstituted aurochsen" living by 1951. The mental characteristics of the aurochs reappeared together with the physical appearance. "Reconstituted aurochsen" are fierce, temperamental, and extremely agile if allowed to run wild. The German experiments have provided a far more convincing reconstruction of a most formidable Pleistocene mammal than any number of skeletal

Fig. 6.9   *A* Bos primigenius *skull from Cambridgeshire, England.*

reconstructions or artists' impressions (Figure 6.10). Hunting habits changed radically at the end of the Pleistocene with the onset of warmer climatic conditions and greater forest cover, causing the retreat of the Arctic fauna, and their replacement by temperate species like the red and roe deer and the elk. Again, hunting activities have changed as drastically in the past century. Richard Lee records how the older Bushmen state that in earlier times there were more game animals and a higher hunting population in the central interior of Botswana.[29] Their forefathers used to hunt in large groups, killing buffalo, giraffe, and elephants. Today their descendents have a predominantly gathering economy, supplemented by the meat of twenty-nine different mammals, mostly those whose carcasses have a relatively high meat yield. Hunting is a common pursuit, the warthog being the most important source of meat, together with small game. This change in hunting habits directly results from the importation of Victorian rifles and early hunting safaris, which decimated the wonderful African fauna within three generations.

Domestic Animals

Apart from identification difficulties, the bones of domestic animals present more problems than those of wild species. If the population is obviously fully domesticated, the characteristics of the species

157

Fig. 6.10 A wild aurochs, as depicted by S. von Heberstain in 1549.

present must be studied to establish distinctions in breeds.[30] With early farming sites, however, where the transition from the wild to domestic state was still in progress, the osteological problems are formidable, for domestication transformed man's relationship with the animals he tamed, his food supplies stabilized, and he made more intensive use of the species involved.[31]

Nearly all domestic animals originated from a social wild species, in other words, a species with an inclination to be sociable, facilitating an association with man. Domestic animals did not all originate in the same part of the world, but were always domesticated in their natural area of distribution in the wild. Scholars have assumed that the domestication of wild animals takes place when a certain level of cultural achievement is reached. Domestication everywhere seems to begin when a growing population changes over to a more settled and culturally higher form of life. A regular food supply is needed for larger groups of people; domestication is dependent on such conditions and, at the same time, is a prerequisite for further cultural progress.

Wild animals lack many characteristics valuable in their domestic counterparts. Thus, wild sheep have hairy coats, but their wool is not the type produced by domestic sheep, which is suitable for spinning; aurochs, ancestors of the domestic ox, and wild goats produce sufficient milk for their young, but not in the quantities so important to man. Considerable changes have taken place during the course of domestication, man developing characteristics in his animals that often render them unfit for survival in the wild.

The history of the domestic species is based on fragmentary animal bones found in the deposits of innumerable caves, rock shelters, and open sites.[32] Osteological studies of wild and domesticated animals are inhibited both by the fragmentary bones in most sites and by the much greater range of sexual and growth variation in domestic, as opposed to wild, populations. Nevertheless, a number of sites have produced evidence of gradual osteological change toward domesticated animals.[33] If the bones of the wild species of prehistoric domesticated animals are compared with those of the domestic animals through time, the range of size variations first increases and eventually a selection in favor of smaller animals and less variation in size appears.[34] This transition is, however, fluid and it is difficult to identify wild or domestic individuals from single bones or small collections. The bones of domestic animals demonstrate that a high degree of adaptability is inherent in wild animals. Man has found it necessary to change the size and qualities of animals according to his need, with corresponding effects on their skeletal remains. Different breeds of cattle, sheep, and other domestic animals have developed since the origins of domestication (Figures 6.11 and 6.12). The humped zebu ox of Asia can be identified in faunal collections from the characteristic bifid spinal process that forms on the neck vertebrae.[35] Humped cattle are pictured in Egyptian tombs (Figure 6.13),[36] and everyone is familiar with the Jersey and Guernsey breeds of modern times.

Slaughter Patterns

The next step after identification of the bones is analyzing the age at which the animals were slaughtered and the butchery techniques used. Age is determined by examining the eruption and wear patterns of teeth, as well as the epiphyses of long bones. The latter may be unfused or partially joined in the case of immature animals, and although these make a useful criterion, it is not so significant in areas like Africa or Asia where the osteology of long bones and other extremities is less well known. Some Near Eastern sites have yielded such large collections that higher proportions of immature epiphyses were used to show the threshold of domestication—the period when the inhabitants of such sites as the Belt Cave in Iran systematically began to kill goats at a younger age than they did when they were hunting the wild species.[37] Most aging is determined by studying the dentition, using complete jaws so that the eruption formulae can be compared. Sometimes single teeth are used, the wear on the cusps being measured by a standard scale, but this method is less reliable.

Fig. 6.11 A Minoan bull and dancers, as painted on the walls of the Palace of Knossos. The ox has a piebald coat and was a domesticated form. (After Arthur Evans.)

The assembled data are then tabulated in graph or table form, ready for interpretation. Some cases of slaughter pattern graphs appear in Figure 6.14—obviously, large samples are essential.

The interpretation of slaughter patterns is fairly straightforward when hunting economies are involved. Most hunting societies were skilled in the chase, taking animals of all ages with a preference for individuals in their prime which yield tender meat (Figure 6.14a). Less able hunters might concentrate on immature or old animals that were easier to trap or run down. Mass game drives of large herbivores like the bison or buffalo yield a more even curve with all ages of beast represented. Hunters tend to select animals with a high meat yield rather than older or younger beasts.[38]

Fig. 6.12 A herd of buffalo grouped around a structure of marsh reeds, from a clay impression of a Sumerian seal.

Fig. 6.13 A stele of Bebwawi, Amarna, Egypt, from the Eighteenth Dynasty, including a zebu bull. (After N. de G. Davies.)

Domestic animals, being a controllable meat supply, are subject to quite different selection criteria. In more advanced agricultural societies, cattle or horses might be kept until old age for draught purposes, surplus males being castrated and females being retained until they stopped lactating or were of no further use for breeding or ploughing. Even if riding or work animals were not kept, the problem of surplus males persists. The ratio of male to female in any cattle population is 1:1, with the result, of course, that there are far too many males for breeding purposes. This male surplus represents an abundant source of prime meat, and was often slaughtered at early adulthood. Cattle stood for wealth in many traditional societies, as they do in some today, but were slaughtered on special occasions like funerals or weddings; the herd surplus was consumed in this manner, and the owner's obligations were satisfied. Thus, a population of cattle jaws found in a site may reveal a characteristic curve (Figure 6.14b) showing that surplus males and females were slaughtered at

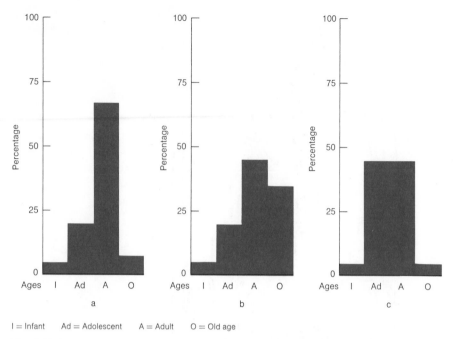

I = Infant   Ad = Adolescent   A = Adult   O = Old age

Fig. 6.14 Aging graphs for hypothetical—and ideal—cases. (a) Hunting population slaughtered by skilled hunters. (b) Typical domestic cattle population. (c) Typical domestic goat population.

different ages. Or perhaps the remains of a herd of goats yield a simple graph (Figure 6.14c), reflecting circumstances in which small stock were slaughtered in their prime for meat purposes. These situations are by no means universal, but offer examples of factors that can affect slaughter pattern data.

Butchery

The fragmentary bones in an occupation level are the end-product of the killing, cutting up, and consumption of domestic or wild animals. To understand the butchery process, the articulation of animal bones must be examined in the levels where they are found, or a close study must be made of the fragmentary body parts. For instance, kill sites occur at Olduvai Gorge and Torralba, Spain, and in the American West, to name only a few. Such areas were occupied by hunters who camped beside their kill, removing the skin and meat from the carcass of a large mammal, and perhaps drying some surplus meat for later consumption. The butchering tools used by the skinners are found in direct association with the bones, so that the excavations preserve the moment of butchery for posterity. Such an incident is illustrated in Figure 6.15 in which the sequence of dismembering a

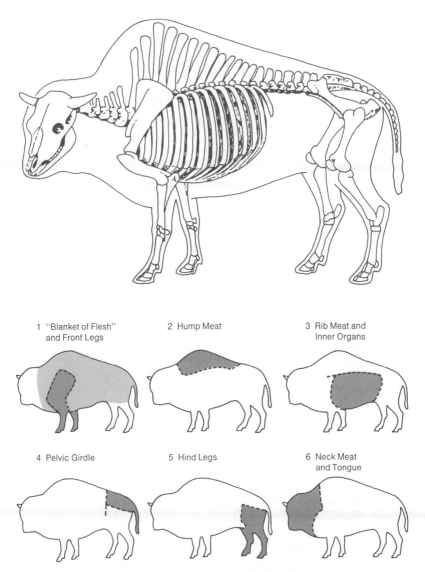

1 "Blanket of Flesh"   2 Hump Meat   3 Rib Meat and
  and Front Legs   Inner Organs

4 Pelvic Girdle   5 Hind Legs   6 Neck Meat
                                                              and Tongue

*Fig. 6.15 Butchering practices of Paleo-Indians at the Olsen-Chubbuck site in Colorado, as recon-
structed from the archaeological evidence and historical butchery data. (From "A Paleo-
Indian Bison Kill," Joe Ben Wheat. Copyright © January 1967 by Scientific American,
Inc. All rights reserved.)*

bison carcass has been reconstructed from an accumulation of bones
at a kill site in Colorado.[39]

Deciphering butchery techniques becomes more complicated at a
base camp or more permanent village where meat was brought onto

the site or slaughtered nearby. In one method, body part distributions are reduced to proportions of the most common bone present.[40] The technique was developed by Theodore White who applied it with success to bison kill sites in the Great Plains, where preservation conditions appear comparatively even. Many sites are larger, however, and soil conditions are such that some more delicate body parts may disintegrate more swiftly than others, to result in a distorted picture of the skeletal remains left on the site by its inhabitants. The bones of the forelimb and extremities are most frequently found, whereas those of the skull, vertebrae, and innominate parts are less common. This pattern is remarkably consistent over many sites and must, to some degree, reflect the selection practices of the butchers. The animal's size may effect how many bones are found at a base site. Goats, chickens, or small deer may be carried to the village as complete carcasses, but usually only small portions of larger beasts are brought in—this is especially true of those with a high meat yield because these are often consumed where killed and every scrap of flesh and entrails utilized.

VEGETAL REMAINS

Gathering and agriculture are two major components of prehistoric subsistence almost invariably underrepresented in the archaeological record. Seeds, fruits, grasses, and leaves are among the most fragile of organic materials and do not survive long unless they are carbonized or preserved under very wet or arid conditions. As early as the mid-nineteenth century, scientists were identifying fruit and cereal crops from the deposits of the Swiss lake dwellings exposed by the especially low waters of the lakes.[41] Some carbonized grains were recorded by Pitt Rivers in his excavations, and plant remains were discovered at an early date in the dry caves of the western United States. Vegetal remains, dried by the arid climate of the Nile Valley, were found in the Desert Fayum by Gertrude Caton-Thompson in the 1920s.[42] Exceptional finds like these helped to found our knowledge of prehistoric food crops. But in recent years, more and more attention has been paid to flotation techniques (see page 166) for recovering large samples of seeds from superficially unproductive sites.[43] Others have used the grain impressions on pots[44] to base a provisional botanical history of Europe; palynology has provided insights into forest clearance dates and agriculture's introduction to many parts of modern Europe.[45]

Carbonized seeds are normally found in cooking pots or among the ashes of hearths where they have been dropped by accident. Though the preservation conditions are not ideal, it is possible to identify both domestic and wild plant species from such discoveries.[46] Much early evidence for cereal cultivation in the Near East comes from carbonized seeds. Many more unburnt vegetal remains occur in waterlogged sites and in dry caves. The Star Carr site in northeastern England yielded a range of fungi and wild seeds, some of which were eaten until recently by European peasants.[47] A Stone Age hunting camp at Gwisho hot springs in central Zambia situated on the edge of a tract of savannah woodland rich in vegetal foods contained quantities of seeds and fruit preserved by the high water table in the springs.[48] Ten thousand identifiable vegetal fragments came from the occupation levels at Gwisho, many of them from six edible species still eaten by southern African hunters; this represents a remarkable continuity of subsistence pattern over more than 4,000 years.

The dry caves of the western United States and Mexico have provided a great quantity of dried vegetal remains. Tularosa Cave in New Mexico is important for its documentation of the transition from the Archaic to Formative stages.[49] Cochise occupants of Tularosa were harvesting primitive corn by 2000 B.C., and their Mogollon successors employed horticulture fully. The dry deposits in the cave contained much organic material, including moccasins, sandals, and hunting implements. The lower levels, occupied by Archaic hunters, yielded the remains of no less than thirty-nine species of wild flora used for food, tools, and raw materials; edible plants included yucca seeds, cacti, walnuts, and various grasses. Tularosa gave a remarkable picture of the introduction of cultigens into the Southwest. Maize, beans, squash, and gourds were found in the Cochise Archaic levels, adding a new dimension to our knowledge of the area's gathering economy. A primitive corn was being grown by the Cochise by 2000 B.C., and a millennium later, squash and beans were being cultivated. Although the origins of agriculture in this area plainly lie to the south in Mexico, the Tularosa finds indicate cultivated crops were introduced into more northerly areas before domestic plants had completed evolving from the wild to the domestic state. The process of economic transition was completed by 300 B.C. when pottery was introduced to Tularosa. Corn has been found even earlier at Bat Cave, northeast of Tularosa, where it has been dated to *ca.* 3500 B.C.[50]

Danger Cave, on the western edge of the Great Salt Lake in western Utah is another large dry cave occupied from about 9000 B.C. until recent times.[51] Over thirteen feet of rich deposit, mostly consisting of dust and chaff, contained one of the most complete cultural inventories ever recovered from the western United States. Sixty-five plant species, all found in the area today, were recovered from the site. Other desert caves in Nevada, such as Lovelock and Gypsum,[52] contain desiccated occupation layers or numerous caches of artifacts. Some hoards include pine nuts, edible seeds, and the raw materials for toolmaking.

The Tehuacán Valley in the state of Puebla, Mexico, has provided a record of continuous human occupation from the earliest times to the Spanish Conquest.[53] Early inhabitants of the valley lived mainly by hunting rabbits, birds, and turtles, but later, about 6700–5000 B.C., their successors subsisted mostly on wild plants like beans and amaranth. These people, who lived in caves during the dry season, began to cultivate squashes and avocados; maize pollen occurs in their cave deposits, and a few small wild maize cobs occur at the end of their occupation. Grinding stones, pestles, and mortars were in use for the first time, indicating that seeds were being ground for food. Richard MacNeish has excavated over a dozen sites in Tehuacán, five of which contained the remains of ancient corn; 80,000 wild plant remains and 25,000 specimens of corn came from the sites, providing a detailed picture of agriculture's origins in highland Mexico. The small wild maize cobs came from the lowest occupation level in San Marcos Cave, and were no more than twenty millimeters (0.78 inches) long. Coxcatlan Cave contained important botanical evidence, too, for by 5000 B.C., although the inhabitants of this and other sites were still gathering most of their vegetal food, 10 per cent of the deposits came from domestic cultivation—gourds, squashes, beans, chili peppers, and corn. A third of Tehuacán subsistence was based on agriculture by 3400 B.C., a period when the domestic dog first appeared; permanent settlement first began soon after this. Pottery was being manufactured by 2300 B.C., and more hybrid types of corn came into use. So many vegetal remains were found in the settlements of Tehuacán that the history of domestic corn in this area can be written in quite astonishing detail (Figure 6.16): abundant at first, wild corn became virtually extinct two thousand years ago, as did the early cultivated varieties, which were superseded by more modern forms. Botanical evidence of this complexity and completeness is unique in the archaeological record.

Flotation techniques have been employed systematically to recover seeds in central Illinois, and also at Ali Kosh in Iran. The method uses water or chemicals to free the seeds, often of microscopic size, from the fine earth or occupation residue that masks them: the vegetal remains float while the residue sinks. Although this technique enables us to recover seeds from many sites where it was impossible before, by no means can it be applied universally, as its effectiveness depends on soil conditions. Through flotation, Stuart Struever and his colleagues recovered over 36,000 fragments of carbonized hickory nut shell from ovens, hearths, and storage-refuse pits in the Apple Creek

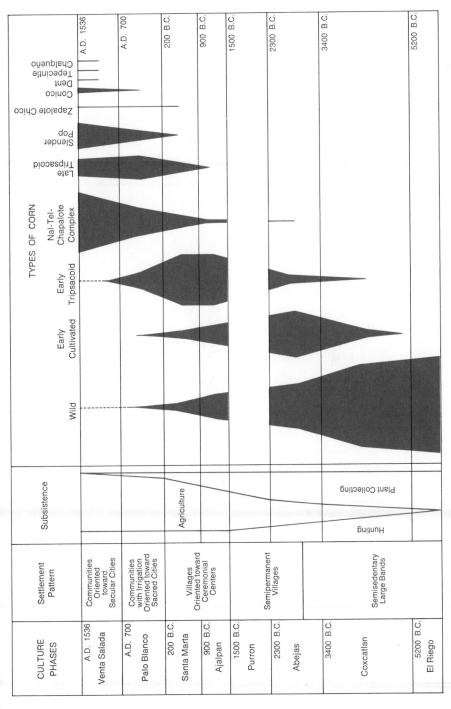

Fig. 6.16 The evolution of maize in the Valley of Mexico.

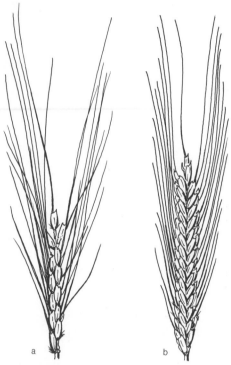

Fig. 6.17 (a) The wild ancestor of einkorn (Triticum boeoticum). (b) Cultivated einkorn (T. monococ-cum). (Both two-thirds actual size.)

site in the Lower Illinois Valley.[54] This Late Woodland settlement also yielded 4,200 fragments of acorn shell, as well as over 2,000 other seeds from at least three species. Few cultivated seeds were found, which indicated that the inhabitants relied on hickory nuts and acorns for much of their vegetable diet.

Frank Hole's experiments with flotation at the Ali Kosh site in Iran were also successful, indeed the results were dramatic.[55] After the first season of excavations, Hole and his colleagues stated confidently that "plant remains were scarce at Ali Kosh." Two years later they used a modified version of Struever's flotation technique and recovered over 40,000 seeds stratified throughout the cultural sequence at the Ali Kosh mound. The data gave a startlingly complete botanical history for the site, showing the increasing importance of emmer wheat and two-row hulled barley and the effects of irrigation (Figure 6.17).

Apart from the seeds themselves, which reveal what the food plants were, grain impressions in the walls of clay vessels or adobe brick help uncover the history of agriculture or gathering. The microscopic

Fig. 6.18 A grain impression from a Neolithic pot at Hurst Fen, Cambridgeshire, England.

casts of grains that adhered to the wet clay of a pot while it was being made are preserved in the firing process and can be identified with a microscope. Numerous grain impressions have been found on European handmade pottery from the end of the Stone Age (Figure 6.18). Indeed, a remarkably complete crop history of prehistoric Europe has been pieced together from grain impressions. The most abundantly cultivated cereal in prehistoric Europe was emmer wheat (*Triticum dicoccum*); wheat was the most important grain during early farming times, but barley rose into prominence during the Bronze Age. Some typical grain impression figures follow:[56]

	Stone Age		Bronze Age		Pre-Roman Iron Age	
	Wheat	Barley	Wheat	Barley	Wheat	Barley
Britain	17	9	23	223	19	15
Denmark	35	54	22	214	1	30

Grain impressions have been studied in the Near East, and western Sahara,[57] whereas some related work on adobe bricks has been carried out in the western United States.[58]

Palynology has been an invaluable tool to study European forest clearance. Many years ago, Danish botanist Johannes Iversen was studying the pollen diagrams from Scandinavian peat sequences when he noticed that there was a remarkably sudden change in the composition of the forests in the beginning of the sub-Boreal period (Blytt and Sernander, zones VII–VIII).[59] The elements of high forest—oak, ash, beech, and elm—simultaneously declined, while, at the same moment, the pollens of grasses increased sharply. At one locality, he found a charcoal layer immediately underlying the zone where forest trees declined. The increase in grass pollens was also associated with the appearance of several cultivation weeds, including *Plantago*, which is characteristically associated with cereal agriculture in Europe and went with European farmers throughout the world, even to North America. Iversen concluded that the tree cover vanished as a direct result of farming activity—man's first major imprint on his environment (Figure 6.19). Similar pollen curves have been plotted from data gathered elsewhere in Europe. The first human clearance of forests has also been dated in Uganda where deep pollen cores from Lake Victoria show a sudden drop in forest cover about 3,000 years ago.[60]

However effective the recovery techniques used for vegetal remains, the picture of either food gathering or agriculture is bound to be incomplete. A look at modern hunters reveals the problem.[61] The !Kung Bushmen of the Kalahari Desert in southern Africa are classic examples of hunter-gatherers who appear in every book on ethnography, and yet until comparatively recently, little was known of their ecology or subsistence patterns. Many early writers on hunters assumed the !Kung relied on game alone and lived in a perennial state of starvation that was relieved periodically by meat-eating orgies. Nothing, in fact, could be farther from the truth. Much subsistence activity of Bushmen and other hunters is conducted by the women who gather the wild vegetable foods that comprise a substantial part of their diet. Many early observers were naturally preoccupied with hunting techniques and more spectacular subsistence activities, for, in former times, many hunting peoples pursued larger game, often cooperating with other bands in the chase.

Today, vegetable foods play a leading part in Bushman diet and have presumably increased in importance as the large game herds have diminished. The Bushmen know of at least eighty-five species of edible fruit, seeds, and plants; of this enormous subsistence base, they eat regularly only some nine species, noticeably the *Bauhinia*.

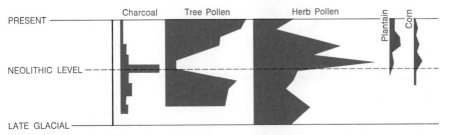

Fig. 6.19 Fluctuation in the frequencies of charcoal and fossil pollen brought by Neolithic coloniza-tion: Ordrup Mose, Denmark. The amount of grass pollen rises sharply as the forest decreases. (After Iversen.)

In a famine year or when prime vegetable food sources are exhausted, they turn to other species, having an excellent cushion of edible food to fall back on when their conventional diet staple is scarce. Theoreti-cally, therefore, the Bushmen can never starve, even if food is scarce at times. Their territory, of course, is delineated in part by available sources of vegetable foods as well as by water supplies; its frontiers in many cases represent a day's walking distance out to the gathering grounds and back to the base camp.

AGRICULTURE AND DOMESTIC AND WILD ANIMALS

Very few subsistence-farming peoples have ever relied on agricultural products or their herds alone to provide them with food the year round. Hunting, fishing, and gathering have always supplemented the diet, and in famine years or times of epidemic the people have fallen back on the natural resources of their environment for survival (Figure 6.20). Since, however, food production has led to increased population densities, famine often ensues because the resource base for farmers remains the same as that which may have supported a smaller hunter-gatherer population in comfort.[62] Even in times of plenty, most food producers rely on game for some of their meat, evidenced by the bones of wild animals in faunal collections where cattle and small stock are also present. The proportions of domestic and wild species in such a collection are considerably important in assessing the roles of hunting and pastoralism in the economy. If such figures are based on how many individuals are represented in the collection, or on some sound formulae, the results can be revealing, especially when a series of collections are available from a cultural sequence extending over several hundred years.

Prehistoric stockbreeding in Europe has been studied intensively,

Fig. 6.20   A woman of the Leya tribe, Zambia, pounding wild nuts for food.

using large bone collections and statistical techniques. Charles Higham[63] used Swiss collections and modern comparative material to document the history of stockbreeding. He combined the faunal analyses with pollen studies and found that the aims of stock-raising were closely integrated with the agricultural methods and technological attainments of prehistoric societies in Switzerland. Higham points out, for example, that bovines and sheep find only limited feeding in mixed oak forest and that a damp, forested environment is difficult for sheep, who are susceptible to blow-fly attacks and other diseases in warm humid weather and who also have a natural antipathy to woodland. Consequently, any diminution in forest acres through agricultural bush clearance encouraged the keeping of domestic herbivores. Higham convincingly argues that any prehistoric tribe, which encouraged stock-raising and agriculture by removing the factors in the environment limiting such activities and by conditioning the "mix" of its herds to the man-modified environment, promoted its chances for survival by increasing its productivity. The earliest Swiss farmers settled near lakes, positioning their villages where the environment best suited their activities. Most sites bordered shores where rich lacustrine soils and a more favorable climate encouraged agriculture. Lake plants gave vital early spring fodder, whereas the undergrowth of the nearby mixed oak forest provided supplemental feed for domestic stock and acorns for pigs.

Early farming was confined to open areas favorable to this activity, but this kind of land rapidly became scarce. Metal tools added a new factor to the situation, and aided in forest clearance. The destruction of forests gave greater areas of pastureland, and removed a major barrier to prehistoric farming. Herbivores became more important because the hay raised in these lands allowed stock to overwinter. In this, as in so many other instances, the economic strategy of the prehistoric farmer integrated with the limiting factors of his environment and his technological abilities to produce a distinct pattern of economic evolution. Behind the proportions of fragmentary bones lie the unconscious and deliberate subsistence strategies of man, the discovery of which is the ultimate goal of the scholar of prehistoric economies.

While one may argue, as Higham does, that the most significant change in prehistoric Europe was the decline in importance of the pig and rise of sheep and horses due to progressive forest clearance, in other areas different factors may affect the content of domestic herds. The inhabitants of the Deh Luran Plain in Iran first began to cultivate cereal crops and keep goats sometime before 7000 B.C. The first food production involved plants and animals introduced from the mountains to the rolling steppe of Deh Luran. As the excavators point out, "What man did, before 7000 B.C., was to domesticate the annuals he could eat, and then domesticate the animals who lived on the perennials."[64] The cultivation system was expanded so that domestic grains increased from 5 per cent of the vegetal remains to about 40 per cent between 7000 and 6000 B.C. But this early domestic plant and animal complex, based as it was on upland-mountain environmental adaptations, inhibited rapid population growth. Even so, the vegetational pattern of the steppe was altered as field weeds were established and land clearance and grazing removed the natural grass covering.

Between 5500 and 5000 B.C., some simple irrigation techniques were introduced that took advantage of the local drainage pattern. Barley cultivation became of prime importance, and the cultivation areas expanded. Sheep increased in importance and cattle were introduced, the latter only assuming a vital role in the economy when ploughs

began to be used around 2000 B.C. Each gradual or rapid change in
the subsistence pattern or environment of Deh Luran instituted by
man led to a complicated chain reaction affecting every sector of the
inhabitants' culture.

The farmers of the Batoka Plateau in southern Zambia were also
cattle owners; abundant grazing grass and good supplies of perennial
water make the region a prime cattle area today. By excavating a
series of settlement sites, the evolution of cattle herding was traced
over a period of 1,300 years.[65] In the seventh century A.D. and in
earlier centuries, the farmers of the plateau had few cattle, relying
on game for much of their protein. By A.D. 1000, cattle represented
about 60 per cent of the food bones at several sites, whereas two
hundred years later they were overwhelmingly dominant in some sites,
and in a single nineteenth-century settlement represented over 90
per cent of the animal bones.[66] The increase in cattle is thought to
be connected with natural increases in herd surpluses rather than
with any major changes in economy or culture, for there has been
a basically similar, mixed farming economy on the Batoka Plateau
since the advent of metallurgy eighteen hundred years ago, and population densities have been too low for major modification of the
vegetational cover.

The rates of herd growth and the importance of pastoralism are
affected by many factors, among them endemic stock disease, the
nutrient qualities of grazing grass, the availability of water supplies,
and, in some areas, the distribution of the dreaded tsetse fly, carrier
of trypanosomiasis which is fatal to cattle and harmful to man.[67] Similar
factors also affect the growth rate of domestic stock, because the size
of cattle or smaller stock can vary widely from one environment to
another.

BIRDS, FISH, AND MOLLUSCA

Bird Bones

Bird bones have been sadly neglected in archaeology, although some
early investigators realized their significance. Japetus Steenstrup and
other early investigators of Danish shell middens took care to identify
birds, including those of migrants.[68] Many Maglemose camps in Denmark have been recognized as summer settlements, where cranes and
mute swans were taken and where winter species are absent. In
contrast, coastal shell middens of the Ertebølle type were occupied
all year, with most fowling taking place in the winter.[69] In 1902 the
famous Peruvianist Max Uhle dug a large Indian mound on the eastern

shores of San Francisco Bay. The site was excavated again in 1926, and Dr. Hildegarde Howard studied a large collection of bird remains from the dig;[70] her report illustrates the potential importance of bird faunas in archaeology. She found that water birds were the predominant species, especially ducks, geese, and cormorants; land birds distinctive of hill country were absent. All the geese were winter visitors, mostly found in the Bay Area between January and April each year. The cormorant bones were nearly all immature, suggesting that the Indians had been robbing cormorant rookeries; most of the cormorant bones equalled an adult bird's in size, but ossification was less complete, equivalent to that in modern birds about five to six weeks old. Dr. Howard examined rookery records and estimated that a date of *ca.* June 28 each year would be the actual time when rookeries could be raided. Thus, from the evidence, she concluded that the Emeryville mound was occupied both during the winter and the early summer, and probably all year.

Bird hunting has often been a sideline in the struggle for subsistence. In many societies, young boys have hunted winged prey with bows and arrows, while training for larger game. A specialized bird-hunting kit is found in several cultures, among them the Post Glacial hunter-gatherer cultures of Northern Europe. Though bows and spears were used in the chase, snaring was obviously practiced regularly. The birds found in some African hunting and farming sites are almost invariably species like guinea fowl who fly comparatively rarely and are easily snared.[71] No traces of the snares have been found in excavations, for they are normally made of perishable materials. Surprisingly little has been written on prehistoric fowling, perhaps because bird bones are fragile and present tricky identification problems.

Fish

Fishing, like fowling, became increasingly important as man began to specialize in different and distinctive economies and as his environmental adaptations became more sophisticated and his technological abilities improved. Evidence for this activity comes from both artifacts and fish bones.

Freshwater and ocean fish can be caught in various ways. Nets, basket traps, and dams were methods in wide use from Post Glacial times on, but their remains rarely survive in the archaeological record except in dry sites or waterlogged deposits. Basket fish traps have been found in Danish peat bogs, dating to the Atlantic vegetational period.[72] The ancient Egyptians employed somewhat similar traps which are depicted in Old Kingdom tomb paintings (2660–2180 B.C.). Nets remain the most popular fishing device and were used in Northern Europe in Post Glacial times, too. Seine nets, which captured surface-swimming fish by surrounding them, have been found in two localities in Finland and Estonia; the damp conditions preserved not only the pine-bark floats, but also parts of the fiber net and stone weights.[73] A large fishweir, constructed of vertical sticks 1.2 to 4.9 meters long (4 to 16 feet), sharpened on one end with a stone axe, enclosed an area of two acres at Boylston Street, Boston.[74] The weir was built about 2500 B.C., and was probably the work of coastal Archaic people. Such traps were evidently widely used along the Atlantic Coast, built in estuary areas where tidal currents were strong. In the Boston weir, brush and flexible withies were placed between the stakes; fish were diverted into the enclosure by "leaders," also made of brush, leading to the trap mouth. Considerable community effort must have been necessary to build this weir, which provided an almost inexhaustible food supply for its designers.

Fishhooks, harpoons, and barbed spearheads are frequent finds in lake- or riverside encampments. The earliest fishhooks had no barbs, but did have a U-shaped profile (Figure 6.21). Post Glacial hunting peoples like the Maglemose folk of Denmark used such artifacts in the seventh millennium B.C., in all probability to hunt the pike, a prized freshwater fish in prehistoric times.[75] Bone and antler harpoon heads, common in Magdalenian deposits from southwest French caves, may sometimes have been used for bottom fishing.[76] The Maglemose peoples of the Baltic Sea area certainly spear fished. Numerous barbed bone points have been recovered from the bottom of an old lake at Kunda in Estonia, two of them associated with pike skeletons. Many pike bones were found at the Mesolithic site of Svaerdborg, Denmark, together with numerous barbed spear-points. North European methods of fishing are vividly described by J. Scheffer in his portrayal of the Lapps: "Their way of fishing alters with the season, in the Summer usually with drag nets, between two boats, or else with spears like tridents, but that they have more teeth. With these they strike pikes, especially when they lie sunning themselves near the top of the water: they do the same by night burning dry wood at the prow, by which light the fish are enticed thither."[77]

Scheffer's words are apt, for artifacts alone tell us little about the role of fish in prehistoric economy or the fishing techniques of prehistoric peoples. Did they fish all year or only when salmon were running? Did they concentrate on bottom fish or rely on stranded whales for fish protein? Such questions can only be answered by examining the surviving fish bones themselves. Unfortunately, piscine remains are among the most fragile in archaeology, and are susceptible to destruction by many corrosive factors. Once recovered, however, fish bones

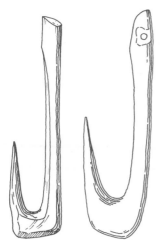

Fig. 6.21 Bone fishhooks of the Maglemosian culture from Northern Europe (two-thirds actual size). (After Clark.)

are readily identified and are often informative. The Stone Age hunters of Gwisho in central Zambia lived near the floodplain of the Kafue River in the third millennium B.C., a vast, seasonally inundated area where fish abound.[78] Each dry season the waters of the Kafue recede, leaving isolated pools that survive long after the river has gone. Many catfish are stranded in the depressions, lurking in the soft mud. The local inhabitants trap the fish or spear them as the pools dry up, eating some of their catch fresh and drying the rest for later consumption. The hunting camps contain catfish bones in overwhelming numbers, whereas other species, normally caught by rod and line or more sophisticated methods, are almost nonexistent. The conclusion reached was that Gwisho hunters were taking bottom fish to the virtual exclusion of other species because they were the easiest to catch, especially as the Kafue's waters were several miles away and other food sources more convenient.

The Chumash Indians of Southern California were remarkably skillful fishermen, venturing far offshore in frameless plank canoes and fishing with hook and line, basket, net, and harpoon. Their piscatory skill is reflected in the archaeological sites of Century Ranch, Los Angeles,[79] where the bones of such deep-sea fish as the albacore and oceanic skipjack were found, together with the remains of large deep-water rockfish that live near the sea bottom in water too deep to be fished from the shore. Five other species normally occurring offshore, including the barracuda, were found in the same midden. The bones of shallow-water fish among them the leopard shark and

California halibut were discovered in the same sites, indicating that both surf fishing and canoe fishing in estuaries with hook and line, basket, or net were also practiced.

The degree to which a community depends on fishing can be impressive. Lake- or seaside fishing encampments tend to be occupied on a more permanent basis than hunting camps, for the food supply, especially when combined with the collection of shellfish, is both reliable and nourishing. The "Later Stone Age" fishing camp at Lothagam in northern Kenya, dating to the fourth millennium B.C., yielded the remains of over 10,000 fish bones, nearly all Nile perch, a species that grows to an enormous size. Only some 250 mammal bones were found in the site, which was certainly occupied over a long period of time.[80]

Mollusca

Shellfish from seashore, lake, or river have formed an important part of prehistoric diet for many thousands of years. Augustin de Beaulieu, who visited the Cape of Good Hope in 1620 with a fleet of ships from Honfleur, France, was a curious and perceptive observer whose wanderings over the Cape Peninsula enabled him to describe the Khoi-Khoi, the indigenous cattle herders and gatherers: "Also they go along the seashore where they find certain shell fish, or some dead whale or other fish, however putrefied it may be, and this they put on the fire for a little and make a good meal of it."[81] The identification of the mollusca in shell middens is a matter for expert conchologists, who possess a mine of information on the edibility and seasons of shellfish. With such data, it was determined that the Khoi-Khoi seem to have depended on shellfish at dry times of the year when inland pastures were parched and vegetable foods in short supply. Other peoples subsisted on mollusca for most of the year, accumulating gigantic piles of shells at strategic places on the shores of lakes or oceans near favored rocky outcrops or tidal pools.

A century ago, the Danes were discussing the distribution of Baltic oysters found in seaside middens near Copenhagen,[82] and the study of prehistoric mollusca has continued since then. Modern midden analysis involves the systematic sampling of the deposits, and the counting and weighing of the various constituents of the soil. The proportions of different shells are readily calculated, and their size, which sometimes changes through time, easily measured. California shell middens have long been the subject of intensive research, with the changes in frequency of mollusca projected against ecological changes in the site areas.

The La Jolla Culture middens of La Batiquitos Lagoon in San Diego are a notable example of such analysis. Claude N. Warren[83] took column samples from one shell mound and found that the remains of five species of shellfish were the dominant elements in the molluscan diet of the inhabitants. The changes in the major species of shellfish were then calculated for each excavated level. They found that *Mytilus*, the bay mussel, was commonest in the lower levels, gradually being replaced by *Chione*, the Venus shell, and *Pecten*, the scallop, both of which assumed greater importance in the later phases of the site occupation, which has been radiocarbon dated from the fifth to second millennia b.c. Warren found that *Ostrea*, the oyster, a species characteristic of a rocky coast, was also most common in the lower levels, indicating that the San Diego shore was rocky beach at that time, with extensive colonies of shellfish. By about 6,300 years ago La Batiquitos Lagoon was silted to the extent that it was ecologically more suitable for *Pecten* than the rock-loving *Mytilus*. Soon afterward, however, the lagoons became so silted that even *Pecten* and *Chione* could no longer support a large population dependent on shellfish, which then had to move elsewhere. Similar investigations elsewhere in California have also shown the enormous potential of mollusca in studying prehistoric ecology.

Both fresh and seawater shells had ornamental roles, too. Favored species were traded over enormous distance in North America, Europe, and Africa. *Spondylus gaederopus*, a mussel native to the Black Sea, the Sea of Marmora, and the Aegean, was widely distributed through human agency as far north and west as Poland and the Rhineland by early Danubian farmers in the fifth millennium b.c.[84] The shells were used as pendants, beads, or bracelets and are ubiquitous in Danubian country. As the Danubians expanded northward and westward into their new territories, they began to trade the shells to perpetuate the ornamental tradition of their homeland. On the other side of the world, baler shells from the coast of Cape York in northern Australia were chipped and ground to form oval ornaments that were passed from hand to hand across the continent to South Australia by hunting bands—a remarkable example of the high value of seashell ornaments to some communities.[85] The *conus* shell, common on the East African coast, was widely traded, finding its way into the African interior and becoming a traditional prerequisite of chieftainly prestige. The nineteenth-century missionary and explorer David Livingstone records his visit to Chief Shinte in western Zambia in 1855: the going price for two *conus* shells at that time was a slave, or five for a tusk of elephant ivory. Archaeological digs have indicated that *conus* shells were handled in the Zambezi Valley seven hundred years earlier, reflecting a long history of trade in such prestigious ornaments (Figure 6.22).[86] Indeed, as late as 1910, enterprising merchants were trading china replicas of *conus* shells to the tribesmen of Central Africa.

Fig. 6.22   Ingombe Ilede burial with conus shells, ca. fifteenth century A.D. (The shells are the circular objects around the neck, numbered 1–4.)

ROCK ART

Rock art is a major source of information on economic activities. Some years ago, African archaeologist J. Desmond Clark published an account of "Late Stone Age" hunting practices in southern Africa in which he drew heavily on the rock art of Rhodesia and South Africa (Figure 6.23). The paintings depict the chase, weapons, collecting, camp life, and sometimes domestic animals. Clark remarked, "In the rock art there is preserved an invaluable record of the people's hunting methods, the different kinds of weapons and domestic equipment they used, their customs and ceremonies."[87]

The rock paintings of Natal, South Africa, provide fascinating information on fishing practices and the boats associated with them. Patricia Vinnecombe recorded a fishing scene in the Tsoelike River rockshelter in Lesotho, southern Africa (Figure 6.24).[88] The fishermen, armed with long spears, are massed in boats, apparently cornering a shoal of fish which are swimming around in confusion. Some boats have lines under their hulls which may represent anchors; the fish cannot be identified with certainty, but may be freshwater catfish or yellowfish. Vinnecombe's paper generated considerable discussion—some authorities argued that the boats in the paintings were probably made of bark.[89] Another famous scene from the Cape Province of South Africa depicts a group of ostriches feeding peacefully,

Fig. 6.23   A running hunter from Ho Khotso, Lesotho, southern Africa, shown in a Late Stone Age drawing painted in purple-red. The figure is 21 centimeters (about 8 inches) high.

and among them lurks a hunter wearing an ostrich skin, his legs and bow protruding beneath the belly of an apparently harmless bird. Such vignettes of prehistoric hunting life add enormous insight to

Fig. 6.24   A rock drawing depicting a fishing scene from Lesotho, southern Africa.

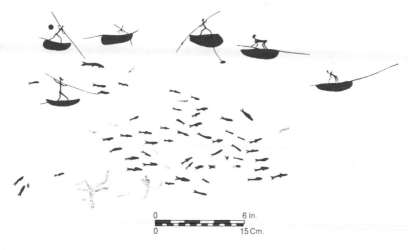

Fig. 6.25   Deer being driven toward bowmen, an Upper Paleolithic wall-painting (dark red) in the Cueva de los Caballos, near Albocácer, Castellón. (After Obermaier.)

data obtained from the food residues recovered from caves and rock-shelters (Figure 6.25).

PREHISTORIC DIET

So far, information on prehistoric subsistence has been that gleaned from various archaeological finds. The ultimate objective of economic archaeology is not only to establish how man obtained his food, but also to reconstruct his actual diet. Dietary reconstruction is difficult, largely because of incomplete economic information. Yet the problems involved are fundamental. What proportion of the diet was meat? How diverse were dietary sources? Did the principal sources of diet change from season to season? To what extent did the people rely on food from neighboring areas? Was food stored? What limitations or restrictions did technology or society place on diet? All these questions lie behind any inquiry into prehistoric subsistence.

The most complete reconstructions of diet come from the remains of meals in the stomachs of prehistoric corpses and from human feces found in dry caves and occupation sites, especially in the western United States. The last meal of a bog corpse from eastern England found in 1911 consisted of blackberry seeds, rose haws, and other wild vegetal remains.[90] The stomach of Tollund man, who was executed around the time of Christ, contained the vegetable remains of a finely ground meal made from barley, linseed, and several wild grasses; no meat was found in the contents.[91]

Many American scholars have studied coprolites from dry caves in the United States and Mexico. Seeds, nuts, deer hair, feathers, and chips of bone have been identified in feces from Danger Cave in Utah, and pollen analysis is now being applied to human excrement.[92] Most analyses have consisted of dry sorting and microscopic analysis, but more advanced techniques are being developed. Robert Heizer and his colleagues have analyzed numerous stratified coprolites from the Lovelock Cave in central Nevada.[93] Most of the 101 coprolites analyzed contained bulrush and cattail seeds; they also showed that Lahontan chub from the waters of nearby Humboldt Lake were regularly eaten. Undoubtedly caught with fiber dip nets found in the cave, they were eaten raw or toasted. One coprolite contained the remains of at least fifty-one chub, calculated by a fish expert to represent a total fish weight of 3.65 pounds. Adult and baby birds, the water tiger beetle, and possibly freshwater gastropods were also eaten. Collecting vegetable foods seems to have been done on a casual basis, and the remains of large mammals were not found in the feces. Unfortunately, however, identifying large mammals is particularly difficult except from hairs or splinters of heavy mammal bones.

Coprolites have been analyzed from stratified cave sequences in the Tehuacán Valley. A diet of grass seeds and a starchy root known as *Ceiba* came into vogue at the beginning of the incipient agriculture stage;[94] this diet continued in use almost up to the Spanish Conquest. Maize is conspicuously absent from the Tehuacán Valley cave coprolites, as though the crop was grown for tribute purposes and not eaten by the inhabitants—or, alternatively, ground so finely that the meal was digested without trace. Coprolites, like other economic evidence, must always be considered in conjunction with other information sources.

Food residues from living floors or occupation levels are less satisfactory. Animal bones, fish bones, or shells, are almost invariably the most common food remains to be found, and tend to be overemphasized in reconstructing an economy, even if accompanied by quite a collection of vegetal remains. Early literature bulges with examples of this emphasis, propounded by investigators who were bemused and delighted by large bone middens; when reinvestigation later revealed that, in fact, collecting or agriculture had formed a major part of the economy. Surprisingly little attention has been paid to prehistoric diet, largely because obtaining the data is difficult. The nutritional factors involved in diet have been seldom studied, and the full potential of this approach to archaeology has not been realized. Californian archaeologists have attempted to study the relative weights of different food sources in shell middens,[95] but the methodological difficulties are considerable. But basically, information on prehistoric diets comes from the analyses and the identification procedures described in this chapter. Since the ultimate objective is explaining how man lived in the past, new theoretical frameworks, systematic use of ethnographic analogy, and quantitative methods will, it is hoped, intensify research on the dietary requirements of prehistoric man.

TRADE

Human subsistence is based on natural resources and on the exploitation of the environment, whether or not man produces food. Many hunting cultures were self-sufficient in their dietary requirements and only used the raw materials within their regular hunting territory. Their knowledge of their environment was detailed and resource-oriented; indeed, trade may have been generated when man moved to a new territory where a formerly abundant raw material did not exist, but was still needed. Contacts between neighboring bands were fleeting and sporadic, and though sometimes based on the exchange of food and raw materials, these contacts could also have a ritual nature. The systematic barter of raw materials may have begun with the exchange of stone for implement-making and stone axes. Several sources of tough stone for axe and adze blades were exploited by Australian stoneworkers, although the extent to which these were traded is a matter for further research.[96] Certainly, stone axes were a primary trade item in early food-producing societies in Western Europe. The yellow nodules, *livres de beurre*, of Grand Pressigny flint are found in early farming sites through France. Petrological analyses of stone axe blades in England have revealed a complex network of quarries and trade routes for the diffusion of tough cutting edges through much of the country.[97]

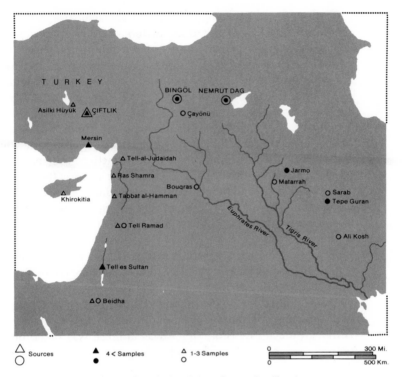

Fig. 6.26 Obsidian trade in the Near East in the sixth and seventh millennia B.C.

With the advent of food production and metallurgy, the demands for raw materials increased and transcended the limited territory of the hunter-gatherer. Skins, hut poles, grain, ornamental materials, and metal ores were soon being handled over enormous distances. British archaeologist Colin Renfrew and a number of colleagues have harnessed scientific technology to study obsidian trade in the Near East.[98] Obsidian is a fine black volcanic glass, eminently suitable for the manufacture of stone tools and mirrors. Only a limited number of obsidian outcrops occur in the Near East and Mediterranean basin (Figure 6.26), and it is possible to identify the source of an obsidian artifact by studying the trace elements both in the source ores and in the finished tools found in sites many miles from the outcrops. Renfrew and his colleagues have reconstructed the history and extent of obsidian trade over the critical period of time when food-producing societies were establishing themselves in the eastern Mediterranean. Obsidian trade helped to widen human perspectives and to develop the complex trade routes so much a part of the growth of urban society and literate civilization.

Trade is normally recognized in the archaeological record by the discovery of objects exotic to the material culture or economy of the host society. Glass, for example, was not manufactured in sub-Saharan Africa before the advent of European rule, yet imported glass beads are widespread finds in archaeological sites of late first millennium A.D.[99] The natural copper outcrops of the Lake Superior region were exploited to make hammered ornaments found in Archaic sites as far away as the southeastern United States.[100] Amber from the shores of the Baltic reached the Mediterranean by regular trade routes as early as the sixteenth century B.C.—the attractive substance was used to adorn wealthy Mycenaeans.[101] The amber trade is thought to have been handled by middlemen who were trading German metal to the vigorous metallurgists of Denmark, southern Sweden, and northern Germany, areas where copper and tin had to be imported for the smiths' use.[102]

Complicated barter networks extended over much of Europe and the Near East in later prehistoric times; the peoples of the African interior knew of and prized seashells from the Indian Ocean. The Hopewell Indians of Ohio traded obsidian, mica, and other exotic raw materials which are found from the Rockies to the Atlantic Coast.[103] Although much prehistoric trade was indirect, was based on prosaic objects, and was bartered between villages, the contacts of early man widened rapidly once regular trade began. The perspectives of farmer and hunter widened as trading became more and more important in supplying raw materials and supporting specialized craftsmen. The transactions between man and his environment and his increased exploitation of the latter were refined and encouraged, as they are today, by intensified local and long-distance trade.

Chapter 7

Technology and Artifacts

"Whatever the ultimate inspiration or the intermediate cause, it was by their hands that the early Europeans dragged themselves out of the primeval mist of savagery, struggled up the long slopes of barbarism and ultimately attained to some kind of civilised existence."[1]* Grahame Clark's words from his classic study of prehistoric Europe provide us with ample justification for studying the technology of the ancients. The tools that man has manufactured throughout his long history were the means by which he augmented his limbs and extended the use of his environment. Other animals beside man use extraneous objects to achieve subsistence objectives and display considerable evidence of behavioral adaptability. But man differs from other animals not only in possessing culture but in the degree to which he has come to depend on it.

Man's physical evolution helped make dependence on his culture possible, but was itself affected by cultural development.[2] Man's success and continued survival has been due to his remaining an unspecialized organism, adaptable—in the main—to changing environmental conditions through his culture and capable of far more rapid change and adjustment to an enormous range of environmental conditions. Biological evolution has proceeded alongside cultural evolution, the two processes interacting with each other. Man adopted an upright posture, freeing his hands for toolmaking and becoming adapted to life in open country where vegetable foods and tree-climbing were

* See pages 332–334 for notes to Chapter 7.

less important. His brain became larger, a trend encouraged perhaps by the use and manufacture of tools. Human awareness and man's culture were shaped by the human brain, working with man's hands to enrich his life experience to an extent unknown in other primates. His technological achievements over the three million years that he has been a toolmaking mammal are both impressive and terrifying. Twentieth-century technology is developing at an almost uncontrollable speed. We can land a man on the moon, transplant human hearts, and build sophisticated computers. Yet our ability to adapt to the quickened technological pace of the 1970s and our society's capability to handle these staggering advances have lagged far behind, nor have we yet developed mechanisms whereby our society can live with twentieth-century technology to the best advantage. Our contemporary armory of computers, atomic bombs, household appliances, and every conceivable artifact designed for a multitude of specialized needs has evolved in a direct, albeit diversely branching, line from the first simple tools made by early man. Archaeologists study the material remains of human activity in their attempts to write culture history and reconstruct cultural process, and artifacts are a primary item they study. Any form of artifact is the end product of well defined and instinctive human behavior. It constitutes its maker's definite idea of the proper way of making the tool concerned, whose form is dictated by definite conventions. In other words, an implement represents not only the level of technological achievement of the society in which its maker lived, but also a vast amount of inherited information and experience passed on to its user from earlier generations. Thus, man's technological achievements are as important to us as his quest for subsistence, and the increasing sophistication of his craftsmanship and increasing diversity and ingenuity of his industrial skills have played a major part in human cultural and physical evolution (Figure 7.1).

STONE TECHNOLOGY

Certain categories of rock have, with bone and wood, been the primary raw materials for man's technology for most of his existence on earth. The advent of metallurgy is but a recent development, and stone tools have provided the foundation for the classification of many prehistoric cultures since scientific archaeology began. The raw material itself has set severe limits on the extent of man's technological achievements for much of his history, and the evolution of stoneworking over the millions of years during which it has been practiced has been infinitely slow—man eventually exploited almost every possibility afforded by suitable rocks for making implements by various techniques.

Fig. 7.1 Australopithecus africanus. *(After extensive research, artist Jay H. Matternes drew this portrait of an* Australopithecus *group.)*

The simplest way of producing a stone that will cut or chop, surely the basic tool produced by prehistoric man, is simply to break it in half and use the resulting sharp edge. But to produce a tool that has a more specialized use or can be employed for several purposes requires slightly more sophisticated flaking technique. First, an angular fragment or smooth pebble of suitable rock can be brought to the

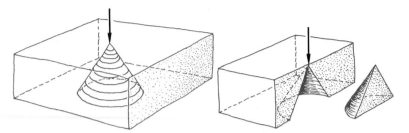

Fig. 7.2   *How stone fractures: (left) when a blow is struck on flinty types of rock, a cone of percussion is formed by shock waves rippling through the stone; (right) a flake is chipped when the block (or core) is hit at the edge and the stone fractures along the edge of the ripple.*

desired shape by systematically flaking it with another stone. The flakes removed from this core or lump are then primarily waste products, whereas the core becomes the implement that is the intentional end product of the stonemaker. Furthermore, the flakes struck from the core can be used themselves as sharp edged knives, or further modified to make more formal artifacts. From this simple beginning, many and complex stone industries have evolved, the earliest tools being simple—many of them virtually indistinguishable from naturally fractured rock.

Identifying man-made implements as distinct from naturally broken rocks is something that can only be learned by experience in handling many artifacts, but here is a generalized description of the principles of stone-implement manufacture.[3] Generally, Stone Age man and other makers of stone tools chose flint, obsidian, and other hard homogeneous rocks to fashion their artifacts. All these rocks break in a systematic way, like industrial glass. A sharp blow directed vertically at a point on the surface of a slab of suitable stone knocks out a solid cone, with its apex at the point where the hammer blow hit the slab. This effects a "conchoidal fracture" (Figure 7.2). When, however, a blow is directed at a stone slab obliquely from the edge and the break occurs conchoidally, a flake is detached. The fractured face of the flake has a characteristic shape, with a bulge extending from the surface of the piece outward down the side. This is known as the "bulb of percussion"—there is a corresponding hollow or flake scar on the core from which the flake has been struck. The bulb of percussion is readily recognized, as the accompanying text figure (Figure 7.3) shows, not only because of the bulge itself but also from the concentric rings that radiate from the center of the impact point, widening gradually away from it. Such deliberate fractures by man are quite different from those produced by natural means like frost,

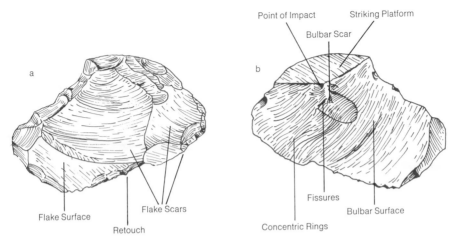

Fig. 7.3   The component parts of a flake tool. (a) Flake surface. (b) Bulbar surface.

extreme heat or cold, water action, or stones falling from a cliff and fracturing on large boulders below.[4] In these cases the rock may sometimes break in a similar manner, but most of the flake scars are irregular, and instead of concentric rings and a bulb of percussion, there is often a rough depressed area on the surface with concentric rings formed around it.

Careful examination is needed to distinguish human and naturally fractured stones one from another, a particularly acute problem with tools of the earliest men.[5] In many cases, their artifacts were made by the simplest of hammerstone techniques, resulting in the removal of two or three flakes from the pebble (Figure 7.4). This produced a jagged edge that was effective, so experiment shows, in dismembering carcasses of game.[6] There have been several famous controversies over alleged "artifacts" found in Lower Pleistocene deposits in Europe and Africa that are contemporary with periods when hominids were already flourishing elsewhere. A celebrated furor arose over a series of alleged tools, named "eoliths," found early in this century in Lower Pleistocene horizons in eastern England.[7] These were championed as early evidence of human occupation for many years until reexamination of the geological contexts and accurate measurements of the flaking angles on the "eoliths" demonstrated that they were probably of natural origin.[8] Under such circumstances, the only sure identification of humanly fractured stone implements is to find them in association with fossil human remains and broken animal bones, preferably on a living floor.

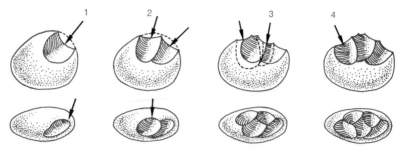

Fig. 7.4   *Chopping tools were made by a simple process. Side view (top row): first, two flakes were struck off (1 and 2); second, the stone was turned over and two more flakes were removed (3); and third, a fifth flake completed the tool, giving it a sharp edge. The bottom row shows the process from above.*

Several different methods of flaking stone were used during prehistoric times. The most common and the earliest used was direct fracturing of the stone with a hammerstone. The core was held in the hand and repeatedly struck with a hammerstone at selected points to produce a steep or sharp edge (Figure 7.5). The angle at which the blow was delivered determined whether the flakes removed were shallow and long or steep and short. In a variant on this technique, the core was swung against an anvil, removing a series of large flakes, a method known as the "block on block." These techniques produced the chopping tools and flakes found at Olduvai Gorge and other Australopithecine living sites (3 million–*ca.* 70,000 B.C.).[9] *Homo erectus* began to make tools flaked on both surfaces (Figure 7.6), such as the Acheulian hand axes of the Middle Pleistocene (400,000–70,000 B.C.), from sites like

Fig. 7.5   *Stoneworking techniques. (a) Using a hammerstone. (b) The anvil technique.*

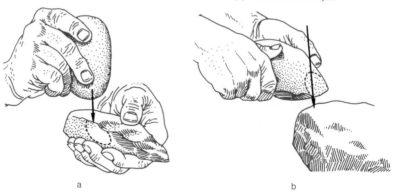

a   b

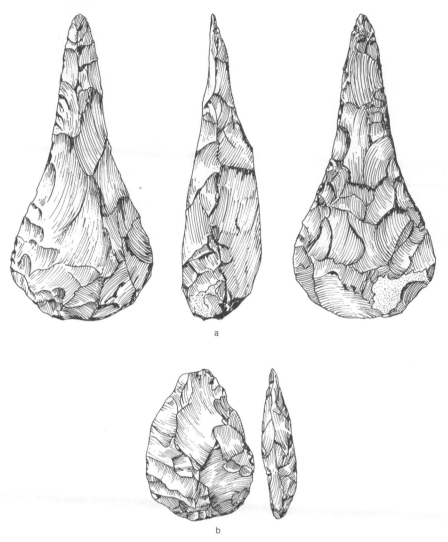

a

b

Fig. 7.6   Two Acheulian hand axes (three views of a, and front and side views of b) from the Thames Valley, England (one-third actual size).

Kalambo Falls, Isimila, Torralba, and Swanscombe.[10] Many later hand axes were finely trimmed by using a piece of hardwood or bone to remove fine skim flakes from the edges of roughly shaped tools. The "cylinder hammer" technique produced sharp tough edges, a refinement from the crude multi-purpose tools of the Lower and early Middle Pleistocene (Figure 7.7).

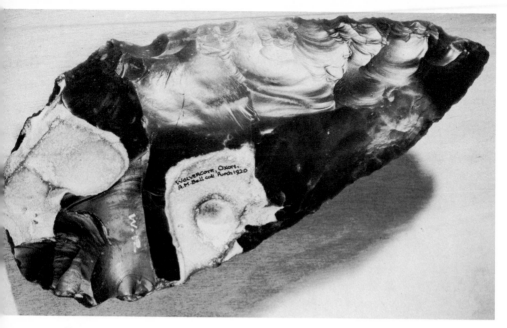

Fig. 7.7   An Acheulian hand axe from Wolvercote, Oxford, England.

During the Upper Pleistocene (later than 70,000 B.C.), man became a more skillful hunter and developed a need for more specialized stone tools. He began to think about shaping cores to produce specific types of flake intended for special purposes such as spearheads. Some people shaped cores to a tortoise shell form so that one flake could be removed from the convex face in a shape ready for immediate use. "Levallois" tortoise cores are widely found in Europe and the Near East where flint was abundant, and were used to produce points and scrapers; the technique was named after a Paris suburb where it was first recognized (Figure 7.8). Other, widely used prepared cores include disc types, where more than one flake was removed from the trimmed core; these have appeared with frequency in Africa, as well as the Near East and Europe, made by Middle Stone Age and Mousterian stoneworkers (ca. 70,000–35,000 B.C.).[11]

Some thirty to forty thousand years ago, man began to make blades with a punch as opposed to the percussion techniques. Many blades were long parallel-sided artifacts produced with great regularity and skill by a punch placed between the hammerstone and the core. Experimental studies indicate that a chest punch could have been used, the core being held between one's feet while resting it on the ground (Figure 7.9). A wooden staff with a hard tip exercised pressure at a specific point on the core's edge, thereby producing a long

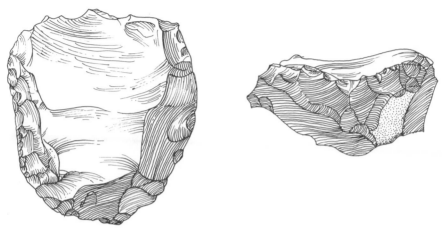

Fig. 7.8 Two views of a Levallois tortoise core from the Thames Valley (one-half actual size).

Fig. 7.9 Two uses of the blade technique, employing a punch.

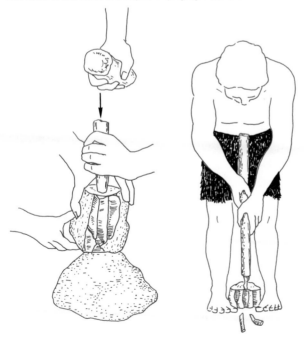

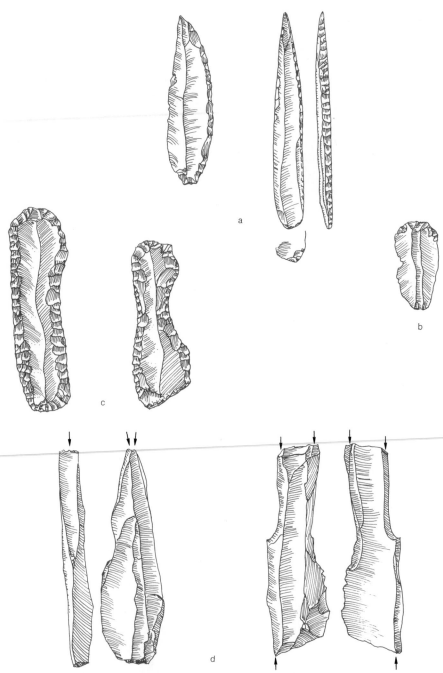

Fig. 7.10   Some major Upper Paleolithic tools (actual size). (a) Backed blades. (b) End-scraper. (c) Sharpened and notched blades. (d) Burins.

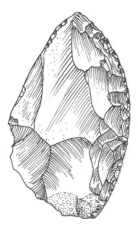

Fig. 7.11 Mousterian side-scraper with step retouch (one-half actual size).

parallel-sided blade. By thrusting his chest down on the punch, the stoneworker could produce a beautiful knife blade of flint or obsidian up to several centimeters long.[12] The knife blades were roughed out and later trimmed to form scrapers, knives, projectile points, and engraving tools—the latter used in Western Europe for carving on antlers and rocks (Figure 7.10). Thus, a much greater variety of specialized tools was made. Developed in the northern parts of Africa, Europe, and southwest Asia, blade tools spread as far as 55° North in European Russia and as far east as Japan and northeastern Siberia; the tools' production was the first stone technology, as far as can be established, to be introduced into the New World and spread there across the Bering Straits.[13]

The secondary trimming of flakes and blades was achieved in numerous ways. In some cases, the blade's side was battered with a stone or a piece of wood to produce fine flake scars to sharpen or blunt the edge. More often, the stoneworker would take a piece of bone or wood, or another stone fragment, and press it against the blade's surface removing short steep step flakes that both sharpened and toughened the working edge (Figure 7.11). Another method was to notch the edge by pressing it against a piece of stone or wood, thereby forming a notched blade or flake that could be used as a hollow scraper for woodworking (Figure 7.12).[14] One way of retouching stone tools was by nibbling the edges with the teeth, a method used by Australian aborigines. But the most famous and most common technique in the later periods of prehistory, especially in the New World, was pressure-flaking. The stoneworker used a small billet of wood or antler and pressed it against the working edge in such a

Fig. 7.12 The stoneworking technique of pressure-flaking.

way that he exerted pressure in a limited direction to remove a fine shallow parallel-sided flake. This formed one of a series of flake scars that eventually covered most of the implement's surfaces (Figure 7.13). The advantage of pressure-flaking is that it facilitates the production of many standardized artifacts with extremely effective working edges in a comparatively short time. In southwest Asia, Europe, and many parts of Africa and south and eastern Asia, small blades were fashioned into minute arrowheads, barbs, and adzes, known as microliths; these

Fig. 7.13 Paleo-Indian pressure-flaked points. (a) Clovis point. (b) Folsom point. (c) Scottsbluff point. (d) Eden point. (Used with permission of McGraw-Hill Book Company and Thames and Hudson Ltd.)

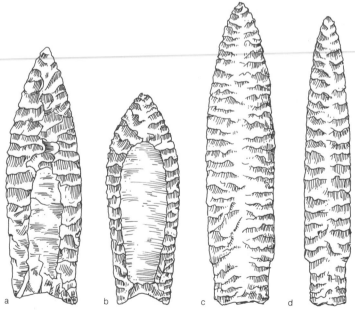

a   b   c   d

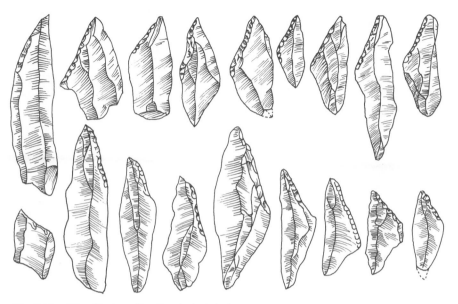

Fig. 7.14   Microliths from Star Carr (actual size).

were often made by a characteristic notching technique (Figure 7.14),[15] and also spread into Arctic America and Australia.

Early farmers began to polish and grind stone to produce implements for use where a sharp working edge was required that would not wear as quickly as one produced by merely flaking the stone (Figure 6.3). The edges were shaped by rough flaking, and then laboriously polished and ground against a coarser rock such as sandstone to produce a sharp tough working edge. Modern experiments have demonstrated the greater effectiveness of polished stone axes in felling forest trees, the toughened working edge taking longer to blunt than that of a flaked axe.[16] Polished stone axes became important in many early peasant societies, especially in Europe, Asia, Mesoamerica (Figure 7.15), and parts of temperate North America. They were not only used in New Guinea, Melanesia, and Polynesia for agriculture, but also in the manufacture of canoes which were essential for fishing and trade.[17]

Early students of Stone Age archaeology were preoccupied with stone tools and their classification. Complicated hierarchies of functional types such as scrapers, arrowheads, points, hand axes, and choppers were carefully erected, and used to study the evolution of prehistoric culture. The French prehistorian Gabriel de Mortillet formulated

Fig. 7.15 Ceremonial Olmec axe head, depicting a god who combines the features of a man and a jaguar. His face is stylized, with flame-like eyes and a drooping mouth.

a sequence of Old Stone Age cultures in 1881,[18] based on evolutionary principles and series of stratified "type fossils." This provincial classificatory scheme had wide acceptance until the 1920s, albeit in modified form, until archaeological research in many other parts of the world showed how parochial de Mortillet's scheme was. The latter was based on finished tools, each cultural stage having certain typological characteristics and type implements associated with it. The various "epochs" of the Stone Age evolved slowly from one into another, the implements changing in each stage. For example, the hand axe or core tool was characteristic of the Acheulian culture in the Lower Paleolithic. In the Middle Paleolithic, there were spearpoints of Mousterian type, which in turn were succeeded by the blade and antler tools of the various stages of the Upper Paleolithic, such as the Aurignacian, Solutrean, and Magdalenian (Table 7.1). The use of "type fossils" continued in the 1920s, and only began to disappear with the development of more sophisticated methods of typological

Table 7.1 Western European Paleolithic Cultures[a]

Paleolithic stages	Cultures	Stages recorded	Approximate dates
UPPER PALEOLITHIC[b] (ca. 35,000– 12,000 years before the present)	Magdalenian	I–VI	15,000 B.C.
	Solutrean	3 to 4 stages recognized	17,000 B.C.
	Later Perigordian	up to 5 variants recognized	25,000 B.C.
	Aurignacian	up to 4 stratified stages known	30,000 B.C.
	Early Perigordian	1 or 2 stages	ca. 35,000– 32,000 B.C.
MIDDLE PALEOLITHIC (ca. 70,000– 35,000)	Mousterian		± 70,000– ca. 35,000 B.C.
LOWER PALEOLITHIC (±2.5–5 million– ca. 70,000)	Acheulian and Clactonian Oldowan (not common in Europe)		ca. 400,000 B.C. ± 2–5 million B.C.

[a] Greatly simplified.
[b] Many archaeologists use another terminology for the Upper Paleolithic of France:

Alternate Terminology	French Terminology
Gravettian	Later Perigordian
Aurignacian	Aurignacian and Perigordian
Chatelperronian	Early Perigordian

The British tend to think of three distinct cultures (alternate terminology) during Aurignacian times, while others think of two contemporary traditions, the Aurignacian dying out as the Perigordian continued.

analysis, as some scholars began to realize that full understanding of stone technology involved the study not only of the finished implements but also of the cores and waste by-products formed by the industrial activity itself.

Their ideas were stimulated by ethnographers who described stone-working techniques among the extinct Tasmanians, the Australian aborigines, American Indians, and South African Bushmen.[19] Gunflint makers were sought out and interviewed; the Brandon flint makers in Suffolk, England, even obligingly made some hand axes.[20] Archaeologists began to experiment with stone themselves; some like the celebrated Monsieur Coutier became expert flint knappers. Dr. Louis Leakey has used hand axes and cleavers to skin antelope, and the French prehistorian François Bordes and his American colleague Don Crabtree have made films documenting the techniques of stone tool manufacture.[21] Because of these and other experiments, stone tool manufacture is understood far better, and the emphasis in analysis has moved toward developing quantitative techniques. Early workers began by calculating the percentages of artifact types in different sites and then comparing the figures. More refined analyses are now fashionable, using cumulative curves[22] and attribute analyses in which different features of stone implements are correlated in clusters with the use of computers.

Other archaeologists have begun to study the edge wear on stone tools as an adjunct to basic typological classification. Soviet archaeologist S. A. Semenov pioneered this field;[23] edge wear is also being studied in Africa as well as the New World.[24] There are several factors that control edge damage. These include the tool's material, the cross section of the edge, and the mode of use together with the material upon which the artifact was used. The unknown variable is normally the material worked by the tool, so it is difficult to say precisely what any artifact's mode of use was. But the study of edge wear does have considerable potential.

With more sophisticated analytical techniques, many classical definitions of Stone Age cultures have been found to be inadequate. Forty years ago, people assumed that many Stone Age cultures, like geological eras, occurred in a standardized form over large parts of the world—the hand-axe culture of Africa, Europe, and Asia, for example, forming one vast monolithic continuum. More detailed studies and analyses, particularly of living floors, have revealed numerous regional variants within this vast distribution of hand-axe sites.[25] These differences are due to variable raw materials, a wide range of differing ecological adaptations, and the infinite variability of human achievement. The study of stone implements is an inquiry into only a part of human behavior, and to draw, as earlier prehistorians did, far-reaching conclusions about the rate of cultural change on the basis of stone tools alone is unwise, for the most durable tools sometimes had lesser significance than other, more perishable aspects of human culture.

WOOD

Nonhuman primates sometimes use sticks to obtain grubs or for other food-getting purposes, so it is logical to assume that since the earliest times man must have used sticks also, and begun to shape them casually into convenient tools. Wooden artifacts form an important part of the material culture of many hunting peoples; occasional, tantalizing glimpses of prehistoric wooden artifacts have come down to us when preservation conditions have been favorable. As mentioned earlier, wooden implements were found on an Acheulian living floor at the Kalambo Falls site in northern Zambia some years ago, in a context that has been radiocarbon dated to about 53,000 years ago.[26] The tools consisted of several pieces of wood, some water worn, including possible digging sticks and a club. In England, a fire-toughened spearpoint was found at the Clacton Channel site which dates to the Mindel-Riss interglacial (*ca.* ?150,000 B.C.) (Figure 7.16). A Middle Paleolithic spear was found at Lehringen, Germany, in association with an elephant skeleton;[27] the creature had been killed by a wooden spear driven into his belly, probably from underneath—a technique sometimes used by the pygmies of the Congo forest. Still another wood artifact was a fragment of a throwing stick which came from the Middle Stone Age site at Florisbad in South Africa.[28] Wooden digging sticks and arrowheads were found at the Gwisho hunting camp in Zambia that dated to *ca.* 2800 B.C.[29] (see Figure 7.17).

Numerous wooden artifacts have been found in dry sites in North America, especially in the Southwest, where Basketmaker settlements have yielded wooden canes, arrow foreshafts with flaked projectiles mounted in them, musical instruments, and other tools.[30] Burials both in the Southwest and in coastal Peru have also yielded wooden artifacts.[31] In addition, the wooden objects found in the Bronze Age graves of Jericho, Ur of the Chaldees, and Tutankhamen's tomb in Egypt are well known.[32]

Normally, however, the use of wood can only be deduced from more durable artifacts. Stone axe blades or arrow barbs are often found, but their wooden hafts have perished; reasonable speculation about the method of mounting the blade or tip is permissible. Thousands of metal axe and adze blades have been found in European

Fig. 7.16 Wooden spearhead from Clacton, England, of the Lower Paleolithic period—76 centimeters (about 30 inches) long.

Bronze Age sites but only a small proportion of them, mostly from northern bogs or the Swiss lake sites, still retain their wooden handles (Figure 6.3).[33] These finds show that the hafting of the bronze heads evolved from a simple binding to the socketed axe in the later Bronze Age.

BONE

Bone as a material for toolmaking probably dates to the very beginnings of human history, but the earliest artifacts apparently consisted of little more than fragments of fractured animal bone used for purposes that could not be fulfilled by wood or stone implements. South African anatomist Raymond Dart has alleged that *Australopithecus* had a fully fledged bone culture and he systematically fractured such bones as jaws and limb bones to form clubs, scrapers, and other artifacts. Dart's[34] "osteodontokeratic"—bone, teeth, horn—culture has been the

Fig. 7.17 A technician demonstrating the use of a Late Stone Age digging stick from Gwisho hot springs, Zambia.

subject of much controversy, and most scholars reject his hypothesis on the grounds that other, natural factors could have caused such systematic bone fractures (Figure 7.18).[35] Formal bone tools are rare on the Olduvai living floors but several bone fragments show systematic utilization as though they were used for scraping skins and similar purposes.[36]

The earliest standardized bone tools date from later prehistoric times. Splinters of bone were sharpened and used as points in many societies, but bone and antler artifacts were especially favored by the Upper Paleolithic Magdalenian peoples of southwestern France some 12,000–14,000 years ago and by Post Glacial hunter-gatherers in Scandinavia.[37] Bone tools dating to as early as 8800 B.C. were found at the Lindenmeis location in Colorado.[38] Many bone tools were either

205

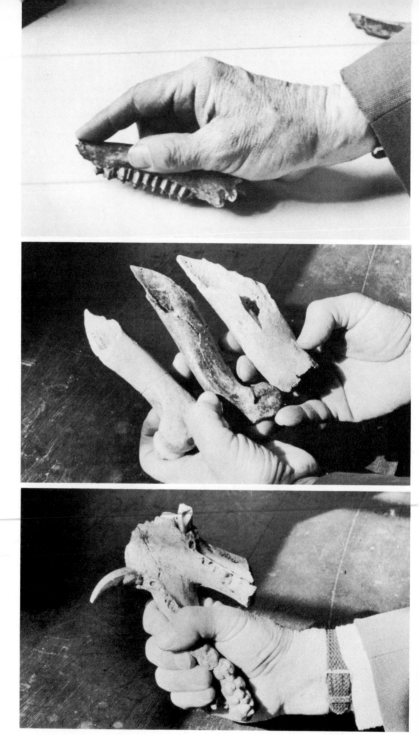

Fig. 7.18   Osteodontokeratic "artifacts" from Makapansgat, South Africa. Raymond Dart believes that
the teeth, limb bones, and tusks of pigs, antelopes, and gazelles were used as tools.

206

ornamental artifacts or formed projectile heads. Splinters from long bones were ground and scraped, as well as being hardened in the fire and polished with beeswax, to produce arrowheads, spearpoints, and other artifacts. Bone was also carved and engraved, especially during Upper Paleolithic times in Western Europe, as was reindeer antler.[39]

Deer antler was an even more important material than bone for some later hunter-gatherers. Fully grown deer antler is particularly suitable for making barbed or simple harpoons and spearpoints. One well known technique involved a beam of reindeer or red deer antler: a series of parallel grooves were made with a suitable stone graver, the resulting splinters being levered from the beam and fashioned into barbed arrowheads or spearheads used for fishing, hunting, and other purposes.[40] Bone and antler were much used in prehistoric times for harpoons for fishing and for conventional hunting. Numerous harpoons are found in Magdalenian sites in Western Europe (Figure 7.19) and also in Eskimo settlements in the Arctic, where they form an invaluable index of cultural development, analogous to that of pottery in the American Southwest.

Fig. 7.19 Magdalenian harpoons from France.

Bone tools do not throw much light on the material culture of peoples to whom the by-products of game animals were not particularly important. In woodland areas where timber is abundant, the tendency is to use wood at the expense of bone and antler. But in the Arctic, bone and ivory are of critical importance, elaborate typological studies have been made of the stylistic and functional changes in such diverse items as the harpoons and the winged ivory counterweights fastened to the butts of harpoons (Figure 7.20). Artifacts include picks made of walrus tusk, and snow shovels and wedges made of ivory and bone—as were drills and domestic utensils. Studying such a range of bone artifacts is complicated by elaborate and variable engraved designs on some artifacts, but H. B. Collins and others have been able to trace the development of the harpoon of the Northern Maritime Eskimo from the elaborate types of the Okvik and Old Bering Sea phases to the simpler forms characteristic of the Punuk phase and modern Eskimo weapons.[41]

With bone tools, functional classification is easier, especially in areas like the Arctic and southern Africa where contemporary ethnographic accounts are available for fruitful analogies. But, as with stone and wooden implements, the study of the by-products is as important as a close scrutiny of the implements, so that one may understand the role of bone technology in the material culture as a whole.

CLAY

Receptacles for carrying food or water must have been in use since the earliest times. Animal skins, bark trays, ostrich eggshells, and wild gourds have also been used in recent times for carrying loads outside the immediate surroundings of a hunting settlement, and must have a long history. Such informal vessels have the advantage of portability and are easy to replace or to improvise with.

The clay pot is one of the most common and imperishable archaeological finds, but has a comparatively recent history. Pottery is almost invariably an attribute of food production, coming into use under conditions where more permanent settlement patterns permit a more elaborate material culture, a more varied diet, and possibly the brewing and storage of fermented gruels or liquids. At one stage it was thought that the advent of pottery coincided with the origins of food production; we now know that agriculture and pastoralism were practiced in the Near East from the eighth millennium B.C., if not earlier, and pottery does not appear until slightly earlier than 6000 B.C. at such early agricultural settlements as Jarmo and Jericho.[42] The inhabitants

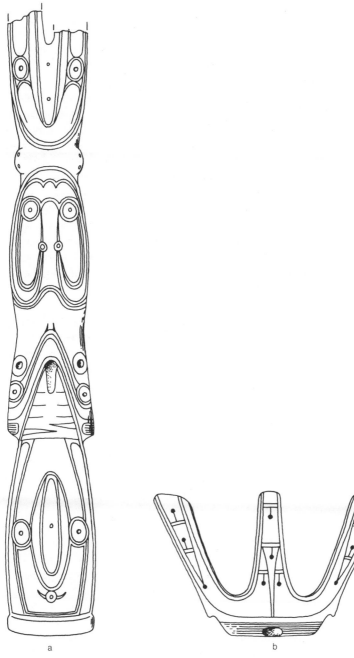

a   b

Fig. 7.20 (a) A socket-piece for a harpoon, Old Bering Sea style, 11.5 centimeters (4.5 inches) long. (b) Eskimo winged ivory object of the Punuk phase, diameter about 12 centimeters (4.7 inches). (Both after Collins, 1937.)

of the Tehuacán Valley in highland Mexico began cultivating crops several thousand years before the first pottery appeared there about 2300 B.C. Pottery was made in Japan by 8000 B.C., occurring in a context which seems to be that of hunters and gatherers.[43]

Serious potsherd archaeology in the New World began with N. C. Nelson in 1914 and A. V. Kidder a few years later, the latter producing refined potsherd stratigraphies from excavations in the rubbish mound at the Pecos Pueblo.[44] Since then, clay vessels have been the basis for innumerable regional surveys of prehistoric culture sequences in the Americas and on the other side of the Atlantic where, however, until recently potsherd archaeology was less well developed. Pottery is normally abundant in those sites where it is found, and is therefore susceptible to statistical treatment, provided that adequate sampling procedures are used in the field. Indeed, detailed analyses of potsherds fill the pages of innumerable archaeological journals; in the past fifty years,[45] an enormous literature has grown up around the subject. The classification of pottery depends on the recognition of numerous attributes found on the potsherds recovered from the ground. Common attributes are shape, dimension, decoration, decorative motif, lip form, and texture (Figure 7.21). The object of such elaborate classifications is to produce a basis for establishing the basic features of a pottery collection, which can then be compared as a whole to collections from other sites close to the original one in space and time.

Functional classification of most prehistoric pottery is an impossible task, unless the anthropological record is sufficiently complete to allow an accurate comparison to be made, or unless the prehistoric vessels are characteristic enough to allow them to be identified as pots of specialized use—perhaps employed for salt-making or some other economic activity. As indicated earlier, many variables act upon the potter and his family. Many African potters, for example, relate the shape of a vessel directly to its function. Bowls are used for cooking vegetables or eating. Pots, with their deeper bodies, are used for storage, water carrying, cooking, or even ritual purposes. Changes in shape may sometimes reflect, indirectly, a change in economic activities, but the economic evidence must be extremely complete before such conclusions can be drawn. At the Isamu Pati Iron Age mound village in Zambia, occupied intermittently for a long period from the seventh to the thirteenth centuries A.D., the uppermost levels contained a much higher proportion of cattle bones than the lower horizons.[46] At the same time, the pottery changed dramatically from a preponderance of simple bag-shaped vessels (Figure 7.22) to an overwhelming dominance of spherical pots with out-turned lips. These

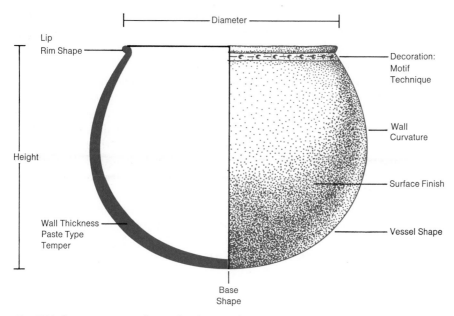

Fig. 7.21 Some common attributes of a clay vessel.

could only have contained liquid, and were tentatively taken to reflect a change in dietary habits, perhaps an increase in milk consumption.

The details of pottery analysis need not concern us here, as they have been well described by Anna Shepard, Frederick Madsen, and others.[47] An amazing amount of information can be conjured from

Fig. 7.22 A Zambian Iron Age pot from the Kalomo culture (one-third actual size).

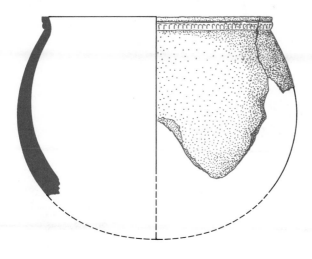

a single potsherd (Figure 7.23). Vessel shapes can be reconstructed from fragmentary potsherds that bear a sufficient portion of the lip profile. Both the techniques and motifs of vessel decoration are important. Decoration often varies according to the pot's shape, and is placed in a regular position on the walls of the vessel depending on its shape. The techniques of adornment are legion: painting, scratching, grooving, incision, stamping, and imprints made with such varied media as the fingernail, cords, or bird bones are all found. Normally, the technique used bears some relationship to the motif, which is restricted to some degree by how it is applied. Variations in technique and motif are reflections of changes both in vessel shape and in fashion, but usually occur gradually.

Another important aspect of ceramic typology is studying the clay's texture and finish, using microscopes and other high-powered instruments as well as elaborate chemical tests. Manufacturing techniques and evidence for trade can sometimes be obtained from detailed

Fig. 7.23 Pots are reconstructed from fragments by a technician through pottery analysis in the laboratory.

studies of clay. In many cases, such deductions can readily be made by linking trace elements in the clay with a particular locality, as in the case of stone axes.[48] Unfortunately, however, these studies only apply where pot-making was a highly developed industry and not merely an activity carried out in a village by people using available resources. There are, however, numerous examples of pottery trading that are reflected in the archaeological record by exotic trade sherds, whose decoration and form lie outside the norm for the industry. Sometimes they can be related to a primary center of pottery distribution in a nearby region.[49] The analysis of potsherds becomes increasingly complex as pottery industries become more elaborate. Particular attention has been paid in the New World and in the Near East to the styles of painted pottery and the techniques for decorating it (Figures 7.24 and 7.25). In some cases, also, a pot that is well made in one locality may be used as a horizon marker for cross-dating in another. The situation becomes much more complex in Classical times when potters, whose names are actually known and whose dates are well established, mass produced vessels that were widely traded in the civilized world and also into neighboring barbarian areas. Such vessels, like Chinese porcelain and glass, can be used to give more accurate dates to sites where no other form of chronology is available.

To assess the significance of ceramic data for cultural studies, not only archaeological evidence but also anthropological sources must be employed, as well as traditions preserved by early explorers of the peoples in the particular area being studied. From the careful use of such accounts it is frequently possible to add valuable information to the basic raw material obtained from the archaeological investigations. Unless ceramic studies lead to a better understanding of the cultural context in which they were found, potsherds form a sterile record of very limited historical value. Morphology and decorative detail are the accepted overriding criteria for establishing the relationship between different ceramic traditions. The actual materials and techniques employed by prehistoric man have only been seriously considered in cases where a particular group of pottery so differs from others in the same archaeological context that it requires detailed analysis.

Potsherds, whether made locally or traded into an area, were originally parts of pots made by inhabitants of a site and used in their daily life. Describing them is an essential part of cataloging prehistoric material culture. The makers were influenced by numerous different factors that are not reflected directly in the archaeological record, such as customs, beliefs, taboos on particular usages, and also the environment and level of economy and technology under which they were made. The closest way to analyzing those factors not reflected

Fig. 7.24 Cylindrical tripod jars from the Early Classic Period at Kaminaljuyú, Guatemala. The decoration is in painted stucco. Left, a Mayoid motif in light green and dark red; right, a Teotihuacánoid motif in buff, light green, and dark red. (After Kidder, Jennings, and Shook, 1946.)

in the record is by analyzing the pottery in its constitutent parts and establishing the norms for each element of these parts, i.e., to produce modes that are the averages of behavior for the potting industry.

Surprisingly little attention has been paid to the social, cultural, and economic settings of pot-making in modern populations. As a result, it is difficult to draw meaningful conclusions, even in areas where the anthropological investigation is comparatively complete. Most descriptions of pottery, both in archaeology and anthropology, deal with techniques and processes of manufacture and with the design elements. They may tell us something about the division of labor in the making of pots, but they reveal little about the potters' status in their own society, their attitudes artistically and in terms of fashion, the economic role of pottery, nor the way in which potters are trained. From the archaeological viewpoint, important factors are the variability found within a potting community and the processes that bring about change in a pottery tradition, as well as stability in it.

Fig. 7.25 Hohokam painted pottery from the southwestern United States. Pots a–c, about 46 centimeters (18 inches) high; remainder, about 14 centimeters (5.5 inches) high. (From Prehistory of North America by Jesse D. Jennings, Fig. 7.9. Copyright © 1968 by McGraw Hill, Inc. Used with permission of McGraw-Hill Book Company.)

METALLURGY: IRON AND COPPER

The study of metallurgy and metal objects found in archaeological sites is limited on one hand by the state of the material's preservation and on the other by our knowledge of primitive metallurgy as a whole.[50] Preservation of metal tools in archaeological horizons is dependent entirely on the soil's acidity. In some circumstances iron tools are preserved perfectly and can be studied in great detail. In other cases, soil acids have completely reduced the iron to a rusty mass that is almost entirely useless. Copper and gold normally survive somewhat better (Figures 7.26 and 7.27). The former was one of the earliest metals smelted by man, for the ore requires a lower melting point than iron does, and is readily shaped into artifacts.

Although native copper was hammered into simple ornaments in the Near East before 5000 B.C., copper smelting and casting only became commonplace in the third millennium, in Pre-Dynastic Egypt and also Sumer.[51] Elaborate castings of stags and cattle were found in the Royal Tombs at Alaca Hüyük, Turkey, dating to the late third millennium B.C. Copperworking was well established in Europe before 2000 B.C., but intensive activity was concentrated in areas where the ore is abundant, namely Spain and Transylvania.[52] In contrast to fine quality stone and iron, copper ores are rare and normally concentrated in well-defined regions. The metal was normally, but not invariably,

Fig. 7.26 *Gold beads from Central Africa were a common trade commodity in later prehistoric times; gold was handled either in the form of dust or finished ornaments.*

alloyed with tin, which is even rarer; bronze produces a harder metal tool and makes casting much easier, so this alloy was more extensively used than the pure metal.

Rich sources of copper ore were rare enough to stimulate constant demand both for the metal and for finished objects. It is thought that the techniques of copperworking spread to temperate Europe through early trading contacts forged with the more sophisticated societies of the Near East.[53] Copper mining and trade formed one foundation of the Luba Kingdom of the Congo in Central Africa whose influence spread far beyond the boundaries of its homeland in the closing centuries of African prehistory.[54] The Indians of Lake Superior in the New World exploited the native copper ore deposits on the southern shores of the lake, and the metal was widely traded and cold-hammered into artifacts in Archaic times (Figure 7.28).[55] During the European Bronze Age, many day-to-day objects, especially spearheads, swords, axes, and brooches were produced and traded (Figure 7.29), but these tools were comparatively valuable, and many people still used stone tools. After the production of iron, bronze was relegated to a more ornamental role but bronze ornaments were still traded.

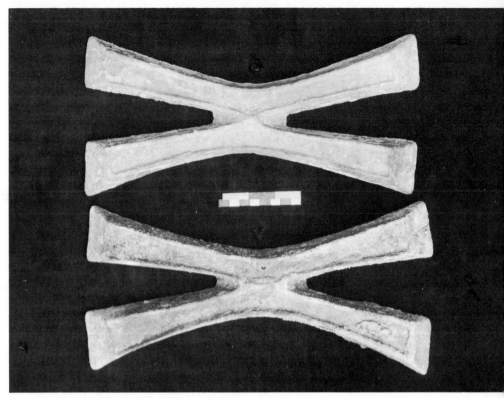

Fig. 7.27 Two copper ingots from a burial in Central Africa. Each weighs about eight pounds (3.6 kilograms), and is of standard form for trading. Presumably they were carried in lots on pairs of sticks wedged into the forks of the ingots. The scale is in centimeters and inches.

Indeed, many prehistoric peoples received copper and iron together, the former being an ornamental or ceremonial metal, the latter more functional.

Much research has been devoted toward the typological classification of copper and bronze artifacts, especially in Europe and the Near East where elaborate classifications of Bronze Age swords, axes, and safety pins dominate the literature. Little is known, however, about the technology of bronzeworking or about how prehistoric man organized the extraction of metal and the production of tools. Analyses of trace elements in the metals, studies of technological variation and of artifact types made by the blacksmiths are as important as the strict archaeological classification of the material. Copper mines were developed in many parts of the Old World and provide a fruitful field for the student of metallurgy to investigate. The most elaborate European workings are in the Tyrol and Salzburg areas,[56] and many

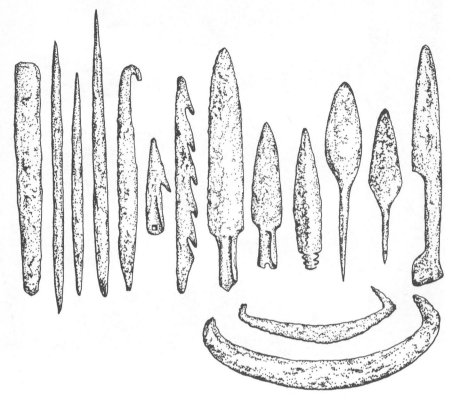

Fig. 7.28   *Copper artifacts from the Archaic period in North America. (After Jesse D. Jennings,* Prehistory of North America, *Fig. 4.8. Copyright © 1968 by McGraw-Hill, Inc. Used with permission of McGraw-Hill Book Company.)*

were oval workings entered by a shaft from above. Fire-setting was used to exploit the lodes of copper ore, and at Mitterburg, Austria, the miners drove shafts into the hillside with bronze picks, extracting the copper by elaborate fire-setting techniques. Many early copper-workings have been found in southern Africa, where the miners followed surface lodes under the ground. Fortunately, the traditional Central African processes of copper smelting have been recorded:[57] the ore was placed in a small furnace with alternating layers of charcoal, and smelted for several hours at high heat maintained with goatskin bellows; the furnace was destroyed after each firing, and the molten copper dripped onto the top of a sand-filled pot buried under the fire.

Iron is a more prosaic metal, lacking the lustrous color of fresh

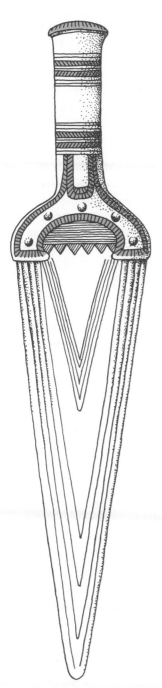

Fig. 7.29 A bronze metal-hilted dagger from Lustenitz, East Germany, second millennium B.C.

copper or bronze, but it yields more effective cutting edges and thus had a far more revolutionary effect on human cultural development than its ornamental relative. Iron tools were first made on a large scale south of the Black Sea in the second millennium B.C., but objects made of the new metal were uncommon for several centuries. The military advantages of the new metal may have been appreciated by the Hittite kings. Even so, iron spread slowly to other areas. Egyptians were working iron by the seventh century B.C., whereas iron artifacts are found in Greece and Crete in eleventh-century B.C. contexts. Iron-working was first established on a large scale in continental Europe in the seventh century B.C. by Hallstatt peoples. In earlier times iron had played a comparatively limited economic role, most artifacts being slavish copies of bronze tools before the metal's full potentials were realized. Weapons like swords and spears were the first artifacts to be modified to the new material, and specialized ironworking tools, such as tongs, and a range of woodworking artifacts began to be used as soon as iron's qualities were recognized.[58]

Iron ore is much more abundant than copper in a natural state, being readily obtained from surface outcrops and bog iron deposits. Once its potentialities had been realized, the metal's use became so widespread that stone and bronze ceased being employed for essential artifacts and were relegated to a subsidiary, often ornamental role. Iron ore was usually obtained from local deposits, and industrial activity tended to be regional until, with the growth of more concentrated settlements, blacksmiths began to congregate in areas of richer outcrops and specialize in iron tool production. The products of Hallstatt peoples of the European Iron Age (sixth century B.C. and later) are particularly famous and brought a rapid acceptance of iron technology by most of prehistoric Europe.

The impact of iron was immense, for it made available abundant supplies of tough cutting tools for agriculture. Charcoal was needed for smelting, and population pressures in temperate Europe meant that man was beginning to clear heavier and more forested soils. With iron tools, essential forest clearance became easier and man achieved even greater mastery over his environment. Ironworking profoundly influenced the development of literate civilizations, which developed more fully the basic technology of early European and Classical smiths. In sub-Saharan Africa, ironworking played an important role in the expansion of Bantu-speaking peoples over much of the subcontinent, but the craft did not reach southern Africa until less than two thousand years ago (Figure 7.30).[59] Some peoples, like the Australian aborigines and the New World Indians, did not discover iron's potential until they came into contact with European explorers.

The functional classification of iron tools is generally a simple matter, for many basic tool types made in prehistoric times are still being used today, either in primitive technology or in our own society. Elaborate typologies of iron artifacts have been formulated, especially in Europe where Hallstatt ironwork has been studied in depth. Iron technology requires many more techniques than the copper or bronze smelting, for high temperatures have to be maintained for many hours to reduce the ore. Prehistoric man normally used an elaborate furnace filled with alternate layers of charcoal and iron ore, which was fired with the use of bellows.[60] The amount of metal produced in a single smelting was comparatively small and the techniques very wasteful in terms of this resulting quantity of iron. Many tools were made by such cumbersome methods, and they were shaped by forging or

Fig. 7.30 An African ironworker using a goatskin bellows.

hammering into simple forms. But tough working edges could only be produced by quenching or tempering the metal or by adding carbon to produce steel.

Surprisingly little is known about the techniques of prehistoric iron technology. Present evidence is inadequate, but Stuart Piggott has postulated that European iron technology remained almost static between 600–700 b.c. and medieval times; tempering and quenching were unknown.[61] Thus, the typological study of iron objects goes much further than merely classifying the artifacts. What was the level of technological achievement? Were the blacksmiths using techniques such as tempering or quenching? Did they strengthen the blades of weapons, and how? Chemical analysis and a careful review of manufacturing techniques can answer most of these questions. Once again, the primary question is not tool types, but the role of the iron artifact in the culture of its makers.

CLASSIFICATION OF ARTIFACTS

Our attitude toward life and our surroundings is one that involves constant classification and sorting of enormous quantities of data. We classify different types of eating utensils: knives, forks, and spoons—each type has a different use and is kept in a separate compartment in the drawer. We group roads according to their surface, finish, and size. A station wagon is classified separately from a truck. In addition to classifying artifacts, life styles, and cultures, we also make choices among them. If we are eating soup, we choose to use a spoon. Some people eat rice with a fork, some use chopsticks, and others have decided that a spoon is more suitable. In this case, there is a variety of available choices, the final decision often dictated by cultural usage rather than functional pragmatism.

Other criteria for choice and classification also exist. Buying an automobile is almost an American national occupation. A visit to a car dealer has all the aura of ritual and gamesmanship associated with religious ceremonies in other societies. Yet the final choice of model and color is dictated by many factors, some of them logical, others less so. The car's size may be affected by the number of people in a family, but one body style may be chosen over another, as may a color, according to the vibrations between the style and color and the family, rather than for any pragmatic reason. The horsepower of the engine and the options added to the car may be partly pragmatic—airconditioning for coolness in a hot climate or a small engine for economy—while others, such as superior upholstery, racing stripes, or revolution tachometers, are added for prestige reasons or simply because custom or tradition has dictated that a car have these accessories. We live in a world of choice and classification, and our sense of choice and classification is constantly being titillated by advertisement, political exhortation, and even education.

CLASSIFICATION IN ARCHAEOLOGY

The archaeologist is an experienced classifier in everyday life and is merely applying to archaeological evidence behavior that, to a considerable extent, is instinctive even though some choices he makes are difficult and are made over a long period of time. In our daily life we habitually use classification as a tool and part of our life style, and like a computer, we should employ it as a servant rather than a master. Sometimes our classifications of good and bad—for example, those based on color of skin or on our definitions of what is moral or immoral, pornographic or acceptable—are made and then adhered to as binding principles of life without ever being questioned or modified, however circumstances may change. Dogmatism and rigidity result from these attitudes and are as dangerous in archaeology as they are in life. In archaeology, classification is a research tool, a means for ordering data, and the objectives of classifications may change according to the problems being investigated.

The archaeologist deals with the fossilized results of human behavior in the form of man's artifacts and in the variations in his tools, so he classifies them as an essential part of archaeological analysis. The classification of archaeological finds proceeds from the simple to the complicated. In the field, the different broad categories of cultural material are classified separately for laboratory analysis. Obviously, animal bones are analyzed in a different manner than stone tools are; glass requires special treatment, as do radiocarbon or pollen samples. This kind of elementary classification is one of convenience for the excavator and laboratory technician, quite divorced from the ultimate goal of discovering the history of the site inhabitants.

An archaeologist's classifications are intended to simplify comparison between tools from different layers or sites. They are designed to help him understand chronological or cultural relationships. Archaeologists erect series of "types" that may cover a bewildering range of artifacts: huts, arrowheads, axes, baskets, fish-spears, shields, bone harpoons, and pots are but a few categories of human remains to have been so classified. F. Hole and R. F. Heizer, in their comprehensive review of archaeology, put the point succinctly: "A *type* is the most frequently used unit of comparison with artifacts. By the word 'type' we mean a particular type of artifact . . . in which several attributes combine or cluster with sufficient frequency or in such distinctive ways that the archaeologist can define and label the artifact and can recognize it when he sees another example."[62] The term "typology" simply refers to the classification of archaeological artifacts. An archaeologist classifies his collection into similar groups, such as projectile points, scrapers, and potsherds, in much the same way as a zoologist would classify a group of bovids as elk, deer, and antelope—and calls each group of artifacts a "type."[63] A list of the types found at a site thus is a description of what has been found there. The value of typology is that it allows the archaeologist to compare what has been found at two different sites or in different levels or areas within a settlement in order to reach some conclusions about the site's nature and its age. The whole process enables comparisons of archaeological types from one site with those from others. Typology, as James Deetz puts it, has as its main aim "classification which permits comparison ... Such comparison allows the archaeologist to align his assemblage with others in time and space."[64] Equivalent assemblages of artifacts from other sites can be equated with those from one's own settlement by typological comparison, using the arbitrary classification used on either site. Sequences of types can be constructed by ordering the assemblages of artifacts through time, and placing collections in relative chronological order.

Using classification as an archaeological tool involves as much research strategy as is needed in the field because of the complex set of variables. A collection of stone tools or potsherds on the laboratory table represents the fossilized remains of human behavior, the products of a prehistoric society and culture which placed a series of complex limitations and technological boundaries around the artifacts. The owners of the tools classified them into different groups for themselves, each one having a definite role in the society. This "functional" classification is the same as ours, i.e., we assign different roles in the eating process to a knife, fork, and spoon. Knives cut meat; the prehistoric arrowhead is employed in the chase. Fish knives are used in eating seafood; one type of missile head is used to hunt deer, another type to shoot birds. Such functional classifications are an intimate part of the culture of the people who made them. The uses of an artifact may be determined not only by convenience and practical considerations, but also by custom or regulation. The light barbed spearheads used by some Australian hunting bands to catch fish are too fragile for dispatching kangaroo; the special barbs enable the impaled fish to be lifted out of the water. Pots are made by women in most African or American Indian societies, which have division of labor by sex; each has formed complicated customs, regulations, or taboos, that, functional considerations apart, categorize clay pots into different types with varying uses and roles in the culture.

Furthermore, each society has its own conception of what a particular artifact should look like. Americans prefer larger cars, Europeans small ones. These preferences reflect not only pragmatic considerations of road width and longer distances in the New World, but also differing attitudes toward travelling and, on the part of many Americans, a preoccupation with prestige and driveway display, manifested in chromium plate and style changes. We think that a car should have a color-coordinated interior and a long hood to look "right." The steering wheel is on the left, hood ornaments are preferred, and a speedometer is required by law. In other words, we know what we want and expect an automobile to look like and possess, even though minor design details change through time—as do the lengths of women's skirts and the widths of ties. So each society, in making its own classifications, has its own "mental template," as Deetz named it,[65] not only of an object's design, but also of its function. Even the Australopithecines must have had a crude conception of what it was to handle a tool and shape it for a definite objective in their quest for food.

The archaeologist seeks to reconstruct cultural history and process and uses artifacts to help do so. Ideally, his classification of the finds should reflect the precise roles and functional classifications made by the members of the society from which they came. Needless to say, such an objective can never be achieved, both because of incomplete preservation and the lack of written records. We have no means of visualizing the complex roles that some artifacts achieved in prehistoric society, nor of establishing the verbal restrictions placed upon their use by the particular society. Although in some cases obvious functional roles like that of an arrowhead for hunting or warfare or of a pot for carrying water can be correctly established in the laboratory, functional classifications are necessarily restricted and limited. For example, we shall consider the case of a Scandinavian flint dagger (Figure 7.31)—a beautifully made, pressure-flaked tool, a copy of the bronze daggers fashionable at that time in Central Europe. This has been classified by generations of archaeologists as a dagger, by implication a weapon of war and defense, worn by Scandinavian farmers who still had no metals and made in a slavish imitation of a more advanced tool. While this instinctive designation may be correct and near the mental template of its owner's expectations and those of his society, we really do not know if our functional classification was correct. Was the dagger actually used in warfare and for personal defense? Was it a weapon or purely an object of prestige for the

Fig. 7.31 A pressure-flaked Scandinavian flint dagger (one-half actual size). (After Oakley.)

owner, perhaps with some religious function? Did it signify the rank of its wearer? What other uses did it have? Did men and boys wear them, but not women? We cannot answer these questions except by using common sense, ethnographic analogy, or various types of multi-variate analyses—sometimes based on the quantification of large samples of major and minor artifact attributes and associations.[66]

The only instances where a classification related to that of the owners themselves can be developed is where the material culture of a modern people shows continuity with the cultural traditions in the archaeological sites excavated. This situation exists in many parts of the world—among the Indians in the southwestern United States and other areas of North America, the hunter-gatherers of the Kalahari Desert in southern Africa, many agricultural peoples of Bantu Africa,

and the Australian aborigines. Even in these cases, functional classification is difficult, for human society is infinitely changeable, and
many complex factors can affect the ways in which people look at
their culture. Each artifact has many attributes or features that identify
it to its owners: these may be the profile or lip of a pot, the decoration
on the shoulder, or a certain shape of handle. While many attributes
may be obvious to us as well, and we may use them to describe
the object, many characteristic features of the artifact in the maker's
eyes may elude us—important to them because of social traditions
or pragmatic functional dictates that never occur to twentieth-century
archaeologists.

How is a category of artifact developed by its owner? What constitutes the variations within one artifact type, and the borders between
one type of clay vessel and another? How does man decide upon
and maintain an artifact "type"? These are questions best considered
by taking an example, succinctly described by James Deetz—the case
of a basket made by the Chumash Indians of Southern California
(Figure 7.32).[67] The mental template of this basket has been reproduced
in tangible form by weaving with plant fibers; the template itself
has been formed in the maker's mind by several factors, the most
important of which is the tremendous reservoir of inherited cultural
experience that the Chumash have acquired, generation by generation,
through the several thousand years they lived in Southern California.
The mental templates of their baskets are almost unconscious, and
relate both to the feeling that such and such a form and a color are
"correct" and traditionally acceptable. But there are more pragmatic

Fig. 7.32   A typical Chumash parching tray.

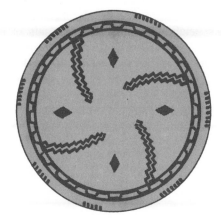

and complex reasons too. This Chumash basket bears a band of decoration around the inside of the rim and rectilinear stepped patterns and diamond patterns on the body of the basket. The basket is flat and circular, with a simple rim. Each feature mentioned above can be described as an attribute of the basket, distinctive ones which combined to give the Chumash receptacle its characteristic form. All these attributes formed part of the mental template of the basket as well. Each has a good reason for its presence, whether traditional, innovative, functional, or imposed by the technology used to make the basket. As Deetz points out, the band of decoration around the rim of the basket is a feature of the decorative tradition of the Chumash and occurs on most of their baskets. Its rich red-brown color, not mentioned before, is caused by the species of reed used in its manufacture—the best material available. The flat round shape is determined by its use, for such trays were used for roasting seeds by tossing them with red embers. While the step-like decoration on the body was dictated by the sewing and weaving techniques of all basketry, the diamond motifs between the steps are unique to this particular basket. The woman who made the diamonds was an innovator; her personal stamp on the basket might be a single occurrence unless it was adopted by others—then over several genera-tions, it might become an integral part of the mental template of the basketry tray made by every woman in the group.

The mental template of this type of Chumash basket and the attributes that comprise the template and the object resulting from it are subject to constant change and are influenced by many factors, some pragmatic, some traditional. The Chumash parching tray is the product of a set of distinctive attributes, and is very similar to others produced by the same mental template of a basket made by other members of the same culture. The baskets of neighboring groups may be basically similar, but the varying attributes of the basket types of the Chumash culture's neighbors reflect different sets of factors and a slightly different mental template. The Chumash example serves as a warning that the variations in human artifacts are both complex and sometimes subtle. Our task as archaeologists is to measure these variations and to establish the causes for and directions of change.[68]

Chapter 8

Ordering and Interpretation

Artifacts and other material remains of the past function within a historical context made up of several variables, the principal of which are time, space, and "culture." Although chronology has been discussed at length in Chapter 2, time and the other variables that affect the finds studied in earlier chapters are explored here.

ARTIFACTS AND TIME

Archaeological contexts have a long history, beginning with Christian Thomsen and the Three-Age System and assuming an increasing importance as early scholars wrestled with problems of stratigraphy, association, and classification. They had a particular concern with ordering of artifacts through time. As early as 1849, Sir John Evans described the *stater* of Philip II of Macedon (Figure 8.1) and its progressive alteration in the hands of British coiners who had little interest in the Greek prototype. Evans noted the degeneration in the design and used it to devise a chronological sequence for the coins.[1]*

Toward the end of the nineteenth century, many scholars, among them the celebrated General Pitt Rivers, began to study the evolution of artifacts. If animals evolved, why not artifacts, they argued. But they soon found that many variables affect changes in tool design, among them improved efficiency, stylistic degeneration, or simply popularity. Pitt Rivers was the first to use the term "typology" to

* See pages 334–336 for notes to Chapter 8.

Fig. 8.1   *The derivation of the British stater from the stater of Philip II of Macedon, as studied by Sir John Evans. The original faces of the Macedonian coin are at the left.*

refer to the employment of methods used in natural science to work out relationships in the form and structure of organisms within an evolutionary sequence, but applied to humanly made objects. Pitt Rivers's typologies were based on another important principle, the fact that certain technological trends are irreversible. To take an obvious example, an aeronautical enthusiast, given the photographs of a series of aircraft types dating from the beginnings of aviation up to the present could place them in approximate order, even if he had no idea of the photographs' dates. But it would be impossible to envisage a typological sequence in which the first aircraft was a supersonic airliner and the latest a Bleriot monoplane of 1912. The modifications needed would be both illogical and incredible.

The humble stone-chopper of the Australopithecines, however, stands in a direct-line relationship to the latest and most sophisticated computers—a platitude, perhaps, although the measurement of technological change over the millennia is a logical step from the study of "types." Early archaeologists like Evans and Pitt Rivers were concerned with a series of objects whose evolutionary direction through time was known; methods of artifact ordering through time were a logical step from their work.

Another scholar, the Egyptologist Sir Flinders Petrie, also contributed much to the early study of artifact chronology. In 1902 he wanted to arrange a large number of Pre-Dynastic tombs from the Nile Valley in chronological order. He eventually placed them in sequence by studying groups of pots found with the skeletons, arranging the vessels in such a way that their stylistic differences reflected gradual change.[2] The handles on the jars were particularly informative, for they changed from functional appendages into more decorative handles, and finally degenerated into a series of painted lines. Flinders Petrie built up a series of pottery stages at Diospolis Parva to which he assigned "sequence dates," the fifty stages running from ST 30 to ST 80. ST 30 was the oldest, for Petrie assumed correctly that the earliest of his wares was not, in fact, the most ancient Egyptian pottery. His sequence dates were subsequently applied over wide areas of the Nile Valley, providing an admirable relative chronology for early Egyptian pottery that remained in use for many years.

Determining the direction of development within a typological series—deciding whether a process of progressive evolution or degeneration is taking place—is not always easy. The flat and flanged axes of the European Bronze Age are obvious examples of tools whose evolution was in the direction of improved efficiency (Figure 8.2). In other cases, the picture can be complicated by deliberate invention, the impact of higher cultures or new economies from outside, and many social restrictions acting on the material culture of its members.

The Law of Association is the key to the study of typological series. Danish archaeologist J. J. A. Worsaae first stated the principle in 1843: the objects accompanying a burial are in most cases things that were in use at the same time.[3] When certain artifact types are found together in grave association after grave association, and when more evolved forms of the same tools are found in association with other burials, the reliability of any typological sequence based on theoretical lines of evolutionary development is enhanced. The basic typology of the European Bronze Age is based almost entirely on the study of grave associations and abandoned hoards of bronze objects buried in times of stress by itinerant merchants or smiths. Many types of hoard are known from European soil—those of traders, religious offerings, votive hoards, and small collections of tools abandoned or lost in a bog or thicket. Merchants' hoards, whose rapid turnover of stock meant a more or less contemporary content, are more useful than religious collections which may contain heirlooms. Grave associations have also been used with success in Peru where a stylistic sequence of spouted pottery bottles found in Moche graves on the north coast confirmed a hypothetical sequence for the Moche pottery style proposed some years earlier.[4] John Rowe and his associates then extended the sequence to other shapes of pottery vessel by means of a complicated series of analyses. Had other types of artifacts been present, such as carvings, textiles, and other tools, they could have proceeded to make typological and chronological studies of a wider range of artifacts until they had a basis for discussing cultural change.

An exemplary case of problem-oriented research into grave-lot chronology using the latest methods of problem-oriented archaeology

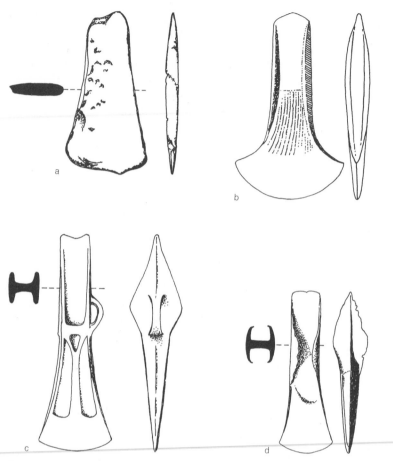

Fig. 8.2   *Bronze axes from Europe (one-third actual size). (a) Flat axe. (b) Axe with step ridges and raised side flanges. (c) Palstave with loop for hafting attachment. (d) Wing-flanged axe.*

has recently been published by British archaeologist Roy Hodson.[5] The Iron Age La Tène cemetery at Munsingen-Rain, Switzerland, lies on a narrow ridge on the Swiss plateau. With lateral space for the cemetery limited, the burials were packed closely in a form of horizontal stratigraphy along the ridge. The earliest, fifth-century B.C. graves are at the north end of the cemetery; the latest, deposited in the second century B.C., in the south. Hodson's study was devoted entirely to distinguishing the successive chronological horizons of the La Tène burials. He did this by laying down some well defined, basic assumptions at the beginning of the project, then carrying out a highly rationalized, formal analysis. Clusters of thoroughly studied artifact attributes were grouped into types, their reliability as chronological horizon indicators assessed carefully, and a refined chronology built up from the groupings. Hodson's study is an example of applying the latest quantitative methods to the study of grave chronology. His refined analyses permitted chronological phases of less than a century to be detectable, admittedly on material that lies at the very end of unwritten history in Europe.

The last fifty years have seen a rapid development in techniques of seriation, or chronological ordering, of artifacts based on Petrie's principles. Recent studies of seriation are based on the assumption that popularity of any artifact or culture trait is a transient thing. The mini skirt becomes the midi or maxi, dancing styles change from month to month, records hit the top forty but are forgotten within a short time, and each year's automobile model, hailed as "brand new," is soon relegated to the secondhand lot. Other traits may have a far longer life. The chopper tools of *Australopithecus* were a major element in early man's tool kit for hundreds of thousands of years. Candles were used for centuries before kerosene and gas lamps came into fashion. But each had its period of maximum relative frequency, or popularity. Figure 8.3 shows how such popularity distributions are made up, using bar graphs plotted against strata or other archaeological associations. Each distribution of artifacts or culture traits plotted has a profile that has been described as resembling a large battleship's hull viewed from the air.

The technique of seriation is based on the assumption that the popularity of pottery types, stone artifact forms, or other culture traits peaks in a "battleship curve," the widest part of the graph representing the period of maximum popularity. Thus, it is argued that sites within a restricted and uniform geographic area showing similar plots of pottery or other artifact types are of broadly the same relative date. A series of sites or surface collections can be linked in a relative chronology, even though, without absolute dates, one cannot tell when they were occupied, provided that the samples of artifacts used are statistically reliable. Edwin Dethlefsen and James Deetz tested the "battleship curve" assumption against some historical data, using a series of Colonial gravestones from a New England cemetery (Figure 8.4).[6] The gravestones, dated by the inscriptions on them, show three decorative styles—death's head, cherub, and urn and willow—that yield an almost perfect series of battleship curves following one upon the other. Seriation is also applied to stylistic change within a single series of artifacts that may in themselves form a "battleship curve";

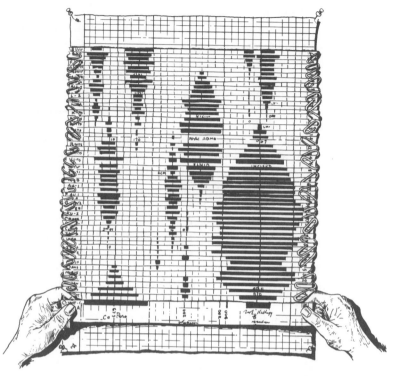

Fig. 8.3   *A seriation graph in the making. Each strip of paper represents a stratigraphic unit, with a bar graph of the pottery counts for each type plotted on it. These are being placed in order to produce the most viable seriated sequence. The strips are placed in position with paper clips on a piece of graph paper pinned to a back board. This diagram is almost complete.*

the same principle, used by Petrie with his Pre-Dynastic jars, applies and a battleship curve results. Deetz and his colleague tested this assumption against dated death's head gravestones (Figure 8.5) and found it valid.

Seriation has become a powerful research tool especially in sites where pottery or other sensitive culture traits are common. A seriated sequence of types or styles from a series of stratified and perhaps dated sites can serve as a yardstick for fitting many surface sites in the same area into a relative sequence. Today's seriators use sophisticated statistical techniques to assess the viability of their conclusions.[7] Sound sampling procedures are obviously essential if seriation is to be used extensively, so it is necessary to establish that the samples collected were selected randomly.[8]

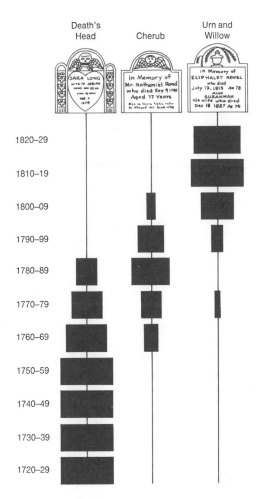

Fig. 8.4   Typical seriated stylistic sequences of New England gravestones from Stoneham, Mass.

ARTIFACTS IN SPACE

Time is a vital dimension of archaeology—so is space. Both represent contexts within which the archaeologist groups his artifacts and other culture traits for purposes of classification and comparison. Space implies distribution and the use of distribution maps.[9] In Chapter 7 we made the basic assumption that most artifacts were used for rational purposes and that characteristic groups of them were used for particular activities like ironworking, butchery, and hunting. Arising from this, similar patterned groups of artifact types may be found on other living sites of the same people, which, although the artifacts

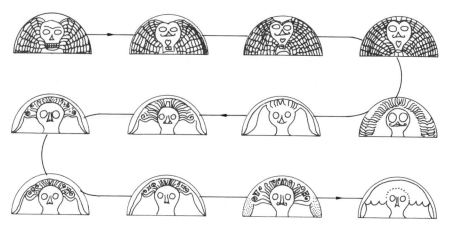

Fig. 8.5   *The seriation of stylistic change within a single New England tombstone motif.*

may differ in detail, obviously resulted from basically similar activities. Provided that the tools from the other sites are in a contemporary context and within a restricted geographic area, archaeologists accept them as being representative of similar "cultures," a term that has come to imply "tribe," although this is a gross generalization. During the earlier millennia of the Stone Age, cultural similarities were widespread—similar hand axes occur in Europe, Africa, and India. But archaeological cultures have proliferated as the man's diversity was accentuated, and considering space in terms of defining cultural boundaries is vital in examining more recent archaeological periods.

ARCHAEOLOGICAL UNITS

Typology is a method of describing the form of one artifact, or a collection of them. The spatial and temporal relationships of the same collections are established by distribution maps on the one hand and by use of absolute and relative chronology on the other. The relationships just mentioned have to be integrated with one another in meaningful terms, a process that is carried out by formulating several archaeological units. The units must be "characteristic, recurrent, and internally consistent, and relate to one another in such a way that one can assume that they are concrete expressions of common social traditions."[10]

Archaeological units[11] are formulated by combining typological data, distributions of sites, and the timespan of the proposed unit. The hardest problem is fixing the dimensions of time and space. The contents of a possible unit formulation have to be defined in terms of earlier and later occupation levels at a site, for the artifacts in this unit may merge into material found in lower or upper levels, whereas earlier or later artifacts may persist or originate in this middle unit. Such problems sometimes must be solved by studying the external relationships of the artifacts to establish their true context. To some extent, of course, the definition of any archaeological unit is arbitrary, and this is acceptable, provided that the archaeologist retains awareness of this and softens the rigidity of his formulations as necessary. The problem, indeed, is the same as that encountered with types.[12]

Many different archaeological units have been utilized by fieldworkers in different parts of the world, for no one has yet succeeded in applying a single terminological scheme to both Old and New World prehistory. Archaeological taxonomy had its origins in the work of Gabriel de Mortillet, J. J. A. Worsaae, and Oscar Montelius in Europe and of Kidder and others in the New World. More attention has been paid to taxonomic problems in North America, where classification became a major preoccupation after the First World War. The present, most commonly used North American terminology had its ancestry in the so-called Midwestern Taxonomic System, and in the work of Willey and Phillips after the Second World War, both attempts to synthesize cultural sequences over large areas of the Americas.[13]

All terminologies of proposed archaeological units are merely suggested labels that try to define groupings of artifacts and other traits in space and time, and represent attempts to reconstruct the prehistoric past by using cultural data. How closely these terminologies relate to actual prehistoric societies is difficult to assess with our present, somewhat crude techniques of reconstructing the past. Much depends on the complexity of the society being reconstructed. Small hunting camps obviously provide an excellent chance to study intact societies, for a single camp was normally occupied by a band of several families enjoying close social relations and a well-knit society. But larger, agricultural settlements offer social situations that are far beyond the capabilities of the archaeologist's spade and interpretative skills because many different factors interact to form a more complex society and there is greater contact between societies which may be trading essential commodities. The archaeologist's *phase, culture, horizon,* and *component* represent, like types, an attempt to organize cultural data as part of the reconstruction of the way prehistoric peoples lived. Archaeological units are also designed to present data in a form suitable for studying prehistoric culture change.

ARCHAEOLOGICAL CULTURES

Definitions of *culture* in anthropology are legion, although everyone agrees that they use it to refer to a distinct human phenomenon. Culture may be qualified to refer to an individual culture such as "Western European," "Middle Class American," or "Nuer." The qualification conjures up certain characteristic attributes or behavior patterns typical of those associated with the cultural label. Each human culture is distinctive, having different features of behavior and artifacts; all cultures are made up of a myriad of tangible and intangible traits, some inherited from earlier generations, others unique to the culture itself—the content of any culture resulting from a complex adaptation to a wider range of ecological, societal, and cultural factors. Human culture is unique because much of its content is transmitted from generation to generation by sophisticated communication systems that permit complex and on-going adaptations to aid man's survival as well as to help rapid cultural change take place—for example, when less advanced societies come into contact with higher civilizations.[14] We would be helpless without our cultural equipment (houses, axes, ploughs, and hunting weapons), and we survive because of our culture. Over twenty-five years ago Clyde Kluckhohn and William Kelly defined culture as "historically created designs for living, explicit and implicit, rational, irrational, and non-rational, which exist at any given time as potential guides for the behavior of man."[15]

Cultures are made up of human behavior and its results, and obviously consist of a complex and constantly interacting set of variables. Human culture is never static, always adjusting to both internal and external change, whether environmental, technological, or societal, and has been referred to as an organized system. Archaeologists study early cultures by working with the tangible remains of human activity, with the artifacts, food residues, and other culture traits discussed in these pages. Archaeological "cultures" are part of terminological usage. They consist of material remains of human culture preserved at a given point in space and time at several sites, in other words "an assemblage of artifacts that recurs repeatedly associated together in dwellings of the same kind and burials of the same rite. The arbitrary peculiarities of all cultural traits are assumed to be concrete expressions of the common social traditions that bind together a culture." Gordon Childe continues, "Artifacts hang together in assemblages, not because they were used in the same age, but also because they were used by the same people, made and executed in accordance with techniques, rites, or styles, prescribed by a social tradition, handed on by precept and example, and modifiable in the same way."[16]

Thus archaeological culture represents a social system, defined in a context of time and space that has come down to us in the form of artifacts and other durable culture traits. Unless we have historical records of the owners, we must give it an arbitrary name—many have proliferated as archaeologists dig up the past. The Acheulian Culture was named after a village in northern France, the Desert Culture after a well-defined geographic area in western North America; others have been called after characteristic tool types. The geographic boundaries of archaeological cultures are arbitrary; so are the artifact classifications of which they consist—it follows that precise definition, not only of the space and time dimensions, but also of content is a prerequisite to comparisons of neighboring cultures or of cultural change in the past. Earlier in this book some methods of analysis and comparison employed to establish the convergence and divergence of different archaeological cultures were reviewed.

CULTURE CHANGE:
INVENTION, MIGRATION, AND DIFFUSION

Although the classification of artifacts and prehistoric cultures in time and space have been discussed, the troublesome subject of cultural change has not. The principal agents of cultural change—invention, migration, and diffusion—are surrounded by a voluminous and often controversial literature,[17] in which people have sought to establish criteria for identifying the three processes in the archaeological record. Some history of archaeological theory is traced in Part 3 of this book, so only a brief consideration of invention, migration, and diffusion as they are recognized in practice is included here.

Invention involves the creation of a new idea, and the transformation of it, in archaeological contexts, into an artifact or other tangible innovation that has survived. Many inventions such as new social institutions, religions, or ideas leave little tangible trace in the archaeological record. An invention implies either the modification of an old idea, or series of ideas, or a completely new concept; it may be made by accident or by intentional research. The atom was split as a result of long and patient investigation with the ultimate objective of fragmentation in view; fire probably accrued to man's armory as a result of accident.[18] Inventions spread, and if they are sufficiently important, spread widely and rapidly. The transistor is in almost universal use because it is an effective advance in electronic technology; ploughs had an equally dramatic effect on agriculture in prehistoric Europe. How inventions spread has been studied extensively by archaeologists and anthropologists. Inventions spread and gain acceptance because of diffusion, a label that refers to the processes by which new ideas or cultural traits spread from one person to another or from one group to another. Diffusion depends greatly on the acceptance of the trait, for new traits must be evaluated in terms of their recipients' needs and social context, with the result that some societies may reject an invention while others accept it avidly. Archaeological finds normally reflect technological development; the acceptance of a diffused cultural trait often depends entirely on its effectiveness as a method of controlling one's environment or raising the standard of living. The advent of ironworking led to more intensive agriculture and the clearance of large woodland areas in Iron Age Europe. Warfare became more effective with iron weapons and a greater factor in political maneuver. Once in use, iron was rapidly recognized as a radical improvement on any other known toolmaking substance, and soon came into common use—a classic example of the rapid diffusion of a significant new invention.[19]

Diffusion is really the spread of ideas that are adopted by other people. It is quite distinct from the spread of commodities or new artifacts from commercial activity, which normally involves the receivers of the new tool using it and not learning to make it themselves. Segmented faience beads were widely traded through Europe from the eastern Mediterranean during the Bronze Age. These objects were made from fine quartz grains cemented together, glazed, and colored blue in XVIIIth Dynasty Egyptian workshops before being brought to Mycene and then onward into barbarian Europe. But the European farmers who received them did not manufacture such beads themselves, obtaining the ornaments by commercial means rather than by diffusion.[20]

One idea may be diffused, or many traits together—perhaps ones that are not even vaguely related. The manufacture of bronze weapons, for example, presupposes that the makers have a knowledge of metallurgy and a conception of the design and use of bronze artifacts. All these traits form a logical pattern of diffused ideas, each dependent on one another. Other traits apparently unconnected may travel together simply because they have been adopted through contact of one group with another; sometimes, indeed, a whole culture may be diffused and adopted by another group, a process described by Alfred Kroeber as "assimilation."[21]

Diffusion often involves the spread of ideas over long distances; these ideas are socially transmitted from individual to individual and ultimately from group to group, but do not involve the actual movement of many people. The process of migration does. A whole society can move, expanding its sphere of influence into new areas. English settlers moved to the North American continent, taking their own culture and society with them; the Spanish occupied Mexico. The results of such population movements were not only a diffusion of ideas, but a mass shift of people, involving social and cultural changes over a wide front. One can argue that these processes are really modified diffusion, but most archaeologists make a distinction between the two.

Distinguishing between independent invention, diffusion, and migration from archaeological evidence is, to put it mildly, a tricky business. Independent invention is usually identified by the isolation of exotic objects in an archaeological component, which cannot have been introduced by trade, and involve a radically new technological concept or idea outside the normal cultural behavior at the time or perhaps related to some earlier experimentation. Many such minor inventions are unusual objects that are made once and then fall into oblivion. A toolmaker may momentarily visualize the possibilities of a new artifact type or raw material, but his product is unacceptable, or he loses interest. Many inventions are believed to have earlier prototypes; clay-lined baskets are thought to have been the forerunners of clay pots in Yugoslavia, Egypt, and other areas, but it is impossible to control the data sufficiently to prove this, and the theories at best are speculative. Examples of revolutionary inventions are legion: bows and arrows, bronze and iron smelting, agriculture, and the domestication of animals are all obvious cases. The evidence for most of these traits is so diffuse that the task of identifying the exact point of invention in time and space is impossible.

Migration and diffusion are equally hard to deduce from archaeological evidence. Both are recognized through evidence of major cultural change within a short period of time at a stratified site. Do these changes result from local invention, diffusion of a cluster of cultural traits that were rapidly adopted, or wholesale population replacement? Distribution maps are a fundamental tool for studying diffusion and migration, but must be used with great care. The plotting of find spots on a map must be carefully controlled, both the exact traits plotted and the chronological range involved. Obviously, a map of a characteristic type of bronze safety pin is useless unless all the pins belong to a narrow segment of prehistoric time, so the artifacts are delineated in space and time.

On the assumption that a trait—let us say swordmaking—was invented in a single village and that the utility of the new design was quickly recognized, we would expect to find the distribution of these swords to expand in a circular pattern on the ground from the village. But time is advancing inexorably, and those settlements at the outer limits of the distribution received the sword at a later date than those in the middle. So the effect is like that of a cone, as the accompanying illustration shows (Figure 8.6). In fact, the cone shape is distorted by many factors like geographical barriers and the degree of acceptance of the new weapon by different peoples. As Deetz urges, the archaeologist in fact looks at distributions in two dimensions, space and time, and the effect is triangular.[22] Under favorable circumstances, with accurate spatial and chronological control, it may be possible to obtain a chronological gradient away from the point of origin. In general terms, for example, food production is accepted as having spread westward into the Mediterranean basin and Europe over a period of several thousand years. The chronological gradient is there, but not nearly as accurate as we would wish.

One of the most famous historical reconstructions based on the diffusion of traits is Leslie Spier's study of the Sun Dance among the Plains Indians of North America.[23] The Sun Dance was a long, important ritual carried out by many North American tribes of the Great Plains and Plateau. Dancers fasted for several days prior to the ceremony. A large center pole was erected in the place designated for the dance and sometimes decorated with buffalo hide. The dancers themselves pierced their backs and chests, making slits through which leather thongs were passed. The thong ends were tied to the center pole or to heavy buffalo skulls that were then dragged after the dancer. Spier divided the Sun Dance into discrete elements such as the decoration of the center pole, use of a specially designated area for the dance, and the amount of fasting beforehand, and he compared individual ceremonies throughout the area where it was in use. He found the most elaborate Sun Dance complex to have been practiced among the Cheyenne Indians and therefore designated the Cheyenne as the originators of the ceremony. Later, archaeologists and ethnographers studied the history of the Cheyenne, and found that they had not moved to the Great Plains until after 1750, a date long after the Sun Dance had been adopted by other Plains groups. Elaboration, then, is not necessarily a good indication of where a culture trait originated.

In cases where such traits as food production have discontinuous distributions, with a development of agriculture in several different areas, the situation is even more controversial. Some say that man is basically an unambitious animal who rarely made drastic discoveries; thus, if he did, the major inventions of mankind were made but once—a school of thought that flourished at the beginning of this century. Scholars like Elliot Smith believed that all civilization derived from the Nile Valley; later discoveries have thrown the basic assumptions of this school of thought into disrepute.

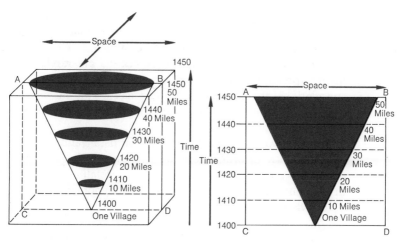

Fig. 8.6 The spread of a culture trait in space and time—the cone effect.

Kroeber, whose knowledge of primitive society was encyclopedic, observed that where two cultures, even those widely separated in time were facing the same problems and were in many degrees similar, they tended to invent new ideas along parallel lines. The similarities may result from environmental patterns or from an ultimate, and often very remote, common origin. Thus, he argued that independent invention of a wide range of significant culture traits is quite possible, and indeed likely. The situation is a flexible one, and requires detailed historical or archaeological information to resolve it, as well as a profound knowledge of the phenomena of culture change. Clearly, speculations based on inadequate archaeological evidence or knowledge of historical connections are doomed to failure.

In archaeological terms, several criteria must be satisfied before we can decide whether a series of artifacts in archaeological sites distant from one another are related to each other in meaningful historical terms. First, the traits or objects must be sufficiently similar in design and typological attributes to indicate that they probably have a common origin. Second, the traits must be shown not to have resulted from convergent evolution. The earlier development of the trait, perhaps as generalized as a form of architecture or a domestic animal, must be carefully traced in both cultures. Third, the distributions of the surviving traits must be carefully studied, as well as those of their antecedents. The only acceptable evidence for the diffusion of a trait, or its transmission by migration, is a series of sites that show, when plotted on a map, a continuous distribution for the trait or perhaps a route along which it spread. Accurate chronological control is essential, with either a time-gradient from either end of the distribution, or one toward the middle. In many cases, the archaeological criteria may be difficult to establish, but the importance of reliable evidence is obvious. These criteria are rarely satisfied, and the interpretation of the prehistoric past suffers as a result. Theoretical speculations are all very well, but may result in completely false conclusions, sometimes supported by uncritical use of scanty archaeological evidence.

How do we distinguish between diffusion and migration in the archaeological record? There are so many different ways in which culture can change. A population may totally replace another by driving out the former inhabitants. This phenomenon is rare, but may occur where two populations live next to each other. Theoretically this may be reflected by a complete change in the material culture, but in practice this is rare. Again, rigid criteria have to be satisfied. Many sites must reflect the same change to demonstrate a population shift over a larger area than one site. Continuous occupation is important, for a vital stage in an evolutionary process may be missing if only a few sites are examined. Every aspect of economic and technological evidence must be examined to avoid a one-sided interpretation of the archaeological record. The more sudden and dramatic the change, the better. Perhaps the most conclusive argument for migration is the abrupt replacement of the existing population by a new racial type; proof of this involves the careful use of data from physical anthropology. A useful indicator of migratory change is evidence of widespread destruction of the earlier occupation by invaders with a completely different material culture. Here again, the evidence must be well-documented and widespread in space. On a wider scope, we must prove that the new culture originated in another area and document the distribution of the new population outside the area of replacement. What migration route did they follow? Were geographical and climatic conditions favorable to the movement of population? In other words, the new and possibly intrusive culture must be viewed within the widest environmental and historical framework to minimize the dangers of unwarranted speculation.

Another common form of migration causing culture change is the movement of a small population group into a new area over which they gain political control, subjecting the indigenous population either by force, economic power, or ritual ability. The native culture may continue to flourish, but the old and new cultures will tend to blend into one, even though rigid social distinctions between the two populations persist. The degree of blending depends on many intangible factors, for each group plays an important role in the total culture and society. Six hundred years ago, the Karanga Kingdom between the Zambezi and the Limpopo rivers in south-central Africa was ruled by a series of hereditary chiefs, who controlled trade and religion, while the indigenous population of farmers mined gold, copper, and other raw materials for long-distance and domestic trade networks. The archaeological record reflects a blending of pottery styles and other culture traits that increased as the kingdom developed after the fifteenth century A.D.[24]

The criteria for studying partial replacement of population are even more rigid than those for total change. Both elements in the blended culture must be isolated by excavation of pure components of each, dating to the time before which the blended culture flourished. In other words, the two populations and their culture must be accurately defined so that the contribution of each to the blended culture can be measured. The intrusive culture must be particularly carefully described, and established as being of nonlocal origin. As with total replacement, the migration route and place of origin must be established. Unless the intrusive culture is well defined, it is only too easy to assign all cultural changes found in a prehistoric sequence to intrusive peoples when in fact they evolved locally without foreign impetus. Another difficulty is demonstrating that the area was settled by foreigners with permanent settlements, and especially to illustrate the gradual process of cultural blending from the archaeological record. To set up these criteria is hard, for the process of blending is often swift and all too few traits are preserved. Accurate dating of individual traits and detailed stratigraphic analyses are essential parts of the criteria, for sometimes one can show that a particular trait, thought to be associated with an intrusive people, in fact appeared at a different time from the others.

Several other migratory situations can occur. Invaders may move into a new area and adopt the material culture of those already there. Families or individuals may move in as settlers, refugees, or perhaps specialist craftsmen; communities of slaves may settle in a new area without having a major impact on the area's native culture.[25] All these processes are subtle ones that are rarely reflected in archaeological sites. The presence of foreign craftsmen might be recognized through a concentration of exotic houses or workshops containing artifacts of foreign design.

Invention, diffusion, and migration are some principal agents of cultural change, and the archaeologist studies them using his observations and analyses as basic raw material. But even if he employs all ecological, archaeological, linguistic, biological, and historical evidence, his data are often inadequate to understand fully the motives of the humans who used the artifacts, structures, and settlements that he has studied. Artifacts result from human behavior, and each one had a definite role in its own culture. Discovering these roles and the part played by innovative traits can at least take us some distance along the route toward understanding the prehistoric past.

SOCIAL ORGANIZATION

The more intangible aspects of human society, including both social organization and religious systems, are difficult to deduce from archaeological data. Many minor differences between prehistoric peoples, those of speech, religion, and social organization, for example, are seldom obvious in the archaeological record—and traditional definitions of culture in archaeology are such that we can only recognize differences when they are detectable in the data obtained through excavation, analysis, and induction. Archaeological cultures are quite different from those of anthropologists and do not necessarily coincide with the boundaries that the owners of a culture may recognize themselves, frontiers imposed by such subtle criteria as hostility, linguistic difference, or diverse religious beliefs.

The starting point for any investigation of social structure must be basically socioeconomic,[26] and consider the minimal economic group—usually the nuclear family—found in the archaeological record. We can hypothesize that the nuclear family occupies a dwelling unit, preserved in the form of floor plans (Figure 8.7) of structures in which

Fig. 8.7   The plan of an Upper Paleolithic hunters' longhouse at Kostenki IV, USSR.

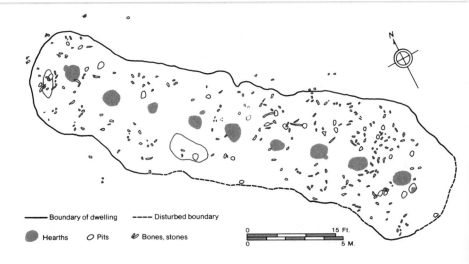

——— Boundary of dwelling   ---- Disturbed boundary

⬤ Hearths   ○ Pits   ✍ Bones, stones

0   15 Ft.
0   5 M.

the minimal unit lived. Unfortunately, so many variables beyond that of the nuclear family, such as kinship, temporary residence, marriage customs, and descent laws, can affect the make-up of a household that the generalization is hardly a reliable one except when a site has a known historical association, or good ethnographic information is available. Lewis Binford was able to make this assumption at the Late Woodland site at Hatchery West, Illinois,[27] and using experimental techniques, he obtained complete data for features at the site and identified the remains of four district communities. The earlier, La Motte, periods of summer and winter occupation were associated with "corporate work areas for the preparation of food."[28] The later, Mississippian settlement was a single-family house, part of a more dispersed settlement pattern than that of the La Motte occupations. The Hatchery West Mississippian occupation was only a segment of a very different community type produced by adaptive changes that resulted in the emergence of the Middle Mississippian in the Midwest.

Binford used artifact patterning as a basis for inferences about prehistoric social systems.[29] Artifact patterning, i.e., combinations of artifacts isolated in excavations, can reflect the activities of individuals or minimal groups of interacting individuals—such as families, lineages, or ironworking teams.[30] The artifact patterning of a whole community is discernible in any single occupation settlement site where structures are present, and the behavioral patterning of an entire society is also best investigated in terms of settlement patterns (Chapter 9).

James Deetz has published a series of papers that deal with artifact patterning in terms of inference of residence and descent in prehistoric societies.[31] His study of the change in patterning of ceramic attributes among the Arikara Indians of the Missouri Valley was based on both archaeological and historical evidence. The excavations revealed three levels of occupation, with the earliest inhabitants of the site having lived in large houses and made fine pots of uniform standard. Such large houses gave shelter to several families who farmed together, the women traditionally doing most of the food production as well as making the pots. But Deetz found that house sizes were smaller in the later levels, and his carefully seriated types from the lower horizon fell into disarray, for styles were much more variable as though the "mental templates" were less rigorously adhered to. The written history of the Arikara provided a possible interpretation, for from the sixteenth century the people had moved more and more frequently as they moved up the Missouri Valley into more open country. As time passed, the men began to act as middlemen in the trade in horses and guns between Plains Indians and white traders, and the role of women changed as farming became less vital. The matrilocal houses of earlier times gave way to mixed settlement, reflected in more variable pottery traditions and other changes in artifact patterning.

Evidence for specialized roles in society and for social stratification is more readily obtained, especially from sites like Harappa or Mohenjodaro where laborers had their own quarters, or from richly furnished graves like those of the Royal Cemetery at Ur or of the Shang chieftains in China.[32] Tattooing, religious objects, or richly ornamented artifacts are all signs of rank, although, unless the associated materials are particularly informative, the amount of additional data obtained is limited.[33]

Much research into social organization in prehistoric societies has derived from studies of relationship and association of artifacts in the field; people are beginning to look at prehistoric social systems within the context of anthropological theory.

RELIGION AND RITUAL

The anonymous cynic who wrote that "religion is the last resort of troubled excavators" hit the nail on the head. Inferences about religion or ritual are bound to be highly speculative, even though artifacts or sites of obvious religious association are found or investigated.[34] Places of worship include Greek and Roman temples, sacred hills, and Mexican religious complexes. The "Venus" figurines of the European Upper Paleolithic have widely been interpreted as fertility symbols,[35] and later human figures have also received similar interpretation[36]—but the ritual associations of such objects are in doubt. The cave art of Altamira and Lascaux has been called a manifestation of "sympathetic hunting magic" by many observers, and new investigative methods are dealing with this interpretation.[37] Burial mutilations, oral tradition, and even astronomy[38] have been used to infer religious activities from archaeological data. Mother Goddess cults, Baal-Astarte rituals, and earth worship are a few of the fascinating manifestations of ritual found in archaeological literature—a delight to the eccentric and entertainment to the serious student of prehistory. Perhaps the best opportunities for the study of prehistoric religion lie in the area of analogy, for example, the case of the red deer antler frontlets from Star Carr.[39]

ANALOGY IN ARCHAEOLOGY

The term "analogy" infers that a relationship exists between two or more phenomena because the same relationship may be observed in similar situations. Our abilities to reason by analogy are often tested in aptitude examinations by such questions as: "A fish is to water as a bird is to: (a) a tree (b) a house (c) air (d) grass seed." Obviously, if we grasp the relationship between fish and water, we will not have any trouble completing the question. Analogy in archaeology involves inferring that the relationship between various traces of human activity in the archaeological record is the same as, or similar to, those of similar phenomena found among modern primitive peoples. Thus, on a very simple level, archaeologists infer that small pointed pieces of stone are projectile points because there are ethnographic records of peoples making small pointed pieces of stone for the tips of lances or arrows. Reasoning by analogy has enjoyed a long history in archaeological interpretation.

In Part 3, the discussion about early unilineal evolutionists shows they considered living tribes to be good examples of successive stages of development in culture history. Each stage of cultural development was correlated with a stage of technology, a form of the family, a kind of religious belief, and a type of political control that could be observed in some living group of people. Because the stages of technology were readily observed in the archaeological record, archaeologists had only to identify the stage of technological development in their sites and then infer by an analogy to some living group the kind of social organization and religion appropriate to the stage, as provided by the unilineal scheme. Thus the Bushmen, Australian aborigines, and Eskimos, who retained a hunting and gathering way of life, manufactured stone tools, and had no knowledge of metallurgy, were considered to be living representatives of Paleolithic peoples. The geologist, W. J. Sollas, made direct analogies between Upper Paleolithic hunters and modern hunting groups.[40] Many early investigators thought that the most primitive Stone Age peoples were matriarchal, had no government, and believed in numerous spirits. The archaeologist who dug a Paleolithic site would interpret his findings by analogy to the unilineal scheme; if he wanted to interpret details not in the scheme, such as the meaning of a particular form of burial, he would turn to the literature of the Bushmen, Australian aborigines, and Eskimos for the "correct" interpretation.

Since the early unilineal schemes have largely been abandoned by Western archaeologists, this kind of simplistic analogy is not often encountered today. In the Soviet Union, however, unilineal schemes of evolution form an important part of Marxist-Leninist doctrine. Even recent Soviet monographs still employ analogy to the "correct stage of development" in order to interpret the social structure of archaeologically known peoples. For example, S. I. Rudenko, writing about the origin of the Eskimo, chides Western scholars for not attempting to describe the development of Eskimo socioeconomic structure. This failure, he writes, "is to be explained by the very simplistic approach of foreign investigators to Eskimo culture, caused by their disregard of the authentic scientific outlook of Marxism-Leninism."[41] Rudenko then postulates that the first stage in Eskimo development was characterized by primitive communism and a matriarchal form of the family. Although he admits that all known Eskimo groups are patrilocal, he sees this as a recent development due to the introduction of trade by American sailors. He then cites the fact that three very important Eskimo spirits are female and leaps to "the conclusion that the Eskimo were matriarchal in the remote past."[42]

Outside of the Soviet Union, the selection and evaluation of appropriate analogies is a far more complicated problem, and one to which several possible solutions have been offered. The thinking of the cultural relativists, especially of the American historical school, is evident in three different approaches to the analogy problem (see Chapters 10 and 11). Cultural relativism proposes that each culture is uniquely composed of ideas and traits and that no two cultures can be compared on any scale due to their uniqueness, a quality that can only be understood subjectively. One relativist approach maintains that all interpretations by means of analogy are assertions that cannot be proved or disproved and for this reason, archaeologists, in order to be scientific, should abandon analogy completely and just report what they find.[43] Thus, finding a small pointed piece of stone is one thing, and calling it a projectile point is quite another. Perhaps, in this particular, archaeologically known culture, such pieces of stone were used as amulets and not as projectile points. Perhaps by calling them projectile points we may be deluded into assuming that they played the same role in the thinking of the people who made them as they do in that of people known from ethnographic literature. Culture relativists would consider this an erroneous conclusion because, since every culture is unique, the role played by an artifact or culture trait in any individual culture must also be unique. It would be a mistake then to infer that a small sharp piece of stone had only utilitarian value to its maker; it may also have been an art object or have had ritual significance. Thus, we cannot use analogy to interpret the ways in which such artifacts are thought of or used in any known culture. The logical conclusion to the relativist view is, of course, that archaeologists cannot interpret anything they find or compare their discoveries to anything else. This train of thought would, if followed to its conclusion, end archaeology completely.

At every step of his investigation, however, the archaeologist must make inferences about human behavior, and these are largely based on analogies with living groups. The very act of distinguishing man-made artifacts from natural objects is guided by analogic reasoning. We know from observations of human behavior that man-made objects are patterned in certain predictable ways. If we did not let this assumption guide our thinking, we could never tell a hand axe from the gravel surrounding it. Abandoning analogy does not seem to be a workable solution to the problem.

The stamp of cultural relativism is also seen in a second approach: archaeological interpretation through analogy should be restricted to the technology of the cultures the archaeologist is studying.[44] Enough small pointed pieces of stone have been found imbedded in the bones of animals and men for us to safely acknowledge that such tools were most likely projectile points. Still, we have no way of knowing if the points were a part of ritual activity as well as the hunt. Similarly, the archaeologist will have information about how houses were constructed and what they looked like, what plants were grown and how these were prepared for food, and perhaps some information on grave furniture. But he will not know what the people who lived at his site *thought* a proper house should look like or which relatives would be invited to help build a house, or what spirits were responsible for making crops grow, or who in the house customarily prepared the food, or whether or not the people believed in life after death. According to the relativist view, the ideas, beliefs, and customs of any people are uniquely their own and not related to either the natural environment or to their hereditary makeup. Although the archaeologist does have direct access to the part of culture that is technological in nature, he has no way of knowing anything about a people's beliefs and ideas; thus, any analogy drawn from the ideas and beliefs of real people is probably incorrect.

This view of archaeological interpretation is implicit or explicit in many archaeological writings. R. H. Thompson, in a widely read article on analogy in archaeology, presents an explicit statement of this viewpoint.[45] He argues that an archaeologist's first inferences *must* be based on technological generalization, and warns that anything beyond this is almost completely subjective and depends on the archaeologist's abilities and competence. But how are we to judge the ability and competence of the archaeologist whose interpretation we are reading? Thompson does not offer a solution to this problem. Under his criteria, archaeologists must then be restricted to talking about technology unless we feel that a particular archaeologist is competent to make other generalizations.

The cultural relativists' third solution is related to that of the historical schools in ethnography as well. European archaeologists typify this as the folk-culture approach;[46] New World scholars call it the direct historical one (see Chapters 10 and 11). On both sides of the Atlantic, this approach uses the simple principle of working from the known to the unknown. In archaeological problems, the known are the living people with written records of their way of life, and the unknown are their ancestors for whom no written records exist. Thus, the archaeologist first excavates historically known sites and determines the inventory of cultural debris in them. Because these are historic sites, the archaeologist freely resorts to written records when he interprets his finds. For example, archaeologists working at the historic site of Fort Raleigh in North Carolina[47] found small lead alloy tokens stamped with the names Hans Schultes and Nuremberg. Normally, without written records, one would not know whether these tokens were pendants, coins, or IOUs for trade with Herr Schultes. The historical records tell us, however, that such lead alloy tokens were used for counting by Elizabethan merchants; the tokens were moved across a board marked off into rows like an abacus. Historians also tell us that Hans Schultes of Nuremberg made lead counters that were very popular on the Continent and in England. The archaeologists who discovered the tokens at Fort Raleigh confidently interpreted their finds as counters, and inferred that the colonists expected to engage in commerce not only with the Indians but with their neighbors and Europe. This kind of archaeological interpretation is often described as "text-aided" research. The only analogy involved is the comparison of the archaeological material to the historical texts of the appropriate period.

Once the historic period is well-known, the archaeologist starts investigating older sites—defined as those most similar to the historic sites in their material content. He continues to draw on the historic material for analogies, but as sites become more and more remote in time from the historical record, his interpretations become less and less reliable. Some archaeologists distinguish between "parahistoric" and "telehistoric" sites to clarify the degree of remoteness of the settlements from historic documents.[48] Parahistoric sites belong to peoples who had no knowledge of writing themselves but who are contemporary with literate societies; their customs or affiliations may be mentioned in the written accounts of their literate neighbors. The Iron Age inhabitants of Maiden Castle in Dorset, although illiterate themselves, were subdued by the legions of a thoroughly literate Roman Empire; the conquerors left numerous traces of their campaigns both in documentary records and in the archaeological record. Sir Mortimer Wheeler's fine description of the investment of Maiden Castle in the first century A.D. owes much to the Roman records of the conquest.[49]

Telehistoric sites are those far removed from written records. Star Carr, the Olsen-Chubbuck bison-kill site in Colorado, and Olduvai Gorge are all "telehistoric," and remote from documentary evidence of the human past. According to proponents of the folk-culture or direct historical approach, confidence in the interpretation of past lifeways diminishes as we move from historic to parahistoric to tele-historic sites; analogies to living peoples become less and less secure the more remote we become from written records. Although this would seem to be a completely sensible attitude, the archaeologist generally infers a great deal about behavior from nondocumentary sources. Is the prehistoric bison kill described by Joe Ben Wheat any less vivid than the siege of Maiden Castle described by Sir Mortimer Wheeler even though the kill site is telehistoric whereas Maiden Castle is parahistoric? Although it would seem that text-aided archaeology is certainly useful, confidence in particular interpretations of past life-ways seems to depend on more than the presence or absence of written documents.

The emphasis on functionalism in ethnology has also influenced archaeological thinking about the use of analogy and behavioral interpretation (see Chapters 10 and 11). Functionalist ethnographies integrate various aspects of culture with each other and with the adaptation of the culture as a whole to its environment. Functionalism stresses the notion that cultures are not made up of a random selection of traits, but that cultural traits are integrated in various ways and influence each other in fairly predictable ways. Functionalist thinking is evident in the way that many archaeologists select analogies from the ethnographic data to help them interpret their archaeological finds. Given that several ethnologically known cultures might provide rea-sonable analogies, functionally oriented scholars suggest selecting those that most closely resemble the archaeological culture in subsis-tence, technology, and environment—and those that are the least removed from the archaeological culture in time and in space. As an example, let us say we wish to find ethnographic analogies for the Desert Culture sites—the term "Desert Culture" refers to the very old (10,000 B.C. to *ca.* 500 B.C.) occupations of the arid western United States.[50] The archaeological remains in these sites—grinding stones, basketry, sandals, cores, choppers, and some stemmed projectile points—indicate a reliance on gathering food and small game hunting; signs of pottery and agriculture are lacking. The desertic environment was harsh but not infertile as food resources. The functionalists would argue that appropriate analogies might be drawn from the literature on the Bushmen of the Kalahari Desert in southern Africa or on the desert Australians, both of whom rely on gathering and small game hunting in desiccated regions. But the Bushmen and the Australian aborigines are far removed from the Desert Culture in both time and space when compared with the modern Pueblo Indians of the southwestern United States who inhabit some of the same territory once occupied by Desert Culture peoples. The Pueblo are, in fact, probable descendents of Desert Culture peoples and might for this reason provide appropriate analogies. But they have adopted pottery, agriculture, and a settled, village way of life, and their entire adaptation to desert conditions differs from that of their desertic, hunter-gatherer ancestors.

We might go so far as to assume that we might use the Bushmen and Australians for analogies regarding subsistence and technology, but for a Desert Culture trait not obviously dependent upon subsistence or technology, the Pueblo Indians might provide the more appropriate analogy. The problem is that we often do not know which aspects of culture are most closely integrated in a functional manner. For example, perhaps we want to know about the role of sandal-making among the Desert Culture people—whether sandals were produced by men, women, individuals on their own initiative, or formal groups working together. If we consider sandal-making an aspect of technology, we might turn to the literature on Bushmen or Australian material culture in which sandals are sometimes featured. Among both the Bushmen and Australian aborigines, domestic tasks are generally done by women working alone or with one or two helpers. The analogy might lead us to argue that sandal-making was regarded as a domestic task by Desert Culture people and carried out by women who usually worked alone. On the other hand, weaving is men's work among the Pueblo Indians and is carried out in special ceremonial rooms; since much ritual performed there today reflects very ancient Pueblo Indian practices, we might be led to infer by analogy that in Desert Culture times, the weaving of sandals was not regarded as a domestic task and was carried out by men. No matter which alternative we chose, we would probably not have much confidence in our choice.

The most recent literature in archaeology reflects a different attitude toward the use of analogy in archaeological interpretation. The selection of possibly appropriate analogies from the ethnological literature is increasingly being seen as only the first step toward interpretation. Once several different analogies are chosen, the implications of each one are explicitly stated and should be tested against the archaeological data.[51] In our example of sandal-making among Desert Culture peoples, the ethnographic literature provided conflicting analogies. If we want to gain confidence in selecting one or the other analogy, we must state explicitly the implications each would have for the archaeological data and then examine the latter again in the light of each implication. If sandal-making were a domestic task done by women working alone, we might expect to find the raw materials for sandal manufacture associated with tools that more surely represent women's work, such as grinding stones for food preparation. We might also expect to find tools for sandal-making (such as awls and scrapers for preparing fiber) among the debris of most domestic sites. We could anticipate that women working alone might introduce more variation into the finished product than might be the case in products made by group effort or by individuals working in the company of other specialists. A contrasting list of implications for the possibility that men produced sandals could also be made, and both sets be tested against the archaeological data.

Devising test implications is not an easy task. For example, to find a measure for the amount of variation in a finished product one would expect under certain production conditions requires sophisticated measurements, various statistical tests, and often experimentation among groups of living people. Archaeologists willing to make the effort entailed in this approach, however, have found that they are able to discover more about ancient societies than was previously thought possible. Reasoning by analogy is, of course, an important part of this process, but it is only one step in the archaeologist's task. Analogies provide the material from which test implications are drawn; they are no longer ends in themselves.

The use of analogy as only one phase of the interpretative process in archaeology is demonstrated by James N. Hill's analysis of room variability at the Broken K Pueblo site in Arizona.[52] Broken K is a ninety-five-room, one-story pueblo that was occupied from A.D. 1150 to 1280. Hill's excavations revealed that three types of rooms were present at Broken K: large rooms containing ventilators, firepits, and mealing bins; small rooms with none of the preceding features; a third type similar to the large room in all respects and with special features like wall niches, benches, and slab-lined floors. Hill turned to the ethnography of living Pueblo peoples and found there were three kinds of rooms in modern pueblos, used for three purposes. Large rooms without special features serve as living areas where most domestic activities are conducted; small rooms are primarily for storage; some large chambers serve as special ceremonial rooms. Hill then hypothesized that the differences among the room types at Broken K reflected the differences in room functions as observed in the modern pueblos. To test this, Hill turned to the ethnographic data for test implications of the functional differences in rooms, and listed sixteen different implications that could be tested against the archaeological data. For example, if the small rooms were used as storage areas, they would be expected to contain large quantities of food remains, such as corncobs, seeds, and pollen; on the other hand, small rooms should not contain evidence of food preparation or eating, such as small grinding stones, animal bones, and charred food remains. If the large rooms were living space, they should contain a greater variety of cultural debris than the small rooms. If the large rooms with special features were ceremonial in function, they should have no evidence of food preparation, although they might contain serving bowls and certainly some traces of ritual paraphernalia. Hill tested each implication of functional difference against the archaeological data and found that most implications were confirmed. Drawing an analogy between Broken K and modern pueblos provided only the clues that then had to be tested by scientific method.

Chapter 9
Settlement Archaeology

The houses of the Latookas are generally bell-shaped, while others are precisely like huge candle-extinguishers, about twenty-five feet high. The roofs are neatly thatched, at an angle of about 75°, resting on a circular wall about four feet high. . . . The town of Tarrangollé is arranged with several entrances, in the shape of low archways through the palisades; these are closed at night by large branches of hooked thorn. . . . The main street is broad, but all others are studiously arranged to admit of only one cow, in single file, between high stockades; thus, in the event of an attack, these narrow passages could be easily defended.[1]*

Sir Samuel Baker was a practical, down-to-earth Victorian explorer who discovered Lake Albert and investigated the sources of the Nile River in the 1860s. He also happened to write good books, and his accounts of the African interior still sparkle with life more than a century after they were penned. Baker wrote of African life, of architecture and village layout, of strange customs, and of diverse ecological adaptations, even though he did not construe them as such. Much of the archaeologist's work is with the reconstruction of prehistoric settlement patterns, environmental adaptations, and house styles—his objective is the piecing together of a far more complete account of the peoples he studies than that of Sir Samuel Baker, which, while vivid, is at best superficial.

Earlier chapters covered observation and organization of archaeological data, including the classification of artifacts, the erection of

* See pages 336–337 for notes to Chapter 9.

257

typologies, and the study of subsistence patterns. Houses, architectural styles, storage pits, temple layouts, and city street plans are recovered from excavations too, and described as individual units in the analysis. But they have a context and a relationship to one another, to the artifacts associated with them, and to the people who built and used them. Settlement archaeology is about these relationships.

Settlement patterns are determined by many factors, by the environment, economic practices, and technological skills.[2] Inherited cultural patterns and established networks of human behavior have an impelling influence on settlement patterns in some societies. The distribution of Bushmen camps in the Kalahari Desert is dependent on the availability of water supplies and vegetable foods; ancient Maya settlements in Mexico were laid out in segments dictated by political and religious organizations. Village layout may be determined by a necessity for protection of stock against animal predators or war parties; other settlements may be strung out at intervals along an important trade artery like a river. Population growth and herd density increases can overload the capacities of hunting grounds or grazing areas, leading to new adaptations and alterations in the settlement pattern. Even the positioning of houses is dictated by a complex variety of social, economic, or even personal factors that may defy explanation, especially when the trowel is the only weapon at the anthropologist's disposal.

Settlement archaeology is part of the analysis of adaptive interactions between man and his environment. Thus, like many problems affecting the study of man, the ones involved are multi-disciplinary and complex. The houses and villages of a prehistoric society, as much as the artifacts found in their settlements and the food residues by their hearths, are part of the settlement pattern. This pattern, by its very nature, involves relationships among people who decided on the basis of practical political, economic, and social considerations to place their houses, settlements, and religious structures where they did. Thus, settlement archaeology offers the archaeologist a chance to examine social organization.

Although archaeologists had long stressed the important role played by environment and technology in determining human settlement patterns, systematic research in this field is a comparatively recent development. Several persuasive scholars had approached settlement archaeology from the archaeological standpoint, making a simplistic assumption that settlement patterns directly resulted from interaction between environment and technology. This form of "ecological determinism" was favored by some scholars but has recently fallen into disfavor as the complex factors involved in settlement archaeology become better understood. Gordon Willey, one of the first to study settlement patterns in the New World, investigated sites in the small Virú Valley in northern coastal Peru soon after World War II.[3] Willey's use of aerial photography to locate the numerous sites in the Valley has already been mentioned. His survey traced the changes in distribution and layout of settlement during several millennia of prehistory during which the Valley's economy changed drastically from early farming times up to the Spanish occupation and beyond. The Virú study related the settlement patterns obtained from aerial photography and ground survey to historical events, economic evidence, and social factors. Willey studied the settlement pattern as a reflection of the environment and the technological level of each Virú population, as well as of its social organization and intercourse, all of which affected the sites built. He realized that the Virú settlement patterns resulted from a far wider spectrum of factors than merely environment and technology, and that the study of broad settlement patterns was not a new approach to archaeology but merely a logical extension of the existing methodology. Settlement archaeology has become a fashionable research objective because of Willey's work and the development of sophisticated computer technology which allows far larger bodies of data to be handled than ever before.

The study of settlement patterns involves examining the degree to which human settlement reflects a society and its technology's adaptation to a specific environment. The social, religious, or political aspects of settlement patterns are also important, and many scholars have not only studied the distribution of sites and the sizes of human settlements, as well as minor details of interior layout within houses or settlements, but also tried to reconstruct the more intangible social factors from archaeological data. This approach involves statistically ordered patterning of artifacts and other culture traits within single settlements, an experimental approach that shows great promise and is dependent to some degree on sophisticated use of computers and other mathematical tools through which the data is not only quantified but also analyzed as to its probable reliability. Bruce Trigger carefully defines three levels of settlement pattern, each of them "shaped by factors that differ in quality or degree from the factors that shape other levels."[4] These are, first, the single building or structure, second, the arrangement of such structures within individual communities, and third, the distribution of communities against the landscape. The object of the exercise is not only to study settlement patterns as a basis for interpreting cultures, but also as an aspect of a total view of prehistoric society. Understanding factors that interact to determine a settlement pattern at any of these three levels of abstraction is vital,

and is best obtained from anthropological analogy with modern societies. At this level of interpretation, opportunities exist for the careful
correlation of archaeological and anthropological data to amplify the
raw facts of prehistory.

STRUCTURES

Studying settlement patterns begins with the individual structure.
Houses, huts, windbreaks, and other dwelling places have infinite
variety, from the crude shelters of grass and sticks used by Stone
Age hunters and Australian bands to the elaborate villas of Imperial
Rome and Henry VIII's palaces. Temples, fortifications, and even cattle
pens are all forms of structures. Domestic architecture may be standardized or differ according to strict modes of variation, some dictated
by society, others by the environment. Both societal and environmental
factors as well as economic pattern are the most vigorous dictates
of single structure design. Rain and snowfall, temperature variation,
wind direction and strength—all play their part in determining house
design. The mammoth hunters of the western Russian plains 20,000
years ago lived in semisubterranean dwellings with roofs made of
skins and mammoth bones, with hearths inside the houses.[5] Theirs
was a treeless and Arctic environment and they made full use of
the by-products of a resource abundantly available to them, the mammoth. On the other hand, the Tonga subsistence farmers of the Middle
Zambezi Valley in Africa live where the midday temperature is often
over 100°F, and the nights are hot most of the year.[6] They spend
more of their lives in the shade of their pole-and-mud huts than
they do in them, the thatched roofs project beyond the walls to form
wide verandas; some houses are built on poles to allow passage of
the wind under them.

Those with nomadic ways of life tend to make less permanent
and elaborate structures. The !Kung Bushmen, hunters of the Kalahari
Desert, Botswana, erect small windbreaks of grass and sticks to protect
themselves from the prevailing winds and provide shade in the hot
months;[7] they abandon the structures when they move camp. The
Plains Indians, on the other hand, have their tepees, which are erected
wherever a new camp is pitched and are sturdy enough to be used
for many years.[8]

Available raw materials are of paramount importance. Mud brick
was used to build the earliest cities in the Mesopotamian delta, for
stone was not available. Ugandan farmers live in huts with thatched
roofs and stake walls, the latter plastered with anthill clay—structures
that survive for many years in the subtropical environment. The clay

renders the walls waterproof and more resistant to the ravages of white ants. Central Eskimos make igloos out of snow blocks simply because it is the most readily available material; their houses are easy to erect and to heat. The Indians of the American Southwest build homes with heavy walls of stone and clay that absorb the sun's heat and insulate the inhabitants against the extreme cold of nighttime. The architectural style of buildings also depends on the builder's skill, the available raw materials, and the general technological level of his society. Some schools, such as the European and suburban American, build houses that, for the most part, have their weight concentrated in the walls, whereas other styles, such as the Far Eastern, support the roof on a framework of beams and use lighter walls that almost hang from the roof.[9]

In many societies, the limited economic opportunities and an even distribution of wealth result in standardized house plans. The building's size or the rooms in it may reflect such groupings as nuclear families. But as societies and cultures become more sophisticated, so do the wealthier citizens, or those of higher rank, who often live in more elaborate structures, and religious activities or specialized trades such as ironworking, trading, or construction work are concentrated in special buildings. In more sophisticated archaeological sites, the recognition of places of worship or special quarters of a town is a fairly easy matter. Many societies had special structures associated with ritual, readily identified in the archaeological record. The temples of the Classic Maya, exemplified by the pyramids at Tikal (Figure 9.1), rise over 60 meters (about 200 feet) above the plaza floors. Small buildings of one to three rooms were placed at the top of the pyramids, which had rectangular plazas enclosed on three or four sides by large mounds. Numerous carved stelae and altar stones were erected in the plazas; the temples surmounting the mounds were elaborately decorated.[10] The ritual purpose of these structures is obvious, but this fact does not reveal the religion, which is a subject in itself. Historical documents and oral traditions may give insights into the character of the religious ceremonies held at a ritual center, but the interpretation of religion from archaeological evidence is a cautious and speculative business.

Some religions, or peoples, do not have conspicuous ritual centers. Many African societies, for example, have monotheistic cults, associated with a supreme being whose priests often have intercessionary powers with him through ancestor cults. Six hundred years ago, the Karanga peoples of what is now Rhodesia worshipped a god named *Mwari*, with whom they communicated through their ancestors. The priests of *Mwari* were the religious and political leaders whose dwell-

Fig. 9.1 *Tikal was the greatest of the Mayan ceremonial centers and was inhabited as early as 600 B.C. This temple dates to the Late Classic, ca. A.D. 700.*

ing places were hilltops upon which they lived in splendid isolation from the common people. Two such hills are the famous archaeological sites of Zimbabwe and Mapungubwe in the Limpopo Valley, where rich finds have been made although much of the *Mwari* cult is lost to the archaeologist.[11] Simple rainmaking ceremonies are often carried out in normal dwellings or in temporary shelters; many African groups build spirit houses—small temporary shelters—that vanish completely from the archaeological record. The extent to which religion can be reconstructed from excavated sites depends greatly on the type of structures with which the religion is associated.

Artisans' houses and trading activities can be identified by concen-

trations of specialized artifacts found in caches in otherwise undistin-
guished structures. Such hoards should include at least a proportion
of unfinished objects to show that toolmakers lived there. In more
elaborate sites, trading and workshop areas and even streets have
been uncovered. At the early town of Hacilar in Turkey, James Mellaart
found potters' workshops in a settlement dating to *ca.* 5435–5250 B.C.[12]
At Thebes and El-Lahun in Egypt, minor craftsmen lived in houses
of two or three rooms within a walled enclosure, depended on others
for their food, and often organized into shifts; information about their
activities has come down to us in records from Deir El-Medina,
Thebes, where generations of workers who built the Pharaohs' tombs
lived for over 400 years.[13] Here again, the historical record allows
amplification of elaborate archaeological finds.

How much can be deduced about social and political institutions
from house architecture? The size and layout of a building may reflect
the family organization of the occupants. Societies may be monoga-
mous or polygamous; in the latter case each wife would have her
own kitchen or even her own hut. Some houses may be occupied
by nuclear families. In South America, long houses are often associated
with lineage organization, and sometimes, with controlled use of
anthropological data, particular house types can be related to particular
forms of family organization. The problem is complex, for even a
standardized house type may have important auxiliary roles, such
as the men's clubs found in parts of Melanesia which are long houses.
The answer to the above question is to consider all the structures
in a site in relation to one another rather than individually, for
relationships between structures are sometimes more significant than
the houses themselves. Within a single house, a family unit can only
be distinguished by interpreting the use of the artifacts found in it,
in order to identify different rooms, especially the individual cooking
areas.

COMMUNITIES

The layout of communities, using the latter word in Murdock's sense
of a "maximal group of persons who normally reside in face-to-face
associations" is a greater problem.[14] Both environment and economy
limit the size and permanence of a settlement because the ability
to gather food and store it is as important as the technology necessary
to transport food and process it into edible units. These two major
factors are vital, for they determine whether a community lives in
one place permanently or must shift camp at regular periods during
the year to subsist. How long Bushmen camps are occupied is limited

by the availability of water, game, and vegetable foods near the site—so the camp moves at regular intervals. Preliterate Uruk and Ubaid city dwellers in Mesopotamia (*ca.* 4000–3000 B.C.) who used irrigation in their agriculture had no need to move regularly to achieve a stable subsistence cycle.[15]

While the permanence of human settlement is affected by subsistence ecology, the layout of a community is greatly determined by social and political factors, particularly by family and kinship considerations. On a large scale, whole sectors of towns may be reserved for religious or ethnic groups living under the protection of the city rulers. Foreign traders may live in their own quarter, reflected in the archaeological record by exotic objects, unusual houses, or many store rooms. Islamic settlements on the East African coast dating to the late first millennium A.D. contain a proportion of indigenous African pottery, reflecting a cosmopolitan population living under the rule of the merchants at Kilwa and elsewhere.[16] Bruce Trigger cites the presence of Huron captives in historic Seneca Indian villages, attested by many Huron-style potsherds among the Seneca materials,[17] but, without the backup of historical records, these might have been described as trade potsherds and their real social significance misinterpreted. The great cities of Harappa and Mohenjodaro flourished in northwestern India during the third and second millennia B.C., with rigid law, standardized architecture, and utilitarian material culture. The agricultural output at Harappa was under municipal control, flour being produced by organized coolie labor housed in rows of identically planned, squalid two-roomed tenements in a special sector of town. The Indus civilization must have been depressingly efficient and slightly terrifying in its standardized heyday.[18] The relationship of one house to another or of a group of structures to other similar groupings forms the basis for interpreting community settlement patterns. Marriage customs may multiply the number of houses associated with one family unit; a father may live in a cattle camp with his sons, and their families occupy houses within his enclosure. Landownership systems may be reflected in community layout, or perhaps the need for mutual protection against animal predators or humans may be uppermost in the minds of the community. The archaeologist looks for systematic and statistically probable associations of settlement attributes—in the same way he looks for artifact attributes—that may indicate a grouping of social units.

A general systems theory context for these types of study only recently developed in archaeology, but it is serving to structure several important settlement pattern studies involving community layouts and the human rationale behind them, as well as the ecological and other factors affecting them. Work along these lines is flourishing in the

New World. George Cowgill and René Millon have begun a detailed mapping and survey project of the urban area of Teotihuacán,[19] the principal ceremonial center and political capital of the Classical Period in the Valley of Mexico. The size and complexity of the site have meant that an enormous amount of information is available from the innumerable features found at Teotihuacán. Records are being built up on all features detected on the surface; the collections of artifacts from 5,000 separate structures are also being correlated with the aid of computer programs. The major aim of the work is a better understanding of Teotihuacán as a going concern throughout its history, and answers to several questions are sought. What were the number and characteristics of the social classes in the city? Were they rigidly delineated? What specialized crafts were practiced and where? What were the social functions and uses of the different artifacts and structures? Discovering the organization, administration, and population grouping of the city is vital, as is the degree of decentralization of ritual, political, and economic power. Also important are the changes taking place through the period *ca* A.D. 100–700 when Teotihuacán flourished.

William Longacre studied the Carter Ranch Pueblo in east-central Arizona[20] in an attempt to determine changes in human adaptation over the period of occupation from A.D. 1050–1200. The Pueblo consists of a U-shaped block of rooms facing a courtyard, containing such facilities as storage areas, cooking places, and religious structures. A mound of trash lies just east of the site and yielded many burials. The Pueblo as a whole is orientated to the east, and the interior features of the site are generally lined up from west to east. There were at least five periods of construction, and the Pueblo expanded for the most part to the east and south. Thousands of potsherds, complete vessels, stone and bone tools, and other cultural remains were found scattered throughout the site. A conventional analysis of the artifacts suggested that Carter Ranch site belongs within the "late Mogollon" culture, but the problem was to "isolate and explain certain organizational features of the sociocultural system as an initial step toward gaining a better understanding of adaptive changes made by the society to environmental stress."[21] Longacre took Lewis Binford's view of culture as a point of basic theoretical assumption, viewing culture as a "systematic whole composed of interrelated subsystems, such as the social system, the technological system, the religious system, etc."[22] Thus, he had to consider the nature and interrelations of the component parts of the sites or cultures under study and relate them to the region's ecology. He was trying to isolate cultural processes and the means by which cultures change or remain stable.

Before analysis of the Pueblo began, the investigators postulated a research design and set up a series of testable hypotheses. Their central argument was that if "there was a residence rule which led to related families living in the same locale through several generations, then ceramic manufacture and decoration would be learned and passed down within the context of this residence unit (assuming female potters). Non-random preference for certain designs might reflect this social pattern."[23] They also assumed that the "patterning of material remains in an archaeological site is the result of the patterned behavior of the members of an extinct society, and that this patterning is potentially informative as to the way the society was organized."[24]

The Carter Ranch study was undertaken to determine more precisely the environmental and cultural changes of the east-central Arizona region between A.D. 1050 and 1200. Palynology has shown small but significant shifts in the vegetational cover to have taken place from A.D. 700 or earlier. The upland regions of east-central Arizona are dotted with prehistoric sites, dating from about A.D. 700–ca. 1000, whose inhabitants cultivated corn. The uplands can now support only marginal agriculture, and cultivation is confined to irrigation in deep stream valleys. Between A.D. 600–1100, the population was scattered in small communities living in hamlets of three to twenty rooms, linked to the arable lands in the many small floodplains in the area. Overpopulation of a particular village led to the creation of a new one on unexploited land. About A.D. 1100 or slightly earlier, a minor shift in rainfall and slight decrease in mean annual temperature is indicated by pollen diagrams, probably resulting in a shorter growing season and making many upland agricultural plots marginal. People began to converge on the deeper valleys where temperatures were higher, and villages coalesced to form larger communities with more than one residence unit. Great kivas, or ceremonial centers, began to appear at a few sites around A.D. 1000–1100, representing an attempt to integrate the separate villages in the single settlement into a more coherent whole by religious or ceremonial means. This process culminated in the development of a few very large pueblos, each composed of many small villages integrated into a single unit. Carter Ranch straddles the period when this was first taking place.

Longacre and his colleagues used relatively sophisticated computer-calculated statistical operations to analyze 175 design elements, and groups of elements were defined, using more than 6,000 potsherds. Then the counts of elements from occupation floors in the rooms examined at Carter Ranch were correlated with each other using a "multiple regression analysis" and an IBM computer. Two distinct clusters of rooms were identified, one at the south end of the pueblo and the second associated with a kiva at the north end. The thirty-four burials found in the midden east of the pueblo were subjected to design element analysis and it was found that the northern burials were related to the northern room cluster, whereas the more southerly skeletons belonged to the southern group. Burials in the center of the midden were mixed as to design distribution, ceremonial grave offerings were common, and the graves contained design elements from both clusters. The investigators considered this area to be a burial ground for high status individuals.

The two clusterings of architectural units were associated with kivas: burial areas and middens. If the hypothesis that women were the potmakers was correct, the distribution of clusters suggested there was postmarital residence near the wife's female relatives, where ceramic decoration was learned and inherited through the residence unit. Stratigraphic analyses of the potsherds in the trash heaps supported the notion of design continuity. The system of postmarital residence suggested by the patterned distributions implied also that rooms, burial rights, and other nonportable objects were inherited within the residence units, probably in the female line. The archaeological evidence, in the form of kivas, associated burial practices, and jointly used storage areas, favored a corporate residential area maintained by a social unit larger than a family. The inference of descent from archaeological data is extremely difficult, but the corporate residence units and pattern of matrilineal inheritance led Longacre to argue that the residence units may represent localized matrilineal descent groups.

The residence unit is a comparatively large social group. But households, the basic economic and landholding unit, are harder to determine from the archaeological record at Carter Ranch Pueblo; they probably consisted of groups of adjoining rooms forming residence areas. Longacre analyzed the rooms' contents thoroughly in an attempt to discover whether the different chambers had specialized functions or were multi-purpose dwelling areas. He studied the correlation of pottery classes with room types and found, for example, that the pottery types found in kivas or other ceremonial structures were less common on household floors. Brown textured jars showed evidence of having been burned over fires—therefore in use as cooking pots—and were very common in rooms with circular floor pits, as were storage pots; perhaps such chambers were used primarily for cooking and storage. The same rooms also contained evidence of general household activities, as though they had one prime purpose, but other uses as well. Painted pottery, on the other hand, showed no signs of smoke, but the bowls, pitchers, and jars made with painted motifs may have served in the preparation and serving of food; they seemed to be associated with rooms having square firepits and mealing bins. Thus, the Carter Ranch rooms appear to have had a multi-functional use, even though different structures had varying primary roles, a pattern found in modern Western Pueblo architecture today. As a result, the household unit is hard to delimit at this site, in contrast to settlements where the rooms' activities tend to be more specialized.

We have dwelt on the Carter Ranch site at some length, for it demonstrates the effectiveness of the new approach to settlement patterns and social organization in archaeology. Carter Ranch dates to a transition period for the farmers of this Southwest region. Statistical analyses have revealed two distinct residence units that have occupied a single site; the farming population has begun to cluster, drawing in from the scattered village units of the previous 500 years. Palynology has given a tentative explanation of the cause—environmental stress—for establishing a settlement pattern of fewer and larger sites. At Carter Ranch, detailed archaeological analysis has documented the first set of adaptive changes that led ultimately toward the cultural system of the modern Western Pueblos.

Analyses of the type used with Carter Ranch and Teotihuacán are in early stages of development, but have tremendous potential in answering some of the obvious and more sophisticated questions posed by settlement patterns. Why were ceremonial Maya pyramids placed where they were in relation to the rest of the settlement around them? Why was the citadel of Harappa in the Indus Valley placed to one side of the city? What effect did political organization have on the growth of specialized communities? Why were fortifications built, and to protect what? What was the importance of trade in the siting of a village or town? Was it built on a particular site to take advantage of raw materials? Was trading the responsibility of some families, or a universal activity? What were the effects of warfare on a high population of animal predators? The archaeologist is only just developing effective methods and techniques to deal with these problems, for, ironically, much basic evidence of use in settlement pattern analysis already appears in scientific monographs or is buried in dusty museum store rooms.

POPULATION DISTRIBUTIONS

The density and distribution of settlements and population are determined to a considerable extent, as is obvious from the Carter Ranch example, by the natural resources of the region under examination and by the economy and technological level of the population. The requirements of hunters differ from those of agriculturalists, and pastoralists have still different preferences—abundant water supplies and grazing grass. In Africa, for example, the distribution of cattle is determined by the zones of tsetse-fly-infested country, for the insect's bite is fatal to stock and dangerous to men; thus, pastoral populations tend to concentrate in fly-free grassland areas where surface water is readily available.[25] The density of agricultural populations is determined by equally critical factors. The shifting cultivator, for example, the Bemba farmer of northern Zambia, has an understanding of his environment that is astonishingly profound; he can rate a plot's fertility and its suitability for one of his crops by examining the vegetational cover and the soil's physical characteristics.[26] Critical factors are the land's staying power, the number of seasons during which it can be cropped with satisfactory results, and the fallow period required before it can be reused. The "climax" vegetation (mature forest cover) indicates fertility, whereas the successive stages of regeneration of vegetation in an abandoned garden show its readiness for recultivation. Farmers and hunters have equally detailed knowledge of their environments, including medicinal and nutritive uses of many plants, and the stock-raiser possesses a remarkable knowledge of the food values of grazing grasses.

The interaction of many complex factors including those mentioned and other, more subtle ones, such as the carrying capacity of agricultural land, provides a backdrop that the student of prehistoric settlement patterns cannot afford to ignore. Archaeologists and geographers have made numerous successful studies of the relationship between prehistoric settlement patterns and environments, such as the Carter Ranch analysis. Sir Cyril Fox made a pioneer study of prehistoric settlement patterns in England on a countrywide scale with his classic monograph *The Personality of Britain*, published in 1932, in which he studied prehistoric population distributions against a base map of the reconstructed vegetation of prehistoric times and modern topography. He distinguished zones of prehistoric population and an increasing penetration of England's highland areas through time. Other studies have skillfully used settlement pattern distributions to correlate, for example, the earliest farming settlement of Central Europe with the loess soils of the plains occupied by Danubian farmers before 3000 B.C. Work on an even larger scale has been carried out in sub-Saharan Africa from which Desmond Clark and his colleagues have produced an *Atlas of African Prehistory;* this plots the distribution of most known Stone Age sites of all periods on translucent sheets that can be laid on base maps of ancient and modern climate, vegetation, and other critical factors. Distribution studies of this magnitude reflect to some degree the distribution of archaeological research rather than of prehistoric settlement patterns, but the ultimate objective is to produce a basic source in which distributional information is available.

Large-scale studies of geographical settlement patterns depend on thorough site survey and are most effective within narrowly defined regions. Several factors may affect the changing settlement patterns of an area. Apart from natural factors like water supplies or game population, a region may change from being self-sufficient to becoming dependent on trade for such basic raw materials as iron ore or ornamental metals. Some inhospitable regions may support flourishing towns purely on the basis of raw materials, and the population relies on trade to exchange its precious materials for food. Trade increased in importance in Central Africa, for instance, as soon as there was a substantial and regular demand for raw materials above the intercommunity level. Traders from India came with the monsoon winds to visit the East Coast of Africa in search of the soft ivory of the African elephant. A regular trade in tusks and metals resulted in exploitation of the far interior, with important trading and religious centers emerging as new centers of population.

Political organization may also affect population distribution, as will warfare. Sotho Chief Mosheshwe of what is now Lesotho in southern Africa saved his people from destruction in the mid-nineteenth century by occupying a fortified hilltop named Taba Bosiu.[27] In preceding decades the Sotho had lived on fertile lowlands west of the Lesotho Mountains. A study of their prehistoric settlement pattern would reflect the major shift in population from the lowlands to the bases and tops of fortified hills like Taba Bosiu because of warfare and political factors. A powerful centralized political organization like that of the Romans is reflected in various types of settlement which, under favorable circumstances, can be related to one another on the basis of architectural style, size, and distribution of population. The size and distribution of Mayan ceremonial centers is an example of archaeological evidence that shows, by the placing of minor ceremonial centers, a relationship between subordinate religious sites and the major one in the center.

SUMMARY

Ecology, warfare, and religion all influence settlement patterns, whether architecture, village or town layout, or wider population distributions. Buildings and town plans are more susceptible to the influence of minor social conventions and whims than the major zone distributions are. A settlement pattern results from a people's adjustment to factors of varying importance that interact with each other.

The three levels of studying settlement patterns—the individual house or structure, the community or settlement as a whole, and the distribution of population within a large zone—yield different data about prehistoric society because of their relationships with each other and the environment. Houses contain information on specialized activities, household units, and family organization. Residence units or communities can be analyzed for data on warfare and trade, religious practices, and even lineage organization and political authority. Larger units of human population add data on the exploitation of natural resources, commerce, and major political groupings. Archaeology is becoming increasingly preoccupied with research projects oriented toward these problems as being essential adjuncts to the analysis of artifacts and occupation residue. The systems approach and new quantitative methods offer exciting prospects for future studies in this field.

Part Three

Frameworks for the Past

The Four Stages of Public Opinion

I (Just after publication)

The Novelty is absurd and subversive of Religion & Morality. The propounder both fool & knave.

II (Twenty years later)

The Novelty is absolute Truth and will yield a full & satisfactory explanation of things in general—The propounder man of sublime genius & perfect virtue.

III (Forty years later)

The Novelty won't explain things in general after all and therefore is a wretched failure. The propounder a very ordinary person advertised by a clique.

IV (A century later)

The Novelty a mixture of truth & error. Explains as much as could reasonably be expected.

The propounder worthy of all honour in spite of his share of human frailties, as one who has added to the permanent possessions of science.

Notes by Thomas Huxley, 1873

Chapter 10
Intellectual Frameworks:
Mercati to Durkheim
(with Linda Cordell)

The archaeological record gives us a broad and tantalizing view of man's diverse adaptations and cultural evolution through the dimensions of time and space. Looking at our long ancestry, we realize that the artifacts of the first toolmaking Australopithecines are the ultimate ancestors of our complex twentieth-century machine tools and computers. We can appreciate the vast amount of time required for man to develop more specialized tool kits, articulate speech, social structure, religious beliefs, and all the other attributes of self-awareness that are distinctively human. More than ever before, in a world of jetliners and instant communication, our knowledge of the unwritten past and of the varied world community combine to reveal the sheer diversity of human experience and life-styles from one end of the world to the other.

This diversity has accelerated in recent millennia. Half a million years ago stone hand axes or chopping tools were in daily use throughout the world of *Homo erectus*. In 1000 B.C., bronze was used by many European societies, iron tools were in use in the Near East, sub-Saharan Africa had no metallurgy and little agriculture, the very early Olmec Civilization was developing in Mesoamerica, and Polynesia was as yet uninhabited by man. Human cultural diversity has mushroomed since then.

The sweeping perspectives of prehistoric time are indeed awesome, and the methods employed to reveal them are well-developed, complex, and widespread. More and more details of man's cultural history are recorded each year, and the pace of discovery threatens to over-

275

whelm us as a "knowledge explosion" occurs in archaeology. Modern cities are constantly expanding as populations increase and man's rapacious demands for living space seek to be satisfied. Housing developments, freeways, dams, pipelines, and other urban phenomena bury the past or destroy it with the blade of a bulldozer. Our knowledge of the past will never be "complete," and if it ever did become so, this objective of archaeology would be insufficient. The facts gleaned from site surveys, excavations, and artifact analyses, and carefully deposited in the pages of learned journals or monographs are meaningless unless they are interpreted, questioned, and tested against general or specific research hypotheses; these, in themselves, form part of the problem-oriented research strategy formulated when site survey or excavation began.

Our discussion so far has been with basic information, the archives of the past that end up in museum storerooms or in excavation notebooks. Regrettably, many archaeological reports go little further than listing facts and cautiously interpreting the finds. Yet these facts should be related to research objectives and conscious hypotheses, for archaeology, as part of anthropology, asks questions about societies and cultures—how they operate, how they change, and what general rules they follow. Archaeologists have an obligation to interpret their data to explain cultural processes and the large- and small-scale changes they detect in the prehistoric past. Indeed, from the beginnings of archaeology, scholars have been trying to reconstruct human history with descriptive models of the past; in this chapter we shall examine more recent attempts to do so. Julian Steward and Frank Setzler posed the question as long ago as 1938: "Shall we hope that the future Darwin of anthropology will interpret the great historical scheme we've erected?"[1]*

RATIONALISM, SCEPTICISM, AND A
NATURALISTIC PHILOSOPHY OF EVENTS

Archaeologists have so far been primarily concerned with "structure"—with the description of forms, be these hand axes, pots, or villages, as they occur in time and space. We have built, like pre-Darwinian biologists, elaborate classifications of prehistoric artifacts based on structural similarities. What then, we may legitimately ask, is the relationship between the different classes of artifacts laboriously erected and actual human behavior? What can we learn of human motives and cultural process? To phrase the question in another way,

* See pages 337–338 for notes to Chapter 10.

we know that human culture has changed in the past three million years, a dazzling palimpsest of stone artifacts, cave art, agricultural societies, and urban complexes—but can we explain how and why this change took place? Archaeologists have addressed themselves to this problem in many different ways and have viewed their role in answering the question in an equally diverse manner.

The interpretation of archaeological data of any kind depended greatly on the notions of the world held by its discoverer. Thus, the medieval peasants who discovered Paleolithic hand axes in the great river valleys of France and England interpreted their finds in the context of their folk beliefs; the hand axes became celestial thunderbolts with magical properties, a reflection of the parochial perspectives of the average peasant and writer of the time. The French farmers knew nothing of the tremendous diversity of mankind that existed beyond the frontiers of their fields and markets, and were shackled by the biblical story of the Creation. Man had fallen; since the Fall in the Garden of Eden when the world was perfect, things had been in a state of decline. Nothing in their world had prepared them to accept the idea that the thunderbolts they cherished were made by men who did not even possess the rather unsophisticated technology of medieval Europe.

The horizons of the European world began to widen very gradually in the eleventh and twelfth centuries. The Crusaders and ambitious travellers, such as Marco Polo (1254–1324), returned with exciting tales of the wonders of the great civilizations of China and the peoples of the Near East. Trade routes, closed since the advent of the Dark Ages, were reopened, with important consequences for the intellectual climate of the later Middle Ages. European scholars were gradually exposed to Muslim scholarship, which had retained an interest in the Classical writers of Greece and Rome, and developed the disciplines of mathematics, geography, and natural sciences far beyond the limited achievements of the Classical civilizations. Trade with the East also stimulated the development of more urban centers in Europe, and an increasingly wealthy urban middle class of merchants emerged. These families found ways to increase their wealth and power outside the rigid frameworks of both the church and the agrarian feudal aristocracy. Intellectually they were far more sceptical than their predecessors, with greater secular concerns and more pragmatic explanations for the past. Thus scholars of the later Middle Ages, such as the Italian Michael Mercati (1541–1593), proposed that the "thunderbolts" found by the European peasants were artifacts produced by men before they knew how to make tools out of iron.[2] The objects themselves, thunderbolts or artifacts, had not changed; they were interpreted differently because man's ideas about his world had changed. Celestial magic was not popular with sceptical fourteenth-century naturalists, although Mercati did not have much evidence to support his interpretations. He did have the writings of Greeks and Romans who speculated about stages in the development of weapons from nails and teeth to stone and wood, to bronze, and finally to iron. A collection of stone artifacts made by American Indians and Asian natives had been brought back to Rome by some explorers and submitted to him for examination. His evaluation of the archaeological finds from European gravels was based on simple analogy rather than supernatural belief.

Today, of course, we have considerably more evidence about the past, much of it based on careful stratigraphic excavations, a battery of dating techniques, and sophisticated laboratory analyses. Yet, perhaps one reason why archaeologists have accumulated evidence in favor of Mercati's interpretation of archaeological finds rather than celestial magic is that we, as scholars, are heirs of the sceptical intellectual climate that sprang up in part from a new awareness of the tremendous diversity of human experience.

Surrounded as we are by the technological accomplishments of twentieth-century technology, it is difficult for us to realize how slowly modern scientific inquiry evolved, and how recently the basic principles of scientific research were developed. The social sciences in particular have been brain children of very recent times, and the archaeologist as a student of human behavior in the past leans heavily upon the research of scholars concerned with the ways in which people behave. Prehistoric research developed hand in hand with the newly fledged field of anthropology, both of them given great impetus by *The Origin of Species*, the acceptance of the Antiquity of Man, and Victorian imperialism, which revealed with even greater clarity the brilliant diversity of man.

Anthropology itself developed out of the radical political and social climate of eighteenth-century Europe. Enlightened writers like John Locke, Thomas Hobbes, Voltaire, and Jean Jacques Rousseau were interested in how they could improve their own society and philosophized about the rules and laws necessary to perpetuate a sophisticated civilization. The naturalistic interpretation of stone artifacts resulted in part from the influence of Newton and Locke who viewed the universe as running like a clock rather than through the hand of God. Did man need despotic government or a minimum of social control? What was the basic nature of man? Man "in a state of nature" did not have the benefits of eighteenth-century European government and civilization. Such peoples' exotic customs and strange appearance were being immortalized by Captain James Cook in the South Seas and Australia and by early travellers in South Africa and North America (see Figures 10.1 and 10.2).[3] The romantics of eighteenth-century Europe depicted contemporary savages in book and lithograph as dancing in Eden-like innocence among pastoral groves. Rousseau particularly glorified the life of "savages," insisting that men would be much better off without the institutions, rules, and repressions of civilization. Hobbes, on the other hand, depicted man in a state of nature as being in constant strife and turmoil; he felt that an absolutist state was necessary for men to live together peacefully. In any case, the eighteenth-century philosophers were aware of mankind's diversity, although their knowledge of other peoples was cloaked in fantasy. The same scholars also questioned their own institutions and held the working assumption that man, thinking rationally, could humanize his government. People like Locke and Anne Robert Turgot (1727–1781) were sceptical of mystical interpretations of the past, and conceived of human society in rational terms. Apparently they were largely motivated by a revulsion against the clerical establishment; they argued both explicitly and implicitly against the church and its interpretation of the world and its history.

By the eighteenth century, European natural science had developed to such an extent that people became aware that the results of science might be applied to the betterment of human life. The explorations of Cook and others had led to some knowledge of primitive societies flourishing at various levels of cultural development. Therefore, a theory of human progress was necessary if men were to improve their lot by formulating better social institutions, and to explain how they had achieved a diversity of life-style far removed from that of the South Sea Islanders.

DEGENERATION AND PROGRESS

Enlightenment thinkers viewed human history in terms of progress, but their ideas were challenged in the closing decades of the eighteenth and the first half of the nineteenth centuries. These were turbulent years, when the French Revolution and campaigns of Napoleon shattered eighteenth-century illusions that man's rational behavior led to improvements in the world. The potency of rational thought was rejected by war-torn and disheartened European intellectuals who doubted the notion of human progress. Scholars like Immanuel Kant (1724–1804), Johann von Herder (1744–1803), and William Godwin (1756–1836) retreated from rationalism in literature, history, and art toward philosophical idealism and romanticism. For the Romantic

Fig. 10.1 A family of Khoi-Khoi pastoralists from the Cape of Good Hope.

writers, the present was not of particular concern; they retreated into an imaginary past when conditions were better and man's behavior was clothed in glory. During the Napoleonic Wars and the uncertainties caused by the rise of a European industrial society, ideas of

Fig. 10.2 An Australian aborigine with his lightweight hunting kit.

progress and evolution dropped out of sight. Philosophers sought "understanding" through emotional introspection, a theme well illustrated by the emotional romantic poetry of early nineteenth-century Europe. This was the philosophical climate into which Darwinism was born, one of considerable introspection, scientific scepticism, and restless scientific inquiry.

The concept of human progress almost disappeared during the Romantic period only to resurge in popularity in the mid-nineteenth century. Orthodox religious interpretations of the past were widely accepted during the 1820s and 1830s, and the decline of man since Adam's Fall was a logical extension of Romantic philosophy. But the Industrial Revolution and the explosion of scientific knowledge in many fields, among them geology and paleontology, gave rise to a renewed scepticism about religious dogma and simplistic explanations of man's early history. This time, there was a difference—the sceptics backed their arguments with scientific fact. They proposed a rational and naturalistic interpretation of events and human affairs in which the concept of progress played an important part. The increased interest in human progress may also have resulted from a general decline in utilitarianism and religious thought.[4] People feared the threat of intellectual and moral anarchy, resulting from the decline in theological leadership.

The concept of progress, and indeed evolutionism itself, may have been a response to this intellectual and moral atmosphere. We have already traced the events that led up to the acceptance of the Antiquity of Man in Chapter 1—they were part of a long and sustained battle between defenders of the church and antievolutionists on the one hand, and the evolutionists, geologists, and archaeologists on the other. But the acceptance of the Antiquity of Man allowed a long time-scale for the diverse panorama of the prehistoric past, which, with Darwinism, led to modern anthropology incorporating both notions of progress and decline in human history. Whereas eighteenth-century cultural historians such as Jacques Turgot and Marquis de Condorcet had reconstructed human history using hypotheses that emphasized man's progress through successively higher stages of development, C. J. Thomsen, Boucher de Perthes, and other archaeologists, as well as the geologists Sir Charles Lyell and William Smith, were confirming notions of human progress in the past. Other scholars such as J. C. Prichard (1786–1848) and Gustav Klemm (1802–1867) were describing many primitive societies; the latter even proposed a three-stage scheme of human cultural development: savagery, tameness, and freedom.[5]

But the early classical works in anthropology were written after *The Origin of Species* had appeared, many dominated by the idea of evolution, even though some authors denied that they had been influenced by Charles Darwin.

EVOLUTION

Steward and Setzler's remark about a future Darwin is apt, for the natural sciences were revolutionized by his coming. The eighteenth-century Swedish taxonomist Carl Linnaeus (1707–1778) started it all by creating a system of ordered relationships for all living creatures in a great hierarchical scheme. His classificatory scheme covered the whole range of life, providing the framework necessary to science before it could advance toward the possibility of physical relationships and multiple creations. Linnaeus published his great *Systema Naturae* in 1735 (a century before Darwin returned from the *Beagle* expedition), basing his classifications on the structural similarities and differences between living organisms. Loren Eiseley has described Carl

Linnaeus as "drunk with the utter wonder of creation,"[6] an apt compliment to a classificatory genius who was, however, publicly committed to a single Creation and fixed modern species.

French paleontologist Jacques Cuvier was one of the first scholars to study mammalian paleontology and to apply Linnaean taxonomy to fossils found in geological beds. The flamboyant Cuvier described and classified thousands of fossilized bones, and yet was an ardent Catastrophist, relegating man to the period of the latest and final Creation. According to men like Cuvier, the great diversity of human and animal life had come about since 4004 B.c., classified by enthusiastic eighteenth-century scientists into a world "teeming with delighted existence."[7]

Darwin's voyage on the *Beagle,* theory of Natural Selection, and *The Origin of Species* provided a theoretical explanation for the diversity of both fossil and living forms that did not rely on supernatural intervention, hypothetical catastrophes, or other improbable and undemonstrable occurrences. Evolution, by means of Natural Selection, does not, of course, entirely explain biological phenomena. Thus, Darwin observed but could not explain variation in all forms of life. Modern genetics and biochemistry have gone a long way to fill in the gaps, even though some problems still await solution. What Darwin was able to do, however, was to describe a single process to account for biological change through time. "As many more individuals of each species are born than can possibly survive, and as consequently there is a frequently recurring struggle for existence, it follows that any being, if it vary however slightly in any manner profitable to itself . . . will have a better chance of surviving and thus be naturally selected," he wrote, propounding his theory of the "Survival of the Fittest."[8] Before Darwin's work was published, people were concerned only with the description of the structures of forms and with erecting classifications based on similarities of structure. Darwin's theory of Natural Selection was developed through his acceptance of the geological theory of uniformitarianism, confirmed by observations of fossil *Megatheria* in the Argentine and from a multitude of vivid field experiences on the *Beagle* expedition (Figure 10.3). He realized that his theories affected human history. "Light," he remarked cautiously, "will be thrown on the origin of man and his history."[9]

The long timespan of prehistory was to the Victorians a period of unknown length. Not until the twentieth century were accurate chronological methods developed. But scholars began to refine the subdivisions of prehistoric time produced by Thomsen. The Stone Age, for example, was divided into a Paleolithic and Neolithic, both of

Fig. 10.3 A Fuegan Indian of the Tekoenica tribe.

these being subdivided into various stages—the Acheulian, Mousterian, Solutrean, and Magdalenian. As these subdivisions were made, people began to ask what they meant. Did the technology, material culture, and society of prehistoric man develop and progress uniformly from the crude tools of the Somme Valley to the sophisticated iron technology of the La Tène culture of Europe? Had there been natural cultural evolution as well as biological evolution in which man had evolved through various stages from savagery to civilization? The doctrines of social evolution were already being propounded by such prolific scholars as Herbert Spencer and others even before the publication of *The Origin of Species*. Human prehistory was seen by many as a logical extension of Darwinism, and Spencer, as long ago as 1850, had said, "Progress is not an accident, but a necessity. It is a fact of nature."[10] In 1867 there were exhibits of prehistoric archaeology at the Paris Exposition, arranged and commented upon by French archaeologist Gabriel de Mortillet, a man who declared passionately, "It's impossible any longer to doubt the great law of the progress of man."[11] He and many colleagues, intoxicated by stone tools and the richness of French archaeological sites, regarded prehistoric man in geological terms, with human culture passing through different epochs according to a universal law of progress in all parts of the world. Indeed, when prehistoric research was first extended beyond the frontiers of Europe, attempts were made to use the same rigid terminology, with, however, limited success.

De Mortillet's view of cultural process was highly evolutionary; yet at the very time it was being set up, others were questioning its validity. As archaeological research extended beyond the confines of Europe and into the New World, the diversity of early human experience began to be revealed in the archaeological record. The great civilizations of the Near East were recovered by Henry Layard[12] and others, and the great Mesoamerican religious complexes were described anew.[13] Upper Paleolithic art was accepted as authentic some years after the discovery of the Altamira paintings in northern Spain in 1875 (Figure 10.4).[14] Yet in many parts of North America and Africa there were no signs of higher civilizations. Furthermore, in the case of the New World civilizations and European cave art, man had apparently regressed. The great religious centers of Mesoamerica had been abandoned, and art equal to that from the French caves (Figure 10.5) did not reappear for many thousands of years. People became less and less certain that there was a common universal prehistory of man. The anthropologist Edward Tylor, whose aim was to sketch a theoretical course of civilization among mankind, was fully prepared to admit that human culture had regressed as well as progressed, and by the 1870s many scholars assumed that there had been regressions in prehistory similar to those in the historical period in which they were more than adequately documented. Tylor was one of many anthropologists and sociologists who were beginning to speculate about the society's development in philosophical terms, developing intellectual frameworks for the study of man.

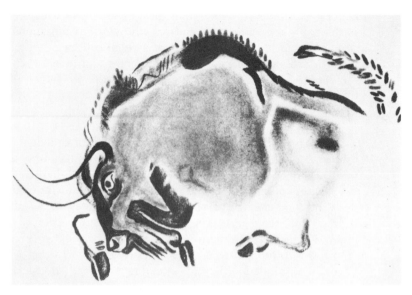

Fig. 10.4 A bison in a polychrome cave painting. The Altamira art represents the ultimate artistic achievement of the Upper Paleolithic hunters of Western Europe.

Fig. 10.5 A giant stag—from a painting in Lascaux Caves, France.

E. B. Tylor

E. B. Tylor (1832–1917) is generally credited with being one of the fathers of anthropology in the English-speaking world.[15] The son of a prosperous manufacturer, he first became interested in the development of human society on a tour of Mexico with the celebrated prehistorian Henry Christy in 1856. Tylor observed the evidence for elaborate prehistoric religion and ritual in the impressive Mayan sites and avidly chronicled the survival of folk customs in modern Mexican peoples, beginning a lifelong study of human culture.[16] At the time he began this work, the serious study of archaeology was gaining tempo, the clerics fighting a rearguard battle against the whole notion of human progress and in particular against the heretical idea that man had evolved from apes and, even worse, a primitive state of humanity comparable to that of modern savages. Tylor and Sir John Lubbock, the articulate author of *Prehistoric Times* and *The Origins of Civilization*, were in the forefront of the battle. The former was an avid supporter of human progress and, like the Enlightenment writers before him, accepted reason as a key to that progress. He took a broad overview of human development from the Paleolithic men of the Somme gravels to Victorian Englishmen, and concluded that life had improved for humanity. Anthropology was an important field of inquiry, for men could free the world from the evils of superstition and barbarism through studying the development of human institutions. Tylor was eloquent in his defense of the study of man:

> The study of man and civilization is not only a matter of scientific interest, but at once passes into the practical business of life. We have in it the means of understanding our own lives and our place in the world, vaguely and imperfectly it is true, but at any rate more clearly than any former generation. The knowledge of man's course of life, from the remote past to the present, will guide us in our duty of leaving the world better than we found it.[17]

Having concluded that man had developed upward from primitive savagery, Tylor then turned his attention to the processes by which knowledge or human skills had been transmitted and studied the causes of culture change, including both invention and diffusion, both major issues of archaeological research in succeeding decades. He sought data from various parts of the world, creating a comparative discipline out of anthropology, comparing one form of an institution with another. This is, by and large, one way in which modern anthropologists work, for they use comparative information in their search for regular associations of cultural phenomena that will help them make general statements about cultural behavior.

Edward Tylor was concerned with the origins and development of "civilized" institutions, particularly those of Victorian England. These he viewed as the highest attainments men had achieved in his day. Their origins, he reasoned, might be found in simpler institutions of ruder peoples. If the stone axes made by the natives of Australia were like the stone axes obtained from the ancient European river terraces, then perhaps the marriage customs of the native Australians were similar to those of the Paleolithic inhabitants of Europe. His data were primarily drawn from two sources: accounts of contemporary primitive peoples and the findings of archaeology. These two sets of data were then ordered to reflect a sequence of development—from the most simple to the most complex. The most complex was, of course, the way the institution existed in Victorian England, the apex of development for Tylor.

Archaeology was crucial to Tylor's search for the origins of European institutions, but little information was available in his time. Archaeologists were busy collecting facts largely obtained from hasty excavations and surface collections without regard to stratigraphic associations. Tylor's scheme of ordering data, from the most simple to the most complex, provided an intellectual framework for these facts and was meant to have universal applicability. This meant that everywhere on earth the development of institutions would be the same except that, in some places, progress had ceased and societies had remained at a lower level. The European sequence from the Paleolithic through the Neolithic to the Bronze and Iron Ages was regarded as an international model. Thus, for example, much time was spent trying to find "the American Paleolithic."[18]

Lewis Morgan

Tylor accepted the Three-Age System but distinguished three different stages of prehistoric development: savagery, barbarism, and civilization. These terms were developed even further by the American anthropologist, Lewis Morgan, who distinguished no less than seven ethnic periods of human progress, outlined in his volume *Ancient Society* in 1877. Morgan's scheme proceeded from a period of Lower Savagery which ended with the discovery of fire, through Middle Savagery culminating in the use of the bow and arrow, and Upper Savagery which achieved the discovery of pottery. Lower Barbarism ended with domestication of animals, whereas iron smelting was the ultimate achievement of Middle Barbarism. Those at a stage of Upper Barbarism invented a phonetic alphabet, and the people of his seventh stage had reached the state of civilization. Morgan has been described as a unilineal evolutionist. His scheme for the progressive cultural evolution of man was based on the assumption that his sequence had developed naturally in different regions, whereas the discoveries of Mayan cities in Yucatan in the early 1840s had precipitated anew issues of diffusion and independent development.

DIFFUSION AND RELATIVISM

Nineteenth-century and much early twentieth-century archaeology was concerned with excavation, discovery, and classification. Scholars were proposing laws of cultural process and were prepared to accept degeneration in cultural experience, and they were doing so increasingly on the basis of the archaeological record. Prehistory was becoming a record of diverse cultural achievement. It was clear that not every prehistoric hunting society had had a period of brilliant artistic achievement and that there were many different regional cultures, societies, and civilizations in prehistoric time widely distributed throughout the known world, each with different distributions, technological achievements, and settlement patterns. By the end of the nineteenth century, archaeology was becoming a record of human cultural achievement set out not as a universal cultural evolution but as a series of numerous and complex regional variations set up in time and space, documenting an immense diversity of human experience.

Cultural relativism began to reemerge as an intellectual concept, replacing the evolutionism of earlier decades. Relativism implied viewing human cultures as having a uniqueness and integrity of their own and not with reference to a single standard of evolution. There was a growth, in other words, of an interest in the specific cultures and societies and a diminishing interest in attempts to build grand schemes of evolution.

The explosion of archaeological knowledge in the late nineteenth century and in America particularly in the early twentieth, led to the gradual realization of human cultural diversity in prehistoric times, but scholars were still faced with the same questions of cultural origin. What were the origins of human culture? When and where was metallurgy introduced? Who were the first farmers? If man did not develop according to evolutionary rules, how then did culture change and cultural diversity come about?

As long ago as the beginning of the nineteenth century, Christian Jurgensen Thomsen and J. J. A. Worsaae had considered the question of cultural process and its effect on the Three-Age System. They had set out a clear role for the process of diffusion in archaeology.[19] The concept of invasions and migrating hordes became especially popular with late nineteenth-century archaeologists who were reacting against the notion of uniform cultural process and who realized that culture change had to be explained in terms of outside influence. The discovery of the new Near Eastern civilizations raised the problems of the origins of such peoples as the Mycenaeans who had been found by Heinrich Schliemann in the 1870s. Many archaeologists began to espouse diffusionist theories, especially when they compared the richness of Near Eastern civilizations with the apparent poverty of European culture. Furthermore, they argued, how could the brilliant New World civilizations of Mexico and Peru have otherwise arisen except through some long distance migration from the civilized centers of the Near East?

Diffusionism found its extreme expression in the hands of Professor Grafton Elliot Smith, who had been greatly influenced by Tylor's writings. The latter pleaded strongly in his widely read books for a study not only of existing preliterate societies, but also of the origins of man and his civilization. Tylor recognized the importance of diffusion in human history and examined in his *Researches into the Early History of Mankind* in 1865 various theories about the origins of civilization and the processes of cultural change. "Sometimes it may be ascribed to the like working of men's minds under like conditions, and, sometimes, it is a proof of blood relationship, or of intercourse, direct or indirect, between the races among whom it is found," he remarked.[20]

By the end of the nineteenth century there were two generalized explanations as to the origin of the cultural changes that appeared in prehistoric times, especially centered around the fact that similar cultural manifestations appeared in different parts of the world widely separated from each other. One theory favored independent invention and development in each area, the same idea as evolution, for evolutionary theory argued that all peoples in all parts of the world developed in a similar fashion, so that similarities are due to similar evolutionary causes. The other theorized that each culture trait had spread from its area of origin to another and so on, diffused by trade, population movement, or cultural contact. Both these theories, that of independent development and of diffusion are, of course, in themselves both entirely acceptable explanations of cultural process in the past. The controversy begins with assessing the relative importance of one or the other; much argument about cultural process in the nineteenth and twentieth centuries has been centered around the role of diffusion as opposed to evolution and the identification of the former or latter in the archaeological record.

Elliot Smith, an eminent anatomist, was the foremost proponent of the diffusionist school. He became Professor of Anatomy at the Government Medical School in Cairo in 1900 and promptly became deeply interested with Egyptology, studying long, unbroken sequences of human culture, in particular the techniques of mummification and embalming, sun worship, and monumental stone architecture. He became obsessed with the complexity of the techniques of Egyptian burial and with other achievements of Nile civilization. In his book, *The Ancient Egyptians*, first published in 1911, he argued that world civilization and much of modern Western culture was diffused from the Nile Valley. He and his disciples, notably W. J. Perry, were the chief supporters of the diffusionist view of the growth of human culture.[21] Both Elliot Smith and Perry envisaged the settlement of the world by small groups of Egyptians who carried out long maritime voyages, colonizing and civilizing the world. They thought that the Mesoamerican civilizations were derived from Egypt and abandoned all pretense at scientific method in their theorizing.

The diffusionist view of human history, like that of universal evolution, is far too simplistic but appears to have appealed widely to archaeologists simply because it was a simple explanation of what was becoming an increasingly complex picture of the human past. It was not until the 1920s that some scholars, notably Gordon Childe, investigated more closely the complexities of culture change in prehistory. The conflict between diffusionists and evolutionists was really precipitated when archaeology began to back away from its predominantly geological concept of the past. Late nineteenth-century anthropology yielded a wealth of descriptions of preliterate peoples in many different environments, and geographers were becoming aware of environment's importance to human culture. Both anthropologists and archaeologists began to realize that they were studying series of human cultures rather than series of geological epochs, the former being distributed through space and time. The early part of the twentieth century was a time of readjustment when archaeologists became preoccupied with the distribution of prehistoric cultures reconstructed through their material remains as preserved in the archaeological record. Diffusion, like relativism, stood in radical opposition to the evolutionism of the nineteenth century.

EMIL DURKHEIM AND FUNCTIONALISM

Emil Durkheim (1858–1917) was a French sociologist of great brilliance whose career began at a time when faith in reason, the order of nature, and social progress was still strong. Durkheim became an active scholar at a time when the evolutionary theories of Darwin and Spencer were the leading scientific ideas of the nineteenth century.[22] Although he espoused the evolutionary hypothesis and the use of the comparative method in both anthropology and sociology, he was critical of both and adopted an "organismic" view of society, which is, in a sense, a manifestation of the relativistic theme in early twentieth-century anthropology. Durkheim's organismic view of society stresses viewing the system as an integral whole. Hence, Durkheim's focus was generally on specific societies or institutions rather than on the total evolutionary frameworks that Tylor, Morgan, and others were attempting to construct. His methodology was aimed at making sociology an empirical study, using research methods employed in the sciences. He tried to work with social facts as "things," using data that could be observed, classified, and explained, rather than merely deduced from arbitrary postulates such as evolution. The "hard" sciences were his research model; his basic assumption was that social institutions are exterior to the individual and exercise constraint over him, and as such, they can be studied as part of the individual world. Thus social facts come to an individual from society, and must therefore be explained in terms of other social facts, not in terms of biological, psychological, or other factors.

Durkheim regarded social facts as those societal items that the individual has in common with others in his group—as society within the individual. Social facts were distinct from the biological consciousness that defines a unique individual. He defined social function: "The 'function' of a social institution is the correspondence between it and the needs of the social organism."[23] The needs of a society are related to, but on a different level from, those of the individuals in that society, and the latter are born into a social world as much as they are into a physical one. Indeed, the conditions of existence of the individual are often different from those for the existence of society, and must be studied separately.

Durkheim has been named the Father of Functionalism in the social sciences, and his functional method, based on the premise that social life is the functioning of social structure, has had a profound effect on the anthropological methodology of the twentieth century. In fact, both diffusionism and functionalism were expressions of this theme of relativity. Diffusionism led to a view of each culture as a distinct phenomenon, a product of so many historical accidents, processes of diffusion, whereas functionalism viewed each culture as a thing that needed investigation in its own terms. Both, then, rejected the single standard of evolutionism that was the hallmark of Tylor, Spencer, and the other evolutionists. Functionalism became popular in the social sciences, and many scholars were influenced by Durk-

heim's theories, among them Robert Lowie, Edward Sapir, Ruth Bene-
dict, A. R. Radcliffe-Brown, and Bronislaw Malinowski.[24] The study
of cultures in their "intertwined state" became a major preoccupation
in anthropology and affected Childe and other archaeologists who
were wrestling with large bodies of archaeological information. Malinowski (1884–1942) was the individual who made the integrated
study of culture a popular method in anthropology, and practiced
and preached functionalism throughout his long career. His view of
functionalism in anthropology was forthright: "The functional view
of culture lays down the principle that in every type of civilization,
every custom, material object, idea and belief fulfills some vital function, has some task to accomplish, represents an indispensable part
within a working whole."[25]

Malinowski had little concern for reconstructions of the past from
archaeological evidence, advocating the functional method for studying
the workings of modern culture. His own fieldwork in the Trobriand
Islands, living as a Trobriander himself, had convinced him that culture
can only be studied by an intimate knowledge of an individual and
his cultural environment. Malinowski stands with Radcliffe-Brown,[26]
a theoretician of the first order, as one of the authors of modern
functionalism.

The combined approaches to the prehistoric past of limited evolutionary reconstruction, diffusionist hypotheses, and to a lesser extent,
functionalism and Boasian cultural relativism led to the urgent necessity for adequate definitions of human culture both in archaeology
and anthropology. This was reflected in a number of integrative
schemes for prehistoric remains, a trend that started with V. Gordon
Childe in the Old World and Alfred Kidder and Max Uhle in the
New. Archaeologists had begun to realize that the days of great overall
theoretical conceptions of the prehistoric past were over, at any rate
until much more information was available.

Chapter 11

Toward Explanation: 1900 to the 1970s
(with Linda Cordell)

FRANZ BOAS AND ARCHAEOLOGY

In the first half of the twentieth century, anthropological writing began to incorporate the idea of diverse cultures, but writers on either side of the Atlantic emphasized different aspects of cultures than those that could be derived by viewing them as wholes. American scholars imbued their writing with a philosophy that was perhaps closer to the romantic and idealistic philosophy of the nineteenth century whose roots had been in European nationalism. Anthropological writings in the Old World tended to reflect not only idealist philosophies but also ideas from biology. Many prominent figures in American anthropology between the two World Wars were men who had emigrated to the United States, their families still possessing nineteenth-century nationalist philosophies.

Franz Boas

Franz Boas (1858–1942) was the dominant figure in American anthropology in the early twentieth century. He was born in Germany, of German-Jewish extraction, and received a liberal education in Europe, a training that brought much idealist, intellectual thought into his anthropological work. After writing a doctoral dissertation in physics, he developed an interest in physical and cultural geography and began his anthropological career with a trip to Baffinland in 1883. His work there was a decisive experience and he described the Eskimo as "a man as we are: that his feelings, his virtues and his shortcomings are based on human nature, like ours."[1]*

Franz Boas was a fanatical worker who trained many enthusiastic and gifted students with whom he undertook the massive task of establishing anthropology as a descriptive science. Boas maintained that anthropology had too many theories, too many broad generalizations, and too little hard data. He had a passion for collecting, classifying, and preserving vast quantities of raw data. His descriptions of such peoples as the Kwakiutl were detailed and carefully marshalled into precise categories.[2] He had a zealous concern that only the strict methods of the sciences be used in anthropological fieldwork; he grew more and more sceptical of theoretical anthropology in his later years and concentrated on intensive research within limited areas.

Boas's influence resulted in a spate of publications that would hardly appeal to the general reader. There were many ethnographies of American Indian tribes in which material cultures were described in almost pitiless detail; monographs contained detailed linguistic studies and, of course, research into culture-trait distributions. Archaeological reports of the 1920s and 1930s emphasized artifact classifications and meticulous examination of archaeological finds, with little behavioral interpretation. Although Boas for the most part was not very interested in archaeology—indeed, through the period his career covered, archaeology and ethnography tended to grow apart—he was, with his student Manuel Gamio, among the first to demonstrate a stratigraphic sequence, at an Aztec site in Mexico.[3] The Boasian influence on archaeology was a healthy one because during this time serious stratigraphic, chronological, and descriptive studies of the pre-Columbian Indian began.

Boasian anthropology tended to draw little from archaeology because archaeologists could only account for culture viewed from the outside, and Boas was interested in understanding cultures from the inside—the criteria, principles, values, and categories of the people themselves. In addition, he was interested in understanding cultures historically, i.e., how they developed. His goal in anthropology was thus twofold: subjective understanding and historical comprehension. His historical technique was that of diffusion, which allowed him to study traits objectively and not subjectively—one need not understand the subjective significance of an artifact to observe its distribution. So Boasian anthropology could expect little from archaeology to contribute to the subjective understanding of peoples, but could expect much from archaeology to understand peoples historically.

* See pages 338–340 for notes to Chapter 11.

Archaeology felt the influence of the Boasian school in a way that inhibited interpretation. The descriptive reports of the 1920s and 1930s resulted from more scientific methodology. These detailed descriptions would have significant implications for anthropology. Boas and his students were involved with publishing a permanent record of the aboriginal cultures of American Indians before they adopted Western ways. Fieldworkers spent much time taking down oral traditions and folktales, as well as enormous lists of such culture traits as types of moccasins, designs of bows and arrows, and hut styles. Much valuable information was, of course, obtained, but the interpretations of aboriginal culture were often fallacious and disproved by archaeological research. For example, American ethnographers of the time regarded the arrival of Europeans and especially of domestic horses as an event of the greatest importance, the Great Plains quickly filling with nomadic buffalo herders and raiders of the type made familiar to us by Hollywood films. The Plains were described as sparsely populated before the arrival of the horse because of a water shortage and a lack of ploughs to till the soil. Yet the work of archaeologists like W. D. Strong, who dug at Signal Butte, Nebraska, revealed that the Great Plains had in fact been inhabited by hunters and horticulturalists for many hundreds of years before the Europeans and their horses turned the plains into a macabre carnival of nomads.[4]

Archaeology, then, became a source of information against which one checked historical reconstructions produced by ethnologists, but the Boasian school considered that archaeology could only yield extremely limited kinds of information about prehistoric culture. Boas and his students, perhaps reflecting the German idealist tradition that was part of their intellectual roots, stressed an understanding of the subjective features of culture rather than its objective or phenomenal features—those that could be directly observed, such as artifacts and house types. In short, they wanted to understand culture from the inside rather than the outside. This placed severe limitations on the value of archaeological data, for the archaeologist could not come into contact with the people he studied, and, therefore, could not be expected to discover much about their subjective life. His finds were limited to the results of technological achievement, subsistence, and settlement patterns. But according to the Boasian point of view, all such cultural traits could vary randomly from culture to culture and give little insight into its spiritual and emotional basis. This approach led archaeologists to view their interpretive tasks in terms of stratified levels that become progressively more difficult to achieve. Technology was seen as easy to describe. Subsistence, at the next level, was thought to require more interpretation and to be a more difficult undertaking. The highest levels of abstraction were those of ideology and belief systems, almost impossible for the archaeologist to reconstruct from his finds.

Another implication of Boasian thinking for archaeological interpretation was reflected in the much greater concern for the construction of typologies from the 1920s onward. Archaeology began to reflect Boas's interest in the history and distribution of individual cultural traits. Descriptive typologies were developed to compare artifacts from one site with those from others; it was no longer enough to know, for example, that two sites hundreds of miles apart both contained obsidian arrowheads. If the distribution of such artifacts was being discussed, far more information was required than merely the evidence of presence at two widely separated locations. Modern typological archaeology owes much of its philosophy and importance to Franz Boas.

One problem central to Edward Tylor's interpretation of the development of institutions and also to the theories of diffusionists was a failure to emphasize that the various institutions in any human culture are normally interrelated. Early anthropologists had little notion of the many diverse cultures in remote parts of the world. In the early twentieth century, anthropological writing began to incorporate the idea of diverse cultures. Boas and his students saw human behavior as a vast spectrum of alternatives from which each group of people might select their own unique complex of behavior. For example, men might make their living by an infinite variety of means. They could, like the Fuegans, be hunters and gatherers, or alternatively, could concentrate on fishing or shellfish collecting. Others might cultivate wheat, oats, and barley, or depend on domestic stock for their livelihood. They might live in a variety of house types ranging from brush shelters to skyscrapers. Their beliefs might encompass one god or ten. The Boasians thought that each human culture selected a different configuration of institutions from the vast array of alternatives, the particular grouping they chose making that culture unique. No one set of alternatives was any better than another. The anthropologist strove to understand the society he was studying by steeping himself in its ideas and subjectively appreciating it. Because each culture was unique, it could not be compared with any others on an objective scale or be considered any better.

This notion of the incomparability of cultures is called "cultural relativism." Each culture selected traits and institutions from numerous alternatives. A given culture could be seen to accept some ideas from one of its neighbors and others from another, many traits being acquired by diffusion. The Boasians were particularly interested in the history of institutions and how these were modified by different groups of peoples; they made many field studies, of which Spier's study of the Sun Dance on the plains is a typical example (see Chapter 10). This type of historical reconstruction is one that can easily lead to erroneous conclusions. Undoubtedly, Boas's greatest contribution to archaeology was in the area of data collection, but his theory of cultural relativism, tinged with a diffusionist flavor, had a considerable effect upon archaeological thinking in the early twentieth century.[5]

V. GORDON CHILDE

Vere Gordon Childe (1892–1957) was an Australian who came to Oxford as a postgraduate student and to archaeology from comparative philology. He began studying European archaeology hoping to find the cradle of the Indo-European peoples and to identify their prehistoric culture.[6] Childe was excited by Sir Arthur Evans's discoveries of Minoan Civilization and by the prehistoric sites of Thessaly, which had been uncovered for the first time in the early decades of this century. After a brief excursion into Australian politics in 1921, Childe turned to his life's work, the study of prehistoric European civilization, a mammoth task that involved him in the identification, classification, and chronological ordering of a multitude of sites and archaeological cultures. He published his first synthesis of European prehistory in 1925, *The Dawn of European Civilization*, the sixth edition appearing in 1957, a few weeks before his death. *The Dawn* was planned to demonstrate by archaeological evidence that Europe "was indebted to the Orient for the rudiments of the arts and crafts that initiated man's emancipation from bondage to his environment and for the foundation of those spiritual ties that coordinate human endeavours."[7] This remarkable book was followed by a series of important publications including *The Most Ancient East* (1928), *The Danube in Prehistory* (1929), *Man Makes Himself* (1936), *What Happened in History* (1942), *Social Evolution* (1951), and *The Prehistory of European Society* (1957). Childe's basic conception of European prehistory was based on diffusionist principles, although he rightly eschewed the grand-scale approach of Elliot Smith and Perry, and the continuing influence of Oriental civilization on European barbarians. He was a brilliant linguist who absorbed from German scholars the concept of an archaeological culture "defined but not constituted by pottery and representing a people,"[8] and based his chronological frameworks on stratigraphic sequences of potsherds in the Danube area and by cross-connections with dated wares in the Aegean. His basic aim was to distill from archaeological remains "a preliterate substitute for the conventional politico-military history with cultures, instead of statesmen, as actors and migrations instead of battles."⁹ Childe's approach to prehistory was founded on Marxist sympathies and a firm conviction that we have meaningful lessons to learn from man's rational, intelligible progress from the earliest stages of his history.

Childe is best remembered by European archaeologists for his innovations in archaeological method, the basis of his encyclopedic syntheses of human progress. He defined cultures based on surviving, characteristic culture traits like pots, implements, house forms, or ornaments, that were constantly associated together. Such cultures were the material expression of "peoples," and might have widespread or limited distribution in time and space, although they were not a chronological concept. These firmly enumerated principles formed the basis of all Childe's work and that of his many students who were soon classifying archaeological cultures not only within Europe and the Near East, but also in widely flung corners of the British Empire where prehistoric research had begun to flourish. Childe had little interest in New World archaeology, so that the impact of his ideas was less profound in North American circles.

The modified diffusionism of Gordon Childe became standard archaeological theory in the 1930s and 1940s—but it was based on the best methodological principles then available. Cultural successions were built up within limited geographic areas and compared to those from neighboring regions, carefully checking those culture traits that have spread from one area to another. Childe's methodology has formed the basis for most modern research in the Old World, except that his diffusionism has been modified by a greater understanding of cultural evolution and independent invention as factors in Old World prehistory. He saw the emergence of food production and, later, urban, literate society in the Near East, perhaps in two great stages, those of the "Neolithic and Urban Revolutions." The modified diffusionism and concepts of Neolithic and Urban Revolutions passed imperceptibly into the textbooks and popular books of a generation of students and interested laymen. Gordon Childe himself was a superb popularizer whose accounts of European prehistory, the origins of civilization, and social evolution were widely read not only by archaeologists but by scientists and many laymen interested in a plausible account of human origins.¹⁰ Yet Childe virtually ignored the New World civilizations, and wrote a prehistory of parts of the Old World rather than a prehistory of man, a task only recently attempted by Grahame Clark and others.¹¹

Gordon Childe distinguished a general evolutionary progression in human economic and social life from the homotaxial stages represented by sequences of archaeological cultures. He visited the Soviet Union in 1934 and discovered the potential of Marxism for explaining the development of prehistoric cultures. He took over some Marxist terms, actually borrowed from Lewis Morgan, and applied them to the archaeological stages separated by his two revolutions: Paleolithic and Mesolithic coincided with savagery; Neolithic was barbarian; the Bronze Age in the Near East was equivalent to civilization.[12] Childe's "Marxism" was mild and basically confined to the idea of the economy being the integrating force in society, the structure of the latter being determined by the mode—the means of production or technology available for achieving society's recognized goals. Later editions of *The Dawn* were as much influenced by Malinowski's functionalism.[13] He lacked the detailed appreciation of the importance of environmental change and ecology in prehistory that characterizes the work of such scholars as Grahame Clark and Stuart Piggott, who followed in Childe's footsteps, although realizing that control of the environment through time was a vital factor in later prehistory.

To a considerable extent, Childe's work ended at the frontiers of the present ecological approach to prehistory. He delivered a series of lectures in Birmingham which later appeared as a book entitled *Social Evolution* (1951). In this provocative volume he sought to discover, by systematic comparisons of prehistoric cultures occupying roughly equivalent levels of development, the regularities of cultural evolution. His comparisons were consciously objective; he made it clear that the technological criteria he derived from Lewis Morgan were taxonomic in nature and not processual. "Revolution," he wrote, "does not purport to describe the mechanism of cultural change. It is not an account of why cultures change ... but of how they change."[14] Thus, he recognized "correlations" between sociopolitical institutions and techno-economic stages, but he did not attempt to choose from these correlations the functionally interrelated institutional structures common to each stage. Childe eschewed simple parallelism in evolutionary development, and emphasized the phenomena of cultural convergence and divergence, thus coming close to the ecological approaches to archaeology characteristic of this decade.

Archaeology is largely a descriptive discipline, and Childe realized that cataloging was useless unless conducted within some frame of reference. Childe's models were really twofold, a technological-evolutionary one, based on the familiar Three-Age System, and an economic model in which the way of getting one's living is a criterion for comparison. He attempted to infer social and political institutions from archaeological data in the full realization that archaeological finds are a limited tool for this purpose. How successful he was must await the judgment of future scholars who work less immediately under his mighty shadow. While his interpretations of the past will provoke discussion, no one can deny his enduring contribution in the areas of classification and chronological ordering and in his insistence upon the relationship between the civilized and barbarian peoples of the Old World. Gordon Childe laid his imprint on the procedures and terminologies of Old World prehistory so firmly that his influence is likely to be felt through our lifetimes.

Those generalizing about cultural process have been concerned for the most part with a form of diluted evolutionism, modified by a modest diffusionism and an admission that independent invention and parallel evolution are sometimes possible. The schemes of V. Gordon Childe or the anthropologist Leslie White[15] are mainly so general that they are hardly significant when faced with the enormous bodies of information now at archaeologists' disposal. Childe tended to consider cultural evolution in terms of autonomous cultural principles and hence tended to ignore the more detailed interrelationships between culture and the environment.

NEW WORLD ARCHAEOLOGY: 1920–1950

In the Old World, Thomsen, Worsaae, and Montelius laid the groundwork for the predominantly stratigraphic and chronological approach to prehistory characteristic of European archaeology, which was further developed by Gordon Childe and other modern scholars. New World archaeologists, whose background was more anthropological and oriented toward data collection and the direct historical approach, had increasing difficulty communicating with one another as more and more regional cultural sequences were developed in the 1920s and 1930s. The term "culture" was used in so many diverse ways that some common yardsticks of comparison had to be devised and formal descriptive terminologies developed. The most widely used was the so-called "Midwestern Taxonomic Method" developed by W. C. McKern and others before the Second World War.[16] The Midwestern taxonomy was based on formal similarities between different assemblages and had no chronological implications. Such terms as "assemblage," "components," "foci," "aspects," and "phases" were a series of hierarchical names used only to classify sites and broader groupings of settlements. Prewar American thinking did not emphasize cultural change, for the great evolutionary sequences of Old World prehistory appeared telescoped in the Americas, where few societies had moved beyond hunting and gathering or simple agriculture. The major preoccupation was with ethnographic description, with classification, and with working backward from known historical sites into prehistory.

This "direct historical approach" probably owes its origin to the Boas school and to W. D. Strong's work in the plains of Nebraska. It involves working from the known, historic period sites to the unknown, prehistoric settlements, preferably those of known peoples. The historical sites provide a fixed datum point to which earlier sequences can be tied, and a series of specific problems that serve to link archaeology and ethnography in the search for solutions to common cultural problems. This approach was applied with success to the Inca Civilization of Peru, where the continuity of prehistoric culture was emphasized rather than its discontinuity, with rewarding results (Figure 11.1).[17]

The regional specializations of the 1930s were less fashionable by 1940 when James Ford, James Griffin, and Gordon Willey began a massive synthesis of unpublished archaeological data from hundreds of sites excavated during the Depression.[18] Their studies of the eastern parts of the United States revealed a steady development of prehistoric material culture over many thousands of years. A series of periods could be distinguished within which broad similarities of prehistoric culture could be discerned, and the periods became developmental stages. This work was extended by Willey and Phillips in an important monograph in 1958,[19] in which they applied essentially the same techniques to the whole of the New World, devising a series of developmental stages for the entire continent. Their stages are defined on the basis of technology, economic data, settlement pattern, art traditions, and social factors, with chronology a less important consideration.

In the 1940s and 1950s, American archaeologists moved away from taxonomy toward the study of cultural processes in the past, viewing millennia of culture history against the complex and ever-changing environment.[20] This move had taken place earlier in the Old World, where prehistory was longer and climatic changes more obvious. The new emphasis on interpretation was based on carefully studied regional culture sequences from which emerge some broad trends in cultural development, showing some resemblance to the theoretical evolutionary stages of earlier archaeology. One conclusion is obvious—man's material culture and social organization have developed from the simple to the infinitely complex. So accounts of world prehistory or broad syntheses of large culture areas must allow for the general notion of progress in prehistory. Much recent archaeological writing has described the progress of man through various stages, in which he had progressively more effective mastery over

Fig. 11.1 An Inca settlement built high in the Peruvian Andes, Machu Picchu was forgotten for 400 years after the site's abandonment when the Spaniards arrived. It was rediscovered by the American explorer Hiram Bingham in 1912, and is a beautiful example of adaptation to a mountain environment.

his environment. Childe with his revolutions,[21] Robert J. Braidwood in the Near East,[22] and Gordon Willey in North America[23] have all attempted to look at culture history from the standpoint of human culture being in constant and dynamic relationship with its environment and other factors interacting with it. Mid-twentieth-century archaeology has come a long way from the taxonomy and classification of earlier decades.

ECOLOGICAL APPROACHES TO ARCHAEOLOGY

We have seen how Gordon Childe's approach to the European past lacked the lively appreciation of the importance of environmental change and cultural ecology that characterizes recent research. But he began, in his latest writings, to move closer to an ecological approach to prehistory.[24] Grahame Clark, who began his career in the study of Post Glacial hunter-gatherers and early farmers in Northern Europe, has long advocated an ecological approach in a series of important articles and books, the most famous of which are his *Prehistoric Europe: The Economic Basis* (1952) and his classic report on the Star Carr excavations.[25] Clark's ecological studies are about people and how they lived, not about things, and now that the chronological problem has to a large extent been solved by the advent of radiocarbon and potassium argon techniques, increasing attention has been paid in the Old World to cultural ecology. The move toward an ecological approach was less self-conscious in Europe than in the New World, where only in the last few years have archaeologists moved away from the direct-historical approach and a major concern with stratigraphy, classification, chronology, and areal studies. American scholars were busy building up local sequences rather than wider syntheses—one detects here some Childean influence and a persistent concern with major evolutionary and mildly diffusionist schemes for the past. Although there had been some attempts at culturally ecological studies before 1950, only recently have such approaches had a real vogue, in part due to great expansion of research in the wake of increased funding for archaeological work, to more rescue campaigns, and to more professional workers in the field. American archaeologists have begun to analyze the processes of culture change that they have been observing for years and to compare them with others. This trend has been strongly stimulated by the training in the theory of cultural and social anthropology given to every American archaeologist.

In 1948, W. W. Taylor published *A Study of Archaeology*, a critique of American archaeology's overriding preoccupation with chronology.[26] Every issue of archaeological journals was crowded with reports of arid pottery chronologies, with little reference to their context or meaning in human terms. Taylor called for a "conjunctive approach" to archaeology, a shift of emphasis from chronological sequences and distributions to detailed studies of individual sites and their features, such as cultural layers, floors, or hearths. The "conjunctive approach" entailed bringing together all possible sources of evidence on a site—technology, style, ecological evidence, architecture, and information on social life—to study the people behind the site and the processes of culture change involved.

A Study of Archaeology was, for its time, a controversial statement and suffered from a lack of examples to support the theoretical polemic.[27] But a number of new departures in archaeology were stimulated by the monograph. Radiocarbon dating provided an opportunity for lesser emphasis on chronology, and settlement pattern archaeology came into vogue in the early 1950s. The potential of settlement archaeology for ecological and social inferences is obvious, but it is, as Gordon Willey has pointed out, a convenient point for the "conjunction" of inquiry into other aspects of prehistoric societies.[28] The last decade has seen the publication of many studies in which settlement patterns of individual structures and whole sites or distributions of settlements have been integrated with detailed analyses of pottery types and other artifacts to throw light on kinship and social organization.[29]

Julian Steward has attempted to develop a methodology for "determining regularities of form, function, and process which recur cross-culturally among societies found in different cultural areas."[30] In contrast to the unilinear evolutionists, who postulated that all societies passed through similar developmental stages, and the cultural relativists, Steward accepted multilinear evolution as a basic assumption—whereby "certain basic types of culture may develop in similar ways under similar conditions but that few concrete aspects of culture will appear among all groups of mankind in a regular sequence."[31] Tylor, Morgan, Childe, and White had all sought to think of cultural development in terms of universal stages, but Steward tried to look for causes of cultural change, developing a method for recognizing the ways in which culture change is caused by adaptation to environment. Steward called this process cultural ecology, arguing that similar adaptive processes occur in other cultures in similar environments—thus the cross-cultural regularities that result are functional. No culture has ever achieved a stable adaptation to its environment, and differences and changes during periods of cultural development in any area are not only more complex, but involve new cultural patterns. Cultural development should therefore be thought of as the emergence of successive levels of sociocultural integration. These, unlike the developmental taxonomies of Tylor, Morgan, and others, are simply regarded as a tool for studying cultures of different complexity.

Steward defined culture types on the basis of cultural features and characteristics represented by a particular developmental level. His cross-cultural regularities are identified on the basis of regular associations of basic cultural features, known as the *cultural core*. These have "similar functional interrelationships resulting from local ecological adaptations and similar levels of sociocultural integration."[32] The traits that make up his culture core have the advantage, from our point of view, in that they often consist of items identifiable in the archaeological record. The culture-core concept is a research device designed to isolate and define distinguishing characteristics of particular culture types abstracted from all data on hand. To Steward, a cultural type consists of core features "that, first, are determined by cross-cultural regularities of cultural ecological adaptation, and second represent a similar level of sociocultural integration."[33] For example, patrilineal bands among the Bushmen, Australians, and Fuegians are a cultural type because the ecological adaptation and level of integration are similar in each case. The environments of these groups differed greatly, ranging from desert to cold and rainy plains, but the practical requirements of the hunting and gathering techniques grouped the people into small patrilocal exogamous bands, each with its own territory. The structure and social function of the bands in each area were very similar, but their adaptations to their environments were similar in terms of function rather than in specific detail. Steward assumed that the existence of a culture trait at a given locality was due to diffusion. He argued that diffusion does not explain the occurrence of certain critical cultural features; one must look rather to the relationship between environment and culture to explain many features of a cultural system. In this sense Steward was carrying a form of functionalism in a direction counter to diffusionism; he was pushing American anthropology to a new view of culture, different from that of Boasian diffusionistic thought. Steward's approach represents a new historical theme that replaces the diffusionist one that dominated American anthropology during the early part of this century.

The acceptance of Steward's theories involves using cultural ecology as both a research problem and a method of interpretation. He asked whether the adjustments of human society to various environments require characteristic modes of behavior and chose those cultural features most closely related to subsistence activities and economic arrangements to answer the question, trying to isolate those aspects of the environment considered by the people themselves as having the greatest importance. Steward recognized as his central thesis that "cultural ecological adaptations constitute creative processes."[34]

Environment has been relegated to a secondary role by Boas and others who believed that the environment is passive and that man's culture has developed because of his selection of certain environmental possibilities while ignoring others. At the other extreme, the environmental determinist believes that forces in nature determine human culture, which is passive. Both approaches have had their advocates among archaeologists and need not detain us here.[35] Steward and the cultural ecologists reject the notion that either culture or the environment is passive, paying closer attention to constant and dynamic interactions between cultures and their environments. Some of the most sophisticated research in archaeology is taking place in this area, as archaeologists wrestle with developing a meeting ground between the necessity for a broad overview of cultural process and the need to look at each particular changing culture in the archaeological record and its micro-adaptation to a dynamic environment. We are as much concerned with the question of why in archaeology as we are with how, the direction in which much energy was expended by earlier scholars.

EXPLANATION AND VERIFICATION

Archaeologists generally agree that there are three basic objectives for their discipline: reconstructing culture history, reconstructing past lifeways, and the study of cultural process. Most of this book has

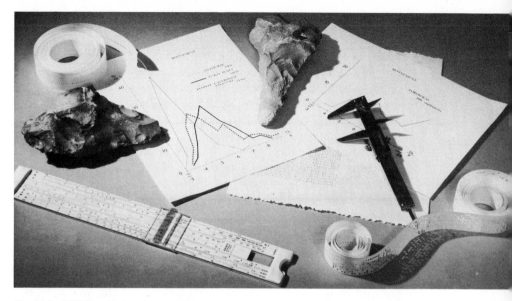

Fig. 11.2 "Still life with hand axes, 1968"—a pleasing group by D. A. Roe showing not only two
hand axes, but also the tools of the modern typologist of Stone Age artifacts.

been taken up with a consideration of the first two aims, and we
have shown how achieving the third has been regarded as unfeasible
by some scholars and as a matter of despair by others. But although
some scholars' curiosity about the past has been satisfied by the
development of new chronologies and a whole battery of sophisticated
aids for studying living floors and prehistoric artifacts, others have
faced the challenge of explaining cultural process and are taking
archaeology in new directions (Figure 11.2). It is safe to say that our
discipline is on the threshold of a new era of discovery in which
explanation of the past is as important, if not more significant, than
description. The concern with explanation is a recent one, for in 1958
Willey and Phillips were able to say that "so little work has been
done in American archaeology on the explanatory level that it's difficult to find a name for it." Although such studies as the Virú Valley
project had been remarkably successful, many scholars were despair-
ing, citing the limitations of archaeological evidence and its fragmentary nature as reasons for avoiding explanation.[36]

Several developments have moved us to new thresholds of investigation. The first has been the discovery by social scientists of Systems
Theory, the second the advent of computers and quantitative methods
for artifact classification, and the third a realization that cultural
ecology—the study of dynamic relationship between culture and environment—was a promising approach to interpreting the past. Several
archaeologists have been particularly active in developing new

307

methods of investigation, among them Lewis Binford, William Long-acre, Stuart Struever, and D. L. Clarke.[37] The 1960s saw a reevaluation of the scientific methods of archaeology, from which it became evident that much archaeological interpretation was unscientific and based on intuition and insufficiently rigorous data. In other words, we needed to develop a more scientific approach to the past that would employ normal scientific procedures in analysis of archaeological data with the objective of attempting explanation as well as description.

Lewis Binford has been the most vigorous advocate of more rigorous scientific testing in archaeology, arguing that statements about the historical, functional, or processual significance of the archaeological record have so far been evaluated on how far our knowledge of contemporary peoples can be projected back to prehistoric contexts and on our judgment of the professional competence and honesty of the archaeologists involved with interpreting the past.[38] Simple induction has been the basis of inferences about the archaeological record, based on guidance from ethnographic data and experimental archaeology. Binford argues that although induction and inferences are perfectly sound methods of understanding the past, independent methods of testing propositions about the past must be developed and be far more rigorous than the time-honored value judgments based on the assessment of professional competence.

Under the normal scientific method, a research problem is approached from a collection of observed data that enables one to pose research hypotheses about the reasons for the observations made from the data. The hypotheses may concern processes of change: Why did barbed harpoons develop larger bases during the occupation of a hunting camp? Why did the Magdalenian culture replace the Solutrean in the Les Eyzies Caves of southwestern France? How and why did the hunter-gatherers of the Near East turn to agriculture and domestic animals for their livelihood? Alternatively, the hypotheses may touch on relationships: What is the relationship between two neighboring but contemporary sites with major differences in food residues and implements of tillage? A new pottery type suddenly appears in a Midwest cultural sequence: Is it the result of trade, population movement, or invention? The artistic style of the ornaments in one Iron Age La Tène cemetery in Central Europe is markedly similar to that of another burial ground hundreds of miles away: What was their stylistic relationship?

Working hypotheses are nothing new in science, and we have been using them unconsciously in archaeology for years. What is new, however, is the development of new research strategies based on verifying propositions through hypothesis testing. These propositions in turn raise others, also subject to proof or disproof. An accepted proposition is one that has been tested against archaeological data and against other alternatives that have been rejected. Once proved, it joins the body of reliable knowledge upon which further hypotheses can be erected which may, in their turn, require additional data or even entirely new approaches to the excavation and collection of archaeological information.

Although the use of scientific method in archaeology is only now gaining ground, the results from its use have been both productive and provocative. Scientific method implies the use of high probability statements rather than generalizations with little quantitative validity, and any proposition is calculated on the basis of the hypotheses and testing procedures used in its formulation. Binford and his colleagues also challenge the assumption that the incompleteness of the archaeological record precludes reliable interpretation of the nonmaterial and perishable components of prehistoric society and culture. All artifacts found in an archaeological site have functioned within a culture and society with reference to many perishable factors like fashion or decorative motifs, each of which has, in itself, a history of acceptance, use, and rejection within the society concerned. The artifacts found in the sites are far more than material items that functioned in the society without reference to the many, often intangible variables determining the form of the objects preserved. Binford argues that "data relevant to most, if not all, the components of past sociocultural systems *are* preserved in the archaeological record."[39] The archaeologist's task is to devise methods for extracting this information that deal with all determinants operating within the society or culture being studied. Accessible or inaccessible phenomena of the past on the basis of empirically tested propositions are the real criteria for recovering the prehistoric past rather than the archaeological record. Thus we lack the methodological sophistication and scientific method and must develop them before much progress in explanation in archaeology can be expected.

SYSTEMS THEORY

In recent years some archaeologists have become aware of systems theory and have introduced some of its ideas and concepts into the study of lifeways in the past. Systems theory involves complicated abstract ideas that are often hard to grasp without a scientific background. Information and games theory which follow on logically from the systems approach are even more mathematical, and although claimed to have some archaeological significance, these are still the province of specialist mathematicians turned archaeologist. Yet some understanding of what systems theory has to offer archaeology is important to any scholar of the past, even if he has no intention of using it. The basic principles of "general systems theory" were enumerated by 1950 and are readily accessible in lucid publications. A system is defined by A. D. Hall and R. E. Fagen as being "a series of objects together with relationships between the objects and their attributes."[40] The components of a machine are a system, as are the neurons forming the brain or the cells forming a living organism. Thus, a system is concerned not only with objects and their individual features but also with the relationships between them. Obviously, the items and relationships within the system that are important will change according to the problem under investigation. The type of rock used to make a stone hand axe is obviously irrelevant in studying the house design and layout of activity areas on a living floor. If all elements in a system interact with one another, then some are clearly more important than others, and the research problem, be it in archaeology, physics, or sociology, concerns only those items in the system that affect, are affected by, or change in response to the way in which the system behaves. "Open systems," those that are dynamic and tend toward growth and diversity, are probably the group to which human society belongs, and offer the best prospect for studying diverse human adaptations through time.

To mention some important concepts of systems theory, we can do no better than quote James Doran's recent able summary:

> Important concepts of system theory are those of *self-regulation* (or *homeostasis*), *positive* and *negative feedback*, *oscillation* and *dynamic equilibrium*. Perhaps the easiest way to convey the meaning of these terms is by an example. Consider a class of school children left by their teacher to work by themselves, and suppose that we are primarily interested in the overall noise level which the class generates. Initially the noise level will be low but it will soon start to climb as each child, hearing more noise around him, makes more noise himself. This tendency of the noise to amplify itself is an example of *positive feedback*. At length, however, we may assume that the noise level will reach such a pitch that the more responsible, or timid, members of the class will attempt to quieten their fellows. Now the greater the noise, the greater the dampening effect, and we have an example of *negative feedback*. The overall effect is that the class will settle to some particular noise level by a process of *self-regulation*. Of course, there will be a certain amount of *oscillation* in the noise level, both in the initial adjustment period, and even afterwards. When the teacher returns he will find that the class has found its way to a state of *dynamic equilibrium* in that although, of course, the individual components of the system (the children in the class) are far from motionless, the system

taken as a whole is unchanging. In fact, the equilibrium is also *stable*, in that any outside intervention which changes the noise level, for example a brief visit from another teacher, will, within limits, have only a temporary effect.

This example gives, of course, only a general impression of the meaning of these forms. It is possible to make them considerably more precise and to construct equivalent mathematical models. These latter, however, will be capable of productive use only in a few of the situations to which the original informal definitions apply.[41]

What relevance does systems theory have to archaeology? Very simply, the basic assumption is made that sociocultural systems are integral whole units. Under this notion, such parts of the system as material culture, social organization, settlement pattern, and economic life are merely subsystems that are arbitrarily abstracted by the research scholar for separate study *as part of the whole system.* The whole sociocultural system is "a unit system in which all the cultural information is a stabilized, but constantly changing network of intercommunicating attributes forming a complex whole—a dynamic system."[42] Clearly, then, material culture and, indeed, all archaeological finds should be studied with reference to their former linkage within a sociocultural system. Lewis Binford, perhaps the most eloquent advocate of explanation, roundly states that "culture is . . . the system of the total extrasomatic means of adaptation. Such a system involves complex sets of relationships among people, places, and things whose matrix may be understood in multivariate terms."[43]

This view of human culture is most useful when we are interpreting or explaining cultural process, settlement pattern, or ecological adaptation. The adaptation theme runs right through this book and through archaeology, the study of fossilized human behavior. Human society is a mechanism, like culture, oriented toward survival and, like the ecosystem of which it is part, will change in response to an alteration in another part of the system to which it belongs. Then, simplistic explanations of culture change in archaeology hardly accurately reflect the actual situation, and clearly no one element in any cultural system is a primary cause of change, since a complex range of different factors—for example, rainfall, vegetation, technology, social restrictions, and population density, interact with one another and react to a change in one element in the system. Human culture is, therefore, from the ecologist's viewpoint, merely one element in the ecosystem, a mechanism of behavior whereby man adapts to his environment.

Kent V. Flannery, who has worked in both the Near East and Mesoamerica, has turned to systems theory to explain culture change. He points out that most archaeologists look at culture as a set of shared beliefs and contends that this view of culture is inadequate to explain culture change; culture changes through time and through space, and therefore shared beliefs must also change. Flannery, along with other system-oriented archaeologists, views human behavior "as a point of overlap (or 'articulation') between a vast number of systems, each of which encompasses both cultural and noncultural phenomena—often much more of the latter."[44] Minor changes may occur in any one of the systems involved and will cause readjustments in the other systems until a new state of equilibrium is reached.

Flannery's systemic view is the point of departure for his discussion of the origins of agriculture in Mesoamerica between *ca.* 8000 B.C. and 200 B.C.—which certainly counts as a major cultural change. The adaptation of the preagricultural peoples of Mesoamerica who later became agriculturalists, Flannery maintains, was not to a given environment or even a microenvironment, but to a few plant and animal genera whose range cross-cut several environments. Using the palynological and faunal analyses of preagricultural sites, Flannery listed the different plants and animals upon which these people depended. The list included maguey (century plant) leaves, the fruits of various cacti, the pods of mesquite trees, white-tailed deer, cottontail rabbits, wild water fowl, and wild grasses including wild corn. Some foods were available the year round, such as the maguey leaves and the cottontails. Others—mesquite pods and deer—were exploited during the dry season, but the cactus fruit and other species were only eaten during the rainy season.

To obtain these foods, the people had to be in the right places at the right times, and the right time depended on the particular plants and animals rather than on the people. Flannery refers to the planning of a group's movements so that it will be in the right place at the right time as "scheduling." The entire food procurement system of a group will then depend both on the seasonality of the particular plant or animal and on the scheduling of the hunters and gatherers. A minor change in any one procurement system will be reflected in the group's scheduling and might preclude exploiting those foods whose seasonality conflicts with the new schedule.

Regulatory factors that prevent exhausting food supplies are obviously important in this connection, too. Genetic changes in two food plants, corn and beans, through time made these plants more important than they had been to the people who used them. Both plants became slightly more productive and this slight increase in productivity acted as positive feedback for their procurement systems. Gradually, more time was spent on corn and beans, and the groups had to reschedule their activities to accommodate this change. Because a group could not be in two places at once, those foods that were procured at times when corn and beans had to be planted or harvested would necessarily be neglected, and negative feedback might be said to have operated in their procurement systems. The role which systems theory plays in the study is rather limited and Flannery does not claim much for it beyond the avoidance of oversimplification in research design and hypothesis testing by attributing major cultural change to a single factor like the discovery that corn could be cultivated.

Another American archaeologist, James W. Judge, recently used a systems theory orientation to discuss the differences and similarities in two types of Paleo-Indian projectile points—Folsom and Midland—found in many sites in North America.[45] In some Southwest and Texan sites, the points have been found in association with an extinct form of bison; they date from about 10,000 B.C. to 7000 B.C., making them among the oldest distinct lithic types in America. Folsom and Midland points are quite similar in appearance and have been found together in a few sites. Both types of points are about 5.1 centimeters (2 inches) long, have concave bases and are beautifully pressure-flaked on both faces (Figure 7.13). Folsom points, unlike Midland ones, have a characteristic flute on each face, produced by the removal of a thin longitudinal flake from each face, and are also somewhat thicker than Midland points. There has been some dispute in the literature about whether Folsom and Midland points should be considered two different archaeological types or not. Judge maintains that in order to explain the differences in the two kinds of points, we must consider the production of each kind as part of a total system; in this way, we see that at each phase of production, constraints are built into the system that affect the form of the finished project.

Judge details the production process involved in making Folsom points, and derives his data from experiments in making points in laboratories as well as from the study of waste-flake material recovered from archaeological sites that contained Folsom points. The first step in Folsom point manufacture is the preparation of a large rectangular, bifacially flaked blank from a suitably large flake (Figure 7.13). One end of this blank is then bevelled by pressure flaking, and a nipple-shaped striking platform is prepared on the other end. The first flute is removed from this platform; the same shape of striking platform is then prepared for a second time and the second flute (on the other face) is removed. The unfluted tip of the point is then snapped off. The basal concavity on the finished point is the result of the platform preparation necessary for the fluting to be completed.

Midland points were produced from thin, unifacially flaked blanks. These were worked by careful pressure flaking until they reached

the characteristic Midland shape. This shape includes a basal concavity, but this was not the result of preparing a striking platform
for removing longitudinal flakes, since Midland points are not fluted.
Judge sees the early step in the production process (preparation of
a striking platform) as a constraint upon the eventual Folsom point
shape. The basal concavity in the Midland points, however, is a final
step in shaping the point. Judge offers two propositions that might
explain the difference between Folsom and Midland points and could
be tested against empirical data. The first proposition is that the
makers of Folsom and Midland points could not control the width
and thickness of the initial flake blanks. If they were wide and thick,
Folsom points were made; if they were thin and narrow, however,
Midland points were produced. This proposition could be tested
through controlled experiments by examining the shape of the cores
used to derive the initial flake and by tests on the kinds of stone
used. His second proposition is that the producers of Folsom and
Midland points could control the width and thickness of the original
flake and that the two kinds of points produced served two different
functions, or were just two different fashionable designs. The empirical
data that would refute the first proposition would lend support to
the second one.

While Judge's analysis of Folsom and Midland points is of great
interest, and his propositions will undoubtedly be tested in the future,
one wonders whether he might not have reached the same deductions
and basic research design without using the terminology and ideas
of the systems approach. As Hole and Heizer have recently pointed
out,[46] systems theory is so new that its potential is largely unrealized
in archaeology. David Clarke and James Doran have both approached
the problem from complicated, mathematically based angles that daunt
the nonscientist, and much basic theoretical inquiry will be needed
before systems theory can replace what David Clarke called "the
murky exhalation which passes for 'interpretative thinking' in archaeology."[47] Certainly archaeological thinking and research will benefit
from such better organized and more objective conceptual frameworks
as, theoretically, systems theory offers. Many elements of human
cultural systems are not capable of being quantitatively tested, nor
is it possible to measure with the necessarily rigorous degrees of
mathematical activity the actual volumes of such concepts as positive
feedback which archaeologists have begun to use in some field studies.
The value of systems theory is that it allows us to put archaeological
situations into a wider systems framework for research purposes,
especially those concerned with behavior, organizations, and ecological
adaptations. Preliminary results, which appear at intervals in these

pages, are promising, and we can expect systems theory to take its place among other diverse research tools of the archaeologist, fenced around, as are other methods, with limitations and restrictions of usage and definition.

Although most archaeologists would agree with Binford and his colleagues that the reconstruction of culture history, ancient lifeways, and the delineation of culture process are central aims of archaeology, there is great disagreement on method and theory. "The major methodological and theoretical points of contrast," says Binford, "involve distinctions between cultural analogies and homologies, between culture viewed as a summation of traits and culture viewed as a system, between units of observation and units of analysis, between inductive and deductive approaches to the archaeological record."[48] What Binford is really arguing for is an elaboration of method and theory using the latest data collection and storage techniques and advanced quantitative analytical methods, which in themselves require a rigorous scientific method and new theoretical ground. "We assume that the past is knowable; that with enough methodological ingenuity, propositions about the past are testable; and that there are valid scientific criteria for judging the probability of a statement about the past,"[49] Binford adds.

The next decades will see the elaboration of a new theoretical structure for much of archaeology based on the systematic application of testable propositions to the archaeological record; the objective will be to study variability in the functioning of cultural systems in the past, with the ultimate aim of formulating some fundamental laws of cultural dynamics. It remains to be seen whether we are on the threshold of a major change in the evolution of archaeology. Certainly the quantitative armory now at the archaeologist's disposal will aid our search for explanations in archaeology.

Chapter 12
Conclusion

"The Professor . . . declared that apes had hippopotamus majors in their brains just as men have. Which was a shocking thing to say."[1]* Many archaeological sites have been dug since the Victorian public learned with shock of its primate origins. The emergence of archaeology as a serious and popular field of investigation has been a cultural phenomenon of this century. Sixty years ago, professional archaeologists were few and far between; now museums, archaeological surveys, and universities are staffed with trained graduates. A flood of monographs and learned journals devoted to antiquity has been accompanied by a spate of popular literature on the subject. Television specials and articles in the *National Geographic* and other periodicals have led to great public awareness of the prehistoric past. Reconstructions of the Australopithecines making their living in the African savannah are commonplace in popular literature and textbooks, and spectacular archaeological discoveries merit prominent headlines in many newspapers.

But why do we study archaeology? Why does it have such widespread popular appeal? The glamour and romance of discovery have often been cited as reasons for lay interest, but this notion of archaeology has become less fashionable as more and more students are exposed to its methods at their schools and universities. The urge to collect and to own is a strong human impulse, one that receives gratifying reward through archaeology. For centuries, the spectacular monuments of the Nile Valley have been raped for their riches, and

* See page 340 for notes to Chapter 12.

modern times have witnessed the systematic plundering of tombs and every type of site, even shell middens, both for valuable finds for the antique market and for "Indian arrowheads." This ruthless exploitation of archaeological sites may gratify profit-hungry dealers or the acquisitively curious, but the damage to human history is incalculable. Fortunately, some nations have implemented rigorous antiquities laws, which have slowed the export of valuable artifacts. But many countries have lagged in this respect, despite UNESCO declarations and the lobbying of professional archaeologists. As a result, much of man's earlier history is lost forever, even though some of his finer artistic achievements are displayed, out of archaeological context, in museums and private collections (Figure 12.1).

Our interest in the remote past stems from philosophical considerations, too. We live in a world of urban environments and crowded humanity, surrounded by sophisticated technology and constant pressure. Our society has yet to create social mechanisms that will allow us to live in harmony in a technological world, using machines for our benefit and that of our polluted and shrinking world. As population pressures increase, and the crisis in cities deepens, we find a nostalgia for the simpler days of the past. The songs of the 1930s are revived; *Time* and *Newsweek* run articles on the "good old days";

Fig. 12.1 Reindeer and salmon engraved on an Upper Paleolithic (Magdalenian) antler fragment from Lorthet, France.

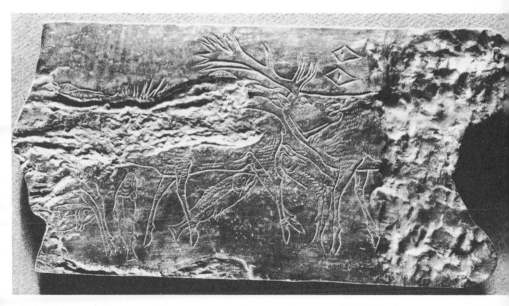

copies of the artifacts of fifty years ago fill boutiques and department stores. Perhaps we are seeking an outlet for our philosophical longings for a less complicated and slower world like that of prehistoric man, where life was determined by the seasons of vegetable food and the movements of game. Our ardent internationalism leads many to study anthropology and the great diversity of mankind—many then proceed to a study of archaeology, to insights into a less complicated world based on subsistence economies and controllable technology. Archaeology has achieved a relevance in many people's eyes simply because it enables them to gain a lengthier perspective on their experience than merely that of the 5,000 years of written history.

Archaeology has a more pressing relevance to many of the world's peoples for whom prehistoric times lasted until the twentieth century. In parts of Africa, Asia, and Latin America, many former colonies have received their independence and developed a fierce and proud nationalism. Like governments throughout history, they seek historical justification for their actions, but the precolonial history of such countries as Kenya or Tanzania has never been written down and can only be recorded through oral tradition or archaeological research. It is no coincidence that African governments are supporting excavations, the results of which sometimes appear in school publications before they do in learned journals.[2] Thus archaeology has a direct relevance to many new nations, and is fulfilling a vital educational role in writing national histories. A distinction should be made here between such activities, based on the latest methods of archaeological research, and attempts to use prehistory for political ends. A notorious example was the racist type of archaeology conducted by some European countries between the wars; more recently, the Zimbabwe Ruins in southern Africa have been the subject of political concern (Figure 12.2).[3] Fortunately, most such attempts are based on unsound reasoning or bad research, but their propaganda value is still regarded by their initiators as useful.

All over the world archaeologists are busy digging up the past and interpreting their findings for their colleagues. Many scholars pay lip service to the educational value of their discoveries, but do little to disseminate their results to schools or the public. Yet archaeologists have a responsibility to do this because research is often supported by public money and the findings may illuminate the history of an Indian community or African population and have a special relevance to their modern descendents. The prehistoric periods of American history may be remote to twentieth-century white Americans, but they are far from irrelevant to the American Indian who may still live in areas inhabited by his prehistoric forebears. Very often his historical education takes no account of the archaeological

Fig. 12.2 The ruins at Zimbabwe, Rhodesia, which was a trading and religious center of the Karanga peoples of south-central Africa in the second millennium A.D. Most of the Great Enclosure, or Temple, was built later than 1400 A.D.

sites he sees every day. Archaeologists have so far failed to rise to this educational challenge, as urgent as that of writing the histories of new nations. We should not allow this vital objective of archaeology to be obscured in the morass of methods and techniques used for reconstructing and explaining the past.

Much of this book has dealt with objects of, and theoretical approaches to the past and with the basic workings of archaeology. The excitement of the subject is difficult to communicate: the pleasure of gaining a new perspective on our long history as human beings, or of handling the artifacts of our forebears, or of visiting the sites where they lived. Secure in our cushioned, twentieth-century world, we forget our awesome and long ancestry among the Australopithecines over five million years ago and, like the Victorians, ignore our primate origins and "primitive" past. Dr. Hastings Banda, the President of Malawi, caused a ripple some years ago by saying that he wished he could erect Stonehenge on the highlands of central Africa to show the world that the British also had a savage past.[4] His remark is apposite. If this book has given you an awareness of the prehistoric past, then it has succeeded in its task.

319

Notes

Chapter 1
INTRODUCTION

[1] For a discussion of the Classical writers' views of the origins of man, see J. H. Plumb, *The Death of the Past*, London, 1969, Chap. 1, and Glyn E. Daniel, *A Hundred Years of Archaeology*, London, 1950, pp. 14–16.

[2] The best accounts of the early antiquarians are in Daniel's *Hundred Years*, already referred to, pp. 16–24, and the same author's *The Origins and Growth of Archaeology*, London, 1967, pp. 33–56.

[3] William Camden is discussed at length by T. D. Kendrick, *British Antiquity*, London, 1950, pp. 134–168.

[4] William Stukeley has been the subject of a delightful biography by Stuart Piggott, *William Stukeley: An Eighteenth-Century Antiquary*, Oxford, 1950. The same author's *The Druids*, London and New York, 1968, is also informative on Druidic cults.

[5] John Aubrey, *An Essay towards the Description of the North Division of Wiltshire*, written between 1659 and 1670.

[6] Glyn E. Daniel's *The Idea of Prehistory*, London, 1962, pp. 1–61, is relevant here.

[7] Richard Colt-Hoare, *History of Ancient Wiltshire*, 1810–1821.

[8] For an illustration of some "thunderbolts," see Michael Mercati's *Metallotheca* (published in 1717—he died in 1593).

[9] The original publication is *Archaeologia*, 1800, p. 204; but there is a reprint in Daniel's *Origins and Growth*, pp. 58–59.

[10] This type of literature is perpetuated in more modern versions by some religious sects. For example, Watchtower Bible and Tract Society, *Did Man Get Here by Evolution or by Creation*, New York, 1967.

[11] These events have been described many times. One good account appears in Daniel's *Idea of Prehistory*, pp. 23–61.

[12] The *Oxford Dictionary* defines a uniformitarian as "One who attributes geological processes and phenomena to forces operating continuously and uniformly."

[13] Alan Morehead's *Darwin and the Beagle*, London, 1961, is "must" reading for everyone interested in Charles Darwin. Michael T. Ghiselin, *The Triumph of the Darwinian Method*, Berkeley, 1969, is an admirable critique of Darwin's published works.

[14] Boucher de Perthes, *De la Création: Essai sur l'origine et la progression des êtres*, Abbeville, 1838–1841; *Antiquités Celtiques et Antédiluviennes*, Abbeville, 1847. These accounts are only for those with a strong interest.

[15] John Evans, "On the Occurrence of Flint Implements in Undisturbed Beds of Gravel, Sand and Clay," *Archaeologia*, 1860, 38:280–308.

[16] T. H. Huxley, *Man's Place in Nature*, London, 1863. Huxley's prose style is justly famous and worth reading for its own sake. A good biography is Cyril Bibby, *T. H. Huxley: Scientist, Humanist and Educator*, London, 1959.

[17] The succinct summary by Gordon R. Willey, "One Hundred Years of American Archaeology," in J. O. Brew (ed.), *One Hundred Years of Anthropology*, Harvard, 1968, pp. 29–55, is probably the best account of the development of New World archaeology available, and it is drawn heavily upon here.

[18] J. L. Stephens, *Incidents of Travel in Central America: Chiapas and Yucatan*, New York, 1841.

[19] Thomas Jefferson, *Notes on the State of Virginia*, Philadelphia, 1801.

[20] Caleb Atwater, "Description of the Antiquities Discovered in the State of Ohio and other Western States," *Transactions and Collections of the American Antiquarian Society*, Worcester, 1820.

[21] *The American Antiquarian and Oriental Journal*, 1884, 6:96–97.

[22] F. H. Cushing, "Preliminary Notes on the Origin, Working Hypothesis and Primary Researches of the Hemenway Southwestern Archaeological Expedition." *Seventh International Congress of Americanists*, Berlin, 1890, pp. 151–152, 163, 167, 170–172.

[23] For a discussion see J. G. D. Clark, *Archaeology and Society*, Cambridge, 1939, pp. 17–37, and James Deetz, *Invitation to Archaeology*, New York, 1967, pp. 1–20.

[24] J. G. D. Clark's *Archaeology and Society* contains much discussion of this point, as does Stuart Piggott's *Approach to Archaeology*, London, 1959, Chaps. 1–2.

[25] For more information see Lewis R. and Sally R. Binford (eds.), *New Perspectives in Archeology*, Chicago, 1968. We return to this subject in Chapter 11.

[26] Bruce Trigger, "Aims in Prehistoric Archaeology," *Antiquity*, 1970, 44:26–37.

[27] Probably the most comprehensive study of theoretical problems in archaeology is D. L. Clarke, *Analytical Archaeology*, London, 1968, though it is not recommended for beginners.

[28] This point is well made by James Deetz in his *Invitation*, pp. 1–2, and by Gordon R. Willey and Philip Phillips, *Method and Theory in Archaeology*, Chicago, 1948, pp. 1–7.

[29] This point was made forcibly by Glyn Daniel in an editorial article in *Antiquity*, 1969, 43:86–87.

[30] J. G. D. Clark, *Archaeology and Society*, Chap. 1.

[31] John Dent, *The Quest for Nonsuch*, London, 1962, and Martin Biddle, "Nonsuch Palace 1959–60: An Interim Report," *Surrey Archaeological Collections*, 1961, 58:1–20.

[32] For two views on analogy, see the articles by Robert Ascher and Raymond H. Thompson reprinted in Brian M. Fagan (ed.), *Introductory Readings in Archaeology*, Boston, 1970, pp. 347–362.

[33] Jan Vansina, *Oral Tradition*, Chicago, 1961, is the standard reference on the methodology of oral history. The same author's *Kingdoms of the Savannah*, Wisconsin, 1966, shows the use of oral records in historical research.

Chapter 2
TIME

[1] Rasmus Nyerup, *Oversyn over Faedrelandets Mindesmaerker fra Oldtiden*, Copenhagen, 1806.

[2] C. J. Thomsen, *Ledestraad til Nordisk Oldkyndighed*, Copenhagen, 1836 (translated by Lord Ellesmere, *A Guide to Northern Archaeology*, London, 1848).

[3] J. J. A. Worsaae, *Danmarks Oldtid*, Copenhagen, 1843.

[4] Edouard Lartet and Henry Christy, *Reliquiae Aquitanicae*, London, 1874.

[5] The Swiss lake dwellings have been described in many publications. Stuart Piggott's *Ancient Europe*, Edinburgh and Chicago, 1965, pp. 57–59, has a short account and bibliography.

[6] For more on this subject, see Glyn E. Daniel's *A Hundred Years of Archaeology*, London, 1950, pp. 85–111, and *The Idea of Prehistory*, London, 1962, pp. 42–61.

[7] N. C. Nelson, *Pueblo Ruins of the Galisteo Basin, New Mexico*, New York, 1914. Manuel Gamio, a student of Franz Boas, carried out stratigraphic excavations in the Valley of Mexico as early as 1909.

[8] Alfred V. Kidder, "An Introduction to the Study of Southwestern Archaeology," *Papers of the Southwestern Expedition,* No. 1, New Haven, 1924.

[9] For some of the latest developments in this field, see Don R. Brothwell and Eric S. Higgs, *Science in Archaeology,* 2nd ed., London, 1969, Sec. 1.

[10] The general question "When was it made?" has been aired by V. Gordon Childe in *Piecing Together the Past,* London, 1956, Chap. 5.

[11] Sir Mortimer Wheeler, *Archaeology from the Earth,* Oxford, 1954, Chap. 4, is the best account of stratigraphy.

[12] Wheeler, *Archaeology,* p. 57 (1956 ed.).

[13] Childe's essay on the "Archaeological Record" in *Piecing Together the Past,* Chap. 3, defines this term.

[14] A good summary of Pleistocene geography and geology for the archaeologist may be found in Karl Butzer, *Environment and Archeology,* London, 1964. Two classic, but somewhat outdated, works are F. E. Zeuner's *Dating the Past,* London, 1946, and *The Pleistocene Period,* London, 1959. K. P. Oakley's *Frameworks for Dating Fossil Man,* London, 3rd ed., 1969, is also very useful. I. W. Cornwall, *Ice Ages,* London and New York, 1970, is a more popular account.

[15] Oakley, *Frameworks,* Chaps. 1–2.

[16] Loess has considerable importance to archaeology, especially to the chronology of the Middle and Upper Paleolithic cultures of Central Europe. Zeuner's *Pleistocene Period,* pp. 24–34, has a good account of periglacial geological phenomena which might serve as a basis for further study.

[17] Oakley, *Frameworks,* Chap. 6.

[18] Coastal shell midden sites are discussed in Chapter 5.

[19] For a summary see C. B. M. McBurney, *The Stone Age of Northern Africa,* Harmondsworth, 1960, pp. 114–121. A later summary of the evidence can be found in P. Biberson's article "Some Aspects of the Lower Palaeolithic of Northwest Africa" in W. W. Bishop and J. Desmond Clark (eds.), *Background to Evolution in Africa,* Chicago, 1967, pp. 447–476.

[20] C. B. M. McBurney and R. G. West, "The Quaternary Deposits at Hoxne, Suffolk, and Their Archaeology," *Proceedings of the Prehistoric Society,* 1954, 20:131–154.

[21] The literature is enormous—F. C. Howell, "Observations on the Earlier Phases of the European Paleolithic," *American Anthropologist,* 1966, 68 (2):88–201 summarizes much of the European material. African sites are covered in part by J. Desmond Clark, *The Prehistory of Africa,* London and New York, 1970.

[22] C. D. Ovey (ed.), "Swanscombe: A Survey of a Pleistocene Site," *Occasional Papers of the Royal Anthropological Institute,* No. 20, 1964.

[23] L. S. B. Leakey, *Olduvai Gorge,* Vol. 1, Cambridge, 1964.

[24] Oakley, *Frameworks,* Chap. 4. An essay on animal bones and the Pleistocene appears in J. M. Coles and E. S. Higgs, *The Archaeology of Early Man,* London, 1969, Chap. 2. For the fluorine dating method see the article by Oakley in Brothwell and Higgs, *Science in Archaeology,* Sec. 1.

[25] Jane Gray and Watson Smith, "Fossil Pollen and Archaeology," *Archaeology,* 1962, 15 (1):16–26.

[26] Oakley, *Frameworks,* Chaps. 3, 11.

[27] Sir Flinders Petrie, "Sequences in Prehistoric Remains," *Journal of the Royal Anthropological Institute,* 1899, 29:295–301. Other relevant literature includes: Childe, *Piecing Together the Past,* Chap. 5, and James Deetz, *Invitation to Archaeology,* New York, 1967, pp. 26–33.

[28] G. W. Brainerd, "The Place of Chronological Ordering in Archaeological Analysis," *American Antiquity,* 1951, 16:301–313.

[29] Owing to space limitations, a number of quite well known but still experimental dating methods have been omitted. See solar radiation in Zeuner, *Pleistocene Period,* pp. 173–207; fission track and obsidian dating, thermoluminescence, in Brothwell and Higgs, *Science in Archaeology,* Sec. 1.

[30] Childe, *Piecing Together the Past,* Chap. 6, contains a detailed account of cross-dating, and "synchronism" in prehistory.

[31] Brian M. Fagan, *Southern Africa during the Iron Age,* London and New York, 1965, contains an account of early trade and the Zimbabwe site.

[32] J. F. Schofield, "Southern African Beads," in Roger Summers, *Inyanga,* Cambridge, 1958, pp. 189–194—a technical article.

[33] J. G. D. Clark, *Prehistoric Europe: The Economic Basis,* London, 1952, pp. 266–269.

[34] B. Bannister, "Dendrochronology," in Brothwell and Higgs, *Science in Archaeology,* pp. 191–205. For an account of the potential of the Bristlecone pine, see G. W. Ferguson, "Bristlecone Pine: Science and Esthetics," *Science,* 1968, 159:839–846.

[35] The literature on thermoluminescence is scattered and mostly technical, but try two articles by D. W. Zimmerman: "Thermoluminescence Dating Using Fine Grains from Pottery," *Archaeometry,* 1971, 13:29–52; and "Thermoluminescent Dating of Upper Palaeolithic Fired Clay from Dolni Věstonice, *Archaeometry,* 1971, 13:53–58. For a brief general account, see E. T. Hall, "Dating Pottery by Thermoluminescence," in Brothwell and Higgs (eds.), *Science in Archaeology,* pp. 106–108.

[36] Discussion of all three techniques will be found in Brothwell and Higgs, *Science in Archaeology,* Chaps. 3–5.

[37] The literature on radiocarbon dating is huge. Try J. R. Arnold and W. F. Libby, "Age Determinations by Radiocarbon Content: Checks with Samples of Known Age," *Science,* 1949, 110:678–680, and also W. F. Libby, *Radiocarbon Dating,* Chicago, 1955, and E. H. Willis, "Radiocarbon Dating" in Brothwell and Higgs, *Science in Archaeology,* pp. 46–57.

[38] The half-life is at present accepted as 5,568 ± 30 by all laboratories, but is liable to correction.

[39] There is a growing literature on this subject. See Hans E. Suess, "Secular Variations of the Cosmic-Ray-Produced Carbon 14 in the Atmosphere and Their Interpretations," *Journal of Geophysical Research,* 1965, 70:23. It has been realized for some time that the radiocarbon dates for historical sites in Egypt were too old (W. F. Libby, "The Accuracy of Radiocarbon Dates," *Science,* 1963, 140:278–280), and the calibration of dendrochronology and radiocarbon dates offers a hopeful way out of the dilemma. The effects of the new research on Old World archaeology have been assessed by Colin Renfrew, "Tree-ring Calibration of Radiocarbon: An Archaeological Evaluation," *Proceedings of the Prehistoric Society,* 1970, 36:280–311. For a typical example of calibration in action, see C. W. Ferguson, B. Huber, and H. E. Suess, "Determination of the Age of Swiss Lake-dwellings as an Example of Dendrochronologically-Calibrated Radiocarbon Dating," *Zeitscrift für Naturforschung,* 1966, 21A, 1173–1177. See also E. K. Ralph and M. C. Han, "Potential of Thermoluminescence in Supplementing Radiocarbon Dating," *World Archaeology,* 1969, 1 (2):157–169.

[40] Potassium argon dating is well covered by W. Gentner, H. J. Lippolt, and J. A. Miller in Brothwell and Higgs, *Science in Archaeology,* Chaps. 6–7. Another useful source is G. Brent Dalrymple and Mason A. Lamphere, *Potassium Argon Dating: Principles, Techniques and Applications to Geochronology,* San Francisco, 1970.

[41] Potassium argon dates for early man are being released with increasing frequency. For a summary of the dates up to 1970, see J. Desmond Clark, *The Prehistory of Africa,* pp. 27–28. New dates are often released in articles in *Nature.* A recent case is *The New York Times* report (February 19, 1971) of a 5.5 million-year-old date for an Australopithecine find—no tools were discovered—from Lothagam, Lake Rudolf, in Kenya. For Old World chronology in general, see Robert W. Ehrich (ed.), *Chronologies in Old World Archaeology,* Chicago, 1965.

[42] R. E. F. Leakey, A. K. Behrensmeyer, F. J. Fitch, J. A. Miller, and M. D. Leakey, "New Hominid Remains and Early Artifacts from Northern Kenya," *Nature,* 1970, 226:223–230. K. P. Oakley, "Pliocene Man," *Antiquity,* 1970, 44 (176):307–308. R. E. F. Leakey, "Further Evidence of Lower Pleistocene Hominids from East Rudolf, Northern Kenya," *Nature,* 1971, 231:245–248. Also F. Vendra, *et al.,* "Preliminary Stratigraphical Studies of the East Rudolf Basin, Kenya," *Nature,* 1971, 231:248–249.

Chapter 3
PRESERVATION AND DISCOVERY

[1] Giovanni Belzoni must be one of the most remarkable characters ever to have turned his hand to archaeology. The quotation is from his *Narrative of the Operations*

and Recent Discoveries within the Pyramids, Temples, Tombs, and Excavations in Egypt and Nubia, London, 1820. A theatrical strong-man turned tomb-robber, Belzoni is well worth an afternoon's reading.

² Brian M. Fagan and F. Van Noten, *The Hunter-Gatherers of Gwisho,* Tervuren, Belgium, 1972.

³ J. Desmond Clark, *The Kalambo Falls Prehistoric Site,* Vol. 2 (in press, 1972).

⁴ P. V. Glob, *The Bog People,* London, 1969, is a popular and fascinating account of the Danish bog corpses.

⁵ Howard Carter, *et al., The Tomb of Tut-ankh-Amen,* London: Vol. 1, 1923; Vol. 2, 1927; Vol. 3, 1933.

⁶ An admirable account of Ancient Egyptian civilization is in Cyril Aldred, *The Egyptians,* London and New York, 1961.

⁷ Jesse D. Jennings, "Danger Cave," *University of Utah Anthropological Papers,* No. 27, 1953.

⁸ Earl H. Morris and Robert F. Burgh, "Basket Maker II Sites near Durango, Colorado." *Carnegie Institution of Washington Publications,* No. 604, Washington, 1954.

For details of the Southwest cultural sequence, see Gordon R. Willey, *Introduction to American Archaeology,* New York, 1966, Vol. 1: *North and Middle America,* Chap. 4, pp. 178–245.

⁹ G. H. S. Bushnell, *Peru,* London, 2nd ed., 1965, gives a succinct and well-illustrated description of Peruvian archaeology.

¹⁰ Herbert W. Dick, "Bat Cave," *School of American Research Monograph,* No. 27, Santa Fe, 1965.

¹¹ R. S. MacNeish, "Ancient Mesoamerican Civilization," *Science,* 1964, 143:531–537.

¹² Bassett Digby, *The Mammoth and Mammoth-hunting in North-East Siberia,* London, 1926.

¹³ The interested reader is referred to Rudenko's monograph for further details: S. I. Rudenko, *Frozen Tombs of Siberia: The Pazyryk Burials of Iron Age Horsemen,* Berkeley, 1970 (translated by M. W. Thompson).

¹⁴ H. B. Collins, *The Archaeology of St. Lawrence Island, Alaska,* Smithsonian Miscellaneous Collections, 96, 1, 1937.

¹⁵ Hedge Larsen and F. G. Rainey, *Ipiutak and the Arctic Whale Hunting Culture,* Anthropological Papers, Vol. 42, American Museum of Natural History, New York, 1948.

¹⁶ A good survey of a wide range of preservative situations is given in J. G. D. Clark's *Archaeology and Society,* Cambridge, 1939, Chap. 3. The examples in the preceding paragraphs are partly drawn from Clark's summary and also from S. J. de Laet, *Archaeology and Its Problems,* London, 1957.

¹⁷ Richard G. Klein, *Man and Culture in the Late Pleistocene,* San Francisco, 1969.

¹⁸ William Camden, *Britannia,* London, 1695 ed., p. 126.

¹⁹ O. G. S. Crawford, *Archaeology in the Field,* London and New York, 1953.

²⁰ O. G. S. Crawford and Alexander Keiller, *Wessex From the Air,* Oxford, 1928, is an early publication on this subject. John Bradford, *Ancient Landscapes: Studies in Field Archaeology,* London, 1957, deals with the Mediterranean area.

²¹ The basic principles of aerial photography in archaeology are enumerated by R. J. C. Atkinson, *Field Archaeology,* London, 1953, pp. 18–29. Infrared photography is still a new technique for archaeology. A sample reference is George J. Gumerman, "Infrared Scanning Images: An Archaeological Application," *Science,* 1969, 164:712–713.

²² Gordon R. Willey, "Prehistoric Settlement Patterns in the Virú Valley, Peru," *Smithsonian Institution, Bureau of American Ethnology, Bulletin* 155, 1953. The relevant passage on aerial photography is on pp. 3–6.

²³ Geoffrey Bibby, *The Testimony of the Spade,* London, 1957, pp. 349–359, has an attractive account of the Gallehus horns. This volume is an interesting introduction to European archaeology and well worth reading.

²⁴ Brian M. Fagan, D. W. Phillipson, and S. G. H. Daniels, *Iron Age Cultures in Zambia—II,* London, 1969, pp. 57–186.

²⁵ The literature is proliferating rapidly, but try Fred Wendorf, *et al., The Prehistory of Nubia,* Dallas, 1968.

[26] L. S. B. Leakey, *Olduvai Gorge, 1931–1951,* Cambridge, 1951, gives an account of early work at Olduvai.

[27] S. J. Laet, *Archaeology and Its Problems,* p. 28.

[28] F. Clark Howell, G. H. Cole, and M. R. Kleindienst, "Isimila. An Acheulian Occupation Site in the Iringa Highlands, Southern Highlands Province, Tanganyika," *Actes du IVe Congrès Panafricain de Préhistoire et de l'étude du Quaternaire, Leopoldville, 1959, Section III—pré- et protohistoire,* Tervuren, Belgium, 1962, pp. 43–80.

[29] Joe Ben Wheat, "A Paleo-Indian Bison Kill," *Scientific American,* January 1967, pp. 44–52.

[30] Brian M. Fagan, *Iron Age Cultures in Zambia—I,* London, 1957, contains a basic description of this area.

[31] The reader is referred to Crawford's *Archaeology in the Field* for further information on field survey. R. F. Heizer's reader, *The Archaeologist at Work,* New York, 1959, contains an important section of examples of site surveys, pp. 186–213.

For techniques of surface collection, see Charles L. Redman and Patti Jo Watson, "Systematic, Intensive Surface Collection," *American Antiquity,* 1970, 35 (3):279–291.

Chapter 4
EXCAVATION

[1] Thomas Wright, "Wanderings of an Antiquary: Part VII," *Gentleman's Magazine,* 1852, p. 569.

[2] Quoted from Glyn E. Daniel's *The Origins and Growth of Archaeology,* London, 1967, pp. 232–233. Some account of the work of Layard, Mariette, and Schliemann can be found in this volume, too.

[3] Carl W. Blegan and others, *Troy,* 4 Vols., Princeton, 1950–58.

[4] General Pitt Rivers, *Excavations in Cranborne Chase,* 1887–98, 4 Vols. Privately printed. His first volume describes his methods.

[5] See Gordon R. Willey's essay in J. O. Brew (ed.), *One Hundred Years of Anthropology,* Harvard, 1968, pp. 29–56.

[6] Sir Mortimer Wheeler's *Archaeology from the Earth,* Oxford, 1954, Chap. 2, contains an arresting account of the history of excavation.

[7] Chapters 4 and 5 are studded with names and examples. Although they all are not referenced, most sites mentioned briefly appear in major works of synthesis.

[8] Handbooks on archaeological excavation include: R. J. C. Atkinson, *Field Archaeology,* London, 1953; R. F. Heizer, *A Guide to Archaeological Field Methods,* Palo Alto, 1966 (3d ed.); and the latest, John Alexander, *The Directing of Archaeological Excavations,* London, 1970.

[9] The Evans family and their work in archaeology have been described by Joan Evans, *Time and Chance,* London, 1943—a fascinating story.

[10] The Minoan civilization is summarized in Sinclair Hood, *The Home of the Heroes: The Aegean before the Greeks,* London and New York, 1967; J. Pendlebury, *The Archaeology of Crete,* London, 1939; M. S. F. Hood, *The Minoans,* London and New York, 1971. Linear B was deciphered by Michael Ventris. See J. Chadwick, *The Decipherment of Linear B.,* Cambridge, 1958.

[11] Wheeler, *Archaeology from the Earth,* 1956 ed., p. 152.

[12] Not covered here are electronic methods of locating subsurface features. Try Alexander, *The Directing of Archaeological Excavations,* pp. 28–30.

[13] This remarkable excavation is mentioned in Chapter 1. See also John Dent, *The Quest for Nonsuch,* London, 1962.

[14] Sampling technique is a comparative newcomer to excavation, but any serious student should read Lewis R. Binford, "A Consideration of Archaeological Research Design," *American Antiquity,* 1964, 29:425–441.

[15] For tools see Atkinson, *Field Archaeology,* pp. 44–49; Alexander, *The Directing of Archaeological Excavations,* pp. 42–45; and Heizer, *A Guide to Archaeological Field Methods,* pp. 32–34.

[16] Recording is admirably covered by Wheeler, *Archaeology from the Earth,* pp. 68–69.

[17] A major controversy arose over Evans's field notes some years ago; see J. Boardman and L. R. Palmer, *On the Knossos Tablets,* Oxford, 1963.

¹⁸ Archaeological surveying is covered in detail by Atkinson in *Field Archaeology*, Chap. 3. Also see Heizer's *Guide*, pp. 21–31.
¹⁹ Wheeler, *Archaeology from the Earth*, pp. 22–37.
²⁰ Excavation organization on a large scale is covered by Wheeler in *ibid.*, pp. 153–177; on a small scale, by Alexander, *The Directing of Archaeological Excavations*, pp. 17–18.

Chapter 5
EXCAVATION PROBLEMS

¹ John Alexander, *The Directing of Archaeological Excavations*, London, 1970, Chap. 6, has published the only guide to living-floor excavation yet available.
² J. G. D. Clark, *Star Carr*, Cambridge, 1954.
³ B. Klima, *Dolní Věstonice*, Prague, 1963. A more general account of Russian finds can be found in Richard G. Klein, *Man and Culture in the Late Pleistocene*, San Francisco, 1969.
⁴ Joe Ben Wheat, "A Paleo-Indian Bison Kill," *Scientific American*, January 1967, pp. 44–52.
⁵ A basic reference on hunter-gatherers of great interest to archaeologists is Richard Lee and Irven DeVore (eds.), *Man the Hunter*, Chicago, 1968.
⁶ For example, the Gwisho settlements in Zambia. Brian M. Fagan and F. Van Noten, *The Hunter-Gatherers of Gwisho*, Tervuren, Belgium, 1972.
⁷ L. S. B. Leakey, *Olduvai Gorge, 1931–1951*, Cambridge, 1951, and F. Clark Howell, *Early Man*, New York, 1965.
⁸ L. S. B. Leakey, *Olduvai Gorge*, Vol. 1, Cambridge, 1965.
⁹ For a more popular account of the Olduvai discoveries see John Pfeiffer, *The Emergence of Man*, New York, 1969, pp. 72–111.
¹⁰ Glynn L. Isaac, "Studies of Early Culture in East Africa," *World Archaeology*, 1969, 1 (1):1–29.
¹¹ J. Desmond Clark, *The Kalambo Falls Prehistoric Site*, Cambridge, 1969 and later.
¹² J. Desmond Clark and C. V. Haynes, "An Elephant Butchery Site at Mwanganda's Village, Karonga, Malawi, and Its Relevance to Palaeolithic Archaeology," *World Archaeology*, 1:390–398.
¹³ F. Clark Howell, G. H. Cole, and M. R. Kleindienst, "Isimila. An Acheulian Occupation Site in the Iringa Highlands, Southern Highlands Province, Tanganyika," *Actes du IVe Congrès Panafricain de préhistoire et de l'étude du Quaternaire, Leopoldville, 1959, Section III—pre- et protohistoire*, Tervuren, Belgium, 1962, pp. 43–80.
¹⁴ J. Desmond Clark, "The Middle Acheulian Occupation Site at Latamne, Northern Syria," *Quaternaria, 9*, 1967, 10, 1969.
¹⁵ Howell, *Early Man*, pp. 85–99.
¹⁶ E. W. Haury, E. B. Sayles, and W. W. Wasley, "The Lehner Mammoth Site, South-eastern Arizona," *American Antiquity*, 1959, 25:2–30.
¹⁷ For evidence of early hunting sites in the New World, see A. D. Krieger, "Early Man in the New World," in J. D. Jennings and E. Norbeck (eds.), *Prehistoric Man in the New World*, Chicago, 1964, pp. 23–84.
¹⁸ Examples are found at Olduvai Gorge.
¹⁹ The Acheulian floor at Kalambo Falls has evidence of these.
²⁰ Kalambo Falls, Isimila, Olduvai, Olorgesaillie are only a few examples.
²¹ Brian M. Fagan and F. Van Noten, *The Hunter-Gatherers of Gwisho*, Tervuren, Belgium, 1972.
²² J. Desmond Clark, *The Prehistory of Southern Africa*, Harmondsworth, 1959, Chaps. 8–10.
²³ John Yellen is in the process of reporting on this important project—he has kindly supplied me with some information in advance of publication.
²⁴ These are vividly illustrated in Howell's *Early Man*, pp. 145–167.
²⁵ D. A. E. Garrod and Dorothea Bate, *The Stone Age of Mt. Carmel*, Vol. 1, Cambridge, 1937.
²⁶ Jesse D. Jennings, "Danger Cave," *University of Utah Anthropological Papers No. 27*, 1957.

[27] Jesse D. Jennings, *Prehistory of North America,* New York, 1968, pp. 140–143.

[28] C. B. M. McBurney, *The Haua Fteah (Cyrenaica),* Cambridge, 1967.

[29] C. B. M. McBurney, "First Season's Fieldwork on British Upper Palaeolithic Cave Deposits," *Proceedings of the Prehistoric Society,* 1959, 25:260–269.

[30] This excavation is described in Howell, *Early Man,* pp. 164–165.

[31] For further examples see Chris Musson, "House-plans and Prehistory," *Current Archaeology,* 1970, 2:267–275.

[32] James Mellaart, *Çatal Hüyük,* London and New York, 1967, p. 62.

[33] For further discussion see John Alexander, *The Directing of Archaeological Excavations,* Chap. 7.

[34] A good example is illustrated in Sir Mortimer Wheeler, *Archaeology from the Earth,* Oxford, 1954, Pl. 5.

[35] For sheer complication, nothing rivals London's archaeology. See W. F. Grimes, *The Excavation of Roman and Medieval London,* London, 1968.

[36] Wheeler, *Archaeology from the Earth,* pp. 91–97.

[37] Stuart Piggott, *Ancient Europe,* Edinburgh and Chicago, 1965, p. 52.

[38] *Ibid.,* pp. 147–148.

[39] *Ibid.,* pp. 179–185.

[40] R. J. C. Atkinson, *Field Archaeology,* London, 1953, pp. 65–67.

[41] Ivor Noël Hume, *Historical Archaeology,* New York, 1968, pp. 140–141.

[42] For a discussion of urban archaeology, start with Alexander, Chap. 8, and then peruse *World Archaeology,* Vol. 2, No. 2, October 1970, which deals with a variety of urban problems.

[43] Robber trenches are discussed by Martin Biddle and Birthe Kjolbye-Biddle in "Metres, Areas and Robbing," *World Archaeology,* 1969, 1 (2):208–219.

[44] Andrew and Wendy Selkirk, "Winchester: The Brooks," *Current Archaeology,* 1970, 2:250–255.

[45] Sir Austin Henry Layard, *Nineveh and Its Remains,* London, 1848.

[46] James Mellaart, *The Earliest Civilizations of the Near East,* London and New York, 1965.

[47] Brian M. Fagan, *Iron Age Cultures in Zambia—I,* London, 1967.

[48] Philip Phillips, James A. Ford, and James B. Griffin, "Archaeological Survey in the Lower Mississippi Alluvial Valley," *Papers of the Peabody Museum of American Archaeology and Ethnology,* 1951, Vol. 25. Also see William H. Sears, "The Southeastern United States," in J. D. Jennings and E. Norbeck (eds.), *Prehistoric Man in the New World,* Chicago, 1964, pp. 259–287.

[49] R. J. Braidwood and B. Howe, "Prehistoric Investigations in Iraqi Kurdistan," *Studies in Ancient Oriental Civilization,* Oriental Institute, Chicago, 1960, 31:39.

[50] Mound excavations are common in many parts of the world. See Seton Lloyd, *Mounds of the Near East,* Edinburgh, 1963.

[51] Sir Mortimer Wheeler, *The Indus Civilization,* Cambridge, 1963, and *Early India and Pakistan,* London and New York, 1959.

[52] Paul Ashbee, *The Bronze Age Round Barrow in Britain,* London, 1960, is a standard work on burial mounds.

[53] Paul Ashbee, *The Earthen Long Barrow in Britain,* London, 1970, is a companion volume on these mounds.

[54] Glyn E. Daniel, *The Megalith Builders of Western Europe,* London, 1958, is a standard work.

[55] This system is described by Atkinson, *Field Archaeology,* pp. 65–68.

[56] M. W. Thompson and Paul Ashbee, "Excavation of a Barrow near the Hardy Monument, Black Down, Portesham, Dorset," *Proceedings of the Prehistoric Society,* 1957, 23:124–136.

[57] Population data is discussed by W. W. Howells and H. V. Vallois in two important papers in R. F. Heizer and S. F. Cook (eds.), "The Application of Quantitative Methods in Archaeology," *Viking Fund Publications in Anthropology,* 1960, 28:158–222.

[58] The excavation of cemeteries is discussed by Alexander, *The Directing of Archaeological Excavations,* pp. 215–20.

[59] A simple manual on skeletal excavation is D. R. Brothwell's *Digging Up Bones,* London, 1965.

[60] As an example, the Ingombe Ilede burials from Zambia; see D. W. Phillipson and Brian M. Fagan, "The Date of the Ingombe Ilede Burials," *Journal of African History,* 1969, 10, 2:199–204.

[61] For techniques of preservation in archaeology generally, see H. J. Plenderleith, *The Conservation of Antiquities and Works of Art,* London, 1956.

[62] For a summary of these cultures, see Jennings, *Prehistory of North America,* pp. 191–214.

[63] Sir Mortimer Wheeler, *Maiden Castle, Dorset,* London, 1943.

[64] W. Dehn and E. Sangmeister, "Die Heuneburg bei Tallhof," *Germania,* 1954, 32:22–59.

[65] Wheeler, *Maiden Castle,* pp. 61–68.

[66] Alexander, *The Directing of Archaeological Excavations,* pp. 224–261.

[67] *Ibid.,* pp. 232–233, 228–230.

[68] *Ibid.,* pp. 255–258. For some interesting experimental archaeology, see P. A. Jewell (ed.), *The Experimental Earthwork on Overton Down,* London, 1960.

[69] The literature is enormous. For the more quantitative aspects of shell midden digging, see S. F. Cook and A. E. Treganza, "The Quantitative Investigation of Indian Mounds," *University of California Publications in American Archaeology and Ethnology,* 1950, 40:223–261.

[70] E. W. Gifford, "Composition of California Shellmounds," *University of California Publications in American Archaeology and Ethnology,* 1916, 12:1–29.

[71] W. Shawcross, "Prehistoric Diet and Economy on a Coastal Site at Galatea Bay, New Zealand," *Proceedings of the Prehistoric Society,* 1967, 33 (7):125–130.

[72] Unfortunately this important excavation is still largely unpublished. Try R. R. Inskeep, "University of Capetown Excavations at Plettenberg Bay," *Scientific South Africa,* 1965, 2:12.

[73] Clement Meighan, "The Little Harbor Site, Catalina Island: An Example of Ecological Interpretation in Archaeology," *American Antiquity,* 1959, 24:383–405.

[74] For example, the Annual Reports of the California Archaeological Survey often contain collections of early records of Pacific Coast Indians.

Chapter 6
ENVIRONMENT AND SUBSISTENCE

[1] The basic principles of ecology are enumerated in Eugene P. Odum, *Ecology,* New York, 1963, and numerous other introductory texts.

[2] J. G. D. Clark's *Aspects of Prehistory,* Berkeley, 1970, is a provocative trilogy of essays on human culture as a product of evolution. It is worth reading in this context.

[3] C. B. M. McBurney's *The Haua Fteah (Cyrenaica),* Cambridge, 1967, is a massive report on this important site. The second chapter by E. S. Higgs (pp. 16–44) summarizes the environmental and mammalian evidence. It is a book for advanced students.

[4] See Jesse D. Jennings, *Prehistory of North America,* New York, 1968, for many examples.

[5] The vegetational changes resulting from agriculture are discussed more fully on pp. 170–171, but see Johannes Iversen, "Land Occupation in Denmark's Stone Age," *Danmarks Geologiske Undersøgelse,* II Raekke, 1941, 66:20–26.

[6] J. G. D. Clark, *Star Carr,* Cambridge, 1954, is the classic monograph. It is drawn on extensively in this book.

[7] J. Desmond Clark, *The Kalambo Falls Prehistoric Site,* Vol. 1, Cambridge, 1969.

[8] An early book was J. G. D. Clark, *Archaeology and Society,* London, 1939.

[9] Chronology and classification were primary concerns. See Chapter 11.

[10] J. G. D. Clark, *Archaeology and Society,* pp. 174–177.

[11] This point has been made by J. G. D. Clark in many publications, notably *Prehistoric Europe: The Economic Basis,* London, 1952—a standard work on economic archaeology.

[12] Rodents are not discussed in this book, but they are a fascinating field of research.

Basic references can be obtained from I. W. Cornwall, *Bones for the Archaeologist*, London, 1956.

[13] This important topic has been discussed by Patricia Daly, "Approaches to Faunal Analysis in Archaeology," *American Antiquity*, 1969, 34 (2):146–153.

[14] Cornwall's *Bones for the Archaeologist* is a classic. Less well known, but useful is M. L. Ryder, *Animal Bones in Archaeology*, Oxford, 1969.

[15] There is no substitute for the actual handling of bones to learn how to analyze them. Students seriously interested in such analysis should express this to an archaeologist who handles bones.

[16] Brian M. Fagan and F. Van Noten, *The Hunter-Gatherers of Gwisho*, Tervuren, Belgium, 1972.

[17] For drawings, see Cornwall, *Bones*, Chaps. 4–5.

[18] An excellent example of a Near Eastern faunal report appears in Frank Hole, Kent V. Flannery, and James A. Neely, "Prehistory and Human Ecology of the Deh Luran Plain," *Memoirs of the Museum of Anthropology, University of Michigan*, 1969, 1:262–330.

[19] Even measurements are inadequate, for numerous factors affect growth rates in cattle and buffalo, to say nothing of sexual dimorphism.

[20] The comment in footnote 19 applies.

[21] The reader is referred to the literature for a review of the question. See, for example, Daly, "Approaches to Faunal Analysis."

[22] Richard B. Lee, "The Subsistence Ecology of the !Kung Bushmen," unpublished Ph.D. thesis, University of California, Berkeley, 1965.

[23] Phillip Smith, *Le Solutréen en France*, Paris, 1966.

[24] J. G. D. Clark, *Star Carr*, Cambridge, 1954.

[25] Howard D. Winters, "The Riverton Culture," *Illinois Archaeological Survey Monograph*, No. 1, 1969.

[26] Gordon R. Willey, *An Introduction to American Archaeology*, Englewood, N.J., 1966, 1:26–77.

[27] For an account of Indian Bison hunting, see John C. Ewers, "The Last Bison Drives of the Blackfoot Indians," *Journal of the Washington Academy of Sciences*, 1949, 39 (11):355–360.

[28] F. E. Zeuner, *A History of the Domesticated Animals*, London, 1963, pp. 203–211.

[29] Lee, *Subsistence Ecology*, p. 116.

[30] Wolf Herre, "The Science and History of Domestic Animals," in Don R. Brothwell and Eric S. Higgs (eds.), *Science in Archaeology*, London, 1969, pp. 257–272.

[31] An important information source on research into domesticated animals is Peter J. Ucko and G. W. Dimbleby (eds.), *The Domestication and Exploitation of Plants and Animals*, London and Chicago, 1969. It has been drawn on extensively here.

[32] For a summary, see Charles A. Reed, "The Pattern of Animal Domestication in the Prehistoric Near East," in *ibid.*, pp. 361–380.

[33] Belt Cave—a much quoted example—is vividly described by Carleton Coon, *Seven Caves*, London, 1957, pp. 129–167.

[34] Herre, "The Science and History of Domestic Animals," p. 261.

[35] In practice, this is harder, for the vertebrae are often very fragmentary.

[36] N. de G. Davies, *The Rock Tombs of El Amarna—V*, Archaeological Survey of Egypt, London, 1908.

[37] P. Duxos, "Methodology and Results of the Study of the Earliest Domesticated Animals in the Near East (Palestine)," in Ucko and Dimbleby (eds.), *Domestication and Exploitation*, pp. 265–276, gives an insight into some of the methodology.

[38] Richard Lee makes this point about the !Kung Bushmen (personal communication to the author).

[39] Some vivid artists' reconstructions of early kills appear in F. Clark Howell, *Early Man*, New York, 1965, pp. 94–99.

[40] Theodore White, "Observations on the Butchering Techniques of Some Aboriginal Peoples," *American Antiquity*, 1953, 19 (2):160–164.

[41] Oswald Heer, "Die Pflanzen der Pfahlbauten," *Mittelungen Antiq. Ges.,* Zurich, 1866, 15:310–317.

[42] G. Caton-Thompson and E. W. Gardner, *The Desert Fayum,* London, 1934.

[43] Stuart Struever, "Flotation Techniques for the Recovery of Small Archaeological Remains," *American Antiquity,* 1968, 33:353–362. A general book on vegetal remains is Geoffrey Dimbleby's *Plants and Archaeology,* London, 1967.

[44] Hans Helbaek has written a series of important papers on grain impressions and food plants. A significant one is his Appendix to the Deh Luran monograph "Plant Collecting, Dry-farming, and Irrigation Agriculture in Prehistoric Deh Luran," Ann Arbor, Mich., 1969, pp. 383–427—a full bibliography is appended.

[45] Johannes Iversen, "Land Occupation in Denmark's Stone Age," *Danmarks Geologiske Undersøgelse,* Copenhagen, 1941, II Raekke, 66:20–26.

[46] See Helbaek, "Plant Collecting."

[47] Clark, *Star Carr,* p. 14.

[48] Fagan and Van Noten, *Gwisho.* Reprinted in Brian M. Fagan (ed.), *Introductory Readings in Archaeology,* Boston, 1970, pp. 168–174.

[49] Paul S. Martin, *et al.,* "Mogollon Cultural Continuity," *Fieldiana: Anthropology,* Chicago, 1952, Vol. 40.

[50] Herbert W. Dick, "Bat Cave," *School of American Research Monograph,* Sante Fe, 1965, No. 27.

[51] Jesse D. Jennings, "Danger Cave," *University of Utah Anthropological Papers,* Salt Lake City, 1957, No. 27.

[52] A general discussion occurs in Jennings, *Prehistory of North America,* pp. 139–150.

[53] The most accessible references are R. S. MacNeish, "Ancient Mesoamerican Civilization," *Science,* 1964, 143:531–537, and "The Origins of New World Civilization," *Scientific American,* 1964, 211 (5):29–37.

[54] Stuart Struever, "Woodland Subsistence-Settlement Systems in the Lower Illinois Valley," in Lewis R. and Sally R. Binford (eds.), *New Perspectives in Archeology,* Chicago, 1968, pp. 285–312.

[55] Hole, *et al., Deh Luran,* pp. 23–28.

[56] J. G. D. Clark, *Prehistoric Europe,* pp. 108–109.

[57] Patrick Munson, "Recent Archaeological Research in the Dhar Tichitt Region of South-Central Mauretania," *West African Archaeological Newsletter,* 1968, 10:6–13.

[58] W. C. Darrah, "Technical Contributions to the Study of Archaeological Materials," *American Antiquity,* 1938, 3:269–270.

[59] Iversen, "Land Occupation."

[60] R. L. Kendall, "An Ecological History of the Lake Victoria Basin," *Ecological Monographs,* 1969, 39:121–176.

[61] Richard B. Lee and Irven DeVore (eds.), *Man the Hunter,* Chicago, 1968. Bushmen diet figures are from Dr. Lee.

[62] Thayer Scudder, *The Ecology of the Gwembe Tonga,* Manchester, 1962, is an excellent study of subsistence agriculture, which is relevant here.

[63] Charles F. W. Higham, "Stock Rearing as a Cultural Factor in Prehistoric Europe," *Proceedings of the Prehistoric Society,* 1967, 33 (6):99–103.

[64] Hole, *et al., Deh Luran,* p. 367.

[65] Brian M. Fagan, *Iron Age Cultures in Zambia—I,* London, 1967.

[66] Brian M. Fagan, D. W. Phillipson and S. G. H. Daniels, *Iron Age Cultures in Zambia—II,* London, 1969, pp. 199–205, 254–255.

[67] For an interesting account of tsetse flies and human settlement, see Frank L. Lambrecht, "Aspects of the Evolution and Ecology of Tsetse Flies and Trypanosomiasis in the Prehistoric African Environment," *Journal of African History,* 1964, V (1):1–24.

[68] Published by Steenstrup in the *Proceedings of the Copenhagen Academy,* 1848–55, as part of a committee report on the middens.

[69] Lord John Avebury, *Prehistoric Times,* London, 1865.

[70] Hildegarde Howard, "The Avifauna of Emeryville Shellmound," *University of California Publications in Zoology,* Berkeley, 1929, 32, 378–383.

[71] Fagan, *Iron Age Cultures,* p. 75. For a review of birds in archaeology, see Elliot

W. Dawson, "Bird Remains in Archaeology" in Brothwell and Higgs (eds.), *Science in Archaeology*, pp. 359-375.

[72] J. G. D. Clark, *Prehistoric Europe*, p. 44.

[73] *Ibid.*, pp. 44-45.

[74] Jennings, *Prehistory of North America*, pp. 125-127.

[75] J. G. D. Clark, *Prehistoric Europe*, p. 47.

[76] For illustrations, see F. Bordes, *The Old Stone Age*, London and New York, 1968, Fig. 59.

[77] J. Scheffer, *The History of Lappland*, Oxford, 1674 (translation).

[78] Fagan and Van Noten, *Gwisho.*

[79] Chester King, Thomas Blackburn, and Ernest Chandonet, "The Archaeological Investigation of Three Sites on the Century Ranch, Western Los Angeles County, California," *California Archaeological Survey Annual Report*, 1968, 10:12-161.

[80] The site has been studied by the author; the report is not yet published.

[81] R. Raven-Hart, *Before Van Riebeeck*, Capetown, 1967, p. 100.

[82] See footnote 61.

[83] Robert M. Crabtree, *et al.*, "Archaeological Investigations at Batiquitos Lagoon, San Diego County," *California Archaeological Survey Annual Report, 1962-3*, Los Angeles, 1963, pp. 319-462.

[84] J. G. D. Clark, *Prehistoric Europe*, pp. 241-243.

[85] D. J. Mulvaney, *The Prehistory of Australia*, London and New York, 1969, Fig. 19.

[86] Brian M. Fagan, "Early Trade and Raw Materials in South Central Africa," *Journal of African History*, 1969, 10 (1):1-14.

[87] J. Desmond Clark, *The Prehistory of Southern Africa*, Harmondsworth, 1959, p. 217.

[88] P. Vinnecombe, "A Fishing Scene from the Tsoelike River, Southeastern Basutoland, *South African Archaeological Bulletin*, 1960, 15:15-19.

[89] J. Desmond Clark, "A Note on Early River-craft and Fishing Practices in South-east Africa," *South African Archaeological Bulletin*, 1960, 15:77-79.

[90] S. H. Warren, "On a Prehistoric Interment near Walton-on-Naze," *Essex Naturalist*, 1911, 16:198-208.

[91] P. V. Glob, *The Bog People*, London, 1969, is a fascinating account of bog corpses in Denmark.

[92] Jennings, "Danger Cave."

[93] R. F. Heizer, "Analysis of Human Coprolites from a Dry Nevada Cave," *Reports of the University of California Archaeological Survey*, 1967, 70:1-20. Also see his "The Archaeology of Prehistoric Great Basin Coprolites," in Brothwell and Higgs (eds.), *Science in Archaeology*, pp. 244-250.

[94] E. O. Callen, "Diet as Revealed by Coprolites," in Brothwell and Higgs (eds.), *Science in Archaeology*, pp. 235-243.

[95] R. F. Heizer, "Physical Analysis of Habitation Residues," in R. F. Heizer and S. F. Cook (eds.), "The Application of Quantitative Methods in Archaeology," *Viking Fund Publications in Anthropology*, 1960, 28:93-102.

[96] An account of early Australian stoneworking occurs in A. W. Howitt, *The Native Tribes of South-East Australia*, London, 1904, pp. 311-312, 340-341. Also see Mulvaney, *Prehistory of Australia*, pp. 170-171.

[97] J. G. D. Clark, *Prehistoric Europe*, pp. 244-251, summarizes research on this topic.

[98] A. C. Renfrew, J. E. Dixon, and J. R. Cann, "Obsidian and Early Cultural Contact in the Near East," *Proceedings of the Prehistoric Society*, 1966, 32, 1-29, and subsequent articles.

[99] Horace Beck and J. F. Schofield, "Beads," in Roger Summers, *Inyanga*, Cambridge, 1958, pp. 180-229.

[100] See Willey, *An Introduction to American Archaeology*, 1:261, for further references.

[101] J. G. D. Clark, *Prehistoric Europe*, pp. 261-266.

[102] Stuart Piggott, *Ancient Europe*, Edinburgh and Chicago, 1965, pp. 137-138.

[103] For this and further examples, see F. Hole and R. F. Heizer, *An Introduction to Prehistoric Archaeology*, New York, 1969, pp. 292-296.

Chapter 7
TECHNOLOGY AND ARTIFACTS

[1] J. G. D. Clark, *Prehistoric Europe*, London, 1952, p. 171.
[2] Parts of this chapter draw again on J. G. D. Clark's *Aspects of Prehistory*, Berkeley, 1970.
[3] The principles of stoneworking have been described in more detail in F. Clark Howell, *Early Man*, New York, 1965, pp. 101–108. Several excellent films on stoneworking have been released; among the best are two produced by the University of California, Berkeley.
[4] An interesting example of this type of natural fracture was described by J. Desmond Clark, "The Natural Fracture of Pebbles from the Batoka Gorge, Northern Rhodesia, and Its Bearing on the Kafuan Industries of Africa," *Proceedings of the Prehistoric Society*, 1958, 24:64–77.
[5] Perfect "pebble tools" have been made by throwing flint cobbles into a cement mixer!
[6] Dr. L. S. B. Leakey has often demonstrated the efficiency of Stone Age tools for dismembering game. See L. S. B. Leakey, "Exploring 1,750,000 Years into Man's Past," *National Geographic*, October 1961, pp. 586–587.
[7] A summary of the controversy occurs in M. C. Burkitt, *The Old Stone Age*, Cambridge, 1955, pp. 103–111.
[8] A. S. Barnes, "Les Outils de l'homme tertiaire en Angleterre. Etude critique," *L'Anthropologie*, 1938, 47.
[9] M. D. Leakey, *Olduvai Gorge*, Vol. 3, Cambridge, 1971.
[10] Four good summary articles deal with hand-axe industries: F. Clark Howell and J. Desmond Clark, "Acheulian Hunter-Gatherers of Sub-Saharan Africa," in F. Clark Howell and François Bourlière (eds.), "African Ecology and Human Evolution," *Viking Fund Publications in Anthropology*, 1963, 36:458–533; J. Desmond Clark, "Acheulian Occupation Sites in the Middle East and Africa: A Study in Cultural Variability," *American Anthropologist*, 1966, 68 (2):202–229; F. Clark Howell, "Observations on the Earlier Phases of the European Lower Paleolithic," *American Anthropologist*, 1966, 68 (2):88–201; D. A. Roe, "The British Lower and Middle Palaeolithic: Some Problems, Methods of Study and Preliminary Results," *Proceedings of the Prehistoric Society*, 1964, 30:245–267.
[11] For a description of this technique, see Howell, *Early Man*, p. 112.
[12] Indian blade- and pressure-flaking has been described by several observers, and a summary of the early literature is in W. H. Holmes, *Handbook of Aboriginal American Antiquities*, Pt. 1, Introductory: The Lithic Industry, Bureau of American Ethnology, Bulletin 60, 1919.
For a lighthearted look at stoneworking, see H. Mewhinney, *A Manual for Neanderthals*, Houston, 1957.
[13] J. G. D. Clark, *Aspects of Prehistory*, pp. 70–79.
[14] Howell, *Early Man*, pp. 114–115.
[15] For the microburin technique, see J. G. D. Clark, *The Mesolithic Age in Britain*, Cambridge, 1932, Appendix 1.
[16] William H. Townsend, "Stone and Steel Tool Use in a New Guinea Society," *Ethnology*, 1969, 8 (2):199–205.
[17] J. G. D. Clark, *World Prehistory*, Cambridge, 1969, Chap. 11.
[18] G. de Mortillet, *Le Préhistorique*, Paris, 1883.
[19] The Bushmen's stoneworking methods were vividly described by George Stow, *The Native Tribes of South Africa*, Capetown, 1905.
[20] The Brandon flintmakers fabricated gunflints for flintlock guns, and were still doing good business until recent years. Rainbird Clark, "The Flint-Knapping Industry at Brandon," *Antiquity*, 1935, 9:38–56.
Another account of gunflint-making is D. W. Phillipson's "Gunflint manufacture in North-western Zambia," *Antiquity*, 1969, 43:301–304.
[21] The films were released by the University of California, Berkeley.

[22] Quantitative methods for studying stone implements have a long history, and the literature is enormous. An early and much used method is that of François Bordes, "Principes d'une methode d'étude des techniques et de la typologie du Paléolithique ancien et moyen," *L'Anthropologie*, 1950, 54:19–34. A. C. Spaulding's essay "Statistical Techniques for the Study of Artifact Types," *American Antiquity*, 1953, 18 (4):305–313, is essential reading for those concerned with this aspect of archaeology. Multivariate analyses are now widely used, and the reader is advised to consult an archaeologist working in this area if he wants up-to-date information. Spaulding's "The Dimensions of Archaeology," in Gertrude E. Dole and Robert L. Carneiro (eds.), *Essays in the Science of Culture in Honor of Leslie A. White*, New York, 1960, pp. 437–456, is also relevant.

[23] S. A. Semenov, *Prehistoric Technology*, London, 1964 (trans. by M. W. Thompson).

[24] Charles M. Keller, "The Development of Edge Wear Patterns on Stone Tools," *Man*, 1966, 1 (4):501–511.

[25] See references in footnote 10.

[26] J. Desmond Clark, *The Kalambo Falls Prehistoric Site*, Vol. 2, Cambridge, 1972.

[27] Illustrated by J. G. D. Clark, *Aspects of Prehistory*, p. 66.

[28] J. Desmond Clark, *The Prehistory of Southern Africa*, Harmondsworth, 1959, pp. 86–89.

[29] Brian M. Fagan and F. Van Noten, *The Hunter-Gatherers of Gwisho*, Tervuren, Belgium, 1972.

[30] A summary occurs in J. D. Jennings, *Prehistory of North America*, New York, 1968, pp. 247–286.

[31] Gosta Montell, *Dress and Ornaments in Ancient Peru*, Goteborg, 1929.

[32] Sir Leonard Woolley's description of the Royal Tombs at Ur-of-the-Chaldees is rightly famous: *Ur Excavations, Publications of the Joint Expedition of the British Museum and of the Museum of the University of Pennsylvania to Mesopotamia*, London, 1934, Vol. 2, *The Royal Cemetery*, pp. 33–38, 41–42.

[33] An introduction to European Bronze Age typology can be obtained from Stuart Piggott, *Ancient Europe*, Edinburgh and Chicago, 1965—where numerous references will be found.

[34] R. A. Dart, *The Osteodontokeratic Culture of Australopithecus prometheus*, Pretoria, 1957.

[35] Donald L. Wolberg, "The Hypothesized Osteodontokeratic Culture of the Australopithecinae: A Look at the Evidence and the Opinions," *Current Anthropology*, 1970, 11 (1):23–38. Also, C. K. Brain, "Bone Weathering and the Problem of Bone Pseudo-tools," *South African Journal of Science*, 1967, 63 (3):97–99; and "Hottentot Food Remains and Their Bearing on the Interpretation of Fossil Bone Assemblages," *Scientific Papers of the Namib Desert Research Station, Pretoria, South Africa*, 1967, 32 (6):1–7.

[36] M. D. Leakey, "Preliminary Survey of the Cultural Material from Beds I and II, Olduvai Gorge, Tanzania," in W. W. Bishop and J. Desmond Clark (eds.), *Background to Evolution in Africa*, Chicago, 1967, pp. 417–446.

[37] F. Bordes, *The Old Stone Age*, New York, 1968.

[38] Gordon R. Willey, *An Introduction to American Archaeology*, New York, 1966, 1:42–43.

[39] P. Graziosi, *Palaeolithic Art*, London, 1960, contains illustrations of the most important pieces.

[40] J. G. D. Clark, *Star Carr*, Cambridge, 1954, pp. 115–119.

[41] H. B. Collins, "The Archaeology of St. Lawrence Island, Alaska," *Smithsonian Miscellaneous Collections*, 1937, 96:1.

[42] A recent summary is Gary A. Wright's "Origins of Food Production in Southwestern Asia: A Survey of Ideas," *Current Anthropology*, 1971, 12 (45):447–478.

[43] For Tehuacán, see R. S. MacNeish, "The Origins of New World Civilization," *Scientific American*, 1964, 211:29–37.

For the remarkable Japanese discoveries, see Richard E. Morlan, "The Perceramic Period of Hokkaido: An Outline," *Arctic Anthropology*, 1967, 4:164–220; Kensaku Hayashi, "The Fukui Microblade Technology and Its Relationships in Northeast Asia and North America," *Arctic Anthropology*, 1968, 5:128–190.

[44] Alfred V. Kidder, *An Introduction to the Study of Southwestern Archaeology with a Preliminary Account of the Excavations at Pecos*, New Haven, 1924.

[45] F. R. Matson, "Ceramics and Man," *Viking Fund Publications in Anthropology*, No. 41, 1965, is a recent corpus on the subject.

[46] Brian M. Fagan, *Iron Age Cultures in Zambia—I*, London, 1967.

[47] Anna O. Shepard, *Ceramics for the Archaeologist*, Washington, D.C., 1965, is a classic on pottery, but definitely a technical monograph.

[48] Nuclear fingerprinting of pottery is another promising method being developed in the United States.

[49] F. Asaro and I. Perlman, "Deduction of Provenience of Pottery from Trace Element Analysis," *Lawrence Radiation Laboratory*, Berkeley, 1967.

[50] Basic references on metallurgy include R. J. Forbes, *Studies in Ancient Technology*, London, 1955–58; R. F. Tylecote, *Metallurgy in Archaeology*, London, 1962.

[51] M. E. L. Mallowan, *Early Mesopotamia and Iran*, London and New York, 1965.

[52] For early metallurgy in Europe, see Piggott, *Ancient Europe*, pp. 71–112.

[53] J. G. D. Clark, *Prehistoric Europe*, pp. 183–204.

[54] Jan Vansina, *Kingdoms of the Savannah*, Madison and London, 1966.

[55] Willey, *An Introduction to American Archaeology*, 1:261.

[56] J. G. D. Clark, *Prehistoric Europe*, pp. 189–194.

[57] Roger Summers, *Ancient Mining in Rhodesia*, Salisbury, 1969.

[58] For the early history of ironworking in the Old World, Stuart Piggott's *Ancient Europe* is a fruitful source of references.

[59] Brian M. Fagan and Roland Oliver, "The Emergence of Bantu Africa," in *The Cambridge History of Africa*, Vol. 2 (to be published).

[60] Iron and copper smelting techniques have not received the attention that they should. Tylecote has summarized some smelting methods, and African metallurgy has been described by several authors. See J. H. Chaplin, "Notes on Traditional Smelting in Northern Rhodesia," *South African Archaeological Bulletin*, 1962, 16 (63):53–60.

[61] Piggott, *Ancient Europe*, pp. 185 ff.

[62] F. Hole and R. F. Heizer, *An Introduction to Prehistoric Archaeology*, New York, 1969, p. 167. V. Gordon Childe's *Piecing Together the Past*, London, 1956, Chap. 7, contains an excellent discussion of classification in archaeology.

[63] The concept of "type" has been the subject of lengthy controversy in New World archaeology, and to a lesser extent in European circles. The literature is bulky and sometimes acrimonious. A few references include Irving Rouse, "The Classification of Artifacts in Archaeology," *American Antiquity*, 1960, 25 (3):313–323; Albert C. Spaulding, "Statistical Techniques"; J. A. Ford, "A Comment on A. C. Spaulding, 'Statistical Techniques. . . ,'" *American Antiquity*, 1954, 19:390–391; J. A. Ford, "On the Concept of Types," *American Anthropologist*, 1954, 56:42–54; A. D. Krieger, "The Typological Concept," *American Antiquity*, 1944, 9:271–288.

[64] James Deetz, *Invitation to Archaeology*, New York, 1967, p. 51.

[65] *Ibid.*, pp. 45–49.

[66] A major discussion of advanced taxonomic methods is found in David Clarke's *Analytical Archaeology*, London, 1968, Chaps. 11–14.

[67] This example drawn from James Deetz's *Invitation to Archaeology*, pp. 45–48, is by far the most articulate discussion of this point so far published.

[68] To learn classification, there is no substitute for actually handling artifacts—interested readers should get involved in some analytical research in a nearby laboratory if possible.

Chapter 8
ORDERING AND INTERPRETATION

[1] John Evans, "On the Date of British Coins," *Numismatic Chronicle*, 1849–50, 12:127.

[2] Flinders Petrie, "Sequences in Prehistoric Remains," *Journal of the Royal Anthropological Institute*, 1899, 29:295–301.

[3] J. J. A. Worsaae, *The Primeval Antiquities of Denmark*, London, 1849 (translation of Danish edition, Copenhagen, 1843).

[4] John Rowe, "Worsaae's Law and the Use of Grave Lots for Archaeological Dating," *American Antiquity*, 1962, 28:129–137.

[5] Frank Roy Hodson, "The La Tène Cemetery at Munsingen-Rain: Catalogue and Relative Chronology," *Acta Bernensia,* V, Bern, 1968.

[6] James Deetz, *Invitation to Archaeology,* New York, 1967, pp. 26–33. Edwin Dethlefsen and James Deetz, "Death's Heads, Cherubs and Willow Trees: Experimental Archaeology in Colonial Cemeteries," *American Antiquity,* 1966, 31:502–510.

[7] See, for example, Robert C. Dunnell, "The Seriation Method and Its Evaluation," *American Antiquity,* 1970, 35 (3):305–319; F. Hole and M. Shaw, "Computer Analysis of Chronological Seriation," *Rice University Studies,* 1967, 53:3; and L. Johnson, "Item Seriation as an Aid for Elementary Scale and Cluster Analysis," *Bulletin of the Museum of Natural History, University of Oregon,* Eugene, 1968, No. 15.

[8] For sampling procedure, see F. Hole and R. F. Heizer, *An Introduction to Prehistoric Archaeology,* New York, 1969, pp. 139–140.

[9] A pungent description of the role of distribution maps in archaeology is in V. Gordon Childe, *Piecing Together the Past,* London, 1956, pp. 115–122.

[10] V. Gordon Childe, *Prehistoric Migrations in Europe,* Oslo, 1950, p. 2.

[11] Fundamental reading on archaeological units is contained in Gordon R. Willey and Philip Phillips, *Method and Theory in American Archaeology,* Chicago, 1958, pp. 11–43. This important book explores the subject in depth and should be read by all students seriously interested in archaeology.

[12] *Ibid.,* pp. 16–17.

[13] W. C. McKern, "The Midwestern Taxonomic Method as an Aid to Archaeological Culture Study," *American Antiquity,* 1939, 4:301–313.

[14] J. G. D. Clark, *Aspects of Prehistory,* Berkeley, 1970.

[15] Clyde Kluckhohn and William Kelly, "The Concept of Culture," in Ralph Linton (ed.), *The Science of Man in the World Crisis,* New York, 1945, pp. 78–106, quote, p. 97.

[16] V. Gordon Childe, "Neolithic House-types in Temperate Europe," *Proceedings of the Prehistoric Society,* 1949, 15:77–86. Quote, p. 81.

[17] This section draws extensively from two works: Childe's *Piecing Together the Past* and Bruce Trigger's *Beyond History: The Methods of Prehistory,* New York, 1968, pp. 26–47. The latter is abundantly referenced.

[18] K. P. Oakley, "Fire as a Palaeolithic Tool and Weapon," *Proceedings of the Prehistoric Society,* 1955, 21:36–48.

[19] Stuart Piggott, *Ancient Europe,* Edinburgh and Chicago, 1965, Chap. 5.

[20] J. G. D. Clark, *Prehistoric Europe,* London, 1952, pp. 266–269. There has been recent discussion about manufacture of British faience beads—some think they were made locally.

[21] Alfred L. Kroeber, *Anthropology,* New York, 1948, is a major corpus of this great anthropologist's work.

[22] Deetz, *Invitation to Archaeology,* pp. 55–59.

[23] Leslie Spier, "The Sun Dance of the Plains Indians," *Anthropological Papers of the American Museum of Natural History,* 1921, 16:7.

[24] Brian M. Fagan, *Southern Africa,* London and New York, 1965, pp. 100–135.

[25] The Indus Civilization made use of coolie labor. See Sir Mortimer Wheeler, *Early India and Pakistan,* London and New York, 1959, Chap. 5.

[26] Hole and Heizer's *An Introduction,* pp. 331–339, has been drawn on here.

[27] Lewis R. Binford, *et al.,* "Archaeology at Hatchery West," *Memoirs of the Society for American Archaeology,* 1970, 24.

[28] *Ibid.,* p. 89.

[29] Another example is the Carter Ranch work by William Longacre, discussed in Chapter 9. See William A. Longacre, "Some Aspects of Prehistoric Society in East-Central Arizona," in Lewis R. and Sally Binford (eds.), *New Perspectives in Archeology,* Chicago, 1968, pp. 89–102.

[30] James Deetz, "The Inference of Residence and Descent Rules from Archeological Data," in Binford and Binford, *New Perspectives,* pp. 41–48.

[31] James Deetz, "The Dynamics of Stylistic Change in Arikara Ceramics," *Illinois Studies in Anthropology,* 1965, No. 4.

[32] The Shang Civilization (1766–1122 B.C.) is discussed by W. Watson, *China before the Han Dynasty*, London, 1961; and Chinese urban archaeology in general, by Paul Wheatley, "Archaeology and the Chinese City," *World Archaeology*, 1970, 2 (2):159–185.

[33] Lewis R. Binford, "Archaeology as Anthropology," *American Antiquity*, 1962, 28 (2):217–225. Brian M. Fagan, D. W. Phillipson, and S. G. H. Daniels, *Iron Age Cultures in Zambia—II*, London, 1969, contains an account of the Ingombe Ilede burials, some of which were adorned with rich grave goods.

[34] John Alexander has described some problems connected with the excavation of such sites. *The Directing of Archaeological Excavations*, London, 1970, Chap. 9.

[35] P. Graziosi, *Palaeolithic Art*, London, 1960.

[36] P. J. Ucko, "The Interpretation of Prehistoric Anthropomorphic Figurines," *Journal of the Royal Anthropological Institute*, 1962, 92:38–54.

[37] A. Leroi-Gourhan, *Treasures of Prehistoric Art*, New York, 1967.

[38] The most famous example of astronomical archaeology is undoubtedly Stonehenge. G. S. Hawkins, *Stonehenge Decoded*, New York, 1965, is a monograph that prompted a lively controversy: R. J. C. Atkinson, "Moonshine on Stonehenge," *Antiquity*, 1966, pp. 212–216.

[39] Clark suggested that some red deer antler frontlets from the site were akin to the headdresses worn by Mongolian shamans. J. G. D. Clark, *Star Carr*, Cambridge, 1954, pp. 168–172.

[40] W. J. Sollas, *Ancient Hunters*, London, 1911.

[41] S. I. Rudenko, "The Ancient Culture of the Bering Sea and the Eskimo Problem," *Arctic Institute of North America—Anthropology of the North: Translations from Russian Sources/No. 1*, University of Toronto Press, 1961, pp. 163–164.

[42] *Ibid.*, p. 165.

[43] M. A. Smith, "The Limitations of Inference in Archaeology," *Archaeological Newsletter*, 1955, 6:3–7.

[44] Among others, see K. C. Chang, "Major Aspects of the Interrelationship of Archeology and Ethnology," *Current Anthropology*, 1967, 8 (34):227–243; and Christopher Hawkes, "Suggestions from the Old World," *American Anthropologist*, 1954, 56:155–168.

[45] R. H. Thompson, "The Subjective Element in Archaeological Inference," *Southwestern Journal of Anthropology*, 1956, 12 (3):327–332. See also Robert Ascher, "Analogy in Archaeological Interpretation," *Southwestern Journal of Anthropology*, 1961, 17 (4):317–325.

[46] See Julian H. Steward, "The Direct Historical Approach to Archaeology," *American Antiquity*, 1942, 7:337–343; Christopher Hawkes, "Archaeological Theory" and W. D. Strong, "Historical Approach in Anthropology," in Alfred L. Kroeber (ed.), *Anthropology Today*, Chicago, 1953.

[47] J. C. Harrington, "Evidence of Manual Reckoning in the Cittie of Ralegh," *The North Carolina Historical Review*, 1956, 33:1.

[48] Hawkes, "Archaeological Theory."

[49] Sir Mortimer Wheeler, *Maiden Castle*, London, 1943, pp. 126–129.

[50] Jesse D. Jennings, "The Desert West," in J. D. Jennings and E. Norbeck (eds.), *Prehistoric Man in the New World*, Chicago, 1964, pp. 149–174.

[51] Lewis R. Binford, "Smudge Pits and Hide Smoking: The Role of Analogy in Archaeological Reasoning," *American Antiquity*, 1967, 32 (1):1–12.

[52] James N. Hill, "Broken K. Pueblo: Prehistoric Social Organization in the American Southwest," *Anthropological Papers, University of Arizona*, 1970, No. 18.

Chapter 9
SETTLEMENT ARCHAEOLOGY

[1] Sir Samuel Baker, *The Albert Nyanza*, London, 1866, 1:150.

[2] The recent volume *Settlement Archaeology*, edited by K. C. Chang (Palo Alto, 1968), has been drawn on extensively in writing this chapter. The book is strongly recommended both for further reading and references.

[3] Gordon R. Willey, "Prehistoric Settlement Patterns in the Virú Valley," *Bureau of American Ethnology, Bulletin No. 155*, Washington, D.C., 1953.

[4] Bruce C. Trigger's important contribution to the Chang volume, "The Determinants of Settlement Patterns," in *Settlement Archaeology*, pp. 53–78, is used to a considerable extent in this chapter. Quote, p. 55.

[5] Good descriptions of such dwellings are to be found in Richard G. Klein, *Man and Culture in the Late Pleistocene*, San Francisco, 1969.

[6] Barrie Reynolds, *The Material Culture of the Gwembe Tonga*, Manchester, 1967.

[7] George Silberbauer, *Bushman Survey Report*, Gaberones, 1965.

[8] C. Daryll Forde, *Habitat, Economy, and Society*, London, 1934.

[9] For discussion, see Trigger, "Determinants," pp. 55–60.

[10] M. D. Coe, *The Maya*, New York, 1967.

[11] Brian M. Fagan, *Southern Africa*, London and New York, 1965, pp. 82–84, 121–122.

[12] James Mellaart, *The Earliest Civilizations of the Near East*, London and New York, 1965, p. 107.

[13] Cyril Aldred, *The Egyptians*, London and New York, 1961, pp. 182–183.

[14] G. P. Murdock, *Social Structure*, New York, 1949, p. 79.

[15] M. E. L. Mallowan, *Early Mesopotamia and Iran*, London and New York, 1965.

[16] Neville Chittick, "Kilwa and the Arab Settlement of the East African Coast," *Journal of African History*, 1963, 4 (2):179–190.

[17] R. S. MacNeish, "Iroquois Pottery Types," *National Museum of Canada Bulletin*, 1952, No. 124.

[18] Sir Mortimer Wheeler, *The Indus Valley Civilization*, Cambridge, 1960.

[19] George L. Cowgill, "Computer Analysis of Archaeological Data from Teotihuacán, Mexico, in Lewis R. and Sally R. Binford (eds.), *New Perspectives in Archeology*, Chicago, 1968, pp. 143–150. Also see René Millon, "Teotihuacán: Completion of Map of Giant Ancient City in the Valley of Mexico," *Science*, 1970, 170:1077–1082.

[20] William A. Longacre, "Some Aspects of Prehistoric Society in East-Central Arizona," in Binford and Binford (eds.), *New Perspectives*, pp. 89–102.

[21] *Ibid.*, p. 89.

[22] *Ibid.*, p. 91.

[23] *Ibid.*

[24] *Ibid.* Final report: *Archaeology as Anthropology*, Tucson, 1970.

[25] For a distribution map of the tsetse fly in Africa, see J. Desmond Clark (ed.), *Atlas of African Prehistory*, Chicago, 1967.

[26] Audrey I. Richards, *Land, Labour and Diet among the Bemba of Northern Rhodesia*, Oxford, 1937, pp. 228–350.

[27] Mosheshwe was a fascinating character. See E. Casalis, *Les Bassoutos*, Paris, 1859, and Leonard Thompson and Monica Wilson (eds.), *Oxford History of South Africa*, Oxford, 1969, 1:398 ff.

Chapter 10
INTELLECTUAL FRAMEWORKS:
MERCATI TO DURKHEIM

[1] Julian H. Steward and Frank M. Setzler, "Function and Configuration in Archaeology," *American Antiquity*, 1938, 4 (1):4–10.

[2] Michael Mercati, *Metallotheca*, 1717.

[3] A delightful account of the discovery of the South Seas and of the "Noble Savage" was written by Alan Moorehead, *The Fatal Impact*, London, 1966. Marvin Harris, *The Rise of Anthropological Theory*, New York, 1968, Chaps. 2–3, has been used extensively in writing this part of the text. His discussion of eighteenth-century thought is valuable.

[4] See J. W. Burrow, *Evolution and Society*, New York, 1966.

[5] Gustav Klemm, *Allgemeine Cultur-Geschichte der Manscheit*, Leipzig, 1843.

[6] Loren Eiseley, *Darwin's Century*, New York, 1958, is an invaluable history of the roots of Darwinism.

[7] See Chapter 1.

[8] Charles Darwin, *The Origin of Species*, London, 1859.

[9] *Ibid.*, p. 275. Many years later, Darwin wrote the *Descent of Man*, London, 1871, in which he explored human evolution.

[10] Herbert Spencer, *Social Statistics,* London, 1855, p. 27.

[11] Gabriel de Mortillet, *Promenades Préhistoriques á l'Exposition Universelle,* Paris, 1867.

[12] Henry A. Layard, *Nineveh and Its Remains,* London, 1849.

[13] J. L. Stephens, *Incidents of Travel in Central America: Chiapas and Yucatan,* New York, 1841.

[14] The most celebrated acceptance of the art was that Emil Cartailhac, "Les Cavernes ornées de dessins: La grotte d'Altamira. Mea culpa d'un sceptique," *L'Anthropologie,* 1901, 12:671.

[15] The descriptions of Tylor, Durkheim, and Boas in this book have been drawn extensively from Abram Kardiner and Edward Preble, *They Studied Man,* New York, 1961.

[16] Edward Tylor, *Anahuac,* London, 1861.

[17] Edward Tylor, *Anthropology,* London, 1881, p. 275 (pagination from Ann Arbor edition, 1960).

[18] Gordon R. Willey, "A Hundred Years of American Archaeology," in J. O. Brew (ed.), *One Hundred Years of Anthropology,* Cambridge, 1968, pp. 29–56.

[19] J. J. A. Worsaae, *The Primeval Antiquities of Denmark,* London, 1849.

[20] Edward Tylor, *Researches into the Early History of Mankind,* London, 1865. Chapter 6 contains a discussion of this point. Quote, p. 3.

[21] Ably discussed by Glyn E. Daniel, *The Idea of Prehistory,* London, 1962, Chap. 5.

[22] Kardiner and Preble, *They Studied Man,* pp. 95–116.

[23] Quoted from *ibid.,* p. 102.

[24] Malinowski was a remarkable character. See *ibid.,* pp. 140–162.

[25] *Ibid.,* p. 151. For an assessment of Malinowski's work, see Clyde Kluckhohn, "Bronislaw Malinowski, 1884–1942," *Journal of American Folklore,* 1943, 56:208–219. Also see Bronislaw Malinowski, *A Scientific Theory of Culture and Other Essays,* London, 1944.

[26] A. R. Radcliffe-Brown, *Structure and Function in Primitive Society,* New York, 1952.

Chapter 11

TOWARD EXPLANATION: 1900 TO THE 1970s

[1] Franz Boas, "The Central Eskimo," *Smithsonian Institution, Bureau of Ethnology, Annual Report No. 6, 1884–5,* 1888, pp. 399–669. Quote, p. 21.

[2] Boas's greatest book was the *Mind of Primitive Man,* New York, 1911. He published a series of his most important papers in *Race, Language and Culture,* New York, 1940. His descriptive work appears in, among other publications, *The Handbook of American Indians,* Washington, D.C. For a biography, see M. J. Herskovits, *Franz Boas: The Science of Man in the Making,* New York, 1953.

[3] Franz Boas, "Archaeological Investigations in the Valley of Mexico by the International School, 1911–12," *Proceedings of the Eighteenth International Congress of Americanists,* London, 1913, pp. 176–179.

[4] W. D. Strong, "An Introduction to Nebraska Archeology," *Smithsonian Miscellaneous Collections,* 1935, Vol. 93, No. 10.

[5] Alfred L. Kroeber was another great gatherer of basic information on the American Indian. One of his most magisterial works was his edited "Handbook of the Indians of California," *Bureau of American Ethnology,* Washington, D.C., Bulletin 78, 1925.

[6] This account of V. Gordon Childe has been drawn from his own "Retrospect," *Antiquity,* 1958, 32:69–74, and Stuart Piggott's "The Dawn and an Epilogue," *Antiquity,* 32:75–79.

[7] V. Gordon Childe, *The Dawn of European Civilization,* London, 1925, Preface.

[8] Childe, "Retrospect," p. 70.

[9] *Ibid.*

[10] J. H. Plumb, *The Death of the Past,* London, 1969, p. 136.

[11] J. G. D. Clark, *World Prehistory: A New Outline,* Cambridge, 1969, and Chester Chard, *Man in Prehistory,* New York, 1968.

[12] For Childe's own assessment of this episode in his life, see "Retrospect," pp. 71–72.

[13] Childe's own admission—see "Retrospect," p. 72.

[14] V. Gordon Childe, *Social Evolution*, London, 1951, p. 3.

[15] Leslie White's work is not discussed in this volume, but see Leslie White, *The Evolution of Culture*, New York, 1959.

[16] W. C. McKern, "The Midwestern Taxonomic Method as an Aid to Archaeological Culture Study," *American Antiquity*, 1939, 4 (4):301–313.

[17] See the essay by Gordon R. Willey, "Horizon Styles and Pottery Traditions in Peruvian Archaeology," *American Antiquity*, 1945, 11:49–56.

[18] J. A. Ford and Gordon R. Willey, "An Interpretation of the Prehistory of the Eastern United States," *American Anthropologist*, 1941, 43 (3):325–363; J. B. Griffin, "Culture Change and Continuity in Eastern United States," in F. Johnson (ed.), *Man in Northeastern North America*, Andover, 1946, pp. 37–95.

[19] Gordon R. Willey and Philip Phillips, *Method and Theory in American Archaeology*, Chicago, 1958.

[20] Again see Gordon R. Willey, "One Hundred Years of American Archaeology," in J. O. Brew (ed.), *One Hundred Years of Anthropology*, Cambridge, 1968, pp. 29–56.

[21] Childe's syntheses are still widely read. Apart from *The Dawn*, the most famous are: *The Most Ancient East*, London, 1928; *The Danube in Prehistory*, Oxford, 1929; *The Bronze Age*, Cambridge, 1930; *New Light on the Most Ancient East*, London, 1934; *Man Makes Himself*, London, 1936; *What Happened in History*, Harmondsworth, 1942; *Prehistoric Migrations in Europe*, Oslo, 1950; *Social Evolution*, London, 1951; *Piecing Together the Past*, London, 1956.

[22] Robert J. Braidwood and B. Howe, *Prehistoric Investigations in Iraqi Kurdistan*, Chicago, 1960. R. M. Adams, *The Evolution of Urban Society*, Chicago, 1966, is another important reference.

[23] Gordon R. Willey, *An Introduction to American Archaeology*, Vol. 1, New York, 1966.

[24] Childe, "Retrospect," p. 74.

[25] J. G. D. Clark, *Star Carr*, Cambridge, 1954.

[26] W. W. Taylor, *A Study of Archaeology*, Menasha, 1948.

[27] See the commentary by Willey in "One Hundred Years," pp. 51–52.

[28] Gordon R. Willey, "Settlement Archaeology: An Appraisal," in K. C. Chang (ed.), *Settlement Archaeology*, Palo Alto, 1968, pp. 208–226, is an important reference, as are the brief comments on p. 52 of "One Hundred Years."

[29] See Chapter 9.

[30] Julian H. Steward, *Theory of Culture Change*, Urbana, 1963, p. 3.

[31] *Ibid.*, p. 4.

[32] *Ibid.*, p. 7.

[33] *Ibid.*

[34] *Ibid.*, p. 34.

[35] One example of the determinist approach is that of Betty Meggers. For a synthesis, see her *Ecuador*, London and New York, 1965.

[36] Stuart Piggott, *Approach to Archaeology*, New York, 1965, pp. 4–5, contains a rather pessimistic statement.

[37] The results of some recent work were summarized in Lewis R. and Sally R. Binford (eds.), *New Perspectives in Archeology*, Chicago, 1968. See also David L. Clarke, *Analytical Archaeology*, London, 1968.

[38] Lewis R. Binford, "Archaeological Perspectives," in Binford and Binford, *New Perspectives*, pp. 5–32.

[39] *Ibid.*, p. 22. Another important reference is by the same author, "Archaeology as Anthropology," *American Antiquity*, 1962, 28 (2):217–225.

[40] A. D. Hall and R. E. Fagen, "Definition of System," *General Systems Yearbook*, 1956, 1:18.

[41] James Doran, "Systems Theory, Computer Simulations and Archaeology," *World Archaeology*, 1970, 1 (3):289–298, quotation from p. 290. This paper is a "must" for all archaeologists, and comes from the pen of a computer scientist concerned with archaeology.

[42] Clarke, *Analytical Archaeology*, p. 43.

[43] Lewis R. Binford, "Systematics and Cultural Process," *American Antiquity*, 1965, 31 (2):209.

[44] The relevant paper is Kent V. Flannery, "Archaeological Systems Theory and Early Mesoamerica," in Betty Meggers (ed.), *Anthropological Archaeology in the Americas*, Washington, D.C., 1968, pp. 67–87. Quote, p. 68.

[45] James W. Judge, "Systems Analysis and the Folsom-Midland Question," *Southwestern Journal of Anthropology*, 1970, 1:40–51.

[46] F. Hole and R. F. Heizer, *An Introduction to Prehistoric Archaeology*, New York, 2nd ed., 1970, p. 385.

[47] In addition to Clarke's book and Doran's paper, the following papers on systems theory may be of interest: Kenneth E. Boulding, "General Systems Theory—the Skeleton of Science," *Management Science*, 1966, 2:197–208. Ludwig von Bertalanffy, "General System Theory," *General Systems Yearbook*, 1956, 1:1–10.

An important paper on explanation in archaeology is Albert C. Spaulding's "Explanation in Archaeology," in Binford and Binford, *New Perspectives*, pp. 33–40.

[48] Binford, "Archaeological Perspectives," p. 26.

[49] *Ibid.*

Chapter 12
CONCLUSION

[1] Charles Kingsley, *The Water Babies*, London, 1863, p. 153 (pagination from 1910 ed.).

[2] *Tarikh*, a journal published in West Africa, is designed to acquaint schoolteachers with the latest results of archaeological and historical research in Africa.

[3] Brian M. Fagan "Review of A. J. Bruwer, *Zimbabwe: Rhodesia's Ancient Greatness*," *Antiquity*, 1970, 3:320.

[4] This remark is attributed to President Banda and is a fitting note upon which to end this book.

Bibliography of Area Archaeologies

To give a comprehensive list of area archaeologies in the limited space available is impossible. In general, English language references predominate, on the assumption most readers of this text are English-speaking. The rate of archaeological publication is such that some works have inevitably been missed. The Ancient Peoples and Places Series (Thames and Hudson, London, and Praeger, New York) is recommended as a source of accurate and scientific information on area archaeology; the volumes are comparatively inexpensive.

WORLD ARCHAEOLOGIES

Chard, Chester. *Man in Prehistory*. New York, 1968.
Clark, Grahame (J. G. D.). *World Prehistory: A New Outline*. Cambridge, 1969.

AFRICA

Clark, J. Desmond. *The Prehistory of Africa*. London and New York, 1970.

ARCTIC

Bandi, M. G. *Eskimo Archaeology*. London, 1969 (originally published in German, 1964).
Giddings, J. L. *Ancient Men of the Arctic*. London and New York, 1967.
Mathiassen, T. *Archaeology of the Central Eskimos*. Copenhagen, 1927.

AUSTRALIA

Mulvaney, D. J. *The Prehistory of Australia.* London and New York, 1969.

CHINA

Chang, Kwang-Chih. *The Archaeology of Ancient China.* New Haven, 1963.
Watson, W. *China.* London and New York, 1959.

EGYPT

Aldred, Cyril. *The Egyptians.* London and New York, 1961.

EUROPE

General Surveys

Clark, J. G. D., and Stuart Piggott. *Prehistoric Societies.* London and New York, 1965.
Roe, Derek. *Prehistory.* London and Berkeley, Calif., 1970.
Thomas, Homer I. *Near Eastern, Mediterranean, and European Chronology.* Lund, 1967.
The archaeological literature of Europe is scattered in publications in many languages. The references given here are those most readily available to Americans. Information on more up-to-date literature should be obtained from archaeologists working in the field.

Stone Age

Bordes, F. *The Old Stone Age.* New York, 1968.
Coles, John, and E. S. Higgs. *The Archaeology of Early Man.* London, 1969.
Both volumes cover other areas of the world as well.

Neolithic and Later

Clark, J. G. D. *Prehistoric Europe: The Economic Basis.* London, 1952.
Piggott, Stuart. *Ancient Europe.* Edinburgh and Chicago, 1965.
Both volumes have some coverage of earlier archaeology.

INDIA AND PAKISTAN

Wheeler, Sir Mortimer. *Early India and Pakistan.* London and New York, 1959.

JAPAN

Kidder, J. E. *Japan.* London and New York, 1959.
The Kidder volume is somewhat outdated. Recent numbers of *Arctic Anthropology* are recommended for information on the pre-ceramic cultures of Japan. It is advisable to contact a specialist before starting a detailed study of Japanese archaeology.

NEAR EAST

Lloyd, S. *Early Highland Peoples of Anatolia.* London and New York, 1967.
Mallowan, M. E. L. *Early Mesopotamia and Iran.* London and New York, 1965.
Mellaart, James. *The Earliest Civilizations of the Near East.* London and New York, 1966.

NORTH AMERICA AND MESOAMERICA

Coe, M. D. *Mexico.* London and New York, 1962.
Coe, M. D. *The Maya.* London and New York, 1966.
Jennings, J. D. *Prehistory of North America.* New York, 1968.
Sanders, William T., and Barbara J. Price. *Mesoamerica: The Evolution of a Civilization.* New York, 1968.
Willey, Gordon R. *Introduction to American Archaeology.* Vol. I: *North and Mesoamerica.* Englewood Cliffs, N.J., 1966.
Wormington, H. M. *Ancient Man in North America.* Denver, 1957.

PACIFIC OCEAN AREA AND NEW ZEALAND

Freeman, J. D., and W. R. Geddes (eds.). *Anthropology in the South Seas.* New Plymouth, N.Z., 1959.
Golson, J., and P. Gathercole. "New Zealand Archaeology." *Antiquity,* 1962, 36:168–174, 271–278.
Sharp, A. *Ancient Voyages in the Pacific.* London, 1957.
Suggs, R. C. *The Island Civilization of Polynesia.* New York, 1960.

SIBERIA

Michael, Henry N. *The Archaeology and Geomorphology of Northern Asia.* Toronto, 1964.
Okladnikov, A. P. *The Ancient Peoples of Siberia and Its Cultures.* London, 1959.

Rudenko, Sergei I. *The Ancient Cultures of the Bering Sea and the Eskimo Problem.* Toronto, 1961.

Rudenko, Sergei I. *Frozen Tombs of Siberia: The Pazyryk Burials of Iron Age Horsemen* (trans. by M. W. Thompson). Berkeley, 1970.

SOUTH AMERICA

Bushnell, G. H. S. *Peru.* London and New York, 1963 (2nd ed.).

Griffin, J. B. "Handbook of South American Indians." *Bureau of American Ethnology Bulletin,* 1946, No. 143.

Lathrap, Donald W. *The Upper Amazon.* London and New York, 1970.

Meggers, Betty J. *Ecuador.* London and New York, 1965.

Willey, Gordon R. *Introduction to American Archaeology,* Vol. 2: *South America.* Englewood Cliffs, N.J., 1971.

SOUTHEAST ASIA

There are numerous articles about this area. See the bibliography in J. G. D. Clark, *World Prehistory,* p. 314.

UNION OF SOVIET SOCIALIST REPUBLICS

Klein, Richard. *Man and Culture in the Late Pleistocene.* San Francisco, 1969.

Mongait, A. *Archaeology in the U.S.S.R.* London, 1959.

Rice, T. T. *The Scythians.* London and New York, 1957.

Sulimirski, Tadeusz. *Prehistoric Russia: An Outline.* London, 1970.

UNITED STATES

General Surveys

Bushnell, G. H. S. *The First Americans.* London and New York, 1968.

Sanders, William T., and Joseph Marino. *New World Prehistory.* New York, 1970.

Glossary

(Those technical terms defined in the text are not included here.)

Absolutist: despotic.
Ake: a shrub (antique English).
Arroyo: a gully.
Articular end: the process at the end of a bone, which serves as the joint.
Artifact: any object manufactured or modified by man.
Assemblage: all the industries at one site.
Attribute: a well-defined feature found on an artifact.

Barrow: a burial mound.
Burin: a blade tool, flaked on either or both ends to form a small chisel or grooving tool.
Byre: a cow shed.

Cambium: a viscid substance lying under the bark of trees, in which the annual growth of wood and bark takes place.
Component: the manifestation of a given archaeological focus at a specific site (*focus* or *phase* in the Willey and Phillips sense—see *Phase*).
Conchologist: one who studies shells.
Coprolite: petrified excrement.
Core: in archaeology, a lump of stone from which humanly struck flakes have been removed.
Cultigen: a cultivable plant.
Cultural anthropology: those aspects of anthropology focusing on cultural facets of human societies—a term widely used in the United States.
Culture: similar assemblages found at several sites, defined in a context of time and space.

345

Culture trait: an item, element, or feature in an archaeological (or anthropological) culture.

Cusp: a projection on the crown of a tooth.

Datum point: a reference point on an archaeological site, normally surveyed onto a large-scale map, and used as a base point for all measurements on the site.

Dendrochronology: tree-ring chronology.

Detritus: debris or droppings.

Downcutting: erosion of a river channel by water action.

Epigrapher: one who studies inscriptions.

Epiphysis: articular end of a long bone, a process that fuses at adulthood.

Escarpment: a hill range or cliff (a geological term).

Ethnography: a descriptive study, normally an in-depth examination of a particular culture.

Ethnology: a cross-cultural study of particular aspects of various cultures, usually theoretically based.

Exogamy: a rule requiring marriage outside a social or cultural unit (*endogamy* means the opposite).

Extrasomatic: outside the body.

Faience: glazed terracotta.

Fibula: a brooch.

Fire setting: a technique for quarrying stone by using fire to shatter the outcrops of rock.

Focus: approximately equivalent to a phase.

Fuller: a clothmaker.

Functional type: an archaeological classification based on the supposed function of the artifact concerned.

Geochronology: geological dating.

Glacial eustasy: the adjustments made in sea levels and the earth's crust as a result of the expansion and contraction of Pleistocene ice sheets.

Heuristic: serving to find out; a means of discovery.

Historiography: the writing of history.

Hominid: a member of the family Hominidae, represented by a single genus *Homo sapiens.*

Homotaxial: strata or cultures that have the same relative position, but are not necessarily contemporaneous.

Horizon: "a primarily spatial continuity represented by cultural traits and assemblages whose nature and mode of occurrence permit the assumption of a broad and rapid spread."—Willey and Phillips, *Method and Theory in American Archaeology,* Chicago, 1958, p. 33.

Hydrology: the scientific study of water—its properties and laws.

Industry: all artifacts of one particular kind (viz., bone, stone, or wood) found at one site, made at the same time, by the same population.
Innominate bones: pelvis and scapula.

Knapper: a stoneworker.

Lactation: the secretion of milk from mammary glands.
Lense: a term used in stratigraphic interpretation to mean a thin line of deposit such as a "sand lense" which is often of minor significance relative to the major layers. On small sites, lenses can sometimes assume greater importance.
Loess: windblown glacial sand.

Matriarchal society: family authority rests with the woman's family.
Matrilocal society: married couples live with or near the wife's mother.
Mica: a mineral, occurring in a glittering scaly form, widely prized for ornamental purposes.
Midden: a deposit of occupation debris, rubbish, or other by-products of human activity.
Monotheistic: a religion recognizing one god.
Moraine: a deposit of debris left by an advancing or retreating glacier.

Obsidian: black volcanic glass.
Ossification: the fusion of a limb bone with its articular end. Also used to imply stagnation, or calcification of soft tissue into bone-like material.
Osteologist: one who studies bones.

Paleobotanist: one who studies prehistoric botany.
Paleoecology: the study of ecology in ancient times.
Paleontology: the study of fossil (or ancient) bones.
Palynology: pollen analysis.
Patrilocal society: married couples live with or near the husband's father.
Pedology: the scientific study of soil.
Periglacial: surrounding a glacial area.
Permafrost: permanently frozen subsoil.
Phase: "an archaeological unit possessing traits sufficiently characteristic to distinguish it from all other units similarly conceived, whether of the same or other cultures or civilizations, spatially limited to the order of magnitude of a locality or region and chronologically limited to a relatively brief interval of time."—Willey and Phillips, *Method and Theory*, p. 22.
Physical anthropology: basically biological anthropology, it includes the study of fossil man, genetics, primates, and blood groups, among other subjects.
Potsherd: a fragment of a clay vessel.

Quaternary era: the last great subdivision of geological time, of which the Pleistocene is a part.

Revetment: a retaining wall supporting an earthwork.

Seriation: ordering.

Social anthropology: the British equivalent for cultural anthropology, but with an emphasis on sociological factors.

Spore: pollen grain.

Stalagmite: a cement-like deposit formed over long periods of time in caves. Stalagmite often seals layers of occupation deposit, especially in limestone caves.

Stela or *stele:* a column or stone slab often with an inscribed or sculptured surface.

Strandlooper: a beachcomber, or shellfish eater.

Superposition: the deposition of one stratum on another.

Tectonic: a term referring to the earth's crust; tectonic movement is an earthquake.

Tell: a mound; a term used to refer to archaeological sites of this type in the Near East.

Tempering: a process for hardening iron blades, involving heating and rapid cooling.

Tradition: in archaeological terms, "a [primarily] temporal continuity represented by persistent configurations in single technologies or other systems of related forms."—Willey and Phillips, *Method and Theory,* p. 37.

Trypanosomiasis: sleeping sickness.

Tsetse: a fly that carries trypanosomiasis. Because of belts of tsetse fly country in Africa, inhabitants are prevented from raising cattle.

Tuff: volcanic lava.

Type fossil: a tool type characteristic of a particular "archaeological era," an outdated concept borrowed from geology.

Typology: classification of artifacts in archaeology.

Unaerated: not exposed to the open air.

Unilineal evolution: evolution in a single direction, without branching.

Unit: in archaeological terms, an artificial taxonomic grouping used for description of artifacts.

Votive: intended as an offering as a result of a vow.

Index

(Page numbers in italics indicate illustrations)

Abbeville, 15–16
Abri Pataud, 105, *107*
absolute dating, 32
accidental discoveries, 70–74
Acheulian, 13, 60, 73, 146, *192–194*, 284
Adena, 131
aerial photography, 68–70
ageing, 159–162
Alaca Hüyük, 215
Ali Kosh, 166
Altamira, 248, *286*
amber trade, 186
American Indians, 3, 17–18, 318–319
analogy, in archaeology, 24, 248–256
Anasazi culture, 62
Ancient Britons, 13
animal drawings, *158, 160, 286, 317*
Antiquity of Man, 9–16, 26, 278, 282
Apple Creek, 166–168
"archaeological animal," 151
archaeological cultures, 238–239
archaeological evidence, 19
archaeological survey, 74
archaeological units, 236–237
archaeologists
  as anthropologists, 21
  as craftsmen, 21
  diversity of, 20
  qualities of, 24

archaeology
  definition of, 21–22, 223–228
  and history, 23
  objectives of, 20, 306–307
  scientific method in, ,309
  study of, 4
archaeomagnetism, 54
area excavation, 85–86
Arikara, 247–248
Arnold, J. R., 55
arrows and spears, *149, 204*
artifacts
  classification of, 222–223
  density of, *103*
  patterning of, 247
assimilation, 240
association, 15
Assurbanipal, King of Assyria,
  frontispiece
Aswan Dam, 72
Atwater, Caleb, 17
Aubrey, John, 6–8
Aurignacian, 107, 201
Aurochs (*Bos primigenius*), *156–157, 158*
Australian aborigines, 28, 197, 202, 220,
  227, 249, 253–254, *281*, 305
Australopithecines, 22, 40, 58, 100, 141,
  189, 192, 204, 230, 275, 316, 319
Avebury, Lord, 6, 136

349

axes and tools, 149, 151, 184, 191–200, 206, 232, 307

Bacon, Francis, 67
Bagford, John, 13
Baker, Samuel, 257
baler shells, 179
Banda, Hastings, 319
Bantu-speaking peoples, 24, 220,
barrows, 78, 122, 125–129
Basketmaker, 62, 203
Bat Cave, 62, 165
Batoka Plateau, 174
Bebwawi, 161
Belt Cave, 159
Belzoni, Giovanni, 59, 80
Bemba, 269
Bent, Theodore, 50
Beresovka mammoth, 62
Bersu, Gerard, 80
Biddle, Martin, 81
Binford, Lewis, 90, 247, 265, 308–311, 315
bird bones, 174–175
Black, Glenn A., 80
Boas, Franz, 294–298, 306
bog corpses, 150
bones
    of extinct animals, 13
    in geochronology, 41–42
    sorting and identification of (animal), 150–155
Bordes, François, 202
Boylston Street (Boston), 176
Brandon (flint makers), 202
bristlecone pine, 52
Britannia, 6
Broken K Pueblo, 255–256
bronzeworking, 217, 219
Brooks site, 118–122
Browne, Thomas, 13
Buckland, William, 15
bulb of percussion, 190–191
burial mounds, 122–129
burials, 130, 132, 180
Bushmen, 100–102, 156, 170–171, 249, 253–254, 258, 263, 305
butchery
    sites, 162–164
    techniques, 159, 163

Cahokia, 123
cambium, 52
Camden, William, 6, 67, 68, 76
Cape York, 179
carbonized seeds, 150
Carnarvon, Lord, 61
Carter, Howard, 61, 80
Carter Ranch Pueblo, 265–268
Çatal Hüyük, 108
Catalina Island, 137
Catastrophists, 14–15, 283
Catherwood, Frederick, 17, 66
Cat Hole, 104
Caton-Thompson, Gertrude, 164
caves, 102–106
    paintings in, 286
cemeteries, 129–131, 232, 308
Century Ranch, 177
Chang, Kwang Chih, 105
Cheyenne Indians, 242
Childe, V. Gordon, 238, 291, 293, 298–301, 303
Christy, Henry, 287
chronological sequence, 53
Chumash Indians, 177, 227–228
Clacton Channel, 60, 203
Clark, Grahame (J. G. D.), 61, 148, 156, 187, 299, 300, 303
Clark, J. Desmond, 180, 269
Clarke, David L., 308, 314
classical antiquities, 5
classification of artifacts, 222–228
Clopton, 119
Cochise, 165
coins, 230
Colchester, 117
Collins, H. B., 208
Colonial gravestones, 233–236
Colonial Williamsburg, 80, 89, 95, 115, 135
Colt-Hoare, Richard, 11
communities, 263
conchoidal fracture, 196
conchologist, 178
cone, of percussion, 190
cone effect, 243
conjunctive approach, 304
context, 82
Conus shell, 179, 180
Conyers, John, 13

Conze, Alexander, 79
copperworking, 215–218
Coutier, J., 202
Cowgill, George, 265
Coxcatlan Cave, 166
Crabtree, Don, 202
Crawford, O. G. S., 67–68
Creation, 3, 10–14, 26–27, 277
Creswellian, 104
crop marks, 69
cross-dating, 49, 51
Cueva de los Caballos, 182
cultural ecology, 305–306
cultural inheritance, 141
cultural process, 20
cultural relativism, 250, 289–291
culture trait, spread of, 243
Cunliffe, Barrie, 81
Curtius, Ernst, 79
Cushing, F. H., 18
Cutler, Reverend Manasseh, 52
Cuvier, Jacques, 14, 283
cylinder hammer technique, 193

daggers, 219, 226
Danger Cave, 62, 103, 165
Danubian, 179, 269
Dart, Raymond, 204–206
Darwin, Charles, 15–18, 282–283, 291
Davis, E. H., 17
de Beaulieu, Augustin, 178
de Condorcet, Marquis, 282
deer antler, 207
Deetz, James, 224–227, 242, 247
Deh Luran Plain, 173–174
Deir El-Medina, 263
Deiringsen-Ruploh, 111
de Mortillet, Gabriel, 199–201, 237, 285
dendrochronology, 51–54, 57
dentition, 153
de Palacio, Garcia, 66
de Perthes, Jacques Boucher, 15–16, 28, 72, 282
Desert Culture, 239, 253–254
Dethlefsen, Edwin, 233
Diaz, Bartholomew, 22
diet (prehistoric), 182–184
diffusion, 239–246, 289–291, 299–301
Dimbleby, Geoffrey, 128–129
direct historical approach, 302

documentary history, 22–23, 31–32
domestication of animals, 157–159, 171–174
Doran, James, 310–311, 314
Dordogne, 28, 102–104
Dorpfeld, Wilhelm, 79
Douglass, A. E., 51
druids, 8
Dugdale, William, 13
Durango, 62
Durkheim, Emil, 291–293
dwellings, 107–115

earthworks, dating of, 133
ecological approaches, 303–306
ecological determinism, 258
ecosystem, 141–142, 148
elephants, evolution of, 42, 43, 44
El-Lahun, 263
Emeryville mound, 175
eoliths, 191
Ertebølle, 174
Eskimo archaeology, 64–65, 207–209
Evans, Sir Arthur, 83–84, 298
Evans, Sir John, 16, 229, 230
evolution, 15, 31, 282–289
excavation, 78, 121
  as destruction, 82
  methods, 81, 85, 109
    grid, 87, 89
    quadrant (*see* quadrant system)
    vertical, 86
  organization, 94–97
  strategy, 83–84
explanation, of cultural process, 306–309

faience beads, 24, 49, 50, 51, 240
Farragut, David Glasgow, 32
Fayum, 164
feces (*see* coprolites)
Fendoch, 134
field archaeology, 7, 8
Fishborne, 81
fishing, 175–178, 181
fission track technique, 54
Flannery, Kent V., 311–313
Florisbad, 203
flotation techniques, 164, 166–168
folk culture approach, 252

Folsom, 156
   points, *198*, 313–314
food residues, 148
Ford, James, 302
fort, Roman, *134*
Fort Raleigh, 252
foundation trenches, 109
Fox, Sir Cyril, 80, 269
Freeman, J. P. Williams, 67
Frere, John, 13, 40
functional classification, 224
functionalism, 253, 291–293

game animals, 158–159
Gamio, Manuel, 295
Galatea Bay, *136–137*
Gallehus, 71
general systems theory (*see* systems
   theory)
Genesis, 3, 10
geochronology, 36–46
Gifford, C. W., 137
Glacial Eustasy, 37–39
glaciations, 37–38
Godwin, William, 279
gold, 215, *216*
grain impressions, 168, *169*
Grand Pressigny flint, 184
gravestones, *235*, *236*
Gravettian, 107
grid excavation, 109
Griffin, James, 302
Gunz, 37
Gwisho, 60, 100, 165, 177, 203, *205*
Gypsum Cave, 165

Hacilar, 263
Hall, Richard, 50
Hallstatt, 220, 221
Harappa, 122–123, 125, *126*, *135*, 248,
   264, 268
harpoons and spears, *204*, *205*, *207*, *209*,
   218
Hatchery West, 247
Haua Fteah Cave, *104*, *105*, 143–145
Haven, Samuel, 17
Heck, Lutz, 156
Heizer, Robert, 183, 223, 314
Henry VIII, 23, 85, 260
Herculaneum, 65
Herodotus, 4
Hesiod, 5

Heuneberg, 133
Higham, Charles, 172
high sea levels, 37–40
Hill, James N., 255
history and archaeology, 22–25
Hittite, 220
Hobbes, Thomas, 278–279
Hodson, Roy, 232
Hohokam, *215*
Hole, Frank, 168, 223, 314
Homer, 5
Homo erectus, 40, 192, 275
Honfleur, 178
Hopewell, 131, 186
Howard, Hildegarde, 175
Howell, F. Clark, 73
houses, *108*, *111*, *115*, *116*, *246*
Hoxne, 13, *40–41*
human behavior, 23
Humboldt Lake, 183
hunting camps, 98
huts, *108*, *112*, *113*
Hutton, James, 14
Huxley, Thomas, 16

imported luxuries, 50
Inca, 62, *303*
Indian, Fuegan, *284*
Indian mounds, 17
Indus civilization, 264, 268
inference, 24
Ingombe Ilede, 71–72, 130, *132*, *180*
inorganic objects, 60
Inskeep, R. R., 39–40
invention, 239, 241, 245
Ipiutak, 65
ironworking, 220–222
Isamu Pati, *113*, 210
Isimila, 73, 100, 193
Iversen, Johannes, 170

Jarmo, 123, 208
Jefferson, Thomas, 17, 79, 82
Jelinek, Arthur, 81
Jericho, 123, 203, 208
Judge, James W., 313–314

Kafue River, 74, 100, 177
Kalambo Falls, 60, 100, 146, 193, 203
Kalomo, *94*, *211*
Kalundu, *96*
Kaminaljuyú, *214*

Kangila, *112*
Kant, Immanuel, 279
Karanga kingdom, 50, 245, 261, *319*
Kariba, 72
Kaushambi, *127*
Kelly, William, 238
Kent's Cavern, 15-16
Khoi-Khoi, 22, 178, *280*
Kidder, A. V., 29, 80, 210, 237, 293
Kilwa, 264
Klemm, Gustav, 282
Kluckhohn, Clyde, 238
Knossos, 76, 83-84, *160*
Koln-Lindenthal, 111
Koobi Fora, 58
Kostenki, *246*
Kroeber, Alfred, 240, 243
Kunda, 176
!Kung Bushmen, 101, 155, 170, 260
Kwakiutl, 295

La Batiquitos Lagoon, 178-179
La Jolla culture, 178-179
lake beds, 40-41
Lake Superior, copper trade, 186, 216
Lake Victoria, 170
La Motte, 247
Lane Fox, A. H. L. (*see* Pitt Rivers, A. H. L.)
Lartet, Edward, 28
Lascaux Caves, 248, *286*
Lassen, Erik, 71
La Tène, 232, 284, 308
Latookas, 257
Layard, Henry, 79, 285
Leakey, L. S. B., 41, 56, 72, 99, 102, 202
Lee, Richard, 157
Lehringen, 203
Les Eyzies, 105, *107*, 308
Lesotho, *181*
Leubingen, *116*
Levallois cores, *194-195*
Leya, *172*
Libby, W. F., 55
Lightfoot, John, 10
Limpopo River, 245, 262
Lindenmeis, 205
Linear B tablets, 84
Linnaeus, Carl, 282
living floor archaeology, 98-102
Livingstone, David, 22, 179
Locke, John, 278-279

loess, 39, 66
Longacre, William, 265, 308
Lorthet, *317*
Lothagam, 178
Lovelock Cave, 103, 165, 183
Luba kingdom, 216
Lubbock, John (*see* Avebury, Lord)
Lyell, Sir Charles, 15, 33, 282

McBurney, C. B. M., 104, 143
MacEnery, J., 15
Machu Picchu, *303*
MacIver, Randall, 50
McKern, W. C., 301
MacNeish, Richard, 62, 199
Madsen, Frederick, 211
Magdalenian, 176, 201, 205-*207*, 284, 308, 317
Maglemose, 174, 176
Maiden Castle, 69, *86-87*, *117*, *132*, *133*, 252-253
maize, 62, 166-168
Malinowski, Bronislaw, 293, 300
mammal bones, 149-150
mammalogists, 152
maps
  general, *39*, *51*, *185*
  of text sites
    Africa, *11*
    Asia, *12*
    Europe, *8*
    Mesoamerica, *7*
    Near East, *10*
    United Kingdom, *9*
    United States, *7*
    Zambia, *75*
Mapungubwe, 262
Marietta, 52
Mariette, August, 79, 82
Marxist-Leninist doctrines, 249-250, 299-300
Maya, 22, *214*, 258, 261, *262*, 268, 270, 289
Megalithic tombs, 125
Meighan, Clement, 137
Mellaart, James, 263
mental template, 225
Mercati, Michael, 13, 277-278
metallurgy, 215-222
microliths, 198
middens, shell, *136-137*
Midland projectile points, 313-314

Midwestern taxonomic system, 237, 301
migration, 240–241
Millon, René, 265
Mindel, 37
Minoan civilization, 83, 160, 298
Mississippian, 123, 247
Missouri Valley, 247
Mitterburg, 218
Miyowagh, 64
Moche, 231
Mogollon, 62, 165, 265
Mohenjodaro, 122–123, 125, 248, 264
mollusca, 148, 178–179
Monomotapa, 49
Montelius, Oscar, 237, 301
Morgan, Lewis, 288–289, 292, 300,
    304–305
Mosheshwe, Chief, 270
mound
    contour plan of, 94
    excavation, 122–125
    formation, 123–124
Mount Carmel, 81, 103
multiple regression analysis, 266–267
Munsingen-Rain, 232
Mwari, 261–262
Mycene, 240

Nabonidus, 4
Nankin porcelain, 49
Natchez, 123
natural selection, 15, 283
Nehalennia, 72
Nelson, N. C., 29, 210
New World archaeology
    history of, 16–19, 21
    outline of, 30
Nile Valley, 61, 72, 316
Nineveh, 122
noble savage, concept of, 6, 278–280
Noël Hume, Ivor, 81
Nonsuch, 23, 85
Nyerup, Rasmus, 27

objects of known age, 49–51
obsidian
    dating, 54
    trade, 185
occupation levels, 35–36
Okvik, 208
Old Bering Sea, 208, 209
Old Kingdom, 175

Olduvai Gorge, 40–41, 56–58, 72, 81, 83,
    99–100, 102, 162, 192, 205, 253
Old World archaeology, 29
Olmec, 200, 275
Olorgesaillie, 100
Olsen-Chubbuck site, 73, 253
Olympia, 79
oral history, 4, 24
Ordrup Mose, 170, 171
organic materials, 60
Origin of Species, 15, 278, 282–283, 285
Ortelius, Abraham, 6
osteodontokeratic culture, 204–206
osteology, 152

palace, 109
paleoecology, 142
Paleolithic cultures, 201
Paley, William, 13–14
palynology, 43–46, 127, 145–146, 170,
    171, 267–268
papyrus texts, 62
parahistoric sites, 252
Pazyryk, 63–64
patination, 60
Pecos Pueblo, 28, 210
Pengelly, William, 16
Perigordian, 107
Perry, W. J., 291, 298
Petrie, Flinders, 47, 50, 79, 80, 230–231
petrological analyses, 184
Peyrère, Isaac de la, 13
Piggott, Stuart, 222, 300
Pitt Rivers, A. H. L., 21, 80–81, 229–230
Plainview, 156
Plantago, 170
Pleistocene, geological events of, 38
Pleistocene faunas, 41–42
Plimoth Plantation, 49
Pliny, 65
Plot, Robert, 13
pollen analysis (see palynology)
pollen diagram, 47
pollen spores, 43–45
Polo, Marco, 277
Pompeii, 65
population distributions, 268–270
porcelain, Chinese, 49–50, 213
Portesham, 128–129
postholes, 109
potassium argon dating, 48, 56–58
pottery, in archaeology, 208–215

prehistoric stockbreeding, 171–173
preservation, 19, 59–66
pressure flaking, 197–198
Prestwich, Joseph, 16
Prichard, J. C., 282
primary silting, 134
Pueblo Indians, 18, 60, 254
Punuk, 208, *209*

quadrant system, 126–127, *128*
Quaternary, 36–37
Queen of Sheba, 50

radiocarbon
    age, 56
    dating, 48, 55–56, *57*
rationalism, 276–279
Reck, Hans, 72
recording, 92–93
relative chronology, 33
Renfrew, Colin, 185
Richborough, 67–68
Riss, 37, 40
river gravels, 40–41
Riverton culture, 156
Robberg, 39, 137
rock paintings, 150, 180–*182*
Rousseau, Jean Jacques, 278
Rowe, John, 231
Rudenko, Sergei, 63, 249–250

Samothrace, 79
sampling, 89–90
San Marcos Cave, 166
Scheffer, J., 176
Schliemann, Heinrich, 76, 79, 290
Schultes, Hans, 252
Scythians, 4
selective excavation, 85
Semenov, S. A., 202
Seneca, 264
Sequoia, 52
seriation, 47, 233–*236*
Setzler, Frank, 276, 282
shadow sites, 69
Shang, 115, 248
Shepard, Anna, 211
Shinte, Chief, 179
Sidi Abderrahmane, 40
Signal Butte, 296
Silchester, 6, 68
site
    diary of, 92

plan, 93
records, 92
Sittard, 112, *115*
skeletons, 129–131
slaughter patterns, 159–162
small finds register, 92–93
Smith, Elliot, 242, 290–291, 298
Smith, William "Strata," 14, 33, 282
snaring, 175
social organization, 246–248
soil marks, 69
solar radiation, 56
Sollas, W. J., 249
Solutré, 156
Solutrean, 201, 284, 308
Somme River, 15, 40, 72–73, 284
Sotho, 270
Speed, John, 6, 17
Spencer, Herbert, 285, 291–292
Speyer, 66
Spier, Leslie, 242, 298
Spondylus, 179
Squier, E. J., 17
Star Carr, 47, 61, 98, 100, *103,* 145–
    147, *151,* 156, 166, *199,* 248, 252,
    303
Steenstrup, Japetus, 174
Stephens, John Lloyd, 17, 66
Steward, Julian, 276, 282, 305–306
stone axes (*see* axes and tools)
Stoneham, *235*
Stonehenge, 6, 68, 319
stone technology, 189–202
storage pits, 115–*118*
Storey's Paddock, *118*
strap-handled vases, 47
stratigraphy
    in archaeology, 33–36
    diagrams of, *34, 35, 41, 42, 95, 96, 97,*
        106, 114, 135
    disruptions in, 36
    interpretation of, 35–36
    recording of, 93
Strong, W. D., 296, 302
structures, 107, 116, 260–263
Struever, Stuart, 166, 308
Stukeley, William, 6, 8
subsistence, 146–150, *172*
Sumer, *160,* 215
Sun Dance, 242
superposition, principle of, 33
Svaerdborg, 176

Svendsdatter, Kirsten, 71
Swanscombe, 41, 42, 142, 193
Swiss lake dwellings, 28, 164
systems theory, 20, 264, 307–315

Taba Bosiu, 270
Talus Slope Village, 62
Tarrangollé, 257
Tasmanians, 202
Taylor, W. W., 304
teeth, eruption and wear patterns, 159
Tehuacán Valley, 166, 167
telehistoric sites, 252
tells, 66, 122–123
temples, 120, 262
Teotihuacán, 214, 265–266
Thames, 40, 41, 73, 142, 193, 195
Thebes, 263
thermoluminescence, 54
Thomas, Cyrus, 18
Thompson, R. H., 251
Thomsen, Christian Jurgensen, 27–28,
    282–283, 289, 301
Three-Age System, 18, 27–29, 289–290,
    300
three-dimensional recording, 88, 93, 121
thunderbolts, 13
Tel'manskaya, 101
Tikal, 261, 262
time perspective, man's sense of, 26
Tollund man, 45, 60–61, 183
Tonga, 260
tools (see axes and tools)
Torralba, 100, 162, 193
Tournal, 19
trade, 184–186
Trigger, Bruce, 259, 264
Troy, 76
trypanosomiasis, 174
Tsoelike River, 180
Tularosa Cave, 62, 165
Turgot, Anne Robert, 279, 282
Tutankhamen, 61–62, 203
Tylor, E. B., 285, 287–288, 290, 292, 297,
    304–305
type fossils, 201
typological analysis, 201–202, 224,
    236–237, 307

Ubaid, 123, 264
Uhle, Max, 67, 174, 293

uniformitarianism, 14
Upper Volta, 72
urban archaeology, 117
Ur-of the-Chaldees, 4, 203, 248
Uruk, 264
Ussher, James, 10, 12, 15, 27

Van Post, Lennart, 43
Vansina, Jan, 24
vegetal remains, 164–171
vegetational zones, postglacial, 46
Venda, 50
Venus figurines, 248
vertebrate fauna (see bones)
vertebrate paleontology, 14
vertical excavation, 85
Viking ships, 66
village, medieval, 119
Vinnecombe, Patricia, 180
Virú Valley, 70, 259, 307
Voltaire, Francois, 278
Von Herder, Johann, 279

Wabash Valley, 156
wagon burials, 112–115
Walcheren, 72
Warren, Claude N., 178–179
Wasserburg, 112
Webb, W. S., 80
Wheat, Joe Ben, 100
Wheeler, Sir Mortimer, 21, 33–34,
    80–81, 84, 252
White, Leslie, 301, 304
White, Theodore, 164
Wiegand, Theodore, 68
Willey, Gordon, 70, 259, 302–305, 307
Wiltshire, 11–12, 128
Winchester, 81, 110, 116, 118, 121, 122
wooden artifacts, 203, 204
Wolvercote, 194
Woodland, 131
Woolley, Leonard, 80
Worsaae, J. J. A., 28, 231, 237, 289, 301
Wright, Thomas, 77
Würm, 37

Yue-Chi peoples, 63

Zambezi, 40, 71–74, 179, 245, 260
zebu ox, 159, 161
Zimbabwe, 50, 263, 318–319
Zuni, 18